SHIPS *of the* WORLD
An Historical Encyclopedia

SHIPS *of the* WORLD
An Historical Encyclopedia

L I N C O L N   P A I N E

With contributions by
James Terry and Hal Fessenden

CONWAY
MARITIME PRESS

Copyright © Lincoln P. Paine, 1997

First published in Great Britain in 1998 by Conway Maritime Press
a division of Batsford Communications PLC
583 Fulham Road
London SW6 5BY

British Library Cataloguing in Publication Data
A record for this title is available on request from the British Library

Hardback Edition
ISBN 0 85177 739 2

Paperback Edition
For sole distribution by The Softback Preview
ISBN 0 85177 770 8

Lincoln P. Paine has asserted his right under the Copyright, Designs and
Patents Act, 1988, to be identified as Author of this Work.

Printed in Hong Kong by Midas Printing Ltd

Book design by Robert Overholtzer

Cover design by Peter Champion

IN MEMORIAM
SIADHAL SWEENEY

———

Navigare necesse est
Vivere non necesse
  — *Pompeius Magnus*

CONTENTS

ILLUSTRATIONS

Photo insert follows page 344

FOREWORD

Long before tales of Homer's wine-dark sea, waterborne vessels of any sort — but most especially deep-draft voyagers — stimulated dreams of adventure and of riches. Of all the conveyances invented by the hand and mind of man, none captures the imagination as firmly as the ship, ancient or modern. We bless ships and give them names; we endow them with human attributes. They have courage, strength of will, pride, resoluteness, and nobility. Their character is often described as faithful, honest, good, or brave according to the quality and tenure of service. When ships die, we mark and remember their loss.

Their shape and ordeals have been modeled and painted, romanced, dramatized, and made into the stuff of song and legend. Steam locomotives had names — most likely they still do — and not a few of them inspired stirring tales, as did pioneering aircraft and today's space vehicles. Today even some passenger aircraft may bear a plate honoring this or that city. But whether wooden hulled or constructed of steel, whether powered by oars or canvas and wind, by coal or oil or nuclear propulsion, the ship is unique among man's creations in the measure of its contributions to human history.

Ships and their movement on the vast oceans of the planet etched the fate of our forebears, and to this day they define the measure of national aspirations. Earth's greatest cities owe their might to safe anchorages, access to the sea, and the power of ships that came to call. In pursuit of trade, exploration, and defense, ships and the sea lanes of communication continue to be the linchpins of national prosperity and, indeed, of survival. By the contents of ships' holds, by their weapons, by their design and seaworthiness, and by the professional capacity and courage of captains and crews the wealth of nations has ever risen or fallen.

Above all else, a ship is defined by the souls who live and work aboard. One of my earliest memories of suspense and hope was listening to radio accounts of Captain Carlson's monumental efforts to save his command, *Flying Enterprise,* and my utter grief when he was forced to abandon the battle to the might of the sea. The saga took place when World War II was still a very fresh memory, when life in Wales and England — where I was raised — meant subsistence on the thin edge of ration stamps, reedy Woodbine cigarettes, and Spam for tea on special days. Inspirational human examples seemed to have left the stage when the last hero fell on the last battlefield in Europe. Carlson's brave example renewed hope in an exhausted people — and in at least one small boy.

The BBC broke through its regular programming time and again to describe the captain's struggle, the evacuation of his crew, and the deteriorating condition of the ship. I listened with my parents, who were as spellbound as I was by the high-seas drama, including my stepfather, who was serving in the Royal Air Force. Although the ship eventually broached and went down, the sheer courage of the attempt gave us all — my family and the whole country — an enormous morale boost. *Flying Enterprise* was never surrendered — she was wrested from her captain and crew. The redeeming grace of extraordinary effort and self-sacrifice was reaffirmed in those broadcasts.

Destiny and the performance of the officers and crew endow the reputation of a ship, but whether bravely fought or shamefully lost, the ship retains a uniquely personal identification. What happens to her can matter not only very deeply and immediately to passengers and crew, but also to whole populations. What happened to *Golden Hind* and *Goeben, Amistad* and *Adventure, Titanic* and *Turbinia,* the little *PT-109, Calypso,* or *Exxon Valdez* affects us all.

This book chronicles the history of more than a thousand of the world's most noteworthy vessels. Many names resonate with the epic events associated with their fates, but not all. A few entries have no identity or documented history, for only the ship's bones and the detritus of long-lost cargo survive to speak to us. But by our study of their construction and purpose we retrieve from antiquity and more recent history details of mankind's reach to discover the world, to unite peoples in trade, and to defend self-interest.

A few select, workaday plain craft of lake and river also find a place in these pages, because certain ships or ship types merit our attention simply by their amazing utility. Some vessels were built to go to places that seem improbable, if not altogether impossible, for a water-borne transport. But if a waterway was at all navigable — if there was enough dew to float a hull of even the most extraordinary design and materials — peoples of widely diverse cultures made every effort to tame the wilderness and seek the horizon.

Some of the ships are included because of the mystery of their eerie disappearance, some because they carried quantities of treasure, and some because of the fashion in which they were handled by their competitive masters. And not a few are here for the breathtaking incompetence that led to their destruction and, often, great loss of life. One way or the other, these are uncommon ships that have remained in mankind's memory. Any encyclo-pedia is open to the challenge of omission, and no doubt there are other ships that might find their way into some future edition. We all have our favorites. Mine are the windships that ventured into distant oceans during the era when commerce and speed reached a kind of salty apotheosis. Nothing afloat ever surpassed the form or splendor of the American extreme clipper, its later adaptations in the British wool and tea clippers and, most spectacularly, in the Flying P Line nitrate racers as epitomized by the five-masted full-rigged ship *Preussen*. These were the mightiest of ships to claw their way westward against Cape Horn gales. We shall never again see their like.

Lincoln Paine has made a determined start within the inherent limitations of the encyclopedia: his selections are outstanding. For anyone with an appreciation of ships and the sea, the attraction of these articles will exceed their use as a reference guide, and the book will become a source of unfailing interest. This work is not just a history of ships; it is a history of the world. Read on.

ERIC J. BERRYMAN
Commander, USNR (Retired)
Trustee, World Ship Trust, London

PREFACE

Ships have always played an important role in shaping human destiny. Whether they ply the waters of the world for peaceful or martial ends, whether engaged in fisheries or trade, carrying passengers for migration or pleasure, or used for geographical or scientific discovery, ships transform the waters of the world from barriers into thoroughfares. Before the age of air travel and satellite communications, ships formed the warp and woof of global communication, and even today they carry the burden of the world's trade.

Evidence of the affection that people have for ships is seen in the fact that ships are named, and when writers invest their vessels with human attributes, the conceit is almost never questioned. For ships are living things and there is a symbiotic relationship between them and their crews that we understand and appreciate intuitively. This obtains whether we are describing a day sailer, an aircraft carrier, or a deep submergence vessel.

Ships of the World: An Historical Encyclopedia is a straightforward work with a simple premise. Individual ships stand out from the crowd, much as people do. This encyclopedia is an attempt to describe more than one thousand of the most important or well-known vessels throughout history. There are no limitations as to size, rig, era, or place of origin (or rediscovery, in the case of archaeological sites). In addition to actual ships, there is an appendix covering a small number of well-known literary ships.

As in any reference work, the criteria for selecting individual vessels, as well as what to say about them, are nominally objective but ultimately subjective. In determining which and what, I have relied not only on my own reading of maritime and general history, but on the advice of dozens of colleagues and friends.

Eric J. Berryman helped refine the idea for the book from its inception and took on the unenviable task of reading every entry as it was written, offering innumerable suggestions and insights that have improved the work in countless ways. Jim Terry, a graceful and scholarly author, interrupted his own writing to contribute about thirty articles on Mediterranean and Western Eu-

ropean archaeological sites. Hal Fessenden taught me much about sailing, and I instinctively turned to him for several articles on shipwrecks and other disasters. Any errors or mistakes that I have introduced in their invaluable contributions are my own.

This work also owes its completion to the advice of and review by countless friends and colleagues who thoughtfully answered my questions, reviewed portions of the manuscript, researched photographs, or otherwise lent a hand. In particular, Norman Brouwer, curator of ships and keeper of the Herman Melville Library at the South Street Seaport Museum, and his assistant, Marie Lore; Frank O. Braynard, executive director of the American Merchant Marine Museum, and our mutual colleague Bill Miller. I also benefited   as have so many others — from the advice of the late Karl Kortum, dean of the historic ship preservation community in the United States, who provided invaluable guidance as I developed the idea for this book.

Others to whom I owe special thanks include George L. Maxwell, Harry Anderson, and Nicole Von Klenke; Captain Richard Bailey, "HMS" *Rose;* David Bell, Imperial War Museum; Liliane Bouillon-Pasquet, Tapisserie de Bayeux; Ian Boreham, Captain Cook Study Unit; David Brink; Lars Bruzelius, Maritime History Virtual Archive; Ian Buxton, University of Newcastle; Eliot Cafritz; Arne Emil Christensen, University of Oslo; Carol City, Plimoth Plantation; John Coates, the Trireme Trust; Jim Delgado, Vancouver Maritime Museum; Margherita Desy, USS *Constitution* Museum; William Dudley, Naval Historical Center; Kathy Flynn, Peabody Essex Museum; Kevin Foster, National Park Service; Bill Gilbert, USS *Long Beach* Association; Jeremy Green, Western Australia Maritime Museum; Edwin Hill and Jodi Erickson, Murphy Library, University of Wisconsin, La Crosse; Olaf Höckmann, Römisch-Germanisches Zentralmuseum, Mainz; Maria Jacobsen, Institute for Nautical Archaeology; Joseph A. Jackson, New York Yacht Club Library; Astrid Johnson, Norsk Sjøfartsmuseum, Oslo; Mark Lardas; Arthur Layton; Nathan Lipfert, Maine Maritime Museum; Tom Lewis; Per

Lofving; Claudia McFall, The Mariners' Museum; Chuck Meide; Bill Middendorf; Dan Moreland; Bob Morse; Tim Newell; Tom Pardo, Amoco Corporation; George Paxton; Michael Phillips; Bob and Dave Poole; Jack Putnam; Tina Shaffer, Bishop Museum; Paul Silverstone; Colin Starkey, National Maritime Museum, Greenwich; Andrew Stathopulos; J. Richard Steffy, Institute for Nautical Archaeology; David Stone, Underwater Archaeological Society of British Columbia; Timothy and Mary Sullivan; Ad van der Zee, Bataviawerf, Lelystad, Netherlands; Stuart Vine, *Mary Rose* Trust; Thomas Wells, AICH; Pam Wuerth, American Sail Training Association; and the librarians of the New York Public Library, Brooklyn Public Library, and Portland (Maine) Public Library.

Few authors can have benefited from such a dedicated back office. After showing me how to write reference books, John Wright acted as my agent for this one. Liz Kubik took no small risk in signing this book, and Harry Foster cheerfully took on the project (and its author) when she left Houghton Mifflin. Managing editor Chris Coffin, senior manuscript editor Larry Cooper, Donna de La Perriere, and Sandra Riley endured countless telephone calls and letters to see the manuscript through production. Katie Blatt did yeoman service as copy editor. I also owe special thanks to Laurie Grace, who translated my view of the world into a set of useful maps.

My mother, Frances McSherry, has provided endless support in all my escapades, this one included. My wife, Allison, and our daughters, Victoria Kaiulani and Madeleine DuGuay, encouraged me to accept this assignment. They have spent much of the past three years looking at my back, though they have never turned their backs on me.

This book is dedicated to the memory of my stepfather, Siadhal Sweeney, from whom I inherited a love of ships and books. No writer ever had such a devoted reader over the shoulder.

LINCOLN P. PAINE
*Brooklyn, New York, and
Portland, Maine, 1994–97*

SHIPS *of the* WORLD
An Historical Encyclopedia

NOTE

Each entry comprises three parts: basic specifications, narrative history, and a source note. Complete publication data for all works cited in the source notes can be found in the Bibliography.

The first paragraph includes basic information about the vessel in question, including:

L/B/D = length, beam, and draft, or depth in hold (dph), given in feet and meters.

Tons = usually given in gross registered tons (grt), displacement (disp).

Hull = hull material, usually wood, iron or steel.

Comp. = complement, including crew and/or passengers.

Arm. = armament, including the number of guns and caliber or weight of projectile, in either standard or metric measurement. Numbers in parentheses indicate the number of turrets and guns per turret: $8 \times 15"$ (4×2) means eight 15-inch guns, in four turrets mounting two guns each.

ASROC = antisubmarine rocket
carr = carronade
dc(p)(t) = depth charge (projector) (track)
how = howitzer
mg = machine gun
pdr. = pounder
quad = quadruple
SAM/AS = surface-to-air missile/antisubmarine
ssm = surface-to-surface missile
TT = torpedo tube(s)

Armor = maximum thickness of belt (or side) and deck armor.

Mach. = machinery, including type of propulsion, horsepower, number of screws, and speed.

Des. = designer.

Built = builder, place, and year of commissioning.

FLEET DESIGNATIONS

CSS = Confederate States Ship
HMAS = Her/His Majesty's Australian Ship
HMCS = Her/His Majesty's Canadian Ship
HMNZS = Her/His Majesty's New Zealand Ship
HMS = Her/His Majesty's Ship
SMS = Seine Majestäts Schiff (Ger.: His Majesty's Ship)
USS = United States Ship
USCGC = United States Coast Guard Cutter

AARON MANBY

Steamship (1f). *L/B/D:* 120′ × 17.2′ (23′ew) × 3.5′ (36.6m × 5.2m (7m) × 1.1m). *Tons:* 116 burthen. *Hull:* iron. *Mach.:* steam engine, sidewheels, 30–50 hp; 7 kts. *Built:* Horseley Ironworks, Tipton, Staffordshire, Eng.; 1821.

One of the first iron-hulled vessels ever, and the first to venture into open water, *Aaron Manby* was built for service on the Seine River in France by an ironmonger of the same name, his son Charles, and Captain (later Admiral Sir) Charles Napier. Fabricated at the Horseley Ironworks, of which Aaron Manby was the master, and assembled at Rotherhithe on the Thames, the flat-bottomed hull was made of quarter-inch-thick iron plate fastened to angle-iron ribs. There was one deck, of wood, and a bowsprit. The vessel's distinctive profile boasted a single 47 foot high funnel. The paddlewheels, designed by Henry Bell, were 12 feet in diameter but only 1.5 feet wide, because the vessel's maximum beam was limited to 23 feet for service on the Seine.

Defying the prevailing wisdom of the day, the iron-hulled vessel not only floated but drew one foot less water than any other steamboat of the day. After trials in May 1822, *Aaron Manby* crossed the English Channel to Le Havre on June 10 before proceeding up the Seine to Paris, where she was based for the next decade. *Aaron Manby* was sold in 1830 and by 1836 she was working on the Loire River out of Nantes. She was not broken up until 1855.

Spratt, "First Iron Steamer."

ABIEL ABBOT LOW

Kerosene launch (1f). *L/B/D:* 38′ × 9′ × 3.8′ (11.6m × 2.7m × 1.2m). *Hull:* wood. *Comp.:* 2. *Mach.:* internal combustion engine, 10 hp, 1 screw; 5 kts. *Built:* William C. Newman, New York Kerosene Engine Co., N.Y.; 1902.

Named for the president of the New York Kerosene Engine Company, *Abiel Abbot Low* was built specifically to showcase that company's kerosene-powered engines. Built under the supervision of William C. Newman, *Low* was launched in the early summer of 1902. On July 9, she departed New York in an attempt to become the first powerboat to cross the Atlantic; she carried 800 gallons of kerosene fuel and provisions for sixty days for Captain Newman and his son. The vessel encountered heavy seas throughout the voyage and was thirty-six days to Falmouth, England, where she arrived on August 14, the first vessel powered by an internal combustion engine to make the passage.

Herreshoff, *Introduction to Yachting*. Kemp, *Oxford Companion to Ships and the Sea*.

ABNER COBURN

Down Easter (3m). *L/B/D:* 223′ × 43′ × 26.7′ (68m × 13.1m × 8.1m). *Tons:* 1,878 reg. *Hull:* wood. *Built:* William Rogers, Bath, Me.; 1882.

Named for a former governor of Maine, the Down Easter *Abner Coburn* was built by William Rogers, who put her in general trade chiefly between the East Coast and the Orient, usually via the Cape of Good Hope and the Indian Ocean. She also sailed on the Cape Horn route between New York and San Francisco. Except for three voyages, from 1882 to 1897 she was commanded by Captain George A. Nichols, who was killed in the Indian Ocean when a wave ripped away the wheelhouse and he was crushed. In the early 1890s, the ship had come under the management of Pendleton, Carver & Nichols, who sold her to the California Shipping Company. This firm sailed *Abner Coburn* in the West Coast lumber trade until 1912, when she was sold to Libby, McNeill & Libby who employed her in their salmon cannery operations around Bristol Bay, Alaska. In the late 1920s, she was intentionally burned in Puget Sound for the scrap metal used in her construction.

Lubbock, *Down Easters*. Matthews, *American Merchant Ships*.

HMS ABOUKIR

Cressy-class armored cruiser (4f/2m). *L/B:* 472′ × 69.5′ (143.9m × 21.2m). *Tons:* 12,000 disp. *Hull:* steel. *Comp.:* 760. *Arm.:* 2 × 9.2″, 12 × 6″, 13 × 12pdr; 2 × 18″TT. *Armor:* 6″ belt. *Mach.:* triple expansion, 2 screws; 21 kts. *Built:* Fairfield Shipbuilding & Engineering Co., Ltd., Govan, Scotland; 1902.

Named for the Egyptian bay in which Rear Admiral Horatio Nelson defeated the fleet of Vice Admiral François Paul Brueys at the Battle of the Nile in 1798, HMS *Aboukir* first saw service on the Mediterranean station before returning to home waters in 1905. At the start of World War I, *Aboukir* was one of four units of Rear Admiral Henry H. Campbell's Seventh Cruiser Squadron based at the Nore. Their role was to support destroyer squadrons of the Southern Force in keeping German minelayers and torpedo boats out of the North Sea approaches to the English Channel. It was an assignment for which the armored cruisers were horribly ill equipped — they were known as the "live bait squadron" — and their deployment to safer waters had been discussed by Admiral of the Fleet Sir John Jellicoe, First Lord of the Admiralty Winston Churchill, and others at a meeting on September 17, 1914. Five days later, at about 0630, *Aboukir* and her sister ships CRESSY and HOGUE were patrolling the Broad Fourteens, an area of the North Sea between Yarmouth and Ymuiden; due to the poor weather, they were without any destroyer escorts. Oblivious to the threat of submarine attack, the three ships were steaming on a steady course at 10 knots when they were attacked by the German *U-9* about 20 miles northwest of the Hook of Holland (30 miles west of Ymuiden). A single torpedo broke *Aboukir* in two and she sank in twenty-five minutes with the loss of 527 men in about 52°18′N, 3°41′E. Captain Drummond ordered *Cressy* and *Hogue* to stand by to pick up survivors, and these ships were also sunk. Only 305 survivors were plucked from the waters of the North Sea by trawlers and Dutch patrol boats and landed at Ymuiden. Less than two months into the war, the Royal Navy had lost 3 ships, 62 officers, and 1,397 ratings in the space of an hour. Moreover, the submarine had established its worth as an offensive weapon with drastic implications for the conduct of surface warfare for the remainder of the war.

Coles, *Three before Breakfast.*

ABRAHAM RYDBERG

(later *Abraham*) Ship (3m). *L/B/D:* 101′ × 22.3′ × 11.4′ (30.8m × 6.8m × 3.5m). *Tons:* 149 grt. *Hull:* wood. *Built:* D. R. Andersson, Karlshamn, Sweden; 1879.

Built as a training ship for the Abraham Rydberg Foundation and named for her benefactor, a prominent Swedish shipowner, the flush-decked *Abraham Rydberg* was among the smallest full-rigged ships ever built. Employed in sail training for thirty-two years, she was not replaced until 1911 when a second steel-hulled ship of the same name was built, and the original ship was renamed *Abraham*. The following year she was sold to A. W. Johannson of Lanna. When *Abraham* was converted for merchant use, the cadet accommodations were removed, increasing her tonnage to 158; in 1917 her tonnage increased again to 168. Between 1926 and 1930 she changed hands three times. Her last owner, H. Palssn of Fortuna, installed an auxiliary engine, and she may have been cut down to a topsail schooner. *Abraham* was hulked at Hälsö in 1935.

Underhill, *Sail Training and Cadet Ships.*

ACHILLE LAURO

(ex-*Willem Ruys*) Liner (2f/2m). *L/B/D:* 631.2′ × 82′ × 47.5′ (192.4m × 25m × 14.5m). *Tons:* 23,114 grt. *Hull:* steel. *Comp.:* 1st 275, tourist 770. *Mach.:* motorship, 32,000 bhp, 2 screws; 22 kts. *Built:* Koninklijke Maatschappij de Schelde, Flushing, Neth.; 1947.

Intended for Royal Rotterdam Lloyd's service between the Netherlands and Indonesia, the *Willem Ruys* was laid down in 1939. Work was suspended during World War II and she did not enter service until 1947. Following Indonesia's nationalization of Dutch assets in 1956, she was put in round-the-world service from Rotterdam, via the Suez Canal to Australia and then on to Port Everglades, in Florida, via the Panama Canal. Sold to Italy's Lauro Lines in 1964 (and named for a former mayor of Naples), she was refurbished with accommodations for 152 first- and 1,155 tourist-class passengers. *Achille Lauro* sailed between Europe and Australia until 1973 when she entered the Mediterranean cruise trade. In 1981, a fire killed two people while the ship was cruising near the Canary Islands, and in 1982–83 she was leased to Chandris Lines after being seized by creditors.

Achille Lauro's eastern Mediterranean cruises generally took her from Genoa to Naples, Syracuse, Alexandria, Port Said, Tartus (Syria), Limassol, and Rhodes. On October 7, 1985, while en route from Alexandria to Port Said — the majority of the passengers had left the ship for sightseeing and were to rejoin the ship at Port Said — she was seized by four Palestinian terrorists. Two days later, after intervention by the Italian and Egyptian governments, the hijackers surrendered at Port Said. Almost immediately it was discovered that one of the hijackers had shot Leon Klinghoffer, a seventy-nine-year-old wheelchair-bound American passenger whose body they threw into the sea. The hijackers were surrendered to a representative of the Palestine Liberation Organization to be flown to Tunis. U.S. jets forced down the Egyptian passenger plane carrying the hijackers at the NATO air base in Catania, Sicily, and they were handed over to Italian authorities to be tried for murder, as the ship was, under international law, Italian territory. The government of Prime Minister Bettino Craxi further outraged public opinion in the United States — and Italy — by proceeding to release the suspects, and Craxi was forced to resign after his coalition government fell over the issue.

Achille Lauro continued in service until 1994 when she caught fire and sank en route from Italy to South Africa. She had just rounded the Horn of Africa on November 30 when a fire broke out in the engine room. Two passengers died and most of the remaining 570 passengers and 407 crew boarded the tanker Hawaiian King before being transferred to other merchant and naval vessels. Achille Lauro sank on December 2 about 150 miles off the coast of Somalia.

Press reports. Bonsor, North Atlantic Seaway.

HMS ACHILLES

Leander-class cruiser (1f/2m). L/B/D: 554.5' × 56' × 19' (169m × 17.1m × 5.8m). Tons: 9,144 disp. Hull: steel. Comp.: 570. Arm.: 8 × 6" (4 × 2), 4 × 4", 12 × 0.5" mg; 8 × 21"TT; 1 aircraft. Armor: 3.5" belt, 1" deck. Mach.: steam turbines, 72,000 shp, 4 screws; 32.5 kts. Built: Cammell Laird & Co., Ltd., Birkenhead, Eng.; 1933.

Commissioned in 1933, the light cruiser HMS Achilles was attached to the Royal Navy's New Zealand Division in March 1936. On August 29, 1939, Captain W. E. Parry received orders to sail for the West Indies. On September 2 the ship was reassigned to cover Allied shipping along the west coast of South America, and in October Achilles joined Commodore Harry Harwood's South American Squadron — HMS EXETER and AJAX — which fought the German pocket battleship ADMIRAL GRAF SPEE on December 13 off the River Plate. When the Royal New Zealand Navy was officially formed, on October 10, 1941, she was recommissioned HMNZS Achilles. In 1948 she was recommissioned as RIN Delhi, flagship of the Royal Indian Navy, and she took part in the seizure of the Portuguese colony of Goa in 1961. She also played herself in the 1956 movie Pursuit of the Graf Spee (in England, Battle of the River Plate) before paying off in 1977.

Pope, Battle of the River Plate.

ADA IREDALE

(later Annie Johnson, Bretagne) Bark (3m). L/B/D: 212.1' × 34.1' × 21.6' (64.6m × 10.4m × 6.6m). Tons: 997 grt. Hull: iron. Comp.: 24. Built: Williamson & Co., Harrington, Eng.; 1872.

Built for Peter Iredale & Company of Liverpool, the iron bark Ada Iredale had made only three or four voyages when in 1876 she sailed with coal from Ardrossan for San Francisco. On October 15, she was about 2,000 miles east of the Marquesas Islands (in 30°30'S, 107°45'W) when she caught fire, probably due to spontaneous combustion. Captain Linton (who was accompanied by his wife) and the crew abandoned ship and eventually made it to San Francisco, and Ada Iredale was written off as a complete loss. Eight months later, a French vessel found the bark drifting in the Pacific and towed her to Tahiti in June of 1877, her cargo still smoldering below decks. Eleven months later she was sold to the San Francisco shipper Captain I. E. Thayer, who gave her a thorough refit in Tahiti before sailing her to San Francisco and selling her to Crawford & Company. Renamed Annie Johnson, she sailed in the Cape Horn trade, doubling the Horn at least thirteen times and proving herself a smart sailer despite the vicissitudes of her early career. In 1912, she was sold to the Matson Steam Navigation Company, also of San Francisco, and rerigged as a four-masted schooner, with an auxiliary engine added in about 1921. Five years later she was sold to Captain L. Ozanne, of Tahiti, who renamed her Bretagne and put her in the interisland copra trade, with twice-yearly voyages between the West Coast and Tahiti. She sank off Cape Flattery while outward bound from Oregon in 1928.

Lubbock, Down Easters. Villiers & Picard, Bounty Ships of France.

ADMIRAL GRAF SPEE

Deutschland-class battleship (1f/3m). L/B/D: 610.1' × 69.9' × 23.9' (186m × 21.3m × 7.25m). Tons: 16,020 disp. Hull: steel. Arm.: 6 × 11" (2 × 3), 8 × 5.9", 6 × 10.5cm, 8 × 37mm, 10 × 20mm; 8 × 21"TT; 1 plane. Armor: 3.2" belt, 1.8" deck. Mach.: diesel, 52,050 shp, 2 screws; 26 kts. Built: Kriegsmarine Werft, Wilhelmshaven, Ger.; 1936.

One of three pocket battleships — the other two being LÜTZOW (ex-Deutschland) and ADMIRAL SCHEER — the Admiral Graf Spee was named for Admiral Graf von Spee, who went down in SMS SCHARNHORST at the Battle of the Falklands in 1914. Under Captain Hans Langsdorff the Graf Spee slipped quietly out of Wilhelmshaven on August 21, 1939, with orders to proceed to the South Atlantic, there to await the coming war. To enable the Graf Spee to remain at sea for the next four or five months, the supply vessel ALTMARK had been sent out ahead to rendezvous.

Graf Spee's mission as a commerce raider was threefold: to sink merchant ships, to force costly changes to the routing of merchant ships, and to draw Allied naval units off their assigned stations in other parts of the world. In the last, at least, *Graf Spee* succeeded brilliantly. As soon as the existence of a surface raider in the South Atlantic was known, twenty-two British and French ships — ten 8-inch cruisers (including EXETER and *Cumberland*), five 6-inch cruisers (including AJAX and ACHILLES), three battlecruisers, and four aircraft carriers — were dispatched to the search. Crisscrossing the South Atlantic, and with one brief foray into the Indian Ocean, *Graf Spee* took nine merchant prizes, though none of great size; not one British crewman died as a result of *Graf Spee*'s actions. Because of the limited facilities for prisoners, Langsdorff periodically transferred his captives to the *Altmark*. *Graf Spee*'s luck ran out after nine prizes, the last being SS *Streonshalh*, taken on December 7, aboard which were confidential papers that suggested the River Plate as the best hunting ground. Unfortunately for Langsdorff, he was anticipated by Commodore Harry Harwood, commanding a squadron that included the *Exeter, Ajax,* and *Achilles.*

The adversaries met at dawn on December 13, in about 34°S, 49°W. After some indecision, Langsdorff decided to concentrate *Graf Spee*'s fire on *Exeter,* which after two hours was forced to break off and retired to the Falklands. Rather than pursue *Exeter* and finish her off or turn on the 6-inch cruisers, Langsdorff made directly for the Plate, trailed by *Ajax* and *Achilles.* She anchored in Uruguayan waters shortly after midnight on December 14. At this point diplomatic forces came into play, and Langsdorff was quickly down to three options — to attempt a breakout, to remain interned, or to scuttle the ship. Even if he could battle his way out of the River Plate against still inferior forces, it is unlikely that he could have sailed his ship to Germany without being brought to decisive battle at some point, and internment was unthinkable. On December 17, having removed all valuable and secret equipment (including radar), Langsdorff sailed *Graf Spee* into international waters and scuttled his ship in 35°11′S, 56°26′W. The next night, in Montevideo, he shot himself.

Pope, *Battle of the River Plate.* Stephen, *Sea Battles in Close-Up.*

ADMIRAL HIPPER

Blücher-class cruiser (1f/3m). *L/B/D:* 675.4′ × 69.9′ × 25.3′ (205.9m × 21.3m × 7.7m). *Tons:* 18,208 disp. *Hull:* steel. *Comp.:* 1,400. *Arm.:* 8 × 8.1″ (4 × 2), 12 × 10.5cm, 12 × 3.7cm, 8 × 2cm; 12 × 21″TT; 3 aircraft. *Armor:* 3.2″ belt, 1.8″ deck. *Mach.:* steam turbines, 133,631 shp, 3 screws; 32.5 kts. *Built:* Blohm & Voss, Hamburg; 1939.

Named for Rear Admiral Franz Ritter von Hipper, commander of the German battlecruiser squadron at Jutland in 1916, *Admiral Hipper* was commissioned just before the start of World War II. She first saw action at the capture of Trondheim during Operation Weserübung, the German invasion of Norway, in the spring of 1940. On April 8, *Hipper* was rammed by HMS GLOWWORM about 100 miles northwest of Trondheim fjord. The British destroyer was sunk, but not before ripping a forty-meter gash in the *Hipper*'s starboard hull, despite which the cruiser completed her assignment. Trondheim fell on April 9 and the *Hipper* was back in Germany on April 12.

In November 1940, *Admiral Hipper* was deployed as a commerce raider, engaging troop convoy WS5A on Christmas Day, and later that day sinking the armed merchant cruiser *Jumna*. Sailing from Brest on February 1, 1941, *Hipper* sank the freighter *Iceland* on February 11, and the next day fell on the nineteen ships of unescorted convoy SLS64 from Sierra Leone; seven ships (32,806 grt.) were sunk and three damaged. High fuel consumption forced her back to Brest, and from there northabout Iceland to Kiel. On December 31, 1941, *Hipper* was part of a fleet that found convoy JW518 in the Barents Sea. The *Hipper* engaged the destroyers HMS *Onslow, Orwell,* and *Achates* (the latter sank), before coming under fire from cruisers HMS SHEFFIELD and *Jamaica,* which scored three hits, one below the waterline, forcing the *Hipper* to retire.

The *Hipper* spent the rest of the war in the Baltic, and was in company with the WILHELM GUSTLOFF when that ship was sunk with the loss of thousands of lives on January 30, 1945. Berthed at Kiel from February 2, *Admiral Hipper* was sunk at dock in the last sortie flown by RAF Bomber Command on May 3, and was broken up later that year.

Gröner, *German Warships 1815–1945.* Whitley, *German Cruisers of World War Two.*

ADMIRAL SCHEER

Deutschland-class battleship (1f/3m). *L/B/D:* 616.3′ × 69.9′ × 23.9′ (187.9m × 21.3m × 7.3m). *Tons:* 15,180 disp. *Hull:* steel. *Comp.:* 1,100–1,300. *Arm.:* 6 × 11″ (3 × 2), 8 × 5.9″, 6 × 8.8cm, 47 × 4.8cm; 8 × 21″TT; 2 aircraft. *Armor:* 3.2″ belt. *Mach.:* diesel, 52,500 shp, 2 screws; 28.3 kts. *Built:* Kriegsmarine Werft, Wilhelmshaven, Ger.; 1936.

One of three *Deutschland*-class pocket battleships, *Admiral Scheer* was named for Admiral Reinhard Scheer, commander in chief of the German Navy during World War I. Although she saw relatively little action at the start of World War II, her antiaircraft gunners were the first to shoot down a British bomber. Originally classed as a pocket battleship, she was designated a heavy cruiser in February 1940, presumably to downplay the importance of the vessel in the wake of the loss of ADMIRAL GRAF SPEE. After an extensive refit, in October 1940 she embarked on a five-month raiding voyage during which she sank sixteen Allied merchant ships totaling over 100,000 tons in the Atlantic and Indian Oceans. Her most celebrated victim was the armed merchant cruiser JERVIS BAY, sunk in defense of a convoy on November 5, 1940. Moved to Norway in 1941, *Admiral Scheer* sank three Soviet tankers in the Kara Sea the following year. Confined to the Baltic Sea from 1943, she was used in support of German ground forces during the retreat from the Eastern Front in the winter of 1944–45. On April 9, 1945, she was hit five times during an RAF raid and capsized in the Deutsche Werke fitting-out basin at Kiel, with the loss of thirty-two crew.

Krancke & Brennecke, *Pocket Battleship.*

ADVANCE

Brigantine. L/B/D: 88' × 21.8' × 8.4' dph (26.8m × 6.6m × 2.6m). *Tons:* 144 tons. *Hull:* wood. *Comp.:* 17. *Built:* New Kent, Maryland; 1847.

Originally built as a merchant ship, *Advance* became the flagship of the first U.S. Arctic expedition in 1850 when she was purchased by New York merchant Henry Grinnell and dispatched with *Rescue* to take part in the search for Sir John Franklin's HMS EREBUS and TERROR. Under command of Lieutenant Edwin J. De Haven, USN, *Advance* departed New York on May 23, 1850, and sailed for Davis Strait and Baffin Bay. From there the ships headed west through Lancaster Sound north of Baffin Island. On August 25, the expedition reached Devon Island where a shore party found the remains of a campsite as well as a number of British ships also engaged in the search for Franklin. In September 1853 the two ships were caught in pack ice with which they drifted through Wellington Channel as far as the northern tip of Devon Island, which they named Cape Grinnell. The ice carried the ships south again to Lancaster Sound and then east to Baffin Bay and Dover Strait before releasing its grip on June 7, 1854. The ships returned to New York, and over the next

twenty months *Advance* was fitted out for a second expedition, this time under Assistant Surgeon Elisha Kent Kane, a veteran of the first voyage.

The Second Grinnell Expedition sailed through Smith Sound at the head of Baffin Bay and into Kane Basin. There the members of the expedition saw Humboldt Glacier, then the largest known, and attained 78°43'N, farther north than any Europeans before them. During their first winter in Rensellaer Harbor all but six of their sled dogs died and the crew members were laid up with scurvy. In March, two men were killed in an attempt (made too early in the season) to establish a forward depot for overland expeditions. A later expedition reached Cape Constitution, which Kane mistakenly believed led to a warmer Open Polar Sea hypothesized by Commander Edward Inglefield in 1852. The latter had sailed in search of the Franklin expedition in the steam yacht *Isabel,* and confirmation of the Open Polar Sea was probably the real object of Kane's mission. Faced with the prospect of another winter aboard *Advance,* eight of the crew attempted to make their way overland to Upernavik. They failed, but with the assistance of Eskimos at Etah and other settlements, returned safely to the ship. The winter was one of horrifying privation, and the expedition's survival was due almost entirely to the Eskimos from whom the men were able to obtain food. Reduced to cannibalizing *Advance* for fuel, the survivors abandoned ship on May 17 and over the next month hauled their three boats, supplies, and four invalid crew 80 miles to open water. Sailing south and east along the coast of Greenland, they reached Upernavik on August 6, 1854, and by October they were back in New York.

Berton, *Arctic Grail.* Kane, *U.S. Grinnell Expedition in Search of Sir John Franklin.* U.S. Navy, *DANFS.*

HMS ADVENTURE

(ex-*Raleigh, Marquis of Rockingham*) Bark (3m). *L/B/D:* 97.3' × 28.4' × 13.2' dph (39.7m × 8.7m × 4m). *Tons:* 336 tons. *Hull:* wood. *Comp.:* 81. *Built:* Fishburn, Whitby, Eng.; 1771.

Within a few months of his return from his first voyage to the South Seas in HMS ENDEAVOUR, James Cook — newly promoted to Commander — was assigned to undertake a second voyage to determine the existence of a southern continent, or Terra Australis, long hypothesized by navigators and geographers. As this would entail an extensive survey of the southern ocean, he was given two ships, RESOLUTION, the flagship, and *Adventure,* which sailed under command of Commander Tobias Furneaux, a veteran of Captain Samuel Wallis's 1766–68 circumnavigation in HMS DOLPHIN. Like *Endeavour* and *Resolution*, *Adventure* was originally a North Sea collier rigged as a bark; she was rerigged by the navy following her purchase in 1771.

The two ships departed from Plymouth on July 13, 1772, and remained in company for seven months, stopping at the Azores, Cape Verde Islands, and Cape Town. In November they departed Cape Town and sailed south. After cruising among the ice fields, the two ships crossed the Antarctic Circle on January 17, 1773, reaching as far south as 67°15′S. On February 8 the two ships separated in a fog, and by prior arrangement Furneaux turned *Adventure* for New Zealand, about 4,200 miles away. They called first at Van Diemen's Land (Tasmania) — visited by Abel Tasman in HEEMSKERCK and *Zeehaen* in 1642 — and charted the southern coast, although they failed to realize that it was an island and not part of New Holland (Australia). (Adventure Bay takes its name from the ship, and Cook named the Furneaux Islands northeast of Tasmania on his third expedition in *Resolution* and DISCOVERY.)

Adventure arrived in Queen Charlotte Sound, New Zealand, on May 7 and was joined ten days later by *Resolution*. The ships' crews traded with the Maori, whom Cook had visited in *Endeavour* in 1769–70. A month later they sailed for Tahiti; en route many of *Adventure*'s crew became ill with scurvy and one died. The ships arrived at Tahiti on August 15 and remained there until September 7. Upon their departure, they embarked a man named Omai, of Huaheine, who returned in the *Adventure* to England and spent two years in London under the patronage of Sir Joseph Banks and Lord Sandwich. Sailing west, the ships called at Tonga (Friendly Islands) before shaping a course for Queen Charlotte Sound.

As they were sailing down the coast of New Zealand at the end of October, the two ships were separated in a storm. Adverse weather prevented *Adventure*'s return to Queen Charlotte Sound until November 30, four days after *Resolution* had sailed. Furneaux decided to return to England alone, but on December 17, one day before their planned departure, ten of the ship's company were sent to gather fresh vegetables for the voyage and were killed in a fight with some Maoris. Five days later the remainder sailed due east, rounding Cape Horn on January 10, 1774, and anchoring on March 19 at Cape Town, where they stayed one month. After a voyage of two years and three days, *Adventure* anchored at Spithead on July 14. Though the voyage was not the success it might have been, *Adventure* had the distinction of being the first ship to circumnavigate the globe from west to east. The ship was subsequently taken over by the navy for use as a storeship in North America until 1783, when she was broken up.

Brock, "Cook's *Endeavour* and Other Ships." Cook, *Journals of James Cook*. McGowan, "Captain Cook's Ships."

ADVENTURE GALLEY

Galley (3m). *L:* ca. 124′ (38m). *Tons:* 285 bm. *Hull:* wood. *Comp.:* 152. *Arm.:* 34 × 12pdr. *Built:* Castle Yard, Deptford, Eng.; 1695.

Adventure Galley was a three-masted ship equipped with thirty-six oars as auxiliary propulsion. In 1696, Captain William Kidd was made captain and, armed with a privateer's commission from William III, set out from England to capture enemy commerce, mainly that of France and Spain. Of obscure background, the Scottish-born Kidd had settled in New York after years as a pirate in the Caribbean. In 1695, Kidd had sailed his merchant ship *Antigua* to London with a view to acquiring a letter of marque that would enable him to sail as a privateer. Kidd's brief also included the right to attack pirates of any nationality, especially those who preyed on the valuable trade routes of the Indian Ocean.

Adventure Galley sailed on April 6, 1696, and captured a French fisherman in the North Atlantic. On September 6, having recruited a further ninety crew in New York, she sailed for the Indian Ocean via Madeira and the Cape Verde Islands, landing at Tulear, Madagascar, on January 27, 1697. En route, Kidd fell in with a squadron of Royal Navy ships and impressed the officers as a would-be pirate rather than a privateer with the King's commission. Rumors of this spread quickly and British merchants kept their distance. After repairs in the Comoros, *Adventure Galley* sailed for the Bab al-Mandab Strait at the mouth of the Red Sea to intercept one of the richly laden ships of the Muslim pilgrim fleet, which sailed under the protection of European traders. On August 15, *Adventure Galley* slipped in among a convoy guarded by two Dutch ships and the East India Company's *Sceptre,* whose captain intimidated Kidd into withdrawing. Kidd then headed for the Malabar Coast of India where he captured a number of prizes, fought off two Portuguese warships from Goa, and had several run-ins with the East India Company. In March 1698, *Adventure Galley* — in company with the prizes *Quedah Merchant* and *Rupparell* — sailed for the island of Saint Marie off the northeast coast of Madagascar. *Adventure Galley* was in wretched condition and eventually sank there. Kidd left the island in *Quedah Merchant,* which ran aground and was burned on Hispaniola after Kidd had sold off what remained of her valuable cargo of textiles.

Upon his return to North America, Kidd was imprisoned and returned to England. A valuable pawn in a political game between William III's Whig supporters, who had backed his venture, and the opposition Tories, who were now in the ascendancy, Kidd was tried for and found guilty of murder and piracy, and then twice hanged (the rope broke the first time). His remains were put on display at Tilbury Point on the Thames as a warning to others.

Ritchie, *Captain Kidd and the War against the Pirates.*

AF CHAPMAN

(ex-*G. D. Kennedy, Dunboyne*) Ship (3m). *L/B/D:* 257′ × 37.5′ × 21.5′ (78.3m × 11.4m × 6.6m). *Tons:* 1,428 grt. *Hull:* iron. *Built:* Whitehaven Shipbuilding Co., Whitehaven, Eng.; 1888.

Laid down during the shipbuilding slump of the mid-1880s, the ship later known as *Af Chapman* was purchased by Messrs. Charles E. Martin & Company, of Dublin, and named *Dunboyne.* After twenty years in service as a merchant ship, she was purchased by Leif Gundersen of Porsgrun, Norway, who sailed her for six years. She was then acquired by the Rederiaklieb Transatlantic (Transatlantic Line) of Sweden, who renamed her *G. D. Kennedy* and sailed her as a cargo/training ship for the company's officer cadets. Sold to the Swedish Navy in 1924 and

The Swedish three-masted training ship AF CHAPMAN *leaving Plymouth, England, in 1928. Courtesy National Maritime Museum, Greenwich.*

renamed *Af Chapman,* in honor of the eminent eighteenth-century naval architect, she was used strictly for sail training, carrying as many as 200 cadets per voyage. During World War II, *Af Chapman* served as a barracks ship; after the war she passed to the Swedish Tourist Union and was opened as a tourist hostel in 1949. She has been on view in Stockholm ever since.

Underhill, *Sail Training and Cadet Ships.*

L'AFRIQUE

Passenger ship (1f/2m). *L/B/D:* 408.5′ × 48.3′ × 27.7′ (124.5m × 14.7m × 8.4m). *Tons:* 5,404 grt. *Hull:* steel. *Comp.:* 127 crew; 458 pass. *Mach.:* triple expansion, 3,000 ihp, 2 screws; 11 kts. *Built:* Swan, Hunter, & Wigham Richardson, Ltd., Wallsend-on-Tyne, Eng.; 1907.

The scene of one of the worst disasters in the French merchant marine, *L'Afrique* was owned by the Compagnie des Chargeurs Réunis and sailed in its service between France and ports in French West Africa. The ship departed Bordeaux for Dakar on January 10, 1920, with a complement of 458 passengers in four classes and 127 crew. One day out, she was caught in a severe gale in the Bay of Biscay and began to experience engine trouble. Captain Le Du radioed for help and *L'Afrique*'s running mate *Ceylan* responded, but because of high seas, *Ceylan* was unable to secure a tow. The next day, the Belgian passenger ship *Anversville* and the Red Star Line's *Lapland* were also standing by as the ship was driven north in the storm. At about 0300 on January 12, *L'Afrique* was driven onto the Roche-Bonnie reefs, about 50 miles from La Rochelle, where she filled and sank. Two of *L'Afrique*'s lifeboats were launched just after midnight, but only thirty-two people — three passengers from third class, and the rest crew members and Senegalese soldiers traveling in steerage — survived to be taken aboard *Ceylan.* In human terms, the loss of *L'Afrique* was France's worst maritime disaster since that of LA BOURGOGNE in 1898.

Hocking, *Dictionary of Disasters at Sea.* Watson, *Disasters at Sea.*

HMS AGAMEMNON

3rd rate 64 (3m). *L/B:* 160′ × 45′ (48.8m × 13.7m). *Tons:* 1,348 bm. *Hull:* wood. *Comp.:* 520. *Arm.:* 26 × 24pdr, 26 × 12pdr, 12 × 6pdr. *Built:* Henry Adams, Buckler's Hard, Eng.; 1781.

HMS *Agamemnon* first saw action in the West Indies with Rear Admiral Richard Kempenfelt's squadron when it captured fifteen ships from a French convoy under Admiral Count Luc Urbain de Guichen, who was bound for the Caribbean. Four months later she was in Admiral Sir George Rodney's squadron at the Battle of the Saintes, April 11, 1782, in which the British defeated the French fleet under Rear Admiral Count François J. P. de Grasse, recouping a little of the glory (but none of the nation) they had lost at the Battle of the Chesapeake the previous summer. When the revolutionary French government declared war on Great Britain in 1793, *Agamemnon* came under command of Captain Horatio Nelson. Nelson sailed with Lord Howe's Mediterranean Fleet in the blockade of Toulon and in the capture of the Corsican ports of Bastia and Calvi, where Nelson lost his right eye. *Agamemnon* remained in the Mediterranean until 1796, a period during which Nelson molded his "band of brothers" and began to establish himself as an innovative, resolute, and daring commander. Nelson was quite fond of his command, and described *Agamemnon* as "without exception the finest 64 in the service."

The following year, *Agamemnon* was with the Channel Fleet when her crew were implicated in the mutiny of the Nore. Present at Nelson's great victory in the Battle of Copenhagen in 1801, her next significant assignment was in 1805 when she sailed with Vice Admiral Sir John Orde's fleet off Cadiz. In July she took part in Admiral Sir Robert Calder's action with the Combined Fleet off El Ferrol. Her squadron later came under the command of Admiral Lord Nelson. During the Battle of Trafalgar against the Franco-Spanish fleet, *Agamemnon* sailed in Nelson's weather column but escaped with relatively few casualties. After further service off Cadiz, she sailed for the West Indies where she took part in several engagements against French naval units and privateers. Over the next few years she sailed variously in the West Indies, the Baltic, off Portugal, and off South America. On June 20, 1809, while putting into the River Plate in a storm, she grounded on an unmarked reef and was lost, though without loss of life.

Hepper, *British Warship Losses*. Mackenzie, *Trafalgar Roll*.

HMS AGAMEMNON

James Watt-class battleship (1f/3m). *L/B/D:* 230.3′ × 55.3′ × 24.1′ (70.2m × 16.9m × 7.3m). *Tons:* 5,080 disp. *Hull:* wood. *Comp.:* 860. *Arm.:* 34 × 8″, 56 × 32pdr, 1 × 68pdr. *Mach.:* Penn trunk engine, 2,268 ihp, single screw; 11.24 kts. *Built:* Woolwich Dockyard; 1852.

Laid down in 1849, launched in 1852, and commissioned the following year, the ship-rigged steam battleship *Agamemnon* was the first warship built with screw pro-

pulsion, though other sailing vessels had been fitted with engines after commissioning. *Agamemnon*'s success was such that she remained the basic model for the first decade of Britain's steam battlefleet. As flagship of Rear Admiral Sir Edmund Lyons's Black Sea fleet (Captain William Mends commanding) during the Crimean War, she took part in the bombardment of Sevastopol on October 17, 1854. She also took part in the shelling of Fort Kinburn, at the mouth of the Dnieper one year later.

In 1857 the British government fitted out *Agamemnon* to carry 1,250 tons of telegraphic cable for the Atlantic Telegraph Company's first attempt to lay a transatlantic telegraph cable. Although this was unsuccessful, the following year the project was resumed. *Agamemnon* and her American counterpart USS *Niagara* spliced their cable ends in midatlantic on July 29 and then sailed for their respective continents. With William Thompson, the future Lord Kelvin, monitoring the progress of the 1,020 miles of cable, *Agamemnon* reached Valentia Bay in County Kerry, Ireland, on August 5, 1858. *Niagara* reached Trinity Bay, Newfoundland, the same day. Eleven days later, Queen Victoria sent a ninety-nine-word message to President James Buchanan, a process that took more than sixteen hours. (Three weeks later the cable failed and service was interrupted for eight years.) After service on the Caribbean and North American stations, *Agamemnon* was paid off in 1862 and sold in 1870.

Clarke, *Voice across the Sea*. Lambert, *Battleships in Transition*.

AGAY WRECK

L/B: 65–80′ × 23′ (20–24m × 7m). *Built:* mid-10th cent.

Situated in the Bay of Agay southeast of Cape Dramont, France (in 43°25′N, 6°52′E), the "wreck of the jars" was first noticed by fisherman who pulled up amphorae in their nets. Lying some 300 meters offshore at a depth of 40–50 meters, the Agay wreck was excavated by Alain Visquis and P. Danneyrol beginning in 1968. The Agay ship was a merchant vessel, probably Arab, and the recovered cargo consisted primarily of amphorae and other jars, most if not all of which are thought to have originated in Spain. Other miscellaneous items included basalt grinding stones, copper vessels, and some 250 bronze ingots. Also found with the larger vessel was the ship's boat, in which lay the remains of a man aged twenty-five–thirty-five years. Both the ship and the boat are early examples of the "skeleton-first" hull construction that originated in this period and which forms the basis of contemporary naval architecture. There are no joints in the planking, which is attached to the frames with iron nails.

Parker, *Ancient Shipwrecks of the Mediterranean*.

A. G. ROPES

Down Easter (3m). *L/B/D:* 258′ × 44.7′ × 28.5′ (78.6m × 13.6m × 8.7m). *Tons:* 2,342 reg. *Hull:* wood. *Des.:* John McDonald. *Built:* I. F. Chapman & Co., Bath, Me.; 1884.

Considered among the finest Down Easters ever built, the three-skysail yard ship *A. G. Ropes* was built by I. F. Chapman & Company for trade between New York, San Francisco, and Great Britain, in which she spent most of her career. The ship was named for Chapman's partner and son-in-law. *Ropes*'s first voyage — under the noted sail carrier Captain David H. Rivers — was celebrated for the rescue of the crew of the bark *Glenperis* off Cape Horn, an act for which *Ropes*'s crew were recognized by the British government. The most curious voyage of *A. G. Ropes* took place in 1889–90. After sustaining damage to the rudder-head off Cape Horn, *Ropes* was forced back to the Falkland Islands. Repairs to the steering gear took eleven days, and when the ship resumed her voyage it was by way of the Cape of Good Hope. The ship finally arrived in San Francisco on February 21, 1900, after a voyage of 204 days from New York and 104 days from the Falklands. *Ropes* was severely damaged in a Pacific typhoon en route from Baltimore to Hong Kong in 1906; after putting into Kobe, Japan, Captain Rivers took his jury-rigged ship back to New York. There she was sold to the Luckenbach Transportation and Wrecking Company and cut down for use as a barge. *A. G. Ropes* sank with the loss of three hands off Forked River, New Jersey, on December 26, 1913.

Lubbock, *Down Easters*. Matthews, *American Merchant Ships*.

AID

Ship. *Tons:* 300. *Hull:* wood. *Comp.:* 115–120. *Arm.:* 2 × 6pdr, 4 × 4pdr, 4 small. *Built:* Deptford Dockyard; 1562.

The Queen's ship *Aid* was one of three built in 1562 as war with France threatened. In the fall of the same year *Aid* was assigned to help supply the English garrison at Le Havre until the capture of the Huguenot-held port by loyalist forces in August 1563. *Aid*'s next important mission came in 1577, when the Adventurers to the North-West for the Discovery of the North-West Passage, or the Companye of Kathai, was formed to follow up Sir Martin Frobisher's discovery of Frobisher Bay on Baffin Island in GABRIEL the previous year. The inlet promised to be the much sought after Northwest Passage, but more important was his discovery of what was widely believed to be gold. *Aid* sailed as flagship of an expedition that included *Gabriel* and *Michael* and about 150 men. Departing in mid-May, the ships arrived at Baffin Island on July 17. They returned home at the end of the summer with three Eskimos — a man and a woman with her child, all of whom died after a month in England — and 200 tons of ore assayed as yielding a profit of £5 in gold and silver per ton.

On the basis of this hopeful but erroneous assessment, Frobisher sailed at the head of sixteen ships with a view to exploring the Northwest Passage, mining ore, and establishing a manned settlement. After taking possession of Greenland — renamed West England — in the name of the Queen, Frobisher and company continued to the west. In 1578 Frobisher Bay was filled with ice and after losing one ship to a floe, they sailed west into what they called Mistaken Strait, now Hudson Strait. The fleet doubled back to Frobisher Bay, where *Aid* was hulled below the waterline by an ice floe and repaired with a sheet of lead. After mining 1,350 tons of ore and erecting a house for future use (immediate plans for leaving a party there through the winter were abandoned), they sailed home. Five years of trying to extract precious metals from the ore brought home on the second and third voyages were fruitless; the Company of Cathay went under and the Baffin Island rocks were "throwne away to repayre the high-wayes."

As tensions between Spain and England worsened, *Aid* was rebuilt and in November 1580 took part in the reduction of Smerwick Fort in Ireland where a combined Spanish-Papal force had taken refuge. Again under Frobisher's command, *Aid* was one of two Queen's ships contributed to Sir Francis Drake's twenty-five-ship expedition to the Spanish West Indies in 1585. In October, the fleet anchored at Bayonne, Spain, where Drake compelled the governor to allow his ships to water and provision before they departed again on October 11. Proceeding to the Cape Verde Islands, Drake put Santiago, Porto Praya, and Santo Domingo to the torch when their inhabitants failed to ransom their towns. The English went on to ransom Santo Domingo and Cartagena, and sacked St. Augustine, Florida. They then sailed for Sir Walter Raleigh's colony at Roanoke, and returned to England with the colonists in July 1586.

Two years later, *Aid* was one of six ships in Drake's western squadron based at Plymouth to await the arrival of the Spanish Armada. She remained with the English fleet from the day of the first action on July 31 through the final defeat of the Spanish ships at the Battle of Grav-elines on August 8. In 1589, *Aid* again sailed with Drake as part of the poorly executed "Counter-Armada." The triple aim of this venture was to destroy the remaining Armada ships in their home ports in Spain and Portugal, restore the pretender Dom Antonio to the Portuguese throne, and seize the Azores as a base from which to attack the Spanish treasure fleets from the West Indies. The overly ambitious plan failed in all its primary objectives and returned to England. In 1590, *Aid* was broken up after a quarter century of service to the Elizabethan navy.

Glasgow, "Navy in the French Wars." Stefansson, *Three Voyages of Martin Frobisher*. Sugden, *Sir Francis Drake*.

HMS AJAX

Leander-class cruiser (1f/2m). *L/B/D:* 554.5′ × 56′ × 19′ (169m × 17.1m × 5.8m). *Tons:* 9,144 disp. *Hull:* steel. *Comp.:* 570. *Arm.:* 8 × 6″ (4x2), 4 × 4″, 12 × 0.5″ mg; 8 × 21″TT; 1 aircraft. *Armor:* 3.5″ belt, 1″ deck. *Mach.:* steam turbines, 72,000 shp, 4 screws; 32.5 kts. *Built:* Vickers-Armstrong, Barrow-in-Furness, Eng.; 1935.

On September 3, 1939, three hours after the British Admiralty broadcast the opening of World War II with the signal "Total Germany," HMS *Ajax* (Captain Charles Woodhouse) intercepted and sank the German merchant ship *Olinda,* the first merchant casualty of the war on either side. On October 27 *Ajax* became the flagship of Commodore Harry Harwood's South America Division. The British knew a German pocket battleship was prowling the South Atlantic, and on December 2 Harwood directed *Ajax* and EXETER to rendezvous with ACHILLES off the River Plate. At daybreak on December 13 they encountered ADMIRAL GRAF SPEE. In a classic cruiser deployment, *Ajax* and *Achilles* sailed together as the First Division to split *Graf Spee*'s fire between them and *Exeter*. At 0725, *Ajax* was straddled by a salvo of *Graf Spee*'s 11-inch shells that knocked out both after turrets; a little later another salvo destroyed the radio aerials. With *Exeter* also heavily damaged, at 0740 Harwood decided to pull back and shadow *Graf Spee* into Montevideo. Four days later, *Graf Spee*'s Captain Hans Langsdorff scuttled his ship in the estuary, and the Battle of the River Plate was over. *Ajax* subsequently was deployed to the eastern Mediterranean and took part in the D-day landings in Normandy on June 6, 1944. Following the war, Ajax was stationed in the Mediterranean, and in 1947 she was part of the flotilla that dogged the refugee ship EXODUS 1947. She was broken up at Cashmore, Newport, in 1949.

Pope, *Battle of the River Plate*.

A. J. FULLER

Down Easter (3m). *L/B/D:* 229.3′ × 41.5′ × 26′ dph (69.9m × 12.6m × 7.9m). *Tons:* 1,849 grt. *Hull:* wood. *Comp.:* 23. *Built:* John McDonald, Bath, Me.; 1881.

Owned primarily by Flint & Company of New York, and named for a shareholder who lived in Bath, Maine, the three-skysail yard *A. J. Fuller* was one of a dozen Down Easters built in 1881. Under the Flint house flag she sailed between New York, San Francisco, and Liverpool for ten years. In 1892, she was put in trade from East Coast ports, where she loaded case oil for the Orient or general cargo or coal to Hawaii, generally returning with sugar cane. It was while she was in that trade that Felix Riesenberg, who later became a master mariner in his own right, sailed in her before the mast. She was sold to the California Shipping Company in 1902 and used in trade between the Pacific Northwest and Australia, exporting lumber and importing coal. In 1912, she was purchased by the Northwestern Fisheries Company of San Francisco, who employed her in their seasonal salmon fisheries — sailing north in the spring with fishermen, cannery workers, and supplies, and returning in the fall with a full load of canned salmon. On October 18, 1918, while inward bound to Seattle in a heavy fog, she was rammed by the Japanese steamship *Mexico Maru* and sank in 40 fathoms.

Matthews, *American Merchant Ships*. Riesenberg, *Under Sail*.

AKAGI

Aircraft carrier. *L/B/D:* 855.2′ × 102.7′ × 28.6′ (260.7m × 31.3m × 8.7m). *Tons:* 41,300 disp. *Hull:* steel. *Comp.:* 2,000. *Arm.:* 66 aircraft; 6 × 8″, 12 × 4.7″, 28 × 25mm. *Armor:* 10″ belt. *Mach.:* geared turbines, 133,000 shp, 4 screws; 31 kts. *Built:* Kure Naval Dockyard, Kure, Japan; 1927.

Named for a mountain northwest of Tokyo, the *Akagi* was laid down in 1920 as one of four *Amagi*-class battlecruisers. These were abandoned in accordance with the Washington Naval Conference of 1922, but the hull of *Akagi* was kept and redesigned as an aircraft carrier, built without an island. (The original *Akagi* was to have received the same treatment but was destroyed in the 1922 earthquake and replaced by KAGA.) *Akagi* was reconfigured in 1935–38, the primary changes being the addition of a full-length flight deck and a small port-side superstructure, the only interruption to her otherwise plain profile.

Akagi saw service in China during the 1930s. In 1941 she was the flagship of Vice Admiral Chuichi Nagumo's First Air Fleet under Captain Kiichi Hasegawa. Training for the attack on the American fleet at Pearl Harbor be-

Flagship of the Japanese fleet at Pearl Harbor, the AKAGI *was one of four Japanese carriers sunk, six months later, at the Battle of Midway, the first decisive American victory of World War II. Courtesy Imperial War Museum, London.*

gan in September 1941. On November 26 a fleet of thirty ships including the carriers *Akagi,* KAGA, HIRYU, SORYU, SHOKAKU, and ZUIKAKU, and the battleships *Hiei* and KIRISHIMA, departed from its staging area at Hitokappu Bay at Etorufu Islands (one of the Kurile Islands subsequently lost to the Soviet Union). The task force sailed east towards a point north of Hawaii before turning south. Shortly after 0600 on December 7, 1941, the first strike of 183 planes lifted from the decks of *Akagi* and the other carriers, then about 220 miles north of Oahu. *Akagi*'s contribution included 15 dive bombers to attack battleship row, 12 torpedo planes to attack battleships, cruisers, and other ships in Pearl Harbor, and 10 fighters to attack Ford, Hickham, Kaneohe, and Wheeler airfields. *Akagi*'s second wave, launched at 0705, consisted of 18 dive bombers and 9 fighters.

At 0753, the flight radioed "Tora, Tora, Tora" ("Tiger, Tiger, Tiger"), signaling that total surprise had been achieved. The destruction was appalling and included 2,403 U.S. dead (2,008 from the Navy alone) and 1,178 wounded. Shipping losses included the complete loss of the battleships ARIZONA, CALIFORNIA, *Nevada, Oklahoma,* and *West Virginia,* the minelayer *Oglala,* and the target ship *Utah* (formerly BB31). In addition, the battleships *Maryland, Pennsylvania,* and *Tennessee,* light cruisers HELENA, *Honolulu,* and *Raleigh,* three destroyers, and four auxiliary craft were lightly damaged. Naval and Army aviation losses amounted to 239 of 447 planes. Japanese losses totaled 9 fighters, 15 bombers, 5 torpedo bombers, and 55 airmen out of 353 sorties flown.

On January 20, 1942, Nagumo's First Air Fleet, including *Akagi, Kaga, Shokaku,* and *Zuikaku,* carried out attacks in support of the Japanese landings at Rabaul, New Guinea, which fell three days later. In April, a force similar to the one that attacked Pearl Harbor, less *Kaga,* attacked Colombo, Ceylon (Sri Lanka), on April 5, and Trincomalee, on April 9. Although the Japanese sank the aircraft carrier HMS HERMES and the County-class cruisers HMS *Dorsetshire* and *Cornwall,* from Admiral Sir James Somerville's British Far Eastern Force, it was a Pyrrhic victory. The loss of 59 aircraft forced *Akagi* and two other carriers back to Japan for planes and new pilots whose inexperience was sorely felt at Midway.

Akagi was once again Nagumo's flagship at the Battle of Midway, fought on June 4–5, 1942. For the first attack on Midway Island, which consisted of land-based targets and not ships, the planes were armed with bombs, but Nagumo took the precaution of having a second wave armed with torpedoes, in case the U.S. fleet appeared. At 0700, strike leader Lieutenant Commander Joichi Tomonaga reported the need for a second attack on Midway itself, and an attack by Midway-based planes five minutes later, though ineffectual, convinced Nagumo that Midway still needed attention. At 0715 he ordered the planes on *Akagi* and *Kaga* to be rearmed with bombs. At 0728, a reconnaissance plane reported a U.S. fleet 240 miles from Midway and at 0809 confirmed this as being five cruisers and five destroyers. At this point Nagumo ordered the second strike on Midway, only to learn eleven minutes later that "the enemy is accompanied by what appears to be a carrier." Nagumo's dilemma — whether to attack Midway, or the carrier (in fact there were three, USS ENTERPRISE, HORNET, and YORKTOWN) — was compounded by the fact that there was probably a carrier-based strike on its way towards him, and only half of his planes were now equipped with torpedoes that he could not launch until he had recovered the first wave of Midway planes, which began landing at 0837. Rejecting the idea of sending torpedo planes from *Hiryu* and *Soryu* because there was no fighter cover available, he scheduled a full-fledged torpedo attack for 1030.

At a little past 0930, 15 torpedo bombers from *Hornet* made a desperate run at the Japanese fleet; none survived. Fourteen torpedo planes from *Enterprise* went in next (4 survived), followed by 17 from *Yorktown* (2 returned). The Japanese fleet remained unscathed. In preparation for the 1030 launch, the Japanese planes were lined up, fully armed, and fueled, when at about 1025 dive bombers from *Enterprise* and *Yorktown* struck from 18,000 feet. The torpedo attacks had forced the Japanese combat air patrol practically down to sea level, and they were not prepared for dive bombers. Within three minutes, *Kaga*, *Akagi*, and *Soryu* had been put out of operation. Nagumo transferred his flag to the light cruiser *Nagara* at about 1100, and at 0455, June 5, the still-burning hulk was torpedoed by the destroyers *Noake* and *Arashi* in position 30°30′N, 179°40′W, and she sank with the loss of more than 270 crew. The outcome at Midway turned the tide of the Pacific war decisively in favor of the United States.

Prange, *At Dawn We Slept; Miracle at Midway*. Stephen, *Sea Battles in Close-Up*.

CSS ALABAMA

(ex-*Enrica*) Auxiliary bark (1f/3m). *L/B/D:* 220′ × 31′9″ × 14′ (67.1m × 9.7m × 4.3m). *Tons:* 1,050 tons. *Hull:* wood. *Comp.:* 148. *Arm.:* 6 × 32pdr, 1 × 110pdr, 1 × 68pdr. *Mach.:* direct-acting engine, 600 ihp, 1 screw; 13 kts. *Built:* Laird Bros., Ltd., Birkenhead, Eng.; 1862.

In the history of commerce warfare, CSS *Alabama* was the most successful raider in terms of numbers of vessels seized — capturing and burning 55 ships, seizing and bonding 10 more. James Dunwoody Bulloch, the Confederate naval agent in Europe responsible for creating a viable high-seas fleet from scratch, ordered Hull No. 290; she was christened *Enrica* and put down the Mersey River on July 29, 1862. Charles Francis Adams, the U.S. minister in London, insisted that the sale of the ship violated Britain's 1861 declaration of neutrality. In a manner of speaking, she did not, for it was not until after the ship had been armed from the supply ships *Agrippina* and *Bahama* off the Azores that Captain Raphael Semmes commissioned her as CSS *Alabama* on August 24, 1862.

Cruising from the Azores, to Newfoundland, and south to the Caribbean, *Alabama* sank 27 ships between September and December of 1862. On January 11, 1863, she sank the auxiliary schooner USS Hatteras of the Gulf Coast Blockading Squadron about 20 miles south of

"*The Fight between the* ALABAMA *and the* KEARSARGE," *a woodcut from the* Illustrated London News *showing the end of the Confederacy's most successful commerce raider off Cherbourg, France, June 19, 1864. Courtesy Library of Congress.*

Galveston. After putting the captured Union crew ashore in Jamaica, *Alabama* continued on her way. On June 20, while cruising off Brazil, she overhauled the Philadelphia merchant bark *Conrad*, which Semmes armed and commissioned as CSS *Tuscaloosa*, Lieutenant John Low commanding. (*Tuscaloosa* cruised in the South Atlantic for six months before being seized by the British in Simon's Bay, South Africa, on December 26.) Visiting South Africa in the autumn of 1863, *Alabama* sailed into the Indian Ocean and as far east as Singapore. Semmes then returned to Europe for an extensive refit, anchoring at Cherbourg on June 11, 1864.

Semmes fully intended to remain at Cherbourg for several months, but the Union government had recently persuaded the French to impose a 24-hour limit on the stay of Confederate-flag ships in French ports. In the meantime, the screw sloop USS *Kearsarge* under Captain John A. Winslow arrived at Cherbourg from Flushing, Belgium, on June 14. Attempting to embark U.S. sailors landed from *Alabama*, Winslow was told he was violating French neutrality and left. Preferring that his ship suffer honorable defeat rather than an ignominious blockade, Semmes is reported to have told his Lieutenant John M. Kell, "Although the Confederate government has ordered me to avoid engagement with the enemy cruisers, I am tired of running from that flaunting rag!" On June 19, *Alabama* sailed out of Cherbourg and, still within sight of the spectators lining the shore, opened fire on *Kearsarge* at 1057. After so long at sea, *Alabama* was no match for *Kearsarge* and was reduced to a sinking condition in an hour. Semmes repeatedly struck his flag, but before *Kearsarge* could act, he and some 40 others were rescued by the British yacht *Deerhound* — a crime for which Semmes was arrested in December 1865 on orders from U.S.

Navy Secretary Gideon Welles. While the sinking of the *Alabama* did not affect the outcome of the Civil War, her loss was a blow to Confederate morale.

The devastation caused by the *Alabama* and her sister raiders, especially FLORIDA and SHENANDOAH, has frequently been cited as one cause of the decline of U.S. international shipping in the latter half of the nineteenth century. An immediate consequence of their efforts was the 900 percent rise in insurance rates for U.S.-flag ships, and the resulting transfer of some 900 ships to foreign registry. Following the war, the United States insisted that Britain be held liable for the destruction wrought by British-built commerce raiders. These proceedings came to be known as the *Alabama* claims, as *Alabama* alone accounted for as much as $5 million in losses. After several false starts, the claims were finally resolved under the Treaty of Washington (1871), by which the United States and Great Britain submitted to arbitration by an international tribunal composed of representatives from Britain, the United States, Italy, Switzerland, and Brazil. The tribunal found that Britain had not exercised "due diligence" and awarded the United States $15.5 million in damages.

Alabama's story did not end there. On November 7, 1984, French divers from the minesweeper *Circé* discovered the remains of the ship lying in about 195 feet of water six miles off Cherbourg. The site is under the protection of a Joint French and American authority.

Guérout, "Engagement between the C.S.S. *Alabama* and the U.S.S. *Kearsarge*." Leary, "'*Alabama*' vs. '*Kearsarge*.'" Robinson, *Shark of the Confederacy*. Semmes, *Memoirs of Service Afloat*. Silverstone, *Warships of the Civil War Navies*.

USS ALABAMA (BB-60)

South Dakota-class battleship. *L/B/D:* 680' × 108.2' × 29.3' (207.3m × 33.2m × 8.9m). *Tons:* 35,000 disp. *Hull:* steel. *Comp.:* 1,793. *Arm.:* 9 × 16" (3x3), 20 × 5", 24 × 40mm, 40 × 20mm. *Armor:* 12.2" belt, 5.8" deck. *Mach.:* geared turbines, 130,000 shp, 4 screws; 28 kts. *Built:* Norfolk Navy Yard, Portsmouth, Va.; 1942.

USS *Alabama*'s first overseas assignment was with the British Home Fleet in the summer of 1943, when she and her sister ship *South Dakota* sailed on Arctic convoys and in diversionary maneuvers aimed at diverting German attention from the Allied landings in Sicily. Detached from this duty in August, she sailed for the South Pacific, arriving in the New Hebrides in September. *Alabama*'s subsequent career in the Pacific theater of World War II fairly mirrors the course of the Allied advance against Japan. She escorted fast carrier forces in operations in the Gilbert Islands in November; the Marshall Islands in late

January and February; the Caroline Islands in March; and on the coast of New Guinea in April 1944. Following a month of repairs in Majuro, Marshall Islands (captured on January 31), *Alabama* rejoined Task Force 58 for the invasion of the Mariana Islands in June, taking part in the Battle of the Philippine Sea, June 19–20, and supporting the landings on Saipan and elsewhere. After upkeep at Eniwetok in the Marshalls, she became flagship of Rear Admiral E. W. Hanson's Battleship Division 9. She supported landings in the Carolines before heading east for the invasion of the Philippines in mid-October. She operated in the Philippines through December. After weathering the typhoon of December 18, in which the destroyers USS *Hull, Monaghan,* and *Spence* were sunk, she returned to Puget Sound, Washington, for overhaul. *Alabama* rejoined TF 58 in May, providing gunfire support against stubborn Japanese positions on Okinawa (five weeks after the American landings on April 1) and supported carrier operations in the Ryukyus and Kyushu, the southernmost of the Japanese main islands. As part of the 3rd Fleet, in July *Alabama* took part in the bombardment of targets in the heart of Japan, including industrial sites only eight miles north of Tokyo.

Following the Japanese surrender on August 15, *Alabama* remained in Japanese waters until September 20, when she embarked 700 sailors en route to San Pedro as part of Operation Magic Carpet. Decommissioned at Seattle in 1947, she remained in reserve until 1962. Two years later she was towed to Mobile, Alabama, where she was opened to the public as a floating memorial and museum ship.

U.S. Navy, *DANFS*.

USS ALBACORE (AGSS-569)

Submarine. *L/B/D:* 203.8' × 27.3' x 18.6' (62.1m × 8.3m × 5.7m). *Tons:* 1,242/1,837 disp. *Hull:* steel. *Comp.:* 36. *Mach.:* diesel/electric, 1 screw; 25/20+ kts. *Built:* Portsmouth Naval Shipyard, Kittery, Me.; 1953.

The third naval vessel (and second submarine) so named, USS *Albacore* was built specifically as a test model for new concepts in submarine design. One of the Navy's primary aims was to develop a hull of optimal hydrodynamic efficiency that could also accommodate a nuclear propulsion plant, the design for which was just under way. Since nuclear power required no oxygen, as diesel engines did, and as there were ways of converting carbon dioxide to oxygen for the crew, this would mean that submarines could operate submerged for almost unlimited periods. One of the most obvious differences between *Albacore* and her predecessors is the rounded surfaces of her hull and the abandonment of deck guns and other fittings that impede hydrodynamic efficiency. This design concept later became universal. World War II submarines, by contrast, looked like narrow boats with pointed bows and flat decks. *Albacore* undertook a variety of cruises to test propeller, rudder, and dive plane configurations, sound reduction materials, sonar and radio systems, and emergency recovery devices. These resulted in faster, quieter, safer, and much more maneuverable submarines. *Albacore* was decommissioned in 1972 and is now on exhibit at the Portsmouth Naval Shipyard.

U.S. Navy, *DANFS*.

ALBATROS

(ex-*Alk*) Schooner (2m). *L/B/D:* 82.8′ × 20.8′ × 9.8′ (25.2m × 6.3m × 3m). *Tons:* 93 grt. *Hull:* steel. *Comp.:* 19. *Mach.:* aux., 1 screw. *Built:* Rijkswerf, Amsterdam; 1920.

Originally named *Alk,* the schooner later known as *Albatros* spent two decades working the North Sea before being purchased by the German government in 1937. Twelve years later she was purchased by Royal Rotterdam Lloyd for use as a training ship for future officers. Her small size made her ideal for this kind of work as the dozen trainees could receive personal attention from the six or so professional crew. While under Dutch ownership she sailed extensively in the North Sea, with occasional voyages as far as Spain and Portugal.

The American yachtsman Ernest K. Gann purchased *Albatros* in 1956, rerigged her as a brigantine, and spent three years cruising in the Pacific. In 1959, Ocean Academy, Ltd., of Darien, Connecticut, acquired the former training ship with the intent of putting her back in that line of work. Over the next three years, Dr. Christopher B. Sheldon and his wife, Dr. Alice Strahan Sheldon, ran programs for up to fourteen students in the Caribbean and eastern Pacific. On May 3, 1961, while en route from Progreso, Mexico, to Nassau, the Bahamas, she was hit by a white squall about 125 miles west of the Dry Tortugas and sank almost instantly, taking with her four students, Alice Sheldon, and the cook. The loss of *Albatros* prompted the U.S. Coast Guard to undertake a thorough review of the stability and design requirements for sailing school ships, the new rules for which were codified in the Sailing School Vessels Act of 1982. *White Squall,* a film based on the ship's tragic loss, was released in 1995.

Press reports. Underhill, *Sail Training and Cadet Ships*. Film: *White Squall.*

ALBENGA WRECK

Hull: wood. *Built:* Mediterranean; ca. 100 BCE.

The Albenga wreck is that of a sailing merchant ship that sank in 44°3′N, 8°15′E — about 1 kilometer east of Albenga, Italy, in the Gulf of Genoa. Lying at a depth of 40–42 meters, the wreck was first located in modern times when fishermen recovered amphorae from the site in 1930. The wreck was further examined in 1950, and systematic archaeological excavations under the direction of Dr. Nino Lamboglia began in 1957. Because the wreck settled into a bed of river silt, the hull and bottom were well preserved. Lamboglia's investigations revealed that the frames were of oak, the planking of soft wood, and the hull was sheathed with lead sheets fastened with copper nails. The main mast, which survived in situ, was square in section as far as the main-beam and round above. The Albenga ship's original carrying capacity has been estimated at 11,000 to 13,500 amphorae, implying a gross tonnage of as much as 500 to 600 tons in modern terms. Approximately 1,200 amphorae were recovered from the wreck, and a red residue found in many of the jars suggests that the main cargo was wine. The jars were wedged in place in the hold with pumice, rather than the usual brushwood. Some fine table wares, found stacked between the amphorae, were also part of the cargo, while coarser cooking pots, jugs, and storage vessels probably belonged to the galley.

Parker, *Ancient Shipwrecks of the Mediterranean*. Taylor, ed., *Marine Archaeology*. Throckmorton, *Shipwrecks and Archaeology*.

ALBERT BALLIN

(later *Hansa, Sovietsky Sojus*) Liner (2f/4m). *L/B/D:* 602.2′ × 78.7′ (183.6m × 24m). *Tons:* 20,815 grt. *Hull:* steel. *Comp.:* 1st 250; 2nd 340, 3rd 1,060. *Mach.:* steam turbines, 2 screws; 16 kts. *Built:* Blohm & Voss, Hamburg; 1923.

In 1913, the Hamburg-Amerika Linie (Hapag) was the largest merchant shipping fleet in the world, thanks in great part to the company's brilliant general director, Albert Ballin, the driving force behind such world-class transatlantic liners as *Imperator* (later the BERENGARIA), *Vaterland* (LEVIATHAN), and *Bismarck* (MAJESTIC). Overwhelmed by the losses of the Great War, Ballin killed himself in 1919. When the company began building new ships for the transatlantic trade in 1923, the first pair were the sister ships *Albert Ballin* and *Deutschland*. (The slightly larger *Hamburg* and *New York* entered service in 1926 and 1927.) *Albert Ballin* made her maiden voy-

Named for the principal architect of Germany's great passenger shipping fleet in the years before World War I, ALBERT BALLIN *is seen here before her first renaming in 1934. Courtesy The Mariners' Museum, Newport News, Virginia.*

age from Hamburg to Southampton and New York in 1923. She underwent several modifications in the late 1920s. Tourist-class accommodations were added in 1928 (the second class was dropped altogether in 1930), and she was reengined in 1929 to achieve a speed of 19 knots. In 1934 she was lengthened to 645′8″ and her speed increased to 21.5 knots. The following year, Germany's newly installed Nazi government ordered her renamed on the grounds that Ballin was Jewish; in 1936 her first-class accommodations were changed to cabin class, tourist, and third class. Her last transatlantic voyage was completed in 1939, after which she served as an accommodation and training ship. Mined off Warnemünde on March 3, 1945, while taking part in the evacuation of Gdynia, she was taken over by the Soviet Union after the war and entered service with one funnel as the *Sovietsky Sojus*, sailing out of Vladivostok. Overhauled in 1971, she was scrapped in 1981.

Bonsor, *North Atlantic Seaway.* Braynard & Miller, *Fifty Famous Liners.*

HMS ALECTO

Steam sloop (1f/3m). *L/B/D:* 164′ × 32.7′ × 12.6′ (50m × 10m × 3.8m). *Tons:* 796 bm. *Hull:* wood. *Mach.:* direct-acting engine, 280 ihp, sidewheels; 8.5 kts. *Built:* Chatham Dockyard; 1839.

Named for one of the furies of Greek mythology, *Alecto* was a brigantine-rigged sidewheel steamer. She served for six years with the Mediterranean fleet. Built at a time when the Admiralty were beginning to believe that screw propulsion was more efficient than paddlewheels, *Alecto* is best remembered for her role in a series of trials against HMS RATTLER, a near sister ship fitted with a single screw instead of paddles. In the spring of 1845, the Admiralty sponsored a series of twelve trials between the two ships. These included races under steam, under sail alone, one under steam towing the other not under power, and the most famous, a tug-of-war held on April 3. In this, the two ships were joined by a line running from stern to stern. *Alecto* got steam up first, towing *Rattler* at about 2 knots before the latter's engines were engaged. Within five minutes, *Rattler* had brought *Alecto* to a standstill and soon managed to pull the sidewheeler stern first at about 2.8 knots. Although the results seem to have been a foregone conclusion, the demonstrations were good publicity for the Admiralty's subsequent adoption of the screw as the preferred means of auxiliary, and later primary, propulsion. At the end of 1845, *Alecto* resumed more regular assignments, including five years on the American station, and several years on the coast of Africa. She was broken up in 1865.

Brown, *Before the Ironclad.*

HMS ALERT

Screw sloop (1f/3m). *L/B:* 160′ × 32′ (48.8m × 9.8m). *Tons:* 751 bm. *Hull:* wood. *Arm.:* 17 × 32pdr. *Mach.:* steam, 1 screw. *Built:* Pembroke Dockyard, Wales; 1856.

Following the search for Sir John Franklin's expedition in the mid-nineteenth century, British interest in Arctic exploration waned. When the British again turned north, it was to conduct research in terrestrial magnetism and the search for the north magnetic pole. In 1875, the Admiralty dispatched HMS *Alert* and *Discovery* under the command of Captain George S. Nares. A veteran of HMS RESOLUTE in the last government-sponsored search for Franklin, Nares was reassigned from command of the CHALLENGER expedition specifically to take charge of the British Arctic Expedition.

The two ships left Portsmouth on May 29, 1875, and after taking aboard dogs in Greenland, proceeded up the Davis Strait as far as Ellesmere Island's Lady Franklin Bay. *Discovery* remained there while *Alert* pressed on to Cape Sheridan (82°24′N), 53 miles to the north — a new farthest-north point. She remained icebound from September 1, 1875, to July 31, 1876. In April 1876, separate parties were sent out to explore. Commander Markham and his men reached 83°20′N — 400 miles shy of the

This photo, by either Thomas Mitchell or George White, shows men from the ALERT *cutting ice blocks during an expedition to Greenland in the 1870s. Courtesy National Maritime Museum, Greenwich.*

North Pole, and Lieutenant Beaumont's expedition to northeast Greenland reached 82°18′N. These parties and the ships' companies were stricken with scurvy, and several men died before the expedition was brought under control. *Alert* began drifting south in July; in August she and *Discovery* got under way again from Discovery Harbor, reaching England in October. The expedition proved that Greenland was an island and laid to rest the theory of an ice-free polar sea. (In honor of *Alert*'s achievement, the world's northernmost permanently manned settlement, on Ellesmere Island, is named Alert.)

Nares again commanded *Alert* in 1878, on a two-year hydrographic survey of the Strait of Magellan. Laid up at Chatham on her return, the ship was refitted and donated to the United States to sail in Captain Winfield Scott Schley's expedition for the relief of the stranded Adolphus Greely expedition on Ellesmere Island.

Nares, *Narrative of a Voyage to the Polar Sea.*

ALFRED

(ex-*Black Prince*) Ship (3m). *Tons:* 440. *Comp.:* 220. *Arm.:* 20 × 9pdr, 10 × 6pdr. *Built:* John Wharton(?), Philadelphia; 1774.

The merchantman *Black Prince* made two voyages to England before being requisitioned for a warship by the Continental Congress on November 4, 1775. Renamed for Alfred the Great, the ninth-century British king credited with building England's first fleet, *Alfred* was put under command of Captain Dudley Saltonstall. She was made flagship of Commodore Esek Hopkins's eight-ship squadron (including *Columbus*, *Cabot*, *Andrew Doria*, Providence, *Fly*, Hornet, and Wasp), which occupied Nassau for two weeks in March 1776. On October 26, Captain John Paul Jones (a lieutenant on her first voyage) left New London for a cruise off Nova Scotia during which *Alfred* captured nine ships before returning to Boston on December 26. The following August, under Captain Elisha Hinman, *Alfred* and *Raleigh* sailed for France for military supplies. Returning via the West Indies, the two ships were engaged by the British ships HMS *Ariadne* (20 guns) and *Ceres* (14) on March 29, 1778. *Alfred* was captured and acquired by the Royal Navy at Barbados. She was sold out of service in 1782.

McCusker, *"Alfred," the First Continental Flagship;* "American Invasion of Nassau in the Bahamas."

ALICE S. WENTWORTH

(ex-*Lizzie A. Tolles*) Schooner (2m). *L/B/D:* 73.2′ bp × 23.7′ × 7.5′ dph (22.3m × 7.2m × 2.3m). *Tons:* 68 grt. *Hull:* wood. *Comp.:* 2. *Built:* South Norwalk, Conn.; 1863.

Built originally for the brick trade between the Connecticut shore of Long Island Sound and the Hudson River, *Lizzie A. Tolles* was purchased by the Stevens family of Wells, Maine, in the 1890s. In 1905, Captain Arthur A. Stevens so thoroughly rebuilt her that was she was documented as new; he also renamed the schooner for his niece. *Alice S. Wentworth* worked in the coastal trades out of Kennebunk and Portland until her purchase by Zebulon Tilton of Martha's Vineyard in 1921. Together, the two went on to become the most celebrated schooner and master of their day.

The trucking industry had already begun to make its presence felt among the working fleets, but there was still money to be made trading in lumber and nails, Long Island oysters, paving oil from New Jersey, plumbing supplies and shingling from New York, and, on one occasion, ten 10,000-gallon fuel tanks, carried two at a time, from New Bedford to Nantucket. Zeb disdained mechanical devices and only acquired an auxiliary yawl boat when it became clear that he could not trade competitively without one. During the depression, he also carried passengers for afternoon cruises. Long popular with celebrities and the well-to-do, the Vineyard offered up an interesting cast of day trippers, including the stars of stage and screen James Cagney and Katherine Cornell.

In 1939, Zeb was in debt and *Wentworth* was seized and sold at a Marshall's auction to Captain Ralph Parker, who formed the Schooner *Alice S. Wentworth* Associates and hired Zeb as captain. Shareholders included not only Cagney, Cornell, and tobacco heir Griswold Lorillard, but shopkeepers and other admirers from New Bedford to Nantucket. Zeb and the *Wentworth* worked together until 1942, when Zeb, age seventy-five, was laid up after an eye operation. By the time he was ready to put to sea again, *Alice S. Wentworth* had been sold to Parker J. Hall, the first of eight owners who would sail her in a variety of trades in Maine waters. From about 1959 she operated as a

passenger boat out of Rockland and later Boston. In 1974, while awaiting restoration, she was destroyed in a gale.

Burroughs, *Zeb.* Leavitt, *Wake of the Coasters.*

ALLIANCE

(ex-*Hancock*) Frigate (3m). *L/B/D:* 151′ × 36′ x 12.5′ (46m × 11m × 3.8m). *Tons:* 900. *Hull:* wood. *Comp.:* 300. *Arm.:* 28 × 12pdr, 8 × 9pdr. *Built:* William & James K. Hackett, Essex, Mass.; 1777.

Launched as *Hancock,* but renamed in recognition of the French entry into the American Revolution against Britain, *Alliance* was one of the most celebrated American ships of the war. Her first mission, under Captain Pierre Landais, was to carry the Marquis de Lafayette to France to plead for more support for the colonists. She left Boston on January 4, 1779. A mutiny by pro-British crew was discovered and suppressed and the ship went on to capture two prizes before landing at Brest after twenty-three days at sea. Benjamin Franklin then assigned the ship to Captain John Paul Jones's squadron. Landais resented the assignment, and he is believed to have deliberately rammed the flagship, BONHOMME RICHARD, during the convoy's passage from Brest to Bourdeaux in June. While taking part in Jones's raiding cruise around the British Isles in August and September, Landais was repeatedly insubordinate though *Alliance* captured three ships before rounding the north of Scotland. During *Bonhomme Richard*'s epic fight with HMS *Serapis* on September 23, Landais at first stood off from the battle and then fired broadsides into the grappled ships that caused as much damage and death to the Americans as to the British. After the battle, *Alliance* sailed with Jones's squadron to the Netherlands, where Landais was relieved of command.

On December 27, flying Jones's flag, *Alliance* slipped the British blockade off the Texel and sailed down the English Channel and then south to La Coruña, Spain, before returning to Brest. Although Franklin urged Jones to load a cargo of arms and supplies and return to the United States at once, Jones delayed and traveled to Paris. While he was away, Landais appeared at Brest and usurped command of his old vessel. Although the French offered to stop *Alliance,* by force if necessary, Jones let the ship sail under Landais, whose shipmates later locked him up because they thought he was insane.

Captain John Barry assumed command of *Alliance* at Boston in September 1780, but the ship was not ready for sea until February 1781. When she sailed for France, her passengers included George Washington's former aide-de-camp Colonel John Laurens and Thomas Paine. After only three weeks at Brest, she sailed for home in company with the former French East Indiaman *Marquis de Lafayette* loaded with arms and supplies for the Continental Army. On April 2, *Alliance* captured the privateer brigs *Mars* and *Minerva*. Prize crews were put aboard both, but again the French proved fickle allies. *Minerva* sailed for France, and *Marquis de Lafayette* later abandoned Barry, only to be captured by the British.

On May 27, still struggling for home, *Alliance* was engaged by the British sloops HMS *Trepassy* and *Atalanta* (both 14 guns). Unmaneuverable in the light airs, *Alliance* could not position herself against the British ships, which pounded her repeatedly from positions astern. Barry was seriously wounded but refused to surrender, and when the wind sprang up he worked his ship between his opponents and forced them both to surrender. *Alliance* finally returned to Boston on June 6.

The American Revolution ended with the surrender of General Cornwallis's army at Yorktown and on December 24, she embarked the Marquis de Lafayette for his return to France, arriving at Brest on January 17, 1782. Two months later, she sailed for home with dispatches from Benjamin Franklin, but contrary weather made for a long crossing to New London, where she arrived on May 13. *Alliance* put to sea again in August and, as peace still was not formally declared, took eight prizes. Two were returned to the United States and the others accompanied *Alliance* to France where they arrived in October. Two months later Barry was ordered to the West Indies for a consignment of gold, only to find that it had already been loaded aboard the American warship *Duc de Lauzan*. Sailing as an escort, *Alliance* fought off an attack by the frigates HMS *Alarm* (32 guns) and *Sybil* (28) and the sloop of war *Tobago* (14) on March 11, 1783. None of the combatants knew that peace had been achieved through the Treaty of Paris in January. These were the last shots of the American Revolution.

Alliance returned to Newport, and in June was ordered by Congress to carry a cargo of tobacco from Philadelphia to France. The ship grounded leaving Newport, but no damage was detected until after she had left the Delaware, when a leak forced her back to Philadelphia. Funds were unavailable for her repair, and the last ship of the Continental Navy was sold out of service in August 1785, to John Coburn, who in turn sold her to Robert Morris, formerly Agent of Marine of the Continental Congress. Morris converted her for merchant service to China and under Captain Thomas Read *Alliance* sailed for Canton in June 1787, becoming only the eighth U.S.-flag vessel to enter that port, on December 22. She returned to Phila-

delphia on September 17, 1788. Her subsequent career is unknown, except that she was finally abandoned on Petty Island on the Delaware River.

U.S. Navy, *DANFS*.

ALOHA

Bark (3m). *L/B/D:* 216′ × 35′ × 16′ (65.8m × 10.7m 4.9m). *Tons:* 659 grt. *Hull:* steel. *Comp.:* 39 crew. *Mach.:* steam, 1 screw. *Des.:* Clinton Crane. *Built:* Fore River Shipbuilding Co., Quincy, Mass.; 1910.

The bark *Aloha* was the second yacht of the name owned by Arthur Curtiss James, a prominent industrialist and commodore of the New York Yacht Club. James's previous yachts included CORONET and the first *Aloha,* a 160-foot steam brigantine in which he had sailed to Japan. He intended to sail *Aloha* on a round-the-world voyage. *Aloha* made several voyages to the Mediterranean and the Red Sea before World War I restricted her to American waters. In 1917, she was transferred to the U.S. Navy and served as the flagship of Rear Admiral Cameron McRae Winslow, Inspector of Naval Districts, East Coast, until 1919.

In September 1921, James and a party of friends embarked on his long-awaited world cruise, sailing from New York to the Caribbean, through the Panama Canal, across the North Pacific to Japan and continuing west across the Indian Ocean, up the Red Sea and to Marseilles, where the passengers' voyage officially ended. *Aloha* met fickle or contrary winds and was forced to motor much of the way, stopping at exotic ports. Following this voyage, she continued to sail on extended cruises to Europe and along the East Coast until she was broken up in 1938.

Robinson, *Legendary Yachts*. U.S. Navy, *DANFS*.

ALTMARK

(later *Uckermark*) Tanker. *L/B/D:* 463′ × 68′ x 27′ (141.1m × 20.7m × 8.2m). *Tons:* 7,021 grt. *Hull:* steel. *Comp.:* 130. *Mach.:* geared turbines; 22 kts. *Built:* Blohm & Voss, Hamburg; 1938.

Named for a region of Germany, *Altmark* was an unarmed German tanker that served as a supply ship and repository for captured seamen for a number of German surface raiders. On August 3, 1939, she sailed from Wilhelmshaven under Captain Heinrich Dau. After refueling in Port Arthur, Texas, she rendezvoused with the pocket battleship ADMIRAL GRAF SPEE near the Azores on August 28. After *Graf Spee*'s loss in December, *Altmark* re-

This painting by Norman Wilkinson, one of the finest British war artists of World War II, shows the British destroyer COSSACK *coming alongside the auxiliary oiler* ALTMARK, *stern to the land, to liberate hundreds of POWs originally captured by the German raider* GRAF SPEE. *Courtesy National Maritime Museum, Greenwich.*

mained in the South Atlantic for a month before making for home and entered Norwegian waters in February. Knowing there were 299 British merchant seamen aboard, HMS *Arethusa* attempted to search the ship, but was prevented from doing so by the Norwegian torpedo boats *Kjell* and *Skarv*. Prime Minister Winston Churchill then ordered the destroyer HMS COSSACK, under Captain Philip Vian, to violate Norwegian neutrality and rescue the men. On February 16, 1940, *Cossack* entered Jössing Fjord near Bergen. A crew boarded *Altmark* with the cry, "The Navy's here!" and rescued their compatriots. Otherwise unscathed, *Altmark* returned to Germany and, renamed *Uckermark,* was assigned to the cruisers GNEISENAU and SCHARNHORST and commerce raider *Michel.* On November 30, 1942, she was berthed at Yokohama, Japan, when she blew up.

Bennett, *Battle of the River Plate.* Frischauer & Jackson, *The Navy's Here!*

ALVIN

Submersible. *L/B/D:* 22′ × 8′ × 7′ (7m × 2.4m × 2.1m). *Tons:* 16 disp. *Hull:* steel sphere; aluminum frame. *Comp.:* 3. *Mach.:* lead-acid batteries, 3 screws; 1 kt. *Des.:* Bud Froelich. *Built:* General Mills, Minneapolis, Minn., and Hahn & Clay, Houston, Tex. (sphere); 1964.

Irked by the fact that oceanographers had no way to observe the workings of the ocean depths except through

what they could measure or capture from the deck of a surface ship, Allyn Vine proposed the development of a submarine with windows. At a meeting of oceanographers held in Washington, D.C., in 1956, Vine, a Woods Hole Oceanographic Institute ocean engineer, observed that

> a good instrument can measure almost anything better than a person can if you know what you want to measure. . . . But people are so versatile, they can sense things to be done and can investigate problems. I find it difficult to imagine what kind of instrument should have been put on the BEAGLE instead of Charles Darwin.

Six years later, the Office of Naval Research and Woods Hole contracted with General Mills/Litton Industries to build the Navy's first Deep Submergence Research Vessel, which was commissioned on June 5, 1964, with the name *Alvin,* for ALlyn VINe.

Though designed specifically for oceanographic research to be operated by Woods Hole, *Alvin* had been paid for by the Navy, for which she has undertaken several search and recovery missions. The first of these was to find a hydrogen bomb lost in the sea about five miles southeast of Palomares, Spain, after a U.S. Air Force B-52 collided with a KC-135 tanker plane during refueling on January 17, 1966. Less than a month later, *Alvin* and the less maneuverable *Aluminaut* began searching for the missing bomb in an area 135 miles square and over 2,600 feet deep. On March 15, during the nineteenth dive, Marvin McCamis, Cal Wilson, and Art Bartlett located the bomb, which was finally recovered from a depth of 2,800 feet on April 7.

In 1985, *Alvin* veteran Bob Ballard began planning a search for RMS TITANIC. On August 31, following initial site research by a French team, cameras on the Argo, a remotely operated vehicle (ROV) tethered to the research ship *Knorr,* located the sunken liner at a depth of 3,780 meters. The next July, Ballard, Dudley Foster, and Ralph Hollis descended in *Alvin,* to which was tethered the ROV Jason Junior. After a three-hour, fifty-minute search on their first dive, they became the first people to see the majestic liner since her tragic sinking on April 14, 1912.

While these two spectacular investigations are the best known of *Alvin*'s research, the submersible has been used in more than 2,000 scientific dives since 1967. Operating first from a makeshift pontoon mother ship named *Lulu* (for Vine's mother), and since 1982 from a variety of other vessels, *Alvin* has served as a vehicle for groundbreaking research of the ocean floor and submarine canyons, examining geological features and gathering biological specimens — including a swordfish that wedged its sword between *Alvin*'s passenger sphere and the outer frame at a depth of 2,000 feet. On October 16, 1968, *Alvin* slipped out of her cradle while being launched and sank in 1,535 meters; she was recovered on Labor Day, 1969, after being located by *Aluminaut*. In 1974 the original sphere was replaced by a titanium one, and the same year *Alvin* conducted joint research of the Mid-Atlantic Ridge with the French vessels *Archimede* and *Cyana* in Project Famous. Three years later *Alvin* undertook her first research in the Pacific, off the Galapagos Rift. Later research has taken her as far north as the Strait of Juan de Fuca, in the Pacific, and the Gulf of Maine in the Atlantic.

Kaharl, *Water Baby.*

ALVIN CLARK

Topsail schooner (2m). *L/B/D:* 105.8′ × 25.4′ × 9.4′ (32.2m × 7.7m × 2.9m). *Tons:* 220 grt. *Hull:* wood. *Comp.:* 7. *Built:* Joseph M. Keating, Trenton, Mich.; 1846.

The Great Lakes schooner *Alvin Clark* was a general trader built for John Pearson Clark of Detroit. She carried a variety of cargoes between ports on the upper lakes, loading lumber for Buffalo and Oswego to the east, returning with salt, barrel staves, and manufactured goods for Whitefish Bay and Two Rivers, Wisconsin. There she would load lumber and shingles for Chicago, or call at Whitefish Bay for wheat or fish. Many smaller communities were also served. On June 29, 1864, *Alvin Clark* was sailing from Chicago to Oconto, Wisconsin, on Green Bay. She had just passed through Death's Door Passage between the Door Peninsula and Plum Island when she capsized in a squall and sank rapidly with three of her five crew.

In November 1967, scuba diver Frank Hoffmann was asked to free a fisherman's net from an obstruction in Green Bay and so discovered the remains of *Alvin Clark,* her masts in place and the hull in excellent shape thanks to the preservative properties of cold (30°–40°F), fresh water. With a permit from the U.S. Army Corps of Engineers, Hoffmann — a sometime janitor and saloon keeper — and a crew of amateur divers began to raise the vessel. Two years later, *Alvin Clark* was towed into Marinette, Wisconsin, greeted by 15,000 people. The Smithsonian Institution's Howard Chapelle wrote:

> This is a true treasure of the Great Lakes. Your recovery of the schooner is of far greater importance than a few gold coins or a hull fragment of a supposed treasure ship. In your find we will now be able to put together in great part the real working craft of the past.

Unfortunately, Hoffmann was prepared neither professionally nor financially to maintain his find. Despite his efforts to find qualified organizations who would reimburse him for his expenses and look after the ship, none was forthcoming. Over the years, the hull began to dry out, and Hoffmann was forced to preserve *Alvin Clark* himself. With no tourist base to draw on in Marinette, the income for the ship's maintenance was far short of the need. By the mid-1990s, the schooner's desiccated remains washed ashore in Menominee, Michigan, just over the border from Marinette.

Spectre, "*Alvin Clark.*"

AMARYLIS

Catamaran (1m). *L/D:* 25′ × 4″ (7.6m × 0.1m). *Hull:* wood. *Des.:* Nathanael G. Herreshoff. *Built:* John Brown Herreshoff, Bristol, R.I.; 1875.

In 1875, Nathanael G. Herreshoff was an employee of the Corliss Steam Engine Company, in Providence, Rhode Island, when he designed the catamaran, *Amarylis.* While the concept of the catamaran was by no means new, Herreshoff

> devised a [patented] system of jointed connections between the hulls and intermediate structure that carried the rig, so the hulls could pitch and dive independently with but little restraint. These catamarans could sail very fast, and would make 20 m.p.h. on a close reach, also 8 m.p.h. dead to windward.

Herreshoff fully intended *Amarylis* to be sailed for cruising, and he was upset when in 1876 the Centennial Regatta race committee in New York disqualified his catamaran — the outright winner — on the grounds that his tent (the peak of which was lashed to the raised boom) did not constitute proper cruising accommodation. Herreshoff attempted to go into business for himself on the strength of the catamaran design, but there was virtually no market and only three such craft were built after he and his brother formed the Herreshoff Manufacturing Company in 1877. *Amarylis* was sold to Fred Hughes but her eventual fate is unknown. In 1933, K. T. Keller, president of the Chrysler Corporation, ordered a near replica named *Amarylis II.* After half a century at the Ford Dearborn Museum, this vessel was given to the Herreshoff Marine Museum in Bristol, Rhode Island.

Bray & Pinheiro, *Herreshoff of Bristol.* Pinheiro, "Herreshoff Catamarans — *Amarylis.*"

AMBROSE (LV 87)

Lightship (1f/2m). *L/B/D:* 135.4′ × 29′ × 12.8′ (41.2m × 8.8m × 3.9m). *Tons:* 683 disp. *Hull:* steel. *Comp.:* 9. *Mach.:* compound engine, 325 ihp, 1 screw; 10 kts. *Built:* New York Shipbuilding Corp., Camden, N.J.; 1907.

In 1823, the U.S. government established its first lightship station off Sandy Hook, New Jersey, to mark the entrance to the port of New York. Six years later, the station was withdrawn from service. Between 1839 and 1967, seven ships were assigned to the station continuously, including both world wars. Known first as the Sandy Hook lightship, in 1908 the station was renamed Ambrose Channel in honor of John W. Ambrose, a New York businessman who was instrumental in getting the federal government to improve shipping channels into and out of the country's busiest port. No less important than channel maintenance was the light marking the approaches to New York; throughout its history, the Ambrose light was an important leading mark for coastwise and transatlantic shipping.

The oldest surviving of the ships that served Ambrose Channel was the fourth, LV 87, which was on the station continuously from 1908 to 1932. Originally (and only briefly) schooner rigged to provide balancing sails for heavy weather, she began her career with oil lens lanterns, which were eventually replaced by incandescent lights with two 375-mm lens lanterns providing 15,000 candle power. In 1921, she became the first lightship equipped with a radio beacon. From 1932 to 1936, she served as a relief vessel out of New York, and from 1936 to 1962 she was assigned to the Scotland lightship station (about 4.5 miles west of Ambrose lightship), except for two years as an examination ship and three years at Vineyard Sound (1944–47). In 1967, LV 87 was donated to New York's South Street Seaport Museum for use as a floating exhibit. The last ship to serve Ambrose Channel, WLV-613, built in 1952 as *Nantucket*, is also used as a floating exhibit at the New England Historic Seaport in Boston.

Brouwer, *International Register of Historic Ships*. Flint, *Lightships of the United States Government*.

AMERICA

(later *Camilla, Memphis, America*) Schooner (2m). *L/B/D:* 101.8′ × 23′ × 11′ (31m × 7m × 3.4m). *Tons:* 180 disp. *Hull:* wood. *Comp.:* 25. *Des.:* George Steers. *Built:* William H. Brown, New York; 1851.

In 1851, the New York shipbuilder William H. Brown conceived a plan to build an oceangoing racing schooner for the express purpose of racing — and beating — English yachts in English waters. To this end he proposed to build such a vessel on the understanding that a syndicate headed by New York Yacht Club Commodore John Cox Stevens purchase the schooner for $30,000 if she proved faster than the local competition, and that Brown would buy her back if she lost in England. Underlying Brown's confident challenge was his desire to build a vessel to represent the United States in races held in conjunction with Britain's Great Exhibition, which opened at the Crystal Palace on May 1, 1851, two days before *America* was launched into the East River.

Designed by the superintendent of Brown's mold loft, the thirty-one-year-old George Steers, *America*'s design represented a significant departure from the traditional, bluff-bowed "cod's head and mackerel-tail" model. As John Rousmaniere describes it, "*America*'s most notable feature was the combination of sharp, wedge-shaped bow tapering very gradually to her widest point about halfway back from the stem, and another subtle taper back to a broad, rounded transom." Her two masts, with a rake of about 2.75 inches to the foot (for an angle of about 14 degrees), carried a mainsail, boomless foresail, and single jib. In trials, *America* lost to *Maria*, a Cox-owned centerboard sloop designed for inshore racing, but the syndicate offered Brown $20,000 for the jaunty schooner. She sailed for France on June 21, bearing a heavy responsibility for her country's honor, for as Horace Greeley declared to syndicate member James Hamilton (the son of Alexander and a former Secretary of State), "The eyes of the world are on you. You will be beaten, and the country will be abused. . . . If you go and are beaten, you had better not return." After fine-tuning in Le Havre, *America* anchored off the Royal Yacht Squadron at Cowes, Isle of Wight, on July 31.

Unfortunately for the syndicate, who hoped to recoup their expenses with winnings from match races, *America*'s mere appearance scared off bettors, and she lay unchallenged until Stevens decided to compete for the Royal Yacht Squadron's £100 Cup on August 22. This was a 53-mile race around the Isle of Wight, without time allowance, and "open to yachts belonging to the clubs of all nations." *America* was the only non-English entrant in the fleet of seven schooners and eight cutters. Despite a bad start at 1000, an hour into the race she was in fifth place. After rounding Noman's Land buoy, the wind picked up and she stepped out in front of the fleet. Although she broke a jibboom (acquired in England), when she passed the Needles at 1750, she had a 7.5-mile lead over the second-place *Aurora*. Fifteen minutes later, *America* dipped her flag as she passed the royal yacht VICTORIA AND ALBERT, an honor returned the following day when the Queen and Prince Consort visited the victorious schooner, which had crossed the finish line at

2053. *America*'s triumph was admired in England and greeted with rapture in the United States. Addressing the Massachusetts House of Representatives, an exultant Daniel Webster declared, "Like Jupiter among the gods, America is first and there is no second!"

With an eye to the bottom line, however, the syndicate sold *America* to Anglo-Irishman John de Blaquiere, who set off on a Mediterranean cruise. In a second Isle of Wight race the next year, *America* came in less than two minutes out of first place. Laid up, she was sold to Henry Montagu Upton in 1856, two years later to shipbuilder Henry Sotheby Pitcher, and then to Henry Edward Decie, who in April 1861 sailed her to Savannah. Renamed *Camilla,* she returned to England with Confederate government agents; Decie raced her a few more times near Cowes before sailing for France in August. By the end of October she was at Jacksonville, Florida, where she was sold to the Confederate government and, possibly renamed *Memphis,* used as a blockade runner. Scuttled in the St. John River, Florida, when the Union Army captured Jacksonville, she was salvaged by Lieutenant John Stevens (no relation to John Cox Stevens). Rerigged and armed with a 12-pdr. muzzle-loading rifle and two 24-pdr. smoothbore guns, USS *America* was commissioned for service with the South Atlantic Blockading Squadron, in which she captured or caused to run aground three Confederate vessels.

After a refit at New York in 1863, she began duty as a school ship for U.S. Naval Academy midshipmen. Laid up at Annapolis in 1866, she was recommissioned four years later in order to compete in the first race for the cup named in her honor. *America* placed fourth in the fleet of twenty-four schooners and centerboard sloops; the race was won by the centerboard sloop *Magic,* and the sole foreign contestant, the schooner *Cambria,* came in tenth. Three years later, she was sold on the grounds that her upkeep was too costly. Nonetheless, her new owner, General Benjamin Butler, raced her for two more decades. As an unofficial contestant in the 1876 America's Cup race, she came in only five minutes behind *Madeleine* and nineteen minutes ahead of the Canadian *Countess of Dufferin.* After Butler's death in 1893, she passed to his grand-nephew Butler Ames, who raced her for the last time in 1901.

Laid up for fifteen years, she was donated to the Naval Academy. Ill-maintained, in 1940 she was hauled and stored under a shed. When the shed collapsed in 1942, *America*'s fate was sealed, though it was not until 1945 that the Navy ordered her broken up. A near replica was built in 1967, and another in 1995.

Rousmaniere, *Low Black Schooner.*

AMERICA

Down Easter (3m). *L/B/D:* 233′ × 43′ × 28′ (71m × 13.1m × 8.5m). *Tons:* 2,054 grt. *Hull:* wood. *Built:* George Thomas, Quincy, Mass.; 1874.

Built for the Boston merchant firm of Thayer & Lincoln, the Down Easter *America* was well known for her clipperlike speed and fine lines. Crossing three skysail yards, *America* made her maiden voyage from New York to San Francisco in 110 days, and from there proceeded to Liverpool. This route, between New York, the West Coast, and Europe, remained her itinerary through the 1880s. After grounding in a storm at San Pedro on February 8, 1887, she was sold to the Pacific Steam Whaling Company, working in that company's Alaskan salmon canneries fleet and in the coal trade. She was later sold to the Northwestern Fisheries Company, of Seattle, and then to James Griffiths for use as a copper ore barge running between Alaska and Tacoma. She was abandoned in False Bay, San Juan Island, after stranding in the summer of 1914. She had a total of seven captains in her career, five as a deepwater merchant ship and two in the coastwise trade; the longest serving was her last, Captain Noah S. Harding, who commanded her for fourteen years.

Lyman, "Largest Wooden Ship." Matthews, *American Merchant Ships.*

AMERICA

(later USS *West Point, America, Australis, America, Italis, American Star, America*) Liner (2f/2m). *L/B:* 723′ loa × 93.5′ (220.4m × 28.5m). *Tons:* 26,594 grt. *Hull:* steel. *Comp.:* 1st 516, cabin 371, tourist 159. *Mach.:* steam turbine, 2 screws; 22 kts. *Des.:* William Francis Gibbs. *Built:* Newport News Shipbuilding & Dry Dock Co., Newport News, Va.; 1940.

Designed for the North Atlantic passenger trade, *America* was intended to take the place of the recently retired LEVIATHAN as the flagship of the United States Lines' prewar fleet. Laid down in 1938, she was launched on August 31, 1939, one day before the German invasion of Poland plunged Europe into World War II. Rather than enter the prestigious North Atlantic passenger trade, *America* first sailed from New York for cruises to the Caribbean and California. Recalled to Newport News in May 1941, she was commissioned as the troopship USS *West Point* (AP-23) in June, with a capacity for 8,750 troops. In November 1941, she sailed as part of a convoy of Canadian troops bound for Singapore via Cape Town, where she arrived two days after Pearl Harbor, and Bombay. She evacuated 1,276 people from Singapore two weeks before the fall of the port in February. Thereafter

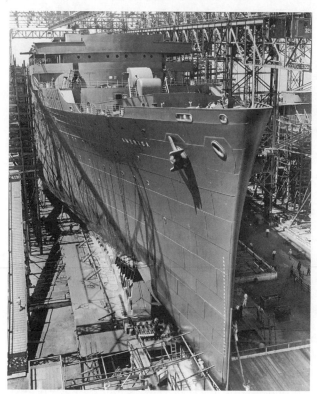

Flagship of the American merchant marine, the passenger liner AMERICA *is seen on the ways during construction at the Newport News Shipbuilding & Dry Dock Co. in 1939. Courtesy The Mariners' Museum, Newport News, Virginia.*

she saw extensive service between the Mediterranean and Australia and New Zealand, followed by trooping duties to the Pacific and Europe.

In 1946 *West Point* was dropped from the Navy list and after a $6 million refit entered the service for which she was originally intended, leaving New York for her first peacetime voyage from New York to Cobh, Southampton, and Le Havre on November 10. *America* later called at Cherbourg and, after 1951, Bremen. But as passenger jets began to cut into North Atlantic passenger traffic, in the early 1960s, *America* was forced to augment her North Atlantic service with cruises to the Caribbean. In 1964 she was withdrawn from North Atlantic service, sold to the Chandris Group's Okeania S/A, and renamed *Australis* for service in the immigrant trade from Britain to Australia. She carried 2,658 passengers in one class, more than any other passenger ship then in service, departing from Southampton and proceeding via Piraeus and the Suez Canal, Australia, the Panama Canal, Port Everglades, and Southampton. (Following the closing of the Suez Canal during the Arab-Israeli War in 1967, she sailed via Cape Town.)

After 1976, the fate of the former flagship of the United States merchant marine became increasingly frenetic. She was transferred from Panamanian to Greek registry, and made her last voyage from Southampton to New Zealand, where she was laid up at Timaru. In 1978, she was sold to New York-based Venture Cruise Lines, which went bust after two incompetently managed cruises of the now renamed *America*. Repurchased by Chandris in 1978, she was renamed *Italis*, her forward dummy funnel was removed, and she entered service as a cruise ship from Barcelona. Laid up for most of the 1980s, she was eventually renamed *American Star* and purchased by Thai interests for conversion to a floating hotel. While under tow to Ahuket in January 1994, she was blown ashore by a hurricane on the island of Fuertaventura, Canary Islands, and split in two.

Bonsor, *North Atlantic Seaway*. Miller, *SS "United States."* U.S. Navy, *DANFS*.

AMERICAN PROMISE

Cutter. *L/B/D:* 60′ × 17.2′ × 10.3′ (18.3m × 5.2m × 3.1m). *Tons:* 38.7 tons. *Hull:* fiberglass. *Comp.:* 1. *Des.:* Frederick E. "Ted" Hood. *Built:* Little Harbor Boat Yard, Marblehead, Mass.; 1985.

In 1983, businessman and veteran solo sailor Dodge Morgan resolved to fulfill a decades-old ambition to sail around the world single-handed. To that end, he enlisted naval architect Ted Hood to design a boat capable of completing "a solo, nonstop, easterly circumnavigation in 180 to 220 days. . . . A boat to bear the rigors of six months' continuous sailing in varied weather conditions; a boat to average 6.25 knots or better over that span of time." *American Promise* was completed in nine months and ready for trials in May 1985. Five months later, on October 14, 1985, Morgan drifted inauspiciously out of Portland in a dead calm. Two nights later *American Promise* was in the teeth of gale, her autopilots failed to work, and after six days at sea Morgan knew he had to put into Bermuda. With the problems solved, he started out again from Bermuda on November 12, 1985.

Virtually every aspect of *American Promise* and the voyage was planned in minute detail. A consummate sailor, Morgan made the most of his advantages to turn in a staggering performance as the thirteenth person (and first American ever) to complete a solo nonstop circumnavigation. First and foremost, the voyage was the fastest time for a single-handed true circumnavigation of only 150 days, 1 hour, and 6 minutes, for an average speed of 7.13 knots, or 171.1 miles per day. This record is a measure of sea time only, and therefore includes circumnavigations with stopovers, including those of Philippe Jeantot in the monohull CRÉDIT AGRICOLE (159 days in 1982–83) and Alain Colas in the trimaran *Manureva* (ex-*Pen Duick IV*; 169 days in 1973–74). Along the way, he broke a number of other records for point-to-point sailing, and day's and week's runs. Morgan's memoir of the voyage and its preparation offers an unusually frank look at the technical and personal aspects of solo voyaging that combines both observations written on board and analyses of various aspects of the undertaking written after the voyage.

Morgan, *Voyage of "American Promise."*

AMERIGO VESPUCCI

Ship (3m). *L/B/D:* 269.5′ × 51′ × 22′ (82.1m × 15.5m × 6.7m). *Tons:* 4,100 disp. *Hull:* steel. *Comp.:* 450. *Mach.:* diesel electric, 1,900 hp, 1 screw; 10.5 kts. *Built:* Royal Shipyard, Castellamare di Stabia, Italy; 1930.

In the late 1920s, the Italian navy began construction of two ships for training their officer cadets at sea, *Cristoforo Colombo* and *Amerigo Vespucci*. The design chosen was that of a seventy-four-gun frigate, though they had steel hulls and carried double topgallants, auxiliary power, and other modern devices. *Amerigo Vespucci* was named for the Florentine explorer for whom the sixteenth-century German cartographer Martin Waldseemüller named the newly discovered landmasses to the west. *Amerigo Vespucci*'s full lines are in sharp contrast to the majority of sail-training vessels, which generally follow the finer model adapted from nineteenth-century merchant ship design. Harold Underhill records a letter from a Norwegian submarine commander about an encounter with the two ships in the 1930s:

> I dived on a northerly course about mid waters of the Skagerrak and went deep for about an hour in order to keep the lunch on the tables. On breaking surface again with the periscope, I took a quick look all round and got a shock. I had gone down in the 20th century and come up again in the 18th, for there, some miles away, were two majestic men-of-war, under a press of canvas and sailing proudly in line-astern.

Following World War II, *Cristoforo Colombo* was acquired by the Soviet Union. *Amerigo Vespucci* resumed her sail-training mission for the Italian navy well into the 1990s.

Underhill, *Sail Training and Cadet Ships.*

HMS AMETHYST

Modified *Black Swan*-class sloop (1f/1m). *L/B/D:* 299.5′ × 38′ × 11′ (19.5m × 6m × 3.3m). *Tons:* 1,430 disp. *Comp.:* 192. *Arm.:* 6 × 4″ (3 × 2), 6 × 40mm; hedgehogs. *Mach.:* geared turbines, 4,300 shp, 2 screws; 19 kts. *Built:* Alexander Stephen & Sons, Ltd., Glasgow; 1943.

Following World War II, HMS *Amethyst* was stationed with the British fleet in the Far East. During the Chinese Civil War between the Communist People's Liberation Army (PLA) and the Nationalist Kuomintang, the British kept a vessel at Nanking on the Yangtze River to look after British interests. On April 19, 1949, *Amethyst* was dispatched to relieve HMS *Consort*. The danger of being brought into the fighting was high, and after anchoring the first night at Kiangyin (Chiang-yin), the ship was piped down for action. PLA forces opened fire with machine guns and artillery at about 0830 the next morning, and at about 0930 a hit on the wheelhouse injured the coxswain, who inadvertently threw the helm to port, grounding *Amethyst* on Rose Island. A second shell mortally wounded Lieutenant Commander B. M. Skinner, after which Lieutenant Geoffrey Weston assumed command. When he was injured, John Simons Kerans took over. Shelling stopped at 1100, and 65–70 ratings left *Amethyst* in hopes of making the Nationalist lines; twenty-two men had been killed and thirty-one wounded. *Consort* was forced back under heavy fire, and the next day the cruiser HMS *London* suffered three killed and fourteen seriously injured before retiring in company with *Black Swan*.

Despite diplomatic overtures to allow her to withdraw from the river, *Amethyst* remained impounded on the Yangtze for another ten weeks. At 2012 on the moonless night of July 30, *Amethyst* slipped her anchor and turned downstream in the wake of the freighter *Kiang Ling Liberation*. After running past batteries at Kiangyin and Woosung (the latter were silent), *Amethyst* was free of the river by 0530 the next morning. Returning to a hero's welcome in Britain, her crew were received by George VI at Buckingham Palace. After a refit at Devonport, *Amethyst* returned to the Far East in 1950. She played herself in a 1957 film called *Yangtze Incident* (also released as *Battle Hell* and *Escape of the Amethyst*). She was scrapped at Plymouth the next year.

Murfett, *Hostage on the Yangtze.*

AMISTAD

Topsail schooner (2m). *L/B/D:* 64' × 19.8' × 6.2' dph (19.5m × 6m × 1.9m). *Tons:* ca. 60 grt. *Hull:* wood. *Comp.:* 5 crew. *Built:* Baltimore; <1839.

In August 1839, reports of a schooner of distinctive Baltimore clipper lines and manned by twenty-five to thirty Africans began circulating around the waterfronts of New York and New England. The vessel had requested food and water from several passing ships, and some of its crew had landed along the eastern end of Long Island. On August 26, as the ship lay at anchor off Culloden Point, the schooner and her crew were seized by the revenue cutter *Washington* under Lieutenant Thomas Gedney.

The ship turned out to be a coastal slave trader of Cuban registry. On June 28, she had embarked fifty-three slaves newly landed at Havana from the Portuguese slave ship *Teçora* and purchased by José Ruiz and Pedro Montes, who hired *Amistad* for the two-day sail to Puerto Príncipe. Under the leadership of a slave named Cinque, who had been captured from his home in Kaw-Mendi in what is now Sierra Leone, the slaves seized the ship, killing the captain and his cook and wounding Montes and Ruiz in the process; two sailors also disappeared, possibly drowning when they leaped overboard. Cinque ordered his erstwhile captors to steer *Amistad* to the east, the direction from which he knew they had sailed in *Teçora;* but by night, Montes and Ruiz sailed north, hoping to make landfall in one of the slave-owning states of the United States.

After seizing *Amistad,* whose name is Spanish for "friendship," Gedney had the ship taken to New London, where, because slavery was still legal in Connecticut, he could claim salvage on the ship and her cargo, including the slaves, who had been purchased for $450 each in Havana. In the opening round of legal proceedings, Ruiz and Montes argued that their property should be handed over to the Spanish consul and that the slaves be charged with murder and mutiny in a Spanish court. In support of their case, they insisted that the slaves were not from Africa, but that they had been slaves prior to the banning of the slave trade. Owning slaves was not illegal under Spanish law, but trafficking in slaves had been since 1817. Gedney brought suit on behalf of himself and his crew seeking compensation for salvage. The plight of the Africans, whose de facto leader was still Cinque, immediately aroused the interest of the abolitionist movement. Their intent was to demonstrate that the Spaniards were guilty of piracy for engaging in the slave trade. The Africans would then be free to return to their homes in Africa.

The abolitionists' biggest obstacle was President Martin Van Buren, who was eager to avoid a confrontation with the Spanish government, which sought a ruling in favor of Ruiz and Montes. More important, he was up for reelection and had no intention of alienating southern voters. Articulating his administration's case was Secretary of State John Forsyth, himself a Georgia slave-owner. A district court ruling found that the Africans had been born as free men and were kidnapped into slavery. However, the court also decided that Cinque and the others should be turned over to the administration to be returned to Africa. Fearing that the Van Buren administration might just as easily return the Africans to Spain, the abolitionists enlisted the services of Representative John Quincy Adams, himself a former president and secretary of state, to argue the Africans' case before the Supreme Court. The high court eventually ruled in favor of the Africans, and in November 1841 the thirty-five survivors of the original fifty-three taken aboard *Amistad* returned to Sierra Leone in the bark *Gentleman,* under the auspices of the American Colonization Society. *Amistad* was returned to Cuba, but the legal entanglements did not end there: although Congress voted $70,000 to be paid to Spain in 1844, reparations were not paid until 1860.

In 1995 the Connecticut Afro-American Historical Society and Mystic Seaport Museum announced plans to build a replica of *Amistad.*

Jones, *Mutiny on the "Amistad."* Smith, "On the Design of the *Amistad."*

AMOCO CADIZ

Tanker (1f). *L/B/D:* 1,095.5' × 167.6' × 85.9' (334m × 51.1m × 26.2m). *Tons:* 109,700 grt; 233,690 dwt. *Hull:* steel. *Comp.:* 44. *Mach.:* diesel, 30,400 hp, 1 screw; 15 kts. *Built:* Astilleros Españoles, SA, Cadiz; 1974.

The very large crude carrier (VLCC) *Amoco Cadiz* was built to carry oil between the Persian Gulf and Europe. In early February 1978, she loaded 121,157 tons of oil at Ras Tanara, Saudi Arabia, and then topped off with 98,640 tons at Kharg Island, Iran. (A ton of crude is 7.3 barrels, or 306.6 gallons.) She left the Persian Gulf on February 7, bound for Rotterdam, via Lyme Bay, England, a customary stop to lighten tankers before the passage up the North Sea. Rounding the Cape of Good Hope on the 28th, she made a fueling stop at Las Palmas on March 11. Three days later *Amoco Cadiz* began to encounter heavy weather, which continued through March 16, by which point she was entering the English Channel, due into

The oil tanker AMOCO CADIZ *lies with her back broken after running aground on the rocky coast of France in March 1978. An estimated 223,000 tons of oil washed up along 125 miles of the rocky Breton coast. Photo by Pim Korver, Rotterdam, courtesy Amoco Corporation.*

Lyme Bay later that day. At about 0916, the tanker was about eight miles north of Ushant when her steering gear failed. Although Captain Pasquale Bandari hoisted the international signal for "Not Under Command" almost immediately, he did not request assistance until 1120, when his engineer determined that the damage was irreparable. The German salvage tug *Pacific,* under command of Captain Weinert, arrived on the scene at 1220. The first tow was secured at 1425 but parted at 1719. As *Amoco Cadiz* drifted toward shore, the port anchor was let go at about 2004, but it did not hold. A second tow was secured at 2023, but the sheer mass of *Amoco Cadiz* in the teeth of Force 10 weather conditions made it impossible for *Pacific* to do more than slow the ship's coastward drift.

At 2104, *Amoco Cadiz* touched bottom for the first time, and her hull and storage tanks were ripped open. Half an hour later she grounded on Men Goulven Rocks in 48°36′N, 4°46′W. Her crew were rescued by helicopter. At 1000 on March 17 the vessel broke in two, spilling 223,000 tons of crude oil. The oil slick spread across 125 miles of the coast of Brittany, destroying fisheries, oyster and seaweed beds, and bathing beaches despite the efforts of 10,000 French soldiers deployed to clean the beaches. The storm continued to pound the ship, and on March 28 she broke into three sections. The French Navy subsequently destroyed the remains of the ship with depth charges. It would be another ten years before the resulting lawsuits were wound up, and in 1988 a U.S. federal judge

ordered Amoco Oil Corporation to pay $85.2 million in fines — $45 million for the costs of the spill and $39 million in interest.

Chelminski, *Superwreck: "Amoco Cadiz."* Hooke, *Modern Shipping Disasters: 1963–1987.*

AMSTERDAM

Ship (3m). *L/B/D:* 157.5′ × 38.2′ × 19.5′ dph (48m × 11.6m × 5.9m). *Tons:* 1,110 disp. *Hull:* wood. *Comp.:* 191 crew; 123 soldiers; 3 pass. *Arm.:* 8 × 12pdr, 16 × 8pdr, 8 × 4pdr, 10 swivels. *Built:* Oostenburg Shipyard (VOC), Amsterdam; 1744.

Between 1602 and 1799, the Verenigde Oostindische Compagnie (United East India Company, or VOC) built 1,700 East Indiamen for the long-distance trade between the Netherlands and the East Indies. *Amsterdam* was one of the largest of the 150-*voet* class approved in 1742. (One *voet* equals 1.05 feet.) Laid down in April of 1744, she was finished in time to join the VOC's autumn fleet to Batavia and loaded in the deep water anchorage off the Texel. Under Captain Willem Klump, she sailed on November 15 but was three times forced back by North Sea gales. On January 8, 1745, she sailed in company with five other ships, only to encounter more gales off the Downs in the English Channel. When the weather cleared, she sailed farther down channel until she grounded and lost her rudder; Klump then anchored off Hastings. Perhaps threatened by mutiny — his sailors had been dying at the rate of about three per day — Klump attempted to run his ship aground in an effort to save her, which he did January 26, off Bulverhithe, just west of Hastings. The passengers and most of the crew landed safely, although within two days fifty more crew had died ashore and many were too ill to leave the ship. *Amsterdam* settled into the beach at the rate of about 6 inches a day, and her keel came to rest about 20 feet below the surface. The wreck was never forgotten, and during the summer of 1969 curious workers laying a sewage pipe began exploring the area with a backhoe and located the ship beneath the sand in 50°50′N, 00°31′E. At this point, thanks largely to the energetic efforts of maritime archaeologist Peter Marsden and others, the ship was legally secured when Britain accepted the Dutch government's right to the wreck. Although much of the ship's contents had been saved (including more than 300,000 florins worth of silver) or plundered at the time of the wreck, *Amsterdam*'s remaining stores, including medical supplies, clothing, wine and beer, and other artifacts of shipboard life provide a fine view of life aboard these lumbering merchantmen that spent more than nine months at sea in a quest for the spices of the Orient. In 1989 the city of Amsterdam launched a full-scale sailing replica of the East Indiaman called *Amsterdam II.*

Friedman, "*Amsterdam II.*" Marsden, *The Wreck of the "Amsterdam."* Van Rooij & Gawronski, *East Indiaman Amsterdam.*

ANDREA DORIA

Liner (1f/2m). *L/B:* 630.1′ × 79.8′ (192m × 24.3m). *Tons:* 29,082 grt. *Hull:* steel. *Comp.:* 1st 218, cabin 320, tourist 703; 563 crew. *Mach.:* geared turbines, 2 screws; 26 kts. *Built:* Ansaldo Societá per Azioni, Genoa; 1953.

Andrea Doria was the first passenger liner built to run in North Atlantic service for the Italia Società per Azioni di Navigazione (Italian Line) after World War II. Named for the sixteenth-century Genoese admiral, the luxury liner entered service between Genoa and New York on July 25, 1953, making intermediate stops at Cannes and Naples. She shared this route with her sister ship *Cristoforo Colombo,* which entered service a year later. On July 17, 1956, *Andrea Doria* departed Genoa on her fifty-first crossing of the Atlantic, and by the evening of the twenty-fifth she was speeding though the foggy approaches to Nantucket Sound when she was rammed by the Swedish-America Line passenger ship STOCKHOLM, outward bound from New York. Although the Swedish-America Line ship had appeared on *Andrea Doria's* radar screen, there was no effort to take evasive action until it was too late. At 2345, *Stockholm* knifed thirty feet into *Andrea Doria's* starboard side and forty-three people aboard the Italian liner were killed instantly. A watertight bulkhead was also destroyed in the collision, and the ship began to list so severely that she was unable to launch her starboard lifeboats. Captain Piero Calamai issued a distress call and by 0430, the 1,663 passengers and crew who had survived the collision had been taken aboard the French Line's ILE DE FRANCE, the freighter *Cape Ann,* the navy transport *Pvt. William H. Thomas,* and *Stockholm.* The pride of the Italian merchant fleet sank at 1009 the following morning. An inquiry into the cause of the disaster was settled out of court between the two lines. In the mid-1980s, Peter Gimbel led a series of dives on the wreck. The ship's safe was salvaged, but more important, his photographs demonstrated that the ship's watertight integrity had been destroyed in the collision and that the ship's loss was not an engineering defect, as some had suspected.

Hoffer, *Saved!*

ANDREW DORIA

(ex-*Defiance*) Brigantine (2m) *L/B/D:* ca. 75′ × 25′ × 10′ (22.9m × 7.6m × 3m). *Tons:* ca. 190 tons. *Hull:* wood. *Comp.:* 112. *Arm.:* 14 × 4pdr. *Built:* <1775.

The Continental Congress authorized the purchase of the merchant brig *Defiance* in October 1775. Armed and renamed *Andrew Doria* in honor of the fifteenth-century Venetian admiral, she was placed under command of Captain Nicholas Biddle. In January 1776 she took part in Commodore Esek Hopkins's capture of Fort Nassau in the Bahamas and returned with the fleet to New London in April. Over the next six months, *Andrew Doria* captured ten ships, including four supply vessels belonging to Virginia's Loyalist governor John Murray, Earl of Dunmore. In October, Biddle took command of the frigate RANDOLPH and was succeeded by Captain Isaiah Robinson who was dispatched to St. Eustatius, Dutch West Indies, for military stores. Her arrival at the port on November 16, 1776, was met with the first salute to the American flag rendered by a foreign power in a foreign port. On the same voyage, *Andrew Doria* captured the British sloop *Racehorse* (12 guns), which entered the Continental Navy as *Surprize,* and a merchant ship. *Andrew Doria* never left the Delaware after her return to Philadelphia. Following the loss of Fort Mercer, New Jersey, Captain Robinson ordered his ship burned to prevent her falling into British hands.

Fowler, *Rebels under Sail.* U.S. Navy, *DANFS.*

ANDREW JACKSON

Clipper (3m). *L/B/D:* 220′ × 41.2′ × 22.2′ dph (67.1m × 12.5m × 6.8m). *Tons:* 1,679 om. *Hull:* wood. *Built:* Irons & Grinnell, Mystic, Conn.; 1855.

Andrew Jackson was launched as *Belle Hoxie* but renamed when purchased by the New York firm of John H. Brower & Company. A medium clipper, she combined comparatively large stowage capacity with very fine lines. She had a round stern, a design element found only in Mystic-built sailing ships in the United States and not used in Britain until the advent of iron in shipbuilding. She made a number of fast passages between New York and San Francisco, averaging 106 days over six voyages as compared with 104 days for *Flying Fish* and only 103 for FLYING CLOUD. She was the only ship to make the run between New York and San Francisco in less than 110 days four years running. This was due to a number of factors, not least her hard-driving Captain John Williams, a veteran of the Black Ball Line of transatlantic packets, who was memorialized in a sea chantey:

> 'Tis larboard and starboard on deck you will sprawl,
> For kicking Jack Williams commands that Black Ball.

On December 25, 1859, Williams dropped the pilot at New York en route for San Francisco. *Andrew Jackson* arrived at the pilot station on the California coast 89 days, 4 hours later, a passage credited as being four hours faster than the record set by Captain Josiah Cressy in *Flying Cloud* in 1854. Upon his arrival at San Francisco, Williams was awarded a commodore's pennant for the fastest run between New York and San Francisco and upon his return to New York, John Brower presented him with a chronometer watch engraved "89 days 4 hours." Although clipper historians Octavius Howe and Frederick Matthews ignited a debate — sixty-six years after the fact — over whether *Andrew Jackson* was entitled to the record, there is no record of any of *Flying Cloud*'s numerous supporters contesting the validity of Williams's claim of a record from pilot to pilot, although *Flying Cloud* holds the record from anchor to anchor. (At the end of her record run, *Andrew Jackson* had to wait until the following morning for a pilot.) It is also worth noting that *Flying Cloud* twice made the passage in under ninety days, and her overall average of 103 days between the two ports is two days better than *Andrew Jackson*'s.

These times remained the fastest by any sailing vessel on the Cape Horn route for 140 years, when a series of purpose-built yachts employing the most sophisticated construction materials and navigation and weather forecasting systems began vying for the honor. The record was broken first by Warren Luhrs's *Thursday's Child,* then by the trimaran George Kolesnikov's *Great American* in 76 days, 23 hours, and again in 1994, by *Eucureuil Poitou-Charentes 2,* a 60-foot monohull skippered by Isabelle Autissier, in 62 days, 5 hours, 55 minutes. The latter time was faster than that of the battleship USS OREGON, which steamed from Seattle to Florida in 1898.

In 1860 *Andrew Jackson* established an uncontested transatlantic record by sailing from Liverpool to Sandy Hook in 15 days (November 3–18). She had also sailed to Liverpool in 15 days — two days shy of the record — at the start of the same voyage, and the *New York Herald* reported that on the voyage out and home she was "only 30 days at sea, including two days of calms, and sailed over 6500 miles, thus averaging nearly 220 miles a day throughout — a rate of speed rarely, if ever, equaled, continuously in a sailing vessel before."

Andrew Jackson made her last passage under the American flag in 1863, carrying spars from Puget Sound for Spain. Sold to H. L. Seligman of Glasgow, she came under command of Captain McCallum and was put in trade to the Orient. On her first voyage under the Red Duster she loaded lumber at New Brunswick for the Orient, returning from Java in 1865. Three years later, while homeward bound from Singapore, she was wrecked on a reef in the Gaspar Straits on December 4, 1868.

Cutler, *Greyhounds of the Sea.* Howe & Matthews, *American Clipper Ships.*

ANGLO-SAXON

Freighter. *L/B/D:* 440.2′ × 58′ × 25.2′ (134.2m × 17.7m × 7.7m). *Tons:* 5,596 grt. *Hull:* steel. *Comp.:* 40. *Mach.:* quadruple expansion, 453 nhp. *Built:* Short Bros., Sunderland, Eng.; 1929.

Anglo-Saxon was a tramp freighter owned by the Nitrate Producers S.S. Company. On August 8, 1940, she sailed from Newport, England, for Bahía Blanca with a cargo of coal in company with Convoy OB195. After the convoy dispersed, she sailed south. At 2020 hours on August 21, she was attacked by the German raider WIDDER; her location was 26°10′N, 34°09′W, about 900 miles WSW of the Canary Islands. The ship was destroyed together with the lifeboats, but seven crew — three seriously injured — found their way to the ship's 18-foot jolly boat. The boat had a lug rig, but it carried a minimum of supplies and no navigational aids. Five of the crew died in the first week of September, leaving only Robert Tapscott and Roy Widdicombe, both of whom had signed on as able seamen. The two men survived without shelter from the elements or sufficient food, until they sighted land on October 30. After seventy days during which they had sailed and drifted 2,775 miles, they managed to put ashore in Eleuthera, the Bahamas. Both men returned to the merchant marine. Tapscott survived the war, but en route home from New York, Widdicombe's ship, *Furness Prince,* was torpedoed off Scotland on February 18, 1941; there were no survivors.

Jones, *Two Survived.* Lund, *Raider and the Tramp.*

ANN MCKIM

Clipper (3m). *L/B/D:* 140.6m × 27.5′ × 13.7′ (42.8m × 8.4m × 4.2m). *Tons:* 493 bm. *Hull:* wood. *Built:* Kennard & Williamson, Baltimore; 1833.

Described as "the longest merchant ship in the United States" at the time of her building, the ship-rigged *Ann McKim* is often said to be the first clipper ship. Built for Isaac McKim of Baltimore, and named for his wife, she had finer lines than any large vessel of her day, although there was nothing especially novel in her design or construction. The celebrated Baltimore clippers of the early nineteenth century were usually brig or schooner rigged; Carl Cutler cites a number of examples of sharp-built ships of the period, from the Virginia-built *Paul Sieman* (1800) to *Corinthian* (1822). Unlike the full-blown clipper ships of the 1850s, built for service to China and California, *Ann McKim* was intended for trade to South America, and on her first voyage sailed for Callao, Peru, and Huasco, Chile, under Captain Martin, sailing out in 89 days and home in 72.

Isaac McKim died in 1837, and the same year she was sold to Howland & Aspinwall. In 1837 and 1838, she demonstrated herself a crack ship, returning from Valparaiso to the Virginia Capes in 59 days and 53 days, respectively. The Baltimore *Sun* was justifiably proud of the accomplishment, noting, "The *Ann McKim* is a Baltimore vessel out and out, built and owned here. Baltimore ship builders against the world for building fleet craft." The next year she made her first voyage in the China trades, in which she would remain for the rest of her career as an American-flag vessel. Her first two voyages were sailed in the off season and as a result were longer than average. In 1842, she sailed from New York to Anjer in the then record time of 79 days, returning in 93 days. Five years later she was sold to Chilean interests who kept her in the Pacific trades. In 1849, she sailed from Valparaiso to San Francisco following the discovery of gold there, and remained on that route until 1852 when she was broken up at Valparaiso.

Cutler, *Greyhounds of the Sea*. Howe & Matthews, *American Clipper Ships*.

ANTIKYTHERA WRECK

Hull: wood. *Built:* ca. 85 BCE.

The Antikythera wreck is a first-century BCE merchant ship lying in 35°52′N, 23°20′E near the island of Antikythera off the northwest tip of Crete. In the spring of 1900, sponge divers from Syme discovered the wreck site at a depth of 50 to 60 meters. The site was the object of one of the earliest underwater excavations, conducted by the sponge divers working under their captain, Dimitrios Kondos, with the assistance of the Greek navy. Provided with only primitive helmet-diving equipment, the divers suffered from the bends and narcosis and could remain on the bottom only for short stretches of time. The effort is better described as a salvage operation than an archaeological excavation. As Peter Throckmorton later wrote,

It was . . . as if the tomb of Tutankhamen had been excavated in five-minute shifts by drunken stevedores who had never seen an Egyptian tomb, working in semi-darkness, dressed in American football pads with coal scuttles on their heads.

Small sections of elm planking from the hull were recovered and stored at the National Museum in Athens; however, the original shape or dimensions cannot be determined. The planks were fastened edge to edge by mortises and tenons, and copper nails were used to attach a sheathing of lead. The wreck site was revisited by Jacques-Yves Cousteau and the crew of CALYPSO in 1953. Using a portable airlift, divers located the well-preserved hull under about 40 centimeters of sand. A second visit by Cousteau in 1976 resulted in the discovery of a treasure of gold bars.

The Antikythera ship's last port of call is unknown, but an intriguing possibility is that she was carrying loot from Pergamon (in what is now western Turkey) to Rome — part of the massive reparations exacted by Rome after her victory in the First Mithradatic War (88–85 BCE). This idea is suggested by Pergamene coins dated 88–86 BCE found during Cousteau's 1976 excavation. The site is best known for its remarkable cargo of bronze and marble sculpture, amphorae from Rhodes, Kos, and Taranto, pottery, glass vessels from Alexandria, and a bronze bedstead decorated with animal heads. The "Antikythera Youth," a larger-than-life-size bronze statue of a nude athlete or hero, dates probably from the 4th century BCE. Already an antique when the ship sank, this work is now a showpiece of the National Museum in Athens. Still more interesting is an astronomical device with a clockwork mechanism used to predict the motion of the sun through the zodiac, the rising and setting of the stars, constellations and planets, and the phases of the moon. Careful study of this artifact, which is the most complex scientific instrument preserved from antiquity, indicates that it was probably made in 82 BCE and "set" in 80 BCE.

Price, "An Ancient Greek Computer." Throckmorton, ed., *Shipwrecks and Archaeology*. Weinberg, "Antikythera Wreck Reconsidered."

AQUITANIA

Liner (4f/2m). *L/B/D:* 901′ × 97′ (274.6m × 29.6m). *Tons:* 45,647 grt. *Hull:* steel. *Comp.:* 1st 618, 2nd 614, 3rd 1,998; crew 972. *Mach.:* steam turbines, 4 screws; 23 kts. *Built:* John Brown & Co., Ltd., Clydebank, Scotland; 1914.

Named for a Roman province in southwestern France, Cunard Line's *Aquitania* was built to complement the transatlantic service between Liverpool and New York

A ship's officer stands near the forward funnel of the British speed queen AQUITANIA *in Bedford Lemère's famous photo of 1914. Note the yawning bells of the ventilator cowls designed to force fresh air below decks, a common sight in all prewar liners. Courtesy National Maritime Museum, Greenwich.*

offered by LUSITANIA and MAURETANIA. It was never intended that she try for the Blue Riband as her older running mates had, but she was half again as large and in time she would be considered the most successful of the great transatlantic liners. Commissioned only three months before the outbreak of World War I, in August 1914 she was requisitioned as an armed merchant cruiser. After she was involved in a collision the same month, the Admiralty decided to put her in service as a troopship and, briefly, as a hospital ship. Laid up for most of 1917, she resumed work as a trooper in 1918.

In June 1919 she reentered the transatlantic passenger trade. During a major overhaul in 1920, her original coal-powered engines were replaced with oil-burning engines and her handsome fittings and furnishings were brought out of storage. Her opulent design included a restaurant in Louis XVI style, a Jacobean smoking lounge modeled on a room in Greenwich Hospital, and a two-deck-high Palladian smoking room. Over the next twenty years she was the most popular ship on the transatlantic run, sailing in tandem with BERENGARIA and *Mauretania,* and she conducted off-season cruises to Mediterranean ports.

From 1936 to 1939 she was paired with Cunard's QUEEN MARY. *Aquitania* was to have retired following completion of QUEEN ELIZABETH in 1940, but the outbreak of World War II gave her a new lease on life and she was refitted as a troop carrier with a capacity for 7,724 passengers. The only pre-1914 ship to work the whole war in this service, she carried more than 300,000 servicemen chiefly between Australia and Suez and between the United States and Britain. In 1948, she was returned to Cunard and made twenty-five voyages between Southampton and Halifax, carrying immigrants, displaced persons, and returning veterans. In December 1949, she steamed into Southampton at the conclusion of her 443rd transatlantic crossing. After thirty-five years of service, the last of the four-stackers was moved to Faslane and broken up in February 1950.

Bonsor, *North Atlantic Seaway.* Braynard, *Lives of the Liners.* Shipbuilder and Marine Engine-Builder, *The Cunard Quadruple-Screw Atlantic Liner "Aquitania."*

ARABIC

(ex-*Minnewaska*) Liner (1f/4m). *L/B/D:* 600.7' bp × 65.5' (183.1m × 20m). *Tons:* 15,801 grt. *Hull:* steel. *Mach.:* quadruple-expansion, 2 screws; 16 kts. *Built:* Harland & Wolff, Ltd., Belfast, Ireland; 1903.

Laid down for the Atlantic Transport Line as *Minnewaska,* this ship was purchased by the White Star Line and launched as *Arabic.* She carried passengers in three classes between Liverpool and either New York or Boston. On August 19, 1915, while en route to New York, *Arabic* was torpedoed and sunk off the coast of Ireland by Lieutenant Rudolph Schneider's *U-24,* with the loss of about forty passengers and crew, including three Americans. The incident followed by less than four months the sinking of LUSITANIA, and it was condemned by the United States as an unprecedented violation of neutral rights. When President Woodrow Wilson threatened to sever diplomatic ties with Germany, Ambassador Count Johann Heinrich von Bernstorff proffered the so-called Arabic Pledge under which German submarines would not attack unarmed passenger ships without warning and would provide for the safety of passengers and crews when they did attack. Wilson accepted the proposal, and Germany affirmed the pledge on October 5 and agreed to pay an indemnity for the U.S. passengers lost. Except for two months in 1916 — during which the French liner SUSSEX was sunk — German submarines refrained from unrestricted submarine warfare until February 1917.

Bonsor, *North Atlantic Seaway.* Halpern, *Naval History of World War I.*

ARCHIBALD RUSSELL

Bark (4m). *L/B/D:* 291.4′ × 43.2′ × 24.1′ (88.8m × 13.2m × 7.3m). *Tons:* 2,385 grt. *Hull:* steel. *Des.:* Scott's Shipbuilding & Engineering Co., Greenock, Scotland; 1905.

Archibald Russell was built for John Hardie & Sons, one of the last British shipping companies to remain in sail and whose other vessels included HOUGOMONT and KILLORAN. The ship was named for a member of the family whose business Hardie had taken over in 1885. The last large square-rigger built on the Clyde, she was one of the few such ships fitted with bilge keels to reduce rolling. On her first voyage she loaded nitrates in Chile and proceeded from there to Australia for wheat, returning to Falmouth in the good time of ninety-three days. She remained in general trade between Europe, Australia, and West Coast (U.S.) ports from Iquique to Tacoma right through World War I.

Laid up in 1923, she was sold to Gustaf Erikson of Mariehamn, Åland, who had previously acquired *Hougomont* and *Killoran.* After her first voyage under the Finnish flag, she was refitted to accommodate cadets, most of whom were Lithuanians training for the merchant marine. A mainstay of the grain race fleets until World War II, in 1929 *Archibald Russell* had the fastest homeward passage of the fourteen ships sailing that year. Seized by the British at Hull in 1939, she was used as a storage ship during the war and returned to Erikson in 1947. The cost of refitting her was prohibitive and she was broken up at Dunston in 1949.

Hurst, *Square-Riggers: The Final Epoch.* Lubbock, *Last of the Windjammers.*

ARCHIMEDES

Dredge. *L/B:* 125′ × 62′ (38.1m × 8.9m). *Mach.:* steam engine, paddlewheels. *Des.:* Henry M. Shreve. *Built:* Dohrman & Humphries, New Albany, Ind.; 1831.

Archimedes was the second snag boat of the same design built for the U.S. Army Corps of Engineers. The first, *Heliopolis,* was a catamaran design consisting of two 125-foot by 25-foot hulls separated by 12-foot beams. Powered by two paddlewheels (one on either hull), the vessel was fitted with a steam pulley, cables, chains, and other devices for snagging tree trunks and other obstacles. The procedure was simple, even primitive: the vessel was driven into a tree, which was then grappled, hauled aboard, and cut into smaller pieces that were then thrown overboard to float downriver. The importance of the snag boats was immense. Steaming times on the Mississippi were cut in half, from as much as fifteen days to only six or seven days between New Orleans and Louisville.

The work for which *Archimedes* is best remembered is clearing the "great raft," a 200-mile-long thicket of trees, mud, and other growth that made inaccessible the upper reaches of the Red River, which flowed from eastern Texas to the Mississippi. That part of Texas was then owned by Mexico but inhabited by a large population of displaced Cherokees and settlers from the United States. Shreve started work on the raft in 1833 and six years later the Red River was opened to navigation along its entire 1,200-mile length to Fort Towson. Along the way, Shreve also helped found Shreveport, Louisiana.

McCall, *Conquering the Rivers.*

ARCTIC

Sidewheel steamship (1f/2m). *L/B/D:* 284′ × 46′ (72′ew) × 7′ (86.6m × 1.9m × (21.9m) 2.1m). *Tons:* 2,856 grt. *Mach.:* side-lever beam engine, 1,000 hp, sidewheels; 13 kts. *Built:* William H. Brown, New York; 1850.

The *Arctic* was one of four sidewheel steamships built for the New York and Liverpool United States Mail Steamship Company, better known as the Collins Line. One passenger described the ship as having "an air of almost Oriental magnificence," and the ship was known as the Clipper of the Seas. On September 20, 1854, the *Arctic* left Liverpool with between 322 and 389 people aboard, including about 150 crew. One week out in reduced visibility, the *Arctic* collided with the French screw steamer VESTA in about 46°45′N, 52°60′W. As water poured into the uncompartmentalized hull, Captain James C. Luce attempted to run for Cape Race about 45 or 50 miles away. The ship sank an hour later, and the undisciplined crew made off with the lifeboats, which were, in any case, inadequate for the number of people aboard the ship. Among the 85 or so survivors — not one woman or child among them — were 11 people, including Captain Luce, who had clung to the remains of a paddlebox.

The *Arctic* disaster led to calls for improvements in navigational practices and for greater corporate responsibility. Mississippi Congressman William T. S. Barry castigated the Collins Line: "If they had spent in lifeboats for that vessel the money which they spent in gingerbread ornaments and decorations, there might have been hundreds of valuable lives saved." Among the safety measures implemented in the wake of the tragedy were the more widespread use of lifeboats and steam whistles and, under the aegis of Lieutenant Matthew Fontaine Maury, the

J. W. Hill's pencil-and-watercolor sketch of the wood-hulled Collins Line steamer ARCTIC, *whose collision with the iron-hulled* VESTA *led to a hideous loss of life and, incidentally, the institution of much-needed reforms in the maritime industry. Courtesy Peabody Essex Museum, Salem, Massachusetts.*

establishment of separate transatlantic lanes for east-bound and westbound steamer traffic.

Brown, *Women and Children Last.*

AREND

Ship (3m). L: 120′ (36.6m). Hull: wood. Comp.: 110. Arm.: 32 guns. Built: Netherlands; <1675.

In 1675, Arend Roggeveen applied to States-General for a charter to search for unknown or unconfirmed lands in the South Pacific. Although he died before he could undertake the mission, in 1721 his son Jacob made a similar proposal to the Dutch West India Company. They fitted him out with *Den Arend* ("The Eagle"), *Thienhoven* (100 feet/30.5 meters, 24 guns, 80 crew), and *Den Afrikaansche Galei* (92 feet/28 meters, 14 guns, 33 crew). In particular, Roggeveen intended to search for Davis's Land, reputedly seen in latitude 27°S about 1,500 miles from the coast of South America by English buccaneer Edward Davis in 1687. The ships sailed from the Texel on July 26, 1721, and after a stop in Brazil rounded Cape Horn. Sailing northwest, Roggeveen's men were the first Europeans to visit Easter Island on April 5 (Easter Sunday), 1722. Thereafter the ships sailed west following the track

laid down by Willem Schouten and Jacob Le Maire in EENDRACHT in 1616. On May 19, the *Galei* was lost on Takapoto Island in the Tuamotu Archipelago, and five sailors deserted the expedition. Having made no substantial discovery, Roggeveen was bound to return home. Deciding that rounding Cape Horn again would be impossible with a sick and disabled crew, he determined to sail west and then north around New Guinea to Batavia, where they arrived on October 3. There, the East India Company confiscated the ships and property of the rival West India Company crews before sending them on to the Netherlands.

Roggeveen, *Journal of Jacob Roggeveen.*

ARETHUSA

Bark (3m). L/B/D: 231′ × 36.1′ × 20.5′ dph (70.4m × 11m × 6.2m). Tons: 1,279 grt. Comp.: 21. Built: Archibald McMillan & Son, Ltd., Dumbarton, Scotland; 1890.

Built as a general cargo carrier, *Arethusa* traded to the Far East, the colonial trade to Australia, and the nitrate trade from Chile. She gained lasting fame when the young Rex Clements, who signed aboard her as an apprentice in about 1901, wrote of his first voyage in her — eighteen months from London to Adelaide, Newcastle, Callao, Pisco, and home again — in *Gipsy of the Horn: A Narrative of a Voyage Round the World in a Windjammer,* published in 1924. *Arethusa* carried on through World War I, until she was intercepted and sunk by a German submarine about 15 miles northwest of Achill Island, on April 24, 1917.

Clements, *Gipsy of the Horn.*

ARGO

Galley (1m). *L/B/D:* 54′ × 9.3′ × 2′ (16.5m × 2.8m × 0.6m). *Hull:* wood. *Comp.:* 20. *Des.:* Colin Mudie. *Built:* Vasilis Delimitros, Spetses, Greece; 1984.

In the early 1980s, Tim Severin decided to retrace the voyage of Jason from the Aegean to Colchis on the eastern shores of the Black Sea. The most comprehensive version of the Golden Fleece myth is recorded in Apollonius of Rhodes' *Argonautica,* from the third century BCE. According to Apollonius, in order to reclaim the throne from his uncle, Jason was sent by Pelias of Iolcus to capture the Golden Fleece from Colchis. His ship was built by Argos and crewed by a number of Greek heroes including Argos and Jason. Passing through the northern Aegean, they traversed the Dardanelles, Sea of Marmara, and Bosporus and proceeded east along the southern shore of the Black Sea to Colchis, in what is thought to be present-day Georgia. There, King Aeetes told Jason that he could have the Golden Fleece only if he yoked two fire-breathing oxen, plowed a field, sowed it with dragon's teeth, and slew the warriors who would spring from the seed on the same day. Aided by Aeetes' daughter Medea, Jason succeeded in his task. According to Strabo (fifth century BCE), the legend of the Golden Fleece originated in the Colchians' practice of using wool to filter gold dust from the rivers.

Working from pictorial and other evidence, Colin Mudie drew plans for a galley from about 1200 BCE. The new *Argo* departed Volos on May 2, 1984, and after crossing the Aegean, she entered the Dardanelles nineteen days later. By June 15 the ship was in the Black Sea, and proceeding under oars alone for most of the time, she made her way slowly eastward. Among the ports of call they could identify with Greek myth were Eregli, near where the River Acheron flows and where Herakles descended into the Underworld to capture Hades' watchdog, Cerberus, and where Idmon the soothsayer and Tiphys, Jason's helmsman, died. Once east of Sinope, *Argo* encountered favorable winds although the storms of the first thirty-six hours tested the mettle of the Bronze Age design and the twentieth-century crew to the utmost. Ten days later they arrived at Giresun Island, known as the Island of Ares, where Jason had met four of his Colchian cousins, who had been shipwrecked en route to Greece and who agreed to accompany him back to their home. On July 19, the new *Argo* departed Hopa, Turkey, the first ship to clear the port for the Soviet Union since World War II. Once into Soviet territorial waters, the crew were greeted by the sail-training bark *Tovarisch* and a crew of professional oarsmen and other athletes who helped row *Argo* the rest of the way to Poti, where the latter-day Argonauts were welcomed by thousands of Georgians for whom the legend of Jason and the Golden Fleece remains very much a part of the popular culture. After several days of celebration, *Argo* was towed and rowed up the Rhioni River (as the Phasis is now known) until she ran aground on a mud bank abreast of Jaladdi, the oldest Bronze Age settlement yet found on the Rhioni River.

Jason's route home varies depending on the version of the myth. Some say he returned the way he came, while others have him ascending the Danube or other rivers and proceeding overland to the Mediterranean. Severin and his crew returned via more conventional means, and *Argo* was eventually taken to the Exeter Maritime Museum in England.

Apollonius Rhodius, *Argonautica.* Severin, *Jason Voyage.*

ARGO MERCHANT

(ex-*Arcturus*) Tanker (3m). *L/B/D:* 641.3′ × 84.3′ × 34.8′ (195.5m × 25.7m × 10.6m). *Tons:* 18,743 grt. *Hull:* steel. *Comp.:* 38. *Mach.:* 16 kts. *Built:* Howaldtswerke, AG, Hamburg; 1953.

The vehicle of what might have been one of the worst ecological disasters in the United States, the tanker *Argo Merchant* was launched as *Arcturus.* She led an uneventful life during her first eleven years at sea, but in 1964 she began to experience chronic problems with her engines, machinery, and crew. Between 1964 and 1973 the ship was involved in fourteen shipping casualties — five and a half times the average — including one collision in Japan and two groundings in Indonesia (under the name *Permina Samudra III*) and Sicily (as *Vari*). In 1973 she was bought by Thebes Shipping, Inc., and renamed *Argo Merchant.* In 1975 she received Bureau Véritas's highest rating, but following small oil spills at Philadelphia and Boston, the commander of the First Coast Guard District recommended barring her from U.S. waters, though that couldn't be done legally.

In early December 1976, *Argo Merchant* loaded 7.7 million gallons of crude oil at Puerto La Cruz, Venezuela, for Boston. Under Captain Georgios Papadopoulos, the ship carried two unqualified crew as helmsmen, a broken gyroscope, inadequate charts, and an inaccurate radio direction finder. At 0600 on December 15, the tanker ran aground on Middle Rip Shoal in position 41°02N, 69°27′W — about 25 miles southeast of Nantucket and more than 24 miles off her intended course. The thirty-eight crew were rescued, but the shallow waters and the season made it impossible to offload the oil or move the ship. On December 21, 1976, *Argo Merchant* broke apart and spilled enough oil to heat 18,000 homes for a year. Northwest winds blew the 60- by 100-mile slick offshore, and coastal fisheries and beaches were spared the worst.

Hooke, *Modern Shipping Disasters.* Winslow, *Hard Aground.*

USS ARGUS

Brig (2m). *L/B/D:* 95.5′ × 27′ × 12.7′ (29.1m × 8.2m × 3.9m). *Tons:* 31 bm. *Hull:* wood. *Comp.:* 142. *Arm.:* 18 × 24pdr, 2 × 12pdr. *Built:* Edmund Hartt, Boston; 1803.

One of two ships, with USS HORNET, authorized by Congress in 1803, USS *Argus* was launched and commissioned the same year and sailed for the Mediterranean station under Lieutenant Stephen Decatur, who relinquished command to Lieutenant Isaac Hull at Gibraltar. *Argus* remained in the Mediterranean for three years and was present at many of the defining moments in the Barbary Wars: the bombardment of Tripoli in August 1804; the ill-fated attempt to destroy the Tripolitan fleet with the bomb ship INTREPID, which she escorted into the port; and the capture of Derna. In 1804, Colonel William Eaton conceived a plan to restore the deposed Pasha Hamet Karamanli to the throne of Tripoli. Raising a mixed force of Greeks, Italians, Arabs, and ten Americans, Eaton marched 600 miles across North Africa from Egypt to Derna where, supported by gunfire from *Argus* and *Hornet,* they captured the fort on April 27, 1805. (This action inspired "The Marine Hymn" verse about "the shores of Tripoli.")

The following year, *Argus* returned to the United States and after a brief lay-up, she was assigned to home waters along the East Coast. She remained in this work through the opening of the War of 1812. In the fall of that year she captured six British prizes. On June 19, 1813, Minister to France William H. Crawford embarked in *Argus* for the voyage to L'Orient, France, where she arrived on July 11. Nine days later, Lieutenant William H. Allen embarked on a commerce-destroying mission in the English Channel and then into the Irish Sea. *Argus*'s crew captured 20

ships — 11 of them after August 10 — of which 13 were sunk and the remainder used as cartel ships, manned and kept. At dawn on the 14th, *Argus* was brought to battle by HM Brig *Pelican* (18 guns), Commander John Fordyce Maples. The contest was brief, *Pelican* gaining the weather gauge and rendering the American unmaneuverable within 15 minutes. *Argus* lost 10 men killed (including Allen) and 13 wounded. She was brought back to Plymouth and sold to an unknown buyer.

Dye, *Fatal Cruise of the Argus.* U.S. Navy, *DANFS.*

ARGUS

Schooner (4m). *L/B/D:* 188.8′ × 32.5′ × 19.5′ dph (63.7m × 9.9m × 5.9m). *Tons:* 696 grt. *Comp.:* 70. *Hull:* steel. *Mach.:* oil engine, 475 hp diesel. *Built:* De Haan & Oerlemans Scheepsbauwerft, Heusden, Neth.; 1939.

Owned by the Parceria Geral de Pescarias of Lisbon, *Argus* and thirty-two other sailing ships were a vital part of the post–World War II Portuguese Grand Banks fishing fleet. Their story is celebrated in Alan Villiers's *Quest of the Schooner "Argus."* With his characteristic respect for ships and men, Villiers records how he sailed under Captain Adolfo from Portugal to the Grand Banks and then north into Baffin Bay. Every day from April until October, *Argus*'s 53 cod fishermen took to 14-foot, flat-bottomed dories from which they paid out and hauled in, by hand, 600-hook long-lines. Eventually converted for side-fishing, *Argus* remained under Portuguese ownership until 1976 when she was sold to Windjammer Cruises for use as a charter boat in the Caribbean. Renamed *Polynesia II,* she remained in that work through the 1980s.

Villiers, *Quest of the Schooner "Argus."*

ARIEL

Clipper (3m). *L/B/D:* 197.4′ × 33.9′ × 21′ (60.2m × 10.3m × 6.4m). *Tons:* 853 net. *Hull:* composite. *Des.:* William Rennie. *Built:* Robert Steele & Co., Greenock, Scotland; 1865.

Ordered by Shaw, Lowther & Maxton for the China tea trade, *Ariel* was built of composite construction, with iron frames and wood planking. Named for "an ayrie spirit" in Shakespeare's *Tempest,* she was considered one of the most beautiful clippers ever built, and her long-time captain John Keay later wrote to Basil Lubbock:

> *Ariel* was a perfect beauty to every nautical man who ever saw her: in symmetrical grace and proportion of hull, spars, sails, rigging and finish, she satisfied the eye and put all in

Pearl Harbor's "Battleship Row" during the surprise attack on the Hawaiian naval base, December 7, 1941. From left to right are USS NEVADA, VESTAL *and* ARIZONA, WEST VIRGINIA *(listing to port after a torpedo hit) and* TENNESSEE, OKLAHOMA *and* MARYLAND, *fleet oiler* NEOSHO *(sunk 5 months later), and, far right,* CALIFORNIA. *Courtesy U.S. Naval Historical Center Foundation, Washington, D.C.*

love with her without exception. The curve of stem, figurehead and entrance, the easy sheer and graceful lines of the hull seemed grown and finished as life takes shape and beauty. The proportion and stand of her masts and yards were all perfect.

It was a pleasure to coach her. Very light airs gave her headway and I could trust her like a live thing in all evolutions; in fact she could do anything short of speaking.

Though her career was short, *Ariel* left an impressive record. Her first return from Foochow, under Keay, established her as one of the fastest clippers. On May 29, 1866, she crossed the bar at Foochow fourteen hours behind FIERY CROSS (though she had finished loading first) and less than a day ahead of *Serica, Taitsing,* and *Taeping.* She carried 615 tons of tea at £5 per ton, with a guaranteed premium of "10s per ton extra if first sailing vessel in dock [at London] with new teas from Foochow." The ships were virtually neck and neck down the China Sea, across the Indian Ocean, and up the Atlantic. *Ariel* was off Deal at 0800 September 6, followed ten minutes later by

Taeping and, later that night, *Serica.* (All three were from Steele's yard.) *Ariel* and *Taeping* split the premium, but the simultaneous arrival of so much tea drove down the market price and the offer of a premium was thereafter dropped.

On her second passage out, *Ariel* left Gravesend on October 14, 1866, and anchored at Hong Kong on January 5, 1867, after a passage of 83 days, the fastest ever made against the monsoon and less than a week off the record of 77 days made by *Cairngorm* in 1853. The average of *Ariel's* other three outward passages was 106 days. Captain Keay's first mate Courtenay took command of *Ariel* in 1868, and four years later she was lost at sea en route from London for Sydney under Captain Cachevaille.

Lubbock, *China Clippers.* MacGregor, *Tea Clippers.*

USS ARIZONA (BB-39)

Pennsylvania-class battleship. *L/B/D:* 608′ × 106.3′ × 28.8′ (185.3m × 32.4m × 8.8m). *Tons:* 36,567 disp. *Hull:* steel. *Comp.:* 915–1,358. *Arm.:* 12 × 14″ (3 × 4), 22 × 5″, 4 × 3″. *Armor:* 13.5″ belt, 4″ deck. *Mach.:* geared turbines, 31,500 shp, 4 screws; 21 kts. *Built:* New York Navy Yard, Brooklyn; 1916.

USS *Arizona* was one of two *Pennsylvania*-class dreadnought battleships built during World War I. Because of the scarcity of fuel oil in Britain, she was unable to serve in Europe and her first wartime service was spent patrolling the East Coast. With Woodrow Wilson's flotilla en route to the ill-fated Versailles peace conference, *Arizona* was later dispatched to the Mediterranean. In May 1919, the ship provided protection for U.S. interests during the Greek invasion of Smyrna. Returning to home waters, *Arizona* spent most of the 1920s attached to the Pacific Fleet at San Pedro. A modernization program in 1930–31 saw the removal of her original tripod masts and the addition of antitorpedo blisters. In 1938–39, she was flagship of Rear Admiral Chester W. Nimitz, Commander of Battleship Division 1.

In April 1940, *Arizona* was part of the fleet sent to Pearl Harbor as a forward deterrent to Japanese expansion in the Pacific. As fate would have it, she became one of the first U.S. casualties of Japanese aggression. On December 7, 1941, USS *Arizona* was one of seven battleships moored along Battleship Row on the southeast shore of Ford Island. (Her sister ship *Pennsylvania* was in dry-dock.) At 0755, the first waves of carrier planes — 81 fighters, 135 dive bombers, 104 high-level bombers, and 40 torpedo planes from 6 aircraft carriers — roared overhead. About one minute into the raid an armor-piercing bomb exploded in her forward magazine and *Arizona* became the first ship sunk in the attack. Although the ship settled quickly, trapping many of her crew below decks, *Arizona* was not abandoned until 1032. The final death toll was 1,103 officers and crew out of 1,358 aboard, including Captain Franklin Van Valkenburgh and Rear Admiral Isaac C. Kidd, Commander of Battleship Division 1, both of whom were killed in the initial explosion. Although Fleet Admiral Isoroku Yamamoto's audacious attack mauled the U.S. fleet severely, the three Pacific-based aircraft carriers USS ENTERPRISE, LEXINGTON, and SARATOGA were at sea and formed the nucleus of the huge armada that would finally defeat Japan three and a half years later.

Although USS *Arizona* was officially listed as sunk by enemy action, the ship was never formally decommissioned. Since 1950, the national ensign has been raised on the ship every day as on any other commissioned ship in the Navy. In 1962, the Arizona Memorial, a white bridge spanning the hull of the sunken ship, was opened and dedicated as a national shrine.

Delgado, "Recovering the Past of USS *Arizona*." Stillwell, *Battleship "Arizona."*

ARK

L/B/D: 300 cubits × 50 × 30 (dph). *Hull:* gopher wood. *Comp.:* 8 people; animals. *Built:* Noah.

The Ark was the vessel that God commanded Noah to build in preparation for the flood, which He sent because "God saw that the wickedness of man was great in the earth, and that every imagination of the thoughts of his heart was only evil continually." God determined to drown all of mankind except for Noah, whom He ordered to build a vessel in which his family and representatives of all the species of the Earth could live for the duration of the flood. God's building instructions were explicit:

> Make thee an ark of gopher wood; rooms shalt thou make in the ark, and shalt pitch it within and without with pitch. And this is the fashion which thou shalt make it of. The length of the ark shall be three hundred cubits, the breadth of it fifty cubits, and the height of it thirty cubits. A window shalt thou make to the ark, and in a cubit shalt thou finish it above; and the door of the ark shalt thou set in the side thereof; with lower, second and third stories shalt thou make it.

After Noah had gathered his wife, his sons Shem, Ham, and Japheth together with their wives, and "living creatures of every kind, two of each kind, male and female" — birds, beasts and reptiles — "and every kind of food that can be eaten," God sent the flood. The rain itself lasted for 40 days and eventually covered the earth with water to a depth of 15 cubits. There remained the problem of figuring out "if the waters were abated off the face of the ground." Noah investigated this by sending out a dove from the Ark. On the first try, she found nothing, and on the second she returned "and, lo, in her mouth was an olive leaf pluckt off." On the third try, she failed to return. Nonetheless, the Ark drifted for 150 days before finally coming to rest on the mountains of Ararat, in what is now eastern Turkey. After one year, one month, and ten days, Noah and his family left the Ark, whereupon God established with Noah the covenant of the rainbow, and his sons went forth to populate the earth.

The historicity of the Ark has been the subject of endless speculation since biblical times, and several expeditions have set out in search of the vessel's remains in the twentieth century. The length-to-beam ratio of 6:1 is plausible for a vessel of the sixth century BCE (the date of the composition of Genesis). But if a cubit is about half a meter (1.5 feet — some estimates put it at about 0.6m, or 2 feet), a length of 140 meters (450 feet) would make the Ark many times bigger than the largest known vessels from antiquity. (A simplified measurement of length times beam times half the beam divided by 100 yields a gross tonnage of about 12,000 tons.)

Of more immediate relevance to historians of later maritime history is the fact that the Ark is the most commonly illustrated vessel in European art. Taken together, these images in frescoes, stone carvings, manuscripts, and other media comprise a visual encyclopedia of shipbuilding that shows the transition from shell-first construction with frames inserted later (clinker in the north, carvel in the south) to the skeleton-first construction that predominated after the fifteenth century.

Genesis 6:1–8:17. Unger, *The Art of Medieval Technology.*

CSS ARKANSAS

Arkansas-class ironclad. *L/B/D:* 165′ × 35′ × 11.5′ (50.3m × 10.7m × 3.5m). *Hull:* wood and iron. *Comp.:* 200. *Arm.:* 2 × 9″, 2 × 9″, 2 × 6″, 2 × 32pdr, 2 × 64pdr. *Armor:* 18″ iron and wood. *Mach.:* low-pressure engines, 900 ihp, 2 screws; 8 mph. *Built:* J. T. Shirley, Memphis, Tenn.; 1862.

CSS *Arkansas* was a powerful casemate ironclad ram distinguished particularly for what she accomplished, despite being so imperfectly and incompletely finished that a junior officer, George W. Gift, described her as a "hermaphrodite iron-clad." Plated over with railroad iron and iron plate, she had a 9-ton ramming beak and was considered fast for her size. Laid down at Memphis and completed at Yazoo City, she was commissioned in May 1862, Lieutenant Isaac Newton Brown commanding. On July 15 she engaged the ironclads *Tyler, Belle of the West* and CARONDELET, the latter being run aground with 35 casualties. She then entered the Mississippi and ran through Flag Officer David Farragut's fleet above Vicksburg to take refuge beneath the batteries of that city. The same night she was again engaged by Farragut's fleet as it put down the river. After repairs, *Arkansas* left for Baton Rouge on August 3, but her engines failed three days later, and she was abandoned and set afire to avoid capture by USS *Essex.*

Milligan, *Gunboats down the Mississippi.* Still, *Iron Afloat.*

ARK ROYAL

(ex-*Ark Raleigh*) Galleon (4m). *Tons:* 694 burden. *Hull:* wood. *Comp.:* 4 × 60pdr, 4 × 30pdr, 12 × 18pdr, 12 × 9pdr, 6 × 6pdr, 17 small. *Built:* Deptford Dockyard; 1587.

Built for Sir Walter Raleigh at Deptford, *Ark Raleigh* was taken over by Queen Elizabeth before completion and renamed. During the Spanish Armada the following year, *Ark Royal* sailed as flagship of Charles Howard, Lord Howard of Effingham. With high stern castles but a cut-down forecastle that made her more weatherly than the high-charged vessels of the previous century, she had four masts; the fore and main were square rigged and set topsails, while the mizzen and bonaventure set single lateen sails.

When the Spanish Armada arrived in the English Channel on July 30, 1588, Howard led his fleet of more than fifty-six ships out of Plymouth. The following day, his ships came astern of the larger, less maneuverable Spanish fleet, and *Ark Royal* was the first English ship to engage the Spanish, attacking the 820-ton *Rata Santa Maria Encoronada* until other Spanish ships could come to her aid. On August 2, the Spanish fleet was caught off Portland Bill between the English fleet and the land. Martín de Bertendona's *Regazona* attempted to board *Ark Royal,* which slipped away. When the wind changed in Howard's favor, he attacked Medina Sidonia's flagship, SAN MARTÍN, though to little effect.

The following three days brought only light winds and the two fleets made their way slowly towards Calais, where they anchored on August 6. The next night, Howard ordered a fleet of fire ships sent down on the Spanish fleet, which escaped in disorder but otherwise relatively unscathed. The next morning, Howard led an English force in boarding the galleass *San Lorenzo,* which had grounded on a sandbar in the escape, and *Ark Royal* missed the main action of the Battle of Gravelines. By the next day, the Spanish fleet was blown past the rendezvous with the land forces of the Duke of Parma and into the North Sea. Although the English could not destroy the Spanish fleet, the elements did.

*Ark Royal'*s next major engagement came in 1596, when she was part of a fleet that attacked the Spanish at Cadiz. She was readied to repel another Spanish threat in 1599, although the anticipated invasion never happened. In 1608, *Ark Royal* was rebuilt as *Anne Royal,* and as such she remained on the navy list until she sank at Tilbury Hope in 1636.

Mattingly, *Armada.* Sugden, *Sir Francis Drake.*

HMS ARK ROYAL

Ark Royal-class aircraft carrier. *L/B/D:* 800' × 94.8' × 22.8' (243.8m × 28.9m × 6.9m). *Tons:* 27,720 disp. *Hull:* steel. *Comp.:* 1,580. *Arm.:* 72 aircraft; 16 × 4.5", 48 × 2pdr, 6 × 20mm. *Armor:* 4.5" belt, 3.5" deck. *Mach.:* geared turbines, 102,000 shp, 3 screws; 30.8 kts. *Built:* Cammell Laird & Co., Ltd., Birkenhead, Eng.; 1938.

The third ship of the name, HMS *Ark Royal* was one of the Royal Navy's most modern aircraft carriers at the start of World War II. Attached to the Home Fleet and under command of Captain A. J. Power in 1939, *Ark Royal* was involved in virtually every major naval campaign during the war's first two years, and many enduring carrier aviation techniques were developed and perfected on her decks. On September 14, 1939, planes from *Ark Royal* scored the first Allied victory against the German submarine corps, sinking *U-39* northwest of Ireland. On the 27th, her Skuas shot down the first German planes of the war over the North Sea. In a retaliatory attack, the Germans claimed — not for the last time — to have sunk the carrier. Soon after, *Ark Royal* and the battleship RENOWN were dispatched to the South Atlantic to look for the pocket battleship ADMIRAL GRAF SPEE, and from October to February 1940 she remained stationed at Freetown, Sierra Leone, patrolling the seas between Brazil and West Africa before returning to Portsmouth.

Ark Royal was next dispatched to the Mediterranean to join the aircraft carrier GLORIOUS at Alexandria. No sooner had she arrived when on April 7 the Germans invaded Norway. Two weeks later she was back in the Clyde and on April 23 she sailed for Norway — Captain C. S. Holland — for the start of ten weeks of operations, ultimately fruitless, intended to keep Narvik from falling into German hands. On June 8, *Glorious* was sunk by SCHARNHORST and GNEISENAU, and four days later *Ark Royal* launched retaliatory strikes against German shipping at Trondheim, losing eight of fifteen planes in an inconclusive raid.

After four days at Scapa Flow, *Ark Royal* returned to the Mediterranean. Following the surrender of France and the advent of the Vichy government of Marshal Pétain, the British realized that they must either capture or destroy the French fleet to prevent it falling into German hands. On July 2, Vice Admiral Sir James Somerville hoisted his flag in the battlecruiser HMS HOOD to form Force H — consisting also of battleships *Valiant* and *Resolution, Ark Royal,* and cruisers *Arethusa* and *Enterprise,* among other ships. The next day Force H arrived off Mers el-Kébir at the start of Operation Catapult, whereby the British intended to neutralize the potential threat posed by the French fleet. In the port just three miles from Oran, Algeria, lay the battlecruisers *Dun-*

kerque, STRASBOURG, battleships PROVENCE and BRETAGNE, seaplane carrier *Commandant Teste,* and six destroyers. Admiral Marcel Gensoul was given a number of options: fight, sail to a British port, the French West Indies, or the United States, or scuttle his ships within six hours. When Gensoul declined to heed the British demands, Somerville opened the attack. *Bretagne* blew up, *Provence* was beached, and *Dunkerque* was damaged and finished off the next day by aircraft from *Ark Royal.* Only *Strasbourg* escaped to Toulon.

With Italy's declaration of war on June 10, 1940, the Admiralty's main priority became the maintenance of its Mediterranean supply line and especially Malta, which lay halfway between Gibraltar and Egypt. In July, *Ark Royal* flew the first of many operations against Italian airfields near Cagliari, Sardinia. In late September, she was sent to West Africa in a failed attempt to land de Gaulle's Free French forces at Dakar, Senegal. In early October she was at Liverpool for several weeks of maintenance, but by November 7 she was back in the Mediterranean attacking Cagliari. At the end of the month, she took part in the Battle of Spartivento, engaging a fleet that included the battleships VITTORIO VENETO and *Giulio Cesare,* although there were no losses on either side. The following spring she was used frequently to deliver planes to the beleaguered garrison at Malta, and in March she briefly took part in the search for the battle-cruisers *Gneisenau* and *Scharnhorst* in the Atlantic.

In April 1941, Captain L. E. H. Maund assumed command. When it was learned that BISMARCK was at large in the North Atlantic, *Ark Royal,* RENOWN, and SHEFFIELD were among the ships of Force H mobilized to search for the crippled German battleship as she made her way towards France. At 0835 on the morning of May 26, ten Swordfish flew off the decks of *Ark Royal,* which was pitching some 50 feet in high winds and seas. At 1115 *Bismarck* was sighted, and from then on until her sinking the next day, British forces were continuously in contact with her. That night, planes from *Ark Royal* scored two torpedo hits that knocked out *Bismarck*'s steering gear, and the next morning she was finished off by British surface units.

Ark Royal returned to the Mediterranean, dedicated especially to the relief of Malta. At 1541 on November 13, she was torpedoed by *U-81* about thirty miles east of Gibraltar. Despite valiant efforts to keep her afloat, *Ark Royal* sank the next morning at 0613, with only one man lost, off Gibraltar in 36°06'N, 5°07'W.

Jameson, *Ark Royal 1939–1941.*

ARKTIKA

(ex-*Leonid Brezhnev*) *Arktika*-class icebreaker (1f/2m). *L/B/D:* 435.3′ × 91.9′ × 30.1′ (148m × 28m × 11m). *Tons:* 18,172 grt. *Hull:* steel. *Mach.:* nuclear reactors, steam turbines, 75,000 shp, 3 screws; 18 kts. *Built:* Baltic Shipbuilding & Engineering Works, Leningrad, USSR; 1974.

The second nuclear-powered icebreaker built by the Soviet Union after LENIN, *Arktika* was the first of five vessels in her class. Originally named for the General Secretary of the USSR, she was designed for the sea routes of the Northeast Passage across the top of the Soviet Union; in 1975 she became the first surface ship to reach the North Pole. Sponsored by T. B. Guzhenko, minister of the merchant fleet of the Soviet Union, the expedition was described simply as a "scientific-practical experimental voyage" intended to test the new icebreaker in more extreme conditions than the ship would ordinarily encounter. Under command of Captain O. G. Pashnin, *Arktika* sailed from Murmansk on August 9, 1975, and reached the North Pole eight days later.

This trip was not repeated for another decade, but since the 1980s, the voyage has become one of increasing popularity for tourists who travel in great comfort to the top of the world aboard Russian, Swedish, German, and other ships.

Gardiner, ed., *Shipping Revolution.*

ASGARD

Ketch. *L/B/D:* 44′ × 13′ × 7.5′ (13.4m × 4m × 2.3m). *Tons:* 18 grt. *Hull:* wood. *Comp.:* 6. *Built:* Colin Archer, Larvik; 1905.

In 1903, flush with the success of his classic espionage thriller *Riddle of the Sands,* which had awakened the English public to the threat posed by a militarized Germany just across the North Sea, Erskine Childers married the Irish-American Mary Osgood of Boston. As a wedding present, her parents gave the Childerses the ketch-rigged yacht ordered from the great Norwegian designer Colin Archer. Over the next decade, the couple cruised around England, Ireland, the North Sea, and the Baltic. In the meantime, they became increasingly involved in Ireland's Home Rule movement. Shortly before the outbreak of World War I, Army of Ulster Volunteers in the North of Ireland brought from Germany 35,000 rifles and 3 million rounds of ammunition. Before the Irish Nationalists might do the same, the British government made such imports illegal. Nonetheless, Childers became involved in a scheme involving mostly Anglo-Irish Protestants like himself to import Mauser rifles and ammunition on be-

half of the Irish Volunteers in the south. On July 3, 1914, *Asgard* sailed from Conway, Wales, with a crew of six including Molly Childers and Mary Spring-Rice, who had suggested the idea to Irish nationalist Roger Casement. After rendezvousing at Cowes with Conor O'Brien in *Kelpie* (with a crew of four), on the night of July 12 the two vessels loaded 1,500 rifles from the German tug *Gladiator* off Ruytigen Lightship near the mouth of the Scheldt. They returned to Ireland unchallenged and the Mausers were distributed to the Irish Volunteers, *Asgard*'s at Kingstown (Dun Laoghaire), and *Kelpie*'s at Kilcoole, Wicklow.

World War I began a week later. A lieutenant in the Royal Navy Volunteer Reserve, Childers was awarded the Distinguished Service Cross for his work as an reconnaissance expert, his first assignment being aboard the seaplane carrier HMS *Engadine*. In 1921, Childers refused to accept the treaty leading to the creation of the Irish Free State and joined the Irish Republican Army. The following year he was arrested by Free State soldiers and, found guilty of a weapons charge, executed by firing squad after first shaking hands with each of its members. (Half a century later, his son became president of Ireland.) Following Childers's death, *Asgard* was used as a sail-training vessel by the Irish government. Declared a national monument, in 1980 she was laid up and preserved ashore at the Kilmainham Museum, Dublin.

Childers, *Howth Gun-Running; Thirst for the Sea.* Leather, *Colin Archer and the Seaworthy Double-Ender.*

HMS ASSOCIATION

2nd rate 90 (3m). *L/B/D:* 165′ × 45.3′ × 18.2′ dph (50.3m × 13.8m × 5.6m). *Tons:* 1,459 bm. *Hull:* wood. *Comp.:* 680. *Arm.:* 26 × 32pdr, 26 × 18pdr, 26 × 9pdr, 18 × 6pdr. *Des.:* Bagwell. *Built:* Portsmouth Dockyard, Eng.; 1699.

The flagship of Admiral Sir Cloudisley Shovell when he was sent out to the Mediterranean in the War of the Spanish Succession, *Association* took part in the capture of Gibraltar on August 4, 1704, and the subsequent battle of Malaga, against the French fleet on August 24. The ship is best remembered for the tragedy that befell Shovell's squadron upon its return from the Mediterranean in the autumn of 1707 under Captain Edmund Loades. After lying-to near the mouth of the English Channel while waiting for a fresh breeze, the 12 ships proceeded on the evening of October 22. However, the ships were off course, and they soon ran aground on the Bishop and Clerks Rocks off the Scilly Isles. *Association* was quickly smashed on the rocks, with the loss of her entire complement of 800 men. Three other ships were also lost that night: the 3rd-rate *Eagle*, Captain Robert Hancock, with more than 500 men; the 4th-rate *Romney*, Captain William Coney, with about 250 crew; and the fireship *Firebrand*, Commander Francis Piercey, from which there were 24 survivors.

Hepper, *British Warship Losses*. Powell, "Wreck of Sir Cloudesley Shovell."

L'ASTROLABE

(ex-*L'Autruche*) Frigate (3m). *Tons:* 450. *Hull:* wood. *Comp.:* 109. *Built:* France; 1781.

L'Astrolabe was the second of two ships in the Comte de La Pérouse's expedition to the Pacific in 1785–88. A former supply vessel, *L'Astrolabe* sailed under command of Paul-Antoine-Marie Fleuriot de Langle. In company with LA BOUSSOLE, she sailed from Brest on August 1, 1785, calling at Brazil, Chile, Easter Island, and Hawaii before making an extensive survey of the Pacific coast of North America from Mount St. Elias to Monterey. The two ships then crossed to Macao and stayed for the first two months of 1787 before sailing to the Philippines, the Sea of Japan, and Sakhalin Island (where de Langle was honored with the name of a bay), and along the Kurile Islands to the remote Russian settlement at Petropavlovsk on the Kamchatka Peninsula.

In September, they sailed south and did not make landfall until December 6, when they landed in the Samoan Islands (which Bougainville had called the Navigators) and anchored at Tutuila. On December 11, de Langle went ashore to get fresh water and was attacked by more than 1,000 Samoans who killed him and 11 of his crew, and wounded 20 others. Although the attack seemed unprovoked, La Pérouse refused to allow any reprisals, carrying out to the letter Louis XVI's injunction that "he will have recourse to arms only as a last extremity, only as a means of defense, and in circumstances when any tolerance would inevitably place the ships and the King's subjects in danger."

La Pérouse appointed Robert Sutton de Clonard to command *L'Astrolabe* and the ships sailed for Botany Bay, Australia, where they arrived on January 24, 1788. The French sent their last dispatches home, announcing their intention to visit Tonga, New Caledonia, the Solomon Islands, the Louisiade Archipelago, and the west coast of Australia before returning to France in June 1789. Nothing was heard from the ships after their departure from Botany Bay in March, and in 1791, the French government dispatched a search expedition under Chevalier

d'Entrecasteaux in *La Recherche* and L'ESPERANCE. No sign of the La Pérouse expedition was discovered until Captain Peter Dillon recovered artifacts from the ships on the island of Vanikoro in 1826.

La Pérouse, *Journal of Jean-François de Galaup de la Pérouse*. Shelton, *From Hudson's Bay to Botany Bay*.

L'ASTROLABE

(ex-*Coquille*) Corvette (3m). *Tons:* 380. *Hull:* wood. *Comp.:* 70–79. *Built:* France; 1811.

Shortly after returning to France from a three-year circumnavigation as lieutenant in Louis de Freycinet's L'URANIE, Louis I. Duperrey and his colleague Jules S. Dumont d'Urville made a proposal for a new circumnavigation to the Minister of Marine, the Marquis de Clermont Tonnerre. The twin aims were scientific — including studies of terrestrial magnetism and meteorology — and geographic, with a view especially to confirming or correcting the position of islands and other landmarks essential to safe navigation. Departing Toulon on August 11, 1822, *Coquille* ("Shell") sailed via Ascension Island, St. Catherine Island (arriving the week that Brazil declared its independence from Portugal), and the Falklands — where the shipwrecked *Uranie* still lay — before rounding Cape Horn. Once in the Pacific, *Coquille* sailed along the coast of South America as far as Paita, Peru, and then headed west through the Tuamotus to Tahiti, arriving on May 3. The expedition continued westward through the Society, Friendly (Tonga), and Fiji Islands. Though bound for Australia, horrendous weather forced them to steer northwest, and they passed the Santa Cruz and Solomon Islands before landing at Louis de Bougainville's Port Praslin, New Britain. From there *Coquille* continued across the top of New Guinea to the Dutch entrepôt at Amboina where the French spent most of October.

Coquille sailed to Port Jackson via the west and south coasts of Australia, and after a two-month layover continued to New Zealand in April 1824. After two weeks visiting with the English missionaries, who had been established there for nine years, the French sailed north through the Ellice and Gilbert Islands and west through the Carolines to New Guinea, where they arrived at the end of July. After a stop at the Dutch settlement of Surabaya, *Coquille* turned for France via the British island of Mauritius — formerly the French Ile de France — and St. Helena, where the British had imprisoned French emperor Napoleon Bonaparte from 1815 to his death in 1821. The ship arrived at Marseilles on March 24, 1825.

Upon returning to France, *Coquille* was renamed *L'As-*

The French frigate L'ASTROLABE *and corvette* LA ZÉLÉE's
aground in the Torres Strait towards the end of L'ASTROLABE's
*third and last circumnavigation, undertaken in 1837–40. The
painting is by Louis Le Breton, official artist of the expedition.
Courtesy Peabody Essex Museum, Salem, Massachusetts.*

trolabe, in honor of one of La Pérouse's ships which had
disappeared in 1788. Under Dumont d'Urville, whose
interests were more geographic and ethnographic than
Duperrey's, *Astrolabe* would undertake two further voyages of discovery. The first, from 1826 to 1829, was concentrated in Australian and western Pacific waters, with a
view especially to locating any trace of the La Pérouse
expedition. After a survey of Australia's south coast, *Astrolabe* sailed to New Zealand, where her crew made extensive ethnographic and zoological studies. The French
continued to Tonga and Fiji Islands, where they charted
120 islands — many of them previously unknown — before heading west to the waters around New Guinea.
After repairs to the ship at Amboina, Dumont d'Urville
sailed east through the Torres Strait and south to Tasmania, where Dumont d'Urville learned that the English
captain Peter Dillon had found relics of La Pérouse's
expedition on Vanikoro. Sailing to the New Hebrides, the
French confirmed these findings and gathered artifacts
with which they returned to Marseilles on February 24,
1829, after further stops at Guam, in the East Indies, and
at Ile de France. (Dillon had returned earlier and Charles
X appointed him to the Legion of Honor.)

Although English and American whalers and sealers
had been hunting in the Southern Ocean for the half century since Cook's 1774 voyage into the ice in ENDEAVOUR, and Bellingshausen had sailed near Antarctica in
1820/21 in VOSTOK and *Mirny,* the French had played no
active role in the exploration of the South Seas. In 1836,
France's Emperor Louis-Philippe decided to mount an
expedition to locate the south magnetic pole, with Dumont d'Urville as its leader in *Astrolabe.* Unlike the ship's

previous two expeditions, she would be accompanied by
La Zélée, under Charles Hector Jacquinot, a veteran of the
previous expedition; between them, the ships embarked
seven scientists and naturalists. Departing Toulon on
September 7, 1837, the two ships sailed via Tenerife and
Rio de Janeiro for the Strait of Magellan where they remained from December through January 1838, taking
aboard a Swiss and an Englishman who had been living
among the Patagonians. On January 22, the ships were
confronted with an impenetrable mass of ice that Dumont d'Urville described as

> a marvelous spectacle. More severe and grandiose than can
> be expressed, even as it lifted the imagination it filled the
> heart with a feeling of involuntary terror; nowhere else is one
> so sharply convinced of one's impotence. The image of a new
> world unfolds before us, but it is an inert, lugubrious, and
> silent world in which everything threatens the destruction of
> one's faculties.

The ships were unable to make much progress southward, although they sighted the previously named Palmer
Peninsula, and sailed for Chile in April 1838, where two
men died of scurvy and twenty-two others either deserted or were too ill to continue. From South America
the expedition sailed through the many of the larger Pacific Island groups — the Marquesas, Tahiti, Samoas, Tongas, Fiji, then northwest through the Santa Cruz Islands,
Solomons, and Carolines before coming to the Spanish
island of Guam. *Astrolabe* and *Zélée* continued to the
Philippines, the Dutch East Indies, and then westabout to
Tasmania where they arrived in November 1839. On the
first of the new year, the two ships sailed south and on
January 19 they saw the part of Antarctica they called
Terra Adélie (for d'Urville's wife), though they were unable to land. They also crossed the path of USS *Porpoise,*
one of the ships in the expedition led by Captain Charles
Wilkes in USS VINCENNES.

After determining approximately the position of the
south magnetic pole, the ships returned to Tasmania
where they reembarked some of their sick crew before
sailing for New Zealand. The French were also chagrined
to find that the English had made significant advances in
settling the land they had once considered for a French
colony. From there the ships made their way back to
France, arriving at Toulon on November 7, 1840. Although twenty-two crew had died, and another twenty-seven had left the expedition because of illness or desertion, the ships had brought back the largest quantity of
natural history specimens ever garnered in a single expedition. Although Dumont d'Urville died before its publication, his account of *Astrolabe*'s third voyage ran to
twenty-three volumes, with five atlases. The ship's pre-

vious two voyages resulted in seven volumes and four atlases by Duperrey and fourteen volumes and five atlases by Dumont d'Urville.

Brosse, *Great Voyages of Discovery.* Dumont d'Urville, *Two Voyages to the South Seas by Captain Jules S-C Dumont d'Urville.* Dunmore, *French Explorers in the Pacific.*

ATAGO

Takao-class cruiser (2f/2m). *L/B/D:* 668.7′ × 59.2′ × 20.1′ (203.8m × 18m × 6.1m). *Tons:* 15,490 disp. *Hull:* steel. *Comp.:* 733. *Arm.:* 10 × 8″, 4 × 4.8″, 2 × 40mm; 8 × 24″TT; 3 aircraft. *Armor:* 5″ belt, 1.4″ deck. *Mach.:* geared turbines, 130,000 shp, 4 screws; 35.5 kts. *Built:* Kure Kaigun Kosho, Kure, Japan; 1932.

One of four heavy cruisers built to the same design, *Atago* and her sister ships underwent a substantial rebuild in 1938–39, emerging with a wider beam, more antiaircraft guns, and a slightly altered profile. *Atago* was the flagship of Vice Admiral Nobutake Kondo's Third Fleet during the invasion of the Philippines on December 8, 1941 (December 7 at Pearl Harbor, Hawaii). Following the success of that invasion, she provided distant cover for Malaya and Borneo operations though January 1942, and then sailed as part of a detached force during operations in the Dutch East Indies through March. In late May 1942, *Atago* sailed as flagship of Kondo's Midway Occupation Force, which was to occupy the strategic island following its reduction by carrier planes from AKAGI, HIRYU, SO-RYU, and KAGA, all of which were sunk by U.S. forces on June 4–5.

After weathering the Battles of the Eastern Solomons (August 23–25) and Santa Cruz Islands (October 26–27), *Atago* was damaged at the Naval Battle of Guadalcanal on November 14 by shelling from the U.S. battleships *Washington* and *South Dakota.* In November 1943, she was one of six cruisers under Vice Admiral Takeo Kurita at Rabaul knocked out of action at Rabaul by planes off USS SARA-TOGA and PRINCETON. Nearly a year later, *Atago* was flagship of Kurita's First Striking Force, the most powerful part of the Japanese Navy at the time: seven battleships, eleven heavy cruisers, two light cruisers, and nineteen destroyers anchored at Lingga Roads near Singapore. On October 18, 1944, this fleet weighed anchor at the start of SHO-1, the defense of the Philippines. Five days later, the ships were followed by the submarines USS *Dace* (Lieutenant Commander Claggett) and *Darter* (Lieutenant Commander McClintock) along the Palawan Passage. At 0632 on October 23, *Darter* torpedoed *Atago* at a distance of 980 yards. Although Kurita survived, his flagship sank 18 minutes later with the loss of 320 lives in 09°28′N, 117°17′E. *Atago*'s sister ships fared no better:

Maya was sunk by *Dace; Takao* was forced back to Brunei after being torpedoed by *Darter* (later scuttled after running onto a reef); and two days later *Chokai* was lost at the Battle off Samar.

Jentschura, Jung, & Mickel, *Warships of the Imperial Japanese Navy.* Morison, *Two-Ocean War.*

ATHENIA

Liner (1f/2m). *L/B:* 526.3′ bp × 66.4′ (160.4m × 20.2m). *Tons:* 13,465 grt. *Hull:* steel. *Comp.:* cabin 516; 3rd 1,000. *Mach.:* steam turbines, 2 screws; 15 kts. *Built:* Fairfield Shipbuilding & Engineering Co., Ltd., Govan, Scotland; 1923.

Athenia was built for the Anchor-Donaldson Limited's service between Britain and Canada, and for most of her career sailed between either Glasgow or Liverpool and Quebec and Montreal, with occasional stops at Halifax and St. John. At the height of the winter season she frequently operated as a cruise ship. In 1935, the Anchor Line went out of business, and her owners became the Donaldson Atlantic Line Ltd.

Athenia was the first British ship sunk by a German U-boat in World War II. Germany had invaded Poland on September 1 and Britain declared war on Germany at 1115 on September 3, shortly after *Athenia* sailed from Glasgow en route to Montreal with 1,100 passengers embarked, more than 300 of whom were American citizens. That afternoon she was spotted by U-30 about 250 miles northwest of Inishtrahull, Northern Ireland. Although German U-boats were supposed to be operating under prize regulations that obliged them to stop and search any potential targets, Lieutenant Fritz-Julius Lemp decided *Athenia* was an armed merchant cruiser and fired two torpedoes without warning. The ship sank with the loss of 112 passengers and crew, but despite the fact that among these were 28 Americans, within hours, President Franklin D. Roosevelt had announced that his government was preparing "a declaration of American neutrality."

Bonsor, *North Atlantic Seaway.* Terraine, *Business in Great Waters.*

ATHLIT RAM

Built: 2nd cent. BCE.

In 1980, while conducting a routine underwater survey near Athlit on the Israeli coast, marine archaeologist Yehoshua Ramon discovered a bronze ram from an ancient warship. The partially covered ram lay about 200 meters offshore at a depth of 3 meters. The ram was lifted, conserved, and is now on permanent display at the National Maritime Museum, Haifa. A team from the University of Haifa later investigated the sea floor in the area, but no ship or related artifacts have yet been found.

The ram measures 2.26 meters long, 0.76 meters wide, and 0.96 meters wide, and weighs about 465 kilograms. The surviving wooden armature to which the bronze was fitted was built up of 16 pieces of cedar, elm, and pine. The central wedge-shaped ramming timber was connected by mortise and tenon to the ship's stem; a second heavy timber, raked aft, formed an angle of 71 degrees with the top of the ramming timber. This armature was enclosed in a bronze jacket averaging 2 centimeters in thickness and fastened with copper nails. The asymmetries of the construction suggest that the bronze piece was custom-cast to fit the preexisting bow timbers.

The Athlit ram is of a type familiar from pictorial representations of the Classical and Hellenistic periods. Three bladelike protrusions run horizontally along each side. At the head the three horizontal blades are crossed down the center by a solid vertical section, forming a gridlike striking surface. Driven by oar power, this ancient "warhead" was designed to smash the enemy ship's planking at the waterline. The ram is decorated with a variety of symbols in relief that have been identified with the Hellenistic kings of Egypt Ptolemy V Epiphanes and his successor, Ptolemy VI Philometor, who reigned 204–164 BCE. A date for the ram in the first half of the second century BCE is supported by tree-ring analysis of the wood.

Casson & Steffy, *Athlit Ram.*

CSS ATLANTA

(ex-*Fingal*) Casemate ironclad (1f). *L/B/D:* 204′ × 41′ × 15.8′ (62.2m × 12.5m × 4.8m). *Tons:* 1,006 grt. *Hull:* iron. *Comp.:* 145. *Arm.:* 2 × 7″, 2 × 6.4″, spar torpedo. *Armor:* 4″ casemate. *Mach.:* vertical direct-acting engines, 3 screws; 8 kts. *Built:* J. & G. Thomson, Govan, Scotland; 1861.

The casemate ironclad CSS *Atlanta* began life as the schooner-rigged Scottish coastal steamer *Fingal.* Chartered by Confederate agent James D. Bulloch, she sailed from Scotland, picked up Bulloch in Holyhead (where she inadvertently rammed and sank the brig *Siccardi*), and sailed for Savannah. Her cargo included 14,000 Enfield rifles, one million cartridges, sabers, uniforms, and other materiel. By the time *Fingal* was ready to return to England with a cargo of cotton, Union forces had blockaded Savannah, and in the spring of 1862 she was purchased by the Confederate government. Cut down to the waterline and converted to a casemate ironclad by Nelson and Asa Tift, she was armed with two 7-inch and two 6.4-inch guns, a ram, and spar torpedo.

Commissioned CSS *Atlanta* in 1862, on June 17, 1863, *Atlanta* (Lieutenant William A. Webb, commanding) attempted to attack the Union fleet in Wassau Sound. As she moved down on the Union monitors *Nahant* and *Weehawken,* she ran aground and came under devastating fire that compelled Webb's surrender. After repairs at Philadelphia, *Atlanta* was commissioned in the Union navy and assigned to the North Atlantic Blockading Squadron in 1864, with which she saw extensive service on the James River below Richmond. Decommissioned after the Civil War, she is believed to have been sold to Haitian interests in June 1869 and, renamed *Triumph,* lost at sea off Cape Hatteras in December.

Silverstone, *Warships of the Civil War Navies.* Still, *Iron Afloat.* U.S. Navy, *DANFS.*

ATLANTIC

Steamship (1f/4m). *L/B:* 435′ × 40.9′ (128m × 12.5m). *Tons:* 3,707 grt. *Hull:* iron. *Comp.:* 140 crew; 1st 166, 3rd 1,000 pass. *Mach.:* compound engines, 600 hp, single screw; 14 kts. *Built:* Harland & Wolff, Ltd., Belfast, Ireland, 1871.

The second ship built for Thomas Ismay's White Star Line — formally known as the Oceanic Steam Navigation Company Ltd. — the luxuriously appointed *Atlantic* sailed between Liverpool, Queenstown, and New York. Although it was intended that she enter service to Chile in January 1873, the company's plans to develop that route were abandoned and she continued in transatlantic service. On March 20, 1873, *Atlantic* left Liverpool on her 19th voyage. Four days out she encountered the first of a succession of severe storms and on April 1 Captain John A. Williams decided to make for Halifax to replenish her coal, as required by company regulations. At 0312 the next morning, *Atlantic* drove hard onto the reefs of Marr's Island, east of Halifax Harbor (44°26′N, 63°44′W). Beaten by the waves, within 10 minutes the ship was heeled over about 50 degrees and passengers took to the rigging to avoid being swept into the sea. In the ensuing chaos, the bosun managed to swim ashore with a line along which an estimated 250 crew and passengers crawled to land. A handful of others got away in one of the ship's lifeboats, and the remainder of the survivors were rescued the following morning by fishermen. Accounts differ as to the number of lives lost, with estimates running from 454 of 981 passengers and crew, to

560 of only 931. Incredibly, not one of the survivors was a woman, and only one was a child. A court of inquiry found Captain Williams negligent for running the ship towards the land at speed and for failing to sound the bottom as he neared shore. However, in recognition of his outstanding conduct during the rescue operations and following the accident, his license was suspended for only two years.

Eaton & Haas, *Falling Star.*

ATLANTIC

Schooner (3m). *L/B/D:* 185' × 29.5' × 17.5' (56.4m × 9m × 5.3m). *Tons:* 303 grt. *Hull:* steel. *Comp.:* 7 + crew. *Mach.:* triple expansion. *Des.:* William Gardner (Gardner & Cox). *Built:* Townsend & Downey S. & R., Co., Shooters Island, N.Y.; 1903.

Built for Wilson Marshall, *Atlantic's* greatest claim to fame came in 1905 when she was one of eleven yachts to compete for the Emperor's Cup put up by Kaiser Wilhelm for a race between New York and Lizard Head, England. Among the eight American, two British, and one German entrants were Lord Brassey's SUNBEAM and the 239-foot full-rigged British ship *Valhalla. Atlantic's* professional captain Charles Barr — a veteran of America's Cup campaigns in *Columbia* (1899 and 1901) and RELIANCE (1903) — drove the powerful schooner through a violent gale to a crossing in 12 days, 4 hours. Her 348-mile day's run on May 23–24 has never been bettered, and her overall time was not beaten until 1968, when Eric Taberly's 58-foot trimaran *Paul Richard* made the passage in 10 days, 5 hours, and 14 minutes. During World War I, Marshall publicly smashed the Emperor's Cup with the intent of donating the gold to the Red Cross; it turned out to be gold-plated pewter worth about $35.

Sold to James Cox Bradley, *Atlantic* saw duty as a subchaser tender, and after World War I she was sold to Cornelius Vanderbilt. Under Gerard B. Lambert, heir to the company that made Listerine, she was a favorite to win the 1928 transatlantic race for the King's Cup sponsored by Alfonso XIII of Spain. She lost to *Elena,* and in the same race, Paul Hammond's NIÑA won the Queen's Cup for smaller boats. In 1935, she escorted Lambert's J-Boat *Yankee* to England for a series of races. *Atlantic* did little racing thereafter and in World War II she was transferred to the U.S. Coast Guard for use in antisubmarine duty. Following the war she was brought to the U.S. Coast Guard Academy for sail training. Towed to the Delaware River for breaking up a few years later, she was saved from the breakers by Ward Bright. His plans to restore the

The three-masted schooner ATLANTIC *during the 1928 transatlantic race sponsored by the King of Spain. Lithograph by Burnell Poole, courtesy the family of Burnell Poole.*

vessel came to naught, but her remains could still be seen on the river's Jersey shore following his death in 1968.

Parkinson, *History of the New York Yacht Club.* Robinson, *Legendary Yachts.* Stevenson, *Race for the Emperor's Cup.*

L'ATLANTIQUE

Liner (3f/2m). *L/B:* 744' × 92.1' (226.7m × 28.1m). *Tons:* 42,512 grt. *Hull:* steel. *Comp.:* 1st 414, 2nd 158, 3rd 584; 663 crew. *Mach.:* geared turbines, 50,000 shp, 4 screws; 23 kts. *Built:* Chantiers & Ateliers de St. Nazaire (Penhoët), France; 1931.

At the time of her launching for the Compagnie de Navigation Sud Atlantique, *L'Atlantique* was the largest and most luxurious ship on the South American run. Built for service between France and Argentina, she made her maiden voyage from Bordeaux to Buenos Aires on September 29, 1931. Unfortunately, her career was destined to be a short one. On January 3, 1933, after scarcely a full year in service, she sailed from Bordeaux to Le Havre for a refit. At 0330 the next morning, she was about 22 miles from the island of Guernsey when a fire of unknown origin broke out in a passenger cabin on E deck. There were no passengers aboard, but the shorthanded crew was unable to contain the blaze. Nineteen of the crew were killed before the order was given to abandon ship at 0800. *L'Atlantique* burned and drifted on the tide without sinking, and on January 6 she was taken in tow to Cherbourg by a small fleet of Dutch, German, and French tugs. The ship was abandoned by her owners, and the burned-out hulk languished at Cherbourg until 1936 when she was sold for scrap to the Port Glasgow firm of Smith & Houston.

Kludas, *Great Passenger Ships of the World.*

ATLANTIS

(ex-*Goldenfels*) Merchant raider (2f/2m). *L/B/D:* 488.1′ × 61.3′ × 31.1′ (155m × 18.7m × 8.7m). *Tons:* 7,862 grt. *Hull:* steel. *Comp.:* 351. *Arm.:* 6 × 6″, 1 × 7.5cm, 1 × 3.7cm, 2 × 2cm, 4 × TT; 2 aircraft. *Mach.:* diesel, 7,600 bhp, 1 screw; 16 kts. *Built:* Bremer Vulcan Schiffbau & Maschinenfabrik, Vegesack, Hamburg; 1937.

Built for the Hansa Line as a freighter, *Goldenfels* was converted to wartime duty in 1939. Known by German intelligence as Schiff 16 and designated Raider C by the British, the Helfskreuzer *Atlantis* became the most successful German merchant cruiser of World War II, credited with the sinking or capture of twenty-two Allied merchant ships totaling 145,697 grt. Sailing under the command of Captain Bernard Rogge on March 31, 1940, the *Atlantis* operated in the Atlantic and Indian Oceans before crossing the South Pacific and returning to the Atlantic. On November 22, 1941, while rendezvousing with *U-126*, the *Atlantis* was scuttled after being engaged by heavy cruiser HMS *Devonshire* in 04°02′S, 18°29′W, about 300 miles northwest of Ascension Island. Fight men were lost; the survivors were ultimately rescued by a succession of German and Italian submarines.

Muggenthaler, *German Raiders of World War II.* Schmalenbach, *German Raiders.*

HMS AUDACIOUS

King George V-class battleship (2f/1m). *L/B/D:* 597.6′ × 89′ × 28.8′ (182.1m × 27.1m × 8.8m). *Tons:* 23,000 disp. *Hull:* steel. *Comp.:* 782. *Arm.:* 10 x 13.5″ (5x2), 16 × 4″, 4 × 3pdr; 3 × 21″TT. *Armor:* belt 12″, deck 4″. *Mach.:* Parsons turbines, 31,000 ihp, 4 screws; 21 kts. *Built:* Laird Bros., Ltd., Birkenhead, Eng.; 1913.

At the outbreak of World War I, HMS *Audacious* was part of the Second Battle Squadron. Fearful of the Grand Fleet's vulnerability to torpedo attack, in September 1914 Admiral Sir John Jellicoe ordered the fleet moved from Scapa Flow to Loch Ewe and then to Loch Swilly. Nonetheless, on October 27, *Audacious* struck a mine laid by the ocean liner-turned-minelayer *Berlin* off Tory Island north of Ireland. Taken in tow by the White Star liner OLYMPIC, *Audacious* sank twelve hours later. Almost immediately, Jellicoe wrote the Admiralty that given the German use of "submarines, mines, and torpedoes . . . [i]f the enemy turned away from us [in a fleet action] I should assume the intention was to lead us over mines and submarines, and decline to be drawn." It was just this fear that underlay his controversial decision to turn his ships away from what might have been a complete rout of the retreating High Seas Fleet at Jutland rather than risk a massed torpedo attack. *Audacious* was in fact the only British dreadnought lost to either mines or submarines during World War I.

Halpern, *Naval History of World War I.* O'Connell, *Sacred Vessels.* Parkes, *British Battleships.*

USS AUGUSTA (CA-31)

Northampton-class cruiser (2f/2m). *L/B/D:* 600.3′ × 66.1′ × 23′ (183m × 20.1m × 7m). *Tons:* 11,420 disp. *Hull:* steel. *Comp.:* 735–1,200. *Arm.:* 9 × 8″ (3x3), 8 × 5″, 32 × 40mm, 27 × 20mm; 6 × 21″TT; 4 aircraft. *Armor:* 3″ belt, 1″ deck. *Mach.:* geared turbines, 107,000 shp, 4 screws; 32.5 kts. *Built:* Newport News Shipbuilding & Dry Dock Co., Newport News, Va.; 1931.

While many ships have been ahead of their time in a technological sense, USS *Augusta* is best remembered for her involvement in incidents that prefigured great events, especially the United States' war with Japan and the founding of the United Nations after World War II. The third ship named for the northern Georgia city, *Augusta* was officially classified as a heavy cruiser following the Washington Naval Conference of 1930. First deployed as flagship of the Scouting Force, she entered the Pacific in 1932 to take part in fleet maneuvers. When these were completed, she and other units remained on the West Coast as a deterrent to Japanese aggression in Manchuria, which had been invaded in 1931. The following year, she relieved her sister ship USS HOUSTON as flagship of the Asiatic Fleet. Operating out of the Philippines, she visited ports in Australia, China, and throughout southeast Asia, where she was known as "Augie Maru." In August 1933, she carried the U.S. delegation to the funeral of Japan's Fleet Admiral Heihachiro Togo, hero of Tsushima and Port Arthur. Flying the flag of Admiral Harry E. Yarnell, in July 1937 *Augusta* was part of the first U.S. fleet to visit the Soviet port of Vladivostok in fifteen years.

Returning to Tsingtao just as hostilities between Japan and China were intensifying, Admiral Yarnell ordered *Augusta* to Shanghai to protect U.S. interests there. Chinese bombers mistakenly attacked the ship on August 14 and six days later a Chinese antiaircraft shell landed on the ship, killing one sailor. *Augusta* remained at Shanghai through the new year, when she carried survivors of USS PANAY, sunk by Japanese aircraft on December 12, to the Philippines. She returned to Chinese waters until late September 1940 before sailing for the United States.

After an extensive overhaul at Mare Island, *Augusta* sailed for Newport, Rhode Island, where Admiral Ernest J. King, Commander in Chief, Atlantic Fleet, broke his flag in her in May 1941. That summer, *Augusta* carried President Roosevelt to the Atlantic Conference, a series of shipboard meetings with Prime Minister Winston Churchill (aboard HMS PRINCE OF WALES) at Placentia Bay, Newfoundland. The leaders discussed greater U.S. involvement against German U-boats, drew up a set of aims for the war (in which the United States was still neutral), and established broad principles for postwar policies. The principles released on August 14 were endorsed by the anti-Axis nations and became the basis of the United Nations Declaration of January 1942.

Augusta saw no combat until October of that year, when she sailed for French Morocco as flagship of Rear Admiral H. Kent Hewitt's Task Force 34 in Operation Torch; among her distinguished complement was Major General George S. Patton. Following this campaign, *Augusta* took part in a number of North Atlantic convoys and other operations between New England, Newfoundland, and Iceland. On June 6, 1944, *Augusta* was one of three U.S. cruisers in the Eastern Naval Task Force supporting British D-day landings on Normandy. General Omar Bradley and his staff were aboard from June 5 until they went ashore on the 10th. *Augusta* then proceeded to the Mediterranean where she took part in Operation Dragoon, the Allied landing around Toulon and Marseilles, during which Navy Secretary James Forrestal joined the ship.

Following V-E Day, which found her once again stateside, on June 13 *Augusta* embarked President Harry S. Truman, Secretary of State James F. Byrnes, and Fleet Admiral William D. Leahy, bound for Antwerp en route to the Potsdam Conference; they re-embarked on July 28 at Portsmouth, England. Decommissioned in 1946, *Augusta* remained part of the reserve fleet at Philadelphia until 1959, when she was sold for scrap to Robert Benjamin of Panama City, Florida.

Morton, *Atlantic Meeting.* U.S. Navy, *DANFS.*

AUGUSTUS

Liner (2f/2m). *L/B:* 711′ × 82.7′ (216.6m × 25.2m). *Tons:* 32,650 grt. *Hull:* steel. *Comp.:* 1st 302, 2nd 504, 3rd 1,404; crew 500. *Mach.:* MAN diesel, 28,000 shp, 4 screws; 20 kts. *Built:* Gio. Ansaldo & Co., Sestri Ponente, Genoa; 1927.

The world's largest passenger motorship, the *Augustus* was built for the Navigazione Generale Italiana (NGI) of Genoa. Although she was intended for the South American run and spent most of her first year sailing between Genoa and the River Plate ports of Montevideo and Buenos Aires, in 1928 she made her first voyage to New York. In 1932, NGI merged with Lloyd Sabaudo and Cosulich to form Italia Flotta Riunite (later Italia SAN), and *Augustus* spent the majority of her time on the North Atlantic, with occasional voyages to South America and in cruise ship service.

In 1934 the ship's passenger accommodations were reconfigured, the most significant change being the division of the third class into tourist and third class with 454 and 766 passengers, respectively. Five years later, *Augustus* was taken out of service in order to convert her to turbine propulsion. The outbreak of World War II led to a cancellation of this plan; but in 1943, she was taken over by the Italian Navy, which wanted to convert her for use as an aircraft carrier to be named *Sparviero*. Work on this project ended with Italy's surrender in June, and in September of the same year she was taken over by the Germans, who in 1944 sank her as a blockship at Genoa. After the war she was raised and broken up.

Kludas, *Great Passenger Ships of the World.*

AURORA

Cruiser (3f/2m). *L/B/D:* 415.7′ × 55′ × 21.5′ (126.6m × 16.8m × 6.6m). *Tons:* 6,823 disp. *Hull:* steel. *Comp.:* 571. *Arm.:* 8 × 6″, 24 × 3″, 8 × 1pdr; 3 × 15″TT. *Armor:* 2.5″ deck. *Mach.:* triple expansion, 11,600 ihp, 3 screws; 19 kts. *Built:* New Admiralty, St. Petersburg, Russia; 1900.

In 1904 *Aurora* was in company with another cruiser and some torpedo boats en route to join Russia's Pacific Fleet at Vladivostok when war with Japan began. Ordered back to the Baltic, she was assigned to the Second Pacific Squadron — 10 battleships, 12 cruisers, 7 destroyers, and other vessels — which sailed for the Far East in September under Vice Admiral Zinovi Petrovich Rozhestvensky. Steaming across the Dogger Bank in the North Sea, the Russian fleet opened fire on what they suspected might be Japanese torpedo boats, but which turned out to be English fishing boats. Russian marksmanship was appalling and only one trawler was sunk, with the loss of two fishermen. However, the Russian guns also fired on each other, and *Aurora* was hit by five shells from the flagship *Kniaz Suvorov.* (Japanese ships were not unknown in European waters. Britain and Japan had been allies since 1902, and the Russians had received reports of Japanese

The cruiser AURORA, *whose guns fired the opening salvo of the Bolshevik Revolution, which overthrew the provisional government of Alexander Kerensky at St. Petersburg in November 1917. The ship is still preserved as a memorial in St. Petersburg. Courtesy Peabody Essex Museum, Salem, Massachusetts.*

torpedo boats in the Baltic and the North Sea. Twelve years later, seventeen Japanese destroyers would be deployed in the Mediterranean during the German submarine campaign against Allied shipping in World War I.)

War with Britain was narrowly averted, and the fleet sailed on, coaling at Tangier, Dakar, Madagascar, Singapore, and Saigon before passing into the Straits of Tsushima. There, in the watery defile between Japan and the Korean peninsula, Admiral Heihachiro Togo's fleet annihilated the Russian fleet. Battle between the two cruiser squadrons was joined at about 1330 on May 27, 1905, and the Russians soon had the worst of it. With ten dead, including Captain Egorev, and eighty-six wounded, *Aurora* retired from the battle with *Zemchug* and squadron flagship *Oleg*. Three weeks later the three ships put into Manila, where they were interned by the United States until the conclusion of hostilities, when *Aurora* returned to European Russia.

Aurora remained in the Baltic through World War I. Following the abdication of Nicholas II and the installation of the provisional government on March 15, 1917, *Aurora* was undergoing repairs at St. Petersburg. The government ordered her to sea for trials as a way of removing her and her revolutionary crew from the capital. These orders were countermanded by the Central Committee of the Baltic Fleet and she took up station on the Neva River. When Lenin staged a coup against Alexander Kerensky's government on November 6 (October 24 in the Russian calendar), *Aurora*'s pro-Bolshevik crew responded by anchoring their ship near the strategic Nikolaevsky Bridge. At 0210 on November 7, *Aurora* fired blanks to signal the Bolsheviks' determination to force the ouster of the government. Guns from the Peter and Paul fortress then opened fire on the Winter Palace, and the government

resigned that day. *Aurora* played no further role in the Russian Revolution, but the Bolshevik government ordered her preserved as a memorial and museum on the Neva, where she is still open to the public.

Mawdsley, *The Russian Revolution and the Baltic Fleet*. Watts, *Imperial Russian Navy*.

AUSTRALIA II

12-meter sloop. *L/B/D:* 63.1′ × 12′ × 8.5′ (19.2m × 3.7m × 2.6m). *Tons:* 21.8 disp. *Hull:* aluminum. *Comp.:* 11. *Des.:* Ben Lexcen. *Built:* Steve E. Ward & Co., Perth, Cottesloe, Australia; 1982.

In 1983, the 12-meter sloop *Australia II*, skippered by John Bertrand, broke the longest-running winning streak in the history of sport by defeating the United States defender *Liberty* and taking the America's Cup from the United States for the first time in 132 years. One of two 12-meters built for a syndicate headed by Australia's Alan Bond (the other was *Challenge 12*), *Australia II*'s design included a radical "winged keel," which enhanced her maneuverability and was the object of considerable controversy during the Cup season. As Ben Lexcen described it,

> The keel is somewhat shorter than a regular keel. . . . It's narrower where it leaves the hull, and long at the bottom. . . . For about half of its length on the bottom it has protrusions that stick out on each side; they poke down at about 20 degrees, and they are about a meter wide and about two or three meters long.

Although *Australia II* was measured for the Twelve Meter Rule in Australia and again after arriving in the United

States, as she chalked up a string of victories against other prospective challengers, the New York Yacht Club began to dispute the legality of the keel's design, the secret of which the Australians guarded jealously, shrouding the underbody of the hull from prying eyes. (NYYC representatives failed to attend the boat's measurement in Newport, as they were entitled, where they could have seen the keel for themselves.) The nub of the problem was articulated by American designer Halsey Herreshoff in a letter to the International Yacht Racing Union: "If the closely guarded peculiar design of *Australia II* is allowed to remain in competition, or is . . . rated without penalty, the yacht will likely . . . win the America's Cup in September." The NYYC was forced to accept independent verification that *Australia II*'s keel was permissible under the International Twelve Meter Rule. As Herreshoff later explained, though, the winged keel was only "the most conspicuous feature" of *Australia II*'s radical design.

> The ballyhoo about that masked the significant facts that *Australia II* was the first boat to go to minimum 12-Meter length and displacement and that she had significantly less wetted surface than any other Twelve; this latter fact won the Cup!

The 1983 challenge included more syndicates than any of the 24 previous Cup races, with *Canada 1, France 3,* Italy's *Azzurra,* Britain's *Victory 83,* and, from Australia, *Australia II, Challenge 12,* and *Advance.* The challenge matches lasted from June 18 to September 5, with the final series being decided between *Victory 83* (which won 30 of 54 races over the summer) and *Australia II* (48 of 54). The first of the seven America's Cup races took place on September 14, with the defender *Liberty,* Dennis Conner at the helm, defeating *Australia II* by a margin of 1 minute, 10 seconds. *Liberty* took the second race with a lead of 1:33, but the third race was called because neither vessel finished within the 5-hour, 15-minute time limit. When the race was called, *Australia II* was nearly 6 minutes ahead of *Liberty.* The next day, *Australia II* won her first race by 3:14, a record margin in Cup competition. The fourth race, which Conner is said to have sailed "perfectly," brought the series to 3–1 in favor of *Liberty.* In race five, *Australia II* posted a commanding lead of 1:47, and in the sixth, she established a new record margin of 3:25. In the seventh and last race, *Liberty* led until the fourth mark, when *Australia II* began to pull away. On the last leg of the race, Conner tried to beat the Australians in a tacking duel — 47 tacks in all — but the chal-

lengers nipped across the line in a time of 4 hours, 15 minutes, and 29 seconds, 43 seconds ahead of *Liberty.* She was the first challenger to take the America's Cup since the schooner for which it was named brought home the Hundred Guinea Cup in 1851. Upon her return to Australia, *Australia II* was exhibited at the National Maritime Museum in Sydney.

Herreshoff, "History of America's Cup Yacht Racing." Levitt & Lloyd, *Upset: Australia Wins the America's Cup.*

L'Avenir

(later *Admiral Karpfanger*) Bark (4m). *L/B/D:* 285.3′ × 45.1′ × 24.9′ (87m × 13.7m × 7.6m). *Tons:* 2,754 grt. *Hull:* steel. *Comp.:* 32–160. *Built:* Rickmers Reismühlen Rhederei & Schiffbau, AG, Bremerhaven, Ger.; 1908.

L'Avenir, whose name means "future prospects," was the third ship owned by the Association Maritime Belge (ASMAR) of Antwerp as a cargo-carrying, sail-training ship. (The first, *Comte de Smet de Naeyer,* was lost on her second voyage in 1906, and the other was *Linlithgowshire.*) A handsome ship, she was similar in design to the Rickmers-built Herzogin Cecilie, and was one of the first sailing ships fitted with a wireless radio. She made six voyages for ASMAR before the start of World War I, which found her at Le Havre. During the war she traded with a regular crew, returning frequently to European waters despite the danger of U-boats and merchant raiders. In 1920 she resumed sail training, carrying as many as eighty cadets per voyage in the 1920s.

In 1932, *L'Avenir* was sold to Gustav Erikson of Mariehamn who put her into the Australian grain trade but also fitted her with accommodations for passengers. Although some people took advantage of the opportunity to sail to Australia, most of her passengers sailed only on the short homeward leg from England to Finland. Too small to be profitable in the bulk grain trade, in 1936 she was sold to the Hamburg-Amerika Linie to train future steamship officers. Renamed *Admiral Karpfanger,* she sailed from Hamburg to Australia without incident. Clearing Wallaroo on February 8, 1938, she radioed her position on March 1, but was posted missing later that year. Wreckage from the ship was found in the vicinity of Tierra del Fuego.

Butlin, *White Sails Crowding.* Underhill, *Sail Training and Cadet Ships.*

B

BADEN-BADEN

Rotor ship (2m). *L/B/D:* 155.8′ × 28.6′ × 12.5′ dph (48.2m × 4m × 3.8m). *Tons:* 497 grt. *Hull:* steel. *Comp.:* 15. *Mach.:* 2 rotor cylinders. *Des.:* Anton Flettner. *Built:* Friederich Krupp AG Germaniawerft, Hamburg; 1920.

The rotor vessel *Baden-Baden* was the invention of German physicist Anton Flettner, founding director of the Institute of Hydro and Aerodynamics. After experimenting with the use of metal sails, which increased sailing ship efficiency by fifty percent, Flettner turned to the use of rotating cylinders. These were a practical application of the Magnus Effect, discovered in 1852, which holds that "a sphere or cylinder spinning in a moving airstrip develops a force at a right angle to the direction of the moving air." When the wind blows at right angles to the cylinders, it creates a vacuum on the forward side of the rotor, and a high (or positive) pressure abaft, so that the vessel is literally pushed forward.

Anton Flettner's experimental "rotor" ship of 1920. Although she is hardly a "tall ship" of the kind envisioned by John Masefield, her clipper bow is a reminder that she, too, is a windjammer. Courtesy Peabody Essex Museum, Salem, Massachusetts.

To demonstrate the practicality of the rotor ship, Flettner stripped the barkentine *Buckau* of her masts and rigging and fitted her with two rotor cylinders fifty feet high and nine feet in diameter. This new rig weighed only seven tons, compared with the thirty-five tons of the sailing rig, and because it was forty-two feet shorter, it also improved the vessel's stability. One difficulty of the rotor ship was that in order to tack, the cylinders (which were powered by 45 hp motors) had to be stopped while the ship was turned across the wind using her auxiliary motors. However, the rotor ship could sail within twenty-five degrees of the direction of the wind, while the barkentine could sail only to within forty-five degrees of the wind.

To demonstrate the feasibility of his new ship, Flettner raced her against her traditionally rigged sister ship *Anon* from Danzig to Leith with a cargo of timber. Although the winds were at one point so strong that the rotors had to be shut down, *Buckau* won. Hamburg-Amerika Linie ordered ten rotor ships (although only one, *Barbara*, was actually built). Flettner eventually acquired full ownership of *Buckau*, which he renamed *Baden-Baden*. On April 2, 1926, she sailed from Hamburg under command of Captain Peter Callsen, and after a stop in the Canary Islands, sailed into New York Harbor on May 9. Although the ship had demonstrated her worth, the abundance of cheap fuel and the demand for steady service condemned the ship to only theoretical success. In 1929, *Baden-Baden* was sold, rerigged as an auxiliary schooner, and traded in the Caribbean until 1931, when she was abandoned at sea.

The potential of the rotor ship had yet to be fully realized. During the oil crises of the 1970s, the idea was rejuvenated by a number of commercial companies and nonprofit groups, the best known of which were the Cousteau Society's Moulin à Vent ("Windmill") and Alcyone.

Rogers, *Freak Ships*.

BALCLUTHA

(ex-*Pacific Queen, Star of Alaska, Balclutha*) Ship (3m). *L/B/D:* 256.3′ × 38.5′ × 22.7′ (78.1m1 × 1.7m × 6.9). *Tons:* 1,862 grt. *Hull:* steel. *Built:* Charles Connell & Co. Ltd., Glasgow; 1886.

Built for Robert McMillan of Dumbarton as a general trader, *Balclutha* was named for a town in New Zealand. She rounded Cape Horn seventeen times in thirteen years; from Europe and the East Coast of the United States, she carried general cargoes, including wine, case oil, and coal. Her ports of call in the Pacific included Chile for nitrate, Australia and New Zealand for wool, Burma for rice, San Francisco for grain, and the Pacific Northwest for lumber. After thirteen years under the Connell flag, she was sold to West Coast interests and carried lumber from the West Coast to Australia, returning with coal. In 1902 she was sold to the Alaska Packers Association of San Francisco and for the next twenty-eight years made the annual trip north to serve as a floating barracks and store ship for the Alaska salmon fisheries. Under the name *Star of Alaska,* each spring she would sail with 300 fishermen and cannery workers (the former were mostly whites and the latter were Chinese) together with supplies, returning in the fall with as many as 78,000 cases of tinned salmon. In 1905, she ran hard aground near Kodiak Island, but the Alaska Packers superintendent at Karluk, 75 miles away, was able to salvage her and patch her up enough for the return to San Francisco without assistance. In 1930, *Star of Alaska* was the last of the Alaska Packers sailing ships to make the Alaska run. *Star of Alaska* was purchased by a carnival promoter named Tex Kissinger who renamed her *Pacific Queen* and used her as a garish waterfront attraction in ports up and down the West Coast. Although it was demeaning work, it kept her from the ship breakers, and when Kissinger died in the early 1950s, she was still in one piece, beached in Sausalito.

On the other side of San Francisco Bay was the fledgling San Francisco Maritime Museum, whose founding president was Karl Kortum, who had sailed before the mast in KAIULANI. With the support of Harry Lundeberg, secretary-treasurer of the powerful Sailors Union of the Pacific, Kortum was able to persuade his board to purchase the ship for $25,000. Over the next year, *Balclutha* was restored to her former appearance, thanks to an estimated 13,000 man-hours contributed by fourteen San Francisco labor unions and supplies donated from businesses around the city. In 1955, her gangway opened to the public, and in her first year as a museum she earned the museum $100,000, firmly establishing the viability of museum ships and helping to pave the way for saving scores of historic ships around the world in the decades since.

Heine, *Historic Ships of the World.* Huycke, "Colonial Trader to Museum Ship"; "The Ship *Pacific Queen.*"

USS BALTIMORE (C-3)

Protected cruiser (2f/2m). *L/B/D:* 335′ × 48.7′ × 20.5′ (102.1m × 14.8m × 6.2m). *Tons:* 4,413 disp. *Hull:* steel. *Comp.:* 386. *Arm.:* 4 × 8″, 6 × 6″, 4 × 6pdr, 2 × 3pdr, 2 × 1pdr. *Armor:* 4″ belt, 4″ deck. *Mach.:* triple expansion, 2 screws; 20kts. 10,750 ihp. *Built:* William Cramp & Sons Ship & Engine Building Co., Philadelphia; 1890.

USS *Baltimore* first gained renown in the so-called *Baltimore* affair, during the Chilean civil war of 1891. Shortly after the start of hostilities in January, *Baltimore* was one of several ships dispatched to Chilean waters to protect American interests. In the spring of that year, the U.S. government detained the steamer *Itata* and a cargo of weapons and ammunition smuggled out of the country by Chilean insurgents, who were led by Admiral Jorge Montt. Somewhat later, the *Baltimore* stood guard while repairs were made to a privately owned submarine cable — an operation also viewed as favorable to President José Manuel Balmaceda. These and similar actions convinced Chilean rebels that the United States favored the Balmaceda regime, which fell in September. Later that fall, the *Baltimore* was ordered to Valparaiso to provide protection for the U.S. legation at Santiago. There, on October 16, a mob attacked 117 sailors on shore leave and two sailors were killed. After a two-month trial, in which three Chileans and one American sailor were sentenced to jail, *Baltimore* was ordered to San Francisco. Diplomatic wrangling between Chile and the United States dragged on until January 1892.

In 1898, amid escalating tension between the United States and Spain, *Baltimore* was dispatched with ammunition to Commodore George Dewey's Asiatic Squadron at Hong Kong, arriving there on April 22. Five days later the squadron sailed for the Philippines, and at the Battle of Manila Bay (May 1), *Baltimore* sank the Spanish *Don Antonio de Ulloa.* Over the next twenty-five years, *Baltimore* was in and out of commission several times. During World War I, she operated as part of the Northern Barrage, the Allied effort to close the 350-mile gap between Orkney and Norway to German submarines. She was sold out of the Navy in 1942.

Goldberg, "*Baltimore*" *Affair.* Hopkins, "Six *Baltimores.*"

BANSHEE

(later *J. L. Smallwood, Irene*) Sidewheel steamship (2f/2m). *L/B/D:* 214′ × 20.3′ × 10′ (65.2m × 6.2m × 3m). *Tons:* 325 grt. *Hull:* iron & steel. *Comp.:* 60–89. *Arm.:* 1 × 30pdr, 1 × 12pdr. *Mach.:* oscillating engines, sidewheels; 12 kts. *Built:* Jones Quiggin & Co., Liverpool; 1862.

Built as a blockade-runner for the Anglo-Confederate Trading Company, *Banshee* was the first steel-hulled ship to cross the Atlantic. Her design set the pattern for about a hundred further paddlewheel blockade-runners, including over thirty built of steel, that followed from British and Scottish shipyards. Captured on her fifteenth trip by USS *Grand Gulf* and the U.S. armed transport *Fulton* bound from Nassau, Bahamas, to Wilmington on November 21, 1863, she was condemned by a prize court and bought by the U.S. Navy on March 12, 1864. Commissioned as USS *Banshee* in June, she was assigned to the North Atlantic Blockading Squadron and took part in the unsuccessful attack on Fort Fisher, North Carolina, on December 24–25. Reassigned to the Potomac River Flotilla in January 1865, she was sold on September 30, 1865, and carried fruit and other cargo under the name *J. L. Smallwood*. Sold again to British interests and renamed *Irene*, she is known to have survived at least as late as 1895.

Silverstone, *Warships of the Civil War Navies*. Spratt, *Transatlantic Paddle Steamers*. Taylor, *Running the Blockade*.

HMS BARFLEUR

2nd rate 90 (3m). *L/B/D:* 177.5′ × 50.2′ × 21′ (54.1m × 15.3m × 6.4m). *Tons:* 1,947 bm. *Hull:* wood. *Comp.:* 750. *Arm.:* 28 × 32pdr, 30 × 18pdr, 30 × 12pdr, 2 × 6pdr. *Des.:* Sir Thomas Slade. *Built:* Chatham Dockyard; 1768.

HMS *Barfleur* was named for the Anglo-Dutch victory over the French at Cape Barfleur in 1692. In September 1780, she was made flagship of Vice Admiral Samuel Hood, second in command to Admiral George Brydges Rodney on the West Indies station. In August 1781, *Barfleur* and 13 ships sailed to New York, Hood now serving as second in command to Rear Admiral Thomas Graves in HMS LONDON (90 guns). Charged with preventing the French Admiral François Joseph Paul de Grasse, flying his flag in the 120-gun VILLE DE PARIS, from cutting off Major General Charles Cornwallis, then dug in on the Yorktown peninsula, the 19 British ships turned south on August 30 and arrived off the mouth of Chesapeake Bay on September 5. Although *Barfleur* was supposed to sail fourth in line, as the French fleet stood out of the bay Graves ordered his ships to wear, so that Hood's squadron was now in the rear. As a result of a cautious adherence to one of two conflicting signals from Graves, few of his ships actually engaged the French fleet, whose continued control of the Bay forced the surrender of Cornwallis six weeks later.

Though American independence was all but assured, war between Britain and France continued in the West Indies. On January 25, 1782, Hood seized the anchorage at Basse Terre from de Grasse, although the English garrison on St. Kitts was forced to surrender on February 12. Two nights later, Hood slipped away from the superior French fleet (29 ships to his 22), and on February 25 he rendezvoused with 12 ships under Rodney. Their objective was to prevent de Grasse from joining a Franco-Spanish force at Haiti, which would have given the latter a fleet of 55 ships of the line and 20,000 troops with which to attack Jamaica. On April 9, the fleets met off Dominica, each about 30 ships strong, but light winds allowed them only a minor skirmish and the French withdrew to protect their convoy. Three days later, the 36 ships under Rodney in *Formidable*, with Hood again second in command, met de Grasse's 31 ships off The Saintes, a group of three islands south of Guadeloupe. At 0700 the French were sailing south in line ahead while the British were sailing north. Battle began at 0740, the two fleets passing each other on opposite tacks. At 0905, the wind hauled to the south southeast, and gaps opened in the French line. Seizing the initiative, Rodney luffed and with six ships passed through the French line four ships astern of *Ville de France*. At the same time, HMS *Bedford* led the 13 ships of Hood's rear squadron through the French line between *Dauphin* and *Royal César*, second and third ships ahead of *Ville de Paris*. Unable to regroup, the French were at the mercy of the concentrated fire of the British ships. At 1800, *Ville de Paris* was surrounded by nine British ships and struck her flag to *Barfleur;* four other French ships followed suit. Though the battle forestalled a French invasion of Jamaica, the overcautious Rodney restrained Hood from capturing more ships and thereby destroying French seapower in the Caribbean.

Peace was achieved in 1783, but ten years later Britain joined the First Coalition against Revolutionary France. *Barfleur* was part of Admiral Richard Howe's fleet at the Glorious First of June, 1794, against France's Rear Admiral Villaret-de-Joyeuse, and on June 23, 1795, she was in Admiral Alexander Hood's action against Villaret-de-Joyeuse off Ile de Groix. *Barfleur* flew the flag of Vice Admiral W. Waldegrave at the Battle of Cape St. Vincent, fought on February 14, 1797. Her last significant action came in 1805, when she took part in the blockade of

Rochefort and, on July 22, 1805, in Vice Admiral Sir Robert Calder's desultory action against Vice Admiral Pierre Villeneuve off Cape Finisterre, Spain. *Barfleur* continued in service for more than a decade, and was broken up in 1819.

Larrabee, *Decision at the Chesapeake*. Mahan, *The Influence of Sea Power upon History*.

HMS BARHAM

Queen Elizabeth-class battleship (2f/2m). *L/B/D:* 645.9′ × 90.6′ × 30.8′ (196.9m × 27.6m × 9.4m). *Tons:* 33,000 disp. *Hull:* steel. *Comp.:* 1,120. *Arm.:* 8 × 15″ (4x2), 14 × 6″, 2 × 3″, 4 × 3pdr. *Armor:* 13″ belt, 3″ deck. *Mach.:* geared turbines, 75,000 hp, 4 screws; 24 kts. *Built:* John Brown & Co., Ltd., Clydebank, Scotland; 1915.

One of five *Queen Elizabeth*-class battleships, HMS *Barham* was the third British ship named for Admiral Charles Middleton, Lord Barham, First Lord of the Admiralty at the time of Trafalgar. Commissioned as flagship of Rear Admiral H. Evan-Thomas's Fifth Battle Squadron, *Barham* was stationed at Rosyth when the Battle of Jutland was fought. The Fifth Battle Squadron sailed in support of Vice Admiral Sir David Beatty's Battle Cruiser Force. During the "run to the north," *Barham* came under fire from the battleships of Admiral Reinhard Scheer's High Seas Fleet, around 1700, and narrowly escaped a massive internal explosion following a hit near B turret.

On duty in the Mediterranean and Atlantic in the interwar period, *Barham* underwent a major refit from 1930 to 1933. In December 1939, she was recalled from Alexandria to the Home Fleet. On the morning of the 12th she was off the Mull of Kintyre when she accidentally rammed the destroyer HMS *Duchess,* which sank with only 24 survivors from her crew of 146. Two weeks later, she was on patrol in the Denmark Strait when she was torpedoed by Fritz-Julius Lemp's U-30, in position 58°34′N, 6°30′W. She proceeded to Greenock under her own power and after three months of repairs she joined the Mediterranean Fleet. In the night action at the Battle of Matapan on March 28–29, 1941, she helped sink the Italian cruiser *Zara* and destroyer *Alfieri.* Two months later (May 27) *Barham* was severely damaged during the German invasion of Crete and sailed to Durban, South Africa, for repairs.

She returned to the Mediterranean and on November 25, 1941, became flagship of Vice Admiral H. D. Pridham-Wippell. During operations against Field Marshal Rommel's North African convoys, at 1625 on November 25, 1941, she was torpedoed off As Sallum, Egypt, by the

German submarine *U-331,* under H. D. Freiherr von Tiesenhausen. Five minutes later *Barham* capsized, exploded, and sank in position 32°34′N, 26°24′E. The official death toll was 862 men, with 487 survivors, Pridham-Wippell among them.

Jones, *Battleship Barham*.

BATAVIA

Ship (3m). *L/B/D:* 150′ × 36′ × 14′ dph (45.7m × 11m × 4.3m). *Tons:* 600 tons. *Hull:* wood. *Comp.:* ca. 300. *Arm.:* 28 guns. *Built:* VOC, Amsterdam, Neth.; 1628.

Named for the Dutch entrepôt on the island of Java, the Dutch East India Company's (VOC's) retour ship (that is, one designed for the roundtrip between the Netherlands and the East Indies) *Batavia* sailed from the Texel in a fleet of eleven ships on October 29, 1628. *Batavia*'s captain was Adriaen Jacobsz, but the overall commander was Fleet President Francisco Pelsaert. The two men disliked each other and there was considerable friction between them, especially after the ship's boatswain was incriminated in the assault of Lucretia Jansdr, a widow who had spurned his advances. After rounding the Cape of Good Hope, VOC ships were ordered to sail east for 2,400 to 3,000 miles (depending on the season) between 36°S and 42°S before turning northeast or north for Java. As there was no way to determine longitude at sea, shipwrecks on the west coast of Australia were inevitable. Jacobsz underestimated his ship's progress, and in the middle of the night on June 4, 1629, *Batavia* ran aground on what Pelsaert described as "the perilous shallows of the Abrolhos, otherwise called by the Dutch the Frederick Houtmann's rocks" — about 28°57′N, 114°10′E. ("Abrolhos" is a corruption of the Portuguese for "Watch out!") Efforts to save the ship were useless, and the ship's company was divided between two nearby islands, with 180 placed on one, and 40 on the other. Two days later, Pelsaert set out to look for water with two of the ship's boats, the smaller of which was lost on the mainland 40 miles away. Finding no water, on June 16 Pelsaert headed for Java and with 48 people in one boat managed to reach Batavia without incident on July 8. A week later, *Sardam* sailed for the Abrolhos with a crew of 26, including some Gujarati divers, but adverse winds kept them at sea until September 17.

In the meantime, a mutiny led by Jeronimus Cornelisz had led to the murder of more than 100 castaways, including 12 women and 7 children. As *Sardam* approached, a boat put out to warn Pelsaert that Cornelisz intended to seize his ship and sail away without the other survivors. The mutineers were captured and immediately tried aboard *Sardam;* 7 of them were hanged on Seal Island on October 2, and 2 more were ordered marooned on the mainland. Of *Batavia*'s original complement, 60 had drowned in the wreck and 125 were murdered. On November 15, *Sardam* sailed with the 74 survivors as well as 9 chests of silver, 2 cannon, and other salvaged items with a combined value of 210,500 guilders.

In 1648, Joost Hartgers published the best-selling *Unhappy Voyage of the Ship Batavia to the East-Indies, sailing under the Hon. François Pelsaert,* but the ship was all but forgotten until various artifacts were found in the Abrolhos in 1960. Divers found the partial remains of the ship itself lodged on Morning Reef. Between 1973 and 1976 archaeologists recovered a large portion of the stern and side of the hull, cannon, and, among other artifacts, 128 sandstone blocks later used in the construction of a portico at the Western Australian Maritime Museum at Fremantle. A replica of the *Batavia* was launched at Lelystad, Netherlands, in 1995.

Drake-Brockman, *Voyage to Disaster.* Green, *Loss of the Retourship "Batavia."* Pelsaert, *The Voyage of the "Batavia."*

BATHYSPHERE

L: 4.8' dia (1.4m). *Tons:* 2.5 tons. *Hull:* steel. *Comp.:* 2. *Des.:* Otis Barton and Cox & Stephens. *Built:* Watson-Stillman Hydraulic Machinery Co.; 1930.

In the late 1920s, the New York Zoological Society began a concentrated study of the ocean depths nine miles off the coast of Nonsuch Island, Bermuda, in 32°12′N,

The Queen Elizabeth-*class battleships — of which* BARHAM *was one — were among the most successful ever built, seeing action in both world wars.* BARHAM *was the only one of the 5 sister ships lost to enemy action, when the U-331 torpedoed her off Egypt, November 25, 1941. Courtesy National Maritime Museum, Greenwich.*

64°36′W. Disappointed with the meager returns from deep-sea trawls, Dr. William Beebe sought to develop a way of observing the deep firsthand. Because pressure increases by 14.7 pounds per square inch for every 33 feet in depth, the observation platform had to be strong, compact, and round, to distribute the pressure evenly. With the help of Otis Barton, a bathysphere (from the Greek for "deep sphere") was built in 1929. It proved too heavy for the tender, *Ready,* and a second was completed in 1930. With a skin 1.5 inches thick and two 8-inch-wide fused-quartz observation windows, the two-man observation ball was attached to a cable and lowered from the tender. A second cable provided electricity and a telephone connection to the surface. Oxygen was supplied by two cylinders, and carbon dioxide and moisture were absorbed by trays of soda lime and calcium chloride, respectively.

The first descent was made on June 6, 1930, to a depth of 800 feet. Five days later *Bathysphere* went down to 1,426 feet, and on August 15, 1934, reached 3,028 feet, the extreme limit of the tether. (The previous record depths were 383 feet for a submarine and 525 feet for an armored suited diver on a Bavarian lake.) However, record depths were only incidental to the work at hand. "Every descent and ascent of the bathysphere," wrote Beebe, "showed a fauna, rich beyond what the summary of all our 1,500 [sampling] nets would lead us to expect." In addition to discovering and photographing weird and hitherto unknown species of eels, lanternfish, squid, and jellyfish, Beebe was fascinated by the amount of light generated by animals in the deep, especially beyond 1,700 feet, the absolute limit to which sunlight penetrated. The last dives in the *Bathysphere* were completed in 1934, and comparable depths were not attained until after World War II, when August Picard developed the first self-propelled bathyscaph ("deep boat"), TRIESTE.

Beebe, *Half Mile Down.*

BATORY

Liner (2f/2m). *L/B:* 525.7′ × 70.8′ (160.2m × 21.6m). *Tons:* 14,287 grt. *Hull:* steel. *Comp.:* tourist 370; 3rd 400. *Mach.:* motorship, 2 screws; 17 kts. *Built:* Cantieri Riuniti dell' Adriatico, Monfalcone, Italy; 1936.

The second of two new ships built for the Gdynia-America Line, *Batory* was named for the sixteenth-century Polish king Stefan Batory. She carried immigrants between Gdynia, Copenhagen, Halifax, and New York, with cruises to the Caribbean during the winter season. *Batory*'s last prewar voyage to New York ended on September 5, 1939, four days after the German invasion of Poland. Laid up at New York, she entered service as an Allied troop ship in 1940, continuing in that work until 1946 when she was refitted at Antwerp. She resumed her prewar schedule from Gdynia, adding a stop at Southampton, but as the Cold War intensified in 1951, American longshoremen refused to handle *Batory.* The now renamed Polish Ocean Line put her in service from Gdynia and Southampton via the Suez Canal to Bombay and Karachi. In 1957, she was reconfigured to carry 76 first- and 740 tourist-class passengers and put on the North Atlantic run between Gdynia, Quebec, and Montreal. Taken out of service in 1968 and replaced by *Stefan Batory* (ex-*Maasdam*), after a few cruises to the Canary Islands and Caribbean, *Batory* was fitted out as a floating hotel at Gdansk. In 1971, she was scrapped in Hong Kong.

Bonsor, *North Atlantic Seaway.* Braynard & Miller, *Fifty Famous Liners.*

HMS BEAGLE

Bark (3m). *L/B/D:* 90.3′ × 24.5′ × 12.5′ (27.5m × 7.5m × 3.8m). *Tons:* 235 bm. *Hull:* wood. *Comp.:* 75. *Arm.:* 5 × 6pdr, 2 × 9pdr. *Des.:* Sir Henry Peake. *Built:* Woolwich Dockyard; 1820.

HMS *Beagle* was originally launched as one of 115 *Cherokee*-class 10-gun brigs built by the Royal Navy between 1807 and 1830 and used in a variety of roles including surveying and antislaver patrols. By the time of her first voyage *Beagle* had been converted to a bark rig. Her first major voyage was from May 1826 to October 1830 with HMS *Adventure,* to chart the straits and passages of the southern tip of South America; it was during this voyage that the Beagle Channel, skirting the southern edge of Tierra del Fuego, was explored and named. Under the stress of arduous conditions in the waters around Tierra del Fuego, Captain Pringle Stokes killed himself in August 1828. Short of provisions and with many of the crew ill, *Beagle* returned to Buenos Aires where Lieutenant Robert FitzRoy took command for the homeward voyage.

FitzRoy commanded *Beagle* on her subsequent circumnavigation during which she was to complete the survey of Tierra del Fuego, the Chilean coast, and a number of Pacific islands, and to carry out chronometric observations — she carried 22 chronometers. Among the 74 crew and passengers were three Fuegians who had been taken to England and were returning home. Also assigned to the ship was a twenty-one-year-old botany student, Charles Darwin, whose professor, J. S. Henslow, considered him not a "*finished* naturalist, but . . . amply qualified for collecting, observing, and noting, anything new to be noted in Natural History." *Beagle* departed

Devonport on December 27, 1831, and after stops in the Cape Verde Islands and Bahía arrived at Rio de Janeiro on April 4. After three months of hydrographic surveys of the Brazilian coast (Darwin was occupied in researching the rain forest), *Beagle* proceeded to Bahía Blanca, Argentina. It was there that Darwin first uncovered fossils that led him to question the relationship of living and extinct species.

On January 19, 1833, *Beagle* arrived at Ponsonby Sound, Tierra del Fuego, where Jemmy Buttons, York Minster, and Fuegia Basket returned home. Richard Matthews, a missionary sent to minister to the Fuegians, quickly abandoned his calling to return to the ship. In February, *Beagle* returned to Uruguay, via the Falkland Islands. The conditions at the southern tip of the Americas required the use of a second ship, and FitzRoy took it upon himself to purchase an American vessel, renamed *Adventure;* the Admiralty later made him sell the ship in Chile. Surveys of the Argentine coast resumed from April through July, when the ship reached El Carmen, on the Rio Negro, then the southernmost outpost in Argentina. Darwin returned overland from there to Bahía Blanca, then up the Rio Paraná to Santa Fe and finally to Montevideo, where he rejoined the ship on October 21. *Beagle* returned to Tierra del Fuego to complete her survey work in January, then surveyed the Falkland Islands in March and April. She sailed through the Strait of Magellan into Chilean waters in June 1834, and arrived at Valparaiso on July 23. As before, *Beagle* conducted coastal surveys while Darwin made overland treks in the Chilean Andes. After visiting the Chonos Archipelago in November 1834, *Beagle* returned to the Chilean mainland in February and surveyed there until July. After stops at Iquique and Callao, Peru, *Beagle* sailed for the Galápagos Islands, 600 miles west of Ecuador.

The ship arrived there on September 17, and though the expedition remained only one month, it was here that Darwin made the observations — particularly of the 13 different species of finches — that proved the foundation for his theory of natural selection. *Beagle* left the Galápagos on October 20 bound for Tahiti. For the remainder of the voyage the expedition's primary mission was to make chronometric observations, though there was much of interest to occupy Darwin at their remaining stops, which included New Zealand, Australia, Tasmania, the Cocos (Keeling) Islands, Mauritius, and Cape Town, and then in the Atlantic, St. Helena and Bahía.

Beagle finally returned to Falmouth on October 2, 1836. Although his *Origin of Species* was not published until 1859, his voyage in *Beagle* (during which he had been badly affected by seasickness) laid the foundation for his theories of evolution and natural selection,

A photo by Amory H. Waite, Jr., of the BEAR *at Discovery Inlet, the farthest point south reached by the ship during Rear Admiral Richard Byrd's second Antarctic expedition, 1932. Courtesy Peabody Essex Museum, Salem, Massachusetts.*

and profoundly affected the course of modern scientific thought. As Darwin himself wrote, "The voyage in the *Beagle* has been by far the most important event in my life and has determined the whole of my existence."

Six months after her return, *Beagle* was off to Australia under the command of Captain John Lord Stokes, a veteran of the FitzRoy-Darwin voyage. After surveying the western coast between the Swan River (Perth) and Fitzroy River (named for his former commander), she sailed around to the southeast corner of the continent. There, *Beagle* conducted surveys along both shores of the Bass Strait, and then in May of 1839 sailed northabout to the shores of the Arafura Sea opposite Timor. Her crew named a number of geographical features, including Port Darwin (for their former shipmate) and the Flinders River, after the indomitable surveyor of HMS INVESTIGATOR. In so honoring his predecessor, Stokes reflected that "monuments may crumble, but a name endures as long as the world."

Her work in Australia done, *Beagle* returned to England in 1843, after 18 years' hard service to her nation and the world. Transferred out of the Royal Navy in 1845, *Beagle* ended her days as the Preventive Service's stationary *Beagle Watch Vessel* (renamed *W.V.7* in 1863) moored at Pagelsham Pool on the coast of Essex. She was sold and probably broken up in 1870.

Darwin, *Diary of the Voyage of H.M.S. "Beagle."* FitzRoy & King, *Narrative of the Surveying Voyages of H.M.S. "Adventure" and "Beagle."* Thomson, HMS *"Beagle."*

BEAR

Barkentine (3m). *L/B/D:* 198.5′ × 29.8′ × 18.8′ (60.5m × 9.1m × 5.7m). *Tons:* 1,675 disp. *Hull:* wood. *Comp.:* 35–40. *Mach.:* steam, 300 ihp, 1 screw. *Built:* Alexander Stephen & Sons, Ltd., Dundee; 1874.

Built for the ten-day-long sealing season — in 1883, her best year, she brought home more than 30,000 pelts — *Bear* was designed for work amid Arctic ice fields. In 1884, she was sold to the U.S. government and took part in the search for the Greeley Expedition, whose seven survivors were found at Cape Sabine. From 1885 to 1927, *Bear* served as a U.S. Revenue Marine cutter stationed in Alaska where she looked out for seal poachers, shipwrecked whalers, and illicit trade with native Alaskans, ferried reindeer from Siberia to Alaska, and served as a floating courthouse. Laid up at Oakland in 1926 and transferred to the city for use as a museum ship, *Bear* starred as the sealer *Macedonia* in the 1930 film version of Jack London's *Sea Wolf*. Rear Admiral Richard Byrd acquired her for his second Antarctic expedition in 1932, and *Bear* sailed there again with the U.S. Antarctic Service in 1938. From 1941 to 1944, USS *Bear* served in the Northeast Atlantic Patrol. Purchased for the sealing trade in 1948, her refit proved too costly and she was laid up in Halifax. In 1963, while in tow to Philadelphia for use as a floating restaurant, she foundered about 250 miles (400 kilometers) east of New York in 42°40′N, 65°11′W.

Bixby. *Track of the "Bear."* Boroughs, *Great Ice Ship "Bear."*

BEAVER

Steamship (1f/2m). *L/B/D:* 100.8' × 20' (33'ew) × 8.5' (30.7m × 6.1m (10.1m) × 2.6m). *Tons:* 187 om. *Hull:* wood. *Comp.:* 31. *Arm.:* 4 brass cannon. *Mach.:* side-lever, 35 hp, sidewheels. *Built:* Green, Wigrams & Green, Blackwall, Eng.; 1835.

In the early 1800s, the powerful Hudson's Bay Company (HBC) had extended its control across Canada to the Pacific coast, and by 1821 it had bought out or merged with its chief rivals, John Jacob Astor's Pacific Fur Company and the Canadian North West Company. From its headquarters at Fort Vancouver (now Vancouver, Oregon) on the Columbia River, it controlled an extensive network of outposts along the coast. The loss of two sailing vessels in 1829 and 1830 forced the company to consider the advantages of steam, and in 1834 Hudson's Bay ordered a paddle steamer from the London firm of Green, Wigrams & Green.

On August 29, 1835, the brigantine-rigged *Beaver* sailed for the Northwest in company with the bark *Columbia.* After stops in the Juan Fernández Islands and Hawaii, they arrived at Fort Vancouver on March 19, 1836. There the engine was assembled and the paddlewheels were mounted, and on May 16, the logbook records, "the engineers got the steam up and tried the engines." Though she had a voracious appetite for wood and coal, the first steamship on the west coast of North America quickly proved her worth, and for seventeen years she served the HBC well, opening remote reaches of the coast to the fur trade and enabling "the Honorable Company" to extend its authority over the Indians with whom it traded.

Although she worked chiefly in the Gulf of Georgia and Puget Sound, in 1840 *Beaver* carried company representatives to Sitka, Alaska, for negotiations with the Russian-American Company. Following the Oregon Treaty of 1846, her homeport was moved from Fort Vancouver to Fort Victoria (now Victoria) on Vancouver Island. In 1853, the company sent out the new screw steamer *Otter,* and *Beaver* was relegated to passenger and cargo work.

Laid up from 1860 to 1862, she was chartered by the Royal Navy for survey work and from 1863 to 1870, she was employed in charting the heavily indented coasts of Vancouver Island and continental British Columbia as far as Alaska under command of Lieutenant Daniel Pender. *Beaver* was laid up again in 1871 and three years later the HBC sold her to a consortium that eventually became the British Columbia Towing and Transportation Company. She towed barges, log booms, and sailing vessels lying off Cape Flaherty until February 1883, when she went aground off Burrard Inlet. Changing hands several times thereafter, *Beaver* was not put back in service until 1888.

That year, on the night of July 25, she ran aground on Prospect Point in the Burrard Inlet in Vancouver.

Citizens of Vancouver recognized the historic importance of the *Beaver,* but despite various appeals the city government failed to act and the ship was gradually stripped of her fittings and machinery, parts of which were melted down. The hulk eventually sank, but the ship's boiler (the last of five fitted during her career) and paddlewheel shafts were salvaged. Divers visited the now submerged vessel in the 1960s and 1980s, and in the 1990s, the wreck site was mapped by the Underwater Archaeology Society of British Columbia.

Delgado, *"Beaver."*

BELEM

(ex-*Giorgio Cini, Fantôme II, Belem*) Bark (3m). *L/B/D:* 162.7' × 28.9' × 11.5' (49.6m x 8.8m × 3.5m). *Tons:* 562 grt. *Hull:* steel. *Mach.:* diesel, 1 screw. *Built:* A. Dubigeon, Nantes, France; 1896.

Built for the Nantes firm of Denis Crovan & Company, for the cocoa trade from Belém, Brazil, to Nantes. Later purchased by the firm of H. Fleuriot & Company, she remained in the same trade (which catered to Parisian chocolatiers) until 1913. In that year, the Duke of Westminster bought her for use as a yacht. Fitted with auxiliary engines, her most obvious external changes were the extension of her deck house forward as far as the foremast and the erection of a distinctive, if uncharacteristic, teak balustrade around the poop.

Ten years later she was sold to Sir A. E. Guinness, the brewer, who renamed her *Fantôme II* and kept her as a yacht until his death in 1950. Thereafter, she was sold to the Fondazione Giorgio Cini in Venice for use as a sail-training ship, chiefly for orphaned boys bound for the Navy. Rerigged as a barkentine, she spent the next three decades in the Adriatic. In the mid-1980s she was purchased by the Paris-based Fondation Belem. Restored to the original rig and name, she is used as a sail-training vessel in European waters.

Brouwer, *International Register of Historic Ships.* Underhill, *Sail Training and Cadet Ships.*

HMS BELFAST

Edinburgh-class cruiser (2f/2m). *L/B/D:* 613.5' × 66.3' × 23.2' (187m × 20.2m × 7.1m). *Tons:* 13,385 disp. *Hull:* steel. *Comp.:* 780–850. *Arm.:* 12 × 6" (4x3), 12 × 4", 16 × 2pdr, 8 × 0.5"mg; 6 × 21"TT; 3 aircraft. *Armor:* 4.5" belt, 3" deck. *Mach.:* geared turbines, 80,000 shp, 4 screws; 32.5 kts. *Built:* Harland & Wolff, Ltd., Belfast, N. Ireland; 1939.

The largest cruiser in the Royal Navy when commissioned in August 1939, HMS *Belfast* was nearly sunk three months later when on November 21 a magnetic mine in the Firth of Forth broke her back. After extensive repairs at Devonport, she was recommissioned in November 1942. As flagship of the Tenth Cruiser Squadron at Scapa Flow, Captain Frederick Parham commanding, *Belfast* covered the Russian convoy route. On December 26, 1942, she took part in the annihilation of the German battlecruiser SCHARNHORST. The following September, *Belfast* sailed in support of the unsuccessful naval aviation attack on the German battleship TIRPITZ in Altenfjord. During Operation Neptune — the naval end of the D-day invasion in June 1944 — *Belfast* was part of Rear Admiral F. H. G. Dalrymple-Hamilton's bombarding force, and for five weeks she hit German shore emplacements at the Sword and Juno landing zones and inland. Prior to the Allied invasion, Prime Minister Winston Churchill had announced his intention to watch the invasion from the decks of *Belfast,* a reckless suggestion that was only dropped when King George V said that if Churchill went, he would too.

Refitted for tropical duty, *Belfast* was dispatched to the Pacific, but she arrived when the war was all but over. From 1946 to 1948 she operated in the Pacific and then returned to home waters for a refit. Assigned as flagship of the British fleet in China during the AMETHYST crisis in 1949, she remained in the Pacific through the Korean War (1950–52), and in two years fired more rounds against enemy shore emplacements than she had in all of World War II. Following several show-the-flag cruises around the world, HMS *Belfast* was paid off in 1963. After several years as an accommodation vessel in Portsmouth, a private citizens' group banded together to save *Belfast* under the auspices of the Imperial War Museum. She has been open to the public in the Thames River, opposite the Tower of London, since 1971.

Watton, *Cruiser "Belfast."*

BELGICA

(ex-*Patria*) Screw steamer (1f/3m). *L/B/D:* 118′ × 25′ × 13.4′ (36m × 7.6m × 4.1m). *Tons:* 336 grt. *Hull:* wood. *Comp.:* 20. *Mach.:* compound engine, 30 nhp. *Built:* K. Jacobsen, Svelvig, Norway; 1884.

Built for the Norwegian seal trade, *Belgica* was acquired and renamed for Commandant Adrien de Gerlache's Bel-

gian Antarctic Expedition, the chief object of which was to determine the position of the South Magnetic Pole. Outfitting the ship took longer than intended, and the ship did not arrive off Palmer Land until January 1898, late in the Antarctic summer. By March, the ship was icebound near Alexander Island, and over the course of the next thirteen months she was held fast, drifting 600 miles along the Antarctic Peninsula shore of the Bellingshausen Sea towards Peter I Island. Unprepared for such an extensive stay in that climate, most of the crew were stricken with scurvy, and command of the expedition devolved temporarily on *Belgica*'s first mate, Roald Amundsen, who was assisted by ship's doctor Frederick A. Cook. In April 1899, the crew used explosives to free the ship from the ice, and *Belgica* returned to Belgium. Although the *Belgica* expedition was only a minor success, being the first to winter in Antarctica, it did set the stage for the swift advances in Antarctic exploration that culminated in Amundsen's ascent to the South Pole from the ship FRAM in 1911.

Acquired by N. C. Halvorsen in 1902, and then by the Duc d'Orléans who embarked in her for research in the Kara and Greenland Seas in 1905, *Belgica* remained in service through 1913.

Cook, *Through the First Antarctic Night.*

BELLE

Barque longue (2m). *L/B:* 51′ × 14′ (15.5m × 4.3m). *Tons:* 45 tons. *Hull:* wood. *Comp.:* 20–30. *Arm.:* 6 guns. *Built:* Honoré Malet, Rochefort, France; 1684.

Discovered in the shallow waters of Matagorda Bay off the Texas coast, *Belle* was the flagship of Robert Cavalier, Sieur de La Salle's ill-fated expedition to establish French colonies at the mouth of the Mississippi. One of the most important French explorers of North America, La Salle prospered as a fur trader on the Great Lakes, and his GRIFFON of 1679 was the first ship built on the Lakes. In 1682, he and Henri de Tonty became the first Europeans to sail down the Mississippi River to its mouth, after which he claimed the territory Louisiana for France. Returning to France, La Salle received the backing of Louis XIV to secure the claim.

On July 24, 1684, he sailed from La Rochelle at the head of a fleet of four ships — *Belle,* a gift from Louis, *Joly* (36 guns), the ketch *St. François,* and the storeship *Aimable.* After a two-month stay in St. Domingue (Haiti) during which *St. François* was seized by pirates, the fleet sailed into the Gulf of Mexico in November. Guided by inaccurate maps, they landed just west of the Mississippi but, uncertain of their position, they pressed on, only to reach Matagorda Bay, 400 miles west of the Mississippi, in January of 1685. The inhospitable land was made almost unbearable by the loss of *Aimable* and the bulk of the expedition's supplies as she entered the bay. Shortly thereafter, *Joly* sailed for France, leaving *Belle* and some 180 ailing and disgruntled settlers. La Salle made several overland expeditions in search of the Mississippi — of which he believed Matagorda Bay to be a branch — but the settlers left at Fort St. Louis (near present-day Port Lavaca) were reduced by disease and in skirmishes with the native inhabitants of the coast.

Belle remained moored in the bay with a crew of about twenty. Running low on water, in January 1686 the captain tried to sail for Fort St. Louis. The ship was blown east across the bay, ran aground, and sank; only six of her crew survived. A year later, with no end of their ordeal in sight, the would-be colonists numbered fewer than forty. La Salle and about half the company set out in search of help, but two months later he was murdered by his own men near the Trinity River. Of this group, only five reached France; the fate of those who remained at Fort St. Louis can only be surmised, as no effort was made to find them.

In the 1970s, the Texas Historical Commission began a systematic effort to find *Belle*. In 1995, while sweeping the bay with a magnetometer, archaeologists led by Barto Arnold found the ship lying in about twelve feet of water just east of the Matagorda Peninsula. A cofferdam was erected around the site and the water pumped out so that what amounted to a dry-land excavation of the site could be carried out. A variety of human remains — including one complete skeleton — and artifacts have been recovered, among them eighty whole or semiwhole casks containing cargo, gunpowder, lead shot, foodstuffs, and pitch; empty casks that once contained wine and water; several boxes containing muskets and trade goods such as beads, rings, combs, and knife blades; one iron swivel gun, two bronze cannon, and a carriage gun; rigging fittings; cooking implements; and personal effects such as a crucifix, bowls, and pipes.

Following the excavation of the smaller items, the remains of the hull were completely disassembled and removed from the site. After careful conservation ashore, they will be completely reassembled and open to public view.

LaRoe, "La Salle's Last Voyage."

LA BELLE POULE

Frigate (3m). L/B: 140' × 38' (42.7m × 11.6m). *Tons:* 902 bm. *Hull:* wood. *Comp.:* 260. *Arm.:* 26 × 12pdr, 4 × 6pdr. *Built:* Bourdeaux; 1768.

Launched during the relatively long peace between the end of the Seven Years' War and the American Revolution, *La Belle Poule* was a fast frigate and one of the first French warships with a copper bottom. By 1778, relations between France and Britain had become strained owing to the former's support for the American colonists' fight for independence. On June 16, a squadron composed of the frigate *Belle Poule* and *La Licorne* and the lugger *Le Coureur* were cruising in the western approaches to the English Channel when it came in sight of Rear Admiral Augustus Keppel's Channel Fleet, which had been ordered to blockade Brest. Rather than close with the superior force, Captain Isaac Jean Timothée Chadeau de la Clocheterie signaled for his consorts to scatter. The fast British frigate *Arethusa* (28 guns) caught up with *Belle Poule* and *Coureur,* and demanded their surrender. When Chadeau de la Clocheterie refused, *Arethusa* opened fire at 1800. The battle lasted five hours as the ships drifted towards the coast of Brittany. *Arethusa* finally withdrew to the safety of the British fleet. The next morning, *Belle Poule* eluded two other British ships and returned to Brest with 40 dead and 61 wounded; *Licorne* and *Coureur* were both captured.

Chadeau de la Clocheterie's success in the unprovoked attack won him instant celebrity at court, and *Belle Poule* was assigned to a new captain. On July 15, 1780, she was captured by HMS *Nonsuch* off the Loire and brought into the Royal Navy rated as a 36-gun, 5th-rate frigate. Sometime after 1781 she became a receiving ship. She was sold out of the service in 1801.

Culver, *Forty Famous Ships.*

HMS BELLEROPHON

Arrogant-class 3rd rate 74 (3m). *L/B/D:* 168' × 46.8' × 19.8' (51.2m × 14.3m × 6m). *Tons:* 1,643 bm. *Hull:* wood. *Comp.:* 550. *Arm.:* 28 × 32pdr, 28 × 18pdr, 18 × 9pdr. *Des.:* Sir Thomas Slade. *Built:* Greaves & Co., Frindsbury, Eng.; 1786.

Named for the mythical Greek hero who was the companion of the winged horse Pegasus, HMS *Bellerophon* was the second ship of the name. Her first fleet action was with Lord Howe at the Glorious First of June, 1794, against the French fleet of Admiral Villaret-de-Joyeuse, during which she forced the 74-gun *Eole* to strike. She

The third-rate 74-gun HMS BELLEROPHON *was the veteran of many naval actions during the Napoleonic Wars. John James Chalon painted her at Plymouth, where she housed the imprisoned Napoleon from July 25 to August 14, 1815, prior to his permanent exile on the remote island of St. Helena. Courtesy National Maritime Museum, Greenwich.*

subsequently distinguished herself in several actions during the blockade off France. In 1797, under Captain Henry d'Esterre Darby, she was assigned to Rear Admiral Horatio Nelson's squadron sent to find the French fleet bound for Egypt. At the Battle of the Nile on the evening of August 1, 1798, *Bellerophon* engaged the 120-gun L'ORIENT. Within the hour she was dismasted and had to disengage, coming under fire from TONNANT (80 guns) as she did so. Her casualties included 193 killed or injured.

Over the next four years, she served variously in the Mediterranean, with the Channel Fleet, and in the West Indies. At the Battle of Trafalgar on October 21, 1805, "Billy Ruffian," as she was known among the lower deck, sailed in the lee division. Inspired by Nelson's signal that "England expects that every man will do his duty," her gun crews chalked on the gun barrels, "*Bellerophon:* Death or Glory." Despite casualties numbering 132, including Captain John Cooke, she took the French *Aigle* (74).

From 1806 to 1809, she sailed with the Channel Fleet and in the Baltic. Following his loss at Waterloo in 1815, Napoleon was compelled to surrender to *Bellerophon's* Captain Frederick Lewis Maitland at Rochefort, and she carried the defeated emperor to England prior to his exile to St. Helena. The following year she became a prison hulk, which she remained until broken up in 1836. Among others who served in *Bellerophon* as young men were Matthew Flinders, a midshipman at the Glorious First of June, who surveyed Australia in HMS INVESTIGATOR (1801–3), and John Franklin, who commanded the ill-fated Arctic expedition in HMS EREBUS and TERROR (1845–47).

Culver, *Forty Famous Ships.* Mackenzie, *Trafalgar Roll.* Schom, *Trafalgar.*

BENJAMIN F. PACKARD

Down Easter (3m). *L/B/D:* 244.2′ × 43.3 × 26.7′ (74.4m × 13.2m × 8.1m). *Tons:* 2,076 reg. *Hull:* wood. *Built:* Goss, Sawyer & Packard, Bath, Me.; 1883.

Named for the junior partner of the yard that built her, *Benjamin F. Packard* was a three-skysail yard Down Easter built for Captain John R. Kelley. In the 1920s and 1930s, promoters seeking to profit from the ship's use as a shore-side attraction created stories about her fast passages in the tea and wool trades. In point of fact, *Packard* never sailed to either Australia or China, and she was a slow ship. Her average runs from East Coast ports to San Francisco with general cargo were 148 days; on the return, she shipped grain from California. She also carried other bulk cargoes, including case oil and lumber, and served ports in England, British Columbia, and Japan. Thanks to Captain Zaccheus "Tiger" Allen, her master from 1889 to 1904, *Packard* had a reputation as a hard ship and was known to some as the "Battleship of the American Merchant Marine." Bought by Arthur Sewall & Company in 1887, she was sold to the Northwestern Fisheries Company of Seattle in 1907, and later to the Booth Fisheries Company, for which companies she sailed in the Alaska salmon fisheries until 1924. She was then sold and towed to New York — via the Panama Canal — with a cargo of lumber. A succession of buyers kept her from the breakers, and in 1927–28, she was loaned to the United States Junior Naval Reserve and moored on the Hudson River at 96th Street in Manhattan. Auctioned out of the estate of marine antique collector Max Williams in 1929, she was sold for $1,000 in an evening in which model ships went for more than twice that. *Packard* was eventually moved to Playland Park on Long Island Sound in Rye, New York. Gaudily decked out as a "pirate" ship, "this last remnant of the great days of American sailing ships" attracted too few visitors to be profitable, and in May 1939, she was towed into Long Island Sound and scuttled in 190 feet of water off Eaton's Neck. Various artifacts had been salvaged from the ship, including the after house, which was dismantled and taken to Mystic Seaport Museum.

Morris, *Portrait of a Ship.*

her maiden name in deference to Wilhelm II's enthusiastic interest in her construction. The largest ship of her day, she was christened by the Kaiser less than six weeks after the loss of TITANIC, and entered service on June 10, 1913, when she departed Cuxhaven for Southampton, Cherbourg, and New York. Elegant though she was, *Imperator* was a top-heavy ship, a flaw corrected that November when her towering funnels (one of which was a dummy) were shortened by nearly 10 feet and some of her heavier fixtures were removed or replaced with those of lighter materials.

The outbreak of World War I found her at Hamburg, where she was laid up and all but abandoned for the duration of the hostilities. Taken over by the U.S. Navy following the Armistice, she was commissioned as USS *Imperator* on May 5 and made three voyages in which she carried 25,000 soldiers and civilians to the United States. In November, *Imperator* was transferred to the British government, and the following year she was given to Britain as reparations. She sailed briefly under lease to Cunard before that company purchased her outright and renamed her *Berengaria,* for the wife of Richard I (Lion Heart). Beginning in 1921 she was given a complete overhaul, and her fuel was changed from coal to oil. As flagship of the Cunard fleet, she resumed weekly service between Southampton, Cherbourg, and New York in concert with AQUITANIA and MAURETANIA.

The Great Depression forced *Berengaria* to supplement her transatlantic work with cruises to Bermuda, the Caribbean, and the Canadian Maritimes. Although Cunard intended to keep her in service until she could be replaced by QUEEN ELIZABETH, a series of fires traced to her deteriorating electrical wiring led to the revocation of her passenger certificate by the American authorities, finally forcing Cunard to sell her in 1938. *Berengaria* was taken to Jarrow in December of that year and cut down; she was not completely broken up until 1946.

Bonsor, *North Atlantic Seaway.* Braynard, *Classic Ocean Liners.*

BERENGARIA

(ex-*Imperator*) Liner (3f/2m). *L/B/D:* 919′ × 98.3′ (268.2m × 29.9m). *Tons:* 51,680 grt. *Hull:* steel. *Comp.:* 1st 908, 2nd 592, 3rd 962, 4th 1,772; 1,180 crew. *Mach.:* steam turbines, 4 screws, 60,000 hp; 22.5 kts. *Built:* AG Vulcan, Hamburg; 1913.

The first of the Albert Ballin–inspired trio of Hamburg-Amerika superliners built to challenge British domination of the North Atlantic passenger trade, *Imperator* was originally to have been called *Europa,* but she was given

BERGENSFJORD

(later *Argentina, Jerusalem, Aliya*) Liner (2f/2m). *L/B/D:* 512.1′ × 61.2′ (161.5m × 18.7m). *Tons:* 10,666 grt. *Hull:* steel. *Comp.:* 1st 100, 2nd 250, 3rd 850. *Mach.:* quadruple expansion, 2 screws; 15 kts. *Built:* Cammell, Laird & Co., Ltd., Birkenhead, Eng.; 1913.

The second ship built for Norwegian America Line, Norway's premier transatlantic passenger line, *Bergensfjord* entered service in September 1913. Her normal service was between Christiania (now Oslo), Kristiansand, Stavanger, Bergen, and New York; thanks to Norway's neutrality, this service continued through World War I. Norwegian America's first ship, *Kristianiafjord,* had wrecked in 1917, and following the war *Bergensfjord* maintained steady service, with *Stavangerfjord,* until 1940. In July 1924, an engine room explosion forced the beaching of the ship near Bergen, and during repairs she was converted from coal to oil fuel.

Bergensfjord's last passage from Norway ended at New York on April 15, 1940, one week after the German invasion of Norway. Pressed into service as a troop ship, she sailed in this work for the duration of World War II. In 1946, Norwegian America sold her to Home Lines, who gave her accommodations for 32 passengers in first class and 969 in tourist class. Renamed *Argentina,* she entered the burgeoning immigrant trade between Italy and Brazil, Uruguay and Argentina; three years later she began sailing to the Caribbean and Venezuela. After brief service to New York and Halifax, Home Lines put the ship into charter work, and on one voyage she carried French Foreign Legionnaires from Algeria to Indochina.

In 1953 *Argentina* was sold to the Zim Israel Navigation Company and entered service between the Mediterranean and New York. From 1955 she sailed between Haifa and Marseilles, and two years later she was renamed *Aliya* when a new *Jerusalem* was commissioned for Zim Lines. Laid up in 1958, she was scrapped at La Spezia the next year.

Bonsor, *North Atlantic Seaway.* Braynard & Miller, *Fifty Famous Liners 2.*

BERKSHIRE

Sidewheel steamer (2f/6m). *L/B/D:* 422.4' × 50.6' × 12.9' (128.7m × 15.4m × 3.9m). *Tons:* 2,918 grt. *Hull:* steel. *Mach.:* beam engines, 5,000 nhp, sidewheels. *Built:* New York Ship Building Co., Camden, N.J.; 1913.

The largest night boat ever to run on the Hudson River, and one of the last to run in that service, *Berkshire* was laid down as the Hudson Navigation Company's *Princeton* but underwent a change of name before launching. All four of the company's last night boats, which also included *C. W. Morse, Rensselaer,* and *Trojan* — had beam engines rather than the more efficient and modern compound or triple expansion engines. Although she was often known as the "mighty" *Berkshire,* or by some equally fitting epithet, her grand size was topped by two dwarf smokestacks. Her staterooms were plain, with bunk beds, a sink, and chamber pot, although deluxe

suites included two twin beds and a private bathroom. The interior decoration was also highly refined and its classical simplicity lacked the ebullience of Fall River Line boats such as PURITAN.

Built for service between New York City and Albany, after World War I, *Berkshire* and her sister ships faced increasing competition from road traffic. In 1926, the company reorganized and was renamed the Hudson River Night Line. This line went bankrupt in 1932 and the ships were in and out of service as they changed hands several times. *Berkshire* was withdrawn from service in 1937, returned the following year as a replacement for *Rensselaer,* and was withdrawn again when night service ended in 1939.

Hilton, *Night Boat.*

BERTRAND

Sternwheel steamer (2f). *L/B/D:* 161' × 32.9' × 5.2' dph (49.1m × 10m × 1.6m). *Tons:* 251 grt. *Hull:* wood. *Built:* Dunlevy & Co., Wheeling, W. Va.; 1864.

The only American steamboat the remains of which have been fully excavated as an archaeological site, the *Bertrand* was a "mountain boat" designed for work on the shallow waters of the western tributaries of the Mississippi River. Mountain boats had an extremely shallow draft — *Bertrand* reportedly drew as little as eighteen inches without cargo — and were equipped with "grasshopper" poles for getting over rapids and shallows. Mounted on either side of the bow, the poles were driven into the riverbed, and then used to hoist the vessel up as it drove forward. The process was repeated until the obstacle was cleared.

Taken to St. Louis, *Bertrand* was sold to the Montana & Idaho Transportation Company, which had five vessels plying the Missouri River between St. Louis and Fort Benton, Montana Territory. (The remote head of navigation lies at an elevation of 3,300 feet above sea level some 3,600 miles from the mouth of the Mississippi River.) In 1864, gold and other mining strikes had created a boom in trade on the Missouri, and a handbill for the Montana & Idaho advertised "1865, 1865! Ho! For the Gold Mines! Through Bills [of] Lading Given . . . to Virginia City, Bannock City, Deer Lodge and All Points in the Mining Districts." Loaded with quicksilver (used for separating gold from its ore) and myriad other supplies for the fledgling upriver communities, *Bertrand* sailed from St. Louis on March 16 under Captain John Jacobs. On April 1, she hit a snag and sank at Portage La Force, about twenty-five miles north of Omaha, Nebraska, and 640 miles from St. Louis.

Although no one was killed, the economic consequences to the mining districts must have been considerable, as *Bertrand* carried about 13 percent of all the goods consigned to Fort Benton in 1865. Much of the deck cargo was apparently salvaged after her loss, but the stern-wheeler eventually disappeared from view as silt from the meandering Missouri buried her. In 1968, two salvors hoping to locate the shipment of quicksilver, as well as whiskey and gold thought to be aboard, discovered the wreck, which by then was covered by twenty-six feet of sediment. Fortunately for posterity, the site was located within the De Soto National Wildlife Refuge. Working under the direction of a National Park Service archaeologist, the salvors excavated the site with the understanding that the government would retain 40 percent of the bulk items as well as "any artifacts (to include all man-made objects or parts thereof) or other valuable historical items."

Although most of the engine and deck structures had been removed, the hull was in remarkably good condition. Most important, however, was the recovery of nearly 2 million individual items from the cargo, about 300,000 of which merited conservation. Included in the hoard was a staggering array of mid-nineteenth-century Americana, from foodstuffs, personal effects, and clothing to mining supplies, tools, and artifacts of iron, leather, and wood, glass and ceramic bottles, textiles, hundreds of cases of wine, ale, champagne, patent medicines, ketchup, and sauces.

Petsche, *Steamboat "Bertrand."*

BESSEMER

Screw steamer. *L/B/D:* 349.6′ × 40.2′ (54′ew) × 11.5′ (106.6m × 12.3m (16.5m) × 3.5m). *Tons:* 1,974 grt. *Hull:* iron. *Mach.:* oscillating steam engines, 800 hp, 4 screws. *Des.:* Sir Henry Bessemer. *Built:* Earle's Co., Hull, Eng.; 1875.

Although he is best remembered today for his invention of the Bessemer process of making steel, the invention for which Sir Henry Bessemer was best known in his own day was a cross-channel steamship designed to reduce as far as possible the conditions that caused seasickness in passengers. The ship was powered by two pairs of paddlewheels mounted 106 feet apart. The most innovative aspect of the ship's design was a 180-ton gimbaled saloon measuring seventy feet long, thirty feet wide and twenty feet high. This was mounted on trunnions and the motion was controlled by hydraulic machinery so that it would remain level relative to the motion of the ship. Lavishly decorated, the saloon was also equipped with forced ventilation to alleviate stuffiness. There were also rows of private cabins on either side of the ship which increased the overall beam to fifty-four feet. *Bessemer* made her maiden voyage between Dover and Calais on Saturday, May 8, 1875, but the results fell far short of expectations. Sir Henry was quickly forced to abandon the gimbaled saloon, and the ship was refitted with more traditional accommodations. She was finally withdrawn from service in 1880.

Rogers, *Freak Ships.*

BETSY

Merchantman (2m). *L/B:* 74.7′ × 23.8′ (22.8m × 7.3m). *Tons:* 171 burthen. *Hull:* wood. *Built:* <1781.

In 1781, British Major General Earl Charles Cornwallis was ordered to establish an ice-free port in Virginia, to which the Royal Navy's main fleet based at New York could withdraw in winter. Although ensconced at Portsmouth and Hampton Roads, Cornwallis decided to shift his base across the peninsula to Yorktown, which provided a better and more easily defended anchorage, though from the landward side it was inferior to his previous position. He had at his disposal a fleet of more than fifty, including seven armed ships and upwards of forty transports and supply ships, prizes, and hired vessels. On September 5, a British fleet under Rear Admiral Thomas Graves in HMS LONDON was defeated by Rear Admiral Comte de Grasse in VILLE DE PARIS, at the Battle of the Chesapeake. This left Cornwallis to face the French fleet and a combined Franco-American force led by General George Washington, with the Marquis de Lafayette and Lieutenant General Count Jean-Baptiste de Rochambeau. In an effort to secure his seaward flank, Cornwallis ordered fifteen vessels scuttled as close to shore as possible, and he deployed his heaviest ships where their guns could bear on the land forces. On October 10, his heaviest ship, the forty-four-gun HMS *Charon,* burned to the waterline under fire from land. Six days later the British tried to withdraw upriver, but they were bogged down in a thunderstorm, and the next day Cornwallis presented a flag of truce. With Cornwallis's surrender on October 19, the United States had won the independence so brazenly declared five years before.

Cornwallis's ships, many damaged by Washington's guns, were handed over to the French, who salvaged a number of the vessels throughout the summer of 1782. About twenty-six of the ships were abandoned. The submerged fleet was the object of occasional interest over the next two centuries. In 1976, divers from the American Institute of Nautical Archaeology began excavation of some recently found wreck sites. The best preserved of those discovered turned out be a relatively small merchantman (Shipwreck 44Y088) lying in 20 feet of water about 500 feet offshore. This ship had been fairly well preserved in silt and clay. In 1982, a cofferdam was erected to isolate the hull from the river and otherwise facilitate the excavation and conservation of the site. As either the British or the French (or both) had stripped the ship prior to its sinking, the surviving artifacts comprise mostly small items, such as coat hooks and pieces of furniture. Nonetheless, the Yorktown ship is one of the best-preserved eighteenth-century merchant ships ever found, and it has thrown considerable light on the details of merchant ship construction in this period.

Broadwater et al., "Yorktown Shipwreck Archaeological Project." Johnston et al., "Cornwallis Cave Shipwreck, Yorktown, Virginia." Sands, *Yorktown's Captive Fleet.*

HMS BIRKENHEAD

Paddle frigate (1f/2m). *L/B/D:* 210′ × 36.7′ (60.5′ew) × 15.8′ (64m × 11.2m (18.4m) × 4.8m). *Tons:* 1,918 disp. *Hull:* iron. *Comp.:* 250 crew. *Arm.:* 1 × 10″, 1 × 68pdr. *Mach.:* side lever steam engines, 536 nhp, 2 paddles; 13 kts. *Des.:* J. Laird. *Built:* Laird Bros., Birkenhead, Eng.; 1845.

Named for the British port, HMS *Birkenhead* was the Royal Navy's first iron-hulled frigate, originally rigged as a brig but converted to a barkentine. On August 27, 1847, she was used to free Brunel's GREAT BRITAIN, which had stranded in Belfast Lough the year before. Gunnery trials led the Admiralty to the conclusion that iron was unsuitable for warship construction because it could be pierced or shattered by shot, and *Birkenhead* was converted to use as a troopship in 1848. In January 1852, under Master Robert Salmond she sailed for South Africa with 487 officers and men of the 74th Highlanders and other regiments commanded by Colonel Alexander Seton, together with 25 women and 31 children. After touching at Cape Town, the ship sailed on to Algoa Bay. At 0200 on the morning of February 26, *Birkenhead* hit a rock in False Bay. Three boats were launched from the ship, and as *Birkenhead* began to break up and sink the soldiers held their ranks in a legendary display of valor and chivalry. In all, 438 men lost their lives; the 193 survivors included all the women and children. The remains of the ship, which had broken into three pieces, were discovered by divers in the 1980s.

Bevan, *Drums of the "Birkenhead."* Brown, *Before the Ironclad.* Hepper, *British Warship Losses.*

BISMARCK

Bismarck-class battleship (1f/2m). *L/B/D:* 813.8′ × 118.1′ × 28.5′ (251m × 36m × 9.9m) *Tons:* 50,300 disp. *Hull:* steel. *Comp.:* 2,065. *Arm.:* 8 × 15.2″ (4x2), 12 × 6″, 16 × 10.5cm, 16 × 3.7cm, 78 × 2cm; 6 aircraft. *Armor:* 12.8″ belt, 4.8″ deck. *Mach.:* geared turbines, 150,170 shp, 3 screws; 30 kts. *Built:* Blohm & Voss, Hamburg; 1940.

Named for Otto von Bismarck, the nineteenth-century Prussian statesman who forged the German nation, *Bismarck* was, with her sister ship TIRPITZ, one of the two largest German warships ever built. Commissioned nearly a year after the outbreak of World War II, *Bismarck's* first combat mission was also her last. On May 18, 1941, under command of Captain Ernst Lindemann and flying the flag of Vice Admiral Günther Lütjens, she sailed from the Baltic seaport of Gdynia with the pocket battleship PRINZ EUGEN on a commerce-raiding mission code-named Operation Rheinübung. Putting into Bergen, the ships were spotted by RAF planes and the British fleet mobilized to prevent their breakout into the Atlantic. Under cover of night and bad weather, the ships slipped into the Norwegian Sea and sailed north and west around Iceland. On May 23, *Bismarck* and *Prinz Eugen* were sighted in the Denmark Strait northwest of Iceland by the British cruisers HMS *Suffolk* and NORFOLK. On May 22, the Battle Cruiser Force of HMS HOOD and PRINCE OF WALES had sailed from Scapa Flow and was now southwest of Iceland about 300 miles away. Vice Admiral L. E. Holland steered an interception course and contact between the two forces was established at 0537 on

The German battleship BISMARCK *sailed on only one combat mission, in May 1941. Only three days after sinking the British battlecruiser* HMS HOOD, *she was herself sunk by a British task force in midatlantic. Courtesy Imperial War Museum, London.*

May 24. *Prince of Wales* opened fire at 0553 at a range of about 12 miles. *Bismarck* engaged *Hood,* and at 0600 a 15-inch shell from her fourth salvo tore through the ship, which split in two and sank with the loss of 1,415 men. *Prince of Wales* was hit repeatedly before breaking off action 13 minutes later, though not before landing three crucial hits on *Bismarck.* With his ship down in the bow and leaking oil, Lütjens decided to make for the French port of St. Nazaire.

Suffolk and Norfolk continued to shadow the Germans, while Admiral Sir John Tovey's Home Fleet — including battleships HMS KING GEORGE V and REPULSE, aircraft carrier VICTORIOUS, and five cruisers — and Force H from Gibraltar — battlecruiser RENOWN, aircraft carrier ARK ROYAL, and cruiser SHEFFIELD — were deployed to intercept. (All told, *Bismarck* was actively pursued by a total of five battleships, two aircraft carriers, nine cruisers, and eighteen destroyers.) During a brief evening action against *Suffolk,* the undamaged *Prinz Eugen* parted company and proceeded alone to Brest. A nighttime air strike from *Victorious* failed to inflict any damage, and all contact with *Bismarck* was lost after 0300 on May 25. She was not located until 1030 on May 26, and in the interval it had been wrongly believed that she had changed course for Germany.

At 2047 that night, torpedo-bombers from *Ark Royal* scored hits that damaged *Bismarck's* steering gear and forced her to steam north northwest, directly towards the oncoming *King George V* and RODNEY and shadowed closely by the cruiser HMS *Sheffield* and five destroyers led by Captain Philip Vian in HMS COSSACK. At this point, with *Bismarck's* speed down to 10 knots, Lütjens radioed to Germany: "Ship no longer maneuverable, we fight to the last shell." Torpedo attacks throughout the night scored no major damage, but the destroyers' persistent harrying exhausted the German crew.

At 0847 on May 27, *Rodney* opened fire at a range of 25,000 yards, *King George V* a minute later, and the cruisers HMS *Norfolk* and *Dorsetshire* somewhat later. The range quickly closed to only 8,600 yards and by 0930 *Bismarck's* main armament had been silenced. *Dorsetshire* was ordered to sink *Bismarck* with torpedoes, though survivors maintained that scuttling charges and not torpedoes sank the ship. Whatever the ultimate cause, *Bismarck* sank at 1036 in 48°10′N, 16°12′W. *Dorsetshire* and the destroyer *Maori* rescued 115 survivors, but a suspected submarine sighting forced them to break off their search. A total of 1,977 of *Bismarck's* crew went down with their ship.

Ballard & Archbold, *Discovery of the "Bismarck."* Müllenheim-Rechberg, *Battleship "Bismarck."* Film: *Sink the "Bismarck"!* (1960).

BLACKFRIARS BARGE

Sailing barge. *L/B:* 50–55′ × 22′ (15–17m x 6.5m). *Tons:* ca. 92 tons. *Hull:* wood. *Built:* England(?); 100–200 CE.

The Blackfriars vessel was a Romano-British sailing barge of the second century, which sank in the River Thames while carrying a cargo of building stone. It is especially noteworthy as an example of the ancient shipbuilding tradition of Celtic northwestern Europe, which differed from the Greco-Roman tradition of the Mediterranean. The wreck was discovered in September 1962 during construction work near the north end of the Blackfriars Bridge in London. Archaeological excavations were carried out by the Guildhall Museum in 1962 and 1963 under the direction of Peter Marsden. The site is approximately 130 yards south of present-day Thames Street, which is thought to represent the line of the Roman-era waterfront. On the basis of Roman potsherds collected from the stratified gravel surrounding the wreck, the excavators believe that the Blackfriars barge sank in the second century.

Like its modern counterparts, the Blackfriars barge is beamy, keelless, and flat-bottomed. The side strakes meet the bottom strakes at a 30–35-degree angle, or chine, rather than curving to form rounded bilges. Unlike contemporary ships from the Mediterranean, the Blackfriars barge was built skeleton first. Strakes were not edge-joined by mortise and tenon but were attached directly to the floor-timbers with iron nails. The nailing technique was complex: first, a hole about three-quarters of an inch in diameter was drilled vertically into the floor timber and an oak peg was inserted. A long nail was then clenched. Gaps in the seams — in places as much as one-half inch wide — were caulked with hazel twigs hammered in from the outboard side.

Cut into the middle of a floor-timber about one-third the length of the ship from the bow, but 5 inches off center, is a socket that marks the approximate position of the mast pillar. The mast itself would have been fitted into a tabernacle at the upper end of the pillar. The position of the mast forward of amidships suggests that the ship was rigged with a single square sail. At the bottom of the socket was a bronze coin of the emperor Domitian, minted at Rome in 88 or 89 CE. The reverse of the coin depicts the goddess Fortuna holding a steering oar.

Immediately abaft the socket, the floor-timbers and side frames were covered by oak planks that formed the bottom of the hold. Overlying this hold area was a pile of Kentish ragstone, used extensively as a building material in Roman London. The stone probably came from the neighborhood of Maidstone, where ragstone was quarried commercially in recent times. The Blackfriars barge thus may have begun its last voyage on the Medway River, near Maidstone, Kent, then followed the Thames estuary to London to deliver its cargo.

Marsden, *Ship of the Roman Period.*

HMS BLOSSOM

Sloop-of-war (3m). *L/B:* 108.5' × 30' (33.1m × 9.1m). *Tons:* 427 bm. *Hull:* wood. *Comp.:* 100. *Arm.:* 18 × 18pdr. *Built:* Guillaum, Northam, Eng.; 1806.

Among the most ambitious nineteenth-century plans to discover the Northwest Passage was a three-pronged venture involving John Franklin, Edward Parry and Commander Frederick William Beechey. While Franklin attempted to complete an overland survey of the Arctic coast from the Mackenzie River to Icy Point (James Cook's farthest north with RESOLUTION and DISCOVERY in 1778), Parry would penetrate the Arctic from the east in HECLA and *Fury,* and Beechey — a veteran of Franklin's *Advance* in 1818 and Parry's *Hecla* in 1819 — would sail through the Bering Strait and eastward to rendezvous with the other parties.

After fitting out for the expedition, Beechey's HMS *Blossom* departed Spithead on May 19, 1825, sailing southwest down the Atlantic with stops at Tenerife and Rio de Janeiro, rounding Cape Horn via the Falklands and Tierra del Fuego. After calling at Concepción and Valparaíso, Chile, she proceeded west to confirm or correct the existence of various islands reported from previous voyages. After visits to Easter Island and Pitcairn Island, *Blossom* continued through the Society Islands to arrive at Tahiti on April 18, 1826. Turning north, they sailed to Onorooroo, Woahoo (Honolulu, Oahu) on May 20, and left from there for Petropavlovsk on the Kamchatka Peninsula, where they arrived on June 29. There they learned that Parry's *Fury* had been crushed in the ice but that her crew had returned to England in *Hecla.* Passing through the Bering Strait on July 19, *Blossom* arrived at Chamisso Inlet in Kotzebue Sound on July 25, 1826, only five days later than the date agreed to in England eighteen months before — an astonishing feat of seamanship. There being no sign of Franklin, Beechey proceeded to explore the coast as far as 70°38'N, 36 miles northeast of Icy Cape, where they arrived on August 15. From there, Thomas Elson took the ship's barge to look for Franklin and on August 23, he reached Point Barrow (71°23'N, 156°21'W), the farthest into the Arctic anyone except Eskimos had ever penetrated and which he named

for Sir John Barrow, the Second Secretary of the Admiralty. (Perhaps discouraged by "the most dreary, miserable and uninteresting portions of the sea coast that can perhaps be found in any part of the world," Franklin turned back to the Great Bear Lake from Return Point five days before Elson reached Point Barrow, 146 miles to the west.)

Sailing from Kotzebue Bay on October 14, *Blossom* headed for Yerba Buena (now San Francisco), where she arrived on November 7. After six weeks in the tiny Spanish port, which Beechey predicted would become "a great naval establishment," the expedition called briefly at Monterey and then crossed the Pacific to Macao, arriving on April 11, 1827. After calling again at Petropavlovsk, they returned to Kotzebue Sound. The ice was worse this season, and there was no news of Franklin. On October 5, Beechey turned for home, calling at Monterey, Yerba Buena, and San Blas, Mexico, en route, and arrived in England on October 12, 1827. In addition to the geographical knowledge gained, the two-year voyage resulted in the publication of two important works on botany and zoology. *Blossom* remained in service as a survey ship until 1833 when she was hulked; she was broken up in 1848.

Beechey, *Narrative of a Voyage to the Pacific and Beering's Strait.* Brock, "Dossier HMS *Blossom* 1806–1848." Peard, *To the Pacific and Arctic with Beechey.*

SMS BLÜCHER

Blücher-class armored cruiser. *L/B/D:* 525.9' x 79.6' × 28.6' (161.8m × 24.5m × 8.8m). *Tons:* 17,500 disp. *Hull:* steel. *Comp.:* 929. *Arm.:* 12 × 8.4" (6 × 2), 8 × 6", 16 × 8.8cm; 4 × 18"TT. *Armor:* 7.2" belt, 2.8" deck. *Mach.:* triple expansion, 38,323 ihp, 3 screws; 25.4 kts. *Built:* Kaiserliche Werft, Kiel, Ger.; 1909.

Named for Gebhard Leberecht von Blücher, Prussian hero of the Battle of Waterloo, SMS *Blücher* was somewhat stronger than the *Scharnhorst*-class but smaller than SMS VON DER TANN and her successor heavy cruisers. These shortcomings proved fatal when on January 23, 1914, Rear Admiral Franz von Hipper sailed with *Blücher* as a replacement for *Von der Tann* in his squadron's sortie to the Dogger Bank. The British mustered an overwhelming force to oppose Hipper, key among them Vice Admiral Sir David Beatty's Battle Cruiser Fleet. The Dogger Bank action opened on the 24th between the light cruisers HMS *Aurora* and SMS *Kolberg,* but suspecting a trap, Hipper turned for home, pursued by the British, who opened fire at 0905. Poor signaling led to British fire being concentrated on *Blücher,* in the rear of the German line, and shortly before noon she succumbed to the concentrated fire of *Indomitable* and *New Zealand* and capsized in position 54°20′N, 05°43′E. The loss of *Blücher* and 792 crew reinforced the German instinct not to risk capital ships in a general engagement.

Halpern, *Naval History of World War I.* Van der Vat, *Grand Scuttle.*

BLÜCHER

Blücher-class heavy cruiser. *L/B/D:* 674.5′ × 69.9′ × 25.3′ (205.9m × 21.3m × 7.7m). *Tons:* 18,208 disp. *Hull:* steel. *Comp.:* 1,400. *Arm.:* 8 × 8.1″ (4x2), 12 × 10.5cm, 12 × 3.7cm, 8 × 2cm, 12 × 21″TT; 3 aircraft. *Armor:* 3.2″ belt, 2.2″ deck. *Mach.:* steam turbines, 131,821 shp, 3 screws; 32.5 kts. *Built:* Deutsche Werke, Kiel, Ger.; 1939.

The ill-fated *Blücher* was the first of a five-ship class of heavy cruisers laid down between 1936 and 1939. Under Captain Heinrich Woldag, *Blücher* took part in the German invasion of Norway in 1940, sailing from Kiel in company with *Emden* and *Lützow*. *Blücher* encountered some resistance upon entering Oslofjord on the night of April 8, but at 0521, while trying to force the Drøbak Narrows, the ship was mauled at point-blank range by 11.2-inch and 6-inch guns and land-based torpedoes. *Blücher* anchored about 2.5 kilometers below Askholmen Island while its turbines were repaired, but successive explosions forced Woldag to abandon ship at 0700. Twenty-three minutes later, *Blücher* capsized and sank in 59°44′N, 10°36′E, the largest of the three surface units — with KARLSRUHE and KÖNIGSBERG — lost in Operation Weserübung. ADMIRAL HIPPER and PRINZ EUGEN were also commissioned in the German Navy; *Lützow* was sold to the Soviet Union in February 1940 and renamed *Petropavlovsk*, and in 1942 an attempt was made to reconfigure *Seydlitz* as an aircraft carrier, although the ship was never completed.

Gröner, *German Warships.* Whitley, *German Cruisers of World War Two.*

BLUENOSE

Schooner (2m). *L/B/D:* 143′ × 27′ × 15.8′ (43.6m × 8.2m × 4.8m). *Tons:* 285 disp. *Hull:* wood. *Comp.:* 22–28. *Des.:* William J. Roue. *Built:* Smith & Rhuland, Lunenburg, Nova Scotia; 1921.

Bluenose was designed specifically to race for the International Trophy, a prize established by W. H. Dennis, publisher of the Halifax *Herald,* to answer the complaint that the America's Cup races were between yachts rather than working vessels that could stand up to a good wind. Her

designer was William J. Roue, a self-described amateur naval architect well known in Nova Scotia. Her first skipper was Angus Walters, one of the most successful fishermen on the Grand Banks, who had acquitted himself well in the trials for the first International Fishermen's Trophy race held in October 1920. (The winner, *Delawana,* lost two races to the Gloucester schooner *Esperanto.*) *Bluenose* beat all comers handily, and she was chosen to represent Canada in the race against the U.S. defender. *Esperanto* had been lost that summer off Sable Island and the Americans tried to put forward the W. Starling Burgess-designed *Mayflower.* Her bid was rejected on the grounds that she was not a working fisherman. The honor fell to *Elsie,* under *Esperanto*'s Marty Welch. *Bluenose* beat *Elsie* by margins of more than two miles in races held on October 22 and 24. The following year, she bested the new Thomas McManus–designed *Henry Ford,* skippered by Clayton Morrissey. The 1923 race was against the Burgess-designed COLUMBIA and ended in a draw. *Columbia* won the first race, and in the second the two boats fouled each other and *Bluenose* won by a minute and a half. She also won the third race, but because Walters failed to round one of the marks to seaward as the committee had ordered, following the earlier collision, he was said to have forfeited the race. But Walters refused to race again and sailed away the next day.

It was eight years before the International Trophy was contested again, but in 1930, *Bluenose* raced the GERTRUDE L. THEBAUD under Captain Ben Pine for the Sir Thomas Lipton Cup and lost. The following year the *Thebaud* challenged for the International Trophy in Halifax and was beaten handily by margins of 29 minutes and 12 minutes. Two years later, the pride of the Canadian fishing fleet sailed to Chicago to represent Canada at the Century of Progress Exposition. There and in Toronto, the pride of the Canadian fishing fleet was visited by thousands of admirers. In 1935 she was again on exhibit, this time in England, where she came in third in a race around the Isle of Wight. One day out of Falmouth, *Bluenose* encountered a Force 11 hurricane and was forced back to Falmouth for repairs, which lasted a month. During the next season diesel engines were installed. Two years later, the last of the International Trophy races was held in Massachusetts. *Bluenose* retired the trophy by winning three races of five against *Thebaud.* With the outbreak of World War II and German U-boats a threat even to the Grand Banks schooners, *Bluenose* was tied up until sold to the West Indies Trading Company in 1942. Under Captain Wilson Berringer, she sailed in the interisland trade until 1946 when she grounded off Haiti, broke her back, and sank.

Although built for racing, first and foremost *Bluenose*

was a working vessel, and she spent the bulk of her career in the long-line cod fisheries on the Grand Banks, racing only when the fishing season was over. Even before World War II, images of the graceful schooner had adorned Canadian stamps and coins, and after her loss her memory remained very much alive in the Canadian imagination. In 1963, the government of Nova Scotia built *Bluenose II,* a replica of the original, which sails as a goodwill ambassador for the province.

Darrach, *Race to Fame.* Merkel & MacAskill, *Schooner "Bluenose."*

LE BON

3rd-rate ship (3m). *L/B:* 135.5′ × 36′ (41.3m × 11m). *Tons:* 850 bm. *Hull:* wood. *Comp.:* 500. *Arm.:* 50 guns. *Built:* Hubac, Brest; 1672.

Built during the expansion of the French Navy under Louis XIV's Minister of Marine Jean-Baptiste Colbert, *Le Bon* ("The Good") first saw action during the Franco-Dutch War of 1672–80. At the two battles of Schooneveldt (June 7 and 14, 1673) and the Texel (August 21), she fought with the combined Anglo-French fleet against the Dutch. She remained in the Brest fleet and was flagship of Vice Admiral François-Louis Rousselet de Châteaurenault in skirmishes with the Dutch off Ushant in 1677 and 1678. Following the Peace of Nijmegen in February 1679, she was stationed with the fleet of Vice Admiral Jean d'Estrées in the French West Indies.

Returning to Europe, in 1683 *Le Bon* sailed under command of Count Ferdinand de Relingue in the Baltic before joining the French Mediterranean squadron. At the time France was at war with Spain, particularly with respect to Spanish territories in Italy. In 1684, the French captured Genoa, and in response, Spain allied with Naples, Sicily, and Sardinia to combat the French threat. On July 10, *Le Bon* and a convoy were becalmed off northern Corsica when a combined fleet of 33 galleys under the Marquis de Centurione surrounded the French warship, 12 lying astern and 21 blocking her advance. In the course of a brilliantly fought five-hour battle, de Relingue outshot and outmaneuvered the galleys, two of which he sank, one by ramming and another by gunfire, and three of which were completely disabled. Badly damaged herself, with 90 of her crew dead, *Le Bon* limped into Livorno pursued by the galleys, who only called off their attack when a Dutch warship threatened to defend *Le Bon.*

The ship's next major engagement was during the French campaign to restore the Catholic James II to the English throne in place of the Dutch Protestant William

II of Orange. On July 10, 1690, she was part of Comte de Tourville's fleet in the French victory over the English at the Battle of Béveziers (Beachy Head). She later joined d'Estrées's Mediterranean squadron, but while en route to rejoin Tourville at Brest before the battles of Barfleur and La Hogue, she wrecked off Ceuta, Spain, in May 1692.

Culver, *Forty Famous Ships.*

BONHOMME RICHARD

(ex-*Duc de Duras*) Frigate (3m). *L/B/D:* 145′ × 36.8′ × 17.5′ (47m × 11.9m × 5.7m). *Tons:* 700 tons burthen. *Hull:* wood. *Comp.:* 322. *Arm.:* 6 × 18pdr, 28 × 12pdr, 6 × 8pdr, 10 swivels. *Des.:* N. Groignard. *Built:* M. Segondat-Duvernet, L'Orient, France; 1765.

Built for La Compagnie des Indes and originally named for one of the French East India Company's shareholders, *Duc de Duras* made two roundtrips to China before the company was dissolved in 1769. Taken over by the French government, she made one voyage to Ile de France as a troop transport before being sold to Sieur Bernier and Sieur Bérard — the latter eventually taking full ownership. During the American Revolution, the Continental Navy officer John Paul Jones — a veteran of the fledgling republic's ALFRED, PROVIDENCE, and RANGER — had been promised a ship by the French government, and in 1778, the merchant Leray de Chaumont intervened with the government to secure *Duc de Duras* for him.

After ordering his ships refit with twenty-eight 12-pdr. and six 8-pdr. guns and ten 3-pdr. swivels, Jones named his ship *Bonhomme Richard* after Benjamin Franklin's own translation of *Poor Richard's Almanac.* On August 14, 1779, *Bonhomme Richard* sailed at the head of a seven-ship squadron, including ALLIANCE (36 guns), *Pallas* (32), and *Vengeance* (12). Jones's squadron spent three weeks raiding merchant shipping in and around the Irish Sea, and then sailed around Ireland and northern Scotland into the North Sea. After sailing into the Firth of Forth to threaten Edinburgh, on September 23, they were off Flamborough Head when they encountered a convoy of 41 merchant ships homeward bound from the Baltic and escorted by HMS *Serapis,* a 44-gun two-deck fifth-rate frigate under Captain Richard Pearson, and by the armed merchant ship *Duchess of Scarborough* (20). Alerted to the presence of enemy ships, the convoy was ordered to scatter. Jones maneuvered *Bonhomme Richard* towards *Serapis* but refused to answer the latter's signals until the two ships were less than 50 meters apart.

The battle erupted with simultaneous broadsides at about 1915. On the second round, two of *Bonhomme*

Richard's 18-pdr. guns exploded and Jones ordered the gundeck cleared. Within half an hour, *Serapis's* repeated 18-pdr. broadsides on the starboard hull and stern had devastated *Bonhomme Richard,* leaving 60 dead and as many wounded, and seven holes along the waterline. At about 2000, the two ships were lying starboard-to-starboard, and realizing that their only advantage lay in keeping *Serapis* close, Jones ordered his men to grapple the British ship. Nonetheless *Serapis* guns continued to fire, so destroying *Bonhomme Richard's* hull that much of the shot passed through the hull without hitting anything before falling into the water. One observer later remarked, "One might have driven in with a coach and six [horses], at one side of this breach, and out the other."

Serapis continued firing with such intensity that both ships were soon ablaze. Meanwhile, the French marines in the tops had effectively cleared the British tops and prevented the British crew from securing the quarterdeck, across which the Americans were now attempting board. At about 2110, *Alliance,* which had been standing off from the action, closed the two ships and fired broadsides of canister and grape shot that inflicted serious injuries on both combatants. Although *Bonhomme Richard* was now effectively reduced to two 18-pdr. guns, when asked by *Serapis's* Captain Richard Pearson if he wanted to surrender, Jones replied, "No. I'll sink, but I'm damned if I'll strike."

At 2200, *Bonhomme Richard's* quartermaster released the 100 or so British prisoners in the hold. At the same time, a grenade thrown into the main hatch of *Serapis* exploded in the gundeck, knocking out the entire battery. Reckoning that he had secured the safety of his convoy, and that further fighting would only result in the needless slaughter of his men — half of whom were already dead — Captain Pearson struck his flag. Jones accepted Pearson's surrender with grace, inviting him to share a glass of wine in what was left of his quarters after three or four broadsides.

Of the 322 crew with which Jones had started the battle, 140 died during or shortly after the battle. *Bonhomme Richard* was so badly holed that Jones transferred his flag to *Serapis* the following morning. On January 25, *Bonhomme Richard* sank in about 200 meters a few miles off Flamborough Head, from which the entire night engagement had been watched. *Serapis* landed at Texel, the Netherlands, on October 4, and from 1779 to 1781 she was on the lists of the French Navy. The victory of *Bonhomme Richard* over *Serapis* was achieved neither by superior tactics, nor superior training, nor certainly better ships. As Captain Edward Beach has written, it was "due to sheer power of will." But of such intangibles are legends made, and above any other achievement, it is for the Battle of Flamborough Head, neither strategically nor tactically significant in itself, that John Paul Jones is remembered as the father of the United States Navy.

There have been two attempts to find the wreck of Jones's command, both funded by the American author Clive Cussler. The first was mounted in 1978 by English historian Sydney Wignall. The next year, an expedition headed by Lieutenant Commander Eric Berryman, USN, "covered ten times as much territory with a cost factor less than half the first effort," according to Cussler. But "even with a top-rated team, we failed to find the elusive *Bonhomme Richard.*"

Boudriot, *John Paul Jones and the "Bonhomme Richard" 1779.* Cussler, *Sea Hunters.* Morison, *John Paul Jones.* U.S. Navy, *DANFS.*

BON PORTÉ WRECK

L: 33′ (10m). *Built:* ca. 550–525 BCE.

This important early wreck was found in the Bay of Bon Porté near St. Tropez, France (43°10′N, 6°39′E). Identified in 1971 by amateur divers at a depth of approximately 50 meters, the ship was first excavated by nautical archaeologist Jean-Pierre Joncheray in 1974, but not before the cargo of Etruscan and Greek amphorae had been extensively looted. The date of the wreck, established on the basis of the ceramic finds, was confirmed by carbon 14 analysis of the wood. The preserved timbers include a 3-meter-long fragment of the keel and 6 ribs. The 9.6-centimeter-high by 6-centimeter-wide keel served to align the frames but added little to the strength of the ship. The frames are widely spaced, the distance between them varying from 0.92 meters to 1.00 meters. The strakes were joined at wide intervals by treenails driven into their edges and further held together by stitches wedged tight by treenails hammered into the stitch-holes. There is no evidence for how the planking was attached to the frames. The small vessel must have had a distinctively rounded profile both athwartships and fore-and-aft.

Basch, "Sewn Ship of *Bon Porté.*" Parker, *Ancient Shipwrecks.*

BORDEIN

River steamer. *Hull:* iron. *Mach.:* steam, sidewheel. *Built:* Bulaq Dockyard, Egypt; 1869.

Built for Sir Samuel Baker's expedition to the Upper Nile in 1869, *Bordein* was subsequently employed as a river ferry on the Nile between Dongala and Khartoum. She was also one of a fleet of steamers used to clear the Bahr el-Jebel for navigation. In 1884, she was pressed into service by Britain's General Charles George "Chinese" Gordon for his ascent up the Nile to Khartoum during the Sudanese War. One of several steamers sent up the Blue Nile on foraging expeditions for food, she became Gordon's only lifeline to the outside world when the Mahdi's forces besieged Khartoum. On November 25, she was sent north for the last time, bearing urgent dispatches about the plight of the garrisons at Omdurman and Khartoum, as well as six volumes of Gordon's journal. On January 25, 1885, she was southbound again with the steamer *Talatwein* and 20 desperately needed Redcoats and 200 native soldiers when the vessel hit a rock at the Sixth Cataract of the Nile about 55 miles north of Khartoum. *Bordein* remained fast for 24 hours and finally reached the vicinity of Khartoum on January 28, two days after the sack of Khartoum by the forces of the Mahdi. She was scuttled by the British, but repaired for service under the Mahdi, until recaptured by the Anglo-Egyptian Army after the Battle of Omdurman in 1898. The steamer continued in service for several years in the Sudan and her hull and paddleboxes were eventually preserved ashore at Khartoum, under the auspices of the River Transport Corporation.

Brouwer, *International Register of Historic Ships*. James et al., *Juan Maria Schuver's Travels*. Nutting, *Gordon of Khartoum*.

USS BORIE (DD-215)

Clemson-class destroyer (4f/2m). *L/B/D:* 314.3′ × 31.8′ × 9.9′ (95.8m × 9.7m × 3m). *Tons:* 1,215 disp. *Hull:* steel. *Comp.:* 154. *Arm.:* 4 × 4″ (2 × 2), 1 × 3″; 12 × 21″TT. *Mach.:* geared turbines, 27,700 shp, 2 screws; 35 kts. *Built:* William Cramp & Sons Ship and Engine Building Co., Philadelphia; 1920.

Named for Adolph Edward Borie, President Ulysses S. Grant's secretary of the navy in 1869, USS *Borie*'s first assignment was to the U.S. Naval Detachment in Turkish waters in the Black Sea. In 1921, she transferred to the Asiatic Fleet where she remained, except for two years with the Atlantic Fleet, until 1939. After work with the Neutrality Patrol, designed to keep European combatants out of American waters, when the United States entered World War II, *Borie* moved to convoy duty in the Caribbean.

On July 30, 1943, she joined the escort carrier USS *Card*, flagship of one of the newly formed hunter-killer antisubmarine groups in the Atlantic. Between August and October, the *Card* group — including also the destroyers *Barry* and *Goff* — sank eight submarines. On November 1, *Borie* was searching for one of a pair of submarines that had escaped the group the night before. At about 0145 that morning she forced a different submarine, *U-405*, to the surface in 49°N, 31°14′W. Lieutenant Commander Charles H. Hutchins rammed the U-boat and *Borie* remained lodged on her foredeck for 10 minutes, the gun crews of the two vessels firing at each other with everything available. Commander Hopman finally freed his submarine, but before she could escape, *Borie* straddled her with three depth charges and the *U-405* sank with the loss of all 49 crew. With 27 of her own men killed, and too badly damaged to be taken in tow in the heavy seas, *Borie* had to be sunk at 0945, on November 2, by USS *Barry*.

Morison, *Two-Ocean War*. U.S. Navy, *DANFS*.

LA BOUDEUSE

Frigate (3m). *L/B/D:* 134.5′ × 35.1′ × 17.7′ (41m × 10.7m × 5.4m). *Tons:* 550. *Hull:* wood. *Comp.:* 214. *Arm.:* 26 × 8pdr. *Des.:* Raffeau. *Built:* Nantes; 1766.

The French were relative latecomers to global circumnavigation and Pacific exploration, but their first major expedition, led by Louis Antoine de Bougainville with the ships *Boudeuse* and *Etoile,* set a new standard. The purpose of the voyage was not only the increase of geographical knowledge, but the study of astronomy, botany, and zoology. The ship's company included the naturalist Philibert de Commerson and astronomer C. F. P. Véron. There were diplomatic and commercial aspects to the voyage as well. *Boudeuse* sailed from Brest on December 5, 1766, arriving at Montevideo on January 31, 1767. From there she sailed with the Spanish frigates *Liebre* and *Esmeralda* to the Falkland Islands where the French colony was formally transferred to Spanish rule. Bougainville had founded the colony in 1764, with a view to establishing a French presence on the Cape Horn route, and the islands were called Les Malouines — corrupted by the Spanish to Malvinas — after the St. Malo merchants who underwrote the enterprise. After rendezvousing with the storeship *Etoile*, which had sailed two months after *Boudeuse*, the ships sailed from Montevideo on November 14. Their passage through the Strait of Magellan took fifty-two days during which the French charted the waters and studied the inhabitants of lower Patagonia and Tierra del Fuego.

Entering the Pacific on January 26, 1768, the ships headed northwest to 20°S before turning west. The ships' first landfall was in the Tuamotus. Unable to anchor, Bougainville called them collectively the Dangerous Archipelago. Continuing west, on April 6, 1768, they arrived at Tahiti, the second Europeans to do so, only ten months after HMS DOLPHIN. Enchanted with the island and its people — especially the women — Bougainville gave it the name New Cythera, for the birthplace of Aphrodite of Greek myth, and claimed it for France. After only nine days, the ships sailed on, the company now including Ahutoru, the brother of the local chieftain, who volunteered to join the expedition and later lived in Paris. Bougainville neglected to discuss the bleaker aspects of Tahitian life, and his reports of the French experience had a profound influence on Enlightenment thinkers such as Rousseau and his concept of the noble savage.

At this point, as Helen Wallis has written, Bougainville became the first explorer "to resist the lure of the safer routes and bear steadily westward from Tahiti, the first, as he claimed, to maintain a westerly course in 15°S into the little-known seas of the south-western Pacific." This course took the French through the Samoan Islands (which they called the Navigators) and on May 22, to the New Hebrides (Vanuatu). These were last seen by Europeans in 1606, when SAN PEDRO Y SAN PABLO and *San Pedrico* had landed there during Pedro Fernández de Quirós's search for the Solomon Islands. As the islanders were not eager for their trade and there were few places to anchor safely, Bougainville claimed the land for France before turning again to the west. Again, unlike any of his known predecessors, Bougainville was intent on determining whether there was a passage between New Guinea and Australia. Although *San Pedrico* had sailed through the Torres Strait in 1605, a description of that voyage remained buried in Spanish archives, and eighteenth-century geographers were ignorant of the fact.

June 4 brought the two ships to the Great Barrier Reef, which in 15°S is about 30 miles from the coast of Australia. Though Bougainville was sure that they were in "the vicinity of a great land . . . nothing less than the eastern coast of New Holland," the danger to his ships was too great to justify the risk of further exploration here: "The sea broke with great violence upon these shoals, and some summits of rocks appeared above water from place to place. This last discovery was the voice of God, and we were obedient to it." They worked to the north and June 10 found them in New Guinea's Gulf of the Louisiade, in which they were embayed for ten days before rounding Cape Deliverance to the east. Another ten days brought them to Choiseul Island, where their reception was far from friendly. Though this was the western Solomons, the elusive islands of Alvaro Mendaña's 1568 voyage in LOS REYES, Bougainville did not realize it, just as Carteret had failed to when he passed the same way in HMS SWALLOW only four months earlier.

Sorely in need of fresh food, the French pressed on to New Britain where they happened to anchor within a few miles of Carteret's camp. Sailing around New Ireland, they shaped a course for the Moluccas and arrived at the Dutch settlement at Boeroe on September 1. By the end of the month they were at Batavia, where Bougainville learned the name of his English predecessor — Carteret — who had departed just twelve days before. Although a secret aim of the expedition had been to obtain spices for transplantation on Ile de France (Mauritius), Batavia was so disease-ridden that Bougainville sailed on October 18 after only a hasty refit. The slower *Etoile* was left to proceed at her own pace. After a more extensive refit at Ile de France, they sailed for the Cape of Good Hope in January. On February 26, *Boudeuse* caught up with *Swallow* and Bougainville inquired discreetly into the particulars of *Swallow*'s voyage while dissembling about his own. In exchange for his offer of help, Carteret "presented me with an arrow which he had got in one of the isles he had found on his voyage round the world, a voyage that he was far from suspecting we had likewise made." Leaving *Swallow* in their wake, the French pressed on to St. Malo where *Boudeuse* arrived on March 16, 1769, having lost only seven men in more than two years at sea. In addition to correcting or adding to charts of the Pacific, the expedition returned with specimens of more than 3,000 species of plants and animals.

Bougainville, *Voyage Round the World*. Brosse, *Great Voyages of Discovery*.

HMS BOUNTY

(ex-*Bethia*) Ship (3m). *L/B/D:* 91′ × 24.3′ × 11.3′ dph (27.7m × 7.5m × 3.5m). *Tons:* 220 burthen. *Hull:* wood. *Comp.:* 46. *Arm.:* 4 × 4pdr, 10 swivels. *Built:* Hull, Eng.; 1784.

In 1775, the Society for West India Merchants proposed that breadfruit trees, native to the South Pacific, be transplanted to the West Indies to be grown as a food staple for slaves. Twelve years later the Royal Navy purchased the merchant ship *Bethia* especially for the purpose of sailing to the Society Islands "where, according to the accounts which are given by the late Captain Cook, and Persons who accompanied him during his Voyages, the Bread Fruit Tree is to be found in the most luxuriant state." After the vessel was approved for the purpose by the botanist Joseph Banks, a veteran of Captain James Cook's first voyage, *Bethia* was purchased from Messrs. Wellbank, Sharp, and Brown in May 1787. At Deptford Dockyard the ship was refitted to carry 300 breadfruit trees, its upper deck being rebuilt "to have as many Gratings . . . as conveniently can be to give air; likewise to have Scuttles through the side for the same reason." Half the trees were destined for Jamaica, and half for the Royal Botanical Garden at St. Vincent; at his discretion Lieutenant William Bligh could take some trees for Kew Gardens on his return to Britain. The Admiralty also ordered the ship sheathed in copper. Three boats were also ordered from naval contractor John Burr, a 16-foot jolly boat, a 20-foot cutter, and the 23-foot BOUNTY LAUNCH.

On August 17, Bligh was appointed to command HM Armed Vessel *Bounty,* as the ship was officially designated. A veteran of Cook's third voyage to the Pacific, during which he served as master of HMS RESOLUTION, Bligh was an accomplished hydrographer. Sailing from Portsmouth on December 23, 1787, *Bounty* went to Tahiti, arriving there on October 26, 1788. After five months in the island paradise, which the crew seem thoroughly to have enjoyed except for Bligh's increasingly harsh discipline, *Bounty* weighed anchor on April 6, 1789, with more than a thousand breadfruit trees. Twenty-two days later, 5 members of the 43-man crew seized the ship in a bloodless mutiny. The ringleader was Fletcher Christian, whom Bligh had appointed the ship's second in command and who now put Bligh and 19 of his supporters into the ship's launch, which Bligh sailed to the Dutch entrepôt at Timor.

Christian attempted a landing on Tubuai, about 400 miles south of Tahiti, where they arrived on May 28. The crew met with a poor reception and soon returned to Tahiti, where they stayed 10 days while they loaded 460 hogs, 50 goats, and embarked 28 Tahitians — 9 men, 8 boys, 10 women, and 1 girl. A second visit to Tubuai was no better, and after a pitched battle with about 700 Tubuaians, 66 of whom were killed, the mutineers and their Tahitian shipmates departed on September 17. Accompanied by the Tubuaian chief Taroa, 3 men, and 12 women, who had befriended them, they arrived back at Tahiti on September 20. Sixteen of the mutineers (some of whom seem to have been unwilling accessories from the start) remained on the island, and the next day Christian sailed with the Tubuaians, a few Tahitians, and 8 of the crew. Navigating with a defective chronometer and in search of an uninhabited island whose published position was 200 miles east of its actual position, the mutineers reached Pitcairn Island in January or February of 1790. The next day, they burned their ship and attempted to settle the island. As the English promptly divided the island among themselves and relegated the Tahitians to second-class status, relations between the men turned violent and several were killed. The survivors gradually acclimated themselves to their new situation. Eighteen years later, on February 6, 1808, Pitcairn was visited by the Nantucket sealer *Topaz* under Captain Matthew Folger. The sole male survivor of the original band of settlers was Alexander Smith, whom Folger gave the new name John Adams, to lessen his chance of arrest should the island be visited by a British warship. Following the publication of Captain Frederick William Beechey's report of his visit aboard HMS BLOSSOM thirteen years after that, Pitcairn came under the protection of the British crown in 1825.

Fourteen mutineers were eventually arrested in Tahiti by the men of HMS PANDORA, which had been dispatched for the purpose. On August 28, 1791, *Pandora* struck the Great Barrier Reef and sank; four of the mutineers were drowned. *Pandora*'s survivors sailed to Timor and the ten surviving mutineers were ultimately brought to trial in England. Thomas Ellison, John Milward, and Thomas Burkitt were hanged. Bligh was also given a second chance to complete his mission, which he did in HMS *Providence* in 1792. (*Providence* was later wrecked, on May 17, 1797, when, under command of Commander William Broughton, she ran aground in the Sakashima Islands east of Taiwan during a surveying voyage of the North Pacific.)

The story of the mutiny on the *Bounty* has inspired countless retellings and fictional accounts. The first of several movies of the mutiny, *The Mutiny on the Bounty,* appeared in 1935, starring Charles Laughton and Clark Gable, and featured the *Lilly* as the *Bounty.* Replicas of *Bounty* were built for the 1962 remake starring Marlon Brando and Trevor Howard and for *Bounty* (1985) with Mel Gibson and Anthony Hopkins.

Barrow, *Mutiny and Piractical Seizure of HMS "Bounty."* Bligh, *Narrative of the Mutiny on the "Bounty."* Knight, "H.M. Armed Vessel *Bounty.*" Smith, "Some Remarks about the Mutiny of the *Bounty.*"

BOUNTY LAUNCH

Launch (1m). *L/B/D:* 23′ × 6.8′ × 2.8′ dph (7m × 2.1m × 0.8m). *Hull:* wood. *Comp.:* 20. *Built:* John Samuel White, Cowes, Isle of Wight, Eng.; 1787.

When Fletcher Christian rallied his supporters to mutiny aboard HMS BOUNTY on April 28, 1789, there was no thought of killing Lieutenant William Bligh. Instead, they put him and 19 supporters into the ship's launch together with 28 gallons of water, 5 bottles of wine, 4 quarts of rum, 150 pounds of biscuit, and 20 pounds of pork. Bligh was also given a sextant and 4 cutlasses. Fully loaded, the 23-foot-long launch had a freeboard of only 7 inches. The day after the mutiny, the launch landed at the nearby island of Tofoa, in the Fiji Islands, but one of the crew was killed by the inhabitants as they prepared to leave the next day. With rations limited to one ounce of bread and four ounces of water daily (later reduced to half an ounce of bread and one ounce of water), Bligh decided to sail direct for the Dutch settlement at Timor, 3,600 miles to the west. The launch passed through the New Hebrides (May 14–15), along the Great Barrier Reef (May 16–June 4), through the Torres Strait between Australia and New Guinea, and on to Timor, arriving on June 12. Miraculously, in sailing 43 days through uncharted waters in an open boat overcrowded with desperately ill-provisioned men, Bligh had not lost a single one of his crew. Recognized then and now as an outstanding feat of navigation, the voyage of the *Bounty* launch remains almost without peer in the history of navigation.

Bligh, *Narrative of the Mutiny on the "Bounty."* Fryer, *Voyage of the "Bounty" Launch.*

LA BOURGOGNE

Liner (2f/4m). *L/B/D:* 494.3' × 52.2' (150.7m × 15.9m). *Tons:* 7,395 grt. *Hull:* steel. *Comp.:* 1st 390, 2nd 65, 3rd 600; crew 220. *Mach.:* compound engine, 1 screw; 17 kts. *Built:* Forges & Chantiers de la Méditerranée, La Seyne, France; 1886.

The fastest of four sister ships built in 1885–86 for Compagnie Générale Transatlantique (French Line) service between France and New York, *La Bourgogne* made her maiden voyage from Le Havre to New York on June 19, 1886. Her service was uneventful until 10 years later when she rammed and sank the Atlas Line steamship *Ailsa* off the U.S. coast. The following year she and her sisters (*La Champagne, La Bretagne,* and *La Gascogne*) were given quadruple-expansion engines and her rig was reduced to two masts. On July 4, 1898, *La Bourgogne* was rammed and sunk by the British square-rigged ship CROMARTYSHIRE off Cape Sable in 43°N, 61°W with the loss of 549 passengers and crew from a total complement of 726 people.

Bonsor, *North Atlantic Seaway.* Gibbs, *Passenger Liners of the Western Ocean.*

LA BOUSSOLE

(ex-*Le Portefaix*) Ship (3m). *Tons:* 450 tons. *Hull:* wood. *Comp.:* 113. *Built:* France; 1781.

Built as the fishery supply ship *Portefaix,* the refitted *La Boussole* ("Compass") was the flagship of Jean-François de Galaup, Comte de la Pérouse, on one of France's most famous eighteenth-century expeditions to the Pacific.

The expedition had its origins in the Anglo-French rivalry for dominance in the Pacific following the American Revolution. The French had already sent out several expeditions to the Pacific, including those of Louis-Antoine de Bougainville's LA BOUDEUSE and *L'Etoile* in 1766–69 and Jean-François de Surville's ST. JEAN-BAPTISTE in 1769–77. By the 1780s, the French had a twofold interest in such a voyage: to investigate commercial possibilities, especially in the Pacific Northwest fur trade; and to expand on Captain James Cook's geographic, scientific, and ethnographic discoveries. Planning for the expedition involved both the French Navy and scientists, including naturalist Leclerc de Buffon, chemist Antoine-Laurent Lavoisier, and mathematician the Marquis de Condorcet. The expedition also had the personal endorsement of Louis XVI.

La Boussole and L'ASTROLABE sailed from Brest on August 1, 1785, calling at Madeira, Tenerife, and Santa Catarina Island near Rio de Janeiro before a calm rounding of Cape Horn. In February at Concepción and Talcahuano, Chile, La Pérouse took careful note of the Spanish administration whose policies he credited with stifling the growth of a country "whose products, if they reached their maximum, could supply half Europe." The ships sailed for Easter Island, where they spent a day, and then sailed on to the island of Maui. Although frequently critical of the habits and traditions of native people, and dismissive of the fashionable idea of the noble savage, La Pérouse was clear in the purpose of his voyage and observed that "modern navigators have no other purpose when they describe the customs of newly discovered people than to complete the story of mankind." Reflecting on his stay in the Hawaiian Islands, he wrote:

> Although the French are the first to have stepped onto the island of *Mowee* in recent times, I did not take possession of it in the King's name. This European practice is too utterly ridiculous, and philosophers must reflect with some sadness that, because one has muskets and canons, one looks upon 60,000 inhabitants as worth nothing, ignoring their rights over a land where for centuries their ancestors have been buried.

After less than two days at Maui, the two ships took their departure from the islands on June 1. Three weeks later they made a landfall off Mount St. Elias, Alaska (first named by Vitus Bering in 1741), and followed the coast east and south about 200 miles to Port des Français (Lituya Bay), where they established a camp on an island purchased from the Tlingit. On July 13, twenty-one sailors and officers were drowned when their boats overturned at the mouth of the bay.

The expedition sailed south on July 30 and arrived at

the Spanish settlement at Monterey on September 14, hugging the coast for much of the way. Ten days later the ships sailed west, naming French Frigate Shoals and Necker Island and stopping at uninhabited Asuncion Island in the Marianas chain before arriving at Macao on January 2, 1787. They remained there for two months, during which the French sold the furs they had collected in the Pacific Northwest and recruited twelve Chinese seamen. After sailing to the Philippines for a brief stay, in April *La Boussole* and *L'Astrolabe* turned north, passing into the Sea of Japan, previously unexplored by Europeans. Sailing up the Strait of Tartary between the mainland and Sakhalin Island, they landed at Ternei, Suffren Bay, and Castries Bay on the Asian coast, and De Langle Bay (named for *L'Astrolabe*'s captain) on Sakhalin. The ships then transited the Strait of La Pérouse between that island and Hokkaido, and sailed up the Kurile Islands to Petropavlovsk on the Kamchatka Peninsula, where they were feted by Russian officials for twenty-four days.

At the end of October, the two ships headed for the South Pacific, though it was not until December 6 that they encountered land again, anchoring off the island of Tutuila, one of a group that Bougainville had named the Navigator Islands and which now forms part of American Samoa. Despite reservations about the islanders' intentions, La Pérouse allowed de Langle to get fresh water from an island creek, a decision that cost the lives of de Langle and 11 others in a seemingly unprovoked attack by more than 1,000 islanders on December 11. There were no reprisals, and having confirmed the position of the remaining islands of the group, the expedition sailed for the English settlement at Botany Bay, New Holland, arriving there on January 26, 1788, just as the British were shifting the outpost to nearby Port Jackson (Sydney).

La Boussole and *L'Astrolabe* stayed on the Australian coast for six weeks. As at Macao and Petropavlovsk, copies of the ships' logs and charts of the voyage were sent home, this time via a British ship. On March 10, 1788, the two ships weighed anchor. The plan was for the ships to sail east as far as Tonga, then west past New Caledonia, the Solomon Islands, then along the northern coast of Australia from Cape York counterclockwise as far as Tasmania, and then west again to Réunion at the end of the year before returning to France in 1789. When they failed to return, a succession of search expeditions were sent out, starting with d'Entrecasteaux in *La Recherche* and L'ESPERANCE in 1791–94. In 1826 Captain Peter Dillon happened on artifacts from the ships on the island of Vanikoro north of New Caledonia. His finds were confirmed by Dumont d'Urville in 1828, and in 1959, a New Zealand diver named Reece Discomb located the remains of the ships in False (Wreck) Passage near Ambi. The

ships apparently had grounded on a submerged coral formation. Local tradition suggests that there were survivors, though their fate is unknown.

[La Pérouse], *Journal of Jean-François de la Galaup de la Pérouse.* Shelton, *From Hudson's Bay to Botany Bay.*

BOWDOIN

Gaff schooner (2m). *L/B/D:* 88′ × 21′ × 10′ (26.9m × 6.4m × 3m). *Tons:* 66 grt. *Hull:* wood. *Comp.:* 7–16. *Mach.:* diesel, 190 hp, 1 screw. *Des.:* William Hand. *Built:* Hodgdon Bros. Shipyard, Boothbay Harbor, Me.; 1921.

Bowdoin was built to designs worked out by Donald B. MacMillan, a veteran of several voyages to the Arctic, including Robert Peary's successful effort to reach the North Pole in 1906 and a four-year stay in Greenland in 1913–17. Named for MacMillan's alma mater, *Bowdoin* was stoutly built, with a steel-sheathed bow, simple pole masts, and no bowsprit. On July 16, 1921, she departed Wiscasset on the first of her twenty-six voyages north. Sponsored by the Carnegie Foundation and planned for a study of terrestrial magnetism and atmospheric electricity, the voyage took *Bowdoin* north along Labrador and west through Hudson Strait and into Foxe Basin. There, on September 21, she entered Schooner Harbor on Foxe Peninsula and quickly became the focal point for a small village of nomadic Inuits who joined her over the winter.

Returning to Maine the following summer, she had a seventeen-month layover before embarking on her first expedition to northern Greenland, under the auspices of the Carnegie Foundation and National Geographic Society. Crossing the Arctic Circle along the coast of Greenland on August 2, 1923, *Bowdoin* and her crew wintered in Refuge Harbor north of Etah, 685 miles from the North Pole. Frozen in for 320 days, they made short trips away from the ship, again in the company of local Inuits, and in April erected a plaque commemorating the men who had died in the Greeley Expedition of 1881–84.

On her next expedition, sponsored by the U.S. Navy and National Geographic Society, *Bowdoin* sailed in company with USS *Peary*. Members of the crew performed experiments with radio communications from the far north, tried to confirm or disprove the existence of lands reported by earlier expeditions, studied barometric pressure, and made the first color photographic record of Arctic flora and fauna. Using three amphibious planes carried aboard *Peary*, Lieutenant Commander Richard Byrd also made the first aerial surveys of western Greenland. In 1929, MacMillan and *Bowdoin* carried supplies to the Moravian mission at Nain, in northern Labrador, beginning a relationship that would last another fifteen years. The next year, on what proved to be her only trip to Iceland, *Bowdoin* carried students for the first time, and from 1934 on she always sailed with students who paid for the privilege of sailing with "Mac" to the high north.

A few years later, MacMillan married, and despite his previous insistence that no woman — even his wife — would (or could) sail to the Arctic, in 1938 Miriam accompanied him as far as Nain and then, at the insistence of the rest of the crew, on to Greenland. (In all, "Lady Mac" would make nine voyages with her husband aboard *Bowdoin*. Her glowing accounts of the voyages tended to gloss over the hardships, and veterans of the northern voyages referred to her book as "Green Seas, White Lies.") The following year, MacMillan sold *Bowdoin* to the Navy. In 1941, he commanded her on a voyage to Greenland where the Navy was building air bases at Sondrestrom on the Arctic Circle and Narsarssuak. MacMillan joined the Hydrographic Service in 1942, but *Bowdoin* returned to Greenland for survey work through most of 1943, after which she was laid up.

In 1946, MacMillan rejoined his old ship, and they resumed their annual trips to Labrador and Greenland. MacMillan made his last voyage in *Bowdoin* in 1954, at the age of eighty, and *Bowdoin* was sold to Mystic Seaport Museum for use as a museum ship. Nine years later, in sad need of repair, she was sold to the Schooner Bowdoin Association and used for chartering in Maine waters. After a lengthy rebuild from 1980 to 1989, she joined the Maine Maritime Academy at Castine and resumed her original educational mission in the Arctic, visiting Labrador for the first time in a quarter century in 1990.

MacMillan, *Etah and Beyond*. MacMillan, *Green Seas, White Ice*. Thorndike, *Arctic Schooner "Bowdoin."*

HMS Breadalbane

Bark (3m). *L/B/D:* 125′ × 24′ × 18′ dph (38.1m × 7.3m × 5.5m). *Tons:* 428 bm. *Hull:* wood. *Comp.:* 21. *Built:* Hedderwich & Rowan, Glasgow; 1843.

Originally built for a consortium of Scottish merchants, *Breadalbane* spent ten years trading between England and Calcutta. In 1853, she was hired by the British Admiralty to carry coal and other supplies to the *North Star,* a depot ship for the ships searching the Arctic for Sir John Franklin's HMS Erebus and Terror. On May 19, 1853, *Breadalbane* sailed with Captain Inglefield's HMS *Phoenix* (the first propeller ship in the Arctic) and arrived at Beechey Island on August 8. The two ships were anchored to an ice floe when, at about 0330 on August 21, "The ice

from the offing closed, and so effectually crushed the transport as to complete her destruction in the short space of fifteen minutes." She sank in thirty fathoms of water about half a mile south of Beechey Island.

While diving beneath the ice in 1975, Joe MacInnis found a fragment of a ship that research subsequently revealed to be from *Breadalbane*. In 1978 he began searching, though it was not until August 11, 1980, that divers working from the Canadian Coast Guard Cutter *John A. Macdonald* found the ship largely intact, two masts still standing and the hull in good condition except where she had been hulled by the ice. Because of the depth and icy conditions on the surface, prolonged work on the site was impossible, although the ship's wheel was recovered and given to Parks Canada for conservation.

MacInnis, *The Land that Devours Ships*.

Brederode

Ship (3m). *L/B/D:* 132′ × 32′ × 13.5′ (40.2m × 9.8m × 4.1m). *Tons:* 800 tons. *Hull:* wood. *Arm.:* 56 guns. *Built:* Rotterdam; 1644.

Named for Johan Wolfert van Brederode, brother-in-law of stadtholder Frederick Hendrick and president of the Admiralty of Rotterdam, *Brederode* sailed as flagship for a succession of admirals in the first Anglo-Dutch War of the mid-seventeenth century. After three years under the flag of Vice Admiral Witte de With, in 1647 she was put under command of Admiral Maarten Harpertszoon Tromp. Four years later, as antagonism between British and Dutch merchants grew, the British instituted the Navigation Acts on October 9, 1651. Among other things, these restricted British goods for British ships and called for foreign ships in the English Channel to dip their flags to British warships as a mark of respect. A few minor incidents occurred over the winter, but on May 18, 1652, Tromp's fleet was in the Channel protecting convoys of Dutch traders when it was forced to seek shelter in the Downs. Ordered to leave, Tromp sailed for France, but the next day saw the English fleet under Admiral Robert Blake bearing down on him. Tromp, his fleet in some disarray, turned to meet the English. He almost had the better of the English until Admiral Bourne arrived with nine ships from the Downs. The Battle of Dover cost the Dutch two ships, but Tromp had carried out his orders, namely, to protect Dutch trade and to do nothing to discredit his own flag.

Shortly before the official declaration of war on July 8, Tromp was relieved of his command for his failure against an English fleet under Admiral Sir George Ayscue. His successor was Michiel Adrienszoon de Ruyter, whom the English naval historian William Laird Clowes described as "the greatest naval leader of his century." Political considerations led to de Ruyter's serving under Witte de With in September, but this move was so unpopular that when the Dutch fleet attacked the British in the Thames estuary on October 8, *Brederode*'s crew refused to allow Witte de With to shift his flag to the ship. The Dutch fought listlessly at the Battle of the Kentish Knock — twenty ships refused to fight altogether — and Blake's fleet sank three Dutch ships and damaged many others. On December 10, with Tromp again at the head of the fleet in *Brederode,* the Dutch attacked a much smaller force under Blake in the Battle of Dungeness. Although his flagship was nearly captured, Tromp took five English ships (out of forty-two) and then shepherded one outbound and one inbound convoy through the English Channel. According to legend, he returned to port with a broom lashed to the mast to signify that he had swept the Channel clean.

Such confidence was short-lived, and on February 18, 1653, the English attacked Tromp as he escorted an outbound convoy past Portland. The so-called Three Days' Fight cost the Dutch four warships captured, five sunk, and three burned, and thirty to fifty merchantmen captured, although Blake was severely wounded in the action. The next and most decisive engagement of the war came at the Battle of the North Foreland on June 2. The Dutch had been off the English coast with about ninety-eight ships and six fireships, and the English off the Dutch coast with more than 100 ships. (The English advantage was greater than the numbers imply, because many of the Dutch ships were converted or hired merchantmen, and Dutch warships tended to be smaller owing to the shallow draft necessitated by the shallow Dutch waters.) The fleets met off North Foreland, England, the English under Admiral Sir William Penn (in the *James*). The battle seems to have taken place between two more or less parallel battle lines, and Tromp is often credited with having developed this tactic, which the English adopted and refined over the next 250 years. The flagships closed with one another, but neither Tromp nor Penn could gain the upper hand. At the end of the day, the Dutch retired to the south, their ammunition almost exhausted, but the next day the English bore down on them in light airs, and by the end of June 3 they had sunk six Dutch ships, burned two, and captured eleven together with 1,350 prisoners. De Ruyter was so disgusted with the outcome that he left the navy until improvements were made.

Tromp refit his fleet in the Maas and on July 24 sailed out to lift the blockade. Two days later, Witte de With left the Texel, whereupon the English moved to prevent a junction of the fleets. Although they failed in this and were outnumbered by about seventeen ships, the English fought well and Tromp was killed. Although both fleets suffered heavily, the Dutch could ill afford their losses, and the Battle of Scheveningen proved the last major fight of the war. The English losses forced them to lift their blockade, although many Dutch merchant ships subsequently fell prey to English privateers, and there were a number of single ship actions before peace was finally concluded in April 1654.

The Dutch had been supported by Denmark, and three years later they sent ships to support Denmark in its war against Sweden's Karl X Gustaf. In the fall of 1658, the Swedes besieged Copenhagen, and the Dutch dispatched thirty-five ships under Jacob Wassenaer van Obdam in *Eendracht*. On November 8, the Dutch and Swedish fleets met in the Battle of the Sound off Helsingør. Although the Dutch lost five ships — *Brederode* among them — to the Swedes' three, Copenhagen was relieved, and the Dutch maintained control of the Sound until peace was negotiated in 1660.

Clowes, *Royal Navy.*

BREMEN

Liner (2f/2m) *L/B/D:* 939.1' × 101.9' (286.3m × 31.1m). *Tons:* 51,656 grt. *Hull:* steel. *Comp.:* 1st 600, 2nd 500, tourist 300, 3rd 600; crew 990. *Mach.:* steam turbines, 4 screws; 27 kts. *Built:* AG Weser, Bremen, Ger.; 1929.

One of two express steamers laid down for Norddeutscher Lloyd's transatlantic passenger service, the sleek-hulled, squat-funneled *Bremen* was launched on August 16, 1928, one day after her sister ship EUROPA. Initially conceived as 35,000-ton ships to sail in consort with NDL's *Columbus,* while still on the ways it was decided to enlarge the ships to 50,000 tons in a direct bid to rival Cunard Line's MAURETANIA, queen of the Atlantic since 1909. *Bremen*'s maiden voyage from Bremen to Southampton, Cherbourg, and New York began on July 17, 1929, and ended five days later, after a crossing from Cherbourg to Ambrose Light at a speed of 27.83 knots (4 days, 17 hours, and 42 minutes) — more than one knot faster than *Mauretania*'s record of twenty years before. She surrendered the westbound honor to *Europa* the following year, but on the return leg of her maiden voyage, she set an eastbound record of 27.91 knots between Ambrose and Eddystone Light, a passage next bettered by herself in 1933, at 28.5 knots. In an effort to further capitalize on their ships' considerable speed, Norddeutscher Lloyd fitted *Bremen* and *Europa* with seaplanes that enabled the two ships to deliver mail as much as forty hours prior to their arrival in port. This extravagant innovation was dropped in 1935.

Bremen's last westbound passage ended at New York on August 28, 1938. Two days later she sailed for Europe without passengers and when war was declared she was diverted to Murmansk; she finally returned to Bremen in December. Although the intent was to use her as a troopship for Operation Sealion, when the German invasion of England was aborted in September 1940, she became an accommodation ship. On March 16, 1941, a disgruntled seaman set a fire that destroyed the ship. *Bremen* was not broken up until after the war, between 1952 and 1956.

Bonsor, *North Atlantic Seaway.* Braynard & Miller, *Fifty Famous Liners.*

BREMEN COG

Cog (1m). *L/B/D:* 77' × 25' × 7.4' (23.3m × 7.6m × 2.25m). *Tons:* 50–56 ton burden. *Hull:* wood. *Built:* Bremen, Ger.; 1379/80.

The most complete extant representative of a ship type once ubiquitous in northern Europe, the fourteenth-century Cog of Bremen was discovered two kilometers below the medieval city of Bremen during dredging operations on the Weser River in 1962. The unballasted vessel appears to have been swept away in a spring flood and come to rest on a sandbar about four kilometers from the shipyard where she was built. Although the hull was essentially complete, work on the sterncastle was not finished. Among the artifacts found in or near the ship were a barrel of tar and a number of shipbuilding tools.

The Bremen Cog is especially important because prior to its discovery, the only available evidence of what cogs looked like came from the official seals of Hanseatic towns and their coinage. The hull form had been evolving for 1,500 years (the earliest evidence is a 200 BCE clay model found at the town of Leese on the Weser), and from the thirteenth to fifteenth centuries the cog dominated trade between the Baltic and North Sea ports of the Hanseatic League. The type was found mostly between England and Bruges in the west and along the southern shore of the Baltic Sea as far as Elbing (now Elblag, Poland) in the east, but cogs also traded to the Mediterranean, and by the early 1300s the type was being copied by shipwrights from Spain to Venice. Like Viking ships, cogs were built hull first, with reinforcing frames added later. In northern Europe, the practice of skeleton-first, carvel-built ships became more common after about 1470. By about 1400, the cog's chief rival was the more full-bodied,

one-masted hulk. The cog seems to have disappeared by about 1450, followed within a half century by the hulk, which was in turn superseded by the three-masted carrack.

Easily distinguished from its better-known Viking contemporaries, the Bremen Cog is a relatively squat, box-like vessel of heavier and more rigid construction. The keel is 15.6 meters long, and there are overhangs of 4.8 meters forward and 2.4 meters aft. The height from keelson to deck is 3.14 meters. With a carrying capacity of little more than 50 tons, the Bremen Cog was not small for her day, although the largest cogs could carry three times as much. Her construction includes a combination of styles of wood joinery. There are twelve strakes on either side of the keel, each made up of three or four planks. Interestingly, Werner Lahn describes that

in the first four strakes we find a unique feature — the cog-builders deemed it necessary to change from the carvel to the clinkered planking method within these strakes. In most cases the change took place not only within one strake, but on a single plank. The foreship is strictly clinker planked, amidships the planking is strictly carvel. Thus on each side of the ship, the first four strakes consist of one clinkered, eight mixed and five carvel planks.

The sides of the hull are continued with four clinker laid strakes on either side. The Bremen Cog's hull is also strengthened by five transverse crossbeams that protrude from either side of the hull. The inner planking is incomplete, but what there is attached to the futtocks and then fastened with treenails that went through to the outer planking. Little of the deck planking — laid crosswise rather than fore-and-aft — is complete. Some of the deck planks would have been nailed down and others kept loose, with finger holes for easy removal to expedite the stowage and offloading of cargo. The cog's propulsion was a single square sail on a single mast stepped amidships. The sails of the Hanseatic League vessels were traditionally patterned with bold, vertical red-and-white stripes. The helmsman manipulated the tiller for the centerline rudder from the main deck just below the sterncastle.

Only the starboard side of the Bremen Cog's sterncastle survived, but it is possible to reconstruct the whole. The deck was trapezoidal, with the narrower part (6.4 meters wide) overhanging the stern and the wider part (6.8m) forward; the length was 4.6 meters. To port and starboard there were extensions measuring about 3.5 meters long and 1.8 meters wide. The area beneath the main castle deck was open and housed the 3.5-meter-long windlass, while the area beneath the starboard deck was enclosed. The castle deck was the only caulked deck on the vessel. Other features of the sterncastle were a small toilet to starboard and a capstan. The capstan and the windlass would have been used for weighing anchor, stepping the mast, loading heavy cargo, and trimming the sail. The workmanship on the capstan and the windlass suggest that these were made by specialist "sub-contractor" suppliers and not the shipwrights.

Excavation of the Bremen Cog under Siegfried Fliedner took from 1962 to 1965, and the preservation and assembly of the more than 2,000 pieces took Werner Lahn's team seven years. In 1982, the remains were soaked in a preservative solution of polyethylene glycol at the Deutsches Schiffahrtsmuseum, Bremerhaven, which was founded in 1971 as a direct result of the Bremen Cog project. Two full-scale replicas of the Bremen Cog have been built. The one in Kiel was constructed employing fourteenth-century techniques to the degree possible. That at Bremerhaven was constructed with a view to contemporary safety standards and has a motor so that it can retrace the old Hanse routes without the assistance of tugs. Both replicas have performed well in a variety of conditions and contributed significantly to our understanding of how these ships were handled.

Gardiner, *Cogs, Caravels, and Galleons*. Lahn, *Die Kogge von Bremen — The Hanse Cog of Bremen*.

BRENDAN

Sailing curragh (2m). *L/B/D:* 36′ × 0.8′ (11m × 2.4m). *Tons:* 2,400 lbs. *Hull:* cowhide on wood frame. *Comp.:* 5. *Des.:* Colin Mudie, based on written evidence. *Built:* Crosshaven Boatyard, Cork, Ireland; 1976.

Brendan was a re-creation of a medieval Irish curragh built by Tim Severin to demonstrate that the Navigatio Sancti Brendan Abbatis — the Voyage of St. Brendan the Abbot — could be a fact-based account of a transatlantic voyage from Ireland to North America made some time between 500 and 1000 CE. On May 17, 1976, with a crew of five, *Brendan* sailed from Brandon Creek, Ireland. Following the Stepping Stone route, the curragh stopped in the Aran Islands, Tory Island, and Ballyhoorisky before crossing to Iona, Tiree, and Stornoway. From the Isle of Lewis, *Brendan* sailed across 200 miles of open ocean to the Faeroe Islands. They sailed from Thorshavn on July 4 and made the 500-mile passage to Reykjavik in 13 days. *Brendan* was hauled and stored for the winter in an airplane hangar. On May 17, 1977, four of the original crew — George Molony, Arthur Magan, Trondur Patursson

(who had joined at Thorshavn), and Severin — sailed from Reykjavik for North America. Crossing the Denmark Strait, they rounded the southern tip of Greenland and sailed into the Davis Strait where they experienced about 10 days of gales. Nearly crushed by ice off the easternmost tip of Labrador, they were able to patch the leather skin and stop the leaking. On June 26, *Brendan* landed on Peckford Island in the Outer Wadham Group, about 150 miles northwest of St. Johns after a 50-day, 1,300-mile journey across the North Atlantic.

Severin, *"Brendan" Voyage*.

SMS BRESLAU

(later *Midilli*) *Magdeburg*-class light cruiser (4f/2m). *L/B/D:* 450.8′ × 43.9′ × 16.9′ (138.7m × 13.5m × 5.2m). *Tons:* 5,281 disp. *Hull:* steel. *Comp.:* 354. *Arm.:* 12 × 10.5cm; 2 × 20″TT. *Armor:* 2.4″ belt, 2.4″ deck. *Mach.:* steam turbines, 33,482 shp, 4 screws; 27.5 kts. *Built:* AG Vulcan, Stettin, Ger.; 1912.

Named for the German city, SMS *Breslau* was a consort for the battlecruiser GOEBEN in Germany's Mediterranean Squadron. *Breslau*'s career paralleled that of her more famous running mate. While making their way eastward towards Constantinople, *Breslau* briefly engaged the British cruiser HMS *Gloucester* on August 7, 1914, but she reached the Ottoman capital unscathed. Renamed *Midilli* (the Turkish for Mitylene, on the island of Lesbos), she first saw action under the Turkish flag on October 29 when she bombarded the Russian port of Novorossisk. She took part in several engagements against the Russian fleet. In April 1916, she was straddled by 12-inch shells from the Russian dreadnought *Ekaterina II* after signals officer Karl Dönitz flashed a message in German, when the distance between the two ships was believed to be safe for such impertinence. In 1916 and 1917 she was rearmed, and in her final configuration her 10.5-centimeter guns were replaced by eight 6-inch guns. At dawn on January 20, 1918, *Goeben, Breslau,* and four Turkish destroyers steamed out of the Dardanelles to harass the Anglo-French blockading fleet. *Breslau* scored several hits on the 14-inch-gun monitor HMS *Raglan* before she was finished off by *Goeben*. *Breslau* then sank the monitor *M28* with a direct hit. About an hour later, *Breslau* struck a succession of mines off Lemnos and was abandoned at 0810 in 40°05′N, 26°02′E with the loss of about 330 men; about 150 of the crew were saved.

Halpern, *Naval History of World War I*. Van der Vat, *The Ship that Changed the World*.

BRETAGNE

Provence-class battleship (2f/2m). *L/B/D:* 551′ × 91.5′ × 29.5′ (168m × 27.9m × 9m). *Tons:* 28,500 disp. *Hull:* steel. *Comp.:* 1,190. *Arm.:* 10 × 13″ (5 × 2), 14 × 5″, 4 × 75mm. *Armor:* 10.8″ belt, 1.6″ deck. *Mach.:* steam turbines, 28,000 shp, 4 screws; 20 kts. *Built:* Forges & Chantiers de la Méditerranée, La Seyne, France; 1916.

Named for the French province of Brittany, *Bretagne* was one of three PROVENCE-class battleships laid down in 1912; the third was *Lorraine.* Completed in 1916, she spent World War I operating against the Austro-Hungarian fleet in the Adriatic. All three ships underwent major conversions during the interwar years, in 1921, 1925, and 1932–34. *Bretagne* emerged from the last conversion with new oil-burning engines that generated 43,000 shp. The start of World War II found *Bretagne* in the Mediterranean, and after the establishment of the Vichy French government, she was sent to Mers el-Kébir, near Oran, Algeria. Fearing a German takeover of the French Navy, the British launched Operation Catapult, designed to give the French commanders at Mers el-Kébir the opportunity either to demilitarize their ships, disperse them to overseas ports, or surrender them outright. Admiral Marcel Gensoul refused to comply with the British ultimatum and began preparing to take his ships to sea, and on July 3, 1940, Vice Admiral Sir James Somerville ordered his ships to engage. Within minutes, *Bretagne* was sunk with the loss of 1,012 lives by fire from the British battleships HOOD, BARHAM, and *Resolution. Provence* and *Dunkerque* were damaged but later returned to Toulon, where they were scuttled in November 1942. STRASBOURG escaped unscathed.

Breyer, *Battleships and Battlecruisers.*

BRIGG BOAT

L/B: 40′ × 7.5′ (12.2m × 2.3m). *Tons:* 7 disp. *Hull:* oak. *Built:* England; 800–650 BCE.

The Bronze Age Brigg boat was discovered by workmen on the bank of the Ancholme River one mile northwest of Brigg, Humberside, in April 1888. After investigation by the county surveyor, a small portion of the hull went to the Lincoln Museum and the remainder was reburied. In 1974, the site was reexamined by Sean McGrail and the remains of the hull were removed to the National Maritime Museum for conservation. Further study of the "raft" revealed that it was constructed of oak planks sewn together with stitches made of willow. The seams were caulked with moss and covered with laths made of hazel. Each plank also has a set of integral cleats (six on each plank survive) through which holes were bored and oak battens inserted to keep the five planks somewhat rigid and flat. Although only one side strake has survived, the finished boat seems to have had the shape of a long, thin topless box, with a depth of 0.34 meters to 0.55 meters. The surviving side strake also has holes on both sides, which suggests that it was attached both to the bottom of the hull and to a second side plank. Various estimates as to the depth of the finished craft are put at between 0.34 meters (for one side plank) and 0.55 meters (for two). The vessel was probably poled as a river ferry, and various calculations suggest that it could carry as many as ten men and forty sheep, or twenty men and thirty cattle, depending on the height of the square sides.

McGrail, "The Brigg Raft." McGrail & Kentley, *Sewn Plank Boats.*

BRILLIANT

Gaff schooner (2m). *L/B/D:* 61.5′ × 14.7′ × 8.8′ (18.7m × 4.5m × 2.7m). *Tons:* 38 disp. *Hull:* wood. *Comp.:* 12. *Mach.:* diesel, 97 hp, 1 screw. *Des.:* Olin Stephens. *Built:* Henry B. Nevins, City Island, N.Y.; 1932.

One of only a few yachts constructed to Lloyd's A-1 specifications, *Brilliant* was built as a gift by Mrs. Walter Barnum for her husband. Barnum's requirements for a cruising boat were exacting, and he wrote to Olin Stephens that "I feel we should always keep before us a mental picture of her hove to in the middle of the North Atlantic, with the wind at 80 miles an hour and seas in proportion." At the same time, he asked that the "hull and rig design be in no way adversely affected by any accommodation requirement." Despite Barnum's avowed intention to use her for cruising, she proved a remarkably competitive boat. In her first season, she placed second behind *Highland Light* in the Bermuda Race, and the following year she sailed to England. En route, she made the transatlantic crossing from Nantucket Lightship to Bishop Rock in 15 days 1 hour 23 minutes, a record for a vessel of her size. She went on to win a number of races in England and elicited the highest praise from *Yachting World*'s Weston Martyr: "I never saw a finer and more honest piece of boatbuilding and rigging in my life."

Barnum sold *Brilliant* in 1939, and she changed hands several times before and during World War II, when she sailed as a Coast Guard picket boat on antisubmarine patrol. Following the war, *Brilliant* was bought by Briggs Cunningham who tried to rerig her for racing, but owing to changes in racing rules *Brilliant* could not stand up to the new breed of racers and measurement rules. In 1952 he donated the schooner to Connecticut's Mystic Maritime Museum for use in the museum's sail-training program, work to which she is admirably suited and which she has advanced for more than half a century.

Gerard, *Brilliant Passage*. Wilson, "Sailing the Schooner *Brilliant*."

BRITANNIA

Liner (1f/3m). *L/B/D:* 212.2′ bp × 30.5′ (17.1′ew) x 16.6′ (64.7m × 9.3m (16.5m) × 5.2m). *Hull:* wood. *Tons:* 1,156 grt. *Comp.:* 115 pass; 89 crew. *Mach.:* side-lever engine (Robert Napier), 440 nhp, sidewheels; 8.5 kts. *Built:* Messrs. Robert Duncan & Co., Glasgow; 1840.

The oldest passenger-ship line in existence today, Cunard Line was among the first to enter the North Atlantic passenger trade, and the first to do so with a view to maintaining regular service provided by a fleet of ships. The man behind this venture was Haligonian entrepreneur John Cunard, who won the British Admiralty's first contract for a mail subsidy tendered in 1838, shortly after the voyages of SIRIUS and GREAT WESTERN had established conclusively the feasibility of transatlantic steam navigation. Although Cunard's line was often known by his name, from 1840 to 1878 it was officially the British and North American Royal Mail Steam Packet Company.

Cunard's first four vessels were *Britannia, Acadia, Caledonia,* and *Columbia,* and the last entered service in January 1841. *Britannia*'s maiden voyage, from Liverpool to Halifax, was made in 12 days, 10 hours, or an average speed of about 8.5 knots; after an 8-hour layover, the ship proceeded to Boston where she arrived after 34 hours. She continued in this trade for 9 years (frequently calling at New York) and performed with remarkable regularity for the line. Such was the imperative of her schedule that when in February 1844 the port of Boston was frozen over, citizens of the town pitched in to help cut a channel through the ice to the sea. Three years later, on September 14, 1847, she stranded at Cape Race, but she was able to continue to New York and reentered service after repairs there. All told, Cunard had an exemplary safety record. Although *Columbia* wrecked near Cape Sable in 1843 (without loss of life), it was not until 1872 that a second Cunard ship was lost — again, without fatalities.

From the outset, Cunard's steamers attracted the dignitaries and celebrities of the day, though not all were favorably disposed to the comparatively meager comforts the ships afforded to even their most celebrated guests. In January 1842, Charles Dickens and his wife took *Britannia* to America for the author's first tour of the United States. Singularly unimpressed with his accommodations, he complained, "Anything so utterly and monstrously

absurd as the size of our cabin 'No gentleman of England who lives at home at ease,' can for a moment imagine. Neither of the portmanteaus would go into it."

By 1849, Cunard's fleet had grown to 16 ships and *Britannia* and *Acadia* were sold to the German Federal fleet and renamed *Barbarossa* and *Erzherzog Johann,* respectively. Transferred to Bremerhaven, *Barbarossa*'s armament consisted of nine 68-pdr. guns. In 1851 her mainmast was removed, in 1873 her remaining two masts were removed, and in the following year she was transferred to the Prussian Navy for use as a barracks ship and guard ship. Thirteen years later, her engines were removed and she remained at Kiel for a further 15 years, during which time her remaining masts were removed. In 1880, she was finally stricken from the lists and used as a target ship. On July 28, she was sunk by the torpedo boat SMS *Zieten.* Her hull was salvaged and broken up at the Imperial Dockyard at Kiel.

Bonsor, *North Atlantic Seaway*. Gröner, *German Warships*.

BRITANNIA

Gaff cutter. *L/B/D:* 100′ × 23.3′ × 12.6′ (30.5m x 7.1m × 3.8m). *Tons:* 221 TM. *Hull:* composite. *Des.:* G. L. Watson. *Built:* D. & W. Henderson Co., Glasgow; 1893.

Built for the Prince of Wales (later King Edward VII) in 1893, *Britannia* was one of the most successful and famous yachts of her day. During her first season, she placed first in twenty races — nine more than her nearest challenger — and over her entire racing career, which lasted off and on until 1935, she won 231 first prizes in 635 starts. Changes in the racing rules made *Britannia* less competitive and in 1897 the Prince of Wales sold her. She passed through several owners until 1902, when, after his ascension to the throne, Edward VII bought her back for cruising. *Britannia* remained in the royal family, passing to George V upon the death of his father. In 1921, she was rerigged for racing, and there followed several modifications until her gaff rig was replaced by a more streamlined marconi (or Bermuda) rig in 1931. Following the death of George V four years later, *Britannia* was towed into deep water off the Isle of Wight and sunk. In her long career she had amassed a racing record of 231 victories and 129 second- or third-place showings in 635 starts.

Kemp, ed., *Oxford Companion to Ships and the Sea*. Underhill, *Sailing Ship Rigs and Rigging*.

One of the great racers of her day, BRITANNIA *was owned by the Prince of Wales, later Edward VII. This photo shows her towards the end of her career in the 1930s. Although her gaff rig was replaced with a Bermuda rig, she still presented a formidable sight. Courtesy New York Yacht Club.*

BRITANNIA

Yacht (3f/1m). *L/B/D:* 412.3′ × 55′ × 15.6′ (125.8m × 16.8m × 4.8m). *Tons:* 5,796 grt. *Hull:* steel. *Mach.:* geared turbines, 12,000 bhp, 2 screws; 22.75 kts. *Built:* John Brown & Co., Ltd., Clydebank, Scotland; 1954.

Conceived of as a replacement for the third *Victoria and Albert* (1899) in the late 1930s, construction of the Royal Yacht *Britannia* was postponed until after World War II. In an effort to counter public opposition to the expense involved in her construction, the ship was designed for easy conversion to a hospital ship in an emergency. (Critics have observed that she was never so employed.) As the personal yacht of first George VI and later Elizabeth II, *Britannia* has been used to show the flag in many remote and not so remote parts of the world, from Australia to Africa, Canada and the United States. The significance

of flags is inherent in her three otherwise anachronistic masts. When the monarch is aboard, *Britannia* flies the flag of the Lord High Admiral (fore), the Royal Standard (main), and Union Jack (mizzen). On one of her last official duties before her retirement in 1997, *Britannia* embarked the outgoing governor of Hong Kong, Chris Patten, following the return of the British colony to Chinese rule.

Morton, *Royal Yacht "Britannia."*

BRITANNIA II

L: 37′ (11.3m). *Hull:* fiberglass. *Comp.:* 2. *Des.:* Uffa Fox. *Built:* England; 1971.

Britannia II was a sophisticated rowing boat designed for John Fairfax who, with Sylvia Cook, sought to make the first crossing of the Pacific Ocean under oars alone. The boat was named for another Fox-designed boat that Fairfax rowed single-handed across the Atlantic. After completion in England, *Britannia II* was shipped to San Francisco, where Fairfax and Cook embarked on April 26, 1971. Stopping at Ensañada, Mexico, in June they then headed west, arriving on October 6 at the all but inaccessible Washington Island. On November 12, they resumed their journey, which was nearly cut short when *Britannia II* wrecked on Onotoa in the Gilbert Islands on January 9, 1972. The boat was towed to Tarawa for repairs and the duo departed on February 7, 1972. Reprovisioned from a ship east of the Santa Cruz Islands, they were nearing Australia a month later when John was bitten on the arm by a shark. A week later they were caught in Cyclone Emily for four days. Having survived that, they crossed the Great Barrier Reef — on which they lost their anchor — and arrived finally at Hayman Island on April 22, 1972.

Even as *Britannia II* was completing this epic passage, Derek King was envisioning a round-the-world voyage. Fairfax and Cook offered him the use of *Britannia II* as soon as she returned from a tour of Australia, and she was refit to accommodate three rowers — the others were Peter Bird and Carol Maystone. *Britannia II* cleared Gibraltar on March 24, 1974, but there was dissension among the three from the start. During a layover at Casablanca, Maystone left the expedition, and King and Bird continued on the 3,545-mile crossing to the Caribbean. Halfway over, the two decided to abandon the project — which they estimated would take three years — once they had crossed the Atlantic. On August 10, after 93 days at sea, they made landfall at St. Lucia.

Fairfax & Cook, *Oars across the Pacific*. King & Bird, *Small Boat against the Sea*.

BRITANNIC

Liner (4f/2m). *L/B:* 852′ bp × 94′ (259.7m × 28.7m). *Tons:* 48,158 grt. *Hull:* steel. *Comp.:* 3,109 patients; 489 medics; 675 crew. *Mach.:* triple expansion & steam turbines, 3 screws; 21 kts. *Built:* Harland & Wolff, Belfast, Ireland; 1915.

The last of the fifteen four-funnel ships laid down for transatlantic passenger service, *Britannic* was a slightly enlarged version of White Star Line's OLYMPIC and TITANIC. Unfinished by the outbreak of World War I, she was requisitioned in November 1915 and commissioned as the hospital ship HMHS *Britannic*. In the next year she made a total of six voyages to the Mediterranean under Captain Charles A. Bartlett, and brought home more than 15,000 soldiers wounded in the Gallipoli, Salonika, and Egyptian campaigns. While outward bound from Naples to Lemnos on her sixth voyage, she struck a mine — probably laid by the German submarine *U-73* — at 0812 on November 21, about four miles west of Kea Island (37°38′N, 24°30′E). She sank in less than an hour with the loss of twenty-one of her crew.

Bonsor, *North Atlantic Seaway*. Mills, "*Britannic.*"

BRITISH ISLES

Ship (3m). *L/B/D:* 308.9′ × 43.9′ × 24.8′ dph. *Tons:* 2,394 grt. *Hull:* steel. *Comp.:* 31. *Built:* John Reid, Port Glasgow, Scotland; 1884.

One of the largest square-rigged ships to come from the Clyde, *British Isles* was the last sailing ship built for the British Shipowners Company, Ltd., of Liverpool. Her builder, John Reid, was given carte blanche to build the best full-rigged ship he could, and no expense was spared in her construction or fittings. Built entirely of steel, including her masts and yards, her hull was divided into three separate compartments as a safety measure when carrying combustible cargoes such as coal. *British Isles* was also capable of a good turn of speed, and in 1898 she sailed from London to Sydney in a record eighty days under Captain J. M. Stott. In 1903, while outward bound in the Bay of Biscay on her first voyage under Captain James P. Barker, she overhauled the five-masted bark PREUSSEN, and on the same voyage she posted her best day's run ever of 383 miles in twenty-four hours.

After fifteen years in general trade for British Shipowners, she was sold to Thomas Shute and Company, of Liverpool, for whom she sailed until 1914. In that year she was sold to Navigazione Generale Italiana for use as a hulk at Genoa. Ten years later she was sold to Argentine interests, and renamed first *Tigre* and then *Olivos*. She ended her days in the River Plate in 1934.

Barker, *Log of a Limejuicer*. Jones, *Cape Horn Breed*. Lubbock, *Last of the Windjammers*.

BRITISH STEEL

(later *British Soldier*) Ketch. *L/B:* 59′ × 12.8′ (18m × 13.9m). *Tons:* 17. *Hull:* steel. *Comp.:* 1–10. *Des.:* Robert Clark. *Built:* Dartmouth, Eng.; 1970.

In 1968, Chay Blyth was one of five sailors who sailed to win the Golden Globe, put up by the London *Sunday Times* for the first person to sail alone around the world without stopping. Although Blyth was certainly up for the voyage — in 1966 he and John Ridgway had rowed from Cape Cod to Ireland in ENGLISH ROSE III — his thirty-foot *Dytiscus* was not, and he pulled out of the race off South Africa. (The sole finisher was Robin Knox-Johnston's SUHAILI.) Nothing daunted, Blyth decided to sail around the world alone, nonstop, from east to west, against the prevailing westerly winds. For this voyage, he built the steel-hulled yacht *British Steel*, named for his primary corporate sponsor.

British Steel left the Hamble on October 18, 1970, bound for Cape Horn on the first leg of his 30,000-mile voyage. Rounding the Horn in a full gale on December 24, he lost his self-steering gear. "Wrong Way" Chay, as the press dubbed him, described *British Steel* as "fantastic at going to windward," and after tacking back and forth against the Roaring Forties, by the beginning of March he was off New Zealand. Two weeks later he had passed Tasmania, and another ten weeks brought him across the Indian Ocean and into the South Atlantic, where he crossed his outward track on June 29. *British Steel* returned to England on August 6, 1971, after 292 days at sea — 21 days faster than Knox-Johnston.

The next year, *British Steel* placed fourth in the Observer Single-handed Transatlantic Race (OSTAR). Blyth later loaned his boat to the British Army for the Whitbread Round the World Race. Renamed *British Soldier*, she was sailed by four interservice crews of ten men, one crew for each leg of the race.

Blyth, *Impossible Dream*.

USS BROOKLYN (AC-3)

Brooklyn-class armored cruiser (3f/2m). *L/B/D:* 400.5′ × 64.7′ × 26.2′ (122.1m × 19.7m × 8m). *Tons:* 9,215 disp. *Hull:* steel. *Comp.:* 516. *Arm.:* 8 × 6″, 12 × 5″, 12 × 6pdr, 4 × 1pdr, 4 × mg, 2 × 3″; 4

× 18″TT. *Armor:* 3″ belt, 6″ deck. *Mach.:* 4 VTE, 18,770 ihp, 2 screws; 22 kts. *Built:* William Cramp & Sons, Philadelphia; 1896.

An improved version of the *New York*–class armored cruiser, USS *Brooklyn* was the first American ship whose contract specified that all major components be made in the United States rather than being imported from abroad — the rule before the country's industrial maturity. Though her hull was distinguished by a pronounced tumblehome and ram bow, *Brooklyn*'s design was innovative in several respects. More heavily armed than other cruisers, she carried eight rather than four 6-inch guns, mounted in turrets forward, aft, and two wing turrets amidships. This configuration enabled her to train six guns forward, aft, or on either broadside. In addition, *Brooklyn* was the first ship to employ electricity to turn the turrets, which were previously trained by either hydraulic or steam power. The experiment was a great success and electric-powered turrets were adopted for subsequent warships.

Commissioned in 1896, *Brooklyn* represented the U.S. Navy at ceremonies marking Queen Victoria's Diamond Jubilee. Returning to the United States, she patrolled on the Atlantic coast and West Indies until 1898, when she became flagship to Commodore W. S. Schley's Flying Squadron during the Spanish-American War. At the end of May, Schley instituted blockades first of Cienfuegos and then of Santiago, where the bulk of Admiral Pascual Cervera's fleet of antiquated cruisers lay. On July 3, Cervera attempted a breakout from the port and, after nearly ramming USS TEXAS, *Brooklyn* led the chase that resulted in the destruction of four armored cruisers and 350 Spanish dead on the Cuban coast. The *Brooklyn* suffered one fatality — the only U.S. crewman killed in the battle.

From 1899 to 1902 she was flagship of the Asiatic Squadron based at Manila, from where she visited China, the Dutch East Indies, and Australia. In 1902, she returned to Havana for ceremonies marking the transfer of government from the United States to a native Cuban government, and thereafter divided her time between the North Atlantic Fleet and the European Squadron. In 1905, she was dispatched to France to receive the remains of Revolutionary War Captain John Paul Jones for entombment at the U.S. Naval Academy in Annapolis. *Brooklyn* was in and out of commission from 1906 to 1914, when she joined the Neutrality Patrol off Boston before a second assignment as flagship of the Asiatic Fleet. She remained in the Pacific until 1921, when she was sold out of the navy.

Emerson, "Armoured Cruiser USS *Brooklyn*." U.S. Navy, *DANFS*.

BROWN'S FERRY VESSEL

L/B/D: 50.4′ × 14′ × 3.8′ dph (15.37m × 4.2m × 1.7m). *Tons:* 25 long tons. *Hull:* wood. *Comp.:* 2–3. *Built:* South Carolina; ca. 1740.

The Brown's Ferry vessel is a small cargo boat found by Hampton Shuping while diving in the Black River at Brown's Ferry, South Carolina, in 1976. Alan Albright arranged for the proper excavation of the site and the conservation of the hull at the University of South Carolina's Institute of Archaeology and Anthropology in Columbia. Dating from 1740, the Brown's Ferry vessel is the oldest extant American-built vessel, about fifty years older than the Revolutionary War gundalow PHILADELPHIA. The bottom of the vessel was flat and consisted of three planks, the keelson being made of one piece; there was no keel. Parts of twelve strakes survive, five to port and seven to starboard, and these were fastened with treenails and iron nails to twenty frames. There were two mast steps in the keelson, one forward and one amidships and it has been conjectured that the vessel sported a spritsail rig.

The vessel's cargo consisted of more than 10,000 bricks weighing a total of 25 tons, together with four millstones, two dozen bottles and three iron pots. There were also a number of personal effects including a pipe, a razor, and a quadrant. Damage from teredo worms in the hull suggests that the vessel operated along the coastal route to Charleston as well as on rivers.

Albright & Steffy, "Brown's Ferry Vessel."

BUCINTORO

State barge. *L/B/D:* 143.7′ × 23.9′ × 27.6′ (43.8m × 7.3m × 8.4m). *Hull:* wood. *Comp.:* 168 oarsmen. *Built:* Arsenale, Venice; 1728.

In 1100, the Venetian Doge Pietro Orseolo began the consolidation of Venetian power with the defeat of Dalmatian pirates who had long infested the Adriatic trade routes. As the power of the Most Serene Republic grew, her annual rite of the blessing of the sea evolved into a more complex and elaborate ceremony by which Venice was spiritually wed to the Adriatic. The *sposalizia* — literally, the wedding — annually took place on Ascension Day, the anniversary of the departure of Orseolo's fleet. The Doge, his retainers, members of the clergy, and the various ambassadors to Venice would put out in the *Bucintoro,* rowed by 168 oarsmen pulling on 42 oars. After the blessing of the ring by the Patriarch of San Elena, the *Bucintoro* would continue past the Lido, and the Doge would drop the marriage ring into the Adriatic with the words: "Disponsamus te, Mare, in signum veri perpetuique dominii" (We wed thee, Adriatic, as a sign of our true and perpetual dominion). The presence of ambassadors ensured that this was no idle covenant, and indeed the Holy Roman Emperor Frederick III, among others, sought permission for his ships to pass through the Adriatic.

Just when the *sposalizia* formally began is unknown. There was a ritual blessing of the Adriatic in Orseolo's time, and this would have taken on added importance following his victory over the pirates. Two centuries later, in 1177, the stature of Venice was further enlarged with Pope Alexander III's official recognition of her role in mediating a long-standing dispute between the papacy and the Holy Roman Empire. "Bucintoro" is also of uncertain origin. One theory is that it refers to a figurehead combining elements of a cow and a centaur. It may also be a corruption for either *ducentorum,* meaning a boat carrying 200 men, or *cinto d'oro,* meaning girdled with gold, as the later vessels certainly were. The last of the state barges to bear the name *Bucintoro* was built in 1728. In addition to the *sposalizia,* she was also used for important ceremonies of state. Her end came in 1797 when the French seized the Republic of Venice. In a rite of ritualistic humiliation, General Napoleon Bonaparte ordered his troops to melt down the gold decoration and destroy the barge's adornments. The hull was spared and fitted out as a floating battery in the Austrian Navy. The renamed *Hydra* may have remained in service until 1824.

Senior, "*Bucentaur.*"

BUFFEL

Turret-ram (1f/2m). *L/B/D:* 205.8′ × 40.4′ × 15.9′ (62.7m × 12.3m × 4.8m). *Tons:* 2,198 disp. *Hull:* iron. *Comp.:* 159. *Arm.:* 2 × 9.2″, 4 × 30pdr. *Armor:* 6.1″ belt. *Mach.:* compound engine, 2,000 ihp, 2 screws; 12.4 kts. *Built:* Robert Napier & Sons, Glasgow; 1868.

Designed for coastal defense service in the North Sea, the turret-ram *Buffel* was one of several such ships built for the Royal Netherlands Navy between 1866 and 1890, and the only one to have survived until the end of the twentieth century. As the name implies, the turret-ram carried two distinct weapons. The submerged bow ram was an instrument the origins of which can be traced to antiquity. Its function was to disable an enemy warship either by making holes in it below the waterline, or by sheering off its rudder. The rotating turret-mounted gun was a new development that increased the arc of fire while providing a protective shelter for the gun and gunners. *Buffel* (the name is Dutch for buffalo) carried no sails, but she was intended for work in home waters within easy reach of coal supplies.

After 17 years in active service, *Buffel* became an accommodation ship berthed first at Gellevoetsluis and later at Den Helder. She survived World War II laid up at Amsterdam, and today she is preserved at the Maritiem Museum Prins Hendrick in Rotterdam.

Heine, *Historic Ships of the World.* Silverstone, *Dictionary of the World's Capital Ships.*

The cruiser USS BROOKLYN *seen at the end of the Spanish-American War in 1898. Though thoroughly modern in her own day, she boasted a number of features that would vanish from warship design within a decade, in particular the pronounced tumblehome, "ram" bow, and mixed armament, including guns of six different calibers and torpedoes. Courtesy U.S. Naval Historical Center, Washington, D.C.*

HMS BULWARK

London-class battleship (2f/2m). *L/B/D:* 431.8′ × 75′ × 26.8′ (131.6m × 22.9m × 8.2m). *Tons:* 15,460 disp. *Hull:* steel. *Comp.:* 780. *Arm.:* 4 × 12″ (2 × 2), 12 × 6″, 16 × 12pdr, 6 × 3pdr; 4 × 18″TT. *Armor:* 9″ belt. *Mach.:* triple expansion, 15,000 ihp, 2 screws; 18 kts. *Des.:* Sir William White. *Built:* Devonport Dockyard, Plymouth, Eng.; 1902.

HMS *Bulwark* was one of five pre-Dreadnought battleships laid down in response to France's turn-of-the-century shipbuilding program. One of the first major units fitted with Marconi wireless telegraph, *Bulwark* served as flagship of the Mediterranean fleet, based at Malta, from 1902 to 1907. Detailed to the Home Fleet, formed as a counterbalance to Germany's North Sea fleet, *Bulwark* served as divisional flagship until 1911 when she was transferred to the Fifth Battle Squadron of the reserve fleet. Mobilized and fully manned upon the outbreak of World War I, she was assigned to the Channel Fleet, which comprised nineteen pre-*Dreadnought* battleships. On November 26, 1914, *Bulwark* was anchored off Sheerness when at 0753 the ship was "rent asunder" by a massive internal explosion caused by the poor storage of cordite charges, some of which were twelve years old. The ship sank instantly, taking with her a full complement of 781 ranks and ratings.

Ball, "Life and Death of an Edwardian Flagship." Parkes, *British Battleships.*

C

USS CAIRO

Cairo-class ironclad gunboat. *L/B/D:* 175′ × 51.2′ × 6′ (53.3m × 15.6m × 1.8m). *Tons:* 512 disp. *Hull:* wood. *Comp.:* 251. *Arm.:* 3 × 8″, 6 × 42pdr, 6 × 32pdr, 1 × 12pdr. *Armor:* 2.5″ casemate. *Des.:* John Lenthall, Samuel M. Pook & James B. Eads. *Mach.:* horizontal engines, center wheel; 9 kts. *Built:* James Eads & Co., Mound City, Ill.; 1862.

Cairo was one of seven river gunboats known as "Pook Turtles" after the designer Samuel M. Pook and completed by James B. Eads for service with the U.S. Army's Western Gunboat Flotilla. Named for the Ohio River port in Illinois, *Cairo* was originally commissioned as a U.S. Army ship but was transferred to the U.S. Navy's Mississippi Squadron on October 1, 1862. The ironclad saw extensive action on the Cumberland and Mississippi Rivers from February on, and on June 6, 1862, *Cairo* was one of seven Union gunboats that sank five and severely damaged one of eight Confederate gunboats during the capture of Memphis. In October 1862, she was transferred to

the U.S. Navy's Mississippi Squadron, and her armament was changed so that she mounted three 42-pdr. guns instead of six, and carried an additional 30-pdr. *Cairo* saw little further action until December, when, as part of an expedition on the Yazoo River under Commander Thomas O. Selfridge, she hit two stationary torpedoes and sank below Haines Bluff, Mississippi, on December 12, 1862. In 1956, the remains of the *Cairo* were found and identified by Edwin C. Bearss of the Vicksburg National Military Park, where the vessel is now on public display.

Bearss, *Hardluck Ironclad.*

USRC CALEB CUSHING

Revenue cutter (2m). *L/B/D:* 100.3′ × 23′ x 9.6′ (30.6m × 7m × 2.4m). *Tons:* 153 disp. *Hull:* wood. *Arm.:* 1 × 32pdr, 1 × 12pdr. *Built:* J. M. Hood, Somerset, Mass.; 1853.

The U.S. revenue cutter *Caleb Cushing* was the last in a long line of captured Union ships that began with the Confederate raider CSS FLORIDA's seizure of the Baltimore-bound brig *Clarence* (ex-*Coquette*) on May 6, 1863. Armed as a commerce raider under Lieutenant Charles W. Read, *Clarence* went on to capture six more ships until Read decided to transfer his crew to the bark *Tacony* (known briefly as *Florida 2*) on June 12. Cruising New England waters, *Tacony* captured fifteen vessels, mostly fishing schooners, over the next twelve days. On June 24, Read transferred his crew to the schooner *Archer* and burned *Tacony*. Learning that the revenue cutter *Caleb Cushing* and a passenger steamer were lying off Portland, Maine, in Casco Bay, Read decided to capture the revenue cutter first, and then to seize the passenger boat. He succeeded in the former effort on July 29, but the next day the presence of a superior Union fleet forced him to burn his prize and take to his boats, although he and his crew were quickly captured. In a curious twist, the revenue cutter's namesake, a distinguished congressman and diplomat who negotiated the Treaty of Whangia opening

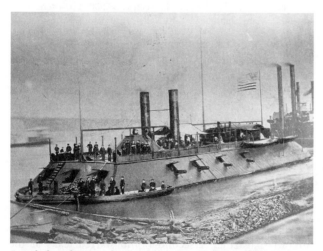

Ironclad gunboats such as CAIRO *were a mainstay of the Union Army's operations on the western rivers during the Civil War.* CAIRO *was lost after less than a year in service, but her remains were discovered in 1956. Courtesy U.S. Naval Historical Center, Washington, D.C.*

Chinese ports to U.S. shipping, later played a leading role in negotiating the settlement of the ALABAMA's claims with Great Britain.

Canney, *U.S. Coast Guard and Revenue Cutters.* Smith, *Confederates Down East.*

CALIFORNIA

Sidewheel steamer (1f/3m). *L/B/D:* 200′ × 33′ × 22′ (61m × 10.1m × 6.7m). *Tons:* 1,057 grt. *Hull:* wood. *Comp.:* 200 pass; 75 crew. *Mach.:* side-lever engine, 250 nhp, 2 paddles. *Built:* William H. Webb, New York; 1848.

In 1847, the Postmaster General of the United States issued the first contracts for mail to be carried by steamship between New York and Chagres, on the Panamanian Isthmus, and in the Pacific, between Panama and Oregon. Early in 1848, the New York shipping company Howland and Aspinwall secured the latter contract, despite the fact that there was then neither coal nor ports to speak of on the West Coast, nor even profits for that matter. The same year, the Pacific Mail Steamship Company was chartered and three sidewheel steamships were ordered, *California* and *Panama* from William H. Webb, and *Oregon* from Smith & Dimon.

Launched on May 19, *California* sailed from New York on October 6 under command of Captain Cleveland Forbes. Although capable of carrying 200, she had only seven passengers, none of whom was going farther than Peru. Once at sea, the engine and piping proved faulty, and the general layout of the ship and machinery did not take into consideration the inconveniences of steam engineering. Nonetheless, progress was steady and twenty-five days out, *California* put into Rio de Janeiro for fuel and provisions. The third steamship to pass through the Strait of Magellan, she arrived at Valparaiso twenty-four days out from Rio. Stopping next at Callao, between 50 and 100 Peruvians embarked in the ship on the strength of rumors that gold had been discovered in California.

When *California* reached Panama on January 17, 1849, she was met by more than 1,500 Americans who formed the first wave of Forty-Niners spurred west by President James K. Polk's official announcement of the California gold strikes earlier that year. Forced to repel some would-be passengers by force, *California* finally sailed with 375 passengers on January 31. The clientele embarked at Panama was a mixed lot, according to Forbes.

[W]e have many on board of very high standing, both in Cabin & Steerage, but we also have many of the scum of creation, Black legs, gamblers, thieves, runners & Drunkards, and if we make the trip without difficulty & great loss to the ship by their acts of pilfering & waste, I will be much surprised . . . all seem to be bound to California with the idea that low conduct & uncouth deportment is necessary to make them appear of importance.

In the event, it was a shortage of coal that contributed most to the superficial destruction of the ship as wood furniture and spare yards were broken up to keep the engines going.

On February 28, 1849, *California* became the first steamship to enter San Francisco Bay, having made the 14,000-mile voyage after 76 days at sea and 144 days overall from New York. The passengers left the ship and to a man the crew deserted for the diggings; Forbes alone remained, but he later resigned for reasons of health and returned East. *California* remained in service on the West Coast for a further forty-six years, sailing under the Pacific Mail flag until 1875, save for eight years with the Mexican Coast Steamship Company (1860–68). She was then bought by Goodall, Nelson & Perkins Steamship Company, who took out her engine and rerigged her as a bark. She sailed with that rig for twenty years until she ran aground at Pacasmayo, Peru, in 1895.

Berthold, *Pioneer Steamer "California."* Somerville, *Aspinwall Empire.*

USS CALIFORNIA (BB-44)

Tennessee-class battleship. *L/B/D:* 624.5′ × 97.3′ × 30.3′ (190.3m × 29.7m × 9.2m). *Tons:* 32,300 disp. *Hull:* steel. *Comp.:* 1,083–2,200. *Arm.:* 12 × 14″ (4 × 3), 14 × 5″, 4 × 3″; 2 × 21″TT. *Armor:* 13.5″ belt, 3.5″ deck. *Mach.:* turboelectric, 28,500 shp, 4 screws; 21 kts. *Built:* Mare Island Navy Yard, Vallejo, Calif.; 1921.

One of four U.S. battleships launched in the months following the end of World War I, USS *California* (the fifth ship to carry that name) served as flagship of the Pacific Fleet and later of the Battle Fleet (Battle Force), U.S. Fleet, for the next 20 years. In 1940, her homeport was moved to Pearl Harbor, and it was there that the planes of Admiral Chuichi Nagumo's Pearl Harbor Striking Force found her on the morning of December 7, 1941. Moored at the southern end of Battleship Row, *California* was preparing for a materiel inspection and her watertight integrity was severely compromised. At 0805, 10 minutes after the first attack began, an armor-piercing bomb exploded below decks setting off an antiaircraft magazine. A second bomb started leaks at the bow, and the ship sank in her berth. When the attack was over, she had lost 98 crew killed, and 61 wounded.

Refloated at the end of March, she sailed for Bremerton for full repairs and improvements in June 1942. Following trials in the spring of 1944, she joined the Pacific Fleet in time for the invasion of the Mariana Islands in June, taking part in the shore bombardment of Saipan, Guam, and Tinian between June and August. That fall, she took part in the Battle of Surigao Strait (October 25) and the invasion of Luzon at Lingayen Gulf (January 9, 1945), where she was hit by a kamikaze that killed 44 crew and wounded 155. After repairs at Bremerton following this action, she returned to duty in time for the bombardment of Okinawa in June and July. Returning to Philadelphia in December, she was placed in reserve the following August and sold for breaking up in 1959.

Morison, *Two-Ocean War*. U.S. Navy, *DANFS*.

CALIFORNIAN

Liner (1f/4m). *L/B/D:* 447.6′ × 54.2′ × 30′ dph (136.4m × 16.5m × 9.1m). *Tons:* 6,223 grt. *Hull:* steel. *Comp.:* 1st 60, 3rd 350; 50 crew. *Mach.:* triple expansion, 1 screw; 13.5 kts. *Built:* Caledon Shipbuilding & Engineering Co., Dundee, Scotland; 1902.

The Leyland Line's freighter *Californian* was built for service between England and Caribbean and Gulf Coast ports, but she sailed occasionally on North Atlantic routes as well. At 2021 on the evening of April 14, 1912, she was en route to Boston when she hove to in a massive ice field in the North Atlantic. About half an hour later, a brilliantly lit vessel appeared on the horizon — the TITANIC, bound for New York on her maiden voyage. *Californian* attempted to contact the unknown ship by radio shortly after 2300 to warn her of ice, but she was brushed off by *Titanic's* harried wireless operator, John Phillips, who was busy transmitting passenger messages to Cape Race, Newfoundland. Half an hour later, at 2340, the precise time that the *Titanic* struck an iceberg, *Californian's* crew noticed that the mystery ship seemed to stop and extinguish some of her lights. At 0015, April 15, just after *Californian* turned off her wireless for the night, Phillips sent the *Titanic's* first distress call.

Californian's Captain Stanley Lord and his crew continued to puzzle over the actions of the steamer on the horizon, particularly when she began to fire rockets — eight in all between 0045 and 0140. Lord and his officers discussed the strange ship, the rockets, her failure to respond to the Morse lamp, and the "queer" way she looked, like she had a "big side out of the water." Yet no one thought to try to raise the mysterious ship by wireless. (After the disaster, all ships were required to man their radios 24 hours a day.) Nor did anyone surmise that the ship was in fact *Titanic*, with which *Californian* experienced such a brusque communication earlier that eve-

ning. At 0240, the crew of *Californian* spotted more rockets (presumably fired from CARPATHIA, which was responding to *Titanic's* distress calls at full speed), but it was not until 0520 that *Californian's* wireless operator was returned to work and learned of the *Titanic's* sinking a scant fifteen miles away.

News of *Californian's* proximity to the disaster created a sensation when the ship docked at Boston on April 19. Lord initially denied that anything unusual occurred on the night in question, but several of his crew testified about seeing the eight rockets. The U.S. Senate Committee investigating the tragedy found that Lord had failed to respond to *Titanic's* rockets "in accordance with the dictates of humanity, international usage, and the requirements of law." The British Board of Trade went further, charging that had Lord responded appropriately, *Californian* "might have saved many if not all the lives that were lost."

Lord claimed in his defense that despite his ship's general proximity to *Titanic*, ice conditions dictated behavior that was unfairly second-guessed. He also said that there was another vessel between his ship and *Titanic*, later identified as the Norwegian sealer *Samson*. (Subsequent research found that *Samson* could not have been in the area at the time.) Despite the censure of the American and British inquiries, Lord had his apologists, led by the Mercantile Marine Service Association and a few well-placed members of the British Parliament and the press. Although he resigned from Leyland Line in August 1912 and spent the rest of his life answering for his conduct during the *Titanic* sinking, he had a long and respected career with the Nitrate Producers Steam Ship Company. *Californian* continued in service as a merchant ship until November 9, 1915, when she was torpedoed in the Mediterranean 61 miles south-southwest of Cape Matapan, Greece.

Reade, *Ship That Stood Still*.

HMS CALLIOPE

Calliope-class corvette (1f/3m). *L/B/D:* 235′ × 44.5′ × 19.1′ (71.6m × 13.6m × 5.8m). *Tons:* 2,770 disp. *Hull:* steel. *Comp.:* 317. *Arm.:* 4 × 6″ (4 × 1), 12 × 5″, 6 mg; 2 × 14″TT. *Mach.:* compound engine, 4,023 ihp, 1 screw; 14.7 kts. *Des.:* Nathaniel Barnaby. *Built:* Portsmouth Dockyard, Eng.; 1884.

One of the last two corvettes powered by steam and sail (she carried a bark rig) in the Royal Navy, HMS *Calliope* was similar to the *Comus*-class corvettes commissioned for long-range commerce protection between 1879 and 1881. Dispatched to the Australian station from 1886 to

1890, she achieved lasting fame in 1889 as the only one of seven warships to escape serious damage when a hurricane hit Apia. *Calliope* had been sent to protect British interests in Samoa in the face of mounting tension between the United States and Germany. On March 14, the weather began to deteriorate, but advised by local pilots that the storm season was over, the fleets prepared to ride out the storm at anchor. The storm continued unabated through the sixteenth, wrecking twelve of the thirteen ships in the harbor, including three German and three American warships. Only *Calliope* was able to get under way and, narrowly missing both the reefs and USS *Trenton,* struggle into open waters. Four days later she returned to a scene of utter devastation; Robert Louis Stevenson described the aftermath: "no sail afloat and the beach piled high with the wrecks of ships and debris of mountain forests."

The "Hurricane Jumper," as she came to be known, returned to Britain in 1890 and was laid up for seven years. After eight years as a tender, she became a reserve training ship in the Tyne in 1906. Renamed *Helicon* from 1915 to 1936, she remained there until broken up in 1951.

Brown, "Seamanship, Steam and Steel." Osbon, "Passing of the Steam and Sail Corvette."

CALYPSO

(ex-*J-826*) Research ship (1f/1m). *L/B/D:* 139′ × 25′ × 10′ (42.4m × 7.6m × 3m). *Tons:* 402 disp. *Hull:* wood. *Comp.:* 27. *Mach.:* diesels, 580 hp, 2 screws; 10 kts. *Built:* Ballard Marine Railway, Seattle; 1942.

Commissioned in 1942, *J-826* was one of 561 yard motor minesweepers (YMS) built during World War II. Turned over to the British, she operated out of Malta, Taranto, and Naples until the end of the war. In 1947 she reverted to U.S. Navy control, but two years later she was sold for use as a ferry operating between Malta and Gozo. Renamed *Calypso,* she had a capacity for 400 people and 11 cars. The next year, she was purchased by Lieutenant Commander Jacques-Yves Cousteau, who had helped found the French Navy's Undersea Research Group in 1945, but who was then on leave to further develop SCUBA (self-contained underwater breathing apparatus) diving and other means of underwater investigation.

Calypso proved an ideal platform for such work. Cousteau and his crews pioneered a wide variety of techniques with which they explored the "silent kingdom" of the world's oceans, coastal waters, and rivers. Their innumerable discoveries focused world attention on the vari-

ety and fragility of the world's ocean environment and that of the surrounding shores. Over the next forty-six years, the ship logged more than one million miles, chiefly in the Mediterranean, the coast of Africa, North and South America, Oceania, the East Indies, and Antarctica. The primary vehicle of France's oceanographic effort until 1966, *Calypso* carried state-of-the-art equipment, including one- and two-person minisubs, diving saucers, and underwater scooters. In addition, the ship was fitted with a "false nose" — an observation chamber ten feet below the waterline — and she carried helicopters and equipment for monitoring meteorological conditions. Perhaps most significant was the Cousteau Society's dissemination of the results of its research through periodicals, books, and documentaries. The first of these, *The Silent World,* took four years to film, and in 1957 Cousteau and his young codirector, Louis Malle, won the Cannes Film Festival's Golden Palm. This was followed by *Beneath the Frozen World* (about Antarctica), *Rediscovery of the World* (about the islands of the western Pacific), and more than sixty others, including the 1960s television series, *The Undersea World of Jacques Cousteau.*

On January 8, 1996, a barge to which *Calypso* was moored broke loose and drove the vessel onto a piling in Singapore Harbor. She was raised, but the near loss of the fifty-six-year-old ship led the Society to proceed with plans to commission *Calypso II,* specially designed as a platform for oceanographic research and powered by diesel engines and a twenty-six-meter-high Turbovoile® — a type of rotor cylinder similar to that designed by Anton Flettner for his BADEN-BADEN in 1920.

Richards, "Sis and *J-826*." Traonouïl et al., "Reviving a Legend."

HMS CAMPBELTOWN

(ex-USS *Buchanan*) *Wickes*-class destroyer (2f/2m). *L/B/D:* 314.4′ × 31.8′ × 9′ (95.8m × 9.7m × 2.7m). *Tons:* 1,090 disp. *Hull:* steel. *Comp.:* 113. *Arm.:* 4 x 4″ (2x2), 1 × 1pdr, 2 × 3pdr, 2 × .30 cal; 12 × 21″TT. *Mach.:* geared turbines, 26,000 shp, 2 screws; 35 kts. *Built:* Bath Iron Works, Bath, Me.; 1919.

Named for Admiral Franklin Buchanan, who served in the U.S. Navy from 1815 until joining the Confederate States Navy in 1861, USS *Buchanan* (DD-131) served with the Pacific Fleet out of San Diego for two decades. At the start of World War II, she was put on the Atlantic Neutrality Patrol designed to keep European combatants out of American waters. Turned over to the British as part of the lend-lease program in September 1940 and renamed HMS *Campbeltown,* she worked as a convoy escort on the Atlantic.

Concerned about the potential threat posed by TIR-PITZ should she break out into the Atlantic, the British launched Operation Chariot, to destroy the Normandie dock (named for the French ocean liner) at St. Nazaire, the only dock large enough to hold the German battleship. Packed with explosives and escorted by commandos in gunboats, motor torpedo boats, and motor launches, on the night of March 28, 1942, *Campbeltown* was driven into the dock caisson. Eleven hours later, the time-delayed explosives destroyed the dock and other port facilities. Only four of the motor launches returned from the chaotic operation, for which five Victoria Crosses were awarded, including one to *Campbeltown*'s Lieutenant Commander S. H. Beattie.

Wingate, *HMS "Campbeltown."*

HMS CAMPERDOWN

Admiral-class battleship. (2f/1m). *L/B/D:* 330′ bp × 68.5′ × 28.4′ (100.6m × 20.9m × 8.7m). *Tons:* 10,600 disp. *Hull:* steel. *Comp.:* 525–536. *Arm.:* 4 × 13.5″ (2 × 2), 6 × 6″, 12 × 6pdr, 10 × 3pdr; 5 × 14″TT. *Armor:* 18″ belt, 3″ deck. *Mach.:* compound engine, 7,500 ihp, 2 screws; 15.7 kts. *Built:* Portsmouth Dockyard, Eng.; 1889.

HMS *Camperdown* — the name celebrates a British victory over a Dutch fleet on October 11, 1797 — was one of four *Admiral*-class barbette ships (later classified as battleships) laid down in 1882–83. *Camperdown* spent six months as flagship of the Mediterranean Fleet and was next flagship of the Channel Fleet until 1892, when she returned to the Mediterranean. On June 22, 1893, *Camperdown* was flying the flag of Rear Admiral A. H. Markham during maneuvers off Tripoli, Lebanon. The ships were steaming in two columns about six cables apart when Vice Admiral Sir George Tryon, Commander in Chief, Mediterranean, ordered the two divisions to turn inwards, a maneuver that most officers on the bridge could see would result in a collision. *Camperdown* rammed VICTORIA, which sank with the loss of 358 of her officers and crew, Tryon among them. *Camperdown* nearly sank, too, but staggered into port. Following repairs she was put into reserve. After a turn as a Coast Guard ship and submarine berthing ship at Harwich, she was broken up in 1911.

Parkes, *British Battleships.*

HMS CANOPUS

Canopus-class battleship (2f/2m). *L/B/D:* 418′ × 74′ × 26.5′ (127.4m × 22.6m × 8.1m). *Tons:* 14,320 disp. *Hull:* steel. *Comp.:* 750. *Arm.:* 4 × 12″, 12 × 6″, 12 × 12pdr, 6 × 3pdr; 4 × 18″TT. *Armor:* 6″ belt; 2.5″ deck. *Mach.:* triple expansion, 13,500 ihp, 2 screws; 18.3 kts. *Built:* Portsmouth Dockyard, Eng.; 1899.

Named for the ancient Egyptian city near Alexandria where Nelson defeated the French at the Battle of the Nile, the *Canopus* was the first of six lightly built pre-Dreadnought battleships ordered in 1896. *Canopus* spent two tours in the Mediterranean (1903 and 1908), and the outbreak of World War I found her laid up and scheduled for scrapping in 1915. The British Admiralty sent *Canopus,* Captain Heathcote Grant commanding, to reinforce Rear Admiral Christopher Cradock's South American squadron against Vice Admiral Graf von Spee's East Asia Cruiser Squadron. But Cradock detached her to escort colliers and she missed the disastrous Battle of Coronel. First Sea Lord Fisher then ordered the ship beached at Stanley as a defense for the Falkland Islands port and on December 8, *Canopus* fired the opening shots of the battle of the Falklands against the scouting GNEISENAU and *Nurnberg.* After service in the Dardanelles in 1915, she was taken out of active service and broken up in February 1920.

Marder, *From the Dreadnought to Scapa Flow.*

CAP ARCONA

Liner (3f/2m). *L/B:* 643.6′ bp × 84.6′ (196.2m × 25.8m). *Tons:* 27,561 grt. *Hull:* steel. *Comp.:* 1st 575, 2nd 275, 3rd 465. *Mach.:* steam turbines, 2 screws; 20 kts. *Built:* Blohm & Voss, Hamburg; 1927.

Built for Hamburg–South American Line's passenger trade between Hamburg, Rio de Janeiro, and Buenos Aires, *Cap Arcona* remained in that trade for her whole civilian career. She generally made the passage between Hamburg and Brazil in 12 days, and in 15 to Argentina. Following the outbreak of World War II in September 1939, *Cap Arcona* was kept at Hamburg until the following year when she moved to Gotenhafen (Gdynia) for use as an accommodation ship. In 1945, she was pressed into active service and was used to repatriate refugees from the collapsing Eastern Front to western Germany. She carried an estimated 25,000 evacuees in her first three voyages. She was sunk in a British bombing raid on Lübeck harbor on May 3, one day after the fall of Berlin and five days before the end of the war in Europe. From among the estimated 6,000 passengers aboard the ship, there were only about 350 survivors.

Bonsor, *South Atlantic Seaway.* Braynard & Miller, *Fifty Famous Liners.*

CAPE GELIDONYA WRECK

L: 26–32′ (8–10m). *Hull:* wood. *Built:* Phoenician; ca. 1200 BCE.

The first Bronze Age shipwreck ever excavated lies off Cape Gelidonya (Gelidonou Burnu, or "Cape of Swallows") on the southwest coast of Turkey, in 36°11′N, 30°25′E. With its strong, unpredictable current and jagged, half-submerged rocks, the area is "extremely hazardous to mariners," as the Roman encyclopedist Pliny noted in the first century CE. A row of five rocky, uninhabited islands extends south from the cape and the remains of the ship lie between the two islands closest to the mainland. She probably wrecked on the north side of the more southerly of these and sank in about 90 feet of water.

The wreck was discovered in 1954 by Kemal Aras, the captain of a sponge boat from Bodrum. In 1959, following directions provided by Aras, Peter Throckmorton located and photographed the site. In the summer of 1960, archaeologist George F. Bass directed an expedition from the University Museum of the University of Pennsylvania to investigate the ship and its cargo. A second expedition was mounted in 1987–88. The Gelidonya ship was the first wreck to be excavated in its entirety on the seabed following archaeological techniques adapted to an underwater site.

Because the ship settled on a rocky bottom covered by only a few inches of sand, little of the structure was preserved. Bass and his team found just a handful of wood fragments, including some pieces that have been identified as ceiling planks, apparently joined to the strakes by treenails. Oak brushwood was used as dunnage, cushioning the hull from the heavy cargo. The length of the ship was estimated from the disposition of the cargo on the bottom, not on the basis of the surviving wooden elements.

The cargo consisted of at least one ton of metal: 88 complete and partial bronze ingots and an indeterminate quantity of tin, along with bronze farm tools (picks, hoes, axes, pruning hooks), weapons (knives, spearheads, a sword), and household objects (a mirror, a spit, fragments of a tripod). Most of the bronze objects were broken, suggesting that they were being transported as scrap. Equipment for metalworking, including a swage block, stone hammers, and whetstone, was found amid the wreckage. Three sets of balance-pan weights and a finely carved hematite cylinder seal were probably the personal possessions of the merchant who owned the ship.

The approximate date of the wreck has been established by study of the small finds and pottery and by carbon-14 analysis of the brushwood. Bass believes the Gelidonya ship was a Phoenician vessel, outbound from a Syrian homeport. Five amulets, perhaps carried by the crew members as good luck charms, appear Syro-Palestinian in form, as is the merchant's cylinder seal. The vessel was most likely sailing west along the Anatolian coast, en route to the Aegean Sea. Its last port of call may have been on the island of Cyprus (about 150 miles to the southeast), a major center for ancient bronze production and distribution.

Bass, "Cape Gelidonya: A Bronze Age Shipwreck"; "Return to Cape Gelidonya." Throckmorton, ed. *Sea Remembers.*

CAP PILAR

Barkentine (3m). *L/B/D:* 117.8′ × 27.5′ × 12.7′ dph (35.9m × 8.4m × 3.9m). *Tons:* 295 grt. *Hull:* wood. *Comp.:* 20. *Built:* G. Gautier, St. Malo, France; 1911.

Built for the French Grand Banks fishing fleet, *Cap Pilar* was purchased from Louis Laisney in 1936 by Adrian Seligman, an English veteran of three years in Gustaf Erikson's ships, including OLIVEBANK. Even before he had a ship, Seligman advertised for six crew to join him and his prospective bride, Jane Batterbury (whom he married shortly thereafter), on a voyage round the world. *Cap Pilar,* named for the promontory at the western end of the Strait of Magellan, was later found in St. Malo. On September 29, 1937, *Cap Pilar* left London with a crew of nineteen — "a few cheerful idiots who like to see God doing the work" — the experienced hands including Seligman and his old Erikson shipmate, Lars Paersch. They sailed down the Atlantic with stops at Madeira, Tenerife, Cape Verde, Rio de Janeiro, Tristan da Cunha, Cape Town, and Simons Town, gaining and losing crew as they went. After running down to Sydney, they began a leisurely transpacific voyage, stopping at Auckland — where Jane gave birth to Jessica Jane, who remained with the ship most of the way home — the Gambier and Marquesas Islands, Peru, and the Galápagos. They then sailed through the Panama Canal, and after calls at Jamaica, the Cayman Islands, New York, and Halifax, *Cap Pilar* landed at Falmouth on September 12, 1938, and returned to London twelve days later.

In 1939, *Cap Pilar* was due to be sold to the Nautical College of Haifa, Palestine, but this project was abandoned at the start of World War II. She never went to sea again, and was left to rot at Wyvenhoe.

Seligman, *Voyage of the "Cap Pilar."*

Originally part of the French Grand Banks fishing fleet, the barkentine CAP PILAR *achieved a certain celebrity for her two-year circumnavigation by "a few cheerful idiots who like to see God doing the work in the late 1930s." Courtesy National Maritime Museum, Greenwich.*

HMS CAPTAIN

Canada-class 3rd rate 74 (3m). *L/B/D:* 170′ × 46.7′ × 20.5′ (52.4m × 14.5m × 6.2′). *Tons:* 1,632 bm. *Hull:* wood. *Comp.:* 550. *Arm.:* 28 × 32pdr, 28 × 18pdr, 18 × 9pdr. *Des.:* William Bately. *Built:* Batson, Limehouse, Eng.; 1787.

The third of six ships to bear the name, HMS *Captain* was launched midway between the American and the French Revolutions. At the start of the latter, she was part of Vice Admiral Samuel Hood's Mediterranean fleet when French Royalists threw open the port of Toulon to the British between August and December 1793. On March 14, 1795, she was heavily damaged off Genoa when 13 ships in Vice Admiral Hotham's squadron bested a French force of 15 ships under Vice Admiral Martin. On June 11, 1796, Commodore Horatio Nelson was transferred from HMS AGAMEMNON into *Captain* on orders of Admiral John Jervis. Nelson's squadron was first deployed off Livorno during Napoleon Bonaparte's march through northern Italy at the head of the Armée d'Italie, and in September he oversaw Britain's strategic withdrawal from Corsica.

By February 1797, Nelson had rejoined Jervis's fleet 25 miles west of Cape St. Vincent at the southwest tip of Portugal, just before it intercepted a Spanish fleet under Admiral Don José de Cordoba on February 14. The Spanish were en route from Cartagena to the English Channel to support a Franco-Spanish amphibious invasion of England; they had planned to stop at Cadiz, but overshot the port and were now doubling back. Jervis's fleet consisted of 15 ships of the line while Cordoba commanded 27 ships. The Spanish crews were inexperienced and poorly trained, which Jervis did not know; but the fleet's disorganization was apparent, and he lost no time in exploiting his advantage.

The battle opened with the British sailing south-southwest to pass between two groups of Spanish ships. The bulk of the fleet was heading north-northwest while eight ships sailed north-northeast with a view to circling behind the British to rejoin the main group. At about 1300, the British line began turning to chase the larger Spanish squadron. Realizing that they were in danger of losing the Spanish fleet to leeward, and to prevent a possible junction with the eight ships to the east, Nelson on his own initiative wore ship — *Captain* was third from the last in line — to intercept the Spanish van. Jervis immediately approved the move by ordering *Excellent,* in the rear of the British line, to join *Captain* against Cordoba's immense flagship, *Santísima Trinidad,* which mounted 136 guns on four decks. The battle quickly became general and *Captain* came under fire from seven Spanish ships, suffered many killed and wounded, and had much of her rigging shot away. At 1530, she was closely engaged with *San Nicolás* (80 guns) when the Spaniard was disabled by a broadside from *Excellent* and ran into *San José* (112). With *Captain* no longer maneuverable, Nelson ran his ship alongside *San Nicolás,* which his crew seized in a boarding action in which he participated. He was preparing to order his men into *San José* when the captain of that ship signaled his intent to surrender. "I desired him," wrote Nelson,

> to call on his officers, and on the quarter-deck of a Spanish first-rate, extravagant as the story may seem, did I receive the swords of vanquished Spaniards, which, as I received, I gave to one of my bargemen, who put them with the greatest sang-froid under his arm.

Later in the evening, Nelson was invited aboard Victory where Jervis, soon to be Earl St. Vincent, embraced him and said "he could not sufficiently thank me, and used every kind expression, which could not fail to make me happy."

Having been responsible for half the Spanish ships captured off Cape St. Vincent, *Captain* was the most severely damaged of the British ships and the only one dismasted. She returned to service following repairs, but her only other battle honors were for her part in the capture of Martinique in 1809. The same year she was put into harbor service, and four years later she burned at Plymouth while undergoing conversion to a sheer hulk.

Bennett, *Nelson the Commander.*

HMS Captain

Captain-class turret ship (1f/3m). *L/B/D:* 334′ × 53.3″ × 25.5′ (101.8m × 16.2m × 7.8m). *Tons:* 7,767 disp. *Hull:* iron. *Comp.:* 500. *Arm.:* 4 × 12″ (2 × 2), 2 × 7″. *Armor:* 7″ belt. *Mach.:* trunk engines, 5,400 ihp, 2 screws; 14.25 kts. *Des.:* Cowper Coles. *Built:* Laird Bros., Ltd., Birkenhead, Eng.; 1870.

HMS *Captain* was the inspiration of the Royal Navy's Captain Cowper Coles, an early advocate of center-line turrets for warships. Unlike the traditional broadside battery, turrets enabled a ship's guns to be brought to bear without changing the ship's heading. Coles's ideas were not readily accepted by the naval establishment, which had modified his ideas in their development of HMS *Monarch.* But public support from the British press and members of parliament finally pressured the Admiralty

into accepting his design for HMS *Captain,* which was laid down by Lairds in 1867.

Although designed with a freeboard of only 8.5 feet — the intent was to minimize the area of hull exposed to enemy fire — *Captain* was so heavily built that her upper deck rested only 6.5 feet above the waterline at full draft, which made her a wet ship in all but the calmest weather. The primary armament was contained in two revolving center-line turrets on the upper deck, but a forecastle and poop on the same deck effectively reduced the arc of fire of the four 12-inch guns to broadside positions. Although Coles was in favor of eliminating sail propulsion altogether — among his other innovations was the adoption of twin screws — the Admiralty insisted that *Captain*'s limited coal capacity be augmented by an auxiliary sail rig for ocean voyaging. For his masterpiece Coles insisted on a rig that spread 50,000 square feet of sail. Tripod masts eliminated a mass of standing rigging, but they virtually guaranteed that the ship would capsize before the masts would break.

With her excessive draft and her lofty and rigid masting, the ship had a maximum stability angle of only 21 degrees — as against more than 60 degrees for virtually all other Royal Navy capital ships. These problems notwithstanding, the ship was accepted and joined the Channel Squadron in the summer of 1870 under Captain Hugh Burgoyne; Coles himself sailed in her as an observer. The squadron sailed to Gibraltar to join Admiral Sir Alexander Milne's Mediterranean fleet for maneuvers in the Atlantic. On September 6, Milne boarded *Captain* in the Bay of Biscay to observe gunnery practice. Towards evening the wind freshened and he returned to his flagship, *Lord Warden.* The fleet was about 20 miles west of Cape Finisterre, Spain, when shortly after midnight a blast of wind whipped through the fleet, blowing out sails aboard all 11 ships in the fleet except *Captain.* She was knocked down and sank with the loss of all but 18 of her 499 crew in about 43°N, 9°06′E.

In the court-martial that followed, blame for the tragedy flowed freely between the Admiralty, Coles and his supporters, and the builders. The court avoided castigating any of the principals involved with the controversial ship. Its muted finding asserted: "the *Captain* was built in deference to public opinion expressed in Parliament and through other channels." Although HMS *Captain* can hardly be said to have vindicated all of Coles's innovations — the Royal Navy has never again used the name for one of its ships — center-line turreted guns quickly became the norm for capital ships.

Ballard, *Black Battlefleet.* Sandler, "'In Deference to Public Opinion.'"

CAP TRAFALGAR

Liner; armed merchant cruiser (3f/2m). *L/B/D:* 612.7' × 27.9' x 27.9' (186.8m × 22m × 8.5m). *Tons:* 18,710 grt. *Hull:* steel. *Comp.:* 1st 400, 2nd 275, 3rd 900; crew 330. *Arm.:* 2 × 10.5cm, 6 × 3.7cm. *Mach.:* triple expansion & steam turbine, 3 screws; 17 kts. *Built:* AG Vulcan, Hamburg; 1914.

Built for the Hamburg–South American Steamship Company, during her brief career between March and August 1914, *Cap Trafalgar* was one of the largest liners on the South American run from Europe. On August 18, two weeks after World War I began, *Cap Trafalgar* sailed from Montevideo for a rendezvous with the German South West Africa–based gunboat SMS *Eber,* from which she received her modest armament and her wartime master, Lieutenant Commander Julius Wirth. Removing her third funnel and disguising herself as a Union Castle Line ship, she took up station on the Brazilian coast. On September 14, while refueling off Trinidad Island, she was surprised by the British merchant cruiser CARMANIA at about 1100. In the ensuing battle, the faster and better armed *Cap Trafalgar* was sunk after 1 hour, 40 minutes. The loss, which could have been avoided, was due in part to the fact that while Wirth ordered his ship's fire directed at *Carmania*'s bridge, *Carmania* aimed at the waterline. *Cap Trafalgar* broke off the fight at 1330 and turned for Trinidad; she sank at 1350, in position 20°10'S, 29°51'W. Seventeen of her crew died, including Wirth; 300 escaped to the collier *Eleonore Woermann* and were landed at Buenos Aires.

Bonsor, *South Atlantic Seaway.* Walter, *Kaiser's Pirates.*

CARMANIA

Liner; armed merchant cruiser (2f/2m). *L/B:* 650.4' × 72.2' (198.2m × 22m). *Tons:* 19,524 grt. *Hull:* steel. *Comp.:* 1st 300, 2nd 350, 3rd 2,000. *Arm.:* 8 × 4.7cm. *Mach.:* steam turbines, 3 screws; 18 kts. *Built:* John Brown & Co., Ltd., Clydebank, Scotland; 1905.

Only the third transatlantic liner fitted with turbine propulsion, Cunard Line's *Carmania* was built for the run between Liverpool, Queenstown, and New York. On August 7, 1914, three days after Britain declared war on Germany, *Carmania* arrived at Liverpool after a regular crossing to New York. She was converted to an armed merchant cruiser mounting eight 4.7-inch guns and sailed on August 16, Captain Noel Grant commanding, for duty in the South Atlantic. While on routine patrol off the coast of Brazil with the cruiser HMS *Cornwall,* *Carmania* was sent to Trinidad Island where, at 1100 on September 14, she found the German auxiliary cruiser CAP TRAFALGAR refueling. *Carmania* opened fire at 1203. The Germans concentrated their fire on *Carmania*'s bridge, but Grant aimed for *Cap Trafalgar*'s waterline. Although *Carmania* was hit 80 times and lost 9 crew, the strategy worked and *Cap Trafalgar* broke off the fight at 1330 and sank at 1350. *Carmania* underwent repairs at Gibraltar. In 1916 she returned to the transatlantic run, continuing in that service through the war and for a further 13 years. She was sold and scrapped at Blyth in 1932.

Bonsor, *North Atlantic Seaway.* Walter, *Kaiser's Pirates.*

CARNEGIE

Brigantine (2m). *L/B/D:* 155' × 33' × 14' (47.2m × 10.1m × 4.3m). *Tons:* 568 disp. *Hull:* wood. *Comp.:* 8 scientists, 17 crew. *Des.:* Henry J. Gielow. *Built:* Tebo Yacht Basin Co., Brooklyn, N.Y.; 1909.

Built for Hamburg–South America Line's passenger service between Germany and South America, during World War I CAP TRAFALGAR was fitted out as an armed merchant cruiser. Courtesy The Mariners' Museum, Newport News, Virginia.

A wooden ship named for a man of steel, the brigantine CARNEGIE *of 1909 was built with the express purpose of investigating variations in the Earth's magnetic field. Courtesy National Maritime Museum, Greenwich.*

The problems of Earth's magnetism have bedeviled navigators ever since the invention of the compass, because the compass points not to the North Pole, or true north, but to the magnetic north pole, the location of which changes over time. (In 1992, the magnetic north pole was located at about 78°24′N, 104°18′W, about 1,000 miles south of the North Pole.) To determine an accurate course with a compass, one needs to know the horizontal angle between true north and magnetic north — known as variation, or declination — which varies according to where one is in relation to the magnetic pole and other variables.

One of the first to examine this problem had been Edmund Halley, in PARAMORE, but by the twentieth century, the problem remained to be addressed fully. In 1904, the Carnegie Institution began a massive survey of magnetic variation with the establishment of observatories the world over. From 1903 to 1908, the institution employed the brigantine *Galilee* to conduct magnetic surveys at sea; but as her hull included some magnetic materials, she proved less than perfect for the assignment. Thus was born the idea for a vessel designed solely for magnetic research. Completely iron-free, her engines, propeller shaft, anchors, and other fittings were of bronze, her anchor hawser was hemp, and she mounted a wooden fisherman's windlass on her foredeck. (It is a nice irony, and speaks volumes of her benefactor and name-

sake's humanitarian vision, that Andrew Carnegie made his fortune in steel.)

Between 1909 and 1921, *Carnegie* made six voyages during which she conducted magnetic surveys across all the oceans of the world from as far north as 80°N and as far south as 60°S. The primary magnetic survey completed in 1922, she was laid up at Washington, D.C. Six years later, she was recommissioned for a three-year cruise the purpose of which was both to check previous magnetic readings and to conduct basic oceanographic research. Equipped with instruments for bottom sampling, meteorological measurements, and other observations, she departed Washington on May 1, 1928, under Captain James Percy Ault, who had commanded her on three previous expeditions. After sailing to Hamburg via Plymouth, England, she recrossed the Atlantic via Iceland and Barbados to Panama. Transiting the Canal, *Carnegie* entered the Pacific in October and sailed for Easter Island. From there the ship sailed east to Peru, and then west again for Yokohama, via Samoa and Guam. From Japan she returned east to San Francisco and then sailed for Hawaii, American Samoa, and Western Samoa. On November 9, 1929, while loading drums of gasoline in preparation for the departure from Apia, the ship was destroyed in an explosion that killed Captain Ault and the cabin boy.

Paul, *Last Cruise of the "Carnegie."*

CAROLINE

(ex-*Carolina*) Sidewheel steamboat (1f). *L/B:* 71′ × 20.5′ (21.6m × 6.2m). *Tons:* 46 grt. *Hull:* wood. *Mach.:* sidewheel. *Built:* New York; 1822.

The diminutive passenger steamer *Caroline* — possibly named for George IV's Queen Caroline — was built for service in New York in the early 1820s. Sold to North Carolina interests for service on Albemarle Sound, by 1834 she was back on the Hudson ferrying between Albany and Troy, New York. Sold again and renamed *Caroline*, she was towed through the Erie and Oswego Canals and put in service on the St. Lawrence River. Still later she passed up the Welland Canal to Lake Erie for service between Buffalo and Port Robinson. On December 1, 1837, William Wells of Buffalo bought *Caroline* and laid her up in the Niagara River.

That year, the first of Queen Victoria's 64-year reign, tensions between the United States and Britain were aggravated by the rising secessionist feeling in Upper and Lower Canada (now Ontario and Quebec, respectively). After a failed attack on Toronto on December 5, the Patriots' leader William Lyon Mackenzie fled to a generally sympathetic Buffalo, New York, and established his headquarters on Navy Island in the Niagara River. The Patriots hired *Caroline* to transport supplies to their base, and so she was hacked out of the ice on December 28. The following day she made several runs to Navy Island before tying up at Schlosser, New York. That night, while 33 people slept aboard, Commander Andrew Drew and 45 men rowed over from Chippewa, Ontario, and attacked. Amos Durfee of Buffalo was killed, and *Caroline* was towed into the stream and burned. Americans were incensed by Britain's violation of American sovereignty and General Winfield Scott was dispatched to maintain calm; nonetheless *Caroline* was avenged in the burning of SIR ROBERT PEEL in May 1837. *Caroline* ran aground before going over Niagara Falls, and her engine and figurehead were eventually salvaged and preserved in the Buffalo Historical Society.

Musham, "Early Great Lakes Steamboats: The *Caroline* Affair."

USS CARONDELET

Cairo-class ironclad gunboat (2f/2m). *L/B/D:* 175′ × 51.2′ × 6′ (53.3m × 15.6m × 1.8m). *Tons:* 512. *Hull:* wood. *Comp.:* 251. *Arm.:* 6 × 32pdr, 3 × 8″, 6 × 42pdr, 1 × 12pdr. *Armor:* 2.5″ casemate. *Mach.:* horizontal beam engines, centerwheel; 4 kts. *Built:* James Eads & Co., St. Louis, Mo.; 1862.

Named for a village in St. Louis County, Missouri, USS *Carondelet* first saw action with the U.S. Army's Western Gunboat Flotilla at the capture of Fort Henry, on the Tennessee River, on February 6, 1862. A week later, she was at the fall of Fort Donelson, on the Cumberland. Moving to the Mississippi, under Commander Henry Walke *Carondelet* contributed to the capture of Island No. 10, Fort Pillow, and Memphis, Tennessee. In July she ran aground and was heavily damaged on the Yazoo River in an engagement with CSS ARKANSAS when that ironclad escaped down the Yazoo and past the Union fleet above Vicksburg, Mississippi. In October 1862, the Western Gunboat Flotilla was transferred to the Navy and became the Mississippi Squadron. *Carondelet* subsequently took part in several engagements on the Yazoo, Mississippi, and Red Rivers aimed at weakening Vicksburg's defenses. By the beginning of 1864, her armament consisted of two 100-pdr., one 50-pdr., one 30-pdr., three 9-inch, and four 8-inch guns. (The 8-inch were later removed.) The surrender of that Confederate stronghold on July 4, 1864, and of Port Hudson, Louisiana, two days later, gave the Union complete control of the Mississippi, and *Carondelet* returned to the Cumberland. Her last major engagement was at Bell's Mill, below Nashville, on December 3, 1864. Sold in November 1865, her hull was later incorporated into a wharf at Gallipolis, Ohio.

Anderson, *By Sea and River*. Silverstone, *Warships of the Civil War Navies*. U.S. Navy, *DANFS*.

CARONIA

Liner (1f/1m). *L/B:* 715′ × 91.4′ (217.9m × 27.9m). *Tons:* 34,183 grt. *Hull:* steel. *Comp.:* 1st 581, cabin 351. *Mach.:* steam turbines, 2 screws; 22 kts. *Built:* John Brown & Co., Ltd., Clydebank, Scotland; 1947.

The second Cunard Line ship of the name, *Caronia* was one of the first ships built for service primarily as a cruise ship. Although many liners had been employed in cruising, this was seasonal work for which North Atlantic passenger ships were not well suited. Painted three shades of green, *Caronia* began summertime service between Southampton, Cherbourg, and New York in 1947, with cruises from New York during the winter. As passenger jets cut into the transatlantic trade, the "Green Goddess" was turned increasingly to cruising, and she was well known for her round-the-world cruises. Among the amenities added were air conditioning, in 1956, and a lido deck — a deck with a pool, named for the resort area near Venice — in 1965. Three years later Cunard sold her to Star Line, and she was renamed *Columbia* and later *Caribia*. Laid up for much of the time, she was not a success for her new owners and was finally sold to Taiwanese shipbreakers. While en route to Kao-hsiung in 1974, she struck the breakwater at Guam and broke apart.

Bonsor, *North Atlantic Seaway*. Watson, *Disasters at Sea*.

CARPATHIA

Liner (1f/4m). *L/B:* 540′ bp × 64.5′ (164.6m × 19.7m). *Tons:* 13,555 grt. *Hull:* steel. *Comp.:* 2nd 204, 3rd 1,500. *Mach.:* quadruple expansion, 2 screws; 14 kts. *Built:* Swan, Hunter & Wigham Richardson, Ltd., Wallsend-on-Tyne, Eng.; 1903.

Named for the region in Central Europe, the Cunard Line's *Carpathia* was originally built for two-class (second and third) passenger service between Trieste and New York, with stops at Fiume, Naples, and Gibraltar. (She later carried three classes.) On April 15, 1912, en route to the Mediterranean with 750 passengers under command of Captain Arthur Rostron, she received the first distress call from TITANIC while 58 miles or 4 hours' steaming from the doomed ship's position. About 1530, an hour after the *Titanic* sank, *Carpathia* came on with the first of the few lifeboats from which she would rescue a total of 706 survivors of the 2,223 passengers and crew who had sailed from Southampton. *Carpathia* put back to New York and arrived there on the evening of April 18. After lowering *Titanic*'s lifeboats at the White Star pier she returned to Cunard's Pier 54 where she was greeted by a crowd of some 30,000 people.

During World War I, *Carpathia* continued in service on the North Atlantic. On July 17, 1918, she was torpedoed by *U-55* about 120 miles west of Fastnet en route from Liverpool to Boston, with the loss of five people.

Bonsor, *North Atlantic Seaway*. Lynch & Marschall, *Titanic*.

USS CASSIN YOUNG (DD-793)

Fletcher-class destroyer (2f/2m). *L/B/D:* 376.5′ × 39.7′ × 17.8′ (114.8m × 12.1m × 5.4m). *Tons:* 2,050 disp. *Hull:* steel. *Comp.:* 320. *Arm.:* 5 x 5″; 10 × 21″TT; 6 dcp, 2 dct. *Mach.:* geared turbines, 60,000 shp, 2 screws; 36 kts. *Built:* Bethlehem Steel Co., San Pedro, Calif.; 1943.

USS *Cassin Young* was named for a naval officer awarded a Medal of Honor for his actions at Pearl Harbor, and a Navy Cross as commander of the cruiser USS *San Francisco* at the battles of Cape Esperance and Guadalcanal,

where he was killed on November 13, 1942. Commissioned on December 31, 1943, she joined Vice Admiral Marc Mitscher's Fast Carrier Force (Task Force 58) as a picket ship in time for the invasion of the Caroline Islands in April, and from June through August, of the Marianas. After the attacks on the Palau Islands (July through October), she sailed with the carriers into what would become the Formosa Air Battle of October 10–13. At the far-flung Battle of Leyte Gulf, *Cassin Young* was part of Task Group 38.3 at the Battle of Cape Engano (October 25) in which four Japanese carriers were sunk. At the end of March 1945, she was at Okinawa where she was used for inshore support and as a radar picket against kamikazes. On April 12, she downed five suicide planes before being hit by one. After repairs at Ulithi, she returned to Okinawa and remained there off and on until July 29, when she was hit a second time and lost 22 dead and 45 wounded in the last kamikaze attack of the war. Placed in reserve from 1946 to 1952, after a round-the-world cruise she spent the remainder of her career in the Atlantic and Mediterranean. Decommissioned again in 1960, *Cassin Young* has been a museum ship at the Charlestown (Massachusetts) Navy Yard since 1978.

U.S. Navy, *DANFS*.

CATALPA

Bark (3m). *L/B/D:* 90′ × 25′ × 12′ dph (27.4m x 7.6m × 3.7m). *Tons:* 260 net. *Hull:* wood. *Comp.:* 22. *Built:* Medford, Mass.; 1844.

Catalpa (the name is that of a species of tree) sailed as a merchant ship for New York owners until 1852, when she was purchased by I. Howland, Jr. & Company (owners of CHARLES W. MORGAN) and put into service as a whaleship. She made two good voyages from New Bedford to the Pacific grounds (1852–56 and 1856–60) before being sold to San Francisco interests for use as a merchant ship in 1862. Four years later she resumed whaling, under the ownership of N. T. Gifford. After one voyage she was sold in 1873 to F. W. Homan of Gloucester, who put her in the lumber trade to the West Indies. The following year he sold her to John T. Richardson of New Bedford.

Though a legitimate whaling agent in his own right, Richardson purchased the bark on behalf of the Clan na Gael, an Irish-American organization whose leadership had a bold plan to rescue six Fenian convicts in Fremantle, Western Australia. Thomas Darragh, Martin Hogan, Michael Harrington, Thomas Hassett, Robert Cranston, and James Wilson, British Army veterans all, had been given life sentences in 1866 for their involvement in a planned uprising by the United Irish Brotherhood, founded by James Stephens in 1858. Fitted out for whaling in the Atlantic, *Catalpa* sailed from New Bedford on August 29, 1874, with a crew of 22. The only man who knew of her true mission was Captain George S. Anthony, a veteran whaler and Richardson's son-in-law. The ship landed 200 barrels of oil at Fayal in October; shortly thereafter Anthony confided his secret mission to his first mate, Samuel Smith, before making for Australia. On February 16, they fell in with the British ship *Ocean Beauty,* whose captain gave Anthony a chart of Australia. He also related to the astonished American that he had used the same chart as captain of *Hougoumont* on that ship's voyage to Australia in 1866–68, with 383 convicts, including the six whom Anthony was to rescue!

In the meantime, John Breslin (mastermind of James Stephens's brilliant escape from Dublin's Richmond Gaol in 1865) and John Desmond had been sent ahead via steamer to lay plans for the actual rescue. They had grown quite anxious over *Catalpa*'s delay when, after 11 months at sea, she landed at Bunbury, about 85 miles from Fremantle, on March 28, 1876. By this time, Breslin and Desmond had been joined by two other rescuers. As the prisoners were on a ticket of leave and free to work outside of the prison each day, the escape itself was relatively easy. On April 17 (Easter Monday), the six men walked away from their various assignments, and were spirited down to Rockingham beach. There the ten embarked in a whaleboat manned by five oarsmen and Anthony. After 28 hours rowing after *Catalpa* while evading a police cutter and the mail steamer *Georgette,* they were brought aboard the whaleship, which promptly hoisted the American flag and stood out to sea.

The next morning, *Georgette,* now armed with a single 12-pdr. gun, resumed the chase. At 0800 she fired a warning shot across *Catalpa*'s bow and ordered her to stop. "You have six escaped prisoners aboard. I give you fifteen minutes to consider, and if you don't heave to, I'll blow the masts out of you." Captain Anthony replied, "That's the American flag. I am on the high seas. My flag protects me. If you fire on this ship you fire on the American flag." After a tense hour and a half, *Georgette* put about for Fremantle and *Catalpa* was on her way.

Anthony was supposed to land his passengers in Fernandina, Florida, and resume whaling, partly to raise money to defray expenses of the voyage. Instead, owing to the rescued men's complaints of illness, poor food, and anxiety should they be captured on the high seas, Anthony steered *Catalpa* for New York, where they landed on August 19, 1876. News of their arrival spread quickly, and when *Catalpa* put into New Bedford five days later, she was greeted with a 71-gun salute representing every state in the Union and every county in Ireland.

Although he was only minimally compensated for his voyage, Anthony was held in special respect by Irish Fenians. On a tour of the United States in 1920, Irish Free State President Eamon De Valera visited Anthony's grave in the company of his widow and daughter. Among the others involved in the Fremantle mission, the six erstwhile convicts settled in the United States, and John Breslin went on to assist in the construction of John Holland's submarine, FENIAN RAM.

Ó Lúing, *Fremantle Mission.* Pease, *Catalpa Expedition.* Starbuck, *History of the North American Whale Fishery to 1872.*

USS CAVALLA (SS-244)

Gato-class submarine. *L/B/D:* 311.8' × 27.3' × 15.3' (95m × 8.3m × 4.6m). *Tons:* 1,526 disp. *Hull:* steel; 300' dd. *Comp.:* 60. *Arm.:* 10 × 21"TT; 1 × 3". *Mach.:* diesel/electric, 6,500 hp; 21 kts. *Built:* Electric Boat Co., Groton, Conn.; 1944.

Named for a species of fish, USS *Cavalla* distinguished herself by earning a Presidential Unit Citation on her maiden voyage war patrol. Leaving Pearl Harbor under Lieutenant Commander H. J. Kossler on May 31, 1944, eighteen days later she made contact with Vice Admiral Jisaburo Ozawa's First Mobile Fleet as it steamed towards the U.S. Fifth Fleet off Guam. In the battle known as the Great Marianas Turkey Shoot, in which Japanese naval aviation was virtually annihilated, *Cavalla* herself torpedoed and sank the carrier SHOKAKU on June 19 in 11°50'N, 137°57'E. Of *Cavalla*'s six wartime patrols, only this and the third were rated successful. In the latter, *Cavalla* sank the destroyer *Shimotsuki* in a surface action near Singapore (2°21'N, 107°20'E) on November 25. On January 5, 1945, she sank two cargo ships in 5°S, 112°16'E. The end of the war found *Cavalla* patrolling off Japan, when she was attacked by a Japanese plane shortly after the cease-fire was announced on August 15. Unscathed, she joined the U.S. fleet at Tokyo Bay during the surrender ceremonies on September 2. Put in reserve in 1946, she was reactivated in 1951 and in 1953 was reclassified as a hunter-killer submarine (SSK-244). In service in the Atlantic through 1963, she was later transferred to the U.S. Submarine Veterans of World War II. Placed ashore, she was opened to the public in 1971.

Roscoe, *United States Submarine Operations.* U.S. Navy, *DANFS.*

C. B. PEDERSEN

(ex-*Svecia, Elsa Ölander, Ferm, Emmanuele Accame*) Bark (4m). *L/B/D:* 289' × 40' × 25' (88.1m × 12.2m × 7.6m). *Tons:* 2,142 grt. *Hull:* steel. *Comp.:* 32. *Built:* Continental Iron Co., Pertusola, Italy; 1891.

One of the most famous Italian square-riggers of the late nineteenth and early twentieth centuries, *Emmanuele Accame* was named for the founder of Emmanuele Accame & Figli of Genoa. The company's only four-masted vessel, she sailed in general trade worldwide. In 1912 she was sold to Marjussen, Jorgensen & Company of Grimstad, Norway, and, renamed *Ferm,* continued in general trade. Between 1916 and 1923 she changed hands (and names) several times, finally winding up with Alex Pedersen of Stockholm, who gave her the name by which she is best remembered.

Manned by twenty-five to thirty cadets and ten crew, *C. B. Pedersen* entered the Australian grain trade, carrying lumber out from the Baltic. Her times were never exceptional, and in 1930 and 1932, she was so badly damaged in storms that she sailed via the Panama Canal rather than by way of Cape Horn, and in 1933 she sailed for Europe via the Cape of Good Hope. In 1934, she collided with the steamer *Halmstad* in the Skagerrak and returned to Gothenburg for repairs. By the time she got to Australia there were no grain charters, so Captain Dahlstrom decided to embark eight passengers, four men and four women; to these was added a woman stowaway who earned her keep as a stewardess. The Swedish Navy dropped their sail-training program in 1936, and the next year *C. B. Pedersen* sailed for Australia with every prospect of being scrapped upon her return. On April 25, about 600 miles southwest of the Azores, she collided with the Elders & Fyffes steamer *Chagres* and sank within twenty minutes in position 35°46'N, 35°48'W. The crew were rescued, but the captain of *Chagres* suffered a heart attack and died.

Bednall, *Strange Sea Road.* Hurst, *Square-Riggers: The Final Epoch.*

CENTAUR

Hospital ship. *L/B/D:* 315.7' × 48.2' × 21.5' (96.2m × 14.7m × 6.6m). *Tons:* 3,066 grt. *Hull:* steel. *Comp.:* 332. *Mach.:* steam turbines, 355 nhp, 2 screws. *Built:* Scott's Shipbuilding & Engineering Co., Ltd., Greenock, Scotland; 1924.

The Blue Funnel Line's passenger-cargo ship *Centaur* was built for regular service between Fremantle and Singapore. Her first wartime experience came in November 1941 when she towed a lifeboat with 62 survivors from the German commerce raider *Kormoran* to Carnarvon. She last called at Singapore in December 1941 and sailed from there six weeks before the island fell to the Japanese. After brief service to Broome, she was moved to the safety of Australia's east coast. In January 1943, *Centaur* was converted to a hospital ship equipped to carry 200 patients. On May 12, she left Sydney on her second trip to Port Moresby with a total complement of 332, the majority of whom were members of the 2/12 Field Ambulance Corps. Against standing orders, Captain Murray followed an inshore route, and at 0410 on May 13 she was torpedoed about 28 miles south of Moreton Island; she broke in two and sank in two minutes. The 64 survivors were rescued by the destroyer USS *Mugford* two days later. The Japanese denied any involvement in the tragedy until publication of the official history of World War II in 1979. *Centaur* had been sunk by *I-177,* whose Captain Hajime Nakagawa served six years in prison for unrelated war crimes.

Plowman & Zammit, "Sinking of the *Centaur.*"

CENTRAL AMERICA

(ex-*George Law*) Sidewheel steamer (1f/3m). *L/B/D:* 278' × 40' × 32' (84.7m × 12.2m × 9.8m). *Tons:* 2,141 grt. *Hull:* wood. *Comp.:* 545. *Mach.:* steam, sidewheels. *Built:* New York; 1853.

The sidewheel steamship *George Law* was built for service between New York and Aspinwall, Panama. From that terminus, gold seekers would cross the Isthmus of Panama to catch another ship northbound for San Francisco. On her return passage, the *Law* invariably carried successful prospectors fresh from the diggings, as well as large consignments of gold bound for the New York money markets. Shortly after being renamed *Central America* in 1857, she began her 44th passage from Panama to New York, via Havana, with passengers and an estimated $1,600,000 worth of gold, then valued at about $20 an ounce. Under command of Captain William Lewis Herndon, she was off South Carolina when, on September 8, she was caught in a hurricane that started a fatal leak in the hull. After three days of furious winds and high seas, she lost all power. The next day, the Boston brig *Marine,* herself badly damaged in the storm, stood by to receive 148 of *Central America*'s complement, including all of the women and children. That night, the ship tipped her bow skyward and sank, taking with her 423 passengers and crew. Although it was the United States' worst maritime disaster to date, *Central America*'s losses were not only counted in human lives, for the loss of the monthly shipment of gold from the San Francisco Mint to New York banks helped trigger the financial panic of 1857.

For the next 130 years, the ship lay undisturbed at a depth of 8,000 feet, 200 miles off the coast of South Carolina. In the 1980s, Tommy Thompson, Bob Evans, and Barry Schatz formed the Columbus-America Discovery Group (named for the trio's hometown). Working from the deck of the research vessel *Arctic Discoverer,* the group found the wreck about 160 miles east of Charleston, South Carolina. Using a remote-operated vehicle called *Nemo,* they recovered an undisclosed quantity of gold, including $20 gold Double Eagles (valued today at $8,000 apiece) and a 62-pound gold bar, together with personal artifacts, including two trunks of clothes and other personal effects. In 1992, a Federal Appeals Court ruled that the salvors did not have clear title to the treasure — valued at about $1 billion — the right to which was contested by eight of the cargo's original insurance companies. Further work on the site was suspended pending a resolution of the dispute.

Delgado, *Murder Most Foul.* Klare, *Final Voyage of the "Central America."*

HMS CENTURION

4th rate 60 (3m). *L/B:* 144′ × 40′ (43.9m × 12.2m). *Tons:* 1,005 bm. *Hull:* wood. *Arm.:* 24 × 24pdr, 26 × 9pdr, 10 × 6pdr. *Built:* Portsmouth Dockyard; 1732.

At the start of the War of the Austrian Succession in 1739, Commodore George Anson took command of a squadron that was given the task of harassing Spanish shipping on the coast of South America and capturing the Manila galleon, the annual shipment of gold and silver from Mexico to the Philippines. His six ships were HMS *Centurion, Severn* (50 guns), *Pearl* (40), WAGER (28), *Tryal* (8), and the supply ship *Anna Pink.* Despite the support of First Lord of the Admiralty Sir Charles Wager, Anson was unable properly to man his ship. Short 300 sailors, Anson was given only 170: 32 from Chatham hospital, and 98 marines, many of them novices. In lieu of a land force of 500 men, he was given "invalids to be collected from the out-pensioners of Chelsea college . . . who from their age, wounds, or other infirmities, are incapable of service in marching regiments." Of these, all but 259 deserted before they were embarked in the ships.

These and other delays postponed the sailing date to September 1740, by which time the Spanish had dispatched to the Pacific a squadron of six ships under Don Joseph Pizarro. After stops at Madeira, Brazil, and Argentina, the British ships were separated in a withering autumn rounding of Cape Horn. Worse, the crews began to suffer from scurvy, and the disease was so virulent that *Centurion*'s lieutenant "could muster no more than two Quarter-masters, and six Fore-mast men capable of working; so that without assistance of the officers, servants and the boys, it might have proved impossible for us to have reached [Juan Fernández] Island, after we had got sight of it" on June 9, 1741. They were joined there by *Tryal, Gloucester* (which had "already thrown over-board two thirds of their complement"), and *Anna Pink.* (*Wager* was lost on the coast of Chile on May 15, though many of her crew survived. *Severn* and *Pearl* turned back from the Horn.) By the time the surviving ships left Juan Fernández, they had lost a staggering 626 of the 961 crew they had sailed with; the remaining 335 men and boys were "a number, greatly insufficient for the manning of *Centurion* alone."

On September 9, *Centurion* left the island and three days later captured the merchantman *Nuestra Señora del Monte Carmelo,* from which Anson learned that Pizarro was still in the Atlantic. Over the next two months, the English took three Spanish merchantmen, one of which, *Nuestra Señora del Arranzazú,* was renamed *Tryal Prize* and used as a replacement for the abandoned *Tryal.* On November 13, they seized Paita, burning the town, sinking five ships and taking one. From there they sailed north to keep watch off Acapulco in the vain hope of capturing the Manila galleon. After destroying their prizes and making what repairs they could manage on the hostile Mexican coast, on May 6, 1742, *Centurion* and *Gloucester* sailed for China. By August 15, the latter was in such a state of decay that she had to be scuttled; eleven days later *Centurion* landed at Tinian, which was in regular contact with the Spanish garrison at Guam. Half of the crew were ashore, Anson included, when a typhoon struck on September 21. The ship's cables parted and *Centurion* disappeared. Believing they might never see her again, Anson and his 113 crew set about to lengthen a small Spanish "bark" in which they planned to sail to China. Three weeks later *Centurion* returned, and on October 21 the reunited crew sailed for Macao, where they arrived on November 12.

As the Chinese looked on all ships not engaged in trade as pirates, fitting out at Macao proved extremely difficult, and *Centurion* was not ready for sea until April 6. Rather than sail directly for England, Anson intended to intercept the Manila galleon off the Philippines. Keeping station off Cape Espiritu Santo for a month, on June 20 they overhauled *Nuestra Señora de la Covadonga* (36 guns) six leagues from the Cape (in about 12°35′N, 125°10′E). The Spanish ship was no match for the determined *Centurion,* and Captain Jerónimo de Montero lost sixty-seven crew killed and eighty-four wounded compared with only two English killed and seventeen wounded. The two ships arrived at Canton on July 11 and Anson's efforts to provision his ship were again frustrated. *Covadonga* was sold for $6,000 to local merchants and *Centurion* sailed for home on December 15, 1743.

Centurion's nearly four-year circumnavigation ended at Spithead on June 15, 1744. Despite the loss of three ships and more than 1,300 crew (only four to enemy action), Anson's capture of the Manila galleon with 1,313,843 pieces of eight and 35,682 ounces of virgin silver outshone any other achievement of England's ten-year war with Spain and was ranked the equal of Drake's circumnavigation in GOLDEN HIND 160 years before. Anson achieved flag rank the following year, and *Centurion* was in a squadron commanded by him at the Battle of Cape Finisterre in which the English defeated Admiral de la Jonquière on May 3, 1747, and captured seven merchantmen, four ships of the line, and two frigates. During the Seven Years' War, *Centurion* was at the capture of Louisburg in 1758, and Quebec the next year. In 1762, she participated in the capture of Havana. She was broken up seven years later. In addition to eyewitness accounts of Anson's circumnavigation, Patrick O'Brian's *The Golden Ocean* is a readable and accurate, though fictional, account of the voyage.

Anson, *Voyage Round the World.*

HMVS CERBERUS

Coastal defense monitor (1f/2m). *L/B/D:* 225′ × 45′ × 15.3′ (68.6m × 13.7m × 4.6m). *Tons:* 3,340 disp. *Hull:* iron. *Comp.:* 155. *Arm.:* 4 × 10″ (2 × 2) *Armor:* 8″ belt, 1.5″ deck. *Mach.:* horizontal steam, 1,369 ihp, 2 screws; 9.75 kts. *Built:* Palmer Shipyard, Jarrow, Eng.; 1870.

Named for the three-headed dog of Greek myth who guards the underworld, HMVS *Cerberus* was one of seven near sister ships designed for coastal defense around the empire. The first British warship designed without masts, she was further distinguished by a low freeboard, breastwork armor, and a central superstructure with turrets fore and aft. *Cerberus*'s main armament consisted of four 10-inch guns mounted in two turrets, forward and aft, which could be trained over an arc of 270 degrees. She also had ballast tanks that could be filled to sink the hull and lower her freeboard to further reduce her profile in battle. Describing the class of ungainly ships, Admiral G. A. Ballard wrote that "no contemporary opponent of their own tonnage . . . would have stood much chance against them. They might be said to resemble full-armed

knights riding on donkeys, easy to avoid but bad to close with."

First assigned to Her Majesty's Victoria (State) Navy and in 1901 to the fledgling Australian Navy, she was intended for the defense of Melbourne's Port Philip Bay. During World War I she was used as a port guard ship and munitions ship. In 1921, renamed HMAS *Platypus I*, she was employed as a submarine depot ship. In 1926, her hull was purchased by the city of Sandringham and sunk as a breakwater for the Black Rock Yacht Club. She remains there in a deteriorated state.

Ballard, *Black Battlefleet.* Herd, *HMVS "Cerberus."*

CHALLENGE

(later *Golden City*) Clipper (3m). *L/B/D:* 224′ × 43′ × 25′ dph (68.3m × 13.1m × 7.6m). *Tons:* 2,006 bm. *Hull:* wood. *Comp.:* 40–60. *Built:* William H. Webb, New York; 1851.

The celebrated, if ill-starred, clipper *Challenge* was designed and built for the California trade by William H. Webb for the New York merchant firm of N. L. & G. Griswold. The largest merchant sailing ship ever launched when she took the waters of the East River on May 24, 1851, she was 27.5 feet longer than USS *Pennsylvania*, the longest ship in the U.S. Navy. Built expressly to dominate the California trade, George Griswold asked Captain Robert Waterman to come out of retirement to take *Challenge* around the Horn to San Francisco, and offered him a bonus of $10,000 if he could do so in the unheard-of time of 90 days or less. Best known for his record passages in NATCHEZ and SEA WITCH, Waterman was planning to settle in California to exploit his considerable real estate investments, but he accepted Griswold's *Challenge.* Waterman supervised the design of her towering rig, the dimensions of which were awesome by any standard: the main truck was 230 feet high, her main yard was 90 feet long, elongated to 160 feet with studding sails set, and she spread 12,780 square yards of canvas.

Ironically, in the period that marked the acme of the American merchant marine, when her visionary designers, determined merchants, and driving captains were the envy of the world, the one thing in perilously short supply was a stock of competent, willing seamen. Once in California, many deserted for the diggings after President James Polk announced the discovery of gold at Sutter's Mill. On July 13, 1851, *Challenge* stood down New York harbor with 56 men whom Waterman later described as "the worst crew I ever saw." Only six had ever taken the helm, half had never been to sea, and a few understood no English. On August 17, when the ship was off Brazil,

A painting of the legendary clipper CHALLENGE *by the Chinese ship portrait and chart painter Hin Qua. Courtesy Peabody Essex Museum, Salem, Massachusetts.*

the first mate, James Douglass, who had a reputation as a brute, was knifed by one of the crew in an attempted mutiny. The ringleader, Fred Birkenshaw, escaped immediate punishment by hiding in a well in the forecastle until after *Challenge* had thrashed her way around Cape Horn. Waterman drove his ship relentlessly to make his westing against the winter gales of the southern ocean, sailing as far south as 75°S in search of a favorable wind.

In the end, *Challenge* arrived at San Francisco on October 29, after a passage of 108 days. (Adding insult to injury, *Sea Witch* had broken the 90-day mark for the first time a scant two months before.) Of more immediate concern, though, within days *Challenge*'s crew had inflamed the waterfront with tales of the officers' brutality — ten of *Challenge*'s crew died from disease, occasionally laced with rough justice, and the elements. Waterman countered with charges of mutiny. The crew were exonerated and Douglass got off with a light sentence. Yet *Challenge* was a marked ship, and Captain John Land had to offer $200 per head for the 40 crew he needed to sail to Shanghai.

Waterman retired from the sea, but *Challenge* sailed on. Dismasted in the China Sea in 1859 en route to Hong Kong, she was sold the following year to Thomas Hunt, who renamed her *Golden City* and sailed her between China and India. In 1866, the London-based shipper Captain Joseph Wilson purchased *Golden City* and sailed her to the Orient for ten years before she went aground near Ushant and sank after being towed off the rocks.

Cutler, *Greyhounds of the Sea*. Whipple, *"Challenge."*

HMS CHALLENGER

Screw corvette (1f/3m). *L/B:* 200′ × 40.5′ (61m × 12.3m). *Tons:* 2,306 disp. *Hull:* wood. *Comp.:* 243. *Arm.:* 20 × 8″, 2 × 68pdr. *Mach.:* compound engine, 1,200 hp, 1 screw. *Built:* Woolwich Dockyard, Eng.; 1858.

In the early 1870s, the Royal Society began pushing for a massive oceanographic expedition to probe all three of the world's major oceans — the Atlantic, Pacific, and Indian. The Royal Navy supplied the screw corvette *Challenger* — the largest vessel used for an oceanographic expedition to date — and a crew under Captain George Strong Nares. The team of six civilian scientists, led by naturalist Charles Wyville Thomson, included H. N. Moseley and John Murray. Fitted with a wide array of equipment for taking soundings of up to 6,000 fathoms (36,000 feet), as well as temperature readings, current measurements, and bottom samples from depths of up to 4,000 fathoms, she sailed from Sheerness on December 7, 1872.

The first ten months of the voyage were spent in the Atlantic, which the ship crossed three times, visiting the Caribbean, Halifax, Bermuda, Madeira, the Canary Islands, Brazil, and Tristan da Cunha. During this time, the scientists established the routine they would maintain throughout their voyage, dredging for animal specimens, taking soundings, and gauging water temperatures and currents, among other measurements, about once every 200 miles. (In the course of the voyage, they made such observations at 362 stations.) Observations were not limited to oceanographic matters alone and, while ashore, extensive findings of flora and fauna were made. After seven weeks at Cape Town, *Challenger* sailed on December 17, 1873, bound for the Southern Ocean.

Nine days later she landed at uninhabited Marion Island, then continued east past the Crozets and on to Kerguelen, roughly midway between South Africa and Australia, in latitude 50°S, and then to Heard Island, 300 miles to the southeast, where she was greeted by some resident sealers. From here *Challenger* sailed south, encountering ice in about 61°S, 80°E, on February 11, 1874. She threaded her way through the ice fields until March 1, when she shaped a course for Melbourne. *Challenger* spent a month in Australia, and another five weeks at Sydney, before crossing the Tasman Sea for Wellington.

From New Zealand the expedition sailed north to Tonga and then headed west calling in the Tonga Islands, at the Cape York Peninsula, Australia. From there scientists and crew made their way north and west through the innumerable archipelagos of the East Indies and Philippines before arriving at Hong Kong. *Challenger*'s stay at the British Crown Colony was marked by the departure of Captain Nares, ordered home to command an Antarctic survey in HMS ALERT and *Discovery,* and the arrival of his replacement Captain Frank Turle Thomson. After backtracking through the Philippines, they sailed east to Humboldt Bay, on the north coast of New Guinea, and the Admiralty Islands, where they named Nares Harbour in honor of their former commander. Turning north for Japan, on March 23, thirteen days out, they recorded their deepest sounding, 4,475 fathoms, in position 11°24′N, 143°16′E. The ship and her company spent two months in Japan, where *Challenger* was dry-docked at Yokosuka.

On June 15, the expedition sailed east to conduct observations along latitude 35°N between Japan and Hawaii. On their passage south to Tahiti, the expedition discovered that the Pacific seabed was covered with manganese nodules, the commercial exploitation of which first came under consideration in the 1950s. From Tahiti, with its rich coral finds, *Challenger* headed for Juan Fernandez Island and then to Chile, where the ship was readied for the passage through the Strait of Magellan. The passage north through the Atlantic Ocean was interrupted only by brief calls at Port Stanley, Montevideo, Ascension, and Vigo, Spain. She dropped anchor at Spithead on May 24, 1876, after a voyage of 68,890 miles in three and a half years. Facilitated in large part by expedition member John Murray, the publication of the fifty-volume expedition report was completed nineteen years later.

The results of the *Challenger* expedition cannot be briefly summarized, but of most general interest were the discovery of more than 4,000 previously unknown specimens of marine life, the first comprehensive study of ocean currents and the terrain and composition of the seabed, and the discovery that the average depth of the Pacific Ocean is significantly greater than that of the Atlantic. *Challenger* herself was hulked in 1880, but remained in naval service until sold to J. B. Garnham in 1921.

Buchanan et al., *Narrative of the Voyage.* Linklater, *Voyage of the "Challenger."*

CHAMPIGNY

(later *Fennia*) Bark (4m). *L/B/D:* 312.1′ × 45.9′ × 23.8′ (95.1m × 14m × 7.2m). *Tons:* 3,112 grt. *Hull:* steel. *Built:* Chantiers de la Méditerranée, Le Havre, France; 1902.

Built for La Société des Long Couriers Français of Le Havre, *Champigny* made eleven voyages from France to the Pacific, calling at Honolulu, Melbourne, Sydney, Newcastle, Valparaiso, Puget Sound, San Francisco, and Vancouver, among other ports. In 1917, she put into Bourdeaux and was sold to the Société Générale d'Armament of Nantes. Sailing for Melbourne, she made two roundtrip voyages to San Francisco before returning to St. Nazaire in 1919. She made one final voyage under the French flag, and was laid up at Nantes in 1922 owing to the postwar shipping glut. The following year she was purchased by the Finnish School Ship Association of Helsinki for use as a cadet training ship. Renamed *Fennia,* she replaced an earlier training ship of the same name. She made two round-the-world voyages carrying diverse cargoes, including nitrate, lumber, and coal. In February 1927, *Fennia* was dismasted off Cape Horn while bound from Cardiff for Valparaiso with a cargo of fuel oil and coke. Captain Ragnar Christersson put back to the Falkland Islands where *Fennia* was written off as a total loss. Purchased by the Falkland Islands Company, she remained at Stanley until 1967 when Karl Kortum acquired her for preservation at the San Francisco Maritime Museum. Repairs to the ship were undertaken at Montevideo, but adequate funding failed and she was broken up in 1977.

Lille & Gronstaad, *Finnish Deep-Water Sailers.* Underhill, *Sail Training and Cadet Ships.* Villiers & Picard, *Bounty Ships of France.*

CHAMPION OF THE SEAS

Clipper (3m). *L/B/D:* 252′ × 45.6′ × 29.2′ (76.8m × 13.9m × 8.9m). *Tons:* 2,447 burden. *Hull:* wood. *Built:* Donald McKay, East Boston, Mass.; 1854.

The second of four large clippers ordered by James Baines for his Black Ball Line of passenger ships running between Liverpool and Australia, the three-decked *Champion of the Seas* entered service in 1854. She was similar in appearance to McKay's LIGHTNING and JAMES BAINES, but unlike those two vessels, she set no sails above the royals. Although she had no record passages to her credit, *Champion of the Seas* is credited with the fastest day's run in 24 hours, 465 miles from noon to noon on December 10–11, 1854, under Captain Alexander Newlands. During the Indian Mutiny of 1857, the British government chartered the three Black Ball clippers to carry troops to Calcutta. Before embarking about 1,000 troops, she and *James Baines* were reviewed by Queen Victoria. Her best known commanders were Newland, John McKirdy, and J. M. Outridge, who joined the ship in 1860 and remained with her for two years after her sale in 1866 to Cassell & Company. Sold again to T. Harrison & Company, Liverpool, in 1873, she was then engaged in general trade. In December 1876, she loaded guano at Pabellon de Pica, Chile, for Cork. On January 3, 1877, she was abandoned off Cape Horn in a sinking condition in 33°40′N, 3°10′W; all hands were saved by the British bark *Windsor.*

Hollett, *Fast Passage to Australia.* Stammers, *Passage Makers.*

USS CHARLES AUSBURNE (DD-570)

Fletcher-class destroyer (2f/2m). *L/B/D:* 376′ × 39.7′ × 17.8′ (11.6m × 12.1m × 5.4m). *Tons:* 2,050 disp. *Hull:* steel. *Comp.:* 273. *Arm.:* 5 × 5″ (5 × 1), 10 × 40mm, 7 × 20mm; 10 × 21″TT; 6 dcp, 2 dct. *Mach.:* geared turbines, 60,000 shp, 2 shafts; 36.5 kts. *Built:* Consolidated Steel Corp., Orange, Tex.; 1942.

USS *Charles Ausburne* was the second ship named for Electrician First Class Charles Lawrence Ausburne, who stayed at the wireless station of the U.S. Army transport *Antilles* when that ship was torpedoed on October 17, 1917. After a voyage as a convoy escort to Casablanca and back, she was assigned as flagship of Destroyer Division 45 and sailed for New Caledonia, her first stop in the long struggle up the Solomon Islands to New Guinea. After a minor engagement off Vella Lavella on September 27–28, during which she sank two troop barges, *Charles Ausburne* became the flagship of Captain Arleigh Burke, whose "Little Beavers" became the most celebrated U.S. destroyer squadron of World War II.

On the night of October 31, Destroyer Squadron (DesRon) 23 bombarded Japanese shore installations at Buna and the Shortland Islands on the eve of Allied troop landings at Empress Augusta Bay. The next night, DesRon 23 helped to repulse a Japanese force sent to disrupt the landings, sinking the cruiser, *Sendai,* and the destroyer, *Hatsukaze.* The Little Beavers continued to support the American forces ashore and carried out periodic attacks against Japanese positions at Bonis. On the night of November 24–25, the five ships of DesRon 23 were sent to intercept a Japanese force off Cape St. George, during which they sank destroyers *Onami, Makinami,* and *Yugiri* and severely damaged a fourth, while emerging from the contest unscathed. *Charles Ausburne* continued in the advance up through Bougainville and New Britain until March 1944, when she was detached to the 5th Fleet. At the same time, her captain, now known as Arleigh "31-Knot" Burke for the high speed at which he conducted his combat operations, became Chief of Staff to Vice Admiral Marc A. Mitscher.

Assigned to Task Force 59, *Charles Ausburne* sailed in support of carrier strikes in the Caroline Islands and at Hollandia, New Guinea. She then joined Task Force 58 for the assault on the Mariana Islands. After overhaul on the West Coast, she returned to the Philippines, helping to sink the destroyer *Hinoki* after the landings at Lingayen Gulf in January 1945. *Charles Ausburne* ended the war on picket duty off Okinawa, but she was spared damage from kamikazes. Awarded the Presidential Unit Citation for her service as flagship of the "Little Beavers," the destroyer was laid up in reserve in 1946. In 1960, she was sold to West Germany and recommissioned as *Z-6.* She remained in service until 1967 and was scrapped in 1969.

U.S. Navy, *DANFS.*

CHARLES COOPER

Packet ship (3m). *L/B/D:* 166′ × 35.8′ × 17.9′ (50.6m × 10.9m × 5.5m). *Tons:* 977 grt. *Hull:* wood. *Comp.:* 260+ pass. *Built:* William Hall, Black Rock, Conn.; 1856.

Built for the South Street merchant firm of Layton & Hurlbut and named for a two-sixteenths-share owner,

Charles Cooper is the only American packet ship to survive in the late twentieth century. The ship's career was long and varied. Her first two years were spent in transatlantic service between New York and Belgium. Eastbound she carried raw goods such as cotton, codfish, mahogany, and tobacco, while westbound she carried passengers and cargo such as wine, glassware, tin, and lead. In 1859, her hull was sheathed in copper and she entered trade to the Mediterranean. The next year, she was sold to Boston merchant Alonzo Hamilton, who kept her in general trade, calling first at New Orleans for cotton and corn before sailing for England. From Liverpool she continued on to Calcutta and made a passage to Ceylon before returning to Boston in 1862. She sailed again for Calcutta the same year, and continued west across the Pacific Ocean to San Francisco, then on to British Columbia to load lumber for Melbourne, before returning to New York via Calcutta in 1866.

Thus ended her last complete voyage. A few months later she sailed for San Francisco via Cape Horn, but on September 25, 1866, she was forced into Port Stanley in a leaking condition. Sold for use as a storage hulk, she survived as a floating warehouse until 1968 when she was purchased by New York's South Street Seaport Museum. A quarter century later, she remains in Port Stanley, preserved as a disused storage hulk close to shore.

Brouwer, *International Register of Historic Ships;* "1856 Packet Ship *Charles Cooper.*"

Charles W. Morgan

Whaleship (3m). *L/B/D:* 111′ × 27.7′ × 13.7′ dph (33.8m × 8.4m × 4.2m). *Tons:* 314 grt. *Hull:* wood. *Comp.:* 26. *Built:* Hillman Bros., New Bedford, Mass.; 1841.

Named for Charles Waln Morgan, who owned half the shares in the new ship, *Charles W. Morgan* became one of the most successful — and eventually the last surviving — American sailing whaleship ever built. Between 1841 and 1886 she made twelve voyages under nine different masters. Sailing from New Bedford, she would round Cape Horn and work her way north through the Pacific in search of sperm whales. (Her later masters also took her out via the Cape of Good Hope and Indian Ocean.) Although she would call on ports in South America, Hawaii, and other Pacific islands, and the West Coast of the United States, these voyages kept the ship and her crews away from home for an average of forty months. It is a testament to the skill with which such ships were sailed that despite the length of the voyages, *Morgan* could be ready for sea again after no more than seven months, and on two occasions in less than six weeks.

Built at a cost of $52,000, she returned from her first voyage with a cargo of whale oil and bone valued at $56,000, and in thirty-seven voyages over eighty years, she grossed over $1,400,000 in profits for her various owners. *Morgan's* most profitable voyage was her sixth. In a voyage lasting three years, seven months, Captain James A. Hamilton returned to New Bedford in 1863 having grossed over $165,000. Edward Mott Robinson had acquired a controlling interest in *Morgan* after the first voyage, and it was at this point, after five voyages, that he sold his shares and the ship came under the ownership of J. & W. R. Wing, who maintained an interest in the ship until 1906. This was not the end of the Robinson family's connection with the *Morgan.* His daughter Henrietta Howland Robinson — known after her marriage as Hetty Green — parlayed her substantial inheritance into a fortune worth more than $100 million, which she guarded with legendary thrift. Her son, H. W. Green, undertook the first effort to preserve *Charles W. Morgan.*

On the next voyage, Lydia Godspeed Flanders, the second wife of Captain Thomas C. Landers, became the first woman to sail in the *Morgan,* which she joined after an overland journey to San Francisco. Flanders's son by his first marriage was lost overboard in July 1864, but Lydia gave birth to another son later that year. Following her return to New Bedford in 1867, the *Morgan* was remeasured according to new government tonnage rules and rerigged as a bark. The following voyage was the worst of her career thus far, grossing less than $50,000. Her next voyage, under John M. Tickham, was her first via the Cape of Good Hope. He had her for two successful voyages, but the following voyage, under Charles F. Keith, was relatively speaking a disaster, grossing less than $27,000 after a voyage of five years, eleven months.

After only three months in port, *Charles W. Morgan* began her thirteenth voyage. By this time, in addition to the increasingly scarce sperm oil, there was a great demand for whalebone from right and bowhead whales, which were most plentiful off the coast of Japan and northeast Asia. After a year's sailing, the *Morgan* offloaded cargo worth $50,000 at San Francisco. That city remained her base for eighteen years, during which she had only five masters; between 1888 and 1904 command was traded fairly regularly between John S. Layton, James A. M. Earle, and Thomas Scullun. The whaling fraternity was always an international one, and among the *Morgan's* crew in this period were men from Cape Verde, New Zealand, the Seychelles, Guadeloupe, and Norfolk Island, the last represented by George Parkin Christian, greatgrandson of BOUNTY mutineer Fletcher Christian.

The *Morgan* left San Francisco for the last time in 1904, arriving at New Bedford in June 1906. Two months later she sailed for the South Atlantic and Indian Oceans, with Port Natal a frequent port of call. By this time, competent and willing crews were scarce and desertions and discharges were frequent. Halfway through his ninth voyage in command of the *Morgan,* Earle quit the ship in 1907; when the voyage ended, under Captain Hiram Nye, only about ten of the original crew remained with the ship. *Charles W. Morgan* completed two more voyages before she was laid up in 1913. Three years later, she got a new lease on life when Captain Benjamin Cleveland acquired a controlling interest in her with the intent of taking her to Desolation Island in the South Atlantic for sea elephants. Shortly before this voyage, he leased the *Morgan* for use as the whaleship *Harpoon* in the silent movie *Miss Petticoats* (1916). The ship changed hands again when she was sold to John A. Cook of Provincetown, where she was registered, and who sailed her on her last three commercial voyages.

In 1922, the *Morgan* was again at work as a movie set, in Elmer Clifton's *Down to the Sea in Ships,* Clara Bow's (the "It" girl's) first film. Still later the *Morgan* was featured in the screen adaptation of Joseph Hergesheimer's *Java Head* (1935). Again laid up, she was saved from oblivion by marine artist Harry Neyland, who persuaded Edward Green, Hetty's well-off heir, to acquire the ship. Green converted her to a floating museum in South Dartmouth, Massachusetts, under the aegis of George Fred Tilton, a veteran whaling captain whose brother Zeb Tilton was the celebrated owner of the schooner ALICE S. WENTWORTH. Following Green's death in 1935, the *Morgan* passed into the hands of a well-intentioned but inadequately funded preservation group called Whaling Enshrined. Three years later, Mystic Museum curator Carl Cutler arranged for the purchase of *Charles W. Morgan,* and the refurbished ship has been on public view in Mystic since November 8, 1941. During a major restoration in the 1970s, the *Morgan* was rerigged as a bark, the rig that she had sported for much of her career.

Leavitt, "*Charles W. Morgan.*" Stackpole, "*Charles W. Morgan.*"

CHARLES W. WETMORE

Whaleback freighter (1f/4m). *L/B/D:* 265' × 38' × 16.4' (80.8m × 11.6m × 5m). *Tons:* 1,399 grt. *Hull:* steel. *Comp.:* 22. *Mach.:* triple expansion, 725 hp, 1 screw. *Des.:* Alexander McDougall. *Built:* American Steel Barge Co., West Superior, Wisc.; 1892.

In 1872, Scottish-born captain Alexander McDougall devised a new freighter hull designed to maximize carrying capacity while at the same time minimizing resistance from wind and water. The hull had a flat bottom and a rounded deck (to shed water), and, because of its appearance when fully laden, the type became known as a whaleback. Other observers, looking head-on at the conoidal bow, dubbed them pig boats. Shipbuilders refused to have anything to do with McDougall's novel design, so he established his own shipyard at West Superior, Wisconsin. The first vessel, launched in 1888, was named *101,* supposedly because a friend had given 10-to-1 odds that the new ship type would not succeed. It did, and by 1898 McDougall had built 17 whaleback ships and 25 barges, mostly for the ore trade, although CHRISTOPHER COLUMBUS was a passenger ship.

Named for one of the financial backers of American Steel Barge, *Charles W. Wetmore* became the first whaleback to operate outside the Great Lakes. In June 1891, loaded with 95,000 bushels of wheat, she sailed from Duluth, shot the St. Lawrence River rapids (she was too big for the locks on the river), and proceeded to England. This voyage removed any doubt as to the seaworthiness of the whalebacks, and it was decided to build them for the transpacific trade. The *Wetmore* loaded materials for building a whaleback at New York, Philadelphia, and Wilmington, rounded Cape Horn, and proceeded north to Puget Sound. On December 6, she lost her rudder off the Oregon coast, but after repairs in Astoria she arrived at Everett, Washington, on December 21. The *Wetmore* grounded and was lost in Coos Bay on September 8, 1892, while outward bound from Tacoma for San Francisco with coal. Two years later, the first and only West Coast whaleback was launched, the 361-foot *City of Everett.* This ship had the distinction of being the first American steamship to transit the Suez Canal and circumnavigate the world. In October 1923, she was lost without trace en route from Havana to New Orleans.

Wilterding, *McDougall's Dream.* Inkster, "McDougall's Whalebacks."

CHARLOTTE DUNDAS

Steamboat (1f/1m). *L/B/D:* 56' × 18' × 8' (17.1m × 5.5m × 2.4m). *Hull:* wood. *Mach.:* horizontal engine, sternwheel; 3.5 kts. *Des.:* William Symington. *Built:* Alexander Hart, Scotland; 1801.

One of the foremost advocates of steam propulsion in the late eighteenth and early nineteenth centuries was the Scottish engineer William Symington. In the 1780s, he had taken out a patent for an engine to be used in a steam-driven carriage. He interrupted this work at the behest of another inventor, Patrick Miller, who was trying to develop paddlewheels as a means of propelling a vessel through the water. In 1788, they built a two-hulled steamboat propelled by two paddlewheels mounted between the hulls. This unnamed vessel worked well in trials in October 1788, and a larger engine drove a Forth and Clyde canal boat at a speed of seven miles per hour in trials in 1789. Miller remained unconvinced of the engine's utility and abandoned the project.

In 1801, Thomas Lord Dundas approached Symington with a view to developing an engine suitable for use by the Farth and Clyde Canal Company, of which he was a governor. Symington devised an engine in which the piston rod was attached by a connecting rod to a crank attached directly to the paddlewheel shaft. This became the standard arrangement to work the paddlewheel shaft. Fitted with these engines, in March 1802 the tugboat *Charlotte Dundas* towed two 70-ton barges from Lock 20 to Port Dundas (19.5 miles) in six hours against a strong headwind. The vessel so impressed Francis Egerton, Duke of Bridgewater, that he ordered eight vessels for use on the canal. His sudden death meant the end of Symington's funding because other canal officials felt that the wash thrown out by steam vessels would erode the banks of the canal. *Charlotte Dundas* was left in a backwater of the canal until 1861, when she was broken up.

Baker, *Engine-Powered Vessel. Dictionary of National Biography.*

CHASSEUR

Schooner (2m). *L/B/D:* 85.7′ keel × 26′ × 12.6′ (26.1m × 7.9m × 3.8m). *Tons:* 356 burthen. *Hull:* wood. *Comp.:* 115. *Arm.:* 16 × 12pdr. *Built:* Thomas Kemp, Fells Point, Baltimore; 1812.

Built as a privateer during the War of 1812, *Chasseur* was the most famous of the so-called Baltimore clippers, sharp, heavily — even dangerously — canvassed, but lightly sparred vessels built around Chesapeake Bay in the late eighteenth and early nineteenth centuries. *Chasseur*'s exploits on both sides of the Atlantic earned her the nickname "Pride of Baltimore." While privateering in English waters, Captain Thomas Boyle impetuously declared a blockade of the British Isles, and on her last cruise of the war, she took 18 prizes. The last was the 16-gun schooner HMS *St. Lawrence* (Lieutenant James Gordon) off Mantazas, Cuba, on February 26, 1815, two months after the Treaty of Ghent had ended the war.

Upon her return to Baltimore, *Chasseur* was sold to the merchants George Patterson and George Stevenson to sail in the China trade. Rerigged as a brig and under command of Captain Hugh Davey, she cleared Baltimore on May 19, 1815. After a stop at Boston to take on more cargo, she sailed for Canton on June 12. Her progress was good, and she passed the equator 25 days out (as against the 35 or 40 days it normally took) and rounded the Cape of Good Hope on August 1. From there she was another 35 days to Java Head (where she stopped briefly for provisions) and was at Whampoa on September 25. After three months in port, she cleared on December 30 and, returning the way she had come, sailed home in a record 95 days from Canton to Boston, and 84 days from Java Head; these records were not bettered until 1832.

Although the voyage was a profitable one, *Chasseur* was sold to Thomas Sheppard for trade to the West Indies. After one voyage to Havana, one of the few Spanish-American ports open to foreign ships during this revolutionary period, *Chasseur* was sold to the Spanish Navy. Armed with 21 guns and manned by a crew of 180, she was renamed *Cazador* (Spanish for *chasseur*, or hunter). Because there was already a *Cazador* in the Spanish Navy, she was carried on the lists as *Almirante*. On August 27, 1816, *Cazador* was part of a squadron that fired on USS *Firebrand*, a New Orleans–based schooner suspected of escorting smugglers in the pay of Mexican revolutionaries. The next year, on June 29, 1817, *Cazador* and *Consulado* attempted to capture *Hotspur* off Morro Castle, but the Colombian privateer managed to escape. The next year, she succeeded in capturing a privateer that had itself just captured a slaver. The whole crew were hanged and the slaves returned to Havana.

Cazador remained on the Spanish lists until 1824; her subsequent fate is unknown. The same year, a Spanish vessel of that name was reported at Charleston in distress, but it is not known if this is the same ship. In 1835, a suspected slaver of the same name was seized at Gibraltar and two years later auctioned by the Royal Navy at Lloyds. However, the connection between the *Cazador/Chasseur* and this vessel has eluded confirmation.

Hopkins, "*Chasseur:* The Pride of Baltimore." Roosevelt, *Naval War of 1812.*

CHAUNCEY MAPLES

Steamer (1f/2m). *L/B/D:* 127′ bp × 20′ × 5.9′ (38.7m × 6.1m × 1.8m). *Tons:* 250 disp. *Hull:* steel. *Comp.:* 12 cabin, 70 deck. *Mach.:* high pressure steam, 200 hp, 1 screw; 8 kts. *Des.:* Alexander Johnson. *Built:* Messrs. Alley & MacLellan, Glasgow; 1899.

The steamer *Chauncey Maples* was named for the late Bishop of Likoma, Lake Nyasa, who worked in the territory of what is now Malawi, East Africa, for two decades. Built in sections in Scotland, she was shipped to Chinde, at the mouth of the Zambesi, and carried from there to Malindi on Lake Malawi. She started life as a steamer for the Universities' Mission to Central Africa (UMCA), as a floating school for the training of clergy and a mobile mission station. In addition, she served as a mail boat and transport. During World War I, she was requisitioned for use as a transport in the campaigns across British and German East Africa and on one voyage carried as many as 500 troops. Armed with a single 1-pdr., her crew twice took part in operations against the German steamer *Hermann von Wissmann*. After the war she resumed her work for the UMCA, who operated her until 1953, when financial difficulties forced them to sell her.

In 1956, *Chauncey Maples* was purchased by a Rhodesian-based firm that operated her as a factory ship for its small fleet of Lake Malawi fishing boats. In 1965, she was sold to the Federation of Rhodesia and Nyasaland to run as a passenger steamer in conjunction with Malawi Railways. Completely overhauled, she was fitted with diesel engines and accommodations for 44 first-class and 180 other passengers.

Garland, *Lady of the Lake*. Mackenzie, "Naval Campaigns on Lakes Victoria and Nyasa."

CHEOPS SHIP

L/B/D: 143′ × 18.7′ × 4.9′ (43.6m × 5.7m × 1.5m). *Tons:* 94 disp. *Hull:* wood. *Built:* Egypt; ca. 2500 BCE.

The oldest, largest, and best-preserved vessel from antiquity, the Cheops ship was found accidentally during the course of a clearance excavation at the Great Pyramid at Giza in 1954. The operation was directed by Kamal el-Mallakh, an architect and Egyptologist working for the Egyptian Antiquities Service. While removing debris just south of the pyramid, excavators discovered two long pits carved in the bedrock and sealed with 14-ton limestone blocks. On opening a small hole into the first pit, el-Mallakh noticed an odor of cedar wood. The first glimpses into the darkness revealed a complete, dismantled boat, superbly preserved in its airtight tomb. According to one investigator, the boat's timbers "looked as hard and as new as if they had been placed there but a year ago." The boat was almost certainly built for Cheops (Khufu), the second pharaoh of the Fourth Dynasty of the Egyptian Old Kingdom. The Great Pyramid was Cheops' tomb, and the cartouche of his son, Djedefre, was found on several of the limestone blocks that sealed the boat pit.

The painstaking process of documentation and excavation followed the initial discovery. More than 1,200 separate pieces of wood were recovered, ranging in size from pegs a few centimeters long to timbers of more than 20 meters. About 95 percent of the ship was built of cedar, probably imported from Lebanon, with the remainder, including acacia, used for cross-bracing in some deck sections, sidder for tenons, hornbeam for oar blades, and sycamore for battens, pegs, and other details.

After the pieces had been removed from the pit and conserved, the complex work of reconstruction began. The jigsaw puzzle was put together over a period of 13 years by Haj Ahmed Youssef Moustafa, director of restoration for the Antiquities Service. The careful recording of each piece in its initial position proved crucial to the reconstruction, since the elements of the ship had been arranged logically in the pit: prow at the west end, stern at the east, starboard timbers on the north side, port timbers on the south, hull pieces at the bottom and sides of the pit, and superstructure elements on top of the pile. Ancient carpenters' marks in the form of symbols in the hieratic Egyptian script gave additional clues about the positioning of individual pieces. In 1982, almost 28 years after the original discovery, the Cheops boat was opened to the public in a specially built museum next to the pyramid.

The Cheops ship is an example of the "shell-first" construction that lasted until about 1000 CE. The builders first put together the hull, adding the internal structural members only after the external shell was complete. The boat has no keel. Instead, the hull is built around a flat bottom made up of 8 timbers, averaging 13 meters in length and 13 centimeters in thickness. Two nearly symmetrical sets of planking form the remainder of the shell, with 11 large planks on each side. These strakes are lashed together from rail to rail, scarfed together at their ends, and further secured with 467 tenons. In the water, the timbers would expand and the rope lashings shrink, resulting in a strong, watertight fit. Thin wooden strips (battens) cover the inboard faces of the seams between the planks. Over the battens are fitted 16 floor timbers — large, curved pieces, each shaped from a single piece of cedar, lashed to the strakes to strengthen the hull. The long sturdy center girder, or spine, runs longitudinally amidships, held up by forked stanchions attached to the floor timbers. The 66 deck beams are supported by the spine and notched sheer strakes. The deck beams, in turn, are dadoed to receive the square and trapezoidal sections of decking.

The hull and deck support three independent structures. On the foredeck, ten slim poles with elegant papyrus-bud finials support a small, lightweight canopy with a plank roof. Aft of midships is the main deck cabin, consisting of an anteroom and main chamber. Its outer walls are constructed of twelve cross-braced wooden panels — five on each side and two at each end. Built directly over and forward of the main cabin is the third superstructure, a canopy believed to have been covered by reed mats. The graceful forms of the high prow and steeply raked stern are derived from rafts of bundled reeds, the earliest form of Nile boat. The stempost is carved in high relief to resemble a bundle of papyrus stalks lashed together with rope.

The boat was equipped with five pairs of oars, varying from 6.58 to 8.35 meters in length. An additional pair of steering oars was mounted on the afterdeck. The positioning of the oars in the reconstruction is conjectural and the question of how the vessel was actually powered has been much discussed. The twelve oars seem an inadequate source of propulsion for a craft this size. It has been suggested that the royal boat would have been towed by smaller craft, with its own oars used only for steering and maneuvering.

There are several theories about the purpose of the boat. Although it has been suggested that the ship was intended only as a "solar barque" to carry the resurrected king with the sun god Re in an eternal circuit of the heavens, some of the battens show clear imprints of ropes; this could only have resulted when the boat was afloat, as the cordage shrank and the wood softened and swelled. It is speculated that the ship was either a funerary barge used to carry the king's embalmed body from Memphis to Giza, or that Cheops himself used it as a pilgrimage boat to visit holy places and that it was buried for his use in the afterlife.

Jenkins, *Boat beneath the Pyramid*. Landström, *Ships of the Pharaohs*. Lipke, *Royal Ship of Cheops*.

USS CHESAPEAKE

Frigate (3m). *L/B/D:* 152.5′ bp × 40.9′ × 13.8′ dph (46.5m × 12.5m × 4.2m). *Tons:* 1,244 bm. *Hull:* wood. *Comp.:* 340. *Arm.:* 28 × 18pdr, 20 × 32pdr. *Des.:* Josiah Fox. *Built:* Gosport Navy Yard, Norfolk, Va.; 1800.

The last and least fortunate of the original six frigates ordered by Congress to deal with the Barbary corsairs in the Mediterranean, USS *Chesapeake*'s construction proceeded fitfully. Laid down in 1795, she was only completed after the start of the Quasi-War with France. The frigates included the heavily built UNITED STATES, CONSTITUTION, and PRESIDENT, rated as 44-gun frigates, and CHESAPEAKE, CONSTELLATION, and *Congress,* rated as 38s and designed to carry twenty-eight 24-pdrs. and eighteen to twenty 12-pdrs.

Chesapeake sailed from Norfolk on June 6, 1800, under Captain Samuel Barron to patrol the West Indies during the Quasi-War with France. She took one French priva-

teer before the cessation of hostilities in 1801. In April 1802, she was flagship of the Mediterranean Squadron under Commodore Richard V. Morris until his replacement by Commodore Edward Preble, in *Constitution*. Among the other complaints leveled against the ineffectual Morris was that he paid more attention to his pregnant wife, who sailed with him, than to prosecuting the war against the corsairs.

Chesapeake was laid up at Washington from mid-1803 to 1807, when she was readied for a two-year assignment as flagship of Commodore James Barron (younger brother of Samuel) in the Mediterranean. In addition to the supplies needed for the lengthy spell on foreign station, the ship carried a number of important passengers and their belongings, which customarily took priority over the battle readiness of American warships not sailing through hostile waters. As the country was at peace, there was little to fear. However, the Royal Navy was hardpressed in its war against Napoleonic France, and in its effort to keep its ships manned had resorted to impressment, first at home and among its merchant fleets, and then among U.S.-flag ships. Shortly before *Chesapeake* sailed, two French ships had sought shelter from a storm in the Chesapeake and a British squadron had anchored in Lynhaven Roads to prevent their escape. In the meantime, five British deserters had joined *Chesapeake* and, despite an apparent diplomatic settlement of the issue (and the fact that four had subsequently deserted *Chesapeake*), HMS *Leopard* had been dispatched from Halifax with orders to take the men from *Chesapeake* when she sailed.

On June 22, *Chesapeake* cleared the bay whose name she carried and *Leopard* followed her past the three-mile limit. When Barron refused to accede to the British demand to have his ship searched for Royal Navy deserters, *Leopard* fired seven unanswered broadsides into the unready *Chesapeake* — only a single gun was fired in reply — killing four men, wounding eighteen, including Barron, and damaging the ship severely. Her boarding party then carried off four men. One was hanged, two died, and the two survivors were returned at Boston in 1812 — shortly after the commencement of hostilities for which their capture was but a distant prelude. After repairs at Norfolk, *Chesapeake* was assigned to patrol New England waters to enforce the embargo laws, under command of Captain Stephen Decatur.

With the outbreak of the War of 1812, *Chesapeake*, Samuel Evans commanding, made an extended cruise against British shipping; between December 1812 and April 1813 she ranged from the West Indies to Africa, taking five British prizes, and through skillful seamanship evading the pursuit of a British 74. Back at Boston, Captain James Lawrence took command and on June 1, put to sea to meet HMS *Shannon,* a crack 38-gun frigate under command of Captain Philip Bowes Vere Broke. Accepting an implicit challenge from Broke (who had actually issued a written one, which Lawrence never received), Lawrence sailed for a rendezvous outside of Boston Harbor and shortly after 1600 came alongside *Shannon.* Meticulously prepared for this battle, *Shannon's* crew killed or fatally wounded most of *Chesapeake's* officers, including Lawrence (whose dying words were "Don't give up the ship"), shot away her head sails, boarded her, and hauled down the American flag to replace it with their own. The bloodiest naval battle of the war, and one of the shortest — it lasted only 15 minutes — had cost the lives of 48 U.S. crew and 30 British, with 98 wounded in *Chesapeake* and 56 in *Shannon.*

Chesapeake was taken to Halifax where she was repaired and brought into the Royal Navy. By a strange twist of fate, she was the site of the court-martial of Captain Edward Crofton, HMS *Leopard* (converted to a troopship in 1812), who had run his ship aground on Anticosti Island in the Gulf of St. Lawrence in June 1814. Later that year, *Chesapeake* sailed for England and ran aground off Plymouth. By mid-1815 she was at Cape Town, where she learned that Britain and the United States were no longer at war. She was sold at Portsmouth and broken up in 1820. The same year, the ghost of the ill-starred *Chesapeake* stirred one last time, when her most disgraced captain, James Barron, killed her most admired, Stephen Decatur, in a duel.

Chapelle, *History of the American Sailing Navy.* Strum, "*Leopard-Chesapeake* Incident of 1807." U.S. Navy, *DANFS.*

was in command of a cruiser squadron operating at the southern entrance to Ironbottom Sound between Savo Island and Guadalcanal. At 0136, a Japanese cruiser force under Vice Admiral Gunichi Mikawa attacked. *Chicago* was hit by a single shell and a torpedo as she raced after a Japanese destroyer, which escaped. The Battle of Savo Island — the first naval battle for Guadalcanal — saw the destruction of the cruisers HMAS *Canberra,* USS *Astoria,* and *Quincy,* and the destroyer USS *Jarvis.* In addition to five major surface units, the Allies lost 1,534 sailors killed and hundreds more severely wounded, all in less than an hour. Fearing for what remained of his Task Force 62, Rear Admiral Richmond Kelly Turner withdrew, temporarily abandoning the 16,000 Marines on Guadalcanal to their fate. Nonetheless, the Japanese failed to capitalize on their victory, and the Americans dug in for the six-month struggle for control of the island, the first bit of territory to be wrested from the Japanese. The losses sustained at Savo Island resulted in large measure from the failure of American command and control. To repair the damage done to Australian-American relations by the loss of the *Canberra,* in April of 1943, the U.S. Navy named a new cruiser for the Australian capital.

By a strange coincidence, the last major naval casualty of the Guadalcanal campaign was none other than the *Chicago.* After repairs at San Francisco, *Chicago* returned to the southwest Pacific in January 1943. Bound for Guadalcanal on the night of the 29th, she was hit by an aerial torpedo and taken in tow. The next evening, nine Japanese planes attacked and sank her off Rennell Island in position 11°25'S, 160°56'E.

Loxton, *Shame of Savo.* U.S. Navy, *DANFS.*

USS CHICAGO (CA-29)

Northampton-class cruiser (2f/2m). *L/B/D:* 600.3' × 66.1' × 23' (183m × 20.1m × 7m). *Tons:* 11,420 disp. *Hull:* steel. *Comp.:* 735–1,200. *Arm.:* 9 × 8" (3x3), 8 × 5", 32 × 40mm, 27 × 20mm; 6 × 21"TT; 4 aircraft. *Armor:* 3" belt, 1" deck. *Mach.:* geared turbines, 107,000 shp, 4 screws; 32.5 kts. *Built:* Mare Island Navy Yard, Vallejo, Calif.; 1931.

The second USS *Chicago* spent most of the 1930s in the eastern Pacific, with occasional cruises in the Caribbean and the Atlantic. Transferred to Pearl Harbor in 1940, the Japanese attack found her at sea with USS ENTERPRISE. From March to August 1942 she operated between New Guinea and New Caledonia, first coming under air attack while searching out the Port Moresby invasion fleet on May 7. Two days after the first American landings on Guadalcanal on August 7, *Chicago's* Captain H. D. Bode

CHILE

Paddle steamer (1f/3m). *L/B/D:* 198' × 29' (50'ew) × 18' (60.4m × 8.8m (15.2m) × 5.5,). *Tons:* 682 tons. *Hull:* wood. *Comp.:* 150 cabin, 150 deck. *Mach.:* side lever steam, sidewheels, 90 hp. *Built:* London; 1840.

Although the first three steam vessels in the Pacific arrived in 1822, 1825, and 1836 respectively, permanent service was not achieved until 1840, only two years after SIRIUS and GREAT WESTERN inaugurated regular steam service on the North Atlantic. In that year, Captain William Wheelwright, entrepreneur and one-time American consul at Buenos Aires, brought out the paddle steamers *Chile* and *Peru* under the flag of the Pacific Steam Navigation Company with the intent of establishing service between Valparaiso and Panama. *Chile* left England on July 2, two weeks ahead of *Peru,* and after stops at Rio de

Janeiro and Port Famine arrived at Valparaiso on October 6. *Peru* continued to Callao, the port of Lima, arriving there on November 3. Service between the Chilean and Peruvian ports opened on November 15, but the first two years were plagued by a variety of difficulties, most significant the lack of coal. Wheelwright established Chile's coal industry near Talcahuano, which helped get the ships on schedule from May 1841, but at the end of the month *Chile* ran aground at Valparaiso. It was several months before she could steam under her own power to Guayaquil, Ecuador, where she was escorted by the Ecuadorian Navy's *Guayas*, the first oceangoing steamship launched in Latin America. A stop at Guayaquil was added briefly to the PSNC route, and in February 1842 *Chile* reached Panama for the first time. By year's end, the service was again limited to the Callao-Talcahuano route, the return voyage taking forty days. Service was put on a more certain footing with the commissioning of the new iron-hulled *Ecuador* in 1845. Seven years later, *Peru* became a total loss after stranding, and *Chile* was sold to General Juan José Flores, the deposed conservative president of Ecuador. *Chile* was seized during an abortive raid on Guayaquil, but she returned to Callao in August of that year. Her subsequent fate is unknown.

Duncan, "*Chile* and *Peru*."

CHITOSE

Chitose-class light aircraft carrier. *L/B/D:* 631.6′ × 68.3′ × 24.7′ (192.5m × 20.8m × 7.5m). *Tons:* 13,647 disp. *Hull:* steel. *Comp.:* 800. *Arm.:* 30 aircraft; 8 × 12.7cm, 30 × 25mm. *Mach.:* geared turbines & diesels, 44,000 shp, 2 screws; 28.9 kts. *Built:* Sasebo Dockyard, Sasebo, Japan; 1938.

Named for a river in Hokkaido, *Chitose* was built as a seaplane carrier and completed in 1938. Modified to carry midget submarines in 1941, she was heavily damaged by aircraft from USS SARATOGA at the Battle of the Eastern Solomons (Guadalcanal) on August 24, 1942, and subsequently converted to a light aircraft carrier, as was her sister ship *Chiyoda*. Struck by two dud torpedoes from USS *Bonefish* in February 1944, she was one of four carriers in Vice Admiral Jisaburo Ozawa's Northern Force at the Battle of Cape Engaño (Leyte Gulf). There she was sunk on October 25, 1944, by carrier planes from USS ESSEX in about 19°20′N, 126°20′E. *Chiyoda* was sunk later the same day by cruiser shell fire.

Morison, *Two-Ocean War.*

CHRISTIAN RADICH

Ship (3m). *L/B/D:* 192.1′ × 32′ × 16′ (58.6m × 9.8m × 4.9m). *Tons:* 676 grt. *Hull:* steel. *Comp.:* 115. *Mach.:* diesel, 450 hp, 1 screw; 8 kts. *Built:* Framnaes Mek. Verstad, Sandefjord, Norway; 1937.

Completed only two years before the start of World War II, the sail-training ship *Christian Radich* was named for a patron of the Christiania (later Oslo) Schoolship Association who left a bequest of 90,000 Norwegian crowns in 1915 for the building of a schoolship. The ship made one short cruise in 1938, followed the next year by her first transatlantic voyage, to New York for the World's Fair. *Christian Radich* returned to Norway in late 1939, only to be taken over by German occupation forces at Horten in April 1940. When the Norwegian Navy refused to run a sail-training program in the Baltic for German naval cadets, the *Radich* was used as a submarine depot ship.

War's end found her capsized at Flensburg, Germany, stripped of virtually all metal and fittings except her shell plating and decks. After £70,000 worth of salvage and repair at her builders in Sandefjord, she resumed sail training in 1947. One of the most regular participants in tall ships races and other events in Europe and North America, by the start of her second half century under sail, *Christian Radich* had been both witness to and a catalyst for the remarkable resurgence of interest in sail training and traditional sail generally worldwide.

Underhill, *Sail Training and Cadet Ships.*

CHRISTOPHER COLUMBUS

Whaleback passenger steamer (1f). *L/B/D:* 362′ × 42′ x 24′ dph (110.3m × 12.8m × 7.3m). *Tons:* 1,511 grt. *Hull:* steel. *Comp.:* 5,000 pass. *Mach.:* triple expansion, 3,040 hp, 1 screw; 18 kts. *Des.:* Alexander McDougall. *Built:* American Steel Barge Co., West Superior, Wisc.; 1893.

The world's only whaleback passenger vessel, *Christopher Columbus* was built for the Chicago World's Fair commemorating the quadricentennial of her namesake's transatlantic voyage in 1492. The intent of her designer, Alexander McDougall, was to publicize his radical new whaleback hull design. The whaleback was so called because with its rounded deck and conoidal bow, which offered little resistance to the elements, the hull resembled a breaching whale. Observers looking at them head-on called them pig boats. Built with four decks — a fifth was added later — *Christopher Columbus* carried nearly two million passengers on the six-mile run between Randolph Street in downtown Chicago and the exposition grounds at Jackson Park. When the fair ended, she was acquired by the Hurson Line for the 170-mile passenger run between Chicago and Milwaukee. Sold to the Goodrich Transit Company in 1909, in 1932–33 she was featured at the Century of Progress exhibition in Chicago. It is estimated that in her forty-four years of service, she carried more passengers than any other Great Lakes passenger vessel ever built before being broken up by the Manitowoc Shipbuilding Company in 1936. Although more than forty whalebacks were built — including the *Meteor,* preserved in Superior, Wisconsin — McDougall's concept never gained widespread acceptance.

Wilterding, *McDougall's Dream.* Inkster, "McDougall's Whalebacks."

CITY OF BENARES

Passenger ship (2f/2m). *L/B/D:* 486.1' × 62.7' × 28.5' (148.2 × 19.1m × 8.7m). *Tons:* 11,081 grt. *Hull:* steel. *Comp.:* 285 pass.; 209 crew. *Mach.:* geared turbines, 1,450 nhp, 1 screw; 15 kts. *Built:* Barclay, Curle & Co., Ltd., Glasgow; 1936.

The largest of Ellerman's City Line ships, *City of Benares* was built for service between England and India, and she remained so engaged until the outbreak of World War II. On Friday, September 13, 1940, she sailed from Liverpool under Captain Landles Nicoll, embarking Rear Admiral Edmund Mackinnon as commodore of OB213, a convoy of nineteen ships bound for Canada. Among her 406 crew and passengers were 101 adults and 90 children being evacuated to Canada by the Children's Overseas Reception Board, or CORB; other CORB destinations were South Africa, Australia, New Zealand, and the United States. Four days out, in about 17°W, the destroyer HMS *Winchelsea* and two sloops left the convoy to meet eastbound Convoy HX71. Despite a standing order to disperse the convoy and let all ships proceed on their own, Mackinnon delayed the order. Shortly after 2200, in position 56°43′N, 21°15′W, *City of Benares* was torpedoed by *U-48* under Lieutenant Commander Heinrich Bleichrodt, one of Germany's most successful submarine commanders on one of his most successful missions. The freighter *Marina* fell victim shortly thereafter, whereupon Mackinnon gave the order to disperse. The order to abandon *City of Benares* came next, but in Force 5 conditions, lowering the boats was difficult and several capsized. Many of those who did not drown outright died of exposure before the destroyer HMS *Hurricane* arrived the next afternoon at 1415. Before dark, 102 people from *Benares* had been rescued — only 7 of them children — and one boat of survivors from *Marina.* A second boat from *Marina* sailed to Ireland with 16 crew, including the

captain, and one boat from *City of Benares* initially thought lost was rescued by HMS *Anthony* on September 26, with 45 people, only 6 of them CORB children. In all, of the 406 people sailing in *City of Benares,* 245 were lost, and of the 90 children, all but 13. Although the CORB scheme was eventually abandoned, one positive result of the tragedy was the decision to have all convoys accompanied by rescue escorts. Collectively, these trawlers, tugboats, and coasting vessels were responsible for rescuing more than 4,000 seamen by war's end.

Barker, *Children of the "Benares."*

CITY OF BERLIN

(later *Berlin, Meade*) Liner (1f/3m). *L/B:* 488.6' bp × 44.2' (148.9m × 13.5m). *Tons:* 5,491 grt. *Hull:* iron. *Comp.:* 1st 170, 2nd 100, 3rd 1,500. *Mach.:* compound engine, 1 screw; 15 kts. *Built:* Caird & Co., Greenock, Scotland; 1875.

The Inman Steamship Company's *City of Berlin* was a remarkable ship in many respects. Most noticeably, she had the highest length-to-beam ratio — 11 to 1 — of any major North Atlantic steamship. (By comparison, her contemporary SCOTIA was about 8:1, and FRANCE/*Norway* is about 9:1.) On her fifth voyage between Liverpool and New York, she twice captured the Blue Riband, crossing from Queenstown to Sandy Hook at 15.21 knots (7 days, 18 hours, 2 minutes; September 17–25, 1875) and returning at 15.37 knots (7 days, 15 hours, 28 minutes; October 2–10). In December 1879, she became the first transatlantic steamship fitted with electric lights for interior spaces. To begin, there were four in the main saloon and two in the steerage compartments. As the *Liverpool Journal of Commerce* reported, the latter "continuously shed a brilliancy hitherto unknown in the steerage part of any vessel." During a major refit by Laird Brothers in 1887, *City of Berlin* was given triple expansion engines and electric lighting was extended throughout the ship. Inman was dissolved in 1893, and *City of Berlin* was sold to the American Line and renamed *Berlin,* though she remained on the same route. Two years later, she passed to the Red Star Line and made seven voyages between Antwerp and New York. In 1898, she sailed a few times between Southampton, Queenstown, and New York, but later in the year she was purchased by the U.S. government and commissioned as the U.S. Army Transport Service ship *Meade.* She saw service in both the Spanish-American War and World War I. Damaged by fire at San Francisco in 1906, she was scrapped in 1921.

Bonsor, *North Atlantic Seaway.*

CITY OF BRUSSELS

Liner (1f/3m). *L/B:* 390' bp × 40.3' (118.9m × 12.3m). *Tons:* 3,081 grt. *Hull:* iron. *Comp.:* cabin 200, 3rd 600. *Mach.:* horizontal trunk engine, 1 screw; 14 kts. *Built:* Tod & MacGregor, Glasgow; 1869.

The first passenger ship to cross the North Atlantic in under eight days, the sleek *City of Brussels* was the first ship designed and built with steam steering gear. (Her owner, the Liverpool, New York and Philadelphia Steam Ship Company, was also known as the Inman Line.) GREAT EASTERN had been retrofitted with this labor-saving device two years before. Following her maiden voyage from Liverpool to New York in October 1869, she was not long in showing her speed. On December 4, she departed Sandy Hook and arrived at Queenstown 7 days, 29 hours, 30 minutes later, having set a new transatlantic record with an average speed of 14.7 knots over 2,771 miles, a half knot faster than *Scotia*'s record of 1863. *City of Brussels* never bettered *Scotia*'s westbound record, which stood until 1872.

Following the debut of the White Star Line in the North Atlantic trade, the two-year-old *City of Brussels* was withdrawn from service in November 1871 for a rebuild. A promenade deck that increased her tonnage to 3,747 grt. was added and her accommodations capacity was increased to 1,000 steerage passengers. Five years later, in 1876, she was given more efficient compound engines. On January 7, 1883, she collided with the steamer *Kirby Hall* in the River Mersey and sank with the loss of ten lives.

Bonsor, *North Atlantic Seaway.*

CITY OF NEW YORK

(later *New York,* USS *Harvard,* USS *Plattsburg*) Liner (3f/3m). *L/B:* 527.6' bp × 63.2' (160.8m × 19.3m). *Tons:* 10,499 grt. *Hull:* steel. *Comp.:* 1st 540, 2nd 200, 3rd 1,000. *Mach.:* triple expansion, 2 screws; 20 kts. *Built:* J. & G. Thomson, Govan, Scotland; 1888.

Built for the Inman & International Steamship Company, *City of New York* remained in the shadow of her illustrious younger sister, CITY OF PARIS, until she captured the Blue Riband for the first and only time, sailing between Sandy Hook and Queenstown at a rate of 20.11 knots (5 days, 19 hours, 57 minutes; August 17–23, 1892). This was the first eastbound crossing in under six days. In 1893, she passed to the American Line and, renamed *New York,* began service between New York and Southampton. (She had previously sailed from London.)

In 1898 *New York* was requisitioned by the U.S. Navy and commissioned as the auxiliary cruiser USS *Harvard.* Assigned to scout and trooping duties, she was present at the destruction of the Spanish fleet off Santiago de Cuba on July 3. The following year *New York* returned to civilian service on the North Atlantic and remained in that work until 1918 when she was commissioned as the troopship USS *Plattsburg.* Following World War I, she was sold to the Franklin Steamship Company, and then to the short-lived Polish Navigation Company. After one voyage to Danzig, she was seized at New York for debt. She passed through a succession of other owners but lay idle until 1922, when she sailed for Istanbul for the American Black Sea Line. She was scrapped at Genoa in 1923.

Bonsor, *North Atlantic Seaway.* U.S. Navy, *DANFS.*

CITY OF PARIS

(later *Paris,* USS *Yale,* *Philadelphia,* USS *Harrisburg*) Liner (3f/3m). *L/B:* 527.6' bp × 63.2' (160.8m × 19.3m). *Tons:* 10,499 grt. *Hull:* steel. *Comp.:* 1st 540, 2nd 200, 3rd 1,000. *Mach.:* triple expansion, 2 screws; 20 kts. *Built:* J. & G. Thomson, Govan, Scotland; 1889.

One of the foremost ocean liners of the nineteenth century, *City of Paris* was one of two ships built for the Inman & International Steamship Company which, from an engineering standpoint, signaled the birth of the true transatlantic steamship. Although steam had been the primary means of propulsion for many ships on the North Atlantic run for decades, *City of Paris* and her sister ship CITY OF NEW YORK were the first twin-screw passenger ships in which the sailing rig was reduced to little more than an ornamental anachronism. On her second voyage from Liverpool to New York, *City of Paris* set new transatlantic records both westbound and eastbound, making the first crossing in under six days with an average speed of 19.95 knots between Queenstown and Sandy Hook, on May 2–8, and the first crossing at better than 20 knots — 20.03 knots — on the return, May 15–22. She captured the Blue Riband for the fifth and final time with a westbound run at 20.7 knots (5 days, 14 hours, 24 minutes; October 13–18, 1892). As it happened, her owners' faith in their technological progress was put to the test in her second year of service. On March 25, 1890, her engine rooms were flooded after her starboard propeller cracked and she had to be towed to Queenstown.

In 1893, the British-flag Inman Line became the American Line, and by an act of Congress, *City of Paris* and *City of New York* were registered in the United States. With their names shortened to *Paris* and *New York,* they continued in service on the North Atlantic, though sailing from Liverpool rather than Southampton.

Antonio Jacobsen's painting of the Inman Line steamer CITY OF PARIS, *one of the first twin-screw ships in transatlantic service. She and her sister ship* CITY OF NEW YORK *introduced a new era on the North Atlantic, and they were so highly regarded that the U.S. Congress approved legislation enabling the foreign-built ships to pass under the American flag. Courtesy Peabody Essex Museum, Salem, Massachusetts.*

At the outbreak of the Spanish-American War, *Paris* was commissioned as the auxiliary cruiser USS *Yale* and put on patrol in the Caribbean between May and Septem ber 1898. The following month she resumed passenger service. On May 21, 1899, she stranded on the Manacles off Land's End, Cornwall, and it was not until July 11 that she could be refloated. Refit at Belfast, she was given quadruple expansion engines and her three funnels were replaced with two; later still her middle mast was removed. In the meantime she was renamed *Philadelphia* and put in service between Southampton, Cherbourg, and New York.

During World War I, *Philadelphia*'s eastern terminus became Liverpool, but she continued in civilian service until again requisitioned by the Navy in May 1918. Commissioned as USS *Harrisburg,* she made ten voyages as a troop transport until decommissioned in 1919. *Philadelphia* was sold to the New York–Naples Steamship Company in 1922. The company proved to be bankrupt and on her first visit to Naples she was seized for debt. She was scrapped at Genoa the following year.

Bonsor, *North Atlantic Seaway.* Braynard & Miller, *Fifty Famous Liners.* U.S. Navy, *DANFS.*

CITY OF ROME

Liner (3f/4m). *L/B:* 560.2′ bp × 52.3′ (170.7m × 15.94m). *Tons:* 8,415 grt. *Hull:* iron. *Comp.:* 1st 125, 2nd 80, 3rd 1,310. *Mach.:* compound engine, 1 screw; 15 kts. *Built:* Barrow Shipbuilding Co., Barrow, Eng.; 1881.

The Inman Steamship Company's *City of Rome* has the distinction of being the first three-funnel steamship to operate on the North Atlantic. (Ships of one, two, four, five, and even six funnels had already made their appearance.) The largest ship built to that date, save for Brunel's GREAT BRITAIN, the bark-rigged liner was widely considered, in the words of Nigel Bonsor, "the most stately and well proportioned steamship ever built." Nevertheless she was a disappointment to her owners, who handed her back to her builders after four roundtrips between Liverpool, Queenstown, and New York. Under Anchor Line management, she sailed first from Liverpool, then Glasgow, and finally Liverpool again until 1898. In that year she was chartered by the U.S. government and used to repatriate 1,667 Spanish prisoners of war. She also sailed under charter to the British government during the Boer War. After a brief return to transatlantic work, she was sold in 1901 and scrapped the following year in Germany.

Bonsor, *North Atlantic Seaway.*

CLEOPATRA

Barge (1m). *L/B/D:* 93′ × 15′ (28.3m × 4.6m). *Hull:* iron. *Comp.:* 9. *Des.:* John Dixon. *Built:* London; 1877.

In 1801, the Khedive of Egypt, Mehmet Ali, offered Great Britain one of the three stone obelisks lying at Alexandria known as Cleopatra's Needles. Weighing some 240 tons, the obelisks were hewn from the rock about 700 miles up the Nile and erected by Thotmes III at Heliopolis, near the Nile Delta, in about 1500 BCE. In about 15 BCE, the Roman Emperor Augustus moved them to Alexandria as a gift to Cleopatra. Many plans were made to transport the Needle to London, but none came to fruition until the mid-1870s. Although the French and Americans moved similar obelisks with comparative ease, the British approach was unnecessarily complicated.

John Dixon, an engineer, designed a cylindrical hull to be taken out to Egypt in sections, built around the Needle, and towed back to England. The cylinder had a vertical stem and stern, a rudder, two bilge keels, a mast for balancing sails, and a deck house. On September 21, 1877, *Cleopatra* was towed out of Alexandria by *Olga* and arrived at Gibraltar sixteen days later. On September 14, five days out of Gibraltar, the ships were hit by a Force 12 hurricane. Six of *Olga*'s crew were lost trying to rescue the crew of the *Cleopatra*. The tow was cast off and Cleopatra's Needle drifted in the Bay of Biscay until towed to El Ferrol by *Fitzmaurice,* an English ship whose master's demand for an exorbitant salvage fee was unmitigated by any sense of patriotic duty. *Cleopatra* was recovered and after repairs arrived at Gravesend on January 21, 1878.

Towed to London, she was dismantled prior to the erection of the obelisk on the Thames Embankment.

Rogers, *Freak Ships.*

CLEOPATRA'S BARGE

Brigantine. *L/B/D:* 83′ × 22.5′ × 11.5′ dph (25.3 × 6.9m × 3.5m). *Tons:* 192 grt. *Hull:* wood. *Built:* Retire Becket, Salem, Mass.; 1816.

Captain George Crowninshield, Jr.'s, *Cleopatra's Barge* was the first seagoing yacht built in the United States. An intriguing blend of seaman and dandy, Crowninshield had acquired *Jefferson* for use as a yacht in 1801, and he sailed her as a privateer during the War of 1812. After the war, Crowninshield commissioned Retire Becket to build him a yacht from scratch. When the ship was launched, he gave her the extravagant name of *Cleopatra's Barge,* all but fulfilling the prediction of his brother Benjamin — then secretary of the navy — that he would choose "some foolish name that would be laughed at." Laugh they might; but when launched, the brigantine attracted thousands of visitors from far and wide, and Crowninshield wrote his brother at the end of December that an "average of over 900 [people] per day" had come to admire his ship.

Opulent and extravagant *Cleopatra's Barge* may have been — the hull was painted with a herringbone pattern to port and multicolored stripes to starboard — but she was nonetheless a swift sailer and smartly handled.

Although the French and Americans managed to transport their ancient "Cleopatra's Needles" on traditional ships, the British opted for a more radical — and nearly disastrous — craft, seen here at Alexandria, August 29, 1877, in a photo by Borgiotti. Courtesy National Maritime Museum, Greenwich.

Built for Captain George Crowninshield, Jr., CLEOPATRA'S BARGE *was the first American pleasure yacht in the grand tradition. George Ropes's painting shows the eccentric herringbone color scheme on the port hull; to starboard were multicolored stripes. Courtesy Peabody Essex Museum, Salem, Massachusetts.*

Armed with some 300 letters of introduction, Crowninshield sailed for Europe on March 30, 1817, visiting sixteen ports in the Azores, Madeira, Gibraltar, North Africa, Spain, France, and Italy, before returning to Salem on October 3. Six weeks later, Crowninshield was dead of a heart attack at the age of fifty-one.

Cleopatra's Barge was sold and, stripped of her finer fittings, sailed as a packet between South Carolina and Boston. In 1821, the brigantine was bought by Bryant & Sturgis and sent out to Hawaii where Kamehameha II bought the ship. Renamed *Haaheo o Hawaii* ("Pride of Hawaii"), the vessel served as a sort of royal flagship until April 4, 1824, when she ran aground on Kaui Island and became a total loss despite prodigious efforts to save her.

Crowninshield, *Story of George Crowninshield's Yacht "Cleopatra's Barge."* Whitehead, "George Crowninshield's Yacht *Cleopatra's Barge.*"

COLORADO

Passenger steamer (1f/2m). *L/B/D:* 314' × 45' × 31.9' (95.7m × 13.7m × 9.7m). *Tons:* 3,357. *Hull:* wood. *Comp.:* 1st 104, steerage 1,500. *Arm.:* 2 × 20pdr, 2 × 30pdr. *Mach.:* steam, sidewheels. *Built:* William H. Webb, New York; 1865.

Built for the Pacific Mail Steamship Company's service between Panama and California, the passenger ship *Colorado* entered service just before the end of the Civil War. At the time, there was still concern over the presence of Confederate raiders in the Pacific, in particular CSS SHENANDOAH, and though her speed was probably as much defense as she needed, she was armed with two 20-pdr. and two 30-pdr. guns. Before the end of the war, steam navigation in the Pacific had been confined to coastal routes in both the Americas and Asia. Sensing an opportunity, Pacific Mail began plans to inaugurate transpacific steamship service between San Francisco and Hong Kong, via Kanagawa, Japan. *Colorado*'s stability was improved and her range increased by the removal of some steerage cabins and the enlargement of her bunkers and water tanks.

Colorado departed San Francisco amid great fanfare on New Year's Day 1867. Three weeks later, she arrived at Kanagawa, and eight days later, on January 30, she was at Hong Kong. The newspapers that she carried were newer by two weeks than those brought via the Mediterranean and Red Sea. Returning eastbound, *Colorado* embarked the entire Japanese embassy then en route to Washington. Although *Colorado* made a few more transpacific runs, she spent the next dozen years mainly in the coastal work for which she was built. She was broken up in 1879. Her successful inauguration of the transpacific route expanded following the launch of a quartet of Pacific steamers — *Celestial Empire, Great Republic, Niphon,* and *America* — with connecting service in China provided by Pacific Mail's *Costa Rica.*

Braynard, *Famous American Ships.*

HMS COLOSSUS

Leviathan-class 3rd rate 74 (3m). *L/B/D:* 172.3' × 48' × 20'8" dph. (52.5m × 14.6m × 6.3m). *Tons:* 1,716 burthen. *Hull:* wood. *Comp.:* 640. *Arm.:* 28 × 32pdr, 28 × 18pdr, 18 × 9pdr, 2 carr. *Built:* Cleverly, Gravesend, Eng.; 1787.

The third-rate ship of the line HMS *Colossus* saw extensive action in the wars with Revolutionary France, including the capture of Toulon in 1793 and the Battle of Groix in 1795. The following year she joined Admiral Sir John Jervis's fleet under Captain George Murray, a friend of Commodore Horatio Nelson. On February 14, 1797, while on blockade of the Spanish coast between the Tagus and Cadiz, *Colossus* was severely damaged at the Battle of

Cape St. Vincent, where Admiral Sir John Jervis with 15 ships of the line overwhelmed a Spanish fleet of 13 ships of the line and 14 frigates.

Her battle damage repaired, *Colossus* joined Nelson's squadron at Naples as an armed storeship. Following the Battle of the Nile on August 1, 1798, *Colossus* was used to transport the wounded, both British and French, as well as the treasure taken from the defeated French fleet. Though victorious, the British ships were badly damaged at the Nile, and *Colossus* herself was so cannibalized that Murray even surrendered his spare anchor to Nelson's VANGUARD.

Ordered home with a convoy of merchant ships, before leaving Naples *Colossus* loaded a cargo of antiquities that had been collected by Sir Edward Hamilton. This was made possible owing both to Hamilton's position as the British minister to Naples, and his and his wife's friendship with Nelson. After stopping at the Tagus for five days, on December 7 Captain Murray led his convoy into the anchorage at St. Mary's Island in the Scilly Islands. Three days later a gale struck, the anchor cable parted, and the sheet and bower anchors would not hold — and there was no spare. *Colossus* went ashore on Southward Well Rock, and the next morning all but one man were rescued. Much of the ship was salvaged soon after, but Hamilton's vases were not. In 1968, Roland Morris began diving on the site (in 49°55′N, 06°21′W) and six years later began recovering fragments from Hamilton's collection. Over the years these were reassembled by the British Museum; the most famous reconstructed artifact is the so-called Colossus Vase dating from fifth-century BCE Athens.

Morris, *HMS "Colossus."*

COLUMBIA

Schooner (2m). *L/B/D:* 141.3′ × 25.8′ × 15.8′ (43.1m × 7.9m × 4.8m). *Tons:* 153 grt. *Hull:* wood. *Comp.:* 22–30. *Des.:* W. Starling Burgess. *Built:* Arthur D. Story, Essex, Mass.; 1923.

In 1921, Nova Scotia publisher William H. Dennis put up a cup for races between the best working schooners in the Nova Scotia and Massachusetts fishing fleets. The first match between Canada's *Delawana* and Gloucester's *Esperanto* was won by the Americans, but the next year, BLUENOSE beat *Elsie* to bring the trophy to Halifax. That fall, Ben Pine, a ship's chandler and schooner operator, formed a group to build a racing fisherman to beat *Bluenose*. Laid down in December, *Columbia* was launched on April 17, 1923, and on May 8 headed for the fishing grounds where she caught 324,000 pounds of cod in her first two months. At the end of the season, she proceeded to Halifax to race *Bluenose*. Although she was defeated in two 40-mile races by margins of less than three minutes each, *Bluenose*'s Captain Angus Walter later said *Columbia* was "the best boat the Americans ever produced." Returning to work as a herring freighter from Newfoundland that winter, *Columbia* resumed hand-lining in the spring, but at the end of 1924 the engineless schooner was laid up. There were no races in 1925, but in 1926 *Columbia* was back on the fishing grounds and beat *Henry Ford* in the Americans' elimination match of 1926, although the Canadians failed to come up with a competitor.

Columbia was fishing about 40 miles west-southwest of Sable Island when a hurricane swept through the fleet on August 24, 1927, and the schooner was lost with all 22 crew. On January 3, 1928, the steam trawler *Venosta* was dragging in 43°24′N, 61°27′W when at 0200 her trawl snagged on what turned out to be *Columbia* herself. The trawl was brought in and the schooner broke the surface before the lines broke. As Captain Myhre later reported, "She was a phantom ship and she came up beside us, and as slowly as she emerged from the water on a perfectly even keel, so did she go back again to the deep."

Story, *Hail "Columbia"!*

COLUMBIA REDIVIVA

Ship (3m). *L/B:* 83.5′ × 24.2′ (25.5m × 7.4m). *Tons:* 212 burthen. *Hull:* wood. *Comp.:* 27–50. *Arm.:* 12 guns. *Built:* Plymouth, Mass.; 1787.

The Pacific Northwest's importance to eastern merchants grew rapidly following the visits to the region by HMS RESOLUTION and DISCOVERY on Captain James Cook's third voyage. Boston merchants quickly saw in the abundance of sea otter pelts a way of breaking into the lucrative China trade, and in 1787 a consortium of six merchants, ship owners, and captains under Joseph Barrell purchased the ship *Columbia Rediviva* and the sloop *Lady Washington*. With John Kendrick in command of *Columbia* (as she was usually known) and Robert Gray in *Lady Washington,* the vessels departed Boston on September 30, 1787. The ships sailed in company until separated in a gale off Cape Horn, and *Lady Washington* was the first to arrive at Nootka Sound — a Spanish settlement on the western side of Vancouver Island and the northern limit of the charted coast — on September 17, 1788, followed on the 24th by *Columbia*. When the Americans arrived they found three ships flying Portuguese colors, although they were actually English ships. The Americans remained there through the winter. In March 1789, Gray sailed in search of skins, meeting with great success, especially at Queen Charlotte Island (which he established was, indeed, an island). Returning to Nootka Sound, Gray found that Kendrick had made no effort to trade for the skins that were the object of the voyage. The two ships sailed to Clayoquot Sound on Vancouver Island where *Lady Washington*'s cargo was transferred to *Columbia*, and Gray and Kendrick traded commands. *Columbia* sailed for Canton, via the Sandwich (Hawaiian) Islands, trading skins for tea. *Columbia* sailed for home on February 12, 1790, via the Cape of Good Hope and on August 9 anchored at Boston, the first ship to circumnavigate the globe under the American flag.

Although Kendrick's desultory command of the expedition ensured it was not a profitable one — to all intents and purposes he commandeered *Lady Washington* and never remitted any profits, if there were any, to the owners — Barrell was sufficiently impressed by Gray to dispatch *Columbia* on a second voyage. Sailing on September 28, 1790 — only six weeks after her return to Boston — *Columbia* returned to Nootka Sound on June 4, 1791, after a passage of only eight months. They traded into the fall before returning to Clayoquot Sound. Over the winter they assembled the sloop *Adventure,* the frames of which they had brought out from Boston. In the spring, while *Adventure* sailed north in search of skins, *Columbia* sailed south. On May 12, 1792, Gray

> saw an appearance of a spacious harbour abreast the Ship, haul'd our wind for it, observ'd two sand bars making off, with a passage between them to a fine river. Out pinnace and sent her in ahead and followed with the ship under short sail, carried in from ½ three to 7 fm. And when over the bar had 10 fm. water, quite fresh.

The existence of Columbia's River, as Gray called it, had long been postulated. In 1775, Bruno de Hezeta (sailing in *Santiago*) had established the location of the river mouth. The land, as John Boit wrote,

> with little labour might be made fit to raise such seeds as is nessescary [sic] for the sustenance of inhabitants, and in short a factory set up here and another at Hancock's River in the Queen Charlotte Isles, wou'd engross the whole trade of the NW Coast (with the help [of] a few small coasting vessels).

The discovery was especially important because it gave the young United States a claim to a region already contested by the Spanish and British, and to which Russia would soon add its voice.

Returning north, *Columbia* resumed the search for sea otter skins with *Adventure* but narrowly missed being wrecked when she struck a rock in Milbanke Sound. At the end of the season, Gray sold *Adventure* to the Spanish and on October 3 sailed for Hawaii and thence to China. Arriving at Macao on December 8, *Columbia* sailed again up the Pearl River on February 2. So ended her career in the Pacific Northwest fur trade. Her exact movements in subsequent years is unknown, but in October 1801 she was broken up, or, as the official register says, "ript to pieces."

Howay, ed., *Voyages of the "Columbia" to the Northwest Coast.*

COMET

Steamboat (1f/1m). *L/B/D:* 43.5′ × 11.3′ × 5.6′ (13.3m × 3.4m × 1.7m). *Tons:* 25 grt. *Hull:* wood. *Mach.:* double-acting, jet condensing engine, 4 nhp, sidewheels; 6 kts. *Built:* John Wood & Co., Glasgow; 1812.

Comet was the first steamboat in commercial service in Europe, and followed by five years the appearance of Robert Fulton's NORTH RIVER STEAM BOAT in the United States. Long interested in steam navigation, the Scottish engineer Henry Bell was familiar with the work of both William Symington, who built CHARLOTTE DUNDAS, and Fulton. He first installed a steam engine in a boat in 1802, and as early as 1803 he was trying to persuade the Admiralty to employ steam propulsion in British warships. Failing to attract their interest and after corresponding with Fulton, Bell ordered *Comet* from the Glasgow firm of Messrs. John Wood & Company, with an engine of his own design built by John Robertson of Glasgow; David Napier built the boiler. Originally built with two paddlewheel shafts turning four paddles, this design was found to be inefficient and one pair of wheels was removed. Another unusual feature of *Comet* was the single tall funnel, which doubled as a mast.

After trials in August 1812, *Comet*'s original service as a ferry between Glasgow and Greenock was not a success, but a tour of Scotland to drum up interest in steamboats was, and by 1815 there were ten steamboats on the Clyde. In 1816, *Comet* herself was sailing on the Firth of Forth, and she was later put into service between Glasgow and the West Highlands. On December 13, 1820, en route to Fort William, she ran aground at Craignish Point. (There is another tradition that she sank in 1825 but was later raised, renamed *Ann,* and sent to work as a coastal schooner until 1875.) Her vertical single-cylinder engine is still preserved at the Science Museum in London.

Baker, *Engine-Powered Vessel.*

COMET

(later *Fiery Star*) Clipper (3m). *L/B/D:* 241' × 41.4' × 22.2' (73.5m × 12.6m × 6.8m). *Tons:* 1,836 om. *Hull:* wood. *Comp.:* 525 pass.; 41 crew. *Built:* William H. Webb, New York; 1851.

Built for the California and China trades, Bucklin & Crane's *Comet* was noted for her fine passenger accommodations, which included a toilet, library, and bathrooms. An extreme clipper ship, she was particularly good sailing to windward. Although her maiden passage to San Francisco was not especially fast (103 days), she continued to Hong Kong and loaded a cargo of teas and silks that proved the most valuable cargo ever imported into the United States to that time. The next year, *Comet* raced *Flying Dutchman,* which left San Francisco one day before her. On three separate occasions the ships were within sight of one another, and *Comet* arrived at New York in 83 days, 18 hours, a day and a half before her Webb-built rival. With freight rates to California low, in 1854 she was dispatched to Liverpool. Still under Captain E. C. Gardner, she proceeded from there to Hong Kong in a record 84 days, 16 hours, anchor to anchor.

Comet continued in general trade through 1862, calling in Australia, the Orient, California, and South America. In 1862, the London-based company of T. M. Mackay purchased her. Renamed *Fiery Star,* she was put in service with the Black Ball Line's immigrant service to Australia. On her first voyage from Queenstown, she carried a total of 525 passengers, 25 in first- and second-class accommodations. Homeward bound from her second voyage out, *Fiery Star* departed Moreton Bay on April 1, 1865, with a cargo of wool. Three weeks out, the ship caught fire and 17 of the crew volunteered to stay with the ship while the captain, 55 passengers, and remaining crew took to the ship's boats. Although the latter were never seen again, the crew of *Fiery Star* were rescued by *Dauntless* only hours before the ship sank.

Cutler, *Greyhounds of the Sea.* Howe & Matthews, *American Clipper Ships.* Stammers, *Passage Makers.*

CONCORD

Bark (3m). *L/B/D:* ca. 39' (keel) × 17.5' × 8' dph (11.9m × 5.3m × 2.4m). *Tons:* 55 tons. *Hull:* wood. *Comp.:* 32. *Arm.:* 4 falconets. *Built:* England; 1590–1600.

In 1602, Bartholomew Gosnold sailed to Norumbega, the land encompassing the area of New England (also known then as the "North Part of Virginia"), to establish an English trading settlement. Apart from *Concord*'s name, her complement — thirty-two men under command of Bartholomew Gosnold of whom twelve were to "remayne there for population" — and the fact that she carried a disassembled shallop capable of carrying twenty-five people, little is known of her dimensions or origins. In 1974, the American naval architect William A. Baker posited a vessel of the dimensions (and armament) given above — a fairly typical vessel of the period, with square foresail, mainsail and main topsail, lateen mizzen, and a spritsail.

Concord sailed from Falmouth on March 26, 1602, and after passing the Azores in mid-April made her next landfall near Cape Elizabeth or Cape Neddick, Maine. There the English met eight Micmacs who had had previous contact with Europeans, probably French fishermen from the north. Their leader was dressed

> in a Wastecoate of blacke worke, a paire of Breeches, cloth Stockings, Shooes, Hat, and Bande. . . . [W]ith a piece of Chalke [they] described the Coast thereabouts, and could name Placentia of the New-found-land, they spake divers Christian words and seemed to understand much more than we, for want of Language could comprehend.

Turning south, *Concord* came next to a place the English initially called Shole-hope, but "where we tooke great store of Cod-fish, for which we altered the name, and called it Cape Cod." They made their way south of the Cape and on May 21 came to "a disinhabited Iland which afterwards appeared unto us: we bore with it, and named it Marthaes Vineyard." After building a small fort on Elizabeths Isle (now Cuttyhunk), they briefly visited the far shore of Buzzards Bay, "the goodliest continent that ever we sawe, promising more by farre then we in any way did expect." Notwithstanding the beauty and bounty of the land, and their friendly dealings with the Indians, the intended settlers refused to be left behind, and on June 18, *Concord* sailed from the Elizabeth Islands and arrived at Exmouth on July 23. Of *Concord*'s subsequent history, nothing is known.

Baker, "Gosnold's *Concord* and Her Shallop." Quinn, ed., *English New England Voyages, 1602–1608.*

HMS CONFIANCE

5th rate 36 (3m). *L/B/D:* 147.4' × 37.2' × 7' dph (44.9m × 11.3m × 2.1m). *Tons:* 1,200 disp. *Hull:* wood. *Comp.:* 270–300. *Arm.:* 27 × 24pdr, 2 × 18pdr, 4 × 32pdr carr., 6 × 24pdr carr. *Built:* Isle aux Noix, Ont.; 1814.

The largest warship ever constructed on Lake Champlain, HMS *Confiance* was built in answer to the American Commander Thomas Macdonough's ambitious shipbuilding program, itself designed to thwart British advances into Vermont and New York during the War of 1812. Captain George Downie's flagship at the Battle of Plattsburg, on September 11, 1814, *Confiance* was forced to strike after a two-hour battle with Macdonough's SARATOGA, during which she sustained at least 105 hits by round shot. Forty of her crew were killed, including Downie, and another 83 wounded. Taken into the U.S. Navy at Whitehall, New York, in 1815, she was never fitted and she was eventually sold out of the Navy in about 1825.

Heinrichs, "Battle of Plattsburg."

CONGRESS

Galley (2m). *L/B/D:* 72.3′ × 19.6′ × 6.2′ dph (22m × 6m × 1.9m). *Tons:* 123 tons. *Hull:* wood. *Arm.:* 1 × 18pdr, 1 × 12pdr, 2 × 9pdr, 6 × 6pdr, swivels. *Built:* Skenesborough, N.Y.; 1776.

The Continental Navy's *Congress* was one of four lateen-rigged galleys — the others were *Washington, Trumbull,* and *Gates* — built for General Benedict Arnold's Lake Champlain flotilla, with which he intended to halt the British advance from Canada to the Hudson River Valley. Launched just five days before the Battle of Valcour Island, on October 11, 1776, *Congress* was severely damaged on the first day of the battle; the same action saw the loss of the schooner *Royal Savage* and the gundalow PHILADELPHIA. The following day she led the retreat south through the British line and around Crown Point. Pursued by the British on October 13, Arnold was forced to run four more gundalows and his flagship aground and burn them. Twenty of *Congress's* crew had died in the three-day running battle. Despite Arnold's losses, though, he had delayed the British advance for the season, and when they advanced the next October, the Americans scored a resounding victory at Saratoga.

Chapelle, *History of the American Sailing Navy.* Fowler, *Rebels under Sail.*

USS CONGRESS

Frigate (3m). *L/B/D:* 164′ × 41′ × 13.3′ (50m × 12.5m × 4.1m). *Tons:* 1,867 disp. *Hull:* wood. *Comp.:* 480. *Arm.:* 4 × 8pdr, 49 × 32pdr. *Built:* Portsmouth Navy Yard, Kittery, Me.; 1841.

The fourth vessel of the name, USS *Congress* saw duty in the Mediterranean and then, in the fall of 1844, protected American interests at the beginning of the eight-year siege of Montevideo by Argentine dictator Juan Manuel

de Rosas. The next year she embarked Commodore Robert Stockton en route to Monterey, where she became flagship of the Pacific Squadron. During the Mexican War (1846–48), she patrolled the coast of California and Mexico and her crew played an active role in defeating Mexico and adding California to the territory of the United States. From 1850 to 1853, she served again on the Brazil station, where she oversaw U.S. interests in South America and enforced bans on the African slave trade. From 1855 to 1857 she was flagship of the Mediterranean Squadron, and 1859 found her again in Brazilian waters until the outbreak of the Civil War.

After her recall to the United States, she was assigned to the North Atlantic Blockading Squadron in 1861. On March 8, 1862, she was on blockade in Hampton Roads when the ironclad CSS VIRGINIA sailed out of Norfolk. After sinking USS CUMBERLAND, *Virginia* turned on *Congress,* whose commanding officer, Lieutenant Joseph Smith, intentionally grounded his ship under the protective fire of batteries near Signal Point. Unfortunately, she could bring only two of her guns to bear against *Virginia's* devastating fire, which claimed the lives of more than 120 of her crew. Unable to take the stranded vessel in tow due to the shallow water, *Virginia* riddled the stricken *Congress* with incendiary shot, and shortly after midnight the resulting fires ignited the magazines and the ship blew up.

Still, *Iron Afloat.* U.S. Navy, *DANFS.*

USS CONSTELLATION

Frigate (3m). *L/B/D:* 164′ bp × 40.5′ × 13.5′ dph (50m × 12.3m × 4.1m). *Tons:* 1,265 disp. *Hull:* wood. *Comp.:* 340. *Arm.:* 38 guns. *Des.:* Josiah Fox, Joshua Humphreys. *Built:* David Stodder, Sterrett Shipyard, Baltimore; 1797.

Known as the Yankee Race Horse, USS *Constellation* was the second frigate completed under the Congressional authorization of 1794. She first saw action during the Quasi-War with France as part of the West Indies Squadron under Captain Thomas Truxton. On February 9, 1799, she captured the frigate *L'Insurgente* (40 guns) in an hour-long engagement off Nevis. Her next major contest was against *Vengeance* (52) in a five-hour night action off Guadeloupe (February 1, 1800) during which the French frigate struck her colors twice but eventually escaped the partially dismasted *Constellation* under cover of darkness. During the Barbary Wars, in 1802, *Constellation* was assigned to the Mediterranean Squadron and took part in the evacuation of Derna and in actions against Tunis in 1805. Blockaded in the Chesapeake during the War of 1812, she returned to the Mediterranean as part of Stephen Decatur's Mediterranean squadron and took part in the capture of the Algerian frigate *Mashuda* in June 1815. From 1819 to 1845 *Constellation* served on a variety of stations, including Brazil, the Pacific, the Mediterranean, the West Indies, and last, as flagship on the East India Squadron during the Opium War. *Constellation* was in ordinary from 1845 to 1853.

There is a great deal of confusion as to *Constellation*'s subsequent fate. It is quite clear that the Navy establishment felt *Constellation* ought to be maintained in some form, and it is possible that some timbers from the ship of 1797 were incorporated in the construction of the sloop of war CONSTELLATION in 1854. But as early as 1872 the historian Admiral George H. Preble wrote that the original *Constellation* was "now represented by a new ship bearing the same name." Until recently the Navy unofficially regarded the *Constellation* of 1854 as a rebuilt version of the frigate of 1797.

Dunne, "Frigate *Constellation* Clearly Was No More: Or Was She?" Randolph, "Fouled Anchors? Foul Blow"; "USS *Constellation*, 1797–1979." Wegner, "An Apple and an Orange." Wegner et al., *Fouled Anchors.*

USS CONSTELLATION

Sloop of war (3m). *L/B/D:* 176′ × 42′ × 19.3′ (53.6m × 12.8m × 5.9m). *Tons:* 1,278 disp. *Hull:* wood. *Comp.:* 227. *Arm.:* 16 × 8″, 4 × 32pdr, 1 × 30pdr, 1 × 20pdr, 2 × 12pdr. *Built:* Gosport Navy Yard, Portsmouth, Va.; 1854.

The last ship built to be driven solely by the wind for the U.S. Navy, the 24-gun sloop of war *Constellation* slid down the ways at the Norfolk Navy Yard in 1854. After a three-year tour of duty in the Mediterranean, the outbreak of the Civil War found her as flagship of the Africa Squadron patrolling against slavers. During the war she was reassigned to the Mediterranean. In 1865 she returned to Newport and was decommissioned. *Constellation* spent the next 75 years as a training and receiving ship. During this period she undertook a number of special assignments. She sailed to Europe for the Paris Exposition of 1878 and the Columbian Exposition of 1892, to Ireland with food aid in 1880, and to Baltimore for the centenary of "The Star-Spangled Banner" in 1914. *Constellation* was renamed *New Constellation* from 1917 to 1925, to free the name for a cruiser that was eventually scrapped under the Washington Naval Agreement of 1922. Recommissioned in 1940, *Constellation* served as relief flagship for the Atlantic Fleet and Battleship Di-

vision Five from 1941 to 1943. Decommissioned and stricken from the Navy lists in 1955, *Constellation* is currently a museum ship in Baltimore.

Dunne, "Frigate *Constellation* Clearly Was No More: Or Was She?" Randolph, "Fouled Anchors? Foul Blow"; "USS *Constellation,* 1797–1979." Wegner, "An Apple and an Orange." Wegner et al., *Fouled Anchors.*

USS CONSTITUTION

Frigate (3m). *L/B/D:* 175′ × 43.5′ × 22.5′ (53.3m × 13.3m × 6.9m). *Tons:* 2,200 tons. *Hull:* wood. *Comp.:* 450. *Arm.:* 32 × 24pdr, 20 × 32pdr, 2 × 24 pdr. *Des.:* Joshua Humphreys, Josiah Fox, William Doughty. *Built:* Edmund Hartt, Boston; 1797.

One of the U.S. Navy's six original frigates, authorized by Congress specifically as a counter to the Barbary corsairs in the Mediterranean, USS *Constitution* was launched in 1797. Though all six were fast, heavily built frigates with a flush spar deck above the gundeck, UNITED STATES, *Constitution,* and PRESIDENT were nominally rated as 44s but mounted thirty 24-pdr. and twenty to twenty-two 12-pdr. long guns (later replaced by short-range 42-pdr. carronades). The slightly smaller CONSTELLATION, CHESAPEAKE, and *Congress,* rated as 38s, carried 28 long guns and 18 to 20 carronades. In the words of James Henderson, an authority on British frigates, "Class for class, they had no superior."

A temporary peace with the Barbary States was achieved before she was finished, but *Constitution* was commissioned in time for the Quasi-War with France, during which she captured a number of smaller ships and privateers in the West Indies. Returning to the Charlestown Navy Yard in 1801, she was placed in ordinary. The United States' next foreign entanglement was with the deys of Algiers, Morocco, Tunis, and Tripoli. In 1803, *Constitution* sailed as flagship of the Mediterranean Squadron maintaining a tight blockade on Tripoli, which was bombarded in August and September 1804, and finally forced the deys of Algiers and Tunis to sign treaties exempting American ships from tribute payments. While the Barbary Wars produced few opportunities for decisive ship-to-ship engagements, the Americans were much admired, and Lord Nelson observed that "there is in the handling of those transatlantic ships a nucleus of trouble for the navy of Great Britain."

Following repairs at New York, in 1809 *Constitution* joined Commodore John Rodgers's North Atlantic Squadron, and the following year Isaac Hull, her most illustrious captain, assumed command. The start of the

War of 1812 found her at Annapolis, Maryland, and she put to sea on July 5. By July 17, *Constitution* was off the New Jersey coast when she spotted ships that all assumed to be Rodgers's squadron. It soon transpired that they were in fact HMS *Africa* (64 guns), the frigates *Shannon*, GUERRIÈRE (38s), *Belvedira* (36), and *Aeolus* (32), and the recently captured U.S. brig, NAUTILUS (12), under command of Captain Sir Philip Broke. In a remarkable 66-hour chase that began in light airs, *Constitution* kept out of range of the British ships by kedging ahead with her anchors, by towing with the ship's boats, and, when the wind finally came up, by what Broke described as "very superior sailing."

On August 19, *Constitution* was cruising the Grand Banks south of Newfoundland when she encountered *Guerrière* in position 41°42′N, 55°48′W. Captain James Dacres was a willing combatant and had only recently invited Rogers to meet "U. States frigate *President . . .* or any other American frigate of equal force for the purpose of having a few minutes tête-à-tête." At 1700, *Guerrière* opened fire at long range; Hull closed the range until 1805 when at a distance of half a pistol shot he gave the order to fire. The first broadside smashed into *Guerrière* and Hull exclaimed, "By heaven, that ship is ours!" Twenty-five minutes later, the dismasted *Guerrière* was wallowing in the heavy seas. *Constitution*'s casualties were seven dead and seven wounded; *Guerrière* had 78 dead and wounded, and was so shattered that Hull ordered her blown up the next day. It was during this battle that *Constitution* earned the nickname "Old Ironsides," after shot was seen bouncing off her hull. *Constitution* returned to a Boston — and a nation — thrilled with the stunning victory. As the *London Times* observed, "It is not merely that an English frigate has been taken, . . . but that it has been taken by a new enemy, an enemy unaccustomed to such triumphs, and likely to be rendered insolent and confident by them."

Family affairs compelled Hull to hand over command to the much maligned William Bainbridge, who had lost USS PHILADELPHIA at Tripoli in 1803. En route to join USS ESSEX and HORNET in the South Pacific, on December 29, 1812, *Constitution* was off the coast of Brazil in 13°6′S, 31°W, when she encountered HMS *Java* (38 guns) under Captain Henry Lambert. Battle was joined at about 1400, and *Constitution* opened fire at about half a mile. *Java* had the better of it at first, but by 1725 *Constitution*'s overwhelming firepower and superior gunnery had reduced *Java* to a mastless hulk, with 124 of her crew killed or wounded, including Captain Lambert. *Constitution*'s casualties were 34 (or 52, according to British estimates) dead and wounded. *Java* was so riddled with shot she had

to be blown up. Dramatic though the victory was, damage to the *Constitution* prevented Bainbridge from continuing his cruise against British shipping.

Constitution put back to Boston where the wounded Bainbridge was replaced by Captain Charles Stewart. After a brief cruise to the Caribbean in early 1814, she put back to Boston where she remained until December 1814 when she again slipped the British blockade. On February 20, 1815 — a week after the war formally ended — she sailed into action against HMS CYANE (22) and *Levant* (20) off Madeira. She forced both ships to strike and both ships were taken as prizes, though *Levant* was recaptured by a British squadron on March 11. *Constitution* arrived at New York on May 15, the most celebrated ship in the U.S. Navy.

Out of commission for the next six years, she returned to the Mediterranean between 1821 and 1828. Two years later she was saved from the scrapyard after a public outcry sparked by the publication of a poetic encomium by Oliver Wendell Holmes. *Constitution* emerged from her rebuilding in 1835 and thereafter sailed on a number of diverse assignments, including the Mediterranean and Home Squadron, and on the South Pacific stations, and, in 1844–46, a 29-month circumnavigation of the world. During the Civil War she saw duty as a navy training ship. Rebuilt in the 1870s, she sailed again as a training ship until 1881, after which she was used as a receiving ship in New Hampshire. In 1897, she was brought to Boston for preservation. She made an extended goodwill voyage in 1931–34, when she was towed to 76 ports along the Atlantic, Gulf, and Pacific coasts. Maintained as a museum ship at Boston, USS *Constitution* is the oldest commissioned ship in the U.S. Navy, and the oldest commissioned warship afloat in the world. To ensure equal weathering on both sides of her hull, she leaves her dock for a turnaround cruise in Boston Harbor on every July 4.

Gillmer, *Old Ironsides*. Martin, *Most Fortunate Ship*. Roosevelt, *Naval War of 1812*.

CONTE DI SAVOIA

Liner (2f/2m). *L/B:* 814.6′ bm × 96.1′ (248.3m × 29.3m). *Tons:* 48,502 grt. *Hull:* steel. *Comp.:* 1st 500, 2nd 366, tourist 412, 3rd 922; crew 786. *Mach.:* geared turbines, 4 screws; 27 kts. *Built:* Cantieri Riuniti dell'Adriatico, Monfalcone, Italy; 1932.

Laid down for Lloyd Sabaudo in the same year as Navigazione Generale Italiana's REX, *Conte di Savoia* actually entered service under the house flag of Italia Flotta Riunite, formed by the merger of Lloyd Sabaudo with Cosulich and Navigazione Generale Italiana. A handsome ship distinguished from the larger *Rex* by a cruiser stern, her most novel feature was a set of gyro-stabilizers that kept her from rolling more than 3 degrees in heavy weather. From 1932 to 1940 she maintained service between Genoa, Villefranche (changed to Cannes in 1938), and New York in company with *Rex* and *Roma*. Her last transatlantic passage was completed in May 1940 just before Italy entered World War II. Laid up at Malamocco near Venice, she was converted to a troopship in 1943. On September 11 of that year, British bombers sank her at Venice. Refloated on October 16, 1945, plans to refit her for service were eventually dropped and she was scrapped at Monfalcone in 1950.

Bonsor, *North Atlantic Seaway*. Kludas, *Great Passenger Ships of the World*.

HMS CONWAY

HM Schoolship *Conway* is the name given to a series of vessels used as stationary schoolships for Britain's Mercantile Marine Service Association. The *Conway* program was designed to prepare students for careers in Britain's merchant navy and the Royal Navy. The curriculum combined the study of liberal arts and nautical science with an Outward Bound segment for the mastery of practical seamanship skills.

The school's first ship was the sixth-rate frigate HMS *Conway*, which was in commission from 1832 to 1857. After a two-year refit, she opened as a schoolship on the Mersey with accommodations for 150 cadets. The institution proved such a success that the Admiralty replaced the *Conway* with the fourth-rate HMS *Winchester*, a *Java*-class frigate of 1822. To preserve a sense of institutional continuity, she was renamed *Conway*. (The original *Conway* was renamed *Winchester* and employed as a naval reserve drillship at Aberdeen.) The program continued to prosper, and in 1875 it acquired the second-rate 92-gun ship HMS *Nile*. This veteran of the Baltic campaign in the Crimean War had a long gestation. Laid down in 1827, she was not launched until 1839 and not commissioned until 1852. Almost immediately she was fitted with an engine and single screw. The new *Conway* opened in 1875 with accommodations for 265 trainees. (The second *Conway* was renamed *Mount Edgecomb* and remained in service with the Devonport and Cornwall Industrial Training Ship Association until 1920.)

The new *Conway* remained on the Mersey until World War II. After several incendiary bombs landed on the ship, she was towed to Plas Newydd, the manor house of the Marquis of Anglesey. She remained there on the Menai Strait after the war. In 1949, the ship was given an extensive refit, and the establishment was expanded to include a shoreside facility. Four years later she was being towed to Liverpool for dry-docking when she stranded in the Menai Strait. The wreck of the last *Conway* burned in 1956.

Fay, "Career of the *Conway*." Masefield, "*Conway*."

LA CORDELIÈRE

(ex-*La Marie Cordelière, La Mareschalle*) Nef (4m). *Tons:* 1,000 tons. *Hull:* wood. *Comp.:* 900. *Arm.:* 16 great guns, 60 lesser guns. *Built:* Morlaix, France; 1448.

La Mareschalle was a nef built at the end of the Hundred Years' War shortly before Charles VII succeeded in forcing the English to relinquish all its French holdings except Calais. More than six decades later, French incursions into Italy under Louis XII brought into being the Holy League, consisting of the Papal States, Venice, Spain, and, in 1512, England's Henry VIII. Among the ships lent to Louis for the defense of the realm was the Breton nef now called *La Cordelière,* commanded by the veteran corsair Hervé de Portznoguer, known also as Primaguet. In August 1512, a fleet of twenty-one ships was gathered at Brest under Admiral René de Clermont. On August 9, Portznoguer was entertaining about 300 people on board *La Cordelière* when an English fleet of some fifty ships under Sir Edward Howard was reported approaching the roadstead. Clermont ordered his fleet to weigh anchor to avoid being bottled up in port, and *La Cordelière* sailed with her guests still aboard and anchored between Capes St. Mathieu and Toulinquet.

The next morning, Clermont ("a worse than bad sailor," according to one French historian) ordered *La Cordelière* and another ship to cover the withdrawal of the French ships as the English attacked. Howard's MARY ROSE was disabled and run aground before three other ships fell on *La Cordelière, Mary James, Sovereign,* and *Regent,* the last commanded by Howard's brother-in-law Sir Thomas Knyvet. Portznoguer ran his ship aboard the *Regent* and Knyvet was killed early in the fighting. The English ships kept up a withering fire until *La Cordelière*'s magazine blew up and the ship sank with the loss of all but 20 of her 1,200 soldiers, seamen, and guests. The old ship did not die entirely in vain, for she was soon followed to the bottom by *Regent,* which also exploded with the loss of all but a few of her men.

Culver, *Forty Famous Ships*. Clowes, *Royal Navy*.

CORIOLANUS

(later *Tiburon, Eugenia Emilia, Lina*) Ship (3m). *L/B/D:* 217.4' × 35.2' × 20.1' dph (66.3m × 10.7m × 6.1m). *Tons:* 1,053 grt. *Hull:* iron. *Comp.:* 30. *Built:* Archibald McMillan & Son, Ltd., Dumbarton, Scotland; 1876.

Built for the London firm of J. Patton, Junior, & Company, *Coriolanus* was considered one of the finest iron clippers ever built and known among her contemporaries as "Queen of the Jute Clippers." Her model received the Gold Medal of the Worshipful Company of Shipbuilders in 1877. Named for the Roman soldier in Shakespeare's play of the same name, on her maiden voyage she sailed from Liverpool to Calcutta in the unequaled time of 65 days. *Coriolanus* sailed well on the wind, as well as before it, which may have contributed to her collision in mid-atlantic on February 4, 1890, with the steamship *Claymore,* whose watch probably underestimated her speed. Both ships were abandoned and *Claymore* sank. *Coriolanus* did not, and after several weeks adrift she was taken in tow to Queenstown by Leyland Line's *Bostonian.* After repairs, she continued to Hamburg to unload her cargo of nitrates.

In 1887 she had been bought by the John Stewart Line, but she was too small, and the line sold her to a Bremen company who also found her unprofitable to run. Thereafter, she changed hands thirteen times, starting with Norwegian interests who cut her down to a bark. The ship's luck held, and she survived a fire at sea in 1896, and six years later a severe grounding during a storm at Algoa Bay, South Africa, which wrecked twelve of the seventeen ships at anchor. In 1921 she went under the Panamanian flag and was renamed *Tiburon.* The following year she lost her main royal mast passing under the Brooklyn Bridge at New York, and she was later impounded at Boston with liquor aboard. Sold into the Cape Verde packet trade, she changed hands a number of times, finally winding up under the Portuguese flag as *Lina.* She returned to the packet trade and plied between New Bedford with cargo and as many as eighty passengers. In 1931 she was sold to the West African Packet Company, which hoped to restore her for trade between Boston and Africa. The company went bankrupt and the old *Coriolanus* was broken up at Fall River in 1936.

Comee, "Last Days of the *Coriolanus.*" Course, *Wheel's Kick and the Wind's Song.* Matson, *Log of the "Coriolanus."*

CORONET

Gaff schooner (2m). *L/B/D:* 133' × 27' × 11.6' (40.5m × 8.2m × 3.5m). *Tons:* 174 grt. *Hull:* wood. *Comp.:* 24. *Des.:* Smith & Terry. *Built:* C. & R. Poillon, Brooklyn, N.Y.; 1885.

One of the most celebrated yachts of the nineteenth century, and as of 1996 the oldest registered yacht in the United States, *Coronet* was built for Brooklyn oil tycoon Rufus T. Bush. Generously appointed with a marble staircase, piano, open fireplace, and six staterooms for the afterguard, *Coronet* was sailed by Captain Christopher S. Crosby for twenty years. Not content with a mere cruising yacht, after a voyage to Europe and back, Bush put up a $10,000 purse for a transatlantic race in 1887. Caldwell Colt accepted the challenge, but his *Dauntless* was no match for *Coronet.* They sailed from Brooklyn on March 12, 1887, and Coronet reached Queenstown in 14 days, 9 hours, and 30 minutes ahead of *Dauntless.* The importance of yachting in this period can be judged by the *New York Times* of March 28, 1887, which devoted the entire first page to the race.

In 1888, Bush made an eastward circumnavigation of the globe via Cape Horn, San Francisco, Hawaii, and Japan, then through the Indian Ocean, Mediterranean, and across the Atlantic to New York, where he sold her. *Coronet* had a succession of owners, the most famous of whom was Arthur Curtiss James, who received the straight stem schooner as a gift from his father in 1894. Described as the perfect vessel for "a young man to learn about seamanship and navigation," the future commodore of the New York Yacht Club made several lengthy voyages in *Coronet,* including one to Japan with scientists from Amherst College. In 1905, *Coronet*'s seventh owner, Louis Bossert, sold her to the evangelical Christian group, The Kingdom. The Reverend Frank W. Sandford sailed her on missionary voyages to the Middle East, Australia, Africa, and the Caribbean. In 1911, the schooner put into Portland, Maine, after a forty-day passage during which six of the ship's company died and many others came down with scurvy. Sandford was convicted of manslaughter. Though *Coronet* was restored to sailing condition, details of her subsequent career are scant. Refurbished and fitted with engines for the first time in 1946, *Coronet* was owned by The Kingdom until 1993. In that year, she was acquired by the International Yacht Restoration School of Newport, which plans to restore her to her former glory.

Campbell, "Until the Owners Return." Murray, "*Coronet:* Whither Away?"

CORSAIR

(later USS *Gloucester*) Screw schooner (2f/1m). *L/B/D:* 241.5' × 27' × 13' (73.6m × 8.2m × 4m). *Tons:* 560 grt. *Hull:* steel. *Mach.:* triple expansion, 2,000 ihp, 1 screw; 17 kts. *Des.:* J. Beavor-Webb. *Built:* Neafie & Levy, Philadelphia; 1890.

The second of four yachts of the same name owned by J. Pierpont Morgan (who owned the first three) and J. Morgan, Jr. (who built the fourth, in 1930), *Corsair* had a celebrated career both as the personal yacht of the financier and philanthropist and as a commissioned ship in the U.S. Navy. During Morgan's tenure as commodore of the New York Yacht Club in 1897–98, *Corsair* served as flagship of that distinguished fleet. It is interesting to note that despite her great size, she was by no means the largest yacht in the club. That same year, there were four vessels longer than 300 feet: W. K. Vanderbilt's *Valiant* (332 feet), Ogden Goulet's *Mayflower* (320 feet) and *Nahma* (306 feet), and Eugene Higgins's *Varuna* (304 feet).

At the start of the Spanish-American War, in April 1898 Morgan presented *Corsair* to the U.S. Navy. She was commissioned as USS *Gloucester* under command of Lieutenant Commander Richard Wainwright. Fitted with four 6-pdr. guns, she joined the Blockading Squadron of the North Atlantic Fleet. At the Battle of Santiago Bay on July 3, she helped sink the Spanish torpedo boats *Pluton* and *Furor*. She was later credited with the single-handed capture of Guanica, Puerto Rico, and aided in the capture of Arroyo. Following the war, *Gloucester* served as a Naval Academy training ship, and between 1902 and 1905 sailed in the West Indies and South America as tender to the Commander in Chief, South Atlantic Squadron. After service with the New York and Massachusetts state militias, *Gloucester* was recommissioned in 1917. Sold out of the service in 1919, she was wrecked in a hurricane off Pensacola, Florida.

Parkinson, *History of the New York Yacht Club*. U.S. Navy, *DANFS*.

HMS COSSACK

Tribal-class destroyer (2f/1m). *L/B/D:* 377′ × 36.5′ × 9′ (114.9m m 11.1m × 2.7m). *Tons:* 2,559 disp. *Hull:* steel. *Comp.:* 190. *Arm.:* 8 × 4.7″ (4x2), 4 × 2pdr, 8 × 0.5″; 4 × 21″TT. *Mach.:* geared turbines, 44,000 shp, 2 screws; 36 kts. *Built:* Vickers-Armstrong, Newcastle-on-Tyne, Eng.; 1938.

Part of the Home Fleet, HMS *Cossack* was at the center of a diplomatic crisis in February 1940, when Norway was still neutral. Her captain, Philip Vian, sailed into Jössing Fjord near Bergen and illegally boarded the German auxiliary tanker ALTMARK to liberate 299 British prisoners of war who had been captured by ADMIRAL GRAF SPEE. Under Commander R. St. V. Sherbrooke, *Cossack* returned to Norway as part of a force of eight destroyers and the battleship REPULSE. During the second battle of Narvik (April 13), she was hit six times by the beached

German destroyer *Diether von Roeder* and drifted ashore; refloated that night, she steamed out of Ofotfjord stern first. Quickly repaired, *Cossack* was one of five destroyers detached from convoy WS8B to join in the search for BISMARCK on May 25–26, 1940, during which *Cossack* reported a torpedo hit on the doomed German battleship. Dispatched to the Mediterranean in 1941, *Cossack* was torpedoed by *U-563* on the night of October 23–24 while escorting convoy HG74 west of Gibraltar; she sank three days later while in tow.

Brice, *Tribals*. Frischauer & Jackson, *Navy's Here!*

COUNTY OF PEEBLES

Ship (4m). *L/B/D:* 266.6′ × 38.7′ × 23.4′ (81.3m × 11.8m × 7.1m). *Tons:* 1,691 grt. *Hull:* iron. *Built:* Barclay, Curle & Co., Ltd., Glasgow; 1875.

As steamships encroached on sailing ships' traditional markets, builders of deep-water square-riggers were forced to build ever larger vessels to remain competitive. But as the hulls grew, so did the need for sail area, a problem best solved by adding a fourth mast. Although a few four-masted ships had been built earlier in the nineteenth century, including *L'Invention* and Donald McKay's GREAT REPUBLIC, the first to have a lasting impact on subsequent shipbuilding was the iron-hulled *County of Peebles*. Built for the Indian jute trade of R. & J. Craig, Glasgow, her successful design led Craig to order a dozen more "four-posters" over the next 20 years. Others followed suit, and about 90 other four-masted ships were built. Even more popular were the four-masted barks, the first of which was launched in 1877, because their manning requirements were significantly less.

County of Peebles traded between European and eastern ports until 1898, when the Chilean Navy bought her. Cut down for use as a coal hulk at Punta Arenas on the Straits of Magellan, she was eventually renamed *Muñoz Gamero*, after a nearby island. In the mid-1960s, she was sunk at Punta Arenas as a breakwater, but her living quarters were later converted to a meeting room with plumbing and electricity. Alongside her are *Hipparchus*, built as a sail-carrying steamer in 1867, and the iron ship *Falstaff* of 1875. The only other extant four-masted ships are the restored FALLS OF CLYDE and *County of Peebles*'s running mate, *County of Roxburgh*, which in 1905 grounded on Takaroa Island in the Tuamotus, where her remains can still be seen.

Brouwer, "Four-Masted Ship *County of Peebles*."

HMS COURAGEOUS

Courageous-class aircraft carrier (1f/1m). *L/B/D:* 786.3′ × 90.5′ × 28.5′ (239.6m × 27.6m × 8.7m). *Tons:* 26,500 disp. *Hull:* steel. *Comp.:* 1,215. *Arm.:* 48 aircraft; 16 × 4.7″. *Armor:* 3″ belt, 1.8″ deck. *Mach.:* geared turbines, 90,000 shp, 4 screws; 31 kts. *Built:* Sir W. G. Armstrong-Whitworth & Co., Ltd., Newcastle-on-Tyne, Eng.; 1917.

Courageous, her sister ship GLORIOUS, and FURIOUS were originally intended as "large light cruisers" tasked with shelling Berlin — more than 80 miles from the Baltic — in support of an amphibious assault on the coast of Pomerania during World War I. The invasion plan was ultimately dropped, and *Courageous* was commissioned with four 15-inch guns rather than the 18-inch guns originally intended. As part of the First Cruiser Squadron, she sustained damage from German light cruisers in the North Sea on November 27, 1917, she but scored no hits on the enemy.

In 1924, it was decided to convert the three ships to aircraft carriers, and *Courageous* emerged from her rebuild to all intents and purposes a new ship. Unfortunately her battle career was short and particularly tragic. Assigned to the Home Fleet at the beginning of World War II, she was on antisubmarine patrol off the southwest coast of Ireland. On September 17, 1939, less than three weeks after the start of the war, she was torpedoed by *U-29* (Lieutenant Commander Otto Schuhart). The first British ship lost in the war, and only the sixth ship of any nationality sunk in action, *Courageous* sank in 50°10′N, 14°45′W, with the loss of 518 crew.

Miller, *War at Sea.* Parkes, *British Battleships.*

LA COURONNE

Ship (3m). *L/B/D:* 165′ lod × 46′ × 19′ dph (50.3m × 14m × 5.8m dph). *Tons:* 2,100 bm. *Hull:* wood. *Arm.:* 68 guns. *Built:* Charles Morieux, La Roche-Bernard, France; 1635.

Laid down in 1629 on the banks of the Seudre River in Brittany, *La Couronne* was the largest French warship built to that time, 25 feet longer and 7 feet broader in the beam than the next largest of the King's ships. As significant, she represented a major shift in French policy, being French-built rather than an import from Holland, as was usual at the time. The inadequacy of contemporary French shipbuilding can be gauged by the fact that *La Couronne* was not launched until 1635. Sometime later she was dismasted, but in the spring of 1639, she was Isaac de Launay Razilly's flagship when the French fleet sailed from Brest for La Coruña, Spain. The French fleet sailed again in June, and after storms arrived at Laredo in July, where they captured an admiral's ship. Subsequently laid up at Brest, *La Couronne* was broken up in 1641, either because too many of her timbers were rotten to make repairs possible, or possibly because a jealous naval officer denied command of the ship arranged for her scrapping.

She was reputedly a good sailer, and much admired in England, Holland, and the other countries she visited in her brief career. Despite her great size, her arming was anachronistic when compared with Dutch and English practice. Although the inadequacy of galleys against larger ships had been confirmed during the siege of the Huguenot stronghold of La Rochelle in 1627–28, *La Couronne* was armed with 12 guns in the stern and 8 in the bows, as protection against the more maneuverable galleys. Moreover, she was lightly armed; England's SOVEREIGN OF THE SEAS (1637) carried 102 guns on a hull about 20 feet shorter than *La Couronne.*

It is interesting to note that the timbers used for construction of *La Couronne* were taken from the forests of the defeated Huguenot leader, Duc de Rohan. Asked her opinion of the new ship, the Duchess de Rohan remarked, with a partisan lack of enthusiasm, "I truly believe that the two forests of Monsieur de Rohan which have been used to build this ship were more beautiful than what I see."

Culver, *Forty Famous Ships.* Hancock, *"La Couronne."*

CRÉDIT AGRICOLE

Sloop. *L:* 56′ (17.1m). *Hull:* aluminum. *Comp.:* 1. *Des.:* Guy Ribadeau Dumas.

Following Robin Knox-Johnston's nonstop, solo round-the-world voyage in SUHAILI in 1968–69, it was only a matter of time before there was enough interest, and expertise, to warrant a round-the-world race. Thirteen years later, the British BOC Corporation stepped forward with the BOC Challenge, which attracted 17 starters. The voyage was conducted in four legs: Newport to Capetown, 7,100 miles; Cape Town to Sydney, 6,900 miles; Sydney to Rio de Janeiro, 8,250 miles; and Rio to Newport, 5,300 miles. The race started on August 28, 1982. Skippered by Philippe Jeantôt, *Crédit Agricole* (named for the French bank that sponsored her) won each of the four legs, with times of 47, 35, 47, and 28 days, respectively. She crossed the finish line off Newport on the morning of May 8, five hours later than expected because Jeantôt hove to in dirty weather. The total elapsed time of 159 days, 2 hours, 26 minutes over 27,550 miles was 12 days ahead of South Africa's Bertie Reed in *Altech Voortrekker* and shaved 10 days off the previous round-the-world record set in 1974 by the late Alain Colas in the trimaran *Manureva* (ex-*Pen Duick IV*). His time was also 28.5 days faster than the previous monohull record set the year before by Australia's Neville Gosson in *Leda Piere One*. Of the remaining fifteen vessels, two sank, two ran aground, and three withdrew because of damage, but no lives were lost.

Press reports.

CREOLE

Brig. Hull: wood. *Comp.:* ca. 150. *Built:* <1841.

On October 27, 1841, the American brig *Creole* sailed from Hampton Roads, Virginia, bound for New Orleans with a cargo of 135 slaves. Early in November, the slaves mutinied, killing a white crew member, taking possession of the vessel, and forcing the pilot to sail for Nassau, Bahama Islands. British authorities arrested nineteen of the ringleaders on criminal charges but freed the rest. Although the United States had outlawed the African slave trade in 1808 (one year after the British), it was still legal to transport slaves between domestic ports in coastal waters. In the meantime, Britain had emancipated slaves within the empire in 1833 and was vigorous in its persecution of the slave trade. Under various international treaties, British ships could stop and search suspected slavers, and in 1841 the United States was the only major maritime nation not committed to helping eradicate the slave trade.

President John Tyler's administration was by no means active in its opposition to slavery, and Secretary of State Daniel Webster demanded that the British extradite the slaves as mutineers, claiming that they were the lawful property of U.S. citizens. He also insisted on an indemnity for the conduct of the officials in Nassau. Britain's rejection of these demands heightened tensions between Washington and London, then in the midst of negotiations over the Webster-Ashburton Treaty. The slaves were not returned and the United States had to be content with an "apology for the necessity of the act." Under the terms of the treaty, signed in 1842, the United States agreed to form a squadron to patrol on the West African Station to suppress the slave trade. In 1855, a joint Anglo-American commission awarded the United States an indemnity of $110,330 for the freed slaves.

Flanders, *Dictionary of American Foreign Policy.*

HMS CRESSY

Cressy-class armoured cruiser (4f/2m). *L/B:* 472' × 69.5' (143.9m × 21.2m). *Tons:* 12,000 disp. *Hull:* steel. *Comp.:* 760. *Arm.:* 2 × 9.2", 12 × 6", 13 × 12pdr, 2 × 18"TT. *Armor:* 6" belt. *Mach.:* triple expansion, 2 screws; 21 kts. *Built:* Fairfield Shipbuilding & Engineering Co., Ltd., Govan, Scotland; 1901.

Named for Crécy, France, where Edward III defeated Philip VI of Valois in 1346, HMS *Cressy* first saw service on the China Station before returning to home waters in 1904. As part of the Grand Fleet's Third Cruiser Squadron based at the Nore, she was sunk, together with her sister ships ABOUKIR and HOGUE, while on patrol against German minelayers and torpedo boats in the Broad Fourteens off the Netherlands. After being hit by a torpedo fired by the German *U-9*, *Aboukir* signaled her consorts to stand by to pick up survivors. The possibility of a submarine torpedo having been the cause of *Aboukir*'s damage was not fully assessed, and *Cressy* and *Hogue* stopped their engines and put out their boats to rescue survivors. The *U-9* launched two torpedoes that split *Cressy*'s hull and ruptured her boilers; the ship sank at 0730 with the loss of 560 crew.

Coles, *Three before Breakfast.*

CROMARTYSHIRE

Ship (3m). *L/B/D:* 248.8' × 38.1' × 22.8' dph (75.8m × 11.6m × 6.9m). *Tons:* 1,462 grt. *Hull:* iron. *Built:* Russell & Co., Greenock, Scotland; 1879.

Thought to be the fastest of Thomas Law's Shire Line ships, one of the largest sailing ship lines of its day, *Cromartyshire* was the first of several Shire vessels ordered from Russell & Company. Her voyaging knew no set itinerary and among the passages found in her logs are London–Sydney, Iquique–Hamburg, Astoria–Queenstown, Barry–Nagasaki, Astoria–Dunkirk, and New Caledonia–Rotterdam. En route from Dunkirk to Philadelphia, Captain O. H. Henderson commanding, on July 4, 1898, she rammed the steel-hulled French passenger steamship LA BOURGOGNE, which sank with the loss of 549 passengers and crew off Cape Sable, in 43°N, 61°W. There were no lives lost in *Cromartyshire*, and after a three-month refit in Halifax she was towed to Philadelphia and there loaded for Valparaiso. On October 24, 1906, under Captain D. Nicholl, who joined her in 1902, she was wrecked at Printabu en route from Australia to Iquique, Chile.

Lubbock, *Last of the Windjammers.*

USS CUMBERLAND

Frigate (3m). *L/B/D:* 175′ bp × 45′ × 22.3′ (53.3m × 13.7m × 6.8m). *Tons:* 1,726 tons. *Hull:* wood. *Comp.:* 400. *Arm.:* 40 × 32pdr, 10 × 64pdr. *Built:* Boston Navy Yard; 1846.

Laid down in 1826, it was not until 1842 that USS *Cumberland* was commissioned as a frigate mounting 50 guns. Her varied service included tours with the Mediterranean Squadron (twice as flagship), and as flagship of the Home Squadron during the Mexican War. In 1856, she was razeed and reclassified as a sloop-of-war mounting 24 guns. She sailed as a squadron flagship twice more with the African Squadron (1857–59) and again with the Home Fleet in 1860.

Shortly after the start of the Civil War, on April 20, 1861, *Cumberland* narrowly escaped destruction at the Norfolk Navy Yard when Union soldiers burned as many ships as they could, including USS *Merrimack,* to prevent their capture by Confederate forces. Assigned to the North Atlantic Blockading Squadron, she captured eight prizes and took part in Silas Stringham's capture of Forts Clark and Hatteras at Hatteras Inlet on August 18–19. On March 8, 1862, she was anchored at the mouth of the James River off Newport News when CSS VIRGINIA — as the salvaged, engined, and iron-clad *Merrimack* was now known — sortied from Norfolk on her destructive maiden voyage. *Virginia* opened fire on USS CONGRESS at 1400 before closing with the more heavily armed *Cumberland,* mounting twenty-two 9-inch and one 10-inch smoothbore guns and one 70-pdr. rifled gun, and under temporary command of Lieutenant George Morris. Ninety minutes later, *Cumberland* sank, her flag still flying. In the interim, *Virginia*'s broadsides had raked the wooden ship's hull with devastating effect, while *Cumberland*'s defiant return fire ricocheted off her opponent. *Virginia* then rammed *Cumberland* on her starboard side. The loss of *Cumberland* and *Congress* that day signaled the beginning of the end of the "wooden walls" from behind which men had fought at sea for all of recorded history.

Selfridge, *Memoirs of Thomas O. Selfridge, Jr.* Silverstone, *Warships of the Civil War Navies.* U.S. Navy, *DANFS.*

CURAÇAO

(ex-*Calpe*) Paddle steamer (1f/3m). *L/B/D:* 130.5′ od × 26.9′ (44.9′ew) × 13.5′ (39.8m × 8.2m (13.7m) × 4.1m). *Tons:* 438 grt. *Hull:* wood. *Comp.:* 42. *Arm.:* 2 × 12pdr carr. *Mach.:* side-lever engines, 150 ihp, sidewheels; 8 kts. *Built:* J. H. & J. Duke, Dover, Eng.; 1825.

The schooner-rigged paddle steamer *Curaçao* was one of the first powered vessels to cross the Atlantic Ocean. She was launched as *Calpe* for service between Great Britain, North America, and the Caribbean. The American and Colonial Steam Navigation Company built the ship but in October 1826, the company sold her to the Netherlands. The first steam vessel in the Royal Netherlands Navy, on April 26, 1827, the renamed *Curaçao* sailed from Hellevoetsluis, near Rotterdam, for Paramaribo, Surinam. The first steamship to operate between Europe and South America, she made one voyage a year to Paramaribo between 1827 and 1829. She made the crossing in between twenty-five and thirty-two days, under steam as much as eighty percent of the time, and carrying as many as sixty-eight passengers. Built by Messrs. Maudslay, Sons and Field, *Curaçao*'s two-cylinder engines were designed so that the shafts could be disengaged and allowed to turn freely when the ship was under sail alone. During the 1830s, she remained in Dutch waters, but from 1840 to 1846 she served on the West Indies station. Laid up for her last four years, she was broken up in 1850.

Spratt, *Transatlantic Paddle Steamers.*

CUTTY SARK

(ex-*Maria di Amparo, Ferreira, Cutty Sark*) Clipper (3m). *L/B/D:* 212.5′ × 36′ × 21′ (64.8m × 11m × 6.4m). *Tons:* 963 grt. *Hull:* composite. *Comp.:* 19–28. *Des.:* Hercules Linton. *Built:* Scott, Linton & Co., Dumbarton, Scotland; 1869.

Among the most famous old sailing ships still extant, *Cutty Sark* was one of the last clippers built for the China tea trade between the 1840s and 1870s. Ordered by Captain John Willis of London, her hull was of composite construction, with teak planking on iron frames. Her design is thought to have been inspired by Willis's *The Tweed,* a Bombay-built, full-rigged ship that first sailed as the paddle steamer *Punjaub. Cutty Sark*'s name is Scottish for "short shirt" and comes from the Robert Burns poem "Tam O'Shanter," in which Tam secretly spies on the witch, Nannie, who is clad in a cutty sark; the reasons for Willis's choice of name are obscure.

Willis's insistence that only the finest materials be used in the construction of *Cutty Sark* resulted in the bankruptcy of her builders before the ship was launched, and her completion was overseen by the firm of Denny Brothers, which took over the Scott & Linton yard. *Cutty Sark*'s first years were disappointing to Willis. She never beat her chief rival, THERMOPYLAE, on the passage home from China. Their most dramatic encounter took place in

1872. Loading together at Shanghai, they sailed on the same tide and were neck and neck down the China Sea. About 400 miles ahead of *Thermopylae* in the Indian Ocean when she lost her rudder in a severe gale, *Cutty Sark*'s crew shipped a makeshift rudder made from spare spars but that too carried away, and they had to fashion a third, with which she completed the 16,000-mile passage in 119 days, behind *Thermopylae* but with the admiration of all London.

The greatest rivalry was not between individual clippers, however, but between clippers and steamships. Using the newly opened Suez Canal, steamers could return from China in only 60 days, thus forcing down the amount the sailing ships could make on their cargoes. By 1871, *Cutty Sark* was able to charge only £3 per 50 cubic feet of tea, less than half the offer in the years before the canal. Steamships had eased clippers out of the general cargo trade from England, too, and *Cutty Sark* had to sail first to Australia with a general cargo and then with coal for Shanghai, which gave her two paying cargoes outbound. Even such desperate measures were not enough, and by 1878 clippers were out of the tea trade. *Cutty Sark* was put to work hauling coal, jute, hemp, wool, and whatever other cargoes were available. She was barely profitable even in general trade because her cargo capacity was small in comparison with the slower, full-bodied sailing ships of the period.

In 1878, she loaded coal in Wales for the U.S. Navy in Shanghai. The voyage was a trying one. The first mate killed one of the hands and left the ship at Anjer before he could be brought to trial. (He was later caught, tried in London, and served seven years' penal servitude for manslaughter. Later he returned to sea and retired as master with the Anglo-American Oil Company.) When *Cutty Sark* was becalmed in the South China Sea, Captain Wallace went mad and leapt overboard. She suffered two more weak captains before coming under command of Captain W. Moore in 1882. After sailing from New York to Semarang with case oil, and then loading such exotic oriental goods as jaggery, myrobalans, and deer horn at Madras, Bimlipatam, and Coconada, she returned to England in 1883.

So began her third and most remarkable career. Sailing for Newcastle, Australia, she loaded a cargo of wool and returned home via Cape Horn in the excellent time of 79 days. As with tea, speed was a critical factor in the wool trade because the wool clip in Australia and the auctions in England were held only at specific times of year. On her second voyage, she again made the return in 79 days, the same time as *Thermopylae*. Moore left the ship and was succeeded by Richard Woodget, who became *Cutty Sark*'s most celebrated master. Except for one more stab

at the tea record — aborted because there was no tea to be had — *Cutty Sark* remained in the wool trade through 1893. Her best run from Sydney to England was 69 days, in 1888, and five years later she overhauled the P & O Line steamer *Britannia* on her approach to Sydney.

Cutty Sark completed her last voyage to Australia in 1895, when she was sold to J. A. Ferreira of Lisbon. As *Ferreira* she took up work in general trade between Lisbon and the Cape Verde Islands, the Gulf Coast, Caribbean, Brazil, and Portuguese East Africa, with occasional runs to British ports. In 1916 she was dismasted in a hurricane and rerigged as a barkentine. Four years later she was sold to the Cia. de Navegacão de Portugal and renamed *Maria di Amparo*. In 1922 she put into Falmouth where she was seen by Captain Wilfred Dowman. Later that year, Dowman purchased her and at his own expense brought her back to England where she was renamed *Cutty Sark* and restored for use as a full-rigged stationary training ship at Falmouth. When Dowman died in 1936, his widow donated the ship to the Thames Nautical Training College and she was moored in the Thames. In 1952, the Cutty Sark Preservation Society came together under the auspices of Frank Carr, director of the National Maritime Museum, and in 1954 she was opened as a museum at Greenwich.

Cutty Sark has had tremendous international renown since 1923 when the London vintners Berry Bros. & Rudd, Ltd., named their blended Scotch whiskey Cutty Sark. Two years after the ship opened to the public, Cutty Sark began its sponsorship of tall-ship races of the Sail Training Association (now International Sail Training Association).

Brettle, *"Cutty Sark."* Fox-Smith, *Return of the "Cutty Sark."* Lubbock, *Log of the "Cutty Sark."*

HMS CYANE

6th rate 22 (3m). *L/B/D:* 110′ × 31.5′ × 17.3′ dph (33.5m × 9.6m × 5.3m). *Tons:* 539 tons. *Hull:* wood. *Comp.:* 180. *Arm.:* 22 × 32pdr, 10 × 18pdr, 2 × 12pdr. *Built:* Bass, Topsham, Eng.; 1806.

Originally named *Columbine,* HMS *Cyane* was one of two frigates taken by the USS CONSTITUTION in a single action while covering a convoy en route from Gibraltar to England in company with HMS *Levant.* Although nominally rated as a 22-gun ship, she mounted a total of 34 guns, while *Levant* mounted 21. On the afternoon of February 20, 1815, while off Madeira, *Cyane* sighted a ship on the horizon and sailed towards her until failure of the unknown ship to answer recognition signals persuaded Captain Gordon Falcon to rejoin *Levant.* The mystery ship, the — nominally a 44, but mounting 50 guns — USS *Constitution,* caught up with the pair at about 1800 and opened fire with her 32-pdrs. well out of range of the British ships' carronades. *Constitution* forced first *Cyane* (6 dead, 29 wounded) and then *Levant* (6 dead, 16 wounded) to strike. Although *Levant* was recaptured by HMS *Acasta* on March 11, *Cyane* returned to the United States and was purchased by the U.S. Navy. From 1819 to 1821 she cruised between the West Indies and the newly founded West African colony of Liberia. She also saw duty in the Mediterranean (1824–25) and on the Brazil station (1825–27). Laid up at the Philadelphia Navy Yard, she was broken up in 1836.

Hepper, *British Warship Losses.* U.S. Navy, *DANFS.*

USS CYANE

Sloop-of-war (3m). *L/B/D:* 132.3′ bp × 36.3′ × 16.5′ (40.3m × 11m × 5m). *Tons:* 792 om. *Hull:* wood. *Comp.:* 200. *Arm.:* 18 × 32pdr, 4 × 24pdr. *Built:* Boston Navy Yard; 1838.

First assigned to the Mediterranean Squadron, the second USS *Cyane* was dispatched to the Pacific Squadron in 1841, a period of strained relations between the United States, Mexico, and Great Britain. Acting on erroneous information, on October 19, 1842, *Cyane*'s Captain William Melville seized Monterey and raised the U.S. flag, only to take it down when he learned there was no war. After a voyage to the East Coast, *Cyane* returned in time to take part in the Mexican War in 1846. On July 6, 1847, *Cyane* again seized Monterey — permanently — and then embarked Lieutenant Colonel John C. Frémont's California Battalion for San Diego. In company with USS *Warren, Cyane* attempted to enforce a blockade along 2,500 miles of Mexican coastline, seizing 30 Mexican vessels and taking part in the capture of Mazatlán on November 11 with USS CONGRESS and INDEPENDENCE. From 1852 to 1857, *Cyane* was assigned to the Home Squadron and cruised between Nova Scotia and Panama. She returned to the Pacific in 1858 and served on the West Coast between Panama and Alaska until laid up at Mare Island in 1871. She was sold in 1887.

Johnson, *Thence Round Cape Horn.* U.S. Navy, *DANFS.*

USS CYCLOPS

Collier. *L/B/D:* 542′ × 65′ × 27.7′ (165.2m × 19.8m × 8.1m). *Tons:* 19,360 disp. *Hull:* steel. *Comp.:* 236. *Mach.:* 15 kts. *Built:* William Cramp & Sons Ship & Engine Building Co., Philadelphia; 1910.

The Navy collier *Cyclops* served in the Navy Auxiliary Service of the Atlantic Fleet and saw duty on both sides of the Atlantic as well as in the Caribbean. During the Mexican troubles in 1914–15, she supported Navy warships stationed off Vera Cruz and also carried refugees from Tampico to New Orleans. Commissioned as a U.S. Navy ship following the American entry into World War I, she made one convoy run to Europe in June 1917 before returning to the East Coast. In January 1918 she was assigned to the Naval Overseas Transportation Service. Still under Lieutenant Commander G. W. Worley, her captain since 1910, she sailed to Brazil to fuel British ships stationed in the South Atlantic. On February 19, she departed Rio de Janeiro, and after calling at Barbados on March 3–4, continued on for the United States. *Cyclops* subsequently vanished without trace in what remains one of the Navy's most mystifying unexplained losses.

U.S. Navy, *DANFS.*

D

DAHSHUR BOATS

In 1893, French archaeologist Jacques de Morgan found six boats buried near the tomb of the Middle Kingdom pharaoh Sesostris III (1878–1842 BCE) at Dahshur, southwest of Cairo. Morgan surmised that these were part of the burial equipment of Sesostris and intended for the pharaoh's journey in the afterlife, as was the CHEOPS SHIP of seven centuries before. The oldest ships known until the discovery of the Cheops ship, two of the boats are exhibited in Cairo, a third is at the Field Museum in Chicago, and a fourth, whose excavation was not formally recorded, was purchased by Andrew Carnegie for the Carnegie Museum of Natural History. Their measurements and construction are similar. The Field boat measures 9.8 meters long by 2.5 meters broad by 1.2 meters deep (32.1 by 8.2 by 3.9 feet); those in the Cairo Museum are 10.2 by 2.2 by 0.9 meters (33.5 by 7.2 by 3 feet), and 9.9 by 2.3 by 0.7 meters (32.5 by 7.5 by 2.3 feet). There are three strakes topped by a bulwark lashed to the sheer strake on either side of the central plank; the planks are fastened along their long edges by mortise-and-tenon joints. There are no ribs, but all the boats had some

Among the oldest ships in the world are those found in the burial tombs of Egyptian pharaohs. The Dhashur boat now in the Field Museum in Chicago is one of four found near the tomb of Sesostris III (1878–1842 BCE). Courtesy Field Museum, Chicago.

decking. In some cases there are peg holes in deck plank ends, but most pieces were simply laid onto the dadoed deck edges; slender stanchions supported the beams in all boats. All the boats had rudder posts topped by falcon heads — a sign of royalty — to support the elaborately painted quarter rudders used to steer the boat. The boats probably were fitted with a baldachin under which a coffin would lie, and decorative elongated bow and stern pieces were probably fitted to give the vessels a papyriform shape, so called for their resemblance to papyrus rafts. Like the Cheops ship, these boats were intended to be towed. The similarity of the design and function of the Sesostris and Cheops boats attests to the continuity of the pharaonic tradition over more than seven centuries.

Ward, *Sacred and Secular*.

HMS DANAE

(ex-*La Vaillante*) 6th rate 20 (3m). *L/B/D:* 119.2′ × 30.9′ × 8.9′ (36.3m × 9.4m × 2.7m). *Tons:* 507 bm. *Hull:* wood. *Comp.:* 155. *Arm.:* 20 × 32pdr, 6 × 12pdr, 6 × 12pdr. *Built:* Bayonne, France; 1796.

The first mission of the French frigate *La Vaillante* was to carry reactionaries arrested in the coup d'état of September 4, 1797, to Cayenne, French Guinea. Sailing on September 24, 1797, she made the passage out in about six weeks, and by January 1798 was back in France. Sent out again on August 6, 1798, with fifty-two *déportés,* including four women and a child, she was captured two days later by Captain Sir Edward Pellew's HMS *Indefatigable.* Taken into the Royal Navy and renamed *Danae* (for a woman in Greek myth), she was rearmed with twenty 32-pdr. carronades, ten 12-pdr. carronades, and two 6-pdr. "longs," the weight of which made her top-heavy.

Although *Danae*'s complement was technically 155, British ships of the era were chronically undermanned and by March 1799 *Danae* had only seventy-one crew. Assigned to operate against French merchantmen and privateers between Le Havre and Brest, she returned periodically to Plymouth, and in November of that year she joined the Channel Fleet to cruise off Ushant. All along, Captain Lord Proby had augmented her crew by signing on men captured from French ships or impressed from English merchantmen and privateers. By the end of February 1800, *Danae*'s crew had grown to 130 crew and marines, including five French prisoners and seven crew claiming U.S. citizenship. On the night of March 14, 1800, about forty of the crew mutinied and seized the ship off Le Conquet, near Brest, and the next morning *Danae* sailed into Le Conquet accompanied by the frigate *La Colombe*. Proby and his loyal crew were exchanged. There were forty-six mutineers, many of American or Irish origin. Most returned to sea and only three were captured by the British and tried. All were found guilty, two were hanged, and one pardoned.

The French considered *Danae* no longer suitable for naval duty and she was sold to a Morlaix merchant named Cooper who chartered her to the French government as a transport. *Danae* made one voyage to Haiti during the uprising led by Toussaint L'Ouverture in 1801. The ship's fate after 1802 is unknown.

Lyon, *Sailing Navy List*. Pope, *Devil Himself*.

DANMARK

Ship (3m). *L/B/D:* 178.8′ × 32.8′ × 13.8′ (54.5m × 10m × 4.2m). *Tons:* 777 grt. *Hull:* steel. *Comp.:* 99. *Mach.:* diesel, 486 hp. *Des.:* Aage Larsen. *Built:* Nakskov Skibs., Nakskov, Denmark; 1932.

Built by the Danish government as a vehicle for training cadet officers for work in the merchant marine, *Danmark* was built along the lines of a traditional merchantman. Praising her graceful lines, Harold Underhill wrote: "She has a perfectly normal profile with poop, fo'castle and deckhouse, and, if one substituted hatches for the cadets' companion, she would be an ordinary trader which is as it should be." Her uneventful career prior to World War II culminated in a voyage to the New York World's Fair in 1939. She was slated to return to Europe in the fall, but her sailing was put off following the start of the war in September and she sailed for the Caribbean. When Germany invaded Denmark in April 1940, she returned to Jacksonville, Florida, where she remained until the United States entered the war, when Captain Knud Hansen offered her to the U.S. government. The Coast Guard welcomed the offer of a training ship and *Danmark* was homeported at the U.S. Coast Guard Academy in New London, Connecticut, serving as a training ship in the relatively protected waters of Long Island Sound for the duration of hostilities. This experience so convinced the

Coast Guard of the value of sail training that, following *Danmark*'s return to Europe after the war, it lobbied for the government to acquire the German training ship *Horst Wessel* — now USCGC EAGLE — as war reparations. *Danmark* resumed her regular sail-training program, and she remains in that work more than half a century later.

Brouwer, *International Register of Historic Ships*. Underhill, *Sail Training and Cadet Ships*.

DAR POMORZA

(ex-*Pomorze Colbert, Prinzess Eitel Friedrich*) Ship (3m). *L/B/D:* 239.2′ × 41.1′ × 20.9′ (72.9m × 12.5m × 6.4). *Tons:* 1,566 grt. *Hull:* steel. *Comp.:* 162. *Mach.:* aux. *Built:* Blohm & Voss, Hamburg; 1910.

After four years as a training ship for Bremen's Deutscher Schulschiff Verein, preparing cadets for the German merchant marine, *Prinzess Eitel Friedrich* was laid up during World War I. Transferred to France as war reparations in 1919, she was laid up at St. Nazaire. Sold in 1922 to the Société des Armateurs Français, three years later she was acquired by the Société de Navigation "Les Navires Ecoles Français" and renamed *Colbert*. Plans to convert the ship to a yacht by Baron de Forest came to nothing, and in 1929 she was sold for the last time, to the government of Poland. Renamed *Dar Pomorza*, she was taken in tow for Nakskov, arriving there in January 1930.

Thus began more than five decades of a career as a schoolship under the Polish flag, sailing every year from the Baltic to the West Indies with between 150 and 200 cadets aboard. Interned in Sweden during World War II, she later returned to service as a sail-training ship under the auspices of the Wyzsza Szkola Morska until 1981. In that year she was replaced by the new *Dar Mlodziezy* and preserved as a stationary museum ship at Gdynia.

Brouwer, *International Register of Historic Ships*. Underhill, *Sail Training and Cadet Ships*. Villiers & Picard, *Bounty Ships of France*.

DARTMOUTH

Ship (3m). *L:* 79′ (24m). *Hull:* wood. *Built:* <1773.

In the spring of 1773, the nearly bankrupt East India Company received permission from Parliament to sell tea directly to the American market, rather than through middlemen in England, at prices that would undercut smugglers who evaded duties by importing from Holland. The question of the surplus tea was itself inconsequential, but the focus of debate quickly became the Townshend duties, an onerous tax that depressed imports into the colonies and netted the Crown only £400. Despite dire predictions from such Parliamentarians as William Dowdeswell — "I tell the Noble Lord now, if he don't take off the duty they won't take the tea" — Prime Minister Lord North refused to repeal the taxes.

Six vessels left for the colonies in the fall of 1773, George Hayley's ships *Dartmouth* (Captain James Hall) and *Eleanor* and brigs *Beaver* and *William* for Boston, and the ships *London* for Charleston and *Polly* for Philadelphia. News of the company's plan reached the colonies before the tea itself, and when *Dartmouth* arrived at Boston on November 28, with 114 chests of tea, Bostonians refused to allow the tea to be landed and demanded that it be returned to England. Above all, the patriots feared that even if the duties were not paid, the authorities would seize the tea and it would eventually be paid for and drunk even by those opposed to the duties, thus weakening their cause. *Dartmouth*'s owner Francis Rotch was unable to get a pass to clear his ship with the tea still aboard. As the tea was liable to seizure by the authorities after 20 days, on the evening of December 16 a group of 30 to 60 unknown patriots calling themselves Mohawks but disguised with nothing more than a blanket, a daub of paint, or blackened faces, descended on the ships, broke open the tea chests aboard *Dartmouth, Eleanor,* and *Beaver* at Griffin's Wharf, and dumped the contents into Boston Harbor. (*William* never made it to Boston, having wrecked on Cape Cod. A replica of the *Beaver* is exhibited at the Boston Tea Party Ship and Museum.)

Despite being eyewitnesses to the event, which lasted three hours, no military authorities took any action against the tea patriots. As John Adams confided to his diary,

> This is the most magnificent Movement of all. There is a Dignity, a Majesty, a Sublimity in this last Effort of the Patriots that I greatly admire. . . . This Destruction of the Tea is so bold, so daring, so firm, intrepid, & inflexible, and it must have so important Consequences and so lasting, that I cannot but consider it as an Epocha in History.

Meanwhile, at Charleston, the consignees refused to pay the duties within the 20-day period and on December 22, *London*'s cargo was seized by the authorities. Stored in government warehouses, it remained untouched until July 1776 when it was sold to raise funds for the patriots' cause.

Labaree, *Boston Tea Party.*

LA DAUPHINE

Ship (3m). Tons: 100 tons. *Comp.:* 50. *Built:* Royal Dockyard, Le Havre; 1517.

Named for the French Dauphin, born the year before the ship's launch, *La Dauphine* was a French royal ship sailed by Giovanni Verrazzano on his westward voyage in search of Cathay and the extreme eastern coast of Asia, or a passage through any land that might lie in his way. Provisioned for eight months, Verrazzano sailed from Dieppe with *La Dauphine* and *La Normande,* which soon returned to France. Taking his departure from the Madeira Islands on about January 17, 1523, *La Dauphine* sailed straight west to near Cape Fear, North Carolina. The ship then sailed south about 225 miles before turning north again. Landing briefly near Cape Fear, *La Dauphine* then sailed along the barrier islands that enclose Pimlico Sound, which Verrazzano initially believed to be the Pacific Ocean, separated from the Atlantic only by the slender Outer Banks. *La Dauphine* next stopped at Arcadia (possibly Kitty Hawk), before sailing offshore until arriving at what is now southern New Jersey. The next identifiable anchorage was New York Bay, where *La Dauphine* anchored the night of April 17 in the Verrazzano Narrows.

Heading east they rounded the tip of Long Island and came into Narragansett Bay, passing Block Island, which Verrazzano compared with the Mediterranean island of Rhodes. (Roger Williams later thought he meant Aquidneck, and in time the name was applied to Rhode Island; Verrazzano had actually named Block Island for the French queen mother, Luisa.) A Wampanoag piloted *La Dauphine* into the future Newport harbor, where Verrazzano anchored for two weeks. After working her way through Vineyard and Nantucket Sounds and rounding Cape Cod, *La Dauphine* next landed among the Abnaki near Casco Bay, and worked east from there along the Maine coast. Here, on the Penobscot River, Verrazzano recorded the Abnaki name "Oranbega." Europeans corrupted this to "Norumbega" and used it to refer to the whole region now known as New England. After skirting Nova Scotia and Newfoundland, where the Portuguese and English had preceded him, he sailed for home, arriving at Dieppe on July 8, 1524. *La Dauphine*'s voyage is important because it was the first to determine that North America was not an extension of Asia. Verrazzano made two subsequent transatlantic voyages, one to Brazil and his last in 1528 when he was killed and eaten by Caribs on Guadeloupe.

Morison, *European Discovery of America: The Northern Voyages.* Wroth, *Voyages of Giovanni da Verrazzano.*

CSS DAVID

Spar torpedo boat. *L/B/D:* 50′ × 6′ × 5′ (15.2m × 1.8m × 1.5m). *Comp.:* 4. *Built:* T. Stoney, Charleston, S.C.; 1863.

Presumably named for the Israelite David in recognition of his battle with Goliath, CSS *David* was built by T. Stroney of Charleston, South Carolina. Shaped like a cigar and designed to operate very low in the water, *David* and the ten other Confederate torpedo boats built at Charleston were intended to sink Federal blockade ships by detonating an explosive charge against the ships' hulls, the explosive being carried on the end of a spar projecting from the bow.

On the night of October 5, 1863, Lieutenant W. T. Glassell commanding, *David* attacked the casemate ironclad steamer USS NEW IRONSIDES. The torpedo detonated under *New Ironsides*'s starboard quarter causing serious damage but throwing up a column of water that extinguished *David*'s boiler fires. All but the pilot, W. Cannon, abandoned ship, though Assistant Engineer J. H. Tomb returned to the vessel. The engines were eventually restarted and *David* made it to safety. (Glassell and J. Sullivan were captured.) *David* is known to have staged two more attacks, neither successful. The first was on March 6, 1864, against USS *Memphis,* and the second was on April 18, when she tried to sink USS *Wabash.* Her ultimate fate is unknown.

Perry, *Infernal Machines.* Silverstone, *Warships of the Civil War Navies.*

DAVID CROCKETT

Clipper (3m). *L/B/D:* 218.8′ × 41′ × 27′ (66.7m × 12.5m × 8.2m). *Tons:* 1,679 bm. *Hull:* wood. *Built:* Greenman & Co., Mystic, Conn.; 1853.

Named for the celebrated American frontiersman and built for Handy & Everett's transatlantic packet trade between New York and Liverpool, the clipper *David Crockett* combined large carrying capacity with good speed and was regarded by some as "almost perfect." As it happened, she made only a few voyages on the transatlantic run before entering the Cape Horn run between New York and San Francisco under the house flag of Lawrence Giles and Company. In this hard trade, *David Crockett* proved one of the most successful clippers ever launched. Having cost $93,000 to build, by the time she quit the Cape Horn trade in 1883, after twenty-five passages from New York to San Francisco, she had earned a net profit of $500,000, and there is no record of any loss to her insurers for any cause. Sold first to Thomas Dunhams Nephew

& Company and then to S. W. Carey, she was rerigged as a bark for service in the Atlantic. In 1890, after nearly four decades under sail, she was sold to Peter Wright & Son, of Philadelphia, and cut down for use as a coal barge "to any port where there is water enough to float her." With leg-of-mutton sails set from stump masts, in this ignominious work she ended her days around the turn of the century. Her figurehead, which was displayed only when in port, survives in the San Francisco Chamber of Commerce.

Howe & Matthews, *American Clipper Ships.*

DE BRAAK

Brig-sloop (2m). *L/B/D:* 84′ × 28.9′ × 11.2′ (25.6m × 8.8m × 3.4m). *Tons:* 255 bm. *Hull:* wood. *Comp.:* 86. *Arm.:* 16 × 24pdr, 2 × 6pdr. *Built:* Britain(?); <1784.

One of the most inept maritime archaeological excavations ever undertaken, the bungled salvage of HMS *Braak* incidentally helped ensure the passage of legislation to develop a rational approach to the preservation of historic underwater sites. The origins of the cutter *De Braak* (Dutch for "The Beagle") are obscure. Although it was long believed that she was Dutch-built, analysis of the hull suggests that she was probably built in Britain. During the 1780s, she sailed against England under the Dutch flag, operating with a Mediterranean squadron out of Toulon, France. In 1793, she took part in the defense of Willemstad, Curaçao, against a French Revolutionary army, and at the end of 1794, *De Braak* was ordered to escort a convoy of East Indiamen to Batavia. Not realizing that their country was again at war with England, the Dutch put into Falmouth where the twenty-four merchantmen and six warships were seized.

Brought into the Royal Navy as HM Sloop-of-War *Braak,* the cutter was rerigged as a brig and rearmed with sixteen 24-pdr. carronades. She entered service under Captain James Drew on June 13, 1797, and remained on duty until dismasted in a storm at the end of the year. Upon her return to service in February 1798, *Braak* joined a convoy bound for the Virginia Capes, but on April 2, off the Azores, she was separated from the other ships. At the end of the month, she captured a Spanish ship worth £160,000 in prize money and on May 25, Captain Drew put into Delaware Bay. Shortly after a pilot boarded off Cape Henlopen, "a sudden flaw of wind" threw the brig on her beam ends and *Braak* sank with the loss of thirty-five of her crew, including Drew, and twelve Spanish prisoners.

Over the years, *De Braak*'s seven-week solo cruise and

the certain fact that she had captured one valuable prize became encrusted with myth. Over the years more than a dozen individuals and groups attempted to find the ship, and by the 1980s estimates of the value of the treasure aboard the humble convoy escort exceeded $500 million. Would-be salvors ran the gamut from salvage experts to charlatans, "sportsmen and socialites," and a convicted felon who initiated his research from the Michigan State Penitentiary. Success of a sort finally came in 1984 when Harvey Harrington's Sub-Sal, Inc., raised a cannon, an anchor, and a ship's bell bearing the name "La Patrocle." Sub-Sal became legal custodian of the wreck on behalf of the U.S. District Court and with a one-year lease began working round-the-clock to retrieve as much as possible from the site. With almost total disregard for archaeological practice, divers tagged a portion of what they recovered and disposed of anything they considered worthless, including human remains, a rare stove, and objects too small to warrant their consideration.

In 1985, Sub-Sal was taken over by a New Hampshire investment group led by L. John Davidson. The state of Delaware began to take a more active interest in the project and assigned Claudia Melson to tag retrieved artifacts, which ultimately included 26,000 items ranging from ship fittings, weapons, and ammunition to toothbrushes, combs, dominoes, a syringe, compasses and dividers, a mahogany telescope, an octant, a sink, 150 shoes, a sailor's "Monmouth" hat, three anchors, storage vessels, and hundreds of specimens of organic foodstuffs including peas, corn, and beans. Determined at all costs to find the ship's treasure, Davidson secured permission to move the 200-year-old hull ashore and excavate the surrounding bottom with a clamshell bucket. During this "historic humiliation," as one archaeologist described it, the hull was raised at a rate of thirty feet per minute (rather than 1.5 feet per minute, regarded as the maximum safe speed). The lifting cables cut into the hull "like a hot knife through butter" and tons of artifact-rich mud and individual artifacts slipped back into the sea. To crown this folly, the surrounding mud was sifted through a road construction rock sorter. All told, the "unmitigated archaeological disaster" of De Braak's salvage cost $2.5 million and yielded a "treasure" of 650 gold, silver, and other coins. The majority of the artifacts were housed in the Zwaanendal Museum in Lewes, Delaware, and the hull was eventually moved to a special facility in Cape Henlopen State Park.

While the underfunded conservation of artifacts continued, the excavation brought to the fore the inadequate state of legal protection for underwater archaeological sites. The law then held that historic shipwrecks and their contents enjoyed no more protection than any other property abandoned at sea; historical value was not considered as it would be in the case of, for example, a Navajo pueblo on dry land. To correct this, archaeologists and preservationists helped draft legislation to protect historic underwater sites. Testifying before Congress in support of the Abandoned Shipwreck Act of 1987, President of the National Trust for Historic Preservation J. Jackson Walter alluded to the De Braak site when he argued that "we would not tolerate a commercial enterprise that bulldozed Gettysburg and then dumped the remains through a sifting machine to recover valuable objects. Yet this is exactly what current law allows treasure hunters to do to our nation's maritime legacy." Signed into law in April 1988, the act gives the federal government title to historic shipwrecks in state waters.

Shomette, Hunt for HMS "De Braak."

HMS DEFENCE

Arrogant-class 3rd rate 74 (3m). *L/B/D:* 168′ × 46.8′ × 19.8′ (51.2m × 14.3m × 6m). *Tons:* 1,630 bm. *Hull:* wood. *Comp.:* 530. *Arm.:* 28 × 32pdr, 28 × 18pdr, 18 × 9pdr. *Hull:* wood. *Des.:* Sir Thomas Slade. *Built:* Devonport Dockyard, Eng.; 1763.

Launched in the last year of the Seven Years' War between France and Britain, HMS *Defence* was the first — and most decorated — Royal Navy ship to bear the name. She did not see action for the first two decades of service, but thereafter her honors include most of the major engagements of the Franco-British contest for supremacy. In 1782, *Defence* was part of Admiral Sir Edward Hughes's fleet at the battle of Cuddalore, India (a subsidiary theater of the American Revolution), against Admiral Pierre de Suffren de St. Tropez. Her first major engagement in European waters was on the Glorious First of June in 1795, when as part of Admiral Lord Howe's Channel Fleet she managed to break the French line under Admiral Villaret-Joyeuse. On February 14, 1797, *Defence* was with Admiral Sir John Jervis's Mediterranean Fleet when it engaged the Spanish fleet under Admiral Don Jose de Cordoba at the Battle of Cape St. Vincent. The following year she was in Rear Admiral Horatio Nelson's fleet at the Battle of the Nile (August 1, 1798), and three years after that at the Battle of Copenhagen (April 2, 1801), as part of Admiral Sir Hyde Parker's squadron. Under Captain George Hope, *Defence* sailed in Admiral Collingwood's lee column at the Battle of Trafalgar on October 21, 1805, where she engaged the French *Berwick* and forced the surrender of the Spanish *San Ildefonso,* which sustained

165 dead and wounded to her own 36. Later detailed to the Baltic fleet, on Christmas Eve 1811, while en route from the Baltic to Britain in company with Rear Admiral Robert Reynolds's flagship, ST. GEORGE, *Defence* ran aground and was lost near Ringkøbing, Denmark; only five of her company survived.

Hepper, *British Warship Losses*. Schom, *Trafalgar*.

DEFENCE

Brigantine. *L/B:* 72' × 20' (21.9m × 6.1m). *Tons:* 170 burthen. *Hull:* wood. *Arm.:* 16 × 6pdr. *Built:* John Cabot and Israel Thorndike, Beverly, Mass.; 1779.

Defence was one of an estimated 1,600 vessels issued with letters of marque and reprisal to sail as privateers against British merchant ships during the American Revolution. Her career was very short-lived, for on her maiden voyage she joined the Penobscot expedition. This disastrous undertaking, led by Captain Dudley Saltonstall in WARREN, was intended to push the British out of their new stronghold on the Bagaduce Peninsula in Penobscot Bay, 175 miles northeast of Boston. Saltonstall's force consisted of forty ships, including *Defence,* whose owners intended to continue from Maine to the rich privateering grounds of the Gulf of St. Lawrence. Despite early successes, on August 13, 1779, Saltonstall's forces collapsed in the face of a powerful British force and burned or scuttled their whole fleet to avoid capture. *Defence* sank into the soft preserving mud of Stockton Bay and remained there undisturbed until 1972. That summer, students from the Maine Marine Academy located the remains of the ship with a homemade sonar device in 44°30'N, 68°30'E. Archaeologists from the Institute of Nautical Archaeology excavated the site for seven seasons during which they recovered extensive amounts of ship fittings and personal possessions. The latter included bottles of French origin, ceramic products of domestic manufacture, five complete mess kits, notions such as buttons and buckles, and shoes and other items that offer a rare glimpse into shipboard life in the late colonial period.

Smith, "Life at Sea." Switzer, "Privateers, not Pirates."

HMS DEFENCE

Minotaur-class armored cruiser (4f/2m). *L/B/D:* 519' × 74.5' × 26' (158.2m × 22.7m × 7.9m). *Tons:* 16,100 disp. *Hull:* steel. *Comp.:* 755. *Arm.:* 4 × 9.2" (2 × 2), 10 × 7.5", 16 × 12pdr; 5 × 18"TT. *Armor:* 6" belt, 2" deck. *Mach.:* triple expansion, 27,000 hp, 2 screws; 23 kts. *Des.:* E. N. Mooney. *Built:* Pembroke Dockyard, Eng.; 1907.

Assigned first to the Home Fleet and then to the China station (1910–12), at the beginning of World War I HMS *Defence* was the flagship of Admiral Ernest Troubridge's First Cruiser Squadron in the Mediterranean. Ordered to avoid a superior force, Troubridge followed, but failed to engage, the German GOEBEN and BRESLAU, which escaped to Constantinople in August 1914. Although cleared by a court-martial, his sea duty was at an end. After duty at the Dardanelles, *Defence* was sent to the South Atlantic. Recalled to home waters, *Defence* became the flagship of Rear Admiral Sir Robert Arbuthnot's First Cruiser Squadron. At the Battle of Jutland on May 31, 1916, Arbuthnot took *Defence* and her sister ships HMS *Warrior* and *Black Prince* to attack the light cruiser SMS *Wiesbaden,* which lay dead in the water between the opposing fleets. Brought under concentrated fire from Rear Admiral Paul Behncke's Third Battle Squadron, *Defence* sank with the loss of all her 893 crew at 1815. *Warrior* and *Black Prince* withdrew, but around midnight the latter blundered back into the German line and was sunk with the loss of 857 men.

Halpern, *Naval History of World War I*. Parkes, *British Battleships*.

HMS DEFIANCE

Elizabeth-class 3rd rate 74 (3m). *L/B/D:* 168.5' × 46.8' × 19.8' (51.4m × 14.3m × 6m). *Tons:* 1,613 bm. *Hull:* wood. *Comp.:* 550–600. *Arm.:* 28 × 32pdr, 28 × 18pdr, 18 × 9pdr. *Des.:* Sir Thomas Slade. *Built:* Messrs. Randall & Co., Rotherhithe, Eng.; 1783.

Launched in 1783, the Royal Navy's tenth HMS *Defiance* was first commissioned, into the Channel Fleet, in 1794. Living up to her name, the ship was involved in three separate mutinies: in 1794, when five of her crew were hanged; 1797, the year of the Spithead mutinies; and 1798, when twenty members of the United Irishmen in her crew were hanged. From 1799 to 1801, *Defiance* sailed with Lord St. Vincent's Mediterranean Fleet. In the latter year she sailed with Admiral Sir Hyde Parker to the Baltic to break up Napoleon's Northern Coalition. On April 2, *Defiance* was part of the British fleet commanded by Rear Admiral Nelson at the Battle of Copenhagen. During the engagement against the Danish fleet and shore batteries, *Defiance*'s casualties included seventy-five dead and wounded.

In 1804 *Defiance* joined Admiral Sir Robert Calder's blockading force off El Ferrol and Cadiz. Under Captain Charles Durham, she took part in the inconclusive action of July 22, 1805, against Vice Admiral Pierre Villeneuve's Combined Fleet off El Ferrol. Nelson replaced Calder in

September, and on October 21 he led his fleet against the Combined Fleet at Trafalgar, *Defiance* in the lee column. After first engaging *Principe de Asturias* (112 guns), she closed with the French *L'Aigle* (74), which struck after a furious engagement that left more than 400 of *L'Aigle's* crew dead or wounded. *Defiance* later captured *San Juan Nepomuceno* (74). Trafalgar cost *Defiance* seventy dead and wounded, and she was all but dismasted in the action.

An interesting postscript to the ship's Trafalgar experience occurred in 1841, when Queen Victoria ordered that surviving members of the lower deck be acknowledged for their service to the Royal Navy between 1793 and 1840. As Robert H. Mackenzie relates,

> Amongst the claimants for the medal and clasp was Jane Townsend, a woman who was present in the ship [at Trafalgar]. As the regulations for the award of the medal contained no reservations as to sex, and as her services were reported as highly satisfactory and useful, her claim was at first admitted; but on reconsideration refused, as it appeared to the Board that complication would arise on account of there being so many other women in the ships of the fleet whose services were reported as equally useful.

Defiance returned to duty in 1806. She sailed in the Bay of Biscay and landed Lieutenant General Arthur Wellesley (later the Duke of Wellington) at La Coruña, Spain, at the start of the Peninsular Campaign in 1808. On February 22, 1809, she took part in an action with three French frigates off Sable d'Olonne and suffered thirty dead and wounded. After repairs, her squadron sailed into Ferrol and captured five Spanish ships, which the British rigged and sailed as prizes to Cadiz. *Defiance* was used as a prison ship at Chatham from 1813 to 1816, when she was broken up.

Kennedy, "Bligh and the *Defiance* Mutiny." Longridge, *Anatomy of Nelson's Ships.* Mackenzie, *Trafalgar Roll.*

USS DELPHY (DD-261)

Clemson-class destroyer (4f/2m). *L/B/D:* 314.4′ × 31.7′ × 9.3′ (95.8m × 9.7m × 2.8m). *Tons:* 1,190 disp. *Hull:* steel. *Comp.:* 120. *Arm.:* 4 × 4″, 2 × 3″; 4 × 21″TT. *Mach.:* geared turbines, 26,000 shp, 2 screws; 35 kts. *Built:* Bethlehem Shipbuilding Corp., Squantum, Mass.; 1918.

Midshipman Richard Delphy served in USS UNITED STATES and ARGUS during the War of 1812, and was killed in the latter ship's engagement with HMS *Pelican.* His namesake's career was no less brief or tragic. Commissioned shortly before the end of World War I, USS

Delphy served briefly in the Atlantic Fleet before transferring to the Pacific Fleet based at San Diego in 1919. On September 8, 1923, she was sailing as the lead ship of Destroyer Division 31, together with 20 other ships bound from San Francisco for San Diego. Steaming at 20 knots, *Delphy* shaped a course down the Santa Barbara Channel. Unbeknownst to anyone in the fogbound fleet, the ships were 30 miles off course. *Delphy* ran onto the rocks of Point Pedernales, about 75 miles north of Santa Barbara. Within minutes, six more destroyers — USS *S. P. Lee, Young, Nicholas, Woodbury, Chauncey* (flag), and *Fuller* — had piled onto the rocks. A total of 22 men died in the disaster. The ships were a total loss and sold for salvage where they lay.

Gibbs, *Shipwrecks of the Pacific Coast.* U.S. Navy, *DANFS.*

DELTA QUEEN

Riverboat (1f). *L/B/D:* 285′ × 58′ × 11.5′ (86.9m ′ × 17.7m × 3.5m). *Tons:* 1,650 grt. *Hull:* steel. *Comp.:* 200 pass. *Mach.:* compound engine, 2,000 ihp, sternwheel. *Built:* California Transportation Co., Stockton, Calif.; 1926.

Prefabricated at the Isherwood Yard on the River Clyde in Scotland, *Delta Queen* and her sister ship *Delta King* were shipped in pieces to Stockton, California. There the California Transportation Company assembled the two vessels for their regular Sacramento River service between San Francisco and Sacramento, and excursions to Stockton, on the San Joaquin River. At the time, they were the most lavishly appointed and expensive sternwheel passenger boats ever commissioned. Driven out of service by a new highway linking Sacramento with San Francisco in 1940, the two vessels were laid up and then purchased by Isbrandtsen Steamship Lines for service out of New Orleans. During World War II, they were requisitioned by the U.S. Navy for duty in San Francisco Bay.

In 1946, *Delta Queen* was purchased by Greene Line Steamers of Cincinnati and towed via the Panama Canal and the Mississippi and Ohio Rivers to be refurbished in Pittsburgh. In 1948 she entered regular passenger service plying the waters of the Ohio, Mississippi, Tennessee, Cumberland, and Tennessee Rivers between Cincinnati, New Orleans, St. Paul, Chattanooga, Nashville, and ports in between. Ownership of the vessel has changed a number of times over the last fifty years, and since 1971, *Delta Queen* has operated with a presidential exemption to the law prohibiting the operation of overnight passenger vessels with wooden superstructures.

Greene, *Long Live the "Delta Queen."* Way, *Way's Packet Directory.*

SMS DERFFLINGER

Derfflinger-class battlecruiser (2f/2m). *L/B/D:* 690.4′ × 95.2′ × 31.2′ (210.4m × 29m × 9.5m). *Tons:* 31,200 disp. *Hull:* steel. *Comp.:* 1,182. *Arm.:* 8 × 12″ (4x2), 12 × 6″, 12 × 3.5″; 4 × 21″TT. *Armor:* 12″ belt. *Mach.:* steam turbines, 63,000 shp, 4 screws; 26.5 kts. *Built:* Blohm & Voss, Hamburg; 1914.

Launched in 1913, SMS *Derfflinger* was not commissioned until just after the outbreak of World War I, on September 1, 1914. She was named for seventeenth-century Brandenburg field marshal Baron Georg von Derfflinger. She first saw action during the bombardment of Scarborough on December 16, 1914, and on January 24, 1915, she was part of Rear Admiral Franz von Hipper's first reconnaissance group at the Battle of Dogger Bank, during which she received one hit. Although she saw action against Russian units in the Gulf of Riga in August, it was more than a year before she sortied again into the North Sea. On April 24, 1916, she took part in the bombardment of Yarmouth and Lowestoft. On May 31, she was part of the High Seas fleet at the Battle of Jutland where, in consort with SMS SEYDLITZ, she sank the battlecruiser HMS *Queen Mary* and, with SMS LÜTZOW, HMS INVINCIBLE. *Derfflinger* herself was struck by seventeen heavy and four medium hits and limped home with 3,000 tons of water in the hold. She underwent repairs at Kiel, but except for a brief sortie into the North Sea in April 1918, her war career was over. Following the armistice, she was interned at Scapa Flow where, on June 21, 1919, she was scuttled, together with the rest of the German fleet, and sank in 150 feet of water. *Derfflinger* was finally raised in 1939. But salvage operations were interrupted by World War II, and she remained moored upside down off Rysa Island until 1948 when she was finally towed to Rosyth and broken up.

Breyer, *Battleships and Battlecruisers.* van der Vat, *Grand Scuttle.*

DE RUYTER

Cruiser (1f/2m). *L/B/D:* 560.1′ × 51.1′ × 16.8′ (170.7m × 15.6m × 5.1m). *Tons:* 7,500 disp. *Hull:* steel. *Comp.:* 435. *Arm.:* 7 × 5.9″ (3 × 2 & 1 × 1), 10 × 40mm, 8 × 12.7mm. *Armor:* 2″ belt, 1.3″ deck. *Mach.:* geared turbines, 66,000 shp, 2 shafts; 32 kts. *Built:* NV Mij Fijenoord, Rotterdam; 1935.

Named for the seventeenth-century Dutch admiral Michiel Adriaanszoon de Ruyter, this light cruiser was flagship of Rear Admiral Karel Doorman's ABDA Striking Force, annihilated at the Battle of the Java Sea in the Allies' desperate effort to stall the Japanese invasion of the Dutch East Indies. Formed February 3, 1942, the fleet

initially consisted of four cruisers of less than 10,000 tons and seven destroyers, all drawn from the Dutch and U.S. fleets. Three weeks later it included five cruisers — *De Ruyter* and *Java*, HMS EXETER, USS HOUSTON, and HMAS PERTH — and nine destroyers. Efforts to stop Japanese landings at Bali and Sumatra were ineffectual. On February 27, Doorman took his fleet out to engage a forty-one-ship convoy supported by Rear Admiral Takeo Takagi's sixteen destroyers, two light cruisers, and two heavy cruisers, almost all equipped with Long Lance torpedoes having a range of 22,000 yards at 49 knots or 44,000 yards at 36 knots. (British torpedoes had a maximum range of 15,000 yards and a maximum speed of 41 knots.) In addition to having fewer, older, and smaller ships, Doorman's fleet was hastily thrown together from four navies with two distinct languages. Moreover, Doorman could expect little air cover and in fact received none at all. Battle was joined at 1612 on February 27 north and east of Surabaya. The ABDA force began to unravel after *Exeter* was hit at 1708 and dropped out of line, confusing the other cruisers. The Japanese fired more than ninety torpedoes, which forced the ABDA ships into nearly constant evasive action. This engagement broke off at 1830, but Doorman continued his pursuit of the transports. By 2130, his active force consisted of only *De Ruyter, Java, Houston,* and *Perth,* three destroyers having been sunk, and six retired, one to escort *Exeter.* At 2300, this squadron encountered the heavy cruisers *Nachi* and *Haguro* whose torpedoes struck first the *Java,* which sank within 15 minutes with only nineteen survivors, and then *De Ruyter,* which sank about three hours later at about 6°10′S, 112°08′E. Only ninety-two of her crew survived; Doorman went down with his ship. *Perth* and *Houston* escaped, to be sunk later at Bantam Bay.

Grove, *Sea Battles in Close-Up.*

DESCUBIERTA

Corvette (3m). *L/B/D:* 109.2′ × 28.7′ × 14.1′ dph (33.3m × 8.7m × 4.3m). *Tons:* 306 toneladas. *Hull:* wood. *Comp.:* 104. *Arm.:* 14 × 6pdr, 2 × 4pdr. *Built:* Cadiz, Spain; 1789.

Flagship of the most important voyage of discovery dispatched by Spain in the eighteenth century, *Descubierta* ("Discovery") was one of two ships — the other was *Atrevida* ("Daring") — built for an expedition conceived of and lead by Don Alejandro Malaspina. Much influenced by the voyages of Captain James Cook and his successors, both English and French, the Italian-born Malaspina planned a "Scientific and Political Voyage Around the World," the twofold aim of which was to increase geographic and scientific knowledge, and to check on the status of Spain's far-flung possessions, particularly those on the Pacific Coast of North America where both Russia and England were expanding their spheres of influence.

Sailing from Cadiz on July 30, 1789, *Descubierta* and *Atrevida* (under Don José Bustamente y Guerra) made first for the River Plate, which they surveyed before following the coast of Patagonia south. After calling in the Falkland Islands (then a Spanish territory), they rounded Cape Horn and called at several ports on the Chilean coast and at Juan Fernández Island. The two ships then separated and made their way independently to Mexico at the end of March. Here Malaspina received new orders from Madrid. Rather than go to the Sandwich (Hawaiian) Islands, he was to proceed north to southern Alaska and survey the coast from Mount St. Elias south to Nootka Sound, where in June 1789 the Spanish commander had arrested two British ships in the fur trade, precipitating the Nootka Sound crisis between Britain and Spain. Departing Acapulco on May 1, 1791, by the end of June the ships were at Yakutat Bay in the shadow of Mount St. Elias and Malaspina Glacier. The ships remained in the area until July 27, exploring as far north and west as Hinchinbrook Island before turning south to arrive on August 12 at the Spanish settlement at Nootka, on the western side of Vancouver Island. After conferring with the local Spanish commander and the Nootkas and dispatching cutters for surveys of the surrounding islands and inlets, the ships sailed south looking for the "Entrada de Hezeta" reported by the Spanish Bruno de Hezeta in 1774. (The mouth of the Columbia River would not be seen or named again until the following year when Robert Gray crossed the bar in his ship COLUMBIA.) After two weeks at Monterey, the ships headed south to Acapulco where they helped prepare the schooners SUTIL and *Mexicana* for a voyage to Nootka before heading west to the Philippines by way of the Mariana Islands.

Continuing their survey work in the Philippines and over to Macao, Malaspina turned southeast, landing first at Espiritu Santo, and then went on to southern New Zealand, calling at Cook's Dusky Sound. From there the ships headed west again to Port Jackson (Sydney), New South Wales, where he landed in March 1793, five years after the arrival of the first colonists. The settlement had learned of a possible visit from England, and the Spanish were welcomed as they set about conducting extensive astronomical, hydrographical, and other experiments and gathering numerous specimens of flora, fauna, and minerals. Malaspina was also thorough in his description of the British settlement, particularly with a view to the potential of its hindering Spanish trade between South America and the Philippines, which had been conducted almost free of interference for more than 200 years. In his report to the Navy minister, he declared that the British government had established its presence in the Pacific — in Australia, the Sandwich Islands, and at Nootka — "in the shades of rights usurped . . . from the other European nations" and established as far back as the Treaty of Tordesillas in 1494.

Descubierta and *Atrevida* left Port Jackson on April 11, sailing northeast for the Friendly (Tonga) Islands and thence east to Callao. From there they sailed south to double Cape Horn and after a stop at Montevideo returned home to Cadiz on September 21, 1793, ending a voyage of more than four years. Unfortunately for Malaspina, his liberal ideas were at odds with the extreme conservatism of Carlos IV and his court, and he was arrested, stripped of his rank (he had been promoted to Admiral on his return), and exiled. As a result, both Malaspina and his achievements were neglected and his *Diario de viaje* was not published in its entirety until 1885.

Cutter, *Malaspina and Galiano*. King, *Secret History of the Convict Colony*. Vaughan, et al., *Voyages of Enlightenment*.

DEUTSCHLAND

Passenger ship (1f/2m). *L/B/D:* 320′ × 42′ × 38′ dph (97.5m × 12.8m × 11.6m). *Tons:* 2,800 grt. *Hull:* steel. *Comp.:* 1st 60, 2nd 120, 3rd 700; 100 crew. *Mach.:* direct-acting, 600 hp, 1 screw; 12 kts. *Built:* Caird & Co., Greenock, Scotland; 1866.

One of four steamships commissioned by Norddeutscher Lloyd between 1865 and 1867, *Deutschland* sailed as part of the company's weekly packet service between Bremen and New York. Built with direct-acting engines, she was refitted with compound engines in 1872. On December 5, 1875, she sailed from Bremen with 113 passengers, most of them German emigrants. Within hours of her departure, the ship encountered a blizzard with gale force winds. Poor visibility forced Captain Edward Brickenstein to reduce speed. Despite every effort with his English pilot to determine the ship's correct position, shortly after 0500 on December 6, *Deutschland* ran aground on Kentish Knock, one of the many treacherous sandbars that guard the mouth of England's Thames River. The ship remained afloat throughout the day, but by evening Captain Brickenstein had ordered the passengers and crew on deck. Some took to the rigging, but many died of exposure in the bitter cold. Help arrived only the next morning, in the form of the steam paddle-tug *Liverpool*, which rescued the survivors. All told, 157 passengers and crew lost their lives in the tragedy, which inspired the young Gerard Manley Hopkins to write his poem "The Wreck of the *Deutschland*."

Street, *Wreck of the "Deutschland."*

DEUTSCHLAND

(later *Victoria Louise, Hansa*) Liner (4f/2m). *L/B:* 684′ bp × 67.3′ (208.5m lbp × 20.4m). *Tons:* 16,502 grt. *Hull:* steel. *Comp.:* 1st 450, 2nd 300, 3rd 350, steerage 1,000; crew 536. *Mach.:* quadruple expansion, 37,800 ihp, 2 screws; 23.5 kts. *Built:* AG Vulcan, Stettin, Germany; 1900.

Built specifically to capture the Blue Riband from Norddeutscher Lloyd's KAISER WILHELM DER GROSSE, Hamburg-Amerika Linie's (Hapag's) *Deutschland* was only the second German ship to establish a record for the fastest crossing of the North Atlantic. The second-largest liner in the world at the time of her building, on her maiden passage to New York, via Plymouth, she steamed from Eddystone Light to Sandy Hook at an average speed of 22.42 knots (5 days, 15 hours, 46 minutes; July 6–12). Her return eastbound was made at an equally impressive 22.46 knots (5 days, 11 hours, 5 minutes; July 18–24). Ultimately, she would increase the speed to 23.15 knots westbound, and 23.51 knots eastbound. Despite her impressive speed and size, *Deutschland* was plagued with

machinery problems. Her engines were extremely loud and prone to such heavy vibration that on April 22, 1902, she lost her rudder and sternpost midatlantic. Despite repairs lasting six months, the problems continued, and she proved to be Hapag's first and only attempt to capture the transatlantic record.

In 1910–11, *Deutschland* was converted to a luxury cruise ship renamed *Victoria Luise*, with accommodations for 487 first-class passengers. At the start of World War I, she was fitted out as an auxiliary cruiser but never used because of the unsatisfactory state of her engines. Due to her poor overall condition, the Allies declined to take her over as war reparations, and in 1920 she was the largest steamship in the German fleet. Renamed *Hansa*, she returned to transatlantic service in 1921. Four years later she was withdrawn from service and broken up at Hamburg.

Bonsor, *North Atlantic Seaway.* Kludas, *Great Passenger Ships of the World.*

DEUTSCHLAND (U-200)

(later *U-155*) Submarine. *L/B/D:* 213.3′ × 29.2′ × 17.4′/42′ (65m × 8.9m × 5.3m/9.3m). *Tons:* 1,503/1,880 disp. (791 grt). *Hull:* steel; 160′ dd. *Comp.:* 30–56. *Arm.:* 6 × 50cm TT. *Mach.:* diesel/electric, 800 ehp, 2 screws; 12.4/5.2 kts. *Des.:* Dr. Techel. *Built:* Flensburger Schiffbau AG, Flensburg, Germany; 1916.

The passenger liner DEUTSCHLAND *shown outward bound from New York, in a 1900 photo by A. Loeffler. Courtesy The Mariners' Museum, Newport News, Virginia.*

Laid down as a "merchant" submarine, the DEUTSCHLAND *was armed only after the United States entered World War I in 1917. Here the captured vessel is seen, looking aft, near Tower Bridge, London, during a postwar tour of Britain in 1919. Courtesy National Maritime Museum, Greenwich.*

Deutschland, an unarmed cargo submarine, was built in response to the crippling British blockade of German ports during World War I. Built ostensibly for the Deutsche Ozean Reederei GmbH (German Ocean Navigation Company), she was under the ultimate authority of the German Navy with the code name U-200 and crewed by veteran submariners under Paul Lebrecht König. Launched on March 28, 1916, *Deutschland* departed on her maiden voyage to Baltimore on March 23, carrying chemical dyes and returning with nickel, copper, and zinc. She returned from her second voyage, to New London, with rubber, oil, and silver, on December 10. Following the interception of the Zimmerman telegram from Germany to Mexico the following January and heightened tensions with the United States, *Deutschland* was converted to a combatant vessel at Wilhelmshaven. Her six deck-mounted 50-centimeter torpedo tubes were replaced by two 50-centimeter bow tubes, and she was armed with two 15-centimeter deck guns. Commissioned as *U-155,* she made three war cruises; although she had good endurance, she was too slow to be very effective and required extensive repairs. From April to August 1917, she sank nineteen ships totaling 53,262 grt. On her second cruise (January to May 1918), she bagged seventeen steamers (50,926 grt), and on her last (August to November),

ber), she sank only seven ships (17,845 grt). On December 2, 1918, *Deutschland/U-155* was taken to England and displayed as a war prize. Sold for scrap in 1921, she was being broken up at Robert Smith and Sons, Birkenhead, when an explosion ripped the ship apart and killed five apprentices.

König, *Voyage of the "Deutschland."* Messimer, *Merchant U-Boat.*

HMS DEVASTATION

Turret ship (2f/1m). *L/B/D:* 285′ bp × 62.3′ x 26.5′ (86.9m × 19m × 8.1m). *Tons:* 9,188 disp. *Hull:* steel. *Comp.:* 400. *Arm.:* 4 × 12″. *Armor:* 12″ belt, 3″ deck. *Mach.:* Penn trunk engines, 800 nhp, 2 screws; 13 kts. *Built:* Portsmouth Dockyard, Eng.; 1871.

By the 1870s, steam power was well established among the world's leading naval powers, and a number of smaller coast defense vessels that relied solely on mechanical propulsion had been built. There had also been an increasing tendency towards turreted guns in place of the broadside arrangement typical of sailing ships of the line. However, so long as seagoing ships relied on masts for even auxiliary power, a turret's arc of fire was necessarily limited. All this changed with the commissioning of HMS *Devastation,* "the first true capital ship under any flag without a single sail, and . . . the first complete application to a sea-going battleship of the principle of mounting the main armament on top of the hull instead of inside it." Her four 12-inch guns — the largest muzzle-loaders ever — were mounted in two turrets each with an arc of fire of 280 degrees. In 1891, these were replaced by 10-inch breech-loaders with twice the range and three times the rate of fire. In the same year, she also received triple-expansion engines the increased efficiency of which enabled her to cross the Atlantic both ways without refueling.

Devastation's first two commissions were divided between home waters and the Mediterranean. After a two-year refit, she spent four years in reserve before being assigned to the First Reserve Fleet in Scotland. She was later made a port guardship at Portsmouth and then at Gibraltar. Retired again in 1902, the first mastless capital ship was broken up in 1908.

Ballard, *Black Battlefleet.*

DIANA

Sloop of war (3m). *L:* 90′ (27.4m). *Tons:* 300 bm. *Hull:* wood. *Comp.:* 67. *Arm.:* 14 × 6pdr, 4 × 8pdr, 4 falconets. *Built:* Sviritsa, Russia; 1807.

One of the most celebrated escapes by ship ever undertaken took place in 1807, when the Russian sloop *Diana*, commanded by Lieutenant Vasilii M. Golovnin, eluded the British fleet at Simon's Bay, South Africa. Assigned as an escort for the storeship *Neva* in the North Pacific, *Diana* did not sail from Kronstadt until July 25, 1807, nine months after *Neva*'s departure for Kamchatka and the Russian American colonies. After attempting to round Cape Horn, Golovnin decided to run east and turn north once past Australia. Unaware that Russia and England had gone to war since his departure from Kronstadt, Golovnin put into Simon's Bay on April 21, 1808. Although he had documents guaranteeing him safe passage by English ships even in the event of war, Commodore Josias Rowley refused to release *Diana* without authorization from England. With neither money for provisions, nor permission to sell anything from the ship to raise money, Golovnin decided he had no recourse but to break his parole and try to escape. After careful study of tidal and wind conditions, at 1830 on May 19, with a fresh northwest wind, Golovnin ordered the two anchors cut and set the storm staysails. As the British had previously ordered the sails unbent and the topmasts

Warship design passed through many phases during the transition from sail to steam. The first oceangoing capital ship built without auxiliary sails was the HMS DEVASTATION, *commissioned in 1873 and seen here off Southend during Queen Victoria's Diamond Jubilee, June 28, 1897. Courtesy National Maritime Museum, Greenwich.*

housed, the next few hours were ones of frantic activity. Golovnin recalled,

> The officers, marines, petty officers and men all without exception worked the topmast and yards. With great pleasure I recall that within two hours, notwithstanding the strong wind, rain and dark of the night, they succeeded in bending the fore and main topsails, in setting them up, hoisting the top-gallant-masts to their places, lifting the topgallant yards and setting up the top[gallant]sails; lifting the studding sail booms to their places, threading through all the studding sail rigging and preparing the studding-sails so that, should the wind permit, we would be able at once to set all the sails.

> By 10 o'clock in the evening we were in the open ocean. And so ended our detention, or rather, arrest in the Cape of Good Hope, which lasted one year and 25 days.

Heading south to 40°S, *Diana* ran her easting down past Tasmania when she turned northward for the New Hebrides, where she anchored at Resolution Harbor (named for Cook's ship) on Tana Island, on June 25. *Diana* finally arrived at Petropavlovsk on September 25, two years and two months out from Kronstadt. From there the ship made a roundtrip to the Russian settlement on Sitka Island, and then spent all of 1810 at Petropavlovsk.

In April 1811, Golovnin was ordered to survey "the Southern Kurile and Shantar Islands, and the coast of Tartary, from latitude 53°38′ north to Okhotsk" between northern Japan and southern Kamchatka. In early July, *Diana* stopped at the island of Kunashir for water and provisions. Despite efforts to establish goodwill with his hosts, on July 11 the xenophobic Japanese arrested the unlucky Golovnin, together with another officer, a midshipman, and four sailors. The Russians remained under arrest in Japan until October 16, 1813, when they embarked in *Diana* — which had escaped from Kunashir following the arrests — after two years, two months, and twenty-six days in captivity. (A keen observer, Golovnin later published detailed descriptions of the people, customs, and history of both the Cape Colony and of Japan.) Golovnin returned to St. Petersburg from Okhotsk seven years to the day after his departure. *Diana* remained in eastern waters and ended her days as a munitions ship at Petropavlovsk.

Golovnin, *Detained in Simon's Bay: Memoirs of a Captivity in Japan.*
Ivashintsov, *Russian Round-the-World Voyages.*

DIRIGO

Bark (4m). *L/B/D:* 312′ × 45.2′ × 25.6′ (95.1m × 13.8m × 7.8m). *Tons:* 3,005 grt. *Hull:* steel. *Comp.:* 32. *Des.:* J. F. Waddington. *Built:* A. Sewall & Co., Bath, Me.; 1894.

After launching his mammoth four-masted bark ROAN-OKE in 1892, Arthur Sewall decided to switch from building wooden ships to building steel-hulled vessels. (Sewall had purchased the British-built, steel-hulled KENIL-WORTH in 1889.) Returning from a research visit to Great Britain, he retooled his shipyard and hired J. F. Waddington to oversee the construction of *Dirigo,* the first American steel-hulled square-rigger, the name for which he aptly borrowed from the Maine state motto, "I lead." *Dirigo* proved a successful vessel, carrying a variety of bulk and general cargoes on an even greater variety of routes between the East Coast, West Coast, Hawaii, Asia, and Europe. Although Sewall built nine steel barks and one schooner, he was sole American builder of steel square-riggers.

Dirigo had a number of unusual voyages. On March 3, 1912, she embarked Jack London, his wife, Charmian, and their servant, Yoshimatsu Nakata. During their 145-day passage from Baltimore to Seattle, Captain Omar Chapman was incapacitated by a fatal stomach cancer and command of the vessel was assumed by the first mate. As Charmian wrote, "Jack London novelized him in 'The Mutiny of the *Elsinore,*' stressing his finer points." Three years later, with international shipping complicated by World War I, Sewall sold *Dirigo* to G. W. McNear & Company of San Francisco. Loaded at Seattle, she sailed for Kalmar, Sweden. About 400 miles west of the Shetland Islands, she was boarded by a British patrol. Although the United States and Sweden were both neutral at the time, the British had reason to suspect that her cargo of barley was ultimately bound for Germany and was therefore contraband. *Dirigo* was later released by a British prize court, but in the meantime she had been sold to the American C. C. Mengel & Brother Company, and then Axim Transportation. On May 3, 1917, she sailed from New York bound for Le Havre; twenty-eight days later she was stopped by a German U-boat six miles southwest of Eddystone Light. As the crew took to their boats (the mate drowned during the transfer), the Germans sank *Dirigo* with gunfire and scuttling charges.

Hennessey, *Sewall Ships of Steel.* Lyford, " 'Long Life and Success.' "

DISCOVERY

Tons: 55–70. *Hull:* wood. *Comp.:* 17. *Built:* England; <1602.

At the beginning of the seventeenth century, England's East India Company was eager to find a sea route to the Indies that was not dominated by the Spanish or the Portuguese. At the time, two of the most promising alternatives were the Northeast Passage, over the top of Russia, and the Northwest Passage across the top of what became Canada. One of the most hard-worked ships in that exploration was *Discovery,* which made six voyages in quest of the Northwest Passage.

In 1602, *Discovery* was one of two "Fly-boates" of 70 tons (the other being *Godspeed*) that sailed under George Weymouth with a combined complement of thirty-five provisioned for eighteen months by "the right Worship-full Merchants of the Moscovie and Turkie Companies." On May 2, they sailed north from the Thames to pass through the Orkneys, then south of Greenland until June 28, when they "descried the land of America, in the latitude of 62. degrees and 30 minutes; which we made to be Warwickes foreland" in the southern part of Baffin Island. Heading south, they approached the entrance to Hudson Strait but were kept out by ice and fog. Turning north, the ships returned to 68°53′ where on July 19 the crew mutinied and "bare up the Helme" for England. On the return south they sailed into Frobisher Bay, past the entrance to Hudson Strait (named for *Discovery*'s next master) and Ungava Bay in northern Quebec. *Discovery* returned to England at the beginning of August and Weymouth reported that "truely there is in three severall places great hope of a passage, betweene the latitude of 62. and 54 degrees; if the fogge doe not hinder it, which is all the feare I have."

Discovery next appeared in sub-Arctic waters in 1610, sailing for the Northwest Company under command of Henry Hudson. The year before, Hudson had sailed in the Dutch East India Company's ship HALVE MAEN to ascend the Hudson River as far as present-day Albany, New York. Back in the employ of his fellow countrymen, Hudson sailed from Gravesend on April 17, 1610, and *Discovery* was the first ship definitely to enter Hudson Strait. Hudson cruised south along the east coast of the bay that bears his name and into James Bay where on November 10, he and his crew were frozen in with scant provisions. Over the harsh winter, the near starving crew became increasingly hostile to Hudson's command and on June 22, 1611, they mutinied. Led by Henry Greene, who "would rather be hanged at home than starved abroad," the mutineers put Hudson, his son, and seven of the infirm crew in *Discovery*'s shallop and sailed away. Hudson was never heard from again. En route home, four of the remaining crew were killed by Eskimos in Hudson Strait — in a rare clash between Eskimos and Europeans — and one more died of starvation before they returned to England under the command of Robert Bylot. Despite the severity of their crime — the masters of Trinity House said "they deserved to be hanged" — none of the mutineers was brought to trial until 1616, partly, it is believed, because of their claim that they had indeed found Hudson Strait.

Backed by the Prince of Wales, the Northwest Company next dispatched an expedition in search of the Northwest Passage under Thomas Button in *Resolution,* accompanied by *Discovery* under John Ingram; curiously, Ingram's orders included no mention of a search for Hudson or his crew. The ships sailed from London on April 14, 1612, retracing the now familiar route. Button named Resolution Island at the entrance to Hudson Strait and then sailed southwest across Hudson Bay to the site of present-day Fort Nelson. Several of the crew died over the hard winter, but in June 1613 the survivors resumed their search for the Northwest Passage, visiting Churchill River, Roes Welcome Sound, and Mansel Island. The ship's next voyage, under William Gibbons, was cut short by unusually severe ice that embayed them for ten weeks at Gibbons Hole (possibly Saglek Bay).

In 1615, the ship was acquired by William Baffin, and on March 15

> againe set forth the *Discovery,* a ship of fiftie five tunnes or thereabouts, which ship had beene the three [sic] former Voyages on the action. The master was Robert Bileth, a man well acquainted with that way: having been employed in the three former Voyages: my selfe [William Baffin] being his Mate and Associate, with fourteen others and two Boyes.

They reached Resolution Island, sailed along the south coast of Baffin Island and Mill, Salisbury, and Nottingham Islands, Foxe Channel, and Southampton Island. Bylot and Baffin also judged, correctly, that Frozen Strait offered no outlet to the west through Hudson Bay. They returned to England on September 8.

The following year, Bylot and Baffin sailed again under the auspices of the Northwest Company and explored western Greenland as far north as Smith Sound. They passed Cary Island and discovered the entrances to Jones and Lancaster Sounds (the true entrance to the Northwest Passage) and reached a farthest north of 77°45′N. This was *Discovery*'s last voyage in search of the Northwest Passage though she remained in service until 1620. Despite Baffin's carefully charting of all the coasts of Baffin Bay over the course of two separate voyages, geographers decided his discoveries were false and the information was gradually removed from maps until John Ross,

sailing in ISABELLA, rediscovered Baffin Bay in 1819. *Discovery*'s farthest north would not be exceeded until Sir George Nares's expedition in the ships ALERT and *Discovery* in 1876.

Cooke & Holland, *Exploration of Northern Canada.* Johnson, *Charting the Sea of Darkness.* Purchas, *Hakluytus Posthumus.*

HMS DISCOVERY

(ex-*Diligence*) Ship (3m). *L/B/D:* 91.4′ × 27.4′ × 11.4′ (27.9m × 8.4m × 3.5m). *Tons:* 299 tons. *Hull:* wood. *Comp.:* 75. *Arm.:* 8 guns, 8 swivels. *Built:* Langbourne, Whitby, Eng.; 1774.

Discovery was the fourth and smallest of the ships assigned to Captain James Cook on his three voyages of discovery. Built as a brig-rigged collier, Cook ordered her rerigged as a ship, as ENDEAVOUR, ADVENTURE and RESOLUTION had been. The purpose of Cook's last voyage was to find a northwest passage between the Atlantic and the Pacific from the Pacific end, for the discovery of which the British Parliament had pledged £20,000. Two ships were required: *Resolution,* flagship of Cook's second voyage, and *Discovery,* commanded by Captain Charles Clerke, a veteran of Byron's circumnavigation in DOLPHIN and the first two Cook expeditions. George Vancouver also sailed as a midshipman.

Discovery sailed on August 1, 1776, and joined *Resolution* at Cape Town on November 10. The ships continued eastward stopping at Van Diemen's Land (Tasmania) and spent three months in the Friendly (Tonga) Islands and at Tahiti. From there, the expedition sailed north. They were the first European ships to visit the Sandwich (Hawaiian) Islands, where they stayed from January 19 to February 2, 1788. Heading northwest, they arrived on the coast of North America on March 7, cruising north until they came to Nootka Sound on the 29th, where they stayed a month. The ships sailed northwest along the Alaska coast, anchoring in Prince William Sound on March 17 and exploring Cook Inlet two weeks later. Rounding the Alaska Peninsula, they sailed into the Bering Sea, north past Cape Prince of Wales and then north and west as far as Icy Cape. Heading east, the ships made the coast of the Chukotski Peninsula on August 29, and then spent from October 3 to 26 at the Russian settlement at Unalaska before returning to the Sandwich Islands for the winter. The ships sailed again on February 4, 1779, but a sprung foremast in *Resolution* forced them back a week later. On the 14th, an altercation between a group of Hawaiians and a shore party led to a skirmish in which four marines and Cook were killed.

Leadership of the expedition fell to Captain Clerke,

who moved to the *Resolution;* John Gore took command of *Discovery.* The ship sailed from Hawaii again on March 22 bound for the Russian outpost at Petropavlovsk on the Kamchatka Peninsula — "a few miserable log-houses and some conical huts." In June they made a second attempt to find the Northeast Passage, sailing past Icy Cape to 71°56′N before abandoning their effort and turning for home on July 24. *Discovery* had been damaged in the ice, and they turned for Petropavlovsk. Captain Clerke died just before they reached Petropavlovsk and was buried there on August 29. Command of the expedition now fell to Gore, a veteran of two expeditions in *Dolphin* as well as Cook's first, in *Endeavour.* James King assumed command of *Discovery.*

Weighing anchor at Petropavlovsk on October 9, they sailed along the east coast of the Kurile Islands and Japan, and then made for Macao, where they arrived December 1. During their six weeks there, members of the crew had sold sea otter pelts gathered in Cook Inlet for such profit that far from wanting to return home — after nearly four years — they wanted to return to Alaska for more. Nonetheless, on January 12 the ships turned for home. After a month in Cape Town, they entered the Atlantic Ocean on May 9. Forced north about Ireland, *Discovery* and *Resolution* landed at Stromness on August 22, 1780, and were back in the Nore on October 4.

Converted to an interyard navy transport, *Discovery* was broken up at Chatham, in October 1797, shortly after the Nore Mutiny.

Cook, *Journals of James Cook.* McGowan, *"Captain Cook's Ships."*

HMS DISCOVERY

Ship (3m). *L/B/D:* 99.2′ keel × 28.3′ × 15.5′ (30.2m × 8.6m × 4.7m). *Tons:* 330 tons. *Hull:* wood. *Comp.:* 100. *Arm.:* 10 × 4pdr, 10 swivels. *Built:* Randall & Brents, London; 1789.

In 1789, the Spanish and English were at loggerheads over control of lands in the Pacific Northwest. In anticipation of a favorable resolution of the Nootka Sound controversy, the English prepared an expedition to sail under Captain George Vancouver. The primary aims were to survey "the direction and extent of all such considerable inlets . . . as may be likely to lead to" a Northwest passage between Cape Mendocino (30°N) and Cook Inlet (60°N), and especially "the supposed straits of Juan de Fuca." The Admiralty furnished two vessels for the purpose, *Discovery* (named for the vessel in which Vancouver sailed as midshipman on Captain James Cook's last voyage to the Pacific), and *Chatham.*

The ships departed Falmouth on April 1, 1791, and

sailing east called at Tenerife and Cape Town, making a landfall at Cape Chatham, Australia, on September 28. They then rounded Tasmania and landed at Dusky Bay, New Zealand, on November 2, 1791. From there they proceeded to Tahiti and, in early March 1792, Kealakekua Bay, where Cook had been killed in 1779. After two weeks in the Sandwich Islands, the ships sailed for North America, arriving off Cape Cabrillo, 130 miles north of San Francisco Bay, on April 17, 1792.

Sailing north, twelve days later *Chatham* and *Discovery* met with Robert Gray's COLUMBIA, the first ship they had seen in eight months, and then sailed into the Strait of Juan de Fuca and proceeded to Discovery Bay about 70 miles east of Cape Flattery for repairs. From that base they explored Puget Sound (named for Second Lieutenant Peter Puget, who commanded *Chatham* from November 25, 1792) and the San Juan Islands. Here they encountered the schooners SUTIL and *Mexicana,* which were conducting surveys of the coast in conjunction with Spanish claims to the area; relations between the English and Spanish were friendly.

In October, Vancouver turned south and, leaving *Chatham* to cross the bar at the mouth of the Columbia River, proceeded to Yerba Buena (now San Francisco) where on November 14 *Discovery* became the first non-Spanish ship to sail into San Francisco Bay. The ships remained on the Spanish coast until January 15, 1793, when they sailed from Mendocino for Hawaii, arriving on February 12. While in Hawaii, Vancouver wanted to punish the murder of two men from the storeship *Daedalus* who had been killed en route to Nootka Sound the previous year. He also wanted to mediate a truce between King Kamehameha and King Kahekili, and to persuade them to accept the protection of the King of England. After *Chatham* sailed for the Northwest, *Discovery* remained in Hawaii making surveys of the islands, including the first of Pearl Harbor.

Discovery returned to Nootka, arriving on May 20, two days after Puget had sailed on an independent survey. The ships continued to survey Queen Charlotte Sound, including Elcho Harbour on Dean Channel just two months before Alexander Mackenzie completed the first crossing of North America north of Mexico on July 21. By the end of the second season, Vancouver's expedition had charted 1,700 miles of coast from 29°56′N to about 56°N. During the expedition's third visit to Hawaii, Vancouver completed his survey of all of the major Hawaiian islands and Kamehameha formally put his islands under the protection of Great Britain.

In mid-March 1794, the ships sailed for Cook's Inlet, Alaska, which Vancouver had visited in 1778. *Discovery* and *Chatham* separated shortly after departing Hawaii and did not find each other until May 6. *Discovery* made a landfall on Chirikof Island and proceeded to Cook's Inlet on April 12. After determining it was not a river — it had been thought a likely candidate for the Northwest Passage — Vancouver sailed around the Kenai Peninsula for a survey of Prince William Sound. Farther east, in Yakutat Inlet, they encountered a party of 900 Russian-led Kodiak Islanders employed in the seal trade. The Yakutat resented the Russians whom they viewed, in the words of the expedition's surgeon-botanist Archibald Menzies, "as intruders in their territories, draining their shores & coasts of Seals Otter & Fish on which their subsistence chiefly Depends & that too without making the least return for their depredations."

In the late summer, they completed charting of the northern end of the Alexander Archipelago, having stopped at Cape Decision at the southern end of Chichagof Island in 1793. The ships sailed for California and finally left Monterey on December 2, 1794. After stops at Maria Magdalena, Cocos Island, the Galapagos, and Valparaiso, they sailed into the Atlantic to arrive at St. Helena on July 3. There they learned that England was at war with Holland, and Vancouver seized the Dutch East Indiaman *Macassar,* which had sailed from Cape Town in ignorance of the fact. *Chatham* was dispatched to Brazil as an escort. *Discovery* sailed on July 15 and Vancouver landed in the Shannon on September 13, 1795. *Discovery* and *Chatham* both arrived at Deptford in late October.

Though Vancouver hoped that his survey would "remove every doubt, and set aside every opinion of a *northwest passage,* or any water communication navigable for shipping, existing between the North Pacific, and the interior of the American continent within the limits of our researches," the search continued. The expedition gave names to scores of places, many of which are in use today. (The city of Vancouver, British Columbia, was not so named until 1886.) Moreover, in the course of the five-year voyage, only five of the *Discovery*'s crew died — only one from disease — and none of *Chatham*'s. Converted to a bomb in 1799, *Discovery* was made a convict ship in 1818 and broken up in 1834 at Deptford.

Fisher, *Vancouver's Charting the Northwest Coast, 1791–1795.* Vancouver, *Voyage of Discovery to the North Pacific Ocean.*

HMS DISCOVERY

Bark (3m). *L/B/D:* 171′ × 33.8′ × 15.8′ 52.1m × 10.3m × 4.8m). *Tons:* 1,570 disp. *Hull:* wood. *Comp.:* 39–43. *Mach.:* triple expansion, 450 ihp, 1 screw; 8 kts. *Des.:* William E. Smith. *Built:* Stevens Yard, Dundee Shipbuilders Co., Dundee, Scotland; 1901.

Despite numerous expeditions to the waters around Antarctica in the 1800s, by the close of the century the continent itself remained all but unknown. To remedy this, Britain's Royal Geographical Society proposed a National Antarctic Expedition to explore the interior by sledge. Private and public funds were raised for the construction of the purpose-built research vessel, which was modeled on the design of the whaleship *Discovery* (ex-*Bloodhound*) that had accompanied the Arctic Expedition of 1875–76. Designed to be marooned in the ice, the new

Built in 1901 for Commander Robert Falcon Scott's expedition to Antarctica, the auxiliary bark HMS DISCOVERY *has had a long and varied career as a research ship, training ship, and now as a floating museum in her homeport of Dundee, Scotland. Courtesy The Mariners' Museum, Newport News, Virginia.*

Discovery had a massively built wooden hull, and was equipped with a hoisting propeller and hoisting rudder. She was also equipped with scientific laboratories and a magnetic observatory.

On August 6, 1901, she sailed from Cowes and after stops at the Cape of Good Hope and Lyttleton, New Zealand, entered the Ross Sea and discovered Edward VII Land in January 1902. Commander Robert Falcon Scott established winter quarters near Mount Erebus on Ross Island, McMurdo Sound, in early February and it was not until the following September 2 that the weather permitted the first sledge journey. Later that Antarctic summer, Scott, Ernest Shackleton, and Edward A. Wilson reached 82°16′S, about 500 miles from the South Pole. *Discovery* remained icebound through 1902–3, but she was resupplied from the support ship *Morning.* Among the expedition's other accomplishments were the first flight in Antarctica, via the tethered hydrogen balloon, *Eva,* on February 4, 1902, and the first use of electricity in Antarctica, generated by a windmill. With help from the supply ships *Morning* (which had visited in 1902–3) and TERRA NOVA, *Discovery* finally broke free of the ice in February 1904, and after stops in the Balleny Islands, Macquerie Island, New Zealand, and the Falklands, arrived at Portsmouth on September 10, 1904.

The following year she was purchased by the Hudson's Bay Company and converted for use as a merchant ship. Between 1905 and 1911 she made seven voyages to Charlton Island, James Bay, at the southern end of Hudson Bay. Laid up from 1912 to 1915, during World War I and into 1920 she traded under charter to European ports from Archangel to the Black Sea, and in 1918–19 she made one last voyage to Hudson Bay. In 1916, the company loaned her to the government to rescue Shackleton's party marooned on Elephant Island after the loss of NIMROD. These men were saved before *Discovery*'s arrival, and she loaded grain in South America for the return passage.

In 1923, she was purchased by the Crown Agents for the Colonies for an expedition to undertake "scientific research in the South Sea." Designated a Royal Research Ship, between 1925 and 1927 she cruised 37,000 miles between Cape Town, Antarctica, and Drake Strait, conducting research on whaling grounds and oceanographic surveys. Two years later, she was employed in the British, Australian, and New Zealand Antarctic Research Expedition (BANZARE), during which Sir Douglas Mawson and Hjalmar Riiser-Larsen agreed on 45°E as the boundary between Norwegian and British claims in Antarctica, and the British claimed sovereignty over all lands between 73°E and 47°E.

Discovery was laid up from 1931 to 1936, when she was acquired by the Boy Scouts Association for use as a stationary training ship and hostel at London. During World War II she was similarly employed by the Admiralty and her engines were scrapped. She reverted to the Sea Scouts in 1946, and from 1955 to 1979 was used jointly by them and the Royal Naval Reserve. Transferred to the Maritime Trust and restored to her 1925 appearance, in 1986 she was opened to the public as a museum ship in Dundee.

Brouwer, *International Register of Historic Ships.* Savours, *Voyages of the "Discovery."*

DOKOS WRECK

The oldest underwater ship-related archaeological site so far discovered is the cargo of a merchant ship dating from about 2200 BCE found at a depth of 18 to 26 meters (60 to 85 feet) off the Greek island of Dokos, about 50 miles southwest of Athens. The existence of a flourishing maritime trade in the Aegean during the Early Helladic period (7000–2000 BCE) was previously known from the presence of obsidian blades from Midos on other islands and at sites on mainland Greece.

The Dokos site in the Bay of Skindos was first identified by Peter Throckmorton in 1975. Subsequent investigations revealed more than 500 clay vases of various shapes and sizes, as well as sauceboats, grindstones for hand mills for grinding grain, amphorae, plates, cups, earthen wine-jars, wineskins, a clay brazier and spit support, and a large vase fragment decorated with multiple concentric circles of a type found in the western Cyclades. Investigation of the island led researchers to conclude that these artifacts did not originate on Dokos and that they must have been from a ship, the remains of which do not survive. Comparison of some objects to similar ones found in Attica suggests that the ship was traveling a well-established sea lane between southern Euobea (north of Attica) and the Gulf of Argos port of Lerna, a city of major importance in the Early Helladic period.

Papathansopoulos, "Dokos Excavation '89."

HMS DOLPHIN

6th rate 24 (3m). *L/B/D:* 113′ × 32′ × 11′ (34.4m × 9.8m × 3.4m). *Tons:* 508 burden. *Hull:* wood. *Comp.:* 160. *Arm.:* 22 × 9pdr, 2 × 3pdr. *Built:* Fellowes, Woolwich Dockyard, Eng.; 1751.

The ninth ship of the Royal Navy to bear the name, HMS *Dolphin* saw duty throughout the Seven Years' War and was part of Admiral John Byng's fleet at the Battle of Minorca (for which the Admiral was court-martialed and executed). The year after the war ended, she was made the flagship of an expedition under Commodore John Byron (a veteran of HMS WAGER). The voyage had several purposes — all redounding to "the advancement of the Trade and Navigation" of Great Britain. Chief among them was to establish a base in the South Atlantic from which Britain might monitor traffic bound for the Pacific.

On June 21, 1764, *Dolphin* and the sloop HMS *Tamar* sailed from Portsmouth and made their way down the Atlantic stopping at the Cape Verdes and Madeira islands before crossing to Rio de Janeiro and down to Port Desire. After provisioning at bountiful Port Famine in the Strait of Magellan, Byron sailed back to the Falkland Islands, which he claimed in the name of George III, not realizing that the French had established a colony there the year before. Returning to Port Famine for provisions, Byron was next to have searched for other islands in the South Atlantic. Instead, he sailed through the Strait of Magellan and into the Pacific from where he had orders to "proceed to New Albion, on the Western Coast of North America" and thereafter search for a Northwest Passage or return to England via the East Indies.

Byron chose to search for the Solomon Islands discovered by Alvaro Mendaña in LOS REYES in 1568. This course took *Dolphin* first to the island of Màs Atuera in the Juan Fernández group, 400 miles off the coast of Chile. Continuing north, in the latitude of the Tropic of Capricorn, Byron turned west northwest and on June 10 came to the island of Takaroa (14°30'S, 143°W) in the Tuamotus. Desperate for fresh provisions, Byron and his crew forced a landing against the inhospitable natives. Here the English found "the carved Head of a Dutch Long boats Rudder," from Roggeveen's *Afrikaansche Galei* which had wrecked in 1721. From here Byron sailed west, jogging to the north just before he hit Tahiti, and continuing until he was in the Tokelaus. On June 28, "Finding there is no such Land as laid down in the [chart by] Neptune François for Solomon's Islands," he hauled to the northward for the Mariana Islands. Sailing through the Gilbert Islands, he turned west again to land at Tinian on July 30, where he spent nine weeks. Now in relatively well known waters, the expedition sailed to the north of the Philippines, through the South China Sea to Batavia and from there, via the Cape of Good Hope, to the Downs, where *Dolphin* arrived on May 9, 1766.

Dolphin was in excellent condition due mostly to the fact that before her sailing, her hull was sheathed in copper "to cause some further experiments to be made of the efficacy of Copper-Sheathing" against teredo worms. Byron had written from Port Famine, "My Opinion of Copper Bottoms is that it is the finest Invention in the World," and this was confirmed by the master shipwright at Deptford who declared her "fit for further Service." *Dolphin* was the second Royal Navy ship fitted with copper (the first was HMS *Alarm,* in 1761), but despite the benefits, copper cladding was not widespread until after 1783.

Almost immediately, *Dolphin* was fitted out for a second voyage, under Captain Samuel Wallis. As *Tamar* had sailed to the West Indies with a damaged rudder, *Dolphin*'s consort this voyage would be HMS SWALLOW, under Lieutenant Samuel Carteret. If Byron had accomplished little else, he had forced a redirection in the Admiralty's exploratory focus to the South Pacific, and when the two ships sailed on August 21, 1766, it was to find "Land or Islands of Great extent . . . in the Southern Hemisphere between Cape Horn and New Zeeland . . . in Climates adapted to the produce of Commodities useful in Commerce."

While the lack of any such lands made this unnecessary, the westerlies that predominate in the southern ocean made it impossible for the ships to sail 100° to 120° of longitude from the Cape "losing as little Southing as possible." Sailing from Plymouth on August 22, 1766, the two ships made a slow passage down the Atlantic and arrived at the Strait of Magellan on December 17. There followed, in the words of J. C. Beaglehole, "one of the longest and most unpleasant passages of the strait of which there is a record . . . four months in almost perpetual danger of shipwreck." No sooner had they entered the Pacific on April 11, 1767, than Wallis lost sight of *Swallow;* and the two ships carried on alone. Forced to the northwest, by June 10 *Dolphin* was in the Tuamotus, and on June 18 she arrived at Tahiti, the first European vessel to do so. Wallis established excellent relations with the queen, Oborea, and the crews spent six idyllic weeks recovering from scurvy and marveling at the people and climate of Tahiti. When they sailed on July 26, it was with promises to return. The European discovery of Tahiti had a profound effect not only on the subsequent exploration of the Pacific — by coincidence, Louis-Antoine de Bougainville's BOUDEUSE and *L'Etoile* arrived at Tahiti only a few months after *Dolphin* — but on the European imagination as well. In his introduction to *The Journals of Captain James Cook,* Beaglehole explains:

> Sailors . . . may well be forgiven for thinking themselves imparadised. So almost suddenly, so overwhelmingly, was the idea of the Pacific at last to enter into the consciousness, not

of seamen alone but of literate Europe. . . . For Wallis had not merely found a convenient port of call. He had stumbled on a foundation stone of the Romantic movement.

The remainder of the voyage paralleled Byron's, although the westward leg was farther to the south, passing through the Society Islands, then between Tonga and Samoa before heading north for Tinian. From there, *Dolphin* sailed on to Batavia, then to the Cape and so to the Downs where she arrived on May 20, 1768. *Dolphin* remained in service as a surveying ship until broken up in 1770.

Byron, *Journal of His Circumnavigation.* Robertson, *Discovery of Tahiti.*

USS DOLPHIN

Dispatch vessel (1f/3m). *L/B/D:* 256.5′ × 32′ × 14.2′ (78.2m × 9.8m × 4.3m). *Tons:* 1,486 disp. *Hull:* steel. *Comp.:* 152. *Arm.:* 1 × 6″, 2 × 6 pdr, 4 × 47mm. *Mach.:* compound engine, 2,255ihp, 1 screw; 16kts. *Built:* John Roach & Sons, Chester, Pa.; 1885.

In 1883, the U.S. Navy convinced Congress that it was time for the nation to develop expertise in the construction of steel warships. To this end it secured authorization for the construction of three armored cruisers, USS *Atlanta, Boston,* and *Chicago,* and the gunboat *Dolphin,* collectively known as the ABCD ships. Although designed in part to demonstrate U.S. technological capabilities, *Dolphin* was built with a very dominant bark rig. Over the years, this was changed to a three-masted, and ultimately a two-masted schooner. The first "New Navy" ship commissioned, *Dolphin* was sent out to the Pacific Station for two years before returning via ports in Asia, the Indian Ocean, and Europe in 1888. She then joined the ABC ships in the "Squadron of Evolution" to develop tactics and maneuvers. In 1895, *Dolphin* was assigned to the Special Service Squadron. After carrying President William McKinley's entourage to the dedication of Grant's Tomb in 1897, she was laid up at New York. Recommissioned in 1898, she sailed on blockade duty during the Spanish-American War, and from 1899 until 1917 *Dolphin* worked as a special dispatch ship for the Navy. Under way to take possession of the Virgin Islands, which Denmark had sold to the United States when the U.S. entered World War I, *Dolphin* remained in the Caribbean as part of the Special Service Squadron until 1922 when she was sold.

Millett, "State Department's Navy." U.S. Navy, *DANFS.*

DONALD MCKAY

Clipper (3m). *L/B/D:* 266′ bp × 46.3′ × 29.5 dph (81.1m × 14.1m × 9m). *Tons:* 2,614 grt. *Hull:* wood. *Comp.:* 1,000. *Built:* Donald McKay, East Boston, Mass.; 1855.

The last of the four great McKay-built clippers built for James Baines, *Donald McKay* sailed under the Black Ball flag for 13 years. The second largest merchant ship in the world at the time of her building, her main yard was 115 feet long, and she set Howes's double topsails. Though not as fast as either LIGHTNING or JAMES BAINES, she nonetheless made excellent passages. On her maiden voyage from Boston to Liverpool, she was a record 12 days to Cape Clear, making the 421-mile run in 24 hours on February 26, 1855; and in six voyages she posted average times to Melbourne of 83 days, and returning in 85. Sold to T. Harrison and Company in 1868, she continued on the Australia run until 1874 when she was sold to J. S. DeWolfe who sailed her in general trade, carrying everything from British soldiers to petroleum. In 1879 she was sold to B. Barling, of Bremerhaven, and sailed between Bremen and New York. Five years later she became a coal hulk at Madeira.

Cutler, *Greyhounds of the Sea.* Hollett, *Fast Passage to Australia.* Howe & Matthews, *American Clipper Ships.* MacGregor, *British and American Clippers.*

DOÑA PAZ

(ex-*Don Sulpicio, Himeyuri Maru*). Passenger ferry. *L/B/D:* 305.4′ × 44.6′ × 26.6′ (93.1m × 13.6m × 8.1m). *Tons:* 2,324 grt. *Hull:* steel. *Comp.:* 1,518; 60 crew. *Built:* Onomichi Zosen K.K., Onomichi, Japan; 1963.

The scene of the worst peacetime maritime disaster in terms of lives lost, *Doña Paz* began her career as the Japanese general cargo/passenger ship *Himeyuri Maru* in Japan. After 12 years of service in general trading around Japanese waters, she was sold to the Sulpicio Lines for service in the Philippines, and renamed *Don Sulpicio.* Three years later, on June 5, 1979, she was en route from Manila to Cebu when a fire broke out forcing her captain to beach her on the coast of Batangas, without loss of life. The ship was declared a constructive total loss, but Sulpicio Line later bought her back from their underwriters, and after a complete refit she reentered her former service under the name *Doña Paz* (Lady Peace).

On December 20, 1987, she was en route from Tacloban, on the island of Leyte, to Manila, via Catbalogan, Samar. At about 2200 she was in the 18-mile-wide Tablas Strait between Mindoro Island and Marinduque Island when she collided with *Vector,* a motor tanker bound from Batangas, Luzon, to Mashate, Central Philippines, with 8,800 barrels of petroleum products. These ignited and caused a fire from which it was virtually impossible to escape. *Vector* had a crew of 13, only 2 of whom survived, while *Doña Paz*'s survivors numbered only 21. Although she was licensed to carry only 1,518 passengers, there were actually 1,586 passengers on the manifest. Based on subsequent interviews with survivors and relatives of passengers not listed on the manifest, the company later put the total number of fatalities at 4,375, about 1,000 of them children; none of the ship's 58 crew survived. The fire was so intense that it all but annihilated the two ships, their cargoes and their passengers and crews. Only 275 bodies washed ashore, and a U.S. Air Force spokesman reported that observer planes found virtually no evidence of the ships: "It was as if it had never happened."

Hooke, *Modern Shipping Disasters.*

DORADE

Yawl. *L/B/D:* 52′ × 10.2′ × 7.6′. *Tons:* 19 disp. *Hull:* wood. *Comp.:* 7. *Des.:* Olin Stephens (Sparkman & Stephens). *Built:* Minneford Yacht Yard, Inc., City Island, N.Y.; 1929.

One of the first yachts designed by young naval architect Olin Stephens, *Dorade* was a racing cruiser ordered by his father. Her inspired design helped launch the careers of both Olin and his brother Rod Stephens, one of the premier yachtsmen of the midcentury. On July 4, 1931, *Dorade* sailed from Brenton's Reef at the start of the Transatlantic Race with a crew that included the Stephens brothers. *Dorade* swept the field of ten boats and arrived off Plymouth's Ram Island on July 21, 16 days, 55 minutes out — two days ahead of any other entrant; on corrected time her margin of victory was four days. Later that summer, *Dorade* won the Fastnet Race. *Dorade* returned to the United States via steamship and upon their return to New York, the crew were given a ticker-tape parade on Broadway from Battery Park to City Hall.

The next year *Dorade* finished first in Class B in the Bermuda Race, and in 1933 Rod Stephens took her back across the Atlantic. After cruising in Norway, she won the Fastnet for a second time before returning to the United States under sail. One of *Dorade*'s most enduring contributions to yacht design is seen not in her hull but in the *Dorade* ventilator, developed over the course of a few seasons, which by means of discontinuous air spouts leading from a traditional cowl ventilator allows air to circulate below while keeping out water.

In 1935, *Dorade* was sold to James Flood of San Fran-

cisco, who sailed her to victory in the 1936 Honolulu Race. She has remained on the West Coast ever since — picking up an auxiliary diesel engine along the way — most recently owned by Mike Douglas of Deer Harbor, Washington.

Kinney, *"You Are First."*

DOVE

Lapworth sloop. *L/B/D:* 24′ × 7.5′ × 4′ (7.3m x 2.3m × 1.2m). *Hull:* fiberglass. *Comp.:* 1. *Built:* 1961.

On July 27, 1965, sixteen-year-old Robin Lee Graham sailed out of San Pedro Harbor, California, to begin a circumnavigation of the globe. Graham had some experience sailing in the Pacific with his family, and he fitted out the secondhand sloop *Dove* with the help of his father. After sailing to Hawaii, he headed southwest for Samoa, stopping en route at Fanning Island. Fifteen miles from Tutuila, *Dove* was dismasted in a squall and Graham ran under jury rig to Apia. After five months in the Samoas, he continued to Tonga and Fiji. There he met Patti Ratterree, whom he later married in South Africa. After sailing to the New Hebrides, Guadalcanal, and Port Moresby, New Guinea, he transited the Torres Straits to Darwin, Australia, where he arrived on May 4, 1967. Two months later, he sailed for the Cocos Islands. Eighteen hours after leaving the Cocos, *Dove* was again dismasted, but with a jury rig, Graham pressed on to Mauritius 2,300 miles to the west. After fitting a new mast, he sailed to South Africa where he spent almost nine months. Sailing from Cape Town on July 13, 1968, he called at Ascension Island, Suriname, and Barbados, where Graham bought a new 33-foot sloop as a replacement for *Dove*. After a year in the Caribbean, Graham sailed *Return of Dove* through the Panama Canal, then southwest to the Galápagos Islands where he spent nearly three months. He headed north to arrive at Los Angeles on April 30, 1970, after a voyage of 30,600 nautical miles.

Graham, *Dove.*

DREADNOUGHT

Clipper (3m). *L/B/D:* 212′ od × 41.5′ × 26.6′ (64.6m × 12.6m × 8.1m). *Tons:* 1,414 om. *Hull:* wood. *Comp.:* 34 crew. *Built:* Currier & Townsend, Newburyport, Mass.; 1853.

The medium clipper *Dreadnought* was built for the "Red Cross Line" of transatlantic packets that carried immigrants westbound between Liverpool and New York. Her

James E. Buttersworth's portrait of the "Red Cross Line" packet ship DREADNOUGHT, *painted shortly after her launch in 1853. The reputation of the smart transatlantic clipper was made under the redoubtable Captain Samuel Samuels. Courtesy Peabody Essex Museum, Salem, Massachusetts.*

first and most celebrated master was Captain Samuel Samuels, who later wrote of her, "She was built for hard usage and to make a reputation for herself and me and that she should do her duty, or that we should both sink." Small wonder, then, that she was one of the most famous ships of the age and earned the nicknames "The Flying Dutchman" and "The Wild Boat of the Atlantic." *Dreadnought* spent nine years under Samuels's command for the Red Cross Line, and in the course of more than 20 recorded voyages (of a career of 31 voyages), she averaged 19 days eastbound and 26 days westbound.

Much of *Dreadnought*'s fame derives from a remarkable passage that began at Liverpool on January 16, 1863. By the 21st, the ship was caught in a furious midatlantic gale in the face of which she carried only a close-reefed maintopsail. (Previously, Samuels never reduced sail to anything less than double-reefed topsails.) One towering wave carried away the rudder, stove the hatches, and, perhaps worst of all, broke Samuels's leg in a compound fracture and killed the carpenter. The crew attempted to rig a rudder, but it was lost. On the fifth day a passing ship attempted to render assistance. The following day, Samuels ordered his second officer (the first officer was incompetent) to sail *Dreadnought* stern first to Fayal, in the Azores, about 350 miles away. The ship covered 183 miles in two days before the seas calmed enough for the crew to hang a jury rudder. Six days later, the ship sailed

into Fayal where Samuels, considerably the worse for wear, recuperated for nearly two months before sailing on April 9 for New York. Further repairs to *Dreadnought* took another two months, and she resumed her voyage for Liverpool on June 9, 1863, under command of Captain Lytle. On the ship's second voyage under Lytle, she was returning from Liverpool in December when bad weather again forced the ship into Fayal, where Lytle died from injuries sustained at sea.

That passage proved the ship's last on the transatlantic run, and in the summer of the following year she made her first voyage to San Francisco and the Pacific. *Dreadnought* completed three voyages in the Cape Horn trade, calling at Honolulu and Callao on the return passages to New Bedford, New York, and, in 1869, Liverpool. On April 28, she sailed for San Francisco with a cargo of finished goods under command of Captain P. N. Mayhew. The voyage proceeded well until dawn of July 4 when the ship ran aground at Cape Peñas on the northeast coast of Tierra del Fuego. There was no hope for the ship, which the crew barely escaped in two boats. Seventeen days later, they hailed the Norwegian bark *General Birch* in the Straits of Le Maire between Tierra del Fuego and Staten Island and were taken to Talcahuano, Chile.

Howe & Matthews, *American Clipper Ships.* Samuels, *From the Forecastle to the Cabin.*

HMS DREADNOUGHT

Dreadnought-class battleship (2f/2m). *L/B/D:* 526′ × 82′ × 29′ (160.3m × 25m × 8.8m). *Tons:* 21,845 disp. *Hull:* steel. *Comp.:* 657–773. *Arm.:* 10 × 12″ (5 × 2), 18 × 12pdr; 5 × 18″TT. *Armor:* 11″ belt, 4″ deck. *Mach.:* steam turbine, 23,000 shp, 4 screws; 21 kts. *Des.:* Sir Philip Watts. *Built:* Portsmouth Dockyard, Eng.; 1906.

The decades following the development of HMS WAR-RIOR in 1861 were a period of experimentation in warship design. Steam propulsion, steel protection, and breech-loading, armor-piercing shells were endlessly tested and refined. As the century wore on, warships shed their rigging and came to rely exclusively on coal-fired compound and triple-expansion steam engines, and they exchanged their broadside batteries for casemates, barbettes, and finally turrets. By the turn of the century, the ideal battleship bristled with a battery of mixed large-caliber guns. The KING EDWARD VII class of 1901 mounted four 12-inch, four 9.2-inch, and ten 6-inch guns, and the *Lord Nelsons* of 1904 carried four 12-inch and ten 9.2-inch guns. At this point, naval thinkers in various countries began to think in terms of an all-big-gun ship — powerfully armed, heavily armored, and fast. With such a ship, the captain could chose when to fight and at what range, the gunnery officer could more easily judge the gunners' accuracy (all the shell splashes would be from guns of the same caliber), and only one size shell would have to be carried.

While he was not the first to conceive of an all-big-gun ship, First Sea Lord Sir John Arbuthnot "Jackie" Fisher was the first to get one built. In December 1904 he formed a committee to refine his basic idea for a ship mounting as many 12-inch guns as possible and capable of 21 knots. Seven weeks later the committee adopted a plan for a ship mounting ten 12-inch guns in five turrets, driven by steam turbines — one of the first large ships so powered — with watertight bulkheads and 11-inch belt armor for protection. The five turrets were laid out in such a way as to allow eight guns to fire broadside, six forward, and six aft. "A" turret was on the raised fore deck, wing turrets "P" and "Q" were situated on either side of the bridge, and "X" and "Y" turrets were mounted on the centerline aft. As the latter two were on the main deck, "X" had only limited arcs of fire to port and starboard. In addition, she carried a light armament of eighteen 12-pdr. guns specifically for use against torpedo boats.

Fisher wanted fast, hard-hitting ships for his navy, and

HMS DREADNOUGHT *of 1906 revolutionized warship design by combining powerful armament, good speed, and thick armor. Precursor of several generations of capital ships,* DREADNOUGHT *was herself obsolete within only a few years. Courtesy National Maritime Museum, Greenwich.*

he led by example. HMS *Dreadnought* was laid down on October 2, 1905, launched on February 9, 1906, and went to sea on October 3, 1906. (Previously the average building time for a capital ship was 33 months, and the record only 31 months.) In January 1906 she sailed for the Mediterranean and then to Port-of-Spain, Trinidad, where far from the prying eyes of domestic critics and foreign rivals, her engines and guns were given a thorough workout by Captain Sir Reginald Bacon. His report showed that in all important respects *Dreadnought* was a success. "No member of the Committee on Designs," he wrote, "dared to hope that all the innovations introduced would have turned out as successfully as had been the case." The Royal Navy's next six battleships were built along essentially the same lines. Returning to Portsmouth, *Dreadnought* became flagship of the Home Fleet. As such she spent most of her time in home waters with occasional cruises to Spain and the Mediterranean.

If optimistic proponents of the all-big-gun ship believed that the *Dreadnought* would give Britain an insuperable lead in naval construction and design, *Dreadnought*'s opponents were wrong to think that Britain could have avoided an arms race by not building an all-big-gun ship. Both groups ignored the determination of other navies and overlooked the general trend towards the development of such ships. The United States had already designed USS *Michigan* and *South Carolina*, which mounted eight 12-inch guns in four centerline turrets, though both were laid down after the *Dreadnought*. Germany responded immediately to the British challenge with orders for four *Nassau*-class ships mounting twelve 11.3-inch guns, and in 1907 Italy laid down the *Dante Alighieri*, the first ship to mount triple-gun turrets.

These developments took place against the backdrop of the Pax Britannica — a world whose innocence, compared to that of our own, can be easily judged from the ease with which the celebrated "*Dreadnought* Hoax" was carried out. In 1911, the ship was lying in Weymouth Bay when a telegram arrived announcing the impending arrival of the Emperor of Abyssinia and his party of five, including two "translators" from the Foreign Office. Conveyed to the ship, they were given a royal welcome and a thorough tour of the *Dreadnought*, the various details of which were explained, via the interpreters, in what turned out to be a mispronounced recitation of part of Virgil's *Aeneid*. His tour complete, the emperor and his entourage departed. Several weeks later, the story of the Abyssinian visit was leaked to the *Daily Mirror* — presumably by the emperor himself, Cambridge University student Anthony Buxton. Among his supporting cast were the painter Duncan Grant, Adrian Stephen, and Stephen's sister Virginia, better known to posterity as Virginia

Woolf, who sported theatrical makeup and a beard for the occasion.

When World War I began, *Dreadnought* had been eclipsed many times over. As a unit of the Grand Fleet's 4th Battle Squadron, her only decisive action against the enemy came on February 18, 1915, when she rammed and sank the German submarine *U-29* in the North Sea. Withdrawn from the fleet because her low speed made it impossible to keep station, she became flagship of the 3rd Battle Squadron at Sheerness, although she returned to the Grand Fleet from March to August 1918. Put in reserve at Rosyth after the war, *Dreadnought* was paid off on March 31, 1920. Sold to T. Ward & Company, she was broken up at Inverness in 1923.

Massie, "*Dreadnought*." Roberts, *Battleship "Dreadnought."* Stephen, "*Dreadnought*" *Hoax.*

SMS DRESDEN

Dresden-class light cruiser (3f/2m). *L/B/D:* 388′ × 44.3′ × 18′ (118.3m × 13.5m × 5.5m). *Tons:* 4,268 disp. *Hull:* steel. *Comp.:* 361. *Arm.:* 10 × 10.5cm, 10 mg, 8 × 5.2cm; 2 × 18″TT. *Mach.:* steam turbines, 18,880 shp, 2 screws; 25 kts. *Built:* Blohm & Voss, Hamburg; 1909.

At the outbreak of World War I, *Dresden* was protecting German interests in war-torn Mexico and carried President Victoriano Huerta into exile in Jamaica. She was due to return to Germany when war came, and after meeting up with SMS KARLSRUHE at Port au Prince, Haiti, she came under the command of Commander Fritz Ludecke. (Another of her officers was Lieutenant Commander Wilhelm Canaris, who became head of German intelligence during World War II.) Turning south, *Dresden* proved a lackluster commerce raider, but in October she joined Vice Admiral Graf von Spee's squadron in the Pacific. She took part in the destruction of the British fleet at the Battle of Coronel on November 1 and she was the only German unit to survive the Germans' crushing defeat at the Battle of the Falklands on December 8. After hiding among the Chilean islands for three months, and an abortive run west across the Pacific, *Dresden* was forced into the Juan Fernández Islands on March 9. Five days later, she was discovered by HMS *Kent* and *Glasgow*. When the British demanded unconditional surrender, Ludecke scuttled his ship at Más Afuera in 33°37′S, 78°48′W. (A second *Dresden* was commissioned in 1918, interned at Scapa Flow, and beached there after being scuttled in 1919. She was broken up for scrap in 1921.)

Walter, *Kaiser's Pirates.*

USS DRUM (SS-228)

Gato-class submarine. *L/B/D:* 311.8′ × 27.3′ × 15.3′ (95m × 8.3m × 4.6m). *Tons:* 1,256/2,410 disp. *Hull:* steel; 300′ dd. *Comp.:* 61. *Arm.:* 10 × 21″TT; 1 × 3″, 3 mg. *Mach.:* diesel/electric, 5,400/2,740 shp, 2 screws; 20/9 kts. *Built:* Portsmouth Navy Yard, Kittery, Me.; 1942.

Named for a type of fish, USS *Drum* was commissioned five weeks before the Japanese attack on Pearl Harbor brought the United States into World War II. Arriving in the Pacific in April 1942, she made a total of thirteen war patrols in all theaters of the Pacific, and had one of the most successful records of any U.S. submarine, credited with sinking fifteen ships for a total of 80,580 gross tons. Her first cruise, off Japan, netted her a seaplane tender and three cargo ships. Her next war patrol was hampered by faulty torpedoes, a common complaint of U.S. submariners throughout the war. On January 24, 1943, on her fourth patrol, *Drum* hit *Ryuho* with two torpedoes, but the carrier refused to sink. Her next four patrols, out of Brisbane, were in the waters around New Guinea, where she sank five ships before a severe depth charge attack forced her stateside for repairs. Her next successful patrol was during the Battle of Leyte Gulf, when she sank three ships in the South China Sea in October 1944. Following the war, *Drum* served as a Naval Reserve training ship in the Potomac River until 1962. Seven years later she was donated to the Battleship Alabama Commission for display as a museum and memorial in Mobile.

U.S. Navy, *DANFS.*

DUKE

Frigate (3m). *L/B:* ca. 80′ keel × 26′ (24m × 8m). *Tons:* 320 tons. *Hull:* wood. *Comp.:* 183. *Arm.:* 30 guns. *Built:* England(?); <1708.

Duke was one of two Bristol-owned privateers — the other was *Duchess* — fitted out for an expedition against Spanish shipping in the Pacific Ocean, still regarded as "a Spanish lake." The ships sailed on August 2, 1708; the officers included William Dampier, veteran of two circumnavigations, including one in ROEBUCK (1699–1700), and Woodes Rogers. After stopping at Cork and the Canary and Cape Verde Islands, the ships came to the island of Grande, off Brazil. About January 15, 1709, they rounded Cape Horn, in the process sailing to 61°53′S, "which for aught we know is the furthest that any one has yet got to the southward." The ships made next for the island of Juan Fernández where on February 1 the castaway Alexander Selkirk greeted them. Four years before, he had sailed as master of the privateer *Cinque Ports* in an expedition commanded by Dampier, who sailed in the *St.*

George. Preferring the uncertainty of exile to work with the *Cinque Ports'* Captain Thomas Stradling, Selkirk was put ashore and left to fend for himself. On Dampier's recommendation, Rogers appointed Selkirk mate in the *Duke*, which sailed next to the coast of Peru. Here Dampier and company captured several ships, including *Havre de Grace*, which they armed and renamed *Marquis*.

On April 22, the English seized the city of Guayaquil and eight ships, which they ransomed for the payment of 30,000 pieces of eight. They cruised between the coast of Peru and the Galapagos Islands until mid-September when they sailed for the Tres Marias Islands, 100 miles south of Mazatlán, Mexico. There they awaited the Manila galleon — Spain's annual shipment of gold and silver from the Americas to the Philippines — until December 21 when they captured one of a pair, *Nuestra Señora de la Incarnacion Disenganio*, which they renamed *Batchelor*. Six days later, they engaged the 450-ton *Bigonia* but could not capture her. From here, the ships turned west across the Pacific. Their run from Port Segura to Guam lasted from January 11 to March 11, 1710; their best day's run was 161 miles, their worst only 41. They were well received by the Spanish governor, and after provisioning, they continued on their long voyage home, with stops at the Portuguese-held Butung Island (May 26), the Dutch entrepôts at Batavia (June 20), and the Cape of Good Hope (December 29). Sailing with a Dutch convoy, Rogers's four ships returned to Erith on October 14, 1711

The voyage of the *Duke* and *Duchess* was a financial success — it grossed about £800,000 for a £14,000 investment — and spurred further incursions into the Pacific. Rogers's *Cruising Voyage round the World* also publicized the remarkable story of Selkirk's stay on Juan Fernández, and became the inspiration for Daniel Defoe's novel *Robinson Crusoe* and William Cowper's "Lines on Solitude," which begins "I am monarch of all I survey."

Rogers, *Cruising Voyage round the World.*

HMS DUKE OF YORK

King George V-class battleship. *L/B/D:* 745′ × 103′ × 29′ (227.1m × 31.4m × 8.8m). *Tons:* 42,237 disp. *Hull:* steel. *Comp.:* 1,543. *Arm.:* 10 × 14″ (2 × 4, 1 × 2), 16 × 5.25″, 32 × 2pdr, 4 rocket projectors; 2 aircraft. *Armor:* 14.7″ belt, 5.9″ deck. *Mach.:* geared turbines, 110,000 shp, 4 shafts; 27.5 kts. *Built:* John Brown & Co., Ltd., Clydebank, Scotland; 1941.

The sixth ship of the name, HMS *Duke of York* was commissioned in November of 1941. The next month she carried Prime Minister Winston Churchill to the United States for the first meeting of the Anglo-American General Staff. In the spring and summer of 1942, she provided distant cover for the Murmansk convoys. After sailing in support of Operation Torch, the Allied landings in North Africa in November 1942, she returned to England for a refit. In October 1943, she resumed operations in Arctic waters. On the morning of December 26, *Duke of York* was providing distant cover for Convoy JW55B when the cruisers HMS NORFOLK, BELFAST, and SHEFFIELD began shadowing the German battleship SCHARNHORST. At 1651, *Duke of York* opened fire; an hour and a half later, at a range of more than 18,000 yards (about 10 miles), she hit *Scharnhorst*'s boiler room. The fatal blow enabled the British ships to close to 3,000 yards, and at 1745 *Scharnhorst* sank in 72°16′N, 28°41′E. *Duke of York* remained in Arctic waters until September 1944. After an eight-month refit, she joined the British Pacific Fleet and took part in the bombardment of the Japanese home islands in August 1945. Placed in reserve in 1949, she was scrapped at Faslane in 1958.

Parkes, *British Battleships*.

DUYFKEN

Jaght (3m). *L/B/D:* 63′ × 17′ × 7′ (19m × 5m × 2m). *Tons:* 30 lasts/60 tons. *Hull:* wood. *Comp.:* 20. *Arm.:* 10 guns. *Built:* Netherlands; <1600.

When the Netherlands declared its independence from Spain in 1581, Philip II retaliated by closing to Dutch merchants the port of Lisbon with its rich trade in oriental spices. The Dutch decided to trade directly with the East, and in 1595 the ships *Hollandia* (400 tons), *Mauritius* (400 tons), *Amsterdam* (200 tons), and *Duyfken* (60 tons) sailed for Java. Although only 80 of the 249 crew survived and *Amsterdam* was lost, the venture was considered successful. In December 1603, another ship called *Duyfken* left the Netherlands under Willem Jansz as part of a fleet of twelve ships. Once in the Indies, Jansz was sent to search out other outlets for trade, particularly in "the great land of Nova Guinea and other East- and Southlands." On November 18, 1605, *Duyfken* sailed from Bantam to Banda and then through the Kai Islands and on to Tanjung Deyong, New Guinea. *Duyfken* rounded False Cape and then crossed the Arafura Sea into the Gulf of Carpentaria (thereby missing Torres Strait) and charted 200 miles of the Australian coast, which Jansz considered part of New Guinea. This is the first recorded visit to Australia by Europeans. Finding the land barren and the people inhospitable (ten of his men were killed on various shore expeditions), at Cape Keerveer ("Turnabout") south of Albatross Bay, Jansz headed home and arrived at Bantam in June 1606, two months before SAN PEDRO transited Torres Strait, thereby establishing that New Guinea was not part of a larger southern continent.

Murdoch, *"Duyfken" and the First Discoveries of Australia*. Sigmond & Zuiderbaan, *Dutch Discoveries of Australia*.

E-9

E-class submarine. *L/B:* 176' × 22.5' (53.6m × 6.9m). *Tons:* 662 disp. *Hull:* steel. *Arm.:* 1 × 12pdr; 5 × 18"TT. *Mach.:* diesel; 15 kts. *Built:* Vickers Ltd., Barrow-in-Furness, Eng.; 1913.

The Royal Navy's E-class submarines constituted one of six classes — A through F — based on the *Holland* prototype developed by John Holland. Between 1906 and 1914, the Royal Navy applied five percent of its shipbuilding budget to submarine construction, and at the start of World War I, it had the largest submarine fleet in the world, though of the Navy's 75 operational boats, only 20 of the D and E class were capable of sustained seagoing cruises. (The other leading submarine powers were France, with 62 in service; Russia, with 36; and Germany, with 28.) The British submarine force began wartime patrols on August 5, 1914. Six weeks later, on September 13, Lieutenant Commander Max Horton's *E-9* claimed the first German victim, sinking the cruiser *Hela* about six miles off Helgoland (in 54°03'N, 7°55'E), with the loss of two dead. On October 6, *E-9* sank the torpedo boat *S-116* off the mouth of the Ems (in 53°42'N, 6°09'E), with the loss of nine crew.

A week later, *E-9, E-1,* and E-11 were dispatched on a special patrol into the Baltic with orders to use the Russian base at Libau. (Engine problems forced *E-11* back to England.) The submarines' arrival was a complete surprise to the Russians, who were never told of the deployment. In May 1915, the Germans occupied Libau and the submarines proceeded to Lipvak on the Gulf of Finland. *E-9* achieved its first Baltic success near the Gulf of Riga when on June 5, she sank the collier *Dora Hugo Stinnes* and damaged the destroyer *S.148,* and on July 2, she damaged Rear Admiral Albert Hopman's armored cruiser *Prinz Adalbert.* (On October 23, 1915, the German flagship was sunk by *E-8* with the loss of 672 crew.) The most important target in the Baltic was the iron ore trade from Sweden, and in October 1915, *E-9* sank three ore ships and damaged a third. By 1916, Germany's use of convoys in the Baltic and the scarcity of spare parts made offensive operations almost impossible, and in 1917 the Russian Revolution further curtailed the naval war. On April 3, 1918, one month after the Russian surrender at Brest-Litovsk, the four E-class and three C-class British submarines at Helsingfors (Helsinki) were scuttled to avoid capture by German troops coming to the aid of anti-Bolshevik White Finnish forces.

Wilson, *Baltic Assignment.*

E-11

E-class submarine. *L/B:* 176' × 22.5' (53.6m × 6.9m). *Tons:* 662 disp. *Hull:* steel. *Arm.:* 1 × 12pdr; 5 × 18"TT. *Mach.:* diesel. *Built:* Vickers Ltd., Barrow-in-Furness, Eng.; 1914.

E 11 was one of fifty-eight British E-class submarines built between 1912 and 1917. Deployed first with Commodore Roger Keyes's Eighth Submarine Flotilla at Harwich, Lieutenant Commander Martin Nasmith's *E-11* took part in a few unsuccessful raids along the German coast. In the last week of December 1914, she was bombed by a Zeppelin while rescuing downed airplane pilots in the North Sea. Unable to sail to the Baltic with *E-1* and E-9 because of engine trouble, *E-11* was one of several British submarines sent out to the Aegean island of Lesbos at the start of the Gallipoli campaign in the spring of 1915.

E-11 entered the Dardanelles for the first of three patrols on May 19, 1915. After sinking a number of naval and merchant vessels in the Sea of Marmara — one carrying a Chicago-based journalist whose reporting transformed *E-11* into eleven submarines — she torpedoed the munitions ship *Stambul* alongside the arsenal at Constantinople. British submarines in the Sea of Marmara could only operate so long as they had supplies and ammunition. To conserve the latter, Nasmith trimmed *E-11*'s torpedoes so that if they missed their target, they would float rather than sink. Once the intended victim was out of sight, he would find the torpedo and members of the crew would jump over the side and push it back into the bow tube. Having sunk six supply and troop ships and a number of sailing vessels in three weeks, Nasmith was awarded a Victoria Cross for his exploits, the third submariner so honored in the Dardanelles campaign.

On her third cruise, *E-11,* together with *E-14,* shelled troop columns marching towards Gallipoli. On August 8, *E-11* torpedoed the Turkish predreadnought *Harridan Barbarossa* (ex-*Kurfürst Friedrich Wilhelm*), which sank with 253 of her 580 crew. Frustrated by the lack of surface targets, Nasmith's crew next attempted to blow up a railway bridge in the Gulf of Izmit. Withdrawn at the conclusion of the Dardanelles campaign in early 1916, the "Scourge of Marmara" was credited with 101 Turkish vessels. *E-9* was broken up at Malta in 1922.

Carr, *By Guess and by God.*

E. A. BRYAN

Liberty ship (1f/3m). *L/B/D:* 441.5′ × 57′ × 27′8″ (134.6m × 17.4m × 8.4m). *Tons:* 7,176 grt. *Hull:* steel. *Comp.:* 81. *Arm.:* 1 × 5″, 10 × 20mm. *Mach.:* triple expansion, 1 screw, 2,500 ihp; 11 kts. *Built:* Kaiser Permanente Yard 2, Richmond, Calif.; 1944.

The deadliest military accident in the United States during World War II resulted from the explosion of two munitions ships at Port Chicago, California, 40 miles northeast of San Francisco on Suisun Bay. On July 17, 1944, munitions handlers were loading the *E. A. Bryan* when the cargo detonated. This was followed by a secondary explosion aboard the Victory ship *Quinault Victory.* The blasts, which were felt as far away as Nevada, leveled much of Port Chicago and killed 321 people, including 69 merchant marine personnel and 203 enlisted men — most of them black — working as stevedores. The sailors were ordered back to work two weeks later, but 258 refused, citing inadequate safety regulations. (The Coast Guard had banned smoking aboard munitions ships only two months before, and it is thought that a careless smoker might have touched off the explosion aboard the *E. A. Bryan.*) Under threat of court-martial, 208 did return to work; 50 were tried and found guilty of mutiny. Sentenced to between 8 and 15 years in prison and given dishonorable discharges, they were released after 16 months. Fifty years later, the Navy rejected a request by four California Representatives to overturn the convictions on the grounds that the sentences were tainted by racial prejudice. While the Navy found that racism contributed to the high proportion of black enlisted men

working as stevedores at the naval base, it denied that race had any influence on the sentences per se, and the appeals were rejected.

Allen, *Port Chicago Mutiny.* Sawyer & Mitchell, *Liberty Ships.*

USCGC EAGLE

(ex-*Horst Wessel*) Bark (1f/3m). *L/B/D:* 277′ × 39.3′ × 17′ (84.4m × 12m × 5.2m). *Tons:* 1,634 disp. *Hull:* steel. *Comp.:* 212. *Mach.:* diesel, 750 hp. *Built:* Blohm & Voss, Hamburg; 1936.

Originally commissioned as a German training ship, the *Horst Wessel* (named for a Nazi thug) was the second of four near-sister ships built by Blohm & Voss in the 1930s. The others were *Gorch Fock* (now *Tovarisch*), *Albert Leo Schlageter* (now *Sagres*), and Romania's *Mircea. Horst Wessel* made only a few training voyages before the start of World War II, when she saw duty in the Baltic as a transport and training vessel. Following the war the United States acquired the ship as part of war reparations and turned her over to the U.S. Coast Guard, which had sailed the Danish training ship DANMARK during the war. Homeported at the U.S. Coast Guard Academy in New London, Connecticut, USCGC *Eagle* (the seventh ship of the name) was for many years one of only a few sail-training ships of any size in the United States. For more than half a century, she has shown the flag in ports throughout the United States, Latin America, and Europe while providing valuable training for Coast Guard cadets. President John F. Kennedy ordered that her hull be given the same orange chevron and blue shield that distinguishes all Coast Guard vessels, and she is readily identifiable in any fleet of ships.

Norton, *"Eagle" Seamanship.* Putz, *"Eagle."*

EASTLAND

Excursion vessel (2f/2m). *L/B/D:* 275′ × 38.2′ × 19.5′ (83.8m × 11.6m × 5.9m). *Tons:* 1,961 grt; 1,218 net. *Hull:* steel. *Comp.:* 1,950–3,300 pass; 70 crew. *Mach.:* triple expansion, 3,500 hp, 2 screws; 24 mph. *Des.:* Sidney G. Jenks. *Built:* Jenks Ship Building Co., Port Huron, Mich.; 1903.

Built for the Michigan Steamship Company's service on the 77-mile run between Chicago and South Haven, Michigan, *Eastland* was the scene of one of the worst shipping disasters in Great Lakes history. *Eastland* was a four-decked vessel originally rated to carry 2,800 people, though actual passenger capacity fluctuated between a high of 3,300 in 1904 and a low of 1,950 in 1908. Access was via five gangways set just above the waterline and the ship had a freeboard of less than two feet when fully loaded; as the doors were usually open, flooding threatened if the vessel listed as little as 10 degrees. In 1907, the Lake Shore Navigation Company bought *Eastland* for service on Lake Erie between Cleveland and Sandusky, Ohio, where she operated for five years without incident. However, rumors of the ship's instability — she tended to list while loading passengers — led the management to offer a $5,000 reward to any competent engineer who could demonstrate that she was unsafe. No challenge came forward.

Eastland returned to Lake Michigan for service with the St. Joseph-Chicago Steamship Company in 1913. Two years later she was chartered by employees of Western Electric for a company picnic in Michigan City, Indiana. Earlier that summer, two decks were reinforced with concrete, and three lifeboats and six life rafts were added to qualify for an increase in passenger capacity to 2,500 people. The resulting decrease in stability went unnoticed for three weeks, during which she carried no more than 1,123 passengers. Passengers for the Western Electric excursion began loading at 0630 on July 24, 1915, and within forty minutes, 2,501 people had embarked. As passengers congregated on the starboard side of the ship, engineers flooded the two port ballast tanks, little realizing that the ship at this point had little or no positive stability. At 0723, as the first lines were cast off and the gangplank was pulled in, water began to flood through the gangways and into the engine room. Five minutes later, with three bow lines still in place, the ship capsized, quietly, "like an egg in the water," according to one observer. Although *Eastland* lay only half submerged in the Chicago River, less than 20 feet from shore, 841 passengers died. The resulting lawsuits, which dragged on for more than twenty years, brought little satisfaction either to the survivors or the victims' families as the courts pinned the tragedy on the engineer and held the company blameless.

Salvage of the ship began immediately, and *Eastland* was righted on August 14. The following year she was auctioned to Captain Edward A. Evers, who sought to use her as a training ship for the Illinois Naval Reserve. In November 1917, the U.S. Navy purchased the ship and converted her to the training gunboat USS *Wilmette*, which served on the Great Lakes until 1945. She was finally scrapped in 1947.

Hilton, "*Eastland*."

EDMUND FITZGERALD

Great Lakes ore boat (1f/1m). *L/B/D:* 729' × 75.1' × 26' (222.2m × 22.9m × 8.1m). *Tons:* 13,632 grt. *Hull:* steel. *Comp.:* 28. *Mach.:* steam turbine, 7,500 shp, 2 screws; 25 kts. *Built:* Great Lakes Engineering Works, River Rouge, Mich.; 1958.

Named for the chairman of the Northwestern Mutual Life Insurance Company of Milwaukee, which owned the ship, at the time of her launch *Edmund Fitzgerald* was the largest ore carrier ever built on the Great Lakes and the largest ship ever assembled from welded prefabricated steel sections. The "Queen of the Lakes" was noted for her first-rate guest accommodations and could carry as many as seven guests in two staterooms. Operated by the Columbia Transportation Company, a division of the Oglebay Norton Company, which leased the ship from Northwestern Mutual, she left on her maiden voyage from Silver Bay, Minnesota, through the Sault Sainte Marie Canals between Lakes Superior and Huron, and on to Detroit, carrying a record 25,000 tons of iron ore. She continued in that trade for 18 years, eventually eclipsed in size and speed by newer ships, but she was always regarded as the epitome of the Lakes ore carriers.

The Great Lakes are notorious for the violence of their winter storms and the speed with which they develop, and navigation on the Lakes all but stops for three months of the year. On Sunday, November 9, 1975, *Edmund Fitzgerald* sailed from Superior, Wisconsin, bound for Detroit — 700 miles along a broad arc to the southeast — loaded with 26,013 tons of taconite. The voyage, under Captain Ernest McSorley, a 44-year veteran of the Lakes who was slated for retirement, was intended as the last of the season. That night, hurricane-force (60–70 miles per hour) winds began blowing from the north, kicking up sharp 30-foot seas into which the fully laden *Fitz* could barely make two miles per hour. Although visual contact was impossible in such conditions, the *Fitz* was in radio and radar contact with other ships throughout the day, including the ore boat *Arthur M. Anderson*, which was about 10 miles astern. A little past 1910, on November 10, *Edmund Fitzgerald* dropped off *Anderson*'s radar scope without warning; she had been about 13 miles north of Whitefish Point, Michigan, and 8 miles west of Copper Mine Point, Ontario (in about 46°58'N, 84°58'N). Despite a desperate air and sea search effort, none of the ship's crew was ever found, either dead or alive. Theories of the ship's loss range from her being capsized when her cargo of iron ore pellets shifted or metal fatigue to flooding.

While the loss of *Edmund Fitzgerald* was dramatic in and of itself, it achieved a more enduring fame than do most shipwrecks when Gordon Lightfoot penned the words to what has become one of the most familiar American ballads of the twentieth century, "The Loss of the *Edmund Fitzgerald.*"

Hemming, *Gales of November.* Ratigan, *Great Lakes Shipwrecks and Survivors.* Film: *The Mystery of the "Edmund Fitzgerald."*

EDNA HOYT

Schooner (5m). *L/B/D:* 224' × 41.1' × 20.8' (68.3m × 12.5m × 6.3m). *Tons:* 1,512 grt. *Hull:* wood. *Built:* Dunn & Eliot, Thomaston, Me.; 1920.

Edna Hoyt was the last of the 58 five-masted schooners built on the East Coast of the United States between 1888 and 1920. Initially engaged in the coal trade between the Chesapeake and New England, first for her builders and later for the Superior Trading and Transportation Company of Boston, in 1929 the *Hoyt* was sold to Foss & Crabtree (also of Boston) and began trading between the East Coast and the Caribbean. Her cargoes consisted of general cargo southbound and sheep guano fertilizer from Venezuela on her return. During the hurricane season, she occasionally sailed only as far south as Florida, for timber. The *Hoyt* remained in these coasting trades until 1937. In August of that year, she loaded a million board feet of lumber at Halifax and sailed for Ireland on her first, and only, transatlantic passage. From Belfast, she proceeded to Newport, Wales, to load coal for Venezuela. While at Newport, her hull was strained when she grounded at low tide, and Captain Hopkins took her to the deeper harbor at Cardiff to complete loading. Sailing on November 2, she was severely knocked about in a storm in the Bay of Biscay. The hull damage sustained at Newport proving worse than realized, she was soon in a leaking condition and was finally taken in tow to Lisbon by the Norwegian freighter *San Amigo.* There the last East Coast five-master was condemned. Sold to J. Vasconcellos in early 1938, she ended her days as a coal hulk in Portugal.

Merriam, *Last of the Five Masters.* Morris, *American Sailing Coasters.*

EDWARD BONAVENTURE

Ship (3m). *Tons:* 160 tons. *Hull:* wood. *Comp.:* 36. *Built:* <1553.

In 1553, the Mysterie [guild] and Companie of the Marchants Aduenturers for the Discoverie of Regions, Dominions, Iland and Places Unknown (headed by Sebastian Cabot) dispatched an expedition under Sir Hugh Willoughby to sail around the top of Norway for China, in search of a Northeast Passage. The three ships were Richard Chancellor's *Edward Bonaventure,* under master Stephen Burroughs, Willoughby's 120-ton *Bona Esperanza,* under William Gefferson, and the 90-ton *Bona Confidentia* under Cornelis Durfoort. The ships put to sea in mid-June and at the end of July became separated in a storm off the Lofoten Islands in northern Norway. *Edward Bonaventure* sailed for Wardhouse (Värdo) and, despite warnings from Scottish merchants, pressed on alone into the White Sea at the beginning of August. The other ships made it to the Lapland coast, where their crews died.

At the mouth of the Dvina River, where the port of Archangel is now situated, Chancellor met with the local governor and through him was invited to the court of Ivan the Terrible at Moscow, 1,500 miles to the south. Cordial relations were established between the czar and Mary Tudor, and, though "robbed homewards by Flemings," Chancellor returned home in the summer of 1554 with a favorable report of his mission, which promised to give the English a firm hold on the valuable fur trade.

In 1555, Chancellor returned to Moscow via the White Sea under a charter from Mary, and English merchants established themselves in Moscow. The following year, Chancellor made a third expedition conveying the first English ambassador to the Russian court, while Burroughs attempted to sail eastward across the Kara Sea in the diminutive *Searchthrift.* In the meantime, Willoughby's two ships had been recovered and Chancellor sailed for England with a total of four ships, conveying the Russian ambassador aboard his own *Edward Bonaventure.* Willoughby's ships sank en route, and *Edward Bonaventure* was wrecked on the coast of Scotland with the loss of Chancellor and his son. The Russian ambassador survived.

Purchas, *Hakluytus Posthumus.*

EDWIN FOX

East Indiaman; ship. *L/B/D:* 160' × 29.8' × 20' (48.8m × 9.1m × 6.1m). *Tons:* 836 reg. *Built:* William Henry Foster, Sukeali (Calcutta), Bengal; 1853.

Built to a design set by the British East India Company (which had dropped its merchant operations in 1834), *Edwin Fox* was built for Thomas Reeves, who owned her for only a year. She subsequently changed hands five times. In 1855, she was employed as a troop transport in the Baltic during the Crimean War, thereafter resuming trading between India and England, and later carrying immigrants out to New Zealand and Australia. Owned by

Shaw, Savill & Company (later Shaw, Savill & Albion Line), from 1873 to 1900 she began service as a "portable bulk freezer" in the New Zealand interisland trade in 1885. Rerigged as a bark in 1887, at some point in the late 1890s refrigeration was installed. In 1905 *Edwin Fox* was purchased by the Christchurch Meat Company of Lyttleton, New Zealand, for use as a storage hulk and landing stage. In 1965 she was acquired by the Edwin Fox Restoration Society, Inc., of Picton, New Zealand. Initial attempts to restore the ship failed, but the effort was resumed in 1986, and the ship is now afloat in Picton harbor and open to the public.

Allen, "Answers." Flackman, "Answers."

Eendracht

Hull: wood. *Built:* Amsterdam, Netherlands; <1616.

The second Dutch ship to reach Australia following *Duyfken*'s voyage of 1605–6, *Eendracht* ("Unity," a popular name for Dutch ships) was en route from the Netherlands to Batavia under the command of Dirck Hartog when she became separated from the rest of the fleet. Tracing the route pioneered by Hendrik Brouwer in 1610, *Eendracht* sailed west across the Indian Ocean from Cape Town before turning north for Java. On October 25, 1615, Hartog arrived at "various islands, which were, however, found uninhabited." These proved to be Dirck Hartog's Island, off Inscription Point near Shark Bay, Western Australia. The point takes its name from the fact that Hartog erected a post and nailed to it a pewter plate commemorating his visit:

> 1616 On 25 October arrived the ship *Eendracht*, of Amsterdam: Supercargo Gilles Miebais of Liege, skipper Dirch Hatichs of Amsterdam. on 27 d[itt]o. she set sail again for Bantam. Deputy supercargo Jan Stins, upper steersman Pieter Doores of Bil. In the year 1616.

Hartog continued north along the coast that now bears his name and eventually reached the Dutch settlement at Batavia. The plate is now at the Rijksmuseum in Amsterdam, having been rescued from Inscription Point by Willem de Vlamingh, who, in command of *Geelvinck*, *Nyptangh*, and *Het Weeseltje*, visited the area (which the VOC called Eendracht's Land) on February 4, 1697, and replaced Hartog's plate with one of his own. This in turn was found by Louis de Freycinet of L'Uranie in 1801, who in 1820 returned in *Le Naturaliste* and took Vlamingh's plate to France. It is now in the Western Australian Maritime Museum in Perth.

Sigmond & Zuiderbaan, *Dutch Discoveries of Australia*.

Eendracht

Tons: 360. *Hull:* wood. *Comp.:* 87. *Arm.:* 19 guns; 12 swivels. *Built:* Netherlands; <1615.

In the early seventeenth century, the Verenigde Oostindische Compagnie (VOC, or United East India Company) had exclusive rights, among Dutch ships, to the Strait of Magellan and Cape of Good Hope. Merchant Isaac Le Maire established the Compagne Australe to trade in the South Seas, the still unexplored Southland (Australia), Japan, and northern Asia, but his ships could do so only if they found an alternative route to the east. This route, Le Maire believed, lay to the south of the Strait of Magellan, and to prove it he fitted out *Eendracht*, under his son Jacob, and *Hoorn*, under Willem Cornelisz Schouten. The ships left the Texel on June 14, 1615, made a stop in Sierra Leone, and then sailed for Port Desire, where they arrived in early December. While careening the ships to clean the bottom growth, *Hoorn* caught fire and was destroyed. Embarking the smaller ship's twenty-two crew, *Eendracht* put to sea again on January 13, 1616. Eleven days later she passed through the Strait of Le Maire between the eastern end of Tierra del Fuego and Staten Island (which the crew named), and on the 29th doubled Cape Horn — named for their hometown — and entered the Pacific.

After calling at Juan Fernández Island in early March 1616, *Eendracht* headed west in about latitude 15°S. The first landfall was in the northern Tuamotus in April, and from there the track passed through the Tongas and on to the Tabat Islands near New Ireland and New Guinea. When *Eendracht* arrived at Bantam, Java, in October the VOC representative did not believe that Schouten and Le Maire had found an alternative to the Strait of Magellan, and he confiscated *Eendracht* and her cargo before sending the crew on to the Netherlands. Perhaps most remarkable in this pioneering voyage around what later centuries would call "Cape Stiff" is that in more than sixteen months at sea, only three sailors died.

Beaglehole, *Exploration of the Pacific*. Villiers, ed., *East and West Indian Mirror*.

Effie M. Morrissey

(later *Ernestina*) Schooner (2m). *L/B/D:* 112′ × 13′ × 24.4′ (34.1m × 4m × 7.4m). *Tons:* 120 grt. *Hull:* wood. *Comp.:* 34. *Des.:* George M. McClain. *Built:* Tarr & James Shipyard, Essex, Mass.; 1894.

Built in the heyday of the Gloucester fishing fleets, the *Fredonia*-style Grand Banks "high-liner" *Effie M. Morrissey* was built for the John F. Wonson Company and Captain William E. Morrissey, for whose daughter she was named. She was a successful fisherman under a variety of captains including Morrissey and his son, Clayton. In 1905, she was sold to Captain Ansel Snow of Digby, Nova Scotia, but continued fishing under the U.S. flag. Nine years later Harold Bartlett of Brigus, Newfoundland, bought her and put her under British registry. In 1925, Bartlett sold *Morrissey* to his brother Bob Bartlett, who had been shipmaster of ROOSEVELT on Commander Robert E. Peary's quest for the North Pole in 1909. Under Bartlett, *Morrissey* was fitted out for Arctic exploration, which hard work she sailed in through World War II. In 1946, she was purchased for use as a yacht, but this plan was dropped after a fire and subsequent scuttling.

Two years later she was purchased by Captain Henrique Mendes who renamed her *Ernestina* and put her in the immigrant trade between the United States and the Cape Verde Islands. *Ernestina* became the last regular Atlantic sailing packet, carrying goods and passengers on twelve 8,000-mile roundtrips from the islands to southern New England until 1965. In 1982, the Republic of Cape Verde gave the schooner to the Commonwealth of Massachusetts to symbolize the close ties between the two lands, with the stipulation that she be used for seafaring education. *Ernestina* was fully restored and certified by the U.S. Coast Guard as an oceangoing sailing-school vessel to undertake a variety of sea education programs.

Thomas, *Fast and Able.*

EGYPT

Passenger liner. *L/B/D:* 499.8′ × 54.3′ × 24.5′ (152.3m × 16.6m × 7.5m). *Tons:* 7,941 grt. *Hull:* steel. *Comp.:* 335. *Mach.:* triple expansion, 1 screw, 1,355 nhp. *Built:* Caird and Co., Greenock, Scotland; 1897.

On May 20, 1922, the P&O passenger ship *Egypt* was on a routine voyage bound from London for Bombay with a complement of 335 passengers and crew under command of Captain Andrew Collyer. Shrouded in dense fog off Armen light, at Finistère, France, she was struck amidships on the port side by the French icebreaker *Seine.* The French ship's reinforced bows knifed through the liner, which sank in only 20 minutes, taking with her 86 passengers and crew in position 48°10′N, 5°30′W. The loss of life was tragic, but public interest focused on the ship's cargo, which included 8 tons of gold ingots and coins, and 43 tons of silver, valued at £1,058,879. Within 10 days of the sinking, Lloyd's had paid off on the insurance claims.

Shortly thereafter, salvors began searching for the wreck, an arduous process that lasted until August 29, 1930, when Commander Giovanni Quaglia, head of the Society for Maritime Recovery (SORIMA), located the ship lying on an even keel about 25 miles south of Ushant (48°06′N, 5°29′W). Despite the loss of many of his best divers (the cargo of a munitions ship lying at a depth of 60 feet had destroyed their salvage ship, *Artiglio*), Quaglia returned to the *Egypt* site the following spring. The ship lay at a depth of 400 feet — the greatest depth at which a salvage operation had yet been attempted — and the only practical way to enter the bullion room was to blow apart the three upper decks and remove the debris. The explosives and the grabs and buckets were manipulated from the surface under the direction of an observer in a pressurized observation chamber known as an iron duke. Work continued through the fall of 1931 and resumed in May 1932. On June 22, Quaglia's team brought up two gold sovereigns, and four days later the team arrived in England with £80,000 in gold bullion. Work continued through 1934, by which time most of the treasure had been salvaged. Proceeds from the recovered treasure were divided among the salvors and the various claimants: SORIMA received 50 percent, Sandberg and Swinburne (who had hired SORIMA on a no cure, no pay basis), 12.5 percent, and the Lloyd's underwriters, 37.5 percent.

Gores, *Marine Salvage.*

EL HORRIA

(ex-*Mahroussa*) Royal yacht (1f/2m). *L/B/D:* 421.5′ × 42.6′ × 17.5′ (128.5m × 13m × 5.3m). *Tons:* 3,762 grt. *Hull:* iron. *Mach.:* steam turbine, 3 screws, 6,500 bhp; 15 kts. *Des.:* O. Lang. *Built:* Samuda Brothers, Poplar, Eng.; 1865.

One of the oldest steam vessels still afloat, *El Horria* was commissioned for the Khedive of Egypt as the royal yacht *Mahroussa.* Completed ten years after the second VICTORIA AND ALBERT (and to plans by the same designer), she remained in the service of the Egyptian royal family until 1951. Her two most significant alterations took place in 1872, when she was lengthened 40 feet, and in 1905 when her two paddle wheels were replaced with triple screws powered by steam turbines, and another 16.5 feet were added. Following the abdication of King Farouk, *Mahroussa* was taken over by the government for use as a naval training ship and renamed *El Horria.* Although she spent most of her career in the eastern Mediterranean, in 1976, at the age of 111, *El Horria* sailed to New York to take part in the International Naval Review held to commemorate the bicentennial of the United States.

Brouwer, *International Register of Historic Ships.* Crabtree, *Royal Yachts of Europe.*

Originally a sidewheel pad-dle steamer, EL HORRIA *has undergone many changes in design since her launch in 1865. Built for the Egyptian ruling family, she later served the government as a training ship. Courtesy Wright and Logan, Portsea, England.*

ELISSA

(ex-*Pioneer, Christophoros, Acheos, Gustaf, Fjeld, Elissa*) Bark (3m). *L/B/D:* 155′ × 28′ × 10′ (47.2m × 8.5m × 3m). *Tons:* 411 grt. *Hull:* iron. *Comp.:* 40. *Built:* Alexander Hall & Sons, Aberdeen, Scotland; 1877.

The long-lived bark *Elissa* first put to sea under the British flag in 1877, sailing for Henry F. Watt of Liverpool — who sailed twice as her captain — with a cargo of coal for Pernambuco, Brazil. Over the next two decades, she spun her web of commerce around the world, to ports in the Pacific, Australia, Southeast Asia, India, and the United States, including twice to her present home in Galveston. On her final voyage under the British flag, she was en route from the West Indies to France with a cargo of mahogany when she was towed into Ventry, Ireland, after sustaining severe damage in February gales. Sold to the Norwegian firm of Bugge & Olsen and renamed *Fjeld,* she remained in service as a bark for fourteen years, when she was sold to a Swede, Carl Johannson. Renamed *Gustaf,* she was rigged down to a barkentine and in 1918 she was given an auxiliary engine. With a progressively simplified rig, she remained in Scandinavian waters for the next forty-two years, changing hands again in 1930, when she came under the Finnish flag as a motor schooner.

In 1960, the ship was sold to Greek interests and renamed *Christophoros* and used as a motorship in the Aegean. There, the following year, maritime archaeologist Peter Throckmorton discovered the ship lying in Piraeus and quickly identified the mastless hull as that of a nineteenth-century merchantman. Six years later, he tried to buy the ship, now renamed *Acheos* and employed as a smuggler in the Adriatic. Two years later, Throckmorton renewed his efforts to buy the ship and in 1970, thanks to the involvement of ship preservationists from around the

United States, particularly the San Francisco Maritime Museum's Karl Kortum, succeeded. Five years later, the Galveston Historical Foundation purchased *Elissa,* and the ship was completely restored to her original rig and put to sea again under sail in 1982. Although she is used chiefly as a dockside attraction, *Elissa* sails several times a year in the Gulf of Mexico. In 1986, she visited ports along the eastern seaboard en route to Operation Sail/Salute to Liberty in New York.

Rybka, "*Elissa* Sails." Stanford, "*Elissa:* The Long Sea Career."

SMS EMDEN

Dresden-class cruiser (3f/2m). *L/B/D:* 388′ × 44.3′ × 18′ (118.3m × 13.5m × 5.5m). *Tons:* 4,268 disp. *Comp.:* 378–394. *Arm.:* 10 × 10.5cm, 10 mgs, 8 × 5.2cm; 2 × 18″TT. *Mach.:* steam turbines, 16,350 ihp, 2 screws; 24 kts. *Built:* Kaiserliche Werft, Danzig, Germany; 1909.

Named for the Ems River city, the light cruiser *Emden* was commissioned in 1910 and assigned to the East Asia Cruiser Squadron stationed at Tsingtao. In August 1913, *Emden* was part of a four-power fleet dispatched to protect U.S., British, German, and Japanese interests on the Yangtze River. As the European crisis approached in 1914, Captain Karl von Müller took *Emden* out of Tsingtao on July 31; World War I began the next day. In the Strait of Tsushima, *Emden* captured the Russian mail boat *Rjasan* on August 4, and returned to Tsingtao two days later. The East Asia Squadron then quit Tsingtao, and on August 12 Vice Admiral Maximilian Graf von Spee steamed east for home waters with SCHARNHORST, GNEISENAU, and *Nürnberg.*

Emden and her supply vessel *Markomannia* threaded

The German light cruiser SMS EMDEN *wreaked havoc on Allied shipping in the Indian Ocean and East Indies during the first three months of World War I. She ran aground on North Keeling Island during an action with* HMAS SYDNEY, *November 9, 1914. Courtesy Imperial War Museum, London.*

their way through the Dutch East Indies and into the Indian Ocean. In the shipping lanes between Burma and India, *Emden* began capturing Allied shipping, sometimes at the rate of two ships a day. On September 21 at 2145, *Emden* stood about a half mile offshore and shelled the Burma Oil Company gas tanks in Madras. After a quick visit to Diego Garcia on October 9, where she narrowly missed an encounter with the armored cruiser HMS HAMPSHIRE and the armed merchant cruiser EMPRESS OF BRITAIN, she resumed raiding. On October 21, *Emden* ran into Penang and torpedoed the Russian cruiser *Yemtschuk;* later that day she also sank the French destroyer *Mousquet.* Next von Müller decided to cut the transoceanic cable at the Cocos Keeling Island northwest of Australia. On November 9, a detachment of about 50 men under Hellmuth von Mücke landed at Direction Island. As they destroyed the radio shack, the radio operators informed them that the Kaiser had honored *Emden*'s crew with Iron Crosses; the operators did not mention that they had reported the news of *Emden*'s arrival. By this time, *Emden* had seized or sunk 16 merchant ships and was the object of a search by more than 75 Allied ships. At 0930, the arrival of the cruiser HMAS SYDNEY forced *Emden* to depart without the landing party. *Emden* opened fire at 0940 at a range of 5,600 yards. *Sydney* was able to keep out of *Emden*'s range, and at about 1115 the helpless German cruiser was intentionally run aground on North Keeling Island. *Emden*'s casualties included 141 dead and 65 wounded; *Sydney* suffered 4 dead and 12 wounded. Von Mücke and his landing party managed to steal the 97-ton copra schooner *Ayesha* and sailed to Pedang. From here they made their way to Istanbul.

Hoyt, *Last Cruise of the "Emden."*

EMPRESS OF BRITAIN

Liner (3f/2m). *L/B:* 790′ × 97.4′ (21.8m × 29.7m). *Tons:* 42,348 grt. *Hull:* steel. *Comp.:* 1st 465, tourist 260, 3rd 470; crew 740. *Mach.:* geared turbines, 66,500 shp, 4 screws; 26.5 kts. *Built:* John Brown & Co., Ltd., Clydebank, Scotland; 1931.

Far and away the largest and fastest passenger ship ever built for the Canadian Pacific Line, or for service between Europe and Canada, *Empress of Britain* made an impressive showing in her first year of service. On her maiden voyage from Southampton to Quebec, she captured the so-called Canadian Blue Riband by steaming between Cherbourg and Father Point in 4 days, 18 hours, 26 minutes — more than 10 hours faster than the previous fastest time set by *Empress of Japan* in 1929. Her eastbound passage was only 17 minutes slower. *Empress of Britain* continued to lower the time between Europe and Canada over her first 6 voyages, and in 1934 made the eastbound crossing in 4 days, 6 hours, and 58 minutes, and the westbound in 4 days, 8 hours flat. This performance was particularly significant because it enabled Canadian Pacific to attract passengers from Chicago, which was closer to Quebec than New York. Launched by the Prince of Wales (later George VI), she was an opulent ship by any standard and the first to have ship-to-shore radio telephones. Her machinery was also designed so that her two outboard propellers could be detached while cruising, an important source of revenue during the winter months as the depression cut into regular passenger trade.

Upon the outbreak of World War II, all Canadian Pacific ships were requisitioned for government duty. On November 25, 1939, *Empress of Britain* began work as a troopship. Homeward bound from Canada with a total of

647 people aboard, on October 26, 1940, she was about 150 miles northwest of Ireland when a German Condor reconnaissance plane flown by Lieutenant Bernard Jope attacked the ship and set her on fire with incendiary bombs. Captain C. H. Sapsworth gave the order to abandon ship, and 598 of the ship's complement were rescued by naval vessels. *Empress of Britain* was taken in tow by the Polish destroyer *Bursa,* but two days later she was torpedoed by *U-32* (Lieutenant Commander Hans Jenisch) and sank in position 55°16'N, 9°50'W. Four days after that, *U-32* was sunk by HMS *Harvester* in 55°38'N, 12°15'W while trying to shell the small freighter *Balzac.*

Seamer, *Floating Inferno.* Shipbuilder and Marine Engine-Builder, *Canadian Pacific . . . Liner "Empress of Britain."* Turner, *"Empress of Britain."*

EMPRESS OF CHINA

(later *Edgar, Clara*) Ship (3m). *L/B/D:* 104.2' × 28.4' × 16' (31.8m × 8.7m × 4.9m). *Tons:* 300–500. *Hull:* wood. *Comp.:* 53. *Hull:* wood. *Arm.:* 10 × 9pdr, 4 × 6pdr. *Built:* John Peck, Boston; 1783.

Built for the Boston merchants Benjamin Guild, Daniel Parker, and others, *Empress of China* became the first American-flag ship to sail to China. The idea for such an expedition was originally suggested by John Ledyard, who had sailed as a marine with James Cook's last expedition in RESOLUTION and DISCOVERY. Ledyard's plan involved collecting fur pelts in the Pacific Northwest for sale in Canton. Telling his idea to anyone who would listen, he eventually secured the attention of Robert Morris, the Philadelphia merchant known as "the financier of the Revolution," and who eventually took a half interest in *Empress of China*'s voyage. The major hurdle facing American traders was that the thirteen colonies produced nothing of value to the Chinese, except ginseng, a root that grew wild throughout the Hudson River Valley and the northeast and which the Chinese regarded as indispensable to medicine. (The Chinese knew about ginseng because it is also native to Central Asia.)

After securing a cargo of 57,687 pounds (29 tons) of ginseng, $20,000 in silver, and 11 pipes of wine and brandy, together with some miscellaneous wares, *Empress of China* left New York on February 22, 1784 — George Washington's birthday — under command of Captain John Green. Sailing as supernumerary, or merchant's representative, was Major Samuel Shaw, who would eventually become the first U.S. consul in Canton. After calling in the Cape Verde Islands, she sailed south, her next landfall being the island of Java, which she reached at the end of July. She finally landed at Whampoa, below Canton on

the Pearl River, on August 28, 1784, after a voyage of 18,000 miles and 128 days. *Empress of China* was one of 34 Western ships to call at Canton that year. After selling their cargo for $291,000 — for a profit of 25 percent to 30 percent — the crew loaded tea, gold, silk, and porcelain for the return voyage, which began on January 12, 1785. On March 9, 1785, they arrived at Cape Town, where Captain Green was interviewed by the captain of the Salem ship GRAND TURK. *Empress of China* finally reached New York on May 11, 1785.

Purchased by the Philadelphia merchant house of Constable, Rucker and Company in July, *Empress of China* made a second voyage to Canton between February 1, 1786, and May 4 of the following year. Sold to William McIntosh and renamed *Edgar,* she sailed to Bordeaux, and then entered regular trade between New York and Belfast. In March 1790, she was sold again, to John Shaw of New York, and renamed *Clara.* On February 24, 1791, she sank in Dublin Bay. There was no loss of life.

Smith, *"Empress of China."*

EMPRESS OF IRELAND

Liner (2f/2m). *L/B:* 570' × 66' (173.7m × 20.1m). *Tons:* 14,191 grt. *Hull:* steel. *Comp.:* 1st 310, 2nd 350, 3rd 800; 420 crew. *Mach.:* quadruple expansion, 2 screws; 18 kts. *Built:* Fairfield Shipbuilding & Engineering Co., Ltd., Glasgow, Scotland; 1905.

The high-speed liners *Empress of Ireland* and her sister ship *Empress of Britain* (1906) were the first ships built for the newly consolidated Canadian Pacific Line. The Empress-class ships had the finest accommodations of the ships running between Liverpool and Quebec; they also made stops at St. John and Halifax. On May 29, 1914, *Empress of Ireland* was outward bound from Quebec with 87 first-class, 253 second-class, and 717 third-class passengers. Shortly after dropping the pilot near Rimouski, at about 0130 on May 30, *Empress* spotted the 440-foot 6,028-ton Norwegian collier *Storstad* inward bound about eight miles off. Suddenly engulfed in a thick fog, the two ships approached each other. Despite last-minute evasive action by both vessels, *Storstad* hit *Empress* amidships, and the liner sank within minutes in 150 feet of water in about 48°30'N, 68°30E. The loss of life was horrendous, with only 217 passengers and 248 crew surviving. The *Storstad* survived the collision, and an official inquiry found the collier entirely to blame.

Vernon-Gibbs, *Passenger Liners of the Western Ocean.* Wood, *Till We Meet Again.*

EMPRESS OF JAPAN

(later *Empress of Scotland, Hanseatic*) Liner (3f/2m). *L/B:* 665.5′ × 83.8′ (203.1m × 25.5m). *Tons:* 26,032 grt. *Hull:* steel. *Comp.:* 1st 400, 2nd 164, 3rd 100, 500 steerage. *Mach.:* steam turbines, 2 screws; 22 kts. *Built:* Fairfield Shipbuilding & Engineering Co., Ltd., Govan, Scotland; 1930.

Formed in 1873 to build a trans-Canada railway, the Canadian Pacific Company established its first service between Vancouver, British Columbia, and Yokohama, Japan, thirteen years later. In 1903, the company inaugurated service on the North Atlantic, creating a wholly British westward "overland" route from Europe to Asia. *Empress of Japan* was one of twenty-nine ships — "Empresses" — built for service on the Pacific run. After a shakedown voyage to Quebec and back, she sailed for Vancouver via the Suez Canal and Hong Kong in 1930 and entered transpacific service in 1931. The fastest and most luxurious liner in the Pacific, the *Empress of Japan* dominated the trade through the 1930s.

In November 1939, she was requisitioned as a troopship and sailed between Australia and Europe. Following Japan's entry into World War II, her name was changed to the *Empress of Scotland*. When finally released from war-related duties in 1948, she was refitted for passenger service on the North Atlantic, sailing between Liverpool, Quebec, and Montreal. She remained in this service until 1957, when she was acquired by Hamburg Atlantic Line and renamed *Hanseatic*. She emerged from a refit with only two masts. For the next eight years she sailed between Cuxhaven, Le Havre, Southampton, and New York. Badly damaged by fire in New York in September 1966, she was towed back to Hamburg and scrapped.

Bonsor, *North Atlantic Seaway.*

ENCHANTRESS

Brig. *Hull:* wood. *Comp.:* 14. *Built:* Baltimore; <1861.

On June 28, 1861, the Confederate privateer brig *Jefferson Davis* (ex-*Putnam*) sailed from Charleston, South Carolina, to cruise against Northern merchantmen. One of her prizes was the brig *Enchantress,* bound from Boston to Santiago de Cuba with general cargo. The ship was seized in 38°52′N, 69°15′W (about 300 miles east of Delaware) and a prize crew was put aboard for the return to Charleston. The only member of the original crew to remain was the black cook, Jacob Garrick. On July 22, the ship was being followed by USS *Albatross* off Hatteras Inlet when Garrick leaped into the sea and began shouting that the vessel was a Confederate prize. The ship's master William Smith had no choice but to surrender, and he and the crew of thirteen were brought to Philadelphia.

The Lincoln administration refused to recognize either the Confederate government or, by extension, letters of marque signed by President Jefferson Davis for Confederate privateers, and Smith and his men were tried for piracy, a capital offense. In anticipation of such a move, the Confederate Congress granted Davis sweeping powers to retaliate, and when Smith and four of his crew were sentenced to die, he ordered a high-ranking Union officer transferred from a prisoner-of-war camp to a common prison, "to be treated in all respects as if [a convicted felon], and to be held for execution in the same manner as may be adopted by the enemy for the execution of the prisoner of war Smith." In February 1862, Lincoln reluctantly remanded Smith and his confederates to a prisoner-of-war camp. Later exchanged for Union POWs, they returned to great acclaim in Charleston.

Robinson, *Confederate Privateers.*

HMS ENDEAVOUR

(ex-*Earl of Pembroke,* later *La Liberté*) Cat-bark (3m). *L/B/D:* 97.6′ × 29.3′ × 11.3′ dph (29.7m × 8.9m × 3.4m). *Tons:* 369 tons. *Hull:* wood. *Comp.:* 85–94. *Arm.:* 6 × 4pdr, 8 swivels. *Built:* Fishburn, Whitby, Eng.; 1764.

In 1768 Lieutenant James Cook was invited to command an expedition to the South Seas sponsored by the Royal Society. (The Society sought the appointment of Alexander Dalrymple, but the Admiralty preferred Cook.) The voyage had a twofold mission. The first was to visit Tahiti to observe (on June 3, 1769) the transit of Venus across the sun, "a phenomenon that must . . . contribute greatly to the improvement of astronomy, on which navigation so much depends." The second mission was to determine whether there was, as suggested by earlier Portuguese and Dutch navigators, a great southern continent, or Terra Australis. The Admiralty's choice of ship for what would turn out to be the first of Captain James Cook's three expeditions to the Pacific Ocean was a bluff-bowed North Sea "cat-built bark" — the name identifies the hull model; the vessel was ship rigged — which was built originally as a collier. Although the Navy Board had earlier considered HMS ROSE and *Tryal,* the type was well known to Cook, who had first gone to sea in just such ships. "From the knowledge and experience that I have had of these sort [*sic*] of vessels," he later wrote, "I shall always be of the opinion that only such are proper to be sent on discoveries to distant parts."

Renamed *Endeavour* and rerigged as a ship (although she was referred to as "H.M. Bark," to distinguish her from another navy ship of the same name), *Endeavour* sailed from Plymouth on August 25, 1768. Her distinguished company included the naturalists Joseph Banks and Daniel Solander, as well as Second Lieutenants John Gore and Charles Clerke, both veterans of HMS DOLPHIN. After calling at Madeira (September 12), Rio de Janeiro (November 14), and the Bay of Good Success in Le Maire Strait (January 15, 1769), she entered the Pacific and arrived at Tahiti on April 13. Cook's crew established good relations with the Tahitians — who had entertained the crews of Bougainville's LA BOUDEUSE and *L'Etoile* the year before — and remained on the island for three full months. When they finally sailed, the ship's company had been augmented by a Tahitian named Tupaia and his servant, Taiata. After calling elsewhere in the Society Islands (so named, as they lay contiguous to one another), they sailed south and then west, and landed on the North Island of New Zealand on October 9. In the course of six months, *Endeavour* established that New Zealand consisted of two main islands — both of which were circumnavigated — separated by Cook Strait, a named suggested by Banks. Abandoning his search for Terra Australis, on March 31, 1770, Cook weighed anchor and sailed due west across the Tasman Sea, hoping to sail into the Indian Ocean via Van Diemen's Land (now called Tasmania for Abel Tasman whose HEEMSKERCK and *Zeehaen* called there in 1642).

The onset of winter drove *Endeavour* off course, and on April 19, the ship arrived off New Holland (Australia). Nine days later, *Endeavour* entered Botany Bay (just south of modern Sydney), which they named "for the great quantity of New Plants & ca" collected there over the next week. *Endeavour* sailed again on May 6, skirting the coast of Australia until June 10, when the ship was holed on the Great Barrier Reef near Cape Tribulation (15°47′S, 145°34′E). "This was," wrote Cook, "an alarming and I may say terrible Circumstance and threatend immediate destruction to us as soon as the Ship was afloat." It took two days to free the ship, and the leak was only stopped by fothering, that is, drawing a sail impregnated with oakum under the ship's bottom to stop the leak. Nine days later, Cook landed at what is now Cooktown. Repairs to the ship lasted six weeks, during which Lieutenant Gore shot and stuffed a kangaroo. After claiming New Holland for the British Crown, Cook sailed *Endeavour* through the Torres Strait, stopping at Savu Island (west of Timor), and then sailing on to the Dutch entrepôt at Batavia (now Jakarta). There, thanks to an "electrical chain" Cook ordered set up for the purpose, *Endeavour* survived a bolt of lightning that did serious damage to a Dutch East Indiaman. The rest of the stay was plagued with difficulty. Further repairs to *Endeavour*'s hull and raging fever and dysentery among the ship's company — seven of whom died, including Tupaia and Taiata — kept the ship at Batavia until December 26, 1770. The voyage across the Indian Ocean saw the death of 23 of the crew from disease contracted in the East Indies. *Endeavour* anchored at Cape Town from March 15 to April 14, 1771, sailed for St. Helena (May 1–4), and anchored in the Downs on July 12, 1771, after a circumnavigation lasting two years, nine months, and fourteen days. Cook was not long at home. Having deposited the "curiosities" gathered in his first epic voyage with Joseph Banks, who later left them to the British Museum, he was promoted to the rank of commander and in July 1772 he sailed again for the Pacific with RESOLUTION and ADVENTURE. His last, ill-fated voyage, with *Resolution* and DISCOVERY, began in 1776.

Following a refit at Woolwich, *Endeavour* made three voyages to the Falkland Islands and was paid off in September 1774. Sold out of the navy on March 7, 1775, *Endeavour* sailed once again as a North Sea collier for fifteen years. She was purchased by French interests in 1790 and as *La Liberté* entered the whale trade. In 1793, she ran aground off Newport, Rhode Island, and was later broken up by James Cahoon. A replica of the ship was commissioned at Fremantle in 1994.

Cook, *Journals of James Cook*. Knight, "H.M. Bark *Endeavour*." McGowan, "Captain Cook's Ships."

ENDURANCE

Barkentine (1f/3m). *L/B:* 144′ × 25′ (43.9m × 7.5m). *Tons:* 300 grt. *Hull:* wood. *Comp.:* 28. *Mach.:* steam, 350 hp, 1 screw; 10.2 kts. *Des.:* Aanderud Larsen. *Built:* Framnaes Mek. Verstad, Sandefjord, Norway; 1912.

Shortly after Roald Amundsen led the first expedition to the South Pole in 1911–12, Sir Ernest Henry Shackleton started planning the Imperial Trans-Antarctic Expedition. A veteran of Robert Falcon Scott's HMS DISCOVERY, and leader of the British Imperial Antarctic Expedition in NIMROD, Shackleton chose as his ship a new barkentine built for tourist cruises in the Arctic. (One of her original owners was Adrien de Gerlache, captain of BELGICA when that ship was the first to winter in Antarctica.) Shackleton intended to land with six men at Vahsel Bay on the Weddell Sea, and from there march via the South Pole to McMurdo Sound, where they would rendezvous with the ship *Aurora*.

On August 8, 1914, three days after Britain entered

"She was doomed: no ship built by human hands could have withstood the strain. I ordered all hands out on the floe." So wrote Sir Ernest Henry Shackleton of the barkentine ENDURANCE, *the ship from which he had planned to launch the Imperial Trans-Antarctic Expedition in 1914. Her loss the next year, after being "nipped" in the ice, was followed by one of the most prolonged and brilliant rescues in the annals of exploration. Courtesy Peabody Essex Museum, Salem, Massachusetts.*

World War I, *Endurance* sailed from Plymouth via Madeira to Buenos Aires, from which they departed on October 26. After several weeks at the Grytviken whaling station on South Georgia, on December 11 *Endurance* entered the pack ice at the unexpectedly low parallel of 59°S. The company maneuvered through the ice for about 1,000 miles until January 19, 1915, when *Endurance* stuck fast in 76°30′S, 31°30′W, within sight of the continent and only sixty miles from her intended destination. At the mercy of the ice, the ship drifted for nine months, first west along the Luitpold Coast and then north again parallel to the Antarctic Peninsula. The ice began to relax its grip during July, but over the next few months, *Endurance* was so battered and strained by the ice that, as Shackleton wrote, on October 27, 1915, "She was doomed: no ship built by human hands could have withstood the strain. I ordered all hands out on the floe."

The crew abandoned ship in 69°5′S, 51°30′W, taking off stores and supplies, including three of the ship's boats — named *James Craig, Dudley Docker,* and *Stancomb Wills,* for contributors to the expedition — the dogs, and 150 glass-plate negatives of pictures taken by Frank Hurley. The party camped near the ruined ship (which finally sank on November 21) and drifted north on the pack ice until April 9, 1916, when there was enough open water for them to take to their boats. Rowing and sailing by day, and sleeping on or tied up to ice floes by night, they worked their way towards uninhabited Elephant Island, where they landed on April 15.

Never one to sit still if he could help it, Shackleton determined to sail *James Craig* — at 22 feet long by 6 feet 6 inches broad, the biggest of the three boats — to South Georgia, and he ordered the ship's carpenter to make the boat somewhat more seaworthy by the addition of a canvas deck. On April 24, six of the men began the 700-mile passage through some of the roughest and least-known seas on the planet. Sailing more or less by dead reckoning, they brought their boat into King Haakon Bay on the south side of South Georgia Island on May 10. Having rested a few days, Shackleton took Captain Frank Worsley and Second Officer Tom Crean with him for the 20-mile trek over uncharted mountains and snow fields towards the whaling station at Stromness, which they reached on May 20, after 36 hours. The next day, the whale catcher *Samson* rescued the other three men and *James Craig,* on the south side of the island, while Shackleton took a whaler to rescue the men on Elephant Island. Unfortunately the pack ice was too thick and he was forced back. Several months of false leads in the Falkland Islands and Latin America ensued before he was able to secure the use of the Chilean lighthouse tender *Yelcho* at Punta Arenas. On August 25, they departed the Strait of Magellan, and after five days Shackleton, Worsley, and Crean arrived at Elephant Island, 128 days after their departure for South Georgia. As Shackleton wrote to his wife on their return to Punta Arenas, "I have done it. . . . Not a life lost and we have been through Hell."

Though he had failed in his purpose, Shackleton's determination and ingenuity on the *Endurance* expedition earned him a unique place in the history of exploration. In the words of Sir Edmund Hillary, "For scientific discovery give me Scott; for speed and efficiency give me Amundsen; but when disaster strikes and all hope is gone, get down on your knees and pray for Shackleton." *James Caird* is preserved at Dulwich College, Shackleton's alma mater.

Huntford, *Shackleton.* Shackleton, *South.*

USS ENGLAND (DE-635)

Buckley-class destroyer escort (1f/1m). *L/B/D:* 306' × 37' × 9.4' (93.3m × 11.3m × 2.9m). *Tons:* 1,400 disp. *Hull:* steel. *Comp.:* 186. *Arm.:* 3 × 3", 1 × 1.1", 8 × 20mm; 3 × 21"TT; 8 dcp, 1 dcp/hh, 2 dct. *Mach.:* turbo-electric, 12,000 shp, 2 shafts; 24 kts. *Built:* Bethlehem Steel Co., San Francisco; 1943.

Named for John C. England, an ensign killed aboard the battleship USS *Oklahoma* (BB-37) at Pearl Harbor, USS *England* first operated out of Espiritu Santo in March 1944. Under Commander W. R. Pendleton, on May 18 she sortied with USS *Haggard* and *Franks* to search for Japanese submarines deployed to prevent the American fleet from advancing on the Mariana Islands. Over the next thirteen days, *England* sank six Japanese submarines: *I-16*, on May 19 (5°10'S, 158°17'E); *RO-106*, May 22 (1°40'S, 150°31'E); *RO-104*, May 23 (1°26'S, 149°20'E); *RO-116*, May 24 (00°53'S, 149°14'E); and *RO-108*, May 26 (00°32'S, 148°35'E). After replenishing her depth charges at Manus, on May 31, she helped sink *RO-105* (00°47'S, 149°35'E). Reflecting on this record, Chief of Naval Operations Admiral Ernest J. King announced, "There'll always be an *England* in the United States Navy!" *England* resumed duty as an escort until April 1945 when she took up station near Kerama Retto, south of Okinawa. On May 9, a kamikaze hit just below the bridge killed 37 crew and injured 25. She returned to Philadelphia in July and was sold in 1946.

U.S. Navy, *DANFS*.

ENGLISH ROSE III

Yorkshire dory. L/B: 20' × 5.3' (6.1m × 1.6m). *Hull:* wood. *Comp.:* 2. *Built:* Bradford Boat Services, Bradford, Yorkshire, Eng.; 1966.

In 1966, British Parachute Regiment Captain John Ridgeway learned of a plan by David Johnstone to row from the United States to England in a boat called *Puffin*. Inspired to do the same, he purchased a 20-foot Yorkshire dory modeled on the seaworthy Cape dories used by Grand Banks fishermen. On June 4, 1966, at 1730, he and his regimental comrade Sergeant Chay Blyth (a novice oarsman) pulled away from Orleans, Massachusetts, on Cape Cod. Although they carried provisions for about two months, their progress was slower than expected: ten days out they were overtaken by Hurricane Alma, and two days later they were only 120 miles from Cape Cod. Although they met several ships en route, they boarded only one, the tanker *Haustellum*, which they met on August 4, in about 46°N, 23°W. On September 3, *English Rose III*

finally landed at Kilronan Pier, Inishmore, one of the Aran Islands off Galway, Ireland, having rowed 3,500 miles in 91 days. The book that resulted from their effort is a frank assessment of the physical and mental toll that such unrelenting labor exacted on the two men. Tragically, Johnstone's *Puffin* was later found overturned in midatlantic. In 1969, Blyth attempted to be the first sailor to complete a solo, nonstop circumnavigation of the world in *Dysticus* (the Golden Globe was won by Robin Knox-Johnston in SUHAILI), and in 1970–71, he sailed BRITISH STEEL on a nonstop circumnavigation from east to west.

Ridgway & Blyth, *Fighting Chance*.

USS ENTERPRISE

Schooner (2m). *L/B/D:* 84.6' lod × 22.5' × 10' dph (25.8m × 6.9m × 3m). *Tons:* 135 bm. *Hull:* wood. *Comp.:* 70. *Arm.:* 12 × 6pdr. *Built:* Henry Spencer, Eastern Shore, Md.; 1799.

The third ship of the name, USS *Enterprise* was built during the Quasi-War with France. On her first cruise she sailed to the Caribbean under Lieutenant John Shaw, and by the end of the war she had captured eight French privateers and freed eleven U.S. merchantmen. In the summer of 1801, *Enterprise* joined the "Squadron of Observation" sent to the Mediterranean to protect American shipping from the Barbary corsairs of North Africa. Although she alternated between assignments as a dispatch vessel, convoy escort, and blockade ship, she fought a number of Tripolitan vessels in single ship engagements and participated in the bombardment of Tripolitan forts. Most notable, on December 23, 1803, *Enterprise* and CONSTITUTION captured the Tripolitan ketch *Mastico*, which was taken into the squadron as USS INTREPID. Rearmed with 12-pdr. guns at Venice in 1804, *Enterprise* remained in the Mediterranean until the winter of 1807.

Laid up from 1809 to 1811, after service on the East Coast, *Enterprise* was refitted as a brig and armed with fourteen 18-pdr. carronades and two 9-pdr. longs, putting to sea just before the start of the War of 1812. On September 5, 1813, off Portland, Maine, she fought HM brig *Boxer* (12 guns), which she took in a 45-minute action that resulted in the death of both commanders, Lieutenant William Burrows and *Boxer*'s Captain Samuel Blyth. *Enterprise* next sailed to the Caribbean in company with USS *Rattlesnake,* but the two were forced to separate in the face of a more heavily armed opponent, and *Enterprise* returned to Wilmington, North Carolina, having jettisoned most of her guns to avoid capture.

Enterprise spent the remainder of the war as a guardship at Charleston. After four months with the newly formed Mediterranean Squadron in 1815, she sailed on the West Indies Station operating against smugglers and slavers until July 9, 1823, when she stranded and broke up on Little Curaçao Island.

Culver, *Forty Famous Ships.* U.S. Navy, *DANFS.*

USS ENTERPRISE (CV-6)

Yorktown-class aircraft carrier. *L/B/D:* 809.5′ × 83′ (86′ew) × 21.5′ (246.7m × 25.3m (26.2m) × 6.6m). *Tons:* 25,500 disp. *Hull:* steel. *Comp.:* 2,919. *Arm.:* 72 aircraft; 8 × 5″ (8 × 1), 16 × 1.1″, 24 × 20mm. *Armor:* 4″ belt, 1.5″ deck. *Mach.:* geared turbines, 120,000 shp, 4 shafts; 32.5 kts. *Built:* Newport News Shipbuilding & Dry Dock Co. Newport News, Va.; 1939.

One of two YORKTOWN-class aircraft carriers, USS *Enterprise* was the seventh ship of the name. Popularly known as "The Big E," she was assigned to the Pacific Fleet shortly after commissioning. On December 7, 1941, she had just delivered a Marine air squadron to Wake Island when the Japanese attacked Pearl Harbor. Sorties from the carrier, still at sea, failed to locate the Japanese fleet, but on December 10, her planes sank the submarine *I-170* northeast of Oahu, in position 23°45′N, 155°35′W.

Enterprise spent the early months of 1942 in convoy operations to Samoa and raids on Japanese strongholds in the Marshall Islands. In April, she escorted USS HORNET for the Doolittle raid on Japan. The two carriers were then sent to support USS LEXINGTON and YORKTOWN at the Battle of the Coral Sea, which was over before they arrived. Recalled to Pearl Harbor, on May 30 *Enterprise* sailed as flagship of Rear Admiral Raymond A. Spruance's Task Force 16 (including *Hornet,* six cruisers, and ten destroyers) as it sortied to meet Vice Admiral Chuichi Nagumo's First Air Fleet, then approaching Midway. Nagumo successfully launched one attack on the island, but as he prepared a second, the U.S. carriers (now augmented by USS YORKTOWN) launched a torpedo plane attack that lost all but 6 of 46 planes and inflicted little damage on the enemy. But the Japanese combat air patrol had been forced down to low altitude and the air patrol was unprepared when dive-bombers from *Enterprise* and *Yorktown* struck from 18,000 feet at 1030. Within three minutes, the carriers KAGA, AKAGI, and SORYU had been put out of operation, and all three eventually sank, as did *Hiryu* and the cruiser *Mikuma,* together with 250 planes and 2,200 airmen and crew. Although the United States lost *Yorktown* and the destroyer *Hammann,* Mid-

way turned the tide of the Pacific war decisively in favor of the United States.

Returning to the southwest Pacific, *Enterprise* joined Task Force 61 for the August 7 Marine landings on Guadalcanal and Tulagi at the start of Operation Watchtower. There followed the Battle of the Eastern Solomons (August 24), where *Enterprise* lost 74 crew killed and 95 wounded to three enemy bombs. After repairs at Pearl Harbor, she rejoined Task Force 61 and *Hornet* in time for the Battle of the Santa Cruz Islands on October 26, where her planes sank Vice Admiral N. Kondo's ZUIHO. Although 44 of *Enterprise*'s crew were killed by bombers launched from ZUIKAKU and *Junyo,* damage to the ship was not severe, and she landed a number of *Hornet*'s planes when *Hornet* was torpedoed. After hasty repairs at Nouméa, she returned to the Solomons for the three-day Naval Battle of Guadalcanal. On November 13, planes from *Enterprise* sank the battlecruiser *Hiei,* damaged in action the day before, among several other ships. *Enterprise* also took part in the Battle of Rennell Island, on January 30, 1943, remaining in the Solomons through the spring before a return to the West Coast for repairs.

"The Big E" was back on active duty in time for the next big push across the central Pacific: the landings in the Gilbert Islands on November 20, and in the Marshall Islands in late January and February 1944, and raids on the Japanese fleet anchorage at Truk, Caroline Islands. There, on February 17, she launched the first carrier-based, radar-directed night bombing operation. Her next major assignments were in support of the landings at Hollandia, New Guinea, on April 21 and, two months later, the struggle for Saipan, Guam, and Tinian in the Mariana Islands. For the carrier forces, the highlight of that operation was the momentous Battle of the Philippine Sea on June 19. In what became known as the Great Marianas Turkey Shoot, Vice Admiral Jisaburo Ozawa's First Mobile Fleet lost the carriers *Taiho* and SHOKAKU (both to submarines) as well as 426 carrier planes and the irreplaceable pilots who flew them. After a respite at Pearl Harbor, *Enterprise* undertook raids against Japanese positions from the Volcano and Bonin Islands in the north, to the Palaus in the south and the Philippines in the west.

During the invasion of the Philippines, on October 20–21 more than 130,000 troops landed at Leyte Gulf. In the ensuing Battle of the Sibuyan Sea, one of four naval engagements that made up the Battle for Leyte Gulf (the others were the Battle of Surigao Strait, the Battle off Samar, and the Battle off Cape Engaño), planes from Admiral Marc Mitscher's Task Force 38 — including *Enterprise, Cabot,* ESSEX, FRANKLIN, INTREPID, and LEXINGTON — flew west from the Philippine Sea across

Luzon to attack ships of Vice Admiral Takeo Kurita's Center Force in the Sibuyan Sea. There they sank the huge battleship MUSASHI and prevented Kurita from joining other units of the Japanese counteroffensive.

Enterprise remained in the Philippines through December when she returned briefly to Pearl Harbor. Returning at the start of 1945, she took part in operations against Japanese shipping in the South China Sea between Indochina, the Chinese coast, and Formosa. From February 10, 1945, *Enterprise* began to focus on the Japanese Home Islands, launching raids against targets on Kyushu, Honshu, and in the Sea of Japan. Her planes also supported the landings on Iwo Jima from February 19 until March 9, at one point keeping aircraft aloft for 174 hours straight. Proceeding next to Okinawa, on March 18 she was hit by a bomb that forced her back to Ulithi for repairs. Back on station for only six days, on April 11 a kamikaze knocked her out of commission again until May 6. Seven days later, a second kamikaze destroyed her forward elevator, killing 14 of her crew and wounding 34. *Enterprise* put back to Puget Sound for repairs, which lasted until war's end.

Following work bringing troops home from Europe in Operation Magic Carpet, *Enterprise* was inactivated in 1946 and decommissioned on February 17, 1947. In 1958 she was sold and broken up at Kearny, New Jersey.

Ewing, *USS "Enterprise."* Stafford, *Big E.*

ENZA NEW ZEALAND

(ex-*Tag*) Catamaran (1m). *L/B/D:* 97′ × 42′ × 6.8′ (29.6m × 12.8m × 2.1m). *Tons:* 10 tons. *Hull:* fiberglass. *Comp.:* 8. *Des.:* Nigel Irens & David Alan-Williams. *Built:* Canadair, Montreal; 1984.

Originally built for Mike Birch, the catamaran *Tag* was selected by Robin Knox-Johnston and Peter Blake for their attempt to win the Jules Verne Trophy, announced for the first boat to circle the world under sail in less than 80 days. Their effort was sponsored by the New Zealand Apple and Pear Marketing Board, and *Tag* was renamed *ENZA New Zealand;* the brand name ENZA is an acronym for Eat New Zealand Apples. In 1993, three boats set out in quest of the trophy. Under Olivier de Kersauson, *Charal* left Brest on January 22, and Bruno Peyron's *Commodore Explorer* (ex-*Jet Services V*) and *Enza* sailed in company on January 31. In mid-February, both *Charal* and *Enza* were forced out of the race after hitting submerged objects and limping back to Cape Town. On April 20, *Commodore Explorer* claimed the trophy after returning to Brest in 79 days, 6 hours, 15 minutes.

Enza had been lengthened five feet in 1992 and she was given another seven feet for her second try. On January 16, 1994, with a crew of eight, she departed Brest in company with *Lyonnaise des Eaux Dumez* (the old *Charal*). *Enza* logged over 400 miles a day for the first fortnight, and on day 6 she covered a record 520.9 miles in 24 hours. The speed was phenomenal and so was the attendant noise, which Knox-Johnston described as "somewhat akin to riding a subway with eight fire hoses trained on the outside." On day 35 they were abreast of New Zealand. In 1969, Knox-Johnston's SUHAILI had taken 161 days to go the same distance. Although she ran under bare poles off Cape Horn, *Enza* entered the Atlantic several hundred miles ahead of *Lyonnaise.* On April 1, *Enza* passed Ushant having logged 26,395 miles in 74 days, 22 hours, 17 minutes, at an average speed of 14.7 knots, or 325 miles per day. *Lyonnaise* finished less than three days behind, with a time of 77 days, 5 hours, 3 minutes. In 1997, Kersauson's 90-foot trimaran, *Sport-Elec,* circumnavigated the globe in 71 days, 14 hours, 2 minutes.

Knox-Johnston, *Beyond Jules Verne.* Lewis & Levitt, *Around the World in Seventy-Nine Days.*

EPPLETON HALL

Steam paddle tugboat (1f/1m). *L/B/D:* 100.5″ × 21′ (33.3′ew) × 10′ (30.63m × 10.13m × 3.05m). *Tons:* 166 grt. *Hull:* steel. *Mach.:* side-lever steam, 500 hp, sidewheels. *Built:* Hepple & Co., South Shields, Eng.; 1914.

Named for a "plain square building of the time of Charles the First" in Yorkshire, the sidewheel steam tug *Eppleton Hall* was originally built for Lambton Collieries, Ltd. She spent the first and longest part of her career on the River Wear and then was acquired by French, Fenwick, Wear & Tyne, Ltd., for work on the River Tyne. She all but ended her days with the Seaham Harbor Dock Company who sold her to Clayton and Davies, Shipbreakers, in 1968, and prepared her for scrapping.

The following year a group of San Francisco ship preservationists, including San Francisco Maritime Museum's Karl Kortum and the newspaper publisher Scott Newhall, learned that the last working steam paddle tug in the world, *Reliant,* was about to go out of service. Newhall flew to Newcastle to buy the tug, only to learn that she had been promised to the National Maritime Museum, who intended to cut her up for display indoors at Greenwich. Newhall offered to trade the working *Reliant* for the derelict *Eppleton Hall,* but there was no interest. A subsequent cloak-and-dagger attempt to buy the

With side-lever paddlewheel engines of a design little changed from the earliest such engines of the 1820s, the British paddle tug EPPLETON HALL *was built in 1914. The saga of her restoration and passage to San Francisco is a credit to the indomitable spirit of ship preservationists. Courtesy National Maritime Museum, Golden Gate National Recreation Area, San Francisco.*

ship out from under the National Maritime Museum ended in a confrontation with officials from Scotland Yard.

The only alternative was to take *Eppleton Hall,* "half sunk, filled with mud, gutted," restore her, obtain a seagoing certificate, and steam her 11,000 miles to San Francisco. As Newhall describes the scene,

> The ship . . . had been completely disemboweled. All the woodwork had been burned out, preparatory to cutting the vessel apart. The deck frames were warped. The paddle floats and paddle boxes had been either rotted or burned. The engines were covered with scum and rust, but were vaguely intact. And the *Eppleton Hall*'s bottom was full of water.

Nonetheless, willing and able workmen at R. B. Harrison & Son, Ltd., completed the refit in four months. The engines were reassembled, new paddle floats installed, paddle boxes built, deck frames fitted, and a steel plate inserted to stiffen her for the ocean passages for which she was never intended. After considerable debate with the Board of Trade, *Eppleton Hall* was classified as a yacht, embarked fourteen crew, and steamed out of Newcastle on September 18, 1969.

The ensuing voyage to San Francisco took *Eppleton Hall* down the coast of Europe, island hopping through the Madeiras, Canaries, and Cape Verdes, across to the north coast of South America, through the Panama Canal and up the coast of Mexico and the United States. The passage lasted six months and seven days, during which she endured breakdowns and severe storms, landed an ill crewman in Guatemala, and, aptly, towed an engineless

fishing boat into San Diego. Her triumphant entry into San Francisco Bay signaled the successful conclusion of one of the most dramatic ship preservation efforts ever. Today *Eppleton Hall* is the only steam tug preserved outside of Europe. Owned by the San Francisco Maritime National Historical Park, she still steams under her own power on San Francisco Bay.

Newhall, *"Eppleton Hall."*

HMS EREBUS

Hecla-class bomb vessel (3m). *L/B/D:* 105' × 28.5' × 13.8' (32m × 8.7m × 4.2m). *Tons:* 372 bm. *Hull:* wood. *Comp.:* 67. *Arm.:* 1 × 13" mortar, 1 × 10" mortar, 2 × 6pdr, 8 × 24pdr. *Des.:* Sir Henry Peake. *Built:* Pembroke Dockyard, Wales; 1826.

Named for the entrance to Hades in Greek myth, *Erebus* was a bark-rigged vessel with a primary armament of two mortars weighing three tons each. After two years in the Mediterranean, she was adapted for work in polar waters and sailed to the Antarctic under a Mr. Rice. In 1839 she came under command of James Clark Ross, a veteran of Arctic expeditions in ISABELLA, HMS HECLA, and VICTORY. Ross's primary mission was to study terrestrial magnetism and locate the South Magnetic Pole, as well as to undertake oceanographic, botanical, and zoological observations.

Erebus and TERROR (under Francis R. M. Crozier) sailed from Chatham on September 30, 1839, and after stops at ports of call in the Atlantic and Indian Oceans, notably Simon's Bay, South Africa, and Kerguelen Island, they arrived at Hobart, Tasmania, in August 1840. The ships departed for Antarctica on November 12 and encountered ice two days after Christmas. On New Year's Day 1841 they crossed the Antarctic Circle south of New Zealand. The ships forced their way southward through the pack ice until January 9, when they reached open water — now known as the Ross Sea — in 68°28'S, 176°31'E. Roald Amundsen, who led the first group to reach the South Pole, wrote:

> Few people of the present day [1912] are capable of rightly appreciating this heroic deed, this brilliant proof of human courage and energy. With two ponderous craft — regular "tubs" according to our ideas — these men sailed right into the heart of the pack, which all previous explorers had regarded as certain death. . . . These men were heroes — heroes in the highest sense of the word.

A few days later, the crew landed on Victoria Land, which they claimed for Great Britain and whose landscape they showered with the names of political figures, scientists, and acquaintances, including Mt. Erebus (an active volcano) and Mt. Terror (a dormant one). On February 1 they encountered a barrier in latitude 78°4′S that, in Ross's words, "was about 160 feet high, and extended as far to the east and west as the eye could discern." In fact, the impenetrable Ross Ice Shelf runs for about 1,000 miles and, as one member of the expedition put it, "we might with equal chance of success try to sail through the Cliffs of Dover." *Erebus* and *Terror* remained in the Ross Sea until the end of February and returned to Hobart in April for a three-month refit.

En route to their second visit to Antarctica, the ships visited Sydney and the Bay of Islands, New Zealand, where Ross obtained a chart of J. S. C. Dumont d'Urville's recent Antarctic voyages in ASTROLABE and *Zélée*. On December 18, they entered the pack ice in about 60°50′S, 147°25′W. Held fast, they drifted south at the mercy of the ice. On January 19, 1842, the ships' rudders were destroyed by ice in a furious gale, and it was not until February 1 that they were in ice-free waters again. After three weeks the expedition reached the Ross Ice Shelf in 78°9′30″S; no ship would sail farther south for nearly sixty years. On March 13, the ships were approaching a heavy ice formation when *Erebus* collided with *Terror*. As the latter ship's bowsprit was swept away, the two ships drifted towards two icebergs separated by 60 feet of open water. *Terror* passed through first, followed by *Erebus*, whose yards struck the iceberg repeatedly before Ross

sailed her through the gap "by the hazardous expedient of the sternboard," that is, stern first with the sails aback — "which nothing could justify during such a gale with so high a sea running, but to avert the danger which every moment threatened us of being dashed to pieces."

The ships returned to the Falkland Islands, made a visit to Tierra del Fuego in September, and then in December sailed south again, this time to the islands of the Antarctic Peninsula. Turning east, the ice prevented them from sailing through the Weddell Sea and they got no farther than 71°30′S, 14°51′W before turning for home. After several stops, they arrived at Folkestone on September 4, 1843, after a voyage of four years, five months. In addition to studies in magnetism, they had also brought back oceanographic data and extensive collections of botanical and ornithological specimens.

The next year, *Erebus* and *Terror* were fitted out with 20-hp engines and single-screw propellers for a new voyage in search of the Northwest Passage. Ross declined command, which went to his old friend Sir John Franklin, who had surveyed Australia in HMS INVESTIGATOR, sailed to Spitzbergen, and made a three-year trek to the Coppermine River in the Canadian Arctic. With Crozier still in command of *Terror*, the two ships sailed from Greenhithe on May 19, 1845. *Erebus* and *Terror* each carried stores for two years, and another two years' worth were carried to the Whalefish Islands in the Davis Strait by the supply ship *Barretto Junior*. *Erebus* and *Terror* were

François Etienne Musin's "HMS EREBUS in the Ice, 1846" depicts Sir John Franklin's flagship one year after the two-ship expedition disappeared into the Arctic wastes while searching for the Northwest Passage. Courtesy National Maritime Museum, Greenwich.

last seen in Baffin Bay near the entrance of Lancaster Sound in August 1845.

The ships sailed through Lancaster Strait and after trying to sail north through Wellington Channel, turned south around Cornwallis Island and headed into Peel Strait and Franklin Strait, to the west of Somerset Island and the Boothia Peninsula. Continuing southwest, the ships became icebound in Victoria Strait between King William Island and Victoria Island. Franklin died of natural causes aboard *Erebus* on June 11, 1847, and by the following spring, twenty-three other members of the crew were dead of starvation or scurvy. On April 22, 1848, the 105 survivors abandoned the ships and attempted to march to Fort Resolution, a Hudson's Bay Company outpost on Great Slave Lake more than 600 miles to the southwest. Over the next twelve years, more than a dozen expeditions were launched to search for survivors, including both military and civilian groups from Britain and the United States. The most successful of these was that of *Fox,* under Captain Francis L. M'Clintock.

The ships' fate was only revealed by the discovery of human remains, diaries, and relics of the expedition found in the course of scores of land and sea searches sent out starting in 1848 and culminating in the 1859 expedition of M'Clintock in *Fox.*

Beattie & Geiger, *Frozen in Time.* Owen, *Fate of Franklin.* Ross, J. C., *Voyage of Discovery and Research in the Southern and Antarctic Regions.* Ross, M. J., *Ross in the Antarctic.*

E. R. STERLING

(ex-*Lord Wolseley, Columbia, Lord Wolseley, Everett G. Griggs*) Barkentine (6m). *L/B/D:* 308.2′ × 42.9′ × 25.1′ (93.9m × 13.1m × 7.7m). *Tons:* 2,518 grt. *Hull:* iron. *Comp.:* 17. *Built:* Harland & Wolff, Ltd., Belfast, Ireland; 1883.

The four-masted ship *Lord Wolseley* was built for the Messrs. Thomas Dixon & Sons, Ltd., of Belfast, popularly known as the Lord Line because its ships were named for Irish Lords. Under that name and rig, she traded between Calcutta, Pacific ports, and Europe. In 1898 she was sold to a German firm and, renamed *Columbia,* converted to a bark. After being dismasted off Cape Flattery in 1903, she was sold to the Victoria & Vancouver Stevedoring Company and returned to her original name. Three years later, she was sold to another Vancouver owner, renamed *Everett G. Griggs,* and converted to a six-masted barkentine, that is, square-rigged on the foremast, and fore-and-aft rigged on the main, mizzen, spanker, jigger, and driver masts.

Although somewhat grandiose, this rig was economical and the ship could be handled by a crew of only seventeen, about half her complement as a four-masted bark. She sailed in the lumber trade between the Pacific Northwest and Australia, even after being sold to E. R. Sterling in 1910. Naming the ship for himself, Sterling furnished the ship to accommodate his family and gave her fittings more common on land than at sea, including electric light, a shipboard telephone, the first radio on a sailing ship, and an automobile for use when in port. His son Ray Sterling took command in 1910 and kept her in the lumber trade through World War I and later in the grain trade. On April 16, 1927, she loaded wheat at Adelaide for London. Twice dismasted between the Falklands and Cape Verde, *E. R. Sterling* was forced into St. Thomas in the Virgin Islands in October. There were no repair facilities, and the Dutch tug *Indus* towed the barkentine to London, arriving on January 28, 1928. With only her jigger and parts of her fore, spanker, and driver masts standing, she was sold for scrap.

Anderson, *Sailing Ships of Ireland.* Rogers, *Freak Ships.*

ERICSSON

Caloric ship (4f/2m). *L/B/D:* 260′ × 40′ × 17′ (79.2m × 12.2m × 5.2m). *Tons:* 2,200 tons. *Mach.:* caloric engine, sidewheels. *Built:* Perine, Patterson & Stack, New York; 1852.

The Swedish-born John Ericsson was one of the great inventors of the mid-nineteenth century. Working in England and the United States, he developed designs for steam engines, screw propulsion, and ships' guns. Among the best-known vessels with which his name is associated are the ROBERT F. STOCKTON, USS PRINCETON, USS MONITOR, and the caloric steamship named for himself. The basic principle of the hot-air (Ericsson preferred the term caloric) engine was to use the expansive force of hot air directly, without heating steam first. The resulting apparatus was theoretically more efficient and safer than a steam engine fitted with a boiler. The chief difficulties resulted from the extreme heat at which the engines operated and the greater weight of the engines. By the 1840s, Ericsson had improved his basic design to the point that he felt ready to "construct a ship for navigating the ocean, propelled by paddlewheels actuated by the caloric engine."

Laid down in April 1852, *Ericsson* made her first trial run only nine months later, on January 4, 1853. The machinery consisted of four single-acting vertical cylinders of fourteen-foot bore and six-foot stroke mounted directly over the furnaces. These were connected to pistons that actuated the walking beams attached in turn to single cranks on either paddlewheel shaft. The vessel underwent successful trials on New York Bay and to Washington, D.C., but the initial estimate of the machinery's worth quickly proved unfounded. A new engine was fitted with two double-acting cylinders six feet in diameter and with a stroke of six feet. During the second trial of the new engine, on April 27, the ship was hit by a tornado, heeled over, and sank. Although she was raised four days later, Ericsson was resigned to the fact that the engines would not perform as predicted. As he later wrote, "The average speed at sea proving insufficient for commercial purpose, the owners, with regret, acceded to my proposition to remove the costly machinery, although it had proved perfect as a mechanical combination."

Ericsson fitted the ship with an inclined-cylinder steam engine of his own design, but this proved too underpowered to drive the ship competitively. Nonetheless, *Ericsson* spent the next five years in transatlantic service sailing for John Kitching and under charter to the Collins Line (as a replacement for their ill-fated PACIFIC), though she was far slower than the fastest ships of the day.

In October 1861, the U.S. Navy chartered the *Ericsson* for use as a transport for its assault on Port Royal, South Carolina, and thereafter she was employed sporadically on various other assignments. From July to November she was chartered to the North American Steamship Company for the run between New York and Panama, carrying as many as 849 passengers per trip. To summarize her career to that date, she had made twenty transatlantic voyages to Liverpool, Bremen, Le Havre, and Antwerp under the house flags of John Kitching, Collins Line, North American Lloyds, Dunham & Company, and William Salem & Company.

In 1867, W. W. Shermann acquired the *Ericsson,* removed her engines, and rerigged her as a three-masted ship. As such she performed wonderfully, posting times comparable to those of fast clippers. In the spring of 1874, she and the William Webb clipper YOUNG AMERICA (also built in 1853) sailed from San Francisco for Liverpool in 103 days — 15 days ahead of Donald McKay's GLORY OF THE SEAS. *Ericsson* called at ports on the West Coast, Europe, Chile, Australia, and the Philippines, carrying bulk cargoes of grain, lumber, and coal for a quarter century. She changed ownership several times; the last time she was sold to Boole & Company of San Francisco, in 1892. On November 19 of that year, she was en route from San Francisco to Nanaimo, British Columbia, in ballast when she stranded on Entrance Island near Barclay Sound on Vancouver Island and sank in 48°49′N, 125°14′W. The site of the *Ericsson*'s loss was positively identified by the Underwater Archaeological Society of British Columbia in 1985.

Griffiths, "Ericsson's Caloric Ship."

ESMERALDA

Barkentine (4m). *L/B/D:* 308.5′ × 42.7′ × 19.7′ (94m × 13m × 6m). *Tons:* 3,500 disp. *Hull:* steel. *Comp.:* 332. *Arm.:* 4 × 5.7cm. *Mach.:* diesel. *Built:* Echevarrieta y Larringa, Cadiz, Spain; 1952.

Originally named for the Spanish commander in chief of the Holy League's fleet at the Battle of Lepanto in 1571, *Juan de Austria* was a near-sister ship of the Spanish training vessel JUAN SEBASTIAN DE ELCANO. Despite the proven success of their four-masted topsail schooner, after a fire destroyed the newly built ship, the Spanish decided not to commission her. (The chief difference between *Esmeralda* and *Juan Sebastian de Elcano* is that the former has no fore-and-aft sails on her foremast.)

In 1952, the Chilean government bought the recently completed ship and named it for a Chilean corvette that had fought in the Nitrate War with Peru in 1879. *Esmeralda*'s work as a sail-training vessel took her to ports around the world. However, during the rule of General Augusto Pinochet Ugarte (1973–88), the ship and her crew were frequently greeted by demonstrators, particularly at significant international gatherings, such as Operation Sail 1976/International Naval Review celebrating the U. S. bicentennial. The protests focused especially on reports that *Esmeralda* was used not just for sail training but as a prison ship on which political prisoners were tortured. With the return of the democracy to Chile, *Esmeralda* is once again best known for her role as one of the largest and most outstanding naval sail-training vessels in the world.

Brouwer, *International Register of Historic Ships*. Schäuffelen, *Great Sailing Ships*. Press reports.

ESPAÑA

(ex-*Alfonso XIII*) *España*-class battleship (1f/2m). *L/B/D:* 458.9′ × 78.1′ × 25.3′ (139.9m × 23.8m × 7.7m). *Tons:* 15,840 disp. *Hull:* steel. *Comp.:* 854. *Arm.:* 8 × 12.2″ (4 × 2), 20 × 10.2cm, 2 × 4.7cm. *Armor:* 8″ belt. *Mach.:* turbines, 15,500 shp, 4 screws; 19.6 kts. *Built:* Sociedad Española de Construction Naval, El Ferrol; 1915.

The smallest battleships of the DREADNOUGHT era and the only ones built by Spain in the twentieth century, the three *España*-class battleships were designed in Britain and built under British supervision in Spain. Commissioned as *Alfonso XIII*, for the king who reigned from 1902 to 1931, she was renamed following the wreck of the original *España* on the coast of Morocco in 1923. She took part in various operations during the Riffian uprising against Spanish holdings in Morocco between 1921 and 1926.

At the start of the Spanish Civil War, *España* was lying in El Ferrol when nationalist rebels seized the ship on July 20, 1936. Throughout the war, the nationalist navy was more effective than that of the republicans, and by November 1937, General Francisco Franco declared a blockade of the entire Spanish coast. In the meantime, on April 2, 1937, *España* took part in the bombardment of republican positions near Bilbao, but on April 30 she sank off Santander after hitting a mine — probably laid by the nationalists — with the loss of few, if any, of the crew. *España*'s sister ship, *Jaime I*, remained in republican hands but was put out of commission after an internal explosion on June 17, 1937; she was scrapped in 1939.

Breyer, *Battleships and Battlecruisers.* Thomas, *Spanish Civil War.*

L'ESPERANCE

(ex-*Truite*) Frigate (3m). *Hull:* wood. *Comp.:* 113. *Built:* France; 1791.

By the beginning of 1789, France had learned that La Pérouse's ships ASTROLABE and BOUSSOLE were overdue at the Ile de France. Even as the French Revolution gathered headway, there was widespread concern among both the nobility and revolutionaries for the fate of the expedition, and plans were put in place for the dispatch of a search party. On September 29, 1791, three months after the arrest of Louis XVI, two converted storeships — *L'Esperance* (ex-*Truite*) and *La Recherche* (ex-*Durance*) — sailed from Brest under command of A. R. J. de Bruni, Chevalier d'Entrecasteaux. The crew of *Recherche* numbered 106, under J. M. Huon de Kermadec. Although the chief object of the voyage was to search for La Pérouse, the expedition carried a full complement of scientists — five naturalists, two hydrographers, two draughtsman, and a botanist.

Orders called for d'Entrecasteaux to sail for New Holland (Australia), but at Cape Town he heard a report that people dressed in French uniforms had been seen in the Admiralty Islands, and he altered his plans accordingly. The ships' progress towards the Moluccas was so slow, however, that he decided instead to make for Van Diemen's Land (Tasmania), arriving on April 21, 1792. The French spent five weeks charting and exploring the

southeast coast before striking northeast across the Tasman Sea towards New Caledonia. Reefs prevented a landing there, so they continued northeast past the Solomon Islands to land on New Ireland for a week. July 26 brought the ships to the Admiralty Islands, but there was no sign of La Pérouse.

After provisioning at the Dutch entrepôt of Amboina, on October 13 *Esperance* and *Recherche* were bound for Van Diemen's Land. Rounding Cape Leeuwin, on the southwest corner of Australia, they came to the Recherche Islands and then explored the barren shore of Nuyts Land in the Great Australian Bight. On January 21, 1793 — the same day as Louis XVI's execution — the ships anchored at Van Diemen's Land. From there they headed to Tongatapu, where La Pérouse was known to have sailed after leaving Botany Bay in 1788. Although they were well received by the Tongans from whom they bought hundreds of pigs, birds, and breadfruit trees, there was no sign of La Pérouse, and they made for New Caledonia where Huon de Kermadec died on May 6. Thirteen days later, they came to a previously unknown island south of Santa Cruz — Vanikoro, the very island on which *Astrolabe* and *Boussole* had wrecked. The inhabitants were hostile, and the French sailed without learning anything of the fate of their countrymen.

Sailing through the Solomons and the Louisiades in May and June, the crews became increasingly ill with scurvy and dysentery. On July 20, d'Entrecasteaux died and command of the expedition fell to the ailing A. Hesmivy d'Auribeau. The French sailed through Torres Strait and on October 19 reached Surabaya, only to learn they were at war with the Dutch. News of the Revolution also divided the officers and crew and the expedition dissolved. The officers were promonarchy and had many of the republican crew arrested by the Dutch. The scientists made their way back to France as best they could, but the officers had sent their collections and manuscripts to England, from which they were returned only after intervention by Sir Joseph Banks — and after all the charts had been copied by the Admiralty.

Brosse, *Great Voyages of Discovery.* Dunmore, *French Explorers in the Pacific.*

USS ESSEX

Frigate (3m). *L/B/D:* 140′ bp × 31′ × 12.3′ dph (42.7m × 9.4m × 3.7m). *Tons:* 850 bm. *Hull:* wood. *Comp.:* 319. *Arm.:* 40 × 32pdr, 6 × 18pdr. *Des.:* William Hackett. *Built:* Enos Briggs, Salem, Mass.; 1799.

Built by the citizens of Essex County, Massachusetts, who presented her to the U.S. government, USS *Essex* was

The frigate USS ESSEX *(left) devastated British merchant interests in the Pacific during the War of 1812. But she stood no chance against the long-range guns of* HMS PHOEBE *and* CHERUB *when brought to battle off Valparaiso in March 1814, as seen in this painting by Captain William Bainbridge Hoff. Courtesy U.S. Naval Historical Center, Washington, D.C.*

commissioned under command of Captain Edward Preble. On her first voyage in 1800, during the Quasi-War with France, *Essex* helped convoy a fleet of Dutch East Indiamen through the Indian Ocean. In 1801, she was one of several ships sent to the Mediterranean to contain the Barbary corsairs harassing American shipping. She sailed first under Captain William Bainbridge and then under Captain James Barron. Following the war, she was laid up from 1806 to 1809.

At the beginning of the War of 1812, under command of Captain David Porter, *Essex* captured ten prizes, including HMS *Alert* (18 guns) between July and September. On October 28, 1812, *Essex* left the Delaware River to rendezvous with USS CONSTITUTION and HORNET for a cruise into the South Pacific. After waiting in vain on the coast of Brazil, in January 1813 Porter took the initiative and continued on his own. By way of encouragement, he told his crew that

> the unprotected British commerce, on the coast of Chili [*sic*], Peru, and Mexico, will give you an abundant supply of wealth; and the girls of the Sandwich Islands, shall reward you for your sufferings during the passage round Cape Horn.

The passage was bleak, but the rewards matched Porter's promise. During the course of 1813, *Essex* virtually destroyed Britain's South Pacific whale fishery, and took fifteen prizes, including the whaleship *Atlantic*, which was armed with ten 6-pdr. long guns and ten 18-pdr. carronades and renamed *Essex Junior*. In October, the two ships sailed to Nuka Hiva in the Marquesas Islands. On February 3, 1814, the ships returned to Valparaiso where the ships were blockaded by Captain James Hillyard's HMS *Phoebe* (36) and *Cherub* (18), which had been dis-

patched to the Pacific for the purpose. On March 28, Porter attempted to break out of Valparaiso, but *Essex* lost her main topmast in a gale. Disregarding Chilean neutrality, Hillyard attacked and, taking advantage of his guns' superior range, slowly but surely reduced *Essex,* whose primary armament consisted only of short-range carronades. Three hours later Porter was forced to strike; one of the last flags flying was one proclaiming "Free trade and sailors' rights" — the slogan that had impelled the United States to war. *Essex* lost 58 killed, 31 drowned, and 70 wounded; British losses were 5 dead and 10 wounded. *Essex* was taken into the Royal Navy as a 42-gun frigate. In 1823 she was made a convict ship, and she was sold in 1837. *Essex Junior* sailed to New York as a cartel ship, where she was sold.

Porter, *Journal of a Cruise*. U.S. Navy, *DANFS*.

ESSEX

Whaleship (3m). *Tons:* 238. *Hull:* wood. *Comp.:* 20. *Built:* <1802.

One of the most remarkable and gripping stories of shipwreck concerns that of the whaleship *Essex,* of Nantucket. This tragedy occurred in 1820; the ship had previously made four voyages, the first in 1802, to the whaling grounds off southern Africa, for whale oil, and to the Pacific for sperm oil. The *Essex* departed Nantucket on August 12, 1819, bound again for the Pacific with a crew of twenty, George Pollard, master. Fifteen months later, on November 20, 1820, the ship was about 2,700 miles west of Ecuador. Two boats were out, and Captain Pollard had harpooned a whale while the boat of first mate Owen Chase had been stove by a whale. He had just returned to the ship when he noticed a sperm whale charging *Essex*. The sperm whale's massive head struck the ship in the bows. "We looked at each other with perfect amazement," wrote Chase, "deprived almost of the power of speech." The whale turned and rammed a second time, staving the bows and forcing the crew to abandon ship.

They managed to salvage two quadrants and two sextants, some food and water, and put out in three clinker-built whaleboats before their ship sank, in 0°40′S, 119°W. On December 20, they landed at Henderson's Island, which lacked either sufficient vegetation or water to sustain them, and after seven days they sailed again leaving three crew behind at their own request. The remaining three boats made first for Easter Island and then to Juan Fernández Island. On January 10, 1821, the second mate died, and two days later, Chase's boat was separated from the other two boats. A second man in his boat died on January 20, and a third on February 8. Desperate for food, they elected to eat the latter's corpse. On the 18th, the three remaining crew were picked up by the London brig *Indian* at 33°45′S, 81°03′ W, and landed at Valparaiso two days later. Meanwhile, the other two boats were separated on January 28, but not before the bodies of four deceased crew were eaten by their shipmates. On February 1, the four survivors in Pollard's boat drew lots to see who would be killed to feed the others. Pollard's cabin boy, Owen Coffin, drew the short straw and was shot. Brazilla Ray died on the 11th, and Pollard and Charles Ramsdale — Coffin's executioner — were rescued off St. Mary's Island by the Nantucket whaleship *Dauphin*. The three castaways who chose to remain on Henderson's Island were rescued by another ship that was at Valparaiso when their shipmates landed there.

The most detailed narrative of these ordeals was that of the first mate Owen Chase, who published his account in 1821 in "the hope of obtaining something of remuneration, by giving a short history of my suffering to the world." Briefer accounts by George Pollard and Thomas Chapple, who remained on Henderson's Island, were also published. In those less sensational times, none of the authors seems to have profited from their ordeal, although certain details of their stories, as well as those of similar wrecks of whaleships, were incorporated by Herman Melville in his quintessential whaling novel, *Moby Dick*.

Chase, *Shipwreck of the Whaleship "Essex."* Starbuck, *History of the North American Whale Fishery.*

USS ESSEX (CV-9)

Essex-class aircraft carrier. *L/B/D:* 872′ × 93′ (147.5′ew) × 28.6′ (265.8m × 28.3m (45m) 8.7m). *Tons:* 34,346 disp. *Hull:* steel; 3″ belt. *Comp.:* 3,448. *Arm.:* 80+; 12 × 5″, 17 × 40mm quad. *Mach.:* geared turbines, 150,000 shp, 4 shafts; 33 kts. *Built:* Newport News Shipbuilding & Dry Dock Co. Newport News, Va.; 1942.

The first class of aircraft carrier built after the expiration of the interwar naval agreements, the *Essex*-class carriers were the largest commissioned during World War II. Entering active service on the last day of the year, USS *Essex* arrived in the Pacific in the spring of 1943 and launched air raids on Marcus and Wake Islands in August and October, respectively. The first of her many operations in support of amphibious landings was during the Gilbert Islands campaign in November, followed up by the Marshalls campaign at the end of January 1944. *Essex* returned to San Francisco for her only wartime overhaul in February, returning to the western Pacific in May. As part of Task Force 58, her planes covered the invasion of Saipan on June 15, and four days later took part in the Battle of the Philippine Sea — "the Great Marianas Turkey Shoot" — in which Japanese naval aviation was annihilated. After the Marianas campaign in August, *Essex* proceeded to the invasions of Peleliu, Palau Islands, in September, and the Philippines at Leyte Gulf on October 24–25. While operating north of the Philippines, on November 25, a kamikaze struck *Essex*, killing 15 and wounding 44 of her crew. After brief repairs, she rejoined the Third Fleet off Mindoro in December. In early 1945, *Essex* made a foray against Japanese shipping in the South China Sea as far south as Hong Kong, and along the coast of China. Assigned to Task Force 58 in February, *Essex* helped press the attack on the Japanese home islands, bombing industrial sites around Tokyo as early as February, supporting landings on Iwo Jima, and keeping station off Okinawa from March to May. It was an *Essex* plane that first spotted YAMATO at the start of the Japanese battleship's last mission on April 7. *Essex* flew her last World War II combat missions on August 15.

Decommissioned in 1947, *Essex* was refit and back in service by 1951. She served three tours of duty during Korea, flying missions in support of United Nations ground forces. On September 16, seven of her crew were killed when a plane was forced to crash-land on deck. Following the war, she received an angled flight deck, and after another fourteen months in the Pacific sailed via Cape Horn to join the Atlantic Fleet. For the next two years she operated in the North Atlantic and Mediterranean where, in 1958, she landed troops at Beirut during the Lebanese intervention. Two years later, *Essex* was reclassified as an antisubmarine warfare carrier and homeported at Quonset, Rhode Island. Decommissioned in 1969, she was broken up in 1975.

Raven, *"Essex" Class Carriers.* U.S. Navy, *DANFS.*

ESTONIA

(ex-*Wasa King, Silja Star, Viking Sally*) Ferry (1f). *L/B/D:* 509.7′ × 79.4′ × 18.4′ (155.4m x 24.2m × 5.6m). *Tons:* 15,566 grt. *Hull:* steel. *Comp.:* 2,000 pass.; 200 crew. *Mach.:* oil engine, 24,000 hp; 21 kts. *Built:* Jos. L. Meyer Schiffwerft, Papenburg, West Germany; 1980.

Originally built for the Rederi AB Sally Viking Line, the vehicle/passenger ferry *Viking Sally* entered service between Åbo/Turku, Mariehamn, and Stockholm in 1980. A decade later she was acquired by the Silja Line and renamed *Silja Star* and then *Wasa King.* In 1993, she was sold to Estline, a company jointly owned by the government of newly independent Estonia, and Nordström and Thulin, a Swedish company. Renamed *Estonia,* she was put in service between Tallinn and Stockholm.

At 1900 on September 28, 1994, she left Tallinn on a regularly scheduled 15-hour run; her captains were Aavo Piht and Arvo Andresson. An hour and a half later she encountered heavy weather, and shortly after midnight an engineer noticed flooding in the car deck. Within minutes the pumps were overwhelmed, but it was not until 0124 on September 29 that the ship broadcast her first distress call. Half an hour later *Estonia* capsized and sank suddenly in about 220 feet of water. Official estimates of the number of people embarked ranged from 982, according to Swedish authorities, to 1,049 (Estonian estimates), not including a number of unregistered children. Although many of the ship's company were asleep in their cabins and had no chance to save themselves, those that got off the ship were at the mercy of the frigid 20-foot-high seas. Only 144 people survived the sinking. Remote videotapes of the wreck showed that the locks on the bow door had failed and that the door had separated from the rest of the vessel. In terms of lives lost, *Estonia's* sinking was Sweden's worst tragedy in over a century.

Bruzelius, Maritime History Virtual Archive. Press reports.

EUREKA

(ex-*Ukiah*) Ferry boat (1f). *L/B/D:* 271′ × 42′/78′ew × 6.5′ (82.6m × 12.8m/23.8m × 2m). *Tons:* 2,564 grt. *Hull:* wood. *Comp.:* 10 trains; 500 pass. *Mach.:* beam engine, 1,500 hp, sidewheels. *Des.:* P. Tiernan. *Built:* Tiburon, Calif.; 1890.

The last surviving walking beam engine steamboat in the United States, the passenger/car ferry *Eureka* began life as the San Francisco & Northern Pacific Railroad Company's train and passenger ferry *Ukiah.* With a capacity for ten railroad cars on two parallel tracks on the main deck, she could accommodate up to 500 passengers on the upper deck. Originally in service on San Francisco Bay between Tiburon and San Francisco, she was also chartered for parties of day-trippers making excursions to various places around the Bay. In 1909, her northern terminus was changed to Sausalito, on which run she steamed about 4,000 miles a month, or about fifteen roundtrips a day. During World War I, *Ukiah* was taken over by the U.S. Railroad Administration and worked harder still, so that in 1920 she began a two-year refit. Now named *Eureka* (for the reorganized Northwestern Pacific Railroad's northern terminus), she could carry 120 automobiles and 2,300 passengers, changes in usage and capacity that reflected the increasing mobility of the Bay Area's population. The opening of the Golden Gate and Oakland Bay Bridges in the mid-1930s signaled the demise of the Bay passenger ferries, and *Eureka* made the last run on February 28, 1941.

Thereafter, *Eureka* was used to bring passengers from the transcontinental train terminal in Oakland across the Bay to San Francisco. Gradually this work fell off in the face of competition from airlines, and *Eureka* was pulled out of commercial service in 1958. The Southern Pacific Company then restored the ship and deeded her to the San Francisco Maritime Museum, where she was opened to the public in 1963. She remains part of the same fleet of historic ships, now under the auspices of the National Park Service.

Cullivan, *"Eureka:* A Centennial Retrospective." Harlan, *San Francisco Bay Ferryboats.*

EUROPA

(later *Liberté*) Liner (2f/2m). *L/B:* 939′ × 101.9′ (285.6m × 31.1m). *Tons:* 49,746 grt. *Hull:* steel. *Comp.:* 1st 723, 2nd 500, tourist 300; 3rd 600. *Mach.:* steam turbines, 4 screws; 27 kts. *Built:* Blohm & Voss, Hamburg; 1929.

Intended to enter service together with her sister ship, BREMEN, Norddeutscher Lloyd's *Europa* was all but gutted by fire at her fitting-out dock in March 1929. Despite this setback, when she finally made her maiden voyage from Bremen to Southampton, Cherbourg, and New York in April 1930, she broke *Bremen's* record with an average speed of 27.91 knots between Cherbourg and

Built for transatlantic service, the handsome German liner EUROPA *of 1929 glides serenely on a flat sea. She ended her days in 1961 as* LIBERTÉ *under the French flag. Courtesy The Mariners' Museum, Newport News, Virginia.*

Ambrose Light. She remained on the transatlantic run until August 1939, and after the start of World War II, she became an accommodation ship at Bremerhaven. In 1940 she was converted for use as a troopship in Operation Sea Lion, the abortive German invasion of England, and in 1942 some thought was given to turning her into an aircraft carrier. However, she survived the war more or less intact and on May 8, 1945, she was seized by the United States and commissioned as troopship USS *Europa* (AP-177). Decommissioned in 1946 and handed over to the French as reparations, after four years of rebuilding at St. Nazaire she made her maiden voyage to New York as French Line's *Liberté* in August 1950. She maintained regular transatlantic service with ILE DE FRANCE and *Flandre* until 1961. The following year she was scrapped at La Spezia.

Bonsor, *North Atlantic Seaway.* Braynard & Miller, *Fifty Famous Liners.*

HMS EXETER

Exeter-class cruiser (2f/2m). *L/B/D:* 575′ × 58′ × 20.3′ (175.3m × 17.7m × 6.2m). *Tons:* 10,490. *Hull:* steel. *Comp.:* 630. *Arm.:* 6 × 8″ (3 × 2), 4 × 4″, 2 × 2pdr; 6 × 21″TT; 2 aircraft. *Armor:* 3″ belt, 1.5″ deck. *Mach.:* geared turbines, 80,000 shp, 4 shafts; 32 kts. *Des.:* Sir William Berry. *Built:* Devonport Dockyard, Plymouth, Eng.; 1931.

HMS *Exeter* was one of two heavy cruisers built after the cost of the first ten County-class cruisers proved prohibitive. In September 1939 she was assigned to Commodore Henry Harwood's Force G to look for the German pocket battleship ADMIRAL GRAF SPEE (Captain Hans Langs-

dorff). On December 12 *Exeter* and the 6-inch cruisers AJAX and ACHILLES rendezvoused off Uruguay, 150 miles east of the broad River Plate estuary. At dawn the next day, Force G encountered *Graf Spee* at 0614, with *Exeter* (Captain F. S. Bell) deployed as the single-ship Second Division. Six minutes later, *Exeter* opened fire in reply to *Graf Spee* at 18,700 yards. *Graf Spee* straddled *Exeter* with six 11-inch shells at 0623, and after eight salvoes scored a direct hit on "B" turret. The same hit killed all but three men — Captain Bell among them — on the bridge. At 0638 "A" turret and the gyrocompasses were also knocked out, although the engines were unaffected and the ship could still make good speed. At this point, Langsdorff decided to concentrate on *Ajax* and *Achilles,* which certainly saved *Exeter* because the "Y" turret ceased to work by 0730. By early afternoon, with the ship steaming at only 18 knots, Bell signaled Harwood, "All guns out of action." She had lost 53 crew.

Exeter returned to Devonport for a 13-month refit during which four 4-inch and sixteen 2-pdr. guns were added. In early 1942, she joined Dutch Rear Admiral Karel Doorman's ABDA (American-British-Dutch-Australian) Striking Force as it prepared to meet the Japanese invasion of the Dutch East Indies. Sailing out of Surabaya on February 26, Doorman's vastly outnumbered striking force headed for Admiral Shoji Nishimura's transport fleet. Early in the Battle of the Java Sea, *Exeter* was hit by a shell that knocked out six of her eight boilers, and she retired to Surabaya. From there she left for Ceylon with destroyers HMS *Encounter* and USS *Pope*. On March 1, while still in the Java Sea, they encountered a Japanese force of four heavy cruisers and five destroyers. *Exeter* was sunk by a torpedo from the Japanese destroyer *Inazuma* at about noon in 4°40′S, 110°E. *Encounter* and *Pope* were also lost.

Grove, *Sea Battles in Close Up*. Pope, *Battle of the River Plate*.

EXODUS 1947

(ex-*President Warfield*) Steamboat. *L/B/D:* 320′ × 56.5′ × 18.5′ (97.5m × 17.2m × 5.6m). *Tons:* 1,814 disp. *Hull:* steel. *Comp.:* 69 crew; 300 pass. *Mach.:* steam engine, 2,800 hp, single screw; 15 kts. *Built:* Pusey & Jones Corp., Wilmington, Del.; 1928.

Built for the Baltimore Steam Packet Company and named for its late president S. Davies Warfield (uncle of Wallis Warfield, the future Duchess of Windsor), *President Warfield* served in Old Bay Line service between Norfolk and Baltimore, except for two seasons in Long Island Sound, until taken over by the War Shipping Administration in 1942. On September 21, 1943, she departed St. John's, Newfoundland, with convoy RB-1. The "Skimming Dish" convoy of shallow-draft passenger vessels lost the *Boston, New York, Yorktown,* and the escort HMS *Veteran* to U-boat action. After serving as a barracks ship in England, she was commissioned as USS *President Warfield* (IX-169) and saw service in England and France.

Teeming with Jewish refugees fleeing Europe in the aftermath of World War II, the former Chesapeake Bay excursion boat EXODUS 1947 *defied British naval might to fulfill her mission at Haifa, Palestine, in May 1947. Courtesy The Mariners' Museum, Newport News, Virginia.*

Decommissioned at Hampton Roads in 1946, the former ferry boat was bought from the Maritime Commission by the Potomac Shipwrecking Company and two days later by the Weston Trading Company of New York. The latter was a front for the Palestine resistance organization Haganah, which had been smuggling Jews from Europe to Israel since before World War II. Renamed *Exodus 1947* and illegally flying the Honduran flag, she sailed from Baltimore on February 25, 1947, Itzak Aronowitz, master, with 25 tons of life preservers and mess kits. At Sète, France, she embarked 4,554 Jewish refugees for Palestine. Trailed by an ever-growing flotilla of British ships, including the cruiser HMS AJAX, five destroyers, and two minelayers, on May 4 out she was forcibly boarded; three passengers were killed and 217 wounded. The ship was towed to Haifa and put up for sale. After refusing passage to France, the refugees were landed at Hamburg on September 7, 1947, in an action that turned the tide of world opinion against Britain's Palestine policy. *Exodus 1947* burned at Haifa on August 26, 1952, and was finally scrapped in 1963.

Holly, "*Exodus 1947.*"

USS EXPERIMENT

Schooner (2m). *L/B/D:* 88.5′ × 23.5′ × 6.1′ dph (27m × 7.2m × 1.9m). *Tons:* 176 burthen. *Hull:* wood. *Arm.:* 2 × 12pdr. *Des.:* William Annesley. *Built:* Washington Navy Yard, Washington, D.C.; 1832.

As traditional framing was expensive, heavy, and took up space, naval architect William Annesley devised a way of planking a ship that would do away with frames and published his research in *A New System of Naval Architecture* in 1822. Nine years later he secured a contract to build a schooner — his fourth vessel — for the U.S. Navy. The hull consisted of five layers of planks, the first, third, and fifth running longitudinally, and the second and fourth running laterally; the deck was laid in a similar fashion. Another departure from normal practice was the elliptical hull shape, which Annesley based on his observation of ducks. Although she sailed well downwind, *Experiment* worked badly to windward. As Linda Maloney observes, "in his admiration for the duck [Annesley] failed to note that speed and seaworthiness are not its foremost attributes." Poorly fastened, she leaked, which heightened her crew's reluctance to sail in a ship without frames. Although her commander, Lieutenant William Mervine, thought her fit for any service, his conservative superiors felt otherwise, and she was confined to coastal survey work. Nevertheless, *Experiment*'s greatest failing was the sheer novelty of her frameless construction. In later years, lamination was used widely in iron, steel, and wood and fiberglass hulls.

Maloney, "Naval Experiment."

EXPRESS CRUSADER

(ex-*Spirit of Cutty Sark*) Cutter. *L/B/D:* 53.1' × 13.1' × 7.3' (16.2m × 4m × 2.3m). *Tons:* 15 disp. *Hull:* fiberglass. *Comp.:* 1–10. *Mach.:* oil engine, 62 bhp, 1 screw. *Des.:* E. G. Van de Stadt. *Built:* Tyler Boat Co. & Southern Ocean Shipyard, Poole, Eng.; 1968.

First owned by Leslie Smith who sailed her in the 1968 OSTAR (Observer Single-Handed Trans-Atlantic Race), *Spirit of Cutty Sark* was later bought by Chay Blyth (who had sailed around the world in BRITISH STEEL) for use as a charter yacht. In 1975, New Zealander Naomi Powers met one of Blyth's captains, Rob James, who taught her how to sail and whom she married. Naomi James then decided to be the first woman to sail around the world single-handed. Blyth offered her the loan of *Spirit of Cutty Sark* and the *Daily Express* newspaper agreed to sponsor the venture. Following a scant five weeks of preparation, James sailed out of Dartmouth on September 9, 1977, her sole companion a cat named Boris. After collecting some spare parts at a rendezvous off Gran Canaria on September 23, she resumed her course to Cape Town, South Africa. Essentially a novice sailor when she started, James perfected her navigation skills and prepared herself and *Express Crusader* for heavy weather sailing in the Southern Ocean. Irreparable damage to the self-steering gear two days before her intended rendezvous off Cape Town forced James to put into port for three days and give up any hope of making a nonstop circumnavigation. Unfortunately, too, Boris fell overboard 52 days out.

The voyage across the Indian Ocean included a knockdown and further damage to the self-steering gear, but James was able to pick up spare parts at a rendezvous off Tasmania on January 14, just before one of the worst gales of the voyage. Sailing south of New Zealand, *Express Crusader* was taking the Southern Ocean in stride until February 24 when — with the boat 2,800 miles from New Zealand and 2,300 miles from Cape Horn — the fitting holding the starboard lower shrouds to the mast sheered off, causing the mast to bend from side to side. Rigging a temporary repair, James contemplated putting back to New Zealand and then finishing her voyage via the Panama Canal. But even after capsizing two days later, she decided to press on via the Horn, which she passed on March 19, after 192 days at sea. Five days later she was at Port Stanley, Falkland Islands. There, HMS *Endurance*'s carpenter repaired the rigging and two days later she was off again.

Just before James's departure from Dartmouth, Rob and Blyth had left England at the start of the Whitbread Round the World Race (a crewed race with four scheduled stops) in *Great Britain II,* which won on elapsed time just before *Express Crusader* put into Port Stanley. On May 23, she met Rob off the Azores and then began the last leg home. Arriving at her rendezvous point off England two days early, she decided to drift around rather than arrive early and spoil the scheduled reception at Dartmouth. On June 8, 1978, *Express Crusader* returned to Dartmouth, 272 days after she set out. James subsequently bought the cutter from Blyth.

James, *Alone around the World.*

EXXON VALDEZ

(later *Exxon Mediterranean*) Tanker. *L/B/D:* 987' × 166' × 38.2' (88' dph) (300.8m × 50.6m × 38.2m (26.8m)). *Tons:* 95,169 grt. *Hull:* steel. *Comp.:* 19. *Mach.:* diesel, 31,650 hp; 16 kts. *Built:* National Steel & Shipbuilding Co., San Diego; 1986.

Exxon Valdez was a very large crude oil carrier (VLCC) owned by the Exxon Shipping Company that plied between the Alyeska Marine Terminal of the TransAlaska Pipeline at Valdez and West Coast ports. At 2112 on March 23, 1989, she was under way from Valdez under Captain Joseph Hazelwood with a cargo of 1,264,155 barrels of crude oil. (A barrel of oil is equal to 42 gallons.) After dropping her pilot, she left the outbound shipping lane to avoid ice. Owing to poor navigation, at 0004 on March 24, the supertanker ran aground on Bligh Reef in Prince William Sound, just 25 miles from Valdez. The grounding punctured eight of eleven cargo tanks, and within four hours 5.8 million gallons had been lost. By the time the tanker was refloated on April 5, about 260,000 barrels had been lost and 2,600 square miles of the country's greatest fishing grounds and the surrounding virgin shoreline were sheathed in oil. Captain Hazelwood, who had a record of drunk driving arrests, was charged with criminal mischief, driving a watercraft while intoxicated, reckless endangerment, and negligent discharge of oil. He was found guilty of the last count, fined $51,000, and sentenced to 1,000 hours of community service in lieu of six months in prison. Following repairs, *Exxon Valdez* reentered service in 1990 as *Exxon Mediterranean,* loading oil in the Persian Gulf.

Alaska Oil Spill Commission, *Spill: The Wreck of the "Exxon Valdez."* Keeble, *Out of the Channel.*

FALLS OF CLYDE

Ship (4m). *L/B/D:* 280′ × 40′ × 21′ (85.3m × 12.2m × 6.4m). *Tons:* 1,809 grt. *Hull:* iron. *Built:* Russell & Co., Port Glasgow, Scotland; 1878.

The first of six four-masted ships built for Wright and Breakenridge's Falls Line, *Falls of Clyde* was built for general worldwide trade. Her maiden voyage took her to Karachi, and her subsequent voyaging took her to Australia, California, India, New Zealand, and the British Isles. After twenty-one years under the British flag, she was purchased by Captain William Matson. *Falls of Clyde* sailed briefly under the Hawaiian flag. When Hawaii was annexed by the United States in 1900, it took a special act of Congress to secure the foreign-built ship the right to fly the American flag. Rigged down as a bark and given passenger accommodations, *Falls of Clyde* carried general merchandise from San Francisco and sugar from Honolulu.

In 1907, the Anglo-American Oil Company bought *Falls of Clyde* and converted her to a bulk tanker with a capacity of 19,000 barrels. In this configuration she sailed from Santa Barbara with kerosene and returned from Hawaii with bulk molasses. Following World War I, she sailed to Denmark, and in 1921 she made her last voyage under sail, to Brazil. Rigged down, in 1925 she was purchased by the General Petroleum Company and began life as an oil barge at Ketchikan Harbor, Alaska. There she remained until 1959 when she was sold to William Mitchell, who intended to make her an attraction vessel at Seattle. This plan fell through and subsequent efforts by Karl Kortum, director of the San Francisco Maritime Museum, and Fred Klebingat, who had sailed in her as chief mate in 1915, to place her in Long Beach and Los Angeles were similarly disappointed.

In 1963, the bank holding the mortgage on *Falls of Clyde* decided to sell her to be sunk as part of a breakwater at Vancouver, British Columbia. At the last minute, Kortum and Klebingat aroused interest in the ship in Hawaii, whose flag she had once flown. Funds were raised to pay for the ship and her transfer to Honolulu where she was put under the auspices of the Bernice P. Bishop Museum and opened to the public in 1968. Her restoration as a full-rigged ship was assisted by the grandson of the original builder, Sir William Lithgow, whose Glasgow shipyard donated masts and other fittings.

Heine, *Historic Ships of the World.* Klebingat, "*Falls of Clyde.*"

FANCY

Sloop. *Hull:* wood. *Built:* New York(?); ca. 1700.

One of the earliest yachts built in the English colonies, and the first illustrated in the visual arts, the yacht *Fancy* belonged to Colonel Lewis Morris, the first Lord of the Manor of a tract of land known as Morrisania north of Manhattan. Morris also owned land in New Jersey, and he probably built *Fancy* to sail between his principal holdings and the flourishing settlement in lower Manhattan. William Burgis's "A South Prospect of ye Flourishing City of New York in the Province of New York in America" depicts a parade of ships prior to the departure of Governor Robert Hunter for Albany in 1717, and a contemporary engraving identifies more than thirty points of interest, including "Collonel Morris's *Fancy* turning to Windward with a Sloop of Common Mould." Referring to the same illustration, J. G. Wilson writes,

> Racing on the water was not much in fashion, though the gentry had their barges and some their yachts or pleasure sail-boats. The most elaborate barge, with awning and damask curtains, of which there was mention, was that of the Governor Montgomerie, and the most noted yacht was the *Fancy* belonging to Colonel Lewis Morris, whose Morrisania on the peaceful waters of the Sound gave fine harbor and safe opportunity for sailing.

Of two other vessels often cited as the first American yachts, one was owned by Johan Printz in 1647, governor of the Swedish settlements along the Delaware River, and the other was a 30- to 40-foot pinnace built for Governor William Penn in 1683.

Wilson, *Memorial History of the City of New York.*

FAR WEST

Sternwheel steamer (1f/1m). *L/B/D:* 190′ × 33′ × 1.7′ (57.9m × 10.1m × 0.5m). *Hull:* wood. *Comp.:* 30 crew; 30 pass. *Mach.:* sternwheel. *Built:* Pittsburgh; 1870.

Built for the Coulsen Packet Line, *Far West* was typical of the boats employed on the shallow, fickle, and obstacle-ridden Missouri River. The river extends deep into the American West — 686 miles from St. Louis to Omaha, 1,610 miles to Bismarck, 1,996 miles to the Yellowstone River, and 2,663 miles to Fort Benton, Montana, the head of navigation in the nineteenth century. (Today, the head of navigation is Ponca, Nebraska, a scant 140 miles past Omaha.) Navigation on the Missouri took boats of exceptionally narrow draft; especially shallow sandbars were overcome with "grasshopper" poles, long spars that

In the mid-19th century, "mountain boats" such as the FAR WEST *helped to open the West to trade and settlement. Designed especially for the treacherous waters of the upper Missouri River,* FAR WEST *was once described as "so built that when the river is low and the sand bars come out for air, the first mate can tap a keg and run four miles on the suds." Courtesy Murphy Library, Univ. of Wisconsin, La Crosse.*

could be pushed into the riverbed and used to pull the boat up and forward. Despite the hazards to navigation, the boats were pushed hard; in 1872 *Far West* ran 2,800 miles from Sioux City, Iowa, to Fort Benton, and back, in 17 days, 29 hours.

The Coulsen mountain boats were often chartered to the U.S. Army for use as transports or to explore tributaries of the Missouri. On May 17, 1876, *Far West* sailed from Fort Abraham Lincoln, across the river from Bismarck, to provide support for the army units moving against the Sioux Chief Crazy Horse. *Far West* was under the celebrated Captain Grant Marsh who pioneered navigation of the Yellowstone in 1873, and who earlier in his career sailed with Samuel Clemens (Mark Twain). On June 7, Marsh rendezvoused with Colonel George Armstrong Custer's 7th Cavalry Regiment at the junction of the Yellowstone and Powder Rivers. The 7th and *Far West* continued up the Yellowstone to the mouth of the Rosebud, where Custer's troops turned south. Having ferried Colonel John Gibbon's infantry south across the Yellowstone, on June 25 *Far West* was ordered up the Bighorn River 53 miles to the junction of the Little Bighorn. She was the first vessel to attempt the 100-yard-wide channel and the ascent was only made with the liberal use of grasshoppers and warping ahead with anchors placed on shore. That night, the crew received the first tentative reports of Custer's annihilation at the Battle of Little Bighorn, and the next day they began to embark other wounded soldiers and the horse Comanche, the only survivor of Custer's last stand, which became the 7th's regimental mascot. They turned south to the Yellowstone where they ferried Gibbons north again before turning downriver. *Far West* reached Bismarck on the night of July 5, having covered 700 miles in only 54 hours under way, a phenomenal speed of just over 13 miles per hour.

Far West was sold to Victor Bonnet and Captain Henry M. Dodds for service on the lower Missouri. On October 30, 1883, she hit a snag seven miles below St. Charles, Missouri, and sank.

O'Neill, *Old West: The Rivermen.* Way, *Way's Packet Directory.*

FELICITY ANN

Cutter. *L/B/D:* 23′ × 7′ × 4.7′ (7m × 2.1m × 1.4m). *Tons:* 4 TM. *Hull:* wood. *Comp.:* 1. *Mach.:* diesel, 5 hp, 1 screw. *Des.:* Sid Mashford. *Built:* Mashford Bros., Plymouth, Eng.; 1949.

Impelled by an adventurous curiosity and "unlimited copy with which to feed the typewriter and incidentally me, for I had degenerated into a writer of sorts," Ann Davison decided to be the first woman to sail across the

Atlantic single-handed. Her qualifications were meager, and she had only a limited knowledge of sailing acquired in the wake of a shipwreck three years before in which her husband was killed. While taking sailing lessons from a Commander Lund, she found the sloop *Felicity Ann* — so named before Davison ever saw her — three years old but never sailed. After fitting out in the builder's yard, she sailed from Plymouth on May 18, 1952. Six days out, with the cockpit half filled with water, Davison accepted a tow into Douarnenez from a French fishing boat. A few weeks later she sailed for Vigo, Gibraltar, Casablanca, and the Canary Islands. The last leg to Las Palmas took twenty-nine days, prompting concerns that *Felicity Ann* had been lost at sea. (Drifting in his raft L'HÉRÉTIQUE the previous August, Alain Bombard made the same passage in only eleven days.) On November 20, she departed Las Palmas bound for Antigua. Faced with prolonged calms, *Felicity Ann* was more than nine weeks at sea before making landfall at Barbados on January 18. Turning northward, on January 24, 1953, *Felicity Ann* dropped anchor in Prince Rupert Bay, Dominica. After a few weeks there, she proceeded via Antigua, Nevis, St. Thomas, and Nassau, and finally Miami, her first port in North America. In November of the same year, she arrived at New York. Davison continued to cruise in *Felicity Ann* until 1958.

Davison, *My Ship Is So Small.*

FENIAN RAM

Submarine. *L/B/D:* 31′ × 6′ × 7.3′ (9.4m × 1.8m × 2.2m). *Tons:* 9 disp. *Hull:* iron. *Comp.:* 3. *Arm.:* pneumatic bow gun. *Mach.:* gasoline engine, 17 hp, 1 screw; 9 kts. *Des.:* John P. Holland. *Built:* Delamater-Robinson, Delamater Iron Works, New York; 1881.

The Irish-born schoolteacher and inventor John P. Holland was a long-time believer in the possibilities of submarine technology and wanted only money to put his ideas into practice. His first opportunity came in 1876 when he met John J. Breslin upon the latter's return to New York from rescuing six Irish convicts from Australia in the bark CATALPA. The Clan na Gael (United Irish Brotherhood) agreed to fund Holland's idea, and on May 22, 1878, Holland launched a 14.5 feet long by 3 feet wide prototype on the Passaic River in Paterson, New Jersey. After remaining submerged for up to an hour and otherwise demonstrating the soundness of her builder's concept, she was scuttled in the Passaic River. (*Holland No. 1* was later raised and exhibited at Paterson.)

Work on his next project began shortly thereafter, and *Fenian Ram,* as it was dubbed by the *New York Sun,* was launched in 1881. The name indicated not only its finan-

cial backers, but the use to which it was expected to be put; Holland's first project had been similarly referred to as a "wrecking boat." Holland modeled the hull for this and his subsequent designs, including USS HOLLAND, on the form of a porpoise, which gave the vessel a submerged speed almost equal to that of its surface speed. (Interestingly, this shape was abandoned until the advent of nuclear submarines in the 1950s. One of the great deficiencies of the submarines of World War I and II was their poor speed under water.) *Fenian Ram* was taken to a depth of 60 feet in and around New York Harbor, and could remain submerged for as long as two and a half hours. Her armament, a single pneumatic gun tube set at an angle, successfully fired an early form of torpedo. Although these were supplied through the offices of the U.S. Navy's forward-looking John Ericsson, who had designed USS MONITOR, Holland had reason to be pessimistic about others in the profession. Reflecting on the skepticism that his *Fenian Ram* elicited from the builders at Delamater Iron Works, he later observed:

> Many objections were raised against her, especially by men who should have known better, but the trouble with them was almost the same as I encountered later among the staff officers of the navy, viz: they were, almost without exception, of English, Welsh, or Scotch descent, experienced in all kinds of shipbuilding.

Destined never to see service against British warships, as had been intended, *Fenian Ram*'s active career was short-lived. Fearing that she might be seized in the course of a court proceeding over money, Breslin arranged for the submersible to be taken to New Haven. There the vessel was laid up until 1916, when she was returned to New York for use as an exhibit to raise funds for victims of the failed Easter Rebellion in Ireland. Later moved to the New York State Maritime Academy, in 1927 she was purchased by Edward A. Browne who put her on exhibit in Paterson.

Morris, *John P. Holland.*

FERRIBY BOATS

L/B/D: 52.2′ × 8.2′ × 1.3′ (15.9m × 2.5m × 0.4m). *Tons:* 6.7 burden. *Hull:* wood. *Built:* Britain; ca. 1300 BCE.

The Ferriby boats are the earliest known planked working boats; the only earlier boats are the primarily ceremonial vessels of the Egyptian pharaohs such as the CHEOPS SHIP. Two brothers, E. V. and C. W. Wright, found the first boat along the shore of the Humber estuary near North Ferriby, England, in 1937. A second boat was found in 1941 and a third in 1963 — all in the same deposit of clay. For more than fifty years the site and the finds have been excavated and studied by E. V. Wright, with assistance from the National Maritime Museum, Greenwich.

Only parts of the three boats survived. Boat 1 is represented by most of the bottom and a short length of the first strake on one side. Of Boat 2 the greater part of the keel plank was preserved, and of Boat 3 a section of the bottom planking and a length of the adjoining side strake remain. Since the three boats are consistent in design, Wright has been able to use the fragmentary evidence to reconstruct a complete boat (the dimensions of this composite are given above). Most of the features of the reconstruction are reliably attested by the remains, but some details are inferred or based on comparison with other ancient finds.

The Ferriby boatwrights used adze-hewn oak planks up to four inches thick. The keel plank was made from two halves of an oak trunk, spilt lengthwise and scarfed amidships, with the thicker ends shaped to curve upwards at bow and stern. An outer bottom strake on either side of the keel plank and three strakes on each side complete the basic structure. The planks were stitched edge to edge with yew withies, the plank-edges beveled and rabbeted to protect the stitches. The joining demonstrates a high standard of workmanship. The joints were caulked with moss and oak laths were slipped under the withies to tension the stitches and seal the joints. The joints were thus progressively tightened, a process completed by swelling after the boat was launched.

The bottom structure was braced by "cleat-systems" — transverse bars passing through cleats left standing on the upper surfaces of the bottom planks. The shell was stiffened by frames, each consisting of one long and one short natural crook. These frames were lodged in slots or against blocks along the keel plank, secured to cleats on the side strakes by lashings, and slotted through holes into rails on the inner top edges of the sheer strakes. Each end of the hull was strengthened by girth-lashings passing through cleats on the underside of the keel plank. Thwarts were probably located at the level of the top edge of the second side strakes, notched over the plank-edges and protruding outside the hull.

The boats were propelled by paddles — one fairly well preserved pine paddle was found not far from Boat 1. Sail power is also a possibility, but there is no firm evidence for this. Tests have shown that with 12 paddlers, a speed of 5.2 knots could be maintained for 30 minutes — sufficient for a crossing of the Humber estuary at slack water.

The presence in the clay deposit of other boat frag-

ments and part of a primitive winch suggests that the North Ferriby site was a boatyard, where river craft were cannibalized and repaired. The three boats may have been deliberately dismantled, which would account for the absence of the upper strakes. Radiocarbon dating provides a middle date for the three boats of about 1300 BCE, that is, the Late Bronze Age, but boatbuilding techniques must have evolved over centuries to reach the level of complexity in these craft.

Wright, *Ferriby Boats;* "North Ferriby Boats — A Final Report"; *North Ferriby Boats — A Guidebook.*

FIERY CROSS

Ship (3m). *L/B/D:* 185′ × 31.7′ × 19.2′ (56.4m × 9.7m × 5.9m). *Tons:* 695 net. *Hull:* wood. *Des.:* William Rennie. *Built:* Chaloner, Liverpool; 1860.

One of the most successful tea clippers of her day, *Fiery Cross* was modeled after and ultimately named for the *Fiery Cross* of 1855, which was lost on Investigator Shoal in the South China Sea in 1860. Built to order of John Campbell, Glasgow, she was, according to Aberdeen shipbuilder Alexander Hall, "the fastest ship in the China trade at present [1862]." Between 1861 and 1865 she won the premium of £1 per ton of tea for being the first ship to dock at London every year but one. She also made excellent times outbound, and in 1863–64 she sailed from London to Shanghai in a record 92 days against the northeast monsoon. However, in the Great Tea Race of 1866, though she crossed the bar ahead of her rivals, she lost her lead somewhere past the Azores and arrived at Deal a full day behind ARIEL, *Taeping,* and *Serica.*

Following this race, Captain Richard Robinson left the ship and was replaced by George Kirkup, whose cook poisoned him at Hong Kong in 1868. *Fiery Cross* remained in the China trade through the mid-1880s, changing hands in 1874, 1877, 1883, and 1887. According to one account she was sold to Norwegian interests and, renamed *Ellen Lines,* sank at Sheerness with a cargo of burning coal in 1889. Other evidence suggests that she survived in the transatlantic trade until 1893 when she was abandoned at Sheerness.

Lubbock, *China Clippers.* MacGregor. *The Tea Clippers.*

FINISTERRE

Yawl. *L/B/D:* 38.6′ × 11.2′ × 3.9′ (11.8m × 3.4m × 1.2m). *Tons:* 11 disp. *Hull:* wood. *Comp.:* 7. *Mach.:* gas engine. *Des.:* Olin Stephens (Sparkman & Stephens). *Built:* Seth Persson, Saybrook, Conn.; 1954.

Conceived by yachtsman Carleton Mitchell as a boat that would serve as well for single-handed sailing as for cruising or winning ocean races, *Finisterre* exceeded her owner's expectations and astounded the yachting world. Even as he was developing his idea for the perfect boat, Mitchell published several articles outlining his plans and the design of *Finisterre,* which was named for the Spanish cape, Land's End. After placing second in the 1954 Southern Ocean Racing Circuit, her first race series, *Finisterre* won the 1955 SORC outright. This was mere preparation for the Bermuda Race of 1956, in which she was entered in Class D (the smallest boats) with a crew of seven crack yachtsmen. The race began in calms, but the wind gradually grew to over 20 knots, and *Finisterre* won the race with a corrected time of 64 hours. Two years later, in a "classic small boat race," she became only the second yacht to win two Bermuda Races, the first having been Henry Taylor's Olin Stephens–designed *Baruna* in 1938 and 1948. By this time, the well-publicized and brilliantly successful *Finisterre* had been emulated in countless other boats, and it was against no meager competition that she sailed to an all-but-unimaginable (and as of 1996 unequaled) third Bermuda Race victory against a fleet of 121 entrants in 1960. Mitchell continued to sail *Finisterre* until 1966 when he sold her to Vaughan Brown of Annapolis, who kept her until 1975, when she passed to owners in the Caribbean.

Kinney, *"You Are First."* Mitchell, "Looking Back on *Finisterre."*

FINNJET

Ferry (2f/1m). *L/B/D:* 692′ × 83′ (210.9m × 25.3m). *Tons:* 24,605 grt. *Hull:* steel. *Comp.:* 1,532 pass. *Mach.:* gas turbines/diesel-electric, 2 screws; 30.5 kts. *Built:* Wartsila Shipyards, Helsinki, Finland; 1977.

Although the collapse of the North Atlantic passenger trade has been considered by many as synonymous with the death of passenger shipping itself, nothing could be further from the truth. Passenger trade in a variety of old and new guises flourishes, from the huge cruise ships of the Caribbean and the Mediterranean to the almost as large passenger ferries of Europe and Asia. The Finns have been a primary exporter of vessels for both these markets, and by the 1970s they were leading innovators in the design of passenger ships, signaled by the launch in 1977 of *Finnjet.* Built for service between Helsinki and Travemünde, West Germany, *Finnjet* covered the 600 miles in 22 hours. Her great speed — 30 knots — was achieved thanks to a gas turbine engine of a type previously restricted to naval vessels and a handful of spe-

cialized freighters and tankers. *Finnjet*'s engines were, in fact, a modified version of the Pratt & Whitney engines used in Boeing 747 aircraft.

In addition to her high speed, *Finnjet* also offered her customers a level of service previously reserved for cruise line passengers. These amenities included a wide variety of shops, restaurants, and bars, as well as sports and related facilities, conference rooms, and special activities for children. Placing her engines well aft, *Finnjet*'s designers decided also to divide the passenger accommodations from the public rooms, putting the latter in the quieter, forward part of the ship, and the public rooms aft.

In 1982, *Finnjet* underwent a refit that included the installation of a diesel-electric drive engine. This engine enables *Finnjet* to operate more efficiently in the winter months when severe weather in the Baltic makes high speed impossible.

Braynard & Miller, *Fifty Famous Liners 3.*

USS FLASHER (SS-249)

Gato-class submarine. *L/B/D:* 311.8′ × 27.3′ × 15.3′ (95m × 8.3m × 4.6m). *Tons:* 1,256/2,410 disp. *Hull:* steel; 300′ dd. *Comp.:* 61. *Arm.:* 10 × 21″TT; 1 × 3″, 3 mg. *Mach.:* diesel/electric, 5,400/2,740 shp, 2 screws; 20/9 kts. *Built:* Electric Boat Co., Groton, Conn.; 1943.

USS *Flasher* (named for a type of fish also known as a tripletail) is credited with sinking 100,231 gross tons of Japanese shipping, more than any other U.S. submarine in World War II. Under Lieutenant Commander R. T. Whitaker, she began her first patrol from Pearl Harbor in January 1944, sinking four ships between January 18 and February 14. After a five-day layover at Fremantle in February, she spent her second war patrol off French Indochina where she sank four ships between April 29 and May 4. Her third patrol, in the South China Sea, began June 19. Nine days later she sank two ships out of a thirteen-ship convoy, following up twelve days later with the cruiser *Oi.* A week later she sank one and severely damaged another tanker, before returning again to Fremantle for a three-week refit. On her fourth patrol, *Flasher* was deployed to the Philippine Sea to help rescue downed aviators during bombing raids in advance of the Allied landings in the Philippines. Nonetheless she again managed to notch up three ships between September 18 and October 4.

Flasher returned to Fremantle on October 20 and command passed to Lieutenant Commander G. W. Grider. At the head of a three-boat wolf pack she entered Vietnamese waters off Camranh Bay. On December 4, she sank the destroyers *Kishinami* and *Iwanami,* together with a tanker they were escorting. On December 21, she located another convoy and, attacking from the shoreward side, sank three tankers. Her last patrol was again off the coast of Indochina. Although Japanese shipping was becoming scarce, she sank two vessels on February 21 and 25. She ended her patrol at Pearl Harbor from where she sailed for the West Coast for repairs. En route to Guam for her seventh patrol when the war ended, she was recalled to New London where she was placed in reserve in 1946.

Roscoe, *U.S. Submarine Operations in World War II.* U.S. Navy, *DANFS.*

FLORENCE

Down Easter (3m). *L/B/D:* 223.1′ × 41′ × 26′ dph (68m × 12.5m × 7.9m). *Tons:* 1,684. *Hull:* wood. *Built:* Goss & Sawyer, Bath, Me.; 1877.

Built for Charles Davenport & Company, *Florence* was named in honor of Captain John R. Kelley's daughter, who was the model for the ship's figurehead. A Down Easter of good speed and crossing three skysail yards, she was built for and spent much of her career in the California trade sailing between ports in Europe and the east and west coasts of North America, with occasional ports of call in South America, Australia, and Asia; her cargoes included coal, wheat, and lumber. Captain Kelley served only one voyage and was succeeded by R. L. Leonard. In 1885, Captain F. C. Duncan took command, living aboard with his wife and five children (two of them born aboard) until the ship was sold thirteen years later. William E. Mighell of San Francisco operated *Florence* in the coal and lumber trades between the Pacific Northwest, Hawaii, and Australia. Four years later, the ship went missing after sailing from Tacoma, Washington, en route for Honolulu with coal; she is believed to have foundered off Cape Flaherty in a storm.

Matthews, *American Merchant Ships.*

CSS FLORIDA

(ex-*Oreto*) Screw steamer (3m schooner). *L/B/D:* 191′ × 27.4′ × 13′ (58.2m × 8.4m × 4m). *Tons:* 700 burden. Hull: iron. *Comp.:* 52. *Arm.:* 2 × 7″, 6 × 6″, 1 × 12pdr howitzer. *Mach.:* horizontal direct-acting steam engines; 9.5 kts. *Built:* William C. Miller & Sons, Liverpool; 1862.

Known as the "Prince of Privateers," CSS *Florida* was the second most successful Confederate raider after ALA-

BAMA. Laid down in June 1861, the Confederacy's first foreign-built commerce raider departed Liverpool on March 22, 1862, and was commissioned at Green Cay, Bahamas, Lieutenant John Newland Maffitt commanding. From there she sailed to Cuba and through the Federal blockade into Mobile where she arrived on September 4. She remained in port until January 16, 1863, when she broke through the blockade to begin a lucrative seven-month cruise during which she captured twenty-two vessels, including the clippers *Red Gauntlet* and *Southern Cross,* and facilitated the capture of another twenty-three, among them the revenue cutter CALEB CUSHING. After a five-month refit in Brest, during which command was transferred to Lieutenant Charles M. Morris, she captured eleven ships before putting into Bahia, Brazil, on October 4, 1864, a few days after USS WACHUSETT. Morris pledged to observe Brazilian neutrality and was granted four days in which to make necessary repairs. The Brazilians, anxious to prevent a confrontation between the *Wachusett* and *Florida,* moored some of their own ships-of-the-line between the two antagonists. But on October 7, *Wachusett* rammed the Confederate raider with the intention of sinking her. Wilson had granted about half his crew leave, and after assessing the situation, Lieutenant T. K. Porter surrendered the ship and the remaining crew, who were put in irons. The ship was towed out of Bahia and back to Newport News, where she sank in a collision with the transport *Alliance.*

Owsley, *CSS "Florida."*

FLYING CLOUD

Clipper (3m). *L/B/D:* 235′ × 40.8′ × 21.3′ (71.6m × 12.4m × 6.5m). *Tons:* 1,782 om. *Hull:* wood. *Built:* Donald McKay, East Boston, Mass.; 1851.

Built for Enoch Train of Boston and sold to Grinnell, Minturn & Company, of New York, *Flying Cloud* was one of the fastest — if not the fastest — clipper ship ever launched. The largest merchant sailing ship afloat until the launch of CHALLENGE shortly before her first voyage, great things were expected of her, as a New York paper reported five days before her first voyage:

> We dined on board yesterday with as fine a "band of brothers" as any man could desire for companions in a *Flying Cloud.* Indeed, so familiar were the voices of many that we could not realize that we had mounted to the nebular regions. Yet all admitted that we actually were inside a *Flying Cloud* whose destination was California, and of which Captain Cressy, over whose keen eye and intelligent face there was assuredly no mist, had command; and we can only say

that more table luxury, more tasteful and costly furniture, more ample ventilation and comfort of every kind, we never knew even in an earth-built packet ship or steamer.

The *Flying Cloud* is just the kind of vehicle, or whatever else it may be called, that a sensible man would choose for a ninety days voyage.

Under command of the hard-driving Josiah P. Cressy, she departed New York on June 2, 1851, and arrived at San Francisco on August 31 after a record run of only 89 days, 21 hours. Only a handful of ships ever made the same passage in under 100 days; the average time for all clipper ships was more than 120 days, and for full-built merchant ships 150 days or more. It was quite remarkable, then, when three years later *Flying Cloud* bettered her own time on the same run by 13 hours. Her time of 89 days, 8 hours, anchor to anchor, stood as the record until 1860 when ANDREW JACKSON sailed the same course in 89 days, 4 hours. (The record of 89 days under sail stood until bettered by the high-performance racing sloop THURSDAY'S CHILD in 1988–89.)

Continuing her fourth voyage, *Flying Cloud* sailed for Hong Kong, as she had on her first two voyages, to load tea. A few days out from Whampoa on her homeward run, she grounded on a coral reef and began leaking at a rate of 11 inches an hour. With the pumps manned continuously, *Flying Cloud* arrived at New York on November 24 with her million-dollar cargo intact. On her next voyage, under Captain Reynard, the ship proved badly strained and put into Rio de Janeiro. After five weeks in port, during which her spars were cut down, she resumed her voyage and went on to post her best day's run — 402 miles — and arrived at San Francisco on September 14, 1856, after 113 days at sea from New York.

Laid up until the next January, she made her last Cape Horn passage in 1857 and then was laid up at New York for nearly three years. In December 1859, she sailed for England and loaded for Hong Kong. After three years in trade between England, Australia, and Hong Kong, *Flying Cloud* was sold to T. M. Mackay & Company, a partner in James Baines's Black Ball Line. Put in the immigrant trade, she plied between England and Queensland carrying as many as 515 passengers outbound, and returning with full cargoes of wool. In 1871, *Flying Cloud* was sold to Harry Smith Edwards of South Shields who put her in trade between Newcastle and St. Johns, New Brunswick, carrying coal and pig-iron out and timber back. In June 1874, she grounded on Beacon Island bar and was forced to return to St. Johns. With her back broken, the following year she was burned for her metal fastenings.

Cutler, *Greyhounds of the Sea*. Howe & Matthews, *American Clipper Ships*. Stammers, *Passage Makers*.

FLYING ENTERPRISE

(ex-*Cape Kumukaki*) C-1B cargo ship. *L/B/D:* 396.5′ × 60.1′ × 25.8′ (120.9m × 18.3m × 7.9m). *Tons:* 6,711 grt. *Hull:* steel. *Mach.:* steam turbine, 1 screw. *Built:* Consolidated Steel Corp., Ltd., Wilmington, Del.; 1934.

Originally managed by the U.S. Maritime Administration out of Los Angeles, *Cape Kumukaki* was purchased by Hans Isbrandtsen in the 1940s and renamed *Flying Enterprise;* all Isbrandtsen Steamship Company ships carried the prefix "Flying." Under the command of Captain Henrik Karl Carlsen, *Flying Enterprise* sailed from Hamburg for New York on December 21, 1951. Just past the English Channel, on December 27, she sailed into a hurricane. A 30-foot wave cracked the hull, put the ship on her beam ends, and knocked out the engines. On the 29th, 40 crew and 10 passengers jumped to safety (one died of exposure) and were taken aboard the SS *Southland* and USMT *General A. W. Greely*. Captain Carlsen remained aboard his ship — inclined 60 degrees to port — until joined on January 4, 1952, by Kenneth Roger Dancy from the British salvage tug *Turmoil*. The next day they finally secured a tow and made for Falmouth. Four days later the cable parted and shortly before 1600 hours on January 10, the men were picked up by *Turmoil*. *Flying Enterprise* sank at 1616, 47 miles from Falmouth. Daily press coverage of the heroic salvage effort made Carlsen world famous, but at a press conference he dismissed the acclaim saying, "I don't want a seaman's honest attempt to save his ship used for any commercial purpose or to get anything out of it." The press replied with a standing ovation.

Dugan, *American Viking*.

FNRS-2

(later *FNRS-3*) Bathyscaph. *L:* 6.5′ dia. *Tons:* 12.5 tons. *Hull:* nickel-chrome molybdenum. *Comp.:* 2. *Built:* Emile Henricot Works, Court Etienne, Belgium; 1948.

The world's first bathyscaph was the creation of Swiss physicist and oceanographer Auguste Piccard. The principle of the bathyscaph — the word was Piccard's coinage, derived from the Greek words meaning "deep boat" — was simple. Piccard wanted a manned vessel fitted with observation portholes yet strong enough to withstand the enormous stresses created at great depths — as much as 8 tons per square inch — and able to descend and rise on its own, without being tethered to a mother ship.

Piccard was already well known for his ascent in a balloon to 50,000 feet in order to study cosmic rays, in

1931. The impetus for the bathyscaph arose from a conversation with King Leopold of Belgium, whose father had founded the Fonds National de la Recherche Scientifique, the organization responsible for much of Piccard's research. Asked how his work was progressing, Piccard, who had long been interested in oceanography, found himself telling the king of his plans to build a bathyscaph for abyssal research.

The design of the first bathyscaph, *FNRS-2* (the original *FNRS* was Piccard's stratospheric balloon), was relatively straightforward. The passenger compartment was a steel sphere large enough to hold two crew and fitted with two portholes. This sphere was attached to an elongated float filled with gasoline, which is lighter than water and therefore more buoyant. (The relationship of gasoline and water is comparable to that of helium and air, and the bathyscaph has been compared to an underwater balloon.) The tank also had provisions for water and iron ballast, which could be jettisoned at the bottom of the dive in preparation for the ascent.

On November 3, 1948, *FNRS-2* made an unmanned trial descent to a record depth of 1.371 meters (4,500 feet) off Dakar, Senegal. Funding difficulties led to the bathyscaph's transfer to the French Navy, and it was officially renamed *FNRS-3*. In 1954, *FNRS-3* descended to a record 4,049 meters (13,284 feet) off Dakar, a depth not exceeded until 1959 during TRIESTE's workup for its assault on the 10,912-meter (35,800-foot) Challenger Deep. In the 1960s, *FNRS-3* was replaced by the French Navy's *FNRS-4*.

Houot & Willm, *2000 Fathoms Down*. Piccard, *Earth, Sky, and Sea*. Piccard & Ditez, *Seven Miles Down*.

than put into port, Captain Humble made sail. Shortly before 0400 on Friday morning, September 7, *Forfarshire* was in the Farnes archipelago when she ran aground and broke her back, drowning six of her crew and stranding thirteen passengers and crew on Big Harcar Rock.

Shortly thereafter Grace Darling, daughter of the keeper of Longstone Light, noticed the ship aground, but it was not until 0700 that she and her father could see any survivors, now numbering only nine. As the lifeboat was too big to manage alone, William Darling asked his daughter to join him, and the two rowed about a mile through the running seas to the rescue. Although word of the wreck and the rescue was slow to travel, Grace Darling soon attained a celebrity status for her part in the rescue. Father and daughter were honored with medals from the Royal Humane Society and the forerunner of the Royal National Lifeboat Institute, and Grace received almost £750 in gifts from grateful institutions and individuals, including £50 from Queen Victoria. She was also the subject of several popular narratives and poems (including efforts by William Wordsworth and Algernon Swinburne), and her exploit was celebrated in Europe and the United States. On the centenary of the *Forfarshire* sinking, the twenty-two-year-old heroine was honored with the opening of the Grace Darling Museum in Bamburgh near the graveyard in which she was buried less than three years after her famous exploit. The Royal National Lifeboat Institute has also named several lifeboats in her honor.

Hornby, "Grace Horseley Darling." Mitford, *Grace Had an English Heart*.

FORFARSHIRE

Steamship (1f/2m). *L/B/D:* 132′ × 20′ × 15′ dph (40.2m × 6.1m × 4.6m). *Tons:* 192 burthen. *Hull:* wood. *Mach.:* 2 cyl. steam engine, 190 hp, sidewheels. *Built:* Dundee, Scotland; 1836.

Built for the Dundee and Hull Steam Packet Company, *Forfarshire* was a medium-size steamer that carried freight and passengers on the North Sea coastal route between Hull and Dundee. Her accommodations included twenty-nine berths for passengers in "main cabin" class, and accommodations for "fore cabin" passengers. Deck passengers, restricted to "common soldiers and sailors," were also embarked. On September 5, 1838, *Forfarshire* departed Hull. The starboard boiler began leaking early the next morning. That afternoon the weather deteriorated and the engines finally stopped altogether. Rather

FORT STIKINE

Freighter. *L/B:* 424.2′ × 57.2′ × 35′ (129.3m × 17.4m × 10.7m). *Tons:* 7,142 grt. *Hull:* steel. *Mach.:* triple expansion, 505 nhp, 1 screw; 11 kts. *Built:* Prince Rupert Dry Dock & Shipyard, Prince Rupert, British Columbia; 1942.

Built under lend-lease agreement, *Fort Stikine* was chartered from the Canadian government by Britain's Ministry of War Transport. On February 24, 1944, the freighter departed Birkenhead, England, bound for Bombay, via Karachi, with a mixed cargo that included disassembled gliders and RAF Spitfires, nearly £1 million in gold, and 1,395 tons of ammunition, among other things. Offloading the gliders and planes at Karachi, *Fort Stikine* took on cotton, lubricating oil, scrap iron, sulfur, and resin for the three-day journey to Bombay, where she arrived on April 12, 1944. Two days later, a fire was discovered in the number-two hold where the explosives were stowed. Despite the efforts of the crew and local firemen to drown the blaze, it burned out of control. At 1530, an explosion tore the bow off the ship; Captain Alexander J. Naismith was among the dead. Dock workers and crew continued hopelessly to battle the fire. A second explosion sank every one of the twenty-seven ships in the harbor; none of the buildings in the harbor vicinity escaped damage. Destruction was not confined to the working port, for gold bars and scrap iron blown more than a mile from the ship killed hundreds of civilians. It took 7,000 Allied soldiers nearly a week to put out the fire, and the final death toll from the explosion was 1,376; more than 3,000 people were injured.

Ennis, *Great Bombay Explosion.*

FOX

Steam yacht (1f/3m). *Tons:* 170 burthen. *Hull:* wood. *Comp.:* 26. *Mach.:* steam; 1 screw. *Built:* Alexander Hall & Co., Aberdeen, Scotland; <1857.

Built as a yacht for Sir Richard Sutton, who made one voyage in her to Norway, *Fox* was purchased from his estate by Lady Jane Franklin who put the ship under command of Arctic veteran Captain Francis Leopold M'Clintock, to search for the remains of Sir John Franklin's HMS EREBUS and TERROR, which had been missing since 1848. *Fox* sailed from Aberdeen on July 1, 1857, and became icebound in Melville Bay in northwest Greenland. During the winter she was pushed south through Davis Strait to Cumberland Sound in southern Baffin Island. In April 1858, she resumed her journey, calling at Godthåb and Beechey Island. From there, M'Clintock intended to descend through Peel Sound between the Boothia Peninsula and Prince of Wales Island, but ice conditions forced him south into Prince Regent Inlet (between Baffin Island and Somerset Island), and then west through Bellot Strait between Somerset Island and the Boothia Peninsula. From winter quarters at Port Kennedy, sledging expeditions traced the southern shore of Prince of Wales Island from Franklin Strait in the east to McClintock Channel in the west, as well as the western shore of the Boothia Peninsula and King William Island.

In May 1859, M'Clintock's expedition found remnants of the Franklin expedition at Victory Point, in northwest King William Island. A dispatch from Graham Gore dated May 28, 1847, indicated that *Erebus* and *Terror* had attempted to sail across what became known as McClintock Channel but were frozen in off Cape Felix at the entrance to Victoria Strait, in 70°5′N, 98°23′W. A year later, Commander James Fitzjames annotated the report. The ships had been frozen in from September 12, 1846; Franklin, eight other officers (Gore among them), and fifteen men had died; the ships were abandoned on April 22, 1848; and the remaining 105 men under Captain Crozier "start on tomorrow the 26th for Back's Fish River." None survived.

With this expedition, from which *Fox* returned to England in September 1859 laden with geological and biological specimens and extensive meteorological data, the search for Franklin was officially over. Although the cost of discovery had been high, as Ernest Dodge wrote, "No

This handsome portrait by an anonymous English painter shows the FOX *in Arctic waters during the yacht's successful attempt to find the remains of Sir John Franklin's ill-fated voyage in* HMS EREBUS *and* TERROR *(1857–59). Courtesy National Maritime Museum, Greenwich.*

doubt remained that the Northwest Passage existed. It had yet to be navigated." That would wait until Roald Amundsen and GJØA in 1906.

Dodge, *Northwest by Sea.* M'Clintock, *Voyage of the "Fox" in the Arctic Seas.*

FRAM

Topsail schooner (1f/3m) *L/B/D:* 127.8′ × 34′ × 15′ (39m × 11m × 4.8m). *Tons:* 402 grt; 307 net. *Hull:* wood. *Comp.:* 16. *Mach.:* triple expansion, 220 ihp, 1 screw; 7 kts. *Des.:* Colin Archer. *Built:* Colin Archer, Larvik, Norway; 1892.

In 1879, George DeLong's attempt to reach the North Pole ended in failure when his ship, JEANNETTE, became lodged in the ice for seventeen months. However, the ship's 600-mile drift in the ice from Wrangel Island almost to the New Siberian Islands suggested to the Norwegian zoologist and explorer Fridtjof Nansen "that a current passes across or very near the Pole into the sea between Greenland and Spitzbergen." Nansen determined to use the current to bring him as far north as possible before setting out across the ice to reach the North Pole. To do this, he wrote,

> I propose to have a ship built as small and as strong as possible — just big enough to contain supplies of coal and provisions for twelve men for five years. . . . The main point

The quintessential polar research vessel FRAM, *photographed in Antarctica during Roald Amundsen's expedition of 1910–12, when he and four companions became the first people to reach the South Pole. Courtesy Norsk Sjøfartsmuseum, Oslo.*

in this vessel is that it be built on such principles as to enable it to withstand the pressure of the ice. The sides must slope sufficiently to prevent the ice, when it presses together, from getting firm hold of the hull, as was the case with the *Jeannette* and other vessels. Instead of nipping the ship, the ice must raise it up out of the water.

Nansen turned to the naval architect Colin Archer, who designed a ship that differed "essentially from any other previously known vessel." *Fram* ("Forward") was a massively built, smooth-sided, double-ended vessel shaped like a pilot boat but without a keel or sharp garboard strakes — "able to slip like an eel out of the embraces of the ice." The stem had an aggregate thickness of 4 feet, the frames were 21 inches wide, and the hull planking — of 30-year-old oak — had a maximum thickness of 13 inches. The beams were reinforced with balks, stanchions, braces, and stays. Rigged as a three-masted schooner and fitted with an auxiliary engine, *Fram* carried enough coal for four months' steaming.

Fram sailed from the northern port of Vardö on July 21, 1893. Heading east across the Barents Sea, she passed south of Novaya Zemlya into the Kara Sea and hugged the Eurasian coast until about 135°E, when she turned north. On September 22, 1893, *Fram* lodged in the ice in about 78°43′N. As predicted, the ship was carried to the northwest until November 1895, when her course shifted to the southwest. All the while, her crew took extensive magnetic, astronomical, hydrographic, and meteorological observations from which they determined, among other things, that the Arctic was covered not with a solid, immobile mass of ice but a continually breaking and shifting expanse of drift-ice. *Fram* finally emerged from the ice on August 13, 1896, off the northwest coast of Spitzbergen, just as Nansen had predicted.

In the meantime, Nansen and Frederik Johansen had left *Fram* on March 14, 1895, when the ship lay in about 84°4′N, 102°27′E, in an effort to reach the North Pole with sleds and kayaks. By April 9 they had reached as far as 86°13′N, 95°E before their way was blocked by uneven ice and they turned south for Franz Jozef Land. Here they wintered in a cave on Frederick Jackson Island (81°30′N, 55°E) from August 1895 until May 19, 1896. On June 17, they arrived at an English camp at Cape Flora, Northbrook Island, from which they returned to Vardö in the supply schooner *Windward.* Several weeks later, the two men reunited with *Fram* and her crew at Tromsö. Despite the lack of fresh food, the extensive periods of perpetual light and dark, and the unrelenting cold — the highest monthly average temperature was about 32°F, and the lowest −35°F — the crew of the Norwegian

Polar Expedition remained in excellent physical and mental health. Nansen cheerfully reported how upon his arrival at Cape Flora he discovered that he had gained 22 pounds, and Johansen 13 pounds, since leaving *Fram*.

In 1898, Otto Sverdrup, who commanded the ship after Nansen left for the North Pole, took *Fram* on a three-year expedition in northwest Greenland. After exploring the west coast of Ellesmere Island and other islands, he returned to Norway with a large collection of natural history specimens.

In 1910, *Fram* was brought out of retirement by Roald Amundsen who wanted to emulate Nansen's attempt to reach the Pole by putting his ship in the ice in the Bering Sea. When he learned that Robert Peary (based aboard the ROOSEVELT) had beaten him to the Pole, Amundsen secretly decided to make for the South Pole, a plan he revealed to his crew only when the ship was at Madeira. *Fram* arrived in the Ross Sea in January 1911, reaching 78°38′S, 163°37′W, about 870 miles from the Pole. Averaging 17 to 23 miles per day, Amundsen, Oscar Wisting, Helmer Hanssen, Sverre Hassel, and Olav Bjaaland set out across the Ross Ice Shelf with four sledges and forty-two dogs. Crossing the Queen Maud Mountains, the Norwegians became the first people to reach the South Pole on December 16, 1911 — thirty-one days before Robert Scott's ill-fated expedition from DISCOVERY. They returned to Framheim, their base camp, on January 25, 1912, and sailed for home five days later.

The intrepid *Fram* was later acquired by the Norsk Sjøfartsmuseum in Oslo where she is on public display.

Amundsen, *South Pole*. Nansen, *Farthest North*. Sverdrup, *New Land*.

FRANCE

Bark (5m). *L/B/D*: 361′ × 48.8′ × 25.9′ (110m × 14.9m × 7.9m). *Tons*: 3,784 grt. *Hull*: steel. *Comp.*: 46. *Built*: D. & W. Henderson Co., Glasgow; 1890.

The first five-masted bark and the largest ship in the world at the time of her building, *France* was ordered for A. D. Bordes et Compagnie's nitrate trade between Chile and Europe. On her first trip out, she carried 5,000 tons of coal and on her arrival at Iquique, she discharged the coal and loaded 5,500 tons of nitrate in the short time of eleven days, thanks in large part to her being fitted with steam winches. A fast ship, her best passage out was made in only sixty-three days, and she had another five passages in under eighty days. On January 27, 1897, while riding at anchor in Dungeness Roads, she was hit by the cruiser

The geometric grace and balance of square rig are well illustrated in the five-masted bark FRANCE *of 1890, the first of two ships of the same name, seen here under tow. Crewmen are barely visible at either end of the foreyard. Courtesy National Maritime Museum, Greenwich.*

HMS *Blenheim*. The British ship had seen two lights — a riding light forward and a stern light — and, assuming that they belonged to two separate vessels, tried to steer between them. *Blenheim* turned at the last minute, but drove into the bark's starboard quarter. An admiralty court ruled "the stern light a source of error, which might cause or contribute to an accident." *France* began her last voyage in March 1901, with coal for Valparaiso, under Captain Forgeard. On May 13 she was hit by a violent pampero that knocked her on her beam ends in about 34°S, 48°W. Her crew abandoned ship and were picked up by the German bark *Hebe*.

Lubbock, *Nitrate Clippers*. Villiers & Picard, *Bounty Ships of France*.

FRANCE

Bark (5m). *L/B/D*: 418.8′ × 55.8′ × 24.9′ (127.7m x 17m × 7.6m). *Tons*: 5,633 grt. *Hull*: steel. *Comp.*: 45. *Mach.*: 2 screws. *Built*: Chantiers de la Gironde, Bourdeaux; 1912.

The second five-masted bark of the name, *France* was the largest sailing ship ever built, with a gross tonnage that even exceeded that of the five-masted ship PREUSSEN. She was not considered as graceful as her predecessor (built in 1890), having a pronounced sheer that Basil Lubbock describes as "so steep you could toboggan down it in wet weather," and sporting a jubilee rig, meaning that she set a course, double topsails, and topgallants, but

The largest sailing ship ever built, the FRANCE *of 1912 was not as well proportioned as her predecessor of 1890. She is especially distinguished by the pronounced sheer of her foredeck. Courtesy The Mariners' Museum, Newport News, Virginia.*

no royals. Built for the Société des Navires Mixtes (Prentout-Leblond-Leroux et Compagnie) for their nickel ore trade from New Caledonia, she made three voyages in that trade, her last ending at Clydebank in October 1916. *France* was then sold to Compagnie Française de Marine et Commerce of Rouen, who fitted her with two 90mm guns. She cleared for Montevideo in February 1917, and a week out was attacked by a German U-boat. Under sail and auxiliary power she escaped from her pursuer, making her way to Montevideo. After a trip to New York, she sailed for Port Adelaide with case oil before heading for New Caledonia. After her return to France in March 1919, her engines were removed and she was towed to Shields, England, to load coal for Baltimore. While under tow into the North Sea on December 1, the tow rope parted and *France* was knocked on her beam ends. The tow boat reported her as in distress, but she was later found and towed into Leith, where her cargo was re-stowed, and she cleared for Baltimore. After three transatlantic voyages, she cleared Newport, England, with coal for Lyttleton, New Zealand. In September 1921, she cleared Wellington for London carrying 6,000 casks of tallow and 11,000 bales of wool, the largest cargo ever shipped in a sailing ship from New Zealand. Arriving at London 90 days later, she loaded cement, trucks, and rails for the New Caledonian mines, arriving at Tchio on May 19 after a passage of 105 days. Two months later, she was

en route to Pouembout for a cargo of ore when she grounded on a coral reef. She was abandoned and her hull was sold for £2,000.

Lyman, "Five-Masted Square-Riggers." Villiers & Picard, *Bounty Ships of France.*

FRANCE

(later *Norway*) Liner (2f/1m). *L/B:* 1,035.2′ × 110.9′ (315.5m × 33.8m). *Tons:* 66,348 grt. *Hull:* steel. *Comp.:* 1st 500, tourist 1,550; crew 500. *Mach.:* steam turbines, 4 screws; 34 kts. *Built:* Chantiers de l'Atlantique, St. Nazaire, France; 1962.

The last French Line passenger ship ever built, *France* also has the distinction of being the longest passenger ship, overall, ever built. (By length between perpendiculars or gross tonnage, she is only the fifth largest.) Launched on May 11, 1960, by President Charles de Gaulle's wife, she entered service just as the jet airplane was beginning to capture the bulk of passenger traffic between Europe and the United States. Commissioned with four-bladed propellers, these were replaced by five-bladed ones in her first season in a procedure that took only twelve days. *France* ran for twelve years on the North Atlantic run between Le Havre, Southampton, and New York, and also called three times at Quebec. Her last departure from New York was on September 5, 1974, but in protest of her forthcoming lay-up, her crew refused to put her into port, and she remained anchored off Le Havre until October 10. In 1979 she was finally sold to the Norwegian-Caribbean Line and renamed *Norway*. With her machinery scaled down and two propellers removed, reducing her speed to 21 knots, she was converted to a cruise ship and remained in that work into the 1990s.

Bonsor, *North Atlantic Seaway.*

USS FRANKLIN (CV-13)

Essex-class aircraft carrier. *L/B/D:* 872′ × 93′ (147.5′ew) × 27′8′ (265.8m × 28.3m × 8.4m). *Tons:* 27,100 disp. *Hull:* steel. *Comp.:* 3,448. *Arm.:* 85 aircraft; 12 × 5″, 68 × 40mm. *Mach.:* geared turbines, 15,000 shp, 4 shafts; 32.7 kts. *Built:* Newport News Shipbuilding & Dry Dock Co., Newport News, Va.; 1944.

Named for the Civil War Battle of Franklin, Tennessee, fought on November 30, 1864, USS *Franklin* entered active service in June 1944. She first took part in raids on the Bonin and Mariana Islands in support of American landings on Saipan and Guam, followed by raids on Japanese positions in the western Pacific. During the invasion of the Philippines, on October 27, her planes helped sink ZUIHO, ZUIKAKU, and *Chiyoda*, three of the four Japanese carriers sunk at the Battle of Cape Engaño. While patrolling off Samar on the 29th, *Franklin* was struck by two kamikazes and lost 56 crew dead and 60 wounded. After repairs on the West Coast, in February 1945 she joined the U.S. fleet off the island of Okinawa. From there she sailed to a station off the Japanese home islands. On March 19, while only 50 miles from Honshu, a lone airplane landed two bombs on *Franklin*. The resulting explosions knocked out her engines and the ship was soon engulfed in flames. Thanks to highly effective damage control measures, though, she took a 13-degree list to starboard, *Franklin*'s crew managed to bring her under her own power to Pearl Harbor, and from there to the West Coast. Before the fires could be brought under control, however, 724 men were killed and 265 wounded. The heroic efforts of *Franklin*'s crew resulted in her men being presented with more medals and commendations than any other unit in naval history, including 2 Medals of Honor, 19 Navy Crosses, 22 Silver Stars, 115 Bronze Stars, and 234 letters of commendation.

   Franklin was undergoing repairs at New York when the war ended, and two years later she was put in the reserve fleet. Twelve years later she was reclassified as an auxiliary air transport (AVT-8). Stricken from the navy list in 1964, she was scrapped at Norfolk in 1968.

Hoehling, *"Franklin" Comes Home.* U.S. Navy, *DANFS.*

FRONTENAC

Sidewheel steamer (2f/1m). *L/B/D:* 170′ od × 32′ × 10′ (51.8m × 9.8m × 3m). *Tons:* 700 grt. *Hull:* wood. *Mach.:* steam engine, 50 hp, sidewheels; 9 knots. *Built:* Henry Teabout & Henry Chapman, Finckle's Tavern, Ontario; 1817.

A contemporary of the American vessel ONTARIO and the first Canadian-built steamer on the Great Lakes, *Frontenac* was built for a consortium of Kingston merchants for service on Lake Ontario and the upper St. Lawrence River. Her hull and paddles (the latter measured 12.8 feet in diameter) were built in Canada, but she was powered by engines imported from the Birmingham, England, firm of Boulton and Watt, who had built the engines for Fulton's NORTH RIVER STEAM BOAT. Although her draft proved too deep for work on the St. Lawrence, *Frontenac* (the French name for Lake Ontario) ran between Kingston, York, Ernesttown, Niagara, and Burlington for ten years before being laid up in 1827. Her last owner, R. Hamilton, Esq., removed her engines for use in *Alcione*, and the hull intentionally burned in the Niagara River.

Musham, "Early Great Lakes Steamboats: The 'Ontario' and 'Frontenac.'"

FUKURYU MARU NO. 5

Fishing boat (1f/2m). *L:* 93′ (28.3m). *Tons:* 100. *Hull:* wood. *Comp.:* 23. *Mach.:* diesel, 250 hp; 7 kts. *Built:* Japan; 1947.

Originally named *Kotoshiro Maru*, the sampan-hulled *Fukuryu Maru No. 5* — "Lucky Dragon" — sailed in the Pacific tuna fisheries out of Yaizu, Japan. On January 24, 1954, she departed on a routine trip to the fishing grounds off Midway Island. Her crew let out their baited long lines (about 50 miles long, all told) but the catch was meager, and they lost a major section of the line. Turning southeast, they began fishing in the Marshall Islands on February 25. At about 0345 on the morning of March 1, crewmen on deck saw a brilliant flash of light and a fireball in the west. Darkness fell again, but seven minutes later the vessel was rocked by the double concussion of an enormous explosion. Suspecting that they might have witnessed an American nuclear test and terrified of running afoul of U.S. naval forces, the crew gathered up their lines and turned for home.

   About two hours after the 15-megaton hydrogen bomb explosion, *Lucky Dragon* was blanketed by a white dust irritating to skin and eyes and inducing nausea. Within days, the crew's skin had turned dark brown and their hair began falling out. Although some suspected this was the result of radiation, they did not learn that the U.S.

had conducted a bomb test at Bikini until they returned to Yaizu. (The test was the first at Bikini since 1946, all those in the interval having been conducted at Eniwetok, 300 miles to the west.) Geiger counter measurements showed that *Lucky Dragon* had been exposed to extremely high levels of radiation, and the crew were admitted to hospitals in Tokyo. Radioman Aikichi Kuboyama died in September, and his twenty-two shipmates were not discharged until May 1955.

When word of the radioactive fish became public, prices fell dramatically. At one point the major markets closed, a national crisis in a country that derived most of its protein from pelagic fish. The United States had dropped atomic bombs on Hiroshima and Nagasaki less than a decade before and the Japanese were suspicious of American intentions. This, coupled with U.S. secrecy about its nuclear testing program, strained relations between the two countries. U.S. officials claimed that the Japanese were exaggerating the amount of harmful radiation in fish. Nonetheless, American companies refused to purchase Japanese fish because the radiation levels were too high for domestic consumers, and the U.S. government paid Japan $9 million in compensation. Radiation in fish catches peaked in November before falling off. Foreign countries expressed muted concern about the blasts, and the U.S. government dismissed protests as the work of leftists; concern about the environment was virtually nonexistent.

The Japanese government eventually purchased *Lucky Dragon*. Decontaminated and renamed *Hayabusa Maru*, she sailed as a University of Tokyo Fisheries School training ship.

Lapp, *Voyage of the "Lucky Dragon."*

FULTON STEAM FRIGATE

Steam frigate. *L/B/D:* 156′ × 56′ × 11′ (47.5m × 17.1m × 3.4m). *Tons:* 2,475 disp. *Comp.:* 200. *Arm.:* 24 × 32pdr. *Mach.:* single-cylinder inclined engine, 120 hp, center wheel; 6 kts. *Built:* Adam & Noah Brown, New York; 1815.

Known also as *Demologos* and *Fulton the First,* the *Fulton Steam Frigate* was the first steam-powered warship built for the U.S. Navy, and the last vessel designed by Robert Fulton. On Christmas Eve 1813, Fulton met with a small but eminent gathering of military men and merchants to present his idea for a floating battery to break the British blockade of New York during the War of 1812. Among the naval officers who endorsed the project were Oliver Hazard Perry and Stephen Decatur. Funds for the frigate

were approved by Congress on March 9, 1814, and on October 28 a crowd of 20,000 New Yorkers watched as the ship was launched into the East River and towed across the Hudson to Fulton's New Jersey workshops.

The ship was of innovative design, consisting of two pontoon hulls that came together at the gun deck; a 16-foot paddlewheel was mounted between them. The pontoons were doubled ended, the engine reversible, and there were two sets of rudders so that the ship could be sailed either end first; even the auxiliary rig was double ended, consisting of a lateen sail and jib at either end.

In February 1815, shortly after news that the Treaty of Ghent was signed, Fulton died of pneumonia. Work on the steam frigate continued, and trials in the summer demonstrated that the principle of a steam-powered warship was entirely sound. Despite suggestions that she be used as a training ship, the *Fulton Steam Frigate* was laid up, except for a brief tour of New York Harbor by President James Madison in 1818. With her engines and armament removed in 1821, she was used as a receiving ship at the Brooklyn Navy Yard until June 6, 1829, when the ship accidentally blew up with the loss of 29 crew and 23 wounded. It was not until 1836 that the U.S. Navy ordered a second steam warship, named *Fulton II.*

Chapelle, *Fulton's "Steam Battery."* Philip, *Robert Fulton.* Tyler, "Fulton's Steam Frigate."

HMS FURIOUS

Furious-class aircraft carrier (3m). *L/B/D:* 743.3′ × 95.8′ × 24′ (226.6m × 29.2m × 7.3m). *Tons:* 23,000 disp. *Hull:* steel. *Comp.:* 1,392. *Arm.:* 36 aircraft; 16 × 4″, 48 × 2pdr, 8 × 40mm, 8 × 20mm. *Armor:* 4.5″ belt, 3″ deck. *Mach.:* geared turbines, 111,000 shp, 3 shafts; 32.5 kts. *Built:* Harland & Wolff Ltd., Belfast, Ireland; 1917.

A near sister ship to HMS GLORIOUS and COURAGEOUS, HMS *Furious* was one of the ships built for First Sea Lord John A. Fisher's aborted Baltic Project for operations on the Pomeranian coast. Designed with two 18-inch guns, as completed she had only one, the forward gun being replaced by a flight deck. In 1917, the aft gun was removed and her flight deck extended. On July 18, 1918, she took part in a successful air raid on the Zeppelin base at Tondern, in Schleswig-Holstein.

Although *Furious* was the first ship regularly used as an aircraft carrier, her truncated flight deck abaft the bridge was an unsuccessful design. From 1921 to 1925, she was converted to a flush-deck aircraft carrier and underwent a second refit in 1931–32. At the start of World War II, she

One of the first Japanese "super-dreadnoughts," FUSO was commissioned in 1915. Originally fitted with two funnels and a forward conning tower of fairly ordinary dimensions, she emerged from a major rebuilding in 1935 with the forward funnel removed and a towering "pagoda" mast of extraordinary height. Courtesy Imperial War Museum, London.

was with the Home Fleet. During the German invasion of Norway in April 1940, *Furious* provided limited support to British destroyers in the Battle of Narvik. In 1942, while assigned to Force H based at Gibraltar, she ferried aircraft to the besieged island fortress of Malta between April and June, and remained in the Mediterranean through the next year. In April 1943, the British mounted a series of attacks aimed at sinking TIRPITZ at Kaa Fjord, Norway, and *Furious* sailed with a succession of operations that lasted through September. Although the German battleship was not sunk, she was damaged beyond repair as an effective seagoing unit. Decommissioned in March 1945, *Furious* was broken up in 1948 at Troon.

Jenkins, HMS *"Furious."* Stephen, *Sea Battles in Close-Up.*

FUSO

Fuso-class battleship (2f/2m). *L/B/D:* 672.7′ × 94.1 × 28.5 (205.1m × 28.7m × 8.7m). *Tons:* 30,998 disp. *Hull:* steel. *Comp.:* 1,396. *Arm.:* 12 × 14″ (6x2), 14 × 6″, 8 × 5″, 37 × 25mm. *Armor:* 12″ belt, 7″ deck. *Mach.:* geared turbines, 75,000 shp, 4 shafts; 24.7 kts. *Built:* Kaigun Kosho, Kobe, Japan; 1915.

The super-dreadnoughts *Fuso* and her sister ship *Yamashiro* were the first battleships built almost entirely with Japanese technology and armament. Bearing an ancient name for Japan, *Fuso* was completed during World War I but saw no action in that conflict. From 1930 to 1935, she and *Yamashiro* underwent extensive refits during which they were lengthened 25 feet, their displacement was increased by 9,000 tons, one funnel was taken away, and they were given tall "pagoda"-turret masts.

During World War II, *Fuso* was used extensively in escort duties, and she was detailed to the diversionary attack on the Aleutian Islands during the Japanese attempt to take Midway Island in June 1942. Two years later, *Fuso* was one of seven battleships in Vice Admiral Takeo Kurita's 1st Striking Force at Lingga Roads in the Strait of Malacca. When American forces landed at Leyte Gulf in the invasion of the Philippines, *Fuso*, her sister ship *Yamashiro*, the heavy cruiser MOGAMI, and four destroyers constituted Force C, under command of Vice Admiral Shoji Nishimura. Sailing from Singapore on October 19, they were ordered to break out into Leyte Gulf via Surigao Strait, north of the island of Mindanao. The ships encountered only minimal aerial resistance in the Sulu Sea, and counting on Japan's proven superiority in night actions, Nishimura pressed on into Surigao Strait. At midnight Force C was attacked by forty PT boats, which harried but did not hit the Japanese ships. At 0230, twenty-eight destroyers attacked, and *Fuso* was torpedoed by USS *Melvin*, a destroyer in Captain J. G. Coward's Destroyer Squadron (DesRon) 54. The battleship was soon burning out of control, and at 0338 she blew up and sank in 10°25′N, 125°23′E with an undetermined loss of life.

In a second wave of destroyer attacks, *Yamashiro* was hit by two torpedoes from the Australian destroyer *Arunta*, and three Japanese destroyers were sunk. Nishimura continued eastward with *Takao, Mogami, Yamashiro*, and the destroyer *Shigure*. Blocking his way were the American battleships *California, Tennessee, West Virginia, Maryland*, and *Pennsylvania*, backed up by seven cruisers. These opened fire at 0400, raining 3,250 shells in the next 20 minutes. Nishimura was killed, and the surviving Japanese ships turned. *Yamashiro* was sunk by a destroyer in 10°25′N, 125°20′E, and *Mogami* was rammed by the Japanese cruiser *Nachi* and sank later that morning. Only *Shigure* survived the last surface action fought exclusively between capital ships.

Grove, *Sea Battles in Close Up*. Jentschura, Jung & Mickel, *Warships of the Imperial Japanese Navy*.

G

GABRIEL

Ship (3m). *Tons:* 20 tons. *Hull:* wood. *Comp.:* 18. *Built:* 1576.

Following John Cabot's ill-fated second voyage to North America in 1498, European interest in a northwesterly route to the Orient was abandoned in favor of the pursuit of the Northeast Passage. But by the 1570s, there was such a mass of hearsay evidence and hypothesis that people began to think again that a Northwest Passage might exist. For the English, the primary motive for finding such a route was to capture part of the lucrative Oriental spice trade from the Spanish and Portuguese. But others, such as Sir Humphrey Gilbert, sought to "inhabit some part of those countries, and settle there such needy people of our country which now trouble the commonwealth and through want here at home are enforced to commit outrageous offenses, whereby they are daily consumed with the gallows."

One of the most fervent believers in the Northwest Passage was Martin Frobisher. With backing from the Muscovy Company, on June 12, 1576, he embarked in the bark *Gabriel* and sailed from Gravesend in company with the 25-ton *Michael* and a pinnace of 10 tons. A storm sank the pinnace and forced *Michael* back to England. *Gabriel* carried on and, after nearly capsizing off Greenland, sailed northwest into Davis Strait and by July 20 was off Resolution Island, between Labrador and Baffin Island. On August 11, *Gabriel* sailed into Frobisher's Bay, which, after covering 150 miles in 15 days, they believed was a strait separating America and Asia. Frobisher and his companions noted that the people "be like to Tartars, with long black haire, broad faces, and flatte noses, and tawnie in color." Unfortunately, five of the English were kidnapped by Eskimos, and in retaliation Frobisher seized an Eskimo who was taken back to England.

The crew also returned with iron pyrites mistakenly thought to be gold. This discovery was more than enough incentive for a second voyage, sponsored by the newly formed Adventurers to the North-West for the Discovery of the North-West Passage, or the Companye of Kathai. In 1577, *Gabriel*, now under Robert Fenton, sailed with

Michael, Queen Elizabeth's own Aid, and a company of about 155 men. Departing in mid-May, the ships arrived at Baffin Island on July 17. They returned home at the end of the summer with three Eskimos — a man, a woman, and her child, all of whom died after a month in England — and 200 tons of ore assayed (again incorrectly) as containing gold and silver. In 1578, *Gabriel* was one of fifteen ships in Frobisher's third expedition during which his ships sailed partway into Hudson Strait. The Company of Cathay spent five years trying to smelt precious metals from iron and eventually went bankrupt; Frobisher took the blame. Creditors seized *Gabriel,* and her ultimate fate is unknown.

Hakluyt, *Principal Navigations.* Stefansson, ed., *Three Voyages of Martin Frobisher.*

GALILEE BOAT

(1m). *L/B/D:* 28.6′ × 8.1′ × 4.1′ (8.8m × 2.5m x 1.25m). *Hull:* wood. *Comp.:* 5. *Built:* Hasmonean/Roman; 1st cent. BCE/CE.

The Galilee Boat was discovered in January 1986 by Moshe and Yuval Dothan. A two-year drought in Israel had lowered the level of the Sea of Galilee (Kinneret, in Hebrew), which is normally 656 feet (200 meters) below sea level. Several hundred meters south of Kibbutz Ginosar, in 32°50′N, 35°31′E, the Dothan brothers identified an elongated oval outline in the mud. Inspectors from the Israel Department of Antiquities noted the mortise-and-tenon joints on the uppermost strake and confirmed that the find was indeed an ancient boat.

Before a full-scale excavation could be planned, rumors of the discovery of the "Boat of Jesus" necessitated a rescue excavation. A temporary cofferdam was built to prevent the lake waters from reflooding the site. After the interior of the hull was excavated, drawn, and photographed, fiberglass supports were inserted between the frames and the hull was sprayed inside and out with polyurethane foam. The wreck was then refloated and, with the help of local volunteers, carefully pushed up the coast to the Yigal Allon Centre at Kibbutz Ginosar. After removal of its polyurethane cocoon, the Galilee Boat was placed in a tank for long-term chemical preservation. The wood had survived well because it had been buried in claylike mud that protected it from oxygen and microorganisms.

Cedar and jujube were used for the keel, cedar and pine for the strakes, oak for the tenons, and oak, willow, hawthorn, and redbud for the frames. The keel, preserved for its entire length of 8.27 meters (26.9 feet), was 9.5 centimeters (3.8 inches) wide, and 11.5 centimeters (4.6 inches) high. The mast appears to have been stepped forward of amidships. The planking was edge-joined with mortises and tenons locked with oak pegs. Iron nails were used to fasten the scarf-joints and some double-clenched nails or staples bridged seams in the planking. The seams were caulked with pitch. A second row of mortise-and-tenon joints was detected on a portion of the keel beneath the present garboards, suggesting that the keel was reused from another boat. The stem and stern posts, mast, and internal structures were missing — probably salvaged in antiquity. Slightly to the northeast of the Galilee Boat were found the remains of two other boats. The lakeside site, then, may have been a boatyard where, with wood in short supply, vessels like the Galilee Boat were cannibalized at the end of their working lives.

The boat was probably powered by both sail and oars and used primarily for fishing. Contemporary pictorial and written evidence suggests that the fishermen used a seine net, and that the Galilee boat had a stern deck from which this was worked. The maximum beam is located quite far aft, resulting in an unusually narrow, tapered bow. The bottom has a shallow, curving deadrise, the turn of the bilge is sharp, and the sides flare outward slightly. On the basis of evidence provided by carbon-14 dating of the wood and artifacts found near the boat, it has been determined that the vessel dates from between 100 BCE and 70 CE. The boat was apparently in use for a long time, as the many repairs in various species of wood attest.

Wachsmann, *Sea of Galilee Boat.*

USS GAMBIER BAY (CVE-73)

Casablanca-class escort carrier. *L/B/D:* 512.3′ × 65′ (108′ew) × 22.3′ (156.1m x 19.8m (32.9m) × 6.8m). *Tons:* 7,800 disp. *Hull:* steel. *Comp.:* 860. *Arm.:* 28 aircraft; 1 × 5″, 16 × 40mm. *Mach.:* geared turbines, 16,000 shp, 2 screws; 19 kts. *Built:* Henry Kaiser Shipbuilding Co., Inc., Vancouver, Wash.; 1943.

Named for a bay in Alaska, then a U.S. territory, in early 1944 USS *Gambier Bay* carried troops to Pearl Harbor and from there ferried planes to USS ENTERPRISE in the Marshall Islands. Assigned to Rear Admiral Hugh M. Sallada's Carrier Support Group 2, she provided close air support for the Marine landings during the Marianas campaign, which began June 15. She remained off Saipan through the Battle of the Philippine Sea and the "Great Marianas Turkey Shoot" before proceeding to Tinian and Guam, through mid-August. *Gambier Bay*'s next operation was in support of landings at Peleliu and Angaur in the southern Palaus. She then took part in the landings at Leyte Gulf, the Philippines, before joining Rear Admiral Clifton A. F. Sprague's escort carrier Task Force 3 — known as Taffy 3 — comprising six escort carriers and seven screening ships.

Following the Battle of the Sibuyan Sea, October 24–25, in which the Japanese lost seven ships, Admiral W. F. Halsey dispatched the Third Fleet north in the belief that Vice Admiral Takeo Kurita's Center Force — including the battleships YAMATO, *Kongo, Haruna,* and *Nagato,* together with eight cruisers and eleven destroyers — no longer posed a threat. At 0648 on October 25, the Center Force opened fire on Taffy 3 off Samar Island. In the ensuing action, which Kurita gravely mishandled, *Gambier Bay* came under relentless fire from four heavy cruisers, principally *Chikuma,* receiving her first hits at about 0810 at a range of 10,000 yards. Despite the courageous intervention by destroyers USS JOHNSTON, *Hoel,* and *Heermann* and air support from Taffy 2, about 30 miles away, *Gambier Bay* rolled over and sank at 0907, in 11°31′N, 126°12′E; there were nearly 800 survivors. Four minutes later, Kurita called off his attack, which had cost him three heavy cruisers. In all, the Battle off Samar cost the United States more than 2,000 sailors dead and wounded, plus the loss of two escort carriers — the other was ST. LÔ — destroyers *Johnston* and *Hoel,* and destroyer escort *Samuel B. Roberts.*

Hoyt, *Men of the "Gambier Bay."* Ross, *Escort Carrier "Gambier Bay."*

GARTHPOOL

(ex-*Juteopolis*) Bark (4m). *L/B/D:* 310′ × 45′ x 25′ (94.5m × 13.7m × 7.6m). *Tons:* 2,652 net. *Hull:* steel. *Comp.:* 28. *Built:* Messrs. Thompson & Co., Dundee, Scotland; 1891.

A four-masted bark sporting a jubilee rig — that is, setting no sails above the topgallants — *Juteopolis* was built for the jute trade between Calcutta and Dundee, in which she sailed under Captain W. Linklater for nearly a decade. In 1900 she was bought by the Anglo-American Oil Company and carried case oil in the Pacific. Sold just before World War I to George Windram and Company, Liverpool, she hauled general cargoes. In 1917, she was acquired by Sir William Garthwaite's Marine Navigation Company, though she was not formally renamed until 1921. On her first voyage as *Garthpool*, Captain Atkinson died at sea en route from Port Lincoln to Falmouth in 1921. With freight rates low, the ship was laid up for two years at the end of that passage. In 1924, her port of registry was changed to Montreal and she sailed again in general trade. Two years later, she changed masters again, sailing under Captain David Thomson in the Australia grain trade between Adelaide and, usually, Hull; she was not a fast ship, and her passages often exceeded 120 days. On October 23, 1929, she was outward bound from Hull in ballast. Among the crew was Stan Hugill, who would later earn international renown as a chanteyman and historian of the last days of sail. On November 11, 1929, *Garthpool* ran aground and was lost at Boavista Island, one of the Cape Verde Islands; all hands survived. Although she is often credited with having been the last British deep-water sailing ship — flying as she did the Canadian merchant ensign — that ultimate honor belongs to WILLIAM MITCHELL.

Course, *Windjammers of the Horn.*

GARTHSNAID

(ex-*Inversnaid*) Bark (3m). *L/B/D:* 238′ × 36.2′ x 21.7′ (72.5m × 11m × 6.6m). *Tons:* 1,312 net. *Hull:* steel. *Comp.:* 23. *Built:* Archibald McMillan & Son, Ltd., Dumbarton, Scotland; 1892.

Built as *Inversnaid* for George Milne's Inver Line, which Lubbock characterizes as "undoubtedly one of the finest fleets of windjammers sailing the sea in the twentieth century," the three-masted bark was acquired by William Garthwaite's Marine Navigation Company at the end of 1916 while lying at Port Talbot, New South Wales. (Her sister ship, *Invercoe,* had been sunk by the German commerce raider *Prinz Eitel Friedrich* in February 1915.) Registered in Montreal and renamed *Garthsnaid,* she flew the Canadian merchant service ensign under Captain James Simpson, sailing in general trade between the British Isles, Brazil, Chile, Portuguese East Africa, and Australia. On her last voyage, she loaded fuel for Port Louis, Mauritius, arriving there on June 4, 1922. She sailed in ballast for Queenscliff, Australia, and after sixteen days in port was ordered to continue to Iquique where she finally loaded nitrate for Melbourne; such was the hard lot of working windships in the early 1920s. On March 30, 1923, she was dismasted, and with a jury rig on her foremast, on April 2, she was taken in tow by the White Star cargo liner *Zealandic.* At Melbourne *Garthsnaid* was

declared a total constructive loss and hulked; she was broken up in the 1940s.

Course, *Windjammers of the Horn.*

GASPÉE

Schooner (2m). *L/B:* 68′ × 20′ × 9′ (20.7m x 6.1m × 2.7m). *Tons:* 102 bm. *Hull:* wood. *Comp.:* 30. *Built:* Canada(?); 1763.

With the conclusion of the French and Indian War (or Seven Years' War), Britain annexed French Canada in 1763. To help patrol against smugglers working in the Gulf of St. Lawrence, the British government purchased six schooners and sloops in 1764, including *Gaspée.* The patrol soon expanded to cover the ports of New England. On June 9, 1772, *Gaspée* ran aground on Namquit Spit seven miles from Providence, Rhode Island, while pursuing the ship *Hannah,* which was suspected of avoiding payment of customs duties. News of the stranded vessel quickly reached Providence and that night eight boatloads of colonists, led by the merchant brothers John and Nicholas Brown, moved to seize the vessel. As the colonists approached, they were ordered to identify themselves, but the only reply was "God damn your blood, we have you now!" *Gaspée* was boarded, and the nineteen crew, including Lieutenant William Dudingston, who was wounded in the attack, were landed before the schooner was put to the torch. A Commission of Inquiry was convened in January 1773, but even the posting of £500 reward failed to produce any reliable witnesses. Hence one of the American colonists' first acts of defiance to the British Crown went unpunished.

May, "The *Gaspée* Affair." Miller, *Sea of Glory.* Staples, *Documentary History of the Destruction of the "Gaspée."*

GELDERMALSEN

Dutch East Indiaman; ship (3m). *L/B/D:* 150′ × 42′ x 18′ (45.7m × 12.8m × 5.5m). *Tons:* 1,110 disp. *Hull:* wood. *Comp.:* 112. *Arm.:* 31 guns. *Built:* Zeeland Chamber, VOC, Netherlands; 1746.

Named for the estate of Verenigde Oostindische Compagnie (VOC, or the United East India Company) director Jan Van Borsele, *Geldermalsen* sailed from Holland to Batavia in 1746. Thereafter, she spent the rest of her brief career in the Far East, sailing between Dutch merchant communities at Canton, Batavia, and India. In the fall of 1751, *Geldermalsen* loaded a cargo of tea, silk, and porcelain for shipment from Canton to the Netherlands. In addition, she carried 147 ingots of gold destined for Batavia. The ship sailed from Canton on December 20, under command of Captain Jan Morel. Fifteen days out, she was sailing through the calm South China Sea when she struck Admiral Stellingwerf Reef off Bintan Island southeast of Singapore. The ship was badly holed, and sank during the night. Only thirty-two of the ship's company survived the shipwreck, and fewer still reached Batavia, eight days later.

In 1986, British ship salvor Michael Hatcher found *Geldermalsen*'s remains. With little concern for the ship's archaeological value, Hatcher's team salvaged 126 bars of gold and 160,000 pieces of porcelain — the largest cargo of Chinese export porcelain ever found — most of which had been mass-produced for the burgeoning market in Europe. Before Hatcher's team had completed the work, the International Congress of Maritime Museums condemned the destruction of the wreck.

> Such an archaeologically important find as the *Geldermalsen* should have been excavated in a scientific way. Correlation of the rather well documented information from the available archives and the excavation information is of utmost importance. This means registration of find places within the wreck, details on the ship structure, environmental information, etc. Without such scientific standards, no excavation should take place, in order not to lose the information, which is very important for a historical point of view. In fact, the cargo of the *Geldermalsen* has been looted without concern for context and its commercial sale will entirely destroy the wreck.

Valued at only 35,000 guilders in the seventeenth century — the tea was then worth 400,000 guilders — the porcelain fetched about £10 million at auction in Amsterdam.

Hatcher, de Rham, & Thorncroft, *"Geldermalsen," the Nanking Cargo.* Jorg, *"Geldermalsen."* Miller, "Second Destruction of the *Geldermalsen.*"

GENERAL ARMSTRONG

Topsail schooner (2m). *Tons:* 246 bm. *Hull:* wood. *Comp.:* 90. *Arm.:* 1 × 24pdr, 8 × 9pdr. *Built:* New York; <1814.

Named for Brigadier General John Armstrong, a distinguished soldier and statesman of the American Revolution during the War of 1812, the topsail schooner *General Armstrong* sailed as a privateer under command of Captain Samuel C. Reid. On September 26, 1814, she was lying in the roads at the neutral port of Fayal, Azores, when a British squadron comprising HMS *Plantagenet* (74 guns), *Rota* (36), and *Carnation* (10) came into the anchorage. That afternoon, British boats approached

General Armstrong and, suspicious of their intentions, Reid warned the British off, opening fire only as a last resort. Reid repositioned *General Armstrong* in shallower waters and prepared for an attack. At midnight, 180 men in seven boats supported by *Carnation* began their assault on *General Armstrong.* The American defense was withering; 2 boats were sunk, 2 captured, and the British claimed 34 dead and 86 wounded for only 2 American dead and 7 wounded. Reid cleared his ship for action the next morning, but after repulsing *Carnation,* he realized that his position was hopeless. Rather than sacrifice his men, he scuttled his ship. *General Armstrong*'s splendid fight is especially notable given that her crew were merchant rather than naval seamen.

Roosevelt, *Naval War of 1812.*

GENERAL BELGRANO

(ex-*17 de Octubre,* USS *Phoenix*) *Brooklyn*-class cruiser (2f/2m). *L/B/D:* 608.3′ × 61.8′ × 22.8′ (185.4m × 18.8m × 6.9m). *Tons:* 12,207 disp. *Hull:* steel. *Comp.:* 868–1200. *Arm.:* 15 × 6″ (5 × 3), 8 × 5″; 8 SAM launchers; 2 helicopters. *Armor:* 5.6″ belt, 2″ deck. *Mach.:* geared turbines, 100,000 shp, 4 screws; 32.5 kts. *Built:* New York Shipbuilding Corp., Camden, N.J.; 1938.

Assigned to the Pacific Fleet in 1939, USS *Phoenix* was at Pearl Harbor during the Japanese attack on December 7, 1941. After convoy duty between Pearl Harbor and the West Coast, she sailed for Australia to serve as a troopship escort in the Dutch East Indies and Indian Ocean. Following a refit at Philadelphia in 1943, she carried Navy Secretary Cordell Hull to the Casablanca Conference before steaming back to the South Pacific. From December 1943, *Phoenix* took part in the Allied advance through New Britain, the Admiralty Islands, and New Guinea. She provided close support for the Allied landings on Leyte on October 20 and was present at the Battle of Surigao Strait. She remained in Philippine waters until July, and the end of the war found her en route to Pearl Harbor for overhaul.

Decommissioned in 1946, five years later she was purchased by the Argentine Navy and renamed *17 de Octubre.* Following the military overthrow of the Peronist government in 1955, she was named in honor of the nineteenth-century Argentine patriot Manuel Belgrano. On April 2, 1982, Argentina attacked the British colony of the Falkland Islands, about 300 miles southeast of southern Argentina. Five days later, the British declared a 200-mile exclusion zone around the islands. On May 2, *General Belgrano* was about 235 miles southwest of Stanley when she was spotted by the hunter-killer submarine

HMS *Conqueror*. The modernized *Belgrano*'s armament included two helicopters and two quadruple Sea Cat surface-to-air missile launchers, and although she was outside of the exclusion zone, the British decided that she posed a threat to British operations. HMS *Conqueror* fired two torpedoes and *General Belgrano* went down in 55°24′S, 61°32′W, with the loss of 368 of her 1,091 crew. The first Argentine loss of the war, she was the largest warship sunk in combat since 1945.

Hastings & Jenkins, *Battle of the Falklands*. Hooke, *Modern Shipping Disasters*.

GÉNÉRAL DE SONIS

Bark (3m). *L/B/D:* 277.5′ × 40.4′ × 22.7′ dph (84.6m × 12.3m × 6.9m). *Tons:* 2,307 grt. *Hull:* steel. *Built:* Chantiers Nantais de Construction Maritime, Nantes, France; 1901.

Built for the Compagnie de Navigation Française, *Général de Sonis* entered the grain trade between Australia and Europe in 1902. Sold to the Société Générale d'Armament in 1904, she continued in the same work for the next decade. Outward bound from Port Victoria in March 1913, she had just rescued the crew of the French bark *Jean Bart* when she was herself driven ashore near Wardang Island. Pulled off by a tug, *Général de Sonis* grounded a second time owing to a confusion of signals. She remained aground for nearly four months, but eventually kedged off and was towed to Melbourne for repairs. Two years later, she was bound up the English Channel under tow of *Homer* when ordered to stop by *U-32*. The tug's captain attempted to ram the German submarine and *Général de Sonis* made good her escape. In later years, in addition to Australian wheat she carried rice from French Indochina, and she was one of twelve French ships that loaded grain at San Francisco in 1921. Sold at the conclusion of that voyage to M. Potet, of Le Havre, she made seven voyages in the West Indies log-wood trade. In 1931, she ran aground in French Guiana. Returning to Le Havre she was laid up and in November 1932, the last of the deep-water merchant square-riggers was purchased by Belgian shipbreakers for 1,000 francs.

Hurst, *Square-Riggers*. Villiers & Picard, *Bounty Ships of France*.

GENERAL SLOCUM

Excursion steamer. *L/B/D:* 236′ × 38′ × 7′ (71.9m × 11.6m × 2.1m). *Tons:* 1,283 grt. *Hull:* steel. *Mach.:* steam, sidewheels; 18 kts. *Built:* Devine & Burtis, Brooklyn, N.Y.; 1891.

The site of one of the worst maritime disasters in U.S. history, on June 15, 1904, the Knickerbocker Steamboat Company's excursion steamer *General Slocum* embarked 1,360 children and their escorts, sponsored by St. Mark's German Lutheran Church, for a trip to Locust Point, the Bronx, where the East River meets Long Island Sound. Under Captain William van Schaick, the dangerously overloaded steamer proceeded up the East River from the Third Street pier. About halfway to its destination, a fire was discovered in a forward storage room littered with combustible materials, including tins of oil. The steamer's safety apparatus was old and defective: water had to be pumped by an auxiliary engine, the cloth hoses ruptured under the water pressure, and, as was later apparent, the ship's ten lifeboats were tied fast to the ship. Rather than run *General Slocum* alongside a dock in Queens, Captain van Schaick tried to run the steamer aground on the sandy beach of North Brother Island; instead, the ship grounded in a rocky bay.

By this time the ship was ablaze from bow to stern; 600 passengers were killed when the decks began to collapse. Others, leaping from the burning wreck, were beaten to death by the still turning paddles or drowned by the life vests, many of which had been filled with granulated cork and brought up to proper weight by the inclusion of iron weights. Other children were simply trampled to death in the panic. According to the U.S. Steamboat Inspection Service, whose head was cashiered by President Theodore Roosevelt, 938 people died in the *General Slocum* catastrophe; the New York City police put the toll at 1,031. The disaster was international news, and references to it even recur as a topic of conversation in James Joyce's *Ulysses*, the setting for which is June 16 in Dublin. Captain van Schaick was later found guilty of first-degree manslaughter and sentenced to ten years in Sing Sing federal penitentiary in Ossining, New York. In 1906, the hulk of *General Slocum* was sold to Peter Hagen, who converted it for use as a barge renamed *Maryland*. On December 4, 1911, while bound from Camden to Newark with a cargo of coke, she sprang a leak off Atlantic City and sank on Ludlam Beach.

Gentile, *Shipwrecks of New Jersey*. Rust, *Burning of the "Governor Slocum."*

LA GÉOGRAPHE

Corvette (3m). *Tons:* 350. *Hull:* wood. *Arm.:* 30 guns. *Built:* France; <1800.

In 1800, a French voyage of exploration was proposed, the goal of which was "to make a detailed exploration of the coasts of the southwest, the west, the northwest, and the north of New Holland [Australia], some of which are still unknown and others imperfectly known." The project was endorsed by First Consul Napoleon Bonaparte and carried the imprimatur of Louis Antoine de Bougainville. Commanded by Captain Nicolas Baudin, a veteran of three other scientific voyages, the expedition included the most impressive array of scientific talent ever sent to sea — twenty-four astronomers, botanists, zoologists, mineralogists, gardeners, and draftsmen. Leaving Le Havre on October 19, 1800, *La Géographe* and her storeship *Naturaliste* sailed along the coast of Africa, rather than the normal, faster route which ran southwest towards Brazil and then turned southeast for the Cape of Good Hope. As a result, it took 145 days to reach Ile de France, where forty of the crew, officers, and scientists quit the expedition, some because of illness, others because they refused to continue with the authoritarian Baudin.

Considerably behind schedule, on June 1, 1801, the ships came to Géographe Bay (which they named), near Cape Leeuwin, Australia. Turning north, the ships became separated in a storm, but *Géographe* landed at various points along the western coast of Australia — including Shark Bay — before heading to the Dutch settlement at Kupang, Timor, in August. (*Naturaliste* spent considerable time exploring the Swan River, Australia, and didn't reach Kupang until September 21.) By the time the ships sailed on November 13, their crews had been further depleted by scurvy, which was cured at Kupang, and dysentery, which was contracted there. The ships headed south again, and then sailed for Van Diemen's Land, arriving on January 13, 1802. Despite the recurrence of scurvy, Baudin pushed west towards Nuyts Land, though as before he was separated from *Naturaliste*. By the end of March, *Géographe* had reached the inhospitable south coast of New Holland, which the French called Terre Napoleon. On April 8, 1802, *Géographe* encountered Matthew Flinders's ship, HMS INVESTIGATOR, in Encounter Bay. Although Flinders gave Baudin a copy of the chart he had just completed, the French captain continued to drive his exhausted crew westward and only put about when the ship was out of fuel and water. (Flinders was later arrested at Ile de France, and before his release the French took credit for his discoveries.) *Géographe* finally arrived at the British settlement at Port Jackson (Sydney) a month later.

The French were not, for the moment, at war with England. They were well cared for at the former penal colony where they were soon joined by *Naturaliste*. Baudin also hired a 30-ton schooner, *La Casuarina*, which was put under command of Lieutenant Louis de Freycinet. On November 18, 1802, the three ships sailed south again. From the Bass Strait, *Naturaliste* sailed direct for France with a large number of scientific specimens. *Géographe* and *Casuarina* continued a slow and deliberate survey of the south, west, and north coasts of Australia as far as Joseph Bonaparte Gulf (the name remains today) before putting in once again at Timor from May 6 to June 3. Although the crew continued to succumb to death and disease, the ships sailed with a large collection of exotic animals. After a quick sweep of the Gulf of Carpentaria, they sailed for home via Ile de France. Here Baudin himself died on September 16. *Casuarina* was sold and *Géographe* continued under Captain Pierre Milius, returning to L'Orient on March 25, 1804.

Initially condemned as a failure because of the human toll, in scientific terms the expedition was anything but. In three and a half years, they had collected "more than 100,000 samples of animals both great and small, . . . and the number of new species is more than 2,500," including two black emus that survived in captivity until 1822, at which point they were extinct in the wild. Five narratives of the voyage were published, the most important being the five-volume work by zoologist François Péron and, following his death, Freycinet.

Brosse, *Great Voyages of Discovery*. Dunmore, *French Explorers in the Pacific*.

GEORGE WASHINGTON

(later USS *Catlin*) Liner (2f/4m). *L/B:* 722.5' bp × 78.2' (213.1m × 23.8m). *Tons:* 25,570 grt. *Comp.:* 1st 520, 2nd 377, 3rd 2,000. *Hull:* steel. *Mach.:* quadruple expansion, 2 screws; 18 kts. *Built:* AG Vulcan, Stettin, Germany; 1909.

One of several German passenger ships named for U.S. presidents in the years before World War I, *George Washington* was the largest of Norddeutscher Lloyd's North Atlantic liners to enter service before 1914. The choice of such names was intended as a lure to German immigrants bound for the United States. Just how significant these people were for the German shipping lines is reflected in the fact that as of 1990, Germans still represented by far the largest block of immigrants to the United States — over 12 percent — since 1820.

George Washington entered service from Bremen to Southampton, Cherbourg, and New York in June 1909. Her last voyage on that route began in Bremen on July 25, 1914, and ended at New York on August 3. With the outbreak of the war in Europe, she was ordered to remain at Norddeutscher Lloyd's Hoboken piers — together with such ships as *Imperator* (later LEVIATHAN) — rather

In the years before World War I, German passenger lines catering to the immigrant trade enticed their passengers by naming ships for famous Americans. GEORGE WASHINGTON *has dressed ship on her approach to New York. Courtesy The Mariners' Museum, Newport News, Virginia.*

than risk capture by French and British naval units patrolling off New York. Following the United States' entry into the war, she was seized on April 6, 1917, and commissioned as the naval transport USS *George Washington* for service between the United States and Europe. Following the armistice in 1919, she was handed over to the U.S. Army, and in March she carried President Woodrow Wilson and his entourage to France for the Versailles Peace Conference.

In 1920, *George Washington* was acquired by the United States Shipping Board. Under contract to United States Mail Lines (later United States Lines), she began service between New York, Plymouth, Cherbourg, and Bremerhaven the following year. During her refit at Hoboken, her tonnage had been reduced to 23,788 grt and her accommodations were changed so that she carried 573 passengers in first class, 442 in second, and only 1,485 in third. She remained in this service until 1931, when her age and the depression forced her retirement, and she was laid up on the Patuxent River, Maryland. There she remained until 1940 when the Navy commissioned her as the transport USS *Catlin*. Turned over to the British in 1941, she was again named *George Washington,* but after one voyage, she was given back to the United States. She emerged from a nine-month rebuild in April 1943 fitted with oil-burning engines and only one funnel, and was handed over to the U.S. Army for transport duty in the Pacific, Mediterranean, and Atlantic. Following her wartime service, she was laid up at Baltimore. Gutted by fire on January 17, 1951, she was sold for scrap to the Boston Metals Company.

Bonsor, *North Atlantic Seaway.* Braynard, *Famous American Ships.* U.S. Navy, *DANFS.*

USS GEORGE WASHINGTON (SSBN-598)

George Washington-class fleet ballistic submarine. *L/B/D:* 381.7′ × 33′ × 26.7′ (116.3m x 10.1m × 8.1m). *Tons:* 5,959/6,709 disp. *Hull:* steel; 985′ dd *Comp.:* 139. *Arm.:* 16 Polaris missiles; 6 × 21″TT. *Mach.:* nuclear reactor, 15,000 shp, 1 screw; 20/30 kts. *Built:* Electric Boat Division, General Dynamics, Groton, Conn.; 1959.

USS *George Washington* was originally laid down as the *Skipjack*-class nuclear-powered attack submarine USS *Scorpion* in 1957. While still on the ways, the hull was cut in two and a 130-foot-long midsection was inserted to accommodate sixteen solid-propellant Polaris ballistic missiles. Commissioned December 30, 1959, USS *George Washington* proceeded to Cape Canaveral, Florida, the following June where she loaded two of the missiles. On July 28, she became the first submarine to launch ballistic missiles from a submerged position to a target 1,100 miles downrange. Commander James B. Osborn's message to President Dwight D. Eisenhower was succinct: "Polaris: From out of the deep to target. Perfect." Further tests continued throughout the summer, and *George Washington* loaded her first complement of sixteen nuclear-tipped missiles in October. Each missile was 28 feet 6 inches long, with a diameter of 4.5 feet, weighed 28,500 pounds, with propellant, and carried a 600-kiloton nuclear warhead. The missiles could land within a mile of their target over a distance of about 1,200 nautical miles.

After an initial cruise lasting 66 days submerged, she proceeded to the submarine base at Holy Loch, Scotland, in 1961, operating from there until 1964 when, having logged 100,000 miles at sea, she was refueled for the first time. Later converted to carry Polaris A-3 missiles (which had a range of 2,500 miles), in 1981 *George Washington* was recommissioned as a nuclear attack submarine (SSN-

598) and her missile tubes were filled with cement. She was decommissioned in 1985 and slated for disposal by 1999 through the Navy's nuclear-powered ship and submarine recycling program.

U.S. Navy, *DANFS.*

CSS GEORGIA

(ex-*Japan*) Commerce raider (1f/2m). *L/B/D:* 212' × 27' × 13.8' (64.6m × 8.2m × 4.2m). *Tons:* 648 grt. *Hull:* iron. *Comp.:* 75. *Arm.:* 2 × 100pdr, 2 × 24pdr, 1 × 32pdr. *Mach.:* steeple condensing engines, 900 ihp, 1 screw; 13 kts. *Built:* William Denny & Bros., Ltd., Dumbarton, Scotland; 1862.

Laid down as a merchant vessel, the unfinished *Japan* was purchased for the Confederate Navy in 1863. Sailing on April 1, 1863, under Commander W. L. Maury (cousin of the celebrated oceanographer Matthew Fontaine Maury, who arranged the ship's purchase), CSS *Georgia* was commissioned at sea eight days later. After a brief cruise that took her to Bahia and the Cape Colony, with nine prizes to her credit she put into Cherbourg on October 28 and was decommissioned. She sailed for Liverpool and was sold there. Seized by USS *Niagara* off Portugal on August 15, she was condemned as a prize at Boston. Resuming service as a merchant ship in 1865, she was sold to Canadian interests in 1870, and lost off Tenants Harbor, Maine, on January 14, 1875.

Silverstone, *Warships of the Civil War Navies.* Stephens, "C.S.S. Georgia."

GERTRUDE L. THEBAUD

Schooner (2m). *L/B/D:* 132.6' loa × 25.2' × 12.2 dph (40.4m × 7.7m × 3.7m). *Tons:* 137 grt. *Hull:* wood. *Comp.:* 31. *Mach.:* aux. engine, 180 hp. *Des.:* Frank Paine. *Built:* Arthur D. Story Yard, Essex, Mass.; 1930.

Built in large part due to the generosity of a Franco-American summer resident of Gloucester, Massachusetts, Louis Thebaud, for whose wife the schooner was named, *Gertrude L. Thebaud* was the last of the Gloucester-built Grand Banks fishing schooners. Although the era of the sailing fisheries was clearly in its twilight, the impetus for *Thebaud* was the prospect of capturing the International Fisherman's Trophy from the Nova Scotia fleet. As were all vessels that sailed in this competition, *Thebaud* was built for fishing. But though fast, well found, and ably skippered, her reputation as a fisherman was modest. She sailed in two series against Gloucester's archrival, *Bluenose.* In 1931, under Captain Ben Pine, she lost in two straight races. Seven years later, in what proved to be the last contest for the trophy, she won two out of five races held between October 9 and 26.

Despite her lackluster career as a sailing fisherman, *Gertrude L. Thebaud* was well liked and proved an outstanding ambassador for the port of Gloucester. In April 1933, she carried a delegation to Washington, D.C., to plead on behalf of the hard-pressed fishing industry before President Franklin D. Roosevelt. When the president visited the ship, he was accompanied by Britain's Prime Minister Ramsay MacDonald. In July of that year, she sailed to Chicago to be part of the Massachusetts state exhibit at the World's Fair. Four years later, she was chartered by the Arctic explorer Donald B. MacMillan and sailed as far north as Frobisher Bay with a crew of thirty-seven professors, students, and professional crew. Chartered to the U.S. Coast Guard during World War II, she served as flagship of their coastal defense fleet.

Sold to William H. Hoeffer of New York in August 1944, she departed Gloucester on May 29, 1945, and ended her days as a cargo vessel in the Caribbean. Nearly three years later, in February 1948, she was driven onto a breakwater at La Guaira, Venezuela, and broke up.

Chapelle, *American Fishing Schooners.* Thomas, *Fast and Able.*

GIGLIO SHIP

Hull: wood. *Built:* central Mediterranean; ca. 600 BCE.

The island of Giglio is situated in the Tyrrhenian Sea off the coast of Tuscany (ancient Etruria). The remains of the ship lie at the north end of Campese Bay at the foot of La Secche (42°22'N, 10°52'E), a submerged rock that almost certainly caused the wreck. The ship settled into a sandy gully at the bottom of a steep slope at a depth of 40 to 50 meters. The site was discovered by R. Vallintine in 1961 and excavated from 1982 to 1986 by Oxford University's Maritime Archaeological Research department under the direction of Mensun Bound. Dating from the late seventh or early sixth century BCE, the Giglio wreck is probably that of an Etruscan ship. The cargo included many Etruscan amphorae, but also amphorae from eastern Greece, Samos, and samples from an unknown Phoenician-Punic center. The containers held pitch that eventually spilled out, partially covering and preserving the ship's timbers.

The keel, both the garboards, and three strakes on one side survive. Stitches were used to assemble the hull, as in the BON PORTÉ WRECK. These were locked in place with pegs. The ship was built of pine, fir, oak, elm, and phillyrea, with treenails of olive, hazel, and phillyrea, and blocks of boxwood and evergreen oak. Unfortunately, these common tree species do not point to any one part of the Mediterranean as the Giglio ship's homeport.

The cargo consisted partly of fine painted pottery from Corinth, including more than twenty small, elegant perfume flasks. Also from Corinth was an impressive bronze helmet, decorated with incised designs. The Corinthian material reflects that city's cultural and commercial importance in the Late Archaic period. Another noteworthy find is a pair of wooden calipers perhaps used by the ship's carpenter to gauge mortises and tenons. Wooden flutes recall the Etruscan fondness for wind instruments, renowned in antiquity. Small nuggets of smelted copper may have served as a form of pre-coinage currency. Other finds include lamps, tools, net weights, arrowheads, iron bars, copper and lead ingots, amber, granite anchor stocks, gaming pieces, fragments or ornate inlaid furniture, a writing tablet and stylus, and an elaborately carved inlaid wooden box lid.

Bound, "Early Observations on the Construction of the Preclassical Wreck at Campese Bay." Bound & Vallintine, "Wreck of Possible Etruscan Origin off Giglio Island."

GIORGIOS AVEROF

Pisa-class armored cruiser (3f/2m). *L/B/D:* 462′ x 69′ × 24.7′ (140.8m × 21m × 7.5m). *Tons:* 9,958 disp. *Hull:* steel. *Comp.:* 670. *Arm.:* 4 × 9.2″ (2 × 2), 8 × 7.5″, 16 × 76mm, 5 × 47mm; 3 × 18″TT. *Armor:* 8″ belt, 2″ deck. *Mach.:* triple expansion, 19,000 ihp, 2 screws; 22.5 kts. *Des.:* Giuseppe Orlando. *Built:* Orlando & Co., Livorno, Italy; 1911.

Laid down as a sister ship to the Italian armored cruisers *Pisa* and *Amalfi*, *Averof* was bought by the Greek Navy while still on the stocks. Named for a Greek millionaire who had bequeathed £300,000 for the improvement of the navy, *Averof* was commissioned as flagship of the Greek Navy in 1911. As such she played a crucial role in the Balkan Wars of 1912–13, in which Greece, Bulgaria, Serbia, and Montenegro tried to throw off Ottoman rule. As the strongest unit in either the Bulgarian or Greek fleets (the only two countries that possessed ships), she was instrumental in defeating the Turkish forces at the Battles of Helli (December 3, 1912) and Lemnos (January 5–6, 1913). The resulting containment of the Turkish fleet in the Dardanelles led to the transfer of five Aegean islands — Chios, Lesbos, Samos, Lemnos, and Thasos — to the Greek flag.

The *Averof* underwent two refits during the 1920s, emerging from the second, at La Seyne, France, with new antiaircraft armament but minus her three torpedo tubes.

The only surviving armored cruiser of the early twentieth century, the Greek GIORGIOS AVEROF *was originally intended for the Italian Navy. After service in World War II, the former Greek flagship was preserved as a museum ship. Photo by Richard R. Weiss, courtesy Norman Brouwer.*

Following the German invasion of Greece in the spring of 1941, she escaped to Alexandria and was thereafter employed as a convoy escort in the Indian Ocean until 1944. Decommissioned in 1946, she remained at Poros, forty miles south of Athens, as an accommodation ship and later a floating museum.

Basch, "Historic Ship, the *Giorgio Averoff.*" Gray, ed., *Conway's All the World's Fighting Ships.*

GIPSY MOTH IV

Ketch. *L/B/D:* 54′ × 10.5′ × 7.′ (16.5m × 3.2m x 2.1m). *Tons:* 11.5 disp; 18 TM. *Hull:* fiberglass. *Comp.:* 1. *Des.:* Illingworth & Primrose. *Built:* Camper & Nicholsons, Southampton, Eng.; 1965.

A pioneer of long-distance flight, Francis Chichester was the second person to fly solo from England to Australia, in a Gipsy Moth airplane. When he later turned to single-handed long-distance sailing, he named his four boats (II to V) for his plane. It was in *Gipsy Moth IV* that he achieved lasting fame for his one-stop solo circumnavigation. Among Chichester's other ambitions was to equal the average passage of the wool clippers outward bound to Australia via the Cape of Good Hope, which he calculated to be 100 days. Although he fell short of this goal, *Gipsy Moth IV* — "about as unbalanced or unstable a boat [as] there could be" — made phenomenally good time. Sailing from Plymouth on August 28, he rounded the Cape of Good Hope 58 days out and entered Sydney Heads on December 12, 1966, after a passage of 14,100 miles in 107 days. This was 20 days better than the average speed for all clippers, not just for the fastest. After 48 days spent refitting and provisioning, he set out again, and after a knockdown in the Tasman Sea, he sped through the roaring forties, rounding Cape Horn 50 days out and returning to a hero's welcome at Portsmouth in an overall time of 274 days. A national hero, Chichester sailed *Gipsy Moth IV* up the Thames and was knighted by Queen Elizabeth II with the same sword that Elizabeth I used to knight Sir Francis Drake for his exploits in GOLDEN HIND, the first English ship to sail around the globe, in 1581. *Gipsy Moth IV* is now on public view at Greenwich, in the shadow of the tea clipper CUTTY SARK, last of the breed that inspired Chichester.

Chichester, *"Gipsy Moth" Circles the World*.

LA GIRONA

Galleass (3m). *Hull:* wood. *Comp.:* 349. *Built:* Naples(?); <1588.

The first Armada shipwreck in Ireland identified and excavated in modern times was that of *La Girona,* one of four galleasses that had sailed in Don Hugo de Moncada's Neapolitan Squadron. Galleasses were oared sailing ships — a cross between a galleon and an oared galley — ill suited to work in the North Atlantic, and *Girona* sustained heavy damage en route from Lisbon to La Coruña. She contributed little to the fighting in the English Channel, but in the retreat home from the North Sea she was forced into the port of Killibegs, in Donegal, Ireland, for repairs to her rudder. While there, she took aboard about 800 survivors from two other Spanish shipwrecks. The Genoese carrack *La Rata Santa Maria Encoronada* had gone ashore in Blacksod Bay, County Mayo, and her crew had embarked in the hulk *Duquesa Santa Ana,* which then went aground at Loughros Mor Bay, Donegal. When *Girona* was repaired, Don Alonso de Leiva ordered her to Catholic Scotland. The next day, October 26, 1588, her jury rudder broke and she was driven violently ashore off Lacada Point, County Antrim, in 55°14′N, 06°30′W; fewer than ten of the estimated 1,300 people aboard survived the last of the twenty-four Armada shipwrecks in Ireland.

In 1967, Belgian archaeologist Robert Sténuit began

excavation on the site, and in the following two seasons divers removed two brass cannon, shot for guns up to 50 pounds, lead ingots carried for the production of small-arms ammunition, navigational instruments, and an abundance of personal jewelry of gold and precious stones. One of the most famous and intriguing pieces is believed to represent a flying lizard from the Philippines, *draco volans,* the scientific discovery of which was not made until 200 years later. In addition, the site contained crosses, reliquaries, cameo portraits, gold and silver coins from Europe, Mexico, and Peru, as well as more everyday items such as pottery and ships' fittings.

Flanagan, *Shipwrecks of the Irish Coast.* Sténuit, *Treasures of the Armada.*

GIULIO CESARE

(later *Novorossisk*) *Conte di Cavour*-class battleship (2f/2m). *L/B/D:* 611.4′ × 91.8′ × 34.1′ (186.4m x 28m × 10.4). *Tons:* 25,086 disp. *Hull:* steel. *Comp.:* 1,000. *Arm.:* 13 × 12.2″ (3 × 3, 2 × 2), 18 × 4.8″, 19 × 7.6cm; 3 × 18″TT. *Armor:* 10″ belt, 6.8″ deck. *Mach.:* Parsons turbines, 31,000 ihp, 4 screws; 21.5 kts. *Built:* Cantieri Ansaldo, Genoa, Italy; 1914.

Giulio Cesare ("Julius Caesar") was one of nine Italian dreadnought battleships in four classes authorized between 1907 and 1914. *Giulio Cesare* saw no action during World War I, and in the 1920s she was used as a gunnery training ship. A massive reconstruction from 1933 to 1937 resulted in a virtually new ship. She was lengthened to 186.4 meters, her maximum displacement grew to 29,100 tons, and her screws were reduced to two, although with geared turbines producing 75,000 shaft horsepower, her speed increased to 27.5 knots. Her primary armament also changed from thirteen 12.2-inch guns in five turrets to ten 12.8-inch guns in four turrets.

During World War II, *Giulio Cesare* saw considerable action against Britain's Mediterranean fleet in the struggle for Malta and North Africa. On July 9, 1940, a 15-inch shell from HMS WARSPITE off Punta Stilo knocked her out of action for six weeks. She again tangled with the British off Cape Teulada on November 27, 1940, and she sustained minor damage during an air raid on Naples in January 1941. Through January 1942, when she was laid up, *Giulio Cesare* took part in a number of inconclusive engagements while providing long-range cover for Axis convoys to North Africa.

Following Italy's surrender in 1943, *Giulio Cesare* was transferred to Allied control, and in February 1949 she was transferred to the Soviet Union as reparations under terms set at the Teheran Conference in 1945. Renamed

Novorossisk (for the Black Sea port) and rearmed with 12-inch guns, she was the most heavily armed ship in the Soviet Navy. Anchored in Sevastopol on October 29, 1955, at 0130 the ship was wracked by an explosion just forward of "A" turret. Nearly three hours later, she turned turtle and sank, taking with her 600 of her 1,600 crew. The sinking itself remained a closely guarded secret until 1988, and the actual cause of the twentieth century's worst peacetime naval disaster has never been determined. The four possibilities most often cited — none of them especially compelling — are that a mine laid during World War II came loose and struck the hull; that the ship was sabotaged by KGB agents seeking to discredit Commander in Chief Admiral Nikolai G. Kuznetsov; that the ship was mined by the Italians prior to the ship's transfer to the Soviet Union; or that Italian neofascist commandos under Junio Valerio Borghese, "The Black Prince," mined the ship where she lay.

Breyer, *Battleships and Battlecruisers.* Huchthausen, "Espionage or Negligence?"

Roald Amundsen's converted fishing vessel GJØA *was the first vessel to transit the Northwest Passage, albeit in stages. Here she is seen at Gjøahaven, on Prince William Island in the Canadian Arctic, where she remained fast in the ice from September 12, 1903, to August 13, 1905. Courtesy Norsk Sjøfartsmuseum, Oslo.*

GJØA

Sloop. *L/B/D:* 70′ × 20.6′ × 7.7′ (21.3m × 6.3m × 2.3m). *Tons:* 67 grt. *Mach.:* "Dan" engine, 13 hp, 1 screw. *Built:* Kurt Johannesson Skaale, Rosendal, Hardanger, Norway; 1872.

Under the explorer Roald Amundsen, *Gjøa* was the first ship to transit the Northwest Passage. Named for the fighting Valkyrie of the Vikings, she was built for the fishing trades, in which she worked for twenty-eight years under Captain Asbjørn Sexe of Hangesund and, from the mid-1880s, Captain H. C. Johanneson of Tromsø. Amundsen bought the shallow-draft *Gjøa* for his intended Arctic voyage in 1900 and spent the following year on trials between Norway and Greenland, after which he gave her 3-inch oak sheathing, iron strapping on the bow, and a small kerosene-fueled internal combustion engine.

On June 16, 1903, *Gjøa* sailed from Christiania (Oslo) with Amundsen and a crew of six. They anchored first at Godhavn on the west side of Greenland, where they embarked sleds, dogs, and kayaks. Crossing Melville Bay, they transited Lancaster Sound, and descended south into Peel Sound between Somerset and Prince William Islands before anchoring at King William Island on September 12, 1903. They spent two years at Gjøahaven (68°39′N, 96°08′W) taking observations in an effort to determine the location and movement of the Magnetic North Pole. On August 13, 1905, they sailed west between continental Canada and the south shore of Victoria Island, and on August 26, off Banks Island (in what is now Amundsen Gulf), they encountered the U.S. whaler *Charles Hanson,* which had sailed from the Pacific. At this point they knew that they had transited the elusive Northwest Passage. They wintered again off King Point, during which one of the crew died. From here Amundsen trekked up the Porcupine and Yukon Rivers to Eagle, Alaska, where he telegraphed the news of his success to the world. *Gjøa* arrived in Nome on August 31, 1906, pausing briefly before pushing on to San Francisco. *Gjøa* passed through the Golden Gate on October 19 and was given a hero's welcome by the city, still recovering from the calamitous earthquake in April.

Despite an invitation to be the first ship to pass through the Panama Canal, at the instigation of the Norwegian community in San Francisco, *Gjøa* was turned over to the city and put on exhibit in Golden Gate Park. She remained there for thirty years, admired but slowly deteriorating. A reconstruction of the ship was attempted in 1939, but World War II intervened, and the work was only completed in 1949. *Gjøa* remained in San Francisco until 1974, when she was returned to Norway and exhibited at the Norsk Sjøfartsmuseum, Bigdøy, Oslo.

Amundsen, *My Life as an Explorer; Northwest Passage.* Baker, "*Gjøa.*"

LA GLOIRE

Broadside ironclad ship (3m). *L/B/D:* 255.6′ × 55.9′ x 27.10′ (77.9m × 17m × 8.5m). *Tons:* 5,630 disp. *Hull:* ironclad wood. *Comp.:* 550. *Arm.:* 36 × 6.4″. *Armor:* 4.7″ belt. *Mach.:* 2-cycle trunk, 2,500 ihp, 1 screw; 12.5 kts. *Des.:* Stanislas Dupuy de Lôme. *Built:* Arsenal de Toulon; 1860.

One of the first tests of the effectiveness of ironclad ships in battle conditions occurred during the Crimean War. Impressed especially by their performance against Russian defenses at Fort Kinburn at the mouth of the Dnieper River, the French Navy embarked on a program of building ironclad warships. In this, it was strongly supported by Napoleon III. Appointed naval constructor in 1857, Stanislas Dupuy de Lôme completed plans for six ironclads in 1858. *La Gloire,* the first of these, was essentially a modification of his design for the world's first steam screw warship, *Napoleon* of 1850. Because of their relatively weak industrial base, the French were unable to build an iron-hulled ship. The compromise reached in *Gloire* was for a wooden hull clad with 4.7-inch iron plate and heavily reinforced with iron fastenings. With a single iron deck, *Gloire* was a single-screw three-masted ship mounting thirty-six 6.4-inch muzzle-loading rifled guns. Designed to operate as a battleship in a traditional battle line, *Gloire* had two sister ships, *Invincible* and *Normandie.* These were joined by the iron-hulled *Couronne* and the ten ships of the *Flandre*-class (one of which, *Heroïne,* had an iron hull), as well as the two-decker ironclads *Magenta* and *Solferino,* mounting 50 guns on two decks.

Laid down in May 1858 and commissioned in July 1860, *Gloire* served in the French fleet for nine years before undergoing a thorough overhaul and refit, emerging with six 9.6-inch and two 7.8-inch muzzle-loading rifled guns. In 1879, she was struck from the navy list and broken up four years later. Far from helping the French achieve naval superiority over the British, *Gloire* prompted the conservative British to undertake the development of their own iron ships. No sooner was *Gloire* laid down than the Admiralty promptly ordered two ironclad and four iron ships of their own. The immediate result was HMS WARRIOR, an all-iron-hull warship that entirely dwarfed *Gloire* and ushered in a new generation of fighting ship.

Baxter, *Introduction of the Ironclad Warship.* Lambert, ed., *Steam, Steel and Shellfire.* Silverstone, *Directory of the World's Capital Ships.*

GLOMAR CHALLENGER

Drill ship (1f/3m). *L/B/D:* 399.9′ × 65.3′ × 20′ (121.9m × 19.9m × 6.1m). *Tons:* 6,281 grt. *Hull:* steel. *Comp.:* 70. *Mach.:* diesel-elec-

tric, 5,100 bhp, 2 screws; 11 kts. *Built:* Levingston Shipbuilding Co., Orange, Tex.; 1968.

Named in honor of the oceanographic survey vessel HMS CHALLENGER (Glomar was an acronym for her owner, Global Marine, Inc.), the distinctive-looking *Glomar Challenger* resembled a floating oil rig, with a 45-meter-high lattice drill derrick situated amidships. The idea for *Glomar Challenger* arose out of the need for a way to extract core samples from the ocean floor to study the climatological and geological evolution of Earth. In the words of Cesare Emiliani, a hole bored on the seabed was necessary because

> geographical, geochemical, micropaleontological, and mineralogical analysis of the cores will yield information of great importance on the conditions prevailing on the ocean floor in the water column above, at the ocean surface, in the atmosphere, in neighboring continents, and even in outer space and in the sun, during the time of sediment deposition, that is during the past 100×10^6 [100 million] years or so.

Emiliani's idea was adopted by the Joint Oceanographic Institutions for Deep Earth Sampling (JOIDES), which comprised the Lamont Geological Observatory, Scripps Institution of Oceanography, Woods Hole Oceanographic Institute, and the University of Miami, which used *Glomar Challenger* first in the Deep Sea Drilling Project, or DSDP.

The technology used in her work was that of the deep-sea drill. Rather than anchoring — an impossibility over the great depths in which she operated — *Glomar Challenger* was kept in position by a "dynamic positioning system" using sonar beacons on the ocean floor that relayed data to hydrophones aboard ship, which in turn activated bow and stern thrusters. Her complement comprised three groups: 24 scientists and technicians, a 12-man drilling team, and the ship's crew. The roughnecks operated the drill, which could bore a 1,000-meter hole in the surface of a 4,000-meter seabed. The drill string consisted of lengths of drill pipe of between 9.5 and 28.5 meters in length, with a tungsten carbide tip at the working end. The only major accident occurred when about 4,000 meters of drill pipe were lost while operating in 20-foot seas and 50-knot winds about 150 kilometers south of Cape Horn, in April 1974. To compound the crew's problems, three days later the ship was seized by an Argentine gunboat whose captain suspected *Glomar Challenger* of being an illegal oil-prospecting ship.

Glomar Challenger's contributions to scientific understanding were of enormous significance. From core samples retrieved on her earliest voyages — which JOIDES called "legs" — geologists were able to establish that Alfred Wegener's theory of continental drift, first advanced in about 1915 and subsequently debunked by U.S. geologists, was in fact correct. Researchers were also able to prove the theory of seafloor spreading and determine the age of the seafloor, which was put at about 38 million years. Later voyages also demonstrated that Earth's magnetic poles have reversed themselves repeatedly over time. During fifteen years of operation, *Glomar Challenger* operated in all the major seas of the world from the Arctic Ocean to the Ross Sea and the Mediterranean and Black Seas. After her ninety-sixth leg, in the Gulf of Mexico, *Glomar Challenger* was scrapped at Mobile in 1983.

Hsu, *Challenger at Sea.*

GLOMAR EXPLORER

(AG-193) (ex *Hughes Glomar Explorer*) Heavy lift ship (3m). *L/B/D:* 618.8′ × 115.7′ × 46.7′ (188.8m × 35.3m × 14.2m). *Tons:* 63,300 disp. *Hull:* steel. *Comp.:* 180. *Mach.:* diesel-electric, 13,200 bhp, 2 screws; 11 kts. *Built:* Sun Shipbuilding & Dry Dock, Chester, Pa.; 1973.

Shortly after a Soviet Golf 2-class ballistic missile submarine sank in mid-Pacific about 750 miles northwest of Hawaii, the Central Intelligence Agency initiated Operation Jennifer, a secret program to raise the wreck from a depth of 4,000 meters. Built ostensibly for Global Marine Development, Inc., a subsidiary of Howard Hughes's Summa Corp., *Hughes Glomar Explorer* arrived at the site on July 4, 1974. Over the next month she managed to raise the forward portion of the submarine, including, it was believed, nuclear-tipped torpedoes. The main body of the submarine, which held SSN-5 ballistic missiles, was left in place. The bodies of six of the submarine's eighty-six crew were also recovered, and buried with full military honors. The project was estimated to have cost about $550 million including the ship, personnel, and salvage equipment.

The Navy purchased and renamed *Glomar Explorer* the next year. The ship was of little use to the Navy, except for a two-year lease to Global Marine for seafloor mining, which proved unprofitable. When the survey ship GLOMAR CHALLENGER was broken up in 1983, it was thought that *Glomar Explorer* might be converted to carry on her work. The effort failed and she remained in the National Defense Reserve Fleet until 1996, when she was again converted for use as an oil-drilling rig for Global Marine.

Burleson, *Jennifer Project.* Polmar, *Ships and Aircraft of the U.S. Fleet.* Varner, *Matter of Risk.*

GLORIANA

Cutter. *L/B/D:* 71′ × 13′ × 10.5′ (21.6m × 4m × 3.2m). *Tons:* 38.5 disp. *Hull:* wood on steel frames. *Comp.:* 6. *Des.:* Nathanael G. Herreshoff. *Built:* Herreshoff Manufacturing Co., Bristol, R.I.; 1891.

Built for New York yachtsman E. D. Morgan, *Gloriana* is considered one of the most revolutionary designs in the history of yachting. *Gloriana* was based on the popular 46-Footer Class (the measurement refers to the waterline length), but in designing her, Herreshoff eliminated the rounded forefoot, giving the bow a straight profile and reducing the waterline length relative to the length overall. In the words of Nathanael Herreshoff,

> *Gloriana*'s design had much longer overall length [about six feet more than the standard 46-Footers] and fuller, more rounding waterlines at each end than was usual, giving a longer body for sailing and the long ends very much decreased the tendency to "hobby horse"; consequently she was a much faster and better boat in a seaway.

L. Francis Herreshoff wrote, "*Gloriana*'s bow was copied throughout the world and in the next ten years it was to be seen on everything from catboats to three-masted schooners." *Gloriana*'s construction was also advanced, employing the lightest possible materials aloft, and a composite construction of wood planking on steel frames.

In her first season, *Gloriana* sailed to a remarkable eight straight victories against other 46-Footers, including eight built the same year. This, combined with the untimely death of Edward Burgess, who had designed the America's Cup defenders *Puritan, Mayflower,* and *Volunteer,* established the Herreshoff name at the forefront of American yacht design. Despite his new boat's remarkable record, Morgan sold *Gloriana* before her second season, but she continued sailing for an additional eighteen years under a number of different owners.

Bray & Pinheiro, *Herreshoff of Bristol.* Herreshoff, *Captain Nat Herreshoff.*

HMS GLORIOUS

Courageous-class aircraft carrier (1f/1m). *L/B/D:* 786′ × 90.5′ × 24′ (239.7m × 27.6m × 7.3m). *Tons:* 22,500 disp. *Hull:* steel. *Comp.:* 1,245. *Arm.:* 16 × 4.7″; 48 aircraft. *Armor:* 3″ belt. *Mach.:* geared turbines, 90,000 shp, 4 shafts; 30.5 kts. *Built:* Harland & Wolff, Belfast, Ireland; 1917.

Originally commissioned as a light cruiser with four 15-inch guns, HMS *Glorious* was converted to an aircraft carrier between 1924 and 1930. Stationed first in the Mediterranean and then with the Home Fleet during

World War II, she made five patrols to Norway during and after the German invasion in April 1940. In early June she aided in the evacuation of northern Norway, sailing from Scapa Flow to carry RAF Hurricanes and Gladiators to Britain; it was one of the first times that high-performance monoplane fighters ever landed on an aircraft carrier, without arrester hooks. At about 0300 on June 8, she sailed for Scapa Flow with the destroyers HMS *Acasta* (Commander Charles Glasfurd) and *Ardent* (Lieutenant Commander J. F. Barker). At about 1600 that afternoon, the German battlecruisers SCHARNHORST and GNEISENAU appeared on the horizon. At 1632, *Scharnhorst* opened fire at 28,600 yards, and scored a hit on *Glorious*'s flight deck with her third salvo; 24 minutes later another shell killed Captain Guy D'Oyly-Hughes and many on the bridge. A smoke screen forced a lull in the fighting between 1658 and 1720, when *Glorious* was hit again in the engine room. She sank half an hour later (in 68°38′N, 4°11′E), with the loss of all but 37 of her crew. *Ardent* had sunk at 1725 (68°56′N, 3°51′E), and *Acasta* went down at 1820 (68°40′N, 4°19′E), though not before she landed a torpedo under *Scharnhorst*'s main after turret. There was only one survivor from each of the destroyers.

Howland, "Loss of HMS *Glorious*." Winton, *Carrier "Glorious."*

GLORY OF THE SEAS

Clipper (3m). *L/B/D:* 240.2′ × 44.1′ × 28′ dph (73.2m × 13.4m × 8.5m). *Tons:* 2,009 nrt. *Hull:* wood. *Comp.:* 38. *Built:* Donald McKay, East Boston, Mass.; 1869.

Glory of the Seas was the last medium clipper built by one of the greatest of nineteenth-century shipbuilders, Donald McKay. Although not as fast as the extreme clippers built by McKay and others, *Glory of the Seas* was sailed well and consistently produced a good turn of speed. Under Captain Josiah Knowles, in 1873–74 she sailed from New York to San Francisco in 95 days, the ninth fastest time by a wooden sailing ship and a record not beaten since by an American sailing ship. The next year she set an all-time record of 35 days between San Francisco and Sydney, a passage also marked by the birth of Thomas Knowles to Mary Eaton Knowles, who often sailed with her husband and their three other children, Mattie, Harry, and Mary.

McKay had banked everything he had on the success of *Glory of the Seas*, and he sailed on her maiden voyage from New York to San Francisco. Unfortunately, his financial woes beat him to San Francisco, and he arrived to find that the ship had been sold to Charles Brigham of Boston to raise money to pay off the debts that McKay had incurred in building his ship. The sale effectively ended McKay's career in shipping. Following her return to Boston, *Glory of the Seas* changed hands again before sailing for Liverpool, where Josiah Knowles assumed command in 1871. He remained in command until 1880 when he was succeeded by Captain Daniel McLaughlin. Two years later she was laid up at San Francisco. In 1884, her owners, Sears & Company of Boston, went out of business, but the next year she was bought by Captain Joshua S. Freeman. He sailed her to Liverpool and then on her last Cape Horn voyage back to San Francisco. Freeman subsequently kept her in the coastwise coal trade until 1902 when she was laid up in Oakland Creek. Three years later she was purchased by Barneson-Hibbard Company to be cut down for a barge. The San Francisco earthquake caused such a demand for shipping that it was decided instead to refit *Glory of the Seas* to carry lumber from the Northwest. Thus reprieved, she remained in sail for a further five years. In 1911, she was sold again and cut down for work as a floating cannery in Alaska. She continued in this until 1917, when she was used as a storage hulk for the Glacier Fish Company of Tacoma. In 1923, she was burned where she lay for her scrap metal.

Matthews, *American Merchant Ships*. Mjelde, *"Glory of the Seas."*

HMS GLOWWORM

"G"-class destroyer (2f/2m). *L/B/D:* 323′ × 33′ x 12.4′ (98.5m × 10.1m × 3.8m). *Tons:* 1,345 disp. *Hull:* steel. *Comp.:* 145. *Arm.:* 4 × 4.7″, 1 × 3″; 5 × 21″TT. *Mach.:* geared turbines, 34,000 shp, 2 screws; 36 kts. *Built:* John I. Thornycroft Co., Ltd., Southampton, Eng.; 1935.

Attached to a British Home Fleet force centered on the battlecruiser HMS RENOWN, HMS *Glowworm* sailed from Scapa Flow on April 5 as a covering force for Operation Wilfred, the British plan to mine the coastal waters of Norway. On April 8, the *Glowworm*'s Lieutenant Commander G. P. Roope was given permission to search for a man overboard. Isolated in rough seas and rain about 100 miles northwest of Trondheim, she encountered the German destroyer *Bernd von Arnim* under Commander Rechel, who radioed for assistance. The cruiser ADMIRAL HIPPER under Captain Helmuth Heye arrived shortly after 0930, opening fire at 0959. Heavily outgunned, *Glowworm* fired two salvos of five torpedoes, but to no effect. When it became clear that he could not outrun the

HMS GLOWWORM, *the intrepid destroyer whose death run at the* ADMIRAL HIPPER *during the April 1940 invasion of Norway put the German cruiser out of action for several months. Courtesy Imperial War Museum, London.*

Hipper, Roope turned and rammed his adversary instead, tearing a 40-meter gash along the starboard bow. *Glowworm* sank and 37 men were rescued by the *Hipper,* though Roope was not among them. After the war, he was posthumously awarded the Victoria Cross.

Grove, *Sea Battles in Close Up.*

SMS GNEISENAU

Scharnhorst-class armored cruiser (4f/2m). *L/B/D:* 474.3′ × 70.8′ × 27.6′ (144.6m × 21.6m × 8.4m). *Tons:* 12,900 disp. *Hull:* steel. *Comp.:* 860. *Arm.:* 8 × 8.4″, 6 × 6″, 18 × 88mm; 4 × 18″TT. *Armor:* 6″ belt. *Mach.:* triple expansion, 26,000 ihp, 3 screws; 22.5 kts. *Built:* AG Weser, Bremen, Germany; 1908.

Named for Count August Neithardt von Gneisenau, a Prussian field marshal of the Napoleonic era, *Gneisenau* was one of two armored cruisers in Vice Admiral Maximilian Graf von Spee's East Asiatic Squadron, the other being the flagship SCHARNHORST. During World War 1, after cruising across the Pacific, *Gneisenau* played a major role in the German victory at the Battle of Coronel, off the coast of Chile on November 1, 1914, which saw the destruction of Rear Admiral Christopher Cradock's HMS GOOD HOPE and *Monmouth.* Spee's squadron then rounded Cape Horn en route home. Six weeks after Coronel, *Gneisenau* was in the van of the German squadron scouting near the Falkland Islands when the British battle-cruisers INFLEXIBLE and INVINCIBLE were spotted the morning of December 8. After a nine-hour chase, *Gneisenau* sank at about 1800 in about 52°45′S, 56°05′W, with the loss of about 650 men, including Captain Maerker; 200 crew were saved.

Yates, *Graf Spee's Raiders.*

GNEISENAU

Scharnhorst-class battlecruiser (1f/2m). *L/B/D:* 234.9m × 30m × 9.9m (772.3′ × 98.4′ × 32.5′). *Tons:* 32,100 disp. *Hull:* steel. *Comp.:* 1,840. *Arm.:* 9 × 11.2″ (3x3), 12 × 6″, 14 × 10.5cm, 16 × 37mm, 22 × 20mm; 6 × 21″TT; 3 seaplanes. *Armor:* 14″ belt, 2″ deck. *Mach.:* geared turbines, 165,390 shp, 3 shafts; 31.5 kts. *Built:* Deutsche Werke, Kiel, Germany; 1938.

Gneisenau's first war cruise, with SCHARNHORST, resulted in the sinking of the armed merchant cruiser RAWALPINDI on November 23, 1939, near Iceland. The two ships supported the German landing at Narvik and on April 9, *Gneisenau* was hit by fire from HMS RENOWN. During the Allied withdrawal from Norway two months later, the ships sank the aircraft carrier HMS GLORIOUS and destroyers *Acasta* and *Ardent* off Narvik. On January 22, 1941, *Gneisenau* and *Scharnhorst* began a commerce-raiding cruise during which they sank 22 ships. They returned on March 23 to Brest where they were later joined by PRINZ EUGEN. After nearly a year in the French port, the ships were ordered back to Germany in Operation Cerberus — the famed Channel Dash — which began on February 11, 1942. *Gneisenau* was mined near the German coast on the evening of the 12th but made it to Kiel, only to be bombed there two weeks later. Transferred to Gotenhafen (Gdansk) in April, she was decommissioned in July. Scuttled on March 27, 1945, she was broken up after the war.

Breyer, *Battleships and Battlecruisers.* Stephen, *Sea Battles in Close-Up.*

SMS GOEBEN

(later *Yavuz Sultan Selim*) *Moltke*-class battlecruiser (2f/1m). *L/B/D:* 612′ × 98.4′ × 30.2′ (186.6m x 30m × 9.2m). *Tons:* 24,999 disp.

Hull: steel. *Comp.:* 1,053. *Arm.:* 10 × 11.2″ (5 × 2), 10 × 6″, 8 × 88mm; 4 × 20″TT. *Armor:* 10.8″ belt, 2″deck. *Mach.:* Parsons turbines, 52,000 shp, 4 screws; 28 kts. *Built:* Blohm & Voss, Hamburg; 1912.

Named for the Franco-Prussian War General August von Goeben, while still on trials *Goeben* was ordered to Constantinople to take part in a multinational defense of the Ottoman capital during the second Balkan War in 1912. Designated flagship of the German Navy's newly created Mediterranean Division, she was the most powerful ship in the Mediterranean with a main armament mounted in five twin turrets (two aft, one forward, and two diagonally displaced on the side decks). When Austria declared war on Serbia on July 28, 1914, *Goeben* (Captain Richard Ackermann) and her consort, the light cruiser BRESLAU, were at Pola, Austria. Rear Admiral Wilhelm Souchon determined to get out of the Adriatic rather than risk being bottled up there for the duration of the impending conflict. By August 1, when Germany declared war on Russia, the ships were at Brindisi, Italy. Two days later, Germany declared war on France, and in the early morning of August 3, Souchon bombarded the French colonial ports of Bône and Philippeville. The same day, he was ordered to Turkey.

Diplomatic events of the same week had a great bearing on *Goeben*'s subsequent career. In 1911, the Turkish government had ordered two battleships from British yards. SULTAN OSMAN I and *Reshadieh* had Turkish crews aboard when First Lord of the Admiralty Winston Churchill requisitioned them for the British government on August 2. The same day, Turkey concluded a secret treaty with Germany. The importance of the Turkish role in the European conflict was all but ignored by both France and Britain, whose primary worries regarding *Goeben* and *Breslau* concerned their possible breakout into the Atlantic, and the harassment of troopships plying between North Africa and France, or linking up with Austria-Hungary's Adriatic fleet. Despite orders to find and engage the German ships and not to convoy troopships, French Vice Admiral Augustin Boue de Lapeyre insisted on convoys and failed to deploy his ships to prevent the Germans from heading east — as they were reported to be doing. Moreover, he did not coordinate properly with his British counterpart, Admiral Sir Archibald Berkeley Milne.

After bombarding Philippeville on August 3, *Goeben* later that day passed HMS *Indomitable* and INDEFATIGABLE; all three ships were cleared for action but their guns were trained fore and aft; their respective nations would not be at war until midnight. As the two British ships turned to follow, Souchon ordered the whole ship's company to help in the boiler room, officers included. He gradually lost sight of the British battlecruisers, but the light cruiser *Dublin* continued to trail the ships. After refueling at Messina, they headed for the Adriatic, followed closely by HMS *Gloucester*, who was engaged by *Breslau* on August 8. The ships then sailed around southern Greece and entered the Dardanelles on the evening of August 10. Rear Admiral Ernest Troubridge, the British second-in-command, was court-martialed for breaking off his chase, an action he justified on the grounds that *Goeben* constituted a "superior force" such as the Admiralty had ordered him to avoid, and that a chase risked letting the Austrian fleet out of the Adriatic.

On August 16, Germany announced the sale of the two ships to the Turkish government, and they were renamed *Sultan Yavuz Selim* (for a sixteenth-century Ottoman ruler) and *Middilli* (Turkish for Mitylene). Eager to force the Turks into the war, Souchon collaborated with the pro-German Minister of War Enver Pasha to organize a raid on Sevastopol on October 29; on November 2, Russia declared war. *Goeben* remained active in the Black Sea for the duration of the war. On May 10, 1915, she narrowly escaped a fleet of 17 Russian ships; on January 8, 1916, she came under fire from the 12-inch guns of the *Imperatriza Maria* after signals officer Karl Dönitz flashed a farewell message to the Russian dreadnought.

On January 20, 1918, *Goeben* and *Breslau*, now under command of Vice Admiral Hubert von Rebeur-Paschwitz, left the Dardanelles for the first time for a raid on Salonika. *Goeben* helped to sink the British monitors HMS *Raglan* and *M28*, but after the loss of *Breslau* and hitting three mines herself, *Goeben* returned to the safety of the straits and was beached near Chanak (now Çannanakale). Refloated on January 26, she sailed to Sevastopol for the surrender of Russia's Black Sea Fleet on May 2. The ship was formerly turned over to the Turks on November 2, 1918, three days after Britain and France signed an armistice with Turkey. She was left near Constantinople until salvaged in 1927. Renamed *Yavuz Selim*, she became the flagship of the Turkish Navy in 1930 and was not retired until 1950. After a quarter century on display as a museum ship, she was scrapped in 1976.

Breyer, *Battleships and Battlecruisers.* McLaughlin, *Escape of the "Goeben."* Van der Vat, *Ship that Changed the World.*

GOKSTAD SHIP

Karvi (1m). *L/B/D:* (23.3m × 5.2m × 2m dph (76.4′ × 17′ × 3m). *Tons:* 20.2 disp. *Hull:* oak. *Comp.:* 64–70. *Built:* Norway; ca. 890-895.

Dating from the late ninth century, shortly after the beginning of the Vikings' long-distance raiding, the Gokstad ship is a large clinker-built boat thought to be of a type known as a karvi, similar in construction to the earlier OSEBERG SHIP. Intended for open ocean sailing, the karvi was smaller than the longboats that represented the apogee of Viking ship construction. The Gokstad ship has sixteen strakes (four more than in the Oseberg ship) built up from either side of the single-piece oak keel and the thirty-two oar holes were fitted with shutters that could be closed to keep out water when the single square sail was set. The shield rack could mount two shields between each oar hole. Unlike the more lavishly carved Oseberg ship, which dates from about three-quarters of a century before, the only ornamentation is a carved animal head on the tiller. After the excavation of the burial mound in which the ship was discovered in 1880, the remains of the vessel were transferred to Oslo. The reconstructed ship has been housed in the Viking Ship Hall at Bygdøy, Oslo, alongside the remains of the Oseberg and Tune ships. In addition to the ship itself, the burial mound near Sandefjord also yielded three smaller boats, the smallest of which was 6.6 meters long. In addition, the site yielded the remains of more than two dozen animals, including twelve horses and six dogs, a bed, and cooking implements. Once thought to have been the grave of Olav Gjerstad, stepson of Queen Åsa, this attribution now seems to be erroneous.

In 1893, a nearly exact replica of the Gokstad ship, named *Viking,* was built at Sandefjord and sailed from Bergen to New York in six weeks with a crew of twelve under Magnus Andersen. *Viking* continued on to the Chicago World's Fair via the Erie Canal and Great Lakes; it has been preserved and is currently in storage in Chicago awaiting new exhibition facilities.

Bonde & Christensen, "Dendrochronological Dating of the Viking Age Ship Burials." Nikolaysen, *Viking Ship Discovered at Gokstad in Norway.* Sjøvold, *Oseberg Find.*

GOLDEN HIND

(ex-*Pelican*) Galleon (3m). *L/B/D:* ca. 70′ bp x 19′ × 9′ (21.3m × 5.8m × 2.7m). *Tons:* ca. 150 burden. *Hull:* wood. *Comp.:* 80–85. *Arm.:* 18 guns. *Built:* Plymouth, Eng.; 1576.

Destined to become one of the greatest seamen of all time, Francis Drake made two voyages to the Spanish Main between 1566 and 1568 in company with his kinsman John Hawkins. Although lured by the profitable slave trade and South American silver, the Protestant

A replica of the GOLDEN HIND, *the galleon in which Sir Francis Drake encompassed the world on the first circumnavigation by an English ship. Photo by Beken of Cowes.*

Drake was further motivated by a fervent anti-Catholicism. His hatred increased after the loss of JESUS OF LÜBECK to Spanish duplicity at San Juan d'Ulua. In 1576, Queen Elizabeth approved, albeit secretly, Drake's captaincy of a mission with a threefold aim: to pass through the Strait of Magellan, reconnoiter the Pacific coast of South America, and, if possible, return via the Northwest Passage; to establish relations with people not yet subject to European princes; and to plunder Spanish shipping.

Drake's command consisted of about 180 men in five ships. The flagship, *Pelican,* carried courses, topsails, and topgallants on her main and foremasts, and a lateen mizzen. The other ships were *Elizabeth* (80 tons, 16 guns) under John Winter; *Marigold* (30 tons, 16 guns) under John Thomas; *Swan* (50 tons, 5 guns) under John Chester; and *Christopher* (15 tons, 1 gun) under Tom Moone. After a false start in November, the expedition cleared Plymouth on December 13, 1577. After stopping at Mogador, Morocco, the crew sailed for the Cape Verde Islands, capturing half a dozen Spanish ships and, more important, the Portuguese pilot Nuño da Silva. His *Santa Maria* was renamed *Mary* and put under command first of Thomas Doughty, one of several "gentlemen adventurers" on the voyage, and then of Drake himself, who exchanged *Pelican*'s command with Doughty. The latter proved a troublemaker and Drake soon relieved him of command altogether.

The ships reached the coast of southern Brazil on April 5, proceeded from there to the River Plate, and then on to Puerto San Julian where they landed on June 20. The fleet remained at anchor for a month, during which the crisis with the mutinous Doughty came to a head. Tried on the spot, Doughty was found guilty and executed in the same place that Ferdinand Magellan had executed the treasonous Gaspar de Quesada in 1520. It was here, too, that Drake delivered his celebrated sermon enjoining the "gentlemen to haul and draw with the mariner, and the mariner with the gentlemen," in order to ensure their mutual success.

After abandoning the other three ships, *Pelican, Marigold,* and *Elizabeth* put to sea on August 17. Three days later, they rounded the Cape of Virgins at the entrance to the Strait of Magellan where Drake rechristened his ship *Golden Hind.* The choice of name was political, for the golden hind was found on the coat of arms of Sir Christopher Hatton, one of the voyage's principal backers and a friend of the late Thomas Doughty. After only fourteen days in the strait, the English flag first flew in the Pacific on September 6, 1578. The ships' luck failed when a furious storm drove them southward, costing the expedition two ships. *Marigold* was lost with her 29 crew, and John Winter turned back to England. Drake, however, established that the Strait of Magellan did not separate South America from Terra Incognita Australis, as was then believed, but that its southern shore was made up of islands to the south of which lay open ocean, now known as Drake Passage.

When the storm abated, the English struck north along the unsuspecting west coast of Spanish America. Looting the small port of Valparaiso on December 5, they pressed on to Arica, where silver from the mines of Potosí was shipped to Panama. When *Golden Hind* arrived at Callao on February 15, word of the English presence had preceded them, although there was little the Spanish could do to detain them. Learning that a treasure ship had sailed only three days before, Drake took off in pursuit and on March 1 captured *Nuestra Señora de la Concepción* — nicknamed the *Cacafuego* — off Cape Francisco, Colombia. Sailing out of the main coastal shipping lane, the English transshipped 80 pounds of gold and 26 tons of silver bars equal in value to about £126,000 — or about

half the English Crown's revenues for a year. Although chiefly interested in returning home with their treasure intact, the English captured a few more ships whose crews were almost unanimous in their respect for Drake's gentility and fairness. Their greatest concern was over his drawings of the coastline, which seemed to suggest that more English would follow, "for everything is depicted so naturally that anyone who uses these paintings as a guide cannot possibly go astray."

In searching for the Strait of Anian, or Northwest Passage, Drake sailed as far as 48°N — just south of the Strait of Juan de Fuca — before turning south. On June 17, 1579, *Golden Hind* anchored in 38°30′N at a "convenient and fit harbor" generally thought to be Drake's Bay, on Point Reyes, California, just north of San Francisco Bay. Drake's dealings with the natives were characteristically evenhanded, and the English found "a goodly countrye, and fruitfull soyle, stored with many blessings fit for the use of man" — fit even to be called New Albion and claimed for his majesty.

On July 25, *Golden Hind* sailed west across the Pacific, making no landfall until September 30, when she landed in either the Palau or Ladrones Islands. By October 16 she was off Mindanao in the Philippines, from where she turned south for the Moluccas. The king of Ternate had recently thrown out the Portuguese, but he allowed Drake to load spices and refit. After a month preparing for the last leg of their journey home, the expedition sailed on December 12 but spent a month caught in the maze of islands and shoals in the Indonesian archipelago. On January 9, *Golden Hind* struck a coral reef and was held fast for a day before the wind shifted and she slid into deep water. After watering his ship at Tjilatjap on the south coast of Java (previously thought to be connected to Terra Australis), Drake weighed anchor on March 26. A nonstop journey of over 9,700 miles — remarkable for its lack of incident — brought *Golden Hind* to Sierra Leone on July 22. The first English circumnavigation of the globe ended on September 26, 1580, when *Golden Hind* sailed into Plymouth after a voyage of 2 years, 10 months, and 18 days with 59 of her crew aboard, a great achievement given the record of many later voyages.

Cautioned to lie low while the diplomatic consequences of his voyage were considered at London, Drake was finally received by Queen Elizabeth. On April 4, 1581, Drake was knighted on the decks of *Golden Hind* at Deptford. Elizabeth also ordered the ship displayed in drydock, and the intrepid ship remained on public view until the 1660s.

Hampden, *Francis Drake Privateer.* Sugden, *Sir Francis Drake.*

HMS GOOD HOPE

Drake-class armored cruiser (4f/2m). *L/B/D:* 529.5′ x 71′ × 26′ (161.4m × 21.6m × 7.9m). *Tons:* 14,100 disp. *Hull:* steel. *Comp.:* 900. *Arm.:* 2 × 9.2″, 16 × 6″, 14 × 12pdr; 2 × 18″TT. *Armor:* 6″ belt. *Mach.:* triple expansion, 30,000 hp, 2 screws; 23 kts. *Des.:* Sir William White. *Built:* Fairfield Shipbuilding & Engineering Co. Ltd., Govan, Scotland; 1902.

Laid down as *Africa* but renamed before launching, HMS *Good Hope* was one of four *Drake*-class armored cruisers ordered in 1898. At the outbreak of World War I, *Good Hope* was mobilized under Captain Philip Franklin to become the flagship of Rear Admiral Christopher Cradock's detached squadron tasked with preventing the destruction of Allied shipping in the South Atlantic by German raiders. When it was learned that Vice Admiral Graf von Spee's Asiatic Squadron, was heading east across the Pacific, the Admiralty dispatched the pre-dreadnought battleship CANOPUS to support Cradock's force, which consisted also of the armored cruiser *Monmouth,* under Captain Frank Brandt, the light cruiser *Glasgow,* and the armed merchant cruiser *Otranto.* Cradock relegated *Canopus* to shepherding his colliers as he sailed into the Pacific in search of Spee. On the afternoon of November 1, about 50 miles off Coronel, Chile, the two fleets encountered one another and Cradock sailed into battle against hopeless odds. Among the other defects of both *Good Hope* and *Monmouth* was that their main-deck 6-inch guns were useless in heavy seas, which meant that the brunt of the offensive action had to be carried by *Good Hope*'s two 9.2-inch guns. Outmaneuvered by Spee's ships, Cradock was brought to battle at about 1900. Silhouetted against the setting sun and unable to close with the German ships, *Good Hope* was hit by at least thiry-five armor-piercing shells from SCHARNHORST, and about an hour after the battle started, she sank with all hands (919 crew) in about 36°59′S, 73°55′W. *Monmouth* was effectively out of commission by 1930, when she came under fire from the light cruiser *Nurnberg,* and she sank just after 2100 with the loss of 735 crew. German casualties were two wounded.

Cradock's attack against such an overwhelming force has been attributed to, among other things, his fear of the consequences of not engaging the enemy. Shortly before Coronel, he wrote, "I will take care not to suffer the fate of poor [Rear-Admiral Sir Ernest] Troubridge," who was court-martialed for not pressing his pursuit of the GOEBEN. (First Sea Lord John Fisher later advised Admiral David Beatty, "Steer midway between poor Troubridge and Cradock and all will be well, Cradock preferred.") Less than six weeks later, Cradock was avenged at the Battle of the Falklands, which saw the loss of four German warships and more than 2,000 German sailors, including Spee.

Bennett, *Coronel and the Falklands.* Marder, *From the Dreadnought to Scapa Flow.*

GOVERNOR COBB

Screw steamer (1f/2m). *L/B/D:* 289.1′ × 54′ × 18′ (88.1m × 16.5m × 5.5m). *Tons:* 1,556 grt. *Hull:* steel. *Comp.:* 440 pass.; 88 crew. *Mach.:* steam turbines, 5,000 hp, 3 screws; 19 kts. *Built:* Eastern Steam Ship Corp., Camden, N.J.; 1906.

The passenger steamer *Governor Cobb* has the dual distinction of being the first American-flag commercial vessel driven by turbine engines and, much later in her career, the first ship ever used as a helicopter carrier. Named for Maine governor William T. Cobb, the first American turbine ship was launched twelve years after Charles Parson's revolutionary TURBINIA. From 1906 until 1917, she sailed for the Eastern Steamship Lines between Boston, Maine, and the Canadian Maritimes. Taken over by the U.S. Shipping Board following America's entry into World War I, she sailed as a training ship. In 1920, the Peninsular & Occidental Steamship Company (P&O Line) purchased her for work in the Caribbean, where she remained until 1934. *Governor Cobb* failed to pass inspection in 1937, and she was laid up until 1942.

In that year, the U.S. Coast Guard requisitioned her for conversion into the world's first helicopter carrier. With her upper works and engine completely overhauled and fitted with a landing platform measuring 38 by 63 feet — big enough for three helicopters — she was commissioned in 1943 as USCGC *Cobb.* By the time she was ready for sea, German U-boats were no longer menacing the East Coast as much as they had been, and her mission was redirected towards search and rescue. The *Cobb* was in constant need of repair, and it was not until June 19, 1944, that she landed her first helicopter. From then until January of 1946, she operated in Long Island Sound. Scrapped five months later, the *Cobb* had nevertheless prove the feasibility and worth of ship-borne helicopters just as she had originally helped proved the practicality of turbine propulsion.

Hilton, *Night Boat.* Scheina, "Twice Unique."

GRACE DIEU

Great ship. *L/B/D:* 218′ oa × 50′ × 21.4′ (66.4m × 15.2m × 6.5m). *Tons:* 1400–1500 tons burthen; 2,750 disp. *Hull:* wood. *Comp.:* 250+. *Built:* William Soper, Southampton, Eng.; 1418.

So far as is known, at her launch *Grace Dieu* was the largest ship ever built in northern Europe; and no English ship exceeded her in size until SOVEREIGN OF THE SEAS more than two centuries later. More than 200 feet long overall, she measured 184 feet (60.3 meters) on deck and 135 feet (41.1 meters) on the keel. For many years it was thought that *Grace Dieu* never put to sea — that the ship was a failure — and that this was due to the fact that clinker hulls could not be built so big. (Her clinker-laid strakes were fastened by clenched nails, and caulked with moss and tar.) Laid down in 1416, she was launched and christened by the Bishop of Bangor in 1418, and put to sea under William Payne in 1420. Her crew seem to have refused to muster, although this was probably due to foul weather, poor provisions, and a policy forbidding shore leave. There is nothing in the record to suggest that the ship handled badly.

Later in 1420, *Grace Dieu* transferred to a berth at Bursledon in the Hamble River with the other royal ships (including her contemporaries *Jesus, Trinity Royal,* and *Holigost*), probably because the ships were extremely expensive to man, and Henry V's navy had swept from the Narrow Seas the very French menace the *Grace Dieu* was designed to meet. This included a number of high-charged Genoese carracks, though none were as lofty as *Grace Dieu,* whose forecastle loomed 52 feet above the waterline, and from which her archers and infantrymen could have carried the day against any opponent.

Although *Grace Dieu* appears never to have returned to active service, in 1430 the royal ships were visited by Luca di Maso degli Albizzi, a Florentine Captain of the Galleys who dined aboard *Grace Dieu* with William Soper. Luca, who later wrote, "I never saw so large and so beautiful a construction," took the only contemporary measurements of *Grace Dieu* to have survived. Among these is the almost incredible figure of 204 feet for the mast, which is nonetheless consistent with pictorial evidence. (The number of masts carried by *Grace Dieu* is not known; it may have been only one or as many as three.) In 1433 she was moved farther upstream and enclosed in a dock. The great ship was struck by lightning on the night of January 6–7, 1439, and burned beyond repair, after which an estimated 7 tons of iron and other fittings were salvaged. *Grace Dieu* has lain where she burned ever since (in 50°51′N, 1°17′W), damaged by enthusiastic, if primitive, nineteenth-century archaeologists, but otherwise protected by the mud and accessible only at spring tides.

Prynne, "Annual Lecture of the Society for Nautical Research"; "Notes: The Dimensions of the *Grace Dieu.*" Rose, "Henry V's *Grace Dieu* and Mutiny at Sea." Turner, "Building of the *Grace Dieu, Valentine* and *Falconer.*"

GRACE HARWAR

Ship (3m). *L/B/D:* 266.7′ × 39.1′ × 22′ dph (81.3m × 11.9m × 6.7m). *Tons:* 1,816 grt. *Hull:* steel. *Built:* William Hamilton & Co., Port Glasgow, Scotland; 1889.

Built for W. Montgomery, *Grace Harwar* sailed in general trade for fourteen years under the British flag. She was never a lucky ship; Alan Villiers later claimed that she killed a man on every voyage. A storm-prone ship, she was twice caught in hurricanes in port: at Mobile, in 1913, and again at Iquique in 1922, where two ships out of twenty-five were wrecked. In June 1919, *Grace Harwar* was caught in a hurricane off Cape Horn that left her with a £13,000 repair bill in Buenos Aires. Three years before, she had joined the fleet of Gustaf Erikson, Åland Island. Although the Erikson ships are best known for their work in the grain trade from Australia in the 1930s, they engaged in a variety of trades, hauling lumber, nitrate, grain, case goods, and other bulk cargoes around the world. By 1929, *Grace Harwar* was the last full-rigged ship in the Cape Horn trade. In that year Villiers and Ronald Walker shipped in her with the intent of making a movie about the voyage. Walker was killed by a falling yard thirty-eight days out, and a month later the second mate went mad and threw himself overboard, though he was saved. No movie was made, but Villiers's account of the voyage, *By Way of Cape Horn,* got many adventurous young men interested in shipping before the mast in the last decade of commercial sail. *Grace Harwar*'s last voyage to Australia was made in 1935, and her passage from Falmouth to London in ninety-eight days, one of her best times. However, she was operating at a loss and Erikson sold her to the shipbreakers at Blyth.

Hurst, *Square-Riggers.* Villiers, *By Way of Cape Horn; Set of the Sails.*

GRANDCAMP

(ex-*Benjamin R. Curtis*) Liberty ship (1f/15m). *L/B/D:* 422.8′ × 57′ × 27.7′ (128.9m × 17.4m × 8.4m). *Tons:* 7,176 grt. *Hull:* steel. *Comp.:* 45–81. *Mach.:* triple expansion, 2,500 ihp, 1 screw. *Built:* California Ship Building Co., Los Angeles; 1942.

The scene of one of the most devastating peacetime explosions in the United States, *Grandcamp* was originally named *Benjamin R. Curtis,* for an associate justice of the U.S. Supreme Court who resigned over the Court's handling of the Dred Scott case. Sold to the French government in 1946, she entered general trade between Europe and Gulf Coast and Caribbean ports. On April 11, 1947, she arrived at Texas City, a city of 15,000 people located eleven miles from the Gulf of Mexico between Galveston and Houston. Five days later, the ship was loading ammonium nitrate, a chemical fertilizer that is also used for making explosives. Bags were being lowered into the cargo hatch when a fire was discovered at about 0800. The crew attempted to extinguish the blaze, but half an hour later they were ordered off the ship. As spectators crowded the docks, *Grandcamp* exploded at 0919, sending up a 4,000-foot-high fireball that knocked a plane out of the sky. Burning debris ignited secondary fires at the nearby Monsanto chemical plant, which made styrene, a highly flammable component of plastic, and in grain elevators and oil refineries up to two miles away. At 0110 the next morning, the ammunition-laden freighter *High Flyer* exploded nearby, destroying the Liberty ship *William B. Keene.* Fires raged through Texas City for three days and the death toll was put at 308, with another 3,000 injured.

Sawyer & Mitchell, *Liberty Ships; Victory Ships.* Press reports.

La Grande Hermine

Ship (3m). *L/B/D:* 78.8′ × 25′ × 12′ dph (24m × 7.6m × 3.7m). *Tons:* 120 tons. *Hull:* wood. *Built:* France; <1535.

French fishermen reached the Grand Banks off Newfoundland earlier in the sixteenth century, but the first French voyage of exploration was dispatched in 1524. In a commission for François I, Giovanni Verrazzano sailed La Dauphine along the coast of North America from North Carolina to Newfoundland. The French did not follow up on this pioneering effort for another decade. In 1534, François I commissioned Jacques Cartier to sail with two ships (their names are not known) on a voyage that took him along the coast of Newfoundland, through the Strait of Belle Isle, to the northern coast of New Brunswick, where he embarked two sons of the Indian chief Donnaconna for the return to France. So promising were the results of this voyage that the king renewed his commission and Cartier was given three ships to make a second voyage "to explore beyond *les Terres Neufves* [and] to discover certain far-off countries." The latter referred specifically to Cathay.

Cartier's ships on this voyage were *La Grande Hermine* (120 tons), *La Petite Hermine* (60 tons), and the pinnace *L'Emerillon* (40 tons). They sailed from Saint Malo in May 1535 and on August 10 put into a small bay on the southern coast of Labrador that Cartier named for Saint Lawrence, whose feast day it was. This name eventually applied to the Gulf of St. Lawrence and the river that flows from Lake Ontario past Montréal and Québec, but

Cartier simply called it La Grande Rivière. Spurred on by descriptions of the riches of Saguenay, Cartier sailed up the St. Lawrence and eventually reached Donnaconna's village near present-day Québec. From there he continued west with *L'Emerillon* as far as Lac Saint-Pierre, and with his longboats touched the village of Hochalega under the hill he called Mont Royal. His way barred by rapids, he returned to Quebec for the winter. The following spring, Cartier kidnapped Donnaconna and several of his tribesmen so that they could relate their tales of Saguenay directly to the French king.

War with Spain postponed the launch of a new expedition until 1541. On May 23, Cartier sailed with *La Grande Hermine* (which François I had given to him), *L'Emerillon,* and three other ships as part of an ambitious attempt to establish a French colony in Canada and reach Saguenay. Donnaconna had died in France and their reception was not as warm as it had been previously. Cartier established a fort at Charlesbourg-Royal, and during the winter thirty-five of their company were killed in Indian attacks. A second fleet, under Sieur de Roberval, was supposed to have joined them, but in May Cartier's group sailed alone for France. They met up with Roberval at St. John's, Newfoundland, but Cartier refused to turn back, and continued to France. The riches of Saguenay with which they returned proved to be nothing more than iron ore and quartz.

Although the lack of material success and a half century of civil war prevented France from mounting further expeditions to Canada, fishermen and trappers continued to visit the area throughout the sixteenth century. The next voyages of political significance would be those in which Samuel de Champlain took part between 1603 and 1635. Although few details of *La Grande Hermine* survive, a full-size model was made for Canada's Expo '67. The dimensions given here are based on that model, which is on display at the Cartier-Brebeuf Park in Quebec.

Morison, *European Discovery of America: The Northern Voyages.*

Grand Turk

Ship (3m). *Tons:* 300 tons. *Hull:* wood. *Comp.:* 120; 15. *Arm.:* 28 guns. *Built:* Thomas Barstow, Hanover, Mass.; 1781.

The first of four famous American merchantmen to bear the name, *Grand Turk* was built by the Salem merchant Elias Hasket Derby as a privateer during the American Revolution. *Grand Turk* was named either for the Ottoman Sultan whose nickname was "Grand Turk," or possi-

The accuracy of this rendering of GRAND TURK — *one of the first ships to fly the American flag in Chinese waters — is open to question. The image is actually a copy of one found on a Lowestoft bowl, which in turn is based on the frontispiece of William Hutchinson's* Treatise on Practical Seamanship, *published in Liverpool in 1777 — four years before* GRAND TURK *slid from the ways. Painting by Mrs. Clive A. Edwards, courtesy Peabody Essex Museum, Salem, Massachusetts.*

bly for Grand Turk Island in the Caribbean. With 28 guns and a crew of 120, in the course of 22 months she made four lucrative cruises against British merchant shipping, three of them under Joseph Pratt, seizing 16 British ships between Ireland and the Caribbean. Following the war, *Grand Turk* was stripped of most of her guns, and her crew was reduced to 15. After a trip to the West Indies, she sailed to the Cape of Good Hope where, in 1785, she met EMPRESS OF CHINA, homeward bound from her historic voyage to China. She returned to Salem via St. Helena and the Caribbean after a highly profitable voyage. Her next voyage was to the French-held Indian Ocean island of Mauritius, where she was chartered for Canton, thus becoming the third U.S.-flag ship to trade in China. She returned to Salem on May 22, 1787, after a voyage of nearly 18 months. *Grand Turk* sailed from Salem for the last time in December 1787, bound again for Mauritius, where she was sold.

The second *Grand Turk,* measuring 560 tons, was built at Salem in 1791. Later sold to Boston interests, she traded to India, China, and Russia. After a long passage from China in 1797, she arrived at Portland, Maine, in deplorable condition. She had lain there two weeks when on January 4, 1798, she was ripped from her moorings and wrecked in a gale.

Peabody, *Log of the Grand Turks.*

GRAN GRIFÓN

Hulk (4m). *Tons:* 650. *Hull:* wood. *Comp.:* 45 crew, 234 soldiers. *Arm.:* 38 guns. *Built:* Rostock (Germany); <1588.

When the Spanish Armada sailed from Lisbon on May 30, 1588, there were twenty-three hulks (or urcas), storeships leased from Hanseatic merchants, in the Baltic. The flagship, under Juan Gómez de Medina, of the hulks was *El Gran Grifón* — the griffin is the emblem of her homeport, Rostock. On August 2, the Armada was off Portland Bill when the *Gran Grifón* fell to weather of the main fleet. In an action that cost her seventy dead and wounded, she was nearly captured by Sir Francis Drake's REVENGE before ships of Juan Martinez de Recalde's Biscayan squadron joined the fray and *Gran Grifón* was towed off by a galleass. On August 6–7, she also took part in the rearguard action off Gravelines before the Spanish turned north, hoping to round Scotland and sail home.

The hulks *Gran Grifón, Barca de Amburg, Castillo Negro,* and the Venetian TRINIDAD VALENCERA were separated from the main fleet north of Scotland on about August 20. *Barca de Amburg* foundered on September 1 and her crew were taken aboard *Trinidad Valencera* and *Gran Grifón.* Three days later the surviving ships separated; *Castillo Negro* disappeared and *Trinidad Valencera* was wrecked in Ireland. On September 27, the leaking *Gran Grifón* made Fair Isle, midway between the Orkney and Shetland Islands. As her crew tried to beach the ship, she wrecked in a rocky bay called Stroms Hellier. Most of her company landed, although fifty died of exposure and starvation before they could sail for Scotland where they secured safe passage home.

The wreck was visited in 1758 by John Row and William Evans, who retrieved two brass cannon. In 1970, divers Colin Martin and Sydney Wignall found the remains of the ship. They recovered all or parts of twelve cannon cast in bronze, cast iron, and wrought iron, which shed new light on the arming of these noncombatant supply ships.

Martin, *Full Fathom Five.*

GRAVENEY BOAT

L/B: 45.9′ × 12.8′ (14m × 3.9m). *Tons:* 7. *Hull:* wood. *Comp.:* 4. *Built:* Britain(?); ca. 930.

The vessel discovered at Graveney, Kent, in 1970, is variously referred to as a boat, because it was probably an open-decked vessel not designed for long-distance voyaging with a large crew, and a ship, because it was quite large for vessel for its time. Preserved beneath a two-meter-thick layer of clay on the shore of a creek about one kilometer inland from the Thames estuary and ten kilometers northwest of Canterbury, she was probably built in about 930 CE and abandoned twenty years later. Whether she was used only for lightering along the Kent Coast and up the Thames, or traded across the English Channel or North Sea, the residual remains found on the site suggest that the vessel was connected with active international trade. Among the remains was a cooking pot made in France or Belgium — possibly the ship's own — and evidence of hops and quernstones from the Rhine Valley. The area of Kent in which she was found also had a rich trade in salt.

Uncovered during a drainage improvement project in the Graveney Marshes, the remains were photographed, recorded, and removed in only thirteen days. The forward end of the strakes (there are eleven on either side of the keel) is no longer extant, but it seems likely that the boat was a double ender. As is typical of the period in northern Europe, she was fashioned shell first, with the overlapping strakes attached to a backbone of stempost, keel, and sternpost and then reinforced with frames. She was fastened with both iron nails and willow treenails. The mode of propulsion is unknown. She would have been large to be propelled by sweeps, and there is no clear evidence of a mast or rigging. *Ottor,* a half-scale model of the vessel built in 1988, demonstrated that she would have been a handy sailing boat capable of carrying a crew of four and a five-ton cargo at a speed of four knots in Force 4 conditions. The Graveney boat is now mounted on display at the National Maritime Museum, Greenwich.

Fenwick, *Graveney Boat.* Gifford, "Sailing Performance of Anglo-Saxon Ships."

GREAT ADMIRAL

Down Easter (3m). *L/B/D:* 215.6′ × 40.2′ × 25.6′ (65.7m × 12.3m × 7.8m). *Tons:* 1,497 net. *Hull:* wood. *Comp.:* 36. *Des.:* W. H. Varney. *Built:* Robert E. Jackson, East Boston, Mass.; 1869.

Built for the Boston firm of William F. Weld & Company, *Great Admiral* was named in honor of the Civil War hero Admiral David G. Farragut. A stout, fast Down Easter, her lines approached those of a medium clipper. In her twenty-eight years under the Black Horse Flag, she was commanded by eight captains, most notably Benjamin Thompson (1874–83 and 1885–86) and James F. Rowell (1883–84 and 1887–96). After his retirement, Rowell reflected on his experience in sail:

> The writer may with propriety claim to be a typical American seaman. Typical, in that he started to sea at the age of

sixteen with a fair common school education and passing through every grade, has commanded in the past twenty-five years the ships *Rainbow, Zouave, Lightning, Thomas Dana* and *Great Admiral.* A seaman, in that he was taught his business when the American ship was the pride of every seaman's heart and when their sails filled every sea.

Great Admiral was a remarkably well-handled ship, and in the course of more than 725,000 miles sailed under Weld ownership, she was involved in no serious accidents. Most of her ports of call were on the East and West Coasts of the United States, the Orient, Australia, and Europe. She never sailed to South America and called at Boston only four times between 1872 and 1895. In the following year, *Great Admiral* was sold to Captain E. R. Sterling, who sailed her in the Pacific coal and lumber trades. On December 2, 1906, she sailed from Port Townsend, Washington, bound for San Pedro, California. Four days out, the ship encountered hurricane force winds in about 46°43′N, 127°58′W. Although the masts were cut away, the ship remained partially submerged and the captain, his wife, and the crew clung to the wreckage of the ship for two nights and two days before being rescued by the British ship *Barcore* in 47°05′N, 128°10′W. The survivors — which included all but two of the crew — were later transferred to the bark *Andrew Welch,* bound for San Francisco.

Matthews, *American Merchant Ships.* Lubbock, *Down Easters.*

GREAT BRITAIN

Screw steamship (6m/1f). *L/B/D:* 322′ × 50.5′ × 16′ (98.1m × 15.4m × 4.9m). *Tons:* 2,936 grt. *Hull:* iron. *Comp.:* 260 pass. *Mach.:* direct-acting steam engine, 1 screw; 11 kts. *Des.:* Isambard Kingdom Brunel. *Built:* Great Western Steamship Co., Bristol, Eng.; 1843.

The SS *Great Britain* was the second ship of the trio designed by the innovative and farsighted engineer I. K. Brunel; the other two were GREAT WESTERN and GREAT EASTERN. On a number of counts, *Great Britain* represents a milestone in the history of shipbuilding. She was by far the largest ship of her day, one-third again as long as the biggest ship of the line in the Royal Navy. She was the first seagoing ship built of iron, and the first to be driven by a screw propeller. Though *Great Britain* was not a commercial success for her builders, many of the ship's innovations were adopted in the years following her launch on July 19, 1843, by Queen Victoria's husband, Prince Albert.

Originally conceived as a companion vessel for the *Great Western* — a wooden paddle steamer to be named *City of New York* — Brunel soon determined that great

Isambard Kingdom Brunel's six-masted screw steamship GREAT BRITAIN, *seen in an anonymous photo dating from about 1844. Today the ship can be seen restored to her former glory at her birthplace in Bristol, England. Courtesy National Maritime Museum, Greenwich.*

economies could be achieved, especially in the stowage of coal fuel, in a larger ship. After assessing the seakeeping qualities of the iron-hulled paddle steamer *Rainbow* in her service between England and Belgium, he changed the hull material to iron. Finding no takers for their ship, the Great Western Steamship Company decided to build the vessel themselves, which entailed the construction of a drydock, known as the Great Western (later Wapping) Dock. The company also decided to build the engines for the enormous paddlewheels intended for the ship, at this stage known as *Mammoth*. In 1840, Brunel studied the screw propulsion system of the *Archimedes* and decided to adopt a single-screw propeller for his new ship. The change to a propeller also meant radical changes to the engines. The final design included four cylinders, each 88 inches in diameter. Operated at 18 revolutions per minute, the engine drove the propeller, to which it was connected via a drive chain, at 53 rpm. The propeller itself, of iron, was 15.5 feet in diameter and weighed more than 3 tons. All told, the engines and boilers weighed 520 tons, while 1,040 tons of iron were in the hull. The ship also carried six masts; all but one, the second from the bow, was fore-and-aft rigged.

Great Britain's accommodations included 26 single and 113 double rooms and a cargo capacity of 1,000 tons; there were bunkers for 1,000 tons of coal. When the ship cleared Bristol's Floating Harbor, it was found that the locks were too narrow, and the company had to widen them. Sea trials began on December 13, 1844, in which

Great Britain achieved 11 knots. After a six-month stay in London where she was visited by thousands of admirers, including Queen Victoria, in June she sailed to Liverpool and loaded cargo for New York. She sailed on July 26 under command of *Great Western* veteran James Hoskens and arrived August 10 after a crossing of 14 days, 21 hours. Her return to Bristol took about the same time.

During her second voyage, most of the propeller blades fell off and a new four-bladed screw had to be fitted. The engines were also reconfigured by Maudslay Sons and Field, and produced 1,663 indicated horsepower, up from 686. Subsequent voyages were marred by technical problems of varying severity, but on her fifth voyage, outward bound from Liverpool with 180 passengers (a record for a North Atlantic steamship), she ran aground on September 22, 1846, in Dundrum Bay south of Belfast Lough in Ireland. Although there was no loss of life, it was not until August 27, 1847, that the ship was freed, with the help of the steam frigate HMS BIRKENHEAD. Unable to pay for the necessary work, the Great Western Steamship Company was forced to sell the ship. It was three years before the ship was purchased, by Gibbs, Bright & Company. With a new three-blade screw driven by a two-cylinder engine with a simple gear drive, and the masts reduced to four (square-rigged on the middle two masts), the ship reentered service on the transatlantic run, transferring to the Australia trade after one voyage.

Leaving the Mersey on August 21, 1852, with 650 passengers, *Great Britain* arrived in Melbourne on November 12, after a run of 82 days. She departed Australia in January with 260 passengers and £550,000 in gold dust. Rerigged again, as a three-masted ship, the vessel was sold to the Liverpool & Australian Navigation Company, and sailed from Liverpool with more than 1,000 passengers. Except for service as a troop transport during the Crimean War (1855–56) and one voyage during the Indian Mutiny in 1857, the *Great Britain* remained in the Australian passenger trade until laid up in Birkenhead in February 1876. Acquired the next year by Antony Gibb, Sons and Company, for bulk trade between Britain and San Francisco, *Great Britain* was stripped of her engines and the hull was sheathed in wood. On her third voyage out, on February 25, 1886, she was forced back to Stanley, Falkland Islands, and condemned. After 47 years as a coal and wool storage ship, the Falkland Islands Company moved her from Stanley to nearby Sparrow Cove, where the ship was abandoned.

In 1967, after an appeal to save the ship was initiated by E. C. B. Corlett — a similar idea had been floated by the San Francisco Maritime Museum — the Great Britain Project Committee was formed to bring the ship back to Bristol for restoration to her original design. In a salvage exercise that would have impressed Brunel himself, on April 24, 1970, the ship was towed from Stanley aboard a pontoon barge, stopping first at Montevideo, and then on to Bristol where she eased into Wapping Dock on July 19,

the anniversary of her launch. There the ship has been restored in all its Brunelian glory, down to replicas of the original four-cylinder engines and boilers.

Rolt, *Isambard Kingdom Brunel*. Rowland, *"Great Britain."*

GREAT EASTERN

Paddle & screw steamship (5f/6m). *L/B/D:* 692′ × 82.7′ (117′ew) × 30′ (210.9m × 25.2m (35.7m) × 9.1m). *Tons:* 18,915 grt. *Hull:* iron. *Comp.:* 1st 200, 2nd 400, steerage 2,400. *Mach.:* oscillating steam engine driving sidewheels & horizontal direct-acting engine, 4,890 ihp, driving 1 screw; 13 kts. *Des.:* Isambard Kingdom Brunel. *Built:* Scott, Russell & Co. and Isambard Kingdom Brunel, Millwall, Eng.; 1858.

Isambard Kingdom Brunel's *Great Eastern* was the superlative ship of the nineteenth century. She was a ship of biblical proportions — contemporary observers pointed out that only Noah's 300-cubit ARK was bigger — and it was not until the OLYMPIC of 1899 that a longer ship was built. A ship of greater gross tonnage did not appear until the *Kaiser Wilhelm II* of 1903. The idea behind *Great Eastern* was a ship that could make the voyage out to Australia without having to stop for coal (the Suez Canal would not open until 1869), a concept that appealed especially to the newly formed Eastern Steam Navigation Company (later the Great Ship Company).

Isambard Kingdom Brunel's paddle and screw steamship GREAT EASTERN *of 1858, photographed at low tide. With four funnels, six masts, outsized paddle wheels and anchors, the leviathan dwarfs everything around her, especially the bluff-bowed trading schooner to the left of the paddle. Courtesy Peabody Essex Museum, Salem, Massachusetts.*

From the first, Brunel worked on the project with the gifted but less scrupulous marine engineer and ship-builder John Scott Russell, who described the ship as "a museum of inventions" and who was awarded the contract to build the vessel on the Isle of Dogs in the Thames. As in his earlier ships, Brunel made sure that the ship had great longitudinal strength and the hull was double-hulled throughout, a fact that saved the ship in 1862 when an unmarked reef off Montauk, New York, tore an 85-by-5-foot gash in the outer hull. (It is not true that a riveter was accidentally shut into the ship's double bottom.) In addition, the ship was designed with bulkheads that divided her into ten watertight compartments. *Great Eastern*'s propulsion machinery included both side paddles and a single screw; with diameters of 56 feet and 24 feet, respectively, these were the largest marine paddles and screw ever built. While this combination was dictated by the limits of engine efficiency of the time, the paddles and screw gave the ship a maneuverability that was invaluable in her eventual career as a cable layer. The sidewheels and propeller were driven by separate engines, too, the sidewheels by a four-cylinder oscillating steam engine built by Russell, and the screw by a four-cylinder horizontal direct-acting engine built by James Watt & Company.

The extraordinary dimensions of the ship dictated that she be built on an inclined way parallel to the river so that she could be launched sideways. Russell's financial incompetence nearly destroyed the project, and only through direct supervision did Brunel bring it to completion, though the effort is said to have killed him. Despite Brunel's reluctance, circumstances dictated that the ship be launched on November 3, 1857, and though it was first attempted on that date, she did not take the water until January 31, 1858. Fitting out lasted until September 1859. In failing health, Brunel was again forced to oversee Russell's work. During trials on September 5 — four days before Brunel's death — there was a disastrous explosion, and repairs forced the postponement of *Great Eastern*'s maiden transatlantic voyage until June 1860.

Great Eastern made ten voyages in the North Atlantic passenger trade, but two accidents (neither of them fatal) that cost the company £130,000 forced her out of that trade, and in 1864 she was sold to the newly formed Great Eastern Steamship Company. After alterations, including the removal of one set of boilers and one funnel, *Great Eastern* embarked on a career as a cable-laying ship. The first transatlantic cable had failed shortly after it had been laid down by HMS Agamemnon and USS Niagara in 1858, and when American inventor Cyrus Field visited England in connection with his plan, Brunel reported-ly pointed to *Great Eastern*'s unfinished bulk and said, "There is your ship."

Under charter to the Telegraph Construction Company, on June 24, 1865, *Great Eastern* lay off southern Ireland with 7,000 tons of cable and 500 crew, including Field. After the European end of the cable was laid near Valentia, Ireland, by the smaller HMS *Caroline, Great Eastern* sailed in company with HMS *Terrible* and *Sphinx*. On August 2, three-quarters of the way to Newfoundland, the cable broke and after several failed attempts to recover it, *Great Eastern* returned to Ireland. Undaunted, the Atlantic Telegraph Company had already ordered 1,990 miles of new cable, and after some alterations to her gear, *Great Eastern* sailed again from Valentia on Friday, July 13, 1866. Twelve days later, in Heart's Content, Newfoundland, communications between Europe and North America had dropped from one month to a few minutes. By the end of August, *Great Eastern*'s crew had recovered the submerged cable from the 1865 expedition, and spliced it to a cable running from Newfoundland. By the end of her career, *Great Eastern* had laid a total of five transatlantic cables, and one between Bombay, Aden, and Suez.

In 1874, she was sold to a French company that sought to use *Great Eastern* for first-class passenger service between New York and France, but the project was abandoned after one voyage. Laid up in Milford Haven from 1875 to 1886, she was sold for use as an exhibition ship in Liverpool. She was broken up at Henry Bath & Sons two years later.

Beaver, *Big Ship*. Clarke, *Voice across the Sea*. Dugan, *Great Iron Ship*. Emmerson, *John Scott Russell*. Rolt, *Isambard Kingdom Brunel*.

GREATER BUFFALO

(later USS *Sable*) Passenger steamer. *L/B*: 519′ x 58′ (158.2m × 17.7m). *Tons*: 6,564 disp. *Hull*: steel. *Comp*.: 1,500. *Mach*.: sidewheels. *Des*.: Frank E. Kirby. *Built*: American Shipbuilding Co., Lorain, Ohio; 1924.

Among the largest and most important American night boat services was the Detroit & Cleveland Navigation Company, which had its beginnings in the Detroit & Cleveland Steamboat Line of 1850. The D & C reached its zenith during the boom in Great Lakes shipping following World War I. Although the line already had a number of impressive night boats in operation, in the early 1920s it ordered *Greater Buffalo* and *Great Detroit*, the largest paddlewheel ships ever built with the exception of Isambard Kingdom Brunel's Great Eastern, which was also fitted with a single screw. *Greater Buffalo* and *Great Detroit* were about 15 percent larger than either the D & C's *Greater Detroit III* or the Fall River Line's largest boat, *Commonwealth,* and they carried more than 1,500 overnight passengers on the 260-mile run across Lake Erie between Buffalo and Detroit. The ships' short peak season lasted only about ten weeks a year, and this combined with their large size made them especially vulnerable to the huge drop in passenger traffic during the Great Depression. They remained in operation with heavy losses until 1938, when they were laid up. After the start of World War II, *Greater Buffalo* was requisitioned by the Navy for use as the training carrier USS *Sable.* Thousands of naval aviators trained on her decks until her decommissioning in November 1945. She was sold for scrap in 1948.

Hilton, *Night Boat.* U.S. Navy, *DANFS.*

GREAT GALLEY

Galleasse (4m). *L/B/D:* ca. 180′ (gundeck) × 34′ × 15′ dph (54.9m × 10.4m × 4.6m). *Tons:* 800. *Hull:* wood. *Comp.:* 800–1,200. *Arm.:* 70 brass guns, 147 iron guns. *Built:* Greenwich, Eng.; 1515.

One of the largest English ships of her day, and one of England's last oared warships, *Great Galley* was built during the reign of Henry VIII, five years after the launch of MARY ROSE. As described by Venetian ambassadors, whose letters form the first written account of the ship, she was as large as one of their first-rate galleys, with 120 oars (60 to a side) and four masts, three with topmasts and topsails, and the main with a topgallant mast and sail. Her complement was considerable by modern standards. The Venetians credit her with 60 gunners and 1,200 fightingmen, while French accounts credit her with 800 fighting men. The number of *Great Galley*'s brass and iron guns varied over the years. She seems to have been launched with 217 guns, 14 of them big guns mounted aft. In 1540 she carried 87 guns, while eight years later she carried 97. The inventory of 1540 demonstrates the variety of armament. Her brass guns included five cannons, two demy culveryns, four sakers, and two falcons, while iron guns numbered twelve port pieces, two single slings, fifty double bases, and ten single (or small) bases.

Great Galley remained in the Thames until war with France was renewed in 1522. Assigned to a fleet commanded by Sir William Fitzwilliam, she was not a success and was given a rebuild at Portsmouth that resulted in what was virtually a new ship. The next year Fitzwilliam wrote that "brigandine intends to break her up and make

her carvel" planked, rather than clenched, "for she was the dangerous ship under water that ever man sailed in." The ship underwent a second rebuild in 1536–37, emerging as *Great Bark.* (There is some confusion because of the tendency for different names to be applied to the same vessel, and the same name to different vessels.) This vessel probably took part in an expedition to Scotland in 1544. Her name appears on a number of ship lists until 1562, and she was probably broken up sometime between then and 1565.

Anderson, "Henry VIII's *Great Galley."*

GREAT REPUBLIC

Clipper (4m). *L/B/D:* 302′ × 48.4′ × 29.2′ dph (92m × 14.8m × 8.9m). *Tons:* 4,555 om; 2,751 nm. *Hull:* wood. *Comp.:* 130. *Built:* Donald McKay, East Boston, Mass.; 1853.

As designed and constructed, Donald McKay's extreme clipper *Great Republic* was the largest merchant sailing ship ever built in the United States, measuring 335 feet long, 53 feet and 38 feet depth of hold, and a capacity of 4,555 gross tons by old measurement. In addition to her great size, *Great Republic* was also luxuriously furnished and appointed. Her launch was much anticipated both in the United States and England, and an estimated 30,000 spectators were on hand when she slid down the ways on October 4, 1853. Towed to New York, she loaded a cargo worth $300,000 for Liverpool. On December 26, just days before sailing, a fire broke out at a nearby bakery. Sparks from the burning building blew into the newly tarred rigging of the great ship, which was quickly ablaze from stem to stern. Though the masts were cut away and the ship scuttled, virtually all her upperworks were burned. McKay decided to take the insurance money and she was sold to A. A. Low & Brother.

Her new owners had the ship rebuilt at Sneeden & Whitlock of Greenpoint, New York. As reconfigured, she had only three decks rather than four, her capacity was reduced to 4,555 tons, and her rig considerably shortened from the 15,653 square feet of canvas in McKay's original plan. Originally intended for the Australia trade (as were McKay's JAMES BAINES, DONALD MCKAY, LIGHTNING, and CHAMPION OF THE SEAS), in 1855 she left New York for Liverpool with 52 crew under Joseph Limeburner, who wrote,

> The ship behaves nobly, and can easily make 400 miles in 24 hours. . . . The ship is tight and strong, and the best ship at sea I was ever in. You would hardly know that you were at sea in a heavy sea; she moves along easily, making no fuss, in fact,

splendidly, and steers like a boat in a pond; a boy can steer her easily.

After a brief charter to the French government to carry troops to the Crimea, in 1856–57 she sailed from New York to San Francisco in 92 days, posting several days runs of better than 400 miles and setting a record run from New York to the equator of 15 days, 19 hours. She remained in the California trade until the start of the Civil War, when in 1861 she was chartered by the federal government for use as a transport. Between 1862 and 1865 she made two more voyages to San Francisco. Under Nova Scotian ownership from 1865 to 1868, she was sold to the Merchants Trading Company of Liverpool in 1869 and renamed *Denmark*. On March 2, 1872, she was bound from Nova Scotia for London when she began leaking. Three days later, her crew were forced to abandon ship, and she sank off Bermuda.

Cutler, *Greyhounds of the Sea.* Howe & Matthews, *American Clipper Ships.* MacGregor, *British and American Clippers.*

Great Western

Paddle steamship (1f/4m). *L/B/D:* 236′ × 35.3′ (59.7′ew) × 16.6′ (71.9m × 10.7m (18.2m) × 5.1m). *Tons:* 1,340 grt; 2.300 net. *Hull:* wood. *Mach.:* side-lever direct-acting steam engine, sidewheels; 8.5

kts. *Des.:* Isambard Kingdom Brunel. *Built:* William Patterson, Bristol, Eng.; 1837.

The first ship built to designs by Isambard Kingdom Brunel, *Great Western* was the direct result of Brunel's suggestion to the company's directors, in 1835, that the Great Western Railway should extend its London–Bristol service to New York via a "steamboat." Although regular and reliable packet service between Europe and North America had been in place since 1816, it was all by sail, not steam. Though taken up by the company, the idea was considered sheer folly, as it was widely believed that the power — and hence its fuel, coal — required to drive a steamship varied in direct proportion to the size of the hull. It was Brunel who devised the elegant formula demonstrating that though a ship's capacity increases as the cube of the hull's dimensions, the power required to drive it increases only as the square of the dimensions.

Considerably larger than any vessel built in Europe, the first of Brunel's ships was built of oak, trussed with iron and wood diagonals, and with considerable attention paid to the longitudinal strength of the hull. (The largest Chinese ships of the fourteenth- and fifteenth-century Ming dynasty, including those of Zheng He's voyage to the east coast of Africa, easily exceeded 300 feet.) The ship's engines were the most powerful yet built, and their development was entrusted to the firm of Maudslay Sons and Field. Laid down on July 26, 1836, the ship was

J. Walter's painting of Isambard Kingdom Brunel's Great Western *of 1838, the first of Brunel's trio of "Great" ships. Courtesy Peabody Essex Museum, Salem, Massachusetts.*

launched on July 19, 1837, and proceeded to London, where Maudslay's 100-ton boilers and other machinery were installed. The proportions of *Great Western*'s accommodations were as noteworthy as her more technical aspects. The ship was designed to carry 148 passengers, and she boasted a main passenger saloon 75 feet long by 34 feet at its widest, again a superlative achievement. Although fitting out took until the following March, it was not for lack of motivation, for in the interim, two firms from Liverpool, Bristol's rival port, had entered the race to be first to offer regular steamship service to New York. These were the British & American Steam Navigation Company and the Transatlantic Steamship Company. The Liverpudlians had laid down or purchased ships for the purpose, but as neither would be ready in time to beat *Great Western,* they leased and modified the Irish Sea steamers Sirius and Royal William, respectively. As it happened, *Sirius* left London on March 28, 1838, three days before *Great Western,* bound for Cork.

Two hours after the ship set off down the Thames under Lieutenant James Hosken, RN, the heat from the boilers ignited the deck beams around the funnel. Hosken ran the ship aground, and Bruncl was nearly killed when a charred ladder into the boiler room gave way. Damage was minimal, however, and the ship sailed on the following tide, arriving at Bristol on April 2. After taking on supplies and bunkering, *Great Western* sailed for New York on April 8, with only seven passengers, more than 50 bookings having been canceled after news of the fire.

Great Western arrived at New York on April 23, scant hours after *Sirius,* which had left Cork on April 2. The smaller ship's crossing was four days slower, although Cork was a full day's steaming closer than Bristol. More important for establishing the feasibility of the undertaking, *Great Western* arrived with 700 tons of coal remaining in her bunkers. Although the great ship's landing was accompanied by the tragic death of the engineer, George Pearne, who was scalded to death, the American public was confident of the ship's safety, and the ship with 68 passengers arrived at Bristol 15 days out from New York. Over the course of the next eight years, *Great Western* made 67 crossings, with a best eastbound crossing of 13 days, 6 hours, and westbound 12 days, 9 hours.

In 1846, following the near loss of Great Britain, *Great Western* was sold to the Royal Steam Packet Company, and was engaged in the West Indies passenger trade out of Southampton, being requisitioned as a troop transport during the Crimean War. The ship was broken up at Castles' Yard, Millbank, in 1856–57.

Rolt, *Life of Isambard Kingdom Brunel.*

USS GREER (DD-145)

Wickes-class destroyer (4f/2m). *L/B/D:* 314.3′ × 30.9′ × 9′ (95.8m × 9.4m × 2.7m). *Tons:* 1,165 disp. *Hull:* steel. *Comp.:* 133. *Arm.:* 4 × 4″, 1 × 3″, 12 × 21″TT. *Mach.:* geared turbines, 24,000 shp, 2 screws; 35 kts. *Built:* William Cramp & Sons Ship and Engine Building Co., Philadelphia; 1918.

Named for Rear Admiral James A. Greer (1833–1904), USS *Greer* spent most of her first year of service in the Atlantic before assignment to the Pacific Fleet in 1919. Transferred to the Asiatic Fleet in June 1920, she cruised as far afield as Shanghai, China, Port Arthur, Russia, and the Philippines. Decommissioned in 1937 at Philadelphia, she was ready for sea again in October 1939, shortly after the start of World War II. In February 1940 she was assigned to the Neutrality Patrol, the intent of which was to keep European belligerents — especially German submarines — from conducting military operations within 300 miles of the American coast. This vaguely pro-England policy was later expanded to one of "all aid short of war," whereby U.S. destroyers escorted British convoys as far as Iceland. On September 4, 1941, *Greer* was en route by herself from Reykjavik to Argentia, Newfoundland, when she was attacked by *U-652.* The attack was not entirely unprovoked, as a British plane in contact with *Greer* had depth-charged the submarine. The undamaged *Greer* replied with nineteen depth charges over three hours. The attack was viewed as a legitimate pretext for ostensibly neutral American warships to shoot first. The U.S. entry into World War II was not long in coming. *Greer* remained on convoy duty in various parts of the Atlantic until 1944, when she was assigned to lighter duties. Decommissioned at Philadelphia in July 1945, she was sold for scrap that November.

U.S. Navy, *DANFS.*

LE GRIFFON

Brig. *Tons:* 45–60 tons. *Hull:* wood. *Comp.:* 34. *Arm.:* 5 guns. *Built:* René Robert Cavalier, Sieur La Salle; 1679.

Although French explorers had reached the western Great Lakes as early as 1634, they traveled in canoes or on foot. It was not until 1679 that René-Robert Cavalier de La Salle built the first sailing ship on the upper lakes, near the junction of Cayuga Creek and the Niagara River at the eastern end of Lake Erie in what is now New York State. Work was completed in midsummer and the brig was christened *Le Griffon,* for the heraldic device of the Comte de Frontenac, governor general of New France. On August 7, 1679, the ship set sail for the west in search of a water route to the Orient. The crew of thirty-four included La Salle and the Jesuit diarist Father Louis Hennepin. In three days *Le Griffon* crossed the length of Lake Erie and turned north into the Detroit River, Lake St. Clair, St. Clair River, and Lake Huron. After weathering a violent fall storm on Lake Huron, *Le Griffon* came to a Jesuit mission on Michilimackinac Bay, off the Straits of Mackinac, and proceeded from there to a trading post on the shores of Green Bay. There La Salle, Hennepin, and a few others left the ship, which was then loaded for the return voyage. On September 18, *Le Griffon* sailed for the east, but she was never seen again.

Braynard, *Famous American Ships*.

GRIPSHOLM

Liner (2f/2m). *L/B:* 574.6′ loa × 74.3′ (175.1m x 22.6m). *Tons:* 17,993 grt. *Hull:* steel. *Comp.:* 1st 127, 2nd 482, 3rd 948; crew 360. *Mach.:* motorship, 2 screws; 16 kts. *Built:* Sir W. G. Armstrong, Whitworth & Co., Ltd., Newcastle-on-Tyne, Eng.; 1925.

Built for Swedish-America Line's service between Gothenburg and New York, *Gripsholm* was the first motorship on the North Atlantic passenger run. Originally designed to carry immigrants to the United States, as immigration quotas tightened in the 1930s, her accommodations gradually changed to satisfy a more tourism-oriented clientele. In the winter months, she was used as a cruise ship between Europe and the West Indies.

Because Sweden remained neutral during World War II, *Gripsholm* and her running mate *Drottningholm* were placed under the authority of the International Red Cross and used for the transport of more than 25,000 civilian internees and prisoners of war between Europe and North America. To avoid misidentification by combatants on either side, SVERIGE (Sweden) was painted along the side of the hull and both ships were brightly illuminated at night.

In 1946, *Gripsholm* resumed regular passenger service. A major overhaul in 1949–50 reduced her passenger list to 976 in two classes, and she was fitted with a bulbous bow that increased her length to 179.8 meters (590 feet). In 1954, *Gripsholm* was sold to the Bremen-America Line and began service between Bremen and New York, via Gothenburg and Halifax. Renamed *Berlin* the following year, she was managed by Norddeutscher Lloyd and represented their first post-World War II transatlantic passenger service. In 1957 she was joined on this run by *Bremen* (ex-*Pasteur*). *Berlin* made her last voyage from New York to Bremerhaven in 1966 and was broken up at La Spezia the same year.

Bonsor, *North Atlantic Seaway*. Kludas, *Great Passenger Ships of the World*.

USS GROWLER (SS-215)

Gato-class submarine. *L/B/D:* 311.8′ x 27.2′ × 15.3′ (95m × 8.3m × 4.6m). *Tons:* 1,526/2,410 disp. *Hull:* steel; 300′ dd. *Comp.:* 66. *Arm.:* 10 × 21″TT; 1 × 3″. *Mach.:* diesel/electric, 5,400/2,740 shp, 2 screws; 20/8.5 kts. *Built:* Electric Boat Co., Groton, Conn.; 1942.

Commissioned under Lieutenant Commander Howard I. Gilmore in the spring of 1942, USS *Growler* (a species of largemouth bass and the third ship of the name) made her first World War II patrol off Dutch Harbor, Alaska, in late June. On July 5, she torpedoed three Japanese destroyers, sinking *Arare* and severely damaging the other two. Twelve days later she returned to Pearl Harbor to prepare for her second patrol, off Taiwan. Between August 25 and September 7 she sank four freighters by torpedoes or gunfire. After a refit, she sailed for the Solomon Islands to look for Japanese ships supporting forces at Guadalcanal, and she sank one ship in January. At about 0100 on February 7, *Growler* made a surface attack on a Japanese gunboat. As the gunboat turned to ram *Growler,* Gilmore turned his submarine to ram the Japanese vessel. Under heavy machine gunfire at point-blank range, the wounded Gilmore ordered *Growler* submerged without waiting to get him off the bridge. For his heroic sacrifice he was posthumously awarded the Medal of Honor.

Following repairs at Brisbane, *Growler* resumed her patrols around the Solomon and Bismarck Islands until ordered to the West Coast for repairs in November 1943. Reporting to Majuro, Marshall Islands, in April she formed a wolf pack with USS *Bang* and *Seahorse,* with which she sank one ship. Her next two patrols were as part of "Ben's Busters," a wolf pack named for *Growler*'s new Commander T. B. Oakley, and including USS *Sealion* and *Pampanito*. On September 12 they sank six ships — *Growler* was credited with the destroyer *Shikinami* and frigate *Hirado* — and returned to Fremantle with 150 Allied prisoners rescued from one of the stricken ships. On October 20, *Growler* left Fremantle in company with USS *Hake* and *Hardhead*. On November 8, the three subs attacked a Japanese convoy near the Philippines and *Growler* was apparently sunk by depth charges. (*Pampanito* survived the war to become a museum ship in San Francisco.)

U.S. Navy, *DANFS*.

USS GUADALCANAL (CVE-60)

Casablanca-class escort aircraft carrier. *L/B/D:* 512' × 65' (108.1'ew) × 22.5' (156.1m x 19.8m (32.9m) × 6.9m). *Tons:* 7,800 disp. *Hull:* steel. *Comp.:* 860. *Arm.:* 28 aircraft; 1 × 5", 16 × 40mm. *Mach.:* geared turbines, 16,000 shp, 2 screws; 19 kts. *Built:* Henry J. Kaiser Shipbuilding Co., Inc., Vancouver, Wash.; 1943.

Despite her name, which celebrates the site of the first major ground campaign by American forces in the Pacific theater of World War II, in the Solomon Islands, USS *Guadalcanal* achieved her greatest fame on the Atlantic. As flagship of Captain D. V. Gallery's antisubmarine Task Group 21.12 based at Norfolk, on her first mission she and her escort ships sank the German *U-544* northwest of the Azores (in 40°30'N, 37°20'W) eleven days out, on January 16, 1944. Continuing east, they replenished at Casablanca and returned to Norfolk. A second trip to North Africa was uneventful, but westward bound they sank *U-515* northwest of Madeira (in 34°35'N, 19°18'W) on April 9, when Lieutenant Commander Werner Henke scuttled his sub after a night of depth charging by *Guadalcanal* planes and destroyer escorts USS *Chatelain, Flaherty, Pillsbury,* and *Pope.* The next night they sank *U-68* with all hands northeast of Madeira in 33°24'N, 18°59'W.

Two weeks into the third patrol, on June 4, *Chatelain* located a U-boat northwest of Dakar and began a series of depth-charge patterns. The crew of *U-505* panicked. Her captain ordered her to the surface and the crew abandoned ship, in 21°30'N, 19°20'W. Gallery immediately ordered a boarding party from *Pillsbury* to enter and secure the submarine by closing the seacocks and trying to find and disarm any scuttling charges that had been set. Luckily, there were none, and Lieutenant A. L. David's crew managed to keep the submarine afloat. A towline was secured and TG 21.12 sailed for Bermuda, where they arrived on June 19. Kept secret for the duration of the war, this unique capture provided the Allies with invaluable information about the design, deployment, and operation of German U-boats.

Guadalcanal made three more patrols between June and October, but by late 1944, U-boat operations had been severely curtailed by the loss of the German bases in western France, and opportunities for even the most zealous antisubmarine force were few. From December 1944 to the end of the war, *Guadalcanal* served as a training ship to qualify pilots for carrier operations. Decommissioned at Norfolk in 1946, she was broken up at New York in 1959. In an odd twist of fate, her prize was preserved as a museum ship in Chicago.

Gallery, *Twenty Million Tons under the Sea.* Gröner, *German Warships.* U.S. Navy, *DANFS.*

GUADELOUPE

Paddle frigate (1f/2m). *L/B/D:* 187' od × 30.1' × 9' (57m × 9.2m × 2.7m). *Tons:* 878 disp; 788 bm. *Hull:* iron. *Arm.:* 2 × 68pdr, 2 × 24pdr. *Mach.:* 2 cyl, 180 nhp, sidewheels; 9 kts.. *Built:* Cammell, Laird & Co., Ltd., Birkenhead Iron Works, Birkenhead, Eng.; 1842.

The world's largest iron ship when built, *Guadeloupe* was built on speculation by John Laird, who intended to sell her to the Royal Navy. The Admiralty was not yet interested in iron warships of such size, and he eventually sold the ship to the Mexican Navy, which at that time was contending with the Texas secessionist movement. When *Guadeloupe* was laid down in 1836, the British were not interested in exploiting the use of iron in shipbuilding because they had not as yet devised a satisfactory way of correcting compass error in iron hulls. (Astronomer George Airey published an explanation of how to do this in 1839.) The ship entered service under command of Captain Edward Phillip Charlwood, a Royal Navy captain then on half pay in Britain's peacetime navy. Following two years of service, he provided British authorities with detailed observations on the advantages of iron over wood in warships. These included greater buoyancy, more room below decks because the hull was thinner and there were fewer frames, and watertight bulkheads. As a fighting ship, *Guadeloupe* provided a steadier gun platform for the two 68-pdr. pivot guns (mounted fore and aft), and when the hull was penetrated, the hole was clean and did not splinter as it did in wooden ships. Splinters and the resulting infection were a primary cause of death from combat in wooden ships.

Brown, "Paddle Frigate *Guadeloupe.*"

USS GUARDFISH

Gato-class submarine. *L/B/D:* 311.8' × 27.2' x 15.3' (95m × 8.3m × 4.6m). *Tons:* 1,256/2,410 disp. *Hull:* steel; 300' dd. *Comp.:* 61. *Arm.:* 10 × 21"TT; 1 × 3", 3 × mg. *Mach.:* diesel/electric, 5,400/2,740 shp, 2 screws; 20.25/8.75 kts. *Built:* Electric Boat Co., Groton, Conn.; 1942.

Among the U.S. Navy's most successful submarines, USS *Guardfish* was one of only three ships to receive two Presidential Unit Citations for service in World War II. Under Lieutenant Commander T. B. Klakring, she was the first submarine to patrol northeast of Honshu Island, Japan, where between August 22 and September 2 she sank five merchant ships. On her second patrol, in the Formosa Strait, she sank two more ships on October 21. *Guardfish*'s third patrol, in the Marshall Islands, brought her continued success including the destroyer *Hakaze.*

During her next three patrols, *Guardfish* undertook special operations, landing and embarking survey teams on Bougainville Island, surveying Empress Augusta Bay, and standing lifeguard duty for downed airmen; in addition, she sank three cargo ships and the destroyer *Umikaze*.

After a ten-week refit at San Francisco in the spring of 1944, she sailed under Captain W. V. O'Brien as part of a four-boat wolf pack known as the Mickey Finns. On her single most successful patrol, *Guardfish* severely damaged one freighter and sank four southwest of Formosa. Her tenth cruise was marred by the mistaken sinking of the salvage ship USS *Extractor* on January 24, 1945, with the loss of six of her seventy-nine crew. *Guardfish* ended the war as a training ship and spent twelve years as a naval reserve training ship before decommissioning in 1960. On October 11, 1961, she was sunk as a target during tests of a new generation of torpedo.

Roscoe, *U.S. Submarine Operations in World War II.* U.S. Navy, *DANFS.*

HMS GUERRIÈRE

5th rate 38 (3m). *L/B/D:* 155.8′ × 39.8′ × 12.8′ (47.5m × 12.1m × 3.9m). *Tons:* 1,092 bm. *Hull:* wood. *Comp.:* 284. *Arm.:* 16 × 32pdr, 28 × 18pdr, 2 × 9pdr. *Des.:* Lafosse. *Built:* Cherbourg; 1799.

The French Navy frigate *Guerrière* ("Warrior") was built during the consulate of Napoleon Bonaparte. In 1801 *Guerrière* escorted a troop convoy dispatched to quell the Haitian uprising led by Toussaint L'Ouverture, and she narrowly escaped capture by a British blockade on her return in 1803. Later engaged in commerce raiding against British shipping, in 1806 she was one of three frigates operating against the Greenland whale fisheries. Three British frigates were dispatched to the Shetland Islands to intercept the French, although HMS *Phoebe* and *Thames* returned prematurely. Captain Thomas Lavie's HMS *Blanche* (36 guns) sailed from the Downs, and at 1030 on July 18 they came in sight of *Guerrière* near the Faeroe Islands. Captain Hubert closed with *Blanche* until he

realized, too late, that she was not one of his ship's own consorts. *Blanche* sailed in pursuit and caught up with *Guerrière* at about midnight and loosed two broadsides before the Frenchmen could reply. After an hour's fight, *Guerrière* had lost her mizzen topmast and struck to the British, who had suffered only four wounded as against twenty dead and thirty wounded as well as heavy damage to the French ship.

Repaired and brought into the Royal Navy as a fifth rate frigate, during the War of 1812 she was assigned to the North American Station at Halifax. On July 17, 1812, she was in a squadron commanded by Captain Sir Philip Broke in HMS *Africa* (64) when it came upon the frigate USS CONSTITUTION off New Jersey. After a remarkable sixty-six hour chase in light winds, *Constitution* escaped. On August 19, a solitary *Guerrière* was cruising the Grand Banks south of Newfoundland in position 41°42′N, 55°48′W when she encountered *Constitution* a second time. Her arrogant captain, James Dacres, had issued a challenge to "U. States frigate *President . . .* or any other American frigate of equal force for the purpose of having a few minutes tete-a-tete" and he was quite pleased by the prospect of an engagement. Opening fire at long range, two of her shot bounced off the hull of *Constitution,* which thereafter was known as "Old Ironsides." Commodore Isaac Hull held his fire until he had closed to a range of less than half a pistol shot before he loosed his first broadside. Twenty-five minutes later, the dismasted *Guerrière* was wallowing in the heavy seas with seventy-eight dead and wounded compared with only seven dead and seven wounded aboard *Constitution.* *Guerrière*'s hull was so shattered that Hull ordered her blown up the next day. The unlucky *Guerrière* was thus the first major British unit lost to the U.S. Navy in the War of 1812. The *London Times* observed, correctly, "It is not merely that an English frigate has been taken, . . . but that it has been taken by a new enemy, an enemy unaccustomed to such triumphs, and likely to be rendered insolent and confident by them."

Allen, *Battles of the Royal Navy.* Roosevelt, *Naval War of 1812.*

H

HMCS Haida

Tribal-class destroyer (1f/1m). *L/B/D:* 377' × 36.5' × 26.5' (114.9m × 11.1m × 8.1m). *Tons:* 2,500 disp. *Hull:* steel. *Comp.:* 240. *Arm.:* 6 × 4.7" (3 × 2), 2 × 4", 1 × quad pompom, 2 × twin oerlikon; 4 × 21"TT; dc. *Mach.:* geared turbines, 44,000 shp, 2 screws; 36.5 kts. *Built:* Vickers-Armstrong, Newcastle-on-Tyne, Eng.; 1943.

Although built for the Canadian Navy, HMCS *Haida* did not enter home waters for more than a year after her commissioning. During that time, she sailed under command of Captain H. G. DeWolf, dividing her time between Arctic waters and the English Channel. After a relief expedition to Spitsbergen, beginning in November 1943 *Haida* was detailed to the treacherous Murmansk convoy run, and she accompanied Convoy JW-55B, in pursuit of which the German battlecruiser SCHARN-HORST was sunk on December 26. Throughout the spring of 1944, she was active in the English Channel during operations preparatory to the D-day invasion. On April 26, *Haida* sank the German fleet torpedo boat *T-29* north of Ile de Batz (in 48°53'N, 3°33'W), and three days later she drove ashore *T-27*, which had been damaged on

the 26th, on the coast of Brittany at Pontusval. The latter engagement was not one-sided and *Haida*'s sister ship *Athabascan* was sunk in the same engagement. On June 24, when in company with HMS *Eskimo*, she helped sink *U-971* south of Land's End in 49°01'N, 5°35'W. She subsequently operated along the French coast of the Bay of Biscay and English Channel, and on August 30, she escorted into Cherbourg the French cruiser *Jeanne d'Arc*, carrying fifty members of the French provisional government.

In late September, *Haida* sailed for Canada where she underwent a three-month refit, but by March 1945 she was operating in support of air attacks on merchant shipping along the coast of Norway.

Following the war, *Haida* took up patrol duties in eastern Canada around Labrador and Hudson Bay. After a three-year modernization, in 1952–53, she sailed for the Far East as part of the UN naval forces engaged in shore bombardment duty during the Korean War. Over the next decade, she remained in service in the Atlantic, taking part in NATO exercises in the Baltic, Atlantic, and Mediterranean, in addition to duty in home waters. Re-

The Tribal-class destroyers were among the most successful British-built escorts of World War II. HMCS HAIDA saw rugged duty as a convoy escort and on patrol in the English Channel during World War II, and in the western Pacific during the Korean War. In 1963 she was preserved as a museum at Toronto. Courtesy Norman Brouwer.

tired in 1963, she was preserved as a memorial and museum at Toronto.

Brouwer, *International Register of Historic Ships*. Johnson, *Bering Sea Escort*.

HALVE MAEN

Vlieboat (3m). *L/B/D:* 65′ lod × 17.3′ × 8′ (19.8m × 5.3m × 2.4m). *Tons:* 80 om. *Hull:* wood. *Comp.:* 17–20. *Built:* Verenigde Oostindische Compagnie (VOC), Amsterdam; 1608.

In the early 1600s, Dutch merchants decided to consolidate their efforts to expand trade to the East by forming the Verenigde Oostindische Compagnie (VOC, or United East India Company). Eager to find a short route to the Indies, they took up the search for a Northeast Passage. Shortly after the failed Barents expedition, the VOC contracted with the English explorer Henry Hudson "to search for a passage by the north around the north side of Nova Zembla, and . . . continue thus along that parallel until he shall be able to sail southward to the latitude of 60 degrees." An amendment to the contract enjoined Hudson "to think of no other route or passage, except the route around the north or northeast, above Nova Zembla. . . . If it cannot be accomplished at that time, another route will be the subject of consideration for another voyage."

The vessel chosen was the bark-rigged *Halve Maen,* a relatively flat-bottomed merchant vessel designed for the shallow waters around Vlieland and Texel at the mouth of the Zuyder Zee. The ship sailed on March 25, 1609, and after rounding the North Cape on May 5, she sailed into the Barents Sea. Two weeks later, Hudson abandoned his eastward search. Turning west, on the 21st the ship redoubled the North Cape. Rather than return to Holland, Hudson sailed for the Faeroe Islands, where he watered his ship before continuing west.

In early July *Halve Maen* encountered a fleet of French fishing boats on the Grand Banks off Newfoundland. On July 12 she was off Nova Scotia and a week later the crew landed at the southern end of Penobscot Bay, where they cut and stepped a new foremast. Turning south, they stopped at Cape Cod, which Bartholomew Gosnold had named during his 1602 visit in Concord. Continuing south and southwest, they arrived off the mouth of Chesapeake Bay on August 18. Although the Jamestown settlement — founded two years before on the James River — was known to Hudson, he did not enter the bay.

On August 27 they were at the mouth of the Delaware (or South) River and seven days later anchored off Sandy Hook. Relations with the Indians were generally good, although one of the ship's company was killed while exploring lower New York Bay on September 5. The surroundings were bountiful, and Hudson wrote that "it is as pleasant a land as one need tread upon; very abundant in all kinds of timber suitable for shipbuilding, and for making large casks or vats." On September 13, *Halve Maen* began a four-day, 147-mile ascent of the North (or Hudson) River as far as the site of present-day Albany. North of that, the river had a maximum depth of only seven feet. Of the surrounding countryside Hudson observed,

> The land is the finest for cultivation that I ever in my life set foot upon, and it also abounds in trees of every description. The natives are very good people, for when they saw that I would not remain, they supposed that I was afraid of their bows, and taking the arrows, they broke them in pieces, and threw them into the fire.

Turning south on September 23, the ship's mate killed an Indian who tried to steal some clothes out of the stern cabin. A more serious incident off Manna-hata (Manhattan) on October 2 resulted in the death of four or five Indians who attacked the ship.

On October 4, *Halve Maen* sailed out of New York Bay and after thirty-three days at sea landed at Dartmouth, England. Hudson's decision to stop in England has led some to speculate that he was actually in the pay of English merchants to whom he intended to report his findings. In the event, *Halve Maen* was kept at Dartmouth until after Hudson had sailed on his next and last expedition in search of the Northwest Passage in Discovery. In 1610, *Halve Maen* was returned to the VOC, together with the ship's papers, though the Dutch crews' reports had already spurred Holland to establish trading posts in the Great River of the Mountains, as Hudson's mate Robert Juet described the Hudson River.

In 1611, *Halve Maen* was dispatched to the East Indies under command of Captain Laureus Reale. Her subsequent fate is not known with certainty, and various reports indicate that she was wrecked off Mauritius in the same year, that she was lost off Sumatra in 1616, or that she was burned at Sumatra by the British in 1618. Two important replicas of *Halve Maen* have been built. The first was built in the Netherlands for the Hudson-Fulton Celebration in New York in 1909, and the second by the New York–based New Netherland festival.

Asher, *Henry Hudson the Navigator*. Hendricks, "Construction of the 1988 *Half Moon*." Johnson, *Charting the Sea of Darkness*.

HAMILTON

(ex-*Diana*) Schooner (2m). *L/B:* 73′ × 20′ (22.3m × 6.1m). *Tons:* 112 grt. *Hull:* wood. *Comp.:* 50. *Arm.:* 1 × 32pdr, 1 × 24pdr, 8 × 6pdr. *Built:* Henry Eagle, Oswego, N.Y., 1809.

Built for Matthew McNair of Oswego, *Diana* was one of several schooners acquired for Captain Isaac Chauncey's Lake Ontario squadron during the War of 1812. Armed and renamed *Hamilton,* in honor of Navy Secretary Paul Hamilton, she joined Chauncey's squadron at Sackett's Harbor, New York, in late October. Under Sailing Master Joseph Osgood, she took part in the attacks on Kingston on November 9, 1812, York (now Toronto) on April 27, 1813, and Ft. George, on the Niagara River, on May 27. On the night of August 8, she was overwhelmed in a squall with the loss of all but four of her crew; the schooner SCOURGE was also lost. In 1973, the *Hamilton* and *Scourge* Foundation of Hamilton, Ontario, located the two schooners at a depth of 300 feet. Photographs showed both vessels to be in a remarkable state of preservation.

Cain, *Ghost Ships.* Nelson, "*Hamilton* and *Scourge.*" Roosevelt, *Naval War of 1812.*

HMS HAMPSHIRE

Devonshire-class armored cruiser (4f/2m). *L/B/D:* 475′ × 68.5′ × 25.3′ (144.8m × 20.9m × 7.7m). *Tons:* 10,750 disp. *Hull:* steel. *Comp.:* 655. *Arm.:* 4 × 7.5″ (4 × 1), 6 × 6″, 2 × 12pdr, 17 × 3pdr; 2 × 18″TT. *Armor:* 6″ belt, 1.5″ deck. *Mach.:* triple expansion engines, 21,000 ihp, 2 screws; 22.5 kts. *Built:* Sir W. G. Armstrong, Whitworth & Co., Ltd., Newcastle-on-Tyne, Eng.; 1905.

Designed primarily for commerce protection, *Hampshire* served in home waters and the Mediterranean before being assigned to the China Station in 1912. At the outbreak of World War I, she was one of the three largest British ships in the Pacific. Deployed to hunt for the commerce raider SMS EMDEN, *Hampshire* almost caught the German cruiser at Diego Garcia. After *Emden* was sunk in November, *Hampshire* was reassigned to the Grand Fleet. Present at the Battle of Jutland on May 31, 1916, the Second Cruiser Squadron to which she was attached saw little action.

Less than a week later, she embarked Britain's Minister of War, Field Marshall Earl Kitchener of Khartoum, and his staff, who were en route to Murmansk for negotiations with their Russian counterparts to keep the Eastern Front from collapsing. On the afternoon of June 5, HMS *Hampshire* and destroyers HMS *Unity* and *Victor* sailed from Scapa Flow and then up the west side of Orkney Island. In the face of gale force winds, Captain Herbert Savill ordered the escorts back to Scapa. The week before Jutland, *U-75,* a long-range submarine commanded by Lieutenant Commander Kurt Beitzen, had laid thirty-four mines in the channels west of Orkney. Owing to the weather, the area had not been swept since then. When *Hampshire* was abreast of Marwick Head, she struck at least one mine and sank fifteen minutes later with the loss of 655 people including Kitchener; there were only twelve survivors.

Halpern, *Naval History of World War I.*

HANCOCK

Frigate (3m). *L/B/D:* 136.6′ × 35.5′ × 11.5 dph (41.6m × 10.8m × 3.5m). *Tons:* 750. *Hull:* wood. *Comp.:* 290. *Arm.:* 24 × 12pdr, 10 × 6pdr. *Built:* Jonathan Greenley & John & Ralph Cross, Newburyport, Mass.; 1776.

One of the thirteen original frigates ordered by the Continental Congress in 1775, *Hancock* was named for John Hancock, president of the Continental Congress from 1775 to 1777. Under command of Captain John Manley, she sailed with the frigate *Boston* (24 guns) on May 21, 1777. After capturing a small merchant ship on the 29th, the following day *Hancock* was chased by HMS *Somerset* (64), which only gave up when *Boston* attacked the convoy of transports she was guarding. On June 21, the two ships took on HMS *Fox* (28), which struck after losing her mainmast. After several days repairing their prize, Manley's squadron resumed cruising off the New England coast. On July 6 they were chased by HMS *Rainbow* (44) and *Victor* (10). By the following morning HMS *Flora* (32) joined the chase, at which point the Americans split up. *Fox* was retaken by *Flora* and *Hancock* by *Rainbow; Boston* escaped.

Taken into the Royal Navy as HMS *Iris,* the Massachusetts-built ship was well admired by her captors who described her as "the finest and fastest frigate in the world." Four years later she captured the American TRUMBULL (24) before being captured by the French at the Battle of the Virginia Capes, on September 11, 1781. After active service in the French Navy, *Iris* was hulked at Toulon, where she was blown up by the British on December 18, 1793.

Chapelle, *History of the American Sailing Navy.* U.S. Navy, *DANFS.*

HANNAH

Schooner (2m). *L/B/D:* ca. 61′ × 17′ × 8′ (18.6m × 5.2m × 2.4m). *Tons:* 78 bm. *Hull:* wood. *Arm.:* 4 × 4pdr. *Built:* Marblehead, Mass.; <1775.

John Glover's fishing schooner *Hannah* is commonly accorded the honor of being the first vessel armed and paid for by the Continental Congress during the American Revolution, and thus with the genesis of the American Navy. The truth is somewhat less certain. *Hannah* was the first hired on the authority of the Continental Army's General George Washington. Put under command of Army Captain Nicholson Broughton, and crewed by men from John Glover's Marblehead regiment, she sailed on September 5, 1775. The next day she seized the small sloop *Unity,* with a cargo of naval stores and other provisions. She sailed again at the end of the month, but she was run aground while fleeing from HMS *Nautilus,* a 16-gun sloop, near Beverly, Massachusetts, on October 10. Saved from destruction by spirited resistance from local patriots, she was soon decommissioned by Washington, who had meanwhile hired vessels more appropriate to the Army's needs.

Fowler, *Rebels under Sail.* Miller, *Sea of Glory.*

USS HARDER (SS-257)

Gato-class submarine. *L/B/D:* 311.8′ × 27.2′ × 15.3′ (95m × 8.3m × 4.6m). *Tons:* 1,526/2,424 disp. *Hull:* steel; 300′dd. *Comp.:* 60–80. *Arm.:* 10 × 21″TT; 1 × 3″. *Mach.:* diesel/electric, 5,400/2,740 shp, 2 screws; 20/8.5 kts. *Built:* Electric Boat Co., Groton, Conn.; 1942.

Named for a species of South Atlantic mullet, USS *Harder* had one of the most brilliant careers of any American submarine in World War II. Her first two patrols were in Japanese home waters where, operating alone, she sank four cargo ships. On her third departure from Pearl Harbor, she sailed in company with her sister ships USS *Pargo* and *Snook* for the Mariana Islands. She sank an escort trawler on November 12, 1943, and a week later she accounted for three cargo ships in one night, whereupon she returned to Mare Island, California.

After several weeks of repairs, *Harder* was dispatched to the Caroline Islands with the task of rescuing downed American airmen. On April 1, 1944, she nosed into a reef off Woleai Island, and several of her crew took a raft onto the beach to rescue an injured pilot. Twelve days later, she sank the destroyer *Ikazuchi* in an action summarized by Commander Samuel D. Dealey: "Expended four torpedoes and one Jap destroyer." Following a three-week lay-

over at Fremantle, on May 26 *Harder* sailed with USS *Redfin* in search of Japanese destroyers in the Celebes Sea north of Borneo. On the night of June 6, she attacked a convoy and sank the destroyer *Minatsuki;* the next day *Hayanami* suffered a similar fate. On the night of June 8, still in the same waters, she sank the destroyer *Tanikaze* and probably one other. Two days later, while investigating a Japanese force including three battleships and four cruisers, *Harder* torpedoed an unidentified destroyer in another one-on-one engagement. This rash of activity by one submarine is credited with upsetting the Japanese battle plan for what became the Battle of the Philippine Sea: Vice Admiral Jisaburo Ozawa's First Mobile Fleet was forced to sail from the anchorage at Tawi Tawi earlier than intended.

On her sixth patrol, "Hit 'em" *Harder* sailed on August 5 in a wolf pack with USS *Hake* and *Haddo* for the South China Sea. There they joined USS *Ray* for an attack that cost a Japanese convoy four cargo ships. *Harder*'s trio followed up the next day with the sinking of three frigates, and on August 23 sank the destroyer *Asakazi.* The following morning, while reconnoitering off Dasol Bay, Luzon, *Harder* was depth-charged by a minesweeper and sank with all hands.

Roscoe, *U.S. Submarine Operations in World War II.* U.S. Navy, *DANFS.*

USS HARRIET LANE

(later *Lavinia, Elliott Richie*) Aux. brigantine. *L/B/D:* 180′ × 30′ × 12.5′ dph (54.9m × 9.1m × 3.8m). *Tons:* 639 grt. *Hull:* wood. *Comp.:* 130. *Arm.:* 4 × 9″, 4 × 32pdr, 9″ pivot gun, 20pdr pivot gun. *Mach.:* inclined, direct-acting engine. *Built:* William H. Webb, New York; 1857.

Designed as a revenue cutter, *Harriet Lane* was named for President James Buchanan's niece, who served as the bachelor president's unofficial First Lady. Originally based out of New York, the ship fired the first shot of the Civil War as she tried to stop a ship inward bound to Charleston on the night before the bombardment of Fort Sumter, on April 12, 1861. Transferred to the U.S. Navy on September 17, she saw duty along the East Coast before being transferred to the West Gulf Blockading Squadron, which took Galveston on October 4, 1862. On New Year's Day 1863, Major General John B. Magruder recaptured Galveston and, in the process, *Harriet Lane,* which was rammed by the Confederate "cottonclad" steamers *Bayou City* (Captain Henry S. Lubbock) and *Neptune* (Captain W. H. Sangster). Five crew were killed,

A lithograph captioned "Surprise and Capture of the United States Steamer HARRIET LANE, *by the Confederates under General Magruder, and the Destruction of the Flagship* WESTWARD*" at Galveston, Texas, on New Year's Day, 1863. Courtesy U.S. Naval Historical Center, Washington, D.C.*

including Commander Jonathan M. Wainwright, and twelve wounded. *Harriet Lane* was sold and converted to a blockade-runner renamed *Lavinia* in 1864. Sunk at Havana on January 18, 1865, she was raised and rerigged as the ship *Elliott Richie,* remaining in service until wrecked off the Pernambuco River in 1884.

Frazier, "Cottonclads in a Storm of Iron." Yanaway, "United States Revenue Cutter *Harriet Lane.*"

USS HARTFORD

Screw sloop (1f/3m). *L/B/D:* 225′ × 44′ × 17.2′ (68.6m × 13.4m × 5.2m). *Tons:* 2,900 disp. *Hull:* wood. *Comp.:* 310. *Arm.:* 20 × 9″, 20 × 20pdr, 2 × 12pdr. *Mach.:* horizontal double-piston rod engines, 1,204 ihp, 1 screw; 13.5 kts. *Built:* Harrison Loring, Boston; 1859.

USS *Hartford's* first assignment was as flagship of the East India Squadron under newly appointed Flag Officer Cornelius K. Stribling, charged with safeguarding U.S. interests in the Philippines, China, and elsewhere in Asia. Ordered home following the start of the Civil War, *Hartford* fitted out at Philadelphia and sailed at the end of 1861 as flagship of Flag Officer David G. Farragut's West Gulf Blockading Squadron. Although the operations of the Union high command embraced the coast from Pensacola, Florida, to Texas, their primary objective was the capture of New Orleans, the first city of the South. Farragut marshaled his forces at Ship Island, off Biloxi, Missis-

sippi, and his deep-water ships crossed the Mississippi River bar in April. Forts St. Philip and Jackson were engaged by Commodore David Porter's mortar schooners and steam gunboats for a week before *Hartford* led the advance past the Confederate batteries on April 24. Nearly rammed by the ironclad CSS *Manassas,* she then ran aground trying to avoid a fireship that landed alongside her near Fort St. Philip. The fires were extinguished, and *Hartford* fought her way upriver. Subsequent resistance was negligible, and New Orleans all but surrendered on April 25.

Farragut's next objective was to secure the Mississippi River. Baton Rouge and Natchez fell easily before the Union fleets. But with its 200-foot-high bluffs crowned by Confederate batteries, Vicksburg, Mississippi, was all but impregnable. Leaving a gunboat force below the city, *Hartford* and the other Union ships returned to New Orleans at the end of May. With orders direct from President Abraham Lincoln, Farragut's force returned to Vicksburg on June 26, and then ran the gauntlet to join the Western Flotilla above Vicksburg on June 28. A month later *Hartford* sailed for Pensacola, via New Orleans, for repairs.

Returning in November, Farragut blockaded the Red River, south of Vicksburg, while General Ulysses S. Grant moved overland to take Vicksburg from the rear. On March 14–15, *Hartford* and *Albatross* ran past Confederate batteries at Fort Hudson, Louisiana, and patrolled between there and Vicksburg, which finally fell on July 4, followed by Fort Hudson, which capitulated on the 9th. In Lincoln's felicitous words, "The father of waters again goes unvexed to the sea" — the Confederacy had been cut in two. Despite the fact that Mobile was, after New Orleans, the Confederacy's largest port, other operations received priority and Farragut's squadron was relegated to blockade duty for the remainder of 1863. *Hartford* returned to New York for an overhaul in August, and was not fit for sea again until January 1864.

In June, *Hartford* was off Mobile with a flotilla reinforced with monitors and ironclads to counter the Confederate ironclad TENNESSEE. The Battle of Mobile Bay finally opened at dawn on August 5. The monitors advanced past Fort Morgan, followed by USS *Brooklyn* at the head of the Union fleet until she fell out of line, and *Hartford* took the lead. Although Farragut's oft-quoted "Damn the torpedoes; full speed ahead" is apocryphal, he was lashed to the rigging, and by leading his column across the Confederate minefield, he quickly got his ships well into Mobile Bay and out of range of Fort Morgan. The only remaining obstacle was *Tennessee,* which at 0845 commenced an attack on Farragut's ships. In the brawl

Two views of the screw sloop USS HARTFORD, *flagship of Admiral David G. Farragut's West Gulf Blockading Squadron. The photo shows her riding at anchor in Mobile Bay in 1864. The lithograph shows the* HARTFORD'*s crew serving a 20-pound gun during her close engagement with the ironclad* CSS TENNESSEE. *Courtesy U.S. Naval Historical Center, Washington, D.C.*

that followed, the Union ships poured fire on the impervious ironclad and attempted to ram her, doing more damage to themselves. Finally, at 1000, with her tiller chains shot away, *Tennessee* was compelled to surrender. The forts surrendered by August 23, 1864. Although the war was over before Mobile fell, as a blockade-runner's haven the port was finished.

Hartford returned to New York for repairs in December 1865 and that July was sent out as flagship of the Asiatic Squadron, with which she served two tours of duty, 1865–68 and 1872–75. In 1887 she became a training ship based at Mare Island, California. Laid up from 1890 to 1899, she resumed work as a training ship in the Atlantic until 1912, when she was moored at Charleston, South Carolina, as a station ship. In 1938 she was moved to Washington, D.C., and after World War II transferred to Norfolk Navy Yard as a "relic." In 1956, she foundered at her berth and was broken up.

Jameson & Sternlicht, *Black Devil of the Bayous.*

USS HATTERAS

(ex-*St. Mary's*) Sidewheel steamer (1f/3m). *L/B/D:* 210′ bp × 34′ × 18′ (64m × 10.4m × 5.5m). *Tons:* 1,126 bm. *Hull:* iron. *Comp.:* 126. *Arm.:* 4 × 32pdr, 1 × 20pdr. *Mach.:* beam engine, 500 hp, sidewheels; 8 kts. *Built:* Harland & Hollingsworth Co., Wilmington, Del.; 1861.

Laid down as a merchant steamship, *St. Mary's* was purchased from her builders by the U.S. Navy in September 1861. Assigned to the South Atlantic Blockading Squadron at Key West, on January 7 she raided Cedar Keys harbor where she sank seven Confederate blockade-runners and burned the railroad wharf. Transferred to Farra-

gut's West Gulf Blockading Squadron on January 26, she engaged CSS *Mobile* the next day, and over the course of the year captured seven runners, including the sloop *Poody,* which Commander George F. Emmons brought into the squadron as *Hatteras Jr.*

On January 6, 1863, *Hatteras,* now under Commander Homer C. Blake, was assigned to blockade duty off Galveston. On January 11, she gave chase to a square-rigger about twenty miles south of the port. When challenged, the ship replied that she was the British *Spitfire.* But as a boarding party approached the ship, her Captain Raphael Semmes broke the Confederate flag and opened fire. *Hatteras* and CSS ALABAMA fought at close quarters for forty minutes before *Hatteras* began to sink. She had lost two dead and five wounded; the remainder of the crew were taken aboard *Alabama* and paroled at Port Royal, Jamaica. *Hatteras* sank in about nine fathoms.

Silverstone, *Warships of the Civil War Navies.* U.S. Navy, *DANFS.*

HMS HAVOCK

"A"-class destroyer (1f/2m). *L/B/D:* 180' × 18.5' × 6.7' (54.9m × 5.6m × 2m). *Tons:* 240 disp. *Hull:* steel. *Comp.:* 42. *Arm.:* 1 × 12pdr, 3 × 6pdr; 3 × 18"TT. *Mach.:* triple expansion, 3,554 ihp, 2 screws; 26 kts. *Built:* Yarrow & Co., Ltd., Poplar, Eng.; 1893.

One of the least heralded developments in nineteenth-century naval warfare was that of the free-running torpedo. Although the compressed air–driven torpedo, developed in 1866 by Robert Whitehead and Austrian Navy Captain Giovanni Luppis, carried only an 18-pound charge at a speed of 6 knots, it was quickly understood that the torpedo was a potent and inexpensive weapon that could easily sink even the strongest ironclad battleships. To increase the offensive power of these short-range weapons, navies developed lithe, fast torpedo boats capable of launching their torpedoes and getting away quickly.

To counter this threat to their battlefleets, European naval powers began developing vessels variously described as torpedo-boat "catchers," "hunters," and "destroyers." Initial designs proved unsuitable for fleet operations on the high seas. In 1892, newly appointed Third Sea Lord Rear Admiral John A. "Jackie" Fisher directed the development of a new class of seagoing "Torpedo Boat Destroyer," six of which were ordered: *Havock* and *Hornet* from Yarrow, *Daring* and *Decoy* from Thornycroft, and *Ferret* and *Lynx* from Lairds. *Havock*'s and the other vessels' trials were a great success. Although *Havock* was sold for breaking up in 1912, several first-generation destroyers were among the 221 in the Royal Navy at the start of World War I.

March, *British Destroyers.*

HAWAIIAN ISLES

(later *Star of Greenland, Abraham Rydberg, Foz do Douro*) Bark (4m). *L/B/D:* 270' × 43.1' × 23.5' (82.3m × 13.1m × 7.2m). *Tons:* 2,179 grt. *Hull:* steel. *Built:* Charles Connell & Co., Ltd., Glasgow; 1892.

Hawaiian Isles was built for A. Nelson of Honolulu to sail under the Hawaiian flag in the sugar trade between Hawaii and South America. She changed hands in 1900, when Welch & Company of San Francisco purchased her (bringing her under the American flag), and again in 1906 when she passed to the Matson Navigation Company. Three years later she joined the Alaska Packers Association fleet as *Star of Greenland* and sailed for seventeen years between San Francisco and the Alaska canning fisheries. Laid up for three years, in 1929 she was acquired

by the Swedish Abraham Rydberg Foundation (Rydbergska Stiftelsen) as a replacement for their steel ship, *Abraham Rydberg.* (The Foundation's second sail-training ship was built in 1912 by Bergsunds M.V. Aktieb, Stockholm. In 1928 she was sold to an American for use as a private yacht named *Seven Seas.*) Captain Sune Tamm sailed her to Dublin with a load of barley for the Guinness brewery, and she was then given a Liverpool house amidships to accommodate forty cadets; her gross tonnage increased to 2,345. Now called *Abraham Rydberg,* she joined the grain trade between Australia and Europe. Following the outbreak of World War II, she sailed between South America and the United States. In 1943 she was sold to Julio Ribeiro Campos of Oporto and traded between Portugal and South America. Given auxiliary diesel engines in 1945, she was gradually down-rigged until she ceased to be a sailing ship. Ten years later she was laid up, and in 1957 she was broken up at La Spezia.

Colton, *Last of the Square-Rigged Ships.* Underhill, *Sail Training and Cadet Ships.*

HAWAI'ILOA

Polynesian voyaging canoe (2m). *L/B/D:* 57' × 19' (17.4m × 5.8m). *Tons:* 17,725 pounds. *Hull:* wood. *Comp.:* 12. *Des.:* Dick Rhodes, Rudy and Barry Choy. *Built:* Wright Bowman, Jr., Honolulu, Hawaii; 1993.

Named for the legendary Polynesian voyager who first discovered the Hawaiian Islands some 2,000 years ago and is the ancestor to all native Hawaiians, *Hawai'iloa* is a replica of the traditional voyaging canoes used by Polynesian islanders in their settlement of Oceania. The largest such canoe built in the twentieth century, *Hawai'iloa* has two hulls shaped from Alaskan spruce logs. (Larger Hawaiian canoes were often made of drift logs that washed ashore on the islands.) The hulls are joined by seven crossbeams fashioned from 'Ohio logs and each hull is built up of koa wood. The sole source of power is two V-shaped sails. Built to reenact the long-distance voyages of the Polynesians, *Hawai'iloa* is navigated by the traditional practice of "wayfinding." This is based on an intimate knowledge of such natural phenomena as the movements of the sun and stars, wind and wave patterns, the color of the sky, and seamarks, including birds or fish with particular attributes.

On February 6, 1995, *Hawai'iloa* embarked on her first major voyage from Hawaii to Papeete, Tahiti, a distance of 2,400 miles covered in less than 22 days. The voyage out was made in company with the Polynesian Voyaging Society's first vessel, the 62-foot *Hokule'a* ("Star of glad-

It was in just such lithe, small vessels as the wishbone-sailed HAWAI'ILOA *that early Polynesians peopled the widely spaced islands of the Pacific. Courtesy Bishop Museum, Honolulu.*

ness," the Hawaiian name for the star Arcturus), built in 1976. They then sailed to Raiatea, 150 miles east of Tahiti, for a gathering of traditional craft; the other vessels were the Hawaiian *Makali'i,* the Maori *Te 'Aurere,* and the Cook Islanders *Te 'Au o Tonga* and *Takitumu.* Following a rededication of the temple of Taputapuatea, a primary center of Polynesian voyaging 600 years ago, the canoes sailed from the Society Islands northeast to Nukuhiva in the Marquesas Islands (thought to be where Hawai'iloa originally came from) and then back to Hawaii. *Hawai'iloa*'s second major voyage came in the summer of 1995 when, again in company with *Hokule'a,* she sailed to the Pacific Northwest for a reunion with the Tlingit and Haida of southern Alaska who donated the spruce logs for *Hawai'iloa*'s hull.

Finney, *Voyage of Rediscovery.*

HD-4

Hydrofoil. *L/B:* 60′ × 5.8′ (15.2m × 1.8m). *Comp.:* 1. *Mach.:* Liberty V-12 airplane engines, 700hp, 2 propellers; 70.86 mph. *Des.:* Alexander Graham Bell, Casey Baldwin. *Built:* Baddeck, Nova Scotia; 1917.

Although Alexander Graham Bell is justifiably best remembered for his work in developing the telephone, he was also interested in powered flight. His investigations in aviation led him, in turn, to consider ways to apply the principles of engined flight to a surface vessel. Working with his colleague Frederick W. "Casey" Baldwin at Beinn

Bhreagh, his home in Baddeck, Nova Scotia, he began designing a boat that could transport heavy loads at high speeds. The driving force was provided by propellers, but they had to overcome the resistance through water, which is denser than air. The best way to achieve this was to bring the vessel out of the water in order to reduce drag, which they accomplished by attaching sets of winglike surfaces — called hydrofoils — to the bottom of the hull. As the boat gathered speed, the water passing around the wings would create lift, in the same way that air creates lift as it passes over an airplane wing. As the vessel was raised out of the water, the resistance lessened, enabling it to go faster still, until it rested only on the bottom tier of wings and the hull was completely out of the water.

Bell and Baldwin developed their ideas through a number of working models and smaller towed boats, but World War I provided further impetus for their research, which they hoped to apply to high-speed sub chasers armed with torpedoes and depth charges. Although the project had to be privately financed by Bell's wife, Mabel, the U.S. Navy provided Bell with two 250-horsepower, 12-cylinder Renault airplane engines fitted with twin-bladed propellers that drove the vessel in excess of 50 miles per hour. Trials with the fourth full-size hydrodrome (Greek for "water runner") began in August 1918. The body of the vessel consisted of a cigar-shaped hull that provided flotation when the vessel was at rest and accommodated the crew, fuel, and payload. The engines were mounted on two outriggers forward, to which were also attached two 20-foot-long floats that helped balance

The HD-4 was the fourth of Alexander Graham Bell's hydrodromes built on Lake Baddeck, Nova Scotia. On September 9, 1919, she established a speed record of 70.86 miles per hour. Courtesy Library of Congress.

the narrow hull. Impressed by the success of the *HD-4*, the Navy furnished Bell and Baldwin with two 350-horsepower, V-12 Liberty engines that drove two four-bladed propellers but weighed 800 pounds less than the Renaults. On September 9, 1919, *HD-4* attained the unprecedented speed of 70.86 miles per hour on Lake Baddeck. This remained an uncontested record for many years. Baldwin continued to experiment with hydrodromes following Bell's death in 1922, but it was not until after World War II that hydrofoils, as they are known today, became commercially viable, used chiefly as high-speed passenger ferries. Today the *HD-4* is preserved at the Alexander Graham Bell Museum in Baddeck, Nova Scotia.

Alexander Graham Bell National Historic Site, Baddeck, N.S.

HMS HECLA

Hecla-class bomb vessel (3m). *L/B/D:* 105′ × 28.5′ × 13.8′ (32m × 8.7m × 4.2m). *Tons:* 372 bm. *Hull:* wood. *Comp.:* 67. *Arm.:* 1 × 13″ mortar, 1 × 10″ mortar, 8 × 24pdr, 2 × 6pdr. *Des.:* Sir Henry Peake. *Built:* Barkworth & Hawkes, North Barton, Hull, Eng.; 1815.

Launched one week after the surrender of Napoleon Bonaparte at Waterloo, Belgium, on July 15, 1815, HMS *Hecla* was designed for war but was born at the start of the near-century-long *Pax Britannica*. Although there were few opportunities for men or ships in the peacetime navy, such heavily constructed bomb vessels (her sister ships included HMS Erebus, *Sulphur,* and *Fury*) were ideally suited for voyages of exploration, and in 1819 *Hecla* was fitted out for an Arctic expedition under William Edward Parry, who had sailed as second in command to John Ross's expedition with Isabella and *Alex-*

ander the year before. Chief among his assignments was to determine whether Lancaster Sound was open, of which Parry was certain, or only an inlet, as Ross believed. Parry sailed from Yarmouth on May 11, 1819, with the ships *Hecla* and *Griper* on the first of his three voyages to the Arctic. By August 1, the two ships were completely through Lancaster Sound, which separates Baffin and Devon Islands, and after a detour south into Prince Regent Inlet, they continued through and named Barrow Strait and Melville Strait as far as 112°51′W. They backtracked a little to Winter Harbour, at the southern end of Melville Island, and on September 22 settled in for the winter. Parry's men suffered no unusual hardship, and in the spring Parry led a two-week expedition to Melville Island, north to the shore of Hecla and Griper Bay, and then south again via the head of Liddon Gulf. On August 1, 1820, they left Winter Harbour and continued west as far as 113°46′W (August 15) and named the land to the southwest in honor of Sir Joseph Banks. The ships returned to England at the end of October and Parry was lionized for having traversed half of the Northwest Passage. The next ship to make it so far west in one season would be the 940-foot icebreaker tanker Manhattan, in 1969.

Parry was adamant in his belief that "should another Expedition be determined on, the attempt must be made in a lower latitude; perhaps about Hudson's or Cumberland Straits." He further cautioned that "*because* so great has been our late success, . . . nothing short of the entire accomplishment of the North-West Passage in to the Pacific will satisfy the Public." Nonetheless, in May 1821 *Hecla* and her sister ship *Fury* sailed for Hudson Bay, annually visited by ships of the Hudson's Bay Company, but seldom explored. The ships traversed Hudson Strait and turned northwest along the coast of Baffin Island and across Foxe Channel to the southern end of Melville Peninsula (nearly 600 miles southeast of Melville Island of the year before). After exploring around Southampton Island, they wintered at Winter Island. The next spring, Parry resumed the search for the Northwest Passage, bringing his ships to the northern end of Foxe Basin where the perennially frozen Hecla and Fury Strait leads west into the Gulf of Boothia. A second winter near an Eskimo settlement on Melville Peninsula brought the English into close contact with the Eskimos, from whom they learned the use of sled dogs and Arctic survival techniques, and who were also able to draw rough maps of the region. Parry's men also conducted scientific observations. The persistence of ice in Hecla and Fury Strait and the onset of scurvy persuaded Parry to return to England in 1823, and the ships arrived in the Shetland Islands in October.

No sooner had he returned than plans were forwarded for a third expedition. Before sailing, Parry was made Acting Hydrographer of the Navy, and more than 6,000 people visited *Hecla* when she was open to the public at Deptford until her next departure, on May 8, 1824. Parry's third expedition returned him to Lancaster Sound, but rather than continue due west, once past the Brodeur Peninsula (the western arm of Baffin Island), they were to turn south into Prince Regent Inlet. This was a bad year for ice, however, and the ships were beset for two months before they entered Lancaster Sound. They resumed their westward progress again only to be caught in the ice at the head of Prince Regent Inlet and driven back almost to the mouth of Lancaster Sound. This ice broke up, too, and the ships sailed as far as Port Bowen, on the western shore of the inlet. During the winter there, they concentrated on the problem of magnetic variation. On August 1, 1825, the ships searched in vain for westward leads in the Gulf of Boothia and were driven ashore by the ice. The badly damaged *Fury* was unloaded and hove down for repairs. Before these could be finished, the ship was further damaged by ice and abandoned on August 25, at which point *Hecla* turned for England.

Though this was the last of *Hecla*'s voyages to the Canadian Arctic, in March 1827 Parry took her north again in an attempt to reach the North Pole. Anchoring *Hecla* at Sorgfjord in northern West Spitsbergen, on June 21 he set out with twenty-four men in two boats with provisions for seventy-one days. The ice conditions, heavy loads, and Spartan diet prevented them from making much progress, and the drifting ice was also pushing them south. On July 21, having reached 82°43′N, 19°21′E, they decided to abandon the effort about 500 miles from the Pole. They returned to *Hecla* and turned for home in August.

Over Parry's objections, *Hecla* was withdrawn from Arctic service and dispatched as a survey vessel to the coast of West Africa. She remained in service there through 1831, when she was sold.

Parry, *Journal of a Voyage for the Discovery of a North-West Passage...*; *Journal of a Second Voyage...*; *Journal of a Third Voyage...*; *Narrative of an Attempt to Reach the North Pole...*

HEEMSKERCK

Jacht (3m). *Tons:* 120 ton (60 lasts). *Hull:* wood. *Comp.:* 60. *Built:* VOC, Netherlands; <1638.

In August 1642, the expansionist Governor General of the Indies Anthonie Van Diemen ordered Abel Jansen Tasman and Franchoys Jacobsen Visscher "to discover the partly known and still unreached South and Easternland" (that is, Australia), not for the sake of geography or science, but specifically "for the improvement, and increase of the [Dutch East India] Comp[an]y's general welfare." Two primary aims were to determine whether there was a passage from the Indian Ocean to the Pacific Ocean — which would allow for an increase in trade with Peru and Chile — and to search for the elusive passage to the Pacific south of New Guinea. To undertake this mission, Tasman was given two vessels, the war jacht *Heemskerck* (named for a Dutch town), which had sailed out to the Indies in 1638, and the fluit, or transport, *Zeehaen.*

On August 14, 1642, the ships left Batavia for Mauritius, where they spent a month repairing *Zeehaen*'s rotten spars and rigging. On October 8, they sailed south to about 50°S before heading east. On November 17, they arrived off "Anthonie Van Diemensland" — Tasmania — where they landed several times and saw smoke, but no people, and claimed the land for the Netherlands and the Dutch East India Company. Unable to sail west through the Bass Strait, they turned east again and after eight days in the Tasman Sea came to the South Island of New Zealand, which Tasman thought a continuation of Staten Island off Cape Horn, some 5,000–6,000 miles to the east. Accordingly, they named it Statenland. Heading north, on December 18 four of the crew were killed by Maoris in Murderer's Bay. From here they sailed east and almost passed through Cook Strait, but adverse weather and seas prevented them from making this singular discovery of the Pacific. They tried but were unable to land near Cape Maria Van Diemen (named for the wife of the Governor General). They then headed northeast, believing themselves to have entered the Pacific — as indeed they had — at last. But Van Diemen disagreed, and wrote to the VOC that "whether on this longitude there now exists a passage through to Chile and Peru, as the discoverers are firmly convinced, is not so sure. . . . This is conjecture and should not be deduced from unfounded evidence."

On January 21, they provisioned at Tongatapu in the Tonga Archipelago. On February 1, they turned north and then west, when they narrowly missed losing their ships among the reefs of the Fiji Archipelago. Over the next seven weeks they sailed only 300 miles, but on March 22 they spotted Onthong Java. From here they followed Schouten and Le Maire's 1616 route in EENDRACHT. The voyage ended at Batavia on June 15, 1643. Although Tasman had established that the Southland — Australia — was an island, they knew nothing of the land per se, which was disappointing to the merchant directors of the VOC, who were eager for new markets.

[Tasman], *Abel Janszoon Tasman's Journal.* Sharp, *Voyages of Abel Janszoon Tasman.*

USS HELENA (CL-50)

Brooklyn-class cruiser (2f/2m). *L/B/D:* 608.3′ × 61.8′ × 22.8′ (185.4m × 18.8m × 6.9m). *Tons:* 12,207 disp. *Hull:* steel. *Comp.:* 868–1200. *Arm.:* 15 × 6″ (5 × 3), 8 × 5″, 18–28 × 40mm, 14–28 × 20mm; 4 aircraft. *Armor:* 5.6″ belt, 2″ deck. *Mach.:* geared turbines, 100,000 shp, 4 screws; 32.5 kts. *Built:* New York Navy Yard, Brooklyn, N.Y.; 1939.

Commissioned only two weeks after World War II began in Europe, USS *Helena* was assigned to the Pacific Fleet based at Pearl Harbor. On December 7, 1941, she was moored at a berth on battleship row normally assigned to USS *Pennsylvania.* Three minutes after the surprise attack began, *Helena* was hit by an aerial torpedo that passed under the minesweeper USS *Oglala* tied up alongside, and she settled on an even keel. After repairs in California, she sailed in support of U.S. operations on Guadalcanal in the late summer of 1942. Part of the task force formed around USS WASP, she took off almost 400 of the aircraft carrier's crew when she was sunk between Espiritu Santo and Guadalcanal on September 15. At the Battle of Cape Esperance on the night of October 11–12, *Helena* sank the cruiser *Furutaku* and destroyer *Fubuki.* The battle for Guadalcanal ground on through the fall, and *Helena*'s next major engagement was the Naval Battle of Guadalcanal, November 12–15. Though she was in the thick of the three-day action, which all but broke the Japanese effort to retake the island, *Helena* emerged little the worse for wear. Total American losses included the cruisers USS JUNEAU and *Atlanta* and four destroyers.

In the spring of 1943, *Helena* was among the U.S. forces detailed to bombard Japanese positions on New Georgia. As the U.S. invasion began at Kula Gulf on July 4, she provided gunfire support for the marine landings until called off to face a run of the Tokyo Express ferrying troops to the relief of Munda. One of three cruisers and four destroyers facing ten Japanese destroyers at 0157 on July 6, *Helena* opened the battle with a barrage so intense that the Japanese claimed she was armed with 6-inch machine guns. But the flash from her rapid fire made her an easy target for the destroyers, and within 10 minutes she had been struck by three torpedoes. She jackknifed and sank. Most of *Helena*'s crew was rescued by U.S. destroyers, but about 200 of her crew remained on the partly submerged bow. Later crowded into ship's boats and some life rafts dropped by rescue planes, these survivors drifted to the island of Vella Lavella where they were finally rescued on July 16. Of her 900 crew, 168 had died. *Helena* subsequently became the first ship honored with a Navy Unit Citation.

Ewing, *American Cruisers of World War Two.* U.S. Navy, *DANFS.*

HENRIETTA MARIE

Ship (3m). *L:* 60′ (18.3m). *Tons:* 120 tons. *Hull:* wood. *Comp.:* 18–20 crew. *Arm.:* 8 guns. *Built:* France?; <1697.

Probably named for the French wife of Charles I, *Henrietta Marie* is believed to have been a French merchantman captured during the War of the League of Augsburg (1689–97) between England, the Netherlands and their Protestant allies, and France. At war's end, the ship was sold and entered service in the lucrative triangular trade. This cartographic euphemism refers to the three-legged voyages that formed the basis of the hideous slave trade for English and colonial merchants. In addition to slaves, taken from Africa to Caribbean and North American ports, the cargoes included cheap trade goods from Britain, or iron and rum from the colonies, taken to Africa, and sugar and molasses taken to the merchants' home-ports, supplemented with fruit and hardwoods for England and hard currency for the colonies.

The most profitable leg of the three was the innocuous-sounding "Middle Passage," in which millions of people were shipped in chains from West Africa to the West Indies. Estimates of the total number of people shipped from Africa to South and North America during the three centuries of the slave trade range from ten to twenty million. Of the total, about 65 percent were shipped to Brazil, Cuba, Hispaniola, and Jamaica. About 30 percent went to other European colonies in the Caribbean and South America, and about 5 percent to Britain's North American colonies and the United States. Britain outlawed the trade only in 1807, followed the next year by the United States; however, it was not until the abolition of slavery, starting with Britain in 1833 and ending with Brazil in 1888, that the traffic in humans finally died out.

Henrietta Marie seems to have first sailed in the slave trade in 1697, sailing to West Africa under Captain William Deacon and unloading her human cargo in Barbados in 1698 before returning to London. In 1699–1700, she made roughly the same voyage under Thomas Chamberlain, offloading in Jamaica rather than Barbados. At the end of 1700, the little three-masted ship sailed for Africa for the third and last time. Embarking an estimated 400 people from throughout West Africa, *Henrietta Marie* began the forty-day crossing of the Atlantic. It is possible that she stopped briefly at Barbados to ship fresh water and supplies, but the majority of her slaves was sold at Jamaica. There she loaded 81 hogsheads (57 tons) of sugar and smaller amounts of logwood, cotton, and tobacco. Sailing for England in early spring, *Henrietta Marie* headed west to round Cuba before turning east again to head through the Strait of Florida. Unfortunately, the ship ran aground on a coral reef in the Dry Tortugas, west of the Florida Keys. There were no known survivors, and the wreck went unnoticed for 270 years.

In 1972, divers looking for the remains of NUESTRA SEÑORA DE ATOCHA located the remains of the *Henrietta Marie,* which they first identified by the presence of cannon and leg irons, some of which were designed specifically for children. Excavation on the site, known simply as the English wreck, didn't begin until 1983. In that year, the ship's bell was discovered. Inscribed "The Henrietta Marie 1699," this is believed to be a replacement watch bell. The positive identification of a ship whose history could be traced in contemporary records led to increased interest in her and the eventual recovery of thousands of artifacts and fragments. Because of its association with the slave trade, the site was of particular interest to African Americans, and in 1992 the National Association of Black Scuba Divers placed a marker at the site "In Memory and Recognition of the Courage, Pain and Suffering of enslaved African people: 'Speak her name and gently touch the souls of our ancestors.'"

Sullivan, *Slave Ship.*

HENRY B. HYDE

Down Easter (3m). *L/B/D:* 290′ × 45′ × 29′ dph (88.4m x 13.7m × 8.8m). *Tons:* 2,580 grt; 2,462 net. *Hull:* wood. *Comp.:* 34. *Des.:* John McDonald. *Built:* Chapman & Flint Co., Bath, Me.; 1884.

Named for the president of the Equitable Life Insurance Company and built for Flint & Company, of New York, the celebrated Down Easter *Henry B. Hyde* is considered to have been the finest American ship of the postclipper era. The largest ship built in Maine to that time, she was strongly found and cross-braced with iron straps throughout. Her average time over her first twelve passages from New York to San Francisco was a brisk 109 days. Her first master was the hard-driving Phineas Pendleton, Jr., who was succeeded by his son, Phineas III, for two voyages. The *Hyde* was sold with the rest of the Flint fleet to the California Shipping Company in 1899. On her first voyage for that company, under Captain W. J. McLeod, she loaded coal at Norfolk for Hawaii. A fire was discovered in her hold, and the *Hyde* put into Valparaiso where the cargo was discharged and partially reloaded. Two years later, en route from Baltimore to San Francisco, she was forced to put into Cape Town in the same condition. After completing her voyage and returning to New York, the *Hyde* was lost on February 19, 1904, while in tow from New York to load at Baltimore. She was driven ashore about ten miles south of Cape Henry; her crew was saved. She broke in two in October 1904.

Lubbock, *Down Easters.* Matthews, *American Merchant Ships.*

HENRY GRACE À DIEU

("Great Harry"; later *Edward*) Carrack (4m). *L/B:* ca. 175′–200′ main deck (125′–135′ keel) × 50′ (53–61m/38–41m × 15m). *Tons:* 1,500 bm. *Hull:* wood. *Comp.:* 700 (1536). *Arm.:* 43 heavy guns, 141 light guns. *Built:* Woolwich Dockyard, Eng.; 1514.

One of Henry VIII's more enduring achievements was his promotion of England's navy. His ambitious shipbuilding program saw the construction of, among others, MARY ROSE (1505), *Henry Grace à Dieu* (often known simply as "Great Harry"), and GREAT GALLEY (1513). One distinguishing characteristic of these ships was that they were built for war rather than as merchant ships that could be converted for martial purposes. The tonnage of the Great Harry is given variously as 1,500 tons and 1,000 tons; her linear dimensions have been inferred from these figures, the larger one yielding the approximate dimensions given above. Her armament consisted mainly of smaller-caliber brass and iron guns, but the large guns were mounted in the waist of the ship, which not only increased the ship's stability, but made the guns more effective against other ships, which could be more easily hulled at or below the waterline. The smaller-caliber guns were designed mainly for use against masts, rigging, and people, and were most effective mounted in the forecastle, which rose four decks high, and the sterncastle, which had two decks.

Although *Henry Grace à Dieu* was born of the continual wars between England and France, the period following her building was one of comparative peace, and she saw no action until 1545. During the French attack on Portsmouth in July of that year (during which the MARY ROSE sank) she was engaged by Admiral Claude d'Annebault's more maneuverable galleys. Upon the accession of Edward VI in 1547, she was renamed for that monarch. She remained in peacetime service until August 23, 1553 (the year of Edward's death), when she was destroyed by fire at Woolwich.

Laughton, "Report: The *Henry Grace à Dieu.*" Robinson, "The Great Harry."

HERALD OF FREE ENTERPRISE

Ro/ro passenger ferry. *L/B/D:* 432.5′ × 76.1′ × 18.7′ (131.9m × 23.2m × 5.7m). *Tons:* 7,951 grt. *Hull:* steel. *Comp.:* 1,300. *Mach.:* diesel, 24,000 bhp, 3 screws. *Built:* Schichau-Unterweser AG, Bremerhaven, Germany; 1980.

Owned and operated by Townsend Car Ferries, Ltd., *Herald of Free Enterprise* operated on the 70-mile run between Zeebrugge, Belgium, and Dover, England. On March 6, 1987, she had just passed the Zeebrugge breakwater when her car deck flooded, causing the ship to capsize in under a minute, at about 1925. Although the water was only 30 feet deep and more than half the ship was above the water, the disaster happened so quickly that 135 of the 543 passengers and crew were killed, making it the worst disaster in the history of English Channel ferry services. An investigation later blamed the sinking on an improperly closed bow door. Raised and renamed *Flushing Range,* she was broken up the following year.

Press reports. Crainer, *Zeebrugge.*

HERBERT FULLER

Barkentine. *L/B/D:* 158.3′ × 35.5′ × 18′ (48.2m x 10.8m × 5.5m). *Tons:* 781 grt. *Hull:* wood. *Comp.:* 10. *Built:* Harrington, Me.; 1890.

Originally rigged as a bark, the merchantman *Herbert Fuller* was owned by Swan & Son of New York. On July 3, 1896, now rigged as a barkentine, *Fuller* sailed from Boston to Rosario, Argentina, with a load of lumber and a single passenger, Harvard College student Lester B. Monks. Ten days out, on the night of July 13, Monks awoke to horrible screams and, leaving his cabin, found that Captain Charles I. Nash, his wife, and Second Mate August Blandberg had been murdered. The next morning, First Mate Thomas Bram ordered the arrest of Charles Brown, the helmsman at the time of the murders. But acting on the suspicions of the purser, Monks arranged for Bram to be seized and then took the ship to Halifax, the nearest downwind port, with the bodies of the three victims in a boat towed astern. The case riveted the country, and although it was found that Brown had once been jailed for attempted murder, the charges against Bram stood. Sentenced to hang at Boston, he appealed and was found guilty a second time, but sentenced to life in prison. Yet his supporters were many and persistent and in June 1919, President Woodrow Wilson granted Bram a full pardon, nine years after *Herbert Fuller* stopped trading under sail.

Tod, *Last Sail Down East.*

HERBERT L. RAWDING

Schooner (4m). *L/B/D:* 201.7′ × 38.5′ × 21.9′ dph (61,5m × 11.7m × 6.7m). *Tons:* 1,219 grt. *Hull:* wood. *Comp.:* 11. *Built:* Stockton Yard Inc., Stockton, Me.; 1919.

Built for a subsidiary of Crowell and Thurlow of Boston, *Herbert L. Rawding* was built in response to the increased freight rates generated by the heavy losses of commercial shipping during World War I. Named for one of Crowell & Thurlow's senior masters, her first voyage took her from Norfolk to the Canary Islands with coal, from there to Buenos Aires for general cargo, then to Lisbon, and back to Boston with salt. Thereafter she worked in the coastal trade on various routes between Nova Scotia and the Caribbean with cargoes as varied as gypsum, lumber, salt, and molasses. Sold to Lewis K. Thurlow in 1928, she continued in the same trade until the Great Depression forced her lay-up in 1931. Five years later she was acquired by Herman Baruch (brother of statesman Bernard Baruch), who sold her to Captain Robert W. Rickson the following year. She continued in the coastwise and West Indies trade under Rickson's command until he retired in 1940. *Rawding* made two more voyages to the West Indies before her acquisition by the Intercontinental Steamship Lines, Inc., a shady outfit that folded in 1944. Purchased in 1945 by Captain Alex Rodway, she made several voyages before Rodway installed two 350-horsepower diesel engines and removed her spanker mast. In January 1947, *Rawding* loaded lumber for Alexandria, Egypt, and Cyprus, which she delivered without incident. After loading a cargo of salt and bunker oil at Cadiz and Gibraltar, on June 10, 1947, she encountered a northeaster and began to leak. Her crew was rescued by the Liberty ship *Robert W. Hart,* and an hour and a half later, the last four-masted cargo schooner on the North Atlantic sank, about 500 miles west of Cape St. Vincent.

Bowker, *Atlantic Four-Master.*

L'HÉRÉTIQUE

Raft (1m). *L/B/D:* 15.4′ × 6.2′ × 1.6′ (4.7m × 1.9m × 0.5m). *Hull:* rubber. *Comp.:* 1. *Built:* M. Debroutelle, France; 1953.

In the early 1950s, French surgeon Dr. Alain Bombard became interested in the problems associated with survival at sea. Despair, he believed, is "a far more ruthless and efficient killer than any physical factor." Conversely, the morale of the shipwreck victim is as vital to survival as is the need for food and water. Analyzing the nutritional composition of seawater, plankton, and pelagic fish, Bombard determined that as a last resort, seawater can be drunk in small quantities for short periods, that plankton is a source of vitamin C, and that potable water — as well as protein — can be extracted from fish. Taking his experiments outside the laboratory, he set out on a transatlantic voyage in a rubber raft fitted with a single sail and named, in honor of his unorthodox methods, *L'Hérétique.*

Starting in southern France, he made a number of short passages before reaching the Canary Islands, which he departed from on October 18, 1952. Subsisting on raw fish, plankton caught in a fine net, and rainwater, Bombard confirmed that his biggest obstacle was not physical but mental. His body adjusted to its new diet, but to combat his solitude, he maintained a rigorous daily routine that included checking the raft for potential leaks, exercising, and writing up his log and a record of his pulse and blood pressure. Because of a colossal navigation error, Bombard underestimated his arrival in the West Indies by several weeks, which he only realized after a chance encounter with a British freighter when he was 53 days out from the Canaries and 600 miles east of Barbados. After 90 minutes aboard the *Arakaka*, during which he had a shower and a light meal (at which his body later revolted), he resumed his voyage. On December 22, he fetched up at Barbados.

After 65 days at sea, Bombard had lost 55 pounds, he was anemic, and he suffered from a variety of minor ailments from which he quickly recovered. He suffered from neither dehydration nor scurvy, the latter having been prevented by his intake of vitamin C in plankton. Bombard's voyage revolutionized the study of survival techniques worldwide, and he continued his research into the physiopathology of sailors. In recognition of Bombard's achievement, *L'Hérétique* was exhibited at the Musée de la Marine in Paris.

Bombard, *Voyage of the "Hérétique."*

HMS HERMES

Hermes-class aircraft carrier (1f/1m). *L/B/D:* 598′ × 70′ (90′ew) × 21.5′ (182.3m × 21.3m/27.4m × 6.6m). *Tons:* 12,900 disp. *Hull:* steel. *Comp.:* 660. *Arm.:* 15 aircraft; 6 × 5.5″, 3 × 4″, 4 × 3pdr. *Armor:* 3″ belt, 1″ deck. *Mach.:* geared turbines, 40,000 shp, 2 screws; 25 kts. *Built:* Sir W. G. Armstrong, Whitworth & Co., Ltd., Newcastle-on-Tyne, Eng.; 1924.

Laid down at the beginning of 1918 and not completed until 1924, HMS *Hermes* was the first ship designed from the outset as an aircraft carrier and not converted from another design either on the ways or after launching.

With a light, cruiserlike hull, she was relatively fast for her size and had an imposing island surmounted by a large tripod mast. Named for the messenger of the gods of Greek mythology, HMS *Hermes* was stationed in the Far East for virtually her whole career, except for two refits in 1927 and 1933–34. Recalled to the Home Fleet just prior to World War II, she remained in the Atlantic until 1942, when the Japanese began their push through Southeast Asia. Based at Ceylon, *Hermes* was damaged at Colombo on April 5, 1942, during a naval air attack launched from Japanese carriers. Two days later, she was at sea when dive-bombers from AKAGI, HIRYU, SHOKAKU, and ZUIKAKU found her off Batticaloa; she was sunk in 7°50′N, 81°49′E with the loss of 307, the survivors being rescued by the hospital ship *Vita*. In addition to *Hermes*, the two Japanese attacks resulted in the loss of the cruisers HMS *Dorsetshire* and *Cornwall*, destroyers HMS *Tenedos* and RAN *Vampire*, the corvette HMS *Hollyhock* and armed merchant cruiser *Hector*.

Beaver, *British Aircraft Carrier.*

HMS HERMIONE

(later *Santa Cecilia*, HMS *Retribution*) *Hermione*-class 5th rate 32 (3m). *L/B/D:* 129′ x 35.4′ × 15.3′ (39.3m × 10.8m × 4.6m). *Tons:* 717 bm. *Hull:* wood. *Comp.:* 170. *Arm.:* 26 × 12pdr, 6 × 6pdr, 12 swivels. *Des.:* Edward Hunt. *Built:* Teast, Tombs & Co., Bristol, Eng.; 1782.

The scene of "the most daring and sanguinary mutiny that the annals of the British Navy can recall," HMS *Hermione* was a Royal Navy frigate built during the tumultuous era of the French Revolutionary Wars. In this period, the Royal Navy was not only on guard against the navies of France and her allies, but there was growing disaffection within its own ranks, as indicated by the mutinies at Spithead and the Nore. Some of the sailors' discontent had spread to the more remote West Indies Station, where the pestilential climate was an enemy more feared than the French or Spanish. On February 6, 1797, *Hermione* came under command of Hugh Pigot, under whom the ship patrolled the Mona Passage between Santo Domingo and Puerto Rico in company with HM Brig *Diligence*. Pigot was a malevolent officer given to frequent, ruthless, and arbitrary punishment of his crew, who quickly grew to resent and fear his violent rages. At about 1800 on September 21, *Hermione* was struck by a squall and Pigot ordered the topsails reefed. As the men were not taking in sail fast enough to suit him, Pigot bellowed into the rigging that he would flog the last man down, and in their haste to avoid punishment, three of the youngest mizzentopmen slipped and fell to their deaths. Pigot ordered, "Throw the lubbers overboard," and when this provoked murmurs of disbelief from the twelve to fourteen men on the maintopyard, he ordered the bosun's mates aloft to flog them.

Shortly before midnight of the same day, the crew mutinied, and within a few minutes four men were dead: Pigot, two lieutenants, and a midshipman. At this point, surgeon's mate Lawrence Cronan assumed control of the mutiny and turned it from a more or less spontaneous act of vengeance into a vehicle for the aspirations of Irish republicans. Cronan's first recommendation was to kill all of the officers, and, although a number of them were eventually spared, the final death toll was ten. The mutineers appear to have numbered no more than sixty-two of the ship's company, and of these eighteen were considered ringleaders, chief among them bosun's mate Thomas Jay and seaman Thomas Leech, who had twice deserted His Majesty's ships only to return of his own volition.

The next day, the mutineers decided to sail for La Guaira, Venezuela, where they arrived on September 27. According to the governor's report, they claimed to have overthrown the tyrannical Pigot and set him adrift in the ship's launch, but the real story gradually leaked out. Its outline was well known to the captain of the Spanish schooner *San Antonio,* which sailed several weeks later only to be captured by *Diligence.* Word reached Sir Hyde Parker, commander of the West Indies squadron, who immediately ordered a hunt for the mutineers. By 1799, fifteen had been arrested and hanged, their rotting corpses displayed as a warning to others. Seven years later, the last of the twenty-four *Hermione* mutineers was executed.

In the meantime, the Spanish had renamed their prize *Santa Cecilia,* which they armed with 40 guns and manned with a crew of about 400 men. Her fate was in the hands of indecisive colonial bureaucrats for two years before it was decided to sail her to Havana. Shortly before her projected departure, on October 25, 1799, Captain Edward Hamilton led 100 men from his 28-gun frigate HMS *Surprise* and cut her out from under the 200 guns of Puerto Caballo. The British losses were a dozen men, as against about 100 Spanish dead. Admiral Parker ordered her renamed *Retaliation,* but he was overruled by the Admiralty and she became HMS *Retribution.* She returned to Portsmouth in 1802 but was paid off shortly thereafter; three years later she was broken up.

Pope, *Black Ship.*

HERO

Sloop (1m). *L/B/D:* 47.3′ × 16.8′ × 6.3′ (14.4m × 5.1m × 1.9m). *Tons:* 44 om. *Hull:* wood. *Built:* Groton, Conn.; 1800.

In 1819, the British sealer William Smith discovered the South Shetland Islands and their abundant rookeries of seals, whose pelts fetched high prices in China. Reports of the discovery spread quickly, and in the same year the first U.S. sealers sailed from Stonington, Connecticut. In 1820, the Americans returned with a fleet of five ships including Captain Nathaniel B. Palmer's *Hero,* whose crew included the discoverer and author Edmund Fanning. The ships were based at Deception Island, and after hearing reports of mountains to the south, the expedition leader Captain Benjamin Pendleton sent Palmer to investigate further. In November 1820, *Hero* sailed south and west until he approached what he took to be a contiguous, snow-capped landmass. There were no seals on the nearby islands, which made their further investigation unprofitable, and Palmer sailed for the South Shetlands. On his return he encountered the Russian navigator Baron F. G. B. Von Bellingshausen who was exploring the southern ocean in VOSTOK and *Mirny.* Bellingshausen later reported Palmer's discovery and gave Palmer's name to the land now known as the Antarctic Peninsula. *Hero* made a second voyage to the South Shetland sealing grounds in 1821–22, after which she was sold at Coquimbo, Chile.

Fanning, *Voyages around the World.* Stackpole, *Voyage of the Huron and the Huntress.*

HÉROS

3rd rate 74 (3m). *L/B/D:* 178.8′ × 46.2′ × 2.3′ (54.5m × 14.1m × 6.8m). *Tons:* 1,800 burthen. *Hull:* wood. *Arm.:* 28 × 36pdr, 30 × 18pdr, 16 × 8pdr. *Des.:* J. M. B. Coulomb. *Built:* Toulon, France; 1778.

Although France began aiding the nominally independent United States in 1776, it was not until February 6, 1778, that a definitive alliance was forged. Britain quickly declared war against France, and she was soon at war with Spain and the Netherlands, too. A conflict that had been confined to North America quickly expanded to include European possessions in the Caribbean, the Mediterranean, and the Indian Ocean. In 1781, the British dispatched a squadron under Commodore George Johnstone to capture the Dutch colony of South Africa. On the way, they were shadowed by a French squadron under Vice Admiral Pierre André, Bailli de Suffren, who had left France at the same time as Comte de Grasse, whose fleet would force the surrender of General Charles Cornwallis in September. In mid-April, the sixteen British ships were taking on water and supplies at Porto Praya, Cape Verde Islands, when Suffren appeared off the port. His squadron included his flagship *Héros,* another 74-gun ship, and three 64s. Both sides were surprised by the chance encounter, and Suffren's attack was poorly executed by his captains. Nonetheless, he was able to reach the Cape before Johnstone, and he prevented the English from seizing the strategic Dutch colony.

Continuing to the French outpost at Ile de France, upon the death of Commodore Comte d'Orves in February, Suffren assumed command of the French naval forces in the Indian Ocean. His fleet of three 74s, seven 64s, and two 40s reached the coast of Madras, in the Bay of Bengal, a week later. There they sighted the fleet of Vice Admiral Sir Edward Hughes, whose flagship was HMS *Superb* and who commanded in all two 74s, one 68, five 64s, and one 50. The English position was complicated by a war with Hyder Ali, Sultan of Mysore, and by the fact that they hoped to defend the Ceylonese port of Trincomalee, which they had just taken from the Dutch.

On February 17, 1782, the French and English met in an indecisive action off Madras. In April, the British were joined by HMS *Sultan* (74) and *Magnanime* (64), which made the two fleets nearly equal, although the British retained the advantage of having access to better ports and supplies. On April 12, Suffren bore down on Hughes as the latter sailed for Trincomalee. The Battle of Providien (off Ceylon) was hotly contested, and the opposing fleets suffered roughly equal casualties — 137 dead on both sides, though the English had slightly more than and the French slightly less than 400 wounded. (The Battle of Providien was fought the same day that, half a world away, the British fleet under Admiral Sir George Rodney defeated de Grasse at the Battle of the Saintes.) The two fleets were too exhausted to continue fighting, and Hughes sailed for Trincomalee while Suffren made for Batacalo, to the south of the English-held port.

In June, the two fleets sailed north, the French to Cuddalore, which had fallen to Hyder Ali, and the English to Negapatam. On July 5, they met off the latter port; Suffren had only eleven ships, as one had been partially dismasted the day before. Casualties were again heavy — 77 English dead, to 178 French — and the capture of two French ships was only narrowly averted. In mid-August, Suffren was reinforced by two new ships at Batacalo, and moving with prodigious speed he laid siege to Trincomalee, which fell on August 31. Two days later, Hughes appeared off the port, now with fourteen ships under his command. As ever, *Héros* was in the thick of the fighting,

and she and the *Illustre* lost their main and mizzen masts, but Hughes failed to press home his advantage. Owing to the onset of the winter monsoon, this was the last battle of the year. Hughes took his fleet to Bombay, on the west coast of India, and Suffren, deprived of adequate supplies at Trincomalee, sailed east for the Dutch port at Acheen, on the island of Sumatra. In the interval, he had lost the *Orient* (74) and *Bizarre* (64) in accidents.

Although the Peace of Versailles had been signed by the following spring, this was not known; yet the strategic picture in the east had changed dramatically. Hughes now had eighteen ships of the line, including the *Gibraltar* (80), to Suffren's fifteen. Moreover, the French ally Hyder Ali had died, and the British decided to retake Cuddalore. Suffren appeared off the port on June 13, 1783. A week of fickle winds prevented either side from engaging, but on June 20 Suffren attacked. The fighting was general, and though no ships were seriously damaged, casualties were high, both sides losing about 100 men dead and 400 wounded. Nonetheless, Suffren had at last won a tactical and strategic victory, his chief object having been to prevent the loss of Cuddalore. Four days later, the frigate HMS *Medea* arrived with news that peace negotiations were under way, and the French and British agreed to end hostilities.

Suffren quit India in *Héros* in October, returning to a hero's welcome in France via Ile de France and the Cape of Good Hope. At the Cape Colony he was met by the captains of six of Hughes's ships, who readily acknowledged his brilliant conduct of a two-year campaign in which he never wavered in pressing home his attack, despite the disadvantages of undermanned ships and inadequate supplies. "The good Dutchmen have received me as their savior," Suffren wrote, "but among the tributes which have most flattered me, none has given me more pleasure than the esteem and consideration testified by the English who are here."

At the start of the French Revolution, *Héros* was at Toulon when royalist officers opened the port to the British Mediterranean fleet under Vice Admiral Sir Samuel Hood. When the British quit the port in December 1793, *Héros* was burned, along with many other ships.

Clowes, *Royal Navy.* Mahan, *Influence of Sea Power upon History.*

HERZOGIN CECILIE

Bark (4m). *L/B/D:* 310′ × 46′ × 24.7′ (94.5m × 14m × 7.4m). *Tons:* 3,242. *Hull:* steel. *Comp.:* 100 approx. (training ship); 22–30 (merchant ship). *Built:* Rickmers Reismühlen Rhederei & Schiffbau AG, Bremerhaven, Germany; 1902.

The "Duchess" was one of the last ships to trade under sail. Here she is lying at anchor at the end of a long voyage. Courtesy National Maritime Museum, Greenwich.

Following the success of their first sail-training ship *Herzogin Sophie Charlotte* (the former merchant ship *Albert Rickmers*), the Norddeutscher Lloyd Steamship Company launched a second, purpose-built sail-training vessel, named for Wilhelm II's prospective daughter-in-law, Herzogin Cecilie von Mecklenburg-Schwerin. *Herzogin Cecilie* — the Duchess — became the most celebrated sailing ship of her day. Built to carry a professional crew of about 23, and 60 trainees, in 1912 she was refitted to carry as many as 90 cadets and her poop was lengthened from 175 feet to 194 feet. *Herzogin Cecilie* plied the familiar routes of the last days of sail, outward bound from Bremerhaven with mixed cargoes, and homeward bound from the Americas or Australia with grain, nitrate, or timber. The Duchess was a smart sailer, and in her first trip out to Chile, under Max Dietrich, in 1904, she was within three days of the five-masted ship PREUSSEN. Dietrich was succeeded by Otto Walther in 1908, and he, in turn, by Dietrich Ballehr, who commanded *Herzogin Cecilie* throughout her long internship in Chile during World War I, first at Guayacan (where she arrived July 25, 1914) and later Coquimbo, where she sat from 1919 to 1920. She finally sailed for Ostend with nitrate, only to be handed over to France for reparations, and subsequently sold, in 1921, to Gustaf Erikson, of Mariehamn, Åland Islands.

In January 1922, the erstwhile training ship sailed with a crew of twenty-six under Reuben de Cloux (an Åland ship master of Belgian ancestry), with Norwegian timber for Melbourne. So began the most illustrious half of her life, in the twilight of merchant sail, as she battled Cape Horn with bulk cargoes of grain, timber, nitrate, and coal coke. The most celebrated member of her crew was able seaman Alan Villiers, whose account of the voyage from Port Lincoln to Falmouth in 1928 is a classic of sea writing. At the conclusion of this passage, the Duchess made her first voyage to her homeport of Mariehamn. De Cloux left the following year and was replaced by Sven Eriksson.

Despite the great economy of cargo carrying under sail, *Herzogin Cecilie* felt the effects of the Great Depression and in the 1930s she began carrying passengers. One of them, Pamela Bourne, married Eriksson and sailed with him on the Duchess's last voyages, which were nonetheless not happy ones. After returning from Port Lincoln and discharging grain at Belfast, two of her crew were killed when a donkey engine exploded. Following repairs at Belfast and Nystad, *Herzogin Cecilie* sailed from Copenhagen on October 15, 1935, and collided with the steamer *Rastede* three nights later. After a quick passage out to Port Lincoln and loading a record 4,295 tons of grain, she was back at Falmouth in eighty-six days, on April 23, 1936. That night she sailed for Ipswich, but due to navigational errors and a heavy fog, at 0350 she grounded on Ham Stone Rock and drifted onto Bolt Head. The loss was world news, and after much of the cargo and gear had been offloaded, she was refloated on June 19, only to ground again outside Salcombe Harbor. All plans to salvage the Duchess came to nothing, and she was later sold for scrap for £225. Her remains still lie in Starhole Bay, though many of her fine accommodations and fittings were saved and are housed in the Ålands Sjöfartsmuseum.

Eriksson, *Life and Death of the Duchess.* Greenhill & Hackman, "*Herzogin Cecilie.*" Villiers, *Falmouth for Orders.*

HESPER

Schooner (4m). *L/B/D:* 210.2' × 41' × 20.4' dph (64.1m × 12.5m × 6.2m). *Tons:* 1,348 grt. *Hull:* wood. *Comp.:* 11. *Built:* Crownin-shield Ship Building Co., South Somerset, Mass.; 1918.

Built for the firm of Rogers & Webb, Boston, *Hesper* was one of several four-masted schooners built for coast-wise trade during World War I, when shipping rates were driven up by the loss of steamships to German U-boats. Cheaply built and inexpensive to build, the big schooners remained profitable through the 1920s, until the Great Depression forced many of them to be laid up. *Hesper* was laid up at Rockport in 1928. In the early 1930s, Frank Winter purchased her and LUTHER LITTLE with the in-tention of reviving the port of Wiscasset, Maine, by homeporting the two cargo vessels there. His plans fell through and the two lay in the Sheepscot River until the 1900s, neglected and decayed, but clearly visible from the main road, Route 1.

Morris, *Four Masted Schooners of the East Coast.* Tod, *Last Sail Down East.*

HESPERUS

Ship (3m). *L/B/D:* 262.2' × 39.7' × 23.5' dph (79.9m × 12.1m × 7.2m). *Tons:* 1,777 grt. *Hull:* iron. *Built:* Robert Steele & Co., Greenock, Scotland; 1873.

The iron clipper *Hesperus* was built for Anderson and Anderson's Orient Line immigrant service between Eng-land and Australia. Described as a Queen of the Iron Age (of ships), she was built for safety and comfort, and though she was neither designed nor driven to be a rec-ord breaker, she was fast. After sixteen years in the immi-grant trade, *Hesperus* became one of the first ships ac-quired by Devitt & Moore to be used for training of merchant officers. With accommodations for twenty-five to forty cadets, in addition to her regular crew and pas-sengers, she sailed to Sydney in ninety-nine days. As a result of a long layover in the port, her apprentices wound up pawning many of their clothes and other be-longings, and, unable to retrieve them, satisfied them-selves with the theft of the pawnbrokers' three brass balls, which they set from the jibboom on their departure.

Hesperus made her last voyage to Australia in 1898–99. On her return, she was purchased by the Odessa Naviga-tion School and renamed *Grand Duchess Nicolaevna* (for the daughter of Czar Nicholas II). She worked as a sail-training ship in the Black Sea until after World War I, when she flew the flag of the Russian Republic. After a voyage between Montreal and Liverpool in 1920, re-counted in Frederick William Wallace's *Under Sail in the Last of the Clippers, Grand Duchess* was transferred to French registry. In 1921, she was sold to the London Steamship & Trading Corporation, Ltd., under the name *Silvana.* After one voyage to Argentina and France, she was sold for scrapping at Genoa in 1924.

Lubbock, *Colonial Clippers.* Wallace, *Under Sail in the Last of the Clippers.*

HIGHBORN CAY WRECK

L/B: ca. 62.3' × 18' (19m × 5.5m). *Tons:* ca. 100. *Hull:* wood. *Arm.:* 2 lombards, 13 swivels. *Built:* Lisbon(?); 16th cent.

Located in the Bahamas' Exuma Islands, the sixteenth-century Highborn Cay wreck site was first visited in 1965 by American amateur divers who removed and recorded briefly what artifacts they could. In 1983, archaeologists from Texas A & M's Institute of Nautical Archaeology relocated the site and began a more in-depth survey. Arti-facts found on the site include two lombards and thirteen swivel guns, rigging hardware, ship fastenings, and three anchors. One of the latter was found with the ballast pile, while the other two — including the heaviest sheet an-chor — were found 100 to 150 meters away, indicating that the ship was at anchor when she sank, possibly in a storm. The remains of the ship's hull were excavated in 1988. It is the earliest discovery-era ship for which the ac-tual dimensions of structural elements are known, in-cluding keel, keelson, stempost, frames, futtocks, and planking. Analysis of the physical evidence and relevant studies of contemporary shipbuilding technique suggest that the vessel was originally 19 meters long, with a beam of from 5 to 5.7 meters. Analysis of the ballast stone suggests the ship may have been built in Lisbon.

Oertling, "Highborn Cay wreck." Smith, et al., "Highborn Cay Wreck."

HIRYU

Soryu-class aircraft carrier. *L/B/D:* 745.9′ × 73.3′ × 25.8′ (229.2m × 22.3m × 7.9m). *Tons:* 20,250 disp. *Hull:* steel. *Comp.:* 1,100. *Arm.:* 73 aircraft; 12 × 5″, 31 × 25mm. *Mach.:* geared turbines, 153,000 shp, 4 screws; 34 kts. *Built:* Yokosuka Dockyard, Yokosuka, Japan; 1939.

Under Captain Tomeo Kaku, *Hiryu* ("Flying Dragon") was one of six carriers involved in the Japanese attack on Pearl Harbor on December 7, 1941; the others were AK-AGI, KAGA, SORYU, SHOKAKU, and ZUIKAKU. She later took part in the capture of Wake Island (December 27). During the campaign for the Dutch East Indies in early 1942, she participated in attacks on Rabaul, Ambon, and the diversionary strike on Darwin, Australia, to cover the February 1942 invasion of Timor. Heavy losses during strikes on Ceylon (April 5 and 9) forced *Hiryu* back to Japan. At Midway, *Hiryu* was spared the devastation of the U.S. attacks that sank *Akagi, Kaga,* and *Soryu* on the morning of June 5, and she launched two air strikes against USS YORKTOWN, which forced that carrier to be abandoned at 1456. Knocked out of action by dive-bombers from USS HORNET and ENTERPRISE at 1703, *Hiryu* stubbornly refused to sink until torpedoed by two Japanese destroyers at 0510 on June 6 in position 31°28′N, 179°24′E. The battle cost her 750 dead.

Prange, *At Dawn We Slept; Miracle at Midway.*

CSS H. L. HUNLEY

(ex-*Fish Boat*) Submarine. *L/B/D:* 30–40′ × 4′ × 4–5′ dph (9–12m × 1.2m × 1.5m). *Hull:* iron. *Comp.:* 9. *Arm.:* spar torpedo. *Mach.:* Hand-cranked propeller. *Built:* Thomas B. Park & Thomas W. Lyons, Mobile, Ala.; 1863.

CSS *H. L. Hunley* was the first submarine to sink an enemy warship in combat. The *Hunley* was actually the third vessel, after CSS PIONEER and *American Diver,* built by a group of investors and inventors lured by the Confederate government's promise of prize money equal to 20 percent of the value of any Union warship sunk. Among the hopefuls were the vessel's namesake, Confederate Army Captain Horace Lawson Hunley. Basically a modified iron cylinder steam boiler, the *Hunley* was steered by one member of the crew and propelled by eight others turning a propeller shaft. The simple armament consisted of a spar torpedo, a mine carried at the end of a long pole that detonated on contact with an enemy ship. Following successful trials at Mobile in August 1863, the *Hunley* was shipped by rail to Charleston, South Carolina.

The original captain was James R. McClintock, a partner in the venture, but his lack of success in attacking Union shipping led to the Confederates' requisitioning the vessel, which was commissioned and crewed by volunteers under Lieutenant John A. Payne. Five of this navy crew were killed when the submarine accidentally sank; another nine people died, Hunley among them, when she sank again on October 15. Despite the ship's predisposition to kill its crews, a third crew was found. On the night of February 17, 1864, CSS *H. L. Hunley* sailed into Charleston Harbor and attacked the screw sloop USS HOUSA-TONIC, which was sunk with the loss of five men.

Killing more of her own crew than enemy sailors, the Confederacy's submarine H. L. HUNLEY *earned such unfortunate sobriquets as "floating coffin" and "deadly trap." Yet she went a long way towards demonstrating the viability of underwater warfare. This view shows the ill-fated vessel at Charleston, South Carolina, on December 6, 1863, two months before her loss in 1864. Courtesy U.S. Naval Historical Center, Washington, D.C.*

Neither the *Hunley* nor its crew returned from this mission, and the remains of the world's first successful submarine were presumed lost forever. That same night, however, Confederate officer Lieutenant Colonel O. M. Dantzler recorded that "the signals agreed upon to be given in case the boat wished a light to be exposed at this post [Battery Marshall] as a guide for its return were observed and answered." Others also reported seeing an exchange of signals forty-five minutes after the sinking of the *Housatonic,* but these facts seem to have escaped the notice of the Office of Submarine Defenses. Captain M. M. Gray, CSA, later wrote, "I am of the opinion that . . . she went into the hole made in the *Housatonic* by the explosion of torpedoes and did not have sufficient power to back out." In 1994, researchers managed to locate the elusive submarine in the waters of Charleston Harbor.

Although *Hunley* was only a qualified success, having killed less than one of the enemy for every four of her own crew, her destruction of USS *Housatonic* ushered in a form of warfare that would find its full, grim expression half a century later in World War I.

Kloepel, *Danger beneath the Waves.* Perry, *Infernal Machines.*

HMS HOGUE

Cressy-class armored cruiser (4f/2m). *L/B:* 472′ × 69.5′ (143.9m × 21.2m). *Tons:* 12,000 disp. *Hull:* steel. *Comp.:* 760. *Arm.:* 2 × 9.2″, 12 × 6″, 13 × 12pdr.; 2 × 18″TT. *Armor:* 6″ belt. *Mach.:* triple expansion, screws; 21 kts. *Built:* Vickers Ltd., Barrow-in-Furness, Eng.; 1902.

Named for the site of an action during the 1692 Battle of Barfleur between an Anglo-Dutch fleet under Admiral Edward Russell and a French force under Admiral de Tourville, HMS *Hogue* spent two years on the China Station, followed by two years in North American waters. At the beginning of World War I, she was assigned to the Grand Fleet's Third Cruiser Squadron. On the morning of September 22, 1914, *Hogue* was on patrol with two of the three other ships of the "live bait squadron" in the Broad Fourteens off the Dutch coast about 20 miles north of the Hook of Holland. ABOUKIR was hit by a torpedo fired from the *U-9* at about 0630, and her captain ordered *Hogue* and CRESSY to stand by to pick up survivors. As she approached the stricken *Aboukir* to retrieve survivors, *Hogue* was hit by two torpedoes and capsized and sank within 10 minutes, with the loss of 327 dead.

Coles, *Three before Breakfast.*

HOHENZOLLERN

Screw steamer (2f/3m). *L/B/D:* 382.6 × 45.9 × 23.1′ (116.6m × 14m × 0.6m). *Tons:* 4,460 grt. *Hull:* steel. *Comp.:* 313. *Arm.* 3 × 10.5cm, 12 × 5cm. *Mach.:* triple expansion, 9,000 ihp, 2 screws; 21.5 kts. *Built:* Stettiner Maschinenbau AG Vulcan, Stettin, Germany; 1893.

Named for the German ruling family, *Hohenzollern* was built for Kaiser Wilhelm II, the imperial architect of the German fleet in the naval race with Britain that preceded World War I. A keen navalist, Wilhelm was not only an admiral of the German fleet, but through the good graces of his maternal grandmother, Queen Victoria, an honorary Admiral of the Fleet in the Royal Navy. Later he told his uncle King Edward VII, while entertaining him aboard his flagship at Kiel,

> When, as a little boy, I was allowed to visit Portsmouth and Plymouth hand in hand with kind aunts and friendly admirals, I admired the proud English ships in those two superb harbors. Then there awoke in me the wish to build ships of my own like these someday, and when I was grown up to possess as fine a navy as the English.

The Reichstag did not share Wilhelm's enthusiasm for yachts, and in order to have her construction paid for, *Hohenzollern* was classified as a dispatch boat in the naval appropriations. Although she sailed mostly in the Baltic and North Seas, with annual cruises to Norway, she was often present at the Isle of Wight for the great British yachting regatta during Cowes Week. She also made several cruises to the Mediterranean and sailed once, in 1902, to the United States. *Hohenzollern* was sold in 1920 and broken up in 1923.

Crabtree, *Royal Yachts of Europe.* Massie, *"Dreadnought."*

USS HOLLAND (SS-1)

Holland-class submarine. *L/B/D:* 53.3′ × 10.3′ × 8.5′/11.4′ (16.2m × 3.1m × 2.6m/3.5m). *Tons:* 63/74 disp. *Hull:* steel; 75′ dd. *Comp.:* 6. *Arm.:* 1 × 18″TT; 1 × 8.4″ pneumatic gun. *Mach.:* gasoline engine/electric motor, 45/150 hp, 1 screw; 8/5 kts. *Des.:* John P. Holland. *Built:* Crescent Shipyard, Elizabeth, N.J.; 1900.

John Philip Holland's sixth submarine boat design — her predecessors included FENIAN RAM — was the first operationally practical submarine commissioned into the U.S. Navy. *Holland* was "the forerunner of all modern submarines," in the words of British submariner and historian Richard Compton-Hall: "the design and the construction were entirely along the lines of submarines today with frames, plating and general arrangements [that] would not be out of place in any submarine drawing

The prototype of the world's first successful class of submarines, USS HOLLAND *was named for her inventor, the engineer John Holland. Courtesy U.S. Naval Historical Center, Washington, D.C.*

office today." A gasoline engine drove the vessel on the surface while an electric motor powered her when submerged. She had diving rudders fitted on either side of her single four-bladed propeller. The primary armament consisted of three 18-inch torpedoes that were fired from a single torpedo tube in the bow. After surface trials and a 30-minute static submergence, *Holland*'s first dive underway was made, on March 17, 1898 — St. Patrick's Day, fittingly enough, given Holland's Irish Republican background — in the waters off Staten Island, New York.

Witnessing her official trials ten days later, Assistant Secretary of the Navy Theodore Roosevelt urged that the Navy purchase the vessel, but it was not until April 11, 1900, that she was formally commissioned as USS *Holland* at Newport. The Navy also ordered an additional six submarines on the same model. Towed to Annapolis, *Holland* was used to train officers and crew of the U.S. Navy's nascent submarine service until sold for scrap in 1913.

Compton-Hall, *Submarine Boats.* Morris, *John P. Holland.* U.S. Navy, *DANFS.*

HOLLANDIA

Retour ship (3m). *L/B/D:* 161.5′ × 44.2′ × 20.4′ dph (49.2m × 13.5m × 6.2m). *Tons:* 750 grt. *Hull:* wood. *Comp.:* 300. *Arm.:* 8 × 12pdr, 16 × 8pdr, 8 × 4pdr, 10 swivels. *Built:* W. T. Bloc, VOC, Amsterdam; 1742.

The second of the 150-*voet* (foot) class of retour ships built by the Verenigde Oostindische Compagnie (VOC,

or Dutch East India Company) for its trade to Batavia, *Hollandia* was lost in the Scilly Isles on her maiden voyage. Rediscovered in 1971, her wreck was the subject of eleven years of excavation and research into this important class of ship. The VOC first attempted to standardize the dimensions of its retour ships in 1697, with the establishment of the 130-*voet* and 145-*voet* classes. (The retour ships were measured over the lower gundeck; one Amsterdam foot equals about 28.25 centimeters.) Modifications in 1714 and 1727 resulted in less seaworthy vessels. Early in 1742, the company created three new classes — 150 *voet*, 136 (later 140) *voet*, and 120 *voet* — and distributed ship plans and molds to the various VOC shipyards.

The first of the largest class, *Eendracht* was laid down in February at Amsterdam and sailed for Batavia in September. *Hollandia* and *Overnes* were next to be launched, and on June 3, 1743, they sailed in company with the smaller *Heuvel.* Ten days later, the ships were nearly through the English Channel when *Hollandia* separated from the others in rough weather. Forced northwest, she apparently struck Gunners Rock off the island of Annet in the Scillies and sank in 49°54′N, 6°22′W. None of the complement of 276 survived. The wreck site was first discovered by English diver Rex Cowan in 1971, who worked the site with professional archaeologists and volunteers for six years, during which they recovered 50,000 silver coins. Cowan subsequently allowed the Rijksmuseum in Amsterdam to recover the remaining artifacts. Virtually nothing of the ship itself survived, but among the hundreds of artifacts recovered are personal possessions including clothing and dice, eating utensils and food containers, navigational instruments, and weapons.

Analysis of this material has yielded a wealth of information about life aboard the ships of one of the world's first modern international trading companies.

Gawronski, et al., *"Hollandia" Compendium.*

HOMERIC

(ex-*Columbus*) Liner (2f/2m). *L/B:* 774.3′ × 83.3′ (228.9m × 25.4m). *Tons:* 34,351 grt. *Hull:* steel. *Comp.:* 1st 529, 2nd 487, 3rd 1,750. *Mach.:* triple expansion, 2 screws; 19 kts. *Built:* F. Schichau, Danzig; 1920.

Laid down as *Columbus* for Norddeutscher Lloyd's transatlantic service in 1913, construction of the ship was interrupted by World War I. Following the war, Norddeutscher Lloyd was forced to hand her over to Great Britain, and she was acquired by the White Star Line in 1920. Renamed *Homeric* — the second White Star ship of the name — she began her first voyage on February 14, 1922, sailing from Southampton for Cherbourg and New York. Sailing in consort with MAJESTIC and OLYMPIC, she had a reputation as being the steadiest passenger ship afloat. In 1923, her coal-burning plant was replaced with an oil-burning one. By 1932, she was significantly outclassed by the newer generation of steamships, and she was put in cruise service to the Canaries, West Africa, and the Mediterranean. Three years later, shortly after the merger of Cunard and White Star, she was withdrawn from service, and in 1936 she was scrapped by T. W. Ward at Inverkeithing.

Bonsor, *North Atlantic Seaway.* Braynard & Miller, *Fifty Famous Liners.*

HMS HOOD

Hood-class battlecruiser (2f/2m). *L/B/D:* 860′ × 104′ × 28.5′ (262.1m × 31.7m × 8.7m). *Tons:* 45,200 disp. *Hull:* steel. *Comp.:* 1,477. *Arm.:* 8 × 15″ (4x2); 12 × 5.5″, 4 × 4″, 16 × 40mm; 6 × 21″TT. *Armor:* 12″ belt, 3″ deck. *Mach.:* geared turbines, 144,000 shp, 4 screws; 31 kts. *Built:* John Brown & Co., Ltd., Clydebank, Scotland; 1920.

Bearing the name of one of the most distinguished families to serve the Royal Navy, including two admirals, one vice admiral, one rear admiral, and one captain, HMS *Hood* was laid down in 1916 in response to Germany's *Mackensen*-class battlecruisers, none of which was ever commissioned. Although *Hood*'s design was modified in light of the loss of the battlecruisers HMS *Queen Mary,* INDEFATIGABLE, and INVINCIBLE (flagship of Rear Ad-

miral Sir Horace Hood) at Jutland, and she was modernized twice, her magazine protection remained one of her weak spots and she carried only 3-inch deck armor. Throughout the 1920s *Hood* was assigned to either the Atlantic or Home Fleets, and she completed a ten-month world cruise with RENOWN in 1923. In 1929 she began a two-year refit. After duty with the Mediterranean Fleet in 1936, she underwent a brief refit in early 1939 before returning to the Home Fleet.

After the outbreak of World War II, *Hood* saw action in a variety of theaters, including the North Sea, the chase of SCHARNHORST and GNEISENAU, and convoy duty. *Hood* was in the attack on the French fleet at the Battle of Mers el-Kébir on July 3, 1940, and then returned to the Home Fleet at Scapa Flow. On May 22, 1941, *Hood* (Captain R. Kerr) sailed as the flagship of Vice Admiral L. E. Holland's Battle Cruiser Force, which included HMS PRINCE OF WALES and six destroyers, to intercept the German battleship BISMARCK and heavy cruiser PRINZ EUGEN. The four heavy units made visual contact at 0537 on May 24, and *Hood* opened fire fifteen minutes later. *Bismarck* and *Prinz Eugen* scored hits on *Hood* and at 0600 there was a massive explosion; the ship split in two and sank four minutes later. *Prince of Wales* quickly broke off the engagement, and destroyers later picked up three survivors from a total complement of 1,418 men. One of the largest warships in the world, *Hood* was destroyed exactly one week shy of the twenty-fifth anniversary of the Battle of Jutland, the lessons of which had been so consciously applied to her design. Although a number of theories about the exact cause of her loss have been advanced, it is widely believed that plunging fire from *Bismarck* penetrated her weak deck armor to ignite one of her magazines.

Hoyt, *Life and Death of HMS "Hood."* Roberts, *Battlecruiser "Hood."*

HOPE

(ex-USS *Consolation*) Hospital ship (1f/4m). *L/B/D:* 520′ × 71.5′ × 24′ (158.5m × 21.8m × 7.3m). *Tons:* 11,141 disp. *Hull:* steel. *Comp.:* 94 crew, 95 medical staff, 230 berths. *Mach.:* oil. *Built:* Sun Shipbuilding and Dry Dock Co., Chester, Pa.; 1945.

Laid down as the Maritime Commission's *Marine Walrus* and acquired the same month for use as a hospital ship, USS *Consolation* entered service just after the end of World War II. After duty in Japan screening returning American prisoners of war, she repatriated troops from around the Pacific. From 1950 to 1954, *Consolation* provided medical assistance in the Korean War, and she was the first hospital ship to use helicopters to evacuate wounded directly from the battlefield. She remained on duty in the Pacific until 1955, taking part in the "Passage to Freedom" evacuation of civilians from North Vietnam following the Communist takeover.

In 1958, President Dwight D. Eisenhower appointed Dr. William B. Walsh to the People to People Health Foundation to make recommendations on how to assist the developing world. Walsh organized Health Opportunity for People Everywhere (HOPE) and chartered *Consolation* from the Navy for use as a civilian hospital ship. Her first mission began in 1960, when she sailed from San Francisco to Indonesia, Hong Kong, and South Vietnam. Over the next fourteen years, *Hope* recruited more than 3,000 volunteers to work in Africa, South America, and East Asia. At each port of call, the ship's staff trained local doctors and nurses in the latest surgical and diagnostic techniques and provided immunizations, x-rays, and medical treatment for hundreds of thousands of patients.

Hope was broken up at Brownsville, Texas, in 1974. While the end of the ship was regrettable, Project HOPE subsequently expanded its mission from only one or two littoral countries per year to as many as thirty to forty countries per year anywhere in the world.

U.S. Navy, *DANFS*. Walsh, *A Ship Called "Hope."*

HORNET

Sloop. *L/B/D:* ca. 64′ × 18′ × 10′ (19.5m × 5.5m × 3m). *Tons:* 75 bm. *Hull:* wood. *Arm.:* 10 × 4pdr. *Built:* Baltimore(?); 1774.

A merchant sloop owned by Baltimore merchant Captain William Stone, *Hornet* was one of the first vessels (with WASP) chartered by Congress for the Continental Navy. On February 18, 1776, she sailed in a squadron under Commodore Esek Hopkins, flying his flag in ALFRED, to capture British gunpowder at New Providence, the Bahamas. Running afoul of *Fly,* she was forced back to the Delaware. On January 30, 1777, *Hornet* (now under James Nicholson) and *Fly* were ordered to escort a merchant convoy bound for Martinique to secure French military stores bound for the Continental Army.

Following General Sir William Howe's capture of Philadelphia on September 26, *Hornet,* ANDREW DORIA, *Wasp,* and *Fly* were part of the fleet that lay on the Delaware River between the British fleet at Chester and Philadelphia, which had fallen to the British. *Hornet*'s ultimate fate is uncertain. Some believe that she was burned, together with *Andrew Doria* and *Wasp,* following the fall of the Delaware River Forts Mifflin and Mercer on November 20, 1777, to prevent their falling into British hands. It is also possible that she escaped the Delaware, only to be captured off Charleston by the British schooner *Porcupine* after loading a cargo of indigo for Martinique.

Fowler, *Rebels under Sail.* Miller, *Sea of Glory.*

USS HORNET

Brig. *L/B/D:* 106.8′ × 31.4′ × 14′ dph (32.5m × 9.6m × 4.3m). *Tons:* 440 bm. *Hull:* wood. *Comp.:* 50. *Arm.:* 16 × 32pdr, 2 × 12pdr. *Des.:* Josiah Fox. *Built:* William Price, Baltimore; 1805.

USS *Hornet* and WASP were two blue-water fighting vessels ordered by Congress in the midst of President Thomas Jefferson's "gunboat navy" building program at the beginning of the nineteenth century. Under command of Commandant Isaac Chauncey, *Hornet* was assigned to the Mediterranean Squadron in 1806–7, after which she was decommissioned at Charleston, South Carolina. Returning to service in 1808, she patrolled the East Coast enforcing the Embargo Act, which forbade export shipping from U.S. ports. Following the repeal of this act, in 1810 she was rerigged as a ship at the Washington Navy Yard, and her beam was increased by 10 inches.

The beginning of the War of 1812 found her with Commodore John Rodgers's squadron at New York. Sailing under Master Commandant James Lawrence, on July 9 *Hornet* seized the British privateer *Dolphin,* which was unfortunately recaptured with her prize crew. On October 30, *Hornet* sailed for the Pacific in company with USS CONSTITUTION. En route, they were to rendezvous with USS ESSEX at Salvador, Brazil. It was at this time that *Constitution* fought her celebrated duel with HMS *Java* and returned to Boston. *Hornet* blockaded British shipping at Salvador until the arrival of HMS *Montagu* (74 guns). On February 24, 1813, off Demerara, British Guiana, she intercepted the HM Brig *Peacock* (18). Lawrence "ran him close on board on the starboard quarter, and kept up such a heavy and well directed fire, that in less than 15 minutes she surrendered (being literally cut to pieces)." In recognition of this decisive action, Lawrence was given command of the frigate USS CHESAPEAKE. Blockaded at New York until 1815, under Lieutenant James Biddle *Hornet* sailed with orders to harass British commerce in the Indian Ocean. Unaware that a peace had been signed, *Hornet* fought HMS *Penguin* (18) in a sharp contest on March 23, 1815, about five miles northeast of Tristan da Cunha. The Americans' superior gunnery destroyed *Penguin,* which was later scuttled, and killed between 10 and 25 of her crew, including Commander James Dickinson.

Hornet arrived at New York on August 23, to great acclaim, despite the fact that the war had been over for eight months. She saw further service in the Atlantic and Mediterranean before assignment to the Caribbean, based at Key West and Pensacola. She remained with the West Indies Squadron until her loss with all hands in September or October 1829 in a gale off Tampico, Mexico.

Aimone, "Cruise of the U.S. Sloop *Hornet* in 1815." Hardin, "Notes." U.S. Navy, *DANFS*.

USS HORNET (CV-8)

Hornet-class aircraft carrier (1f/2m). *L/B/D:* 809.5′ × 83.1′ (114′ew) × 21.5′ (246.7m × 25.3m/34.7m × 6.6m). *Tons:* 25,500 disp. *Hull:* steel. *Comp.:* 2,919. *Arm.:* 81–85 aircraft; 8 × 5″, 16 × 1.1″, 24 × 20mm. *Armor:* 4″ belt, 1.5″ deck. *Mach.:* geared turbines, 120,000 shp, 4 shafts; 120,000 shp. *Built:* Newport News Shipbuilding and Dry Dock Co., Newport News, Va.; 1941.

Commissioned under Captain Marc A. Mitscher less than two months before the Japanese attack on Pearl Harbor brought the United States into World War II, USS *Hornet* spent four months training out of Norfolk before sailing for San Francisco. There she embarked sixteen Army Air Force B-25 bombers and their crews, under command of Lieutenant Colonel James H. Doolittle. Steaming east, she was met near Midway by a task force centered around USS ENTERPRISE. At about 0900 on April 18, 1942, 600 miles west of Japan (and 200 miles west of the intended launch position), the Tokyo Raiders flew off for their historic raid on Tokyo, Nagoya, and Kobe. *Hornet*'s role in the unprecedented operation was kept secret for a year, and President Franklin D. Roosevelt would only say that the planes had taken off from "Shangri-La," the fictional setting of James Hilton's *Lost Horizon.*

On April 30, *Hornet* and *Enterprise* were sent to support USS LEXINGTON and YORKTOWN at the Battle of the Coral Sea, which was over before they arrived. Two days after returning to Pearl Harbor, they were deployed to meet the Japanese carrier fleet at Midway, where 15 of her torpedo planes were launched and shot down by Japanese fighters; her dive-bombers failed to find the enemy fleet. In pursuing the routed Japanese, which had lost the carriers AKAGI, HIRYU, KAGA, and SORYU, planes from *Hornet* sank the cruiser *Mikuma* and damaged MOGAMI almost beyond recognition.

Two months later, *Hornet* sailed with Task Force 17 in support of operations on Guadalcanal in the Solomon Islands, where from mid-September she was the only U.S. carrier in service. At the Battle of the Santa Cruz Islands, on October 26, *Hornet* and *Enterprise* were pitted against a Japanese force comprising the carriers SHOKAKU (heavily damaged by planes from *Hornet*) and ZUIHO. Combined torpedo and bomb attacks by Japanese planes so severely damaged *Hornet* that Captain Mason had to order the burning ship abandoned. Despite more than 10 torpedoes in her hull and 400 rounds of 5-inch shells from U.S. destroyers USS *Mustin* and *Anderson,* the abandoned hulk was finally sunk by Japanese destroyers on October 27, 1942, in 8°38′S, 166°43′E.

Rose, *Ship that Held the Line.*

HOUGOMONT

Bark (4m). *L/B/D:* 292.7′ × 43.2′ × 24′ dph (89.2m × 13.2m × 7.3m). *Tons:* 2,428 grt. *Hull:* steel. *Built:* Charles Scott & Co., Greenock, Scotland; 1897.

Named for the Belgian chateau occupied by the British during the Battle of Waterloo in 1815, *Hougomont* was built for J. Hardie & Company of Glasgow. She carried a variety of cargoes to ports around the world, calling on her first voyage at New York, San Francisco, Yokohama, Astoria, and Falmouth. On February 26, 1903, she ran aground in Solway Firth in a heavy storm; refloated two weeks later, she was eventually repaired at Greenock and sailed for Australia in October. In 1908, *Hougomont* was bound from Coquimbo for Tocopilla in ballast but was carried past the port by the fast-running Humboldt Current. Four hundred miles later, the captain tore up his charter and quit the coast of Chile for Australia. In 1914, *Hougomont* ran aground on Fire Island, New York, but without serious damage. Hardie retained ownership of *Hougomont* until 1924, when she was sold to Gustaf Erikson, who had previously purchased Hardie's ARCHIBALD RUSSELL and KILLORAN. *Hougomont* ended her days with the Finnish grain fleet, plying yearly between Australia and Europe in the grain races. Her last voyage was troubled from the start. After taking a month to get out of the English Channel, she was about 530 miles south of Cape Borda on April 20, 1932, when she was dismasted in a brief but ferocious squall of hurricane force. As Alex Hurst describes the remarkable scene,

> Before anything could be done, the fore upper topgallant yard, with four men on it, buckled and broke. Two of the men succeeded in sliding down the back-stays though, as the fore-mast, main and part of the mizzen all came down concurrently — the main snapping off some six feet clear of the deck — one can only record that they were incredibly lucky, and that is gross understatement! The other two men, overbalanced by the broken yard, were flattened against the rig-

ging by the force of the wind, and thus saved momentarily from falling into the sea. They too escaped and got down all right, remarkable as it may seem.

Declining a tow from a passing steamer, Captain R. Lindholm sailed *Hougomont* under jury rig to Port Adelaide, where she was condemned and broken up.

Hurst, *Square-Riggers.* Lubbock, *Last of the Windjammers.*

HOUQUA

Clipper (3m). *L/B/D:* 142.3′ × 29.1′ × 16.7′ (43.4m × 8.9m × 5.1m). *Tons:* 583 om. *Hull:* wood. *Built:* Brown & Bell, New York; 1844.

Built on account for A. A. Low & Brother of New York, *Houqua* was named for Canton's preeminent Hong merchant, who died in 1843. Although Low intended to sell their ship to the Chinese for use as a warship (her bulwarks were pierced for sixteen guns), she proved too small for the work and remained in Low's China trade her entire career. Built at the outset of the clipper era, *Houqua* elicited what Carl Cutler has described as "the first of a series of semi-poetical effusions that were to greet the more noteworthy of the new ships for the next decade." Typical of these effusions was that written by James Gordon Bennett for his *New York Herald:*

> One of the prettiest and most rakish looking packet ships ever built in the civilized world is now to be seen at the foot of Jone's Lane on the East River. . . .
>
> We never saw a vessel so perfect in all her parts as this new celestial packet. She is about 600 tons in size — as sharp as a cutter — as symmetrical as a yacht — as rakish in her rig as a pirate — and as neat in her deck and cabin arrangements as a lady's boudoir.
>
> Her figure is a bust of Houqua, and her bows are as sharp as the toes of a pair of Chinese shoes.

Houqua made consistently good times on the China run, starting with her first voyage from New York to Macao, 85 days out and 90 days back, under Captain Nathaniel B. Palmer. He was succeeded in command by his brothers Alexander Palmer and Theodore D. Palmer, and had four other captains besides. Rerigged as a bark in 1857, she remained in the China trade, with occasional trading passages to Japan and other Oriental ports. On August 15, 1864, she sailed from Yokohama under William Cartwright, her captain since 1855, and was never seen again.

Cutler, *Greyhounds of the Sea.* Howe & Matthews, *American Clipper Ships.*

An unknown Chinese artist painted the American clipper ship HOUQUA, *dismasted in a hurricane. Courtesy Peabody Essex Museum, Salem, Massachusetts.*

USS HOUSATONIC

Ossipee-class screw sloop (1f/2m). *L/B/D:* 205′ bp × 38′ × 16.6′ (62.5m × 11.6m × 5.1m). *Tons:* 1,934 disp. *Hull:* wood. *Comp.:* 160. *Arm.:* 1 × 100pdr, 2 × 30pdr, 1 × 11″, 2 × 32pdr, 2 × 24pdr hwz, 1 × 12pdr hwz. *Mach.:* horizontal direct-acting engines, 715 ihp, 1 screw; 12 kts. *Des.:* John Lenthall. *Built:* Globe Iron Works, Boston; 1862.

One of four *Ossipee*-class unarmored screw sloops laid down after the start of the Civil War, the bark-rigged *Housatonic* joined the South Atlantic Blockading Squadron in September 1861, stationed off Charleston Harbor. The largest ship on station at the time, her first engagement took place on January 31, 1863, when she helped fight off an attack by the ironclad rams *Chicora* and *Palmetto State,* which had inflicted serious damage on USS *Mercedita* and *Keystone State.* Their attack was provoked by the recent capture of the blockade-runner *Princess Royal,* inward bound with "the war's most important single cargo of contraband," including two marine engines, ordnance, and ammunition.

That summer, the Union ships adopted a more aggressive posture and began shelling Fort Morgan and other shore installations. On the night of February 17, 1864, while *Housatonic* was moored just off Charleston Harbor, the officer of the watch saw what he later described as "a plank moving in the water." He ordered the anchor slipped and the engine reversed, but two minutes later, the spar torpedo of the Confederate submarine H. L. HUNLEY detonated on the starboard hull just forward of

The ironclad turret ship HUASCAR *is one of only a few warships surviving from the mid-19th century. In addition to an increased preference for steam over sail, this critical period saw the first experiments with the turreted, centerline guns that would become a mainstay of 20th-century capital ship design. Courtesy Norman Brouwer.*

the mizzen mast. *Housatonic* filled rapidly and sank with the loss of five of her crew. Although *H. L. Hunley* was the first submarine to sink another ship in combat, she and her crew were lost following the attack. The remains of the *Hunley* were not discovered until 1995.

Silverstone, *Warships of the Civil War Navies.* U.S. Navy, *DANFS.*

USS HOUSTON (CA-30)

Northampton-class cruiser (2f/2m). *L/B/D:* 600.3′ × 66.1′ × 23′ (183m × 20.1m × 7m). *Tons:* 11,420 disp. *Hull:* steel. *Comp.:* 735–1,200. *Arm.:* 9 × 8″ (3 × 3), 8 × 5″, 32 × 40mm, 27 × 20mm; 6 × 21″TT; 4 aircraft. *Armor:* 3″ belt, 1″ deck. *Mach.:* geared turbines, 107,000 shp, 4 screws; 32.5 kts. *Built:* Newport News Shipbuilding and Dry Dock, Newport News, Va.; 1929.

In 1941, USS *Houston* was the heaviest ship in Admiral Thomas C. Hart's small Asiatic Fleet, which had transferred from China to the Philippines in 1940. Ordered south to the Dutch East Indies following the Japanese invasion on December 8, the American ships were absorbed into the ABDA (American-British-Dutch-Australian) Striking Force under Dutch Rear Admiral Karel Doorman in HNMS DE RUYTER and based at Surabaya, on the island of Java. *Houston* had her "X" turret knocked out in a failed operation against the Japanese fleet coming down the Makasar Strait. At the Battle of the Java Sea, on February 27, *Houston* and HMAS PERTH survived the destruction of the ABDA force and retired to Batavia on

Doorman's orders. The following night, en route to the Sunda Strait, the two heavy cruisers decided to wreak what revenge they could on the Japanese forces landing at the northwestern tip of Java. After an hour in the narrow confines of Bantam Bay under withering fire from Japanese heavy cruisers and destroyers, both Allied cruisers were sunk. *Houston* slipped beneath the waves at about 0036 on March 1. The Netherlands East Indies surrendered to the Japanese eight days later.

Winslow, *Ghost that Died in Sunda Strait.*

HUASCAR

Ironclad turret ship (2m). *L/B/D:* 200′ lbp × 35.5′ x 16′ (37.8m × 10.2m × 3.4m). *Tons:* 1,870 disp. *Hull:* iron. *Comp.:* 193. *Arm.:* 2 × 300pdr, 1 × 10″, 2 × 40pdr, 1 × 12pdr. *Armor:* 4.5″ belt. *Mach.:* Maudslay return connecting rod engine, 300 hp, 1 screw; 12 kts. *Des.:* Cowper Coles. *Built:* Laird Bros., Ltd., Birkenhead, Eng.; 1865.

Ordered by the Peruvian Navy during the war with Spain, *Huascar* was named for the son of the Incan emperor Huayna Capac. The third of the seagoing turret ships conceived by Captain Cowper Coles, *Huascar*'s primary armament was housed in a 22-foot-diameter turret mounted abaft the foremast. She had a 138-degree arc of fire on either beam. *Huascar* joined the Peruvian-Chilean squadron under Chile's Rear Admiral Manuel Blanco Encalada and proceeded to Callao to take part in Peru's final revolution against Spain, but arrived after hostilities with Spain were over.

In 1877, *Huascar* was seized by supporters of Nicolas de Piérola, and under command of Manuel M. Carrasco, she raided as far as Pisagua, Bolivia, before being engaged by HMS *Shah* and *Amethyst* off Ilo, Peru, on May 29. Piérola surrendered the ship to Peruvian authorities the following day. In April 1879, Peru entered the War of the Pacific as Bolivia's ally against Chile. Under Commander Miguel Grau, on May 21 *Huascar* and the ironclad frigate *Independencia* attempted to raise the Chilean blockade of Iquique by the gunboat *Covadonga* and the twenty-year-old screw corvette *Esmeralda,* which *Huascar* sank by ramming. On October 8, *Huascar* encountered the Chilean ships *Cochrane* and *Blanco Encalada* off Agamos Point near Antofagasta. In the hour-and-a-half battle, which pitted Coles's turret ironclad against Edward J. Reed's broadside battery ships, *Huascar* was hit with an estimated 70 rounds that knocked out her steering, penetrated her turret, and killed 64 of her 193 crew, including Grau. Captured and commissioned in the Chilean Navy, *Huascar* was put on blockade duty for the remainder of the war. In 1901 *Huascar* was stricken from the active list, but she served as a submarine tender from 1917 to 1930. She was opened to the public as a museum ship at Talcahuano in 1952. (Several years after her engagement with *Huascar, Blanco Encalada* was the first ship sunk by a self-propelled torpedo, during the Chilean revolution.)

Seeger, "The Ten-Cent War." Wood, "Ironclad Turret Ship *Huascar.*"

HMS HUSSAR

Mermaid-class frigate (3m). *L/B/D:* 124′ × 33.5′ × 11′ dph (37.8m × 10.2m × 3.4m). *Tons:* 613 bm. *Hull:* wood. *Comp.:* 200. *Arm.:* 24 × 9pdr, 4 × 3pdr, 12 swivels. *Des.:* Sir Thomas Slade. *Built:* Inwood, Rotherhithe, Eng.; 1763.

During the American Revolution, HMS *Hussar* sailed as a dispatch boat on the North American station. By mid-1779, the British position in New York was precarious as a French army had joined forces with General George Washington's troops north of the city. When Admiral Sir George Brydges Rodney took his twenty ships of the line south in November, it was decided that the army's pay roll be moved to the anchorage at Gardiner's Bay on eastern Long Island. Over his pilot's better judgment, on November 24 *Hussar*'s Captain Charles Pole decided to sail from the East River through the treacherous waters of Hell Gate between Manhattan Island and Long Island.

Just before reaching Long Island Sound, *Hussar* was swept onto Pot Rock and began sinking. Pole was unable to run her aground and she sank in 16 fathoms of water. The British immediately denied there was any gold aboard the ship, but despite the difficulty of diving in the waters of Hell Gate, reports of $2 to $4 million in gold were the catalyst that prompted many salvage efforts over the next 150 years. This continued even after the U.S. Army Corps of Engineers "blew the worst features of Hell Gate straight back to hell" with 56,000 pounds of dynamite in 1876. *Hussar*'s remains, if any survive, are now believed to lie beneath landfill in the Bronx.

Hepper, *British Warship Losses.* Rattray, *Perils of the Port of New York.*

I

I-26

Junsen Type B submarine. L/B/D: 350′ × 30.5′ × 16′ (106.7m × 9.3m × 4.9m). *Tons:* 2,584/3,654 disp. *Hull:* steel; 333′ dd. *Comp.:* 105. *Arm.:* 6 × 21″TT; 1 × 5.5″. *Mach.:* diesel/electric, 12,400/2,000 hp; 23.5/8 kts. *Built:* Mitsubishi Zosen Kaisha, Kobe, Japan; 1941.

Completed the year Japan entered World War II, *I-26* was one of the largest and the most successful Japanese submarines. Intended for transpacific operations, the Junsen Type B boats carried a floatplane launched from the foredeck. Deployed as part of the Submarine Reconnaissance Unit north of Hawaii during the attack on Pearl Harbor, on December 8, 1941, *I-26* torpedoed the 2,140-ton lumber freighter *Cynthia Olsen.* She later took up station off Cape Flattery, Washington, one of nine submarines deployed as far south as San Diego. During a second mission off British Columbia in the summer of 1942, she sank a freighter and bombed a radio station on Vancouver Island, but overall these coastwise operations achieved negligible results.

During the American landings on Guadalcanal, on August 31, 1942, *I-26* torpedoed USS SARATOGA. (The carrier had been undergoing repairs since January after an attack by *I-6.*) As the struggle for the Solomon Islands continued, on November 13, *I-26* sank the light cruiser USS JUNEAU in 10°34′S, 161°04′E with all but ten of her crew, including the five Sullivan brothers.

As part of a campaign by both Germany and Japan to undermine Britain by fomenting unrest in India, in the fall of 1943, *I-26* landed a dozen Indian revolutionaries on the coast of Pakistan. Returning from this otherwise ineffectual assignment, she sank two cargo ships and damaged a third. Her next battle assignment came following the Battle of the Philippine Sea, when *I-26* was deployed with the First Submarine Group as part of Sho-Go 1, Japan's campaign for the defense of the Philippines. Rather than form picket lines, units of the First Submarine Group patrolled an assigned sector east of Mindanao. As the Battle of Leyte Gulf unfolded, *I-26* shifted to a position east of Leyte, and during the Battle off Samar on October 25, 1944, she was sunk by the destroyer escort *Richard M. Rowell* (DE-403).

Boyd & Yoshida, *Japanese Submarine Force and World War II.*

I-124

I-121-class mine-laying submarine. L/B/D: 279′ × 24.5′ × 14.5′ (85m × 7.5m × 4.4m). *Tons:* 1,383/1,768 disp. *Hull:* steel. *Comp.:* 80. *Arm.:* 4 × 21″TT; 1 × 5.5″; 42 mines. *Mach.:* diesel-electric. 2,400/1,200 hp, 14/9.5 kts. *Built:* Kure Shipyard, Kure, Japan; 1928.

One of four *I-121*-class mine-laying submarines built by the Japanese in the 1920s, *I-124* has been implicated in one of the great unsolved mysteries of World War II. In November 1941, three weeks before Japan entered the war, the Australian cruiser HMAS SYDNEY was sunk in an engagement with the German raider *Kormoran* off the west coast of Australia. Because the battle-tested *Sydney* was sunk virtually without a trace, it has long been assumed that she was sunk by either a German or Japanese submarine that was refueling or rearming from the *Kormoran.* Since Japan was not yet at war with Britain or Australia, no acknowledgment of such an attack could have been made. Unfortunately, no conclusive evidence has surfaced since the war.

By January 1942, the Japanese were pushing their southern flank to Australian waters. On January 20, the *I-124* attacked the fleet oiler USS *Trinity* near Darwin, the most important port on the north coast of Australia. The three torpedoes missed their target; a counterattack by the escort destroyer USS *Alden* was also unsuccessful. Later the same day, the corvette HMAS *Deloraine* was dispatched to the scene. Nearly torpedoed herself at 1335, *Deloraine* located and depth-charged the *I-124,* which surfaced once about 90 minutes later before sinking. All 80 of her crew died, including her commanding officer, Lieutenant Commander Kouichi Kishigami, and his division commander, Captain Keiyuu Endo. Over the next few weeks, a number of efforts were made to find the wreck, but work was suspended following the Japanese carrier attack on Darwin on February 19.

The Royal Australian Navy's first submarine kill lay undisturbed until 1972, when the first of several groups of divers located the ship. *I-124* was eventually given some protection from treasure seekers by her designation as a war grave.

Lewis, *Sensuikan "I-124."*

ILE DE FRANCE

(later *Furansu Maru*) Liner (3f/2m). *L/B/D:* 792.9′ × 91.8′ (241.7m × 28m). *Tons:* 43,153 grt. *Hull:* steel. *Comp.:* 1st 537, 2nd 603, 3rd 646; 800 crew. *Mach.:* steam, quadruple screw; 23 kts. *Built:* Chantiers & Ateliers de St. Nazaire (Penhoët), St. Nazaire, France; 1927.

Ile de France was the first ship to employ on a grand scale the art deco "ocean liner" style that characterized the interiors of the great transatlantic passenger ships of the mid-twentieth century. Her spacious public rooms included a three-deck-high restaurant, a four-deck-high grand foyer, and a Gothic chapel adorned with fourteen pillars; for the benefit of her Prohibition-weary American passengers, she sported a bar thought to be the longest in any passenger ship. Launched by the Compagnie Générale Transatlantique (French Line) as a passenger-mail liner in 1926, *Ile de France* entered service the following year between Le Havre and New York. Two years after her launch, a seaplane catapult was fitted so that mail could be flown ashore before the ship reached port, but this innovation was dropped in 1930. In 1932 her accommodations were altered and first class was enlarged to 670 passengers, second class was changed to cater to 408 tourist-class passengers, and third class was reduced to 508 passengers. In 1940, *Ile de France* was sent from Marseilles to Saigon with war materiel but was diverted to Singapore. Seized by the Royal Navy, she was converted to a troopship and sailed under the flags of Great Britain and Free France. Reverting to French ownership after the war, she emerged from a refit with only one funnel and reentered regular commercial service between France and New York in 1949. In 1956, *Ile de France* rescued 750 survivors from the Italian passenger liner ANDREA DORIA after that ship was rammed by the STOCKHOLM off Nantucket Island on July 26. The following year *Ile de France* was sold to Japanese shipbreakers and renamed *Furansu* ("France") *Maru.* Her passage to the breakers was interrupted so that she could play the role of the ocean liner *Claridon* in the film *The Last Voyage* (1959), for which she was intentionally sunk. Later raised, she was broken up at Osaka.

Bonsor, *North Atlantic Seaway.* Braynard & Miller, *Fifty Famous Liners.*

Flagship of the French Line from 1926 until the commissioning of the ultra-chic superliner NORMANDIE *in 1935,* ILE DE FRANCE *epitomized the rakish elegance of the transatlantic liners between the wars. Courtesy The Mariners' Museum, Newport News, Virginia.*

HMS ILLUSTRIOUS

Illustrious-class aircraft carrier (1f/2m). *L/B/D:* 753.5′ × 95.8′ × 28′ (229.8m × 29.2m × 8.5m). *Tons:* 23,200 disp. *Hull:* steel. *Comp.:* 1,392. *Arm.:* 36 aircraft; 16 × 4.5", 48 × 2pdr. *Armor:* 4.5" belt, 3" deck. *Mach.:* geared turbines, 110,000 shp, 3 screws; 31 kts. *Built:* Vickers-Armstrong, Ltd., Barrow-in-Furness, Eng.; 1940.

The fourth Royal Navy ship of the name, HMS *Illustrious* was the first of a four-ship class of aircraft carriers commissioned in 1940 and 1941; her sister ships were HMS *Formidable, Indomitable,* and VICTORIOUS. The British had a very conservative approach to the uses of carrier aviation, and the ships were heavily armored and carried relatively few aircraft. (Their smaller contemporaries USS WASP and HORNET had a capacity for 86 aircraft.) Nonetheless, to *Illustrious* belongs the distinction of being the first ship to launch a major carrier strike against an enemy fleet.

When Italy declared war on Great Britain in June 1940, ten days before the fall of France, the immediate problem for Admiral A. B. Cunningham was to protect the vital sea lanes between Gibraltar and Malta, and from Malta to Alexandria, Egypt. In the 1930s, Admiral Sir Dudley Pound had begun entertaining a plan for a preemptive aerial attack on the navy base at Taranto, at the top of the heel of the Italian boot. One of the most vigorous proponents of this plan was Rear Admiral A. L. St. G. Lyster, who joined Cunningham in the Mediterranean when *Illustrious* arrived in August 1940. In planning his attack, he had at his disposal two carriers, the other being HMS *Eagle,* with eighteen aircraft. The operation was planned originally for October 21 (Trafalgar Day), but it had to be postponed after a fire aboard *Illustrious* destroyed two aircraft and damaged five others. *Eagle* was subsequently found unfit for service, and five of her Swordfish were transferred to the *Illustrious,* which now had a total complement of twenty-four Swordfish torpedo-spotter reconnaissance aircraft to carry out the mission.

To mask his intentions, Cunningham initiated a weeklong series of fleet operations in support of four convoys. On November 6, *Illustrious* departed Alexandria with a convoy escort force bound for Malta. Although three Swordfish crashed on November 10 and 11, at 1945 on the evening of the 11th, the carrier launched her first twelve-plane strike 170 miles southeast of Taranto. The British did not achieve anything like complete surprise, but despite a heavy barrage of antiaircraft fire, three torpedoes hit home, one on the battleship CONTE DI CAVOUR and two on the newly commissioned LITTORIO, and only one aircraft was lost (both her crew survived). The start of the second strike was marred by an on-deck collision between two aircraft, only one of which flew in the attack. This strike managed to score a third hit on the *Littorio* and one on the battleship *Caio Giulio,* also for the loss of only one aircraft.

Considering the meager force allocated to the operation, the raid on Taranto was impressive. Half of the Italian Navy's battleships were severely damaged — *Conte di Cavour* never returned to service and *Littorio* and *Caio Giulio* were out of service for nearly half a year — and the remainder of the ships at Taranto were transferred to more remote bases on the west coast of Italy. The raid on Taranto signaled the coming of age of carrier aviation, and it was carefully studied by the Japanese in planning their attack on the U.S. Navy base at Pearl Harbor, Hawaii.

Illustrious herself was vulnerable to aerial attack. On January 10, 1941, she was badly damaged by land-based German dive-bombers while escorting a convoy east of Sicily. Putting in at Malta, she was hit a second time before she sailed to the Norfolk Navy Yard in Virginia for repairs.

Upon her return to service in 1942, *Illustrious* was dispatched to the Indian Ocean, and in May she and *Indomitable* covered troop landings at Diego Suarez, Madagascar, from which Vichy French forces could threaten convoys rounding South Africa. In 1943, she returned to the Mediterranean for operations with Force H, based at Gibraltar, and helped cover the Allied landings in Sicily. The following year she joined Admiral Sir James Somerville's Eastern Fleet and participated in raids on the Japanese-held Indonesian islands of Palembang and Sabang. Three months later, the British Pacific Fleet — including carriers *Formidable* and *Victorious* — operated in support of the landings on Okinawa.

Following World War II, *Illustrious* was used as a training carrier. Refitted in 1948, she was decommissioned in 1954 and broken up two years later at Faslane.

Schofield, *Taranto.* Stephen, *Sea Battles in Close-Up.*

HMS IMPLACABLE

(ex-*Duguay-Trouin,* later HMS *Lion*) 3rd rate (3m). *L/B/D:* 181.5′ × 48.9′ × 22′ (55.3m × 14.9m × 6.7m). *Tons:* 1,896 bm. *Hull:* wood. *Comp.:* 670. *Arm.:* 30 × 32pdr, 12 × 32pdr carr, 30 × 18pdr, 2 × 12pdr. *Built:* Rochefort, France; 1801.

Named for one of the greatest French admirals, René Duguay-Trouin (1673–1736) — who as a privateer in 1711 captured and ransomed the city of Rio de Janeiro — the 74-gun ship *Duguay-Trouin* was launched just after the establishment of Napoleon Bonaparte's consulate in

France. In 1801, she helped convoy General C. V. E. Leclerc's army to Santo Domingo for the suppression of the slave rebellion led by Toussaint L'Ouverture. While in the Caribbean she became flagship of Vice Admiral Louis-René Levassor de Latouche-Tréville. On April 15, 1803, *Duguay-Trouin* grounded off the port of Jérémie, and she could only be refloated after Captain Pierre l'Hermité jettisoned twenty of her heaviest guns, each weighing more than three tons.

Illness in the fleet forced the return of three ships to France, and on July 24, 1803, *Duguay-Trouin, Guerrière* (Captain Louis-Alexis Beaudouin), and *Duquesne* (Commodore Querangal) attempted to run the British blockade, though the latter was captured. On August 29, *Duguay-Trouin* was engaged by the Royal Navy frigate *Boadicea* off El Ferrol, Spain. In an effort to determine how well manned she was, Captain Maitland engaged the larger ship until he was satisfied that the French could fight their lower deck guns. *Duguay-Trouin* was then engaged by Sir Edward Pellew's squadron, which chased her so closely that Pellew's HMS *Culloden* came under fire from shore batteries at La Coruña.

Duguay-Trouin eventually passed under command of Claude Touffet, but remained at La Coruña until August 11, 1805, when she sailed with the Comte de Villeneuve's fleet for Cadiz. Although ordered to Naples by Napoleon, Villeneuve feared an engagement with the British fleet, first under Vice Admiral Sir Cuthbert Collingwood and then under Vice Admiral Lord Nelson in VICTORY. When he learned that Napoleon was relieving him of his command, he took his eighteen French and fifteen Spanish ships of the line out of Cadiz, and on October 21 turned to fight Nelson. As the ships sailed into battle, *Duguay-Trouin* was one of the ten ships in the van under Rear Admiral Pierre Dumanoir Le Pelley in *Formidable.* Except for a few ships whose captains fought as they should in defiance of his orders, Dumanoir kept his squadron out of battle until 1500 — three hours after battle was joined. *Formidable, Duguay-Trouin, Mont Blanc, Scipion,* and the Spanish *Neptuno* sailed to the assistance of Villeneuve's BUCENTAURE. But too late to aid the beleaguered flagship, Dumanoir quit the battle with four of his ships, *Neptuno* having been captured by HMS *Minotaur* and *Spartiate.*

Two weeks later Dumanoir was cruising in the Bay of Biscay when they sighted the British frigate *Phoenix.* The chase brought them right into the fleet of Sir Richard Strachan on November 4, and the four French ships were overwhelmed by Strachan's superior force. Aboard *Duguay-Trouin,* Touffet and all his lieutenants were killed or injured and the ship was surrendered by Ensign de Vaisseau Rigodet.

Taken into the Royal Navy, the 74-gun ship was renamed HMS *Implacable.* In 1808, she sailed under Captain Thomas Byam Martin as part of Sir James Saumarez's Baltic expedition. Detached to the Swedish fleet, on August 26 *Implacable* and Rear Admiral Samuel Hood's *Centaur* engaged, captured, and blew up the Russian *Vsevolod* (74) practically within range of the whole Russian fleet. Laid up following the Napoleonic Wars, *Implacable*'s next action was with the Mediterranean fleet, when she sailed as part of a combined British, Austrian, and Turkish force in an action off the coast of Syria to prevent an Egyptian advance into Turkey.

From July 1855 she served as a Royal Navy training ship at Devonport, and in 1871 she was renamed *Lion.* In 1912, the Navy loaned her to Mr. J. Wheatley Cobb for use as a training ship, and her name reverted to *Implacable.* A major overhaul was undertaken in 1925 and she remained a private training ship until World War II. Drydocked at Portsmouth in 1943, she was commissioned as a training ship and renamed *Foudroyant;* she was paid off for the last time in 1947. A survey of the ship showed that deterioration of the hull during the war was so extensive as to make her restoration prohibitively expensive — more than £200,000 in 1948. As a result, on December 2, 1949, she was towed into the English Channel and scuttled. The loss of the ship galvanized a small fraternity of preservationists, chief among them Frank Carr, director of the National Maritime Museum in Greenwich, who established the World Ship Trust. Today, *Implacable* lives on in the mission of the Trust: "to advance the education of the public by the preservation and display of historic ships and associated artifacts."

Mackenzie, *The Trafalgar Roll.* Schom, *Trafalgar.* Wyllie, "H.M.S. *Implacable.*"

HMS INDEFATIGABLE

Indefatigable-class battlecruiser (3f/2m). *L/B/D:* 590′ × 80′ × 27′ (179.8m × 24.4m × 8.2m). *Tons:* 22,080 disp. *Hull:* steel. *Comp.:* 800–1,021. *Arm.:* 8 × 12″ (4 × 2), 14 × 4″, 4 × 3pdr; 2 × 18″TT. *Armor:* 6″ belt, 2.5″ deck. *Mach.:* Parsons turbines, 33,000 ihp, 4 screws; 25 kts. *Des.:* W. T. Davis. *Built:* Devonport Dockyard, Plymouth, Eng.; 1911.

The first of a three-ship class, HMS *Indefatigable* was only a slight improvement over the first battlecruiser class named for HMS INVINCIBLE. As in the earlier ships, she had four turrets, one forward, one aft, and two displaced diagonally on either side of the ship. After duty with the Home Fleet, in 1913 she was transferred to the Mediterranean Fleet. In August 1914 she took part in the hunt for

SMS GOEBEN and BRESLAU, and was later stationed on the Dardanelles blockade. Recalled to home waters in February 1915, she joined Vice Admiral Sir William C. Pakenham's Second Battle Cruiser Squadron. At the Battle of Jutland on May 31, 1916, during the "run to the south," the first engagement between the British and German battlecruisers, *Indefatigable* was in the rear, opposite SMS VON DER TANN. After 27 minutes, a hit on the fore turret penetrated the magazine spaces and blew the ship in half, and she sank at 1605 with the loss of 1,017 crew; there were four survivors.

Parkes, *British Battleships.*

USS INDEPENDENCE

Ship of the line (3m). *L/B/D:* 190.8′ bp × 54.6′ × 24.3′ (58.2m × 16.6m × 7.4m). *Tons:* 2,257 bm. *Hull:* wood. *Comp.:* 790. *Arm.:* 90 × 32pdr. *Built:* Edmund Hartt and J. Barker, Boston, Mass.; 1814.

By 1814, the course of naval operations in the War of 1812 made it apparent that a fleet comprised of nothing larger than 44-gun frigates, no matter how well fought, was no match for the largest units of the all-too-effective British blockade. To rectify this, the U.S. Navy ordered three 74-gun ships of the line: USS *Independence, Franklin,* and *Washington.* Launched in June 1814, *Independence* was quickly armed and stationed off Boston Harbor. The war was soon over, and in June 1815 she sailed as flagship of a squadron under Commodore William Bainbridge to the Mediterranean, where she arrived after a new peace had been concluded with the Barbary corsairs. *Independence* returned stateside the same year and remained in service until 1822.

Poorly designed as a three-decker, *Independence* had only three and a half feet of freeboard at her lower gun deck, which made it all but impossible to use those guns in battle. She remained in ordinary at Boston until 1835–36 when she was razeed — that is, her spar deck was removed — and she was recommissioned as a 54-gun frigate. "Thus," in the words of Howard Chapelle, "a ship considered a failure and useless for almost twenty-two years became one of the best ships in the Navy."

Her first assignment after recommissioning in 1837 was to convey to Kronstadt the U.S. minister to Russia George Dallas, en route to his new post at St. Petersburg. *Independence* then sailed from the Baltic to Rio de Janeiro where she served as flagship of the Navy's Brazil Squadron, responsible for safeguarding U.S. interests along the east coast of South America. Two years later she became flagship of Commodore Charles Stewart's Home Squadron. Following the outbreak of the Mexican War in 1846,

Sailmaker's plan for the American 74-gun ship of the line USS INDEPENDENCE *prior to the removal of her spar deck in 1836, when she was reconfigured as a 54-gun frigate. Courtesy U.S. Naval Historical Center, Washington, D.C.*

she sailed for Monterey, California, and Commodore William B. Shubrick broke his flag aboard *Independence* in January 1847. The Pacific Squadron, which also comprised the frigate *Congress* (44) and three sloops, seized the ports of Guaymas (October 20) and Mazatlán (November 11). En route home in 1848, *Independence* called at Honolulu. A mild outbreak of measles among her crew quickly spread to the Hawaiian people with devastating effect: the ensuing epidemic is believed to have killed 10 percent of the native population.

Independence spent three years as flagship of the Mediterranean Squadron, returning to New York in 1852 and placed in ordinary. Two years later she sailed for Valparaiso to take up assignment as flagship of the Pacific Squadron for a second time, her duties taking her north to San Francisco and east to Hawaii. On October 2, 1857, she entered the Mare Island Navy Yard at San Francisco and became a receiving ship. Sold in 1914, her hardwood was salvaged and the remainder burned to recover her metal fittings.

Chapelle, *History of the American Sailing Navy.* Johnson, *Thence Round Cape Horn.* U.S. Navy, *DANFS.*

INDIANA

Screw steamship (1f/1m). *L/B/D:* 146.5′ × 23′ × 10.8′ (44.7m × 7m × 3.3m). *Tons:* 349 grt. *Hull:* wood. *Comp.:* 18 crew. *Mach.:* vertical steam engine. *Built:* Joseph M. Keating, Vermilion, Ohio; 1848.

Built for a consortium of Ohioans and a New Yorker as a cargo-passenger boat, and homeported at Sandusky, Ohio, *Indiana* worked primarily on Lake Erie with occasional trips to Lakes Michigan and Huron. In 1852, she was sold to Buffalo interests and chartered first to the Union Steamboat Company and then the Clipper Line. Sold to Francis Perew of Cleveland in 1854, *Indiana* was probably cut down to one deck and given a second mast. On June 16, 1858, she was bound from Marquette, Michigan, to Sault Sainte Marie, when the propeller's stuffing box broke, causing an irreparable leak. The ship's crew and three passengers abandoned the ship, and *Indiana* sank with her 280 tons of iron ore in 120 feet of water about 3.6 miles (5.8 km) off Crisp Point, Michigan.

The wreck site was located by John R. Steele in 1972, and the Smithsonian Institution soon became interested in recovering *Indiana*'s remarkably well-preserved machinery for the National Museum of American History in Washington, D.C. Since 1979, divers have recovered the complete 18-foot-high vertical steam engine, the 15-foot 7-inch boiler, the 9-foot 7-inch four-bladed propeller, the steering quadrant and related machinery, as well as the ship's safe, among other items.

Johnston, "Downbound."

USS INDIANA (BB-1)

Indiana-class pre-dreadnought battleship (2f/1m). *L/B/D:* 350.1′ × 69.3′ × 27′ (106.7m × 21.1m × 8.2m). *Tons:* 11,688 disp. *Hull:* steel. *Comp.:* 650. *Arm.:* 4 × 13″ (2 × 2), 8 × 8″; 4 × 6″, 20 × 6pdr, 6 × 1pdr. *Armor:* 18″ belt, 3″ deck. *Mach.:* VTE engines, 9,000 ihp, 2 screws; 15.5 kts. *Built:* William Cramp & Sons Ship and Engine Building Co., Philadelphia; 1895.

Authorized in 1890, USS *Indiana* was the name ship of the U.S. Navy's first class of battleships; the others were USS *Massachusetts* and OREGON. Classified as coastal defense battleships, they had more powerful guns and thicker armor than their contemporaries and, in the words of a British naval architect, they were "distinctly superior to any European vessels of the same displacement, and . . . quite a match for any ships afloat." In 1898, *Indiana* was one of ten ships in Admiral William T. Sampson's squadron sent to intercept a Spanish fleet of four antiquated cruisers and lighter units en route to Cuba. After shelling San Juan, Puerto Rico, on May 12, she withdrew to Key West before proceeding to Santiago, Cuba. When Admiral Pascual Cervera y Topete attempted his desperate breakout on July 3, *Indiana, Gloucester* (ex-CORSAIR), and *Iowa* shattered the destroyers *Pluton* and *Furor*.

From 1905 to 1914, *Indiana* worked as a training ship. Decommissioned from 1914 to 1917, she resumed training duty following the U.S. entry into World War I. In 1920, she was sunk as a target ship during tests of aerial bombs.

U.S. Navy, *DANFS.*

USS INDIANAPOLIS (CA-35)

Portland-class cruiser (2f/2m). *L/B/D:* 610.3′ × 66.1′ × 17.4′ (186m × 20.1m × 5.3m). *Tons:* 12,775 disp. *Comp.:* 551–1,269. *Hull:* steel. *Arm.:* 9 × 8″ (3 × 3), 8 × 5″ (4 × 2), 24 × 40mm, 16 × 20mm; 4 aircraft. *Armor:* 3″ belt, 2.5″ deck. *Mach.:* geared turbines, 107,000 hp, 4 screws; 32.5 kts. *Built:* New York Shipbuilding Corp., Camden, N.J.; 1932.

The second ship of the name, USS *Indianapolis*'s peacetime years were distinguished by her frequent passages with President Franklin D. Roosevelt aboard. The most extensive of these was a "Good Neighbor" cruise to South America (November 18–December 15, 1936) under Captain H. K. Hewitt. The log for Tuesday, November 24, relates the ceremony for crossing the equator:

> Made all necessary preparations to receive his Royal Majesty Neptunus Rex, Ruler of the Raging Main and Kin of all creatures in and of the Deeps of the Seven Seas, with honors fitting and proper. . . . The Royal Party took their posts on the quarter deck and proceeded to hold court, commencing with the trial of the most "ratey" Pollywog, the President of the United States. The sentences and punishments were administered and executed without faltering until the last victim had paid his penalty at 1515.

The outbreak of World War II found *Indianapolis* in the Pacific. She was assigned to Task Force 11 and took part in operations in the waters around New Britain and New Guinea in early 1942. She saw action in the Aleutian Islands from August 1942 to the spring of 1943. Later in the year she flew Vice Admiral Raymond Spruance's flag in the Gilbert Islands (November 1943), the Marshalls (January 1944), Carolines (March and April), and Mariana Islands (through September). Later detailed to Vice Admiral Marc A. Mitscher's fast-carrier attack force in operations against the Japanese Home Islands (March 31) off Okinawa, *Indianapolis* was hit by a kamikaze's bomb that exploded after passing through the bottom of the hull. She returned to San Francisco under her own power. With repairs complete, she was ordered to carry to Tinian Island the operative parts of the atom bomb destined for Hiroshima. Under Captain Charles B. McVay III, she sailed from Farallon Light to Diamond Head in a record 74½ hours. After stopping briefly for fuel and stores at Pearl Harbor, she reached Tinian on July 26. Her top-secret cargo discharged, she departed for Guam and Leyte. Shortly before midnight on the second day out,

An aerial view of the handsome cruiser USS INDIANAPOLIS *arriving at Buenos Aires during President Franklin D. Roosevelt's goodwill cruise to South America, November 30, 1936. Courtesy U.S. Naval Historical Center, Washington, D.C.*

she was spotted by the Japanese submarine *I-58,* under Commander Machitsura Hashimoto. Hashimoto fired six torpedoes at 0015 on July 30. (Some reports suggest that manned midget submarines called kaitens were used.) One blew off the bow and the other hit just below the bridge. *Indianapolis* sank in about ten minutes in 12°02′N, 134°48′E, taking an estimated 400 of her crew with her; they were the lucky ones. A series of radio transmission errors resulted in there being no overdue message posted, and in the course of the next few days, 500 of the crew died, many of them eaten by sharks. Finally, on August 2, a patrol plane happened to notice groups of survivors drifting in the sea. Over the next six days, 316 men were rescued.

As if the "routine stupidity and unnecessary suffering," as Samuel Eliot Morison described it, of the Navy's second-greatest loss of life from a single ship were not enough (only USS ARIZONA had more casualties), the Navy proceeded to court-martial Captain McVay for failing to order a zigzag course (a fact he freely acknowledged) and for not abandoning ship sooner. Incredibly, among the prosecution's star witnesses was none other than *I-58*'s Commander Hashimoto. McVay was found guilty of the first charge and acquitted of the second.

Lech, *All the Drowned Sailors.* U.S. Navy, *DANFS.*

HMS INFLEXIBLE

Brig-rigged turret ship (2f/2m). *L/B/D:* 320′ × 75′ × 26.5 (97.5m × 22.9m × 8.1m). *Tons:* 11,880 disp. *Hull:* steel. *Comp.:* 440. *Arm.:* 4 × 16″ (2x2), 6 × 20pdr. *Armor:* citadel 16–24″, bulkheads 14–22″. *Mach.:* inverted compound engine, 8,400 ihp, 2 screws; 14.75 kts. *Des.:* Sir Nathaniel Barnaby. *Built:* Portsmouth Dockyard, Eng.; 1881.

The most progressive British battleship to follow HMS WARRIOR, HMS *Inflexible* incorporated a number of innovative design elements, many of which became standard features of later warship architecture. She was the first ship to use an underwater armor deck in place of vertical armor along the waterline, and the 24-inch armor used in the 110-foot-long central box citadel was the thickest ever used in a British warship. *Inflexible*'s 16-inch guns — carried in two turrets mounted en echelon — were also the largest fitted to that time. These muzzle-loading rifles could only be loaded from outside the turrets, a relatively awkward maneuver achieved by depressing the muzzles into a built-up portion of the armored deck directly above the magazines. *Inflexible* was the first ship fitted with electric light. However, because of the labyrinthine division of the hull spaces that ensured the stability and survivability of the ship, her first captain, John Arbuthnot Fisher, devoted several months to color-coding the passageways and using other devices to enable the crew to maneuver efficiently below decks, in darkness if need be. Nonetheless, it was not until the crew had perfected its sail handling — the auxiliary rig was never intended for use in battle — that *Inflexible* was rated "the best ship in the Fleet." The sails were replaced by fighting tops in 1885.

Seven and a half years under construction, upon her commissioning, *Inflexible* was the most powerful warship in the world. Joining the Mediterranean Fleet in 1881, she was part of the British force sent to Alexandria during the abortive uprising by the Egyptian General Ahmed Arabi (Arabi Pasha) against the pro-European Khedive of Egypt. During the bombardment of July 12, *Inflexible* lost five men killed and forty-four wounded from enemy fire. (Under Fisher, her shore parties later improvised the first armored train for patrolling the outskirts of the city.) She remained in the Mediterranean until 1885 and emerged from a refit to be placed in reserve. She was again in commission in the Mediterranean from 1890 to 1893 and thereafter served as a guard ship at Portsmouth. She was broken up in 1903.

Massie, *"Dreadnought."* Parkes, *British Battleships.*

HMS INFLEXIBLE

Invincible-class battlecruiser (2m/3f). *L/B/D:* 567' × 78.5' × 26.8' (172.8m × 23.9m × 8.1m). *Tons:* 17,250 disp. *Hull:* steel. *Comp.:* 784. *Arm.:* 8 × 12" (4 × 2); 16 × 4"; 1 × 3"; 5 × 18"TT. *Armor:* belt 6", deck 2.5". *Mach.:* Parsons turbines, 41,000 hp, 4 screws; 25 kts. *Built:* John Brown & Co., Clydebank, Scotland; 1908.

One of the first three battlecruisers built, HMS *Inflexible* served in the Home Fleet and Channel Squadron before becoming flagship of the Mediterranean Fleet in 1912. In August 1914, she shadowed SMS GOEBEN and BRESLAU prior to their escape to Constantinople. Recalled to home waters, in November she and HMS INVINCIBLE were ordered to the South Atlantic after the defeat of the British squadron at the Battle of Coronel. The ships arrived at the Falkland Islands on December 7, and the next morning Vice Admiral Maximilian Graf von Spee's East Asiatic Cruiser Squadron was spotted. With their longer range, the British were able to sink SMS SCHARNHORST and GNEISENAU without damage to themselves. After serving as Vice Admiral Sir Sackville Carden's flagship at the Dardanelles, where she was bombed and mined on March 18, 1915, *Inflexible* was assigned to the Third Battle Cruiser Squadron. She survived the Battle of Jutland (May 31, 1916) unscathed. In 1921, *Inflexible* was sold and broken up in Germany.

Halpern, *Naval History of World War I*. Parkes, *British Battleships*.

INTELLIGENT WHALE

Submarine. *L/B/D:* 28.7' × 7' × 9' dph (8.7m x 2.1m × 2.7m). *Tons:* 4,000 lb. *Hull:* iron. *Comp.:* 6–13. *Mach.:* hand crank, single screw; 4 kts. *Des.:* Scovel S. Meriam. *Built:* August Price, Cornelius S. Bushnell, American Submarine Co.; 1863.

The immediate impetus for the development and construction of the experimental submarine *Intelligent Whale* was triggered by Union fears excited by the success of similar vessels in the Confederacy during the Civil War. CSS H. L. HUNLEY and PIONEER were two outstanding examples. Meriam's design called for a manually operated vessel. To dive, water was admitted to the ballast chambers; to surface, the water was expelled again by means of pumps and compressed air. A hand-crank geared to a single propeller was the sole means of forward propulsion. Only six people were required to operate the vessel, though it could carry as many as thirteen at one time. *Intelligent Whale* carried no armament per se, but she was intended as a vehicle for sneak attack. In her only known operational test, she was submerged to a depth of sixteen feet, whereupon a General Sweeney exited the hull in a diver's suit, attached an underwater mine to the hull of an anchored barge, and returned to the submarine. The mine was detonated by pulling a lanyard leading to a friction primer on the mine. This trial was only completed in 1872, the Navy having purchased *Intelligent Whale* from the American Submarine Company in 1864. Although the scow was sunk, the Navy was not impressed with the undertaking and declined either to test *Intelligent Whale* further or to pay the fee due on acceptance of the craft. Placed on exhibit at the Brooklyn Navy Yard, the submarine was transferred to the Washington Navy Yard's Navy Memorial Museum in 1966.

Delgado & Clifford, *Great American Ships*. U.S. Navy, *DANFS*.

USS INTREPID

(ex-*Mastico*, *L'Intrepide*) Ketch (2m). *L/B:* 60' × 12' (18.3m × 3.7m). *Tons:* 64. *Hull:* wood. *Comp.:* 64. *Arm.:* 4 guns. *Built:* France; 1798.

Built for Napoleon's Egyptian campaign in 1798, following the defeat of the French fleet at the Battle of the Nile, the bomb-ketch *L'Intrépide* was sold to Tripoli. On October 31, 1803, the renamed *Mastico* took part in the capture of USS PHILADELPHIA when the frigate ran aground off Tripoli Harbor. Two months later, while en route to Constantinople, she was captured by USS ENTERPRISE, under Lieutenant Stephen Decatur, and taken into the American fleet as *Intrepid*. To deny Tripoli any chance of refloating *Philadelphia* themselves, Commodore Edward Preble decided to burn the ship. Renamed *Intrepid* and commanded by Decatur, *Intrepid* slipped into the harbor on the night of February 16, 1804. Sixty of her crew overwhelmed *Philadelphia*'s token crew and set the ship ablaze, with no casualties to themselves. Hearing of the brilliant feat, England's Lord Nelson proclaimed it "the most bold and daring act of the age." *Intrepid* lay idle at Syracuse until August, when it was decided to use her as a "floating volcano" to destroy the Tripolitan fleet at anchor. Packed with gunpowder and manned by twelve volunteers under Lieutenant Richard Somers, *Intrepid* entered the harbor on September 4. The ketch exploded prematurely, and there were no survivors.

U.S. Navy, *DANFS*.

USS INTREPID (CV-11)

Essex-class aircraft carrier (1f/1m). *L/B/D:* 872' × 93.2' (147.6'ew) × 28.6' (265.8m × 28.4m (45m) × 8.7m). *Tons:* 34,364 disp. *Hull:* steel. *Comp.:* 3,448. *Arm.:* 12 × 5", 68 × 40mm. *Armor:* 3" belt. *Mach.:* geared turbines, 150,000 shp, 4 screws; 33 kts. *Built:* Newport News Shipbuilding & Dry Dock Co., Newport News, Va.; 1943.

The fourth U.S. Navy vessel and the first of two aircraft carriers of the name, USS *Intrepid* was commissioned almost halfway through World War II. Her first assignment was to join with carriers Essex and *Cabot* for the invasion of the Marshall Islands, where the carriers operated off Kwajalein from January 29 to February 2, 1944. Sailing from there as part of the armada bound for Truk, about 1,000 miles to the east, her planes took part in the destruction of that Japanese anchorage on the 17th. That night *Intrepid* was hit by an aerial torpedo, her first hit of the war. A makeshift sail of hatch covers and odd canvas had to be jury rigged to bring her head around before she could return to Pearl Harbor en route to the West Coast for repairs.

Returning to service in June, in September she took part in the invasion of the southern Palaus and preliminary attacks on the Philippines. When the invasion of Leyte began, one of *Intrepid*'s flyers was the first to locate the Japanese fleet on October 24. At the Battle of Surigao Strait, the Third Fleet sank the Japanese battleship Musashi and damaged Yamato, *Nagato,* and *Haruna.* Pursuing the Japanese north, *Intrepid*'s pilots took part in the Battle of Cape Engaño, which cost the Japanese the carriers Zuiho, *Chitose,* Zuikaku, and *Chiyoda.* On October 30, *Intrepid* was hit by a kamikaze while launching attacks against Clark Field near Manila, although she was able to remain on station. On November 25, as the Americans tried to prevent Japanese reinforcements from landing on Luzon, the "Evil I," as she was becoming known, was crashed by two kamikazes that killed 65 of her crew and forced her to San Francisco for repairs. No sooner was she back in service, off Kyushu, than she was hit yet again by a kamikaze, though with only mild damage, on March 18. Seven days later, she was part of the Okinawa invasion force. On April 16, she was hit by her fifth kamikaze and forced back to San Francisco for repairs that lasted until July 29.

In 1946, *Intrepid* was laid up at San Francisco. Four years later she was converted to an attack aircraft carrier (CVA-11) and was the first American carrier fitted with steam catapults. Her waterline beam grew to 101 feet, while her extreme width was 191.9 feet. For the next seven years she sailed in the Atlantic, Caribbean, and Mediterranean. Recommissioned as an antisubmarine warfare support carrier in 1961, she was the lead ship in the recovery of astronaut Scott Carpenter after splashdown from his Mercury mission on May 24, 1962, and three years later of John Young and Virgil Grissom on their return from the first manned Gemini flight on March 23, 1965.

After a modernization, *Intrepid* returned to the western Pacific for operations during the Vietnam War, where she served from 1966 until 1968, when she returned to duty in the Atlantic and Mediterranean. Decommissioned in 1974, eight years later she was opened to the public as the centerpiece of the Intrepid Sea-Air-Space Museum in New York City.

Roberts, *Aircraft Carrier "Intrepid."* U.S. Navy, *DANFS.*

INTREPID

12-meter sloop. *L/B/D:* 65.2′ × 11.9′ × 9.1′ (19.9m × 3.6m × 2.8m). *Tons:* 58,000 disp. *Hull:* wood. *Comp.:* 11. *Des.:* Olin Stephens. *Built:* Minneford Yacht Yard, Inc., City Island, N.Y.; 1967.

In 1967, the Royal Sydney Yacht Squadron issued its second challenge to the New York Yacht Club for the America's Cup. (In 1962, Australia's *Gretel* lost 4–1 to *Weatherly.*) In response, the Americans formed the Intrepid Syndicate, which included Bus Mosbacher, *Weatherly*'s former skipper, and designer Olin Stephens. Among *Intrepid*'s other innovations were the placement of the winches — and their handlers — below deck to reduce the center of gravity, and a steering system that included a steering rudder detached from the fin keel. There was also a trim rudder on the rudder that reduced her turning radius significantly and enabled her to point higher. After sweeping the trial races against a host of previous Cup defenders, *Intrepid* was the hands-down favorite against *Dame Pattie* (under Jock Sturrock), whom she bested in four straight races with a margin of victory that equaled about 11 seconds per mile over all four races.

Three years later, *Intrepid* was brought out of retirement to defend a second time. This time, she faced tough competition in the trials, as Stephens had designed a new boat for the Valiant Syndicate. After modifications by Britton Chance, Jr., under skipper Bill Ficker, *Intrepid* sailed to a 22–5 record in trials, thus giving her the right to defend against Australia's *Gretel II,* who had herself won a 4–0 series against rival challenger *France,* owned by Baron Bich. The series proved the longest and one of the most highly charged to date. In the first race, *Gretel II* showed herself quite *Intrepid*'s equal but lost a man overboard whose rescue cost her about five minutes. Just before the beginning of the second race, one of *Intrepid*'s crew was stung by a bee and had to be airlifted to a hospital. Then, *Gretel*'s victory was disqualified because she had hit *Intrepid* just after the starting gun. The third race went to *Intrepid,* but the Australians kept the best-of-seven series alive with a clean win in the fourth, only to lose in the fifth race.

In the 1974 trials, the seven-year-old *Intrepid* put her aluminum successor to the test in a 4–5 series before

Courageous earned the right to defend the Cup against *Southern Cross*. *Intrepid* was eventually sold to Baron Bich.

Robinson, *Legendary Yachts.*

HMS INVESTIGATOR

(ex-*Xenophon*) Ship-sloop (3m). *L/B:* 100.5′ × 28.5′ (30.6m × 8.7m). *Tons:* 334 bm. *Hull:* wood. *Built:* Sunderland, Eng.; 1795.

In 1798, Matthew Flinders served as lieutenant of HMS *Norfolk* during George Bass's expedition along the southeast coast of Australia, during which the ship passed through Bass Strait to confirm that Tasmania was an island. Three years later, Flinders applied to Sir Joseph Banks for support in mounting a voyage around Australia. The Admiralty endorsed the plan and Flinders was supplied with *Xenophon,* a stout North Country ship that "in form resembled the description of vessels recommended by Captain Cook as best calculated for voyages of discovery." Departing Spithead on July 18, 1801, the renamed HMS *Investigator* called at the Cape of Good Hope before setting out across the Indian Ocean. *Investigator* arrived off Cape Leeuwin at the southwest corner of Australia on December 6. After putting into King George Sound, the expedition began a running survey of the Great Australian Bight, which stretched 3,200 kilometers to Spencer Gulf. Among the other objects of their search was a passage that led north to the Gulf of Carpentaria, for Australia was then believed to be divided by a strait. At the entrance to Spencer Gulf, seven of the ship's company were lost when a small boat capsized. Flinders surveyed Port Lincoln, which he named for his home county. Working their way east, *Investigator's* crew next charted Kangaroo Island, Yorke Peninsula, and St. Vincent Gulf. On April 8, at Encounter Bay, they were surprised to meet LA GÉOGRAPHE under Nicolas Baudin, with whom Flinders had several cordial meetings, despite the fact that their two countries were then at war. Sailing eastward through Bass Strait, Flinders visited King Island and Port Philip (Melbourne) before arriving at Port Jackson on May 9.

Investigator took aboard twelve new men, including an aborigine named Bongaree, with whom Flinders had sailed previously and who served as an intermediary with other aborigines encountered on the voyage. The expedition was also joined by *Lady Nelson,* a centerboard brig designed for surveying in shallow water; she proved a sluggish sailor and eventually returned to Port Jackson. Following in the wake of Cook's ENDEAVOUR, *Investigator* hugged the east coast of Australia before passing through the Great Barrier Reef and then transiting Torres Strait, which Flinders had previously sailed through with Captain William Bligh in HMS *Providence.* While surveying the Gulf of Carpentaria, *Investigator's* timbers were found to be in a dismal state, and the ship's carpenter reported that the ship would not last much more than six months. Flinders sailed to the Dutch settlement on Timor, but as there was no prospect of obtaining another ship, he decided to sail westabout around Australia for Port Jackson, setting "all possible sail day and night" and reluctantly abandoning his survey of the north and west coasts.

Investigator reached Port Jackson in June 1803 and Flinders sailed for home in the storeship *Porpoise,* only to be shipwrecked on the Great Barrier Reef. Placed in command of *Cumberland,* he was forced to put into Ile de France, not knowing that England and France were again at war. Detained until 1810, he returned to England broken in health and lived barely long enough to see his memoirs in print. Meanwhile, *Investigator* had been repaired and returned to England; she was hulked in 1810.

Flinders, *Voyage to Terra Australis.* Ritchie, *Admiralty Chart.*

HMS INVESTIGATOR

Ship (3m). *L/B/D:* 118′ × 28.3′ × 18.9′ (36m × 8.6m × 5.8m). *Tons:* 422 bm. *Hull:* wood. *Comp.:* 66. *Built:* Charles Scott & Co., Greenock, Scotland; 1848.

On May 12, 1848, Sir James Clark Ross led the Admiralty's first expedition in search of HMS EREBUS and TERROR. The very same ships with which he had spent four years exploring Antarctica were now lost in the Canadian Arctic under command of Sir John Franklin. HMS *Investigator* and *Enterprise* sailed through Lancaster Sound and Barrow Strait to Somerset Island; from here sledges were dispatched in search of Franklin. One one of them, Ross and Francis L. M'Clintock descended Peel Sound to within 70 miles of *Erebus* and *Terror* before they were forced to turn back. After only one winter, *Investigator* and *Enterprise* returned to England in 1849.

On January 31, 1850, Captain Richard Collinson, in *Enterprise,* and Lieutenant Robert McClure, in *Investigator,* sailed from England in an attempt to discover whether Franklin's ships had actually completed the Northwest Passage. The ships rounded Cape Horn and were separated in the Pacific. Rather than wait for Collinson at Bering Strait, McClure sailed *Investigator* east into the Beaufort Sea and then northeast into the Prince of Wales Strait between Banks Island and Victoria Island, but by September *Investigator* was fast in the ice. In October, McClure set out by sledge up the strait to the shore of Viscount Melville Sound, to which William E. Parry had sailed in HMS HECLA in 1819–20, and thereby confirmed the existence of a Northwest Passage, however choked with ice.

The next season, McClure worked *Investigator* south and around the western and northern shores of Banks Island, through McClure Strait towards Melville Sound. Heavy ice prevented their making for Winter Harbor, about 175 miles to the east, and on September 23, 1851, *Investigator* put into Mercy Bay on northeast Banks Island. In 1852, a sledging expedition visited Winter Harbor and left a note describing the desperate situation at Mercy Harbor, where the ship's crew was subsisting on daily rations of a half pound of beef and twelve ounces of flour. The note was discovered by the crew of HMS RESOLUTE, then thirty-five miles east of Winter Harbor, and on April 6, 1853, a sledge party reached Mercy Bay. McClure reluctantly abandoned *Investigator* in late May, and her surviving crew marched east to *Resolute*. They did not return to England until 1854.

Dodge, *Northwest by Sea*. McClure, *Discovery of the North-West Passage by H.M.S. "Investigator."*

HMS INVINCIBLE

Invincible-class battlecruiser (3f/2m). *L/B/D:* 567′ × 78.5′ × 29.6′ (172.8m × 23.9m × 9m). *Tons:* 19,940 disp. *Hull:* steel. *Comp.:* 730–1,032. *Arm.:* 8 × 12″ (4 × 2), 16 × 4″, 1 × 3″; 5 × 18″TT. *Armor:* 6″ belt, 2.5″ deck. *Mach.:* steam turbines, 41,000 shp, 4 screws; 25.5 kts. *Built:* Sir W. G. Armstrong, Whitworth & Co., Ltd., Newcastle-on-Tyne, Eng.; 1908.

Conceived of by First Sea Lord Admiral John Arbuthnot Fisher in the same year as the revolutionary battleship DREADNOUGHT, *Invincible* was intended not as a ship fit to fight in the line of battle, but as a commerce protector. With great hitting strength, her defense against larger ships was predicated on superior speed rather than thick armor, a flaw that was to doom many battlecruisers. Originally classified as a "large armoured cruiser" (the designation "battlecruiser" came in 1913), *Invincible* was ordered the same year as HMS *Dreadnought*. She mounted eight 10-inch guns (as opposed to *Dreadnought*'s ten guns) in four turrets, one forward, one aft, and two en echelon amidships. Longer and faster than *Dreadnought*, the role of the battlecruisers was defined as follows: "to engage the enemy battle cruisers in a fleet action, or, if none are present, by using their speed to cross the bow of the enemy and engage the van of his battlefleet."

The battlecruiser HMS INVINCIBLE *carried eight 12-inch guns in four turrets, one forward, one aft, and two diagonally offset side turrets. The latter two, turned to a broadside position, are visible between the second and third funnels. (Note the diagonal shadows of the starboard guns along the hull.) Inadequately protected, three battlecruisers including* INVINCIBLE *were sunk at the Battle of Jutland in 1916. Courtesy Imperial War Museum, London.*

Part of the First Cruiser Squadron from 1911 to 1913, *Invincible* served briefly in the Mediterranean before returning to the Home Fleet. After taking part in action in the Heligoland Bight on August 28, 1914, she was reassigned to the Grand Fleet's Second Battle Cruiser Squadron. Following the Battle of Coronel, she became the flagship of Admiral Sir Frederick Doveton Sturdee and was dispatched with her sister ship INFLEXIBLE to intercept Vice Admiral Graf Spee's squadron. The ships reached the Falklands on December 7, 1914. The following morning, von Spee's ships appeared off Stanley, and in the ensuing engagement, *Invincible* and *Inflexible,* the light cruisers *Glasgow, Kent,* and *Cornwall,* and armed merchant cruiser *Otranto,* sank the armored cruisers SCHARNHORST and GNEISENAU, the light cruisers *Leipzig* and *Nürnberg,* and two colliers. *Invincible* was hit twenty-two times, but there were no fatalities. Returning to the Second Battle Squadron in March 1915, in May she became flagship of Rear Admiral the Honourable Horace Hood's Third Battle Cruiser Squadron.

At the Battle of Jutland on May 31, 1916, *Invincible, Indomitable,* and *Inflexible* were steaming ahead of Admiral Sir John Jellicoe's Grand Fleet when *Invincible* came under sustained fire from the German battleships DERFFLINGER, LÜTZOW, and *König.* At 1833 a shell scored a direct hit on Q turret. The antiflash devices between turrets and magazines were inadequate and there was an almost instantaneous explosion that blew the ship in half in 57°2′N, 6°7′E. There were only six survivors; 1,021 crew were lost. Following the loss of INDEFATIGABLE and *Queen Mary,* whose combined survivors numbered only twenty-two people, the loss of *Invincible* led Rear Admiral David Beatty to remark simply, "There seems to be something wrong with our bloody ships today."

Tarrant, *Battlecruiser "Invincible."*

USS IOWA (BB-61)

Iowa-class battleship (2f/2m). *L/B/D:* 887.3′ × 108.2′ × 37.8′ (270.4m × 33m × 11.5m). *Tons:* 55,250 disp. *Hull:* steel. *Comp.:* 1,570–2,800. *Arm.:* 9 × 16″ (3 × 3), 20 × 5″, 60 × 40mm. *Armor:* 12.4″ belt, 5.5″ deck. *Mach.:* geared turbines, 212,000 shp, 4 screws; 33 kts. *Built:* New York Navy Yard, Brooklyn, N.Y.; 1943.

Authorized by Congress in 1938, the *Iowa*-class battleships were the largest and last battleships built in the United States, and with a speed of 33 knots, they were the fastest battleships the world has ever seen. Only Japan's YAMATO and MUSASHI exceeded them in tonnage or weight of shell. Although six of these superships were originally planned, only four were built: *Iowa,* MISSOURI, *New Jersey,* and *Wisconsin.* Experience gained in World War II dictated that priority be given to other types of ships, especially the mortal enemies of the battleship — aircraft carriers and submarines. (Nor were the *Iowa*s the largest U.S. battleships planned. Five *Montana*-class, 58,000- to 65,000-ton ships were ordered in 1940, but none was laid down.)

Built in only thirty-two months, *Iowa*'s career spanned nearly half a century, though she was actually in commission for only eighteen years. After two months of training off Newfoundland in anticipation of a breakout by the German battleship TIRPITZ, in October 1943 *Iowa* carried President Franklin D. Roosevelt to Casablanca en route to the Teheran Conference with Prime Minister Winston Churchill and Premier Joseph Stalin. In January 1944, she sailed for the Pacific as flagship of Battleship Division 7 for the invasion of the Marshall Islands later that month. She also supported amphibious operations in the Caroline Islands, the Marianas, and New Guinea. In June she sailed with Fast Carrier Task Force 58 at the Battle of the Philippine Sea. Following the invasion and securing of the Philippines in the fall, she returned to San Francisco for overhaul, but returned in time for the landings on Okinawa and to bomb targets on the Japanese mainland.

Following the end of World War II, *Iowa* remained with the Pacific Fleet until 1949 when she was laid up. Recommissioned as flagship of the Seventh Fleet in 1951, she sailed in support of UN forces in Korea from April to October 1952, before joining the Atlantic Fleet. She remained as part of this Fleet until 1958, during which time she did a stint in the Mediterranean as flagship of the Sixth Fleet. Part of the Atlantic Reserve Fleet at Philadelphia for the next twenty-six years, *Iowa* was recommissioned — along with her sister ships — to take her place in the "600-ship Navy" of the defense-minded President Ronald Reagan. Her secondary armament included twelve 5-inch guns and four 20-millimeter quad Phalanx guns.

Iowa's subsequent career showing the flag, especially in the waters around the Middle East during the Iran-Iraq War, was short-lived. On April 19, 1989, an explosion in Number 2 turret killed forty-seven of her gun crew; twenty ammunition handlers six decks below survived the blast. The official Navy investigation blamed the accident on a crew member, claiming that he had intentionally set off the explosion in despair over a homosexual relationship. The family denied the accusations and the Navy later retracted its claim, which many considered a cover-up for a more basic mechanical failure. The Navy formally decommissioned *Iowa* in 1990. Her sister ships soon followed.

Polmar, *Naval Institute Guide to Ships and Aircraft of the U.S. Fleet.* Sumrall, *"Iowa"-class Battleships.* U.S. Navy, *DANFS.*

HMS IRON DUKE

Iron Duke-class battleship (2f/2m). *L/B/D:* 622.8′ × 90′ × 29.5′ (189.8m × 27.4m × 9m). *Tons:* 30,380 disp. *Hull:* steel. *Comp.:* 1,022. *Arm.:* 10 × 13.5″ (5 × 2), 12 × 6″, 2 × 3″, 4 × 3pdr. *Armor:* 12″ belt, 2.5″ deck. *Mach.:* steam turbines, 29,000 shp, 20.7 kts. *Built:* Portsmouth Dockyard, Eng.; 1914.

The name ship of the first class of battleship built with antiaircraft guns, *Iron Duke* was commissioned just after the start of World War I and immediately became flagship of Admiral John Jellicoe's Grand Fleet. She was named in honor of the Duke of Wellington, hero of the Napoleonic Wars. In the first years of the war, the Germans had launched a number of "tip and run" raids across the North Sea to bombard coastal cities such as Scarborough. On May 30, 1916, British intelligence learned that the German fleet was sailing from Wilhelmshaven, and that evening *Iron Duke* sailed from Scapa Flow at the head of a powerful force comprising twenty-four dreadnoughts, three battlecruisers, twelve light cruisers, eight armored cruisers, five flotilla leaders, forty-six destroyers, and a minelayer.

The plan was to rendezvous with Vice Admiral Sir David Beatty's six battlecruisers, fourteen light cruisers, twenty-seven destroyers, a seaplane carrier, and four dreadnoughts to stop the anticipated German raid. In fact, the Germans hoped to lure the British into a line of submarines lying off the British naval bases, and then into the grasp of Admiral Reinhard Scheer's High Seas Fleet, comprising sixteen dreadnoughts, six pre-dreadnoughts, five light cruisers, and thirty-one destroyers. Beatty's German counterpart was Rear Admiral Franz von Hipper, in SMS LÜTZOW with five battlecruisers, four light cruisers, and thirty destroyers and torpedo boats.

The Battle of Jutland began between light units of Beatty's and Hipper's respective fleets at about 1430 on May 31. By 1530, the two fleets were within sight of one another, and Hipper wheeled to the south in an effort to draw Beatty into range of the German High Seas Fleet about forty-six miles away. During the "run to the south," Beatty lost the battlecruisers HMS INDEFATIGABLE and *Queen Mary,* and his flagship LION was heavily damaged. By 1700, the leading British ships were within range of the High Seas Fleet and turned for the north, drawing the Germans towards Jellicoe. At 1815, Beatty and Jellicoe joined forces and Jellicoe deployed his battleships so that they would "cross the T" of the German line of advance and bring the majority of their guns to bear. The Germans managed to sink first Rear Admiral Sir Robert Arbuthnot's armored cruiser DEFENCE and shortly thereafter, Rear Admiral the Honourable Horace L. A. Hood's battlecruiser INVINCIBLE. Nonetheless, the Germans also came under withering fire from the British, and Hipper's *Lützow* had to be abandoned. At 1833, Scheer ordered

Mounting six 13½-inch guns in three turrets, the super-dreadnought IRON DUKE *sailed as Admiral Sir John Jellicoe's flagship at the Battle of Jutland in May 1916. This picture shows her just before the start of World War I. Courtesy Imperial War Museum, London.*

his celebrated *Gefechtskehrtwendung,* a 180-degree "battle turn," while his ships were closely engaged by the enemy. Jellicoe ordered his fleet to pursue, though at less than top speed. Half an hour later, the German fleet turned back towards the British in what became known as the "death ride of the battlecruisers," during which DERF-FLINGER and SEYDLITZ took the brunt of the fighting. At 2035, Scheer broke off the engagement for the last time, though skirmishes between destroyers and light cruisers continued through the night.

Jutland cost the British three battlecruisers, three cruisers, a flotilla leader, and seven destroyers. The Germans lost one battlecruiser, one pre-dreadnought, four light cruisers, and five torpedo boats. However, after Jutland the German High Seas Fleet never again attempted to engage the British battle fleet, and the battle proved to be the last between battleships fought without naval air power or submarines.

Transferred to the Second Battle Squadron in November 1916, *Iron Duke* was sent to the Mediterranean in 1919 and was briefly assigned to the Black Sea during the Russian Civil War. From 1926 to 1929, she was with the Atlantic Fleet, but under the terms of the London Naval Treaty of 1930, she was downgraded to a gunnery training ship. By the start of World War II, she was a depot ship at Scapa Flow. Although hit by German bombers on October 17, 1939, she remained in service until broken up in 1946.

Halpern, *Naval History of World War I.* Parkes, *British Battleships.*

ISABELLA

L/B: 110′ × 28′ (33.5m × 8.5m). *Tons:* 383 bm. *Hull:* wood. *Comp.:* 57. *Built:* Hull, Eng.; 1786.

With the end of the Napoleonic Wars, British interest in scientific exploration began to widen and in 1818, the Admiralty launched two expeditions to take up the long-dormant search for northern routes to the Pacific. In search of the Northeast Passage, bound for the waters around Spitzbergen, was Captain John Buchan in the hired whaleship *Dorothea,* and Lieutenant John Franklin in *Trent.* The more notable expedition, for the Northwest Passage, was under Commander John Ross in *Isabella,* sailing in company with *Alexander,* under William Parry. The two converted whaleships rounded the southern tip of Greenland and then sailed into Davis Strait. These waters were well known to the whalers from Hull and other British whaling ports, though only as far as Disco Island, and Ross's two ships were in company with forty-five of them around Hare Island. Ross pressed on past

75°N through the Davis Strait and Baffin Bay as far as Melville Bay on Greenland's west coast — the first ships to do so since William Baffin in DISCOVERY in 1616. The expedition then crossed to the southern end of Ellesmere Island and sailed south past the eastern entrances to Jones Sound and Lancaster Sound. Ross decided that neither provided an outlet to the west. In particular, he believed that Lancaster Sound was blocked by a range of mountains, the "Croker Mountains." This mirage vanished the next year when Parry sailed through Lancaster Sound and about halfway through the Northwest Passage in HECLA and *Griper.* In the twentieth century, Lancaster Sound was the preferred eastern channel of the Northwest Passage.

Isabella returned to the Hull whaling fleet in 1819 and continued whaling for many seasons, bringing home as much as 250 tons of oil in a good year. On August 26, 1833, the ship was in Lancaster Sound just west of Navy Board Inlet when she was approached by three long boats. In these were none other than the survivors from Captain John Ross's exploration ship VICTORY, which had left England in 1829 and wrecked in 1831. The next year, on May 12, 1833, *Isabella* was lost on the Greenland coast.

Lubbock, *Arctic Whalers.* Ross, *Voyage of Discovery; Narrative of a Second Voyage in Search of a North-West Passage.*

ISIS

(1m). *L/B:* 180′ od/114′ keel × 45′ + (54.9m/34.7m × 13.7m). *Tons:* 1,200–1,300 burden. *Hull:* wood. *Built:* 2nd cent. CE.

In *The Ship, or The Wishes,* the Greek writer Lucian of Samosata (about 120–180 CE) describes a giant ship, part of the fleet that carried Egyptian grain from Alexandria to Rome. Blown off course, *Isis* put in at Piraeus, the port of Athens, where it drew a crowd of onlookers. Though the passage occurs in a work of fiction, it is likely that *Isis* was a real ship. The appearance of this huge grain-carrier apparently created a minor sensation in Athens, and provided Lucian with a topical setting for his satire. The description is put in the mouth of Samippus, one of the characters in Lucian's story:

> What a big ship! A hundred and twenty cubits long, the shipwright said, well over a quarter as wide, and from the deck to the deepest part of the bilge, twenty-nine. And what a tall mast, what a yardarm to carry! What a forestay to hold it up! How gently the stern curves up, with a little golden goose below! But at the opposite end, the prow juts right out, with the goddess Isis — after whom the ship is named — on

either side. And the other adornments, the paintings, and the owner's pennant bright as fire! In the bow the anchors, capstans and windlasses, and on the poop the cabins — it all seems wonderful to me. You'd guess that the crew numbers a legion. They say she carries enough grain to feed all Attica for a year.

The captain tells another character how the ship ended at Piraeus after seventy days of foul winds and storms. As Lionel Casson points out, the passage provides important information on the route normally taken by the grain fleet: north northeast from Alexandria, passing to the west of Cyprus, then westward along the south coast of Asia Minor as far as Rhodes or Cnidus. From there, the captain meant to sail south of Crete, avoiding dangerous Cape Malea, then presumably west northwest towards Malta then north through the Straits of Messina. The captain explained that *Isis* "should have been in Italy by now," if they had "kept Crete to starboard and sailed beyond Malea."

Lucian gives fairly specific dimensions: the *Isis* is 120 cubits (180 feet) in length, more than a quarter of that (45 feet) in beam, and 29 cubits (43.5 feet) from the deck to bottom of the hold at its deepest. Based on these figures, Casson has calculated her capacity at 1,200 to 1,300 tons — a figure not at all improbable given the scale of the Roman grain trade, the skill of Roman shipwrights, and the collateral evidence from excavated underwater sites such as the ALBENGA WRECK. After the fall of Rome, merchant vessels of this size were not built again in the west until the carracks of the sixteenth century.

Casson, "The *Isis* and Her Voyage." Lucian of Samosata, *The Ship, or The Wishes.*

J

JAMES BAINES

Clipper (3m). *L/B/D:* 266' loa × 44.9' × 29' dph (81.1m × 13.6m × 29m). *Tons:* 2,275 reg. *Hull:* wood. *Comp.:* 700 pass.; 100+ crew. *Built:* Donald McKay, East Boston, Mass.; 1854.

The third of the Donald McKay–built clippers ordered for James Baines & Company's Black Ball Line in 1854–55, *James Baines* was a three-deck ship built for the Australian passenger trade. She set single topsails, royals, and skysails, with a moonsail on the mainmast, and studding sails on the fore and main. Her life was brief but brilliant. Under Captain Charles McDonnell, she sailed from Boston to Liverpool in a record 12 days, 6 hours, though her best day's run was only 342 miles. Her maiden voyage to Australia, with 1,400 tons of cargo, 691 passengers (74 in first class), and upwards of 100 crew, was 65 days, and she returned in 69½ days. Among the stores shipped for this crowd, the Melbourne *Argus* of February 13, 1855, reported that there were "in addition to the usual stores, 73 sheep, 25 of which are preserved in ice; 86 pigs, 6 of which are in ice; and 100 dozen of fowls, 30 dozen of which are in ice, the live stock being reserved for use after the vessel has crossed the line."

In 1857, *James Baines* was one of three Black Ball ships chartered to carry troops out to India. While lying in Portsmouth with CHAMPION OF THE SEAS, she was reviewed by Queen Victoria and the Prince Consort. "On taking her leave," reported the *European Times,*

> Her Majesty expressed herself much gratified by the visit. She had no idea there were such vessels in the merchant service, and complimented Mr Mackay [a shareholder of James Baines & Co., not the builder] and the Captain individually on the size and equipment of the *James Baines* and the *Champion of the Seas* generally.

James Baines sailed for India with about 1,000 men of the 97th Regiment; she returned from Calcutta the following spring laden with jute, linseed, rice, and hides. While she was lying at Husisson Dock, Liverpool, a fire broke out in her forward hole on the morning of April 21, 1858, and she was burned irreparably.

Hollett, *Fast Passage to Australia.* Howe and Matthews, *American Clipper Ships.* Stammers, *Passage Makers.*

JAMES MONROE

Packet ship (3m). *L/B:* 118' × 28.3' (36m × 8.6m). *Tons:* 424 bm. *Hull:* wood. *Comp.:* 200 pass. *Built:* Adam Brown, New York; 1817.

The Black Ball Line of three ships was established in April 1817, with the ships originally intended to sail in succession, though not, like the later packets, on a fixed schedule. The addition of *James Monroe* as a fourth ship, on October 24, 1817, led to the announcement of the first regular transatlantic ship service: "To sail on their Appointed Days, full or not full." The fifth of the month was fixed as the departure date from New York, while ships were to sail from Liverpool on the seventeenth, beginning in January 1818. The proprietors of what came to be known as the Black Ball Line were Isaac Wright & Son, Francis Thompson, Benjamin Marshall, and Jeremiah Thompson, all Quakers of New York. Coming only four years after the opening of the first scheduled packet service in the United States — between Albany and New York City — this was an extraordinarily bold and uniquely American initiative that sought to capitalize on the new need for more reliable and faster service for passengers and smaller (though more numerous and hence more lucrative) consignments of various nonbulk cargoes, both of which would generate increased revenues. The start of regularly scheduled sailings encouraged the development of ever faster ships, both sail and steam, and initiated a revolutionary way of serving customers, seen today in the myriad companies offering "next-day" delivery virtually anywhere in the commercial world.

Named for the newly elected president, *James Monroe* inaugurated this service on January 5, 1818, when she departed New York under Captain James Watkinson with eight passengers and a cargo consisting of apples, flour, cotton, cranberries, hops, and wool; her holds were only about three-quarters full. She arrived at Liverpool on

February 2, a respectable time for the season, especially when compared with the majority of other ships sailing at the same time. The return passage started on March 3, but the ship was forced to return to Liverpool for repairs after a storm in the Irish Sea. *James Monroe* returned to New York only a week before her next scheduled sailing. Overall, in their first year of operation the Black Ballers averaged 25 days eastbound and 43 days westbound. Because of a shipping glut on the North Atlantic, profits were low for the first three years of service, and it was not until 1821 that the next regular packet service was established by the New Line, or Red Star Line. Sold to E. Malibran in the early 1820s, *James Monroe* changed hands again in the financial panic of 1825–26. The ship remained in service until 1850, when she was wrecked in Tasmania.

Albion, *The Rise of New York Port; Square-Riggers on Schedule.* Cutler, *Queens of the Western Ocean.*

JEANNETTE

(ex-*Pandora*) *Philomel*-class gun vessel (1f/3m). *L/B/D:* 145′ × 25.5′ × 15′ (44.2m × 78m × 4.6m). *Tons:* 244 grt. *Hull:* wood. *Comp.:* 33. *Mach.:* steam, 200 hp, 1 screw. *Built:* Pembroke Dockyard, Wales; 1861.

After fourteen years as a Royal Navy gunboat, HMS *Pandora* was sold to Sir Allen Young, who made two voyages in search of the Northwest Passage via Peel Sound. In 1876, Young sold *Pandora* to Lieutenant George W. De Long, USN, acting on behalf of the flamboyant New York newspaper publisher James Gordon Bennett, who wanted to sponsor an expedition to reach the North Pole. Congress passed legislation to put the expedition under the Navy's jurisdiction while Bennett footed the bill and generated publicity. The premise of the expedition was that beyond the Arctic ice so far encountered by explorers, the north polar region comprised a warm, open sea fed by the Gulf Stream in the Atlantic and the Kuro Shio Current in the North Pacific. For this reason, the rechristened *Jeannette*, named for Bennett's sister, was to sail through the Bering Strait, the first polar expedition to use that route since Lieutenant Robert McClure in HMS INVESTIGATOR in 1850–51.

Strengthened for work in the ice, *Jeannette* departed San Francisco on July 8, 1879. After stops at Unalaska, St. Michael, where the crew took aboard sleds and forty sled dogs and two Inuit drivers, and Lavrentia, Siberia, where they recoaled for the last time, they sailed through the Bering Strait on August 28. They made several stops along the Siberian coast and made for Wrangell Island. Nine days later, *Jeannette* was stuck fast, even as the U.S.

Coast and Geodetic Survey published a report on Bering Sea currents, concluding that "nothing in the least tends to support the widely spread but unphilosophical notion that in any part of the Polar Sea we may look for large areas free from ice."

The course of *Jeannette*'s drift in the ice took her well west of Wrangell Island, but it was erratic, and by January 1881 the ship had meandered 1,300 miles but was only 250 miles northwest of her position when originally beset. Few of the experimental devices worked as they should, the hull leaked badly, and navigator John Danenhower required repeated operations for an eye condition brought about by syphilis. In May 1881, the ship was within sight of Henrietta Island where a team led by Engineer George W. Melville deposited an account of the voyage thus far. (The precaution of placing written accounts of an expedition's progress in various locations was common among Arctic explorers intent on securing credit for their discoveries, or directing parties sent out to search for them. Melville's account was recovered by Soviet scientists in 1938.) Shortly thereafter, the ice bore down on the ship, and on the morning of June 12, 1881, *Jeannette* was crushed in position 77°08′N, 153°25′E, about 250 miles from Siberia.

The crew managed to take off two cutters, a whaleboat, eight sleds, and sled dogs. At first, the drift of the ice carried them three miles northwest for every mile they made southwest, but by July 29 they were in the New Siberian Islands. Setting out again, they encountered more open water. On September 12, about 100 miles from the Siberian coast, the boats were separated in a gale. Lieutenant Charles Chipp and his seven crew disappeared, while the boats commanded by De Long and Melville landed about 125 miles apart in the Lena River delta. Melville's party of 11 reached safety at a Tungus village and later dispatched search parties to look for the others. According to De Long's diary, by October 30, 140 days after the loss of the *Jeannette*, De Long and all his men were dead. The scientific failure of the expedition and heavy loss of life led to a congressional hearing. At a time when the United States was beginning to emerge as a world power, the prestige of the Navy was on trial, and the hearing became a forum for the rehabilitation of the *Jeannette*'s officers and crew.

Gutteridge, *Icebound.*

JEREMIAH O'BRIEN

Liberty ship (1f/3m). *L/B/D:* 441.5′ × 57′ × 27.8′ (134.6m × 17.4m × 8.5m). *Tons:* 7,176 grt. *Hull:* steel. *Comp.:* 65. *Arm.:* 1 × 5″, 10 × 20mm. *Mach.:* triple expansion, 2,500 hp, 1 screw; 11 kts. *Built:* New England Shipbuilding Corp., South Portland, Me.; 1943.

Named for the "Machias Admiral" responsible for the capture of the British armed sloop *Margaretta, Jeremiah O'Brien* is one of more than 2,751 so-called Liberty ships built as part of a war emergency shipbuilding program during World War II. Of welded, prefabricated construction, the ships that President Franklin D. Roosevelt dubbed "The Ugly Ducklings" were turned out in huge numbers from shipyards around the country. Cheaply and quickly made, scores were lost during the war, but on more than one occasion, the Libertys and their crews proved astonishingly rugged. The best-preserved surviving Liberty ship, *Jeremiah O'Brien* saw service in the Atlantic, Pacific, and Indian Oceans during World War II, and during the D-day invasion in June 1944, she made eleven roundtrips between English ports and the Normandy invasion beaches.

The *O'Brien* was laid up in the reserve fleet at Suisun Bay, California, in 1947, together with hundreds of other Libertys; hundreds more were similarly gathered in reserve fleets around the country. In 1978, thanks largely to the efforts of Rear Admiral Thomas J. Patterson, USMS, the National Liberty Ship Memorial was founded to preserve the ship as a memorial to the merchant marine, which played a crucial but infrequently heralded role in World War II. After a year of work, the ship proceeded to her new berth at San Francisco under her own power in 1980. Since that time, she has made annual cruises around San Francisco Bay, and in 1994, she steamed to France to take part in the fiftieth anniversary celebrations of D-day.

Jaffe, *Last Liberty.*

HMS JERSEY

4th rate 60 (3m). *L/B/D:* 144' × 41.5' × 16.9' (43.9m × 12.6m × 5.2m). *Tons:* 1,068 bm. *Hull:* wood. *Comp.:* 400. *Arm.:* 24 × 24pdr, 26 × 9pdr, 10 × 6pdr. *Built:* Devonport Dockyard, Plymouth, Eng.; 1736.

Built during a period of relative peace in England, HMS *Jersey* was soon in battle. Her first encounter came in Admiral Edward Vernon's failed attack on the Spanish port of Cartagena, Colombia, at the start of the War of Jenkins's Ear in October 1739. (The war was so called because the *casus belli* was the detention of the merchant brig *Rebecca* and the loss of the master's ear to a Spanish officer's knife.) *Jersey*'s next major action came during the Seven Years' War (or French and Indian War). On August 18–19, 1759, Admiral Edward Boscawen's British fleet of fifteen ships of the line at Gibraltar gave chase to twelve ships under Admiral M. de la Clue Sabran sailing from

the Mediterranean to the Atlantic. Five French ships escaped to Cadiz, but the others were brought to battle east of Cape St. Vincent, Portugal. One French ship sank, two escaped, and four were run ashore in Lagos Bay where Boscawen, disregarding Portuguese neutrality, attacked them the next day. De la Clue's flagship *Ocean* and *Redoutable* were burned, and *Téméraire* and *Modeste* were captured.

In March 1771, *Jersey*'s masts and spars were removed and she was officially classed as a hospital ship moored in Wallabout Bay, later the site of the Brooklyn Navy Yard. During the American Revolution, she was used as a prison ship for captured Continental Army soldiers, and her name is synonymous with the squalor and deprivation to which American prisoners were subject. Thousands of prisoners were crammed below decks where there was virtually no natural light or fresh air and few provisions for the sick. Political conditions only made things worse, as the British had no interest in legitimizing the cause of independence by exchanging prisoners, and General George Washington had no interest in surrendering professional British soldiers for his ragtag volunteers. The ghastly statistics speak for themselves. While between 4,400 and 6,800 soldiers and sailors are believed to have died in combat during the American Revolution, another 18,500 died in captivity, of disease, or from other causes. The estimated number of fatalities aboard the New York prison ships stands at between 4,000 and 11,000. It was recorded that as many as seven or eight corpses a day were buried from *Jersey* alone before the British surrendered at Yorktown in September 1783. When the British evacuated New York two months later, *Jersey* was abandoned.

Jackson, "Forgotten Saga of New York's Prison Ships." Kemp, ed., *Oxford Companion to Ships and the Sea.*

JERVIS BAY

Liner (1f/2m). *L/B/D:* 530.6' × 68.3' × 12.15' (161.7m bp × 20.8m × 39.9m). *Tons:* 13,839 grt. *Hull:* steel. *Comp.:* 1st 12, 3rd 712; 216 crew. *Arm.:* 8 × 6". *Mach.:* geared turbines, 9,000 shp, 2 screws; 15 kts. *Built:* Vickers Ltd., Barrow-in Furness, Eng.; 1922.

Named for a bay about 85 miles south of Sydney, Australia, *Jervis Bay* was one of five sister ships built for the Australian Commonwealth Line's monthly service between Brisbane and London. In 1928, the Bay liners came under the aegis of Lord Kylsant's White Star Line, Ltd., a holding company that collapsed five years later when the ships were taken over by the newly formed Aberdeen & Commonwealth Line. In September 1939, *Jervis Bay* was

War artist Charles Pears captures the start of the JERVIS BAY *action, November 5, 1940, as the vastly inferior armed merchant cruiser turns against the German battleship* ADMIRAL SCHEER *(far right), to allow heavily laden members of the convoy to scatter. Courtesy National Maritime Museum, Greenwich.*

at London, where she was requisitioned by the British government for use as an armed merchant cruiser. Fitted out with eight 6-inch guns, she was assigned to convoy duty on the North Atlantic. At about 1500 on November 5, 1940, *Jervis Bay* was convoying thirty-seven ships eastbound when they came under attack by the German pocket battleship ADMIRAL SCHEER about halfway between Newfoundland and Ireland (52°26′N, 32°34′W). Captain S. E. Fogarty Fegen turned his ship to charge the overwhelming *Admiral Scheer* in an effort to allow the other ships to escape. Within 15 minutes, *Jervis Bay* was dead in the water; she sank at about 2000 with the loss of 190 of her 259 crew. Although *Admiral Scheer* sank five other ships, the toll would doubtless have been higher were it not for *Jervis Bay*'s valiant charge, in recognition for which Captain Fegen was awarded a posthumous Victoria Cross.

Pollock, *"Jervis Bay."* Savill & Haws, *Aberdeen and Aberdeen & Commonwealth Lines.*

JESUS OF LÜBECK

Round ship (4m). *Tons:* 700 tons. *Hull:* wood. *Comp.:* 300. *Arm.:* 26 guns. *Built:* Germany(?); <1544.

Built for trading under the auspices of the Hanseatic League, administratively headquartered in the Baltic Sea port of Lübeck, *Jesus of Lübeck* was a round ship designed chiefly for work in the waters of northern Europe and not for oceanic voyaging. A large and imposing vessel, she had high stern- and forecastles from which her crew could repel boarders. But these same features caught the wind, making her unresponsive to the helm and straining the hull. Henry VIII purchased her in 1544 during his naval build-up, but she was poorly maintained in the decades that followed. In 1564, Queen Elizabeth lent *Jesus of Lübeck* to John Hawkins for an expedition during which he sold African slaves illegally in the Spanish Caribbean. (Slavery was legal, but trading without the proper papers was not.)

Two years later, Hawkins sailed again with six vessels, the royal ships *Jesus of Lübeck* and *Minion* (300 tons), *William and John* (150 tons), *Swallow* (100 tons), *Judith* (50 tons), and *Angel* (33 tons). Clearing Plymouth on October 2, 1567, they arrived on the coast of Guinea in mid-November. After two months spent gathering slaves, either by theft from Portuguese slavers or by trade and conquest, the English sailed for the Caribbean, arriving off Dominica on March 27, 1568. Restrictions on trade made it difficult for Hawkins to offload his cargo, but after selling most of the slaves near Cartagena, he was ready to return to England. Hit by a hurricane in the Gulf of Mexico, *Jesus of Lübeck* was so strained that Hawkins ordered part of the upperworks cut away, a fortuitous move that may have been the genesis of the race-built, weatherly galleons Hawkins promoted for the English Navy in the years before the Spanish Armada. Putting into San Juan de Ulloa, Mexico, near Vera Cruz, on September 15, Hawkins hoped to repair his ships before the arrival of the Spanish *flota*, which appeared two days later bearing the new Viceroy of Mexico, Don Martin Enríquez. Negotiating an armistice, the English continued their repairs, but on September 23, the Spanish launched a surprise attack, sinking *Jesus of Lübeck, Angel, Swallow,* and two Portuguese prizes — though not before the flagship had sunk two Spanish ships. Only *Judith,* by now under command of Francis Drake, and *Minion* survived the voyage, returning to Plymouth in late January 1569 with barely 70 of the 400 men with which the expedition began.

Hampden, *Francis Drake Privateer.* Sugden, *Sir Francis Drake.*

JHELUM

Ship (3m). *L/B/D:* 123.1′ × 27.1′ × 18.1′ (37.5m × 8.3m × 5.5m). *Tons:* 428 grt. *Hull:* wood. *Comp.:* 14–21. *Built:* Joseph Steel & Son, Liverpool; 1849.

Built for general trading between India and England, *Jhelum* was named for a tributary of the Indus River and the site of a battle between English and Indian forces the

The merchantman JHELUM *in 1976, more than a century after she was condemned at Stanley and taken over as a floating warehouse, a fate shared by several other ships. Part of the bulwarks have been cut away to allow for easy access by wagons. Such surgery weakened the ships and hastened the collapse of hulls in an environment otherwise favorable to long-term preservation. Courtesy Norman Brouwer.*

year before her launch. Her owner and builder, Joseph Steel, kept her in that trade for only one voyage before he sent his ship to South America. Carrying general cargo out, *Jhelum* returned from Arica with nitrate (fertilizer from bird droppings). This was the first of thirteen such voyages to Chile, Peru, or Ecuador until Steel sold his interest in the ship in 1863. Her European terminus was always Liverpool, although she called one time each at Hamburg and Baltimore en route home. Her average times were about 100 to 110 days between South America and England.

Cut down to a bark rig in 1858, five years later she came under the ownership of John Widdicombe and Charles Bell, among others, who kept her in the same trade between England and Latin America, though she mostly shipped coal outbound. On August 18, 1870, after a rough passage round Cape Horn, Captain Beaglehole put his ship into the Falkland Islands in a leaking condition. Her crew refused to sail *Jhelum* any further and a survey found her unfit for sea. The ship was eventually transferred to J. M. Dean & Company but not before Beaglehole had spent nine months at Stanley. He finally left the port in HMS *Charybdis* on May 27, 1871. *Jhelum* ended her days as a floating warehouse for wool storage, as did many of the other ships condemned at Stanley, including VICAR OF BRAY, which also put into the port in distress in 1870. *Jhelum*'s remains are still visible, though rapidly deteriorating.

Stammers & Kearon, *"Jhelum": A Victorian Merchant Ship.*

USS JOHNSTON (DD-557)

Fletcher-class destroyer (2f/2m). *L/B/D:* 376.5′ × 39.7′ × 17.8′ (114.8m × 12.1m × 5.4m). *Tons:* 2,700 disp. *Hull:* steel. *Comp.:* 273. *Arm.:* 5 × 5″ (5 × 1), 10 × 40mm, 7 × 20mm; 10 × 21″TT; 6 dcp, 2 dct. *Mach.:* geared turbines, 60,000 shp, 2 shafts; 36.5 kts. *Built:* Seattle Tacoma Shipbuilding Co., Seattle, Wash.; 1943.

Named for John Vincent Johnston, a Union gunboat captain on the Mississippi River during the Civil War, USS *Johnston* entered service on October 27, 1943. At her commissioning, Commander Ernest E. Evans echoed John Paul Jones when he told his crew, "This is going to be a fighting ship. I intend to go in harm's way." He was as good as his word. Three months later, *Johnston*'s first action was during the invasion of the Marshall Islands where she bombed targets on Kwajalein and Eniwetok. She next sailed for the Solomon Islands where she sank the Japanese submarine *I-176* on May 15 off Bougainville Island. After taking part in the invasion of Guam in July, *Johnston* joined an escort carrier group for operations in the Palau Islands.

After replenishing at Manaus, she joined Rear Admiral Clifton A. F. Sprague's Task Force 3, comprising six escort carriers, three destroyers, and four destroyer escorts. A few days later, Taffy 3, as the unit was known, was on patrol in the Philippine Sea east of Samar Island. On the morning of October 25, much to the surprise of all concerned, Vice Admiral Takeo Kurita's Center Force — battleships YAMATO, *Kongo, Haruna,* and *Nagato,* seven cruisers, and twelve or more destroyers — came into range of the "Baby Flattops." Sprague immediately ordered his carriers southwest at flank speed — 17.5 knots — while destroyers *Johnston, Hoel* (DD-553), and *Heermann* (DD-532) were ordered to frustrate the Japanese advance. This they did by laying smoke and then wheeling into the on-rushing Japanese force.

Johnston was outranked for the first 20 minutes of the battle, but began firing her 5-inch shells at the rate of 40 minutes as soon as she could. Firing 10 torpedoes into a line of cruisers, she sank *Kumano.* Minutes later she was hit by three 14-inch shells, followed quickly by three 6-inch shells in an exchange that her gunnery officer likened to "a puppy being smacked by a truck." With one engine and three 5-inch guns knocked out, *Johnston* ducked into a rain squall and gained a brief respite. She emerged to find herself on a collision course with *Heermann,* which she missed by less than 10 feet. At this point, the smoke was so thick that Evans ordered no guns fired unless the gunners could see their targets. At 0820, *Kongo* was 7,000 yards away hurling 14-inch shells over the destroyer. In an effort to draw fire from escort carrier GAMBIER BAY, Evans ordered an attack on the cruiser *Chikuma,* only breaking off the unequal duel to avoid a Japanese destroyer squadron. *Hoel* had sunk at 0855, *Gambier Bay* at 0907, and by 0930, *Johnston*'s remaining 5-inch guns were knocked out and she was dead in the water. Fifteen minutes later, Evans gave the order to abandon ship, which sank at 1010 in 11°40′N, 126°20′E. There were only 141 survivors — Evans was not among them — one of whom reported that he saw a Japanese destroyer captain salute the ship as she went down. Despite the Americans' losses — escort carriers *Gambier Bay* and ST. Lô, *Johnston, Hoel,* and the destroyer escort *Samuel B. Roberts* — Taffy 3 had sunk two cruisers and denied the Japanese a significant victory.

Morison, *History of the United States Naval Operations in World War II.* U.S. Navy, *DANFS.*

JOLIBA

Schooner. *L/B/D:* 40′ × 6′ × 1′ (12.2m × 1.8m × 0.3m). *Hull:* wood. *Comp.:* 6. *Built:* Sansanding, Bambara (Mali); 1805.

In 1805, the Scottish explorer Mungo Park set out to travel the length of the Niger River to the sea, a feat not yet accomplished by any European. Although the source of the Niger was known, the river's mouth had been a mystery to Europeans as long ago as Herodotus in the fifth century BCE. The Niger was variously believed to drain into the Sahara, descend under the desert to emerge in the Mediterranean, flow into the Nile or Congo Rivers, or empty into the Atlantic — as in fact it does, at the end of its 2,600-mile course to the Gulf of Guinea. On his first expedition to West Africa (1794–97), Park had seen the Niger near Ségou (in what is now Mali), where the river flows east. Eight years later, now aged thirty-four, Park embarked on his second journey. Ascending the Gambia River with forty-four men at the start of the rainy season in April, he reached Ségou in September with only three men left. There King Mansong gave him two canoes that he cobbled together into what he hopefully called "His Majesty's Schooner *Joliba.*" On November 20, 1805, Park, his surviving companions, and three servants set out down the Niger. After passing Tombouctou, they had traveled to within 600 miles of the river mouth when they were killed at Bussa, in what is now Nigeria. The journey was completed in 1830 by John and Richard Lander.

de Gramont, *Strong Brown God.*

JOLIE BRISE

Gaff cutter. *L/B/D:* 56.2′ × 15.8′ × 10.2′ (17.1m × 4.8m × 3.1m). *Tons:* 44. *Hull:* wood. *Comp.:* 12. *Built:* M. Paumelle, Le Havre; 1913.

One of the most celebrated yachts of the twentieth century, *Jolie Brise* was built as a French pilot cutter, but the start of World War I curtailed her use in that work. In 1917, she was sold to interests in Concarneau and sailed in the tuna fisheries for three years before being laid up. *Jolie Brise* was purchased by Evelyn George Martin in 1924 and converted into a cruising yacht. The next year, Martin helped establish the Royal Ocean Racing Club's first Fastnet Race, which *Jolie Brise* won. (The 610-mile race runs from Ryde, Isle of Wight, around Fastnet Rock off southwest Ireland, and back to Plymouth.) The next year, Martin sailed to Newport, Rhode Island, for the start of the Bermuda Race, which *Jolie Brise* won in her class before returning home for the second Fastnet Race. Martin then sold *Jolie Brise* to Robert "Bobby" Somerset, under whose command she won the 1929 Fastnet Race and the first race to Santander, Spain. She made a poor showing in the next year's Fastnet — her last for more than sixty years — but Somerset entered her in the 1932 Bermuda Race, the only one to begin from Montauk

Point, New York. *Jolie Brise* distinguished herself the first night out when she was run alongside the burning *Adriana* to retrieve her crew, all but one of whom leaped to safety on the cutter.

This was *Jolie Brise*'s last major race, and from 1932 to 1939 she was used exclusively for cruising between Britain and the Mediterranean. Requisitioned by the Royal Navy, she saw no service during World War II, and in 1946 she was acquired by a group that planned to take her to New Zealand under the name *Pleasant Breeze*. (*Jolie Brise* is the French equivalent of moderate breeze, Force 4 on the Beaufort Scale.) This effort failed, and she was purchased at Lisbon by Luis Lobato, who sailed her in Portugal and the Mediterranean for two decades. During Portugal's socialist revolution in 1975, Lobato sold *Jolie Brise* to the International Sailing Craft Association at the Exeter Maritime Museum, under whose auspices she continues to cruise, and occasionally race, throughout northern Europe.

Bryer, *"Jolie Brise."* Rolt, "Eighty Years a Gaff Cutter."

Joseph Conrad

(ex-*Georg Stage*) Ship (3m). *L/B/D:* 110.5′ × 25.2′ × 12′ (33.7m × 7.7m × 3.7m). *Tons:* 212 grt. *Hull:* iron. *Comp.:* 23–90. *Mach.:* aux. diesel, 265 hp, 1 screw. *Built:* Burmeister & Wain, Copenhagen; 1882.

The original training ship built for the Stiftelsen Georg Stages Minde, *Georg Stage* was named in memory of the son of Frederick Stage, the program's founder. Used for training merchant ship cadets, she sailed in the waters of the Baltic and North Seas during the summer months, and spent the winters laid up in Copenhagen. In 1905, she sank with the loss of twenty-two cadets following a collision with the British steamer *Ancona of Leith*. Raised and refitted, and with her engine removed, she continued as a training ship for the Danish merchant marine for another twenty-nine years, when a new *Georg Stage* was built.

The same year, the Australian journalist-turned-seaman Alan Villiers (then thirty-two) purchased the ship and renamed her *Joseph Conrad* in honor of the great sea writer. Villiers fitted her out for a circumnavigation that began at Ipswich, England, on October 22, 1934. In the course of the voyage, the *Conrad* called at New York, Rio de Janeiro, and Cape Town, then crossed the Indian Ocean before turning north to sail through the East Indies. Heading west as far as the Solomon Islands, she turned south for Sydney. After additional stops in New Zealand, northwest again to New Guinea, back to New Zealand, and on to Tahiti, *Conrad* rounded Cape Horn and returned to New York on October 16, 1936, after a voyage of 57,000 miles. At the end of it Villiers was broke, and he sold the *Conrad* to Huntington Hartford, who converted her to a yacht. Villiers also published two accounts of the voyage, *The Cruise of the "Conrad"* and *Stormalong*, told from the perspective of an apprentice who signed on at the age of fourteen. Four years later she passed to the U.S. Maritime Commission for use as a merchant training vessel out of St. Petersburg. Following World War II, she was laid up until presented to the Marine Historical Association as a floating museum and stationary training vessel at Mystic, Connecticut, where she arrived in 1948. She remains in that work today at the Mystic Seaport Museum.

Villiers, *Cruise of the "Conrad"*; *Stormalong*.

Joshua

Ketch. *L:* 39.5′ (12m). *Hull:* steel. *Comp.:* 1+. *Des.:* Jean Knocker. *Built:* France; 1961.

Named for the first single-handed circumnavigator, Joshua Slocum, Bernard Moitessier's ketch was built with the proceeds of *To the Reefs*, a book about his adventures en route from French Indochina to the Caribbean. In the course of this extended passage, the junk *Marie-Thérèse* was wrecked in the Indian Ocean, and her successor *Marie-Thérèse II* was wrecked in Trinidad. After using *Joshua* as a sailing school in the Mediterranean, Moitessier decided to sail to French Polynesia. He remained there for several years, and when he decided to return he did so in a nonstop run from Tahiti to Alicante, Spain, whereupon he wrote an account of his prolonged circumnavigation, *The First Voyage of Joshua*.

In 1969, the *Sunday Times* announced its sponsorship of the Golden Globe, to be awarded to the first person to sail single-handed around the world without stopping. Moitessier was easily the most experienced single-hander of the entrants, who included Robin Knox-Johnston in Suhaili and Donald Crowhurst in Teignmouth Electron. One of the later starters, the powerful *Joshua* gained steadily on *Suhaili*, and many thought it possible she would win the Golden Globe, though as Moitessier carried no radio, no one knew for sure. After rounding Cape Horn, the iconoclastic Moitessier decided to throw the race. Communicating his intention via slingshot to a passing tanker near the Cape of Good Hope, he wrote, "I continue non-stop toward the Pacific Islands because I am happy at sea and, perhaps, to save my soul." And so, without stopping, *Joshua* arrived at Papeete having covered 37,455 miles in 10 months without a single stop.

Joshua sailed faster than *Suhaili* by about 15 miles per day. Moitessier and *Joshua* remained in Tahiti until 1980, when he decided to try his hand on the American lecture circuit. After two years in California, Moitessier chartered *Joshua* to actor Klaus Kinski and sailed with him to Mexico. There, in December 1982, *Joshua* was blown ashore and wrecked on Cabo San Lucas.

Lesure, "Unlikely Legend." Moitessier, *First Voyage of the "Joshua"; Long Way.*

J. T. WING

(ex-*Oliver H. Perry, J. O. Webster, Charles F. Gordon*) Schooner (3m). *L/B/D:* 139′ × 33.7′ × 12.7′ (42.4m × 10.3m × 3.9m). *Tons:* 431 grt. *Hull:* wood. *Comp.:* 8. *Built:* Beazley Bros., Weymouth, Nova Scotia; 1919.

Built to carry mahogany from West Africa to Canada, *Charles F. Gordon* was sold in 1922 to Alexander and

Lewis Stockwell, who put her under the American flag and renamed her *J. O. Webster.* During the Florida building boom of the mid-1920s, she freighted lumber from New England and was part of the last big fleet of windjammers in Biscayne Bay. In 1934, she ran aground near Noank, Connecticut, and was seized for rum-running. The next year she was sold to the J. T. Wing Company, a Detroit chandlery. Renamed *J. T. Wing,* she freighted logs from Rimouski, Quebec, to Port Huron, Michigan. For two years she was a familiar sight at ports on Lakes Huron and Michigan, but her deep-sea hull was ill suited to the requirements of Great Lakes navigation.

From 1939 to 1941, she was owned by the Great Lakes Sea Scouts and named for Oliver Hazard Perry. Sold to the Chippewa Lumber Company of Sault Ste. Marie in 1941, *J. T. Wing* was laid up from 1943 to 1946. In the latter year, the Great Lakes' last commercial sailing vessel was donated to the city of Detroit and opened as an exhibit of the Dossin Great Lakes Museum. She was con-

Under a low sky, a typical Great Lakes ore carrier steams by the Nova Scotia–built schooner J. T. WING *at Marine City, Michigan. Built for the Atlantic coastwise trade, the three-masted* J. O. WEBSTER *spent part of her career on the Great Lakes, first as the Boy Scout training ship* OLIVER H. PERRY *and later in trade again as the* J. T. WING. *Author's collection.*

demned in 1956, and as the cost of rebuilding was prohibitive, she was broken up in 1958.

Fraser-Lee, "Bluenose on the Great Lakes."

JUAN SEBASTIAN DE ELCANO

Topsail schooner (4m). *L/B/D:* 308.7′ × 42.9′ × 22.2′ (94.1m × 13.1m × 6.8m). *Tons:* 3,750 disp. *Hull:* steel. *Comp.:* 265. *Arm.:* 4 × 6pdr. *Mach.:* diesel, 500 bhp, 1 screw; 9.5 kts. *Des.:* Camper & Nicholsons, Ltd., Southampton. *Built:* Echevarrieta y Larrinaga, Cadiz, Spain; 1927.

Although Ferdinand Magellan is often credited with being the first man to circumnavigate the globe, he was killed in the Moluccas in 1521 when his ship VICTORIA was only about halfway around the world. His pilot Juan Sebastian de Elcano took command of the vessel and arrived back at Spain with a crew of only nineteen men after a voyage of three years. De Elcano is thus a fitting choice of name for a Spanish sail-training vessel, and his four-masted namesake has served the officers and cadets of the Spanish Navy in that capacity for almost three-quarters of a century. Whether flying the flag of a monarchy, Franco's fascist dictatorship, or parliamentary democracy, *Juan Sebastian de Elcano* has sailed both as a training vessel and as a goodwill ambassador for Spain, and always as a vivid reminder that Spain once ruled supreme at sea.

Underhill, *Sail Training and Cadet Ships.*

USS JUNEAU (CL-52)

Atlanta-class cruiser. *L/B/D:* 541.5′ × 53.2′ × 20.5′ (165m × 16.2m × 6.2m). *Tons:* 8,340 disp. *Hull:* steel. *Comp.:* 623. *Arm.:* 16 × 5″ (8 × 2), 16 × 1.1′; 8 × 21″. *Armor:* 3.8″ belt, 1.3″ deck. *Mach.:* 75,000 hp, 2 screws; 32 kts. *Built:* Federal Shipbuilding Co., Kearny, N.J.; 1942.

One of eight *Atlanta/Oakland*-class cruisers, the only American cruisers to carry dual-purpose 5-inch guns for their primary armament, USS *Juneau* spent several months on the East Coast before being sent to the South Pacific in the fall of 1942. On September 10, she joined a task force centered on USS WASP and was assigned to ferrying planes and troops to Guadalcanal; five days later, *Juneau* helped rescue survivors from the stricken aircraft carrier. Over the next several months, she took part in the brutal defense of Guadalcanal. At the Battle of the Santa Cruz Islands (October 26–27) *Juneau* was part of the screen for USS HORNET, whose captain was forced to give the order to abandon ship, whereupon *Juneau* joined

the escort screen for USS ENTERPRISE. On November 8, *Juneau* departed Nouméa, New Caledonia, in a convoy bound for Guadalcanal. The transports and cargo ships arrived on the 12th. Shortly before 0200 the next morning, the American Landing Support Group engaged a numerically superior Japanese fleet. In the closely fought Naval Battle of Guadalcanal, *Juneau* was forced to withdraw after a torpedo knocked out one of her screws. The next morning, as the battered American fleet retired, *Juneau* was torpedoed again by the Japanese submarine *I-26*. She sank in less than a minute (in 10°34′S, 161°04′E), taking with her all but ten of her crew. Among the dead were Captain Lyman K. Swenson and the five Sullivan brothers, ages twenty-two to twenty-eight. Their loss forced a change in Navy policy, under which brothers were no longer allowed to serve in the same ship. The destroyer USS THE SULLIVANS was also named in their memory.

U.S. Navy, *DANFS.*

JUNIOR

Whaleship (3m). *L/B/D:* 115′ × 27′ × 13.5′ dph (35.1m × 8.2m × 4.1m). *Tons:* 378 disp. *Hull:* wood. *Comp:* 23. *Built:* East Haddam, Conn.; 1836.

Owned by David R. Greene and Company of New Bedford, *Junior* was the scene of one of the most notorious mutinies of the American whaling fleet. Under Captain Archibald Melen, Jr., the ship sailed for the Pacific whaling grounds on June 21, 1857. The crew lived in appalling circumstances with brutal, incompetent officers and stores that included casks of rotting meat purchased in Hawaii on the ship's previous voyage. By Christmas Day the ship was about six days from Australia, having gone six months without spotting one whale. Fortified with Christmas spirits and led by malcontent boat steerer Cyrus Plummer, a group of the crew killed the captain and third mate, and wounded the first and second mates. Ten of the mutineers left the ship near Cape Howe; eight crew were eventually caught and returned to New Bedford as prisoners aboard their old ship. At the highly publicized trial, the defense cited the inhumane conditions before the mast as mitigating circumstances for their act, and only Plummer was found guilty of murder. (President James Buchanan commuted his death sentence to life in prison.) *Junior* made one more voyage before being sold to New York in 1862, and she was sold foreign in 1865.

Harris, "Mutiny on *Junior*." Starbuck, *History of the North American Whale Fishery.*

JYLLAND

Steam frigate (3m). *L/B/D:* 210.3′ × 43′ × 19.7′ (64.1m × 13.1m × 6m). *Tons:* 2,450 disp. *Hull:* wood. *Comp.:* 437. *Arm.:* 44 × 30pdr, 1 × 18pdr, 1 × 12pdr, 3 × 4pdr. *Mach.:* horizontal steam engine, 400 nhp, 1 screw; 12 kts. *Built:* Nyholm Naval Shipyard, Copenhagen; 1860.

The Danish steam frigate JYLLAND, *minus her masts, in 1979. From a distance the white stripe might mask the hogged hull (the fact that she is lower at the bow and stern than amidships), but the gently arching row of gunports reveals the curvature of the deck. Courtesy Norman Brouwer.*

The development of the steam engine and auxiliary power in the nineteenth century helped to revolutionize navigation and naval warfare. However, paddle machinery was vulnerable to enemy fire and took up so much space formerly given over to guns that it was more of a liability than an asset. The widespread adoption of screw propulsion in the 1840s made steam warships a more realistic alternative to windships. *Jylland* (Jutland) was built for the Danish Navy in 1860. Initially sailed as a cadet-training ship, on May 9, 1863, she was severely damaged in the Battle of Helgoland between a Danish fleet under Admiral Edouard Suenson and an Austro-Prussian force under Admiral Wilhelm von Tegetthoff. Hostilities had begun after King Christian IX attempted to formally annex the duchies of Schleswig and Holstein — historically Danish but with a large German population — into Denmark. On the pretext of enforcing the Treaty of London of 1852, which forbade any such annexation, Prussia's Chancellor Otto von Bismarck — with an Austrian alliance — forced the Danes to back down in 1864.

Denmark, which surrendered the two duchies only to see them annexed by Prussia after the Austro-Prussian War of 1866, remained at peace through the end of the nineteenth century. *Jylland*'s role was largely one of showing the flag, mostly in European waters but also in the Danish West Indies (now the U.S. Virgin Islands). From 1892 to 1908, *Jylland* was used as a stationary barracks and training ship. In the latter year, the government decided to save the ship as a museum, although she was used as a barracks during and just after both world wars. The last survivor from the era of wooden-hulled, screw-driven warships has been undergoing restoration in a permanent dry dock at Ebeltoft since 1984.

Brouwer, *International Register of Historic Ships.* Kjølsen, "Old Danish Frigate." Schäuffelen, *Great Sailing Ships.*

K

KADIRGA

Galley. *L/B:* 121.2' × 18.7' (36.9m × 5.7m). *Hull:* wood. *Comp.:* 144 oarsmen. *Built:* Imperial Shipyard, Kasimpasha, Turkey; 16th-17th cent.

The *Kadirga* is the largest of twenty-nine state caïques (or barges) preserved at the Maritime Museum in Istanbul. Although some traditions hold that she was actually a Byzantine galley captured at the fall of Constantinople in 1453, the best estimates of her date of build range between the reigns of Sultan Mehmet II (1451–81) and that of Mehmet IV (1648–87). The later date is based on her similarity to Western galleys of the same period, in which the sternpost is set at an angle to the keel rather than framed in a continuous curve.

The *Kadirga* (which is simply the Turkish word for "galley") is a 48-oared galley *a scaloccio,* that is, with three men on a bench pulling a single oar. (In a galley *alla sensile,* each rower on the bench pulled his own oar.) The steersman stands on the raised stern holding a centerline rudder. Just forward of this position is a canopied cabin (in Turkish, a *köshk,* or kiosk), supported by four silvered columns and "worked in ivory and mother-of-pearl, and decorated with rock crystal and turquoise stones." From there the hull descends in a gentle sheer down to the rowers' deck, and the bow ends in a long tapered ram.

Used chiefly for ceremonial occasions, the *Kadirga* may have been used for extended voyages, including the 125 miles (200 kilometers) east across the Sea of Marmara. The *Kadirga* was used as late as the reign of Mahmut II (1808–39), after which she was laid up at Topkapi Palace. In 1913, the entire fleet of imperial caïques was rowed or towed to the Naval Arsenal at Kasimpasha, where they remained until 1956. In that year, *Kadirga* was moved to Beshiktash, near the Bosporus, and then to the Naval Museum in 1970, where she has been on exhibit ever since.

Basch, "*Kadirga* Revisited." Brookes, "The Turkish Imperial State Barges." Lehmann, "Turkish Imperial State Barges."

KAGA

Kaga-class aircraft carrier. *L/B/D:* 812.5' × 106.6' × 31' (247.7m × 32.5m × 9.4m). *Tons:* 42,541 disp. *Hull:* steel. *Comp.:* 2,020. *Arm.:* 90 aircraft; 10 × 8", 16 × 5", 30 × 25mm. *Armor:* 11" belt. *Mach.:* geared turbines, 4 shafts, 127,400 shp; 28.5 kts. *Built:* Yokosuka Dockyard, Yokosuka, Japan; 1928.

Laid down and launched as a battleship, work on the *Kaga* (named for a city in Japan) was stopped in accordance with the terms of the Washington Naval Treaty of 1922. The following year, work to finish her as an aircraft carrier began, and *Kaga* was completed on March 31, 1928. One of the six carriers in Vice Admiral Chuichi Nagumo's First Air Fleet sent against Pearl Harbor on December 7, 1941, *Kaga* later took part in operations against the Dutch East Indies and New Guinea. One of four carriers in Admiral Nagumo's fleet at the Battle of Midway, *Kaga* was sunk (in 30°23'N, 179°17'W) by dive-bombers from USS ENTERPRISE at about 1026 on June 4, 1942, with the loss of 800 crew.

Stephen, *Sea Battles in Close-Up.* Silverstone, *Directory of the World's Capital Ships.*

KAISER WILHELM DER GROSSE

Liner; auxiliary cruiser (4f/2m). *L/B:* 191.2m bp × 20.1m (627.4' × 66'). *Tons:* 14,349 grt. *Hull:* steel. *Comp.:* 1st 332, 2nd 343, 3rd 1,074. *Arm.:* 6 × 10.5cm; 2 × 3.7cm. *Mach.:* triple expansion, 14,000 ihp, 2 screws; 22 kts. *Built:* AG Vulcan, Stettin, Germany; 1897.

The German merchant marine's first bid to enter the race for supremacy on the North Atlantic passenger run, Norddeutscher Lloyd's *Kaiser Wilhelm der Grosse* — named for the grandfather of the reigning Wilhelm II — was designed to be the largest and most powerful ship afloat. The first ocean liner with four funnels (only fourteen were built), arranged in two pairs rather than being evenly spaced, the sumptuously decorated ship initiated the era of the superliner. Her prodigious speed was evident from the first, when she made the fastest crossing of

Undated postcard of the German express liner KAISER WILHELM DER GROSSE *entering the lock at Bremerhaven. Courtesy The Mariners' Museum, Newport News, Virginia.*

any maiden voyage — Bremen to New York via Southampton — in September 1897. Two months later she became the first German ship to capture the Blue Riband by sailing from Sandy Hook to the Needles at an average speed of 22.27 knots. The following March, she set a westbound record with a speed of 22.29 knots. (Both times were bettered by Hamburg-Amerika's DEUTSCHLAND in 1900.)

In June 1900 she narrowly avoided destruction when a fire broke out at the Norddeutscher Lloyd piers in Hoboken, New Jersey. The fire was the worst in the history of the port of New York, and while she escaped relatively unscathed, her consorts *Bremen, Main,* and *Saale* were badly damaged; the last had to be sold. Six years later *Kaiser Wilhelm der Grosse* was rammed by the British freighter *Orinoco* off Cherbourg in a collision in which five passengers were killed.

Owing to the profitability of the emigrant trade, in 1914 *Kaiser Wilhelm der Grosse* was reconfigured to carry only third- and fourth-class passengers, and her few remaining voyages between Bremen and New York were direct. Her last voyage from New York began on July 21 and she was safely back in Bremen at the outbreak of World War I.

Fitted out as an armed merchant cruiser, she sailed from Bremerhaven in the first week of August under command of Captain Max Reymann with a crew of 584. Over the course of the next two weeks she encountered five ships, three of which she sank and two of which she released as they were full of passengers. Starved for fuel, on August 21 she entered the neutral port of Rio de Oro, Spanish Sahara. While refueling from three colliers, she

was surprised by HMS *Highflyer*. After a brief pounding by the cruiser's 6-inch guns, Reymann ordered his ship scuttled, and *Kaiser Wilhelm der Grosse* sank in 23°34′N, 16°2′W. There were at least 480 survivors and an unknown number of casualties.

Bonsor, *North Atlantic Seaway.* Walter, *Kaiser's Pirates.*

KAIULANI

(ex-*Star of Finland, Kaiulani*) Bark (3m). *L/B/D:* 250′ × 42′ × 19.2′ (76.2m × 12.8m × 5.8m). *Tons:* 1,699 grt. *Hull:* steel. *Comp.:* 17 crew; 16 pass. *Des.:* J. A. Hargan. *Built:* A. Sewall & Co., Bath, Me.; 1899.

The last square-rigger to sail in regular commercial service under the American flag, *Kaiulani* was named for Princess Victoria Kaiulani, the last heir apparent to the Hawaiian throne, who died in 1899, the year of her namesake's launch and one year after the Republic of Hawaii was annexed by the United States. The white-hulled bark was built by Arthur Sewall, Maine's celebrated "Maritime Prince," for A. Hackfield & Company's Hawaiian (or Planters) Line. *Kaiulani* carried passengers and mixed cargo from San Francisco to Honolulu, returning to the West Coast with sugar. In the off-season she sailed on different routes that took her as far afield as Australia.

In 1908, *Kaiulani*'s owners were taken over by the Matson Line, and two years later she was retired from the San Francisco–Honolulu route. Sold to the Alaska Packers Association and renamed *Star of Finland,* every spring she sailed from San Francisco freighting supplies and crews for the lonely salmon fisheries sprinkled along the Alaskan mainland. There she would remain through the fall, when she would return with a full cargo of tinned salmon. This work was one of the last bastions of sail, and the Alaska Packers maintained a sturdy fleet of iron- and steel-hulled English and American ships, including five from Sewall's yard. *Star of Finland* made the voyage every year until 1927, when she was laid up at Alameda. Although the other ships were sold off, she remained in San Francisco Bay through the 1930s, sailing briefly, as both the bark *Vigilant* and ship *William Brown,* in the Gary Cooper film *Souls at Sea* (1937).

As World War II threatened to involve the United States, virtually all available shipping was put back in service. *Star of Finland* was no exception, and in 1941 she was purchased by the Hammond Lumber Company, who gave her back her old name. *Kaiulani* was chartered to the Danish East Asiatic Company to carry 1.6 million board feet of lumber from Gray's Harbor, Washington, to Dur-

Named for Hawaii's last princess, the three-masted, steel-hulled bark KAIULANI *was built for service between San Francisco and Hawaii. By the time this picture was taken, by O. Beaton in 1912, she was hard at work in the Alaska fisheries. Pressed into service during the shipping shortage at the start of World War II, she became the last American square-rigger to round Cape Horn, in 1941. Courtesy Special Collections Division, University of Washington Libraries, Seattle.*

ban, South Africa. Under command of Captain Hjalmar Wigsten and with a crew that included future ship preservationists Karl Kortum and Harry Dring, she sailed on September 25, 1941, becoming the first American square-rigger to double Cape Horn in twenty-one years, and possibly the last merchant square-rigger ever to do so. While roaring through the southern ocean, her crew picked up radio transmissions from which they learned of the Japanese attack on Pearl Harbor on December 7.

Arriving at Durban on January 29, 1942, *Kaiulani* discharged her lumber, but cargoes for square-riggers were few and far between, and it was not until May 7 that she cleared for Sydney, Australia, with 190 tons of freight, including explosives. After learning of submarine activity off Sydney, Wigsten decided to sail instead for Hobart, Tasmania, where she arrived in June. The U.S. Army learned of the ship's presence in Australian waters, and *Kaiulani* was sailed to Sydney. Here she was stripped down for use as a coal barge to provide fuel for "MacArthur's Navy" as the Allies worked their way along the coast of New Guinea and the Philippine archipelago. War's end found her at Manila, and in 1948 she was sold as surplus to the Madrigal Shipping Company. For the next seventeen years she hauled mahogany logs from Mindanao to Manila.

In 1963, a group of Americans formed the National Maritime Historical Society to preserve the last known Yankee square-rigger as a public exhibit at Washington, D.C. The Philippines' President Diosdado Macapagal formally donated *Kaiulani* to President Lyndon B. Johnson on behalf of the American people in 1964. Unfortunately, efforts to raise funds to complete her restoration for return to the United States were unsuccessful, and *Kaiulani* was broken up in 1974. A portion of her forefoot was subsequently acquired by the National Park Service for display at the National Maritime Museum in San Francisco.

Hutchinson, "*Kaiulani*." Nerney, *History of Williams, Dimond and Company.* Wittholz, "Aloha *Kaiulani!*"

SMS KARLSRUHE

Karlsruhe-class light cruiser (4f/2m). *L/B/D:* 466.4′ × 45′ × 18′ (142.2m × 13.7m × 6.3m). *Tons:* 6,191 disp. *Hull:* steel. *Comp.:* 373. *Arm.:* 12 × 4.1″, 2 × 20″TT. *Mach.:* steam turbines, 37,885 shp, 2 screws; 28.5 kts. *Built:* Friedrich Krupp AG Germaniawerft, Kiel, Germany; 1914.

Named for the city on the Rhine River, at the start of World War I, *Karlsruhe* was the newest cruiser in the German Navy, having been commissioned only three months before. Arriving on the West Indies station in July, with war imminent, Captain Erich Köhler slipped out of Havana on July 30 to await orders. On August 6, *Karlsruhe* rendezvoused with the passenger ship KRONPRINZ WILHELM in the remote cays of the Bahamas to exchange ammunition for provisions. Interrupted by HMS *Sussex,* flying the flag of Rear Admiral Sir Christopher Cradock, *Karlsruhe* fled the slower ship only to find herself that night within range of HMS *Bristol,* from whom she also escaped. After coaling quickly at San Juan, Puerto Rico, and Curaçao, Köhler took his ship into the sea lanes off Brazil, which, from the British standpoint at least, was preferable to the North Atlantic. *Karlsruhe*'s success was limited initially, but between August 31 and October 24 she captured fifteen ships, and the British had no report of her whereabouts between September 28 and October 22. Köhler now decided to try an attack on Barbados and Martinique similar to SMS EMDEN's attack on Penang. On November 4, *Karlsruhe* and the supply ships *Rio Negro* and *Indrani* were about 300 miles southwest of Barbados in 11°07′N, 55°25′W when a huge explosion — subsequently attributed to the spontaneous combustion of unstable ammunition — suddenly blew off her bows, killing 263 of her officers and crew. The survivors returned to Germany in December, and the secret of her loss was so well kept that the British continued to hunt for her until they learned of her loss from debris washed up on the island of St. Vincent in April 1915.

Yates, *Graf Spee's Raiders.*

The German light cruiser KARLSRUHE, *one of three ships lost during the invasion of Norway in 1940, seen from the decks of the American aircraft carrier* USS LANGLEY *at San Diego, California, March 28, 1934. Note that she carries nine 6-inch guns in three turrets, one forward and two aft. Courtesy U.S. Naval Historical Center, Washington, D.C.*

had his crew taken off, and at 2250 he ordered the torpedo-boat *Greif* to sink his ship, in 58°04′N, 8°4′E. She was one of three heavy surface units lost in the invasion of Norway, with BLÜCHER and KÖNIGSBERG.

Gröner, *German Warships.* Whitley, *German Cruisers of World War Two.*

KARLSRUHE

Königsberg-class cruiser (2f/2m). *L/B/D:* 570.7′ × 49.9′ × 20.7′ (174m × 15.2m × 6.3m). *Tons:* 7,700 disp. *Hull:* steel. *Comp.:* 820–850. *Arm.:* 9 × 6″ (3 × 3), 6 × 8.8cm, 8 × 3.7cm, 4 × 2cm; 12 × 21″TT; 2 aircraft. *Mach.:* steam turbines, 68,200 shp, 2 screws; 32.5 kts. *Des.:* Constructional Advisor Ehrenberg. *Built:* Deutsche Werke, Kiel, Germany; 1929.

One of three "K"-class light cruisers designed as commerce raiders in the 1920s, *Karlsruhe* first saw wartime duty off Spain during the Spanish Civil War. On April 7, 1940, *Karlsruhe* (Captain Rieve) and sister ship *Köln* were deployed to Bergen as part of Operation Weserübung. Later sent to Kristiansand in southern Norway, after overcoming the battery at Odderoy, *Karlsruhe* disembarked troops and munitions as planned before sailing for home waters at 1900, on April 9. About an hour later, *Karlsruhe* was hit by up to three torpedoes fired from the submarine HMS *Truant,* under Lieutenant Commander C. H. Hutchinson. With his ship in a sinking condition, Rieve

USS KEARNY (DD-432)

Gleaves-class destroyer (1f/1m). *L/B/D:* 347.4′ × 36.1′ × 11.8′ (105.9m × 11m × 3.6m). *Tons:* 2,060 disp. *Hull:* steel. *Comp.:* 208. *Arm.:* 4 × 5″, 12 × .50 cal., 2 × 10″TT, 2 dct. *Mach.:* geared turbines, 44,000 shp, 2 shafts; 36.5 kts. *Built:* Federal Ship Building & Dry Dock Co., Kearny, N.J.; 1940.

Named for Lawrence Kearny, a naval officer whose diplomatic acuity in the 1840s improved U.S. relations with China and reversed Britain's annexation of Hawaii, USS *Kearny* was first assigned to the Neutrality Patrol, intended to keep European belligerents out of the Americas. Following an expansion of U.S. policy to one of "all aid short of war" in support of England, *Kearny* began escorting British convoys between Newfoundland and Iceland. On October 16, 1941, a German submarine sank three merchant ships in a convoy that *Kearny* was escorting, and *Kearny* was struck by a torpedo that wounded 22 sailors and killed 11 others, the first U.S. fatalities of World War II. She limped into Reykjavik but was not ready for sea again until after the U.S. declaration of war.

Kearny returned to duty in April 1942, escorting convoys to England, the Caribbean, South America, and North Africa, where she took part in Operation Torch, the invasion of Morocco, in November 1942. After two months as part of escort carrier USS *Core*'s hunter-killer task group, *Kearny* sailed for the Mediterranean, providing fire support for forces bogged down at Anzio, Italy, in March 1944, and in August for the Allied landings near St. Tropez, France. Following convoy duty in the Mediterranean and Atlantic, *Kearny* transferred to the Pacific in August 1945, arriving at Pearl Harbor after the Japanese surrender. Decommissioned in 1946, she ended her days in the reserve fleet at Orange, Texas.

U.S. Navy, *DANFS*.

Two officers pose next to one of USS KEARSARGE*'s two 11-inch pivot guns. It is June 19, 1864, the day the screw sloop sank the Confederate raider* CSS ALABAMA *off Cherbourg, France. Courtesy U.S. Naval Historical Center, Washington, D.C.*

USS KEARSARGE

Mohican-class screw sloop (3m). *L/B/D:* 198.5′ bp × 33.8′ × 15.8′ (60.5m × 10.3m × 4.8m). *Tons:* 1,550 disp.; 1,031 burden. *Hull:* wood. *Comp.:* 160. *Arm.:* 2 × 11″, 4 × 32pdr. *Mach.:* horizontal back-acting engines, 842 ihp, 1 screw; 11 kts. *Built:* Portsmouth Navy Yard, Kittery, Me.; 1862.

Ordered under the emergency war program of 1861, USS *Kearsarge* (named for a New Hampshire mountain) had a rather commonplace career in the European Squadron of the U.S. Navy. Under Captain Charles W. Pickering, she departed Portsmouth, New Hampshire, on January 24, 1862, and took part in the blockade of CSS SUMTER at Gibraltar; *Sumter*'s commander, Captain Raphael Semmes, thereupon left the ship. Thereafter *Kearsarge* patrolled the western Atlantic in pursuit of Semmes's new ship, CSS ALABAMA, and other raiders. In June 1864, *Kearsarge* was at Flushing, Holland, under Captain John A. Winslow, when word arrived that the notorious Confederate raider had put into Cherbourg on June 11. Three days later, *Kearsarge* arrived off the French coast. Local officials told him that any attempt to embark U.S. sailors put ashore from *Alabama* would violate French neutrality, so Winslow — a shipmate of Semmes before the war — put to sea to await *Alabama*'s inevitable departure. On the morning of June 19, *Alabama* stood out of Cherbourg and opened fire on *Kearsarge* at 1057. Fitted with protective chain cables and fighting with better-quality munitions, *Kearsarge* was more than a match for the war-weary *Alabama,* which began to sink after an hour. *Kearsarge* rescued most of *Alabama*'s crew except for Semmes and about forty others, who escaped aboard a British yacht. This single engagement against the Confederacy's most notorious commerce raider made *Kearsarge* one of the best-known ships in the U.S. Navy.

After an unsuccessful effort to locate CSS FLORIDA, *Kearsarge* proceeded to the Caribbean and from there to Boston where she was decommissioned for repairs. *Kearsarge* continued in service for another thirty years, seeing service in virtually every sphere of U.S. interest around the world: the Mediterranean, South America, the Pacific, and the China Station. She wrecked on Roncador Reef off Central America while en route from Haiti to Bluefields, Nicaragua, on February 2, 1894, without loss of life. Deemed unsalvageable, she was stricken from the Navy list the same year.

Guérout, "Engagement between the C.S.S. *Alabama* and the U.S.S. *Kearsarge*." Leary, "*Alabama* vs. *Kearsarge*."

KENILWORTH

(later *Star of Scotland*). Bark (4m). *L/B/D:* 300.2′ × 43.1′ × 24.2′ (91.5m × 13.1m × 7.4m). *Tons:* 2,308 grt. *Hull:* steel. *Comp.:* 20. *Built:* John C. Reid & Co., Glasgow, Scotland; 1887.

Kenilworth was the last of five ships built for Williamson and Milligan's so-called Waverly Line, whose ships were named for characters in Sir Walter Scott's Waverly novels: *Ivanhoe, Roderick Dhu, Lammermoor,* and *Cedric the Saxon.* Built to carry bulk cargoes, the ship was damaged by fire in 1889 in San Francisco, and sold to Arthur Sewall & Company (though only after a special act of Congress), becoming the first steel-hulled U.S.-flag-sailing merchant ship. She continued in her long hauls, calling in Australia, Shanghai, Calcutta, and elsewhere.

One routine passage wound up taking almost two years from port to port, and kept the ship at sea for a total of fourteen months. Sailing from Philadelphia for San Francisco with coal on August 15, 1906, *Kenilworth* spent fifty-five days beating against Cape Horn before putting back to Montevideo in early 1907 where she underwent seven weeks of repairs to her steering gear and rigging. On her next attempt at the Horn, she was at sea for 152 days before being forced back again, this time with leaking bows, which were patched with cement at Rio de Janeiro. She finally arrived at San Francisco in July 1908, eighty-eight days out from Rio. Sold to the Alaska Packers' Association and renamed *Star of Scotland,* she spent the next twenty-two years as a depot ship in the Alaska salmon fisheries. (During World War I she traded briefly between California and Hawaii under the auspices of the U.S. Shipping Board.)

In 1930 she was sold for use as a fishing barge in Los Angeles. Her career took a decided twist in 1938 when she was acquired for use as a floating casino, renamed *Rex,* and moored in international waters just outside the three-mile limit. This short-lived enterprise — remembered in Raymond Chandler's novel *Farewell, My Lovely* — came to a close in 1940 when she was sold again, to Frank A. Hellenthal. Rerigged as a six-masted schooner, on January 20, 1942, she sailed with a cargo of lumber from Aberdeen, Washington, to Cape Town. Bound for Paranaguá, Brazil, in ballast, she was sunk by *U-159* about 900 miles off the coast of South-West Africa (Namibia) on November 13. One of the crew was killed, and the remaining fifteen reached Angola eighteen days later.

Lyman, "*Star of Scotland,* ex-*Kenilworth,*"

KILLORAN

Bark (3m). *L/B/D:* 261.5′ × 39.5′ × 22.7′ (79.7m × 12m × 6.9m). *Tons:* 1,757. *Hull:* steel. *Built:* Ailsa Shipbuilding Co., Glasgow; 1900.

Owned by James Browne of Glasgow from 1900 to 1909 and by Messrs. J. Hardie & Company until 1924, *Killoran* spent most of her career under the British flag trading to the west coast of North and South America and Australian ports. Although the origin of her name is uncertain, the most likely origins are Kiloran Bay, on the Isle of Colonsay, or an Irish village named Killoran. Despite the risk of sinking by German U-boats, she sailed during World War I and is credited with saving more than 80 survivors from the freighter *Trevean* in 1917.

One of the last steel-hulled general traders to fly the British flag, *Killoran* was laid up at Sunderland in 1921. Three years later, the Finnish shipowner Gustaf Erikson purchased her, and after two voyages in general trade to Canada and Chile, he put her in the Australian grain trade. She remained in this work from 1927 until 1940, although she occasionally loaded other cargoes in South America and elsewhere. On July 13, 1939, *Killoran* left Port Lincoln, Australia, and called at Queenstown for orders on November 29 with the last cargo of prewar grain to reach Europe. Under Captain Karl Leman, three months later she sailed from Cardiff for Buenos Aires. Departing from there on June 15, 1940, with a cargo of maize and sugar for Las Palmas, Canary Islands, on August 10 she was stopped by the German merchant raider WIDDER. After examining the neutral ship's papers, Commander Hellmuth von Ruckteschell ordered bombs set, and *Killoran* sank at 1539, in position 33°06′N, 24°19′W. Ironically, within a year, Finland was allied with Germany and Erikson's PAMIR and LAWHILL would be seized in New Zealand and South Africa, respectively.

Ferguson-Innes, "*Killoran.*"

HMS KING EDWARD VII

King Edward VII-class battleship (2f/2m). *L/B/D:* 453.8′ × 78′ × 26.8′ (138.3m × 23.8m × 8.2m). *Tons:* 17,009 disp. *Comp.:* 777. *Hull:* steel. *Arm.:* 4 × 12″ (2 × 2); 4 × 9.2″, 10 × 6″, 14 × 12pdr; 14 × 3pdr; 4 × 18″TT. *Armor:* 9″ belt. *Mach.:* triple expansion, 18,000 hp, 2 screws; 18.5 kts. *Des.:* Sir William White, Sir Philip Watts. *Built:* Devonport Dockyard, Plymouth, Eng.; 1905.

The first of a class of eight pre-*Dreadnought* battleships nicknamed the "Wobbly Eights" (Italian naval constructor Vittorio Cuniberti referred to them as "monsters with short legs") because of problems with their balanced rudders, *King Edward VII* was commissioned as flagship of the Atlantic Fleet from 1905 to 1906, followed by service in the Channel Fleet (1907–9) and Home Fleet (1911–12). Well out of date by the time World War I began, the class comprised the third battle squadron during the war. *King Edward VII* was mined off Cape Wrath (in 58°43′N, 4°4′W) on January 6, 1916, in a minefield laid by the German raider MÖWE. All the crew was transferred to destroyers before the ship rolled over and sank at 2000. None of the class engaged a German ship during World War I, although HMS *Britannia* was sunk by *U-50* off Cape Trafalgar on November 9, 1918. The remaining ships were sold out of the service by 1921.

Parkes, *British Battleships*.

HMS KING GEORGE V

King George V-class battleship (2f/2m). *L/B/D:* 745′ × 103′ × 35.5′ (227.1m × 31.4m × 10.8m). *Tons:* 44,460 disp. *Comp.:* 1,314–1,631. *Hull:* steel. *Arm.:* 10 × 14″ (2 × 4, 1 × 2); 16 × 5.2″, 64 × 2pdr; 2 aircraft. *Armor:* 15″ belt; 4″ deck. *Mach.:* geared turbines, 110,000 shp, 4 screws; 27.5 kts. *Des.:* Sir Arthur Johns. *Built:* Vickers Ltd., Barrow-in-Furness, Eng.; 1940.

Named for the reigning British monarch, HMS *King George V* was the first of a five-ship class that was criticized because it was weaker than the most powerful German battleships then afloat or building. Designed within the limits established by the 1936 London Naval Limitation Treaty, their relatively weak primary armament comprised 14-inch guns rather than the 16-inch guns mounted by HMS NELSON and RODNEY, or the 15-inch guns of BISMARCK or TIRPITZ. After sailing in support of the Lofoten Islands commando raids on March 4, 1941, *King George V* became the flagship of the Home Fleet under Admiral Sir John Tovey. In late May she was involved in the pursuit of *Bismarck,* and on the morning of the 27th, she and *Rodney* poured endless rounds into the doomed battleship. Earlier in the chase, lack of fuel had forced home PRINCE OF WALES and aircraft carrier VICTORIOUS, but destruction of the German ship was of such paramount importance to Prime Minister Winston Churchill that he ordered the following extraordinary — and irresponsible — message sent: "We cannot visualize the situation from your signal. *Bismarck* must be sunk at all costs and if to do this it is necessary for *King George V* to remain on the scene she must do even if it subsequently means towing *King George V*." As it happened, the message was not received until after BISMARCK was sunk, and Tovey later asserted that he would have ignored it anyway.

Active in northern waters through mid-1943, *King George V* collided with and sank the destroyer HMS *Punjabi* while on convoy duty in the spring of 1942. After covering the invasion of Sicily, she carried Churchill home from the Tehran Conference in December. She served with the British Pacific Fleet from 1944 and was present at the surrender of Japan in September 1945. Recommissioned as flagship of the Home Fleet in 1946,

she was decommissioned three years later and scrapped at Dalmuir in 1958.

Dumas, "*King George V* Class." Miller, *War at Sea*.

KIRISHIMA

Kongo-class battlecruiser (3f/2m). *L/B/D:* 704′ × 92′ × 26.9′ (214.6m × 28m × 8.2m). *Tons:* 32,200. *Hull:* steel. *Comp.:* 1,221–1,437. *Arm.:* 8 × 14″ (4 × 2), 16 × 6″, 8 × 3.1″, 4 × 3″, 7 mg; 8 × 21″TT; 3 aircraft. *Armor:* 8″ belt, 2″ deck. *Mach.:* geared turbines, 64,000 shp, 4 screws; 27.5 kts. *Built:* Mitsubishi Zosen Kaisha, Nagasaki, Japan; 1915.

One of four KONGO-class battlecruisers laid down before World War I, in 1933–34 *Kirishima* was lengthened 24 feet, her speed was increased to 30 knots, and she was reclassified as a battleship. In December 1941, she sailed as part of Rear Admiral G. Mikawa's Support Force at Pearl Harbor. During the Japanese mopping up of the Allied forces in the Dutch East Indies, together with *Hiei* she sank the destroyer USS *Edsall* on February 17, 1942, south of Java. She escorted Japanese carriers during their raids on Ceylon the next month. At the Naval Battle of Guadalcanal, on November 13–15, 1942, the Japanese fleet hoped to block the reinforcement of the U.S. garrison on Guadalcanal. On the night of the 13th, the two fleets blundered into each other. Though the Japanese sank more ships at the outset, *Hiei* was crippled and later sunk by U.S. aircraft. In the meantime, the battleships WASHINGTON and *South Dakota* were brought up, and on the morning of November 15, they encountered the Japanese north of Savo Island. *Kirishima* and the cruisers ATAGO and *Takao* engaged USS *South Dakota*, but *Washington*'s 16-inch guns quickly reduced *Kirishima* to a flaming wreck, and Vice Admiral Nobutake Kondo ordered her scuttled at 0320 in 9°05′S, 159°42′E.

Breyer, *Battleships and Battlecruisers*. Morison, *Two-Ocean War*.

KØBENHAVEN

Bark (5m). *L/B/D:* 368.9′ × 49.3′ × 26.9′ (112.4m × 15m × 8.2m). *Tons:* 3,901 grt. *Hull:* steel. *Comp.:* 50–60. *Mach.:* diesel, 500 hp, 1 screw. *Built:* Ramage & Ferguson, Ltd., Leith, Scotland; 1921.

In 1914, the Danish East Asiatic Company ordered a five-masted bark from the English shipbuilders Ramage & Leith, for use as a sail-training vessel for prospective officers. World War I began shortly after the hull was finished, and it was purchased on the stocks by the Royal Navy, renamed *Black Dragon*, and towed to Gibraltar for use as an oil hulk. The war did not dampen the Danes' enthusiasm for a sail-training scheme, and in 1921 the second *Københaven* was launched. Powerfully rigged, she set double topsails and double topgallants, with royals above, and as originally sparred set double gaffs on the spanker mast. Her deck layout had four structures: a topgallant forecastle, a midship house abaft the mainmast, another house abaft the mizzen, and a poop running from abaft the jigger mast to the stern.

Her oceanic voyaging took her from Europe to ports in South America and Australia, and her cargoes included timber, nitrate, and grain. Although regarded as an excellent sailer, *Københaven* had a short career. On December 14, 1928, she cleared Buenos Aires for Melbourne in ballast with 60 crew under Captain H. F. Anderson. Although equipped with radio, after passing Montevideo, Uruguay, she was never seen or heard from again. Two theories of her demise are that she was overwhelmed by a pampero (a sudden storm occurring off the pampas of Argentina), or that she sank after hitting an iceberg.

Underhill, *Sail Training and Cadet Ships.*

KOMAGATA MARU

(ex-*Sicilia, Stubbenbuck*) Liner (1f/2m). *L/B:* 329′ × 41.5′ (100.3m × 12.7m). *Tons:* 2,922 grt. *Hull:* steel. *Comp.:* 1st 10, 3rd 620. *Mach.:* triple expansion, 265 hp, 1 screw; 11 kts. *Built:* Charles Connell & Co., Ltd., Glasgow, Scotland; 1890.

Built for Dampfschiff Rederei, Hansa's service between Germany and Canada, the passenger ship *Stubbenbuck* was acquired by Hamburg-Amerika Linie in 1892. Renamed *Sicilia,* she continued in transatlantic service, with eastern ports of call ranging from the Mediterranean to the Baltic. In about 1904, she was sold to the Japanese firm of Kisen Goshi Kaisa and renamed *Komagata Maru.*

In 1908, Sikh businessman Gurdit Singh chartered the ship in an effort to challenge Canada's racial immigration policies. Singh recruited 376 passengers — 340 Sikhs, 12 Hindus, and 24 Muslims — at Hong Kong, Shanghai, and Moji, Japan, and the ship arrived at Vancouver on May 23, 1908. Immigration authorities prevented the passengers from disembarking on a variety of pretexts, and a test case in the courts resulted in the legal defeat of the immigrants. Nonetheless, the ship remained at anchor through the summer and the passengers were threatened with the use of force. *Komagata Maru* finally sailed on July 23, arriving in Japan on August 12. Still her passengers' troubles were far from over. After five weeks in port, she sailed for Calcutta, but she was detained at the town

of Budge Budge on the Hooghly River on September 29. About 250 passengers believed to be pro-independence agitators were rounded up by the police, and in confused circumstances twenty people were killed, sixteen of them Sikhs. Twenty-seven escaped, including Singh, who surrendered to authorities seven years later after consultations with Mahatma Gandhi. *Komagata Maru* was eventually returned to her owners, and resumed regular service. She was renamed *Heian Maru* in 1925, and wrecked near Cape Soidomai, Japan, on February 11, 1926. In 1951, Singh persuaded India's first Prime Minister, Jawaharlal Nehru, to erect a memorial to the people of the *Komagata Maru.* Coincidentally, Canada began tentatively to liberalize its immigration policies shortly thereafter.

Bonsor, *North Atlantic Seaway.* Johnston, *Voyage of the "Komagata Maru."*

SMS KÖNIGSBERG

Königsberg-class light cruiser (3f/2m). *L/B/D:* 378.2′ × 43.3′ × 17.4′ (115.3m × 13.2m × 5.3m). *Tons:* 3,814 disp. *Hull:* steel. *Comp.:* 322. *Arm.:* 10 × 10.5cm; 10 × 3.7cm; 2 × 18″TT. *Armor:* 4″ belt, 3.2″ deck. *Mach.:* triple expansion, 13,918 ihp, 2 screws; 24.1 kts. *Built:* Kaiserliche Werft, Kiel, Germany; 1907.

After four years of service in home waters followed by a three-year refit, SMS *Königsberg* was dispatched to the East African Station under Captain Max Looff. Arriving at Dar Es Salaam on July 6, 1914, she slipped out of port on July 31, just ahead of a British Cape Squadron blockading force. *Königsberg* captured and sank *City of Winchester* on August 6 off Somalia, an event that disrupted British shipping in the Indian Ocean. On September 20, Looff sank the antiquated cruiser HMS *Pegasus.* In need of maintenance, Looff took his ship into the Rufiji River delta about 150 miles south of Dar Es Salaam. The British located *Königsberg* in October, but their deep-draft ships could do no more than keep station off the Rufiji. Relief finally came in the form of the shallow-draft monitors HMS *Severn, Mersey,* and *Madeira.* On June 11, 1915, they ran the gauntlet of *Königsberg*'s light guns, which had been set up in the approaches to the delta, and sank the cruiser at long range in 7°51′S, 39°15′E. *Königsberg* lost 30 of her crew, but her 10.5-centimeter guns were salvaged and used on land in German East Africa for the duration of the war. *Königsberg*'s remains were broken up in 1965.

Gröner, *German Warships.* Walter, *Kaiser's Pirates.*

KÖNIGSBERG

Königsberg-class light cruiser. *L/B/D:* 570.7' × 50.2' × 20.7' (174m × 15.3m × 6.3m). *Tons:* 8,350 disp. *Hull:* steel. *Comp.:* 820–850. *Arm.:* 9 × 6" (3 × 3), 6 × 8.8cm, 8 × 3.7cm, 4 × 2cm; 12 × 21"TT; 2 aircraft. *Armor:* 2.8" belt, 1.6" deck. *Mach.:* steam turbines, 68,000 shp, 2 screws; 32.5 kts. *Des.:* Constructional Advisor Ehrenberg. *Built:* Reichsmarinewerft, Wilhelmshaven, Germany; 1929.

One of three "K"-class light cruisers designed as commerce raiders in the 1920s, *Königsberg* (named for the German city) first saw wartime duty off Spain during the Spanish Civil War. On April 7, 1940, *Königsberg* and its sister ship *Köln* were deployed to Bergen as part of Operation Weserübung. The ship was later hit by 8-inch guns on Kvarven, one of which put an 11-foot hole in the hull. Although able to continue fighting, the ship was not able to return immediately to Germany, and on April 10, Fleet Air Arm Skua fighter-bombers based in the Orkney Islands attacked *Königsberg*, which capsized at dockside, one of three major naval casualties in Germany's invasion of Norway — Hitler's "zone of destiny" — along with BLÜCHER and KARLSRUHE. The ship was refloated in 1942, but despite repeated efforts to right the vessel, she remained in Byfjord until broken up after the war.

Whitley, *German Cruisers of World War Two.*

KON-TIKI

Raft (1m). *L/B:* 45' × 18' (13.7m × 5.5m). *Hull:* balsa wood. *Comp.:* 6. *Des.:* traditional. *Built:* Callao, Peru; 1947.

In 1937, Norwegian zoologist Thor Heyerdahl went to live on the island of Fatu Hiva in the Marquesas Islands. Heyerdahl was intrigued by the presence in Polynesia of plants indigenous to South America, and especially by legends on Easter Island that echoed those of the Inca tradition in Peru. Tiki, the son of the sun, who was ancestor of the Easter Islanders, seemed to be the same as Kon-Tiki, the mythical head of a white race who, expelled by the Incas from around Lake Titicaca, sailed west across the Pacific. After World War II, Heyerdahl tried to circulate his theory of American colonization of the Pacific, but he was snubbed by the scholarly community. The basis for his rejection was the certainty that "none of the peoples of South America got over to the islands in the Pacific [because] they couldn't get there. They had no boats." Heyerdahl determined to demonstrate the feasibility of crossing 4,000 miles of the Pacific using pre-Columbian raft-building techniques.

The balsa logs were felled in the mountain jungles of Ecuador, floated downriver to Guayaquil, and shipped from there to the naval dockyard at Callao, Peru. The design of the vessel was based on Spanish descriptions of Inca rafts at the time of the conquest. The longest of the nine logs, which formed the center of the raft, was 45 feet; shorter and shorter logs were laid symmetrically on either side so that the sides were only 30 feet long. These were lashed together with 1¼-inch-thick hemp, and fir planks driven between big gaps in the logs acted as centerboards to prevent the raft from drifting to leeward. The mast consisted of two mangrove poles angled toward each other and lashed at the top; from this was set a square sail on a bamboo yard. A 19-foot steering oar rested between two tholepins on a large block astern. Lighter bamboo logs were laid crossways on the raft and covered with a bamboo decking. Aft there was a bamboo cabin.

On April 28, 1947, *Kon-Tiki* was towed 50 miles northwest of Callao by a tug and cast adrift. After a day of calms, the crew encountered 60 hours of rough weather in the Humboldt Current that pushed them far to the northwest. They struggled with the unwieldy steering oar for several weeks before they discovered that the most effective way to regulate the direction of the raft was with the centerboards, which the Incas, according to a Spanish account, "pushed down into the chinks between the timbers." Another concern was the rate at which the balsa wood initially absorbed water, leading each crew member in turn to wonder whether the raft would sink before reaching land. Early on in the planning of the expedition, Heyerdahl had estimated that it would take at least 97 days to reach land, but on July 30 — only 93 days from Callao — the company sighted the island of Puka Puka in the Tuamotus. They were unable to close with the land, but four days later they were off Angatau, though again prevented from landing. Four days after that, *Kon-Tiki* was washed onto the Raroia reef. After a week on an uninhabited island, they were visited by islanders from across the lagoon and through them began the slow return to civilization. The schooner *Tamara* was dispatched from Tahiti to bring the raft and crew to Papeete, whence they proceeded to the United States aboard the Norwegian freighter *Thor-I.*

The raft returned to Oslo and was made the centerpiece of the Kon-Tiki Museum, devoted to the story of the voyage itself and related aspects of American and Polynesian ethnography. As Heyerdahl himself acknowledged:

My migration theory, as such, was not necessarily proved by the successful outcome of the Kon-Tiki expedition. What we *did* prove was that the South American balsa raft possessed qualities not previously known to scientists of our time, and that the Pacific islands are located well inside the range of prehistoric craft from Peru.

The *Kon-Tiki* expedition proved to be the first of several similar ventures Heyerdahl would undertake to demonstrate the abilities of prehistoric navigators, chief among them being the transatlantic RA II expedition in 1970, and the TIGRIS expedition from the Persian Gulf to the Red Sea in 1978.

Heyerdahl, *Kon-Tiki.*

KRONAN

1st-rate ship (3m). *L/B/D:* 197' × 43.5' × 16' (60m × 13.3m × 4.9m). *Tons:* 2,140 disp. *Hull:* wood. *Comp.:* 500 crew, 300 soldiers. *Arm.:* 124–128 guns. *Des.:* Francis Sheldon. *Built:* Skeppsholmen, Stockholm; 1672.

The wreck of the seventeenth-century Swedish flagship *Kronan* ("Crown") was discovered in 1980 by Anders Franzén, fourteen years after his discovery of WASA. The ship's loss was well documented, having occurred about four miles off the southeast coast of the island of Öland on June 1, 1676, during the Battle of Öland, when the Swedish fleet was defeated by a combined Danish-Dutch force. The battle, the worst naval defeat in Swedish history, also saw the loss of the first-rate ship *Svärdet* ("Sword"), and the death of 1,400 of the ships' crews. Designed by the English shipwright Francis Sheldon, whom Karl X Gustaf recruited from England in 1654, *Kronan* was the first three-decked ship built for the Swedish Navy. Laid down and launched in 1668 but not completed until 1672, she became flagship of the Swedish Navy in 1675.

Kronan's loss was not due to battle damage but rather to improper ship handling. On May 25, the Swedes had allowed a Danish fleet to escape in a battle fought between Bornholm and Rügen. Hoping to gain an advantage by fighting closer to home, the fleet of sixty ships was running northward before a gale with the combined Danish and Dutch fleet in pursuit when a signal was given to turn and close with the enemy. *Kronan* apparently turned without taking in sail. The ship heeled sharply to port. A sudden explosion blew out the starboard side of the hull. She sank quickly, taking with her all but 42 of the crew of 850, including Admiral Baron Lorentz Creutz. One survivor reported that Creutz's last order was "In the name of Jesus, make sure that the cannon ports are closed and the cannon made fast, so that in turning we don't suffer the same fate as befell the *Wasa*." Archaeological evidence shows that this order was not carried out in time. Eight cannon were found on the seabed about 100 meters from the ship, and the lower deck gunports were open.

The remains of the vessel, found at a depth of 26 meters, consist of the aftermost two-thirds of the port side of the hull from the orlop deck to the upper deck. Unlike *Wasa,* which was lost on her maiden voyage in 1628, *Kronan* had been in service for a number of years and the site has yielded a great range of artifacts from the battle-tested ship and her crew. In the first ten years of excavation, 20,000 separate objects representing 6,518 artifacts were identified. *Kronan* was armed with between 124 and 128 bronze cannon (some of which may have been recovered from *Wasa*), 60 of which were salvaged during the 1680s. Between 1981 and 1990, another 43 were raised, the largest of which were 36-pdrs.; 25 were of Danish origin, 8 Spanish, 6 Danish, and 4 German. The oldest of these was a German gun cast in 1514; the newest was cast in Sweden in 1661. Personal possessions included remains of clothing, eating utensils, musical instruments, and navigational instruments including compasses, sundials, and dividers. Of the coins, some originating from as far away as Egypt and Turkey, the oldest dates from the 1400s. *Kronan* has also yielded a large number of sculptural carvings.

In the course of the modern excavation, divers also made and used a replica seventeenth-century diving bell. This consisted of a weighted platform suspended by iron rods from a bell shaped like a lampshade. The reserve air within the bell allowed the diver to conserve air on the descent to the bottom — in this case, 26 meters — and to increase his working time on the seafloor.

Einarsson, "Royal Ship *Kronan.*" Franzén, "*Kronan:* Remnants of a Mighty Warship."

KRONPRINZESSEN CECILIE

(later USS *Mount Vernon*) Liner (4f/3m). *L/B:* 707' × 72.2' (215.3m × 21.9m). *Tons:* 19,360 grt. *Hull:* steel. *Comp.:* 1st 740, 2nd 326, steerage 740; crew 602. *Mach.:* quadruple expansion, 45,000 ihp, 2 screws; 23.6 kts. *Built:* AG Vulcan, Stettin, Germany; 1907.

The last of four express liners ordered by Norddeutscher Lloyd between 1897 and 1907, *Kronprinzessen Cecilie* was named for the Kaiser's daughter-in-law. Although she was powered by the largest reciprocating steam engine ever used in a ship, she was no match for her running mates, and especially not for Cunard's LUSITANIA and MAURE-

Combining elements of neoclassical, baroque, and art nouveau design, the lavish decorations in this first-class sitting room aboard the German express liner KRONPRINZESSEN CECILIE *were characteristic of the most luxurious transatlantic liners in the years before World War I. Courtesy The Mariners' Museum, Newport News, Virginia.*

TANIA, which entered service the same year. Over the next seven years, *Kronprinzessen Cecilie* ran with the express liners KAISER WILHELM DER GROSSE, KRONPRINZ WILHELM, and *Kaiser Wilhelm II,* maintaining weekly service between Bremen and New York, via Southampton and Cherbourg.

The start of World War I found *Kronprinzessen Cecilie* homeward bound from New York with a cargo that included 40 million marks ($2 million) in gold. Rather than risk capture or sinking by the British, she returned to the United States, where she was interned first at Bar Harbor and later at Boston. When the United States entered the war against Germany in April 1917, the ship was seized and commissioned as the troop transport USS *Mount Vernon.* On September 5, 1918, she was about 200 miles from Brest homeward bound in convoy when she was attacked by *U-82.* A single torpedo knocked out half her boilers and killed 36 of her crew, but the ship returned to

Brest for repairs. She continued in service through 1919. The following year she was turned over to the United States Shipping Board, but plans to put her in service with the U.S. Mail Lines or the United States Lines fell through, and from 1924 to 1940 she was laid up in the Chesapeake. When the British government declined to purchase the ship in 1940, she was broken up at the Boston Iron and Metal Company in Baltimore.

Bonsor, *North Atlantic Seaway.* Kludas, *Great Passenger Ships of the World.* U.S. Navy, *DANFS.*

KRONPRINZ WILHELM

(later USS *Von Steuben*) Passenger liner (4f/2m). *L/B/D:* 637.3′ × 66.3′ (194.2m × 20.2m). *Tons:* 14,908 grt. *Hull:* steel. *Comp.:* 1st 367, 2nd 340, 3rd 1,054; as cruiser, 402. *Mach.:* quadruple expansion, 36,000 ihp, 2 screws; 22 kts. *Built:* AG Vulcan, Stettin, Germany; 1901.

A successor to Norddeutscher Lloyd's KAISER WILHELM DER GROSSE, *Kronprinz Wilhelm* quickly established herself as one of the fastest passenger liners on the North Atlantic. In September 1902 she won the Blue Riband for the fastest crossing from Cherbourg to New York — 5 days, 11 hours, 57 minutes. Named for the son of Germany's Kaiser Wilhelm II, *Kronprinz Wilhelm* ran between Bremen, Southampton, Cherbourg, and New York for thirteen years. On July 29, 1914, she arrived at Hoboken piers, two days before Germany declared war on Russia. Previously designated for service as a front-line auxiliary cruiser, she sailed from New York Harbor two days later and rendezvoused with the light cruiser SMS KARLSRUHE northwest of the Bahamas on August 6. She shipped two 88-millimeter guns, and Lieutenant Commander Paul Wolfgang Thierfelder came aboard as her wartime commander before the two ships were surprised by HMS *Bristol; Kronprinz Wilhelm* escaped to the south. Despite repeated Allied broadcasts that she had been sunk, torpedoed, or interned, between September 4, 1914, and March 28, 1915, she captured or sank fifteen ships (60,522 grt) — ten British, four French, and one Norwegian — off the east coast of South America. Without friendly ports in which to refuel, *Kronprinz Wilhelm's* mission was an impossible one, and on April 11, she entered Newport News, Virginia, where she was interned until the United States entered the war. On June 9, 1917, *Kronprinz Wilhelm* was commissioned USS *Von Steuben* — in honor of the German hero of the American Revolution. She sailed as a troop transport between the United States and Europe until 1919, and for five years thereafter she was operated by the United States Shipping Board, first as *Baron Von Steuben* and later as *Von Steuben*. She was broken up in 1923.

Bonsor, *North Atlantic Seaway.* Hoyt, *Ghost of the Atlantic.* Niezychowski, *Cruise of the "Kronprinz Wilhelm."*

KUNGSHOLM

M/S liner (2f/2m). *L/B/D:* 609.2′ × 78.2′ (185.7m × 23.8m). *Tons:* 21,532 grt. *Hull:* steel. *Comp.:* 1st 115, 2nd 490, 3rd 970. *Mach.:* motorship, 2 screws; 17 kts. *Built:* Blohm & Voss, Hamburg; 1928.

Built for Swedish-America Line, *Kungsholm* sailed between Gothenburg and New York through the 1930s. The start of World War II found her in New York, where her owners put her in the Caribbean cruise trade. In January 1942, the U.S. War Shipping Administration purchased *Kungsholm* and, renamed *John Ericsson,* she served as a troopship under United States Lines management. After the war she plied between New York and Southampton, with stops at Le Havre and Cobh, until she was badly damaged by fire at New York in March 1947. She was bought back by Swedish-America Line in July and then sold to the Panamanian-flag Home Lines in December. Renamed *Italia,* she emerged from a major refit at Genoa with accommodations for 226 first-class, 296 cabin, and 800 tourist passengers. She made her first voyage from Genoa to South America in 1948, but the immigrant trade for which she was intended dropped off quickly, and she resumed service between the Mediterranean and New York. From 1952 Hamburg-Amerika Linie operated her between Germany, New York, and Canada, and from 1960 to 1964 she cruised from New York to the Bahamas and the Mediterranean. Sold to Freeport Bahama Enterprises in 1964, she became the floating hotel *Imperial Bahama.* The next year she was broken up at Bilbao, Spain.

Bonsor, *North Atlantic Seaway.* Kludas, *Great Passenger Ships of the World.*

KYRENIA SHIP

L/B: 44.6′ od × 14.4′ (13.6m × 4.4m). *Tons:* 25 tons burden; 14 disp. *Hull:* wood. *Comp.:* 4. *Built:* Eastern Mediterranean; 4th cent. BCE.

The Kyrenia ship, the best-preserved ancient Greek merchant vessel ever found, was discovered by diver Andreas Cariolou in 1967 and excavated from 1968 to 1969 under the direction of Michael Katzev. The wreck site is off the north coast of Cyprus in 35°20′N, 33°19′E, not far from the port of Kyrenia. The ship lay on a flat, sandy bottom at a depth of 27 meters. Sixty percent of the total structural area and 75 percent of the ship's representative timbers survived, buried under a mound of amphorae.

The hull was built mostly of Aleppo pine, with oak tenons and lead sheathing below the waterline. Twenty tons of cargo were found, including almost 400 amphorae, mostly of Rhodian type, and some 10,000 almonds, which were distributed in clumps as if they had been stowed in sacks. Twenty-nine millstones of volcanic stone from Nisyros were used as ballast. Four sets of pottery plates, bowls, and cups, and four wooden spoons, were also found, indicating the size of the crew on the ship's last voyage. Because excavators uncovered no evidence of a galley or hearth, the crew presumably cooked their food ashore. Finds of lead net-weights suggest that the sailors fished to supplement a diet of olives, pistachios, almonds, hazelnuts, lentils, garlic, herbs, grapes, and figs.

Coins of Antigonos the One-Eyed and Demetrios the Besieger found on the site suggest that the wreck of the Kyrenia ship occurred about 310–300 BCE. At the time of sinking she was an old and often-repaired vessel, with a hull that had been patched on at least two occasions. Carbon-14 tests on the almonds yielded a date range of 288 BCE, ±90 years, but similar tests gave dates a century earlier for the cutting of the trees for the ship's timbers. Eight iron spearheads were recovered from the site, some of them embedded in the outer surface of the hull, and one theory holds that the ship was captured by pirates, looted, and scuttled.

After conservation, the recovered timbers were reassembled and mounted for display in the Crusader Castle of Kyrenia, and a full-scale sailing replica called KYRENIA II was completed in 1985.

Katzev, "Last Harbor for the Oldest Known Greek Ship"; "Resurrecting the Oldest Known Greek Ship." Steffy, "The Kyrenia Ship."

KYRENIA II

Replica trader. *L:* 44.5′ (13.6m). *Tons:* 25 grt. *Hull:* wood. *Comp.:* 5. *Built:* Perama, Greece; 1985.

Kyrenia II is a full-scale sailing replica of the KYRENIA SHIP, a small Greek merchantman of the fourth century BCE. The reconstruction was possible thanks to Richard Steffy's intensive study of the unusually well-preserved original wreck. His collaborators in the project were Harry Tzalas, President of the Hellenic Institute for the

Preservation of Nautical Traditions, Manolis Psaros, a shipyard owner at Perama near Athens, and master shipwright Michaelis Oikonomou.

The keel, planking, frames, and interior scantlings were constructed from *Pinus brutia* from the island of Samos. The keel of the original ship was hewn from a single naturally curved tree, and it took four attempts to find a perfectly curved log of the proper size for the replica. After the keel was laid, construction proceeded according to the shell-first method. More than 4,000 oak tenons and 8,000 mortises were cut to fit the strakes. In the complex framing system, floors alternate with half-frames, futtocks continue the arms of the floors, and top-timbers extend beyond the ends of the half-frames. Hand-forged nails of pure copper were used to secure the frames to the hull. The nails were driven in from outside the hull through drilled holes, then bent and clenched over to bite into the frame tops.

In the bow a nearly vertical cutwater is dovetailed into the end of the stempost and reinforced with a substantial knee (this configuration is conjectural, as the original stempost did not survive). A bulkhead in the stern supports an afterdeck, from which the helmsman steers and the crew handle the brails. The Kyrenia site yielded 176 lead brail rings. In the reconstruction, brail rings were sewn in vertical rows on the leeward side of the single square sail, enabling it to be raised and lowered like a Venetian blind. In addition to the afterdeck, *Kyrenia II* has a small foredeck from which to lower anchors and handle the sail. Although the pine mast step was well preserved in the original ship, no trace of mast or yard was found. These were reconstructed in silver fir on the basis of literary sources, artistic representations, and the shipwright's practical experience. No evidence of caulking was found in the original Kyrenia ship. When the uncaulked *Kyrenia II* was launched, she was awash after two hours in the sea, but the next day the wood had swelled enough to close the seams, and she floated high and dry. The lower hull was later coated with a mixture of pitch, pig fat, and soot to retard weed growth.

In the summer of 1986, *Kyrenia II* was shipped to New York to sail in Operation Sail 1986/Salute to Liberty, and in September of the same year she made a historic 26-day passage from Piraeus, Greece, to Paphos, Cyprus, sailing over 400 nautical miles at an average speed of 2.95 knots. On her return voyage in April 1987, she reached speeds of 12 knots and sailed 138 nautical miles in one 24-hour period. In lighter winds, she was able to sail close-hauled 50–60 degrees off the wind and make over 2 knots. The voyages of *Kyrenia II* demonstrated that small ancient vessels could ply Mediterranean trade routes in rough weather and complete long open-water passages even without consistently favorable winds.

Katzev, "*Kyrenia II*"; "Voyage of *Kyrenia II*." Katzev and Katzev, "*Kyrenia II*." Spathari et al., *Voyage into Time and Legend aboard the Kyrenia Ship*.

LACONIA

Liner (1f/2m). *L/B/D:* 601.3′ × 73.7′ (183.3m × 22.5m). *Tons:* 19,860 grt. *Hull:* steel. *Comp.:* 1st 350, 2nd 350, 3rd 1,500. *Mach.:* steam turbines, 2 screws; 16 kts. *Built:* Swan, Hunter & Wigham Richardson, Ltd., Wallsend-on-Tyne, Eng.; 1921

The Cunard Line ship *Laconia* was built for transatlantic passenger and cargo service between England and New York, with occasional stops at Hamburg. In 1923 and 1924, *Laconia* undertook two world cruises (the first by a Cunard ship), calling at twenty-three ports over the course of four months. Thereafter she returned to North Atlantic service, in which she remained for the next fifteen years. Her most significant peacetime accident occurred on September 24, 1934, when, en route from Boston to New York, she rammed the freighter *Pan Royal.* Although both ships sustained heavy damage, they were able to proceed under their own power.

When World War II started in September 1939, *Laconia* had just departed New York. Upon reaching England she was requisitioned and converted for service as a merchant cruiser armed with eight 6-inch and two 3-inch guns. After transporting a load of gold bullion to Halifax, she was put on convoy escort duty. In late 1941, she began sailing between England and the Middle East, via South Africa. On September 12 she was en route from Freetown, Liberia, with a large contingent of Italian POWs when she was torpedoed by *U-156* at 2010 about 500 miles north of Ascension Island. A great many of the prisoners were probably killed in the initial explosion, and because *Laconia* was sinking, Captain Sharp gave the order to abandon ship.

Rather than leave the survivors — more than 1,000 people, including women and children — to their fate, the *U-156* began rescuing them. Captain Werner Hartenstein summoned two other U-boats, the Italian submarine *Capellini,* and Vichy French warships to the scene, and he broadcast his peaceful intentions on an international emergency radio frequency. The rescue operation went on for several days, but on September 16, an American bomber flew overhead. Disregarding the display of a large Red Cross flag and the fact that the submarine had embarked 200 survivors and had four lifeboats in tow, the B-24 bombed the *U-156* and sank a boatload of Italian POWs. Captain Hartenstein ordered the *Laconia* survivors over the side, although the other vessels eventually saved about 1,250 people.

Upon learning of the rescue operation carried out by his U-boats, Grand Admiral Karl Dönitz issued the "*Laconia* order," by which German submarines were prohibited from attempting any similar efforts because the risk was too great:

1. All attempts at rescuing members of ships that have sunk, including attempts to pick up persons swimming, or to place them in lifeboats, or attempts to upright capsized boats, or supply provisions or water, are to cease. The rescue of survivors contradicts the elementary necessity of war for the destruction of enemy ships and crews.
2. The order for the seizure of commanding officers and chief engineers remains in force.
3. Survivors are only to be picked up in cases where their interrogation would be of value to the boat.
4. Be severe. Remember that in his bombing attacks on German cities, the enemy has no regard for women and children.

Given the tactical and logistical considerations involved — submarines cannot accommodate more than a handful of additional bodies — the order made little practical difference to the conduct of the submarine war. This fact was acknowledged at the Nuremberg War Crimes Tribunal, where Dönitz was charged with war crimes in connection with the "*Laconia* order." He was spared the death penalty by a deposition from Admiral Chester Nimitz, who testified that U.S. submarines made no effort to rescue their victims.

Burdick, *Our World Tour, 1922–23.* Miller, *War at Sea.* Peillard, *The "Laconia" Affair.*

USS LAFFEY (DD-724)

Allen M. Sumner-class destroyer (2f/1m). *L/B/D:* 376.5' × 41.1' × 12.5' (114.8m × 12.5m × 3.8m). *Tons:* 2,220 disp. *Hull:* steel. *Comp.:* 336. *Arm.:* 6 × 5" (3 × 2), 11 × 20mm, 4 × 40mm; 6 × 21"TT; 6 dcp, 2 dct. *Mach.:* geared turbines, 60,000 shp, 2 screws; 36.5 kts. *Built:* Bath Iron Works, Bath, Me.; 1943.

Named for Bartlett Laffey, who was awarded a Medal of Honor for his help in repulsing a Confederate assault near Yazoo City, Mississippi, in 1864, USS *Laffey* was the second destroyer of the name to see action in World War II. The first, a *Bristol*-class destroyer (DD-459), was a veteran of the Solomons campaign and was sunk at the Naval Battle of Guadalcanal on November 13–14, 1942.

Commissioned in February 1944, the second *Laffey* escorted a transatlantic convoy in May and covered the Allied landings on D-day (June 6), where she pounded German shore positions at Utah Beach, Baie de la Seine, near Cherbourg, France. At the end of June, she sailed for the United States and then for the Pacific, where she joined Task Force 38 in November. She took part in the invasion of the Philippines, screening aircraft carriers and covering landings at Ormoc Bay and Mindoro in December, and Lingayen Gulf in January. As part of Task Force 54, in March she took part in the invasion of Okinawa. On April 14, *Laffey* was assigned to radar picket duty about 30 miles north of Okinawa, together with two landing craft support ships, *LCS-51* and *LCS-116*. Radar picket ships were responsible for detecting and engaging enemy aircraft as far as possible from ground troops, and they came under intense attack from kamikazes and

other aviators throughout the Okinawa campaign. *Laffey*'s first two days on the picket line were relatively quiet, but at 0744, on April 16, the first Japanese plane appeared, only to be driven off by *Laffey*'s guns and sunk by a U.S. fighter from combat air patrol. The next contact was made at 0829, when four Japanese dive-bombers were splashed by *Laffey*'s gunners. Over the course of the next 62 minutes, *Laffey* came under direct attack from 18 more Japanese planes. Ten were shot down, but *Laffey* was hit by 5 kamikazes, and took bomb hits and near misses from 8 more before the attack was over. With 32 crew dead and 71 wounded, *Laffey* limped back to Okinawa and eventually made her way back to Puget Sound for rebuilding.

"The ship that would not die" returned to duty in the Pacific in October 1945. Put in reserve from 1947 to 1951, she joined Task Force 77 in the Korean War through 1952. Transferred to Norfolk, she spent the remainder of her career in the Atlantic and Mediterranean until decommissioned in 1975. Six years later, she was opened to the public as a museum ship at the Patriots Point Maritime Museum in Mt. Pleasant, South Carolina.

Becton, *Ship That Would Not Die.* U.S. Navy, *DANFS.*

LAKE CHAMPLAIN

(later *Ruthenia, Choran Maru*) Liner (1f/4m). *L/B:* 446' bp × 52' (135.9m × 15.85m). *Tons:* 7,392 grt. *Hull:* steel. *Comp.:* 1st 100, 2nd 80, 3rd 500. *Mach.:* triple expansion, 2 screws; 13 kts. *Built:* Barclay, Curle & Co. Ltd., Glasgow, Scotland; 1900.

"The ship that would not die." On April 16, 1945, the destroyer USS LAFFEY *was hit by five kamikaze planes and took bomb hits and near misses from eight others while stationed off the embattled island of Okinawa, in the Ryukyu Islands south of Japan. Courtesy U.S. Naval Historical Center, Washington, D.C.*

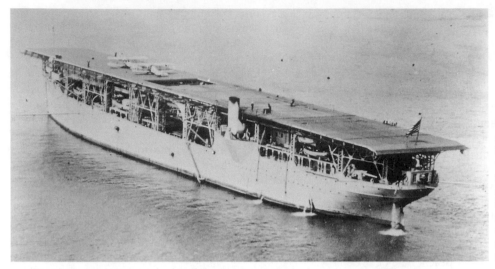

The U.S. Navy's first aircraft carrier, the flush-deck USS LANGLEY, *was converted from the collier* USS JUPITER. *In this picture, dating from 1922–24, two biplanes are on the flight deck forward of the elevator. Courtesy U.S. Naval Historical Center, Washington, D.C.*

Launched for Elder Dempster Line's run between Liverpool, Quebec, and Montreal, in 1901 *Lake Champlain* became the first merchant ship ever fitted with a wireless telegraph. In 1903, *Lake Champlain* and fourteen of her passenger and cargo running mates were bought by Canadian Pacific Steamships, Ltd., when that line expanded its service to the North Atlantic. *Lake Champlain* was a stolid immigrant ship, reconfigured in 1906 to carry 150 second-class passengers and 1,000 third-class. In 1913, she was renamed *Ruthenia* and, with her sister ship *Lake Erie* (renamed *Tyrolia*), transported Austro-Hungarian immigrants between Trieste and Canada. In January 1914, she briefly resumed service between London and Canada.

Later the same year she was converted to a dummy battleship, HMS *King George V.* In 1915 she became a storeship and in 1916 a naval oiler. Taken out to Singapore in 1929 for use as an oil hulk, she was captured there by the Japanese in 1942 and renamed *Choran Maru.* She survived the war intact, but in 1949 her long and varied career came to an end when she was towed to Dalmuir and scrapped.

Bonsor, *North Atlantic Seaway.*

USS LANGLEY (CV-1)

(ex-USS *Jupiter*) *Langley*-class aircraft carrier (2f). *L/B/D:* 542' × 65' × 18.9' (165.2m × 19.8m × 5.8m). *Tons:* 11,500 disp. *Hull:* steel. *Comp.:* 468. *Arm.:* 55 aircraft; 4 × 5". *Mach.:* turbine-electric, 7,152 shp; 15 kts. *Built:* Mare Island Navy Yard, Vallejo, Calif.; 1913.

The U.S. Navy's first turboelectric ship, USS *Jupiter* (AC-3), was commissioned as a fleet collier shortly before World War I. After brief duty in the Pacific during the Vera Cruz crisis, she became the first ship to transit the Panama Canal from west to east, on Columbus Day, 1914. She remained in the Atlantic for the duration of World War I, after which she returned to the West Coast.

Following the Royal Navy's commissioning of HMS FURIOUS, the world's first aircraft carrier, in 1919 the U.S. Navy decided to convert *Jupiter* for the same use. Named for the late aviation pioneer Samuel Pierpont Langley, USS *Langley* was commissioned in 1922. As rebuilt, *Langley* had a flush flight deck on top of an open trusswork erected on her upper deck, which was used for aircraft maintenance and storage. Fitted with two funnels (she had one, briefly) that folded down during flight operations, she originally carried eight aircraft; this was later increased to forty-two planes. After fourteen years as a training ground for naval aviators, by 1936 *Langley* was too small to accommodate the new generation of naval aircraft and she was converted to a seaplane tender, with the forward third of her flight deck removed. (This conversion also freed up the tonnage available for the construction of new aircraft carriers under the Washington Naval Treaty.)

Assigned to the Aircraft Scouting Group in 1937, *Langley* was at Cavite, the Philippines, on December 8, 1941 (local time), when the Japanese attacked Pearl Harbor and Manila. Narrowly escaping the Japanese invasion, she arrived at Darwin, Australia, on January 1, 1942, and briefly conducted antisubmarine operations from there. Assigned to the American-British-Dutch-Australian (ABDA) Striking Force under the overall command of Rear Admiral Karel Doorman, on February 22 *Langley* was sent from Fremantle to Tjilatjap, Java, with thirty-two Curtiss P-40 aircraft for the defense of the Dutch East Indies. Five days later, *Langley,* USS *Whipple* (DD-217), and *Edsall* (DD-219) were attacked by land-based Japanese bombers about 50 to 75 miles south of her destination. Hit five times, *Langley* lost all headway. At 1332, less than two hours after the first attack, the order was given to abandon ship, whereupon she was deliberately torpedoed by her escorts; sixteen of her crew died in the battle.

Messimer, *Pawns of War.*

LAWHILL

Bark (4m). *L/B/D:* 317.3′ × 45′ × 25.1′ (96.7m × 13.7m × 7.6m). *Tons:* 2,816 grt. *Hull:* steel. *Comp.:* 18. *Built:* W. B. Thompson, Dundee, Scotland; 1892.

A sister ship of GARTHPOOL, *Lawhill* was built for Charles Barrie of Dundee for general trade. Seven years later she was purchased by the Anglo-American Oil Company (of London) and sailed for them until 1911. (In 1904 she was dismasted and rerigged with her topgallant masts stepped abaft the topmasts and crossing only one yard so they could be easily shipped, a configuration shared by few other ships.) Her last British owner was G. Windram & Company (Liverpool), who held her for three years before selling her to A. Troberg of Mariehamn, Åland, in 1914. Three years later she entered the fleet of Marichamn's Gustaf Erikson, with whom she attained her greatest renown.

At first, *Lawhill* carried timber from the Baltic, coal from Australia, and nitrate from Chile, but in 1927 she entered the Australian grain trade. She remained in that work for the rest of her career under the Finnish flag. Though not a particularly fast ship, she took part in the annual grain races from Australia to Europe. Sailing under a number of distinguished Åland captains, she is nonetheless best remembered for the accounts written of her by members of the crew, most prominently Alan Villiers, whose *Set of the Sails* recounts his work as an able-bodied seaman in 1921 en route from France to Australia. At the end of a sixty-four-day passage from Bourdeaux, *Lawhill* ran aground off Port Lincoln, and Villiers was thrown from the fore lower topsail yard and had to be paid off.

In 1941, *Lawhill* sailed to East London, South Africa. Because Finland had invaded the Soviet Union as an ally of Germany, she was seized by the government. Under control of the Allied war effort, she continued in the grain trade between Australia and South Africa for the duration of the war. She was subsequently purchased by Marcio de Silva Jor and sailed under the Portuguese flag from what is now Maputo, Mozambique. In 1958 she was bought by Japanese shipbreakers and broken up.

Graham, "Queries: The *Lawhill* Figurehead." Sheridan, *Heavenly Hell.* Villiers, *Way of a Ship; The Set of the Sails.*

LEHG II

Ketch. *L/B/D:* 31.2′ × 10.8′ × 5.6′ dph (9.5m × 3.3m × 1.7m). *Hull:* wood. *Comp.:* 1. *Built:* Manuel M. Campos, Argentina; 1934.

Lehg II was a double-ended marconi-rigged ketch designed specifically for her owner, Vito Dumas, a veteran ocean navigator who had sailed his international 8-meter

The four-masted bark LAWHILL *riding light in light airs off Falmouth, England. In this photo, thought to have been taken May 16, 1929, one can see the unusual arrangement of her topgallant masts, stepped abaft the topmasts. Courtesy National Maritime Museum, Greenwich.*

Lehg from France to Brazil in 1931. On June 26, 1942, while tens of millions of people lived and died in the shadow of World War II, Dumas, a farmer by profession, set out from Buenos Aires to circle the world and to be the first person to round Cape Horn single-handed. After calling in Montevideo he was 55 days to Cape Town. He stayed there for three weeks before setting out on the longest leg of his journey, 7,400 miles across the Indian Ocean and south of Tasmania to Wellington, a passage of 104 days. After a month in port, he sailed for Valparaiso, where he stayed five weeks waiting for the most opportune moment to make his assault on Cape Horn. After 38 days he was back at Mar del Plata, where he remained for five weeks before continuing to Montevideo. After two days off, he went on to Buenos Aires, another day's sailing, arriving on September 7, 1943. Dumas had sailed 20,420 miles in 272 days at sea. Although his achievement did not go entirely unrecognized — he received a congratulatory telegram from the Royal Cruising Club in London — his fame was modest compared with what it might have been in a world not engulfed in war. From September 1945 to January 1947, Dumas sailed *Lehg II* on a voyage north. After three months in Havana, he began a 7,000-mile, 106-day "periplus [circumnavigation] without landfall" of the North Atlantic, passing by New York and the Azores, Canaries, and Cape Verde Islands, before putting into Brazil.

Dumas, *Alone through the Roaring Forties.*

LENIN

Icebreaker (2m). *L/B/D:* 439.7′ × 90.7′ × 34.1′ (134m × 27.6m × 10.4m). *Tons:* 13,366 grt. *Hull:* steel. *Comp.:* 220. *Mach.:* nuclear reactors, steam turbines, 30,200 shp, 3 screws; 18 kts. *Built:* Baltic Shipbuilding and Engineering Works, Leningrad, USSR; 1957.

Although Russia borders on four major seas — the Pacific and Arctic Oceans and the Baltic and Black Seas — internal maritime trade has long been complicated by the fact that except for the eastern Arctic and northern Pacific, none of these is contiguous to any other. The only ice-free sea routes between European and Asiatic Russia are around Africa and Asia via the Cape of Good Hope (15,902 miles from St. Petersburg/Leningrad to Vladivostok), or via Cape Horn (18,624 miles). Of even greater significance to the Soviet Union in the mid-twentieth century was its growing reliance on maritime transportation to the remote but resource-rich territories of northern Siberia, where land transport was inadequate.

The Russians began to invest in icebreaking technology in the late nineteenth century in an effort to open the Northeast Passage — pioneered by Adolf Nordenskiöld's VEGA in the 1870s — to maritime trade. The Russians' single greatest innovation came in 1959 when they commissioned the *Lenin,* the world's first nuclear-powered surface ship. Nuclear power is theoretically an ideal technology for vessels operating in such remote and inaccessible places because it obviates the need for regular supplies of fuel. *Lenin* escorted her first convoy of merchant ships in 1960, and she made it possible for freighters to service the ports of Dikson and Dudinka on a regular basis. With a service speed of 18 knots in open water, she could make 2 knots through ice 1.4 meters thick.

During the 1966–67 season, a nuclear accident resulted in the deaths of thirty of her crew. Abandoned for a year, she was towed to Murmansk for repairs and reentered service with a new nuclear plant rated at 44,000 shp in 1972. Despite the inherent hazards, the Soviets built eight more nuclear-powered icebreakers, including ARKTIKA, which became the first surface ship to reach the geographic North Pole. The *Lenin* was decommissioned in 1989 to serve as a stationary power station.

Brigham, "Arctic Icebreakers." Gardiner, ed., *Golden Age of Shipping.* Polmar, *Naval Institute Guide to the Soviet Navy.*

LEONARDO DA VINCI

Liner (1f/1m). *L/B:* 233.9m × 28.1m (767.3′ × 92.2′). *Tons:* 33,340 grt. *Hull:* steel. *Comp.:* 1st 413, cabin 342, tourist 571. *Mach.:* steam turbines, 2 screws; 23 kts. *Built:* Ansaldo Società per Azioni, Genoa, Italy; 1960.

Built as a replacement for Italia's ANDREA DORIA, *Leonardo da Vinci* is considered one of the best ships ever to sail under the Italian flag. She entered service as an express liner between Genoa, Cannes, Naples, and New York in 1960. But as with all new liners of that era, from the start her greatest competition was not from other ships but from passenger jets, though Italia added *Michelangelo* and *Raffaello* to its fleet in 1967. She remained on the North Atlantic run until 1976, though a variety of other ports were added (and dropped) from time to time, and she also undertook a fair amount of cruising. Heavily subsidized by the Italian government, she was finally withdrawn from service and laid up at Genoa. In 1977 she was taken over by Costa Line for use as a cruise ship, but she proved uneconomical to run; she was laid up again in 1978, and offered for sale. *Leonardo da Vinci* was destroyed by a fire and scuttled at La Spezia in July 1980, and she was broken up in 1981–82.

Bonsor, *North Atlantic Seaway.* Braynard & Miller, *Fifty Famous Liners 2.*

HMS LEOPARD

Portland-class 4th rate 50 (3m). *L/B/D:* 146′ × 30.5′ × 17.5′ (44.5m × 9.3m × 5.3m). *Tons:* 1,045 tons. *Hull:* wood. *Comp.:* 350. *Arm.:* 22 × 24pdr, 22 × 12pdr, 4 × 6pdr, 2 × 6pdr. *Des.:* Sir John Williams. *Built:* Sheerness Dockyard, Eng.; 1790.

HMS *Leopard* was laid down at Portsmouth Dockyard in 1775, but ten years later, still in frame, she was taken to Sheerness, where she was finally launched in 1790. She saw action in various theaters during the French Revolution and the Napoleonic Wars, including the Mediterranean and North American stations. She was on duty with the latter in early 1807 when a number of sailors, both British and American citizens, deserted from HMS *Bellisle, Bellona, Triumph, Chichester, Halifax,* and *Zenobia,* then blockading the French 74s *Patriote* and *Eole* in Chesapeake Bay. A number of the sailors joined the crew of the 36-gun frigate USS CHESAPEAKE, and Vice Admiral Sir George Berkeley, commander in chief of the North American Station, dispatched HMS *Leopard* to search the frigate.

On June 22, 1807, Captain Salisbury Pryce Humphreys was stationed off Cape Henry, Virginia, when he hailed USS CHESAPEAKE, outward bound for the Mediterranean under Commodore James Barron. A boat was sent over with a copy of Berkeley's order, but Barron refused a request to search his ship and at the same time ordered the gun deck quietly cleared for battle. The order came too late, for no sooner had the boarding party returned to *Leopard* than the British opened fire. Three broadsides followed, to be answered by only a single cannon shot before Barron surrendered his unready ship. Humphreys refused to accept the surrender but dispatched a boarding party to look for deserters, taking three Americans and the British sailor, who was tried and hanged at Halifax.

Although many subsequently saw in the *Chesapeake-Leopard* affair a prelude to the War of 1812, at the time it did little more than strain diplomatic relations between the United States and Britain. But even as late as 1843 Allen could regret that, "as has in too many instances been the case, the spirited conduct of Vice Admiral Berkeley and of Captain Humphreys was disavowed by the British government; the British right of search was given up, and Vice Admiral Berkeley recalled from the North American command."

Leopard remained on the North American station until 1812 when she was converted to a troopship. On June 28, 1814, she was en route from England to Quebec with 475 men of Royal Scots Guards when she grounded on Anticosti Island in the Gulf of St. Lawrence in heavy fog. The ship was a total loss, although none of the crew or soldiers was lost.

Allen, *Battles of the Royal Navy.* Hepper, *British Warship Losses.* Strum, "*Leopard-Chesapeake* Incident of 1807."

LEVIATHAN

(ex-*Vaterland*) Liner (3f/2m). *L/B/D:* 950′ × 100′ × 35′ (276.7m × 30.6m). *Tons:* 54,282 grt. *Hull:* steel. *Comp.:* 1st 752, 2nd 535, 3rd 850, steerage 1,772; 1,234 crew. *Mach.:* turbines, 60,000 shp, 4 screws; 23.5 kts. *Des.:* Albert Ballin. *Built:* Blohm & Voss, Hamburg; 1914.

Laid down for Hamburg-Amerika Linie as *Europa,* the second of Hapag chairman Albert Ballin's trio of superliners — the other two being *Imperator* (BERENGARIA) and *Bismarck* (MAJESTIC) — was launched as *Vaterland* at the suggestion of Kaiser Wilhelm II. Originally to have been built by Harland & Wolff, the contract for *Vaterland* was eventually won by Blohm & Voss, which introduced a number of refinements. Among the most admired were the split uptakes from the engine room to the first two funnels (the aftermost was a dummy) that allowed for uninterrupted public spaces of 300 feet and forced draft ventilation that all but eliminated the need for deck funnels. *Vaterland* was also built with double bottoms and watertight bulkheads, features that were by no means innovative but which had attained a new importance in the wake of the loss of the TITANIC in 1912. The largest ship in the world at the time of her building, she was launched by Prince Rupprecht of Bavaria on April 13, 1913, before 40,000 spectators.

Vaterland's maiden voyage from Hamburg to Southampton, Cherbourg, and New York began at Hamburg on May 14, 1914, but her career as a German passenger ship was brief. As she prepared to sail from New York to Hamburg at the end of July, World War I began, and the German government ordered Commodore Hans Ruser to keep his ship at her Hoboken pier rather than risk seizure by British and French cruisers lying off New York. She thus became the largest of the thirty-five Hapag ships interned in the United States, seven of which were at New York. Many of the ship's crew remained aboard until the United States entered the war on April 6, 1917, when the ship was officially seized by the United States. Two months later she was turned over to the U.S. Navy for conversion to use as a troop carrier and in July she was commissioned as USS *Leviathan* — a name chosen by President Woodrow Wilson — with the designation SP-1326. In her new capacity, the ship made sixteen voyages to Brest and three to Liverpool between 1917 and 1919; overall she carried 119,000 American Expeditionary Force troops to Europe.

The ship was decommissioned in October 1919, and

The product of German design and enterprise, after service as an American troop transport in World War I, LEVIATHAN *sailed in the livery of the United States Lines and was well known as the flagship of the American merchant marine. Courtesy The Mariners' Museum, Newport News, Virginia.*

title passed to the U.S. Shipping Board, which expected to sell *Leviathan* to J. P. Morgan's International Mercantile Marine. The sale was blocked by opposition orchestrated by William Randolph Hearst, who maintained that the IMM was a British concern and the United States was selling off its greatest ship to "Anglo–Wall Street" interests. In 1920 *Leviathan* was chartered to the United States Mail Steamship Company. A three-year refit was carried out at Newport News under the auspices of William Francis Gibbs, the premier American naval architect of the twentieth century, and *Leviathan* emerged with an inflated gross tonnage calculated at 59,965 tons, 5,000 more than *Majestic*. Large tonnages were prestigious but they increased port dues, and in 1931 she was remeasured at 48,943 gross registered tonnage.

In 1923, *Leviathan* resumed transatlantic passenger service, operated by the United States Lines on behalf of the Shipping Board, departing New York on July 4 for Cherbourg and Southampton. *Leviathan* was one of the preeminent ships of the postwar era, and the flagship of the U.S. merchant marine. Despite being run by a quasi-governmental concern and not being allowed to sell or serve alcohol to her passengers during Prohibition, she remained a very successful ship throughout the 1920s. In 1925, *Leviathan* added a "tourist third cabin" class, which appealed especially to students crossing to Europe and was eventually adopted by the North Atlantic Passenger Conference. Financial losses on the North Atlantic led to

her lay-up in 1933, but she was put back in service the following year at the insistence of the U.S. Department of Commerce. The losses continued and after only five roundtrips she was withdrawn from service in 1934. Three years later *Leviathan* was sold to Metal Industries Ltd. She sailed from New York for the last time to Rosyth, Scotland, where she was scrapped in 1938.

Braynard, "*Leviathan*."

LEXINGTON

(ex-*Wild Duck*) Brigantine (2m). *L/B/D:* 94′ loa × 24.5′ × 11′ (28.7m × 7.5m × 3.4m). *Tons:* 210 bm. *Hull:* wood. *Comp.:* 110. *Arm.:* 14 × 4pdr, 2 × 6pdr, 12 swivels. *Built:* Philadelphia(?); ca. 1773.

Purchased by Abraham van Bibber for the Maryland Committee of Safety at St. Eustatius, the merchantman *Wild Duck* sailed from the Dutch West Indies to Philadelphia with a cargo of gunpowder in February 1776. Purchased by the Continental Congress's Marine Committee and renamed *Lexington*, in honor of the site of the first battle of the American Revolution on April 19, 1775 — "the shot heard round the world" — she was fitted out as a warship under Joshua Humphreys and put under command of Captain John Barry. According to the report of a British spy, she was distinguished by "two topgallant yards and royals, square tuck, painted yellow and a low round stern painted lead color, black sides and yellow mouldings."

On April 7, *Lexington* captured the tender *Edward* in the Continental Navy's first victory in a single-ship action. Over the next six months, *Lexington*'s crew captured two sloops and helped rescue a cargo of gunpowder from the stranded merchantman *Nancy*. Under Captain William Hallock, *Lexington* was captured by HMS *Pearl* (32 guns) en route from the Caribbean to Philadelphia. Seventy of her crew were confined below decks, but they managed to overwhelm the prize crew and return *Lexington* to Baltimore.

Under Captain Henry Johnson, *Lexington* sailed for France on February 20, 1777, seizing two prizes en route. Together with *Reprisal* and *Dolphin,* she embarked on a cruise during which the three vessels captured thirteen ships in the Irish Sea between June 18 and 25. Two days later, *Lexington* was forced into Morlaix, Brittany, where she remained until ordered out of France on September 13. Becalmed off Ushant on September 19, *Lexington* was brought to battle by HMS *Alert* (14), being forced to surrender when her powder was exhausted.

Millar, *Early American Ships.* U.S. Navy, DANFS.

USS LEXINGTON (CV-2)

Lexington-class aircraft carrier. *L/B/D:* 888′ × 105.5′ (130′ew) × 24.2″ (270.7m × 32.2m (39.6m) × 7.4m). *Tons:* 33,000 disp. *Hull:* steel. *Comp.:* 2,122–2,951. *Arm.:* 8 × 8″ (2 × 4), 12 × 5″, 48 × 1.1″, 18 × 20mm. *Armor:* 7″ belt, 2″ deck. *Mach.:* turboelectric, 180,000 shp, 4 screws; 34 kts. *Built:* Fore River Shipbuilding Co., Quincy, Mass.; 1927.

The U.S. Navy's fourth *Lexington* was originally laid down as a battlecruiser in 1921. At the same time, the near universal disgust at the carnage of World War I had led to calls for limitations on naval arms. The Washington Naval Conference called that fall led to agreements limiting the tonnage of battleships and battlecruisers. Under the so-called 5:5:3 formula, by 1934 the United States and Britain were to reduce their capital tonnage to 525,000 tons each (down from 1,178,300 tons and 1,296,540 tons, respectively) and Japan would reduce to 315,000 tons, down from 569,600 tons. (France and Italy were both restricted to 175,000 tons.) In addition, the United States and Japan each would be entitled to convert two battlecruisers currently under construction to aircraft carriers. The overall restrictions on carrier tonnage were 135,000 tons each for the United States and Britain, and 81,000

tons for the Japanese. Built solely for carrying airplanes, they could not mount guns larger than 8 inches.

Conversion of *Lexington* and SARATOGA was authorized on July 1, 1922, but the ships were not completed for nearly six years. Unlike later carriers, they had enclosed hangar decks, and unlike their British counterparts, which had armored flight decks, the *Lexington*-class ships had flight decks of wood planking over steel. With the most powerful engines of any contemporary U.S. warships, these ships were also the largest aircraft carriers built until after World War II, with the exception of Japan's desperate end-of-war conversion, *Shinano*. In addition to her 8-inch and 5-inch gun batteries (which were augmented by increased antiaircraft protection as time went on), *Lexington* was originally intended to carry 90 aircraft; and despite the dramatic increase in the size of carrier aircraft, by the opening of World War II, she still carried 88 planes.

During the 1930s, *Lexington* conducted operations and tactical exercises in the Pacific, Caribbean, and Atlantic in which she more than demonstrated the value of carrier aviation over traditional surface operations. In the fall of 1941, she was deployed to the Hawaiian Islands, one of three U.S. carriers in the Pacific at that time. Japan's December 7 attack on Pearl Harbor found her ferrying aircraft to the Marine garrison at Wake Island. It took several weeks for the Americans to get their footing in the aftermath of Pearl Harbor. But on January 11, 1942, *Lexington* sailed for the Coral Sea as flagship of Vice Admiral Wilson Brown's Task Force 11 in an effort to thwart Japanese advances against supply routes to Australia. On February 20, *Lexington*'s planes accounted for seventeen of eighteen Japanese planes that attacked the ship, and Lieutenant E. H. "Butch" O'Hare was awarded the Medal of Honor for downing five of them. (O'Hare was killed in 1943, and Chicago's O'Hare International Airport is named for him.) On March 6, she joined YORKTOWN to launch a surprise attack on Japanese forces at Rabaul, New Britain.

After two weeks at Pearl Harbor, the two carriers again left for the Coral Sea on May 1. Six days later, *Lexington*'s aircraft sank the light carrier SHOHO east of New Guinea, and then fended off attacks launched from the heavy carriers SHOKAKU and ZUIKAKU. On the morning of May 8, *Lexington*'s planes successfully attacked *Shokaku*, but at 1100, she was herself hit by two aerial torpedoes and three bombs that inflicted heavy damage. The resulting fires were brought under control, but at 1247 gasoline vapors trapped in her hangar deck exploded. Unable to contain the resulting fires, at 1707 Captain Frederick C. Sherman gave the order to abandon ship. Three hours

Laid down as a cruiser, USS LEXINGTON (CV-2) *was the second aircraft carrier commissioned by the U.S. Navy. In this photo, taken in 1929, she is flying off Martin T4M torpedo biplanes.* LEXINGTON *and her sister ship* SARATOGA (CV-3) *were the biggest carriers built until after World War II. Note the differences in general deck arrangement between* LEXINGTON *and her predecessor,* USS LANGLEY (CV-1). *Courtesy U.S. Naval Historical Center, Washington, D.C.*

later, the blazing hulk was torpedoed by USS *Phelps* and sank in position 15°20′S, 155°30′E. In addition to resulting in the first American carrier loss of World War II, the Battle of the Coral Sea was the first naval engagement in which opposing surface units never made visual contact.

Hezlett, *Aircraft and Seapower*. Stephen, *Sea Battles in Close-Up*. U.S. Navy, *DANFS*.

USS LEXINGTON (CV-16)

Essex-class aircraft carrier. *L/B/D:* 872′ × 93′ × 28.6′ (265.8m × 28.3m × 8.7m). *Tons:* 27,100 disp. *Hull:* steel. *Comp.:* 3,448. *Arm.:* 12 × 5″ (4 × 2, 4 × 1), 68 × 40mm, 52 × 20mm; 103 aircraft. *Armor.:* 4″ belt, 2.5″ deck. *Mach.:* geared turbines, 15,000 shp, 4 screws; 32.7 kts. *Built:* Bethlehem Steel Co., Quincy, Mass.; 1943.

The fifth ship of the name, USS *Lexington* was originally laid down as *Cabot*, but she was renamed following the loss of her predecessor at the Battle of the Coral Sea in 1942. After five months of trials she was dispatched to the Pacific theater and took part in operations against Tarawa, Wake, and the Gilbert Islands. After launching a successful attack against Kwajalein on December 4, she was hit by a torpedo that knocked out her steering gear and forced her back to Bremerton for repairs.

As flagship of Rear Admiral Marc Mitscher's Task Force 58, she took part in operations against Hollandia, Truk, and Saipan in May and June 1944. At the Battle of the Philippine Sea (June 19–20), *Lexington*'s planes contributed significantly to the destruction of Japan's naval air power in the "Great Marianas Turkey Shoot" west of Guam. The first day of the battle cost Vice Admiral Jisaburo Ozawa's First Mobile Fleet 346 planes and the carriers SHOKAKU and *Taiho* (sunk by the submarines USS CAVALLA and *Albacore*, respectively); the Americans lost 130 planes.

In the Battle of Leyte Gulf, her planes helped sink the battleship MUSASHI, the heavy cruiser *Nachi*, and the carriers *Chitose*, ZUIKAKU, and ZUIHO, but *Lexington* was herself hit by a kamikaze. After operations in the South China Sea in January, *Lexington* turned north for operations against Tokyo and Iwo Jima in February, before returning to Puget Sound for an overhaul.

She returned to action in July, launching air strikes against naval and air bases and industrial centers. Following her service in World War II, for which she received a Presidential Unit Citation and eleven battle stars, *Lexington* was decommissioned from 1947 to 1955, during which time she was given an angled flight deck and redesignated CVA-16. She remained in Pacific waters until 1962 when she was reassigned to Pensacola for work as the training aircraft carrier CVS-16 (later CVT-16). She was finally decommissioned in 1991.

Morison, *Two-Ocean War*. U.S. Navy, *DANFS*.

LIBERDADE

Sampan-rigged "canoe" (3m). *L/B/D:* 35′ × 7.5′ × 2.5′ (10.7m × 2.3m × 0.8m). *Tons:* 6 disp. *Hull:* wood. *Comp.:* 4. *Built:* Paranaguá, Brazil; 1888.

In the mid-1880s, Joshua Slocum purchased the bark *Aquidneck* for general trade and in 1886 sailed from New York for Montevideo with case oil. The ship's complement included his second wife and two of his sons by his first marriage: Victor, age 18, who sailed as mate, and Garfield, 6. *Aquidneck* subsequently traded between Uruguay, Argentina, and Brazil, but she was wrecked near Paranaguá, Brazil, shortly after Christmas 1887. With no other prospect for returning to the United States, Slocum designed and built a 35-foot-long "canoe" whose model, he writes, "I got from my recollections of Cape Ann dories and from a photo of a very elegant Japanese *sampan* which I had before me on the spot." The hull had the fine, lithe lines of a New England fishing dory, but the three masts carried the distinctive sails of an oriental junk — "the Chinese *sampan* style, which is, I consider, the most convenient boat rig in the whole world." The finished vessel was launched on May 13, 1888, the same day that Princess Isabel of Brazil signed the Golden Law freeing the country's 700,000 slaves. (*Liberdade* is Portuguese for "liberty.")

After some difficulties in getting outward clearance for their little vessel, which many thought could not make the proposed voyage, the Slocums set out on June 24. Hugging the coast of Brazil, they made several stops, including Santos, Rio de Janeiro, and Bahia. From Pernambuco they sailed direct to Barbados, covering 2,150 miles in 19 days, then to Puerto Rico and Cape Roman, South Carolina, where they arrived on October 28, having covered 5,510 miles without mishap in 53 days. Because of their frequent stops, *Liberdade*'s voyage had been widely reported in the press, and the Slocums were well received upon their return to the capital. After wintering in Washington, D.C., they sailed to Boston; the next year, *Liberdade* returned to Washington where Slocum abandoned her at the Smithsonian Institution. Slocum's lively account, *Voyage of the "Liberdade,"* was published in 1894, the year before he set off on his historic solo circumnavigation in the SPRAY.

Slocum, *Sailing Alone around the World; Voyage of the "Liberdade."*

LIBERTY

Sloop. *L/B:* 64′ × 18′ (19.5m × 5.5m). *Tons:* 85 bm. *Hull:* wood. *Built:* Massachusetts(?); <1768.

On June 10, 1768, Bostonians opposed to the Townshend Acts and intent on preventing customs commissioners from collecting duties on imported goods locked an official in the cabin of John Hancock's merchant sloop, *Liberty,* while the ship's cargo of Madeira wine was being landed. Hancock's ship was towed away from the dock by crew from the HMS *Halifax.* Although the protesting citizens of Boston forced the customs officials to take refuge in Castle William in Boston Harbor, the affair was eventually resolved in favor of the Crown, and *Liberty* was confiscated from Hancock.

The following April, *Liberty* was outfitted in Boston and, under Captain William Reid, patrolled off Rhode Island to inspect colonial vessels for customs violations. When the ship's crew abused Captain Joseph Packwood in Newport on July 19, 1769, the outraged citizens boarded the ship, cut her free, and scuttled her. The ship was later burned at Goat Island in the first open defiance of British authority in the colonies. An account written, but not published, at the time invited Reid to "determine for the future to enter upon some employment worthy of a man and no longer disgrace and degrade himself by continuing to be an infamous detested tool, pimp and informer to a Board whose imperious arbitrary behavior have rendered them ridiculous and contemptible." The guilty parties were never caught.

Millar, *Early American Ships.* Sherman, "Accounting of His Majesty's Armed Sloop *Liberty.*"

USS LIBERTY (AGTR-5)

(ex-*Simmons Victory*) Technical research ship. *L/B/D:* 455′ × 60′ × 23′ (138.9m × 18.3m × 7m). *Tons:* 7,275 disp. *Hull:* steel. *Comp.:* 358. *Built:* Oregon Shipbuilding Corp., Portland, Oreg.; 1945.

Built as a Maritime Commission Victory ship, *Simmons Victory* operated under charter to the Coastwise (Pacific Far East) Line of San Francisco. Apart from brief service during World War II and nine voyages as a supply ship during the Korean War, she worked as a merchant cargo ship until laid up in the National Defense Reserve Fleet at Olympia, Washington, in 1958. The U.S. Navy subsequently acquired her for use as a technical research ship for testing and evaluating electronics and communications equipment, which duty she began in 1963. Two years later she was transferred to the East Coast, and continued her work in the North and South Atlantic.

On June 2, 1967, *Liberty* sailed from Rota, Spain, to the eastern Mediterranean, where she arrived on June 8, four days after the start of the Six-Day War between Israel and

Egypt. She was stationed thirteen miles off the coast of Al-Arish, on the Sinai Peninsula, when, at about 1403, Israeli fighters attacked the ship with fragmentation bombs and rockets. Twenty minutes later, three torpedo boats joined the attack, sending a torpedo into the starboard side. The Israelis later claimed that the attack on the well-identified ship was a case of mistaken identity, although this seems unlikely given the alacrity with which the Israeli government presented an apology to the White House, barely two hours after the attack began. Nonetheless, the Israeli apology was accepted and the U.S. government released few details of the attack, during which 34 crew were killed and 169 wounded — including Commander W. L. McGonagle, who received the Medal of Honor for his actions. *Liberty* herself was awarded a Presidential Unit Citation. After a month of repairs at Malta, *Liberty* returned to Norfolk. The following June she was put into the Atlantic Reserve Fleet, and in 1970 she was sold for scrap to the Boston Metals Company.

Ennes, *Assault on the "Liberty".* Sawyer & Mitchell, *Victory Ships and Tankers.*

LIEMBA

(ex-*Graf von Götzen*) Steamer (1f/1m). *L/B/D:* 232′ × 33′ × 9′ (70.2m × 10.1m × 2.7m). *Tons:* 1,575 disp. *Hull:* steel. *Comp.:* 18 1st, 16 2nd, 350 3rd; *Mach.:* triple expansion, 500 ihp, 2 screws. *Built:* Jos. L. Meyer, Papenburg, Germany; 1914.

Graf von Götzen was a government steamer built for service on Lake Tanganyika in what was then the colony of German East Africa. Her prefabricated parts were built in Germany, shipped to Tanganyika (now Tanzania), and then carried 800 miles overland to Kigoma where they were assembled. At the start of World War I, *Graf von Götzen* was one of three German steamers and a gunboat on the 600-mile-long lake, all of which were either sunk or run aground. (The British success was the basis for C. S. Forester's novel *The African Queen,* which was later made into a movie of the same name starring Humphrey Bogart and Katharine Hepburn.) To prevent her capture by the British, the Germans sank *Graf von Götzen* in July 1916 off the entrance to the Malagarassi River, having first carefully greased all her working parts to prevent corrosion. After the war, she was raised by the Belgians but sank near the entrance to Kigoma. In 1924, the British Railway Administration recovered her, and after a lengthy refurbishing, she was put back in service as *Liemba,* the Kirungu word for "lake." As a passenger-cargo ship, she linked numerous communities along the lake, which separates Congo (Zaire) and Tanzania. She underwent a major refit in 1952, and thereafter began fortnightly service between Kigoma, Tanzania, and Mpulungu, Congo, making seven stops along the way. She is now owned and operated by Tanzania Railways and homeported at Kigoma.

Spies, "*Liemba.*"

LIGHTNING

Clipper (3m). *L/B/D:* 243′ × 44′ × 23′ dph (74.1m × 13.4m × 7.0m). *Tons:* 2,083 reg. *Hull:* wood. *Comp.:* 87 crew; 370 pass. *Built:* Donald McKay, East Boston, Mass.; 1854.

Lightning was the first of the magnificent quartet of clippers built by Donald McKay for James Baines's Black Ball Line of passenger ships for the run between Liverpool and Australia. She was originally a two-decked ship, but her poop was later extended to join the midships house and topgallant forecastle. She crossed a skysail on the main, but could set moonsails above the fore and mizzen royals, and above the main skysail. Under James Nichol Forbes, formerly master of MARCO POLO, in February 1854, *Lightning* sailed from Boston to Liverpool in the record time of 13 days, 20 hours, and in one 24-hour period logged 436 miles. *Lightning*'s other record passages include 63 days from Melbourne to Liverpool in 1854, on the second leg of a passage in which she sailed round the world in a record 5 months, 8 days, and 10 hours, including time in port. This was followed the next year by a Melbourne–Liverpool run of 67 days under Anthony Enright. In March 1857, *Lightning* averaged 17 knots over 48 hours to sail more than 790 knots. *Lightning* was not considered as beautiful as her consorts JAMES BAINES or CHAMPION OF THE SEAS. But according to the London *Times,* "in capacity for stowage and as a safe and rapid vessel, the *Lightning* is considered without a rival." That year, the British government chartered the three Black Ball ships to carry troops for the suppression of the Indian Mutiny, and at a testimonial dinner aboard *Lightning* on the eve of her departure, Benjamin Disraeli tried to persuade Captain Enright to stay with the ship. He declined, and *Lightning* sailed to Bombay under Captain Byrne in 87 days, two weeks faster than either *James Baines* or *Champion of the Seas.* Sold in 1867 to T. Harrison & Company of Liverpool, *Lightning* burned at Geelong, Australia, on October 31, 1869, while fully loaded and preparing to sail for London. She was scuttled and later broken up.

Cutler, *Greyhounds of the Sea.* Hollett, *Fast Passage to Australia.* Howe & Matthews, *American Clipper Ships.*

LIMMEN

Jacht (3m). *Tons:* 120 gross. *Hull:* wood. *Comp.:* 56. *Built:* VOC, Netherlands; <1639.

While Abel Tasman's first voyage around Australia with HEEMSKERCK and *Zeehaen* in 1642–43 confirmed his ability as a navigator, the councilors of the Verenigde Oostindische Compagnie (VOC, or Dutch East India Company) observed, rightly, that "no riches or things of profit but only the said lands and apparently good passage [toward Chile] were discovered." They could not immediately pursue the route to the Americas, but instead they sent Tasman to southern New Guinea "in order to find out whether the known Southland [Australia's Cape York Peninsula] is continuous with it, or in fact separated." If there was a passage, he was then to circumnavigate Australia clockwise and find out whether Van Diemen's Land (Tasmania) was separate from Australia, and look for the wreck of the retour ship BATAVIA. To fulfill this goal, Tasman was given the jachts *Limmen* (a place name) and *Zeemeeuw* ("Seagull," 100 tons, 41 crew) and the galiot *Bracq* (14 crew), to be used for inshore exploration. Sailing from Banda in February 1644, Tasman failed utterly — perhaps inexcusably — to find Torres Strait (as it would later be known, for the Spaniard who had first traversed it, in SAN PEDRO in 1605). He then skirted lightly along the western Cape York Peninsula and across the Gulf of Carpentaria to follow the coast of Australia as far as Port Hedland (about 120°E), where he turned north. Although Tasman failed the VOC in the particulars, he established that the Southland was a vast landmass, and as Governor-General Anthonie Van Diemen wrote to the VOC, "That such a big country, covering different climates — i.e., that southeast at 43½ degrees S. Lat. going down to 2½ degrees — should not have anything of advantage, is hardly plausible. Compare the big Northern areas of America." But with Van Diemen's death the next year, organized Dutch exploration of Australia came to a close.

Sharp, *Voyages of Abel Janszoon Tasman.*

LINDBLAD EXPLORER

Passenger ship (1f/1m). *L/B/D:* 250′ × 46′ × 15′ (76.2m × 14.0m × 4.6m). *Tons:* 2,500 grt. *Hull:* steel. *Comp.:* 100 pass.; 60 crew. *Mach.:* twin diesels, 3,800 hp, 1 screw; 14 kts. *Built:* Nystad Varv Shipyard, Helsinki, Finland; 1969.

Built specifically for "expedition cruising," to take small groups of adventurous travelers to remote or inaccessible places, *Lindblad Explorer* was named for her creator, Lars-Eric Lindblad. She was commissioned in 1969; her maiden voyage was marred by a shipboard fire off Senegal, and she later grounded twice in the Antarctic. Although these were unwelcome accidents, the ship, commonly known as "The Little Red Boat," was built to sustain much of the punishment of the seas of the world, having been constructed to the most stringent U.S. Coast Guard requirements, with a view especially to cruising in polar waters. Her staff of academics and scientists varies depending on the itinerary. Although best known for her cruises to Antarctica and the islands of the Southern Ocean, in 1984 *Lindblad Explorer* became the first passenger ship to traverse the Northwest Passage, and she has reached farther north (82°12′N) and south than any other passenger vessel. Her voyages have also taken her to remote islands of the Pacific from the Galápagos to the East Indies, as well as up the Amazon River.

Shackleton, *Wildlife and Wilderness.* Snyder & Shackleton, *Ship in the Wilderness.*

HMS LION

Lion-class battlecruiser (3f/2m). *L/B/D:* 700′ × 88.5′ × 28.8′ (213.4m × 27m × 9m). *Tons:* 26,350 disp. *Hull:* steel. *Comp.:* 997. *Arm.:* 8 × 13.5″ (4 × 2), 16 × 4″, 4 × 3pdr; 2 × 21″TT. *Armor:* belt 9″, deck 2.5″. *Mach.:* geared turbines, 70,000 shp, 4 screws; 26 kts. *Built.* Devonport Dockyard, Plymouth, Eng.; 1912.

Laid down in direct reply to the challenge posed by MOLTKE, the *Lion*-class battlecruisers — "the splendid cats" — were the biggest and fastest capital ships ever laid down, and the first with all 13.5-inch turrets mounted on the centerline rather than en echelon. As flagship of Rear Admiral Sir David Beatty's First Battle Cruiser Squadron, *Lion*'s first major action was at the Battle of the Dogger Bank on January 24, 1915. There Beatty (with *Tiger, Princess Royal, New Zealand,* and *Indomitable*) surprised Rear Admiral Franz von Hipper's battlecruiser squadron as it attempted to make a third raid on British North Sea towns. *Lion* — and so Beatty — was forced out of the inconclusive battle by two waterline hits received early on.

At Jutland on May 31, 1916, *Lion* was in the van of Beatty's six-ship squadron during the battlecruisers' "run to the south" that opened the battle. The fleets opened fire at 1548, and twelve minutes later, *Lion* only escaped a ship-killing explosion after a direct hit on the midships ("Q") turret thanks to the dying act of Officer of the Turret Major Harvey, who flooded the magazines. Two minutes later, INDEFATIGABLE blew up with the loss of 1,017 crew, followed twenty-four minutes later by the loss of *Queen Mary* with 1,266 men. Before pressing home his attack on Rear Admiral Franz Hipper, Beatty turned to his Flag Captain, A. E. M. Chatfield, and observed, "There seems to be something wrong with our bloody ships today."

Though she was quickly repaired following the battle, *Lion* saw little further action before war's end, except providing cover for an attempt to destroy the German mine-sweeping forces and their escorts off Helgoland on November 17, 1918. In 1924, she was broken up at Jarrow under the terms of the Washington Naval Treaty of 1922.

Bassett, *Battle-Cruisers.* Halpern, *Naval History of World War I.*

HMS LITTLE BELT

(ex-*Lille Belt*) Corvette, 6th rate (3m). *L/B/D:* 116.3′ × 30.3′ × 12.5′ (35.4m × 9.2m × 3.8m). *Tons:* 460 bm. *Hull:* wood. *Comp.:* 121. *Arm.:* 2 × 9pdr, 18 × 32pdr. *Des.:* Hohlenberg. *Built:* Copenhagen, Denmark; 1801.

Throughout the Napoleonic Wars, when not neutral, Denmark was drawn into alliance with France, which resulted in her being invaded by the Royal Navy twice, first in 1801 and again in September 1807. In that year, a fleet of sixty-five warships under Vice Admiral James Gambier accompanied by 29,000 soldiers under General Lord Cathcart arrived off Copenhagen. After a four-day bombardment, the city surrendered and the British seized sixteen ships of the line, ten frigates, and forty-three other vessels; among these was *Lille Belt,* which was commissioned as HMS *Little Belt.*

Put on service on the North American station, in 1811 she became the focus of an incident between the United States and Great Britain that nearly brought about the War of 1812 a year early. In 1807, the Royal Navy had outraged American opinion by firing on Commodore James Barron's frigate USS CHESAPEAKE and forcibly removing members of her crew, some of whom were former British sailors. Four years later, the frigate HMS GUERRIÈRE impressed an American seaman, and Commodore John Rodgers was ordered to sea with the frigate USS PRESIDENT in mid-May. Although he failed to find the *Guerrière,* on the night of May 17, 1811, the Americans caught up with and engaged *Little Belt* about 45 miles from the mouth of Chesapeake Bay. Two broadsides were exchanged, and *Little Belt* was all but dismasted, with thirteen dead and nineteen wounded, before Captain Bingham broke off the engagement. Upon her return to Halifax, *Little Belt* was condemned as "almost a wreck" and sold. The vastly superior *President* survived the battle with hardly a mark, prompting Lord Howard Douglass to observe in his *Naval Gunnery:*

If a vessel meet an enemy of even greatly superior force, it is due to the honor of her flag to try the effect of a few rounds; but unless in this gallant attempt she leave marks of her skill upon the larger body, while she, the smaller body, is hit at every discharge, she does but salute her enemy's triumph and discredit her own gunnery.

Roosevelt, *Naval War of 1812.*

HMS LITTLE BELT

Sloop. *L/B/D:* 59′ bp × 16′ × 7′ dph (18m × 4.9m × 2.1m). *Tons:* 90 bm. *Hull:* wood. *Comp.:* 18. *Arm.:* 1 × 12pdr, 2 × 6pdr. *Built:* Fort Erie, Ontario; 1812.

Built for Captain Robert H. Barclay's Lake Erie squadron, the second HMS *Little Belt* was named for the 18-gun sloop of war that had engaged USS PRESIDENT (38 guns) in 1811 in an incident that presaged the outbreak of the War of 1812. On September 10, 1813, *Little Belt* was one of five vessels in Barclay's line when it sailed against the fleet of Master Commandant Oliver Hazard Perry at the Battle of Lake Erie, off Put-In Bay. *Little Belt* was captured by the schooners *Scorpion* and *Chippeway* while trying to flee the scene of the disastrous battle, which spelled the end of British control of the Great Lakes. Following repairs, *Little Belt* joined the American fleet in time to help transport the army of General William Henry Harrison to Buffalo following its victory over the British at the Battle of the Thames on October 5. Blown ashore at Black Rock, New York, in a gale on December 8, *Little Belt* was burned by the British three weeks later.

Hepper, *British Warship Losses.* U.S. Navy, *DANFS.*

LITTORIO

Vittorio Veneto-class battleship (2f/2m). *L/B/D:* 780′ × 107.4′ × 31.4′ (237.7m × 32.7m × 9.6m). *Tons:* 45,237 disp. *Hull:* steel. *Comp.:* 1,920. *Arm.:* 9 × 15″ (3 × 3), 12 × 6″, 4 × 4.7″, 12 × 3.5″, 20 × 37mm, 24 × 20mm; 3 aircraft. *Armor:* 14.2″ belt, 6.7″ deck. *Mach.:* geared turbines, 128,200 shp, 4 screws; 30 kts. *Built:* Cantieri Ansaldo, Genoa, Italy; 1940.

Littorio (the Italian word for *lictor,* a Roman official who carried the *fasces*) was commissioned five weeks before Italy declared war on France and Britain on June 10, 1940. She operated against the Malta convoys from August through October. While lying at Taranto on November 12, she was hit by three aerial torpedoes during the attack launched from HMS ILLUSTRIOUS. Out of commission until August 1941, on December 13 she engaged a British force tasked with breaking up an Italian convoy to Benghazi, Libya (which got through), and escorting an Allied convoy to Malta (which also made it). In March 1942, flying the flag of Admiral Angelo Iachino at the Battle of Sirte, *Littorio* was forced to withdraw in the face of torpedo attacks from Rear Admiral Philip Vian's destroyers, who were escorting a Malta convoy, in an action for which Vian was knighted. Knocked out of commission by British planes on June 16, 1942, *Littorio* was hit during a U.S. air raid on La Spezia a year later. Following Italy's surrender in 1943, she was renamed *Italia*. En route to Malta, she was hit by German bombs, and she spent the remainder of the war interned at Lake Amaro, Egypt. She was broken up at La Spezia in 1948.

Breyer, *Battleships and Battlecruisers.* Grove, *Sea Battles in Close Up.* Stephen, *Sea Battles in Close-Up.*

LIVADIA

Circular steam yacht (3f). *L/B/D:* 235′ × 163′ × 6.8′ (71.6m × 49.7m × 2.1m). *Tons:* 3,900 disp. *Hull:* steel. *Mach.:* triple-expansion engines, 10,500 ihp, 3 screws; 16 kts. *Des.:* Andrei Aleksandrovich Popov. *Built:* Fairfield Shipbuilding & Engineering Co., Ltd., Govan, Scotland; 1881.

Livadia was the third and last of three circular ships designed by the Russian Rear Admiral Andrei Aleksandrovich Popov. Unlike his two earlier battleships, REAR-ADMIRAL POPOV and *Novgorod*, *Livadia* was ordered by Czar Alexander II as a royal yacht. She differed in other crucial respects, too. Most significant, while the other Popovkas had almost perfectly round hulls, *Livadia* was something of a hybrid. The lower hull was shaped like a flounder — with a beam that was narrow relative to the length — while the vessel's superstructure was more shiplike in appearance, though it was wide enough for the funnels to be situated three abreast. Though Popov's design was intended for relatively calm waters, *Livadia* weathered the 25-foot seas of the Bay of Biscay en route to the Black Sea without difficulty. Little is known of her career in the Black Sea (Alexander was assassinated only nine months after her launch), but she ended her days as a repair ship and was not broken up until 1926.

Donald, "*Livadia.*" Martelle, "*Novgorod* and *Rear-Admiral Popov.*"

LIVELY LADY

Cutter. *L/B/D:* 36′ × 9.2′ × 6.6′ (11m × 2.8m × 2m). *Tons:* 13.75 disp. *Hull:* wood. *Comp.:* 1. *Des.:* Frederick Shephard. *Built:* S. J. P. Cambridge, Calcutta, India; 1948.

Lively Lady was a cruising yacht built for and by S. J. P. Cambridge in India in 1948. Her second owner was greengrocer Alec Rose, who bought her in 1963 to compete the following year in the second solo transatlantic race from England to the United States. *Lively Lady* placed fourth with a crossing of thirty-six days. Two years later Rose embarked on a solo circumnavigation, his intent — like that of Sir Francis Chichester in GIPSY MOTH IV — being to complete the passage with only one stop. Rerigged by Illingworth and Primrose, *Lively Lady*'s primary new feature was the addition of a boomless mizzen mast from which to set a mizzen staysail. After several false starts in the spring, he departed Portsmouth on July 16, 1966. *Lively Lady* made good time, passing the Cape of Good Hope on October 8 and arriving at Melbourne on December 17. After a month-long layover, he sailed on January 14. On the eleventh day out, a masthead fitting parted and he was forced to put in to the southern New Zealand port of Bluff for repairs that lasted five days. He rounded Cape Horn on April 1, and returned to Portsmouth on July 4, 1968. Like Chichester before him, Rose was knighted for his achievement by Elizabeth II.

Rose, *My Lively Lady.*

HMS LONDON

London-class 2nd rate 90 (3m). *L/B/D:* 176.5′ × 46.5′ × 21′ (53.8m × 14.2m × 6.4m). *Tons:* 1,871 bm. *Hull:* wood. *Comp.:* 750. *Arm.:* 28 × 32pdr, 30 × 18pdr, 30 × 12pdr, 2 × 9pdr. *Built:* Chatham Dockyard, Eng.; 1766.

Built during the long peace between the SEVEN YEARS' War and the American Revolution, HMS *London* was the eighth ship of the name. Her chief distinction lies in her role as Rear Admiral Thomas Graves's flagship during the Battle of the Chesapeake, where the Royal Navy's defeat resulted in the end of the American Revolution. In August 1780, Graves sailed in *London* with six ships of the line as reinforcements for Vice Admiral Marriott Arbuthnot, commander of the North American station. On March 16, 1781, *London* was present in a skirmish with a French squadron under Chevalier Destouches off Chesapeake Bay, and in July Graves succeeded Arbuthnot. On August 28 he was joined by a fourteen-ship squadron under Rear Admiral Samuel Hood. With only five of his own ships ready for sea, Graves and Hood turned south for Chesapeake Bay to prevent a French squadron under Rear Admiral Count François Joseph Paul de Grasse from entering Chesapeake Bay and cutting off Major General Charles Cornwallis — then dug in on the Yorktown peninsula — and from landing reinforcements and provisions for General George Washington.

En route from the Caribbean, Hood had reconnoitered Chesapeake Bay on August 25 but found no sign of the French. De Grasse's fleet of twenty-seven ships arrived four days later and anchored off Cape Henry, where Graves and Hood found them on the morning of September 5. Rather than bear down on the French fleet while it was in disarray, Graves ordered his ships in line ahead formation, as called for in the *Fighting Instructions,* with *London* in the middle of the line, Hood's Barfleur (90 guns) fourth in line, and Rear Admiral Francis S. Drake's *Princessa* (70) sixteenth in line. The French got under way at about noon, and at 1405 Graves ordered his captains to wear ship, changing course from west to east so that they paralleled the French on the same tack and putting *Princessa* in the van and *Barfleur* to the rear. Shortly after 1600, Graves raised the signal "to bear down and engage close," but he neglected to take down the signal for "line ahead," with drastic consequences. The van of the British line took the brunt of the French broadsides, and the middle squadron was closely engaged, but the seven ships in Hood's division barely took part in the battle. According to a published account, a conversation afterwards took place between Graves, Hood, and Drake:

> Admiral Graves asked Admiral Hood why he did not bear down and engage? The answer was: "You had up the signal for the line." Admiral Graves then turned to Admiral Drake, and asked him how he came to bear down? He replied: "On account of the signal for action." Admiral Graves then said: "What say you to this, Admiral Hood?" Sir Samuel answered: "The signal for the line was enough for me."

The fighting stopped by about 1815. Although both fleets intended to renew the engagement, light airs over the next few days made this impossible, and on the ninth Graves lost sight of the French fleet, which had doubled back towards the Chesapeake. The next evening, De Grasse rendezvoused in the bay with Comte de Barras de Saint-Laurent, who had arrived from Newport with eight ships. Graves returned to New York where, over the next month, he was reinforced by six more ships of the line. On October 19, he sailed for the Chesapeake with 25 ships of the line and 7,000 troops. The same day, General Washington accepted Cornwallis's surrender at Yorktown. Graves arrived at the Chesapeake five days later, but upon hearing of the defeat, he returned to New York.

On November 10, *London* sailed for Jamaica but took no part in the British defeat of De Grasse and the capture of his Ville de Paris at the Battle of the Saintes in April 1782. The only other battle for which *London* received battle honors was the action off the Ile de Groix on June 23, 1795. In this engagement, Vice Admiral Alexander Hood, Viscount Bridport's Channel Fleet squadron captured three ships from Rear Admiral Louis Thomas Villaret de Joyeuse in a running battle off Brittany. *London* remained in service until broken up in 1811.

Larrabee, *Decision at the Chesapeake.*

USS Long Beach (CGN-9)

Long Beach-class nuclear-powered guided-missile cruiser. *L/B/D:* 721.3′ × 73′ × 30.6′ (219.8m × 22.3m × 9.3m). *Tons:* 15,540 disp. *Hull:* steel. *Comp.:* 1,160. *Arm.:* 2 × 5″, 1 Talos, 2 Terrier, 1 ASROC; 6 × 12.8″ TT. *Mach.:* nuclear reactor, steam turbines, 80,000 hp, 2 screws; 30 kts. *Built:* Fore River Shipbuilding Co., Quincy, Mass.; 1961.

The world's first nuclear-powered surface warship was commissioned five years after the first nuclear-powered submarine, USS Nautilus, and four years after the Soviet Union's icebreaker Lenin. The last American ship designed from the keel up as a cruiser, as originally armed she carried only missiles; guns were added later. After trials to test the effectiveness of her complex propulsion and weapons systems, and goodwill visits to Europe and the Caribbean, USS *Long Beach* joined the Sixth Fleet for operations in the Mediterranean in 1963. At the end of the year, she participated in exercises with two of the Navy's newest nuclear-powered vessels, aircraft carrier USS *Enterprise* and frigate *Bainbridge*. Comprising the first all-nuclear task group, on July 13, 1964, the three ships embarked on Operation Sea Orbit, a circumnavigation without benefit of normal replenishment that, despite goodwill port visits along the way, clearly demonstrated the flexibility afforded by nuclear propulsion. Transferred to the Pacific Fleet and homeported at her namesake city, she conducted operations off Vietnam from 1966 through 1969. In 1968, with a Talos missile she shot down a North Vietnamese jet 70 miles away, the first time an American surface-to-air missile downed an enemy aircraft. After her second refueling and refit in 1970–71, *Long Beach* returned to the western Pacific and was deployed in Vietnamese waters through the end of the American involvement in Southeast Asia.

"The Gray Lady" underwent major weapons changes in the 1980s. Her Talos missile system was replaced with Harpoon missiles and she was fitted with two close-in weapon systems (CIWS), essentially huge Gatling guns designed to shoot down at close range missiles that have escaped other countermeasures. In 1985, she was also armed with Tomahawk cruise missiles. In 1990, and again in 1993–94, she participated in drug-interdiction operations in the Caribbean. En route to the Persian Gulf during Operation Desert Storm in 1991, she helped evacuate 1,200 people from the American naval base at Subic Bay following the eruption of Mount Pinatubo. *Long Beach* was decommissioned and defueled in 1995.

U.S. Navy, *DANFS*.

LONG SERPENT

Longship (1m). *Hull:* wood. *Comp.:* 200. *Mach.:* 68 oars. *Built:* Norway; ca. 1000.

At the end of the tenth century, southern Norway was ruled loosely by Olaf Tryggvason, "the most spectacular viking of the age," and a Christian. In the year 1000, he sailed from Nidaros on the west coast of Norway with a fleet of sixty warships the largest of which was *Long Serpent,* "the most powerful ship in northern waters." Available accounts describe a vessel more akin to a massive floating garrison designed to dominate the battle line in home waters than the sort of vessel that carried the Vikings coursing through the seas and rivers of Europe. Sailing into the Baltic, Olaf visited with Boleslav the Pole at the mouth of the Oder River in Wendland. There he may have recruited eleven vessels from Boleslav to join him in a campaign against the combined forces of Svein Forkbeard of Denmark, the Swedish Olaf Sköttkonung, and Erik, Jarl of Lade, whose father Olaf Tryggvason had earlier deposed as leader of the Norwegians. On Olaf's return home, his fleet encountered that of his confederated enemies somewhere in the narrow Øresund, not far from modern Copenhagen, or near an otherwise unknown island of Svold off Rügen. Sources for the actual battle differ in detail, but in the end, Olaf leaped into the sea "and never again returned to his kingdom in Norway," which passed under Erik.

Jones, *History of the Vikings.* Snorri Sturluson, *Haemskringla.*

LORD OF THE ISLES

Clipper (3m). *L/B/D:* 210′ × 27.8′ × 18.5′ dph (64m × 8.5m × 5.6m). *Tons:* 691 nm. *Hull:* iron. *Built:* Charles Scott & Co., Greenock, Scotland; 1853.

One of the first iron-hulled clippers, *Lord of the Isles* was built for Maxton & Company of Greenock for the China tea trade. An advantage of iron construction was that it allowed for finer lines, and upon her arrival in China she was described as "the finest [ship] ever seen at Shanghai — unmatched for symmetry of form and beauty of model." But her fine lines made her a wet ship and she was known as "The Diving Bell." Her maiden voyage to Melbourne took only 74 days, with a best day's run of 428 miles. She carried a mixed cargo and 17 passengers; on subsequent voyages she would carry more than 300 immigrants. Her performance in the tea trade was uneven. She had three passages in under 100 days, the fastest being 90 days from Shanghai to London under W. Jamieson, her second of three captains. The other five passages were between 118 and 141 days. Her most celebrated voyage was in 1856, the first year that London merchants offered a premium of £1 per ton for the first ship of the season to arrive from China with tea. *Lord of the Isles* departed Foochow on June 10, one day after the American *Maury.* The two ships arrived off Gravesend on October 15. Thanks to a better tug, *Lord of the Isles* docked first and claimed the premium. Her career was cut short on July 24, 1862, when en route to Hong Kong she was lost to fire, caused by spontaneous combustion, in 12°N, 115°E.

Baker, *Running Her Easting Down.* MacGregor, *Tea Clippers.*

LOS REYES

Galleon (3m). *Tons:* 250 bm. *Hull:* wood. *Built:* <1567.

Although Ferdinand Magellan's VICTORIA crossed the Pacific Ocean in 1521, subsequent transpacific voyages were few and far between. In 1565, the Spanish founded a settlement in the Philippines, and in the same year the seaman-friar Fray Andres de Urdaneta discovered that favorable winds for sailing east across the Pacific could be found in latitude 40°N. At the same time, in Peru, Pedro Sarmiento was planning a westward voyage in search of lands rich in gold and silver. Two arguments favored the existence of such a land. European geographers had long postulated a huge southern Terra Australis to counterbalance the earth's northern land masses. According to Inca tradition, Tupac Yupanqui had sailed to the west and returned with gold, silver, and slaves. Sarmiento received permission for such an expedition, and *Los Reyes* ("The Kings") and *Todos Los Santos* ("All Saints") were outfitted for the voyage. Unfortunately, the fabled land was thought to lie only 600 leagues (1,800 miles) from Peru, and the ships were provisioned accordingly, although the 150 crew were bound on a voyage that would take them 7,000 miles across the Pacific.

On November 22, 1567, the expedition sailed from Callao "for islands to the west, called Solomon," under command of twenty-five-year-old Alvaro Mendaña, nephew of the Viceroy. The crew first sailed west southwest to 15°S and then turned to the northwest until latitude 6°S, when they headed west. They made their first landfall in the Ellice Islands on January 15, 1568, but were swept past the islands by the current. Seventeen days later brought them to Ongtong Java in the northern Solomon Islands. Blown southward in a storm for six days, on February 7 they came into Bahia de Estrella on Ysabel Island, which they first took to be a continent. Mendaña's men immediately began to build a brigantine in order to explore the surrounding coasts.

On April 7, the brigantine began its first voyage of exploration with thirty men under senior pilot Hernan Gallego. Sailing east along Santa Isabel, they crossed to Guadalcanal, then returned to Santa Isabel and completed a tour of the coast. Relations with the islanders had deteriorated as Spanish demands for food grew, so Mendaña moved his ships to Guadalcanal on May 12. It was no better with the cannibals of Guadalcanal, and on one watering trip, nine Spaniards were killed and mutilated. Reprisals left forty natives dead or wounded before June 13, when Mendaña moved again, to San Cristobal Island, which had been found on the brigantine's second trip when the explorers also visited the islands of Malaita and Ulawa. On San Cristobal, the Spanish stole food, burned villages, and killed and kidnapped locals. Though most of the prisoners escaped when the ships were careened for three weeks, six sailed with the ships on August 11.

Although Mendaña was supposed to colonize his islands, he was overruled by Gallego and the others, who urged him to return to Peru. Sailing north of the equator, they made landfall in the Marshall Islands, but they could find nothing useful on them. With food and water in short supply, they passed waterless Midway Island on October 2, and on October 16 the ships were separated just before a furious storm hit "with such fury as I had never before seen," wrote Gallego, "although I have been forty-five years at sea, and thirty of them a pilot." Both ships were dismasted and *Los Reyes* only reached Sebastián Vizcaíno Bay in Baja California on December 20, 1568. A few weeks later, at Santiago de Colima (19°5'N), *Todos Los Santos* appeared. By the time they reached Callao on July 26, 1569, only 100 of those who set out were still alive. Despite the exertions of the best navigators, the existence of Mendaña's Solomon Islands would not be confirmed until D'Entrecasteaux visited them in *Recherche* and L'ESPERANCE in 1792.

Amherst & Thomson, *Discovery of the Solomon Islands by Alvaro de Mendaña in 1568.*

LOUISIANA

Casemate ironclad. *L/B:* 264′ × 62′ (80.5m × 18.9m). *Tons:* 1,400 tons. *Hull:* iron. *Arm.:* 2 × 7″, 3 × 9″, 4 × 8″, 7 × 32pdr. *Armor:* 4″ casemate. *Mach.:* 2 centerline paddlewheels, 2 screws. *Built:* E. C. Murray, New Orleans, La.; 1862.

CSS *Louisiana* was one of two ironclads ordered for the defense of New Orleans (the other was CSS *Mississippi*). She was laid down in October 1861 and launched in February 1862, but inadequate supplies and labor delayed her completion. By April 19, when Flag Officer David G. Farragut began shelling Forts Saint Philip and Jackson at the mouth of the Mississippi, Commander John K. Mitchell ordered the still unfinished ship to the defense of the Mississippi. Although with the sides of her casemate set at a 45-degree angle she looked imposing, her arming and iron plating were incomplete. Moreover, the screw propulsion was not hooked up, and she had to be towed the ninety miles to the mouth of the river. Much to the consternation of his subordinates and superiors, Mitchell attempted to complete *Louisiana*'s fitting out upriver of the forts rather than use her with his other ships against the Union mortar boats. On the morning of April 24, 1862, Farragut began his run past the forts. Although *Louisiana* took part in the engagement, Farragut's fleet anchored at New Orleans the next day. On April 28, as the river ports were surrendering, Mitchell set *Louisiana* on fire and she blew up.

Still, *Iron Afloat.* U.S. Navy, *DANFS.*

LST-507

Landing ship; tank (1f/1m). *L/B/D:* 328′ × 50′ × 3.8′ (100m × 15.2m × 1.2m). *Tons:* 2,100 grt. *Hull:* steel. *Comp.:* 260 crew, 160 troops. *Arm.:* 7 × 40mm, 12 × 20mm. *Des.:* John Niedermair. *Mach.:* diesel, 2 screws. 10 kts. *Built:* Jeffersonville Boat & Machine Co., Jeffersonville, Ind.; 1944.

Despite their use in the front line of amphibious assaults in all theaters of World War II, only 26 of the 1,051 LSTs built during the war were lost to enemy action. Two of these were lost in the early morning of April 28, 1944, during Operation Tiger, a mock landing at Slapton Sands by the U.S. Army 4th Division, destined for Utah Beach. On April 27 troops had embarked at Torquay and gone ashore at Slapton Sands more or less as planned. That night, a support convoy of eight LSTs was steaming through Lyme Bay. Though the convoy was supposed to be escorted by the destroyer HMS *Scimitar* and corvette *Azalea,* the former had been rammed during the exercise and was detained at Plymouth.

At 2200 that night, six E-boats from the 5th Schnellboote Flotilla, under Captain Rudolf Peterson, and three E-boats from Lieutenant Commander Freiherr von Mirbach's 9th Flotilla raced out of Cherbourg at 36 knots. At about 0130 on April 28, *S-136* and *S-138* fired torpedoes at *LST-507*, the last ship in the column, carrying 282 soldiers of the 1st Engineer Special Brigade together with 16 trucks, 22 amphibious DUKWs, and 165 crew. Although clearly seen ablaze, owing to the fog of war, it was initially assumed that the ship on fire was not connected with the convoy. The LST was abandoned by 0230, but at 0218 the Germans had attacked *LST-531*, which also sank. *LST-289* was hit by a torpedo that did not detonate. All told, 197 sailors and 552 troops were killed and buried in a field in a part of South Devon that had been evacuated the previous December. Owing to the extremely high secrecy requirements for all aspects of D-Day planning, the casualty figures were combined with those for the Normandy invasion, which began June 6.

Hoyt, *Invasion before Normandy.* Morison, *History of the United States Naval Operations in World War II.* U.S. Navy, *DANFS.*

RMS LUSITANIA

Liner (4f/2m). *L/B:* 787′ × 87.8′ (239.9m × 26.8m). *Tons:* 31,550 grt. *Hull:* steel. *Comp.:* 1st 563, 2nd 464, 3rd 1,138; 900 crew. *Mach.:* steam turbines, 4 screws; 25 kts. *Des.:* Leonard Peskett. *Built:* John Brown & Co., Ltd., Clydebank, Scotland; 1907.

Although *Lusitania* is best remembered for her tragic sinking by the German submarine *U-20* on May 7, 1915, this horrific event has overshadowed *Lusitania*'s place in the dramatic history of turn-of-the-century passenger shipping. To counteract the demise of the U.S. merchant marine, in 1904 American financier J. P. Morgan formed the International Mercantile Marine, which acquired a controlling interest in a number of major shipping companies, including Germany's Hamburg-Amerika Linie and Norddeutscher Lloyd and Britain's White Star Line. Alarmed at this trend, which threatened to rob England of a valuable wartime auxiliary fleet, the British government approached Cunard Line with the offer of a £2,600,000 loan and an annual mail subsidy of £75,000 per ship for the construction of two passenger liners, provided that the company remain wholly British for twenty years and that the ships could be requisitioned as auxiliary cruisers in wartime. Thus enriched, Cunard built *Lusitania* — named for the Roman province of what is now Portugal — and MAURETANIA, the largest, fastest, and most luxurious liners of their day. *Lusitania*'s maiden voyage from Liverpool to New York began on

September 7, 1907, and the next month she crossed between Daunt's Rock and Sandy Hook at a record speed of 23.99 knots. The same month she set an eastbound record of 23.6 knots. *Lusitania*'s fastest crossing was westbound at 25.7 knots (4 days, 16 hours, 40 minutes; August 8–12, 1909). In her day, only *Mauretania* was faster.

Owing to the infeasibility of maintaining a close blockade of Germany, on November 3, 1914, Britain illegally declared a "military area" in the North Sea and all the waters bounded by Iceland, Norway, and Scotland. Germany responded with the equally illegal declaration of "an area of war" around the British Isles and Ireland, and advised the world community — the United States especially — that the sinking of neutral shipping, or passengers, might not be avoidable. The German government knew that the loss of American lives to a submarine attack — even on a British ship — might draw the United States into the war on the side of the Allies. Following the sinking of *Falaba* on March 28, 1915, the German embassy in Washington authorized publication of a warning advising that "in accordance with formal notice [of a declared war zone] given by the Imperial German Government, vessels flying the flag of Great Britain . . . are liable to destruction in those waters and that travellers sailing in the war zone on ships of Great Britain . . . do so at their own risk." The notice first appeared on May 1, the day *Lusitania* sailed from New York with 1,965 passengers and crew, under command of Captain William Thomas Turner.

Five days later the ship entered the war zone. Although the British Admiralty was fully aware of the presence of German submarines off southern Ireland — *U-20* sank three ships on May 6 — no escort was provided for *Lusitania*, whose safety was her speed. Captain Turner had been issued explicit orders to steam a zigzag course and to remain in midchannel well away from headlands and ports. By the afternoon of May 7, *Lusitania* was steaming at between 15 and 18 knots along a straight course only 12 miles south of the Old Head of Kinsale, near Queenstown (Cork) — or 25 miles north of "midchannel." At 1320 she was spotted by Lieutenant Commander Walter Schwieger in *U-20*. Twenty minutes later, at a range of 700 meters, *U-20* fired one torpedo that hit abaft the bridge on the starboard side. The ship listed 15 degrees within seconds, and sank 18 minutes later in 315 feet of water. Only 6 of the ship's 48 lifeboats survived the sinking — many crushed the passengers for whom they were intended — and only 764 people survived; 1,201 passengers and crew died, including 128 Americans. Many survivors testified that there was a second explosion, and some claimed they saw a second torpedo. Although Schwieger fired only one, he wrote in his log that "the explosion of the torpedo must have been followed by a second one (boiler or coal powder)." While some have argued that *Lusitania* must have been carrying munitions detonated by the torpedo — her manifest shows 51 tons of shrapnel and 10 tons of .303 ammunition — the subsequent explosions were probably caused by the rupture of boilers and high-pressure steam lines, the subsidiary cause of the loss of many ships torpedoed in World War I. According to one study, about half of these ships sank in 10 minutes or less.

A great deal has been written about *Lusitania*'s wartime service. At one extreme is the claim that the British — and First Lord of the Admiralty Winston Churchill in particular — deliberately put *Lusitania* in harm's way in the hope that the loss of American lives would drag the United States into the war. At the other extreme is the claim that the sinking was just another in a long line of German atrocities. In fact, the Germans reined in their U-boat campaign and the United States would not enter World War I until 1917. The most that can be said with certainty is that *Lusitania*'s dead were casualties of war.

Ballard & Archbold, *Exploring the "Lusitania."* Ryan & Bailey, *"Lusitania" Controversy.* Shipbuilder and Marine Engine-Builder, *Cunard Express Liners "Lusitania" and "Mauretania."*

LUTHER LITTLE

Schooner (4m). *L/B/D:* 204.5′ × 40.9′ × 19.6′ dph (62.3m × 12.5m × 6m). *Tons:* 1,234 grt. *Hull:* wood. *Comp.:* 11. *Built:* Read Bros. Co., Somerset, Mass.; 1917.

Built for the firm of Rogers & Webb, Boston, *Luther Little* was one of the more than 450 four-masted schooners built for coastwise trade between the 1880s and 1921. The last resurgence of schooner building came during World War I, when shipping rates were driven up by the loss of steamship tonnage to German U-boats. Cheaply built and inexpensive to man, the wooden schooners — the majority of which operated without auxiliary engines — remained profitable through the 1920s, until the Great Depression forced many of them to be laid up. *Luther Little* was laid up for the last time in 1936, and eventually abandoned, on the Sheepscot River at Wiscasset, Maine, side by side with another Rogers & Webb schooner, HESPER. More than half a century later, the abandoned hulks of the last two four-masted schooners built for trade on the Atlantic still survived, though little of them remained.

Morris, *Four-Masted Schooners of the East Coast.* Tod, *Last Sail Down East.*

LUTINE

Frigate (3m). *L/B/D:* 143.2′ × 38.8′ × 12.2′ (43.6m × 11.8m × 3.7m). *Tons:* 951 bm. *Hull:* wood. *Comp.:* 240. *Arm.:* 6 × 24pdr, 26 × 12pdr, 10 × 6pdr. *Des.:* Joseph M. B. Coulombe. *Built:* Toulon, France; 1779.

La Lutine ("The Sprite") was commissioned in the French Navy in 1785, just four years before the start of the French Revolution. On December 18, 1793, she became one of sixteen ships handed over to a British fleet under Vice Admiral Samuel Hood by French Royalists who preferred that the ships go to their historical enemy rather than the revolutionary Republicans. Later the same year she was commissioned in the Royal Navy as HMS *Lutine* and stationed on the North Sea.

In the fall of 1799, a consortium of London merchants anxious over the worsening conditions in Europe prevailed upon the Admiralty to allow them to ship a cargo of some £2 million in gold bullion, some of it intended for payment of British soldiers, to the continent. It was a tense time for merchants and military strategists alike, as the Anglo-Russian coalition against the French in Holland was on the verge of collapse. *Lutine* sailed for Cuxhaven under Captain Lancelot Skynner on October 9. At about midnight that night she was blown ashore in a gale on the coast of Vlieland, near the Zuider Zee, and lost with all hands but two, both of whom died shortly thereafter. Despite many attempts, little of the ship's cargo has ever been recovered. In 1859, the bell was found, however, and because Lloyd's of London, the association of insurance underwriters, had taken an enormous loss when *Lutine* sank, the bell was returned to them. It has hung ever since in the Underwriting Room at Lloyd's, where it is rung just before an important announcement. Traditionally, one ring preceded the announcement of the loss of a vessel, and two rings the arrival of a vessel previously reported overdue or missing.

van der Molen, *Lutine Treasure.*

SMS LÜTZOW

Derfflinger-class battlecruiser (2f/2m). *L/B/D:* 690.1′ × 100′ × 31.5′ (210.4m × 29m × 9.6m). *Tons:* 26,741 disp. *Hull:* steel. *Arm.:* 8 × 12.2″ (4 × 2), 12 × 6″, 12 × 8.8cm; 4 × 20″TT. *Armor:* 12″ belt, 3.2″ deck. *Mach.:* steam turbine, 63,000 shp, 4 screws; 25.5 kts. *Built:* F. Schichau, Danzig, Germany; 1915.

Named for Freiherr Adolf von Lützow, a Prussian officer of the Napoleonic era, the battlecruiser *Lützow* joined Rear Admiral Franz von Hipper's First Scouting Group in March 1916. After SEYDLITZ hit a mine near Norderney, *Lützow* became flagship of the German fleet during the raid on Lowestoft and Yarmouth on April 24–25. A month later, Admiral Reinhard Scheer conceived a bold plan to destroy British merchant and naval shipping in and around the Skaggerak. Hipper's First Scouting Group — *Lützow*, DERFFLINGER, *Seydlitz*, MOLTKE, and VON DER TANN — a Second Scouting Group of four light cruisers, and thirty destroyers sailed for the Norwegian coast as a diversionary force.

At about 1330, on May 31, Hipper's fleet came into sight of Rear Admiral David Beatty's Battle Cruiser Squadron. Hipper's ships wheeled and the "run to the south" began at 1348, *Lützow* coming under the combined fire of LION and *Princess Royal*. A hit by *Lützow* on the former ship's "Q" turret knocked Beatty's flagship out of the battle at 1600. After Hipper rendezvoused with Admiral Reinhard Scheer's High Seas Fleet, the British turned towards Jellicoe, at about 1638. *Lützow* was badly damaged on the "run to the north." When Admiral Jellicoe's Grand Fleet joined the fray shortly after 1800, the tide of battle turned once again. Rear Admiral the Honourable Horace L. A. Hood's Third Battle Cruiser Squadron joined Beatty, and *Lützow* sustained heavy damage from HMS INVINCIBLE until Hood's flagship erupted in flames and sank with the loss of all but six hands. Just before 1900, Hipper transferred his flag from *Lützow*, although he spent two hours of the battle aboard the destroyer *G 39* before being put aboard *Moltke*. The stricken *Lützow* was taken in tow, but efforts to save her were abandoned after midnight. Her crew were transferred to destroyer *G 38*, and at 0145 June 1, she was torpedoed in position 56°05′N, 05°53′E, the most powerful ship on either side lost during the Battle of Jutland.

Gröner, *German Warships*. Halpern, *Naval History of World War I*.

The German battleship DEUTSCHLAND *(later* LÜTZOW*) is trailing her sister ship* ADMIRAL GRAF SPEE *through the Strait of Dover prior to World War II. Clearly visible are the stern turret housing three 28-centimeter guns and the eight 53.3-centimeter torpedo tubes in quadruple mountings.* DEUTSCHLAND *was renamed* LÜTZOW *after the loss of the* GRAF SPEE *at the Battle of the Plate in December 1939. Courtesy Imperial War Museum, London.*

LÜTZOW

(ex-*Deutschland*) *Deutschland*-class battleship (1f/3m). *L/B/D:* 610.1' × 67.9' × 23.9' (186m × 20.7m × 7.3m). *Tons:* 15,900 disp. *Hull:* steel. *Comp.:* 926. *Arm.:* 6 × 11.2" (3 × 2), 8 × 6", 6 × 8.8cm, 9 × 5.3cm; 8 × 21"TT. *Armor:* 3.2" belt, 1.6" deck. *Mach.:* diesel, 55,400 bhp, 2 screws; 26 kts. *Built:* Deutsche Werke, Kiel, Germany; 1933.

The namesake of three *Deutschland*-class Panzerschiffs, or pocket battleships, *Deutschland* served as flagship of the German Navy and first saw action as part of the four-nation Naval Non-Intervention Patrol during the Spanish Civil War. On the night of May 26, 1937, she was bombed by two Spanish republican aircraft (flown by Russian pilots) while lying at Ibiza; 31 crew were killed and 64 wounded. The Germans responded by sending *Deutschland*'s sister ship ADMIRAL SCHEER to bomb Almería and withdrawing, temporarily, from the naval patrol.

Active in the Atlantic in 1939, *Deutschland* was renamed *Lützow,* for Freiherr Adolf von Lützow, a Prussian officer of the Napoleonic era. Following the loss of ADMIRAL GRAF SPEE, she was redesignated a heavy cruiser in February 1940. During the invasion of Norway, *Lützow* was damaged by torpedoes from HMS *Spearfish* in the Kattegat on April 11. Transferred to Norwegian waters in 1942, after ineffectual participation in the Battle of the Barents Sea in December, she returned to the Baltic and in 1944–45, she helped cover the German retreat from the east. Sunk by British planes on April 16, 1845, at Swinemünde, *Lützow* was salvaged by the Soviet Union and broken up at Leningrad in 1946. (A BLÜCHER-class heavy cruiser named *Lützow* was laid down in 1937 but sold to the Soviet and renamed *Petropavlovsk*. She served variously as a floating battery and barracks ship until 1960.)

Breyer, *Battleships and Battlecruisers.* Thomas, *Spanish Civil War.*

M

HMS Macedonian

Lively-class 5th rate 38 (3m). *L/B/D:* 154′ × 39.4′ × 13.5′ dph (46.9m × 12m × 4.1m). *Tons:* 1,082 bm. *Hull:* wood. *Comp.:* 362. *Arm.:* 14 × 32pdr, 28 × 18pdr, 4 × 9pdr. *Des.:* Sir William Rule. *Built:* Woolwich Dockyard, Eng.; 1810.

HMS *Macedonian* has the distinction of being the only British warship captured and returned to an American port during the War of 1812. On October 25, 1812, she encountered Captain Stephen Decatur's larger and more powerful USS UNITED STATES (44 guns) about 500 miles south of the Azores. The battle opened at about 0920, and by noon, *Macedonian* was shattered both in hull and crew. With 104 dead and wounded (as against only 12 American casualties), Captain John Surman Carden surrendered his vessel. After two weeks of repairs in mid-Atlantic, the two ships were able to proceed to New York, where they arrived in December. Purchased by the government and commissioned as USS *Macedonian*, in May 1813 she slipped out of New York with *United States* and the sloop HORNET; but the three ships were forced into New London, where they remained until war's end. In 1815, *Macedonian* joined the ten-ship Mediterranean squadron sent to stop the harassment of U.S.-flag shipping by Barbary pirates, and on June 17, she helped capture the Algerian frigate *Mashuda*.

In 1819 *Macedonian* became the first ship to serve on the Pacific station. Under Captain John Downes (first mate of USS ESSEX in 1813), she ranged as far north as Acapulco, protecting U.S. commerce in South America during a period of widespread revolt against Spanish rule led on the naval side by Chile's Scottish-born Admiral Lord Cochrane. Relieved by USS CONSTELLATION (Captain Charles G. Ridgely), *Macedonian* returned to the Atlantic seaboard in 1821. After five years in the West Indies, she returned for another year in the Pacific. In 1828, she was broken up at the Norfolk Navy Yard. As was the custom, some of her timbers were used in a second ship of the same name. This second *Macedonian* continued in service until 1875; some of her timbers eventually ended up in a City Island, New York, restaurant called Macedonia House.

de Kay, *Chronicles of the Frigate "Macedonian."*

MACHAULT

Ship (3m). *L/B/D:* ca. 131.2′ × 36.1′ × 18′ (40m × 11m × 5.5m dph). *Tons:* 500–550 burthen. *Hull:* wood. *Comp.:* 150. *Arm.:* 28 × 12pdr, swivels. *Built:* Bayonne, France; 1758.

The Battle of the Restigouche, June 22 to July 8, 1760, was the last naval engagement between French and British forces in the Seven Years' War, their struggle for primacy in North America. Although fought between minor units, the battle was a prelude to the French defeat in the war (also known as the French and Indian War). In November 1759, *Machault* was sent from Quebec to France with an urgent plea for the relief of Montreal. The government's response was tepid; in lieu of 4,000 troops requested, 400 were sent, along with as many supplies as could be found. On April 10, 1760, *Machault* sailed from Bourdeaux under Captain Giraudais at the head of a six-ship fleet. Two days out, two ships were captured by Boscawen's blockading fleet, and a third later sank. On May 16–17, Giraudais's ships captured seven merchantmen off the Gaspé Peninsula. Learning that a British force had preceded him up the St. Lawrence, rather than head for the Caribbean or Louisiana as his orders dictated, Giraudais sailed into Chaleur Bay because the area was a gathering place for displaced French Acadian refugees.

In the meantime, two British fleets were looking for the French, one under Captain John Byron in HMS *Fame* (74 guns) from Louisbourg, Nova Scotia, and the other from Quebec. Byron located the French force on June 22, but three days later *Fame* ran aground, and the French failed to capitalize on their advantage before she got off again. Over the next week, Byron's men searched for the channel, which they finally secured by July 1. Giraudais retreated upriver sinking blockships and establishing shore batteries, but by July 8 three ships were within range of *Machault*. Giraudais struck at 1100 and an hour later blew up his ship near what is now Campbelltown. About thirty more sloops and schooners were sunk, burned, or captured.

Between 1969 and 1972, Canadian archaeologists under Walter Zacharchuk excavated the *Machault* site. Although little of the ship survived, large quantities of wine glasses, together with stoneware, cooking implements, personal possessions, ship's fittings, and other artifacts were recovered.

Beattie & Pothier, "Battle of the Restigouche." Sullivan, *Legacy of the "Machault."*

USS MADDOX (DD-731)

(later *Po Yang*) *Allen M. Sumner*-class destroyer (2f/1m). *L/B/D:* 376.5′ × 40.8′ × 15.8′ (114.8m × 12.4m × 4.8m). *Tons:* 3,320 disp. *Hull:* steel. *Comp.:* 336. *Arm.:* 6 × 5″ (3 × 2), 11 × 20mm; 6 dcp; 10 × 21″TT. *Mach.:* geared turbines, 60,000 shp, 2 screws; 34 kts. *Built:* Bath Iron Works, Bath, Me.; 1944.

Named for William T. Maddox, a Marine Corps veteran of the Seminole and Mexican Wars, USS *Maddox* saw duty in three Pacific wars. First assigned to the Third Fleet in support of the landings in the Philippines in World War II, she was the victim of a kamikaze attack on January 21, 1945. After repairs, she returned to duty in the Japanese islands, including three months on station off Okinawa. Following the war, she served briefly in support of occupation forces in China and Korea before returning to San Diego.

In 1950, she returned to the western Pacific and during the Korean War her assignments alternated between support of fast carriers off the Korean peninsula, shore bombardment duty, and work with the Taiwan Patrol Force, which had been formed to deter an anticipated invasion of Taiwan by Communist China. *Maddox* remained in the western Pacific after the war until 1962, when she returned to San Diego.

Maddox rejoined the Seventh Fleet in March 1964 and took up station off Vietnam in May. The U.S. Pacific Fleet had been carrying on reconnaissance of North Vietnam and other countries, including the Soviet Union and

The Tonkin Gulf incident in August 1964, involving the destroyers USS MADDOX *(photographed in 1959) and* TURNER JOY, *was the* casus belli *that plunged America into the tragic, undeclared war against North Vietnam. Courtesy U.S. Naval Historical Center, Washington, D.C.*

China, off and on since 1962. In July 1964, *Maddox* was ordered to undertake a patrol that brought her to within five miles of North Vietnamese territory. On August 2, three North Vietnamese torpedo boats were ordered to sortie against her. At about 1400 that afternoon, *Maddox* reported that an attack appeared imminent and withdrew from the coast at high speed. By 1600, the North Vietnamese *T-336*, *T-339*, and *T-333* had closed to within about 9,000 yards of *Maddox,* which fired three warning shots before engaging the three vessels. The ships exchanged gunfire, and the North Vietnamese fired three torpedoes, all evaded by *Maddox;* two of their vessels were hit by return fire. At this point *Maddox* was about 25 miles off the coast. The action was broken off by 1630, at which point four Navy jets engaged the retreating torpedo boats; *T-339* sank and *T-336* had to be towed home. (The flight leader was Commander — later Vice Admiral — James P. Stockdale, who became a prisoner of war, and in 1992 ran for the vice presidency as Independent Ross Perot's running mate.)

On August 4, Vice Admiral Thomas H. Moorer, commander of the Pacific Fleet, ordered *Maddox* and TURNER JOY to "assert [our] right of freedom of the seas and resume Gulf of Tonkin operation earliest." Destroyer leader Captain Herrick expressed the opinion that apparently North Vietnam "has cut down the gauntlet and now considers itself at war with U.S. . . . U.S. ships in the Gulf of Tonkin can no longer assume that they will be considered neutrals exercising the right of free passage. They will be treated as belligerents and must consider themselves as such."

The White House adopted Moorer's view and instructed the Joint Chiefs of Staff to resume operations in the Gulf of Tonkin. Two days later, *Maddox* and *Turner Joy* believed themselves to be engaged by North Vietnamese vessels in a foul-weather night action that lasted two and a half hours. There were no visual sightings of enemy vessels and it is possible that the destroyers were firing at and avoiding radar echoes caused by freak atmospheric conditions. Nonetheless, the following day, naval air units from USS *Constellation* (CVA-64) and *Ticonderoga* (CVA-14) struck Navy installations inside North Vietnam. Of more lasting significance, President Lyndon B. Johnson submitted to Congress the Tonkin Gulf Resolution, giving him the authority to retaliate against North Vietnam without a declaration of war. The measure passed overwhelmingly two days later; it would be eight and a half years before the last U.S. combat troops were withdrawn from South Vietnam.

Maddox returned to the United States in November but was back in the western Pacific from December 1966 to February 1968. In 1972, she was sold to Taiwan and renamed *Po Yang*. She remained in service until broken up in 1985.

Marolda & Fitzgerald, *United States Navy and the Vietnam Conflict.* U.S. Navy, *DANFS.*

MADRAGUE DE GIENS WRECK

L/B: ca. 131.2′ × 29.5′ (40m × 9m). *Tons:* 375–400 tons burden. *Built:* ca. 75 BCE.

In 1967, French navy divers stumbled onto a large Roman wreck lying about 350 meters off the north coast of the Giens peninsula at a depth of about 18 to 20 meters, near the fishing village of La Madrague de Giens (43°2′N, 6°6′E). Divers from the Archaeological Institute at Aix-en-Provence thoroughly excavated the site from 1972 to 1982. The project, directed by André Tchernia and Patrice Pomey, was the first truly scientific, large-scale underwater excavation carried out in France.

The French team found the remains of a very sizable merchantman, only slightly smaller than the ALBENGA WRECK. The hold had space for 7,000 to 8,000 amphorae and much of the cargo consisted of Italian wine contained in Dressel 1B amphorae (produced in the region of Terracina). Crates of black-gloss tableware and coarseware pottery — several hundred pieces in all — were stacked on top of the amphorae as a secondary cargo. The latest datable coins found were two silver *denarii* of 75 BCE, suggesting that the ship went down not long thereafter. Examination of the hull showed that the ship was double-planked and sheathed with lead. The external planking was fir, the frames and mast-step oak. The ship was constructed in the conventional "shell-first" technique: the keel and strakes were assembled first, and frames were inserted later. A distinctive aspect of the design was a concave prow, a feature known from some artistic representations of Roman merchantmen, but never before found in a wreck. Tchernia reported that the sharply angled hull and the deep keel would have prevented the ship from drifting very much to leeward.

A unique result of the excavation was the documentation of a successful ancient salvage operation. It appears that shortly after the ship went down, divers working from a boat recovered a significant part of the sunken cargo. Two pieces of evidence substantiate this. First, the wreck site was littered with large stones. Geological analysis suggests that these came from the Giens peninsula, perhaps from the north coast near the town of Hyères. As sponge divers have done for centuries, the ancient salvors would have used the stones to speed their descent to the seabed. Second, excavation photos and plans revealed that while three layers of amphorae were still in place on the port side, only one layer remained to starboard — a situation that could not have arisen from "natural causes." The massive investment in both ship and cargo documents the scale and organization of the Mediterranean wine trade in Roman times.

Parker, *Ancient Shipwrecks of the Mediterranean and the Roman Provinces*. Tchernia, "Madrague de Giens Wreck"; "Roman Divers' Salvage at La Madrague de Giens."

MADRE DE DIOS

Carrack (4m). *L:* 165′ (50.3m). *Tons:* 1,600 burthen. *Hull:* wood. *Built:* Portugal; <1591.

At the end of the sixteenth century, Portugal had been brought under the Spanish flag, and Iberian fleets were bringing untold riches from the Americas and the Orient to Europe. *Madre de Dios* was one such ship that made the long voyage to the East. On April 4, 1581, she sailed at the head of a six-ship fleet from Lisbon for Goa, India, under command of Fernão de Medoça. At Goa they loaded a cargo of spices, gems, and other commodities — later estimated at about 4 million ducats or £1 million — and sailed for home in company with four other ships.

In this period following the defeat of the Spanish Armada, the exercise of English sea power was based more on speculation and free enterprise than on formal government policy. This was seen best in the numerous privateering expeditions against the Crown's enemies, especially Spain. Financed by moneyed "adventurers," including Queen Elizabeth, these fleets consisted largely of privately owned ships, though Elizabeth would on occasion hazard some of her own. In the summer of 1592, six ships were assembled at Plymouth to raid Spanish ships in the West Indies. The fleet included Elizabeth's *Garland,* commanded by Sir Martin Frobisher, and *Foresight,* Sir Walter Raleigh's *Roebuck, Galleon Raleigh,* and Sir John Hawkins's *Dainty.* Just before their departure, they learned of the imminent arrival of the Portuguese fleet from India. Shaping their course accordingly, the fleet split into two squadrons, one to cruise off southern Spain and the other off the Azores. On August 3, Captain Thomson's *Dainty* spotted the carrack *Madre de Dios* off Flores and brought the huge ship under fire. She was soon reinforced by *Roebuck, Foresight,* and Captain Christopher Newport's *Dragon,* homeward bound from the West Indies. Engaged at close quarters, the guns of the high-charged carrack were ineffective against the smaller English ships. The difference in size also made it extremely difficult for the English to board *Madre de Dios,* which was taken only after two hours of fierce fighting during which the English lost at least 30 crew.

A prize crew of 52 was put aboard the ship — which was significantly larger than any English ship of the day — and returned to Dartmouth on September 7. The privateers plundered the cargo of the precious stones, including diamonds, rubies, and pearls, and about 400 slaves who had been purchased in Angola were landed on Flores Island. Nonetheless, when the cargo was finally secure and the proceeds divided among the adventurers, it was found to be worth £150,000. "To give you a taste (as it were) of the commodities," wrote Richard Hakluyt,

the spices were pepper [300 tons], cloves, maces, nutmegs, cinnamon, greene ginger; the drugs were benjamin, frankincense, galingale, mirabolans, aloes, zocotrina, camphire: the silks, damasks, taffatas, sarcenets, altobassos, that is counterfeit cloth of gold, unwrought China silke, sleaved silke, white twisted silke, curled cypresse. . . . There were also canopies, and course diaper-towels, quilts of course sarcenet and of calico, carpets like those of Turkey; whereunto are to be added the pearle, muske, civet and amber-griece. The rest of the wares were many in number, but less in value; as elephants teeth, porcellan vessels of China, coco-nuts, hides, ebenwood as black as jet, bedsteads of the same, cloth of the rindes of trees very strange for the matter, and artificial workmanship.

This did not include precious stones "which were no doubt of great value, though they never came to light," having been plundered by the privateers. Nor did it include a sheaf of reports and maps outlining the scope and conduct of Portuguese trade in the Indies, which authorities did secure. Although the English had already mounted one expedition to the East (the tattered remnants of which would return two years later), these documents and the hard evidence of the ship's cargo turned "those secret trades and Indian riches . . . into the broad light of full and perfect knowledge," and provided the final catalyst for the development of English trade directly with the East.

Bovill, "*Madre de Dios*." Boxer, "Taking of Madre de Dios." Hakluyt, *Principal Navigations*.

MAGDALENE VINNEN

(later *Kommodore Johnsen, Sedov*) Bark (4m). *L/B/D:* 357.8′ × 48′ × 26.7′ dph (109.1m × 14.6m × 8.1m). *Tons:* 3,476 grt. *Hull:* steel. *Comp.:* 33. *Mach.:* aux. diesel. *Built:* Friedrich Krupp AG Germaniawerft, Kiel, Germany; 1921.

Still afloat under the Latvian flag as the SEDOV, *the four-masted bark* MAGDALENE VINNEN *was one of the few square-riggers built for commercial trade after World War I. Courtesy National Maritime Museum, Greenwich.*

Built for F. A. Vinnen, Bremen, to replace a prewar schoolship of the same name (a four-masted bark originally built as *Dunstaffnage*), *Magdalene Vinnen* sailed in the commercial nitrate and grain trades from Chile and Australia to Europe. After sixteen years in this commerce, Vinnen sold her to Norddeutscher Lloyd, for whom she continued to sail as a training ship for future officers of the steamship firm. Renamed *Kommodore Johnsen,* she resumed the Australian grain trade until the start of World War II, during which she was confined to the Baltic. Laid up at Flensburger Fjord at the end of the war, in 1949 she was given to the Soviet Union as reparations. Renamed *Sedov,* in honor of Russian polar explorer Georgi J. Sedov, who died in 1914, she remained in service as a training ship under the auspices of the Soviet Ministry of Fisheries. Following the dissolution of the Soviet Union in 1990, she passed to the government of Latvia whose government she has since represented at tall ships events in Europe and overseas.

Brouwer, *International Register of Historic Ships.* Underhill, *Sail Training and Cadet Ships.*

SMS MAGDEBURG

Magdeburg-class light cruiser (4f/2m). *L/B/D:* 454.9′ × 44.3′ × 17.1′ (138.7m × 13.5m × 5.2m). *Tons:* 4,570 disp. *Comp.:* 354. *Hull:* steel. *Arm.:* 12 × 10.5cm; 2 × 20″TT. *Armor:* 2.4″ belt, 2.4″ deck. *Mach.:* steam turbines, 29,904 shp, 3 screws; 27.6 kts. *Built:* AG Weser, Bremen, Germany; 1912.

The nameship of a four-ship class of light cruisers (including BRESLAU, *Strassburg,* and *Stralsund*), SMS *Magdeburg* was stationed in the Baltic Sea and attached to the Torpedo Research Command, under Captain Habenicht. On August 2, 1914, she fired the opening salvos of World War I in a dawn raid on Libau (now Liepaja, Latvia). Her career was short-lived, however. On August 26, while engaged in a mine-laying operation in the Gulf of Finland, *Magdeburg* ran aground on Odensholm Island (59°18′N, 23°21′N). Despite efforts to pull her free, the Germans abandoned her when the Russian cruisers *Pallada* and *Bogatyr* opened fire. *Magdeburg* was partially scuttled at 0910; 15 crew died. Of far greater consequence, in searching the wreck, the Russians recovered the German signals book, which they turned over to the British. The Admiralty's Room 40 was established to break the code, which enabled them to keep very close watch on the German Navy's movements for the duration of the war.

Gröner, *German Warships.* Halpern, *Naval History of World War I.*

MAHDIA WRECK

(1m?). *L/B:* ca. 133.2′ × 45.3′ (40.6m × 13.8m). *Tons:* 300. *Hull:* wood. *Built:* 1st cent. BCE.

The Mahdia shipwreck was first seen by sponge divers off the village of Mahdia, Tunisia, in 1907. Lying at a depth of about 40 meters, the site was excavated before World War I, then by Philippe Tailliez and Jacques-Yves Cousteau in

1948, and by a Franco-Tunisian team in 1954–55. The wreck dates from between 90 and 60 BCE. Numerous architectural and sculptural pieces found in the wreck include 60 to 70 marble columns, Corinthian and Ionic capitals, votive reliefs dating from the fourth century BCE, as well as marble and bronze statues. All seem to be of Greek manufacture, and the ship was probably en route from Piraeus to Ostia (the port of Rome) when it was blown off course and sank on the Tunisian shore. It is difficult to determine the ship's rig, but she was well found and widely traveled; there were amphorae from Kos, Italy, southern Spain, and Tunisia. Much of the cargo seems to have been purchased cheap for resale in Rome after the sack of Athens by Sulla in 86 BCE. The affinity of the architectural fragments with similar works at Pompeii and Herculaneum has led scholars to revise their thinking about the source of the columns found in the two southern Italian cities, previously believed to have been of local Italian manufacture rather than of Greek origin.

Ridgway, review of *Das Wrack*.

USS Maine (BB-2/C)

Maine-class second-class armored battleship (2f/2m). *L/B/D:* 324.3′ × 57′ × 21.5′ (98.8m × 17.4m × 6.6m). *Tons:* 6,682 disp. *Hull:* steel. *Comp.:* 374. *Arm.:* 4 × 10″ (2 × 2), 6 × 6″, 7 × 6pdr, 8 × 1pdr; 4 × 18″TT. *Armor:* 11″ belt, 4″ deck. *Mach.:* vertical triple-expansion engine, 9,000 ihp, 2 screws; 17 kts. *Built:* New York Navy Yard, Brooklyn, N.Y.; 1895.

Laid down in 1888 as an armored cruiser and later designated as a second-class battleship, USS *Maine* was originally rigged as a bark, but the mizzen mast was removed in 1892. The ship's completion was delayed due to a lack of available armor plate. Her primary armament was housed in two turrets, one starboard side forward, the other aft and to port. Assigned to the North Atlantic Squadron at the end of 1895, she cruised along the east coast of the United States from Maine to Key West.

In 1897, U.S. attention was focused on Cuban revolutionaries seeking independence from Spain. At the same time, navalists led by Under Secretary of the Navy Theodore Roosevelt sought to remove the threat of an extension of Japanese influence in the Pacific, especially with respect to the Spanish colony of the Philippines. Then, in response to escalating violence between Cuban revolu-

In 1895, New York Journal publisher William Randolph Hearst dispatched Frederic Remington to illustrate the Cuban revolution against Spanish rule. When the insurgency failed to materialize, Remington asked to leave. Hearst cabled back, "You supply the pictures and I'll supply the war." Three years later — on February 15, 1898 — an explosion ripped through the battleship USS MAINE *as she lay anchored in Havana Harbor. With only part of the* MAINE*'s superstructure rising grimly above the still waters, Hearst finally had the picture he needed to rally America to what he proudly described as "The* Journal*'s war." Courtesy U.S. Naval Historical Center, Washington, D.C.*

tionaries and the Spanish authorities, President William McKinley ordered the North Atlantic Squadron moved to winter quarters at Key West, while the Mediterranean Squadron shifted to Lisbon, from where it could track any Spanish fleet movements towards the Caribbean. Finally, *Maine* was dispatched to Havana to show the flag and protect American interests.

Sailing from her homeport at Norfolk on December 11, 1897, *Maine* called at Key West four days later and departed there on January 24, 1898, arriving in Havana the following day. Tensions were so high that the crew were not permitted any liberty, and the ship remained at anchor in the center of the harbor off Morro Castle. At about 2140 on February 15, the forward part of the hull was destroyed in a huge explosion that left 252 people dead and missing. Although Captain Charles D. Sigsbee's initial report cautioned that "public opinion should be suspended until further report," Richard Wainwright, director of the Office of Naval Intelligence, put forth the suggestion that the ship had been blown up. A U.S. naval court of inquiry led by Captain William T. Sampson concluded that the explosion was the result of an underwater mine, although it was "unable to obtain evidence fixing responsibility for the destruction of the Maine upon any person or persons."

Fueled by a jingoist press in the full bloom of yellow journalism, American popular opinion wanted a war with Spain, and Congress declared war on April 21, 1898. By the end of the Spanish-American War, Spain had lost the Philippines to the United States, and Cuba had gained its independence. Twelve years later, *Maine* was raised, to be sunk at sea with full military honors on March 12, 1914.

Debate over the cause of the explosion continued for the next century. A Spanish investigation suggested that an internal explosion destroyed the ship, an opinion supported by, among others, Commodore George W. Melville, chief of the Bureau of Steam Engineering. But when the ship was raised in 1912, a follow-up investigation supported the finding of Sampson's original board of inquiry. However, in 1975, civilian Navy researchers prepared a technical examination concluding that "the available evidence is consistent with an internal explosion alone. . . . The most likely source was heat from a fire in the coal bunker adjacent to the 6-inch reserve magazine."

Blow, *Ship to Remember*. Rickover, *How the Battleship "Maine" Was Destroyed*. U.S. Navy, *DANFS*.

MAINZ SHIPS

Discovered during excavation for a new hotel in the 1980s, the fourth-century Mainz ships consist of nine major hull fragments from five different vessels. They were originally part of a Roman flotilla situated at the fortress of Mogontiacum (Mainz), the capital of the Roman province of Germania Superior on the Rhine River, about halfway between the North Sea and modern Basel, Switzerland. It appears that the site (located in 50°N, 8°16′E) was actually a breaker's yard, and the ships seem to have been stripped of useful fittings. Construction details of the lightly built hulls are similar. The oak strakes are less than 1 inch thick, excluding mortise-and-tenon joinery. The hulls were apparently built in two stages. First, the thin strakes were fastened by wooden pegs to the "moulding frames" of a temporary skeleton, thus forming a shell into which permanent frames could be inserted in the conventional Mediterranean "shell-

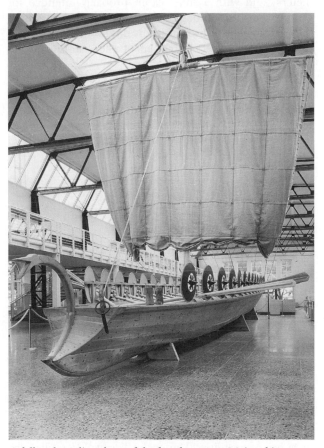

A full-scale replica of one of the fourth-century Mainz ships excavated in the Rhine River city during the 1980s. Courtesy Museum für Antike Seefahrt, Mainz.

first" fashion. The moulding frames were then removed, and the strakes were fastened to the permanent frames by iron nails clenched on the frames' inner surfaces.

Five vessels of two types have been identified. (The numbering is confused because several fragments identified as being separate ships were later found to be part of the same one.) Ships 1, 4, 7, and 9 are slender, open vessels called *lusoriae,* general-purpose cutters used extensively on the Rhine and Danube Rivers. About 21 meters long, 2.5 meters wide, and 1 meter deep (69 feet by 8 feet by 3 feet), they were ideally suited for various types of work, including ramming German dugouts, supplying outposts along the river, and amphibious operations. They had a single mast but were normally propelled by 30 oarsmen at a top speed of 10 knots. The ships were steered by a pair of oars mounted about 2.1 meters forward of the sternpost and held in place by a transverse beam. Ship 3 is a *navis cubiculata* or *iudiciaria* (an inspection boat), shorter and wider (16 meters by 3 meters) and with a small cabin probably intended for visiting officials. Although the vessel probably had a mast, the exact means of propulsion is unknown. One conjecture is that there were outriggers of a sort, and that it was rowed by standing oarsmen.

The vessels were uncovered during a construction project in 1981–82 and later excavated under the supervision of Dr. G. Rupprecht. They are now displayed at the Museum für Antike Seefahrt (Museum of Ancient Shipping) in Mainz, together with reconstructions of the two ship types represented by the finds.

Höckmann, "Late Roman Rhine Vessels from Mainz, Germany"; "Late Roman River Craft from Mainz, Germany."

MAJESTIC

(ex-*Bismarck,* later HMS *Caledonia*) Liner (3f/2m). *L/B/D:* 291.3m loa × 30.5m (955.8′ loa × 100.1′). *Tons:* 56,551 grt. *Hull:* steel. *Comp.:* 1st 700, 2nd 545, 3rd 850; crew 1,000. *Mach.:* steam turbine, 4 screws; 23 kts. *Des.:* Albert Ballin. *Built:* Blohm & Voss, Hamburg; 1919.

The third of Albert Ballin's trio of pre–World War I superliners — the other two were *Vaterland* (LEVIATHAN) and *Imperator* (BERENGARIA) — *Majestic* was laid down in 1913 and launched in June 1914 as Hamburg-Amerika Linie's *Bismarck.* The beginning of World War I prevented her completion, and she was mothballed for the duration of hostilities. Under the Treaty of Versailles, she was handed over to the British government. The world's largest passenger ship was completed in Hamburg and on May 10, 1922, *Majestic* finally sailed from Southampton

to Cherbourg and New York on her maiden voyage for White Star Lines. She remained in regular weekly service with OLYMPIC and HOMERIC, with occasional cruises from New York to Halifax during the lean years of the Depression and Prohibition in the United States. Following the merger of Cunard and White Star in 1934, *Majestic* was sold for scrap in 1936, but the British Admiralty bought her for use as the training ship HMS *Caledonia* at Rosyth. Slated for conversion as a troop transport, on September 29, 1939, *Majestic* was burned beyond repair and sank; she was scrapped by T. W. Ward between 1941 and 1943.

Bonsor, *North Atlantic Seaway.* Braynard, *Classic Ocean Liners.*

MALABAR X

Topsail schooner (2m). *L/B/D:* 58.3′ × 14.2′ × 8.1′ (17.8m × 4.3m × 2.5m). *Tons:* 30.85 disp. *Hull:* wood. *Comp.:* 7. *Mach.:* gas engine, 40 hp, 1 screw. *Des.:* John G. Alden. *Built:* Hodgdon Bros., East Boothbay, Me.; 1930.

Named for a spit of land off Monomoy Point, Cape Cod, that disappeared in the eighteenth century, *Malabar* was the name given to thirteen cruising yachts designed by John Alden. The first three of a series begun in 1921 were schooners of just under 42 feet in length. *Malabar*s four through eight were cruiser-racers of between 47 and 54 feet, intended to be raced with one paid hand, and number nine was intended to be sailed with two paid hands. *Malabar X,* also designed for two paid hands, was the largest of the *Malabars* and the last to be schooner rigged.

Malabar X placed second in the 1930 Bermuda Race, but in the 1932 Bermuda Race — sailed from Montauk, New York, rather than New London, Connecticut — *Malabar* came in first in a dramatic finish for Alden, whose *Grenadier, Water Gypsy,* and *Teragram* finished second, third, and fourth, respectively, on corrected time. *Malabar X* was also the third Alden design to win the biennial classic, *Malabar IV* having done so in 1923 and *Malabar VII* in 1926.

In 1933, Alden sold *Malabar X* to John P. Wilson of Grand Haven, Michigan, and she remained a fixture on the Great Lakes through the 1940s with fine showings in top races. In 1951, she was sold to E. Jo Chamberlain and returned to the East Coast. After a few seasons in the Caribbean, she was sold to William Lee Pryor III, who moved her to New York in the 1980s. Alden built three more boats in the *Malabar* series; *Malabar XI* was a yawl, and *XII* and *XIII* were ketches.

Carrick & Henderson, *John G. Alden and His Yacht Designs.*

CSS MANASSAS

(ex-*Enoch Train*) Ironclad ram (1f). *L/B/D:* 143′ × 33′ × 17′ (43.6m × 10.1m × 5.2m). *Tons:* 387. *Hull:* wood. *Comp.:* 36. *Arm.:* 1 × 32pdr, 1 × 12pdr, 4 × double-shot. *Armor:* 1.5″ belt. *Mach.:* 1 low-pressure & 1 high-pressure engine, 1 screw; 6 kts. *Built:* Paul Curtis & Harrison Loring, Medford, Mass.; 1855.

Built as a river towboat for service on the Mississippi River, in 1861 the single-screw steamer *Enoch Train* was purchased by Captain J. A. Stevenson for use as a privateer. Clad with 1.5-inch iron plate over a concave frame and armed with a 32-pdr. gun and an iron ram, *Manassas* (named for the site of a Confederate victory) had a freeboard of only 1.5 inches and presented an extremely low target. Resembling a floating cigar, the "hellish machine" was both unmaneuverable and slow, traits common to most southern ironclads. Shortly after her conversion, she was appropriated by the Confederate Navy for use on the lower Mississippi. Under Lieutenant A. F. Worley, she took part in an attack on the Union blockade at Head of Passes on October 12 and lost her ram in an attack on USS *Richmond.* When Flag Officer David G. Farragut's fleet forced its way past Forts Jackson and St. Philip on April 24, 1862, *Manassas* rammed USS MISSISSIPPI and *Brooklyn,* though neither decisively. Trailing Farragut's force upriver, she came under withering fire from *Mississippi.* Run aground and abandoned by her crew, she was set on fire, drifted free, and blew up.

Still, *Iron Afloat.* U.S. Navy, *DANFS.*

MANHATTAN

Tanker (1f/3m). *L/B/D:* 940′ × 132′ × 52′ (286.5m × 40.2m × 15.8m). *Tons:* 115,000 dwt. *Hull:* steel. *Comp.:* 60–126. *Mach.:* steam turbine, 43,000 shp, 2 screws; 17 kts. *Built:* Bethlehem Steel Co., Quincy, Mass.; 1962.

Prompted by the discovery of oil in Prudhoe Bay on the North Slope of Alaska in 1968, the Humble Oil & Refining Company and Atlantic Richfield Company decided to test the feasibility of transporting oil via ship through the Northwest Passage. They chartered the tanker *Manhattan* and sent her to the Sun Shipyard at Chester, Pennsylvania, for conversion to an icebreaker. The world's largest commercial ship when commissioned, *Manhattan* had had a checkered career as a tanker because her deep draft forced her either to sail light or to transship her cargoes outside of port. In preparation for her Arctic voyage, *Manhattan* was cut into four sections, each of which was modified for work in the ice. When reassembled, the ship had grown 65 feet in length and 16 feet in beam.

On August 24, 1969 (exactly one month after *Apollo 11* returned to Earth from the first manned lunar landing), *Manhattan* sailed from Chester with 112 crew, scientists, and journalists. Escorted by the Canadian icebreaker *John A. Macdonald,* on September 5 she sailed west across the top of Baffin Island into Lancaster Sound. Stopped by the ice about 50 miles into McClure Strait between Melville and Banks Islands, on September 10, *Manhattan*'s Captain Arthur W. Smith executed a U-turn and headed south to pass through Prince of Wales Strait between Banks and Victoria Islands and entered Amundsen Sound on September 14. Turning west along the coast of continental Canada, *Manhattan* arrived five days later at Prudhoe Bay where she took aboard a symbolic cargo of one barrel of oil. On the 21st, she reached Point Barrow, her western terminus. During the return voyage, engineers conducted tests to determine the machinery requirements needed for commercial navigation through the ice. Exiting Lancaster Sound on October 30, *Manhattan* returned to New York on November 12. Although her success showed that the voyage was physically possible, the route was neither environmentally nor economically sound, and it was decided to build a trans-Alaska pipeline to Valdez on Prince William Sound. *Manhattan* resumed regular service again until 1987. Laid up off Yosu, South Korea, she was scrapped after grounding in a typhoon.

Smith, *Northwest Passage.*

MAPLE LEAF

Steamboat (2f/3m). *L/B/D:* 181′ × 24.7′ (44′ew) × 10.6′ (55.2m × 7.5m (13.4m) × 3.2m. *Hull:* wood. *Mach.:* walking beam engine, 2 sidewheels. *Built:* Marine Railway Yard, Kingston, Ont.; 1851.

Built for trade on Lake Ontario between Rochester, New York, and Canadian ports, the sidewheel steamer *Maple Leaf* was sunk by a Confederate spar torpedo on the St. Johns River, Florida. Her remains are now one of the premier riverine archaeological sites in the United States. As trade on the Great Lakes waned in the late 1850s, *Maple Leaf* was put into service as an excursion vessel. With the coming of the Civil War, Boston investors purchased the ship and chartered her to the U.S. Army for service as a transport. On April 1, 1864, she was carrying three infantry regiments (the 112th and 169th New York, and 13th Indiana) under Brigadier General Foster when she hit a mine and sank near Mandarin Point, 12 miles above downtown Jacksonville. A hazard to navigation, her upperworks were dismantled by the U.S. Army Corps of Engineers after the war.

Maple Leaf was rediscovered in 1984 by divers of St. Johns Archaeological Expeditions, Inc., and since 1988 the site has been excavated by them and by the state of Florida, East Carolina University, and the U.S. Army. The ship is well preserved thanks to the river's sediment, which is so thick that divers work in conditions of near-zero visibility and employ portable cofferdams to divert the flow of water and silt. In addition to details about Great Lakes shipbuilding techniques and walking-beam machinery, the site has yielded considerable amounts of military material as well as textiles, rubber, wooden musical instruments, and other personal effects, many of which can be identified with respect to the regiment, company, and in some cases individual owner.

Cantelas & Rodgers, "*Maple Leaf.*"

USS MARBLEHEAD (CL-12)

Omaha-class cruiser (4f/2m). *L/B/D:* 555.5′ × 55.3′ × 17′ (169.3m × 16.9m × 5.2m). *Tons:* 7,050 disp. *Hull:* steel. *Comp.:* 675. *Arm.:* 10 × 6″ (1 × 2, 8 × 1), 4 × 3″, 6 × 21″TT. *Armor:* 3″ belt, 1.5″ deck. *Mach.:* steam turbines, 90,000 hp, 4 screws; 35 kts. *Built:* William Cramp & Sons Ship and Engine Building Co., Philadelphia, Pa.; 1924.

USS *Marblehead*'s first deployment to hostile waters was in 1927 when she sailed for Nicaragua to help bolster the government of Emiliano Chamorro. Later that year, she helped safeguard American interests in Shanghai and Hankow during the Chinese civil war. Returning to the United States, *Marblehead* spent five years with the Atlantic Fleet, followed by service with the Pacific Fleet from 1933 to 1938, when she was assigned to the Asiatic Fleet.

Following the Japanese attack on Pearl Harbor on December 7, 1941, *Marblehead* was assigned to the joint American-British-Dutch-Australian (ABDA) command and helped cover the withdrawal of American forces from the Philippines to the Dutch East Indies. On February 2, the ABDA force sortied from Surabaya to intercept a Japanese convoy. Shortly before 1000, the ships were attacked by Japanese bombers. *Marblehead* took two direct hits that knocked out her steering gear and holed her below the waterline. When the fight broke off, her casualties included 15 dead and 34 wounded. With only minimal repairs, *Marblehead* sailed for New York via Java, Ceylon, South Africa, and Brazil. After five months in refit, she was attached to the South Atlantic until February 1944. *Marblehead* then spent five months on convoy duty in the North Atlantic. In August 1944, she joined Operation Anvil to provide gunfire support for amphibious landings near Saint Raphael in southern France. Decommissioned in November 1945, she was scrapped in early 1946.

U.S. Navy, *DANFS.*

MARCO POLO

Packet ship (3m). *L/B/D:* 184.1′ × 36.3′ × 29.4′ dph. *Tons:* 1,625 reg. *Hull:* wood. *Comp.:* 60 crew; 750 pass. *Built:* James Smith, Courtenay Bay, St. John, New Brunswick, Can.; 1851.

Although she was named for the famous fourteenth-century Venetian explorer, "the most celebrated of all Cana-

Seen here in San Diego in the 1930s, the eight-inch cruiser USS MARBLEHEAD *saw duty in the Caribbean, Far East, Indonesia, Mediterranean, and North Atlantic. Courtesy U.S. Naval Historical Center, Washington, D.C.*

dian-built sailing ships" had modest origins and was never intended for more than commonplace merchant work. *Marco Polo*'s building was attended by a series of accidents. When launched into Marsh Creek, she ran aground on the opposite shore and was freed only after considerable effort. As a result her hull was somewhat hogged, and her departure on May 31, 1851, was greeted with relief by her builders. After sailing to Liverpool with a cargo of lumber and scrap iron, she proceeded to Mobile, Alabama, for cotton.

On her return to Liverpool, she was sold to James Baines, Thomas Miller Mackay (28 shares each), and Captain James Nichol Forbes (8 shares). Refitted to carry passengers on the Australia run, she sailed on July 4, 1852, with 749 emigrants in her three decks — 48 more than she was licensed to carry. Armed with a copy of the *Sailing Directions* compiled by the U.S. Navy's Lieutenant Matthew Fontaine Maury, the hard-driving "Bully" Forbes reached Melbourne on September 18, after a passage of only 76 days. The roundtrip was completed in only 175 days (5 months, 21 days), including time in port. As the average passage out to Australia was 123 days from London and 110 days from Liverpool, her owners were quick to capitalize on *Marco Polo*'s claim to the title of "fastest ship in the world." Despite Forbes's professed intention "to astonish God almighty," her second voyage was made in 6 months even, and her third in 6 months, 4 days.

Marco Polo remained in the Australian passenger trade until 1874, when she was sold to Wilson & Blain of South Shields. Cut down as a bark, she entered trade as a general cargo carrier but then spent almost twenty months on the coast of Chile waiting for a cargo of guano. As she left the coast, her crew decided to fish for a 16-foot shark. It put up such a struggle on deck that it crashed through the cabin skylight, and it was only killed after a violent struggle with the ax-wielding ship's carpenter in which the cabin was all but destroyed. In 1880 *Marco Polo* was sold under the Norwegian flag and entered the lumber trade. On July 22, 1883, en route from Quebec to Europe, she was run ashore in a leaking condition at Cape Cavendish, Prince Edward Island. So she ended her days as she had begun, and not far from her birthplace.

Hollett, *Fast Passage to Australia*. Wallace, *In the Wake of the Wind Ships*.

MA-ROBERT

Steamboat (1f/2m). *L/B:* 75′ × 8′ (22.9m × 2.4m). *Hull:* steel. *Comp.:* 17. *Mach.:* steam, sidewheels. *Built:* MacGregor Laird, Birkenhead, Eng.; 1858.

Following the appointment of missionary-explorer David Livingstone as consul for East Africa at Quelimane, Mozambique, the British government ordered a paddle steamer to be built for his use on the Zambesi River. The first steam vessel built of steel, she was called *Ma-Robert*, the name by which the Makalolo called Mrs. Livingstone after the birth of her first son. The vessel was sent out to Africa in sections and assembled at the mouth of the Zambesi River in the summer of 1858. *Ma-Robert* sailed up the Zambesi to Tete, but proved inadequate for the task. Livingstone condemned her as "a wretched sham vessel" and deplored especially her engines, which were, he wrote, "evidently made to grind coffee in a shop window." Worse yet, her draft was too deep for good river work, and her poor-quality steel hull rusted out and had to be caulked with mud. In 1859, Livingstone took her 200 miles up the Shire River, and with his staff and porters trekked overland to the source of the Shire, becoming, in September, the first Europeans to view Lake Nyasa. In December 1860, Livingstone took *Ma-Robert* up the Kongoni River, where on the 21st she grounded and sank. In the meantime two new vessels, *Pioneer* and *Lady Nyasa*, had been sent out. Nonetheless, in May 1863 Livingstone hoped to salvage *Ma-Robert*, only to find that she had been burned three months before.

Jeal, *Livingstone*.

MARY

Yacht (1m). *L/B/D:* 52′ (keel) × 19.1′ × 7.6′ dph (15.8m × 5.8m × 2.3m). *Tons:* 100 burthen. *Hull:* wood. *Comp.:* 28 crew; 50 pass. *Arm.:* 2 × 4pdr, 6 × 3pdr, 1 × 1.5pdr. *Built:* Amsterdam; < 1660.

Although the British have cultivated yachting to a higher degree than any other nation, the concept of the yacht was originally imported from the Netherlands in the seventeenth century. England's sea-minded Charles II had a ready appreciation for good ships, and when he sailed from Breda to Rotterdam on the first leg of his return from ten years of exile in Europe, he expressed his admiration for the luxuriously appointed Dutch *jacht* that had been put at his disposal. Amsterdam's Burgomeister Van Vlooswick thereupon arranged for his city to give a vessel of similar construction to the king. Named for Charles's sister, who was also the widow of William II of Orange, *Mary* spent a year as the official royal yacht. The word derives from the Dutch word for "hunt."

The one-masted *Mary* drew only 5 feet (1.5 meters) but was fitted with leeboards that gave her a maximum draft of about 10 feet (3 meters). This arrangement was typical of the vessels designed for work in the shallow waters of the Dutch coast, but it was not well suited to English sailing. After a year *Mary* was transferred to the Navy for service as a dispatch boat and transport for members of court and other officials. But the idea of pleasure yachts had taken hold, and four yachts of similar design — though of deeper draft and without leeboards — were ordered from the Royal Dockyards in 1662–63. Pepys described *Katherene,* designed by Peter Pett, as "one of the finest things that ever I saw for neatness and room in so small a vessel." Other yachts soon followed, and by 1686, twenty-six had been commissioned. It is interesting to note that the practice of gaudy names is as old as yachting itself: Charles built *The Folly,* Prince Rupert built *Fanfan,* and *Jamie* was named for the Duke of York.

In the meantime, *Mary* was stationed in the Irish Sea, mainly sailing between Holyhead, on the island of Anglesey, and Ireland. During the second (1665–67) and third (1672–74) Anglo-Dutch Wars, she also engaged in anti-privateering duty in the Irish Sea. At about 0200 on March 25, 1675, she was en route from Dublin to Chester when she struck a rock in the Skerries about seven miles from Holyhead and sank with the loss of 35 of her 74 passengers and crew. The ship remained undisturbed where she sank (53°25'N, 4°36'W) until July 1971, when two groups of divers from the British Sub Aqua Club independently discovered the wreck site. Among the artifacts recovered were six English and two Dutch bronze guns, coins from the reigns of Elizabeth, Charles I, and Charles II, gold lockets, and various wares in silver and pewter.

Heaton, *Yachting: A History.* McBride, "Mary."

MARY CELESTE

(ex-*Amazon*) Brigantine. *L/B:* 99.3' × 25.3' (30.3m × 7.7m). *Tons:* 198 grt. *Hull:* wood. *Comp.:* 10. *Built:* Joshua Dewis, Spencer's Island, Nova Scotia; 1861.

The first vessel launched at the small shipbuilding community of Spencer's Island, Nova Scotia, on the Bay of Fundy, *Amazon* was built for trade on the North Atlantic and to the West Indies and Mediterranean. She remained under local ownership through the mid-1860s, but after grounding on the shores of Cape Breton, she was salvaged by the New York firm of Winchester & Leeds, who put her under the American flag and renamed her *Mary Celeste.* She later underwent a major rebuilding, lengthened to 103 feet and with a capacity enlarged to 282 gross tons.

On November 7, 1872, *Mary Celeste* cleared New York bound for Genoa with a total complement of ten people, including Benjamin S. Briggs, his wife, and two-year-old daughter Sophie, two officers, a steward, and four crew. On December 4, the British brigantine *Dei Gratia,* which had left New York for the Mediterranean on November 15, encountered *Mary Celeste* sailing in a westerly direction under fore lower topsail, foretopmast staysail, and jib. Found between the Azores and Portugal in position 38°20'N, 17°15'W, the ship seemed otherwise abandoned, and Captain David R. Morehouse ordered his mate and two crew to board the mysterious ship. They quickly confirmed that no one was aboard. The fore hatch had been removed, and some fittings and rigging showed evidence of storm damage, although there was no way of telling whether it occurred before or after the ship was abandoned. Although the ship's boat was missing, Briggs's navigation equipment was in his cabin, and there was nothing amiss in any of the other crew's quarters. The last recorded log entry was "Monday, November 25. At 8.00 Eastern point bore S.S.W., 6 miles distant," Eastern Point being on St. Mary's Island in the Azores.

The ship was sailed to Gibraltar for salvage, but the Attorney General of Gibraltar, Frederick S. Flood, grew suspicious of the crew's disappearance. He developed two implausible theories. The first was that the crew had become drunk, killed the captain and his family, and stolen the ship's boat. He later determined that James Winchester had conspired against his partner and ordered the killings himself. While Flood's speculations about *Mary Celeste* prolonged the investigation and public interest in the mystery, in 1884 Arthur Conan Doyle published a short story entitled "J. Habakuk Jephson's Statement," which some consider as "more responsible than anything for the flood of romantic tales and explanations that has descended on the case of the *Mary Celeste* through the years."

The most likely explanation of the crew's mysterious disappearance has to do with the ship's cargo. She had loaded alcohol in casks at New York, and in the warmer weather around the Azores, Captain Briggs may have ordered the holds opened and ventilated. The expansion of the alcohol in warmer weather may have caused a suspicious rush of alcohol when the fore-hatch was removed. The crew then took to the ship's boat, using the main peak halyard as a painter, but the painter broke and the ship was lost in a squall.

After three months of deliberations, *Mary Celeste* was eventually released and continued to Genoa. She changed hands several more times and was lost on the Reef of the Rochelais, off Haiti, in 1885. Even this accident was deemed suspicious and the captain was indicted for trying to defraud the insurers.

Bradford, *Secret of the "Mary Celeste."* Doyle, *"J. Habakuk Jephson's Statement."* Fay, *"Mary Celeste."*

MARY POWELL

Sidewheel steamboat. *L/B/D:* 294′ × 34.5′ (64′ew) × 6′ (89.6m × 10.5m (19.5m) × 1.8m). *Tons:* 820 grt. *Comp.:* 250 pass, 18 crew. *Mach.:* vertical beam engine; sidewheel paddles. *Built:* Michael S. Allison, Jersey City, N.J.; 1861.

Mary Powell was the inspiration of her first master, Captain Absalom L. Anderson, who named her for the widow of Thomas Powell, a prominent businessman whose namesake steamboat he had commanded. (Mary Ludlow Powell was the sister of Lieutenant Augustus C. Ludlow, who was killed on the USS CHESAPEAKE in the War of 1812.) The graceful, elegant, and fast *Mary Powell* ruled as "Queen of the Hudson" between Rondout (above Poughkeepsie) and New York City, a run of a little more than five hours each way. The *Mary Powell*'s consistently high reputation over her 53-year career is explained in part by the fact that she was owned by either Captain Anderson or his son for all but three years (1869–72) of her career. The father retired in 1882 and A. E. Anderson took the helm in 1886, a post he held until his death in 1914. *Mary Powell* was sold to Poughkeepsie shipbreakers with the stipulation that she "not be made the subject of any fire or destruction for the production of moving picture films or destroyed in any such manner as shall be deemed . . . prejudicial to the public estimate of the safety of steam navigation." She changed hands twice more, but after six years in a mudbank near Kingston, she was scrapped in June 1920.

Ringwald, *"Mary Powell."*

MARY ROSE

Carrack (4m). *L/B/D:* 105′ (keel) × 38.3′ × 15.1′ (32m × 11.97m × 4.6m). *Tons:* 600 burthen; after 1536, 700. *Hull:* wood. *Comp.:* 415. *Arm.:* 78; after 1536, 91. *Built:* Portsmouth Dockyard, Eng.; 1510.

At the beginning of the sixteenth century, ships were used primarily for moving troops and sea fights consisted of pitched battles at close quarters where crew and soldiers fought for the capture of the enemy ship. Even after the development of cannon in the fourteenth century, naval guns were essentially for use against opposing soldiers and sailors massed in preparation for a boarding action. Fighting ships tended to have towering "castles" fore and aft, from which gunners and archers could fire down onto their opponents. The evolution of antiship gunnery became possible with the development of guns of increased range and weight of shot. Because of stability requirements, these could only be mounted low down in the ship, and this only after watertight gunports were developed in the early 1500s.

The oldest extant ship in which these converging technologies is seen is *Mary Rose,* Henry VIII's carvel-built flagship (named for his younger sister), and one of the first English purpose-built warships. Constructed at Portsmouth, she was armed at London with guns manufactured by the Belgian Hans Poppenreuter, among others. One indication of the increasing importance of antiship gunnery is the fact that *Mary Rose* carried 200 sailors, 185 soldiers, and 30 gunners, while her predecessors generally carried more soldiers; the larger *Sovereign,* for instance, carried 300 sailors and 400 soldiers. *Mary Rose* was not just an impressive gun platform, but she also handled well. In 1513, Admiral Sir Edward Howard reported to the king, "Sir, she is the noblest shipp of sayle and grett shipp at this hour that I trow be in Christendom. A shipp of 100 tonne wyl not be soner . . . abowt then she."

In 1511, *Mary Rose* sailed as flagship of Howard's fleet of twenty ships patrolling, with a Spanish fleet, between Brest and the then-English port of Calais. The next year, Henry joined the Holy League of the Papal States and Venice in an effort to contain France's Louis XII. On August 10, 1512, Howard attacked the French fleet at Brest where he took or destroyed thirty-two French ships and captured 800 prisoners. The French flagship, LA CORDELIÈRE, lost all but six of her 1,500 crew when she and the English *Regent* caught fire, the latter losing all but 180 of her 700 crew. In April 1513, Howard was killed at the blockade of Brest, and Henry named his older brother Sir Thomas Howard as his replacement. That summer, *Mary Rose* helped bring an English army to Calais (later victorious at the Battle of the Spurs) and then sailed north to Scotland, where Howard took part in the defeat of James IV at the Battle of Flodden Field. *Mary Rose* continued in service until 1536 when Henry embarked on a rebuilding program. She emerged from this armed with ninety-one guns — some newly made — including bronze culverins, demi-culverins, sakers, and falcons.

In 1544, *Mary Rose* was used in Henry's operations against France. In 1545, Francis I mounted an invasion of Portsmouth with a force of 30,000 troops carried in 235 ships. Henry's defensive fleet consisted of only sixty ships at Portsmouth, with forty more en route, manned by a total of 12,000 crew. On July 18, the French fleet arrived between the Isle of Wight and Portsmouth, and the English fleet weighed anchor. *Mary Rose* came under Vice Admiral Sir George Carew, who had been appointed that same day. Although Admiral Claude d'Annebault's flagship, *La Maîtresse,* sprang a leak and sank off St. Helen's, the French fleet was tactically well positioned. The following morning, French galleys advanced on the English fleet, taking *Great Harry* under fire. Then the wind sprang up from the north and the English fleet advanced. Unfortunately, her undisciplined crew — Carew's last known words, to a passing ship: "I have the sort of knaves I cannot rule" — had neither secured the guns nor closed the gunports. Suddenly *Mary Rose* heeled, flooded, and sank, with the loss of all but 35 of her complement. Despite the loss, and the fact that the French landed troops both on the Isle of Wight and on the coast of Sussex four days later, the French campaigning was indecisive, and by August 17 d'Annebault's fleet was back at Le Havre. That the French force was equal in determination and superior in execution to the Spanish Armada of 1588 is a fact little known today.

Efforts to salvage *Mary Rose* started immediately, but resulted only in the salvage of some guns. In 1836, the pioneering divers John and Charles Deane investigated the wreck. They recovered four bronze and four complete wrought-iron guns (and broken pieces of several others) before they stopped work in 1840. After this, the site of *Mary Rose* was again forgotten. In 1965, military historian Alexander McKee began Project Solent Ships to investigate the wrecks of HMS *Boyne*, Royal George, and *Mary Rose,* the last being the chief object of his search. The ship was positively identified in 1970, lying in 50°45′N, 1°06′W. Twelve years later, after careful excavation and preparation under the guidance of Margaret Rule and with the active participation of Prince Charles, the remaining starboard portion of her hull was raised and housed at Portsmouth Naval Base where it is on public display. Among the chief points of archaeological interest is the fact that, in McKee's words, "The *Mary Rose* represents a day in the life of Tudor England. You cannot get that sort of information from libraries; you cannot get it from excavating a land site. . . . What you have in the *Mary Rose* is a four- or five-storey structure complete with everything it contained on that day in 1545." This includes artifacts used by surgeons, archers, and navigators as well as clothing and other objects in daily use. (Certain organic material, such as linen and horn, does not survive.) The ship is also important to the study of naval architecture, as her construction antedates the use

of drawn plans. The surviving pictorial and written record of Tudor-era ships is otherwise scarce.

Bradford, *Story of the "Mary Rose."* McKee, *King Henry VIII's "Mary Rose."* Rule, *"Mary Rose."*

MAS-15

Torpedo boat. *L/B/D:* 52.5′ × 8.6′ × 3.9′ (16m × 2.6m × 1.2m). *Tons:* 16 disp. *Hull:* wood. *Comp.:* 8–18. *Arm.:* 2 × 18″TT; 3 × 6.5mm, 4 dc. *Mach.:* gasoline/electric, 450/10 hp, 2 screws; 25 kts. *Built:* Società Veneziana, Automobile Nautiche, Venice; 1916.

In 1915, the Italian navy began building a fleet of motor torpedo boats — *motobarco armata silurante* (MAS) — which were destined to play an important role in the naval war in the Adriatic Sea. In addition to powerful gasoline engines, they had auxiliary electric engines for silent running. Italy entered World War I in 1916 on the side of the Allies and the MAS boats were employed almost immediately against the Austro-Hungarian fleet. The torpedo boats were especially successful in hit-and-run operations against merchant and naval shipping. One of their most notable successes came on the night of December 10, 1916, when *MAS-9* under Lieutenant Luigi Rizzo and *MAS-11* under Capotimoniere Ferrarini slipped into Trieste and sank the second-class battleship *Wien.*

On June 10, 1918, Rizzo was in command of *MAS-15* while on mine-sweeping duties with *MAS-21* on the Croatian coast opposite Ancona, when the Italians encountered the Austrian battleships Szent István and *Tegetthof.* Rizzo torpedoed *Szent István* at about 0330, and the battleship sank at about 0600, thus forcing the Austrians to abandon an attack on the Otranto Barrage. *MAS-15* remained in service for eighteen years after World War I. Decommissioned in 1936, she was laid up and preserved at the Vittoriano Museum in Rome.

Brouwer, *International Register of Historic Ships.* Halpern, *Naval History of World War I.*

USS MASON (DE-529)

Evarts-class destroyer escort (1f/1m). *L/B/D:* 289.4′ × 35.1′ × 8.3′ (88.2m × 10.7m × 2.5m). *Tons:* 1,360 disp. *Hull:* steel. *Comp.:* 156. *Arm.:* 3 × 3″, 4 × 1.1″, 9 × 20mm; 2 × dct, 8 × dcp, 1 HH. *Mach.:* diesel, 6,000 hp, 2 shafts; 20 kts. *Built:* Boston Navy Yard; 1943.

Named for Ensign Newton Henry Mason, a Navy aviator shot down during the Battle of the Coral Sea, USS *Mason* achieved fame as the first Navy combat unit manned by a predominantly black crew. Although African-Americans had served with distinction in U.S. naval forces since the Revolution, in the first half of the twentieth century the service had been so thoroughly segregated that by 1943 — the second year of U.S. participation in World War II — the Navy was 98 percent white. Of the 28,000 blacks in the service, more than 19,000 were stewards, 2,000 were Seabees, and 6,600 were in general service.

In an effort to integrate blacks into the service, the Navy decided to man a destroyer escort with blacks under Lieutenant Commander William M. Blackford, Jr., USNR, and other white officers. In all, *Mason* made eight transatlantic crossings as a convoy escort. The most celebrated of these — the Battle of the Barges — was Convoy NY-119, a collection of unwieldy tugboats, Harbor tankers, and barges en route from New York to Portsmouth. On October 18, 1944, *Mason* was detached to lead twenty of the faster vessels into Falmouth in Force 8 conditions. As the ship entered Falmouth Harbor, a welded seam ripped open. Despite the storm, the crew managed to repair the deck under way, and having deposited their charges safely, they put back to sea to rendezvous with the rest of the convoy. Weather conditions were so severe that two Royal Navy ships detailed to accompany *Mason* had to put back. Convoy Commander Alfred Lind recommended that each crew member of USS *Mason* receive a letter of commendation for his outstanding performance. The request was ignored for fifty years, until February 16, 1994, when Secretary of the Navy John H. Dalton issued letters to eleven of *Mason*'s surviving crew.

Mason made one more convoy run to northern Europe, followed by three to Oran and Gibraltar. After the German surrender in May 1945, she worked as a training and test ship. Decommissioned in 1945, she was scrapped in 1947.

Kelly, *Proudly We Served.*

USS MASSACHUSETTS (BB-59)

South Dakota-class battleship (2f/1m). *L/B/D:* 680′ × 108.2′ × 36.3′ (207.3m × 33m × 11.1m). *Tons:* 46,200 disp. *Hull:* steel. *Comp.:* 1,795. *Arm.:* 9 × 16″ (3 × 3), 20 × 5″, 24 × 40mm. *Armor:* 12.2″ belt, 6″ deck. *Mach.:* geared turbines, 130,000 shp, 4 screws; 27 kts. *Built:* Bethlehem Steel Co., Quincy, Mass.; 1942.

The fifth ship of the name, USS *Massachusetts* was one of four *South Dakota*-class battleships built and, with USS ALABAMA, one of two still extant in the 1990s. Commissioned into the full fury of World War II, following trials, *Massachusetts* was flagship of Rear Admiral H. Kent Hewitt's Western Naval Task Force during Operation Torch, the Allied landings in Morocco and Algeria. While

steaming off Casablanca on the morning of November 8, 1942, she was taken under fire by the 15-inch guns of *Jean Bart*. *Massachusetts*'s 16-inch guns silenced the French battleship within a few minutes, and then sank the destroyers *Fougeux* and *Boulonnais* before turning to shell shore positions.

From North Africa, *Massachusetts* was dispatched to Nouméa, New Caledonia, where she arrived on March 4, 1943. After convoy duty in the South Pacific, in November she joined the fast carrier forces for landings in the Gilbert Islands and, in late January 1944, the Marshalls. She then took part in raids on the Mariana and Caroline Islands and supported Allied landings at Hollandia, New Guinea. Following a refit at Puget Sound, she rejoined Task Force 38 for the invasion of the Philippines in October 1944. She then took part in operations against Japanese supply lines between Saigon and Hong Kong before turning north for the final assault on the Japanese home islands, including preinvasion strikes against Iwo Jima in February. After providing shore support for the landings on Okinawa off and on between March and June, *Massachusetts* shelled industrial complexes at Kamaishi and Hamamatsu north of Tokyo.

Laid up in the Atlantic Reserve Fleet following the war, "Big Mamie" was decommissioned in 1947. In 1962, she was transferred to the state of Massachusetts and opened as a memorial and museum ship at Fall River in 1965.

Morison, *History of the United States Naval Operations in World War II.* U.S. Navy, *DANFS.*

MATARÓ

Round ship model (2m). *L/B/D:* 4.1′ × 1.5′ × 0.8′ (1.2m × 0.5m × 0.2m). *Hull:* wood. *Built:* Mataró, Spain; ca. 1450.

In 1929, a small ship model dating from the first half of the fifteenth century was offered for sale at a New York art gallery. Originally a votive model hung from the ceiling of a church in Mataró near Barcelona, Spain, the Mataró ship was purchased by a Dutch collector, who loaned it to the Maritiem Museum Prins Hendrik in Rotterdam. As the best exemplar of a Spanish ship of the period, it became the object of extensive scholarly research. In the 1980s, further examination of the hull using an endoscope revealed many details of the internal construction. The degree of detail of the votive model suggests that it could only have been made by an experienced, if anonymous, shipwright. Study of the model has done much to advance understanding about the design and construction of ships in the fifteenth century, a crucial period in the evolution of European ships, just before the rounding of the Cape of Good Hope and the crossing of the Atlantic. The vessel has a rounded stern and comparatively sharp bow. The hull comprises fifteen beams, the foremost five of which end flush with the planks, while the aftermost beams project through the planking. There are eleven strakes on either side of the keel, laid edge to edge, carvel fashion, and caulked with hemp fiber and paid with pitch. Two additional strakes abaft the waist form a raised half deck, and there is also a raised foredeck. The main deck and half deck are both cambered. The Mataró ship was apparently rigged originally with two masts — a main and mizzen — although a third was later added to the foredeck.

Culver & Nance, "Contemporary Fifteenth Century Ship." Pastor, "Replica of the Nao Catalana (Catalan Vessel) of 1450." Van Nouhuys, "Model of a Spanish Caravel."

MATHEW

Caravel (3m). *L/B/D:* 73′ × 20.5′ × 7′ (22.3m × 6.2m ×2.1m). *Tons:* 85 disp. *Hull:* wood. *Comp.:* 18. *Built:* <1493.

Identified as a *navicula,* or small ship, England's first ship of exploration was probably a caravel no larger than NIÑA, the smallest ship to sail with Christopher Columbus on his first transatlantic voyage in 1492. *Mathew's* captain, John Cabot, was of Italian (perhaps even Genoese) birth and possibly an acquaintance of Columbus. A veteran of the spice trade in the eastern Mediterranean — he lived in Venice and traded to Mecca — sometime after the return of Columbus's first expedition, Cabot began seeking sponsorship for a northerly voyage to the Orient. (At this point, no one realized that Columbus's voyage had brought him not to Asia but to a previously unknown continent.) Rebuffed by Spain and Portugal, Cabot turned to England's Henry VII, who in 1496 granted him letters patent "to seeke out, discover, and finde, whatsoever iles, countreyes, regions or provinces of the heathen and infidelis, whatsoever they bee, and in what part of the world soever they be, whiche before this time have beene unbeknowen to all Christians."

Though Cabot was granted permission to sail with five ships, only one could be had for the expedition, and on May 20, 1497, the solitary *Mathew* sailed from Bristol. Particulars of the voyage are not known with certainty. According to Samuel Eliot Morison, the ship rounded the south of Ireland and took departure from Dursey Head to sail due west on about latitude 51°N. After thirty-five days at sea, she was in soundings and on June 24 fetched up off Cape Dégrat at the northern end of Newfoundland. (Other conjectured landfalls include Cape Bonavista, Newfoundland, and Cape Breton, Nova Scotia.)

Probably deterred by ice from sailing north or west, Cabot turned south and, after one landing, followed the east coast of Newfoundland, exploring Trinity Bay, rounding Cape Race, and sailing into Placentia Bay before doubling back to Cape Dégrat. From there, *Mathew* turned for home on July 20 and arrived at Bristol on August 6.

Cabot brought no objects of trade with him, but on the basis of his report, Henry VII granted him additional patents, and in May 1498 Cabot sailed from Bristol with five ships. One of these put back, but the other four and their crews disappeared. *Mathew* was apparently not among these, and in 1504 she was still listed in the Bristol records. She sailed to Ireland under Edmund Griffeth and made separate trips to Bordeaux and Spain under William Claron, but her ultimate fate is not known. In 1996, a replica of *Mathew* designed by Colin Mudie was launched in Bristol and sailed to North America for the 500th anniversary of Cabot's voyage. (The dimensions given above are those of the replica, the design of which was based on careful analysis of the best contemporary evidence available.)

Morison, *European Discovery of America: The Northern Voyages.* Williamson, *Cabot Voyages.*

MAURETANIA

Liner (4f/2m). *L/B:* 790′ × 88′ (240.8m × 26.8m). *Tons:* 31,938 grt. *Hull:* steel. *Comp.:* 1st 563, 2nd 464, 3rd 1,138; crew 812. *Mach.:* steam turbine, 4 screws; 25 kts. *Built:* Swan, Hunter & Wigham Richardson, Ltd., Wallsend-on-Tyne, Eng.; 1907.

By the turn of the century, the prestige of Britain's merchant marine was under threat from two sides. Since 1897, German passenger ships had outpaced the British with a succession of fast and elegant transatlantic liners, most notably KAISER WILHELM DER GROSSE, DEUTSCHLAND, KRONPRINZ WILHELM, and *Kaiser Wilhelm II.* To the west, American financier J. P. Morgan's International Mercantile Marine had acquired a controlling interest not only in Germany's Hamburg-Amerika Linie and Norddeutscher Lloyd, but also in Britain's White Star Line. In response to the latter development especially, the British government offered Cunard Line a loan of £2,600,000 for the construction of two passenger liners, provided that the company remain wholly British for twenty years and that the ships could be requisitioned in wartime. In addition, Cunard was guaranteed a mail subsidy of £75,000 per ship per year.

The immediate result was the construction of the ill-fated LUSITANIA and her no less magnificent sister ship, *Mauretania,* the largest, most luxurious, and fastest liners of their day. On the return leg of her maiden voyage, *Mauretania* — named for the Roman province in North Africa — captured the Blue Riband from her sister with an eastbound crossing from Sandy Hook to Queenstown at an average speed of 23.69 knots. Although *Mauretania* would not wrest the westbound record from *Lusitania* until September 26–30, 1909, her record speed of 26.06 knots from Queenstown to Ambrose (4 days, 10 hours, 51 minutes) would stand for twenty years, when it was finally eclipsed by Norddeutscher Lloyd's BREMEN. Eastbound, *Mauretania* beat her own record seven times, the last August 20–25, 1924, with a speed of 26.25 knots (5 days, 1 hour, 49 minutes) from Ambrose to Cherbourg.

A favorite of passengers of all classes and nationalities, *Mauretania* remained on the transatlantic run until just after the outbreak of World War I in 1914. Shortly thereafter, she was converted to use as a troopship for service between England and the Mediterranean. After brief service as a hospital ship to bring home wounded soldiers from the Gallipoli campaign, she reverted to trooping duty in 1916, ferrying Canadian and later U.S. troops to Europe. She remained in this work until shortly after the Armistice, and finally reentered commercial passenger service in 1919.

Following a fire at Southampton in July 1921, Cunard replaced *Mauretania*'s coal-burning engines with oil fuel, and adjusted her accommodations to account for the decline in steerage passengers occasioned by the imposition of U.S. immigrant quotas. As reconfigured for transatlantic service, she could carry 589 passengers in first class, 400 in second, and 767 in third. As the depression worsened and increased competition from other British and European ships began to eclipse *Mauretania,* she was gradually withdrawn from transatlantic service and entered the cruise trade in both the Mediterranean and Caribbean. Her last departure from New York was on September 26, 1934. Sold the following year to ship breakers, she was scrapped at Rosyth in 1936.

Bonsor, *North Atlantic Seaway.* Braynard & Miller, *Fifty Famous Liners.* Shipbuilder and Marine Engine-Builder, *The Cunard Express Liners "Lusitania" and "Mauretania."*

MAYAGÜEZ

(ex-*Sea, Santa Eliana, White Falcon*) Container ship. *L/B/D:* 504.1′ × 74.2′ × 25.4′ (153.6m × 22.6m × 7.7m). *Tons:* 10,485 grt. *Hull:* steel. *Comp.:* 40. *Mach.:* steam turbines, 6,600 shp, 1 shaft. *Built:* North Carolina Shipbuilding Co., Wilmington, N.C.; 1944.

Built as a C-2 general-purpose cargo ship for the North Atlantic convoy run, following World War II, *White Falcon* was sold by American Export Lines to Grace Lines and entered service to South America. In 1959 she was one of the first ships converted to carry modular containers and was lengthened 45 feet. The development of containerized shipping dramatically reduced the time and labor needed to load and unload cargo. Sold to Sea-Land Service, Inc., she was renamed *Sea* and then *Mayagüez* (for the Puerto Rican port). Following service in the Caribbean, in 1974 she entered service between Hong Kong, Saigon, Sattahip (Thailand), and Singapore. On May 12, 1975, between Saigon and Sattahip, *Mayagüez* was seized by a Cambodian gunboat of Pol Pot's Khmer Rouge government, which had come to power on April 17 (the same month that Saigon fell to the North Vietnamese) and extended Cambodia's territorial waters to 90 miles. President Gerald Ford ordered U.S. forces to seize the ship and her crew, who had been transferred to Lompong Son on the mainland. On May 16, the destroyer USS *Harold E. Holt* seized the abandoned *Mayagüez* and towed her out of Cambodian waters. The crew had been released on a Thai fishing boat, but before this was known, USS *Coral Sea* launched air strikes on Ream airfield and U.S. Marines landed on Koh Tang Island; 18 marines were posted dead or missing and 50 were wounded.

Rowan, *Four Days of "Mayagüez."*

MAYFLOWER

Galleon (3m). *L/B/D:* ca. 90′ × 26′ × 11′ dph (27.4m × 7.9m × 3.4m). *Tons:* 180 burden. *Hull:* wood. *Comp.:* 101 pass.; 20–30 crew. *Built:* Leigh, Eng.; 1606(?).

Although the little ship that brought the Pilgrims to Plymouth Rock in 1620 is one of the most celebrated vessels in U.S. history, facts concerning her origins and end are obscure. While the vessel may be the same *Mayflower* as one mentioned in London port documents of 1606 belonging to Robert Bonner of Leigh, the record becomes clearer in 1609 when there is mention of a *Mayflower* of London, Christopher Jones master and part owner. This ship plied the seas chiefly between England and the French Biscay ports of La Rochelle and Bordeaux. Outbound she carried such items as cloth and rabbit skins, returning with her hold filled with wine and brandy. She is also recorded as having shipped furs from Norway and silks from Hamburg.

While this doughty trader and hundreds like her etched their wakes in the sea lanes of northern Europe, the still young Church of England had seen the development of various schismatic groups who considered Anglicanism more Popish than Protestant. Puritans believed

Anglicanism could be reformed from within, while Separatists believed in neither the authority of the Church of England nor, in spiritual matters, the monarch as head of the Church. In 1607, several groups of Separatists managed to move their "unlawful religious gatherings" to the Netherlands, but ten years later they were eager to settle in the New World, under English Crown, if not religious, authority.

Direct appeals to the Company for Virginia, which had established the Jamestown colony in 1609, came to nothing. *Mayflower*'s charter was eventually arranged through the Merchant Adventurers, which included representatives of the Virginia Company, the London Company, and the Plymouth Company, all of which could make land grants in the Americas. The dissenters worked most closely with Thomas Weston and John Pierce, who had secured a patent from the Virginia Company to settle within its domains, in "the neighborhood of Hudsons River in the northern part of Virginia."

The Separatists sailed from Leyden in *Speedwell* for a rendezvous with *Mayflower* at Southampton towards the end of July 1620, and the ships sailed in company on August 5, with ninety Pilgrims aboard *Mayflower* and thirty more in *Speedwell*. The latter was in no condition to make a transatlantic passage, and after her leaks forced the two ships into first Dartmouth and then Plymouth, the crews realized they could use only Captain Jones's larger ship. Overcrowding was alleviated somewhat when about eighteen or twenty of the company decided to stay in England, and *Mayflower* finally sailed from Plymouth on September 6 with 50 men, 20 women, and 34 children, about half of them Separatists and the others members of the Church of England. (William Bradford was the first person to refer to the Separatists as Pilgrims, in 1630, by which he meant only that they had traveled in and to foreign lands. The first child born to a woman in the group after landing at Cape Cod was named Peregrine, or "pilgrim.")

The first half of the passage was rough, but thereafter the weather was good, and on November 9 they saw land at Truro, Cape Cod, 200 miles north of the Virginia Company's domains, which extended about as far north as New York. Jones attempted to sail south, but contrary winds and the approach of winter forced the ship back around the tip of Cape Cod, and on November 11, 1620, they anchored at Provincetown Harbor. In sixty-seven days at sea one of the group had died, and one child was born, named Oceanus Hopkins. Before going ashore, forty-one of the company signed the "Mayflower Compact," the document by which all members of the ship's company would be ruled.

On November 15, Miles Standish led a small group of Pilgrims on their first foray along the neck of Cape Cod. At the end of the month, they made a second expedition, by shallop (which had to be assembled after *Mayflower*'s arrival), to the Pamet River near Truro, and a third expedition took them across Massachusetts Bay. Here was a good place for wintering, and on December 16 *Mayflower* arrived at "the harbour . . . which is apparently, by Captain John Smith's chart of 1614, no other than the place he calls 'Plimouth' thereon."

Although the first winter was hard, in the spring they met an English-speaking Indian. Squanto had been to England and sold into the slave market in Spain in 1614. Somehow he made his way back to England and enlisted as an interpreter on a ship bound for Newfoundland. Now living with Massasoit, Great Chief of the Wampanoags, Squanto provided inestimable help to the fledgling Pilgrim settlement. By April the weather had moderated, but half of the *Mayflower*'s crew had died. She took her departure on April 5, 1621, and arrived in the Thames estuary after a run of only thirty-one days.

Mayflower's history after that point becomes something of a mystery. She is last mentioned in connection with Jones's name on December 18, 1621, unloading at London the last of a cargo from La Rochelle that included 1,930 pounds of cotton yarn, "yards of Turkey grograine," and twelve hundredweight of currants. In 1624, a vessel of the same name, in which Josian Jones, the captain's widow, was a part owner, was surveyed at Rotherhithe and valued at £128 8s 4d. What happened thereafter is unknown.

In 1956, naval architect William A. Baker designed a replica of *Mayflower* based on scholarly interpretation of the few facts known about the Pilgrims' *Mayflower* and the design of other contemporary ships. With a lateen mizzen, she sets courses and single topsails on the main and foremasts, and in place of fore-and-aft headsails (a later development), she set a single square spritsail from the bowsprit. In 1957, a crew of thirty-three under square-rigger veteran Alan Villiers sailed the replica from Plymouth, England, to Plymouth, Massachusetts, in fifty-three days. She has been on exhibit at Plimoth Plantation ever since.

Baker, *"Mayflower" and Other Colonial Vessels; New "Mayflower."* Caffrey, *"Mayflower."* Hackney, *"Mayflower."* Villiers, "How We Sailed *Mayflower II* to America."

MEDUSA

Transport (3m). *L/B/D:* ca. 150′ × 40′ × 12′ (45.7m × 12.2m × 3.7m). *Tons:* 1,000 burthen. *Hull:* wood. *Comp.:* 365. *Arm.:* 14 × 18pdr. *Built:* St. Nazaire, France; 1810.

Théodore Géricault's idealized rendering of the raft of the shipwrecked MEDUSA at the moment of discovery by an approaching ship, in the far distance. For many at home, the loss of the French transport on the coast of West Africa symbolized the venality and corruption of French society under the newly restored Bourbon monarchy. Courtesy Réunions des Musées Nationaux, Paris.

Named for the hideous gorgon of Greek mythology, *Medusa* was originally built as a 44-gun frigate. With the end of the Napoleonic Wars in 1815, she was converted to a troop transport, and 30 of her guns were removed. On June 16, 1816, *Medusa* sailed as flagship of a four-ship convoy dispatched to establish a garrison in Senegal, which had been repatriated to France as part of the peace settlement negotiated after the defeat of Napoleon Bonaparte at Waterloo and after the return of the Bourbon monarchy to the French throne. The captain of the convoy, Viscount Hughes de Chaumareys, was a royalist with no previous command experience. Pressured for a quick passage by the new governor of Senegal, Colonel Julien-Désiré Schmaltz, de Chaumareys disregarded the Naval Ministry's orders first by sailing ahead of his squadron and then by crossing the treacherous and poorly charted Arguin Bank off the coast of West Africa.

On the afternoon of July 2, sailing in good weather, *Medusa* ran aground roughly 50 kilometers off the coast of the Sahara Desert and 250 miles north of Saint-Louis, Senegal. De Chaumareys's efforts to refloat the ship failed because he refused to jettison any of her fourteen 3-ton cannon. A gale on July 5 only worsened the ship's plight. De Chaumareys proceeded to abandon ship, but rather than ferry the passengers ashore systematically, he allowed everyone to clamber pell-mell into the ship's six boats. These could only accommodate about half the ship's complement, and 150 people, mostly soldiers and sailors, were ordered onto a raft, hastily thrown together from spars, planks, barrels, and loose rigging, and poorly provisioned. De Chaumareys and Schmaltz planned to tow the raft, but it was so sluggish that they soon abandoned it. Those in the boats eventually made it to Saint-Louis.

Conditions on the overloaded raft were terrible to start with and worsened fast. Over a two-week period, drowning, starvation, burning heat, violent mutiny, and widespread cannibalism reduced the original complement to 15, including the ship's doctor, J. B. Henri Savigny, and geographical engineer Alexandre Corréard. On July 17, the delirious survivors were rescued by the French ship *Argus.* Seven weeks after the shipwreck, four more men were found aboard the *Medusa,* the last of 17 men who had chosen to remain with the ship.

News of the catastrophe quickly reached Paris. Savigny and Corréard's account condemning de Chaumareys and Schmaltz for their incompetence, callousness, and cowardice achieved wide circulation at home and abroad. Bonapartists seized on the tragedy to embarrass the Naval Ministry's nepotistic command structure and to attack the monarchy. De Chaumareys was tried on five counts but acquitted of abandoning his squadron, of failing to refloat his ship and save her cargo of gold, and of abandoning the raft. He was found guilty of incompetent and complacent navigation and of abandoning *Medusa* before all her passengers were off. The last verdict carried the death penalty, but De Chaumareys was sentenced to only three years in jail. The trial was widely denounced as a whitewash and confirmation of Bourbon corruption, and by 1818, public opinion had forced the resignation of Governor Schmaltz and the unprecedented passage of the Gouvion de Saint-Cyr law legislating for the first time a meritocracy in the French military.

Perhaps the best-known legacy of the *Medusa* shipwreck, though, was a painting by Théodore Géricault, first exhibited at the Paris Salon in September 1819. Popularly known as "The Raft of the *Medusa,*" the painting is entitled simply "Scene of Shipwreck" and portrays the survivors at the moment of their seeing salvation on the horizon in the form of the *Argus.* In 1980, the remains of the ship itself were identified by divers on the Arguin Bank some 50 kilometers off the coast of Mauritania.

McKee, *Death Raft.* Savigny & Corréard, *Narrative of a Voyage to Senegal.* Weeks, "Notes and News."

MEDWAY

(ex-*Ama Begonakoa*) Bark (4m). *L/B/D:* 300′ × 43.2′ × 24.8′ (91.4m × 13.2m × 7.6m). *Tons:* 2,516 grt. *Hull:* steel. *Comp.:* 62. *Built:* Archibald McMillan & Co., Ltd., Dumbarton, Scotland; 1902.

Built as a cargo-carrying training ship for the Spanish Compania Sota y Anzar, *Ama Begonakoa* was owned in Spain but registered at Montevideo and flew the Uruguayan flag. After nine years sailing for her Spanish-Uruguayan owners, she was sold to the British company of Devitt & Moore to augment their officer sail-training program, then carried out in the four-masted bark *Port Jackson.* Renamed *Medway* and manned by thirty-two officers and crew and twenty to thirty cadets, she sailed between Britain and Australia. Following the loss of *Port Jackson* to a German U-boat in April 1917 only 180 miles from Fastnet, *Medway* was restricted to routes between Australia and South America. Despite the importance attached to her sail-training work by both Devitt & Moore and the Admiralty — most World War I–era cadets entered the Royal Naval Reserve — in 1918 the Ministry of Shipping requisitioned *Medway.* Taken to Hong Kong, she was cut down for use as an oil barge, though she never sailed for the government in that capacity. In 1920 she was reclassed as a twin-screw schooner owned by the Anglo-Saxon Oil Company. Renamed *Myr Shell* two years later, she worked as an oil tanker in the Far East until 1933, when she was broken up in Japan.

Course, *Painted Ports.* Underhill, *Sail Training and Cadet Ships.*

USS MEMPHIS (CA-10)

(ex-*Tennessee*) *Tennessee*-class armored cruiser (4f/2m). *L/B/D:* 504.4′ × 72′ × 25′ (153.7m × 21.9m × 7.6m). *Tons:* 13,712 disp. *Hull:* steel. *Comp.:* 887. *Arm.:* 4 × 10″ (2 × 2), 16 × 6″, 22 × 3″, 4 × 3pdr; 4 × 21″TT. *Armor:* 5″ belt, 5″ deck. *Mach.:* vertical triple expansion, 23,000 ihp, 2 screws; 22 kts. *Built:* William Cramp & Sons Ship and Engine Building Co., Philadelphia; 1906.

Shortly after her commissioning, USS *Tennessee* made the first of two trips to Panama for presidential inspections of work on the Panama Canal, as escort to USS *Louisiana* during President Theodore Roosevelt's visit. On her second trip, in 1910–11, she flew the flag of President William Howard Taft. In the meantime, she sailed with the Special Service Squadron in France and, in 1908–10, with the Pacific Fleet. In November 1912, *Tennessee* was dispatched to Smyrna, Turkey, to safeguard the interests of American citizens during the First Balkan War. In 1915, she sailed with the American Relief Expedition to Europe, returning with gold from the Bank of England for safekeeping in Canada.

In January 1916, *Tennessee* was sent to Haiti at the start of the nineteen-year U.S. occupation of the island nation. That May, she was renamed *Memphis* to release the state's name for a new battleship (BB-43). The next month, *Memphis* was dispatched to the Dominican Republic at the start of the eight-year military occupation of that country. On August 29, she was anchored at Santo Domingo with the gunboat *Castine* when the Caribbean was hit by a submarine earthquake. At about 1515, it was noticed that the ship was rolling heavily in the anchorage. Even as preparations were under way to get steam up and leave the harbor, a huge yellow-green wave estimated at 75 feet in height was seen on the horizon. At about 1605, a boat returning from shore was capsized in the now heavy surf inside the harbor; 25 of the 31 aboard drowned. *Castine* tried to back down to rescue survivors, but the surf was too high and she ran for the open sea.

Although the surface of the water around *Memphis* was unbroken, the huge swells buried her foredeck under masses of water unlike anything her officers or crew had ever seen. At 1635, the ship was hit by three seismic waves in succession, the last of which, about 50 feet higher than the bridge (itself 40 feet above the waterline), wrenched the ship about 100 yards from her anchorage. The troughs of the waves were so deep that, though the normal depth of the anchorage was 55 feet, *Memphis* hit bottom repeatedly. Half an hour later, she came to rest on the shore in only 12 feet of water. Her massive engines were unseated and her hull punctured and stove in. In all, 40 of her crew were killed and 204 injured, but the survivors counted themselves lucky.

A court-martial found Captain Edward L. Beach guilty of "failing to keep sufficient steam on his vessel to get under way 'on short notice.'" After World War I, Secretary of the Navy Josephus Daniels overturned Beach's punishment. His decision hinged on the fact that "the storm [*sic*] which occasioned the loss of Captain Beach's vessel was volcanic in origin and of such unusual severity that it may properly be considered an act of God which it was humanly impracticable to foresee and to make adequate preparation to meet." In the meantime, *Memphis* had been stricken from the Navy list. Sold for scrap in 1922, she was not broken up until 1937. (The authoritative account of the disaster was written by Captain Beach's son of the same name.)

Beach, *Wreck of the "Memphis."*

MERCATOR

Barkentine (3m). *L/B/D:* 209.7′ × 35′ × 16.8′ dph (63.9m × 10.7m × 5.1m). *Tons:* 770 grt. *Hull:* steel. *Comp.:* 100. *Mach.:* aux.

diesel; 1 screw. *Des.:* G. L. Watson Ltd. *Built:* Ramage & Ferguson Ltd., Leith, Eng.; 1932.

Mercator was built as a sail-training ship for the Belgian government — which at the same time canceled the subsidies for L'AVENIR, forcing the sale of that ship to Hamburg-Amerika Linie. On her four-day maiden voyage from Leith to Ostend, *Mercator* limped into the harbor with sagging rigging and down by the head as a result of flooding of a forward compartment. She had originally been rigged as a topsail schooner, carrying a fore course, single topsail, and single topgallant, as well as a fore-and-aft foresail, but she emerged from repairs at a French yard rigged as a barkentine, shorn of her foresail, and given double topsails and topgallants. During the 1930s, she made twenty sail-training voyages, including several transatlantic runs. In February 1940, she called in the Belgian Congo en route from South America. As Germany had just invaded Belgium, she was kept in West Africa and used for hydrographic work on the West African coast. Transferred to the Royal Navy for use as a submarine depot ship at Sierra Leone in 1943, she did not return to Belgian control until 1948. She resumed sail training in 1951 and kept at it for ten years, when she was opened as a museum ship administered by the Belgian Transport Authority, first at Antwerp and later at Ostend.

Brouwer, *International Register of Historic Ships.* Underhill, *Sail Training and Cadet Ships.*

MERESTEYN

Ship (3m). *L:* 145′ (44.2m). *Tons:* 160 lasten. *Hull:* wood. *Comp.:* 200. *Built:* VOC, Amsterdam; 1693.

Meresteyn was a typical Dutch East India Company (Verenigde Oostindische Compagnie, or VOC) ship built for trade between the Netherlands and the Dutch East Indies. On October 4, 1701, she sailed from the Texel bound for Batavia. The passage out took longer than expected, and by late March forty of the crew were so ill that on April 3, 1702, Captain Jan Subbingh put into Saldanha Bay for fresh provisions rather than sail the extra 70 miles to the Dutch settlement at Cape Town. After anchoring off Jutten Island, the ship was soon carried shoreward by the strong current. *Meresteyn* grounded on the rocks and sank, taking with her forty of her complement, including two women, five children, and Subbingh. A few survivors reached the mainland the next day and returned with a meager supply of water and food for the ninety-nine survivors. A week later, all but ten of the crew were taken off the island by a relief vessel, those remaining being assigned to look for remains of the ship and her cargo, which included silver for the purchase of goods in Asia.

This effort was abandoned in May, and *Meresteyn*'s cargo lay undisturbed until divers discovered and sold off coins from the wreck in 1971. A subsequent collection of more than 3,200 ducatoons and schellings dating from between 1583 and 1684 was cataloged and put up for auction in 1975. Other finds include pistols, swords, wood and glass containers, shoes, eating utensils, and carpenter's tools.

Marsden, "Meresteyn."

METEOR

Survey ship (1f/2m). *L/B/D:* 233.2′ × 33.5′ × 13.1′ (71.1m × 10.2m × 4m). *Tons:* 1,504 disp. *Hull:* steel. *Comp.:* 138. *Mach.:* triple expansion, 1,550 ihp, 2 screws; 11.5 kts. *Built:* Reichsmarinewerft, Wilhelmshaven, Germany; 1924.

One of the most important oceanographic expeditions of the twentieth century was that undertaken in the survey ship *Meteor*. Laid down as an *Iltis*-class gunboat and launched in 1915, *Meteor* remained incomplete at the end of World War I. With vigorous naval backing, Dr. Alfred Merz developed a program for a systematic description of the meteorological, chemical, and topographic attributes of the Atlantic Ocean. Fitted with a brigantine rig to reduce the reliance on fuel, *Meteor* was complete in 1925, and the expedition departed in April 1925. Unfortunately, Dr. Merz had to be landed in Buenos Aires where he later died of a lung condition. Thereafter, the ship traversed the Atlantic Ocean fourteen times to generate profiles of the ocean between 20°N and 55°S. Working at 310 hydrographic stations, her scientists used 67,400 echo soundings to map the topography of the ocean floor and made 9,400 measurements of temperature, salinity, and chemical content at varying depths. Analysis of the latter established the pattern of ocean water circulation, nutrient dispersal, and plankton growth. The expedition was also the first to make extensive studies of surface evaporation.

After her return to Germany in 1927, *Meteor* was used for research and fisheries protection. After World War II, she was taken over by the Soviet Union and renamed *Ekvator*. As late as 1972, she was still in service as a barracks ship in the Baltic.

Gröner, *German Warships.* Spiess, *"Meteor" Expedition.*

METEOR III

(later *Nordstern, Aldebaran*) Gaff topsail schooner (2m). *L/B/D:* 161′ × 27′ × 16′ (49.1m × 8.2m × 4.9m). *Tons:* 412 disp. *Hull:* steel. *Comp.:* 52. *Des.:* H. G. Barber, A. Cary Smith. *Built:* Townsend & Downey S. & R. Co., Shooter's Island, N.Y.; 1902.

Germany's Kaiser Wilhelm II was a maternal grandson of Britain's Queen Victoria, and from this side of his family, he inherited an enduring love of things maritime. This was manifest in his support of Admiral Alfred von Tirpitz's expansion and modernization of the German Navy, as well as in his love of yachting. Between 1887 and 1914, Wilhelm bought or built five exceptional yachts — all named *Meteor* — which he raced vigorously against the finest British, Continental, and American yachtsmen of the day. His competitive zeal at Cowes Regatta Week so irked his uncle the Prince of Wales that the future Edward VII gave up racing altogether and sold his yacht BRITANNIA.

Wilhelm's first *Meteor* (ex-*Thistle*) was British-built, as was the second. *Meteor III*, the only one of the five built in the United States, was christened by Alice Roosevelt Longworth. Her father, President Theodore Roosevelt, topped the list of 3,000 attendees (all in evening dress for the 1030 launching), which included Vanderbilts, Morgans, and Rockefellers. Among the schooner's refinements were an Imperial bedroom suite, two saloons (one for ladies), and a dining room that seated twenty-four. In emulation of the Cowes Regatta, Wilhelm had initiated a similar function at Kiel, and in 1904, he was as arrogant to his guests as he ever had been to his uncle. In the first race of the 1904 series, *Meteor III* was sailing in a fleet of fifteen yachts, including Morton F. Plant's *Ingomar*, captained by Charlie Barr. At the start of the race, the American boat began to overtake *Meteor III* on the starboard tack, but the Kaiser refused to give way. "Closer and closer the yachts came together," recorded Brooke Anthony Heckstall-Smith, who was sailing in the afterguard.

> Our gigantic Oregon bowsprit was pointing straight at the *Meteor*'s bow.... There was a fine breeze; we had every stitch of canvas on, including the jib topsail.... It was a silent, tense, and terrible moment. Then Barr's voice rang out to me: "Mr. Smith, Rule!" It was my duty to declare the Rule in a tight place; Barr knew it as well as I did, but it was a definite agreement between us that the responsibility was mine. "*Ingomar*, right!" I replied instantly. "Mr. Robinson, what am I to do?" shouted Barr. [Charles Robinson, Vice Commodore of the New York Yacht Club, was *Ingomar*'s racing skipper.] "Hold on!" came Charlie's instant decision. . . . I was prepared for a deuce of a crash. I heard old Morton F. Plant shout to his friend who was representing

him: "By God, Charlie, you're the boy. I'll give way to no man!"

> At that moment, the *Meteor*'s helm was put down. Our bowsprit was within three feet of her rigging. Our helm was jammed down hard also, as quickly as the wheel would turn. Both vessels ranged alongside one another as they shot into the wind.

After the race Wilhelm was compelled to apologize for his poor sportsmanship.

The Kaiser grew tired of *Meteor III* after five years. Finally confident of native naval architecture, he ordered *Meteor IV*, the first of his yachts designed, built, and crewed entirely by Germans. *Meteor V* was built just before World War I. In the meantime, *Meteor III* was sold to Dr. Carl Dietrich Harries, the inventor of synthetic rubber, who renamed her *Nordstern* and installed a diesel engine. She remained in German hands until after World War I, when Maurice Bunau-Varilla, part-owner of the French newspaper *Le Matin,* bought her and renamed her *Pays de France II.* Bunau-Varilla sold her to the Italian rayon king, Baron Alberto Fassini, who renamed her *Aldebaran* and kept her from 1926 to 1932, when he sold her to his French counterpart, Edmond Gillet. The latter had no enthusiasm for yachts and quickly sold her to the London-based American Francis Taylor. An experienced steam yachtsman, Taylor so enjoyed sailing his refurbished yacht in the English Channel during the winter of 1934 that he went on a five-year cruising vacation in the Pacific.

In 1939, the future movie star Sterling Hayden took an option on the boat with a view to starting a sailing school based in Boston. Following a bad storm, he put in to Charleston, South Carolina, and Taylor took her back. *Aldebaran* changed hands several more times, winding up with the War Shipping Administration in 1942. Even with the wartime shipping emergency she went unused and languished at her birthplace, Shooter's Island, until 1946, when she was bought for scrap by a Staten Island shipbreaker, John J. Witte.

Heckstall-Smith, *Sacred Cowes.* Ross, "Where Are They Now?"

MIKASA

Predreadnought battleship (2f/2m). *L/B/D:* 432′ × 76′ × 27′ (131.7m × 23.2m × 8.3m). *Tons:* 15,440 disp. *Hull:* steel. *Comp.:* 773. *Arm.:* 4 × 12.2″ (2 × 2), 14 × 6.1″, 20 × 7.6cm, 12 × 47mm; 5 × 18″TT. *Armor:* 9″ belt, 3″ deck. *Mach.:* vertical triple expansion, 15,000 ihp, 2 screws; 18 kts. *Built:* Vickers Sons & Maxim, Barrow-in-Furness, Eng.; 1896.

Japan began expanding its Navy in the early 1890s, turning first to France and later England for large warships for which it did not have the industrial capacity. In 1893 and 1894, the navy ordered six battleships from British yards, the largest of which was *Mikasa*, a ship similar in design to Britain's own *Majestic*-class battleships and, for a few months after her building, the largest warship in the world. Although the original impetus for Japan's military build-up had been friction with China, Japan defeated China at the Battle of the Yalu in 1894 and went on to occupy Korea and, briefly, Port Arthur in Manchuria. Forced to relinquish this naval base by pressure from European countries, Japan was galled when Russia occupied the Liaotung Peninsula and Port Arthur (Lüshun, China) in 1898.

On February 8, 1904, *Mikasa* was Admiral Heihachiro Togo's flagship during the Japanese surprise attack by destroyers on the Russian Far Eastern Fleet at Port Arthur. This was followed the next day by a bombardment of the port, during which *Mikasa* was hit several times. Although only three of eighteen torpedoes hit their targets, the Russians had lost the initiative. On August 10, Admiral Vitgeft attempted a breakout to Vladivostok, on the Sea of Japan opposite Hokkaido. Although *Mikasa* was hit twenty-three times and had to undergo extensive repairs, the Battle of the Yellow Sea was a clear defeat for the Russians. Vitgeft was killed when his flagship *Tsarevich* was hit by a 12 inch shell, and the Russian fleet quickly retired to Port Arthur in disorder. (*Tsarevich* escaped to the German-occupied port of Tsingtao, where she was interned.) In December, the Japanese took Port Arthur from the landward side, and by the end of January 1905, the Russians had lost all seven battleships of the Far Eastern Fleet.

Meanwhile, in September 1904 Admiral Zinovi Petrovich Rozhestvensky had left Kronstadt with the Baltic Fleet at the start of an 18,000-mile voyage round the Cape of Good Hope to Vladivistok. As his fleet steamed through the narrow Korea Strait on May 27, 1905, they were attacked by the Japanese fleet near the island of Tsushima. Rozhestvensky's force included four new and four older battleships, four coast defense ships, and six cruisers (including AURORA). Togo had only four battleships, two armored cruisers, and six cruisers. But what the Japanese lacked in numbers they made up for in speed, experience, and morale.

Togo used his battleships' six-knot superiority in speed to outflank the Russian fleet, concentrating first on the flagship. *Kniaz Suvarov* was quickly knocked out of line and eventually sank. Within five hours, the new battleships *Imperator Alexander III* and *Borodino* were also

sunk with the loss of all but one of their 1,692 crew, while *Orel* was captured. Total Russian losses included ten ships sunk (including six battleships) and four captured; three ships were interned and one escaped. The Japanese lost no ships. *Mikasa* was hit thirty-two times by Russian shells but suffered only eight dead.

On September 12, a magazine explosion killed 114 of *Mikasa*'s crew and left her sunk at her moorings. In August 1906, she was refloated, but her fighting days were over. On September 20, 1923, she was stricken from the list of commissioned ships and preserved as a memorial. At the end of World War II, she was stripped of her fittings in a compromise between the USSR, who wanted her scrapped, and the United States. Fifteen years later, she was restored as a memorial at Yokosuka, thanks in large part to help offered by Admiral Chester Nimitz, USN.

Breyer, *Battleships and Battlecruisers*. Heine, *Historic Ships of the World*.

MISCHIEF

Bristol Channel pilot cutter (1m). *L/B/D:* 45′ × 13′ × 7.5′ (13.7m × 4m × 2.3m). *Tons:* 29 Thames measurement. *Hull:* wood. *Comp.:* 5. *Mach.:* aux. *Built:* Thomas Baker, Cardiff, Wales; 1906.

Built for work in the Bristol Channel of southwest England, pilot cutter *Mischief* was owned by William "Billy the Mischief" Morgan for fifteen years before he sold her and she became a yacht, a not uncommon fate for such handsome, sturdy craft. She changed hands ten times before 1954, at which time she was purchased by Major H. William Tilman. The veteran mountaineer and explorer was no ordinary yachtsman. His first voyage in *Mischief* was with a small crew on a 20,000-mile voyage to Valparaiso via the Strait of Magellan. The year after returning to Lymington (whose river comprised the only waters for which Tilman felt it was necessary to carry insurance), Tilman sailed around Africa via Brazil, South Africa, the Comoros, Suez, and Gibraltar. In 1959–60 *Mischief* sailed for the southern Indian Ocean, where her name is remembered in Mount Mischief in the Crozet Islands, and in Cap Mischief, Kerguelen Island.

In the next three seasons, Tilman sailed *Mischief* to West Greenland, exploring Baffin Bay and Lancaster Sound and naming Mount Mischief overlooking Baffin Island's Exeter Sound. When in 1963 *Mischief* was condemned for long voyages, Tilman had her frames doubled and then sailed her twice to East Greenland. In 1966, they headed south again, through the Strait of Magellan to Punta Arenas, then on to the South Shetland and

South Georgia Islands. Her next voyage proved her last; after stops in the Faeroe Islands and Akureyri, *Mischief* stranded on Jan Mayen Island. Taken in tow, she sank 30 miles east of Jan Mayen. Though Tilman "felt like one who had first betrayed and then deserted a stricken friend," the next year he was back at sea in the 1899 pilot cutter *Seabreeze*. Three years later she was lost in an accident the lesson of which was "not to mess about in Greenland fjords without an engine, especially when they are full of ice." After two seasons with the 1902 pilot cutter *Baroque*, Tilman retired from the sea at age seventy-seven.

Tilman, *Ice with Everything; Mischief Goes South; Mischief in Greenland; Mischief in Patagonia; Mostly Mischief.*

USS MISSISSIPPI

Mississippi-class sidewheel steamer (1f/3m). *L/B/D:* 229′ × 40′ (66.5′ew) × 21.8′ (69.8m × 12.2m (20.1m) × 6.6m). *Tons:* 3,220 disp. *Hull:* wood. *Comp.:* 257. *Arm.:* 2 × 10″, 8 × 8″. *Mach.:* sidelever engines, 700 nhp, sidewheels; 11 kts. *Des.:* John Lenthall, Hartt & Humphries. *Built:* Philadelphia Navy Yard; 1841.

One of the first sidewheel steam frigates ordered for the U.S. Navy, USS *Mississippi* was built under the personal supervision of Commodore Matthew Perry, formerly commander of USS *Fulton II* and a strong advocate of steam propulsion. Rigged as a bark, *Mississippi* was used extensively to test the utility of steam for naval operations. As with all paddle frigates, her greatest deficiency was that the placement of her paddles interfered with the guns, and her engines were vulnerable to enemy fire.

In 1845 she sailed as Perry's flagship in the West Indian Squadron during the Mexican War, and she took part in the blockade of Mexican Gulf and Caribbean coast ports, as well as in the capture of Vera Cruz, Tuxpan, and Tabasco in 1847. With the return of peace, *Mississippi* cruised in the Mediterranean from 1849 to 1851. Calling at Constantinople in the latter year, she embarked Hungarian nationalist Lajos Kossuth and fifty fugitives from the Austrian government, and returned to the United States.

Placed once more under Perry's command, in 1852 she sailed for the Far East with his mission, which was charged specifically with opening trade with Japan. His first visit to Edo (Tokyo) in July served to awe the Japanese with his "black ships" (the other was USS *Susquehanna*) — the first steamships to visit Japan. Perry returned the following year and concluded the Treaty of Kanagawa on March 31, 1854. Except for a visit to the

United States in 1855–56, *Mississippi* remained in the Orient until 1860, supporting French and British vessels in the bombardment of Taku on June 25, 1859, and landing marines to protect U.S. interests at Shanghai in August.

Mississippi returned to Boston in 1860, and remained there until assigned to blockade duty off Key West in June 1861. Joining Flag Officer David G. Farragut's fleet for the assault on New Orleans, on April 7, 1863, she became the largest vessel to cross the bar of the river whose name she bore. As the Union fleet ran past Forts Jackson and St. Philip, *Mississippi* destroyed CSS *Manassas* before proceeding to New Orleans where she remained until 1863. Farragut then ordered her to take part in the run past Port Hudson, the largest Confederate fort below Vicksburg, in company with the screw steamers USS HARTFORD, MONONGAHELA, and *Richmond*. On March 14, 1863, she had just passed Port Hudson when she ran aground. Still within range of the Confederate batteries, she came under devastating fire that killed 64 of her crew. Despite efforts of his crew and officers, including his executive officer George Dewey, Captain Melancthon Smith ordered her set afire and abandoned.

Anderson, *By Sea and by River*. Hagan, *This People's Navy*. Perry, *Narrative of the Expedition of an American Squadron to the China Seas and Japan*. U.S. Navy, *DANFS*.

USS MISSOURI (BB-63)

Iowa-class battleship (2f/2m). *L/B/D:* 887.3′ × 108.2′ × 34.8′ (270.4m × 33m × 8.8m). *Tons:* 57,430 disp. *Hull:* steel. *Comp.:* 1,795. *Arm.:* 9 × 16″ (3 × 3), 20 × 5″, 80 × 40mm, 49 × 20mm. *Armor:* 13.5″ belt, 6.2″ deck. *Mach.:* geared turbines, 212,000 shp, 4 screws; 33 kts. *Built:* New York Navy Yard, Brooklyn, N.Y.; 1944.

The fourth ship of the name, USS *Missouri* was the last battleship commissioned in the U.S. Navy. *Missouri* reached the Caroline Islands in January 1945, and the next month joined Task Force 58 for raids on the Japanese home islands. After gunfire support operations during the landings on Iwo Jima, against shore positions south of Tokyo, and against positions on Okinawa, *Missouri* became flagship of Admiral William F. Halsey, Jr. Following the announcement of the Japanese surrender, *Missouri* sailed into Tokyo Bay on August 29. There, on September 2, Allied and Japanese representatives, including General of the Army and Supreme Allied Commander in the Pacific Douglas MacArthur, Fleet Admiral Chester Nimitz, Admiral Sir Bruce Fraser, RN, and Foreign Minister Mamoru Shigemitsu, signed the formal articles of surrender ending World War II.

It was a close call, but gunners aboard USS MISSOURI *managed to splash this Japanese kamikaze before it hit their ship, April 28, 1945. Four months later, World War II came to an end when, on September 2, Japan's Foreign Minister Mamoru Shigemitsu signed surrender terms on the deck of the "Mighty Mo" in Tokyo Bay. Courtesy U.S. Naval Historical Center, Washington, D.C.*

Transferred to the Atlantic Fleet, in the spring of 1946 *Missouri* sailed for Istanbul bearing the remains of the late Turkish Ambassador Mehmet Munir Ertegun. From there she called at Piraeus in a demonstration of U.S. support for anti-Communist forces during the Greek Civil War. In 1947, *Missouri* sailed for Rio de Janeiro, where the Rio Treaty was signed on her decks and President Harry S. Truman embarked for his return to the United States. On January 17, 1950, the only U.S. battleship in commission left the Hampton Roads Navy Yard after repairs and grounded near Old Point Comfort, where she remained fast for two weeks.

Missouri did two tours of duty in Korea, from September 1950 to March 1951 and September 1952 to March 1953, providing gunfire support for UN ground forces on the peninsula. Decommissioned in 1955, the "Mighty Mo" remained in reserve until 1982, when she and her sister ships — IOWA, *New Jersey,* and *Wisconsin* — were reactivated during President Ronald Reagan's defense build-up. After modernization, she mounted only twelve 5-inch guns and the twenty 40-millimeter quad mounts were removed; the 20-millimeter antiaircraft guns had been taken out in the 1950s. The new armament consisted of four Vulcan Phalanx 20-millimeter Gatling guns, four quadruple Harpoon antiship missiles, and eight quadruple Tomahawk armored box launchers. *Missouri* and *Wisconsin* saw action during the Persian Gulf War in 1991, but the Pentagon later determined that the ships were prohibitively expensive, and they were decommissioned in the early 1990s. As of 1997, *Missouri* was slated to open as a museum ship at Ford Island, Pearl Harbor.

Stillwell, *Battleship "Missouri."*

MOGAMI

Mogami-class cruiser (1f/2m). *L/B/D:* 661′ × 59.1′ × 18.1′ (201.5m × 18m × 5.5m). *Tons:* 11,169 disp. *Hull:* steel. *Comp.:* 850. *Arm.:* 10 × 8″ (5 × 2), 8 × 5″, 8 × 25mm; 12 × 21″TT; 3 aircraft. *Armor:* 2.5″ belt, 2″ deck. *Mach.:* geared turbines, 90,000 shp, 4 screws; 33 kts. *Built:* Kaigun Kosho, Kure, Japan; 1937.

The first of four *Mogami*-class cruisers laid down under the terms of the London Naval Treaty, *Mogami* and her three sister ships were designed with fifteen 6.1-inch guns in triple turrets. These were replaced by ten 8.1-inch guns in 1939 in twin turrets, but following her near destruction at the Battle of Midway in June 1942, the two after turrets were removed to make way for an increased number of floatplanes. At the start of World War II in the Pacific, *Mogami* was part of Rear Admiral Takeo Kurita's

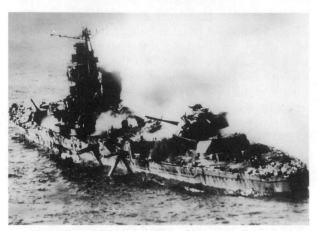

American flyers inflicted tremendous damage on the MOGAMI *at the Battle of Midway in June 1942. Incredibly, the Japanese heavy cruiser made it home and returned to active duty. The battle-scarred veteran was finally sunk at the Battle of Leyte Gulf, October 1944. Courtesy Imperial War Museum, London.*

7th Cruiser Squadron in the South China Sea. From December 1941 through April 1942, she helped cover Japan's eastward movement through landings in Malaysia, Java, Sumatra, and the Andaman Islands. On February 29, 1942, she took part in the Battle of the Sunda Strait during which HMAS PERTH and USS HOUSTON were sunk, and in early April, she raided merchant shipping in conjunction with operations against Ceylon.

On May 27, *Mogami* sailed from Guam as part of the covering force for the invasion of Midway. On June 5, 1942, she and her sister ship *Mikuma* collided while trying to evade submarine USS *Tambor,* and the next day they were attacked by American dive-bombers from USS ENTERPRISE and YORKTOWN. *Mikuma* was sunk, but despite horrendous damage, *Mogami,* under Captain Sato, escaped to Truk. She saw no action for the next year, but on November 3, 1943, refurbished *Mogami* had just entered Rabaul, New Guinea, when she was bombed by planes from USS SARATOGA and PRINCETON.

The next spring, she was part of the Japanese fleet assembled at Tawi-Tawi for Operation A-GO, the defense of the Mariana Islands. This culminated in the disastrous Battle of the Philippine Sea on June 19, 1944, when Japan lost more than 400 planes and aviators. On October 22, 1944, *Mogami* sailed as part of Vice Admiral Shoji Nishimura's Southern Force at the Battle of Leyte Gulf. On the night of October 24, battleships *Yamshiro* and FUSO, *Mogami,* and four destroyers entered Surigao Strait. They evaded a series of PT-boat attacks, but at 0200 the next morning, Captain Jesse G. Cowards's De-

stroyer Squadron (Desron) 54 launched a torpedo attack in which FUSO was blown up and sunk. This was followed at 0353 by an eruption of heavy gunfire from Rear Admiral Jesse B. Oldendorf's battleships USS *West Virginia, Tennessee,* CALIFORNIA, *Maryland, Mississippi,* and *Pennsylvania,* which had crossed the "T" of the Japanese advance. *Mogami* wheeled almost immediately, only to be hit by cruiser *Portland.* As she retired to the south, accompanied by destroyer *Shigure, Mogami* collided with Nishimura's battleship *Nachi.* Later that morning, "burning like a city block," she came under renewed fire from American cruisers and fought off a PT-boat attack. At 0845, under attack from dive-bombers in the Mindanao Sea, the cruiser finally sank in 9°40′N, 124°50′E.

Rohwer & Hummelchen, *Chronology of the War at Sea.* Whitley, *Cruisers of World War Two.*

MOLASSES REEF WRECK

L/B: ca. 6.3′ × 19.7′ (19m × 6m). *Tons:* ca. 100. *Hull:* wood. *Arm.:* 2 bombardetas. *Built:* Spain(?); ca. 1510.

One of the oldest known shipwrecks in the Americas is that of an early sixteenth-century vessel that sank on Molasses Reef in the Caicos Islands. The otherwise unidentified Spanish vessel is thought to have gone down within twenty years of Christopher Columbus's first voyage to the Americas. While the surviving material of the wreck is spread over a wider area, the pile of ballast stones measured 11.5 meters by 3 meters and was about half a meter deep. Originally thought to be the remains of Columbus's PINTA, the site was first identified by a treasure-hunting group licensed to examine the site by the government of Turks and Caicos.

Archaeologists from Texas A & M's Institute of Nautical Archaeology began excavation in 1982, but not before treasure seekers had used explosives to loosen artifacts. Archaeologists found parts of six strakes and located twenty-four frames or frame positions. Hardware finds included iron bolts and nails, three rudder gudgeons, and various rigging fittings. In addition there were seventeen pieces of artillery, 100 ceramic fragments, and an anchor. Based on an analysis of the remains, including the weight of the ballast, it has been estimated that the ship had a capacity of about 100 tons, with a length of about 19 meters and a beam of 6 meters, and that the ship was built either in Spain or by shipwrights working in a style common to Spain at the time.

Keith et al., "Molasses Reef Wreck." Oertling, "Molasses Reef Wreck Hull Analysis."

SMS MOLTKE

Moltke-class battlecruiser. *L/B/D:* 612′ × 96.4′ × 30.2′ (186.6m × 29.4m × 9.2m). *Tons:* 25,400 disp. *Comp.:* 1,158. *Hull:* steel. *Arm.:* 10 × 11.2″ (5 × 2), 12 × 6″, 12 × 8.8cm; 4 × 20″TT. *Armor:* 10.8″ belt, 2″ deck. *Mach.:* Parsons turbines, 85,782 shp, 3 screws; 28.4 kts. *Built:* Blohm & Voss, Hamburg; 1911.

Commissioned in 1911, SMS *Moltke* was named for Franco-Prussian War hero Helmuth von Moltke; she was also a sister ship of SMS GOEBEN. Part of Rear Admiral Franz von Hipper's First Scouting Group, *Moltke* took part in the December 16, 1914, shore bombardment of Hartlepool and Whitby. She was also at the Battle of the Dogger Bank on January 24, 1915, but escaped the engagement relatively unscathed. During the German campaign to close the Gulf of Riga, *Moltke* was torpedoed on August 19 by the British submarine *E-1*. Damage was slight, and the next month *Moltke* was flagship of Vice Admiral Ehrhard Schmidt's task force in Operation Albion, to seize Russia's Ösel and Moon Islands.

Moltke next saw action at the Battle of Jutland on May 31, 1916. During the battlecruiser action with Vice Admiral Sir David Beatty's Battle Cruiser Fleet, *Moltke* took several hits, including one 15-inch shell, but was the least damaged of the German cruisers, and Hipper transferred his flag to *Moltke* after the loss of LÜTZOW. In the German Navy's last sortie of the war, April 24, 1918, *Moltke* was part of an unsuccessful task force sent to intercept a convoy sailing from Norway to Britain. On the return from the Norwegian coast, *Moltke* was torpedoed by the British submarine *E-42*, but she limped back to port. Interned at Scapa Flow on November 21, 1918, she was scuttled there on June 21, 1919. Raised on June 10, 1927, *Moltke* was broken up two years later at Rosyth.

Gröner, *German Warships.* Halpern, *Naval History of World War I.*

USS MONITOR

Monitor. L/B/D: 179′ × 41.5′ × 10.5′ (54.6m × 12.6m × 3.2m). *Tons:* 987 disp. *Comp.:* 49. *Arm.:* 2 × 11″ (2 × 1). *Armor:* 4.5″ belt, 8″ turret. *Hull:* iron. *Mach.:* vibrating-lever engines, 320 ihp, 1 screw; 6 kts. *Des.:* John Ericsson. *Built:* Continental Iron Works, Green Point, N.Y. (hull), Novelty Iron Works, New York (turret), and Delamater & Co., New York (engine); 1862.

Shortly after the start of the Civil War, U.S. Navy Secretary Gideon Welles learned of Confederate plans to raise the hull of USS *Merrimac,* which Federal forces had burned and sunk in their flight from Norfolk's Gosport Navy Yard, and to convert it into an ironclad. To counter the threat posed by such a vessel, he authorized research into the feasibility of an armored steamship clad in either iron or steel. Despite the fact that the French and British had already commissioned LA GLOIRE and HMS WARRIOR, respectively, most American naval architects of the day considered the project impracticable. "No iron-clad vessel of equal displacement [to a wooden vessel]," they argued, "can be made to obtain the same speed as one not thus encumbered." Welles's advisory board nonetheless proposed that three different designs be tried — two broadside ironclads, which became USS NEW IRONSIDES and the poorly armored *Galena,* and one with a revolving turret.

John Ericsson had designed such a vessel for Napoleon III during the Crimean War. Although the inventor had washed his hands of any involvement with the U.S. Navy following its treatment of him after the tragic explosion aboard USS PRINCETON in 1844, his colleague Cornelius S. Bushnell (then building *Galena*) introduced Ericsson to Welles. Welles then invited Ericsson to Washington to present his model to President Abraham Lincoln and the Navy board. On October 4, 1861, he was given a contract for the ship, with the stipulation that all monies be refunded to the Navy if construction were not completed in 100 days. In the course of her construction, Ericsson reportedly devised no less than forty patentable inventions. He also chose the name, asserting that "to the Lords of the Admiralty the new craft will be a monitor, suggesting doubts as to the propriety of completing those four steel ships" (harmless blockade-runners) — he was a master of self-promotion — then building for the Confederacy in English yards.

The finished product was revolutionary in the extreme. The iron vessel consisted of two parts, a hull (122 feet by 34 feet) upon which rested an iron "raft" (172 feet by 41 feet), the dual function of which was to protect the hull from ramming and to provide the vessel with stability in a seaway. Within the hull were living spaces for 41 crew, an engine room (where the temperature reportedly reached 178°F/81°C), and storage spaces for coal and ammunition. Visually and technologically, *Monitor*'s most distinguishing feature was the rotating turret, built up of eight layers of one-inch iron plate and measuring 20 feet in diameter and 9 feet high. Mounted on a steam-powered spindle, the circular turret mounted two 7-ton Dahlgren smoothbore guns. Also protruding from the deck were two ventilation pipes and two funnels aft, and forward a pilot house with 9-inch armor. She was the first warship built without rigging or sails.

Laid down on October 25, 1861, and launched January 30, 1862, USS *Monitor* was commissioned on February 25 under Lieutenant John L. Worden. It was originally in-

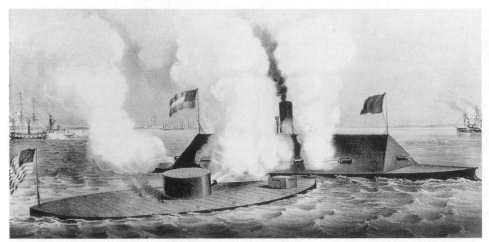

A Currier and Ives lithograph showing "The Terrific Combat Between the MONITOR 2 Guns and MERRIMAC 10 Guns: The first between iron clad ships of war, in Hampton Roads, March 9, 1862, in which the little MONITOR whipped the MERRIMAC and the whole 'school' of rebel steamers." At far left, the USS MINNESOTA; at far right, the Rebel steamers. Courtesy U.S. Naval Academy, Annapolis, Maryland.

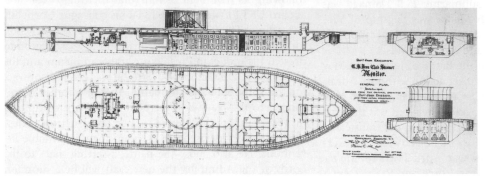

A general plan of the "iron clad steamer" USS MONITOR "deduced from the original drawings of Capt. John Ericsson and from actual measurements taken from the actual vessel." The barrels of the eleven-inch guns can be seen in the center turret, which is almost as deep as the hull. The ship was conned from the smaller forward turret, accessed via a ladder. The machinery, aft, led to a single propeller. Courtesy U.S. Naval Historical Center, Washington, D.C.

tended that *Monitor* would join Flag Officer David G. Farragut's West Gulf Blockading Squadron at New Orleans, but Farragut sailed before she was ready. Instead, she was sent to Washington, D.C., leaving New York on March 6 in tow of the screw steamer *Seth Low*. Two days later, she entered Chesapeake Bay just as CSS VIRGINIA — the former *Merrimac* — was attacking the wooden USS CONGRESS and CUMBERLAND in Hampton Roads. That night, Captain Morston, the senior officer at Hampton Roads, ordered *Monitor* to assist the beleaguered USS *Minnesota*.

On the morning of May 9, as *Virginia* approached to finish off the grounded frigate, *Monitor* slipped out of the shadow of the larger ship to challenge the Confederate ironclad. *Monitor* and *Virginia* battled each other for four hours but neither was able to inflict serious damage on the other. Worden used his ship's superior maneuverability to avoid ramming and shelling by his adversary, but

even so her turret was hit twenty-four times. The two ships were well matched, and although *Virginia* was hard aground for an hour, *Monitor*'s and *Minnesota*'s shot could not penetrate her iron plate. At about 1130, fragments from one of *Virginia*'s shot flew through the eyeslit of *Monitor*'s pilot house. The partially blinded Worden ordered gunnery officer Lieutenant S. D. Greene to take *Monitor* into shallow waters, which he did forty-five minutes later. *Virginia* also broke off the engagement, and so the first battle between ironclad ships ended, and with it the age of the wooden fighting ship.

As long as *Virginia* remained in commission, the Union had no choice but to leave *Monitor* where she was as a deterrent. The Confederates were forced to destroy their ironclad on May 11 when they abandoned Norfolk in the face of General George McClellan's offensive up the Yorktown Peninsula towards Richmond. In company with USS *Galena* and *Naugatuck*, *Monitor* then proceeded up the James River to Drury's Bluff, about eight miles below the Confederate capital. Their way stopped by obstructions in the river and heavy Confederate artillery, the ironclads withdrew on May 13. *Monitor* remained in the vicinity through the end of the year, covering the Union retreat after the Seven Days Battle in June and serving on blockade duty at Hampton Roads thereafter.

On December 29, USS *Rhode Island* towed her out of Hampton Roads bound for the blockade off Wilmington, North Carolina. At about 0130 on December 31, 1862, *Monitor* foundered in a storm off Cape Hatteras, taking with her four officers and twelve crew. Her exact location remained unknown until scientists aboard the research ship *Eastward* located her remains on August 27, 1973. Designated a National Marine Sanctuary in 1975, *Monitor* lies in 225 feet of water at about 35°N, 75°23′E, sixteen miles south-southeast of Cape Hatteras Light.

Cox & Jehle, *Ironclad Intruder.* Delgado, *Symbol of American Ingenuity.* Miller, *USS Monitor.* Nash, "Civil War Legend Examined." U.S. Navy, *DANFS.*

MONKBARNS

Ship (3m). *L/B/D:* 267′ × 40.1 × 21.5 (91.4m × 12.2m × 6.6m) *Tons:* 1,771 grt. *Hull:* steel. *Built:* Archibald McMillan & Son, Ltd., Dumbarton, Scotland; 1895.

Built for D. Corsar and Sons of Liverpool for general trading, *Monkbarns* (a Scottish place name) had an unusual rig, setting double topgallants on her fore and mainmast, but a single topgallant on her mizzen. Under Corsar's Flying Horse Line she was put to the test on more than one occasion, most notably in 1904, when she was caught in ice south of Cape Horn for sixty-three days while en route to San Francisco. In 1911 *Monkbarns* was sold to John Stewart & Company for whom she carried a variety of cargo, including nitrates, grain, and cement. In November 1914 she passed Admiral Graf von Spee's fleet just before the Battle of Coronel, where the German fleet sank HMS GOOD HOPE and *Monmouth.* The following spring she was only five miles from RMS LUSITANIA when the passenger liner was torpedoed on April 12, 1915. *Monkbarns* sailed on, her crew sure that any delay would result in their sinking, too. (Well over 200 British sailing ships were sunk during World War I, and by 1919 there were only four sailing ships still under the British flag.) Despite the war, *Monkbarns* — herself frequently mistaken for the German raider SEEADLER — continued in trade, returning twice to Britain. In 1917, she sailed from Australia for New York with flour for the U.S. Navy. During the trip, eight of the crew refused duty on the

grounds that the food was inadequate. Captain James Donaldson (age seventy-six) put into Rio de Janeiro flying the signal "The crew have mutinied and threatened to kill the Captain." Six of the crew were brought to trial aboard HMS *Armadale Castle,* and five were sentenced to jail before the ship continued on her way.

There was little work for *Monkbarns* during the 1920s, and she made only two voyages out from Europe, punctuated by two and a half years tramping in the Pacific. *Monkbarns*'s last voyage began in 1923, and took her to Australia and Chile. In 1926 she sailed from Valparaiso for London, and became the last British full-rigger to round Cape Horn. The voyage was interrupted by a stop at Rio de Janeiro, where Captain William Davies was hospitalized; he died the next day. The ship was saluted on her return to Gravesend on July 10, for many knew she would be the last London-owned limejuicer to enter the Thames. She was sold to the Norwegian whaling firm of Brun & Van der Lippe of Tonsberg in 1927. She ended her days as a coal hulk for the Ballenera Española at Corcubion, Spain.

Course, *Wheel's Kick and the Wind's Song.* Naylon, "Full-Rigged Ship *Monkbarns.*"

USS MONONGAHELA

Sloop of war (1f/3m). *L/B/D:* 225′ bp × 38′ × 15.1′ (68.6m × 11.6m × 4.6m). *Tons:* 2,078 disp. *Hull:* wood. *Comp.:* 176. *Arm.:* 1 × 200pdr, 2 × 11″, 2 × 24pdr, 4 × 12pdr. *Mach.:* horizontal back-acting engines, 532 ihp, 1 screw; 12 kts. *Built:* Merrick & Sons, Philadelphia; 1863.

Commissioned in 1863 with a barkentine rig, the auxiliary screw sloop USS *Monongahela* was named for the Pennsylvania tributary of the Ohio River. After service in the North Atlantic and with Flag Officer David G. Farragut's West Gulf Blockading Squadron off Mobile, Alabama, in March 1863 she began duty on the Mississippi River, when she attempted to run past Fort Hudson. In October, she sailed for the Texas coast and took part in the capture of Brazos Santiago and Brownsville at the beginning of November. In the spring of 1864, she resumed blockade duty off Mobile. On August 4, she sailed with Farragut's fleet at the Battle of Mobile Bay. After running past Fort Morgan, she was the first ship to ram CSS TENNESSEE, though she did more damage to herself than to the Confederate ironclad.

Monongahela remained with the West Gulf Squadron through the end of the Civil War, after which she was assigned to the West Indies Squadron. On November 18, 1867, while lying off Frederiksted, St. Croix, she was

An illustration of the eight-gun sloop of war USS MONONGAHELA *as originally constructed, with three pivot guns and no bowsprit. She was rerigged and rearmed in 1865. Courtesy U.S. Naval Historical Center, Washington, D.C.*

swept a mile and a half inland on a tsunami. The ship was refloated four months later and towed to New York for repairs. In 1873, she sailed for a three-year tour of duty on the South Atlantic Squadron. After duty as a training ship, she sailed for the West Coast and converted to an engineless, bark-rigged supply ship in 1883. Seven years later she returned to the East Coast, where she was converted to a full-rigged training ship. *Monongahela* ended her days as a storeship at Guantánamo Bay, Cuba, from 1904 until her destruction by fire in 1908.

Silverstone, *Warships of the Civil War Navies.* U.S. Navy, *DANFS.*

MONT BLANC

Freighter. *L/B/D:* 320′ × 44.8′ × 15.3′ (97.5m × 13.7m × 4.7m). *Tons:* 3,121 grt. *Hull:* steel. *Mach.:* triple expansion, 1 screw, 247 nhp; 7.5 kts. *Built:* Sir Raylton Dixon & Co., Middlesborough, Eng.; 1899.

First owned by the firm of E. Anquteil, Rouen, in 1915, the freighter *Mont Blanc* was purchased by the Compagnie Générale Transatlantique (CGT), which had lost many ships to the German U-boat campaign. Normally used to carry general war supplies between North America and Europe, on November 25, 1917, *Mont Blanc* began loading a cargo of explosives. This included 2,300 tons of picric acid, 200 tons of TNT, 10 tons of gun cotton, and as a deck cargo, 35 tons of benzole, a type of gasoline. As his ship was too slow to sail in convoy from New York, on December 1, Captain Aimé Le Medec was ordered to take *Mont Blanc* to Halifax where she was

either to join a slower convoy or proceed independently to France.

At 0730 on December 6, *Mont Blanc* entered Halifax Harbour under command of Pilot Francis Mackay. At the same time, the Norwegian tramp steamer *Imo* (formerly the White Star Line's *Runic* but now owned by the South Pacific Whaling Company and the Belgian Relief Commission) was outward bound from Halifax to New York in ballast under Pilot William Hayes. Forced to get out of the way of another incoming tramp, *Imo* was slightly out of her channel and probably going a little faster than she ought to have been when she made visual contact with *Mont Blanc* at a distance of about three-quarters of a mile. *Imo* was on an intercepting course, so Mackay brought his ship closer to the Dartmouth shore and reduced speed to dead slow, and a minute or two later gave the order to stop engines. When *Imo* refused to get out of the way, Mackay tried to change his course to pass starboard to starboard with *Imo,* but it was too late, and at 0845, *Imo's* bow tore a hole in the starboard side of *Mont Blanc's* hull.

The benzole caught fire immediately and as there was no fire-fighting equipment aboard the ship, Le Medec's crew could do nothing to stop the fire — even scuttling would have taken too long. Fully aware of the danger to themselves, the crew abandoned ship and rowed for the far shore leaving *Mont Blanc* in the stream, her blazing deck attracting spectators along the shore as she drifted into Halifax's Pier 6. Almost immediately, sailors from protected cruiser HMS *Highflyer,* training ship *Niobe,* and harbor tug *Stella Maris* attempted to secure a hawser

CHEOPS SHIP

Victor R. Boswell, Jr., copyright National Geographic Society

OLYMPIAS REPLICA

Courtesy Hellenic Navy and the Trireme Trust, photo by Alexandra Guest

USS IOWA

and pull her into the stream. At the same time, a fire alarm was sent out. At 0906, *Mont Blanc* erupted.

The largest manmade explosion ever detonated before the first atomic bomb was dropped on Hiroshima in 1945 annihilated *Mont Blanc*. But the greatest devastation was to the city of Halifax itself. The neighborhood of Richmond was virtually obliterated, and within a sixteen-mile radius of the explosion, 1,630 buildings were destroyed and 12,000 damaged, leaving 25,000 people without adequate shelter, 6,000 of whom had lost their houses entirely. According to the Halifax Relief Commission, 1,963 people were killed (others put the figure at more than 3,200) and 9,000 wounded, not including 199 blinded by glass from imploding windows. The seismic disturbance caused a thirteen-foot tidal wave in the channel that tore ships from their moorings and rang church bells sixty miles away. *Imo,* with both her captain and pilot dead, was hurled across the channel with most of her superstructure ripped away. Initial rescue efforts were hampered by a blizzard that hit the following morning, but contributions for the relief of Halifax poured in from around Canada, the United States, and Britain.

A court of inquiry was convened the next week and held hearings for more than a month. The initial findings put most of the blame on *Mont Blanc*'s pilot and master, who were found "responsible for violating the rules of the road . . . guilty of neglect of the public safety in not taking proper steps to warn the inhabitants of the city of a probable explosion." The court also found that "the regulations governing the traffic in Halifax harbour in force since the war . . . do not satisfactorily deal with the handling of ships laden with explosives." This was confirmed in a series of lawsuits and appeals by the vessels' owners, although the Lords of the Judicial Committee of the Privy Council in London were more critical of *Imo*'s handling and declared themselves "clearly of the opinion that both ships are to blame for their reciprocal neglect."

Four months after the explosion, *Imo* was refloated and towed to New York for repairs. Originally recommisioned as the White Star Line's *Runic* and later named *Tampican,* in 1920 she was put to work as the whale oil tanker *Guvernoren.* On December 3, 1921, she hit a rock off the Falkland Islands and sank.

Kitz, *Shattered City.* Ruffman & Howell, eds., *Ground Zero.*

MORA

Knorr (1m). *Hull:* wood. *Built:* Normandy, France; <1066.

Flagship of one of the most important amphibious invasions in history, *Mora* was a single-masted vessel built in the Viking tradition. A gift from Matilda to her husband, William, Duke of Normandy — which takes its name from the Norse men who settled there — *Mora* was probably a clinker-built knorr intended for transporting men and animals. The best source of information about the shape and rig of William's ships is the Bayeux tapestry, a 70-meter-long, half-meter-wide scroll embroidered by the defeated English. The tapestry recounts the story of the Norman invasion, starting with William's securing an oath of loyalty from Harold (the earl of Wessex who later succeeded Edward the Confessor as king of England), William's preparation for the invasion during the summer of 1066, and the invasion itself.

William assembled a fleet of about 400 large and 1,000 smaller transports, embarking by some estimates 65,000 crew, soldiers, and other personnel, as well as horses and supplies. On September 14, the fleet assembled at the port of St. Valéry-sur-Somme, where they awaited a fair wind for two weeks. On September 27, the Normans sailed 65 miles across the English Channel to land unopposed at Pevensey. At the same time, Harold was defeating an invasion by the Danish Harald Haardraade at Stamford Bridge, in Yorkshire. Marching south again, Harold's exhausted army met the Normans at Hastings (or Senlac) on October 14, 1066. Harold was killed, struck by an arrow in his eye, the Normans defeated the English, and William the Conqueror introduced a host of beneficial reforms that permanently altered the culture of England.

The origin of the ship's name is unknown, and it is found in only one nearly contemporary written account. The same account describes the bow as adorned with a gilt statue of a boy holding a trumpet to his lips in his left hand, with his right hand pointing — towards England. In the tapestry, the boy is found on the stern.

Wilson, *Bayeux Tapestry.*

MORRO CASTLE

Liner (2f/2m). *L/B:* 508′ × 70.8′ (154.8m × 21.6m). *Tons:* 11,520 grt. *Hull:* steel. *Comp.:* 1st 500, 3rd 50. *Mach.:* turboelectric, 2 screws; 21 kts. *Built:* Newport News Shipbuilding & Dry Dock Co., Newport News, Va.; 1930.

A well-found, luxurious, and thoroughly modern ship, *Morro Castle* was the scene of one of the U.S. merchant marine's most inexplicable and tragic disasters. Built for the Ward Line's run between New York and Havana and named for the fortress that guards the approach to Havana Bay, the ship had a varied cruise itinerary that included stops in Nassau and Miami as well. On the eve-

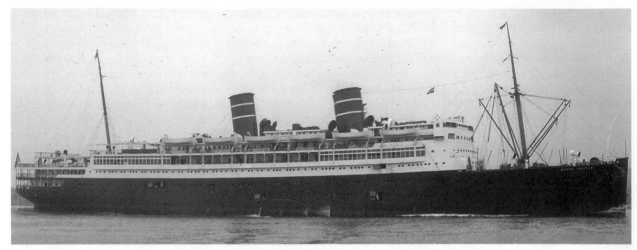

The ill-fated steamer MORRO CASTLE *was typical of the smaller passenger ships built in the interwar period. Courtesy The Mariners' Museum, Newport News, Virginia.*

ning of September 9, 1935, en route from Havana to New York, Captain Robert Wilmott suffered a heart attack in his bathtub and died; command of the ship passed to First Officer William Warms. At about 0245, a fire was found in a closet by the writing room on the promenade deck. The flames spread quickly, but although Warms attempted to maneuver the ship to lessen the effect of the wind, he refused to send out an SOS — to save the company the expense of a salvage fee. Acting on his own initiative, the radio officer sent out one distress call at 0324. Seven minutes later, the ship lost all power and crew began lowering lifeboats, for themselves; of the first 98 to reach shore (the ship was just off Atlantic City, New Jersey), only six were passengers. Those left behind began to leap from the burning ship at about dawn; 71 people were taken aboard *Monarch of Bermuda,* 21 aboard *Andrea S. Luckenbach,* 65 aboard *City of Savannah,* and 67 aboard *Paramount,* a local fishing boat. A total of 137 passengers and crew died. In an effort to shake the negative publicity, the Ward Line was renamed the Cuba Mail Line. Congressional hearings following the wake of the disaster led to the adoption of more stringent safety regulations in U.S.-flag ships, and to U.S. acceptance of the International Convention for the Safety of Life at Sea (SOLAS), first convened in 1914.

Burton, *"Morro Castle."*

MOSHULU

(ex-*Dreadnought, Kurt*) Bark (4m). *L/B/D:* 335.3′ bp × 46.8′ × 26′ (102.1m × 14.3m × 7.9m dph). *Tons:* 3,116 grt. *Hull:* steel. *Comp.:* 33. *Built:* William Hamilton & Co., Port Glasgow, Scotland; 1904.

The second-largest merchant sailing ships built in Britain (only KØBENHAVN was bigger), the sister ships *Kurt* and *Hans* were built for the Hamburg firm of G. J. H. Siemers & Company. *Kurt* spent ten years in the nitrate trade between Germany and Chile, with two passages to Australia and Santa Rosalia, Mexico. In August 1914 she was ordered to Portland, Oregon, for grain; but Siemers decided to keep her there for the duration of World War I. In 1917, she was requisitioned by the U.S. Shipping Board, renamed *Dreadnought* and then *Moshulu,* and put in service to Australia and the Philippines. After the war she was acquired by Charles Nelson Company of San Francisco and entered the lumber trade. She was laid up on Puget Sound from 1928 to 1935, when Gustaf Erikson bought her for the Australian grain trade as a replacement for GRACE HARWAR.

After fitting out, *Moshulu* sailed for Port Victoria, returning to Queenstown in 112 days. After one roundtrip voyage from Åland to Australia, in 1937 she loaded lumber for Lourenço Marques (now Maputo), Mozambique, before sailing for Port Victoria and then home. In the last of the celebrated grain races, *Moshulu* sailed from Port Lincoln to Queenstown in 91 days (March 2 to June 28, 1939), the best time of the thirteen ships that sailed that year. Flying the still neutral Finnish flag, in October 1939 *Moshulu* sailed for Buenos Aires for grain. Upon her arrival in Norway in May 1940, she was rigged down at Horten, and thereafter used as a floating granary around

Scandinavia until 1970. (A plan to fit her out for sail training in consort with PAMIR and PASSAT in 1952 came to nothing.) In 1970 she was bought by Specialty Restaurants of Los Angeles, and after receiving new masts in Amsterdam was towed first to New York and then to Philadelphia. In 1989, she was damaged by fire. After repairs at Camden, New Jersey, she opened as a floating restaurant in Philadelphia.

Colton, *Windjammers Significant.* Newby, *Last Grain Race.*

MÖWE

(ex-*Pungo,* later *Ostsee, Greenbrier, Oldenburg*) Commerce raider (1f/2m). *L/B/D:* 408.4′ × 47.2′ × 22.3′ (124.5m × 14.4m × 6.8m). *Tons:* 4,788 grt. *Hull:* steel. *Comp.:* 235. *Arm.:* 4 × 6″, 1 × 10.5cm; 2 × 20″TT. *Mach.:* triple expansion, 3,200 ihp, 1 screw; 14 kts. *Built:* J. C. Tecklenborg, Geestemünde, Germany; 1914.

The most successful German commerce raider of World War I was one of two ships built by F. Laeisz specifically for the banana trade between the German colony of Cameroons and Germany. Shortly after her launch, though, *Pungo* was leased to the German Navy and fitted out for wartime duty as *Möwe* (seagull). Under Commander Nikolaus Graf Burggraf zu Dohna-Schlodien, she left Kiel in December 1915 and on January 1, 1916, laid mines in the western approaches to the Pentland Firth. Five days later, one of these mines accounted for the loss of battleship HMS KING EDWARD VII. More mines were sowed off La Rochelle before *Möwe* began taking prizes. The first three were seized on January 11 about 150 miles west of Cape Finisterre; two more were taken on the 15th, and a sixth the following day. Only one, liner *Appam,* was spared sinking, and sent to a U.S. port with captives. On January 27 a squall barely allowed *Möwe* to escape from cruiser HMS *Glasgow.* By February, Dohna-Schlodien decided to make for home, and *Möwe* returned to Kiel on March 4, with 14 ships to her credit.

Already the most successful of the German cruisers, she was renamed *Vineta* and undertook three short cruises in the Baltic during which she sank one ship. Renamed *Möwe* once again, she left Wilhelmshaven for the Atlantic on November 22, one week before WOLF and a month before SEEADLER. Her second cruise was even more successful than the first, and accounted for a fur-

ther 25 ships, including one that was sailed home under a prize crew. *Möwe* finally returned to Kiel on March 22, 1917. All told, she had taken 41 ships — 36 British, 3 French, 1 Norwegian, and 1 Japanese, and her mines had accounted for several more.

Withdrawn from raiding work, *Möwe* ended the war as the minelayer *Ostsee.* In 1920 she became the Elders & Fyffes Company's *Greenbrier.* Sold to the Deutsche Seeverkehrs AG in 1933, and renamed *Oldenburg,* she almost survived World War II. She was finally sunk by British planes in Søgnefjord on April 7, 1945, in position 61°12′N, 5°50′E. She was raised and broken up in 1953.

Hoyt, *Phantom Raider.* Rohrbach et al., *Century and a Quarter of Reederei F. Laeisz.* Walter, *Kaiser's Pirates.*

MUSASHI

*Yamato-*class battleship. *L/B/D:* 862.6′ × 127.6′ × 34.1′ (263m × 38.9m × 10.4m). *Tons:* 72,809 disp. *Hull:* steel. *Comp.:* 2,500. *Arm.:* 9 × 18.4″ (3 × 3), 12 × 6.2″, 12 × 5.1″, 24 × 25mm. *Armor:* 16.4″ belt, 9.2″ deck. *Mach.:* geared turbines, 150,000 shp, 4 screws; 27 kts. *Des.:* Hiraga Yuzuru and Fukuda Keiji. *Built:* Mitsubishi Zosen Kaisha, Nagasaki, Japan; 1942.

Named for a province in east central Honshu, *Musashi* was the second *Yamato-*class battleship commissioned by the Japanese Imperial Navy. She saw relatively little action during World War II, but served as the flagship of Admiral Mineichi Koga when he succeeded Admiral Isoroku Yamamoto as commander in chief of the Combined Fleet in 1943. On March 29, 1944, *Musashi* was torpedoed off Palau Island by the submarine USS *Tunny* and returned to Kure for repairs. At the Battle of Leyte Gulf — Japan's effort to disrupt the American landings in the Philippines — YAMATO and *Musashi* formed the core of Vice Admiral Takeo Kurita's Force A. While crossing the Sibuyan Sea in the central Philippines on October 24, 1944, Force A was intercepted by aircraft from Vice Admiral Marc A. Mitscher's Task Force 58, including carriers USS INTREPID, ESSEX, and ENTERPRISE. Hit by 20 aerial torpedoes and 17 bombs, plus 16 near misses, *Musashi* sank in position 12°50′N, 122°35′E, with the loss of 1,039 men, including Captain Toshihei Inoguchi.

Breyer, *Battleships and Battlecruisers.* Grove, *Sea Battles in Close Up.* Morison, *Two-Ocean War.*

N

NADEZHDA

Ship (3m). *Tons:* 450 bm. *Hull:* wood. *Comp.:* 85. *Built:* England; <1803.

Although the Russian-American Company first established a presence in the Alaskan fur trade in 1799, because of the inadequacy of Russia's maritime industry, all supplies had to be shipped overland across Siberia and then across the North Pacific from Petropavlovsk, with pelts returning the same way. The one-way journey could often take as long as two years. The English-trained Russian naval officer Lieutenant J. A. von Krusenstern had long agitated for the opening of a sea route to Alaska, and in 1803 he was given command of the English-built ships *Nadezhda* ("Hope") and *Neva* (named for the St. Petersburg river) to carry supplies to the North Pacific. His crew included Lieutenant Baron von Bellingshausen and Cadet Otto von Kotzebue, who would go on to lead their own expeditions in VOSTOK and RURIK, respectively. Before he left, his mission was expanded to include the delivery of the first Russian embassy to the Japanese court. The mission was further elaborated by the addition of an astronomer and two naturalists to the ship's company.

On August 7, 1803, the ships sailed via Copenhagen for Falmouth where they took on last-minute supplies. En route from the Canary Islands to St. Catherine's, Krusenstern recorded:

> On the 26th November, we crossed the equator at about eleven in the morning in 24° 20′ W. longitude, after a passage of thirty days from Santa Cruz. Under a salute of eleven guns we drank the health of the Emperor, in whose glorious reign the Russian flag first waved in the southern hemisphere. The usual farce with Neptune could not well be represented, as there was nobody on board the ship, except myself, who had crossed the equator.

After calling at St. Catherine's, where they replaced *Neva*'s rotten fore and mainmasts, the ships rounded Cape Horn and entered the Pacific in late February. Because of the delays, Krusenstern was forced to abandon his exploration of the South Seas and proceed as quickly as possible for Kamchatka. The ships were separated, and *Neva*, under Yuri Lisianski, called briefly at Easter Island before rendezvousing at Nuku Hiva, in the Marquesas Islands, in early April. From there they headed to Hawaii where they split up, *Neva* heading for the Russian factory at Kodiak and *Nadezhda* proceeding to Petropavlovsk on the Kamchatka Peninsula. *Nadezhda* spent July 2 to August 27 offloading supplies at Petropavlovsk, and repairing and reprovisioning the ship.

The second phase of the voyage, the delivery of the Russian embassy to Japan, was a diplomatic fiasco. After weathering a typhoon nearly within sight of Japan, *Nadezhda* put into Nagasaki on September 26. Although it was the Japanese who had first suggested the establishment of more formal relations with Russia ten years before, much had changed in the interval. The ship's crew and diplomatic staff alike were kept at arm's length by petty officials for five months, at the end of which the Emperor declined not only to receive the emissaries but even to receive the gifts from Emperor Alexander I.

On April 5, 1805, *Nadezhda* sailed round Kyushu Island and proceeded up the Sea of Japan to further the hydrographic research conducted by Jean-François Galaup de La Pérouse aboard ASTROLABE and BOUSSOLE in 1787. Sailing through La Pérouse Strait, the ship skirted the eastern edge of Sakhalin Island (which Krusenstern still took to be a peninsula), before crossing the Sea of Okhotsk and rounding up to Petropavlovsk on June 5. Here the emissary and his retinue left the ship to make their way overland to St. Petersburg, and on June 23 *Nadezhda* sailed again for further exploration of the Sea of Okhotsk and Sakhalin.

Returning to Petropavlovsk for the last time on August 19, the ship was prepared for the return to Europe, and on September 23, *Nadezhda* sailed. Her first port of call was Canton, on November 6, two days before *Neva*'s arrival with a cargo of furs from the Russian settlements at Kodiak and Novo Arkhangelsk (Sitka). After considerable delays only terminated through the intervention of the English commercial representative in Canton, *Nadezhda* and *Neva* sailed on February 9, 1806, passing through the Straits of Sunda. Midway across the Indian Ocean, on April 3, they were separated by a fog and proceeded independently for home. Alerted to the renewed hostilities between France and Russia, Krusenstern sailed west and north of the British Isles and in late July called at Copenhagen. *Nadezhda* finally dropped anchor at St. Petersburg on August 7, 1806, after a voyage of three years, twelve days, during which not a single man of the ship's company died.

Ivashintsov, *Russian Round-the-World Voyages.* Krusenstern, *Journey round the World.*

Nantucket Lightship

(LV-117) (1f/2m) *L/B/D:* 133.3′ × 30′ × 13′ (40.6m × 9.1m × 4m). *Tons:* 630 disp. *Hull:* steel. *Comp.:* 11. *Mach.:* diesel-electric, 350 shp, 1 screws; 10 kts. *Built:* Charleston Drydock & Machine Co., Charleston, S.C.; 1930.

From 1854 to 1983, a glimpse of the Nantucket Shoals lightship from a ship bound from Europe to New York was the first indication that land was near. Known officially as Nantucket New South Shoal from 1854 to 1896, the station was commonly referred to as South Shoal. Twelve different vessels marked the southern extremity of the shoals lying east and south of Nantucket Island, one of the most exposed lightship stations in the world. The most ill-starred of these was the eighth, LV-117, assigned to the station (in 40°37′N, 69°37′W) in 1931. On June 27, 1933, her anchor chain parted in a gale and despite all efforts to maintain the station under power, she was blown 32 miles downwind before the weather moderated. Six months later, on January 6, 1934, she was sideswiped in a heavy fog by the liner SS *Washington,* though without serious damage to either ship. LV-117's luck ran out at 1006, on May 15, 1934, when the Cunard-White Star liner Olympic rammed the Nantucket lightship in a dense fog. Four of the eleven crew were killed instantly, and three more died of exposure or injuries after their rescue by *Olympic*'s crew. South Shoal was the last of the lightship stations maintained by the U.S. Coast Guard. As of 1996 three of the ships that served the station at one time or another were still extant: LV-112, the replacement for LV-117, paid for by the British government in 1936; WLV-612, built for the San Francisco station in 1950; and WLV-613, built for the Ambrose Channel station in 1952.

Flint, *Lightships of the U.S. Government.*

Narcissus

(later *Isis*) Ship (3m). *L/B/D:* 235′ × 37.1′ × 22′ (71.6m × 11.3m × 6.7m). *Tons:* 1,336 grt. *Hull:* iron. *Built:* Robert Duncan & Co., Port Glasgow, Scotland; 1876.

Narcissus was built to order for Robert R. Paterson Company, Greenock, for general trade. In 1884, after a passage from Penarth to Bombay, seven of the crew left the ship. Among their replacements were Joseph Conrad, a Polish seaman who signed on as second mate, and Joseph Barron, an American black from Charlton County, Georgia. The ship left Bombay on June 3, 1884, bound for Dunkirk. On September 24, 1884, just two weeks from the French port, Barron died. The story of his illness and death formed the core of Conrad's triumphant novel *The Nigger of the Narcissus,* first published in 1898. (*Narcissus* was the only one of the nineteen ships Conrad sailed in whose real name he used in his fiction.) Conrad and the rest of the crew paid off the day after the ship arrived at Dunkirk. Two years later *Narcissus* was bought by C. S. Caird, under whose flag she traded another thirteen years. In 1899, she was sold to Captain Vittorio Bertoletto di Lazzaro of Camogli, Italy. Condemned and hulked at Genoa in 1907, *Narcissus* was given a new lease on life when in 1916 she was sold to P. Passos of Rio de Janeiro. Rigged as a bark and renamed *Isis,* she sailed between the United States and Brazil. Sunk in a collision in 1922, she was sold to E. G. Fontes & Company and continued sailing for three more years, when she was finally scrapped, having outlived Conrad by one year.

Allen, *Sea Years of Joseph Conrad.*

CSS Nashville

(later *Thomas L. Bragg,* CSS *Rattlesnake*) Commerce raider (1f/2m). *L/B/D:* 215.5′ × 34.5′ × 21.9′ dph (65.7m × 10.5m × 6.7m). *Tons:* 1,221 tons. *Hull:* wood. *Comp.:* 40. *Arm.:* 2 × 12pdr. *Mach.:* side-lever engine, sidewheels. *Built:* Thomas Collyer, New York; 1853.

The steamship *Nashville* was built for general service between New York and Charleston, South Carolina. On April 12, 1861, she entered the latter port at the end of her last peacetime passage. As she did so, she was fired upon by USS Harriet Lane, which had come to the relief of Fort Sumter. Seized, and commissioned as a commerce raider in October, CSS *Nashville* sank the clipper *Harvey Birch* before putting into Southampton for repairs on November 21, 1861, the first Confederate warship in European waters. Successfully eluding USS *Tuscarora* at Southampton, *Nashville* returned to Beaufort,

North Carolina, on February 28, 1862, having captured the schooner *Robert Gilfillan.* Escaping Beaufort, on March 17, 1862, she was sold for use as a blockade-runner, renamed *Thomas L. Bragg,* and ran between South Carolina and the Bahamas before being blockaded in Warsaw Sound, Georgia, for eight months. Recommissioned as the privateer CSS *Rattlesnake,* on February 28, 1863, she was destroyed in the Ogeechee River by the monitor USS *Montauk* as she tried to run the blockade.

Chance, et al., *Tangled Machinery and Charred Relics.*

NATCHEZ

Ship (3m). *L/B/D:* 130.3′ × 29.8′ × 14.8′ (39.7m × 9.1m × 4.5m). *Tons:* 514 om. *Hull:* wood. *Built:* Webb & Allen, New York; 1831.

Natchez was designed for trade between New Orleans and New York and as such was built with a flat floor to enable her to cross the shallow bar at the mouth of the Mississippi River. Far from reducing her sailing qualities, as such a hull form was expected to do, *Natchez* and her sisters proved fast ships. In addition to the New York–New Orleans trade (in which she regularly made twelve-day passages), *Natchez* also sailed farther afield, to Le Havre in 1835, and to Valparaiso in 1840. Originally owned by a consortium of New York and New Orleans merchants, she was later purchased by Howland & Aspinwall, who put her under command of Captain Robert H. Waterman, a hard-driving veteran of the transatlantic packet trade.

In 1842, *Natchez* entered the China trade. On her first trip out, she crossed the Pacific from Mazatlán to Canton in a brisk 41 days and returned from Canton in 92 days, two days off the record as it then stood. In 1844, she made the same run in 94 days. On her next voyage, the fourteen-year-old packet romped home from Canton to New York in the phenomenal time of 78 days — January 14 to April 3, 1845 — a feat that made the ship, Waterman, and Howland & Aspinwall world famous. On the strength of this voyage, Howland & Aspinwall ordered SEA WITCH expressly for Waterman's command; she was the only ship that ever bettered *Natchez*'s Canton–New York record, in 1849.

The veteran packet made two more China voyages, one under Waterman and one under Captain Land. In 1850, she sailed for San Francisco in a sluggish time of 150 days. The next year she was sold to S. Thomas & Company of New Bedford and entered the Pacific whaling trade. On her first voyage, under Worthen Hall, she cruised the North Pacific from October 1851 until April 1855. On her second voyage, under Dexter Bellows, she sent home 535 barrels of oil and 6,500 pounds of whale bone before being wrecked in Potter's Bay, Sea of Okhotsk, on October 7, 1856.

Albion, *Square-Riggers on Schedule.* Cutler, *Greyhounds of the Sea.* Howe & Matthews, *American Clipper Ships.* Starbuck, *History of the American Whale Fisheries.*

NATCHEZ

Sidewheel steamer (4f/2m). *L/B/D:* 301′ × 42.6′ × 9.8′ dph (91.7m × 13m × 3m). *Tons:* 1,547 grt. *Hull:* wood. *Comp.:* 125+. *Mach.:* high-pressure engines, sidewheels. *Des.:* Saunders Hartshorn. *Built:* Cincinnati Marine Ways, Cincinnati, Ohio; 1869.

Between 1846 and 1889, Captain Thomas P. Leathers owned seven steamboats named *Natchez.* The sixth of these, the first built after the Civil War, designed for speed and carrying capacity, was an ungainly looking boat, and on her maiden arrival in Natchez, a journalist wrote, "She lay looped up over against the shore like a sick mule to a board fence." She soon developed a reputation for speed and in 1870 steamed the 1,039 miles from New Orleans to St. Louis in 92 hours, 57 minutes — 1 hour, 12 minutes faster than the record set by *J. M. White* in 1844.

One of the best known and bitterest rivalries on the river at the time was between Leathers and Captain John W. Cannon, master of the fast steamer ROB'T. E. LEE. The two vessels ran on the cotton route between Vicksburg and New Orleans, but generally sailed on different days so that comparisons between them were difficult. However, shortly after her record St. Louis run, the two vessels began loading at New Orleans for departure to St. Louis on the same day. Though their captains denied any intention of racing, their preparations were the talk of the river, and government inspectors fixed seals on the safety valves to discourage tampering. Nominally bound for Louisville, the *Lee* departed St. Mary's Market at about 1648, and the *Natchez,* bound for St. Louis, was away 3 minutes, 15 seconds later. Both steamboats loaded coal or pine knots from barges lashed alongside as they continued upriver, but *Natchez* landed at various ports along the way to embark or offload passengers. About an hour north of Vicksburg, *Natchez* was also forced to land to repair a cold-water pump, which took another half hour, but thereafter she gained on her opponent. North of Cairo she entered a heavy fog that enshrouded her for several hours and in the end arrived at St. Louis 6 hours, 33 minutes behind *Lee*'s new record of 3 days, 18 hours, 14 minutes. Although neither boat carried any cargo, and *Natchez* had about ninety passengers aboard, plus her crew, Leathers made few concessions to racing, and it is estimated that he lost a total of 7 hours in stops for passengers. As a result, supporters of the *Natchez* still consider the race an inconclusive test of the two boats' comparative speed.

Natchez remained in service until the end of the decade, and in 1874 she carried a record 5,511 bales of cotton to New Orleans. She was dismantled at Cincinnati in 1879 and her hull was later used as a wharf boat at Vicksburg.

Barkhau, *Great Steamboat Race.* Way, *Way's Packet Directory.*

USS NAUTILUS

Schooner (2m). *L/B/D:* 76.5′ × 23.7′ × 9.8′ dph (23.3m × 7.2m × 3m). *Tons:* 185 disp. *Hull:* wood. *Comp.:* 103. *Arm.:* 12 × 6pdr. *Built:* Henry Spencer, Eastern Shore, Md.; 1799.

Built as a merchant schooner and purchased by the U.S. Navy in 1803, USS *Nautilus*'s first assignment was with the Mediterranean Squadron, then close to war with the corsairs of Algiers, Tunis, and Tripoli. Following the capture of USS PHILADELPHIA in September 1803, *Nautilus* sailed on blockade between Tripoli and Tunis through 1805, using bases at Messina, Syracuse, Malta, and Leghorn (Livorno) for repairs and reprovisioning. In August and September 1804, she took part in attacks on Tripoli, and between April 27 and May 17, 1805, helped in the capture of Derna by the forces of Hamet Caramanli, the Bashaw of Tripoli. The war ended in June of that year and *Nautilus* remained on station until 1806. Laid up at Washington, she reentered service along the East Coast from 1808 to 1810. She was then rerigged as a brig and given a battery of twelve 18-pdr. short-range carronades before joining Commodore Stephen Decatur's squadron. Shortly after the start of the War of 1812, *Nautilus* sailed from New York, and on July 17, 1812, she was captured by an overwhelming British force consisting of HMS *Africa* (64 guns), *Shannon* (38), and *Aeolus* (32). It is believed that she was taken into service by the Royal Navy, but her subsequent fate is unknown.

U.S. Navy, *DANFS.*

NAUTILUS

Submersible (1m). *L/B:* 21.3′ × 6.4′ (6.5m × 2m). *Hull:* wood, copper, iron. *Comp.:* 4. *Arm.:* torpedo (mine). *Mach.:* hand crank, screw. *Des.:* Robert Fulton. *Built:* J. C. Périer, Paris; 1801.

Although Robert Fulton is best remembered for his development of the NORTH RIVER STEAM BOAT in the United States, he first gained international attention with his experiments in submarines. When he began developing his ideas for a submarine is unclear, but on December 13, 1797, he submitted to France's Executive Directory a proposal for a system of submarine warfare. This in-

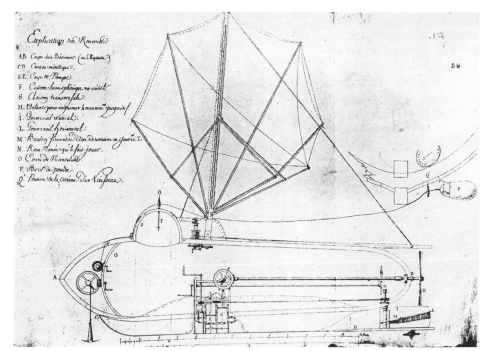

Robert Fulton's original plan for the submarine NAUTILUS *shows the metal bottom (CD), conning tower dome (F) and auger (O), transverse bulkhead (G) with cranks to control the anchor and powder keg (P), propeller (M), vertical (I) and horizontal (L) rudders, the means of attaching the powder keg to a ship's hull (P & Q), and a collapsible mast and sail for operating on the surface. Subsequent modifications included the addition of compressed air tanks and a porthole. Courtesy The Mariners' Museum, Newport News, Virginia.*

cluded a rate schedule for the destruction of English ships: "4000 Livers [livres] per Gun for each British ship over 40 Guns . . . and 2000 Livers per Gun for All vessels of war under 40 tons [*sic*]." In many respects, *Nautilus* resembled the submarines developed a hundred years later. The hydrodynamic hull was a cylinder with a pointed bow and slightly tapered stern. A conning tower doubled as a hatch, there was a periscope, and thin tubes could be used to admit air when the vessel was just below the surface. As originally designed, the oxygen supply was sufficient for four men to remain submerged with two candles burning for three hours. In 1802, Fulton tried experiments with a compressed air canister, and to do away with the need for candles, he inserted a three-quarter-inch glass porthole that admitted enough light to read a watch at a depth of 25 feet. Diving and surfacing was regulated by water in ballast tanks, admitted by valves and expelled with compressed air. Propelled by a hand crank attached to a single, four-bladed propeller, *Nautilus* traveled at two knots. The submarine was steered by means of a vertical rudder and a forward horizontal diving plane. When surfaced, she had an auxiliary sail that could be collapsed on deck.

Fulton's original design had an auger sticking up through the conning tower. This was to have drilled a hole in the hull of a ship, to which an explosive charge would then be fixed. On September 12, 1801, Fulton and three crew departed Le Havre for Cap La Hogue, a distance of 70 miles that *Nautilus* covered in five days. He attempted to close with two English brigs, but both sailed off, though whether by coincidence or because they had seen the curious vessel is unknown. The next year, at Brest, *Nautilus* trailed an explosive charge at a distance of 200 meters which succeeded in destroying a target ship, but the charge could have been set without a submarine. First Consul Napoleon Bonaparte was impressed with the possibilities of such mines, however, and asked if he could see the *Nautilus*. He was informed that Fulton had dismantled it, ostensibly because of rot, but more likely to prevent its design being copied without appropriate compensation.

Fulton eventually made his was to England and managed to interest Prime Minister William Pitt in his ideas, but he never built another submarine. In the optimistic belief that his device would bring an end to naval warfare, Fulton referred to his submarine as "A Curious Machine for Mending Politics." Contemporary French and British naval officers deemed Fulton's devices inappropriately destructive. In the long run, neither view prevailed.

Philip, *Robert Fulton.*

NAUTILUS

(ex-*O-12*) *O*-class submarine. *L/B/D:* 175′ × 16.5′ × 14′ (53.3m × 5m × 4.3m). *Tons:* 491/566 disp. *Hull:* steel. *Comp.:* 29. *Mach.:* 14/11 kts. *Built:* Lake Torpedo Boat Co., Bridgeport, Conn.; 1918.

One of sixteen *O*-class submarines commissioned by the U.S. Navy during World War I, *O-12* was originally armed with four 18-inch torpedo tubes and a 3-inch deck gun. She spent six years with submarine Division 1 based at Coco Solo, Panama, before being placed in reserve. Slated to be scrapped under the terms of the London Naval Treaty of 1930, she was given a reprieve when Australian polar explorer Captain George Hubert Wilkins secured her for an attempt to travel under the ice cap to the North Pole. Modifications included sealing the torpedo tubes and reinforcing the bow, fitting the conning with an augur to drill through the ice, and attaching a wooden "sled deck" to the hull to enable the submarine to glide along the underside of the ice.

After fitting out at New York, the submarine was christened *Nautilus,* in honor of the submarine of the same name in Jules Verne's novel *Twenty Thousand Leagues under the Sea.* On July 4, 1931, *Nautilus* sailed from New York for Spitsbergen where, after considerable engine problems, she arrived in August. She sailed again on August 19 and on September 1 disappeared under the ice, sailing to within 500 miles of the Pole. Much of the equipment designed for the voyage didn't work and some was badly maintained; crew members reluctant to travel beneath the ice sabotaged the diving planes. Nonetheless, scientists aboard the submarine conducted valuable underwater surveys between Greenland and Norway. No other submarine sailed beneath the ice until the nuclear-powered USS NAUTILUS reached the North Pole in 1955. At the end of the expedition, Wilkins's *Nautilus* was sunk in Bergenfjord in accord with the disarmament treaty.

Cross, *Challengers of the Deep.* Wilkins, *Under the North Pole.*

USS NAUTILUS (SSN-571)

Nautilus-class submarine. *L/B/D:* 323.8′ × 27.7′ × 22′ (98.7m × 8.4m × 6.7m). *Tons:* 3,533/4,092 disp. *Hull:* steel; 700′dd. *Comp.:* 116. *Arm.:* 6 × 21″TT. *Mach.:* nuclear reactor, steam turbine, 13,200shp, 2 screws; 23 kts. *Built:* Electric Boat Co., Groton, Conn.; 1955.

The brainchild of Hyman G. Rickover, who eventually rose to the rank of admiral, USS *Nautilus* was the world's first nuclear-powered submarine and the first vessel of any description to cross the North Pole — 90°N. A veteran of the Bureau of Ships, Rickover first considered

The nuclear-powered submarine USS NAUTILUS *surges along the surface during sea trials off the New England coast. By the middle of the 20th century, design and engineering practices were equal to the vision of such 19th-century thinkers as Robert Fulton and Jules Verne. In the summer of 1958,* NAUTILUS *completed a transit of the Northwest Passage while submerged. Courtesy U.S. Naval Historical Center, Washington, D.C.*

nuclear propulsion for ships while on assignment to the Atomic Energy Commission's reactor complex at Oak Ridge, Tennessee, in 1946. Later assigned to head the Bureau of Ships' Nuclear Power Division, and concurrently the Naval Reactors Branch of the Atomic Energy Commission, Rickover quickly developed plans for what became USS *Nautilus,* the fourth vessel of the name. The chief advantage of atomic power over traditional diesel power is that it produces heat to create steam through fission rather than fire; without the need for external sources of air or oxygen, a nuclear-powered submarine can stay submerged almost indefinitely. The space required to store the uranium — *Nautilus* carried about a pound — is much less than that needed for diesel fuel, which means there is more room for weapons and crew.

Laid down by President Harry S. Truman in 1955, the world's first nuclear submarine was launched two years later by First Lady Mamie Eisenhower. On January 17, 1955, under Commander E. P. Wilkinson, USS *Nautilus* cast off her lines from Groton and signaled "under way on nuclear power." On her first voyage, to Puerto Rico, she sailed 1,381 miles in 89.8 hours, the longest submerged distance covered by a submarine to that time, and

achieved the highest underwater speed. By the following year, plans were being developed to send *Nautilus* under the polar ice. In purely military terms, the endurance of nuclear submarines made them ideal candidates to hide beneath the ice in anticipation of a missile attack against the Soviet Union. As a public relations exercise, sending a submarine to the North Pole would confirm American technological superiority. In 1957 *Nautilus* made her first forays under the ice cap under Commander William R. Anderson. Sailing from New London in company with USS *Trigger,* she probed under the ice north of Jan Mayen Island during the first week of September. Just before reaching 86°N, a gyroscope fuse failed and she had to turn back. After participating in NATO war games in the North Atlantic, she returned to duty along the East Coast.

The following spring she was sent to the Pacific in preparation for Operation Sunshine, a top-secret voyage from the Pacific to the Atlantic via the North Pole. Departing Seattle on June 9, 1958, *Nautilus* first attempted to enter the Bering Sea via the western passage running between St. Lawrence Island and Siberia. When that proved too shallow, she doubled back around St. Lawrence Island and headed through the Bering Strait. Just shy of 70°N, *Nautilus* encountered ice more than 60 feet deep, in water that was barely deep enough to allow the sail to pass beneath. Reluctantly, the mission was aborted and the ship returned to Pearl Harbor, still with top-secret clearance.

After a month of shuttling between Washington, New London, Alaska, and Hawaii by key members of the crew, *Nautilus* resumed Operation Sunshine on July 22. By this time, the ice had shifted significantly and *Nautilus* was able to approach the Bering Strait via the western door. Passing the point at which she had been forced to turn back the previous month, *Nautilus* sailed for the deep Barrow Sea Valley and on August 1, laid a course for the Pole. She passed over the top of the world at 1115 EDT, cruising about 400 feet below the surface. Two days later, after 1,830 miles under the ice, *Nautilus* surfaced near Spitsbergen Island and broadcast the message confirming her successful transpolar passage: "Nautilus 90° North." In recognition of this achievement, she became the first ship ever to receive a Presidential Unit Citation in peacetime.

Nautilus's subsequent career included assignment as the first submarine with the Sixth Fleet in the Mediterranean, and she was used extensively in the development of new antisubmarine warfare techniques, the old procedures having been rendered all but obsolete by the advances afforded by nuclear propulsion. In 1962 she took part in the naval blockade during the Cuban Missile Crisis and later she operated with the Second Fleet. During her operational lifetime, *Nautilus* had three nuclear cores that drove her more than 300,000 miles. She was not decommissioned until 1980. Five years later she was opened to the public as part of the Nautilus Memorial and Submarine Force Library and Museum in Groton, Connecticut.

Anderson, *"Nautilus" — 90 North*. U.S. Navy, *DANFS*.

HMS NELSON

Nelson-class battleship (1f/2m). *L/B/D:* 710′ × 106′ × 30′ (216.4m × 32.3m × 9.1m). *Tons:* 38,000 disp. *Hull:* steel. *Comp.:* 1,361. *Arm.:* 9 × 16″ (3 × 3), 12 × 6″, 6 × 4.7″, 8 × 2pdr, 2 × 20mm, 8 × 0.5″; 2 × 24.5″TT. *Armor:* 14″ belt, 6.25″ deck. *Mach.:* geared turbines, 45,000 shp, 2 shafts; 23 kts. *Built:* Sir W. G. Armstrong Co., Ltd., Newcastle-on-Tyne, England; 1927.

Named after Vice Admiral Lord Nelson, the hero of Trafalgar, HMS *Nelson* was built to designs that evolved out of the negotiations at the Washington Naval Conference of 1921. *Nelson* and RODNEY were the most heavily armed British capital ships, mounting 16-inch guns in three triple turrets forward of the bridge tower; 6-inch guns were mounted in double turrets aft. Flagship of the fleet from 1927 to 1941, shortly after the start of World War II, she was damaged by a mine at Loch Ewe on December 4, 1939; she did not rejoin the Home Fleet for nine months. On September 27, 1941, *Nelson* was hit by an aerial torpedo while sailing in support of the Malta Convoy in Operation Halberd and was out of action for another eleven months. In August 1942, she became flagship of Admiral Syfret's Force H — which comprised also *Rodney,* three aircraft carriers, seven cruisers, and thirty-two destroyers — at Gibraltar. As such, she sailed in support of the Malta convoys, the North African landings during Operation Torch in November 1942, and the invasion of Sicily, Operation Husky, in July 1943. On September 29, General Dwight D. Eisenhower and Marshal Pietro Badoglio signed the Italian armistice aboard *Nelson* at Malta.

The following July, she was damaged by a mine in the English Channel and underwent six months of repairs at Philadelphia. On her return to service, she joined the East Indies Fleet for operations against Japanese forces in Malaya, which formally surrendered aboard *Nelson*. Returning to England at the end of 1945, *Nelson* remained as flagship of the Home Fleet in 1946. She was scrapped at Inverkeithing in 1948.

Careless, *Battleship "Nelson."* Raven, *Battleships "Rodney" and "Nelson."*

NEMESIS

Paddle frigate (1f/2m). *L/B/D:* 184′ × 29′ (41′ew) × 6′ (56.1m × 8.8m (12.5m) × 1.8m). *Tons:* 660 bm. *Hull:* wood. *Comp.:* 60–90. *Arm.:* 2 × 32pdr, 4 × 6pdr. *Mach.:* 2 cyl, 120 nhp, sidewheels; 8 kts. *Built:* Cammell Laird & Co., Ltd., Birkenhead, Eng.; 1839.

Although the first iron-hulled steamship, AARON MANBY, was launched in 1821, a number of practical considerations prevented the widespread adoption of iron hulls. The most important of these was overcome in 1839, when Astronomer Royal Sir George Airey determined how to compensate for the effect of iron on the ship's compass. The same year, the Honourable East India Company ordered the paddle gunboat *Nemesis* for service in China. While wooden ships of the same size drew 13 feet, *Nemesis* drew only 6 feet of water fully loaded, which gave her a decided advantage in riverine operations. When under sail, her crew could lower two seven-foot drop keels to improve weatherliness, that is, her ability to sail to windward. Although *Nemesis* carried Airey's compass correctors, these were improperly fitted and on her maiden voyage she ran aground off St. Ives and stove in several iron plates.

In March 1840, *Nemesis* sailed for India under Captain William Hutcheon Hall. (Although never commissioned in the Royal Navy, *Nemesis* was usually under the command of Royal Navy officers.) The first iron steamship to round the Cape of Good Hope, she was forced into Delagoa Bay for repairs to some plates that fractured when the ship broached off South Africa. Continuing on to China, she arrived off the Bogue Forts in November. *Nemesis* played a significant role in the First Opium War and typified the technological advantage that Britain had over the Chinese. In the words of a contemporary British account, she was

> as much admired by our countrymen as dreaded by the Chinese. Well may the latter offer a reward of 50,000 dollars for her, but she will be difficult to take. They call her the devil ship, and say that our shells and rockets could only be invented by the latter. They are more afraid of her than all the Line-of-Battle ships put together.

Nemesis was in the thick of the fighting at the Bogue Forts, Amoy, and Ningpo in 1840 and at Woosung in 1842. Upon her return to Bombay in 1843, it was found that she had suffered much less damage than her wooden counterparts, and Captain Hall's official report to the Admiralty on the ship's performance contributed to their ordering more iron ships. After repairs at Bombay, she began cruising between Bombay, Karachi, and Bassein. She was sold in 1852.

Brown, "*Nemesis*: The First Iron Warship." Hall, *Narrative of the Voyages and Service of the "Nemesis."* Mallard, "Ships of India, 1834–1934."

NEMI SHIPS

About 30 kilometers south of Rome, in the Alban Hills 500 meters above sea level, lies Lake Nemi. According to the Roman historian Suetonius, the emperor Caligula (37–41 CE) built two ships at his imperial villa on the lake, and the memory of the sunken ships lingered in the tradition of the local fishermen. In 1446, the Renaissance Cardinal Don Pospero Colonna, Lord of Nemi, became the first man in modern times to attempt to raise the ships. Others followed until a systematic effort was begun by Eliseo Boghi in 1895. His efforts were so successful that the government intervened to stop his work and assumed direction of the search. It was finally decided to recover the ships by lowering the level of the lake, an effort undertaken between 1929 and 1932. In the words of Lieutenant Commander G. C. Speziale, the project "promised to be both difficult and costly, but very necessary from the point of general culture."

The two ships were found about 200 meters apart, lying at depths of 5 to 12 meters and 15 to 22 meters, respectively. The first galley measured 71.2 meters (239.5 feet) overall, 67.3 meters (220.7 feet) on the waterline and 20 meters in beam (65.6 feet), with a rounded bilge. The end of the stem curved back towards the stern of the ship, while the stern finial was in the shape of a fish tail. In general form, this vessel most closely conformed to what is known of Roman ships of the imperial period. The second galley was more rectangular in shape, measuring 73 meters overall (239.4 feet), 68.9 meters (226 feet) on the waterline, and 14.4 meters (47.2 feet) in beam. Ships of these dimensions were quite remarkable, exceeding by far the size of any known ships prior to the modern period. Tests on models of the two hulls demonstrated that they had low coefficients of friction for low-velocity ships intended to be sailed or rowed. Never intended for sailing on open water, they were lightly constructed, although the hulls were carvel built, with the planks joined edge to edge. To inhibit rot and fouling, the planking was covered by a layer of tar-impregnated wool clad in a thin sheathing of lead.

Among the artifacts found with or near the ships were interior decorations, including a bronze lion, leopard and fox heads originally fitted to the ends of bollards and beams, hinges, and fragments of porphyry, serpentine, mosaics, tesserae, and glass. Technological curiosities were an anchor with movable jaws of a type later developed by Lord Nelson in the eighteenth century, and two types of bearings: the larger, a type of bronze ball bearing, and the smaller, a needle bearing made of wood.

The discovery of so much material intended for ornament — coupled with Caligula's reputation as a libertine — led archaeologists to believe that the ships were intended simply as pleasure yachts. Other theories held that they were used for mock battles (though nothing of a martial character has been found at Nemi), that they were intended for secret naval experiments, and that they were somehow related to the temple of Diana Aricina. (The Romans called the lake Speculum Dianae.) A more recent theory holds that the ships were connected in some way with the mystery cult of Isis to which Caligula was an adherent. According to this explanation, the ships were intentionally sunk after the emperor's assassination as part of a policy to eradicate all memory of his rule.

Removed to shore facilities, the ships were the object of intense scholarly study during the 1930s, when several models of the vessels were made. During World War II, the ships were burned (probably intentionally) on the night of May 31, 1944, during the Allied advance on Rome. By 1996, a group called Dianae Lacus was developing plans to build full-scale replicas of the Nemi ships.

Denham, "Caligula's Galleys." Rubin de Cervin, "Mysteries and Nemesis of the Nemi Ships." Speziale, "The Roman Anchors Found at Nemi"; "Roman Galleys in the Lake of Nemi."

USS NEOSHO

Cimarron-class oiler. *L/B/D:* 553′ × 75′ × 32.3′ (168.6m × 22.9m × 9.9m). *Tons:* 7,470 disp. *Hull:* steel. *Comp.:* 304. *Arm.:* 1 × 5″, 4 × 3″. *Mach.:* geared turbines, 13,500 shp, 2 screws; 18 kts. *Built:* Federal Shipbuilding & Drydock Co., Kearny, N.J.; 1939.

Named for a tributary of the Arkansas River, the fleet oiler USS *Neosho* was the second ship of the name. For the Maritime Commission, she began transporting aviation fuel from the West Coast to the Ford Island Naval Air Station at Pearl Harbor in July 1941. December 7 found her at Pearl Harbor. Commander John S. Phillips fought his ship well throughout the Japanese surprise attack, which was concentrated on Battleship Row, and *Neosho* was credited with shooting down one Japanese plane. Following Pearl Harbor, she was sailed in support of various aircraft carrier task forces. In April she joined Task Force 17, centered on USS YORKTOWN, then marshaling in the Coral Sea to thwart an anticipated invasion of Australia and New Zealand. On May 7, *Neosho* and USS

Sims were detached from the main fleet and bound for Nouméa, New Caledonia, when Japanese reconnaissance planes misidentified the pair as an aircraft carrier and her escort. Attacked by sixty-one planes in three waves, *Sims* was sunk and *Neosho* took direct hits from seven bombs and one dive-bomber that crashed into her. On May 11, the destroyer USS *Henley* took off *Neosho*'s 123 survivors and sank the crippled hulk in 15°35′S, 155°36′E.

U.S. Navy, *DANFS*.

NEPTUNE'S CAR

Clipper (3m). *L/B/D:* 216′ × 40′ × 23.6′ (65.8m × 12.2m × 7.2m). *Tons:* 1,616 om. *Hull:* wood. *Built:* Page & Allen, Portsmouth, Va.; 1853.

One of a very few clippers built outside of New York and New England shipyards, and probably the only large clipper built in Virginia, *Neptune's Car* was built for the New York firm of Foster and Nickerson. Though intended for the Cape Horn trade, her first voyage was a transatlantic run and she did not arrive at San Francisco until February 1854. Returning to New York via Singapore and Calcutta, the ship was put under command of Captain Joshua Patten, who was accompanied by his eighteen-year-old wife, Mary Ann Patten. On her first voyage under his command, *Neptune's Car* was 101 days to San Francisco — arriving within hours of the clipper *Westward Ho,* which had sailed from Boston the day before she cleared Sandy Hook. As was common in the clipper age, *Westward Ho*'s Captain Hussey offered a wager on the outcome of a race between the two ships to Hong Kong. Patten declined, but the ships sailed on the same day and *Neptune's Car* made the passage in fifty days, as against *Westward Ho*'s sixty-one. Loading tea for the London market, *Neptune's Car* returned to New York in 1856.

On July 2, *Neptune's Car* cleared New York for San Francisco, the same day as *Romance of the Seas* and *Intrepid* (on her maiden voyage) on a passage unique in the annals of the Cape Horn trade. Captain Patten was suffering from tuberculosis, and before the ship had even reached the Falkland Islands, he was unconscious with fever. As Patten had arrested his first mate, Keeler, for insubordination, command of *Neptune's Car* fell to the pregnant Mary Patten, the only other person aboard ship who knew navigation. Rounding Cape Horn took six weeks of driving against the prevailing winds, and *Neptune's Car* finally reached San Francisco on November 15, 1856, after a passage of 134 days, three weeks longer than *Romance of the Seas* but eleven days faster than *Intrepid.* Although Captain Patten survived the voyage, he died the

next year. For her crucial role in bringing the ship safely to port, Mary Patten was awarded $1,399 by the insurance company. Her child was born in early 1857, but she herself died of tuberculosis in 1861. She is remembered in the name of the hospital at the U.S. Merchant Marine Academy in Kings Point, New York.

Following her arrival at San Francisco, *Neptune's Car* came under command of Captain Bearse, who had her until 1860, when she came under command of Caleb Sprague. On his only New York–San Francisco voyage, Sprague was forced to arrest a number of the crew for mutiny. He was then forced to put into Callao for repairs, only to have the ship seized by U.S. authorities because she was partially owned by Southern interests. Sold to Barclay & Company of Liverpool, *Neptune's Car* traded under the British flag until at least 1870.

Howe & Matthews, *American Clipper Ships*.

USS NEW IRONSIDES

Ironclad (1f/3m). *L/B/D:* 232′ × 57.5′ × 15.7′ (70.7m × 17.5m × 4.8m). *Tons:* 4,120 disp. *Hull:* wood. *Comp.:* 460. *Arm.:* 2 × 150pdr, 2 × 50pdr, 14 × 11″, 1 × 12pdr, 1 × 12pdr. *Armor:* 4.5″ belt, 1″ deck. *Mach.:* horizontal direct-acting engine, 700 hp, 1 screw; 6 kts. *Des.:* Merrick & Sons. *Built:* William Cramp & Sons Ship and Engine Building Co., Philadelphia; 1862.

Named in honor of USS CONSTITUTION, who earned the nickname "Old Ironsides" during her engagement with HMS GUERRIÈRE, USS *New Ironsides* was one of three ironclads ordered shortly after the start of the Civil War. Modeled on contemporary European designs, she was one of the most powerful ships afloat. Never regarded as sea-kindly, she had a pronounced tumblehome; originally rigged as a ship, her masts were later cut down. *New Ironsides* entered service as flagship of Rear Admiral Samuel du Pont's South Atlantic Blockading Squadron in August 1862. Stationed off Charleston, South Carolina, on April 7 she took part in the bombardment of Forts Moultrie and Sumter; hit 55 times, she suffered no serious damage. Flying the flag of Rear Admiral John A. Dahlgren, *New Ironsides* took part in the bombardment of Morris Island between July and September, receiving 214 hits, again with only negligible effect. Of more serious concern were attacks by spar torpedo boats. *New Ironsides* avoided the first of these on August 21, but on October 5, 1863, she was attacked by CSS DAVID, which managed to detonate a mine on her starboard quarter. The damage was insignificant and *New Ironsides* remained on station until May 1864, when she returned to Philadelphia. Joining the North Atlantic Blockading

Squadron in October, she took part in the bombardment of Fort Fisher, North Carolina, on Christmas Eve and again on January 13–15, 1865, when the fort was finally captured. Decommissioned on April 7, 1865, two days before the Confederate surrender at Appomattox, *New Ironsides* was laid up at League Island, Philadelphia. She was destroyed by fire on December 16, 1866.

Anderson, *By Sea and by River*. Silverstone, *Warships of the Civil War Navies*. U.S. Navy, *DANFS*.

New Orleans

Steamboat (1f/2m). *L/B:* 116′ × 20′ (35.4m × 6.1m). *Hull:* wood. *Mach.:* steam, sidewheels. *Des.:* Robert Fulton. *Built:* Nicholas J. Roosevelt, Pittsburgh, Pa.; 1811.

In 1808, Robert Fulton sent Nicholas J. Roosevelt to Pittsburgh to investigate the prospects for steamboat service on the Ohio and Mississippi Rivers, for the steam navigation of which he and his partner Robert R. Livingston had secured a monopoly. Founder of the first engine works in the United States, Roosevelt had first worked with Livingston in 1797. His favorable report — he descended to New Orleans on a flatboat and returned to New York via sea — resulted in the formation of the Ohio Steam Navigation Company to build *New Orleans,* a boat similar to Fulton's NORTH RIVER STEAM BOAT and thus better suited to the Hudson than to the Mississippi. After trials on the Monongahela River in April 1811, the sidewheel paddle steamer set off down the Ohio with a complement of eight, including Mrs. Roosevelt, who gave birth at Louisville where, to celebrate, Mr. Roosevelt embarked a group of distinguished if disbelieving citizens for a short trip upriver, against the current. Because of the rapids below Louisville, they could not leave until November rains had raised the river enough for the deep draft *New Orleans* to make the passage safely. But no sooner had they left Louisville then the Mississippi and her tributaries were thrown into chaos by the New Madrid earthquake, which made the river unfamiliar to even the most knowledgeable pilots.

At Natchez, an adventurous merchant consigned a load of cotton to the vessel, and on January 12, 1812, *New Orleans* became the first steamboat to call at the port for which she was named. She plied between there and Natchez until July 1814, when she sank near Baton Rouge after hitting a snag. By then, there were already three more steamboats in operation on the river, Fulton's *Vesuvius* and two vessels built by Daniel French — in a direct challenge to the Livingston-Fulton monopoly — *Comet* and Henry Shreve's *Enterprise,* the first sternwheeler. In

1814, there were twenty-one steamboat arrivals recorded at New Orleans; nineteen years later there were 1,200. By 1840, New Orleans was the fourth-busiest port in the world and by the end of the century, more than 4,000 steamboats would be built to serve the Father of Waters.

Carter, *Rivers of America*. Flexner, *Steamboats Come True*.

USS Niagara

Brig. *L/B/D:* 109.8′ × 30′ × 4.7′ dph (33.5m × 9.1m × 1.4m). *Tons:* 493 bm. *Hull:* wood. *Comp.:* 142. *Arm.:* 2 × 12pdr, 18 × 32pdr. *Built:* Adam & Noah Brown, Presque Isle, Pa.; 1813.

USS *Niagara* was one of two sister ships built under the supervision of Master Commandant Oliver Hazard Perry, who was given responsibility for the all but nonexistent Lake Erie fleet during the War of 1812. Chief credit for giving shape to this ad hoc fleet fell to the New York shipbuilders Adam and Noah Brown, who would later have a hand in the building of FULTON STEAM FRIGATE and WALK-IN-THE-WATER, the first Great Lakes steamboat. Noah Brown had been sent to Lake Erie by the Navy Department. Wood was abundant, but skilled labor, naval stores, and guns all had to come overland. Nonetheless, by July 1813 Brown had built the brigs *Niagara* and *Lawrence,* and the schooners *Ariel* and *Ohio,* and had helped in the building or reconstruction of a handful of other vessels. In the words of Howard Chapelle,

> The amount of work that Brown accomplished with about 200 men, without power tools, and in a wilderness during the worst winter months, makes some of the modern [World War II] wartime production feats something less than impressive.

Perry's function was to contain the British advance along the northern frontier from Canada. His fleet was initially blockaded at Presque Isle (now Erie), Pennsylvania, by Captain Robert Barclay, who lifted the blockade on July 30. Three days later, Perry sailed to the western end of Lake Erie where he established a base at Put-in Bay in the Bass Islands north of present-day Sandusky, Ohio. His fleet comprised nine ships: USS *Lawrence, Niagara* (20 guns), *Ariel* (6), *Caledonia* (3), *Somers* (2), *Scorpion, Porcupine, Trippe,* and *Tigress* (1). With his supply lines from Lake Ontario cut, Barclay — a veteran of Trafalgar — was forced to bring the Americans to battle, and on September 10, he sailed from Fort Malden, Ontario, with his fleet of six ships: HMS *Detroit* (20), *Queen Charlotte* (16), *Lady Prevost* (13), *Hunter* (10), *Little Belt* (2), and *Chippewa* (2).

Approaching each other in parallel battle lines — the

engagement was the only traditional fleet action of the war — the two squadrons engaged each other at 1145. Perry's flagship was *Lawrence,* named for his good friend Captain James Lawrence, who had died on June 1 in the battle between USS CHESAPEAKE and HMS *Shannon,* and whose dying words — "Don't give up the ship" — were emblazoned on a pennant flying from the masthead. *Lawrence* took the brunt of the fighting from *Detroit* and *Queen Charlotte,* and by about 1430 had suffered 84 dead and wounded. With 19 of his crew, Perry transferred his flag to *Niagara,* whose captain, Jesse D. Elliott, had kept her out of the fray. Perry immediately sailed through the center of the British line, crossing the "T" and sending raking broadsides the length of Barclay's two biggest ships. Barclay, who had lost an arm in the battle, was forced to strike, thus becoming the first British commander in history to surrender an entire squadron.

That afternoon, Perry wrote to General William Henry Harrison, "We have met the enemy and they are ours. Two Ships, two Brigs one Schooner & one Sloop." The battle at Put-in Bay was a turning point in the War of 1812, for in securing control of Lake Erie, Perry removed the British threat to the Northwest Territory. On September 23, *Niagara* sailed in support of Harrison's attack on Fort Malden, and then covered the Army's recapture of Detroit before going back to Presque Isle for the winter. The following year she captured four British ships on Lake Erie before returning again to her homeport, where she remained as a receiving ship until 1820. The same year her hull was intentionally sunk in Misery Bay, whose cold, fresh water acted as a preservative.

Raised in 1913, she was restored and put on exhibit at various ports along the middle lakes for the Battle of Lake Erie centennial. Kept on permanent exhibit at Erie, she was restored again in 1939 and 1963. A replica of the brig built by Melbourne Smith for the Pennsylvania Historical and Museum Commission was launched in 1988.

Chapelle, *History of the American Sailing Navy.* Roosevelt, *Naval War of 1812.* U.S. Navy, *DANFS.*

NIGHTINGALE

Clipper (3m). *L/B/D:* 185′ od × 36′ × 20′ dph (56.4m × 11m × 6.1m). *Tons:* 1,066 om; 722 nm. *Hull:* wood. *Comp.:* 250 pass. *Built:* Samuel Hanscom, Jr., Portsmouth, N.H.; 1851.

Named for Jenny Lind, the famous singer who made her American debut under the auspices of showman P. T. Barnum in 1850, the clipper ship *Nightingale* was adorned with two likenesses of "the Swedish Nightingale," a bust figurehead on the bow and a stern carving showing her in a reclining position with a nightingale

perched on her finger. Originally to have been named *Sarah Cowles,* before her launch the ship advertised for passengers for a "Grand Trans-Atlantic Excursion to the World's Fair" in England. All told she was designed to carry 250 passengers. Unfortunately, her owner was dissatisfied with her construction, and in the financial tangle that ensued, *Nightingale* was auctioned to the Boston ship brokerage of Davis and Company in early September, who then sold her to Sampson and Tappan. Far from conveying New England gentry to the Crystal Palace Exhibition in London, on October 17 *Nightingale* cleared Boston for Melbourne in one of the first passages to transport miners to the newly discovered Australian gold fields. Sailing to Canton and Shanghai, she entered the lucrative tea trade to London, loading in China on each of her next four voyages, which also included another passage to Melbourne and, in 1859, her first Cape Horn voyage from New York to San Francisco.

Upon her return, *Nightingale* sailed for Rio de Janeiro where she was sold and apparently put in the slave trade under command of Captain Francis Bowen, known as "the Prince of Slaves." Her exact movements in 1860 are difficult to trace, but by the end of the year she was again flying the American flag, though still commanded by Bowen and sailing as a slave ship. Searched by British patrols in the West Indies in January 1861, three months later she was off Cabinda at the mouth of the Congo River — waiting to take slaves aboard — when a boarding party from the sloop of war USS *Saratoga* found 971 slaves in her hold. The slaves were returned to Monrovia, Liberia, though not before 160 had died from tropical fever. Allowed to escape by Lieutenant Guthrie, himself a slave owner, Bowen later commanded the gunrunning steamer VIRGINIUS.

In July 1861, the U.S. Navy purchased *Nightingale* and put her to work as a supply- and storeship for the Gulf Coast Blockading Squadron until 1864. Sold out of the Navy at the end of the Civil War, she sailed from Boston to San Francisco where the Western Union Telegraph Company purchased her for operations in connection with laying a submarine cable across the Bering Strait. After several voyages from San Francisco to Petropavlovsk, she was sold back into merchant trade and began more or less regular work for a succession of different owners between New York, San Francisco, and China. In 1876, *Nightingale* was purchased by Norwegian interests and cut down as a bark for work in the lumber trade out of Krageroe. On April 17, 1893, she was abandoned at sea en route from Liverpool to Halifax, her crew being rescued by a passing vessel.

Cutler, *Greyhounds of the Sea.* Howe & Matthews, *American Clipper Ships.*

NIMROD

Barkentine (1f/3m). *L/B/D:* 136′ × 26.9′ × 16′ (41.5m × 8.2m × 4.9m). *Tons:* 334 grt. *Hull:* wood. *Comp.:* 14. *Mach.:* compound engine, 60 hp, 1 screw. *Built:* Alexander Stephens & Sons, Ltd., Dundee, Scotland; 1865.

Built for rugged work in the Arctic and Antarctic, sealer *Nimrod* was purchased by Ernest Henry Shackleton for his British Imperial Antarctic Expedition. *Nimrod* sailed from Torquay on August 7, 1907, and reached the Ross Sea via New Zealand in January 1908. After searching in vain for a landing site on King Edward Land, *Nimrod* was forced to go to Ross Island at McMurdo Sound, despite a promise to his old captain and rival, Robert Falcon Scott (with whom he had sailed in DISCOVERY), that he would stay west of 170°E. Establishing a base at Hut Point, where *Discovery* previously lay from 1901 to 1904, Shackleton attempted to reach the geographic South Pole 1,725 miles away. Crossing the Ross Ice Shelf, his team ascended to the 10,000-foot-high Polar Plateau but had to turn back at 88°23′S, 162°E — a new farthest south, yet still 97 miles from their goal. In the meantime, Douglas Mawson, T. W. Edgeworth David, and A. F. Mackay reached the South Magnetic Pole, then located at 72°25′S, 155°16′E about 190 miles west of the Ross Sea. *Nimrod* returned to England in June 1909 and Shackleton used her as a floating museum of his voyage before selling her for funds in 1910. Shackleton's most famous Antarctic expedition was his third, in ENDURANCE.

Shackleton, *Heart of the Antarctic.*

NIÑA

Caravela redonda (3m). *L/B/D:* 50′–70′ × 16′–20′ × 7′ dph (15–21m × 5–6m × 2m dph). *Tons:* 55–94 toneladas. *Hull:* wood. *Comp.:* 24. *Arm.:* 9cm lombard, 4.5cm falconets. *Built:* Palos, Spain(?); <1492.

One of the three ships in Christopher Columbus's first voyage of discovery that would take him to the Caribbean islands, *Niña* was a *caravela latina* — that is, lateen rigged on three masts, the largest sail and foremost sail being set nearly amidships. Owned by Juan Niño de Moguer and officially named *Santa Clara*, she is known to history as *Niña* because it was Spanish custom to give ships the feminine form of the owner's surname. Requisitioned by Columbus in satisfaction of a fine owed by the citizens of Los Palos to Ferdinand and Isabella, *Niña* was put under command of Captain Vicente Yáñez Pinzón, whose brother Martín Alonso was master of PINTA. *Niña* sailed from Palos in company with SANTA MARÍA and *Pinta* on August 3, 1492. The latter experienced rudder trouble, so

the other two ships sailed as far as the island of Gomera to wait for their consort. When she did not arrive, they sailed back to Las Palmas. There, Pinzón took advantage of the delay (it had taken *Pinta* two weeks to make port) to alter *Niña*'s rig from that of a *caravela latina* to a *caravela redonda*. With her new rig, she retained her lateen mizzen, set a square sail on her mainmast (the old foremast), and set a square foresail on a new mast stepped near the bow. This made her much better suited to running before the trade winds that would carry her across the Atlantic, and she became Columbus's fastest ship, as well as his favorite.

Resuming the voyage on September 6, the ships met favorable winds for the first two weeks of the voyage, followed by several days of adverse winds and calms between September 20 and 30. On the 25th, Pinzón claimed to have sighted land, though the ships were barely halfway across the Atlantic. By the second week of October, there was increasing evidence that land was near — flocks of migrating birds and flotsam in the form of a piece of carved wood and tree branches. Land was finally sighted at about 0200 on October 12, and they landed later that morning. Though it is not absolutely certain what the island was, it was definitely located in what is now the Bahamas, probably San Salvador or Samana Cay; the Taino inhabitants called it Guanahaní.

Convinced that he was very near Cipango or Cathay (Japan or China), whose gold was the chief object of his voyage, Columbus led his three ships through the Bahamas and south to Cuba, the northeast coast of which he explored for about six weeks. On November 22, *Pinta* departed from the other two ships to explore Great Inagua Island. Vicente Yáñez remained with Columbus, and a few days later, at Puerto Cayo Moa, *Niña* received a new mizzen mast. The two ships crossed the Windward Channel to Hispaniola on December 6, sailed along its northwest coast, and skirted the south coast of Tortuga. Early Christmas morning *Santa María* grounded on a coral reef. After salvaging what they could from the ship, it was clear that her forty crew could not possibly embark in *Niña* for the return voyage, so a fort was erected from *Santa María*'s timbers and thirty-nine men volunteered to stay.

Columbus transferred his flag to *Niña* and proceeded east along the coast on January 4, 1493. Two days later, he was making his way to open water when a lookout saw *Pinta* in the distance. Putting about, the ships rendezvoused at Isle Cabra. On January 8, they began working their way down the coast, getting as far as Cape Samana in what is now the Dominican Republic. Abandoning plans to visit additional islands of which he had heard from various Arawaks — ten of whom he had picked up along the way either to serve as interpreters, for conversion to Christianity, or as certain proof that he had visited a distant land — on January 16 he turned the ships for Spain.

The first month was smooth sailing, but on February 12, *Niña* and *Pinta* were separated in a three-day storm (the first of the voyage) near the Azores, which belonged to Portugal. Although they were in sight of Santa Maria Island on the 15th, it took them three more days to reach the island, which had no secure anchorage. There, while offering penitential prayers for their deliverance from the storm in a chapel at Anjos, half the crew were arrested on suspicion of having plundered Portuguese possessions on the Guinea Coast. Columbus had received his early seafaring education from Portuguese mariners and his wife was Portuguese, and within a few days he had won his crew's release and they sailed again on February 21. Five days out they were overcome by another storm, possibly of hurricane force, which lasted five days. On the night of March 3, they were perilously close to land, which turned out to be just down the coast from the Tagus River. The next morning they sailed into Lisbon. While there, Columbus was summoned to the court of Dom João, the Portuguese king who had declined his request for sponsorship for his planned voyage as early as 1484–85. When Dom João heard Columbus's account of his voyage, complete with presentations by the Caribbean natives, he was more than a little chagrined to realize what he had lost in not sponsoring the Genoese captain himself.

Lisbon was only a two-day sail from Los Palos, and *Niña* nosed into the Rio Tinto on March 15, only hours before *Pinta* — thirty-two weeks from port to port. Within three weeks, he had exchanged correspondence with Ferdinand and Isabella, then holding court 700 miles away at Barcelona, receiving from them confirmation that he was now Admiral of the Ocean Sea. This was among the honors he had been promised, as well as support for a second voyage, preparation for which got under way almost immediately.

Niña was too small to sail as Columbus's flagship, which honor was reserved for a new *Santa María,* nicknamed *Mariagalante.* The new fleet consisted of seventeen ships and more than 1,200 sailors, colonists, and other supernumeraries. Sailing from Cadiz on September 25, the fleet called again at the Canaries, remaining there for about a week before leaving sometime between October 7 and 10. The voyage over was uneventful, and on Sunday, November 3, they made their first landfall, at Dominica. For the next three weeks, they sailed north along the Leeward Islands, giving names that endure today to many of the islands. On November 23, they were

back on the north coast of Hispaniola where they learned that the entire thirty-nine-man garrison left at Navidad had been killed. On January 2, 1494, Columbus and his ships decided to establish a base at Isabela, Hispaniola, to be near the gold at Cibao, in the interior.

On April 24, Columbus chose the caravels *Niña* (of which he now owned half), *San Juan,* and *Cardera* for an exploring expedition. This took them first to the southeast coast of Cuba (including Guantánamo Bay and Santiago), then across to northern Jamaica, back to Cuba as far as Bahia Cortez, and then again along the southern shores of Jamaica and Hispaniola. The ships returned to Isabela on September 24, after an absence of four months. Columbus remained at the ill-managed colony for another eighteen months, during which he worked to establish a trade in Taino slaves. On March 10, 1496, *Niña* and *Santa Cruz* sailed for Spain, embarking between them about 255 people. (*Santa Cruz* had been built at Hispaniola after a hurricane in June 1495 destroyed all Columbus's remaining ships save *Niña.*) A month later they were still in the Caribbean, calling at Guadeloupe in April, where they attempted to reprovision in the face of hostile Caribs. On April 20, 1496, they weighed anchor again, but it was not until June 11 that they fetched up again in the Bay of Cadiz.

Traffic between Spain and the Caribbean was not confined only to Columbus's fleets, and several ships had arrived at Hispaniola while Columbus was there and before his return. While Columbus made preparations for his third voyage to the New World, *Niña*'s Captain Alonso Medel decided to do some trading to Rome on the side, only to be captured by Sardinian pirates. The ship was recaptured by her crew, and returned to Cadiz in time to sail from Sanlúcar on January 23, 1498, under Captain Pedro Francés, shortly before Columbus's main fleet sailed on his third voyage. Her subsequent career in the Caribbean is not known, and the last written record of her is in 1501.

Morison, *Admiral of the Ocean Sea.* Pastor, *Ships of Christopher Columbus.* Philips, "Evolution of Spanish Ship Design."

NIÑA

Staysail schooner (2m). *L/B/D:* 59′ × 15′ × 10′ (18m × 4.6m × 3m). *Hull:* wood. *Comp.:* 12. *Des.:* W. Starling Burgess. *Built:* Reuben Bigelow, Monument Beach, Mass.; 1928.

Commissioned by Elihu Root, Jr., and Paul Hammond expressly for the transatlantic race to Spain of 1928, *Niña*

The Starling Burgess–designed staysail schooner NIÑA *easing along under full sail in the summer of 1965. Built for the transatlantic race of 1928, under her third owner, DeCoursey Fales,* NIÑA *was a two-time Bermuda Race winner, in 1962 and 1964. Courtesy New York Yacht Club.*

was so named because two of the other race entrants were named *Pinta* and *Santa Maria*. In addition to being the smallest boat in her maiden race, *Niña* was the only non-gaff-rigged vessel and sailed with an amateur crew. Nonetheless, she won handily, and as she crossed the finish line, the race's sponsor, Alfonso XIII, cheered from his launch, "Well sailed, *Niña!* I congratulate you! I am the king of Spain." Shortly thereafter, *Niña* sailed for England and, with Sherman Hoyt at the helm, entered and won the Fastnet Race with an elapsed time of 20 days, 15 minutes, 20 seconds. After winning the 1929 race from New London, Connecticut, to Gibson Island, Maryland, she was laid up. In 1933, Bobby Somerset, the English owner of JOLIE BRISE, purchased *Niña*. While en route from New York to the Bahamas, her dried-out hull leaked so badly that she almost sank and had to put into Bermuda for repairs. Somerset put her up for sale, and her future seemed in jeopardy until she was purchased by DeCoursey Fales in 1935.

Slowly but surely Fales restored *Niña* to her former

glory. She won a handful of races before World War II, and afterwards dominated the Vineyard Race and a number of others on the East Coast. The contest that all but eluded her was the biennial Bermuda Race, which she first entered after the war. In 1962, however, the thirty-four-year-old schooner followed the ketch *Stormvogel* over the finish line, and *Niña* was declared the winner on corrected time. She sailed the Bermuda Race once more under Fales in 1964, but two years later while his "Old Girl" was halfway to Bermuda, the seventy-eight-year-old Fales died in New York. *Niña* was donated to the U.S. Merchant Marine Academy for use as a training vessel. Several years later she returned to private ownership and in 1993 was based in Florida.

Robinson, *Legendary Yachts.*

NIPPON MARU

Bark (4m). *L/B/D:* 307′ × 42.5′ × 22.5′ (93.6m × 13m × 6.9m). *Tons:* 2,285 grt *Hull:* steel. *Comp.:* 150 200. *Mach.:* aux. diesel, 2,600 hp. *Built:* Kawasaki Dockyard Co., Kobe, Japan; 1930.

In the late 1920s, the Japanese Ministry of Transport ordered the four-masted barks *Nippon Maru* and *Kaiwo Maru* for the Kokai-Kunrensho (Institute for Nautical Training), which already operated the four-masted bark *Taisei Maru* and the four-masted barkentine *Shintoku Maru*. Their work for the merchant marine is reflected in their names. *Maru*, which signifies wholeness or unity, is an almost universal suffix for Japanese merchant-ship names. *Nippon* means Japan, and *Kaiwo* is the mythological king of the seas, equivalent to Neptune or Poseidon. Commissioned in 1930 and 1931, respectively, the barks were described by Harold Underhill as "imposing rather than beautiful." Their very high freeboards reflected a desire to maximize the amount of natural light admitted to the crew spaces below decks, while their comparatively shorter yards and smaller sails were designed to accommodate the relatively small stature of the average Japanese before World War II.

Before World War II, the ships' training voyages carried them throughout the Pacific, and *Nippon Maru* made four voyages to the United States, five to Hawaii and seven elsewhere in the Pacific. During World War II her yards were sent down and she was used as a motor-training vessel in the Home Islands. Repatriating Japanese soldiers and civilians after the war, she was rerigged in 1952 and resumed training, making her first cruise to the United States in 1954, and her first to the East Coast in 1960. Both *Nippon Maru* and *Kaiwo Maru* remained active training ships until the 1980s, when they were replaced by new ships with the same names.

Brouwer, *International Register of Historic Ships*. Schäuffelen, *Great Sailing Ships*. Underhill, *Sail Training and Cadet Ships*.

NONSUCH

Ketch. *L/B:* 50' × 15' (11m × 4.3m). *Tons:* 43 bm. *Hull:* wood. *Comp.:* 12–24. *Arm.:* 8 guns. *Built:* Wivenhoe, Essex, Eng.; 1650.

An eight-gun navy ketch from 1654 to 1667, when she was sold to Sir William Warren, the diminutive *Nonsuch* was the vehicle responsible for the founding of the Hudson's Bay Company. Prior to that she had a varied career, being built as a merchant trader and purchased by the Navy in 1654. Captured by two Dutch privateers while escorting a merchant ketch through the English Channel on February 3, 1659, she was retaken two months later. In the meantime, the Huron allies of the French fur traders Médard Chouart, Sieur des Groselliers, and his brother-in-law Pierre Esprit Radisson had been defeated by the Iroquois (allied with the English), and thus their trade via the St. Lawrence River and Great Lakes was jeopardized. To make up for this, Chouart and Radisson proposed to open direct trade with the "fur belt" via Hudson Bay. Angered by the high rates at which their furs were taxed and denied any redress from France, they went to England, where they were introduced to the court of Charles II by the chemist Robert Boyle.

By 1667, the nucleus of the Hudson's Bay Company had formed around these two men, and on June 5, 1668, the vessels *Nonsuch* and *Eaglet* (loaned for the venture by Charles II) sailed from London. The ships' primary cargo was "wampumpeage," small marine shell beads widely used as a medium of exchange among eastern Indians. *Eaglet* was damaged in midatlantic and returned to England with Radisson, but *Nonsuch* sailed into Hudson Bay and south to the shores of James Bay. On September 29, 1668, the adventurers landed and began to build Charles Fort (later named Rupert's House) on the Rupert River. After almost a year of trading with the Indians, Groselliers returned to England in October 1669 with a cargo of furs. The following year the Hudson's Bay Company was formally incorporated and given by king's grant an area equivalent to nearly forty percent of modern Canada. The later fate of the *Nonsuch* is unknown. A near replica of the vessel, designed by Alan Hinks in 1968, is on exhibit at the Manitoba Museum of Man and Nature in Winnipeg.

Rich, *History of the Hudson's Bay Company*.

HMS NORFOLK

Norfolk-class cruiser (2f/3m). *L/B/D:* 632.7' × 66' × 20.1' (192.8m × 20.1m × 6.1m). *Tons:* 14,600 disp. *Hull:* steel. *Comp.:* 710. *Arm.:* 8 × 8" (4 × 2), 8 × 4", 16 × 2pdr, 8 × 0.5"; 8 × 21"TT. *Armor:* 5.5" belt, 1" deck. *Mach.:* geared turbines, 80,000 shp, 4 screws; 31.5 kts. *Built:* Fairfield Shipbuilding & Engineering Co., Ltd., Govan, Scotland; 1930.

The fourth ship of the name, HMS *Norfolk* first attracted attention outside the Royal Navy during the so-called Invergordon mutiny of September 1931, during which several hundred sailors in ships throughout the fleet staged a two-day strike. In 1925, the Navy instituted a two-tier wage structure under which new recruits were paid 25 percent less than veterans; six years later, veterans' pay was aligned with the lower wage. The sailors' action succeeded in reducing the proposed pay cut to about 10 percent. Although there were Communist sympathizers among the organizers aboard *Norfolk,* one of whom moved to the Soviet Union, the mutiny reflected an economic rather than an ideological schism in the fleet.

Norfolk spent virtually the whole of World War II as an escort for the Arctic convoys. She took part in the search for the pocket battleships SCHARNHORST and GNEISENAU in November 1939, and — in midatlantic — in that for ADMIRAL SCHEER at the end of 1940. Equipped with Type 286P radar, on May 23, 1941, she and *Suffolk* made contact with PRINZ EUGEN and BISMARCK amid the ice and fog of the Denmark Strait northeast of Iceland. They did not close with the more powerful ships, but on the morning of May 27, *Norfolk* was the first ship to establish visual contact with the now crippled *Bismarck,* and she helped sink the battleship that day. Apart from an assignment to the covering force during Operation Torch, the North Africa landings in October 1942, *Norfolk* remained in the grueling Arctic convoy duty. At the end of December 1943, she hit and was hit by *Scharnhorst* before the German battlecruiser was sunk by a barrage of shells and torpedoes by the superior British force in the Battle of the North Cape. The Royal Navy gradually moved to the offensive in northern waters, and in January 1945 *Norfolk* sailed with a cruiser force that knocked out two freighters and sank a minesweeper in a German convoy. The cruiser remained on the list until sold for scrap in 1950.

Hill, *Oxford Illustrated History of the Royal Navy*. Stephen, *Sea Battles in Close-Up*. Wincott, *Invergordon Mutineer*.

NORGE

(ex-*Pieter de Coninck*) Liner (1f/3m). *L/B:* 340.3' × 40.8' (103.7m × 12.4m). *Tons:* 3,310 grt. *Hull:* iron. *Comp.:* 1st 50, 2nd 150, 3rd

900; 80 crew. *Mach.:* compound engine, 1 screw; 11 kts. *Built:* Alexander Stephen & Sons, Ltd., Glasgow; 1881.

The passenger ship *Pieter de Coninck* was built for the Belgian Engels Line, founded by Theodore C. Engels in 1859 for service between Belgium and South America. By the 1870s, Engels had begun to concentrate more heavily on the Antwerp–New York route, and he built the barkentine-rigged screw steamers *Pieter de Coninck* and *Jan Breydel* for joint service with the White Cross Line. Although intended as passenger-cargo steamers, the sister ships were quickly detailed to carry freight only, and in 1889 they were sold to Denmark's Thingvalla Line, which was taken over by the Scandinavian-American Line in 1898. Under its flag she sailed between Copenhagen, Christiania (Oslo), Kristiansand, and New York.

On June 24, 1904, *Norge* sailed from Denmark with 700 passengers and 80 crew under Captain Waldemar Gundal. Over the course of the next few days, the ship drifted about 375 miles off course, and on June 28, she struck the island reef of Rockall, about 5 miles long and 75 feet at its highest, located about 250 miles northwest of Ireland in 57°35′N, 13°48′W. As the ship was backed off the rock, she was holed badly and quickly sank. Of the 780 people aboard, about 550 went down with her. The survivors were picked up six days later by an eastbound German tanker, although several more people died after their rescue.

Bonsor, *North Atlantic Seaway.* Hocking, *Dictionary of Disasters at Sea.*

NORMAN COURT

Clipper (3m). *L/B/D:* 197.4′ bp × 33′ × 20′ (60.2m × 10.1m × 6.1m). *Tons:* 855 grt. *Hull:* composite. *Comp.:* 22. *Des.:* William Rennie. *Built:* A. & J. Inglis, Glasgow; 1869.

One of the later generation of tea clippers, *Norman Court* was launched just before the opening of the Suez Canal threw open the highly competitive China tea trade to steamships, which could make the same passage in almost one-third the time of even the fastest clippers. Considered William Rennie's masterpiece, *Norman Court* was of a sharper model even than his FIERY CROSS of 1860, and was of composite construction with wood planking on iron frames. An idea of the stresses on even the most well found ships can be had from a description of *Norman Court* by her sometime captain, Andrew Shewan.

> Though so staunch and tight, yet at times the whole fabric [of the ship] would tremble like a piece of whalebone. When we were driving her into a head sea, I have noted, as I lay on

the after lockers, that after a heavy plunge as she recovered herself the after end would vibrate like a diving board when the pressure is released.

Built for the firm of Baring Brothers, *Norman Court* struggled against falling rates in the tea trade through the 1870s, and she was downrigged to a bark in 1877 to reduce manning costs. In 1880 she was sold to Grieve & Company, of Greenock, for the Java sugar trade, in which speed was less important. On March 29, 1883, *Norman Court* wrecked on Anglesey while bound from Queenstown to Greenock on her return from Batavia.

Lubbock, *China Clippers.* MacGregor, *Tea Clippers.*

NORMANDIE

Liner (3f/2m). *L/B:* 1,029.4′ × 118.1′ (313.8m × 36m). *Tons:* 79,280 grt. *Hull:* steel. *Comp.:* 1st 828, tourist 670, 3rd 454; crew 1,345. *Mach.:* steam turbine, 4 screws; 29 kts. *Des.:* Vladimir Yourkevitch. *Built:* Chantiers & Ateliers de St. Nazaire (Penhöet), St. Nazaire, France; 1935.

Following the success of their ILE DE FRANCE, Compagnie Générale Transatlantique (French Line) determined to build the largest and most beautiful ship in the world. Design of the ship eventually fell to Russian émigré naval architect Vladimir Yourkevitch. Although he was then laboring in obscurity as a Renault factory worker, before World War I Yourkevitch had been responsible for the hull form of the innovative *Borodino*-class battlecruisers, laid down in 1912 but never finished. *Normandie*'s hull was narrow at both ends and wide amidships, with a bulbous bow below the waterline. (After World War II, the latter feature was widely adopted in the design of navy and commercial ships.) To create an impression of speed, Yourkevitch enclosed all the deck machinery so that there was an unencumbered vista along her decks, and in so doing he redefined the aesthetic that would characterize new ocean liners until they were eclipsed by jet passenger planes in the 1960s. Designed for deluxe trade, *Normandie* was appointed in a lavish art deco style that also helped redefine the aesthetic of the liner age. As Albert Ballin had done with *Vaterland* (later LEVIATHAN) in 1913, Yourkevitch used split uptakes to create massive public spaces that further lightened the appearance of the ship.

Owing to the tremendous rivalry with Cunard, who were planning the as yet unnamed QUEEN MARY, *Normandie* was built amid great secrecy. She was launched in 1932 and began her maiden voyage from Le Havre to Southampton and New York on May 29, 1935 — in the process capturing the Blue Riband for the fastest crossing

French Line's NORMANDIE *revolutionized passenger-ship design both above and below decks. There are no cargo booms or ventilator cowls, and anchor chains and capstans forward have been decked over to give the ship a streamlined appearance. She has three funnels, receding in height from bow to stern, the aftermost being a dummy — a common stylistic device even with four-funnel ships. The interior was a celebration of the art deco style, elegant in its simplicity and a far cry from the gaudy opulence of the prewar generation, as seen in the interior view of the* KRONPRINZESSEN CECILIE. *Courtesy The Mariners' Museum, Newport News, Virginia.*

between Bishop Rock and Ambrose Light, at a speed of 29.98 knots (4 days, 3 hours, 2 minutes). On her return passage she became the first ship to cross the Atlantic at better than 30 knots — 30.31 knots from Ambrose to Bishop Rock (4 days, 3 hours, 25 minutes). Both runs were bettered by *Queen Mary* the following year, though in 1937 *Normandie* recaptured the Blue Riband in both directions, with a westbound crossing of 30.58 knots (July 29-August 2, 1937; 3 days, 23 hours, 2 minutes) and an eastbound record of 31.20 knots (August 4–8; 3 days,

22 hours, 7 minutes). Initially subject to terrible vibrations, a common defect in the search for speed on passenger ships, this was corrected by replacing three-blade screws with four-blade ones.

Normandie's last westbound voyage began on August 23, 1939, and she was held at New York upon the outbreak of World War II. Following the U.S. entry into the war, the government seized her on December 12, 1941. Many competing plans were put forth by private shipbuilders and by the various service branches — some wanted her for an aircraft carrier, others for a troop transport, and still others for a combination carrier-transport — but she was finally converted for use as a troop transport. On February 9, 1942, just before she was to have made her first voyage under the American flag as USS *Lafayette*, a fire broke out when a spark from a welder's torch ignited a bundle of highly flammable and poorly stowed kapok life vests. Flames swept through the ship and in a matter of hours she was all but gutted. Because of poor coordination in fighting the fire, more water than necessary was pumped into the ship and she turned turtle at the pier. Her salvage provided invaluable training for hundreds of Navy salvage experts, and she was eventually refloated. As her machinery was of no use, she was mothballed for the remainder of the war, following which she was sold to ship breakers and broken up at Newark, New Jersey.

Ardman, *"Normandie," Her Life and Times.* Foucart, *"Normandie."* Shipbuilder and Marine Engine-Builder, *The French Line . . . Steamship "Normandie."*

NORONIC

Cruise ship. *L/B/D:* 362′ × 59.6′ × 24.8′ (110.3m × 18.2m × 7.6m). *Tons:* 6,905 grt. *Hull:* steel. *Comp.:* 524 pass.; 171 crew. *Mach.:* triple-expansion; 14 kts. *Des.:* Eric Tornoos. *Built:* Western Dry Dock & Shipbuilding Co., Port Arthur, Ont.; 1913.

Named for the NOrthern Navigation Company, and Richelieu & ONtario Line, which had recently merged to form Canada Steamship Lines (Northern Navigation ships traditionally ended in *-nic*), the ill-fated *Noronic* had an inauspicious start. Her maiden voyage, scheduled for November 7, 1913, was postponed because of the "Great Storm," which flayed the Great Lakes for six relentless days like no gale in memory. Unstable as built (she had five decks rather than the four in the original design), false sides were added to increase her beam and she was reballasted. Homeported at Sarnia, *Noronic*'s normal route was a seven-day run between Detroit and Duluth, with stops at Sault Ste. Marie and Port Arthur–Fort William. Her running mates on this run were *Huronic* and *Hamonic.* Under command of Captain William Taylor, on September 16, 1949, the "Queen of the Inland Seas" arrived for an overnight pierside stay at Toronto on a special postseason run from Detroit to Prescott, Ontario, on the St. Lawrence River via the Welland Canal.

At 0230 on September 17, a fire was detected in a linen closet on C deck. Because of her age, *Noronic* was exempted from regulations requiring fire-resistant and fire-retarding bulkheads, and within fifteen minutes the fire had ignited her rich wood paneling from stem to stern.

The low, flat lines of the ill-fated passenger steamer NORONIC *typify the design of passenger ships on the Great Lakes in the early 20th century. Author's collection.*

Most of the passengers and crew were asleep, and the intensity of the flames and panic led to the death of 118 people, only one of whom drowned. Although the cause of the fire was not determined, the board of inquiry attributed the huge loss of life to the "complete complacency [that] had descended upon both the ship's officers and the management." Several weeks later, *Noronic* was towed to Hamilton and broken up.

Craig, *"Noronic" Is Burning!*

USS North Carolina (BB-55)

North Carolina-class battleship (2f/2m). *L/B/D:* 728.8′ × 108.3′ × 35.5′ (222.1m × 33m × 10.8m). *Tons:* 46,770 disp. *Hull:* steel. *Comp.:* 1,890. *Arm.:* 9 × 16″ (3 × 3), 20 × 5″, 16 × 1.1″; 12 × .50 cal; 2 aircraft. *Armor:* 18″ belt, 6.3″ deck. *Mach.:* geared turbines, 121,000 shp, 4 screws; 27.6 kts. *Built:* New York Navy Yard, Brooklyn, N.Y.; 1941.

The first U.S. battleship commissioned since 1923, USS *North Carolina* received so much attention during her trials that she earned the nickname "Showboat." Closely involved in the invasion of Guadalcanal, she took an active part in the Battle of the Eastern Solomons on August 23–25. Torpedoed by the Japanese submarine *I-19* near Espiritu Santo on September 15, she underwent repairs at Pearl Harbor before resuming operations in the South Pacific. From November 1943 through May 1944, *North Carolina* supported carrier forces in the Gilbert and Marshall Islands, and the Allied landings at Hollandia, New Guinea. Following the Battle of the Philippine Sea, she returned stateside for repairs, rejoining the fleet shortly after the invasion of the Philippines. During 1945 she took part in raids on Luzon, Taiwan, and occupied China before heading for Japan. There she alternated between shore support for landings on Iwo Jima and Okinawa, where she was hit by friendly fire on April 6, and shelling the home islands of Kyushu and Honshu.

Decommissioned in 1947, "Showboat" remained in reserve until 1961, when she was transferred to the State of North Carolina for use as a naval memorial and museum in Wilmington.

Silverstone, *Directory of the World's Capital Ships*. U.S. Navy, *DANFS*.

Northern Light

Clipper (3m). *L/B/D:* 171.4′ × 36′ × 21.9′ dph (67m × 13.1m × 5.8m). *Tons:* 1,021 reg. *Hull:* wood. *Des.:* Samuel K. Pook. *Built:* E. & H. O. Briggs, South Boston, Mass.; 1851.

In the cemetery at Eastham, Massachusetts, is the gravestone of Captain Freeman Hatch, upon which is inscribed: "Freeman Hatch, 1820–1889. He became famous making the astonishing passage in clipper ship *Northern Light,* from San Francisco to Boston in 76 days, 6 hours — an achievement won by no mortal before or since." More than a century later, that record still stands. The second master of the medium clipper *Northern Light* (Boston-owned for all of her ten years), Hatch accomplished this remarkable feat on the ship's second voyage. Departing San Francisco, she sailed within two days of the clippers *Trade Wind* and *Contest,* which arrived at New York in 84 days and 79 days, respectively. Her next five voyages took her to Calcutta, Manila, and the East Indies. She then made one more voyage on the California run, followed by a voyage that took her to Shanghai, Manila, San Francisco, and Acapulco, before returning to Boston. In 1860, *Northern Light* sailed on her first transatlantic run, to Le Havre. On Christmas Day 1860, she departed Le Havre for New York. Eight days later, she was in collision with the French brig *Nouveau St. Jacques,* which sank first but whose crew and that of *Northern Light* were saved by the vessels *Norma* and *Bremerhaven.*

Cutler, *Greyhounds of the Sea*. Howe & Matthews, *American Clipper Ships.*

Northern Light

Down Easter (3m). *L/B/D:* 219.7′ × 43.1′ × 19′ dph (52.2m × 11m × 6.7m). *Tons:* 1,795 reg. *Hull:* wood. *Built:* George Thomas, Quincy, Mass.; 1873.

The three-skysail yard Down Easter *Northern Light* was owned for her first three years by W. F. Weld & Company, of Boston. Sold to W. H. Kinsman & Company, she sailed for ten more years in general trade between the East Coast, the West Coast, the Orient, and Europe. Her last master under the American flag was Captain Joshua Slocum, who later achieved fame for his exploits in LIBERDADE and SPRAY. In 1882, *Northern Light* had just left New York for Yokohama when a damaged rudder forced her into New London. Her crew mutinied and the first mate was stabbed. The ringleader was arrested but Slocum decided to continue with his old crew. On the return from Manila, *Northern Light* sailed through the pumice-laden Sunda Straits only two days after the explosion of the Krakatoa volcano. Damage to the rudder near Cape Horn forced the ship into Port Elizabeth, South Africa, where the new first mate fell ill and left the ship. His replacement turned out to be an ex-convict whom Slocum clapped in irons after discovering that he had arranged with some of the crew to kill Slocum and seize the ship. In 1885, *Northern Light* was sold to Norwegian interests and renamed *Mathilda.* Under that name she carried oil and timber and sailed in the transatlantic trade for 20 years.

Matthews, *American Merchant Ships.*

NORTH RIVER STEAM BOAT

(aka *Clermont*) Steamboat (1f/2m). *L/B/D:* 146′ × 14′ × 4′ (44.5m × 4.3m × 1.2m). *Tons:* 79 grt (1808: 100 disp.). *Hull:* wood. *Comp.:* 90 pass. *Mach.:* vertical steam engine (24″ × 4′), 20 hp, 2 × 15′ sidewheels; 5 mph. *Des.:* Robert Fulton. *Built:* Charles Browne, Corlear's Hook, N.Y.; 1807.

Known to later generations as *Clermont,* Robert Fulton's *North River Steam Boat* has no claim to being the first steamboat either in the Americas or anywhere else. However, it represents the culmination of years of experiment in Britain, France, and the United States by Fulton, a keen and ambitious student of the advances in steam technology made by his peers and predecessors. What ensured the vessel's success was the savvy with which Fulton and his partner, Robert R. Livingston, pursued their mechanical, political, and financial advantage over potential rivals. The American-born Fulton began his career as a jeweler and painter; it was not until he was living in England in the 1790s that he began his career as an engineer and inventor. In 1797 he moved to France and began developing his ideas for a submarine. Although Fulton's NAUTILUS was technically successful, neither the French nor, later, the British could see any future for such a device.

Fulton next turned his energies to designs for steam-powered ships. While so engaged he met Livingston, then U.S. Minister Plenipotentiary in Paris, who between 1797 and 1801 had designed some boats with his brother-in-law, Colonel John Stevens, and the iron founder Nicholas Roosevelt. Since 1798, Livingston had also held a New York State monopoly on steam navigation between New York City and Albany. The two men were drawn to each other by their mutual interest, though their relationship would be complicated by the patent status of various elements of Fulton's design and Livingston's existing contractual obligations to Roosevelt and Stevens. By October 1802, though, the two men had drafted a contract calling for construction of a passenger steamboat not to exceed 120 feet in length, 8 feet in beam and 15 inches in draft, powered by a Boulton and Watt steam engine, and capable of carrying sixty passengers.

On August 9, 1803, Fulton's first model (powered by an engine built by Étienne Calla) made a flawless demonstration run at Paris before an audience that included such luminaries as Louis de Bougainville, veteran of a circumnavigation in LA BOUDEUSE. Though glowing press reports estimated that steam navigation would reduce the transit time for barges between Nantes and Paris from four months to two weeks, and that it would have "important consequences for the commerce and internal navigation in France," First Consul Napoleon Bonaparte was unimpressed. In the spring of 1804, Fulton went to England, ostensibly to oversee the construction of his steam engine, and he did not return to New York until the end of 1806.

In April 1807 he contracted with Charles Browne to build the hull, which was rigged with two masts, a foremast with square sails and a gaff sail aft. He also arranged for mounting the engine, which had arrived from England the year before, and paddle wheels. The first trial of the as yet unnamed boat took place on the East River on August 9, 1807, and a week later Fulton moved the vessel, deprecated as "Fulton's Folly," from Corlear's Hook to a berth on the North River (better known today as the Hudson). The next day, August 17, she sailed for Albany with Fulton, captain Davis Hunt, engineer George Jackson, and Dr. William McNiven, dean of England's Ripon Cathedral. Setting out at 1300, under steam alone the boat easily passed the broad-canvassed Hudson River sloops to arrive 24 hours later at Livingston's Clermont estate, having covered the 110 miles at a brisk 4.5 miles per hour. From there, she covered the remaining 40 miles to Albany at just under 5 miles an hour.

The steamboat was enrolled at New York on September 3, and the next day at 0642 she departed for Albany, arriving at 1127 on September 5; she returned two days later with four passengers. By stagecoach, the trip from New York to Albany took 57 hours and cost $10. As it took 30 to 35 hours and cost only $7 by *North River Steam Boat* (the fare rate was $1 per 20 miles), once the vessel's safety had been proven, her success and that of the technology that drove her were assured.

That winter Fulton enlarged the hull and at the start of the 1808 season, *North River Steam Boat*'s dimensions were 150 feet in length, 15 feet in beam, and 2 feet in draft (45.7m × 4.6m × 0.6m), with a 4-foot depth of hold. Boiler pressure was increased to 5 pounds per inch, and three cabins were added, with sleeping accommodations for 54 people, women and children being segregated from the men. By midsummer she was carrying up to 140 passengers per trip. A revealing indication of the steamboat's threat to the established order was the fact that several times during the fall, she was deliberately rammed by sloops that then dominated trade between New York and Albany.

In April 1808, Livingston enrolled *North River Steam Boat* at Clermont, and that fall Fulton and Livingston ordered a second steamboat, *Car of Neptune.* By 1809, Livingston and Fulton engaged Nicholas Roosevelt to survey the Ohio and Mississippi Rivers to determine the feasibility of running steamboats between Pittsburgh and New Orleans. In the meantime, rather than directly challenge his brother-in-law's Hudson River monopoly, John Stevens opened steam navigation on the Delaware River with his Phoenix. In 1811, there were rival boats on the Hudson, and Roosevelt's New Orleans steamed from Pittsburgh to her namesake city. By the time that *North River Steam Boat* was retired from service on July 8, 1814, steamboat service had expanded also to Long Island Sound and the Potomac River.

The Fulton-Livingston monopoly incidentally had almost as dramatic an impact on American law as the steamship did on navigation. Aaron Ogden, a former governor of New Jersey, purchased from Livingston's brother the right to operate a steamboat between New York and New Jersey. His partner, Thomas Gibbons, offered a complimentary service exclusively in New Jersey waters. The two men split and Gibbons began to run his *Bellona* between New Jersey and New York, a tricky enterprise ably undertaken by his young captain, Cornelius Vanderbilt. Ogden sued Gibbons and the New York State court found that while Congress had the right to license vessels engaged in interstate commerce, that license did not necessarily confer a right to be so employed. Gibbons's lawyers Daniel Webster and the U.S. Attorney General William Wirt (acting in this instance as a private citizen) argued their case before the Supreme Court. Confirming the broad potential of the Constitution's commerce clause, in *Gibbons* v. *Ogden* the Court decided in favor of Gibbons and pronounced that individual states could not restrain interstate commerce in any way.

Albion, *Rise of New York Port.* Philip, *Robert Fulton.* Ridgely-Nevitt, "The Steam Boat." Ringwald, "First Steamboat to Albany."

Nuestra Señora de Atocha

Galleon (3m). *L/B/D:* 110' × 33' × 14' (33.5m × 10.1m × 4.3m). *Tons:* 550 tons. *Hull:* wood. *Comp.:* 260. *Arm.:* 20–24 guns. *Built:* Alonso Ferrera, Havana, Cuba; 1620.

Nuestra Señora de Atocha was the object of one of the most valuable, and possibly most contentious, treasure wrecks ever found. One of four convoy escorts built in 1619–20 specifically for the protection of the Spanish treasure fleets that plied between Havana and Spain, *Atocha* was named for the Virgin associated with one of the most revered shrines in Madrid. Reportedly built of less than the best materials, on her first voyage, *Atocha* sprung her mainmast en route from Havana to Sanlúcar, and on her return to Cuba she leaked badly in the bows. Sailing to Portobello, Panama, *Atocha* was designated the *almiranta,* or second in command, of the treasure fleet returning to Spain. She embarked silver and gold shipped from the mines of Potosí (in Bolivia), Peru, and Colombia, together with forty-eight passengers returning to Spain. Departing Panama on July 22, 1622, the treasure fleet called first at Cartagena for tobacco and emeralds, and then sailed north for Havana, where they arrived on August 22 to load raw copper and indigo. In addition to whatever was smuggled aboard to evade taxes, *Atocha* carried 35 tons of silver (901 ingots and 255,000 coins) and 161 pieces of gold — a cargo valued at one million pesos.

Despite the threat of hurricanes at that time of year, the twenty-eight-ship fleet sailed six weeks later than planned, on September 4. The next morning, a hurricane hit and the ships were driven north towards the Florida Keys. Twenty-one of the ships passed to the west of the low-lying islands, but *Atocha, Nuestra Señora de Santa Margarita,* and four others did not. Early Tuesday morning, *Atocha* was dashed on a reef off Key West and sank in 55 feet of water with only her mizzen mast visible. Five survivors from the ship's complement of 260 were rescued by the merchantman *Santa Cruz.* All told, the storm had sunk six ships with their 550 passengers and crew.

Santa Cruz returned directly to Havana and officials immediately prepared to recover what they could from the ships. Divers discovered *Atocha's* hatches were still fastened and could not be forced without explosives, but before they could return, the mizzen mast snapped off in another storm, and the ship was lost. Government efforts to find the ships continued until 1623, without success. In 1626, a Havana merchant named Francisco Núñez Melián obtained a salvage contract and on June 26, 1623, using a primitive diving bell, one of his divers recovered a silver ingot from *Santa Margarita.* Altogether, the site yielded 313 silver ingots, 100 sheets of copper, 8 bronze guns, and 64,000 coins. Subsequent efforts were not as well rewarded, though Melián continued to search for *Atocha* off and on until 1643.

In 1970, chicken farmer–turned–treasure hunter Mel Fisher formed a company called Treasure Salvors, Inc., and began looking for *Atocha.* Working with a permit from the State of Florida, in 1971 Treasure Salvors recovered the first artifacts, including an anchor and a gold chain. Employing such crude devices as the "mailbox," which directed prop wash to clear away sand and whatever else overlay the object of their search, over the next four years the company recovered about $6 million worth of gold and silver, as well as a large number of rapiers, muskets and small arms, storage jars, and coins. Of the ship itself, only some rudder pintles and an anchor were found. In 1973, in an attempt to improve their standing with potential investors and the State of Florida, Treasure Salvors hired Duncan Mathewson as staff archaeologist.

On July 13, 1975, Dirk Fisher located five of the ship's bronze guns lying in 39 feet of water. A week later diving was suspended when he, his wife, and another member of the crew drowned after their dive boat capsized in a storm. The next five years revealed little new material from *Atocha,* although in 1980 Treasure Salvors divers relocated the remains of *Santa Margarita,* which they salvaged for two years. The search for *Atocha* continued until July 20, 1985, when the salvors found the hull of the ship, piles of silver ingots, and chests of silver. Salvors made some attempt to excavate the site properly, but the main effort was in the recovery of treasure, as the company name, and its designation of the site as "the motherlode," suggested.

In the meantime, the *Atocha* site had been the object of increasing criticism by nautical archaeologists who considered Treasure Salvors' techniques crude and destructive, and the Florida government moved to take control of the site. The Supreme Court eventually found in favor of Fisher's group on the grounds that its title to the wreck was supported by admiralty law precedent, despite the historical value of the site. Nonetheless, a movement was afoot to protect submerged archaeological sites from treasure hunters in the same way that comparable sites on land are. Concern for these irreplaceable troves of archaeological and anthropological information spread slowly, but aided in part by the outcry over the disastrous handling of the archaeologically priceless but commercially worthless DE BRAAK site in Delaware Bay, preservationists were able to force passage of the Abandoned Shipwreck Act of 1987, which moved historic shipwrecks out of the jurisdiction of standard admiralty law.

Lyon, *"Santa Margarita"; Search for the "Atocha."* Mathewson, *Treasure of the "Atocha."*

NUESTRA SEÑORA DE LA CONCEPCIÓN

Nao (3m). *L:* ca. 140′ (42.7m). *Tons:* 600. *Hull:* wood. *Comp.:* 500. *Arm.:* 40 guns. *Built:* Havana, Cuba; 1620.

Built as a merchantman, the details of the first twenty years of the ship known officially as *Nuestra Señora de la puria y limpia Concepción* are little known. In 1639, the Casa de la Contratación ("House of Trade") in Seville

chartered the ship to sail as *capitana* of the twenty Spanish ships bound for Vera Cruz. Armed with forty guns and carrying a total complement of five hundred men, women, and children, *Concepción* made the westward crossing in sixty-four days. As was the custom, the ships unloaded at San Juan de Ulloa, the port of Vera Cruz, and remained there over the winter.

When the return fleet sailed on July 23, 1641, *Concepción* carried between one and four million pesos (35 to 140 tons) of silver, some gold, and 1,200 bales of cochineal and indigo. Although Don Juan de Villavicenio requested permission to have the ship repaired at Havana, he was overruled, even after the fleet was forced back so a leak in *Concepción* could be repaired. The fleet departed again on September 20, a month after the last ships normally sailed for Spain, in order to avoid the hurricane season.

Eight days out, a hurricane hit the fleet off the coast of Florida. All told, nine ships were lost and only two continued to Spain. The storm blew out on October 1 and she turned south for Puerto Rico. On October 31, the damaged ship grounded on Abrojos reef, north of Hispaniola in 20°43′N. She broke up two days later; thirty-three men in the surviving ship's boat landed on Hispaniola, and about 240 more people reached the island on makeshift rafts constructed from *Concepción*'s timbers.

Several expeditions were mounted to find the wreck, but it was not until 1688 that Captain William Phips discovered the site. Between February 7 and April 19, divers recovered twenty-five tons of silver, seven guns, and some gold — a treasure worth £250,000. In 1976, American treasure hunter Burt Webber rediscovered the wreck and excavated millions of dollars in silver.

Earle, *Wreck of the Almiranta.*

NUESTRA SEÑORA DE LA CONCEPCIÓN

Galleon (3m). *L/B/D:* 147.6′ × 49.2′ × 19.7′ dph (45m × 15m × 6m). *Hull:* wood. *Comp.:* 350–400. *Arm.:* 40 guns. *Built:* Cavite, Manila; <1636.

One of the largest ships of her day, *Nuestra Señora de la Concepción* was built for the trade between Manila and Acapulco. Along this route, the Manila galleons carried Mexican silver to be traded for Oriental porcelain, silks, gold, and spices. *Nuestra Señora de la Concepción* made one voyage in 1636. She set out on her second, in company with the galleon *Ambrosia,* on August 10, 1638. Caught in a storm off the Ladrones (Mariana) Islands, the two ships became separated. *Nuestra Señora de la*

Concepción was dismasted and driven ashore on Agingan Point, Saipan, on September 20. There were only twenty-eight Spanish and an undetermined number of other survivors. *Ambrosia* sailed north around Saipan, only to be lost the next year.

Concepción's cargo was looted by the islanders, and two decades later the Spanish salvaged thirty-six cannon from the wreck. As no cargo manifest existed, there was little incentive to do more. In 1987–88, Pacific Sea Resources negotiated with the government of the Mariana Islands for permission to salvage and record the remains of the wreck. Although nothing of the ship remained, the divers found more than 1,300 pieces of carat gold jewelry, as well as Chinese porcelain and storage jars. The collection was purchased for display in Saipan by Apex, Inc., a Japanese company with extensive holdings in the Marianas.

Recovery of the Manila Galleon the "Nuestra Señora de la Concepción."

NUESTRA SEÑORA DEL ROSARIO

Galleon. Tons: 1,150 toneladas. *Hull:* wood. *Comp.:* 443. *Arm.:* 51 guns. *Built:* Ribadeo, Galicia, Spain; 1587.

Built for the *carrera de las indias,* the trade between Spain and the Americas, *Nuestra Señora del Rosario* was fitting out at Cadiz on June 20, 1587, when she was seized in the name of Philip II for use in the Spanish Armada. On November 17, she was designated as flagship of the Andalusian Squadron under the accomplished seaman Don Pedro de Valdés. Thanks to his efforts, when the Armada sailed from Lisbon on May 9, 1588, she was the most heavily armed ship in the fleet, boasting 51 guns. Her complement comprised 117 crew and 300 soldiers, as well as servants, priests, and other supernumeraries, and she carried about 50,000 escudos, a third of the money earmarked for operations in England. The fleet departed La Coruña on July 22 and seven days later was off the Scilly Islands. Fighting between the English and Spanish fleets began on June 30. Trying to help other ships that had been badly damaged, *Rosario* lost her foremast and bowsprit, and the Spanish fleet pressed on leaving Valdés to fend for himself. That night, Sir Walter Raleigh approached in *Margaret and John* but sailed off with the rest of the fleet.

The next day, Sir Francis Drake appeared, having left his comrades for the sake of a fat prize. Although *Rosario* was larger and more powerfully armed and manned than REVENGE, rather than risk a fight with England's most celebrated seaman, Valdés accepted Drake's terms and surrendered. So far as Elizabeth's government was concerned, the most valuable aspect of the capture was the money (about half may have been pocketed by Valdés, Drake, or both), followed by *Rosario*'s gunpowder. In 1589, the *Rosario* sailed from Dartmouth to Chatham and then to Deptford. The prisoners were finally freed on November 24, 1590. Whether *Nuestra Señora del Rosario* ever sailed again is unknown but it seems unlikely. In 1618, still in Deptford, she was cleaned "of all the slubb, ballast and other trash within board, making her swim and removing her near into the mast dock where she was laid and sunk for the defense and preservation of the wharf there."

Martin, *Spanish Armada Prisoners.*

NYDAM BOAT

L/B: 75′ × 10.5′ (22.9m × 3.2m). *Hull:* wood. *Comp.:* 30+. *Built:* Germany; 350–400 CE.

The oak-hulled Nydam boat is one of two vessels discovered in 1863 in a bog off Als Sound in Schleswig-Holstein, about 50 miles north of Kiel. Dating from the fourth century CE, she represents a transitional phase in the development of northern European shipbuilding towards the end of the period of Roman occupation and influence. In the first century, the Roman historian Tacitus wrote of the Germans:

> The shape of their ships differs from the normal in having a prow at both ends, which is always ready to be put in to shore. They do not rig sails or fasten their oars in banks at the sides. Their oarage is loose, as one finds on some rivers, and can be shifted, as need requires, from side to side.

The Nydam boat is clearly an extension of this tradition. A very large double-ender, she was clinker built with five strakes on either side of the keel. Some of the oak planks were as long as 45 feet, and they were joined to each other by clenched bolts and to the frames by bast ropes; there is also clear evidence of caulking between the planks. There is no indication that the boat carried a mast or rigging for sails, but there were 15 thole pins on either side of the hull, as well as oars, thwarts, poles, and a 9-foot-long steering oar. Although the evidence is only circumstantial, it is likely that the Nydam boat represents the kind of vessels in which the Anglo-Saxons crossed the North Sea to settle in England, starting in the fifth century. Her lines also seem to anticipate those of the seventh-century SUTTON HOO ship found in England.

Holes had been cut in the bottom of the hull, suggesting that the Nydam boat was intentionally sunk to prevent her cargo from being captured. In and around the boat were hundreds of weapons and other artifacts, including 107 swords, 552 spearheads, 70 knives, bows, arrows, quivers, wooden shields, bronze and iron ornaments, as well as the skulls of several horses and one of a cow and 34 Roman coins dating from between 69 and 217 CE. The hull and contents of the Nydam boat were initially housed at a museum in Kiel, but today they are displayed at Schloss Gotorp in the town of Hedeby, Schleswig-Holstein. A smaller fir boat found at the same time and thought to be of Scandinavian origin was probably used for firewood by soldiers during the war between Prussia and Denmark in 1865.

Arenhold, "Nydam Boat at Kiel." Tacitus, *On Britain and Germany.* Throckmorton, ed., *Sea Remembers.*

O'HIGGINS

Frigate (3m). *Hull:* wood. *Comp.:* 600. *Built:* <1817.

In 1817, Thomas Lord Cochrane was invited by General Bernardo O'Higgins, Supreme Director of the Republic of Chile, to assume command of his fledgling country's navy in the struggle against Spanish rule. Something of a maverick within the service, Cochrane had recently been implicated in a stock scandal and dismissed from service, and he readily accepted the new assignment. Turning down a comparable offer to serve the Spanish against the Chileans, he assumed the rank of Vice-Admiral of Chili, Admiral and Commander-in-Chief of the Naval Forces of the Republic. Arriving at Valparaiso towards the end of 1818, Cochrane hoisted his flag in a captured Spanish ship renamed *O'Higgins*. In January 1819 he took a small squadron comprising his flagship, *Lautaro* (44 guns), *San Martin* (56), and *Chacabuco* (20) to blockade Callao. After his men silenced a shore battery and captured a gunboat, the Spanish dubbed Cochrane "El Diablo." The blockade was lifted in March, and the Chileans captured a number of valuable prizes along the Peruvian coast before returning to Callao in September.

Illness forced the breaking of the blockade for a second time, and the fleet split up, Cochrane taking *O'Higgins* south to the heavily fortified port of Valdivia, Chile, which was still held by the Spanish. After reconnoitering the port, he requisitioned a schooner and a brig to strengthen his force. Returning to Valdivia, *O'Higgins* hit a rock and the ammunition was ruined by water. Cochrane calmed his men and insisted they carry out their mission with bayonets. On February 3, 1821, they succeeded in capturing 8 forts, killing 100 men, capturing another 100, and putting 800 to flight. This victory strengthened the Chileans strategically and so shifted the balance of power that the government was able to raise £1 million in London.

At the end of September, Cochrane returned with 7 ships and 4,500 soldiers to Callao, which he blockaded for five weeks. At 2200 on November 5, he led 240 men in 14 boats to cut out the Spanish frigate *Esmeralda*. Although they failed to achieve complete surprise, in only fifteen minutes the Chilean crew took the ship, together with 210 officers and men; they suffered only 11 dead against 160 Spanish. As an English observer aboard HMS *Conway* wrote,

> The loss was a death-blow to the Spanish naval forces in that quarter of the world; for although there were still two Spanish frigates and some smaller vessels in the Pacific, they never afterwards ventured to show themselves, but left Lord Cochrane undisputed master of the sea.

Cochrane refused to allow the prize to be named for himself, and the captured ship was renamed *Valdivia*. After taking the town of Pisco in March, Cochrane shifted his flag to *San Martin,* which was lost at Callao when General José Francisco de San Martin insisted that she be brought too close to shore to offload a cargo of wheat. Lima capitulated shortly thereafter, and Cochrane returned to Valparaiso in *O'Higgins*.

In 1823, Cochrane was invited to render similar services for Brazil, then seeking independence from Portugal, where he again performed with distinction. Three years later, his erstwhile flagship *O'Higgins* was lost at sea en route from Chile to Buenos Aires.

Twitchett, *Life of a Seaman.*

OHIO

Tanker (1f/1m). *L/B/D:* 513.1′ × 68′ × 28.5′ (156.4m × 20.7m × 8.7m). *Tons:* 9,264 grt. *Hull:* steel. *Mach.:* steam turbine, 10,000 shp, 1 shaft; 16 knots. *Built:* Sun Shipbuilding & Dry Dock Co., Chester, Pa.; 1940.

One of the most desperate and disastrous convoy actions of World War II was that fought between the ships of Operation Pedestal and Italian and German air and naval units in the narrow defile that separates North Africa and the Italian islands of Sardinia and Sicily. By the summer of 1942, a lack of supplies had pushed the British colony of Malta to the brink of surrender. Located nearly halfway between Gibraltar and Alexandria, Egypt, the island fortress was a crucial staging ground for the defense of Britain's 2,000-mile-long Mediterranean convoy route and for attacks against ships and planes ferrying supplies to Field Marshal Erwin Rommel's Afrika Korps in North Africa.

By the summer of 1942, everything from food to antiaircraft ammunition was being rationed, and it was estimated that the island could hold out no longer than the end of August. Operation Pedestal was the name given to a relief convoy of fourteen ships that sailed from Liverpool on August 3. The single most important ship was the welded-hull fast tanker *Ohio*, which had been transferred to the British flag after a direct request from Prime Minister Winston Churchill to President Franklin D. Roosevelt, and which sailed under command of Captain Dudley Mason.

On August 10, the convoy was joined at Gibraltar by a force of more than forty Royal Navy vessels, including the battleships HMS RODNEY and NELSON, the aircraft carriers HMS *Victorious, Indomitable, Eagle,* and FURIOUS, seven cruisers, twenty destroyers and eight submarines. The following afternoon, *U-73* torpedoed and sank HMS *Eagle* with the loss of 300 of her crew, and that evening German bombers attacked the convoy, without success. On the night of August 12, further attacks south of Sardinia resulted in damage to the freighter *Deucalion* (which was later sunk) and the loss of the destroyer *Foresight*. At this point, the remaining carriers and battleships also returned to Gibraltar with their escorts, reducing the convoy to thirteen merchant ships, three cruisers, and ten destroyers. The same night, the Italian submarine *Axum* sank the antiaircraft cruiser HMS *Cairo*, and damaged *Ohio* and the cruiser HMS *Nigeria,* which turned for Gibraltar. This was followed by a bomber attack that resulted in the loss of *Empire Hope* and *Clan Ferguson,* and damage to *Brisbane Star,* which eventually made it to Malta on her own. A second submarine attack by the Italian *Alaki* struck HMS *Kenya*.

As the ships sailed through the Skerki Channel at 0130 on August 13, they were set upon by ten torpedo boats that sank the cruiser *Manchester* and the merchantmen *Glenorchy, Wairangi, Almeira Lykes,* and *Santa Elisa*. Repeated air attacks that day resulted in the loss of *Waimarama* in the morning and the disabling of *Dorset* and *Ohio,* and Captain Mason transferred his crew to a destroyer until about 1800. Heavily damaged, *Rochester Castle, Port Chalmers,* and *Melbourne Star* limped into Valetta at 1630 that afternoon. In the meantime, *Ohio* and *Dorset* came under renewed attack that evening. *Dorset* was sunk, and Captain Mason again ordered his crew off the ship. Although within sight of Malta by the following

morning, *Ohio*'s freeboard was less than three feet, and even with two destroyers lashed to her, she could proceed at no more than one knot. She finally limped into Grand Harbour on August 15 but was so severely damaged that she was intentionally sunk at dockside so that she would not break up while her precious cargo was unloaded. *Ohio* remained at Valetta until 1946 when she was towed out of the harbor and sunk in deep water.

Smith, *Pedestal: The Malta Convoy of August 1942.*

OLIVEBANK

(later *Caledonia, Olivebank*) Bark (4m). *L/B/D:* 326′ × 43.1′ × 24.5′ (99.4m × 13.1m × 7.5m). *Tons:* 2,824 grt. *Hull:* steel. *Comp.:* 21. *Built:* Mackie & Thompson, Glasgow; 1892.

One of two sister ships — the other was *Cedarbank* — built for Andrew Weir and Company, which later became the Bank Line, *Olivebank* was employed in general trade for twenty-one years under the British flag. During this time she carried general cargoes between Europe and Pacific ports, including wheat, nitrate, and coal. In 1913, she was sold to Akties Olivebank of Norway for whom she traded for three years. Between 1916 and 1922, she changed hands three more times. After renaming her *Caledonia,* her last Norwegian owners laid her up at Sandefjord for eighteen months. Her luck turned in 1923, when she was sold to Captain Gustav Erikson of Mariehamn, who ran the last big fleet of square-rigged ships. Erikson gave her back her old name and put her in the Australian grain trade. A dull sailer, during the 1930s *Olivebank* was twice reported overdue, but she was much liked and considered "a ship with a great personality." In the late 1920s, she carried cadets for the Lithuanian merchant marine. She remained in the grain trade until she became one of the first casualties of World War II. Homeward bound off Jutland, on September 8, 1939, she hit a mine and sank with the loss of fourteen of her crew, including her captain and chief mate.

Appleyard, *Bank Line and Andrew Weir and Company.* Lubbock, *Last of the Windjammers.* Muncaster, *Rolling round the Horn.*

USS OLYMPIA (C-6)

Olympia-class cruiser (2f/2m). *L/B/D:* 344.1′ × 53′ × 21.5′ (104.9m × 16.2m × 6.6m). *Tons:* 5,586 disp. *Hull:* steel. *Comp.:* 411. *Arm.:* 4 × 8″ (2 × 2), 10 × 5″, 4 × 6pdr, 6 × 1pdr; 6 × 18″TT. *Mach.:* triple-expansion, 18,000 hp, 2 screws; 20 kts. *Built:* Union Iron Works, San Francisco; 1895.

The cruiser USS OLYMPIA *at San Francisco Harbor in 1895. Note her pronounced ram bow, cruiser stern, and mixed armament of 8-inch, 5-inch, 6-pdr., and 1-pdr. guns. The flagship of Commodore George Dewey's victorious squadron at the Battle of Manila Bay in 1898 survives today at Philadelphia. Courtesy U.S. Naval Historical Center, Washington, D.C.*

Named for the capital of Washington State, USS *Olympia*'s first commission was as flagship of the Asiatic Fleet. In 1898, she came under command of Captain Charles V. Gridley and flew the flag of Commodore George Dewey. At the time, Spanish-American relations were strained by Spain's treatment of Cuban nationalists, and the loss by explosion of USS MAINE at Havana Harbor was seen by many as an excellent pretext for a war. In the Far East, such a war would be centered on the Spanish colony of the Philippines, the seizure of which would further enhance America's position as a world power.

War began on April 25 and two days later Dewey received orders to proceed to Manila. In addition to *Olympia,* he had under his command the cruisers BALTIMORE, *Raleigh,* and *Boston,* and the gunboats *Petrel* and *Concord.* Manila was weakly defended by a poorly maintained, inadequately trained Spanish squadron consisting of Rear Admiral Patricio Montojo's flagship, the cruiser *Reina Christina,* which mounted six 6.2-inch guns and was only half as big as *Olympia,* together with the wooden cruiser *Castilla* and five gunboats. After slipping unseen into Manila Bay on May 1, Dewey's ships came under fire at a range of about 9,000 yards. As he later recalled: "At 5:40

when we were within a distance of 5,000 yards, I turned to Captain Gridley and said, 'You may fire when you are ready Gridley.' . . . The very first gun to speak was an 8-inch . . . of the *Olympia.*" The gunnery was appalling on both sides — in Dewey's fleet, only 2.4 percent of the 5,859 shells expended hit their targets — but after two hours, the two largest Spanish ships had been sunk and most of the rest were either sinking or burning. Dewey resumed shelling at 1100, and Montojo surrendered at 1230. Only one American sailor was killed. Returning to Hong Kong on May 20, *Olympia* sailed for New York by way of the Suez Canal and the Mediterranean and arrived to a hero's welcome on October 10, 1899.

Three years later, *Olympia* became flagship of the Caribbean Division, North Atlantic Squadron, and later alternated between assignments in the Atlantic, Mediterranean, and Caribbean. Withdrawn from service in 1906, except for midshipmen cruises from Annapolis between 1907 and 1909, in 1912 she became a barracks ship at Charleston, South Carolina. As war with Germany threatened, she was recommissioned in 1916 and sailed on convoy duty in the North Atlantic. Following the Brest-Litovsk Treaty between Russia and Germany and the start of the Russian Revolution, *Olympia* was dispatched to Archangel and Murmansk to help garrison those northern ports against Bolshevik intrusion. With the end of World War I, *Olympia* moved to the Mediterranean, and between 1918 and 1920 spent most of her time helping to quell disturbances along the Adriatic coast of Yugoslavia, which had come into being with the collapse of the Austro-Hungarian Empire. *Olympia*'s last overseas mission was to carry the remains of World War I's Unknown Soldier from Le Havre to Washington, D.C., for interment at Arlington National Cemetery. Decommissioned and preserved as an historic ship at Philadelphia in 1922, she was taken over by the Cruiser *Olympia* Association in 1957.

Beach, *United States Navy.* Emerson, "USS *Olympia.*" U.S. Navy, *DANFS.*

OLYMPIAS

Trireme (2m). *L/B/D:* 120.7' × 17.7' × 11.8' dph (36.8m × 5.4m × 3.6m). *Tons:* 45 disp. *Hull:* wood. *Comp.:* 196. *Des.:* John F. Coates, John Morrison. *Built:* Piraeus; 1987.

Among the largest, and certainly the fastest, warships in classical antiquity was the trireme, a long, narrow vessel propelled by 170 oars and fitted with a large bow ram with which to punch holes in enemy ships. Triremes — in Greek, *trieres* — evolved from the triacontor and pentecontor, oared ships propelled by 30 and 50 oars, respectively. These smaller vessels probably served chiefly as transports, and when enemy ships engaged each other, the crews would attempt to capture their opponents' ships in a boarding action. However, the most effective way to disable an enemy ship was to ram it. This tactic was one to which the faster and more maneuverable trireme was ideally suited. It is estimated that the trireme was as much as 30 percent faster than a pentecontor, which remained the standard vessel for smaller city-states lacking the resources to build, much less man, triremes. In the years prior to Xerxes' invasion of Greece in 480 BCE, the Athenians built 200 triremes; but at the Battle of Salamis they had to draw on their Plataean and Chalcidian allies to man their ships, each of which required 170 oarsmen, a helmsman, and up to 30 auxiliaries for a total of 40,000 people.

Although large numbers of triremes were built, few details of their design and construction remain. Pictorial and sculptural evidence, though relatively abundant, is inexact, and written descriptions are scant. Archaeological evidence is also slight and likely to remain so. Being unballasted, triremes did not sink; they could be towed

away from battle even if badly damaged, and if they were beyond salvage, they would simply drift at sea until they broke up. The primary evidence for the trireme's dimensions comes from the excavation of the trireme sheds at Zea, near Piraeus. These were capable of housing vessels up to 40 meters in length and 5.6 meters in width. The written record also attests to the materials and method of construction. The primary woods employed for planking were fir, pine, and cedar, fir being lighter and therefore preferable, while the keels were of oak, which was better suited to being hauled ashore. The hull was of shell-first, mortise-and-tenon construction typical of Mediterranean ships of antiquity.

One of the most dedicated students of the trireme is John Morrison, who spent more than half a century researching the evolution, dimensions, manning, and tactical use of triremes. In the 1980s, he and John Coates, retired Chief Naval Architect of the Royal Navy, collaborated on the design of a trireme based on the available evidence. Having determined the basic dimensions, the most complex design issue was the arrangement and size of the oars. Triremes had three banks or files of oars, each pulled by one man. On the uppermost bank were 62 oarsmen, called thranites, 31 on either side, while the lower two tiers held 54 zygians and 54 thalamians, respectively. The thranites' oars pivoted on a short outrigger set out from the hull so that they wouldn't interfere with those of the lower two tiers. The thalamians' oar ports were less than half a meter above the waterline and were covered with leather sleeves to prevent water from entering.

There were two sizes of oars: 9 cubits (4 meters), used by oarsmen at the bow and stern, and 9.5 cubits (4.22 meters), used by oarsmen — who sat on fixed seats — in the middle of the vessel. Although triremes carried two masts, sails were probably not used when the vessel was being rowed because if the wind were coming from anywhere but dead astern, the vessel would heel too much for the oars to work. Even over fairly long periods, rowing could be faster than sailing. Thucydides records one nonstop voyage from Piraeus to Mytilene in 427 BCE in which a trireme was rowed 184 miles in little more than 24 hours (about 7.5 knots) and Xenophon describes the 129-mile run from Byzantium to Heraclea on the Black Sea being covered in about 18 hours (about 7 knots).

In 1982, Coates and David Moss built a mock-up of a trireme oar system, and in 1984 the Hellenic Navy expressed its interest in building a full-scale replica, which took two years to complete. Approximately two millennia after her ancestors last plied the Mediterranean, the trireme *Olympias* took to the waters at Piraeus. Manned by volunteer rowers of both sexes from around the world,

Olympias proved a dramatic success. Although there was much to be learned about the preferred practices in rowing and steering a trireme, *Olympias* attained sprint speeds of 7 knots in the first season. Three years later, after learning a lot about how to row the ship and modifying the oars, speeds of 8.5 knots were achieved in a short sprint.

The trireme seems never to have been improved upon for speed. Larger vessels were apparently built, such as the Roman quinquireme and later large polyremes, but the root words "three," "four," and "five" apply not to the number of banks of oars but to the number of oarsmen (*remex*) on each side of the ship. In a trireme, there was one oar on each of three levels, and one oarsman to each oar. In a quinquireme, the oars on the top two levels were pulled by two men each, and the smaller oars on the bottom level were pulled by one man, so that there were five files of oarsmen on each side of the ship. In the larger and later polyremes, there were only two levels of oars, with each oar pulled by four men (in an octoreme, or "eight") or five men (in a decareme, or "ten"). It is likely that the oars manned by three or more men were at least partly worked by the "stand-and-sit" stroke of the later medieval galleys. Oared vessels continued to evolve and survived in European navies as late as the eighteenth century. The last naval engagements in which oared ships played a significant role were fought in the Russo-Swedish War of 1788–90.

Casson, *Ships and Seamanship in the Ancient World.* Coates, "Trireme Sails Again." Morrison, ed., *Age of the Galley.* Morrison, *Greek and Roman Oared Waships.* Morrison & Coates, *Athenian Trireme.*

OLYMPIC

Liner (4f/2m). *L/B:* 883′ × 92.5′ (269.1m × 28.2m). *Tons:* 45,324 grt. *Hull:* steel. *Comp.:* 1st 735, 2nd 674, 3rd 1,026; crew 860. *Mach.:* triple expansion/steam turbine, 3 screws; 21 kts. *Built:* Harland & Wolff, Belfast, Ireland; 1911.

The biggest ship in the world when launched, *Olympic* was the first of an ill-fated trio of superliners that included BRITANNIC and TITANIC. Ordered for White Star Line, then part of J. P. Morgan's International Mercantile Marine, *Olympic* was intended to be the transatlantic liner par excellence, combining great size and comfort with a moderate turn of speed. Her maiden voyage, under Captain Edward J. Smith, from Southampton to New York via Cherbourg and Queenstown on June 11 took 5 days and 16 hours. That September *Olympic* collided with HMS *Hawke* in the Solent when her triple screws caused such massive suction that the cruiser was pulled into the larger ship's stern. *Olympic* was held to blame, and after

repairs at Belfast resumed service on November 30. Following the loss of her sister ship *Titanic* (then under *Olympic*'s erstwhile Captain Smith), *Olympic* underwent a massive "safety-first" rebuild including the installation of an inner skin and the installation of enough lifeboats to accommodate all passengers and crew.

Following the start of World War I, on October 27 *Olympic* attempted to take in tow the battleship HMS *Audacious,* which had struck a mine off Tory Island, north of Ireland. In September 1915, *Olympic* was converted for use as a troopship, in which role she performed admirably, even sinking the German *U-103* off the Lizard on May 12, 1918. *Olympic* continued as a troopship for about a year after the armistice before she was withdrawn from military duties in August 1919.

Prior to her return to civilian service, *Olympic* was converted from coal to oil fuel. In addition to being cleaner and less bulky, oil fuel was less labor-intensive: engine room staff were cut from 246 to 60 men.

On June 25, 1920, she resumed passenger service between Southampton, Cherbourg, and New York. Still the overbearing ship's ill luck continued, and on March 22, 1924, she collided with Furness Lines' *Fort St. George* near New York, damaging her own sternpost in the process. Her passenger accommodations were reconfigured to suit the changing face of transatlantic travel during the depression, first in 1928 and again in 1931. The superliner's worst collision occurred on the morning of May 16, 1934. Steaming towards New York at high speed in a dense fog, at 1006 she rammed and sank the NANTUCKET LIGHTSHIP. Four of the eleven crew were killed instantly, and three more died of exposure or injuries after their rescue by *Olympic.*

Later the same year, White Star was absorbed by Cunard Line and in the drive for greater efficiency, *Olympic* was withdrawn from service after her last voyage from Southampton on March 27, 1935. Laid up at Southampton upon her return, she was scrapped at Jarrow and Inverkeithing.

Martin, *Other Titanic.* Shipbuilder and Marine Engine-Builder, *White Star . . . Liners "Olympic" and "Titanic."*

OMEGA

(ex-*Drumcliff*) Bark (4m). *L/B/D:* 311.3′ × 43.2′ × 24.2′ dph (94.9m × 13.2m × 7.4m). *Tons:* 2,471 grt. *Hull:* steel. *Built:* Russell & Co., Greenock, Scotland; 1887.

Drumcliff was one of nine "Drum-" ships built for the firm of Gillison & Chadwick. She sailed for them in general trade until sold in 1896 to Rhederei A/G von 1896 of Hamburg, who renamed her *Omega.* She continued in

Photographed here in the early years of the 20th century when under German ownership, as befitted her name the four-masted bark OMEGA *of 1887 was the last square-rigger in commercial sail. Courtesy National Maritime Museum, Greenwich.*

general trade under that flag, ranging as far afield as Australia for wheat, Peru for nitrate, and the U.S. East Coast for case oil. Caught on the coast of Peru at the start of World War I, she was seized and used as a training vessel for the Peruvian Navy. Later acquired by the Compania Administradores del Guano Ltd. of Lima, except for a few voyages to Europe in the early 1920s, she spent the next four decades hauling guano from the Islas de Peru to the mainland, long after the trade in nitrate to Europe had dried up. By 1953, there were only three square-rigged vessels at work in this — or indeed any other — trade: *Omega* and the three-masted barks *Tellus* and *Maipo*. In that year, Frederick Wilhelmsen and his brother sailed in *Omega* for two months. Three years later, *Tellus* and *Maipo* were sold to the breakers. *Omega* survived them by two years, sinking en route from the Pachacomec Islands to Huacho on June 26, 1958, with a cargo of guano. As befitted her name, she was the very last square-rigger in commercial sail.

Hurst, *Square-Riggers*. Wilhelmsen, *"Omega."*

ONTARIO

Sidewheel steamer (1f/2m). *L/B/D:* 140′ × 24′ × 6′ (42.7m × 7.3m × 1.8m). *Tons:* 237 grt. *Hull:* wood. *Mach.:* beam engine, side-wheels; 5 kts. *Built:* Sackett's Harbor, N.Y.; 1817.

After securing permission to operate a steamboat on the Great Lakes — a monopoly that the New York State legislature had granted to Robert Fulton and Robert R. Livingston — the Lake Ontario Steamboat Company was incorporated in 1816 with a view to developing general steamboat service on Lake Ontario. The first U.S.-built steamer on the Great Lakes and a contemporary of the Kingston, Ontario-based FRONTENAC, the schooner-rigged *Ontario* entered service at Sackett's Harbor, New York, on April 11, 1817. She plied between that port, the Genesee River, Ogdensburg, and Niagara until withdrawn from service in 1832.

Musham, "Early Great Lakes Steamboats: The *Ontario* and *Frontenac*."

OREGON

Liner (2f/4m). *L/B:* 501′ bp × 54.2′ (152.7m bp × 16.5m). *Tons:* 7,375 grt. *Hull:* iron. *Comp.:* 1st 340, intermediate 982, 3rd 110, steerage 1,000. *Mach.:* compound engine, 1 screw; 18 kts. *Built:* John Elder & Co., Glasgow; 1883.

Oregon was the last of fifteen ships built for the Liverpool and Great Western Steamship Company, known as the Guion Line for its founder, American shipping executive Stephen Guion, whose ambition was to have the finest and fastest ships afloat. Between 1879 and 1884, his

Fr. Goth's naive painting "The Arrival of the Steamship OREGON at Portland, Maine, on January 21, 1884." Despite the natural advantages of a well-protected deep-water port, Portland could not compete with Boston or New York for transatlantic trade. Courtesy Peabody Essex Museum, Salem, Massachusetts.

Alaska, Arizona, and *Oregon* held sway on the Atlantic. *Oregon* captured the Blue Riband from *Arizona* by crossing from Sandy Hook to Queenstown at 17.12 knots in March 1884 and returning at a speed of 18.56 knots (6 days, 10 hours, 10 minutes; April 13–19). She improved her westbound performance three more times that year, although her last two records were for Cunard, to whom she had been sold to pay off Guion's debts. *Oregon's* fastest Queenstown-to-Sandy Hook crossing was at 18.39 knots (6 days, 11 hours, 9 minutes; September 3–10). Two years later, disaster struck when, at 0420 on March 14, 1886, she collided with a vessel believed to be the schooner *Charles Morse,* eighteen miles east of Long Island. Badly holed, she sank about three hours later. There were no casualties, the majority of her 852 passengers and crew being taken off by Norddeutscher Lloyd's *Fulda.*

Bonsor, *North Atlantic Seaway.* Braynard & Miller, *Fifty Famous Liners.*

USS OREGON (BB-3)

Battleship (2f/1m). *L/B/D:* 351.2′ × 69.3′ × 24′ (107m × 21.1m × 7.3m). *Tons:* 10,288 disp. *Hull:* steel. *Comp.:* 473. *Arm.:* 4 × 13″, 8 × 8″, 4 × 6″, 20 × 6pdr, 6 × 1pdr; 6 × 18″TT. *Armor:* 18″ belt; 3″ deck. *Mach.:* triple expansion, 9,000 hp, 1 screw; 15kts. *Built:* Union Iron Works, San Francisco; 1896.

The only battleship assigned to the Pacific Fleet, on February 16, 1898, USS *Oregon* was just coming out of dry-dock in Bremerton when news reached her of the sinking of the battleship USS MAINE at Havana, the day before. Ordered to San Francisco, she arrived there on March 9 and received orders three days later to join Admiral William Sampson's Atlantic Battle Squadron in Florida. *Oregon* sailed on March 19; she stopped for coal at Callao on April 4, entered the Strait of Magellan on April 17, stopping at Punta Arenas, and arrived at Rio de Janeiro on April 30. There the crew learned that war with Spain had been declared on April 21. Disregarding rumors of a Spanish torpedo boat on the South American coast and of an intercepting squadron en route from the Cape Verde Islands, Captain Charles E. Clark proceeded to Bahia, Barbados and, finally, Jupiter Inlet, Florida, arriving there on May 24. Despite boiler trouble in the Pacific, adverse winds and currents in the South Atlantic, and a bunker fire that lasted two days between Bahia and Barbados, *Oregon* made the 14,000-mile journey in a record sixty-six days. Joining Admiral Sampson's fleet on May 28, *Oregon* took part in the destruction of Admiral Pascual Cervera's fleet at Santiago Bay on June 3. *Oregon's* journey demonstrated both that heavy battleships could stand up to adverse conditions for extended periods and that a canal across the Central American isthmus was vital to U.S. national security. (The Panama Canal opened in 1914.)

After a refit in New York, *Oregon* was assigned to the Asiatic Station where she took part in the suppression of the Philippine Insurrection. Dispatched to China during

The battleship USS ORE-GON, *departing New York for Manila on October 12, 1898, only months after her legendary dash round Cape Horn from Seattle to the Caribbean on the eve of the Spanish-American War. It is interesting to contrast* OREGON *with her smaller contemporary, the cruiser* USS OLYMPIA. *Courtesy U.S. Naval Historical Center, Washington, D.C.*

the Boxer Rebellion, she did not return stateside until 1906, when she was decommissioned in Puget Sound. In and out of commission through World War I, in 1918 she was briefly attached to the American Siberian Expeditionary Forces sent to aid anti-Bolshevik Czechoslovak forces in Vladivostok. A preservation effort to save *Oregon* began in 1921, but in 1942 she was struck from the Navy list and sold for scrap. In 1944, the hull of *Oregon* was requisitioned for use as a hulk at Guam. In 1956, *Oregon*'s remains were sold to a Japanese firm and the ship was scrapped at Kawasaki.

Bradford, "And *Oregon* Rushed Home." Sternlicht, *McKinley's Bulldog.* Webber, *Battleship Oregon.*

L'ORIENT

1st rate 120 (3m). *Hull:* wood. *Arm.:* 120 guns. *Built:* Toulon; 1791.

Originally named for the heir apparent to the French throne, following the death of Louis XVI in 1792, *Le Dauphin Royal* was renamed *Sans Culotte,* the name given to lower-class extremists during the French Revolution. Stationed at Toulon, in March 1795 she flew the flag of Admiral Martin during his skirmish with Vice Admiral William Hotham's Mediterranean Fleet. Three years later, *L'Orient* sailed as flagship of an armada assembled at Toulon under command of Vice Admiral François Paul Brueys d'Aiguïlliers. Bound ultimately for Egypt, where

the French intended to establish a bridgehead from which they could invade British India (the ship's new name suggests the tendency of French strategic thinking), some 75 warships, 400 transports, 10,000, sailors and 36,000 soldiers led by General Napoleon Bonaparte slipped out of port on May 20, 1798. The same day, a blockading force under Rear Admiral Horatio Nelson was blown off station in a gale. On June 10, the French were at Malta, which they captured on the 12th. Continuing via Crete, they reached Egypt on July 1, seizing the port of Alexandria the next day and Cairo three weeks later. In the meantime, Brueys stationed his fleet off the island of Aboukir in the Nile Delta east of Alexandria. On August 1, his thirteen ships were anchored in line ahead and many of the crew getting water ashore when Nelson finally caught up with him in midafternoon. Brueys made two miscalculations: that Nelson would not attack until the next morning, and that his ships need not clear for action the shoreward-facing guns as Nelson would attack only from the sea. He was disappointed on both counts.

Five of Nelson's ships passed between the van of the French line and the shore, while another six, led by Nelson's HMS VANGUARD, ranged themselves on the seaward side of the French line. The battle began at 1830, with the 74-gun BELLEROPHON opposite Brueys's *L'Orient.* By 2000, the British ship was forced to disengage, but *L'Orient* was ablaze and Brueys and Captain Louis de Casabianca were mortally wounded. HMS *Swiftsure* and *Alexander* pressed home the attack on the French flagship, and at about 2200, *L'Orient's* magazine exploded and the ship blew apart. Only about seventy-five of the French crew survived, including Casabianca's ten-year-old son, Jacques, whose steadfast loyalty was commemorated in Felicia Heman's 1829 ballad, which begins, "The boy stood on the burning deck / Whence all but he had fled."

With the loss of *L'Orient,* the six ships in the French van and center quickly surrendered. The British ships had anchored by the stern, and with a favorable wind, they now continued down the French line to capture or destroy all the French ships except *Généreux, Guillaume Tell,* and two frigates, which escaped under Rear Admiral Pierre Charles de Villeneuve. Two other ships of the line were sunk, three were beyond repair, and six were brought into the Royal Navy. The Battle of the Nile was the first decisive defeat of the French in years, and Nelson was lionized throughout Europe, not least by his own officers and crew. Among his many tributes was a casket made from the main mast of *L'Orient* presented to him by *Swiftsure's* Captain Benjamin Hallowell and in which he was buried after his death aboard HMS Victory at the Battle of Trafalgar in 1805.

Culver, *Forty Famous Ships.*

ORION

(ex-*Kurmark*) Merchant raider. *L/B/D:* 463.5′ × 61.1′ × 27′ (141.3m × 18.6m × 8.2m). *Tons:* 7,021 grt. *Hull:* steel. *Comp.:* 377. *Arm.:* 6 × 5.9″, 1 × 75mm. 2 × 37mm, 4 × 20mm; 6 × 21″TT. *Mach.:* steam turbines; 14.8 kts. *Built:* Blohm & Voss, Hamburg; 1930.

Built as a steamship for Hapag East Asia service between Germany and the Orient, at the start of World War II *Kurmark* was requisitioned by the German Navy for use as a merchant raider. Designated Schiff 36 and renamed *Orion* by Lieutenant Commander Kurt Weyher (whose previous command was the bark *Horst Wessel,* now USCGC Eagle), she slipped into the North Atlantic in March 1940, with orders to mine the waters around New Zealand. Although she would spend the next 18 months at sea, longer than any other German raider, she accounted for only 12 Allied ships (73,477 tons). On April 24, she sank the steamer *Haxby* in midatlantic before rounding Cape Horn on May 21. On the night of June 13–14, *Orion* laid 228 mines in the Hauraki Gulf off Auckland, one of which accounted for the Union Steamship Company of New Zealand's liner *Niagara,* bound for Canada with 10 tons of gold bullion. (In early 1941, salvage experts recovered 94 percent of the gold from the

wreck, which lay at 438 feet, 40 feet deeper than Egypt.) The raider spent the next few months in the South Pacific and Indian Oceans, but she sank only three more ships before rendezvousing with *Komet* in the Marshall Islands. Together the two raiders sank the 16,710-ton *Rangitane* on November 27, the largest prey to any raider, and five ships off Nauru (whose phosphate plants and oil reserves *Komet* later destroyed).

Over the next seven months, *Orion's* greatest enemy was her own oil-fired engines, which needed constant repairs. Back in the Atlantic, on July 29, 1941, she torpedoed the English freighter *Chaucer.* (The father of *Chaucer's* Captain Charles Bradley had lost his ship to the raider Möwe in World War I.) Finally, on August 23, 1941, *Orion* limped into Bourdeaux, France, after a voyage of 510 days. She later saw a variety of assignments in European waters, concluding with the evacuation of German forces from the eastern Baltic in April 1945.

Muggenthaler, *German Raiders of World War II.* Weyher & Ehrlich, *Black Raider.*

HMS ORPHEUS

Screw corvette (1f/3m). *L/B/D:* 254′ × 41′ × 19′ (77.4m × 9.4m × 5.8m). *Tons:* 1,706 bm. *Arm.:* 16 × 8″, 1 × 7″, 4 × 40pdr. *Built:* direct-acting horizontal engines, 400 hp, 1 screw; 12 kts. *Built:* Chatham Dockyard, Eng.; 1861.

Commissioned in 1861, HMS *Orpheus* was a flush-deck warship intended for service as flagship of the Australasian Naval Station. Under Captain William Farquharson Burnett, she sailed for Sydney, where Burnett broke his commodore's pennant. On January 31, 1863, *Orpheus* sailed for Auckland to join HMS *Niger* and *Harrier* at Manukau Harbour. Of immediate military concern was the conduct of the Second Maori War. Approaching Manukau Harbour under sail and steam on the clear morning of February 7, 1863, *Orpheus's* officers failed to heed semaphore signals from Manukau Heads indicating the proper approach — across Manukau bar — into Auckland. At about 1230, *Harrier's* Quartermaster Frederick Butler, who was aboard under arrest for desertion, pleaded to share his local knowledge with the sailing master. He quickly discovered that *Orpheus's* chart was not current; but despite an immediate course change, the ship hit hard two minutes later. With no assistance available to her in the treacherous shoal waters, the ship was quickly battered to a hulk. Of the ship's complement of 258, only 69 survived what remains to this date New Zealand's worst maritime disaster.

Hetherington, *Wreck of H.M.S. "Orpheus."*

OSCAR II

Passenger ship (1f/2m). *L/B/D:* 500.5′ × 58.4′ (152.6m × 17.8m). *Tons:* 10,012 grt. *Hull:* steel. *Comp.:* 1st 130, 2nd 140, 3rd 900. *Mach.:* triple expansion, 8,500 ihp, 2 screws; 16 kts. *Built:* Alexander Stephen & Sons, Ltd., Glasgow; 1902.

Named for the reigning King of Sweden, *Oscar II* was one of three sister ships built for Scandinavian-American Line's passenger service between Copenhagen, Christiania (later Oslo), Kristiansand, and New York. The line continued transatlantic service under the neutral Danish flag during World War I, although its ships were frequently detained at Kirkwall by the Royal Navy to ensure against their carrying contraband from the United States to Germany. In 1915, the industrialist Henry Ford chartered *Oscar II* to carry a peace mission to Norway for the purpose of establishing a Neutral Conference for Continuous Mediation. The mission's prime mover was Rosika Schwimmer, a Hungarian journalist and peace activist who tried to get President Woodrow Wilson to mediate an end to hostilities. Promising to get "the boys out of the trenches by Christmas," the Ford entourage embarked on "The Peace Ship" at New York on December 4, 1915. After a brief detention at Kirkwall, Orkney, the ship arrived in Christiania on the 19th. Although Ford was against the war on economic grounds, the man who believed that "history is more or less bunk" was widely ridiculed for his efforts. *Oscar II* remained in service through 1931 and was broken up at Blyth in 1933.

Bonsor, *North Atlantic Seaway.* Kraft, *Peace Ship.*

OSEBERG SHIP

Karvi. *L/B/D:* 70.8′ × 16.7′ × 5.2′ dph (21.6m × 5.1m × 1.6m). *Tons:* 11 disp. *Hull:* wood. *Comp.:* 35. *Built:* Norway; ca. 815–820.

Dating from the beginning of the period of Viking expansion, the Oseberg ship was found in 1904 in a burial mound located on a farm of the same name at Slagen, about 70 miles south of Oslo. The Oseberg ship is a karvi, a large, clinker-built open boat with 12 strakes per side, each riveted to the one below it. The planking was fastened to the 17 ribs by baleen or whale-bone lashings, a technique that made the boat highly elastic. There are 15 oar holes beneath the shield racks on either side of the ship, and the oars themselves measure between 3.7 meters and 4 meters. The rudder, really an enlarged oar, was fitted on the starboard (or steering board) side aft. Evidence suggests that the mast would have stood about 13 meters high and set a single square sail. The ship's one-meter, 7-kilo anchor was made of forged iron with an oak anchor stock. Although the Oseberg ship is estimated to have been about fifteen to twenty years old when it was buried, the ship probably served more as a chieftain's private vessel rather than as a warship. Its low freeboard also suggests that it was built for coastal rather than offshore sailing.

Despite a long-standing belief that the Oseberg mound was the burial place of Queen Åsa, grandmother of Harald Comely-Hair, the evidence is only conjectural. The mound was probably looted in the Middle Ages at which time the ship's bow was damaged; many of the ship's timbers had also collapsed under the weight of the rocks placed in and around the ship when it was buried. The excavation and preservation of the burial site was led by Gabriel Gustafson, who oversaw the removal of thousands of wood fragments that were treated with creosote and taken to Oslo, where they were painstakingly reassembled. In 1926, the ship was moved to the Viking Ship Hall at Bygdøy, Oslo, where it is housed together with remains of the GOKSTAD and Tune ships. Thanks to the blue clay of the Slagen area, the Oseberg horde yielded a great many well-preserved wooden artifacts, including, in addition to the items noted above, a bailing bucket, figureheads, beds, tents, and the remains of more than 10 horses, oxen, and cows.

Sjøvold, *Oseberg Find and the Other Viking Ship Finds.*

SMS OSTFRIESLAND

Helgoland-class battleship (3f/2m). *L/B/D:* 548.9′ × 93.5′ × 29.3′ (167.3m × 28.5m × 8.9m). *Tons:* 24,700 disp. *Hull:* steel. *Comp.:* 1,112. *Arm.:* 12 × 12.2″ (6 × 2), 14 × 6″, 14 × 8.8cm; 6 × 20″TT. *Armor:* 12″ belt, 3.2″ deck. *Mach.:* triple expansion, 31,258 ihp, 3 screws; 20.8 kts. *Built:* Kaiserliche Werft, Wilhelmshaven, Germany; 1911.

Named for a region of Germany bordering on the North Sea, *Ostfriesland* was one of four *Helgoland*-class battleships commissioned in 1911–12. During World War I, she was attached to the first Battle Squadron of the High Seas Fleet and took part in operations in the North Sea and Baltic in 1915–16. Mined while returning to port from the Battle of Jutland in early June 1916, following repairs she made only a few more tentative sorties into the North Sea. In 1920, *Ostfriesland* was turned over to the United States as reparations and prepared for use as a target ship.

During World War I, a number of proposals had been advanced to use airplanes against capital ships, but all were dropped. In 1920, Brigadier General William "Billy" Mitchell began training air crews to demonstrate the superiority of air power over battleships and the Navy reluctantly agreed to provide targets. After sinking three U-boats, a destroyer, and a cruiser, on July 20, 1921, Martin bombers were loaded with 230-pound and later 600-pound bombs to use against *Ostfrieland*, 60 miles off the Virginia coast. These had little effect, but the next day they returned from Langley Field armed with 1,000- and 2,000-pound bombs. Hit below the waterline by six 1-ton bombs, *Ostfriesland* sank 21 minutes after the attack began. Popular lore had it that pro-battleship admirals wept to see the ship go down, but the full power of planes against capital ships would not be felt until 1941, with the British attack on Taranto, and the Japanese attacks on Pearl Harbor and on the battleships HMS PRINCE OF WALES and REPULSE.

Lyman, "Day the Admirals Wept." O'Connell, *Sacred Vessels*.

OTAGO

Bark (3m). *L/B/D:* 147′ × 26′ × 14′ dph (44.8m × 7.9m × 4.3m). *Tons:* 346 grt. *Hull:* iron. *Built:* Alexander Stephen & Sons, Ltd., Glasgow; 1869.

Built for Grierson & Company, of Adelaide, Australia, *Otago* was named for a bay near Dunedin, New Zealand. Although a small bark that would spend most of her career trading around Australia and the East Indies, *Otago*'s maiden voyage was an eighteen-month circumnavigation from England via Adelaide, Sydney, and San Francisco. Sold in 1871, her career is distinguished by the fact that Joseph Conrad sailed in her first as second mate and then as captain. On August 8, 1887, *Otago* sailed from Newcastle, Australia, bound for Haiphong, then part of French Indochina. From there *Otago* sailed for Bangkok, but en route Captain John Snadden died and temporary command fell to the first mate. When the ship arrived in Thailand, Mr. B— (as Conrad refers to him in *The Mirror of the Sea*) was passed over in favor of the twenty-nine-year-old Conrad.

On February 9, 1888, *Otago* sailed for Sydney with a cargo of teak. The three-week passage down the Gulf of Siam was marred by stifling calms, illness among the crew, and the mate's antipathy. But as he recalled in *The Shadow Line,* his fictional account of his first and only command in sail, Conrad was instantly enamored of his ship.

> At the first glance I saw that she was a high-class vessel, a harmonious creature in the lines of her fine body, in the proportioned tallness of her spars. Whatever her age and her history, she had preserved the stamp of her origin. She was one of those craft that in virtue of their design and complete finish will never look old. Amongst her companions moored to the bank, and all bigger than herself, she looked like a creature of high breed — an Arab steed in a string of cart horses.

Six new crew joined the ship at Singapore before *Otago* sailed again. From Sydney, Conrad took her on a series of short passages along the Australian coast before sailing her northabout through the Torres Strait en route to Mauritius. *Otago* returned to Melbourne in January 1889, and Conrad resigned his command at the end of March.

Otago continued trading under a variety of owners before she was converted to a coal hulk by Huddart, Parker & Company. By 1924, she was lying at Hobart, Tasmania, and seven years later she was sold to a ship breaker. Still, it was not until 1960 that she was finally broken up on the Derwent River. Her association with Conrad conferred on her a certain immortality, and, like some medieval saint, her corporal remains are found around the world: the ship's wheel at the headquarters of the Honourable Company of Master Mariners in London, a portion of the stern with the National Park Service in San Francisco, and a portion of the hull near Hobart.

Conrad, *Mirror of the Sea; Shadow Line*. Lubbock, *Last of the Windjammers*.

P

PACIFIC

Steamship (1f/3m). *L/B:* 281′ × 45′ (85.7m × 13.7m). *Tons:* 2,707 grt. *Hull:* wood. *Comp.:* 200 1st, 80 2nd; 140 crew. *Mach.:* side-lever, sidewheels; 12 kts. *Built:* Jacob Bell, New York; 1850.

In the 1840s, transatlantic steam service was dominated by British ships. The U.S. government sought to promote competition among American companies by offering a subsidy for carrying mail between the United States and Europe. In 1847, it awarded a subsidy — $385,000 for guaranteed, year-round, fortnightly sailings — to Edward Knight Collins, founder of the Dramatic Line of sailing packets in the previous decade. Officially named the New York & Liverpool United States Mail Steamship Company, the firm was known simply as Collins Line. The company showed great promise, launching a quartet of fast and elegant sister ships: *Atlantic, Pacific,* ARCTIC, and *Baltic.* On her maiden voyage, *Pacific* became the first American steamship to cross the Atlantic faster than a British one, steaming from Liverpool to New York at 12.5 knots (10 days, 4 hours, 45 minutes; September 11–21, 1850). The next spring, she set a new eastbound record, crossing at 13 knots (9 days, 21 hours, 14 minutes; May 10–20, 1851) with 240 passengers, a record for steamships at that date. Although the Collins ships carried more passengers than Cunard, their closest British competitor, they ran at a loss and in 1852 Congress agreed to increase their subsidy by half a million dollars.

The following year, personal and professional disaster struck Collins when *Arctic* collided with the French screw steamer VESTA and sank near Cape Race with the loss of more than 300 passengers, including his wife and two children. On January 23, 1856, *Pacific* sailed from Liverpool with 80 passengers. Despite exhaustive searches, no trace of her was ever found, and it was generally assumed that she had foundered in midatlantic. However, in the

Samuel Waters's painting of PACIFIC *rescuing the crew of the bark* JESSE STEVENS *in 1852. Four years later, the Collins Line steamer departed Liverpool and vanished. Courtesy Peabody Essex Museum, Salem, Massachusetts.*

early 1990s, divers led by J. L. Smart (who had worked the ROYAL CHARTER wreck site) discovered the remains of a ship tentatively identified as *Pacific,* lying in the Irish Sea about 12 miles northeast of Anglesey. Further investigation remains to determine whether the site represents the bones of *Pacific* and, possibly, why she sank without trace.

Bonsor, *North Atlantic Seaway.* Sloan, "Wreck of the Collins Liner *Pacific."*

PADUA

(later *Kruzenstern*) Bark (4m). *L/B/D:* 320.5′ × 46.1′ × 25.4′ (97.7m × 14.1m × 7.7m). *Tons:* 3,064 grt. *Hull:* steel. *Comp.:* 40 cadets. *Built:* J. C. Tecklenborg, Geestemünde, Germany; 1926.

Built for Reederei F. Laeisz, *Padua* was one of the last large square-rigged ships built to trade under sail. Under

Built for commercial service after World War I, the stately, power- ful PADUA *was one of the last clippers of her age. Of her kind, Harold Underhill wrote, they were "built to sail and be sailed — ships which could take all the driving their master cared to give them, and . . . keep it up voyage after voyage." She is seen here in later years as the Soviet Union's training ship* KRUZENSTERN. *Photo by Beken of Cowes.*

the hard-driving J. Hermann Piening, she made some of the fastest passages of the postwar era, including a 1928 run from Hamburg to Talcahuano in 71 days and a return from Mejilones to Terneuzen, Holland, in 72 days. Five years later, she sailed from Hamburg for the Spencer Gulf in 63 days, one day behind *Priwall,* whose passage was the record time. Her last deep-water voyage for Laeisz was from Bremen to Valparaiso, Port Lincoln, and, in the last grain race, back to Glasgow, where she arrived on July 3, 1939. Having discharged her cargo of grain, she sailed to Hamburg in ballast and arrived there on August 8, less than a month before the start of World War II.

In 1946 *Padua* was seized by the Soviet Union and renamed *Kruzenstern,* in honor of the Russian admiral who led the *Neva* and NADEZHDA expeditions in 1803. Operated by the Ministry of Fisheries as a sail-training ship with a complement of 230 cadets and crew, *Kruzenstern* was active in European waters and visited New York for the U.S. bicentennial in 1976 and the Statue of Liberty Centennial in 1986. With the break-up of the Soviet Union in the early 1990s, she came under the authority of the Estonian Ministry of Fisheries.

Rohrbach, et al., *FL: A Century and a Quarter of Reederei F. Laeisz.*

PAMIR

Bark (4m). *L/B/D:* 316′ × 46′ × 23.4′ (96.3m × 14m × 7.1m). *Tons:* 3,020 grt. *Hull:* steel. *Comp.:* 30; 52 cadets. *Built:* Blohm & Voss, Hamburg; 1905.

Ordered by Reederei F. Laeisz for its Flying P Line of nitrate clippers and named for the Central Asian mountain range, *Pamir* was built to sail in the hard-driving nitrate trade between Europe and Chile via Cape Horn. Leaving Chile in July of 1914, when Captain Max Jürgen Heinrich Jürs learned that war had broken out, he put into Santa Cruz in the Canary Islands, where the German ship and crew remained for over five years. Allocated to Italy as reparations, she was laid up at Castellamare and Genoa until 1922 when she was sold back to Laeisz, returning to the nitrate trade until July 1931. Bought by Gustaf Erikson of Mariehamn, Åland Islands, in Finland, she entered the grain trade from Australia, occasionally carrying timber and other bulk cargoes from Europe. In 1941, Finland was in a state of war with Great Britain, and *Pamir* was seized at Wellington. She made ten voyages under the New Zealand flag from New Zealand and Australia to the United States.

Restored to Finnish ownership in 1948, she was the last sailing ship chartered to carry grain from Australia to Europe. She left Port Victoria on May 28, 1949, three days before her near-sister ship, PASSAT, and dropped anchor in Falmouth 128 days later. (*Passat* was 110 days to Queenstown.) Sold to ship breakers in Antwerp, the two ships were saved when Heinz Schliewen of Lübeck purchased *Pamir* and *Passat* as cargo-carrying sail-training ships with accommodations for 52 cadets. The ships later passed to a consortium of 40 German ship owners (Laeisz was not among them), the Stiftung *Pamir* und *Passat*, Lübeck, to train and trade between Europe and South America. On her fifth voyage, in 1956, she sailed from Buenos Aires on August 10 bound for Hamburg with 3,780 tons of barley and a complement of 86. On September 21, about 600 miles west-southwest of the Azores, she sailed into a hurricane. Her inadequately stowed cargo shifted in the high wind and sea, and after transmitting two distress calls, she sank at about 1600 in the afternoon in approximately 35°57′N, 40°20′W. There were only six survivors.

Churchouse, *"Pamir" under the New Zealand Ensign.* Tunstall-Behrens, *"Pamir": A Voyage to Rio.* Waters, *"Pamir."*

Built to protect American interests in China during that country's civil war, in 1937 the doughty gunboat USS PANAY was sunk by Japanese planes in an event that prefigured the Japanese attack on Pearl Harbor four years later. Courtesy U.S. Naval Historical Center, Washington, D.C.

USS PANAY (PR-5)

River gunboat. *L/B/D:* 191′ × 29′ × 5.3′ (58.2m × 8.8m × 1.6m). *Tons:* 474 disp. *Hull:* steel. *Comp.:* 59. *Arm.:* 2 × 3″; 8 × .30 cal. mg. *Built:* Kiangnan Dockyard & Engineering Works, Shanghai, China; 1928.

Named for a Philippine island, USS *Panay* was one of several vessels built for the Yangtze River patrol to protect U.S. interests during the Chinese civil war. Japanese forces invaded China in July 1937, and on December 11, the last officials at the U.S. Embassy in Nanking were evacuated aboard *Panay,* commanded by Lieutenant Commander James J. Hughes. Avoiding the sharp conflict in and around the capital, *Panay* and the Socony-Vacuum Oil Company tankers *Mei Ping, Mei Hsia,* and *Mei An* sailed upriver, notifying the local Japanese commander of their intention to do so. The next day, the Japanese ordered the destruction of all shipping on the Yangtze above Nanking. At 1327, Japanese dive-bombers attacked the clearly marked American flotilla about 27 miles from Nanking. *Panay* was abandoned after an hour and sank at 1554 with the loss of 2 killed and 48 wounded. *Mei An* was sunk with the loss of her skipper, Captain Carl H. Carlson, and several dozen of her crew. The United States lodged a formal protest, and although the claim that the attack was accidental was incredible, Japan's apology and payment of indemnities were accepted.

Grover, *"Panay" Revisited.* Koginos, *"Panay" Incident.* Perry, *"Panay" Incident.*

HMS PANDORA

6th rate 24 (3m). *L/B/D:* 114.5′ × 32′ × 16′ (34.9m × 9.8m × 4.9m). *Tons:* 520 bm. *Hull:* wood. *Comp.:* 160. *Arm.:* 22 × 9pdr, 2 × 3pdr. *Built:* Adams & Barnard, Deptford Dockyard, Eng.; 1779.

HMS *Pandora* was named — some might say aptly — for the woman of Greek myth who let escape from a box all the evils to which mankind is subject, save hope, which lay, inexplicably, at the bottom. On November 7, 1790, she sailed from Portsmouth under Captain Edward Edwards in search of the mutineers from HMS BOUNTY. Calling at Tenerife and Rio de Janeiro, she rounded Cape Horn in January 1791 and arrived at Tahiti on March 23, 1791. Within the week the fourteen "mutineers" — some of whom had been kept aboard *Bounty* against their will — remaining at Tahiti were arrested. Having also acquired some breadfruit trees (the object of *Bounty*'s voyage) as well as a schooner named *Resolution* built by the mutineers, *Pandora* sailed six weeks later. The prisoners were confined in "Pandora's Box," an 11-by-18-foot hutch erected on the quarter deck. Sailing westward, the ship searched in vain for *Bounty* and the other mutineers among the islands of Polynesia, losing one boat and four of her crew off Palmerston Island, and then *Resolution*, with nine men, for which she searched the Friendly (Tonga) Islands for almost a month.

Passing within sight of Vanikoro, in the Santa Cruz Islands, where La Pérouse's BOUSSOLE and ASTROLABE had wrecked three years before, on August 26 *Pandora* entered Endeavour Strait between New Guinea and Australia. Two nights later she struck a reef. The following morning she sank in sixty feet of water; thirty-one crew and four prisoners were drowned. On August 31, the ninety-nine ill-provisioned survivors put to sea in the four ship's boats and sailed for the Dutch settlement at Kupang, Timor, 1,100 miles to the west. They arrived on September 13; three weeks later, they sailed for Batavia in the East Indiaman *Rembang.* At Semarang they were reunited with the crew of the long-lost *Resolution,* which had arrived a few weeks before without a man lost during its 5,000-mile voyage. A few days later they arrived at Batavia, where Edwards and company embarked in four Dutch traders. They arrived at Table Bay on March 18, 1792, where they joined HMS *Gorgon,* which finally landed at Spithead on June 20. In the subsequent trial of the nine *Bounty* mutineers who survived the journey, four were acquitted, two pardoned, one reprieved, and three hanged. *Pandora*'s remains were discovered by divers in the 1980s and excavation began in 1993.

There is an interesting sidebar to the *Pandora* story. While at Timor, Edwards had been forced to take responsibility for eight men, a woman, and her two children. The adults were convicts who had stolen a small boat from the British penal colony at Botany Bay and sailed 3,254 miles in sixty-nine days without the loss of a single life. The woman, Mary Bryant, had been transported in 1786 and given birth to a girl en route. She later bore a son, who was still at her breast on the voyage to Timor. He died at Batavia and her daughter died aboard *Gorgon.* Her case came to the attention of James Boswell, who visited her and the four other surviving convicts in Newgate Prison, and later secured for them a pardon and bestowed an annuity on Bryant of £10 per year.

McKay & Coleman, *24-Gun Frigate "Pandora."* Marden, "Wreck of H.M.S. *Pandora.*" Rawson, *"Pandora"'s Last Voyage.*

PANTANO LONGARINI WRECK

Merchantman. *L:* 100′ (30m). *Tons:* 200–300. *Hull:* wood. *Built:* Greece or S. Italy; 7th cent.

In 1973, workers draining a field on the south coast of Sicily west of Cape Passero came upon the timbers of a ship approximately 600 meters (1,800 feet) from the shoreline. Samples of the wood were taken to a nearby shipwright, who in turn notified the Department of Antiquities in Syracuse. Formal excavation of the site was turned over to Gerhard Kapitän, who led excavations of the site in 1964 and 1965 working with grants from the University of Pennsylvania. Preliminary tests indicated that the surviving timbers — oak frames and cypress planking and wales — date from between 350 and 650 CE. Although it later turned out that workers had destroyed as much as 15 meters of planking on the starboard side, the surviving timbers were about 12 meters long, and it is estimated that the ship was originally as long as 30 meters. The ship is similar in construction to the seventh-century YASSI ADA WRECK. The hull was built first and the frames inserted later. One interesting detail previously known only through representations of Roman ships is the way in which the longitudinal beams were tucked, or hooked, over the wales. It is theorized that the ship was blown ashore in a sirocco, and that part of the hull was broken up for firewood or scrap shortly after its loss.

Throckmorton & Kapitän, "Ancient Shipwreck at Pantano Longarini."

PANTHER

Iltis-class gunboat (2f/2m). *L/B/D:* 219.4′ × 31.8′ × 11.8′ (66.9m × 9.7m × 3.6m). *Tons:* 1,193 disp. *Hull:* steel. *Comp.:* 130. *Arm.:* 2 × 10.5cm, 4 × 8.8cm, 6 mg. *Mach.:* vertical triple expansion, 1,344 ihp, 2 screws; 13.5 kts. *Built:* Kaiserliche Werft, Danzig, Germany; 1902.

Panther was a gunboat designed for service in Germany's far-flung overseas possessions from Southwest and East Africa to Tsingtao in China. In the summer of 1909, she was homeward bound up the Atlantic when she became the instrument of a diplomatic intrigue in Morocco that involved Germany, France, and Great Britain. The seeds of the Agadir Crisis were sown in 1905 when Morocco was in the throes of political upheaval. France, which had long harbored colonial ambitions in the North African state, sought to assert its supremacy but was challenged by Germany's insistence on an "open door" policy. The Morocco Crisis of 1905 was partially resolved by the Algeciras Conference (attended by thirteen governments), the most significant outcome of which was the strengthening of Anglo-French diplomatic ties under the Entente Cordiale.

Four years later, Germany's colonial ambitions had increased substantially, and it sought to acquire southern Morocco or another African colony. As Morocco veered towards civil war, the French ordered troops to the region; in response, Germany ordered the gunboat *Panther* to protect German interests at Agadir, a small port on the Atlantic coast about 260 miles south of Casablanca, where she arrived on July 1. The only German in the vicinity was a Herr Wilburg, resident at Mogador 75 miles away. Poor roads prevented "the Endangered German," as he was described, from getting in position to have his interests defended until July 4. As before, Britain moved to reaffirm its commitment to France in the face of German gunboat diplomacy. Negotiations between France and Germany resulted in a de facto French protectorate in Morocco in exchange for German acquisition of Cameroon — a 100,000-square-mile piece of French Equatorial Africa.

Panther finally departed Agadir in November. She remained in European waters through World War I and served as a coastal defense vessel. Disarmed in 1921, she performed survey work until 1926 and was broken up at Wilhelmshaven in 1931.

Gröner, *German Warships*. Massie, *"Dreadnought."*

HMS PARAMORE

Pink (3m). *L/B/D:* 64' od (52' keel) × 18' × 9.6' (19.5m (15.8m) × 5.5m × 2.9m). *Tons:* 89 bm. *Hull:* wood. *Comp.:* 24. *Built:* Fisher Harding, Deptford Dockyard, Eng.; 1694.

Edmund Halley, who would later have a comet named after him, was the first master and commander of HM Pink *Paramore,* the first ship built specifically for surveying. The first of Halley's two expeditions "to improve the knowledge of the Longitude and the [magnetic] variations of the Compasse" left Portsmouth on November 29, 1698. The ship visited Madeira, Fernando de Noronha, Brazil, Barbados, and Anguilla, and returned to England on June 22, 1699. After cashiering his refractory lieutenant, Halley sailed again on September 16. The second voyage ventured as far south as 52°24'S, which was reached on February 1, 1700. There they encountered "great islands of ice, of so incredible a height and magnitude that I scarce dare write my thoughts about it." After sighting Tristan da Cunha, a landing was made at St. Helena (where Halley had spent from February 1677 to January 1678 cataloguing stars of the southern skies). They then sailed to Trinidad Island off Brazil (which Halley tried to claim for Britain), Pernambuco, and from there northward through the Caribbean to Newfoundland. *Paramore* returned to England on September 7, 1700. Halley's third voyage, in 1701, was a four-month cruise crisscrossing the English Channel to observe tidal currents. The same year he published the first magnetic charts of the Atlantic and Pacific Oceans. Refitted as a

bomb ketch, HMS *Paramore* sailed under Captain Robert Stevens in Sir George Rooke's Mediterranean squadron in the 1702 war against France. She was sold to Captain John Constable in 1706.

Thrower, *Three Voyages of Edmund Halley.*

PARIS

Liner (3f/2m). *L/B:* 764.3' × 85.3' (232.9m × 26m). *Tons:* 34,569 grt. *Hull:* steel. *Comp.:* 1st 565, 2nd 460, 3rd 1,100; crew 648. *Mach.:* steam turbines, quadruple screw, 46,000 shp; 21 kts. *Built:* Chantiers & Ateliers de St. Nazaire (Penhöet), St. Nazaire, France; 1921.

Paris was one of a quartet of luxury liners intended for Compagnie Générale Transatlantique (CGT)'s North Atlantic trade in the years before World War I. Laid down in 1913, work was suspended following the outbreak of war, but in 1916 she was launched to free up her slipway and laid up at Quiberon Bay. One of the first new ships to enter transatlantic passenger service after the war, *Paris* embarked on her maiden voyage between Le Havre and New York in June 1921. Nearly half again as big as the next largest CGT ship, *France* (1912), she was known as the "Aristocrat of the Atlantic." (The third and fourth ships of the foursome, originally planned for delivery by 1920, were ILE DE FRANCE and *Lafayette*, commissioned in 1927 and 1930, respectively.) Severely damaged by fire at Le Havre in 1929, *Paris* reentered service the following year, but during the next decade, she was used increasingly for cruising. On April 19, 1939, she again caught fire at Le Havre and, in a disaster that prefigured the loss of CGT's NORMANDIE at New York in 1942, capsized in her berth after too much water was pumped onto the flames. The outbreak of World War II in September made salvage impossible, and she was broken up after the war.

Bonsor, *North Atlantic Seaway*. Kludas, *Great Passenger Ships of the World.*

PARMA

(ex-*Arrow*) Bark (4m). *L/B/D:* 327.7' × 46.5' × 26.2' (99.9m × 14.2m × 8m). *Tons:* 3,090 grt. *Hull:* steel. *Comp.:* 32. *Built:* A. Rodger & Co., Port Glasgow, Scotland; 1902.

Arrow was built for the Anglo-American Oil Company for trade between New York, the Far East, and Australia. Her primary cargo outbound was case oil, returning with wool and grain. In 1911, she was sold to Ferdinand Laeisz's Flying P Line. Renamed *Parma,* she entered the

Hard at work in the business district of a square-rigger, the crew of PARMA *furl the fore upper topgallant sail, in a photo by Alan Villiers. Courtesy National Maritime Museum, Greenwich.*

nitrate trade between Chile and Europe. The start of World War I found her at Iquique, where she was interned for the duration of the war with her fleet mate PASSAT. In 1921, she was allocated to the British government as war reparations and returned to Europe, only to be sold back to Laeisz the same year. The market for square-rigged shipping contracted in the depression, and in 1931 Laeisz sold *Parma* to an Åland Island–based syndicate headed by Reuben de Cloux, whom Alan Villiers (his partner in the venture) would later describe as "the outstanding Ålands master-mariner." At the time she was the only Finnish-flag sailing ship in the grain trade not owned by Gustaf Erikson. In 1933 *Parma* sailed from Australia to Falmouth in eighty-three days, the best time of the century, despite the fact that many of her crew thought that the presence of two women — the captain's daughter, Ruby de Cloux, and Betty Jacobsen, an American apprentice — would bring her bad luck. In 1936, *Parma* was damaged at Glasgow while being handled by two towboats. The cost of repairs being prohibitively ex-

pensive, she was sold to German ship breakers. She was rigged down as a hulk at Hamburg and towed to Israel after the war.

Greenhill & Hackman, *Grain Races*. Jacobsen, *Girl before the Mast*. Potts, *Wind from the East*. Rohrbach et al., *FL: A Century and a Quarter of Reederei F. Laeisz*. Villiers, *Last of the Wind Ships; Voyage of the "Parma."*

PASSAT

Bark (4m). *L/B/D:* 322′ × 47.2′ × 22′ (98.1m × 14.4m × 6.7m). *Tons:* 3,091 grt. *Hull:* steel. *Built:* Blohm & Voss, Hamburg; 1911.

A sister ship of PEKING, *Passat* ("Trade Wind") was built for the nitrate trade between Chile and Europe. A fast ship, in her four voyages before World War I she averaged seventy-nine days out to Valparaiso, and ninety days back. Held at Iquique during World War I (with her running mate PARMA), in 1921 she was surrendered to France as reparations only to be sold back to Laeisz at the end of the year. Resuming her old trade, during the 1920s she was involved in two serious accidents in the English Channel: in 1928, she rammed and sank the French steamer *Daphne*, and the following summer she collided with another steamer. In both instances, she was forced back to Rotterdam for repairs.

The depression and the development of synthetic fertilizers made the nitrate trade unprofitable, and in 1931 Laeisz sold *Passat* to the Åland Island ship master, Captain Gustaf Erikson. Under his flag she took part in the grain races between Australia and Europe through the start of World War II. In 1949, she and PAMIR sailed from Australia to Europe for the last time, a passage recorded in Holger Thesleff's *Farewell Windjammer*. Sold to German interests for use as a merchant-training vessel, she sailed between Argentina and Europe with grain. Withdrawn from that work in 1957, she has been preserved as a floating camp at Lübeck since April 1966.

Rohrbach et al., *FL: A Century and a Quarter of Reederei F. Laeisz*. Thesleff, *Farewell Windjammer*.

PATRIA

Liner (3f/2m). *L/B:* 489.7′ × 56.7′ (149.3m × 17.3m). *Tons:* 11,885 grt. *Hull:* steel. *Comp.:* 1st 140, 2nd 250, 3rd 1,850. *Mach:* triple expansion, 2 screws; 17 kts. *Built:* Forges & Chantiers de la Méditerranée, La Seyne, France; 1914.

Launched in 1913 for the Compagnie Française de Navigation à Vapeur Cyprien Fabre & Compagnie (Fabre

Line), *Patria* entered service between Marseilles and New York in April 1914. She made only three voyages before the start of World War I, but despite the submarine threat, she maintained fairly regular service. In the 1920s, she frequently called at Providence, Rhode Island, a Fabre stop that was more convenient for French emigrants bound for Canada. The U.S. Congress passed more stringent immigration laws in 1921, and Fabre's passenger traffic fell by nearly half. Three years later, *Patria* was put in the cruise trade from New York with calls in the Azores, Madeira, and Mediterranean ports as far east as Constantinople and Alexandria. The depression forced Fabre to charter *Patria* to Messageries Maritime in 1932, and she was sold to that line at the beginning of 1940.

That fall, the British government chartered *Patria* for a scheme to relocate to the Indian Ocean island of Mauritius 1,771 Jewish immigrants who had been detained while trying to enter Palestine from Europe illegally. The underground Jewish resistance group Haganah was opposed to British policy in Palestine generally and to this plan in particular. In an effort to dramatize the plight of the Jewish illegals housed aboard the ship, on November 25, 1940, they attempted to scuttle the ship while she lay in Haifa Harbor. Unfortunately, the explosives used were too powerful, and *Patria* rolled over and sank in 12 minutes, taking with her 202 passengers and 50 crew and police. Her shattered hulk lay in Haifa Harbor until broken up in 1951 in La Spezia, Italy.

Bonsor, *North Atlantic Seaway*. Holly, *"Exodus 1947."* Steiner, *Story of the "Patria."*

USS PEACOCK

Sloop of war (3m). *L/B/D:* 117.9′ × 31.5′ × 16.3′ (35.9m × 9.6m × 5m). *Tons:* 509 bm. *Hull:* wood. *Comp.:* 140. *Arm.:* 2 × 12pdr, 20 × 32pdr. *Des.:* William Doughty. *Built:* Adam & Noah Brown, New York; 1813.

Named to commemorate the victory of USS HORNET over HMS *Peacock,* on February 24, 1813, USS *Peacock* departed for the southeastern United States in March 1814. While cruising off Cape Canaveral on April 29, she encountered the eighteen-gun HMS *Epervier* and a merchant ship bound from Havana to Bermuda. She fought the British brig for forty-five minutes before Commander Richard Wade, RN, was forced to strike. After putting into Savannah with her prize (which served in the Mediterranean Squadron under the same name until her disappearance in 1815), *Peacock* set out on her second cruise during which she took fourteen prizes between the Grand Banks, the coasts of Ireland and Spain, and the West Indies. On January 23, 1815, she began her third cruise, to the Indian Ocean, where she captured the East India Company's cruiser *Nautilus* on June 30, only to release her upon learning that the War of 1812 was over.

Peacock sailed with the Mediterranean Squadron from 1816 to 1821. The following year she began service with Commodore David Porter's anti-piracy "Mosquito Fleet" in the West Indies. In 1824, she joined the Pacific Squadron with which she sailed under Master Commandant Thomas ap Catesby Jones. Over the next three years she ranged around the Pacific working to protect U.S. commercial interests threatened by revolution in Spain's South American colonies, as well as in the Pacific islands frequented by American whalers. *Peacock* was the first U.S. warship to visit Tahiti, where Jones drew up an agreement for the safety of shipwrecked American sailors. In 1826 he visited the Hawaiian Islands and negotiated a more comprehensive treaty with King Kamehameha III — never ratified by the United States — relating to both the treatment of U.S. sailors and favorable trading rights for American merchants. En route home, *Peacock* was nearly stove by a whale. She was broken up shortly after her return to New York in 1826.

Johnson, *Thence Round Cape Horn*. U.S. Navy, *DANFS*.

PEGGY

Schooner (2m). *L/B:* 26.4′ × 7.7′ (8.1m × 2.3m). *Hull:* wood. *Des.:* George Quayle. *Built:* Castletown, Isle of Man, UK; 1789.

Named for Margaret Quayle, wife of Captain George Quayle, *Peggy* is the world's oldest surviving yacht. Quayle was an early exponent of the sliding keel (as the earliest centerboards were known), first developed by Captain Shank at Boston, Massachusetts, in about 1775. *Peggy* was one of several multipurpose workboats ordered by Quayle in 1789. Rigged with two masts and fitted with six oar ports, her hull form was apparently common on both sides of the Atlantic in the late 1700s. During her construction, Quayle decided to fit *Peggy* with sliding keels, which made impractical her employment in either fisheries or general trade, and Quayle used her as his private yacht. In 1796, he sailed *Peggy* from the Isle of Man to the English mainland and carted her overland to a regatta on Lake Windermere. Quayle described his reception there with evident pride and wrote that

the long bolsprit [bowsprit] and sliding keels have already produced strong symptoms of scisme [divided opinion] among the devotees of freshwater sailing. Captain Heywood's boat is the second best in the Lake — modesty prevents me from saying who bears the bell.

Quayle also spoke highly of *Peggy*'s performance in the rough return to Man. After deciding not to run before the storm for Liverpool or Wales,

> We put down the Slidg Keels and *that* inabled us to stand on now & then lettg fly the Fore Sail continuing our tacked we fetched abt. 3 Leagues to the Leeward of the Calf — the Wind now changed to the Westward & by one tack we made this Bay. . . . The Quarter Cloths were of the greatest protection, without them I believe we had gone to Davy Jones' Locker — & without the Slidg Keels we cd not have carried Sail enough.

At some point thereafter, *Peggy* was walled up in the cellar of a boathouse built by Quayle on Castletown Harbor. There she remained until the 1930s, when she was rediscovered; documents relating to her history and use also came to light. Preserved as the only surviving two-masted vessel dating from the seventeenth century, *Peggy* has been the centerpiece of the Maritime Folk Museum at Castletown, Isle of Man, since the 1970s.

Brouwer, *International Register of Historic Ships*. Greenhill, "Schooner *Peggy*."

PEKING

(ex-*Arethusa*, HMS *Peking, Arethusa, Peking*) Bark (4m). *L/B/D:* 320.1′ × 46.9′ × 15.4′ (97.8m × 14.3m × 4.7m). *Tons:* 3,100 grt. *Hull:* steel. *Comp.:* 31 crew; 43 trainees. *Built:* Blohm & Voss, Hamburg; 1911.

Built by the Reederei F. Laeisz Company — the Flying P Line — of Hamburg for the 11,000-mile haul from Germany to Chile via Cape Horn, *Peking* carried general cargo from Europe, returning with nitrate, the best and cheapest fertilizer until the advent of chemical fertilizers in the 1920s. *Peking* was laid up in Valparaiso for seven years during and after World War I. Given to Italy as reparations in 1921, two years later she was bought back for her original trade by Laeisz, who in 1926 began carrying merchant marine cadets.

In 1929 a young American named Irving Johnson joined *Peking*, then under command of Captain Max Jürgen Heinrich Jürs, for a voyage from Hamburg to Valparaiso. The result was twofold: *The "Peking" Battles Cape Horn*, a splendid account of his ninety-three-day voyage published in 1933, and an astonishing sixteen-millimeter film of the voyage, including footage taken from the main royal yard in a full hurricane off Cape Horn. He showed his movie to the Honorable Company of Master Mariners, which promptly asked for a copy of this singular visual record to be given to the British Museum.

Built in 1911, the steel bark PEKING *achieved immortality when in 1929 Irving Johnson filmed his passage in her from Germany to Chile.* Around Cape Horn *contains some of the most dramatic footage of a windjammer under sail ever filmed. After a career as a training ship,* PEKING *moved to New York's South Street Seaport Museum. Courtesy Norman Brouwer.*

Laeisz sold *Peking* to the Shaftesbury Homes and Arethusa Training Ship in 1932, and she was used as a stationary schoolship for the next four decades. (During World War II, she was requisitioned by the Royal Navy for use as an accommodation ship at the Chatham Dockyard in Devon.) In 1974, she was acquired by the South Street Seaport Museum for use as a museum ship in New York, where she has been since 1975.

Johnson, *"Peking" Battles Cape Horn*. Rohrbach et al., *FL: A Century and a Quarter of Reederei F. Laeisz*. Film: Johnson, *War with Cape Horn*.

PÉREIRE

Screw steamer (1f/3m) (later *Lancing*, ship, 4m). *L/B/D:* 345' × 43.5' × 29' dph (113.4m × 13.3m × 6.9m). *Tons:* 3,015 grt. *Hull:* iron. *Comp.:* 1st 226, 2nd 98, 3rd 31. *Mach.:* vertical engine, 3,390 ihp, 1 screw; 13 kts. *Des.:* Sir William Pearce. *Built:* Robert Napier & Sons, Glasgow; 1865.

Originally intended as a bark-rigged sidewheel steamer, the Compagnie Générale Transatlantique steamer *Péreire* was converted to a single-screw steamship while still on the stocks. Named for the president of the French Line, she was built for transatlantic service and sailed between Le Havre, Brest, and New York. She was a remarkably fast vessel from the start, and in 1868 made the passage from Brest to New York in 8 days, 10.5 hours, an average speed of 14.5 knots, faster than the time posted by Cunard's SCOTIA between Queenstown and New York in 1863. Except during the Franco-Prussian War in 1870–71, she remained in this service without interruption until 1882, when she was fitted with compound engines and a second funnel. The following year she entered service to Mediterranean, Caribbean, and Gulf of Mexico ports.

In 1888 she was sold to G. A. Hatfield of Nova Scotia, who converted her to a four-masted full-rigged ship renamed *Lancing*. Her new dimensions were 356 feet by 43.8 feet, with a depth of hold of 27.25 feet and a gross tonnage of 2,678; her crew numbered around 27 men. With a length-to-beam ratio of nearly 8 to 1, *Lancing* proved extremely fast under sail. She once logged an average 18 knots over 72 hours, faster than she ever steamed, and in 1916 she sailed from Scotland to Newfoundland in 6 days, 18 hours, land to land. Even more outstanding, while running her easting down from Melbourne in 1890–91, she logged 22 knots over 15 consecu-

tive hours, a speed never equaled by a commercial ship under sail. Though she initially sailed under the Canadian flag, *Lancing* was managed by A. E. Kinnear & Company, of London. She was sold to Norwegian interests in 1893, and then to Canadian interests. From 1901 to 1920, she was owned by Akt. Lancing, Johansen & Company of Christiania (Oslo). Her last Norwegian owners were Melsom & Melsom, who operated her until 1925, when — still carrying the 100-A1 classification at Lloyd's — she was sold to Italian ship breakers.

Craig, *Boy Aloft.*

HMAS PERTH

Sydney-class light cruiser (2f/2m). *L/B/D:* 562' × 56.7' × 19.5' (171.3m × 17.3m × 5.9m). *Tons:* 8,850 disp. *Hull:* steel. *Comp.:* 682. *Arm.:* 8 × 6" (4 × 2), 8 × 4", 12 × 0.5"; 8 × 21"TT; 1 aircraft. *Armor:* 3" belt, 1.3" deck. *Mach.:* geared turbines, 72,000 shp, 4 shafts; 32.5 kts. *Built:* Portsmouth Dockyard, Eng.; 1936.

Commissioned as HMS *Amphion*, this cruiser spent two years as flagship of the Africa Station. Transferred to the Royal Australian Navy and renamed HMAS *Perth,* she represented Australia at the New York World's Fair before sailing for home. While still in the Caribbean, on August 26, she was put under Admiralty orders in anticipation of the start of war in Europe. She remained in Atlantic and Caribbean waters through February 1940 when she returned to Australia. Detailed for service in the Mediterranean in December 1940, *Perth* took part in the Battle of Cape Matapan and the evacuation of Greece and Crete before returning to Australia at the end of 1941.

In early February 1942, *Perth* joined the American-

A Currier and Ives lithograph of the bark-rigged single-screw steamship PÉREIRE, *which went on to a successful career as the four-masted ship* LANCING. *She is flying the French flag at the stern, the U.S. courtesy flag at the fore truck, and, at the main truck, the French Line flag: a red circle and the legend "Cie. Gle. Transatlantique" on a white field. Courtesy The Mariners' Museum, Newport News, Virginia.*

British-Dutch-Australian (ABDA) force cobbled together to stop the Japanese advance through Indonesia. Following the disastrous Battle of the Java Sea, *Perth* and USS HOUSTON were ordered to Tjilatjap. After refueling they sailed from Batavia in the early evening of February 28. At 2245 the two ships ran into a Japanese convoy escorted by an aircraft carrier, seven cruisers, and twenty destroyers. Struck by four torpedoes, *Perth* was sunk off Bantam Bay at 0025 with the loss of 352 crew, including Captain H. M. L. Waller. (Another 111 died as POWs.) The ship's remains were discovered by Australian diver David Burchall in 1967.

Burchell, *Bells of Sunda Strait.* Payne, *H.M.A.S. "Perth."*

PHÉNIX

Redoutable-class submarine. *L/B/D:* 302.5′ × 27′ × 16′ (92.2m × 8.2m × 4.9m). *Tons:* 1,379/2,060 disp. *Hull:* steel. *Comp.:* 67. *Arm.:* 11 × 21.7″TT, 1 × 37mm, 1 mg. *Mach.:* diesel/electric, 6,000/2,500 hp, 2 screws; 17/10 kts. *Built:* C. H. Dubigeon, Nantes, France; 1927.

A member of one of the most successful submarine classes built by France before World War II, *Phénix* was stationed in French Indochina. On June 15, 1939, she was on routine patrols with her sister ship *L'Espoir* and the cruiser *Lamotte-Picquet,* when she sank with all hands eight miles northeast of Cam Ranh in 365 feet of water. There were seventy-one officers and crew aboard under Lieutenant Commander D. M. Bouchacourt. Following so close on the loss of the submarines USS SQUALUS (May 23) and HMS THETIS (June 1) and against a background of rising tension in Europe and the Far East, the tragedy excited suspicions of conspiracy and sabotage. One journal questioned, "Can this be the law of averages — that three democracies lose three submarines in less than a month?" American industrialist Henry Ford blamed the sinkings on "a scheme by financial war-makers to get the country into war. Of course they will blame Germany, but I don't think the Germans are the responsible parties. The real trouble is that wars are over with and the financial war-makers don't know it." Efforts to recover *Phénix* by the salvage vessels *Valeureux* and USS PIGEON were abandoned after a cable looped around the submarine snapped on July 13.

Chesneau, ed., *Conway's All the World's Fighting Ships.* Press reports.

PHILADELPHIA

Gundalow (1m). *L/B/D:* 53.3′ × 15.5′ × 3.8′ dph (16.3m × 4.7m × 1.2m). *Hull:* wood. *Comp.:* 45. *Arm.:* 1 × 12pdr., 2 × 9pdr. *Built:* Skenesborough, N.Y.; 1776.

During the American Revolution, one of Britain's primary objectives was to sever New England from the rest of the colonies, by attacking down Lake Champlain, between New York and Vermont, and into the Hudson River Valley. To counter this threat, General Benedict Arnold assembled a small army of soldiers and shipbuilders at Skenesborough, New York, and, in the course of a few months, threw together a fleet of three galleys, one cutter, and eight gunboats, one of which was *Philadelphia.* The lightly armed, flat-bottomed gundalows set two square sails on a single mast, although the ships' primary means of propulsion was probably sixteen oars. On October 11, 1776, Arnold's fleet was moored off southwest Valcour Island about fifty-five miles north of Fort Ticonderoga, when Captain Thomas Pringle's fleet — five warships, twenty gunboats, and twenty-eight longboats — rounded the southern end of the island. In the ensuing action, the two-masted galleys *Congress* and *Washington* were run aground and captured, and *Philadelphia* was sunk by a single round of 24-pdr. shot. The four-day battle was a tactical defeat for the revolutionaries. Nonetheless, with his ammunition depleted, Pringle was forced to postpone his drive south until the following spring. In the meantime, the Continental Army reinforced its position enough to inflict a stunning victory against the British at Saratoga, considered a turning point in the American Revolution.

In 1934, Colonel Lorenzo F. Hagglund, a salvage engineer, found the remains of *Philadelphia* in ten fathoms of water, her mast still standing. Remarkably preserved after 158 years in the cold, fresh water of Lake Champlain, the hull was raised on August 1, 1935, and exhibited in New York until 1961. *Philadelphia* then underwent four years of restorative work before being exhibited at the Smithsonian Museum of American History in Washington, D.C.

Fowler, *Rebels under Sail.* Lundeberg, *Continental Gunboat "Philadelphia."*

USS PHILADELPHIA

Frigate (3m). *L/B/D:* 157′ × 39′ × 13′ (47.9m × 11.9m × 4m). *Tons:* 1,240 bm. *Hull:* wood. *Comp.:* 307. *Arm.:* 26 × 18pdr long, 16 × 32pdr carr. *Des.:* Josiah Fox. *Built:* Samuel Humphreys, Nathaniel Hutton & John Delavue, Philadelphia; 1800.

One of six frigates built with funds provided by merchants during the Quasi-War with France, USS *Philadelphia* was commissioned under Captain Stephen Decatur, Sr., towards the end of the war. Considered one of the fastest ships of her day, on her first tour of duty off Guadeloupe, she captured five French armed vessels and recaptured six U.S. vessels. Returning to the United States in March 1801, *Philadelphia* was prepared for service in the Mediterranean where U.S. merchant vessels were being harassed because of the government's refusal to pay tribute to the rulers along the Barbary Coast of North Africa. Sailing under command of Captain Samuel Barron in a squadron led by Commodore Richard Hale in USS PRESIDENT, *Philadelphia* sailed on blockade duty off Tripoli for a year before returning to the United States at the end of July 1802. The following spring, she returned to the Mediterranean under Captain William Bainbridge. On August 26, 1803, she captured the Moroccan ship *Mirboka* (24 guns) together with her American prize, the brig *Celia*, and brought them both into Gibraltar.

Proceeding to blockade duty off Tripoli, on October 31 *Philadelphia* hit an uncharted reef in the harbor. Under fire from shore batteries and gunboats, the ship remained fast and Bainbridge was forced to surrender his ship and crew. Shortly after the new year, Captain Stephen Decatur, Jr. — son of her first commander — proposed to Commodore Edward Preble a plan to destroy the ship where she lay, and so prevent the enemy from refloating her for their own use. On February 16, 1804, Decatur slipped past the Tripolitan ships in the gunboat INTREPID. The volunteer crew of sixty boarded *Philadelphia*, overpowered her small crew, and set fire to the ship, all without any American casualties. Upon hearing of the exploit, Britain's Vice Admiral Lord Nelson declared it "the most bold and daring act of the age."

Chapelle, *History of the American Sailing Navy*. U.S. Navy, *DANFS*.

PHOENIX

Steamboat (1f/2m). *L/B/D:* 101′ × 16′ × 6.4′ (30.8m × 4.9m × 2.1m). *Hull:* wood. *Comp.:* 40. *Mach.:* low-pressure engine, side-wheels; 5.5 kts. *Des.:* John Stevens. *Built:* Perth Amboy, N.J.; 1808.

Designed and built by Colonel John Stevens, who first became interested in steam engines when approached by John Fitch in 1787, *Phoenix* was the first steamboat built after Robert Fulton's NORTH RIVER STEAM BOAT entered service on the Hudson River. Stevens had made several overtures to Fulton and his partner Robert Livingston, who happened to be his brother-in-law and one-time collaborator, but was rebuffed. Similar to Fulton's boat in many respects, the biggest improvement in *Phoenix* was that the engine mounting distributed the weight more evenly and minimized pressure on the hull. Launched in April 1808, *Phoenix* was put in service between Perth Amboy and New Brunswick. Fulton and Livingston rejected any offer to go into business with Stevens

on the Hudson, and after Fulton put *Raritan* in direct competition with his ship, Stevens decided that *Phoenix* could be more profitably operated on the Delaware River. This meant a passage of 150 miles along the Jersey shore of the Atlantic Ocean.

On June 10, 1808, she sailed under command of Robert Livingston Stevens (Colonel Stevens's son), stopped for a few days at the Quarantine station, then ran south for three and a half days until forced into Cranberry Inlet for repairs to a paddlewheel. *Phoenix* also put into Barnegat Bay, Cape May, and Newcastle before reaching Philadelphia thirteen days out. Although the trip could only be described as tentative, it was the first sea journey of any steamboat. *Phoenix* entered service between Philadelphia and Trenton, New Jersey, the last leg of the journey from New York, which included a sail from New York to New Brunswick and an overland passage to Trenton. Her first captain on the eight-hour run on the Delaware was Moses Rogers, who later commanded SAVANNAH when that steamer made the first transatlantic crossing in 1819. *Phoenix* remained in service on the Delaware until retired in 1815.

Turnbull, *John Stevens*.

USS PIGEON (ASR-6)

Lapwing-class minesweeper. *L/B/D:* 187.8′ × 35.4′ × 13.4′ (57.3m × 11.2m × 4.1m). *Tons:* 1,400 disp. *Hull:* steel. *Comp.:* 85. *Arm.:* 4 mg. *Mach.:* triple-expansion, 1,400 shp, 1 screw; 14 kts. *Built:* Baltimore Dry Dock & Shipbuilding Co.; 1919.

First commissioned as a minesweeper, USS *Pigeon* spent her entire career in the Pacific. Homeported at Pearl Harbor from 1920 to 1922, she was recommissioned as a gunboat in 1923 when she joined the Yangtze River Patrol Force at Shanghai, attached to Submarine Division 16. Six years later, she was reclassified as submarine rescue vessel ASR-6, and fitted out with deep-sea diving equipment and other apparatus for salvaging or rescuing submarines in distress. In 1939, she took part in the brief effort to raise the French submarine PHÉNIX, which sank off the coast of Vietnam.

In the last days of November 1941, *Pigeon* was assigned to escort American forces withdrawing from Chinese waters in the face of Japanese forces sweeping over northeast China. The American force returned to Manila Bay on December 4. Hearing of the Japanese attack on Pearl Harbor three days later, Commander Richard E. "Spittin' Dick" Hawes loaded the ship with as many supplies as she could hold. Most of the American fleet had left by the time the Japanese first bombed Cavite Navy Yard on December 10. *Pigeon*'s crew managed to save USS *Seadragon* — which went on to make twelve wartime patrols against Japanese shipping — for which they were honored with the first Presidential Unit Citation.

Even as Cavite burned, *Pigeon*'s crew salvaged deck guns, munitions, and other equipment from the base. As the Japanese advanced on Manila Bay, *Pigeon* shuttled between U.S. forces at Manila, Corregidor Island, and Bataan, earning, in the process, her second Presidential Unit Citation. Command of *Pigeon* passed to Lieutenant Commander Frank Alfred Davis. Unable to leave Manila Bay because of the Japanese fleet in the South China Sea, *Pigeon* continued to support the last U.S. forces on Bataan and Corregidor until sunk by a dive-bomber on May 4, only two days before Major General Jonathan Wainwright was forced to surrender his forces to Lieutenant General Homma Masaharu.

U.S. Navy, *DANFS*.

PILGRIM

Brig. *L/B/D:* 86.5′ × 21.6′ × 10.8′ dph (26.4m × 6.6m × 3.3m). *Tons:* 181 bm. *Hull:* wood. *Comp.:* 15. *Built:* Sprague J. James, Medford, Mass.; 1825.

Built for Joshua Blake, Francis Stanton, and George Hallett of Boston, *Pilgrim* was a typical trading brig of her day. Between 1831 and 1834 she changed hands four times, finally winding up under the ownership of Bryant, Sturgis & Company. On August 15, 1834, she sailed from Boston for the West Coast to trade finished goods for hides. Sailing as a foremast hand was Richard Henry Dana, son of a Boston lawyer, who had been suspended from Harvard for his part in a student protest. He then contracted measles, which severely affected his eyesight, and in an effort to both improve his health and alleviate the boredom of his "rustication," he decided to sail before the mast in a ship bound for the remote coast of California — fifteen years before the gold rush. "Our cargo," Dana wrote,

> was an assorted one; that is, it consisted of everything under the sun. We had spirits of all kinds, (sold by the cask,) teas, coffee, sugars, spices, raisins, molasses, hard-ware, crockery-ware, tin-ware, cutlery, clothing of all kinds, boots and shoes from Lynn, calicoes and cottons from Lowell, crapes, silks; also, shawls, scarfs, necklaces, jewelry, and combs for the ladies; furniture; and in fact, everything that can be imagined, from Chinese fire-works to English cart-wheels — of which we had a dozen pairs with their iron rims on.

Pilgrim arrived on the California coast on January 13, 1835, and after some trading at Monterey, the capital

of Upper California, turned south for Santa Barbara. There the crew began to load dried hides, which they carried through the surf on their heads to a small boat that was then rowed out to *Pilgrim*. The crew soon realized that the voyage, which they originally believed would take eighteen months, would be extended until they collected 50,000 hides. "Here we were, in a little vessel, with a small crew, on a half-civilized coast, at the ends of the earth, and with a prospect of remaining an indefinite period, two or three years at the least." The routine of life in California consisted of sailing between the small mission towns along the coast in search of hides. On August 25, 1835, Bryant, Sturgis & Company's *Alert* arrived at San Diego, and Dana, whose father was anxious that he resume his studies, was allowed to transfer to the ship, which was due to sail for Boston before *Pilgrim*. Nonetheless, *Alert* remained on the coast until the following May. Shorthanded, she had a rough time of it rounding Cape Horn in July, the dead of winter in southern climes. *Alert* arrived at Boston on September 20, 1836.

Dana returned to Harvard, his eyesight much improved, and graduated at the head of his class in June 1837. While attending law school and teaching elocution at Harvard, he also wrote his narrative of his experiences; *Two Years Before the Mast* was published in 1840. A frank and unromantic narrative of life at sea, the book is often regarded as a polemic on the brutality of life afloat. Dana's concern for the welfare of seamen was genuine, and he devoted his admiralty law practice to the advocacy of seamen's rights. Although Dana was revolted by flogging and the caprice that seemed to animate *Pilgrim*'s master, Francis A. Thompson — he regarded *Alert*'s Edward H. Faucon as a better seaman and captain — Dana appreciated the shipboard hierarchy and his sympathy for the welfare of sailors did not extend to overturning the existing order.

> I have no fancies about equality on board ship. It is a thing out of the question, and certainly, in the present state of mankind, not to be desired. I cannot conceive of any rational man's troubling his head about it. I never knew a sailor who found fault with the orders and ranks of the service; and if I expected to pass the rest of my life before the mast [as in fact he had contemplated], I would not wish to have the power of the captain diminished an iota.

Moreover, Dana leavened his account with his observations about the customs of Mexicans and Indians, the crews of the handful of other ships — Mexican, British, American, and Russian — encountered in the same trade, and the geography. He was more than a little prescient when he declared, of San Francisco Bay, "If California ever become a prosperous country, this bay will be the centre of its prosperity."

Two Years Before the Mast was an instant success both in the United States and abroad, and it has been in print continuously for more than 150 years. (Ironically, the young advocate sold all rights to his publisher for $250 and he received no royalties for 28 years.) *Pilgrim* eventually returned to Boston, and between 1837 and 1841 she changed hands several times. In the latter year she was sold to Robert Haley of Boston, for whom she traded until 1856 when she burned off the coast of North Carolina. A replica of the brig was built in 1945 and is now operated by the Orange County Marine Institute in Dana Point, California.

Dana, *Two Years Before the Mast.*

PINTA

Caravela redonda (3m). *L/B/D:* 55′–74′ × 18′–21′ × 7′ dph (17–23m × 5–7m × 2m dph). *Tons:* 75–116 toneladas. *Hull:* wood. *Comp.:* 26. *Arm.:* 9cm lombard, 4.5cm falconets. *Built:* Los Palos, Spain(?); <1492.

The smallest and least known of Christopher Columbus's three ships on his first voyage to the Americas in 1492–93, *Pinta* was a *caravela redonda,* a trading vessel setting a single square sail on the fore and main masts, and a single lateen sail on the mizzen. As was the case with NIÑA, Columbus requisitioned the ship for the voyage in satisfaction of a fine levied by Spain's Ferdinand and Isabella. Acquired from Cristóbal Quintero, who sailed as a seaman on the voyage, she was put under the command of Martín Alonso Pinzón and sailed from Los Palos in company with SANTA MARÍA and *Niña* on August 3, 1492. Three days out, *Pinta* had trouble with her rudder, which could not be permanently repaired until Pinzón put into Las Palmas, on Grand Canary Island. Columbus pressed on to Gomera, in hopes of finding a replacement vessel, and when they returned to Las Palmas on August 25, two weeks later, *Pinta* had been there barely a day. With repairs to *Pinta* complete, and *Niña* sporting a new rig, the little fleet sailed on September 1, and after two days at Gomera, they resumed their westward voyage on September 6.

Pinzón, one of the leading seamen of Palos whose brother Vicente Yáñez Pinzón commanded *Niña,* was in large part responsible for Columbus's success in recruiting crew and outfitting his ships, and he seems to have chafed somewhat at being second in command. The Genoese Columbus was, after all, a foreigner, and his Enterprise of the Indies was not one to which people thronged,

even though it had royal backing. On September 25, Pinzón claimed a landfall, which proved false — they were in midatlantic — and on October 6, he advised Columbus that he thought they had already overshot Cipango (Japan), their intended destination. By the second week of October, flotsam indicated that land was near. At about 0200 on October 12, *Pinta*'s lookout Rodrigo de Triana made the first verifiable sighting of land. Nonetheless, on the basis of having seen a light some hours before (when they were probably 30 miles from land), Columbus claimed the first sighting — and the 10,000 *maravedís* promised by Ferdinand and Isabella — for himself.

The island, which Columbus named San Salvador, was the Taino Indian island of Guanahaní, in what is now the Bahamas. (Though the exact landing place is unknown, the leading candidates for the island are San Salvador and, about 60 miles southwest, Samana Cay.) The three ships explored the Bahamas between October 12 and 26, and then headed south to the northeast coast of Cuba.

On November 20, the three ships made a tentative foray in the direction of the Bahamas, but while trying to return to Cuba, Pinzón took off in *Pinta* to investigate Babeque (now Great Inagua Island) in hopes of finding gold, and probably to assert his independence from Columbus. The effort proved fruitless, and he sailed south to the northern coast of Hispaniola, spending about three weeks in a harbor to the east of where *Santa María* and *Niña* were exploring. From his base (possibly Puerto Blanco), Pinzón explored the interior and claimed to have visited the gold-rich region of Cibao. Hearing of the wreck of *Santa María* on Christmas Day, he attempted to rejoin Columbus, and he did so at Isla Cabra on January 6, 1493, just as Columbus was beginning his voyage home in *Niña.*

After two days of repairs and provisioning, the two ships sailed for Spain. They remained in company until February 13 when they were separated in a storm. *Pinta* made her way to Bayona, north of the Portuguese border, probably by the end of February. While there, Pinzón sent letters to Ferdinand and Isabella requesting permission to report to them in person on the successful completion of the voyage. Rebuffed, he was forced to return to Los Palos, where he arrived only hours after Columbus. Ill and despondent at being bested by Columbus, Pinzón made his way home and died soon thereafter. *Pinta*'s subsequent fate is unknown.

Morison, *Admiral of the Ocean Sea.* Pastor, *Ships of Christopher Columbus.* Philips, "Evolution of Spanish Ship Design."

CSS PIONEER

Submarine. *L/B/D:* 30′ × 4′ × 6′ dph (9.1m × 1.2m × 1.8m). *Tons:* 4 tons. *Comp.:* 2. *Arm.:* clock-work torpedo. *Mach.:* manual screw. *Built:* J. R. McClintock, New Orleans, La.; 1862.

Designed and built by New Orleans machinist J. R. McClintock, the cigar-shaped *Pioneer* was the first of three submarines built in the Confederacy during the Civil War. (Her successors were the five-man *Pioneer II* and the celebrated H. L. HUNLEY.) Commissioned as a privateer in March 1862, J. K. Scott commanding, on trials *Pioneer* reportedly completed several successful dives and sank a schooner and several smaller vessels by means of a clock-work torpedo designed to be screwed into the enemy ship's hull. Before she could see action against the enemy, *Pioneer* was scuttled in Bayou St. John to avoid capture by Flag Officer David Farragut's forces after the fall of New Orleans on April 25, 1862. Raised after the war, *Pioneer* was displayed at the Louisiana Home for Confederate Soldiers. In 1954 she was moved to the Louisiana State Museum in New Orleans.

U.S. Navy, *DANFS.* Silverstone, *Warships of the Civil War Navies.*

USS PLUNGER (SS-2)

(later *A-1*) *Holland*-class submarine. *L/B/D:* 63.9′ × 11.9′ × 10.6′ (19.5m × 3.6m × 3.2m). *Tons:* 107/123 disp. *Hull:* steel. *Comp.:* 7. *Arm.:* 1 × 18″TT. *Mach.:* gasoline engine, 150 bhp, 1 screw; 8/7 kts. *Des.:* John P. Holland. *Built:* Crescent Shipyard, Elizabeth, N.J.; 1902.

The first submarine of the name, USS *Plunger* was the second submarine commissioned into the U.S. Navy, after the HOLLAND. Used primarily to examine the mechanics of submarine technology and tactics, she also trained many of the men who would go on to crew the fledgling submarine fleet. Among those especially interested in the new technology was President Theodore Roosevelt. Never one to shy from adventure, the former Secretary of the Navy boarded *Plunger* for a test dive near his home in Oyster Bay, N.Y., on August 23, 1905. His reflections on the experience shed some light on both his own motives as well as on what many considered the prospects for the newest advance in naval architecture.

> I went down in it chiefly because I did not like to have the officers and enlisted men think I wanted them to try things I was reluctant to try myself. I believe a good deal can be done with these submarines, although there is always the danger of people getting carried away with the idea and thinking that they can be of more use than they possibly could be.

Fifty-six years and 598 very useful submarines later, the Navy commissioned the GEORGE WASHINGTON–class nuclear-powered fleet ballistic submarine USS *Theodore Roosevelt.*

Decommissioned for two years, *Plunger* was assigned to the First Submarine Flotilla at New York where, in 1909, Ensign Chester W. Nimitz took command. The future Fleet Admiral, who would deploy submarines to brilliant effect against the Japanese merchant marine and navy in World War II, later described *Plunger* and her ilk as "a cross between a Jules Verne fantasy and a humpbacked whale." Renamed *A-1* in 1911, she was stricken from the Navy List the following year. Used as a target ship, she was sold for scrap in 1922.

U.S. Navy, *DANFS.*

USS POLARIS

(ex-*Periwinkle, America*) Schooner-rigged screw tug (1f/2m). *L/B/D:* 140′ × 28′ × 10.5′ (42.7m × 8.5m × 3.2m). *Tons:* 387 burden. *Hull:* wood. *Comp.:* 16–37. *Arm.:* 2 × 24pdr. *Mach.:* steam, 1 screw. *Built:* Neafie & Levy, Philadelphia; 1864.

Originally named *America,* the screw tug USS *Periwinkle* first saw duty on Chesapeake Bay and the Rappahannock River with the U.S. Navy. She was laid up at the Norfolk Navy Yard from 1867 to 1870, when the Navy loaned her to Charles Francis Hall's North Polar Expedition. Renamed *Polaris* (for the North Star), after fitting out for work in the Arctic ice, she sailed from the New York Navy Yard in July 1871. That season, the northern reaches of Baffin Strait were remarkably clear of ice and by August 30, *Polaris* was on the edge of the Lincoln Sea at 82°11′N, a record farthest north. *Polaris* was stopped by the ice and pushed south while Hall established winter quarters at Thank God Harbour, Greenland, on September 10. On November 8, Hall died following a suspicious illness. (A 1968 autopsy found high levels of arsenic, although whether he was poisoned deliberately or accidentally — patent medicines of the day were rich in arsenic — was never determined.) Command of the expedition devolved on Sidney O. Budington, who dispatched an expedition to try for the Pole in June 1872. This was unsuccessful and *Polaris* turned south. On October 12, the ship was beset by ice in Smith Sound and was on the verge of being crushed. Nineteen of the crew and Eskimo guides abandoned ship for the surrounding ice and fourteen crew remained on the ship. *Polaris* was run aground near Etah and crushed on October 24. After wintering ashore, the crew sailed south in two boats and were rescued by a

The U.S. Navy's second submarine, the USS PLUNGER *of 1902 had the dual distinction of hosting President Theodore Roosevelt on a test dive on Long Island Sound and of being an early command of Chester Nimitz, who as Fleet Admiral signed a copy of this photo. At left,* PLUNGER *is tied alongside* USS SHARK. *Below, the officer rising from the conning tower gives an idea of just how small the first submarines were. Courtesy U.S. Naval Historical Center, Washington, D.C.*

whaler, returning home via Scotland. Miraculously, the nineteen icebound castaways, including Eskimo women and children, drifted 1,500 miles, migrating from floe to floe as their temporary homes threatened to break up, and were rescued by the whaler *Tigress* on April 30, 1873.

Loomis, *Weird and Tragic Shores.* Silverstone, *Warships of the Civil War Navies.*

POLITICIAN

(ex-*London Merchant*) Cargo ship. *L/B/D:* 450.4' × 58.1' × 38.5' (137.3m × 17.7m × 11.7m). *Tons:* 7,939 grt. *Hull:* steel. *Mach.:* steam turbine, 1,004 hp, 1 screw. *Built:* Furness Shipbuilding Co., Ltd., Haverton Hill-on-Tees, Eng.; 1923.

Popularly known as *Polly,* the steamship *Politician* was a break-bulk freighter owned by the Charente Steamship Company. During World War II, Britain employed a variety of strategies to raise hard currency to buy war materiel for the fight against Nazi Germany, including the export of spirits. On February 3, 1941, *Politician* sailed under Captain Beaconsfield Worthington from Liverpool for Kingston, Jamaica, and New Orleans with a cargo that included Jamaican currency and about 22,000 cases of duty-free Scotch for the U.S. market. Two days out, *Polly* ran aground on Eriskay Island in the Outer Hebrides. Salvage efforts recovered 13,093 cases of whiskey. Another 2,000 cases were "saved" by islanders who hid them in crofts and houses across the island. Several of the islanders were later prosecuted for theft by the tax authorities, but after the war, their story was recounted in *Whisky Galore,* a novel by the Scottish author Compton Mackenzie. The first best-selling novel with a Scots Gaelic title (a rough translation is "abundant whiskey"), the book was later made into a movie of the same name, released as *Whiskey à Go-Go* in France, and because American censors would not allow "whiskey" in the title, as *Tight Little Island* in the United States. (Humorist James Thurber later observed that the proper American title should have been *Scotch on the Rocks*.)

Hutchinson, *Polly*.

POLLY WOODSIDE

(ex-*Rona*, *Polly Woodside*) Bark (3m). *L/B/D:* 192.2′ × 30′ × 17′ (58.6m × 9.1m × 5.2m). *Tons:* 678 grt. *Hull:* iron. *Comp.:* 15 + 10 trainees. *Built:* Workman Clark & Co., Belfast, Ireland; 1885.

Polly Woodside was built for William J. Woodside of Belfast, who named her for his wife. From 1884 to 1904, she was registered as a single-ship company. Her primary cargoes were coal from the United Kingdom and, chiefly, nitrate or wheat from South America. Her seventeen voyages in this period each lasted about a year, although in 1893–95, she called in Santos, Chittagong, Trinidad, New York, Rio de Janeiro, and Rosario before returning to King's Lynn.

In 1904 she was sold twice, the second time to Arthur Hughes Turnbull of Christchurch, New Zealand. From 1905 to 1921, renamed *Rona* (a Maori name), she carried various bulk cargoes between ports in Australia, New Zealand, and Tasmania, with a few passages to San Francisco during World War I. In 1917 she was fitted out to carry ten apprentices. Ending her sailing career in 1921, she was acquired by the Adelaide Steamship Company, Ltd., for use as a coal hulk. She stayed in that rough work under various owners until 1962. During World War II she was requisitioned by the Royal Australian Navy for use in New Guinea.

Active interest in preserving the ship began in 1962, initiated by Karl Kortum in San Francisco and Dr. E. Graeme Robertson, who became chairman of the *Polly Woodside* Restoration Committee. The ship was transferred to the National Trust of Australia (Victoria) in 1968. Nine years later, she was opened to the public at Old Duke's and Orr's Dry Dock in Melbourne.

Darroch, *Barque "Polly Woodside" ("Rona")*.

PORTICELLO WRECK

L: ca. 53′–56′ (16–17m). *Tons:* ca. 30 burden. *Hull:* wood. *Built:* ca. 400 BCE.

The Porticello wreck lies in the Straits of Messina just off the town of Porticello, Calabria, in about 38°14′N, 15°40′E. The site was found by a diver in 1969, and local fishermen looted the wreck of table pottery, anchors, and about 100 amphorae before the police intervened, whereupon the looters were arrested, convicted, and jailed, and the antiquities found in their possession confiscated. At the request of the Superintendent of Antiquities for Calabria, David Owen of the University Museum at the University of Pennsylvania organized a team of divers and archaeologists to begin excavation the following year.

The wreck lay 225 meters offshore, at a depth of 33 to 37 meters. After sinking, the ship probably broke up rapidly on the boulders, and the scouring action of the current swept most of the hull away. However, some elements of the vessel and her cargo preserved in the hollows between the boulders provided archaeologists with clues about the ship and its last voyage. The modest remains of the hull included tenons and a fragment of mortised timber that show that the strakes were edge-joined — the commonest method of ship construction in the ancient Mediterranean. Long copper nails, several dozen of which were recovered, were used to fasten strakes to frames. Excavators also found several rectangular strips of lead with tack holes at intervals along the edges used to patch leaks in the hull. The find of a wooden cleat is unique among ancient Mediterranean wrecks. A square bolt driven through the center of the cleat would have fastened it to the mast or cap rail. Also of interest is an hourglass-shaped toggle — a device known from the Kyrenia and other ancient wrecks — that may have been used as part of an antiluffing system for a square sail, and suggests that the Porticello ship was square-rigged. The ship carried composite anchors with wooden shanks, wooden arms with bronze teeth, and wooden stocks with lead cores. The most unexpected finds from the cargo were twenty-two pieces of cast-bronze sculpture, including a well-preserved, strikingly realistic male head, probably of Greek origin, dating from between 450 and 420 BCE. The head has been described as a portrait of a philosopher or poet, or perhaps the centaur Chiron.

The wreck can be dated reliably to about 400 BCE on the basis of the finds of Attic pottery used by the crew. In addition to the sculpture, the cargo included wine from Byzantium on the Bosporus and Mende in the northern Aegean, salt fish from a Punic site, and lead ingots from the Laurion mines near Athens. Looting of the site made it difficult to reconstruct the ship's route on the basis of artifactual clues, but one possibility is that she started her voyage at Athens, where the lead and possibly the bronze statues were produced, and where wine from the north-eastern Mediterranean was readily available. Her intended destination was certainly somewhere in the western Mediterranean.

Eiseman, "Porticello Shipwreck." Eiseman & Ridgway, *Porticello Shipwreck*. Owen, "Excavating a Classical Shipwreck"; "Picking Up the Pieces."

PORTLAND

Passenger steamer (2f/2m). *L/B/D:* 280.9′ × 42.1′ × 15.5′ (85.6m × 12.8m × 4.7m). *Tons:* 2,283 grt. *Hull:* wood. *Comp.:* 700 pass. *Mach.:* vertical beam engine, sidewheels; 13 kts. *Built:* New England Shipbuilding Corp., Bath, Me.; 1890.

In 1890, the Portland Steam Packet Company commissioned the sidewheel passenger steamer *Portland* for its overnight service between Portland and Boston. A handsome, well-found boat, she remained on this run without serious mishap for eight years. At about 1900 on November 26, 1898, the Saturday after Thanksgiving, *Portland* departed Boston with between 160 and 190 passengers and crew aboard. Although the Portland Steam Packet Company later claimed to have wired Captain Hollis H. Blanchard to postpone his departure until 2100, in view of the weather, prudence should have dictated a delay. Many other ships scheduled to depart New England ports that night remained at the dock.

Two vessels later reported seeing *Portland* in Massachusetts Bay, but the following night, remains of the ship and her passengers began washing ashore on Cape Cod. The exact number of dead was never determined because the only passenger manifest was lost with the ship. (Ships were thereafter required to make a copy to be left ashore at sailing.) Although some 400 boats and ships of various descriptions were lost along the coast that night, the storm has been known ever since as the Portland Gale. In 1989, divers with the Maritime Historical Group of New England located the wreck lying about 20 miles north of Cape Cod in 300 feet of water.

Cooke, "Divers Report Mystery Ship Found." Humiston, *Windjammers and Walking Beams*.

KNIAZ POTEMKIN TAVRICHESKI

Potemkin-class battleship (3f/2m). *L/B/D:* 378.5′ × 73′ × 27′ (115.3m × 22.3m × 8.2m). *Tons:* 12,582 tons. *Hull:* steel. *Comp.:* 741. *Arm.:* 4 × 12" (2 × 2), 14 × 6", 5 × 457mm TT. *Armor:* 229mm belt, 76mm deck. *Mach.:* triple expansion, 10,600 ihp, 2 screws; 16 kts. *Built:* Nikolaiev Admiralty Yard, Nikolaiev, Russia; 1903.

Immortalized in Sergei Eisenstein's classic silent film *Battleship Potemkin* (1925), the pre-dreadnought battleship *Kniaz Potemkin Tavricheski* was named for Prince Grigory Aleksandrovich Potemkin, who under Catherine the Great annexed the Crimea and built Russia's first fleet on the Black Sea in the late eighteenth century. *Potemkin* was the last and largest of eight Russian capital ships commissioned between 1886 and 1900 for the Black Sea Fleet, one of three dictated by Russia's peculiar maritime geography. Under the Treaty of Berlin (1878), Russian warships were denied access to the Turkish-held Bosporus, and the Black Sea Fleet had to operate independently of the Baltic and Far East Fleets. When the Baltic Squadron dispatched to the Pacific during the Russo-Japanese War was destroyed in the Strait of Tsushima on May 27, 1905, *Potemkin* was the most powerful ship in the Russian Navy's only cohesive naval force.

Russia's humiliation in the Far East demoralized the military and was accompanied by a worsening economic situation and widespread antigovernment unrest among reform-minded intellectuals and factory workers. A peaceful march outside the Winter Palace in St. Petersburg was brutally suppressed by Cossacks on January 22, 1905, known as Bloody Sunday. The Black Sea port of Odessa remained relatively unaffected by these developments until the spring, when strikes were called. On June 26, workers in nearby Peresyp clashed with Cossacks, and the local army commander, General Kokhanov, established martial law.

Social Democrats had been active in the fleet since 1903, and in June 1905 they planned for a general mutiny during gunnery trials off Tendra Island. Sympathy for reform varied from ship to ship, and *Potemkin*'s crew was viewed as among the most loyal, but after the ship sailed for Tendra, on June 27 the men refused to eat maggot-infested meat that had been brought aboard. Captain Yevgeny Golikov tried to assure his crew that the meat was edible, but Commander Ippolit Giliarovsky, his second in command, was intent on asserting his authority. He ordered twelve sailors chosen at random ranks to be executed — though some feel he may have been bluffing. When a firing squad appeared, Torpedo Quartermaster Afanasy Matushenko, a Social Democrat agitator, reportedly shouted, "Don't shoot your own comrades — you can't kill your own shipmates." This was followed by shouts to seize the ship, and some of the men rushed the armory. Within half an hour, seven officers had been killed and thrown overboard, including Giliarovsky and Golikov; among the mutineers, Able Seaman Grigory Vakulinchuk was mortally wounded.

Matushenko ordered the ship to Odessa, and a People's Committee was established to run the ship. The mutineers threatened to bombard the city if met with resistance. As the most powerful weapon in Russia's arsenal was in the hands of insurrectionists, the threat was real enough, and Czar Nicholas declared "a state of war" to exist with the mutineers. The mutineers landed Vakulinchuk's corpse on the quay near the foot of the majestic Richelieu Steps, where it became a focal point for Odessa's revolutionaries. That afternoon, demonstrators on the steps were caught between two detachments of Cossacks. The massacre of hundreds of civilians went unnoticed aboard the *Potemkin* because of the noise and dust of coaling operations. Yet when apprised of the tragedy, the mutineers refused to turn their guns against the city because they could identify no specific targets. That night, Odessa was engulfed in riots, and an estimated 6,000 people were killed by soldiers and looters.

When news of the mutiny reached Sevastopol, *Georgi Pobiedonsets* ("George the Victorious"), *Tri Sviatitelia* ("Three Saints"), and *Dvenadtsat Apostolov* ("Twelve Apostles") were dispatched to Odessa. As the ships approached, *Potemkin* sailed out with a signal ordering "Surrender or we fire," and Rear Admiral Vishnevetsky turned for Tendra to join the flagship *Rotislav* and *Sinop*, while *Potemkin* returned to Odessa, flush with victory. The strengthened squadron returned to Odessa, and shortly after noon on June 30 *Potemkin* sailed out to meet the ships. Not gunfire but cheers met the ship as she twice steamed through the fleet, and the captain of *Georgi Pobiedonsets* surrendered his command to mutineers aboard his ship, which returned to Odessa with the *Potemkin*. (When the remaining ships returned to Sevastopol, the Black Sea Fleet's Admiral Chukhnin dismissed 5,000 ratings and ordered the engines of the remaining battleships disabled.)

Georgi Pobiedonsets's crew were not committed revolutionaries, and on July 1 the ship weighed anchor to leave port. Under threat of bombardment by *Potemkin* at point-blank range, she came about but was driven hard aground on the harbor mole, thus putting her powerful guns at the disposal of the military authorities in Odessa. With the tables turned against them, *Potemkin*'s crew voted to sail for Constanta, Romania, where they arrived the following day.

Romania's King Carol was wary of offending his giant neighbor to the north and refused the ship more than a day's provisions, and on July 3 *Potemkin* sailed for Feodosiya in the Crimea, where she arrived on July 6. Army patrols killed a number of sailors as they attempted to steal coal barges. Faced with the lack of food, fuel, and fresh water, the mutineers reluctantly returned to Constantsa, where a majority of the crew accepted the offer of Romanian citizenship. Before leaving the ship, Matushenko ordered her scuttled in the shallow harbor. Two Russian battleships reached Constanta the next day, and by July 11 *Potemkin* had been pumped out and was in tow back to Odessa. The mutiny that prefigured the Russian revolution by twelve years was over.

On October 9, Czar Nicholas ordered the ship renamed *Panteleimon* in honor of a Russian Orthodox saint whose feast day is also the anniversary of the Russian victory over the Swedes at the Battle of Gangut (in Swedish, Hangø) on July 27, 1714. The pre-dreadnoughts of the Black Sea Fleet remained in service through World War I, though they were superseded by three *Imperatritsa Maria*-class dreadnoughts commissioned in 1915. In April 1917, the newly installed Provisional Government renamed the ship *Potemkin* and a month later *Boretz zu Svobodu* ("Fighter for Liberty"). The old ship changed hands several times over the next two years as control of Sevastopol passed to the independent Ukraine, the German army, counterrevolutionaries (who scuttled her on April 25, 1919), and Bolsheviks. She was finally broken up in 1923.

Hough, *The "Potemkin" Mutiny*. Silverstone, *Directory of the World's Capital Ships*.

USS POTOMAC (AG-25)

(ex-*Electra*) Presidential yacht. *L/B/D:* 165′ × 23.8′ × 8.1′ (42.6m × 9.5m × 2.5m). *Tons:* 416 disp. *Hull:* steel. *Comp.:* 45. *Mach.:* diesel; 13 kts. *Built:* Manitowoc Ship Building Co., Manitowoc, Wisc.; 1934.

The fourth ship of the name, USS *Potomac* originally saw service as the Coast Guard cutter *Electra* operating against rumrunners on the East Coast during Prohibition. Transferred to the Navy in 1935, she was refurbished as Franklin D. Roosevelt's presidential yacht *Potomac* the next year. Slated for replacement by a larger vessel in 1940, the start of World War II prevented this and she continued in service through 1946. Replaced by USS *Williamsburg*, *Potomac* was transferred to the state of Maryland's Tidewater Fisheries Commission until 1960. Her subsequent career included service as a ferry between San Juan, Puerto Rico, and St. Thomas, U.S. Virgin Islands, and as a floating Roosevelt museum. In 1964 Elvis

Presley purchased *Potomac* and donated her to St. Jude's Children's Hospital in Memphis. Later sold, she was seized by the U.S. Custom Service in a San Francisco drug raid and later sank at the dock. Purchased by the Port of Oakland in the 1990s, she was undergoing restoration at this writing.

Crockett, *Special Fleet.*

POURQUOI PAS?

Screw bark (1f/3m). *L/B/D:* 139.7' × 31.2' × 15.4' dph (77.4m × 13.7m × 5.6m). *Tons:* 449 reg. *Hull:* wood. *Comp.:* 42. *Mach.:* compound engine, 1 screw. *Built:* Ed Gautier, St. Malo, France; 1908.

Whimsically named by France's foremost Antarctic explorer, the name of Jean-Baptiste Charcot's *Pourquoi Pas?* translates simply, "Why not?" The veteran leader of France's first Antarctic expedition in *Français* (1903–1905), Charcot departed Le Havre on his second expedition on August 23, 1908. After calling in various South American ports, he sailed from the Norwegian sealing port at Deception Island, South Shetland Islands, on Christmas Day. Charcot was disappointed in his ambitious expectation of sailing farther south than anyone before him, and *Pourquoi Pas?* wintered at Point Circumcision, on Petermann Island, until November. Despite a cursory survey at Deception Island that revealed damage to the stem, *Pourquoi Pas?* sailed for a second winter in the Antarctic. On this trip, she sailed between 69°S and 70°S, as far west as 122°W. Among other achievements, the Charcot expedition surveyed 1,250 miles of Antarctic coastline, made extensive hydrographic surveys — including a 225-day study of tides — meteorological studies, bacteriological experiments, and magnetic observations. On January 7, 1910, the expedition also discovered Charcot Land, which Charcot named for his father, an esteemed physician.

Returning to France in June 1910, *Pourquoi Pas?* was handed over to the École Pratique des Hautes Études for use as a training ship, sailing in northern latitudes. Laid up at the beginning of World War I, in 1916 she was requisitioned by the French Navy for work as a training ship stationed at L'Orient. Following the war, Charcot resumed command of his ship, sailing her to Iceland and the Faeroe Islands nearly every summer. In 1925, she made her first visit to Greenland's Scoresby Sound, and the next year she carried ninety Eskimos from Angmagssalik to Rosenvinge Bay to establish an Eskimo colony at Scoresby Sound.

In 1928, *Pourquoi Pas?* was dispatched in a vain search for Roald Amundsen, the Arctic explorer whose plane had disappeared during a search for Umberto Nobile's airship *Italia.* In 1931, she was back at Scoresby Sound to establish an observation post at Rosenvinge Bay, and she returned there every year until 1936, the last year in which the sixty-nine-year-old Charcot would be eligible to sail. Departing Saint Servan on July 16, *Pourquoi Pas?* spent a month in the remarkably ice-free waters of Greenland, her crew engaged primarily in correcting charts. On August 30, a coal dust explosion forced her to accept a tow into Reykjavik. Following repairs, *Pourquoi Pas?* sailed for France on September 15. Despite the fine weather that day, a storm of unusual violence came up that night and *Pourquoi Pas?* narrowly missed going ashore on Akranes Point. An hour and forty minutes later, the mizzen mast went by the boards, and at 0515 she hit a submerged rock off Bargafjord, north of Reykjavik. There was only one survivor, a seaman named Gonidec, among the forty-two officers and crew.

Charcot, *Voyage of the "Pourquoi Pas?"* Oulié, *Charcot and the Antarctic.*

USS POWHATAN

Sidewheel steamer (3m). *L/B/D:* 253.8' × 45' × 18.5' (53.3m × 13.5m × 4m). *Tons:* 3,479 disp. *Hull:* wood. *Comp.:* 289. *Arm.:* 1 × 11", 10 × 9", 5 × 12pdr. *Mach.:* inclined engine, 1,500 ihp, sidewheels; 11 kts. *Built:* Gosport Navy Yard, Portsmouth, Va.; 1852.

Named for the Indian chief who ruled the coastal area of eastern Virginia in which the English colony of Jamestown was settled in 1607, the bark-rigged USS *Powhatan* was the largest and one of the last of the U.S. Navy's paddle frigates. After two years as flagship of the Navy's Home Squadron, in 1853 she joined the East India Squadron. Commodore Matthew C. Perry had arrived in the Orient the year before with instructions to effect a treaty to open Japan to American trade and to guarantee the protection of shipwrecked American sailors. Perry's first visit to Edo (Tokyo) Bay with the steamers *Mississippi* and *Susquehanna* preceded the arrival of *Powhatan,* but during his second visit, the Treaty of Kanagawa was signed on her decks on March 31, 1854. En route back to the United States, in the summer of 1855 she joined the Royal Navy screw frigate HMS RATTLER in freeing a number of ships being held by pirates at Kulan.

Two years later *Powhatan* joined the West Indies Squadron, and she remained in active service through the Civil War. Under Lieutenant David Dixon Porter, in 1861 she took part in the relief of Fort Pickens, Florida, and helped establish blockades off Mobile and the Mississippi. From 1863 to 1864 she operated off Charleston and with the West Indies Squadron, and in the winter of

Lexington Susquehannah Powhatan Macedonian Mississippi Vandalia Saratoga Southampton Supply

One of the last sidewheel steamers built for service with the Navy, USS POWHATAN *served as flagship of Commodore Perry's famous mission to "open" Japan in 1854. This primitive painting shows the ships' boats — American flags flying — approaching the shore, with the fleet anchored offshore.* POWHATAN *is flying the Commodore's pennant. Courtesy The Mariners' Museum, Newport News, Virginia.*

1864–65, she took part in the reduction of Fort Fisher, North Carolina. After the war, she was Rear Admiral John A. Dahlgren's flagship in the South Pacific. Returning to the Home Squadron in 1869, she remained in Atlantic waters until decommissioned in 1886. She was broken up the following year in Meriden, Connecticut.

Canney, *Old Steam Navy.* U.S. Navy, *DANFS.*

PREDPRIYATIYE

Sloop of war (3m). *Hull:* wood. *Comp.:* 122. *Arm.:* 24 × 6pdr. *Built:* St. Petersburg; 1823.

Built specifically for service between Kamchatka and Russia's North American colonies in what is now Alaska, *Predpriyatiye* ("Enterprise") sailed from Kronstadt on July 28, 1823, under command of Otto von Kotzebue, a veteran of circumnavigations in NADEZHDA (1803–6) and RURIK (1815–18). Although the purpose of the voyage out was to deliver goods to Kamchatka, Kotzebue was also under orders to confirm old discoveries — or make new ones — along his route. After rounding Cape Horn,

with a stop in Valparaiso, *Predpriyatiye* sailed through the Tuamotu Archipelago, where Kotzebue found several previously unseen islands, one of which he named for his ship. The Russians continued first to Tahiti and then Samoa before turning northwest to sail through the Radak Chain to Petropavlovsk, where they arrived on June 9, 1824. Arriving in Novo Arkhangelsk (Sitka) in October, Kotzebue learned that his ship was not needed on station until the following spring, so he sailed for Yerba Buena (now San Francisco), where the Russians spent a month before sailing for the Sandwich (Hawaiian) Islands. *Predpriyatiye* returned to Novo Arkhangelsk (Sitka) on February 24, 1825, and remained in Alaskan waters for five months conducting extensive surveys of the approaches and surrounding waters. The return voyage via Hawaii and the Radaks resulted in the discovery of Bikini Island (initially named for Johann F. Eschscholtz, one of two naturalists aboard). After two months at Manila, *Predpriyatiye* sailed for Kronstadt, where she arrived on July 10, 1826, after several stops en route.

Ivashintsov, *Russian Round-the-World Voyages.* Kotzebue, *New Voyage Round the World.*

Portrait of the frigate USS PRESIDENT *riding out a gale at anchor off the coast of Marseilles. Note how her topmasts and yards have been sent down to reduce windage. Courtesy U.S. Naval Historical Center, Washington, D.C.*

USS PRESIDENT

Frigate (3m). *L/B/D:* 175′ × 44.3′ × 13.1′ (53.3m × 13.5m × 4m). *Tons:* 1,576 bm. *Hull:* wood. *Comp:* 450. *Arm.:* 32 × 24pdr, 22 × 42pdr, 1 × 19pdr. *Des.:* Joshua Humphreys, Josiah Fox, William Doughty. *Built:* Christian Bergh, New York; 1800.

One of the U.S. Navy's original six frigates, USS *President* was authorized by Congress to combat the Barbary corsairs of North Africa. Laid down in 1795, work on *President* was suspended following the peace with Algiers, only to be resumed at the start of the Quasi-War with France three years later. Completed in 1800 under the direction of Naval Constructor William Doughty, *President* was considered the fastest ship of her class in the world. The frigate put to sea in August 1800 under Commander Thomas Truxton, but hostilities with France ended the next month. In 1801, she sailed as flagship of Commodore Richard Dale's Squadron of Evolution (which included UNITED STATES, PHILADELPHIA, and ESSEX) sent to the Mediterranean to protect American merchantmen from renewed attacks by corsairs. *President*

remained in the Mediterranean until the following year, returning again in 1804–5. Put in ordinary upon her return, she was reactivated in 1809 as the British continued impressing American seamen into the Royal Navy.

Following the impressment of one such sailor on May 1, 1811, by HMS GUERRIÈRE, *President* was ordered to sea on the twelfth under Commodore John Rodgers, and after a long chase, five days later she engaged HMS LITTLE BELT (18 guns) about forty-five miles off the Chesapeake. The night action broke off after fifteen minutes; *President* had one man injured and suffered slight damage to the rigging, as against thirteen killed and nineteen wounded on *Little Belt,* which was condemned as "almost a wreck" upon her return to Halifax. In many respects the incident resembled the CHESAPEAKE-LEOPARD affair, and it might have brought on the start of an Anglo-American war a year early but for Rodgers's restrained handling of the incident.

The United States declared war on June 18, 1812, and three days later *President* sailed as flagship of a squadron that included *United States, Congress,* HORNET, and AR-

GUS on a North Atlantic cruise. Two days later *President* fell in with HMS *Belvedira,* but after an eight-hour chase the British ship escaped after one of *President*'s bow chasers blew up, killing and wounding several of the crew, including Rodgers, whose leg was broken. *President* made three more cruises to European waters and the Caribbean, but with lackluster results. Returning to New York on February 18, 1814, she was forced to remain there by the British blockade for almost a year.

At the end of 1814, she came under command of Captain Stephen Decatur. Although the Treaty of Ghent had been signed on December 24, the news had not yet arrived, and on January 14, 1815, Decatur tried to slip the blockade. *President* grounded on a sandbar several hours later, breaking her keel and straining her hull. The next day, HMS *Endymion* (50) gave chase until Decatur turned for a broadside action. *President* had the advantage until HMS *Pomone* and *Tenedos* arrived on the scene. Vastly outgunned and with fifty of his crew dead or wounded, Decatur struck. *President* was taken to Bermuda and seized as a war prize. Too damaged for further work, she was broken up at Portsmouth in 1817, but not before her lines were taken off and used for a new ship of the same name and reputation for speed.

Roosevelt, *Naval War of 1812.* U.S. Navy, *DANFS.*

PRESIDENTE SARMIENTO

Ship (3m). L/B/D: 265′ × 43′ × 18.5′ (80.8m × 13.1m × 5.6m). *Tons:* 2,750 disp. *Hull:* steel. *Comp.:* 294. *Arm.:* 2 × 4.7″, 2 × 4″, 2 × 6pdr; 3 TT. *Mach.:* compound engine, 2,800 ihp, 1 screw; 15 kts. *Built:* Laird Bros., Birkenhead, Eng.; 1898.

One of the first ships built by a government for naval sail-training, *Presidente Sarmiento* was named for President Domingo Sarmiento (1868–74), one of the fathers of modern Argentina and founder of the country's naval academy. Between 1898 and 1938, she trained more than a thousand prospective officers under sail in thirty-seven long-distance voyages, including seven circumnavigations. In the course of these training cruises, she represented Argentina at coronations and presidential inaugurations in England, Spain, the United States, Chile, and Mexico. In contrast to most naval sail-training ships, which generally employ saluting cannon, *Presidente Sarmiento* carried two 4.7-inch, two 4-inch, and two 6-pdr. guns, as well as three deck-mounted torpedo tubes. Laid up in 1938, she served as a shoreside training ship for another twenty-three years, when she was finally decommissioned. Since 1961, *Presidente Sarmiento* has been a museum ship in Buenos Aires, together with the bark-

rigged former hydrographic survey ship *Uruguay,* originally commissioned in 1874 as the corvette *Parana.*

Underhill, *Sail Training and Cadet Ships.*

PRESIDENT MONROE

(ex-*Panhandle State;* later *President Buchanan, Emily H. M. Weder*) *Liner (1f/2m). L/B:* 501.8′ bp × 62.3′ (153m × 19m). *Tons:* 10,533 grt. *Hull:* steel. *Comp.:* 1st 78. *Mach.:* triple expansion, 2 screws; 14 kts. *Built:* New York Shipbuilding Corp., Camden, N.J.; 1920.

The passenger-cargo ship *Panhandle State* (the nickname for West Virginia) was the first ship built for the short-lived United States Mail Steamship Company. After only eight roundtrips between New York, Boulogne, and London, U.S. Mail folded and its ships were transferred to United States Lines. Renamed *President Monroe* in 1922, the following year she was sold to the Dollar Steamship Line of San Francisco and, from 1924, put in round-the-world service: New York, Havana, the Panama Canal, Los Angeles, San Francisco, Honolulu, Kobe, Shanghai, Hong Kong, Manila, Singapore, Penang, Colombo, the Suez Canal, Naples, Genoa, Marseilles, and Boston — a voyage of 105 days from New York to New York. From 1931 to 1937 she ran between New York and Manila, before resuming her circumnavigation. Dollar folded in 1939 and many of her ships were taken over by the American President Lines. Renamed *President Buchanan* when a new *President Monroe* was commissioned in 1940, she entered general service. During World War II, she served as a troopship until 1943 and then as the hospital ship *Emily H. M. Weder.* Sailing again as *President Buchanan* after World War II, she remained in service until 1957, when she was scrapped at San Francisco.

Bonsor, *North Atlantic Seaway.*

PREUSSEN

Ship (5m). L/B/D: 407.8′ × 53.6′ × 27.1′ (124.3m × 16.3m × 8.3m). *Tons:* 5,081 grt. *Hull:* steel. *Comp.:* 48. *Built:* J. C. Tecklenborg, Geestemünde, Germany; 1902.

The second ship of the name built for Reederei F. Laeisz, *Preussen* (Prussia) was one of only four five-masted square-riggers, the only five-masted ship, and the largest ship without auxiliary engines ever to sail. (The only bigger square-riggers were the barks *R. C. Rickmers* and FRANCE.) Built for the nitrate trade between Europe and Chile, the Pride of Germany's 5 masts and 30 yards set 43 sails with a total area of 59,848 square feet. Although five-masted vessels could carry more cargo than four-masted ones, the ship rig offered little increase in speed over the bark, and because they required larger crews, these ships were definitely more expensive to man. Notwithstanding such relative economies, *Preussen* was a fast ship, especially under Captain Boye R. Petersen, her master from 1902 to 1909. *Preussen* sailed from Europe to Chile twelve times with average passages of sixty-five days; her thirteen returns were completed in seventy-three days on average. In 1903, she was a record fifty-five days from the English Channel to Iquique. Five years later, under charter to Standard Oil Company, she sailed from New York to Yokohama via the Cape of Good Hope, and in one eleven-day period she reeled off 3,019 miles, an average speed of over eleven knots.

On November 7, 1910, outward bound to Chile under command of J. Heinrich H. Nissen, *Preussen* rammed SS *Brighton*. The cross-channel steamer was making seventeen knots in foggy conditions; *Preussen* was logging four knots. As *Brighton* turned to cross in front of *Preussen*, the ship's bowsprit sheered off one of the steamer's two funnels and ripped a hole in the steamer's hull. With her bows stove in, *Preussen* was taken in tow by the steam tug *Alert*. Eighteen miles from Dover, Nissen tried to anchor in the lee of Dungeness, but the ship's anchor chains parted in a squall and Nissen was forced to run for Dover. Standing into Dover escorted by three tugs — *Alert, Albatross,* and *John Bull* — *Preussen*'s top hamper created so much windage that the tow lines parted. Setting sail in an effort to back out of the shallows, *Preussen*'s bow snagged on a reef in Crab Bay. All attempts to free the huge five-master failed, and the ship ended her days where she lay. (Laeisz's first *Preussen*, a steel ship of 1891, had been renamed *Posen* when this ship was built. Outward bound with a cargo of gunpowder, she exploded and burned in the South Atlantic on October 14, 1909.)

Rohrbach, et al., *FL: A Century and a Quarter of Reederei F. Laeisz.*

Prince of Wales and HMS HOOD intercepted the Germans south of the Denmark Strait and opened fire at 0553. Seven minutes later *Hood* exploded and sank. *Prince of Wales* was hit seven times — four shells failed to explode — before retiring at 0613, but not before scoring three hits on *Bismarck*. Towards evening, *Prince of Wales* engaged *Bismarck* briefly before returning to Scapa.

Prince of Wales carried Prime Minister Winston Churchill to Argentia Bay, Newfoundland, for the August 9–12, 1941, Atlantic Conference with President Franklin D. Roosevelt, at which they signed the Atlantic Charter creating the United Nations. The same summer, the Admiralty began planning for the defense of the Far East, and *Prince of Wales* and REPULSE were dispatched to Singapore as the nucleus of the Eastern Fleet under Admiral Sir Tom Phillips. They arrived on December 2; by the eighth, the Japanese had attacked Pearl Harbor and begun moving into Southeast Asia. That afternoon Force "Z" — the two capital ships and destroyers HMS *Electra, Express,* and *Tenedos,* and HMAS *Vampire* — sortied to attack Japanese forces in southern Thailand. Sighted by submarine *I-68* the next afternoon, Force "Z" avoided further detection until 0220 on December 10. Shortly before dawn, the Japanese launched thirty-four high-level bombers and fifty-one torpedo-bombers, which attacked the two capital ships at 1115. *Prince of Wales* was hit by seven or eight torpedoes and bombs before sinking at 1318 with the loss of 325 crew, including Admiral Phillips and Captain John Leach; the survivors were rescued by *Express*. In 1959, *Prince of Wales* was located in position 3°34′N, 104°27′E. The sinking of *Prince of Wales* and *Repulse* was the worst British naval defeat of World War II and the first unqualified demonstration of the vulnerability of capital ships to coordinated air attack on the high seas.

Middlebrook & Mahoney, *Battleship.* Morton, *Atlantic Meeting.*

HMS PRINCE OF WALES

King George V-class battleship (2f/2m). *L/B/D:* 745′ × 103′ × 29′ (227.1m × 31.4m × 8.8m). *Tons:* 43,786 disp. *Hull:* steel. *Comp.:* 1,560. *Arm.:* 10 × 14″ (2 × 4, 1 × 2), 16 × 5.25″, 32 × 2pdr, 3 rocket projectors; 2 aircraft. *Armor:* 14.7″ belt, 6″ deck. *Mach.:* geared turbines. 4 shafts, 100,000 shp; 28 kts. *Built:* Cammell Laird & Co., Ltd., Birkenhead, Eng.; 1941.

Less than two months after commissioning, HMS *Prince of Wales* was part of the Battle Squadron Force sent from Scapa Flow to cover the expected breakout of BISMARCK and PRINZ EUGEN. Two days later, on May 24, 1941,

PRINCESS VICTORIA

Ferry. *L/B/D:* 309.8′ × 48.1′ × 11.5′ (94.4m × 14.7m × 3.5m). *Tons:* 2,700. *Comp.:* 60 crew; 172 pass. *Hull:* steel. *Mach.:* Sulzer diesels, 2 × screws; 19.6 kts. *Built:* William Denny & Bros., Ltd., Dumbarton, Scotland; 1947.

The British Transport Commission's *Princess Victoria* operated on the Irish Sea between Larne, Northern Ireland, and Stranraer, Scotland, from 1947 to 1953. The ferry was a replacement for an earlier vessel of the same name which had been requisitioned as a minelayer and lost in 1940. In addition to carrying passengers, *Princess Victoria* was also designated to carry milk from Northern Ireland to Scotland, a special service held over from the lean years of World War II. On January 31, 1953, *Princess Victoria* left Stranraer at 0745 under Captain James Ferguson, sailing into the teeth of a northerly gale with snow squalls gusting over 60 miles per hour. Shortly after clearing Loch Ryan, a wave stove in one of her doors and flooded the car deck. Hove to and not under command, at 1034 she broadcast her first SOS call. The destroyer HMS *Constant* was dispatched from Rothesay, four hours distant, and *Sir Samuel Kelly*, the RNLI lifeboat at Portpatrick, Scotland, was launched. At 1358, *Princess Victoria* was on her beam ends; she was abandoned about five miles east of Copelands, at the mouth of Belfast Lough. A number of merchant ships joined the search for survivors, and 44 people were rescued; 128 passengers and crew died.

MacHaffie, *Short Sea Route*. Pollock, *Last Message 1358*.

USS PRINCETON

Sloop of war (1f/3m). *L/B/D:* 164′ × 31.5′ × 17′ (50m × 9.3m × 5.2m). *Tons:* 954 disp. *Hull:* iron. *Comp.:* 166. *Arm.:* 2 × 12″, 12 × 42-pdr. *Mach.:* semicylindrical reciprocating engines, 220 hp, 1 screw; 10 kts. *Built:* John Lenthall, Philadelphia Navy Yard; 1843.

A warship of innovative design and armament, USS *Princeton* was built "under the patronage of Captain Robert F. Stockton and the superintendence of [John] Ericsson." The two had previously collaborated in the building of ROBERT F. STOCKTON, the first ship to carry a direct-acting screw engine, the primary advantage of which was that the engines could be placed below the waterline and out of the line of fire. Built by Merrick and Towne of Philadelphia, *Princeton*'s propulsion consisted of a semicylindrical reciprocating steam engine driving a single helicoidal screw — that is, one with a single blade that spirals around the shaft. Arriving at New York, on October 19, 1843, *Princeton* beat Brunel's side-wheeler GREAT WESTERN over a twenty-one-mile course.

The following January she received her two 12-inch shell guns, the British-built "Oregon," designed by Ericsson, and the New York–built "Peacemaker," modeled on Ericsson's gun but designed by Stockton. In February 1844, the ship sailed to Washington, D.C., with a view to persuading Congress to approve the fitting out of more ships with more heavy guns, a measure endorsed by President John Tyler. Her third Potomac cruise, on February 29, was attended by 300 to 400 people including officials and their families and, for the second time, Tyler. During the demonstration of the "Peacemaker" the gun exploded, killing eight people. Among them were Secretary of State Abel P. Upshur and Secretary of the Navy

One of the U.S. Navy's worst peacetime tragedies was the explosion of USS PRINCETON's *12-in. gun, the "Peacemaker," during an official cruise on the Potomac River, February 28, 1844. President John Tyler was below when the explosion occurred, but Secretary of State Abel P. Upshur and Secretary of the Navy Thomas Gilmer — one third of his cabinet — were killed. Courtesy U.S. Naval Historical Center, Washington, D.C.*

Thomas Gilmer; nine were wounded, including Stockton and Senator Thomas Hart Benson.

Following repairs, *Princeton* was deployed with the Home Squadron in 1845, serving on blockade duty in the Mexican War and carrying to Galveston the Congressional resolution annexing Texas. After service in the Mediterranean in 1848–49, where she was admired by European observers, she returned to Boston Navy Yard in 1849 and was broken up. Some of her timbers and Ericsson's engine were used in the construction of USS *Princeton* of 1851, the second of five vessels so named.

Baxter, *Introduction of the Ironclad Warship*. Tucker, "U.S. Navy Steam Sloop *Princeton*."

USS PRINCETON (CV-23)

Independence-class light aircraft carrier. *L/B/D:* 622.5′ × 71.5′ (109.2′ew) × 26′ (189.7m × 21.8m (33.3m) × 7.9m). *Tons:* 11,000. *Hull:* steel. *Comp.:* 1,569. *Arm.:* 45 aircraft; 26 × 40mm. *Mach.:* steam turbine, 100,000 shp, 4 screws; 31 kts. *Built:* New York Shipbuilding Corp., Camden, N.J.; 1943.

Laid down in June 1941 as the light cruiser USS *Tallahassee*, after the United States entered World War II, it was decided to complete the hull as the aircraft carrier USS *Princeton*. After commissioning, she sailed for the

Pacific in August 1943 and joined Task Force 11. In September she was flagship of a force that seized Baker Island, about 1,700 miles southwest of Hawaii. After supporting the November invasion of the Gilbert Islands, she proceeded to the southwest Pacific where she mounted operations against Japanese airfields during the Allied landings at Empress Augusta Bay. After repairs on the West Coast, she joined Task Force 58 for the attack on the Marshall Islands in January and February 1944. Following raids in the Caroline Islands, *Princeton* sailed for New Guinea, where her planes provided air cover for the April landings at Hollandia.

Princeton next took part in the invasion of the Mariana Islands. During the Battle of the Philippine Sea on June 19, the so-called Great Marianas Turkey Shoot, her aviators were credited with downing thirty Japanese planes. Thereafter, *Princeton* alternated between attacks on Japanese positions in the Palaus, the Philippines, and Taiwan. During the October 20 landings at Dulag and San Pedro on Leyte Island, *Princeton*'s Task Group 38.3 provided air cover from the Sibuyan Sea off Luzon, about 200 miles north. Four days later, TG 38.3 was attacked by land-based aircraft. At 1100, a bomb crashed through *Princeton*'s flight deck and hangar deck. Enveloped in smoke and flames, her crew tried to save the ship, assisted by a number of other ships. At 1524, a magazine explosion blew off her stern and after flight deck, killing 237 and wounding 436 crew on the cruiser *Birmingham*, which was alongside at the time. With 200 of her own crew dead, *Princeton* was abandoned at 1406, and finally sank in 15°12′N, 123°37′E after being torpedoed by the destroyers USS *Irwin* and *Reno*.

Morison, *Two-Ocean War.* U.S. Navy, *DANFS.*

PRINZ EUGEN

Prinz Eugen-class heavy cruiser (1f/2m). *L/B/D:* 681.3′ × 71.8′ × 26.1′ (207.7m × 21.9m × 8m). *Tons:* 18,750 disp. *Hull:* steel. *Comp.:* 1,600. *Armor:* 3.2″ belt, 2″ deck. *Mach.:* steam turbines, 133,631 shp, 3 screws; 32.5 kts. *Arm.:* 8 × 8″ (4 × 2), 12 × 4″, 12 × 3.7cm, 8 × 2cm; 12 × 21″TT; 3 aircraft. *Built:* Friedrich Krupp Germaniawerft AG, Kiel, Germany; 1940.

A modified *Admiral Hipper*-class cruiser, *Prinz Eugen* was named for Eugene of Savoy, who fought for Leopold I of Austria, to symbolize Austro-German unity. Under Captain Helmuth Brinkmann, *Prinz Eugen* sailed with Bismarck in May 1941, making contact with the radar-equipped First Cruiser Squadron, HMS Norfolk, and *Suffolk* amid the ice and fog northeast of Iceland on May 23. An intercepting battlecruiser squadron including HMS Hood and Prince of Wales opened fire at 0553 on May 24. The four ships exchanged fire and *Hood* was sunk by *Bismarck*. *Prinz Eugen* remained unscathed and later that day parted company with the doomed *Bismarck*. On June 1 *Prinz Eugen* arrived at Brest, joining Gneisenau and Scharnhorst for several months of inaction.

Hitler ordered the ships home via the English Channel, and Operation Cerberus — the Channel Dash — began on February 11, 1942. *Prinz Eugen* made it safely to Brunsbüttel with a minimum of distraction from the RAF or destroyers. A week later, she was dispatched to Norway with Admiral Scheer. On February 23, near Trondheimfjord, HMS *Trident* (Lieutenant Commander Sladen) torpedoed *Prinz Eugen,* knocking out the steering gear. Following repairs and a stint as a training ship, in June 1944 *Prinz Eugen* (Captain Reinicke) was ordered to the Gulf of Finland to provide support against Soviet land targets for the German withdrawal from the collapsing Eastern Front, and for the evacuation of German forces from Finland. In October 1944, the ship collided with the light cruiser *Leipzig,* nearly cutting the smaller ship in two. After the war *Prinz Eugen* entered the lists of the U.S. Navy as *IX300.* Used in the nuclear bomb tests at Bikini Atoll in July 1946, the hull was severely strained and finally gave out on December 22, when the ship capsized at Kwajalein Atoll in 9°22′N, 167°09′E.

Whitley, *German Cruisers of World War Two.*

PRISCILLA

Sidewheel steamer (2f/4m). *L/B/D:* 440′ × 52.3′ × 18.3′ (134.1m × 15.9m × 5.6m). *Tons:* 2,673 grt. *Hull:* steel. *Comp.:* 1,500 pass.; 200 crew. *Mach.:* inclined compound engines, 8,500 hp, sidewheels; 22 kts. *Des.:* George Peirce. *Built:* Delaware River Iron Ship Building & Engine Works, Chester, Pa.; 1894.

Known variously as the "Queen of Long Island Sound" and the "Mauretania of Inland Waters," the Fall River Line's night boat *Priscilla* was one of the largest vessels ever built for service on Long Island Sound, being surpassed only by her running mate, *Commonwealth,* in 1908. Before the opening of the Cape Cod Canal to passenger steamer service in 1916, travelers from New York to Boston sailed in night boats in the early evening. After a stop at Newport, the boats would continue up to Mount Hope Bay and Fall River, where passengers would board the 0710 train to Boston, ninety minutes farther on. That night, the boats would depart Fall River, and after a stop at Newport would arrive at New York at 0700 the next morning. Named for the fair Puritan maiden immortalized by Longfellow, *Priscilla* was one of six similar steamboats built for the Fall River Line between 1883 and 1908. In addition to size and speed, she was well known for her opulent interiors, which included a 130-foot-long main saloon decorated in northern Italian Renaissance style, while her dining room boasted Indo-Moorish motifs.

Apart from work during special events such as the America's Cup races, *Priscilla* worked as a Fall River night boat for forty-three years. The most dramatic departure from her routine came on the night of July 21, 1924, when she raced at top speed through heavy fog to pick up survivors of her rival, the steamer *Boston,* after that vessel's collision with the tanker *Swift Arrow.* The only significant alterations to *Priscilla* were to improve safety following the TITANIC and MORRO CASTLE disasters in 1912 and 1934, respectively.

By the 1930s, the night boats were facing stiff competition, for both freight and passengers, from railroads, trucks, and cars. Three years later, the Fall River Line ceased operations and sold off its remaining boats — *Priscilla, Plymouth, Providence,* and *Commonwealth.* All four were scrapped at Baltimore, and with them died the age of the "floating palaces" that dominated transportation in New England for a century.

Brouwer, "Queen of Long Island Sound." McAdam, *"Priscilla" of Fall River.*

PROVENCE

Provence-class battleship (2f/2m). *L/B/D:* 551′ × 91.5′ × 29.5′ (168m × 27.9m × 9m). *Tons:* 28,500 disp. *Hull:* steel. *Comp.:* 1,190. *Arm.:* 10 × 13″ (5 × 2), 14 × 5″, 4 × 75mm. *Armor:* 10.8″ belt, 1.6″ deck. *Mach.:* steam turbines, 28,000 shp, 4 screws; 20 kts. *Built:* Arsenal de Brest, France; 1916.

Named for the French province, *Provence* was the first of three *Provence*-class battleships laid down in 1912; the others were BRETAGNE and *Lorraine.* After completion in 1916, she was made flagship of the Allied naval forces in the Mediterranean, whose primary objectives were to contain the Austro-Hungarian fleet in the Adriatic and combat the U-boat menace. During the Russian civil war, in December 1918 French forces operating in concert with White Russians occupied Odessa, Ukraine, and in early 1919 *Provence* was dispatched to the Black Sea to provide additional support to the counterrevolutionaries.

In 1937, *Provence* sailed on neutrality patrol during the Spanish civil war. The start of World War II found her in the South Atlantic, and she took part in the search for the German pocket battleship ADMIRAL GRAF SPEE before returning to the Mediterranean. Following the armistice between France and Germany and the establishment of the Vichy government, *Provence* was sent to the port of Mers el-Kébir, near Oran, Algeria, together with *Bretagne* and the battlecruisers *Dunkerque* and PROVENCE. Fearing a German takeover of the French fleet, the British launched Operation Catapult to co-opt or destroy the French fleet. On July 3, 1940, Vice Admiral Sir James Somerville's Force H arrived off Mers el-Kébir with the battleships HMS HOOD, BARHAM, and *Resolution* and aircraft carrier ARK ROYAL. When Admiral Gensoul refused to demilitarize his ships, disperse them to overseas ports, or surrender them outright, the British ships opened fire. *Bretagne* was sunk outright and STRASBOURG escaped. *Provence* and *Dunkerque* were both damaged, but they later returned to Toulon where they were scuttled in November 1942. *Provence* was raised by the Germans, sunk again as a blockship in 1943, and finally broken up in 1949.

Breyer, *Battleships and Battlecruisers.*

PROVIDENCE

(ex-*Katy*) Topsail sloop (1m). *L/B/D:* 67′ × 20′ × 9′ (20.4m × 6.1m × 2.7m). *Tons:* 95 bm. *Hull:* wood. *Comp.:* 52–90. *Arm.:* 12 × 6pdr, 10 swivels. *Built:* Providence, R.I.; ca. 1768.

Originally owned by Providence merchant John Brown, the merchant sloop *Katy* was one of two sloops chartered by the Rhode Island General Assembly in June 1775 to protect Rhode Island shipping from British warships, in particular HMS ROSE. Abraham Whipple, *Katy*'s first captain, captured the sloop *Diana* during the summer and was then ordered to capture a store of gunpowder at Bermuda, an unsuccessful operation. Purchased by the General Assembly on her return, *Katy* sailed for Philadelphia and, renamed *Providence,* entered the Continental Navy under Captain John Hazard.

On February 17, 1776, *Providence* sailed for the Bahamas, again in search of gunpowder, as part of a squadron commanded by Esek Hopkins in ALFRED. The Americans occupied Nassau in early March but failed to capture the gunpowder. Hopkins's ships returned to New London, where *Providence* became John Paul Jones's first command. After carrying soldiers from New London to New York and escorting a convoy of colliers to Philadelphia, *Providence* sailed on an independent cruise on August 1. Jones quickly captured a whaleship and a merchant ship and dispatched his prizes to Philadelphia. He then turned for Nova Scotia, where he burned or captured eight fishing schooners and recruited new crew to replace those he had put aboard his captured ships.

Returning to Rhode Island on October 9, Jones took command of *Alfred*. The two ships, with *Providence* now under Captain Hoysted Hacker, took the merchantmen *Active* and *Kitty* and the armed transport HMS *Mellish,* before *Providence* was forced back to Newport for repairs. In February 1777, *Providence* ran the British blockade off Narragansett Bay and captured another transport off Cape Breton. Put under Captain John P. Rathbun, *Providence* made two more coastal cruises before sailing again for the Bahamas in early 1778. Through a series of brilliant stratagems, Rathbun took and held the town for three days (January 27 to 30) during which time he spiked the guns of Fort Nassau, seized 1,600 pounds of gunpowder (at last), took 6 British prizes, and freed 30 American prisoners, all without bloodshed. She returned to Rhode Island unscathed on January 30, 1779.

Providence followed up this action with the capture of HM Brig *Diligent* (12 guns) off New York on May 7. The latter was taken into the Continental Navy and repaired in time to take part in the disastrous Penobscot expedition under Commodore Dudley Saltonstall in WARREN, together with *Providence* and thirty-seven other ships. On August 13, *Providence* and all but two of the American ships were run aground and burned to avoid capture by a superior British fleet that had appeared in Penobscot Bay.

In 1976 a fiberglass replica of *Providence* was built to commemorate the U.S. Bicentennial. Based at Newport, Rhode Island, she was used for sail training through the 1990s.

Miller, *Sea of Glory.* Morison, *John Paul Jones.* Rider, *Valour Fore and Aft.*

PT-109

Patrol torpedo boat. *L/B/D:* 80′ × 20.8′ × 5′ (24.4m × 6.3m × 1.5m). *Tons:* 45 tons. *Comp.:* 13. *Arm.:* 1 × 40mm; 2 × 20mm; 4 × 21″TT. *Hull:* wood. *Mach.:* Packard marine engines, 4,050 bph; 40 kts. *Built:* Elco Naval Division, Electric Boat Co., Bayonne, N.J.; 1942.

One of the more than 500 lightweight, fast torpedo boats built during World War II, *PT-109* entered service in the Pacific on July 10, 1942. Transferred to Motor Torpedo Boat Squadron 5 in September 1942, she came under command of Lieutenant John F. Kennedy. Active throughout the Solomons campaign, on the night of August 1–2, 1943, *PT-109* was one of fifteen PT boats patrolling the Blackett Strait south of Kolombangara Island. In the words of Samuel Eliot Morison, the action was "unsuccessful in a military sense, but important to a future President of the United States." At about 0230, *PT-109*

was cut in half by the *Amagiri*, a *Fubuki*-class destroyer under Commander Hanami, and sank in about 8°03′S, 156°58′E. After the war, the story of Lieutenant Kennedy's efforts to rescue the injured and bring about the rescue of his crew (two of the thirteen died in the collision) were magnificently exploited to further his political career. It is interesting to note that one of the authors of the official report on Kennedy's conduct was Lieutenant Byron S. White, whom Kennedy would later appoint to the Supreme Court of the United States.

Bulkley, *At Close Quarters.*

USS PUEBLO (AGER-2)

Environmental research ship (1f/2m). *L/B/D:* 176.5′ × 32′ × 9.3′ (53.8m × 9.8m × 2.8m). *Tons:* 850 disp. *Hull:* steel. *Comp.:* 81. *Mach.:* 12 kts. *Built:* Kewaunee Shipbuilding & Engineering Co., Kewaunee, Wisc.; 1944.

Built as a supply ship for the U.S. Army Transportation Corps, *FP-344* served as a harbor craft in the Philippines from 1944 to 1954, when she was laid up on the West Coast. Transferred to the U.S. Navy in 1966, she was renamed *Pueblo* and commissioned as an environmental research ship the following year. Homeported at Yokosuka, Japan, she was assigned to intelligence and oceanographic research work in the Sea of Japan, possibly under the authority of the highly secretive National Security Agency (NSA). Seized by the North Koreans on January 23, 1968, several versions of what happened and why have been advanced. According to a study by Robert A. Liston published in 1988, the NSA intended for the *Pueblo* to be seized by the North Koreans in the hopes that they would find and use an encoding machine that would enable U.S. intelligence to monitor traffic between North Korea and China. This plan was superseded after the *Pueblo* intercepted messages indicating that the Soviet Union was planning an invasion of China. After leaking a report of the intercept to both Chinese and Soviet intelligence agents, the NSA ordered *Pueblo* back to sea, knowing that both the Soviets and Chinese would be on the lookout for the ship.

Pueblo was cruising in international waters between Japan and Korea when a North Korean patrol boat ordered her to heave to and she was boarded. According to Liston, Chinese troops had boarded when a Soviet ship came within range and fired on *Pueblo* in hopes of keeping her out of Chinese hands. One of the American crew was killed, and the ship was eventually taken to Wonsan, where the Americans were charged with violating North Korea's territorial waters. Although U.S. naval forces took up station, there were no reprisals. The crew — four of whom had been wounded in the attack — were detained for eleven months before their release on December 22, after a contrived agreement under which a U.S. representative to the Mixed Armistice Commission signed a document stating that *Pueblo* had been engaged in espionage. With the agreement of the North Koreans, the confession was promptly denounced as false. Though *Pueblo*'s capture has been described by one intelligence officer as "the greatest intelligence coup of modern times," owing to the secrecy in which the Navy's investigation of the incident was carried out, it is unlikely that all the facts of the case will be brought to light.

Liston, *"Pueblo" Surrender*. U.S. Navy, *DANFS*.

PUNIC (MARSALA) SHIP

Liburnian. *L/B:* ca. 110′ × 16′ (33.5m × 4.9m). *Hull:* wood. *Comp.:* ca. 75. *Built:* Tunisia(?); <241 BCE.

In 1969, a commercial dredger working in the harbor of Marsala in western Sicily uncovered the remains of several shipwrecks. The following summer, Honor Frost led a team of underwater archaeologists to the site, which over four seasons yielded a pile of ballast stones, a forty-foot length of keel, together with about one-third of the original port side of the hull and fragments of the starboard side. Most significant was the recovery of a portion of the sternpost from which archaeologists were able to determine the shape of the hull. The fact that the stern had been driven into the relatively hard bottom of seaweed and sand indicated that the ship had sunk stern first, probably after being rammed. This, combined with the presence of ballast stone and the absence of amphorae, suggested that she was a warship.

Those crew who could get off took with them their personal weapons — the ship's primary armament was the bow ram — but they left ample evidence of what they ate. Food remains show that the crew had an excellent diet that included deer, goat, horse, ox, pig, and sheep, as well as olives, nuts, and fruit. Most unexpected was the recovery of the stems of plant material, which botanical testing showed to be hops, nettles, or cannabis. Circumstances suggest the latter, and that possibly it was chewed during long-distance rowing or before going into battle, just as the Royal Navy later issued rum to its crews. Mixed in with the ballast stones were the bones of a dog and a human, possibly an injured crewman trapped by the shifting ballast.

The vessel is believed to have been a "long ship" known as a Liburnian, an oared vessel with seventeen sweeps on either side, each pulled by two oarsmen. Small and swift, Liburnians were employed for carrying messages and for scouting. All other known wrecks of the period have been of "round" cargo ships. The presence of this wreck at Marsala is historically significant, because it was near this port — then known as Lilybaeum — that Rome defeated Carthage in the Battle of the Aegates (Egadi) Islands, sinking about 50 ships and capturing another 70 from a fleet of 220 ships. This battle concluded the first Punic War and forced the Carthaginians to give up their hold in western Sicily. In the first millennium BCE, Mediterranean trade was dominated by three great powers in turn. First were the Phoenicians, whose chief ports were Sidon and Tyre in what is now Lebanon, from the eleventh to the eighth century. They were succeeded by their colonial offspring, Carthage, in what is now Tunisia, who lost to Rome after a succession of three Punic Wars, fought from 264 to 241 BCE, from 218 to 201 BCE and, finally, 149–146 BCE.

One of the most fascinating discoveries about Carthaginian shipbuilding was the high degree of literacy and organization associated with it. Careful examination of the Punic ship showed that the builders had written on the various members to mark their placement in relation to one another. Archaeologists and historians of shipbuilding concur that "the findings on the Punic ship show a degree of planning and organization that is without parallel until the Industrial Revolution."

Tragically, despite the enormous historical, archaeological, and cultural value of this find, the Punic Marsala ship has been all but abandoned. After several years of neglect, in 1992 the Sicilian parliament voted to designate funds for repair and conservation of the ship's remains, which had been raised and housed in Marsala. Three years later, before any money had been spent, the parliament annulled the grant.

Frost, "How Carthage Lost the Sea"; Frost et al., "Marsala Punic Ship"; *Punic Ship*.

PURITAN

Sidewheel steamer (2f/4m). *L/B/D:* 403.5′ × 52.5′ × 8.1′ (123m × 16m × 2.5m). *Tons:* 3,075 grt. *Hull:* steel. *Comp.:* 364 staterooms. *Mach.:* walking beam engine, 7,500 hp, sidewheels; 20 mph. *Des.:* George Peirce. *Built:* Delaware River Iron Ship Building & Engine Works, Chester, Pa.; 1888.

One of the Fall River Line's last quartet of night boats that carried passengers between New York and Fall River, Massachusetts, for the train to Boston, *Puritan* was driven by the biggest walking-beam engine ever built. Designed by Andrew Fletcher, the compound engine weighed 46 tons, the low-pressure cylinder measured 110 inches in diameter with a 9-foot stroke, and the high-pressure cylinder measured 75 inches with a 14-foot stroke. This machinery was carried in the Fall River Line's first steel hull, which rose four decks high: the engine was all but hidden, the beam enclosed on the hurricane deck and the paddlewheels shielded by ordinary joinery work rather than ornately decorated paddle boxes. The overall effect was elegant, and it was said that "when under way she was the most beautiful steamer of her day." This was reflected also in *Puritan*'s interior, which was a celebration of northern Italian Renaissance style, hardly in keeping with her name.

After two decades in service, *Puritan* was superseded by a new quartet of Fall River boats, *Commonwealth*, *Plymouth*, Priscilla, and *Providence*. After seven years as a reserve vessel at Newport, in 1915 she was sold for scrap to the Scott Wrecking Company of New London.

McAdam, *Old Fall River Line*.

PYROSCAPHE

Steamboat (1f). *L/B:* ca. 130′–140′ × 14′ (40–43m × 4.3m). *Tons:* 163 tons. *Hull:* wood. *Mach.:* horizontal, double-acting steam engine, sidewheels. *Des.:* Marquis Claude de Jouffroy d'Abbans. *Built:* Ecully, France; 1783.

In the late eighteenth century, European and American inventors began to consider ways of applying the steam engine to transportation on land and sea. One of the first working steamboats was developed in France by the Marquis Claude de Jouffroy d'Abbans. In 1782, Jouffroy built a forty-three-foot steam-powered boat propelled by two flapped paddles, but the machinery was inadequate to the task. The next July, Jouffroy built *Pyroscaphe* (from the Greek for "fire boat"), a vessel driven by a horizontal double-acting engine that drove two 13.1-foot sidewheels each equipped with eight paddles. The engine was devised by Messieurs Frères Jean et Compagnie of Lyons and consisted of a 25.6-inch-diameter cylinder with a 77-inch stroke. On July 15, 1783, *Pyroscaphe* steamed up the Saône River for fifteen minutes before the engine gave out. The Academy of Lyons endorsed Jouffroy's experiment, but his application for a fifteen-year monopoly to build steamboats in France was rejected after a furious debate in the Academy of Sciences. Political events overtook Jouffroy, and he did not build a second vessel, *Charles-Philippe*, until 1816, long after steam had been successfully developed elsewhere.

Baker, *Engine Powered Vessel*. Flexner, *Steamboats Come True*.

Quanzhou wreck

Fu-ship (3m). *L/B/D:* 111.5′ × 32.1′ × 9.8′ (34m × 9.82m × 3m). *Tons:* 374.4 disp. *Hull:* wood. *Built:* South China; 13th cent.

In 1975, workers dredging a canal on Quanzhou Bay (24°91′N, 118°59′E) in Fujian Province, China, uncovered the remains of what turned out to be a thirteenth-century ship dating from the end of the Southern Song Dynasty. Over the course of the summer, the remains of the vessel were completely excavated and taken to Quanzhou for conservation and study. The remains of the hull, which has a V-shaped bottom, includes the keel and the remains of thirty strakes, fourteen to port and sixteen to starboard. There were steps for two masts, the placement of which forward and amidships suggests the existence of a third mast in the stern. Although the remaining vessel members are only 24 meters in length by 9 meters wide, interpretation of the finds suggests that the ship originally measured 34.6 meters by 9.82 meters, with a loaded draft of 3 meters. The hull is solidly constructed, with two layers of planking below the waterline — the first eleven strakes from the keel — and three above, using a combination of clinker and carvel joinery that Australian archaeologist Jeremy Green has described as "complex rabbeted carvel-clinker."

The first pair of strakes out from the keel is joined by a "rabbeted carvel joint" in which the edge between the strakes is rabbeted with simple lap joints. The second and third strakes are joined by a "rabbeted clinker joint" in which a rabbet is cut in the inside lower edge of the third plank, which is fitted against the uncut upper edge of the second. The third, fourth, and fifth strakes are joined by the rabbeted carvel joint, and the fifth and sixth by the rabbeted clinker joint, and so on. This innermost layer of planking is sheathed by a second layer of strakes that are edge-joined to one another. However, as these are laid directly on top of the inner layer, the third, sixth, ninth, and thirteenth strakes are clinker laid over the second, fifth, eighth, and twelfth, respectively. The third layer of planking is carvel laid from the thirteenth to the seventeenth strakes.

Twelve bulkheads divide the ship into thirteen compartments; there are waterways cut into the base of all but the aftermost and foremost bulkheads, which were watertight. The bulkheads were fastened to the inner layer of planking with iron braces and iron nails, the latter being set and covered with *t'ung* putty as a preservative. Another interesting find is the placement in the keel of seven coins in the pattern of the constellation of Ursa Minor, and a bronze mirror, both of which were thought to bring the vessel good luck. While the underbody of the hull tapered towards the bow, the upper decks fore and aft were probably trapezoidal.

The cargo reveals that the Quanzhou wreck was originally a "spices and pepper ship" or a "spice junk." The cargo included medicinals and 2,300 kilograms of spice-woods including laka-wood, sandalwood, and black pepper from Java, garu-wood from Cambodia, betel nuts from Indonesia, frankincense from central Arabia, ambergris from Somalia, and tortoiseshell. It is not clear from this manifest that the Quanzhou ship actually sailed as far afield as Africa, but it does attest to the importance of the port of Quanzhou (on mainland China opposite Taiwan), whose merchants began trading with Africa and the Middle East in the sixth century. Comparing Quanzhou with the great Mediterranean entrepôt, Marco Polo wrote,

> The quantity of pepper imported there is so considerable, that what is carried to Alexandria, to satisfy the demand of the western parts of the world, is trifling in comparison, perhaps no more than the hundredth part. It is indeed impossible to convey an idea of the number of merchants and the accumulation of goods in this place, which is held to be one of the largest ports in the world.

The ship has been dated based on evidence provided by the hoard of 504 coins, the latest of which were struck in 1273, about the time the ship is thought to have sunk. Today the reassembled hull is on display at the Quanzhou Museum of Overseas Communication History.

Green, "Song Dynasty Shipwreck at Quanzhou." Keith & Buys, "New Light on Medieval Chinese Seagoing Ship Construction."

Li Guo-Qing, "Archaeological Evidence for the Use of 'Chu-Nam' on the Thirteenth-Century Quanzhou Ship." Merwin, "Selections from *Wen-wu* on the Excavation of a Sung Dynasty Seagoing Vessel."

QUEEN ANNE'S REVENGE

(ex-*Concorde*) Ship (3m). *L/B/D:* 103′ × 24.5′ × 13.3′ (12.8′ dph) (31.4m × 7.5m × 4.1m). *Tons:* 200 tons. *Hull:* wood. *Comp.:* 125. *Arm.:* 20–40 guns. *Built:* Britain; ca. 1710.

Queen Anne's Revenge was the name given to the French merchant ship *Concorde* after her capture in 1717 by the pirate Edward Teach, popularly remembered as Blackbeard. *Concorde* is believed to have been built in England in about 1710 and sailed to Rio de Janeiro. In 1713, she was sold to Spanish interests and spent several years trading on the Pacific coast of South America. Sold to a M. Mountaudin in 1717, she was put in the slave trade between Senegal and Martinique. The same year, she was captured by Bahamas-based pirates led by Benjamin Hornigold, who gave Teach command of the ship. Parting amicably from Hornigold, Teach named his ship *Queen Anne's Revenge,* in honor of the British monarch who ruled from 1702 to 1714.

Increasing the armament of his ship to forty guns, many of which were probably short rail guns that could be handled by one man, Teach spent the next year raiding merchant ships in the Caribbean Islands, the Bay of Honduras, and the southeast coast of North America. By the spring of 1718, he had four vessels under his command, including the captured merchantmen *Revenge* and *Adventure,* and an unnamed sloop. In May, Teach captured about eight or nine vessels at Charleston, South Carolina, and demanded as ransom a supply of medicine — some believe because syphilis was rife among his crew. Departing Charleston, he sailed north along the coast of North Carolina. Turning into Topsail (now Beaufort) Inlet, *Queen Anne's Revenge* and *Adventure* were lost on a sandbar. The remains of a ship thought to be *Queen Anne's Revenge* were located in the spring of 1997.

On December 3, 1718, Teach was killed in an attack by forces dispatched by Virginia's Governor Alexander Spottswood. Although he had captured no major prizes during his short career as a pirate, Teach achieved lasting infamy as the ruthless and sadistic drunk, Blackbeard, of Daniel Defoe's highly colored *General History of the Robberies and Murders of the Most Notorious Pyrates,* published in 1724.

Lee, *Blackbeard the Pirate.* Rankin, *Pirates of North Carolina.*

HMS QUEEN CHARLOTTE

Umpire-class 1st rate (3m). *L/B:* 190′ × 52.3′ × 22.3′ (57.9m × 15.9m × 6.8m). *Tons:* 2,279 bm. *Hull:* wood. *Comp.:* 850. *Arm.:* 30 × 32pdr, 28 × 24pdr, 42 × 12pdr. *Des.:* Edward Hunt. *Built:* Chatham Dockyard, Eng.; 1790.

Named for the consort of George III, HMS *Queen Charlotte* was built during a period when Britain was not actively at war with her traditional enemies. But an uneasy peace ruled and the Navy was on a war footing. *Queen Charlotte* spent several years as flagship of Admiral Richard Howe, during the Nootka Sound Controversy with Spain in 1790, and again during the French Revolutionary Wars starting in 1793. In May 1794, she sailed from Portsmouth with thirty-two ships of the line to intercept a grain fleet bound from North America to France. A French fleet under Rear Admiral Villaret-Joyeuse sailed from Brest to provide protection for the convoy, and on June 28, the two fleets made their first contact. A partial action resulted in the dismasting of the French *Révolutionnaire,* which lost about 400 men dead and wounded but escaped capture that night. HMS *Audacious* was also dismasted and forced home. The next day, Howe nearly captured three French ships before Villaret-Joyeuse ceded the weather gauge advantage to rescue them. Two days of fog prevented a further engagement. But on June 1 Howe ranged his fleet to windward of the French and signaled for each of his ships to steer for her French counterpart, pass under her stern, and engage her on the lee side. A few minutes before 1000, *Queen Charlotte* passed below Villaret-Joyeuse's *Montagne* and poured in a succession of broadsides. Engaged by both *Montagne* and *Jacobin, Queen Charlotte* lost her fore topmast, but *Montagne* escaped with her stern stove in and 300 of her crew dead or wounded. Howe's tactic was so successful that the battle was over by noon and six prizes were taken. Howe was too enervated to follow up his tactical victory with a strategic one, and the French grain fleet continued unscathed to Brest. Nonetheless, the battle was known as the Glorious First of June.

On June 23, 1795, *Queen Charlotte* flew the flag of Admiral Alexander Hood, Viscount Bridport, when he engaged another fleet under Villaret-Joyeuse in the Battle of Groix, during which the French lost three ships in a general chase off Brest. Two years later, the men of *Queen Charlotte* took part in the Nore mutiny, which was resolved thanks in large part to the intervention of Viscount Keith, who hoisted his flag in her as second in command of the Channel Fleet. She was Keith's flagship in the Mediterranean three years later when on March 17, 1800,

Philippe-Jacques de Loutherbourg's depiction of the "Battle of the Glorious First of June 1794," showing Admiral Lord Howe's HMS QUEEN CHARLOTTE *with her topmast by the boards, closely engaged by Rear Admiral Villaret-Joyeuse's* MONTAGNE. *Though the French fleet lost six ships, the grain fleet under their protection reached France, giving Villaret-Joyeuse a strategic victory. Courtesy National Maritime Museum, Greenwich.*

she caught fire about twelve miles off Livorno. Keith was ashore at the time, but his ship sank with 690 of her crew.

Dictionary of National Biography. Hepper, *British Warship Losses.*

HMS QUEEN ELIZABETH

Queen Elizabeth-class battleship (2f/2m). *L/B/D:* 645.9′ × 90.6′ × 30.8′ (196.9m × 27.6m × 9.4m). *Tons:* 33,000 disp. *Comp.:* 1,120. *Hull:* steel. *Arm.:* 8 × 15″ (4 × 2), 16 × 6″, 2 × 3″, 4 × 3pdr. *Armor:* belt 13″, deck 3″. *Mach.:* Parsons turbines, 75,000 hp, 4 screws; 24 kts. *Des.:* E. N. Mooney & W. H. Gard. *Built:* Portsmouth Dockyard, Eng.; 1915.

The five *Queen Elizabeth*-class battleships, which included BARHAM and WARSPITE, were long considered "the most perfect example of the naval constructor's art . . . put afloat." They were the first battleships to use oil for fuel or mount fifteen-inch guns, and they were the fastest yet built. As flagship of the East Mediterranean Squadron, HMS *Queen Elizabeth* supported the Gallipoli landings. Recalled to the Grand Fleet in 1915, she was Admiral Sir David Beatty's flagship from 1916 to 1918, and the surrender of the German Fleet was concluded on her decks.

Queen Elizabeth later served in the Atlantic and Mediterranean and underwent extensive alterations between 1937 and 1941. While with the First Battle Squadron in Alexandria, Egypt, she and her sister ship *Valiant* were damaged by limpet mines planted by three Italian two-man submarines on December 19, 1941, and repairs had to be completed in the United States. From 1943 she was flagship of Admiral Sir James Somerville's Eastern Fleet and supported Allied landings in Indonesia and Burma through the end of the war. She was sold in 1948.

Halpern, *Naval History of World War I.* Parkes, *British Battleships.*

QUEEN ELIZABETH

(later *Seawise University*) Liner (2f/2m). *L/B:* 1,030.6′ × 118.5′ (314.2m × 36.1m). *Tons:* 83,673 grt. *Comp.:* 1st 823, cabin 662, tourist 798; crew 1,318. *Hull:* steel. *Mach.:* steam turbines, 4 screws; 29 kts. *Built:* John Brown & Co., Ltd., Clydebank, Scotland; 1940.

In the midst of the great rivalry for preeminence on the North Atlantic run, Cunard Line was determined to maintain weekly service between Southampton and New York with just two ships, the record-setting QUEEN MARY — whose ultimate rival for speed proved to be NORMANDIE — and *Queen Elizabeth.* Laid down in 1936, *Queen Elizabeth* was launched two years later. Benefiting from careful, and in the case of Cunard rivals, clandestine observation of the other greyhounds of her era, the twin-funneled *Queen Elizabeth* was a top priority for her builders until shipyard facilities began to be turned over to military vessels in 1939.

In the opening months of World War II, there was increased concern about her vulnerability to German bombers, and in February 1940, as yet unfinished, it was announced that she would proceed to Southampton for fitting out. Instead, she made her secret maiden voyage to New York. There work was continued until the following November, when she was dispatched to Singapore for fitting out. Some thought was given to converting her to an aircraft carrier, but she was finished as a troopship instead, and plied the Indian Ocean routes between Australia, India, and Suez. In 1942 she was back in New York and her capacity was increased from a mere 5,600 troops to 15,000. Though she was never as fast as her older consort, her speed was her greatest defense, and she worked the submarine-infested Atlantic alone for the duration of the war.

Returned to peacetime service, she made her first voyage in the passenger trade for which she was intended — between Southampton, Cherbourg, and New York — in 1946. Between them, *Queen Elizabeth* and *Queen Mary,* the two largest passenger ships to survive the war, became the most profitable pair of ships ever put in service, even after the commissioning of the world's fastest ocean liner, UNITED STATES, in 1952, and ten years later, CGT's FRANCE. But by that time, commercial jetliners had made their presence felt and the transatlantic passenger-ship trade began quickly to erode. Between 1957 and 1965, traffic plummeted from an all-time high of more than one million passengers to only 650,000, while airline passengers had quadrupled to four million. Still, the *Queens* held their own as countless other ships were withdrawn from service.

To make up for lost revenues, *Queen Elizabeth* was put into cruise service from New York in the winter months. She proved so successful that in 1965 she was given something of a reprieve when she was reconditioned and fitted out with a lido deck with outdoor swimming pool and air conditioning. Still, it was not enough. In 1968, she was withdrawn from service, sold to an American company called Queen, Inc., and laid up in Port Everglades, Florida, as a tourist attraction. Two years later, she was auctioned off to Taiwan shipping magnate C. Y. Tung, renamed *Seawise University* (Seawise being a pun on Tung's first two initials), and sailed for Hong Kong to be converted into an oceangoing university. After a $6 million refit, a fire of suspicious origin broke out and she capsized in Hong Kong Harbor. Salvage proved impossible, and she was scrapped where she lay.

Bonsor, *North Atlantic Seaway.* Braynard & Miller, *Fifty Famous Liners.*

QUEEN ELIZABETH 2

Liner (1f/1m). *L/B:* 963′ × 105.3′ (293.5m × 32.1m). *Tons:* 65,863 grt. *Hull:* steel. *Comp.:* 1st 564, tourist 1,441; crew 906. *Mach.:* steam turbines, 3 screws; 28.5 kts. *Built:* Upper Clyde Shipbuilders, Glasgow; 1969.

Even as the jet age signaled the demise of the great transatlantic steamships that had carried tens of millions of immigrants from Europe to the Americas, Britain's veteran shipping concern Cunard Line decided that its great liner QUEEN MARY should have an heir. In 1959, it began formulating plans for her successor, known first as Q3, and later, when the designs had been radically changed, Q4. In so doing, Cunard did not entirely ignore economic reality. Her design both paid homage to her owner's roots on the North Atlantic and anticipated the expanding clientele of the cruise ship industry. The last of the superliners was launched in 1967 as *Queen Elizabeth 2,* named after Cunard's first *Queen Elizabeth* and not for the sovereign, Queen Elizabeth II.

The *QE2*'s maiden voyage was scheduled for January 1969, but repeated problems with her engines and other defects forced Cunard to refuse delivery until April, and she did not sail on her maiden voyage until May 2. Although a popular ship, she has run at a deficit almost from the outset of her career. Her fame has also been something of a liability, and throughout her career she has been the target of several scares and hoaxes. The first of these came in a transatlantic crossing in 1972 when the Royal Air Force parachuted four bomb disposal experts to her in response to a bomb threat. In April 1973, while under charter for a cruise to Israel in commemoration of that country's twenty-fifth anniversary, she was threatened by terrorist attack, and it was later reported that Libyan leader Muammar Qaddafi had intended to torpedo the ship in the Mediterranean. Despite these and other difficulties, including one crippling engine failure that left her adrift in midatlantic in 1974, she has improved steadily with age.

In the best traditions of the British merchant marine, during Britain's war with Argentina over the Falklands/Malvinas Islands in 1982, she performed yeoman's service as a troop transport together with P&O Line's *Canberra*. She has also circled the world many times without incident. After returning to service, she remained out of the headlines until 1992, when she suffered hull damage after grounding off Cuttyhunk Island, Massachusetts. As of 1997, *Queen Elizabeth 2* was still going strong, very much the last of an era.

Bonsor, *North Atlantic Seaway.* Braynard & Miller, *Fifty Famous Liners.*

QUEEN MARY

Liner (3f/2m). *L/B:* 1,019.4′ loa × 118.6′ (310.7m loa × 36.1m). *Tons:* 80,774 grt. *Hull:* steel. *Comp.:* cabin 776, tourist 784, 3rd 579; crew 1,101. *Mach.:* steam turbines, 160,000 shp, 4 screws; 31.7 kts. *Built:* John Brown & Co., Ltd., Clydebank, Scotland; 1934.

International rivalry for supremacy on the North Atlantic reached its zenith in the early 1930s. British ships had reigned supreme from the 1850s to 1898, when Norddeutscher Lloyd's KAISER WILHELM DER GROSSE became the first German ship to win the Blue Riband for the fastest Atlantic crossing. She was followed by Hapag's DEUTSCHLAND and NDL's KRONPRINZ WILHELM; but Britain returned with sister ships LUSITANIA and MAURETANIA, which between them held the record from 1907 to 1929. From that year until 1938, the Blue Riband would change hands eight more times between five ships from four different countries: Germany's BREMEN and EUROPA, Italy's REX, France's NORMANDIE, and ultimately Britain's *Queen Mary.*

Considered by many the apogee of British passenger shipbuilding, Cunard–White Star Line's *Queen Mary* was laid down just as the Great Depression began to take hold

in Europe, a circumstance that held up her construction between 1931 and 1934. A stately ship, built along the same lines as its pre–World War I beauty AQUITANIA, she was the second 1,000-foot ship to enter service, following the French Line's sleek *Normandie.* The legend surrounding her name is well known. Cunard ships' names customarily ended in *-ia,* and it was widely reported that Cunard sought King George V's permission to name its greatest ship after England's greatest Queen — meaning, presumably, Queen Victoria. The King, the story continues, replied that his wife would be greatly honored, and so hull "534" became *Queen Mary.* A more prosaic explanation for the choice of name is that Cunard intended to break with tradition to accommodate its 1934 merger with White Star, whose ships' names generally ended in *-ic.*

Queen Mary entered service between Southampton, Cherbourg, and New York in 1936, and quickly wrested the Blue Riband from *Normandie* with a westbound voyage between Bishop Rock and Ambrose Light at a record speed of 30.14 knots (4 days, 27 minutes; August 20–24), followed immediately with an eastbound record of 30.6 knots (3 days, 23 hours, 57 minutes). *Normandie* reclaimed both records the following year, only to have *Queen Mary* reply with speeds of 30.99 knots (3 days, 21 hours, 48 minutes; August 4–8, 1938) westbound, and 31.7 knots (3 days, 20 hours, and 42 minutes; August 10–14) eastbound. Although the record for the fastest transatlantic crossing had been known as the Blue Riband since the 1890s, in 1935 British parliamentarian Thomas K. Hales offered a silver trophy to the steamship company whose ship held the current record. Cunard refused to recognize the honor, which fell to only three other companies — Italia (*Rex*), Compagnie Générale Transatlantique (*Normandie*) and, from 1952, United States Lines (UNITED STATES).

Queen Mary's speed made her one of the most popular ships afloat, and she earned handsome profits for her owners until the outbreak of World War II, which found her at New York. After lying idle for six months, she entered service as a troopship in March, sailing unescorted from New York for Sydney, via Cape Town. She ferried troops between Australia and Suez until the United States entered the war, when she began braving the North Atlantic with only her speed to protect her from German submarines, whose commanders were reportedly offered a reward of $250,000 for sinking her. Faster than any warship afloat, she was known as "the Gray Ghost." So great was the imperative for speed that when, on October 2, 1942, she rammed HMS *Curacoa,* she could not stand by to rescue the cruiser's 364 crew, only 26 of whom survived. *Queen Mary* carried on average more than 15,000 troops eastbound, and in 1943 she embarked 16,683 soldiers and crew on one voyage, more than any other ship has ever carried. Over the course of the whole war, she and her consort, QUEEN ELIZABETH, carried more than 1.6 million people between them, including 37 percent of the 875,000 U.S. troops who sailed for Europe.

Queen Mary was released from military duty in 1946, and after refurbishment by her builders she left Southampton on her first peacetime crossing to New York on July 31, 1947. Her postwar tonnage was given as 81,237 gross registered tonnage; the only other major modification was the fitting of Denny-Brown stabilizers in 1958. The two *Queen*s maintained weekly service between Southampton, Cherbourg, and New York, and in 1960 *Queen Mary* posted an impressive 30-knot crossing between Ambrose and Cherbourg. By this time, though, the jet airliner had already signaled the twilight of the transatlantic liner. In 1963, *Queen Mary* began a series of occasional cruises, first to the Canary Islands and later to the Bahamas. However, without central air conditioning, outdoor pools, or other amenities now commonplace on cruise ships, she proved ill suited for the work. In 1967, she was withdrawn from service after more than 1,000 transatlantic crossings.

The same year, *Queen Mary* was sold to the city of Long Beach, California, for use as a maritime museum and hotel. After a farewell departure from Southampton, she sailed via Lisbon, Las Palmas, Rio de Janeiro, Callao, Balboa, and Acapulco to arrive at Long Beach on December 9, 1967. There, the third-largest passenger ship ever to sail the North Atlantic seaway — and the largest to survive — remains (as of 1997) one of the last reminders of the technological and aesthetic genius that dominated the North Atlantic Ocean for more than a century.

Bailey, *Down the Burma Road.* Shipbuilder and Marine Engine-Builder, *Cunard White Star . . . Liner "Queen Mary."* Steele, "*Queen Mary.*"

R

Ra II

Reed raft (1m). *L/B/D:* 39′ × 16′ × 6′ deep (11.9m × 4.9m × 1.8m). *Hull:* papyrus reed. *Comp.:* 8. *Des.:* traditional. *Built:* Safi, Morocco; 1970.

Intrigued by the strong resemblance between various aspects of ancient Egyptian and pre-Columbian culture, Thor Heyerdahl set out to demonstrate that the sources of New World technology and belief could have come from across the Atlantic. A crucial point of similarity was the design of reed boats shown in Egyptian tombs and found on Lake Chad, the Andean Lake Titicaca, and Easter Island, to which he had sailed in the balsa raft KON-TIKI in 1947 in the Pacific. Heyerdahl hired Chadian reed boat builder Abdullah Djibrine and two Buruma colleagues to build a *kaday* from papyrus cut on Lake Tana, the source of the Blue Nile in Ethiopia. The design was worked out in consultation between Djibrine and Björn Langström, a Swedish authority on ancient Egyptian boat design.

The finished *Ra* — named for the Egyptian sun god — made entirely of papyrus and rope was taken by truck and ship to the Moroccan port of Safi where she was launched. The polyglot crew consisted of Heyerdahl, Djibrine, Yuri Alexandrovich Senkevich (Soviet Union), Norman Baker (United States), Carlo Mauri (Italy), Santiago Genoves (Mexico), and Georges Sourial (Egypt). Provisions for the voyage were carried in 160 amphorae made according to a 5,000-year-old example in the Cairo Museum. The voyage began on May 25, 1969. Although *Ra* made it most of the way across the Atlantic, covering about 60 miles a day (2.5 knots), the crew were forced to abandon *Ra* near Barbados, because much of the stern had sagged and the raft was breaking up.

Convinced only that he had chosen the wrong design, Heyerdahl arranged to build *Ra II,* a Moroccan *madia* whose design more closely resembled that of the reed rafts on Lake Titicaca. Four Aymara reed builders from Bolivia were brought to Morocco for the project, which again used reeds from Lake Tana. Though 10 feet shorter than *Ra, Ra II* carried eight crew, Madanni Ait Ouhanni

(Morocco) and Kei Ohara (Japan) sailing in place of Djibrine. The second attempt, in 1970, was a success, the voyage from Morocco to Barbados being completed in only 57 days.

Heyerdahl, *"Ra" Expeditions.*

Rainbow Warrior

(ex-*Sir William Hardy*) Research vessel (1f/2m). *L/B:* 131′ × 27.5′ (48.8m × 8.4m). *Tons:* 418 grt. *Hull:* steel. *Comp.:* 23. *Mach.:* oil engine, 600 bhp; 11 kts. *Built:* Hall, Russell & Co., Aberdeen, Scotland; 1955.

Built as a research vessel for Britain's Ministry of Fisheries and Agriculture, *Sir William Hardy* was named for an eminent marine scientist. In 1977 the all but abandoned trawler was bought by the international activist environmental group Greenpeace and renamed *Rainbow Warrior.* She spent two seasons harassing Icelandic and Spanish whaleships and Norwegian sealers in the North Atlantic, and in 1979 was detained for following the nuclear waste dump-ship *Pacific Swan* into Cherbourg. The next year she was arrested at El Ferrol by Spanish authorities and her engines were stripped pending a trial. Greenpeace smuggled enough engine parts aboard for *Rainbow Warrior* to make a daring night escape into international waters. After repairs in England, she proceeded to Newfoundland to stop sealers, then protested development of oil reserves off New England and toxic waste dumping in the New York bight. Greenpeace next dispatched *Rainbow Warrior* to prevent Japanese fishermen from collecting dolphins in their tuna catch, and to protest development of oil reserves off the coast of California. The ship's most audacious act came in July 1983, when she entered Soviet waters and her crew landed at Lorino, Siberia, to photograph an illegal Soviet whaling operation.

Attention then turned to French nuclear testing on Muroroa Atoll in French Polynesia, about 700 miles southeast of Tahiti. The French first used the test site in 1966, and the first shipboard protest was initiated by David McTaggart, who objected to the French closing to navigation of 100,000 square miles of ocean for security reasons. The first year his 38-foot ketch *Vega* was rammed by a French naval vessel, and the next year — when New Zealand sent HMNZS *Otago* and *Canterbury* to protest the tests — French security forces assaulted the crew. In 1985, Greenpeace dispatched *Vega* and *Rainbow Warrior* — now rigged with two masts — to the area. En route, *Rainbow Warrior* helped transport 320 Rongelap Islanders displaced by U.S. nuclear testing in the 1950s to Mejato on Kwajalein Atoll. The ship arrived at Auckland on July 7 to prepare for the protest at Muroroa. Three days later, at 2338 on June 10, two bombs went off, scuttling the ship at the dock and killing Greenpeace photographer Fernando Pereira. The subsequent finding that the bombs had been set by members of the French Office of External Security (Direction Générale de la Sécurité Extérieure) led to the resignation of French Defense Minister Charles Hernu, among others. Beyond repair, *Rainbow Warrior* was stripped and scuttled at sea.

Dyson, *Sink the "Rainbow"!*

HMS RAMILLIES

(ex-*Royal Katherine*) 2nd rate 90 (3m). *L/B:* 153′ × 40′ (46.6m × 12.2m). *Tons:* 1,086 bm. *Hull:* wood. *Comp.:* 888. *Arm.:* 90 guns. *Built:* Woolwich Dockyard, Eng.; 1664.

The name *Royal Katherine* was first given to an 84-gun ship built in 1664 which saw considerable action in the Second and Third Anglo-Dutch Wars. She took part in the English victory at the Battle of Lowestoft (June 3, 1665), the English defeat in the Four Days' Battle (June 1–4), and their subsequent victory at Orfordness (July 25, 1666). When war with the Dutch was renewed a few years later, *Royal Katherine* (sometimes spelled *Catherine*) was part of the Anglo-French fleet defeated by the Dutch at Solebay on May 28, 1672, and again at the two battles of Schooneveld on May 28 and June 4 the next year. During the War of the League of Augsburg, *Royal Katherine* was part of the Anglo-Dutch fleet that defeated the French at the three-day Battle of Barfleur, on May 19–22, 1692.

In age of sail, in order to obtain funding for new ships from a parsimonious Parliament, the Admiralty would request funding to "rebuild" an old one. Despite appearances to the contrary, the result was in essence the same. So it was that the "rebuilt" *Royal Katherine* emerged from the yard in 1702. During the War of the Spanish Succession, she was present at the siege of Gibraltar on July 24, 1704, and at the siege of Vélez Málaga, Spain, on August 13, she flew the flag of Admiral of the Fleet Sir George Rooke.

Two years later, the ship was renamed for the site of the Duke of Marlborough's victory over the French in Belgium. The next half-century was relatively uneventful for the *Ramillies*.

At the start of the Seven Years' War, the Marquis de la Galissonière captured Minorca, in the western Mediterranean, in April 1756. Ordered to the relief of the besieged garrison at Port Mahon, Vice Admiral the Honourable John Byng was dispatched from Portsmouth with thirteen ships of the line and three frigates. On May 20, 1757, he engaged La Galissonière's fleet about thirty miles from Port Mahon. When the French withdrew, Byng failed either to pursue the fleet or to relieve Port Mahon, which soon surrendered. Instead, he retired to Gibraltar to await reinforcements. Vice Admiral Sir Edward Hawke was sent out to try to recapture Minorca, but the English had lost the island for good.

Although there was widespread condemnation of Byng for failing in his mission, as his court-martial progressed aboard HMS St. George, it became clear that he was being made the scapegoat for a failure of government policy. Sentenced to a firing squad, Byng was executed on the deck of HMS *Monarch* on March 14, 1757. Condemnation of the punishment was widespread. In England it was said that "the unfortunate Admiral was shot because Newcastle [the Prime Minister] deserved to be hanged." But the French had the last word. When Voltaire's fictional Candide visits Portsmouth, he asks why an admiral has been sentenced to die. "In this country," he is told, "it's considered a good idea to kill an admiral from time to time, to encourage the others."

Ramillies did not long survive Byng. In 1760 she was returning to Plymouth before an approaching gale when a combination of poor piloting and inadequate ship handling led to the ship's piling up on the rocks off Bolt Head on the evening of February 15. Only 26 of the 725 crew survived.

Clowes, Hepper, *British Warship Losses.* Pope, *At Twelve Mr. Byng Was Shot.*

RANDOLPH

Frigate (3m). *L/B/D:* 132.8′ × 34.5′ × 18′ (40.5m × 10.5m × 5.5m). *Tons:* ca. 690. Hull: wood. *Comp.:* ca. 200. *Arm.:* 32 guns. *Des.:* Joshua Humphreys. *Built:* John Wharton & Joshua Humphreys, Philadelphia; 1776.

Named for Peyton Randolph, a prominent Virginia delegate to the First Continental Congress, USS *Randolph* was one of the first frigates ordered by Congress for the fledgling Continental Navy. As his ship was launched during an acute manning shortage, Captain Nicholas Biddle recruited a large number of his crew from among imprisoned British seamen. During her first cruise, she lost her mainmast and a large number of crew died of fever, before she put into Charleston, S.C., on March 11. She lost two more masts to lightning before departing on September 1. Two days later she captured four rich prizes, which were taken into Charleston. While there, John Rutledge, President of the South Carolina General Assembly, suggested that *Randolph* lead a flotilla of South Carolina Navy ships to escort a number of merchant ships through the British blockade. The ships sailed on February 14, 1778, and got away unscathed. The colonial warships sailed for the Caribbean but captured no significant prizes. On the evening of March 7, *Randolph* engaged HMS *Yarmouth* (64 guns) off Barbados. The battle was going well for Biddle's ship when its magazine blew up, destroying the ship and killing all but four of her complement.

Jamieson, "American Privateers in the Leeward Islands." McCusker, "American Invasion of Nassau in the Bahamas." U.S. Navy, *DANFS*.

RANGER

Ship sloop (3m). *L/B/D:* 131.4′ (berth deck) × 28′ × 11′ dph (40.1m × 8.5m × 3.4m). *Tons:* 697 bm. *Hull:* wood. *Comp.:* 140. *Arm.:* 18 × 6pdr. *Built:* James K. Hackett, Portsmouth, N.H.; 1777.

The Continental Congress appointed John Paul Jones as master of the newly built ship *Ranger* on June 14, 1777. (On the same date, coincidentally, Congress resolved "that the flag of the thirteen United States be thirteen stripes, alternate red and white; that the union be thirteen stars, white in a blue field, representing a new constellation.") *Ranger* sailed for France on November 1 and arrived at Nantes on December 2, having taken two English prizes en route. On February 14, 1778, Admiral LaMotte Piquet's flagship *Robuste* became the first foreign ship to salute the Stars and Stripes after *Ranger* rendered honors to the French fleet at Quiberon Bay.

Ranger departed Brest on April 11 and took or burned four vessels in the Irish Sea. On the night of April 22, Jones entered Solway Firth and the next morning took forty men in two boats to raid Whitehaven, from which Jones had sailed to America at the age of thirteen. The rebels spiked the guns of the English fort and set fire to a collier. Jones then crossed the bay to Scotland with a view to capturing the Earl of Selkirk to help effect a prisoner exchange. Selkirk was away, and the shore party contented itself with stealing some silver from Lady Selkirk. Jones was appalled and later purchased it from his crew

Recruiting poster advertising positions aboard "the ship RANGER, *of Twenty Guns, (for France) now laying in Portsmouth, in the State of New Hampshire, commanded by John Paul Jones Esq." There are no known pictures of the ship in which Jones first took the American Revolution to the shores of England in the spring of 1778. Courtesy U.S. Naval Historical Center, Washington, D.C.*

and returned it, with apologies. On April 25, *Ranger* fought HMS *Drake* (20 guns) off Carrickfergus, Ireland, in an engagement described by Jones as "warm, close and obstinate." The poorly manned *Drake* lost five killed (including Captain George Burdon) and twenty injured. A prize crew was put aboard and the two ships returned to Brest, capturing a storeship en route. *Ranger* returned to the United States under Lieutenant Thomas Simpson in company with *Boston* and *Providence,* arriving at Portsmouth with three prizes on October 15, 1778.

Between February and November 1779, *Ranger* sailed with *Queen of France* and, variously, WARREN or *Providence,* capturing eighteen prizes (three were later retaken) valued at more than $1 million. On November 23, 1779, *Ranger* joined Commodore Abraham Whipple's squadron bound for Charleston, South Carolina. On January 24, 1780, *Ranger* and *Providence* captured three supply transports off Tybee Island before returning to the defense of the port. When Charleston fell on May 11, 1780,

Ranger, Providence, and *Boston* were captured and commissioned into the Royal Navy. HMS *Halifax* (ex-*Ranger*) was sold the next year.

Miller, *Sea of Glory.* Sawtelle, *John Paul Jones and the "Ranger."*

USS RANGER

(later USS *Rockport, Nantucket, Bay State, Emery Rice*) Screw steamer (1f/3m). *L/B/D:* 177.3′ × 32′ × 12.8′ (54m × 9.8m × 3.9m). *Tons:* 1,120 disp. *Hull:* iron. *Arm.:* 1 × 11″, 2 × 9″, 1 × 60pdr. *Mach.:* compound engine, 560 ihp, 1 screw; 10 kts. *Built:* Harland & Hollingsworth, Wilmington, Del.; 1876.

First deployed with the Asiatic Fleet, after two years at Hong Kong USS *Ranger* began a twenty-two-year career as a hydrographic survey vessel and as a protector of the American seal fisheries. From 1905 to 1908 she sailed as a schoolship with the Philippine Nautical School, and in 1909 she was loaned to the Massachusetts Maritime Academy. She remained under its control until 1940, except for the years 1917–20 when (renamed first USS *Rockport* and then *Nantucket*) she was used as a gunboat and a training ship. In 1940, *Nantucket* was transferred to the Maritime Administration's new U.S. Merchant Ma-

rine Academy at Kings Point, New York. Renamed *Emery Rice,* for the master of the merchant ship *Mongolia* — the first U.S. vessel to fire on a U-boat in 1917 — she was withdrawn from sea duty in 1944. Fourteen years later she was broken up for scrap. Although it was impossible to preserve the ship, the San Francisco Maritime Museum's Karl Kortum saved the sixty-one-ton horizontal back-acting compound-condensing main propulsion steam engine (known in England as a return connecting-rod engine). After a quarter century in storage, this engine was put on display at the American Merchant Marine Museum in Kings Point.

McCready, "*Emery Rice* Engine." U.S. Navy, *DANFS.*

The barkentine-rigged screw steamer USS RANGER *drying sails, probably off the Mare Island Navy Yard, California, in December 1899, towards the end of her two-decade tour of duty as a fisheries protection vessel. Courtesy U.S. Naval Historical Center, Washington, D.C.*

USS RANGER (CV-4)

Ranger-class aircraft carrier (3m/6f). *L/B/D:* 769′ × 81.7′ (86′ew) × 19.7′ (234.4m × 24.9m (26.2m) × 6m). *Tons:* 14,500 disp. *Hull:* steel. *Comp.:* 1,788–2,461. *Arm.:* 76 aircraft; 8 × 5″, 40 mg. *Armor:* ?″ belt; 1″ flight deck. *Mach.:* geared turbines, 53,500 shp, 2 shafts; 29 kts. *Built:* Newport News Shipbuilding & Dry Dock Co., Newport News, Va.; 1934.

The sixth USS *Ranger* was the fourth American aircraft carrier built, but the first to be designed as such from the keel up. Among her other innovations was the addition of a gallery deck for the defensive armament just below the flight deck. Her most distinctive attribute was her six funnels, three on either side of the flight deck aft, which could fold down during flight operations. Though substantially larger than the escort carriers built during World War II, *Ranger* was too light and too slow to be effective as a fleet carrier.

Ranger began her career in the Atlantic before transferring to the Pacific, where she remained until 1939. She then returned to the Atlantic for duty with the Neutrality Patrol, designed to keep European belligerents from operating in American waters. After the Japanese attack on Pearl Harbor on December 7, 1941, *Ranger* commenced four months of patrols in the South Atlantic. Following maintenance in Norfolk, she carried a total of 140 Army Air Force planes on two voyages to Accra, West Africa. In November 1942, she took part in the Allied invasion of North Africa. From November 8 to 11, her planes flew 496 combat sorties over targets between Rabat and Casablanca, destroying 85 enemy planes, scores of tanks and other vehicles, and disabling the French destroyer *Albatros. Ranger*'s losses totaled 16 planes.

In February 1943, she carried 75 planes to Accra and, after patrols along the East Coast, *Ranger* was attached to

Britain's Home Fleet in August. In October, she took part in raids on German shipping near Bodö, Norway. Returning stateside in January, *Ranger* convoyed a further 76 planes to Casablanca in April. Refitted for service as a night-fighter-interceptor training carrier, she proceeded to the Pacific in July 1944. Decommissioned in 1946, she was sold for scrap the next year.

U.S. Navy, *DANFS*.

RANGER

J-class cutter. *L/B/D:* 135.5′ × 20.7′ × 19′ (41.2m × 6.4m × 2.3m). *Tons:* 128 grt. *Hull:* steel. *Comp.:* 24. *Des.:* W. Starling Burgess & Olin Stephens. *Built:* Bath Iron Works, Bath, Me.; 1937.

The finest and fastest of the towering Bermuda-rigged J-boats that competed for the America's Cup in 1930 (SHAMROCK V vs. *Enterprise*), 1934 (*Endeavour* vs. *Rainbow*), and in 1937, *Ranger* was designed by the team of Starling Burgess and the twenty-nine-year-old Olin Stephens. Named for John Paul Jones's command, her owner was Harold S. Vanderbilt, the first sole owner of a Cup defender since General Charles J. Paine, whose *Volunteer* had been designed by Burgess's father, Edward, in 1887. En route from Bath to Marblehead, *Ranger* lost her 165-foot duraluminum mast as she rolled in a quartering sea. It took three weeks to make a new mast, but even rigged with *Rainbow*'s smaller mast as a temporary replacement, *Ranger* easily won the right to defend the Cup with twelve straight victories in match races. As an anonymous observer wrote, "W. Starling Burgess and Olin J. Stephens, in designing *Ranger,* hit on something that jumped over some twenty years of normal progress in yacht design and came down with a boat whose speed, compared with her contemporaries, is nothing short of phenomenal." To avoid her thirteenth race being the first of the Cup series, she raced twice more, losing to T. O. M. Sopwith's 1933 challenger, *Endeavour,* and to *Yankee*. The Cup series began on July 31, and *Ranger* swept Sopwith's *Endeavour II,* setting five course records in as many races. Her overall record consisted of thirty-two victories in thirty-four races completed with an average margin of victory of 7 minutes, 42 seconds; the two losses were by an average of only 45 seconds. *Ranger*'s career was as brief as it was brilliant, and she was broken up for scrap in 1941.

Snow, *Bath Iron Works*. Taylor, "*Ranger*, the American Defender."

CSS RAPPAHANNOCK

(ex-HMS *Victor, Scylla*) Commerce raider (2f/3m). *L/B/D:* 201′ (lbp) × 30.3′ × 14.5′ (61.3m × 9.2m × 4.4m). *Tons:* 1,042 tons. *Hull:* wood. *Comp.:* 100. *Arm.:* 2 × 9″ *Mach.:* reciprocating engines, 350 nhp, 1 screw; 11 kts. *Built:* Mare & Co., Blackwall, Eng.; 1856.

Laid down and launched as a screw gunship, HMS *Victor* saw service in the Royal Navy during the Crimean War but was put in ordinary after only two years in commission. Sold to a Confederate naval agent who claimed to want her for the China trade, British authorities seized the renamed *Scylla* when it became clear she was intended for service in the Confederate Navy as a replacement for CSS GEORGIA. With her refit still incomplete, on November 24, 1863, her crew took her out of Sheerness with riggers and machinists still aboard. Commissioned at sea and named for the Virginia river, her engines burned out and she put into Calais for repairs. In February 1864 the French government, afraid of compromising its neutrality, refused to allow her departure, and she spent the balance of the war as a supply vessel. Following the war, she was turned over to the U.S. government.

Spencer, *Confederate Navy in Europe*.

HMS RATTLER

Screw sloop (1f/3m). *L/B/D:* 176.5′ × 32.7′ × 11.8′ (53.8m × 10m × 3.6m). *Tons:* 1,112 disp. *Hull:* wood. *Arm.:* 1 × 68pdr, 4 × 32pdr carr. *Mach.:* vertical "Siamese" engine, 519 ihp, 1 screw; 9.1 kts. *Des.:* Isambard Kingdom Brunel & Francis Petit Smith. *Built:* Sheerness Dockyard, Eng.; 1843.

Following a series of demonstrations of the feasibility of screw propulsion by John Ericsson (with the 45-foot launch *Frances B. Ogden*), Francis Petit Smith (with the 34-launch *Francis Smith* and the 237-ton *Archimedes*), and others in the late 1830s, the Admiralty Board ordered the construction of its first screw steamer in 1840. With machinery designed by Isambard Kingdom Brunel (who had changed the propulsion of GREAT BRITAIN on the strength of the *Archimedes* trials) and Smith, *Rattler* easily attained 8¾ knots and proved herself in races with her paddle-driven half-sister *Polyphemus*. Between February 1844 and January 1845, the designers experimented with thirty-two different propellers of two, three, and four blades. The most successful of these was a Smith two-blade propeller with a diameter of 10 feet 1 inch, a pitch of 11 feet, and a length of 1 foot 3 inches.

The ultimate contest between screw and paddle propulsion was actually a series of races between *Rattler* and

Alecto, another paddle half-sister. Starting on March 30, 1845, the two ships raced each other in a variety of conditions and using various combinations of propulsion: steam or sail only, or both together. The most celebrated contest fell on April 4, when *Rattler* and *Alecto* engaged in a tug-of-war. *Alecto* was given a significant advantage by towing *Rattler* stern-to at 2 knots before *Rattler*'s engines were engaged. Five minutes later, *Rattler* had pulled *Alecto* to a standstill and was soon pulling the paddle-driven vessel at 2.8 knots. Although this is frequently cited as the turning point in the Admiralty's thinking about screw propulsion, it had already ordered seven screw frigates, as well as other smaller ships, and the first screw battleship, HMS *Ajax,* was about to be laid down.

HMS *Rattler* was finally commissioned in 1849, when she joined the antislavery patrol off Africa under Commander Arthur Cumming. Two years later she was dispatched to the East Indies station, where the Royal Navy was active in the suppression of piracy along the coasts of China and Malaysia. In July 1855, under Commander William Fellowes, she was joined by HMS *Eaglet* and crew from the USS Powhatan in freeing four ships taken by pirates at Kulan, China. An estimated 500 pirates were killed and another 1,000 taken prisoner, with the loss of only six British and four American lives. *Rattler* returned to Britain shortly thereafter and was broken up at Woolwich in 1856.

Brown, "Introduction of the Screw Propeller into the Royal Navy." Lambert, ed., *Steam, Steel, and Shellfire.* Phillips, *Ships of the Old Navy.*

RAWALPINDI

Passenger ship. *L/B/D:* 547.7′ × 71.3′ × 18.9′ (166.9m × 21.7m × 5.8m). *Tons:* 16,619 grt. *Hull:* steel. *Mach.:* quadruple expansion, 2 screws. *Built:* Harland & Wolff, Ltd., Belfast, Northern Ireland; 1925.

One of four so-called R-class passenger ships built for the Peninsular and Oriental Steam Navigation Company in the mid-1920s (her sisters were *Rajputana, Ranchi,* and *Ranpura*), *Rawalpindi* was built for the company's trade between Great Britain and India via the Mediterranean, Suez Canal, and Red Sea. Requisitioned for wartime service on August 24, 1939, one week before the German invasion of Poland ignited World War II, *Rawalpindi* was the first P&O ship converted for service on the Northern Patrol to intercept German merchant ships and to escort Allied convoys. On the afternoon of November 23, *Rawalpindi* (named for a tributary of the Indus River) was steaming between Iceland and the Faeroe Islands when she encountered the German battlecruisers Scharnhorst and Gneisenau. Fitted with only eight 6-inch guns and crewed largely with naval reservists, *Rawalpindi* was no match for her opponents, both of which had a primary armament of nine 11-inch guns. Nonetheless, Captain E. C. Kennedy steered his ship directly for the enemy. A quarter of an hour later, *Rawalpindi* was sinking and 54 of her crew of 365 were dead. The heroic action was not a complete loss, for the ship alerted the Home Fleet and the German battlecruisers were forced to abort their first wartime cruise and return to port.

Edwards, *Salvo!* Howarth & Howarth, *Story of P&O.*

REALE

Galley (3m). *L/B/D:* ca. 131′ × 18′ × 4.5′ (40m × 5.5m × 1.5m). *Tons:* 170 disp. *Hull:* wood. *Comp.:* 700. *Arm.:* 1 × 36pdr, 2 × 9pdr, 8 × 4.5pdr. *Built:* <1571.

Reale, or Royal, is the name given to Don Juan of Austria's flagship at the Battle of Lepanto in 1571. The last great battle between oared ships, Lepanto pitted a combined fleet of Venetian, Papal, and Spanish galleys against a unitary Turkish fleet. In 1570, the Turks demanded that Venice cede control of Cyprus, and when the Venetians refused they besieged the port of Nicosia. Venice appealed to other Christian powers for help, and found allies in Pope Pius V, who ignored the Papacy's traditional rivalry with Venice in northern Italy, and Spain's Philip II, who was indifferent to Venetian troubles in the east but irritated by Muslim pirates in the western Mediterranean. Fleets from the three unlikely allies sailed to Crete at the end of August, but by the end of September they had split up and returned home. Meanwhile, the Turks captured Nicosia and besieged Famagusta. Though prospects for joint action were dim, Venice, Spain, and the Papacy hammered out a Treaty of Alliance in May 1571. Don John of Austria, son of Emperor Charles V and half-brother of Philip II, was designated Captain General, while Sebastiano Veniero, Venice's general at sea, and Marc Antonio Colonna, the papal commander in chief, reported to him.

In September 1571, the fleets assembled at Messina, Sicily, and sailed from there on September 16. Skirting the coast of Italy, they crossed the Adriatic to arrive ten days later at Corfu, opposite the Gulf of Patras. The Turkish fleet had been raiding Venetian outposts along the Dalmatian coast of the Adriatic, and with the fall of Famagusta in August, Ali Pasha was ordered to find and destroy the Christian fleet. On the day the enemy left Messina, he sailed for Lepanto (in Greek, Navpaktos) on the strait between the Gulfs of Patras and Corinth. Reconnaissance missions by both the Christians and the Turks underestimated each other's strength, and by October 7, 1571, both sides were eager for battle.

To ensure that the Christian fleet would fight as one, ships of all nationalities were mixed through the different squadrons, and Don John, Veniero, and Colonna sailed side by side at the head of the 62 galleys in the center squadron. Juan de Cardona sailed with 7 galleys in the van, Agostino Barbarigo of Venice on the left flank with 53 galleys, Andrea Doria of Genoa with 50 galleys on the right, and, in reserve, the Marquis of Santuz with 30 galleys. Six Venetian galleasses commanded by Antonio Duodo sailed ahead of the main squadrons. The Christians had about 44,000 men and 30,000 soldiers, most of the latter relying on guns rather than bows and arrows as their chief weapon.

Opposing the Christians was a slightly larger Turkish force under Ali Pasha in the center with 90 galleys, Uluch Ali with 61 galleys and 32 galliots on the left wing, and Mohammed Scirocco with 55 galleys on the right. In addition there were about 30 vessels in reserve; total Turkish manpower was about 75,000. Although the Turks had a numerical superiority in ships and their line was a mile longer than the allied one, Turkish galleys tended to be more lightly built; nor did they have anything equivalent to the heavy firepower of the Venetian galleasses, which mounted a heavier broadside armament than galleys, carried on a deck above the rowers.

The power of these hybrid ships told early, and they sank a galley of Scirocco's squadron at about 1030 and disrupted the Turkish line as it passed and veered towards the shore. Ali Pasha's division attacked the Christian center and had the advantage until a Papal galley attacked the Turkish flagship. By 1300, the Turkish standard was captured and Ali Pasha dead, and the Turkish center was disintegrating. The course of battle on the southern flank was the subject of much discussion. Uluch Ali tried to outflank Doria, but the Genoese moved south to prevent him from doing so, until Uluch Ali wheeled and attacked the center again. Venetian resentment of the Genoese Doria was so great that he was later accused of trying to flee the battle. In fact he acquitted himself bravely.

By the end of the battle, the Turks had lost 80 ships sunk or damaged beyond repair and another 130 captured. Casualties totaled 30,000 dead and wounded, about 7,000 taken prisoner, and about 10,000 Christian galley slaves freed. Against these, the Christians had lost 12 ships and about 7,700 men, with another 14,000 wounded. Although defeat could have spelled disaster for Christian Europe, the victory was most important as proof that the Turks were not invincible. The Christian allies pursued a tiresome campaign in 1572 during which they captured a single Turkish ship, and that winter Venice signed a treaty under which its merchants were allowed to resume their trade to Alexandria. It mattered little, for the old spice route to the East (upon which Venetian prosperity rested) was going the way of the oared galley, replaced by Portuguese carracks trading directly with the Indies via the Cape of Good Hope.

Rodgers, *Naval Warfare under Oars.*

REAR-ADMIRAL POPOV

Circular battleship (2f). *L/D:* 120.0′ × 14.8′ (36.6m dia. × 4.5m). *Tons:* 3,550 disp. *Hull:* steel. *Comp.:* 206. *Arm.:* 2 × 12.2″. *Armor:* 1.8″ belt. *Mach.:* compound engines, 4,500 ihp, 6 screws; 8 kts. *Des.:* Andrei Aleksandrovich Popov. *Built:* New Admiralty Yard, St. Petersburg, Russia; 1874.

The larger and better known of two circular battleships built by the Russian Imperial Navy in the 1870s, *Rear-Admiral Popov* was laid down as *Kiev* but later renamed in honor of her designer, Rear Admiral Andrei Aleksandrovich Popov. Popov's idea was to create a stable platform for large-caliber guns to guard the shallow coastal waters around the Black Sea ports of Odessa, Nikolayev, and Ochakov. The ships mounted two 11-inch guns (they may have been fitted ultimately with 12-inch guns) mounted on a revolving turntable that could turn in an arc of thirty-five degrees on either side of the centerline. *Novgorod,* the first of the two ships, was constructed at St. Petersburg in 1872 and then taken apart and put on trains for reassembly at Nikolayev, where she was completed in 1874. *Kiev* was built from the keel up at Nikolayev. After reviewing the results of *Novgorod*'s trials, Popov recommended that the second ship's diameter be enlarged by almost six meters. *Kiev* was renamed in honor of Popov before her launch, and by imperial decree both ships were designated as Popovkas, as was LI-VADIA, a yacht of similar design. Both *Rear-Admiral Popov* and *Novgorod* performed well in their assigned roles, and during the Russo-Turkish War, the two ships served with the Danube Flotilla. Designated Coastal Defense Armor-Clad Ships in 1892, they later served as storeships until stricken from the naval lists in 1903. They were not scrapped until 1912.

Martelle, "*Novgorod* and *Rear-Admiral Popov.*"

The curiously designed Russian circular iron-clad REAR-ADMIRAL POPOV *lying in the Nikolaiev Depositing Dock, South Russia. The design concept was an interesting one, but it fell short of expectations. Courtesy Peabody Essex Museum, Salem, Massachusetts.*

REBECCA

Brig. *Hull:* wood. *Built:* England(?); <1731.

An otherwise obscure merchant brig that sailed between the West Indies and England, *Rebecca* was detained by a Spanish patrol off the coast of Havana on April 9, 1731. The Spanish Captain Fandino, who was known for his excesses, pillaged the ship and abused the crew, going so far as to slice off the ear of Robert Jenkins, *Rebecca*'s master. Although the Spanish intent was that the ship "should perish in her passage," she arrived at London on June 11, 1731. Jenkins's case gained widespread attention, and he was summoned before George II. There the matter lay for seven years. Relations between English merchants and Spanish authority continued to deteriorate, and in 1738 Parliament called Jenkins to testify about his experience. His patriotic testimony — "I committed my soul to God and my cause to my country" — and the display of what he claimed were the remains of his ear made it inevitable that the ensuing conflict with Spain become known as the War of Jenkins' Ear. This rapidly evolved into the more complex War of the Austrian Succession (1739–48), best remembered in naval history for Commodore George Anson's circumnavigation in HMS CENTURION and the loss of HMS WAGER in the same voyage.

Dictionary of National Biography.

RED JACKET

Clipper (3m). *L/B/D:* 251.2′ × 44′ × 31′ (76.6m × 13.4m × 9.4m). *Tons:* 2,305 reg. *Hull:* wood. *Comp.:* 98 crew; 650 passengers. *Built:* George Thomas, Rockland, Me.; 1853.

Named for the Seneca chief Sagoyewatha, known as Red Jacket for the British Army officer's coat he wore, the clipper *Red Jacket* was built for Seacombe and Taylor, Boston, who intended to put her in the California trade. Under Captain Asa Eldridge, she sailed from New York to Liverpool and made the passage in 13 days, 1 hour, and 25 minutes, dock to dock, a sailing ship record that stands to the present day. Chartered by Pilkington & Wilson's White Star Line — chief rival of James Baines's Black Ball Line — for service to Melbourne, under Captain Samuel Reid she made the passage in 69 days, 11 hours, and 15 minutes. After a return passage of 73 days, she was purchased by White Star. She was considered the smartest-looking ship in the British merchant fleet, and one of the fastest. After some runs to India, she was sold to Wilson & Chambers, Liverpool, and then to H. Milvain, Newcastle, for the timber trade between Quebec and London. In 1883, she was sold to Turner & Company, London. She was hulked in the Cape Verde Islands in 1886.

Cutler, *Greyhounds of the Sea*. Hollett, *Fast Passage to Australia*. Howe & Matthews, *American Clipper Ships*.

RELIANCE

Cutter. *L/B/D:* 144′ × 25.8′ × 19.6′ (43.9m × 7.9m × 6m). *Tons:* 189 disp. *Hull:* bronze plate on steel frames. *Comp.:* 66. *Des.:* Nathanael G. Herreshoff. *Built:* Herreshoff Manufacturing Co., Bristol, R.I.; 1903.

The largest single-masted vessel ever built, Captain Nat Herreshoff's fourth America's Cup defender, *Reliance,* was one of the earliest examples of a racing machine. Built for a syndicate headed by New York Yacht Club Commodore C. Oliver Iselin, below deck *Reliance* was an open, unfinished hull with exposed frames. She was the first America's Cup racer to employ winches below deck, giving her a decided advantage over the challenger, Sir Thomas Lipton's *Shamrock III,* which relied on unassisted manpower. Above all it was her massive sail plan that caught the eye. *Reliance* had a sparred length of 201 feet 6 inches from the tip of the bowsprit to the after end of the boom, her topmast towered 199 feet 6 inches above the waterline, and her spinnaker pole was 83 feet 9 inches long. Her 17,730 square feet of sail — equivalent to that

Nat Herreshoff's celebrated America's Cup defender RELIANCE *of 1903. Her 17,730 square feet of sail include a main, gaff topsail, fore staysail, jib, and jib topsail. Lithograph by Burnell Poole, courtesy the family of Burnell Poole.*

of about eight 12-meter yachts — drove *Reliance* at speeds reaching 17.5 knots on her maiden voyage, faster than most of the steam yachts that sailed out to watch her.

Under the redoubtable Captain Charlie Barr, in the trial races *Reliance* easily defeated *Columbia,* which had defended the Cup against Lipton's *Shamrock* in 1899 and *Shamrock II* in 1901. In the first race against Lipton's third challenger, the William Fife–designed *Shamrock III,* in August 1903, *Reliance* sailed the thirty-mile course in 3 hours, 32 minutes, 17 seconds, winning with a margin of 7 minutes, 3 seconds. Lipton closed the gap in the second race, losing by only 1 minute, 18 seconds, against *Reliance*'s time of 3 hours, 14 minutes, 54 seconds. The third race was sailed in light airs and neither boat finished within the allotted time.

Reliance finished her first and only season undefeated, for the next year she was broken up. By this point, the "90-footer" America's Cup boats — so called for their waterline length — were so extreme, costly, and even dangerous that Herreshoff was asked to devise a new rating rule. The Universal Rule was first employed in the next America's Cup challenge, held between *Resolute* and *Shamrock IV* in 1920.

Herreshoff, H. C., "A History of America's Cup Yacht Racing." Herreshoff, L. F., *Captain Nat Herreshoff.*

HMS RENOWN

Repulse-class battlecruiser (2f/2m). *L/B/D:* 794.2′ × 90′ × 25.8′ (242.1m × 27.4m × 7.8m). *Tons:* 32,727 disp. *Hull:* steel. *Comp.:* 1,180. *Arm.:* 6 × 15″ (3 × 2), 17 × 4″, 6 × 3pdr; 2 × 21″TT; 4 aircraft. *Armor:* 9″ belt, 5.8″ deck. *Mach.:* geared turbines, 126,000 shp, 4 shafts; 32.6 kts. *Built:* Fairfield Shipping & Engineering Co., Ltd., Govan, Scotland; 1916.

Laid down in January 1915 and completed twenty months later, *Renown* was one of two very fast battlecruisers ordered by the Admiralty on the strength of the success of the INVINCIBLE-class ships over Admiral Graf von Spee's squadron at the Battle of the Falklands. Despite their speed, they were fitted with only six 15-inch guns and they were weakly armored. The latter deficiency was never threatened during World War I, but during *Renown*'s two interwar refits (1923–26 and 1936–39), an effort was made to improve her defense against torpedo and aircraft attack.

Assigned to the Home Fleet at the start of World War II, on April 8, 1940, *Renown* engaged SCHARNHORST and ADMIRAL HIPPER. From 1940 to 1943 she saw action with Force H in the Mediterranean, sailing as a convoy

For ships at war, the common enemy is the weather. Here the powerful battlecruiser HMS RENOWN *is seen laboring in a storm, in a photo taken from the aircraft carrier* ARK ROYAL *when the two ships were part of Force H, based at Gibraltar in 1940–41. It was in just such conditions that* ARK ROYAL *launched ten Swordfish during the hunt for the* BISMARCK *in May 1941. Courtesy National Maritime Museum, Greenwich.*

escort and taking part in the bombardment of Genoa in February 1941. In 1943, she embarked Prime Minister Winston Churchill on his return from Canada, and en route to the Teheran Conference. In December she joined the Eastern Fleet for operations against the Japanese in the Dutch East Indies. Returning to home waters in March 1945, *Renown* finished the war at Devonport. She was sold and broken up in 1948.

Parkes, *British Battleships*. Smith, *Hit First, Hit Hard*.

REPUBLIC

Liner (1f/4m). *L/B:* 585' × 67.8' (178.3m bp × 20.7m). *Tons:* 15,378 grt. *Hull:* steel. *Comp.:* 1st 250+, steerage 230+; crew 300. *Mach.:* quadruple expansion, 10,000 ihp, 2 screws; 16 kts. *Built:* Harland & Wolff, Ltd., Belfast, Ireland; 1903.

Built for the Dominion Line's service between Liverpool and Boston, *Columbus* made only two voyages before that company's Liverpool–Boston and Boston–Mediterranean

routes were taken over by White Star Line, the dominant company of the International Mercantile Marine Company of which Dominion was also a part. Renamed *Republic,* the ship sailed on the North Atlantic run in the spring, and between Boston, Naples, and Genoa in the fall and winter. In 1902, Elder Dempster's LAKE CHAMPLAIN had become the first passenger liner fitted with Marconi wireless radio, and *Republic* was one of the first ships to be similarly outfitted. On January 23, 1909, she was outward bound from New York with relief supplies for victims of a catastrophic earthquake in southern Italy. At about 0530, in position 40°17′N, 70°W, she collided with the Lloyd Italiano liner *Florida* (Captain Angelo Ruspini), whose passengers included 838 earthquake survivors. *Republic's* Captain William Inman Sealby ordered radioman John R. Binns to begin broadcasting the CQD distress signal in the first emergency use of a radio on the high seas. (Popularly thought to stand for "Come quick, danger," CQD comprised two elements: CQ was the signal for "all stations attention" and D meant "urgent." SOS had been formally adopted as the international distress call in 1908, but it was not yet in wide use.) *Republic's* passengers were transferred first to *Florida* and then to White Star's *Baltic* (Captain John R. Ranson) when she arrived shortly after 1800. Other ships responding to *Republic's* distress calls, relayed via a radio station on Nantucket, included *La Lorraine, City of Everett, Furnessia, Lucania,* and the revenue cutters *Gresham* and *Seneca. Florida* limped on to New York under her own power, while *Republic* was taken in tow by *Gresham* and *Furnessia* in the hopes of beaching her on Martha's Vineyard. Shortly after 2030 on January 24, she sank south of the island. In all, three of *Republic's* passengers and three of *Florida's* crew died as a result of the collision.

Eaton & Haas, *Falling Star.* Kludas, *Great Passenger Ships of the World.*

HMS REPULSE

Repulse-class battlecruiser (2f/2m). *L/B/D:* 794.2' × 90' × 27' (242.1m × 27.4m × 8.2m). *Tons:* 38,300 disp. *Hull:* steel. *Comp.:* 1,180. *Arm.:* 6 × 15" (3 × 2), 17 × 4", 6 × 3pdr; 2 × 21"TT; 4 aircraft. *Armor:* 9" belt, 5.8" deck. *Mach.:* geared turbines, 120,000 shp, 4 shafts; 31.5 kts. *Built:* John Brown & Co., Clydebank, Scotland; 1916.

HMS *Repulse* was one of two very fast battlecruisers ordered by the Admiralty in 1915 on the strength of the success of the INVINCIBLE-class ships over Admiral Graf von Spee's squadron at the Battle of the Falklands; the other was RENOWN. In World War I, *Repulse's* combat service with the Battle Cruiser Squadron was limited to a skirmish with German light cruisers in the Helgoland Bight on November 17, 1917. Following the war, her belt armor was increased to nine inches. During the inter-war period she made several long cruises, including one around the world, and she served with the Home and Mediterranean fleets.

When World War II began, *Repulse* served on convoy duty in the Atlantic, and in April 1940 she took part in various actions during the German invasion of Norway. In October 1941, she was sent to the Far East with HMS PRINCE OF WALES as the nucleus of the Eastern Fleet under Admiral Sir Tom Phillips. They arrived at Singapore on December 2. Six days later, the Japanese attacked Pearl Harbor and began their drive into Southeast Asia. Also on December 8, Force "Z" — the two capital ships and destroyers HMS *Electra, Express,* and *Tenedos,* and HMAS *Vampire* — sortied to attack Japanese forces in southern Thailand. Force "Z" was sighted by submarine *I-68* the next afternoon, but avoided further detection until 0220 on December 10. Shortly before dawn, the Japanese launched thirty-four land-based bombers and fifty-one torpedo-bombers, which attacked the two capital ships at 1115. The planes made three separate attacks, and *Repulse* sank at 1235, an hour before *Prince of Wales.* The remains of the ship were located in 1959 lying in 3°37′N, 104°20′E. The loss of the two ships was the first unqualified demonstration of the vulnerability of capital ships to coordinated air attack on the high seas.

Parkes, *British Battleships.* Middlebrook & Mahoney, *Battleship.*

RESOLUTE

(ex-*Refuge, Ptarmigan*) Bark (3m). *L/B/D:* 115′ × 28.3′ × 11.5′ (35.1m × 8.6m × 3.5m). *Tons:* 424 bm. *Comp.:* 61. *Hull:* wood. *Built:* Smith(?), Shields, Eng.; 1849.

Built as the merchant ship *Ptarmigan* and purchased by the Royal Navy in 1850, HM Discovery Ship *Resolute* was one of six vessels sent out that year under command of Captain Henry Austin in search of Sir John Franklin's HMS EREBUS and TERROR. The expedition also included the Royal Navy's bark *Assistance,* the steamers *Intrepid* and *Pioneer,* and the privately owned brigs *Lady Franklin* and *Sophia.* The ships wintered in Lancaster Sound and returned to England in the fall of 1851, having found no trace of Franklin's ships.

The four Navy ships sailed again for the Arctic in April 1852. The expedition was led by Sir Edward Belcher in *Assistance,* with Captain Henry Kellett in *Resolute,* Captain Sherard Osborn in *Pioneer,* and Captain Francis L. McClintock in *Intrepid.* Leaving the supply ship *North Star* at Beechey Island in Lancaster Sound, *Assistance* and *Pioneer* turned north into Wellington Sound (between Devon and Cornwallis Islands) where they were iced in off Griffith Island. *Resolute* and *Intrepid* sailed west towards Melville Island and reached Winter Harbor on September 5 before withdrawing to Dealy Island, thirty-five miles east. From there, various sledging expeditions set out in search of both the Franklin expedition and that of Leopold McClure's INVESTIGATOR and Richard Collinson's *Enterprise* — the "search for the searchers." Returning to Winter Harbor, a sledge party found a note from McClure's party indicating that *Investigator* was at Banks Island, 175 miles southwest across Melville Sound. The following April, a rescue party was sent out and the survivors of the *Investigator* returned to *Resolute.*

Having exhausted any hope of finding Franklin's expedition in Barrow Strait or Melville Sound, Kellett decided to return to Beechey Island. The ice was impenetrable, and *Resolute* and *Intrepid* wintered off the southeast of Bathurst Island. In the summer of 1854, Belcher sent orders for Kellett to abandon his ships and march his men to Beechey Island. Kellett reluctantly complied. On August 26, 1854, *North Star* turned for home with a total complement of 263 men, comprising the crews of six ships, including her own. The same day, she fell in with the supply ships *Phoenix* and *Talbot,* and the men were divided between the three ships for the return to England.

Though acquitted for his poor handling of his ships, none of which was at risk of sinking when abandoned, Belcher was publicly disgraced. A year after his return to England, the American whaler *George Henry* came upon *Resolute* drifting in the Davis Strait 1,100 miles east of where she was abandoned. Captain James Buddington took the ship in tow to New London, Connecticut. The U.S. government purchased the vessel and after a refit presented her to the British government. The ship was eventually laid up at Chatham, but before she was broken up in 1879, Queen Victoria ordered a table made from her timbers and presented to President Rutherford B. Hayes. In 1961, President John F. Kennedy had the desk moved to the Oval Office of the White House.

de Bray, *Frenchman in Search of Franklin.* M'Dougall, *Eventful Voyage of H. M. Discovery Ship "Resolute."*

HMS RESOLUTION

(ex-*Drake, Marquis of Granby*) Ship-sloop (3m). *L/B/D:* 110.7′ × 30.5′ × 13.2′ dph (33.7m × 9.3m × 4m). *Tons:* 461 tons. *Hull:* wood. *Comp.:* 112; 12 civilians. *Arm.:* 12 × 6pdr, 12 swivels. *Built:* Fishburn, Whitby, Eng.; 1770.

Shortly after returning to England from his first voyage of discovery in ENDEAVOUR, Commander James Cook was given two ships for a voyage to determine the existence of a great southern continent. Cook's flagship was *Resolution* while Commander Tobias Furneaux was the senior officer aboard ADVENTURE; originally bark-rigged North Sea colliers, the two were rerigged as ships. The ships departed Plymouth on July 13, 1772. After a stay at Cape Town, in November they sailed south to become the first ships known to have crossed the Antarctic Circle, on January 17, 1773, reaching as far south as 67°15′S. The two ships were separated by fog on February 8, and after failing to find *Adventure,* Cook continued exploring the fringes of the southern ice pack until March 17, when he turned for New Zealand. They arrived at Dusky Sound on South Island on March 25 and rendezvoused with *Adventure* at Ship Cove in Queen Charlotte Sound on the south side of Cook Strait on May 18.

A month later they sailed east, looking for land, then turned for Tahiti, staying there from August 15 to September 7. Sailing west, the two ships called in the Tonga Islands, which Cook named "the Friendly Archipelago as a lasting friendship seems to subsist among the Inhabitants and their Courtesy to Strangers intitles them to that Name," before heading again for New Zealand, where they arrived at the end of October. *Resolution* and *Adventure* were separated in a storm and after waiting at Cook Strait until November 26, *Resolution* headed south. The ship crossed the Antarctic Circle for the second time and ultimately reached as far as 71°10′S, 106°30′W (east of the Palmer Peninsula). After stopping at Easter Island, she continued east through the Marquesas, to Tahiti, where Cook and his crew were warmly entertained for six weeks. *Resolution* sailed again on June 4 and after exploring Espiritu Santo (Vanuatu), New Caledonia, and Norfolk Island, she arrived again at the Cook Strait.

A month later, *Resolution* shaped a course for Cape Horn on November 9. She explored Tierra del Fuego and Staten Island from December 17 to January 3, 1775, and then sailed east, discovering uninhabited South Georgia Island on January 14 and the South Sandwich Islands a few days later. Having sailed the length of the Southern Ocean, but "having failed to find a southern continent" — as Cook explained to the Admiralty — "because it does not lie in a navigable sea," she sailed for Cape Town. After several Atlantic stops, *Resolution* arrived at Spithead on July 29.

No less remarkable than this expedition's extraordinary contribution to geographic knowledge is the fact that, thanks to Cook's strict regimen for cleaning and airing the ship and the antiscorbutic diet (including "sour krout") he insisted on to prevent scurvy, in the course of a 70,000-mile voyage lasting three years and eighteen days, only four of *Resolution*'s crew died, and only one of them to sickness.

Promoted to the rank of Post Captain, Cook was soon off again on a voyage to find the Northwest Passage, for the discovery of which the British Parliament had pledged £20,000. *Resolution* was retained for the purpose, this time paired with DISCOVERY under Captain Charles Clerke. Among *Resolution*'s crew on this voyage were Lieutenant John Gore and William Bligh, who sailed as master, and Omai, who was returning to Tahiti after two years in London, where he had traveled in *Adventure*. *Resolution* sailed on July 14, 1776, and was joined by *Discovery* at Cape Town on November 10.

The ships continued eastward, stopping at new and familiar lands, including three months in Van Diemen's Land, Tonga Islands, and Tahiti. The expedition left the South Pacific and headed north. After stopping in the Sandwich (Hawaiian) Islands in January 1778, they sailed northwest, arriving on the coast of North America on March 7 and at Nootka Sound on the 29th. There *Resolution* received a major overhaul, including new mizzen, fore topmast, and foremast. Departing again on April 26, the ships sailed northwest along the Alaska coast, anchoring in Prince William Sound on May 12 — "520 leagues to the westward of any part of Baffins or Hudsons bay" — and two weeks later, Cook Inlet. Rounding the Alaska Peninsula, they sailed into the Bering Sea, calling along the coast before passing Cape Prince of Wales — the east side of the Bering Strait — and then north and west as far as Icy Cape, 126 miles southwest of Point Barrow, on August 18. The ships made the coast of the Chukotski Peninsula on the 29th, and then spent from October 3 to 26 at the Russian settlement at Unalaska before proceeding back to the Sandwich Islands. Anchoring at Hawaii, they remained through the winter, Cook being venerated as a chief (some people believe as a divinity called Orono). The ships sailed again on February 4, 1779, but a sprung foremast in *Resolution* forced them back a week later. On the 14th, an argument between a group of Hawaiians and a shore party led to a skirmish in which four marines and Cook himself were killed. So died "one of the most celebrated Navigators that this or former ages can boast of."

Command of the expedition, and *Resolution*, fell to Captain Clerke; *Discovery* was under command of Lieutenant John Gore. The ships sailed from the Sandwich Islands on March 23 bound for Petropavlovsk on the Kamchatka Peninsula and, after a second foray past Icy Cape to 71°56′N, the crew abandoned their effort to find a northern passage to the Atlantic. Captain Clerke died on August 22 and was buried at Petropavlovsk, where the ships landed two days later. Command of the expedition now fell to Gore, a veteran of two expeditions in HMS DOLPHIN as well as Cook's first, in *Endeavour*. James King was promoted to command the *Discovery*. The ship sailed southwest to trace the coast of Japan (though storms hindered them greatly) and called in at Macao. She then sailed for Cape Town, avoiding Batavia. Forced north about Ireland, the ships landed at Stromness on August 22, 1780, and were back in the Nore on October 4, after a voyage of four years, two months, and twenty-two days.

Resolution subsequently became a Royal Navy transport and sailed for the East Indies in March 1781. On June 10, 1782, she was captured by the French ships *Annibal* and *Sphinx* northwest of Trincomalee. Admiral Suffren later intimated that she either sank or was recaptured by the British, but her ultimate fate is unknown.

F. S., "Cook's *Resolution*." Freeston, "His Majesty's Sloop *Resolution*, 1772." McGowan, "Captain Cook's Ships."

RESOLUTION

Ship (3m). *L/B:* 100.3′ × 26.2′ (30.6m × 8m). *Tons:* 291 tons. *Hull:* wood. *Built:* Fishburne & Broderick, Whitby, Eng.; 1803.

Among the most influential families in the history of Arctic exploration was that of William Scoresby, Senior, and Junior, who hailed from Whitby, North Yorkshire, one of the premier English fishing and whaling ports. In 1803, the elder Scoresby took command of the whaleship *Resolution*, in which his son rose from apprentice to first mate and, in 1810, captain. English whalers in this period routinely made annual voyages to Arctic waters, and collectively they had contributed more to the scientific understanding of the region than anyone else. On May 25, 1806, the Scoresbys sailed *Resolution* to a record high latitude of 81°30′N. Eleven years later, the younger Scoresby would relay to Sir Joseph Banks the fact that Arctic conditions were moderating — the sea was "perfectly devoid of ice" as high as 80°N and the Greenland shore was ice-free. This information set in motion the parade of government-sponsored voyages in search of the Northwest Passage. Although Scoresby sought to command the first expedition, and was backed by Banks (a veteran of Captain James Cook's first voyage in HMS ENDEAVOUR), the command fell to Captain John Ross, with ISABELLA and *Alexander*. Scoresby sold his interest in *Resolution* in 1813, but the ship remained under Whitby ownership until 1829 when she was sold to Peterhead interests.

Berton, *Arctic Grail*. Lubbock, *Arctic Whalers*.

USS REUBEN JAMES (DD-245)

Clemson-class destroyer (4f/2m). *L/B/D:* 314.3′ × 30.5′ × 8.6′ (95.8m × 9.3m × 2.6m). *Tons:* 1,090 disp. *Hull:* steel. *Comp.:* 101. *Arm.:* 4 × 4″ (2 × 2), 1 × 3″; 4 × 21″TT. *Mach.:* geared turbines, 27,700 shp, 2 screws; 35 kts. *Built:* New York Shipbuilding Corp., Camden, N.J.; 1920.

Named for a veteran of the Quasi-War with France, the Barbary Wars (during which James was credited with saving Stephen Decatur's life aboard INTREPID), and the War of 1812, USS *Reuben James* was a World War I–era flush-deck destroyer. Commissioned just after World War I, she was assigned to the Atlantic Fleet and took part in postwar relief activities in the Adriatic, Mediterranean, and at Danzig under the auspices of the American Relief Administration. Homeported at New York from 1922, in 1926 she was stationed off Nicaragua to prevent arms from reaching General Agustino Sandino's forces during his uprising against President Emiliano Chamorro. From September 1933 to January 1934, she patrolled Cuban waters following a coup led by Fulgencia Batista. Transferred to San Diego in 1934, she remained in Pacific waters until recalled to the Atlantic in January 1939. In March 1941 *Reuben James* was assigned to the escort force based at Hvalfjordur, Iceland, to provide cover for eastbound British convoys between Newfoundland and Iceland. On October 23, she sailed from Argentia, Newfoundland, with four other destroyers escorting convoy HX-156. Shortly before dawn on October 31, the convoy was attacked by *U-562*, and at 0525, *Reuben James* was struck by a torpedo that detonated her magazine. The ship sank quickly and only 44 of her 159 crew survived. Though the destroyers USS GREER and KEARNY had engaged U-boats before, *Reuben James* was the first U.S. Navy vessel sunk in World War II. Her loss inspired one of the first antiwar songs of World War II, "Reuben James."

U.S. Navy, *DANFS*.

REVENGE

Ship (3m). *L/B/D:* 92′ (keel) × 32′ × 16′ dph (28m × 9.8m × 4.9m). *Tons:* 441 tons burden. *Hull:* wood. *Comp.:* 250. *Arm.:* 2 demi-cannon, 4 cannon-periers. 10 culverins, 6 demi-culverins, 10 sakers, 2 falcons, 2 portpieces, 4 fowlers, or 6 bases. *Built:* Deptford Dockyard(?), Eng.; 1577.

Revenge was one of the first galleons, built to a new model recommended by Sir John Hawkins and Matthew Baker and characterized by a narrow length-to-beam ratio, a lower freeboard, and a square stern. These so-called race-built ships were faster and more maneuverable than the high-charged ships, with towering fore and stern castles, that then predominated in European navies. Depicted as having three masts — though she may have carried a bonaventure mizzen on occasion — her upperworks were painted in a green-and-white harlequin pattern. Commanded by some of the greatest captains of the Elizabethan navy, *Revenge* is perhaps the most famous of the ships to fight in the Spanish wars.

In September 1580, she was part of the English fleet dispatched to root out a combined Papal-Spanish force that had landed in Munster, Ireland, and taken refuge in Smerwick Castle. In the winter of 1587, *Revenge* became the flagship of a squadron commanded by Sir Francis Drake and organized in anticipation of the Spanish Armada. Although Drake attempted to sail against the Spanish fleet after its first departure from Spain in the spring, he was frustrated in this effort by contrary winds in June and July.

After returning to Plymouth, Drake finally got his chance on July 31, when *Revenge* took part in the first action between the English and Spanish fleets. With Hawkins's *Victory* and Frobisher's *Triumph*, *Revenge* engaged Juan Martínez de Recalde's *San Juan de Portugal*, the largest of the Spanish galleons, between Fowey and Plymouth. With their longer-range culverins, the English ships were able to hit their opponent from a distance of about 300 yards, out of range of the Spanish guns, until the appearance of *El Gran Grin*, when the English retired. That night, *Revenge* was the lead ship in the English squadron as it trailed the Spanish fleet, but Drake doused his stern light and sailed off in pursuit of some unidentified ships, leaving ARK ROYAL and some others trailing what turned out to be the bulk of the Spanish fleet. The next morning Drake captured Don Pedro de Valdés's NUESTRA SEÑORA DEL ROSARIO, which had been damaged the previous day in collision with another ship. This turned out to be the biggest prize of the campaign.

On August 3, *Revenge* and other ships fell on Juan Gómez de Medina's *El Gran Grifon*, which had fallen behind the rest of the fleet. Though the English surrounded their prey, the Spanish fleet managed to rescue their comrade, which was taken in tow by a galleass. Drake continued the pursuit of the Spanish fleet to their anchorage at Calais, where the English fireships forced them into disorder. On August 8, Drake briefly engaged Medina Sidonia's flagship SAN MARTÍN before sailing after the bulk of the Spanish fleet as it headed into the North Sea. The English continued after the Spanish until leaving them to their fate to put into the Firth of Forth for badly needed supplies on August 12.

The next year *Revenge* was again Drake's flagship in the so-called counter-armada, with which the English hoped to destroy whatever Spanish ships had survived the return from England, establish the pretender Don Antonio on the throne of Portugal at Lisbon, and then seize the Azores as a base from which to intercept the all-important Spanish treasure fleet from the Americas. The ill-conceived expedition was not a success and the English fleet returned much the worse for wear after two months, with only about 2,000 of the 10,000 soldiers originally embarked fit for duty. In 1590, *Revenge* sailed as Sir Martin Frobisher's flagship in his unsuccessful attempt to intercept the Spanish treasure fleet near the Iberian peninsula.

In August 1591, Lord Thomas Howard (in *Defiance*) led a similar expedition comprising about a dozen other Queen's ships and armed merchantmen, including *Revenge,* now flying the flag of Vice Admiral Sir Richard Grenville. Unbeknownst to the English, the Spanish had dispatched a fleet of fifty-five ships under Don Alonso de Bazan to rendezvous with the *flota*, which had left Havana with about seventy ships of all kinds. On September 7, Don Alonso learned that Howard's fleet was anchored north of Flores in the Azores. On the morning of the 8th, he divided his fleet to encircle the island and come at the English pincer fashion. Taken by surprise and vastly outnumbered, Howard ordered his fleet northeast. Grenville preferred to fight and weighed anchor only after embarking some men who had been sent ashore for water.

At about 1700, *Revenge* was boarded by the thirty-seven-gun *San Felipe* and *San Bernabé*, followed by *San Cristobál, Asunción,* and *La Serena*. The grappled ships fought through the night, and both *Asunción* and *La Serena* eventually sank. Mortally wounded by musket fire, Grenville ordered his ship blown up, in the words of a contemporary account, "that the Spaniards should never glory to have taken a ship of her majesty's." But after fourteen hours of battle — only three fought in daylight — and repeated boardings, the captain and master surrendered, and the Spanish put a prize crew aboard the devastated ship. According to Sir Richard Hawkins, *Revenge* wallowed

> like a logge on the seas . . . the masts all beaten over board, all her tackle cut asunder, her upper worke altogether rased, and in effect evened she was with the water, but the very foundation or bottom of a ship, nothing left over head either for flight or defence.

The surviving English crew were taken prisoner and transferred out of the ship, and Grenville died a few days later. The treasure fleet rendezvoused with Don Alonso's fleet soon after, and the combined fleet of some 120 ships sailed for Spain. En route, they were overtaken by a weeklong storm during which *Revenge,* about fifteen Spanish warships, and scores of merchant ships were lost.

Earle, *Last Fight of the "Revenge."* Tennyson, "Last Fight of the *Revenge."*

REX

Liner (2f/2m). *L/B:* 879.9′ × 97′ (268.2m loa × 29.6m). *Tons:* 51,062 grt. *Hull:* steel. *Comp.:* 1st 640, special 378, tourist 410, 3rd 866; crew 810. *Mach.:* steam turbines, 4 screws; 28 kts. *Built:* Gio. Ansaldo & Co., Sestri Ponente, Italy; 1932.

Launched for Italia, *Rex* was the only Italian ship ever to hold the Blue Riband for the fastest crossing of the Atlantic. Launched in 1932 for Italy's Navigazione Generale Italiana, that line merged with rival Lloyd Sabaudo, builders of her future running mate CONTE DI SAVOIA, and Italia Flotte Riunite Cosulich to form Italia the same year. The two ships were intended as rivals for the current Atlantic champions, Germany's EUROPA and BREMEN. Despite every promise of a record-breaking maiden voyage from Genoa to Naples and New York, engine problems forced her into Gibraltar for three days, during which 730 of her 2,030 passengers jumped ship in search of another way across. Things were soon put to rights. In July 1933, *Europa* had broken her own record for the second time, but the next month, *Rex* improved on her performance by a full knot, steaming from Gibraltar to Ambrose at 28.92 knots (4 days, 13 hours, 58 minutes; August 11–16). She never set an eastbound record, but together with *Conte di Savoia* she did a great deal to popularize first-class travel to the Mediterranean. *Rex* remained in service through the opening months of World War II, sailing between Genoa and New York until May 1940.

Italy declared war on France and Britain the next month, and *Rex* was laid up at Pola, in what is now Slovenia, where she remained out of harm's way until 1944. That summer, it was decided to scuttle *Rex* at Trieste to impede the Allied advance. As she was being moved into position on September 8, 1944, she was sunk by British bombers off Cape d'Istria just south of Trieste. After the war, Italia briefly considered raising the ship and refitting her for service; but she lay on the wrong side of the new international boundary. She was scrapped by the Yugoslavs in 1947–48.

Bonsor, *North Atlantic Seaway.* Braynard, *Lives of the Liners.*

RICKMER RICKMERS

(ex-*Santo André, Sagres, Flores, Max*) Ship (3m). *L/B/D:* 259.3′ × 40.4′ × 19.7′ (79m × 12.3m × 6m). *Tons:* 1,980 grt. *Hull:* steel. *Comp.:* 300 (as training ship). *Mach.:* diesel, 350 hp. *Built:* R. C. Rickmers, Bremerhaven, Germany; 1896.

Built for the trading house of R. C. Rickmers for trade to the Far East, on her maiden voyage in 1896, *Rickmer Rickmers* sailed with coal for Hong Kong and returned from Saigon with rice and bamboo, the latter being a common material in household furnishings at the turn of the century. This remained her primary route under the German flag, although she also made at least one passage to Chile and one transatlantic run. Rigged originally as a ship, in 1905 she lost several spars from the mizzen mast and her owners took advantage of this to rerig her as a bark, which required a smaller crew. In 1912 she was sold to C. Krabbenhoft, Hamburg, who put her in the nitrate trade. Homeward bound in 1916, she put into Horta, in the Azores.

The Portuguese government had recently joined the Allies and seized the ship, which they renamed *Flores* and put in transatlantic trade. Although laid up during the postwar shipping slump, she resumed service as a merchantman until 1924, when the Portuguese Navy bought her for use as a training ship. The figurehead of Rickmer Rickmers was replaced with one of Prince Henry the Navigator, and the ship was named *Sagres,* for the southwestern promontory on which he established his school of navigation in the fifteenth century. As a training ship she was distinguished by large red crosses on all her square sails. In 1962, she moved to Alfeite as a stationary schoolship and renamed *Santo André* so that Portugal's new sail-training ship could be named SAGRES. In the mid-1980s, the old *Rickmer Rickmers* was purchased by Windjammer für Hamburg who restored her to her original outward appearance. As a dockside attraction in Hamburg, her interior spaces now include exhibit halls and a restaurant.

Brouwer, *International Register of Historic Ships.* Schäuffelen, *Great Sailing Ships.* Underhill, *Sail Training and Cadet Ships.*

RISDAM

Fluit (3m). *L/B:* ca. 121′ × 31′ (37m × 9.5m). *Tons:* 100 last. *Hull:* wood. *Comp.:* 162. *Built:* VOC, Hoorn, Netherlands; 1713.

The wreck of the Verenigde Oostindische Compagnie's (Dutch East India Company or VOC) *Risdam* is the only known example of an eighteenth-century *fluit.* Built for the company's trade between the Netherlands and the

Indies, *Risdam* completed one voyage to Batavia and back between September 27, 1714, and July 30, 1718. On the passage out she carried 119 passengers and crew, while on the return she carried 87. She sailed again with 162 people aboard on November 16, 1718, and arrived at Batavia on August 31, 1719. Thereafter she was put in general trade between the VOC's various ports in Indonesia and Southeast Asia. In the last stages of her last passage, *Risdam* sailed to Ligor, Malaysia, where she loaded 12.8 tons of tin, then north to Ayutthaya for sappanwood, ginger, *achar* (a type of pickled relish), and lime. She left the Thai port on December 8 and headed south. Leaking badly, she was run aground near the island of Pulau Batu Gajah opposite Mersing, on New Year's Day, 1727. Divers discovered the site in the early 1980s, and the Malaysian government began excavation in 1985. In addition to the items listed on the manifest, the site also yielded more than 100 elephant tusks.

Green, "Survey of the VOC *fluit Risdam*."

ROANOKE

Down Easter (4m). *L/B/D:* 350′ × 49.2′ × 27′ (106.7m × 15m × 8.2m). *Tons:* 3,539 tons. *Hull:* wood. *Comp.:* 32. *Des.:* William Potter Pattee. *Built:* A. Sewall & Co., Bath, Me.; 1892.

The largest wooden square-rigged vessel built in the United States (with the exception of McKay's original GREAT REPUBLIC), *Roanoke* was one of a quartet of huge Sewall Down Easters that included the ship *Rappahannock* and the four-masted barks *Shenandoah* and *Susquehanna.* Although these ships were intended to herald a revival of American merchant sail, in many ways they represented the swan song of the age of "wooden ships and iron men." *Roanoke* was the last wooden ship built by Arthur Sewall, who from this time on launched only steel deepwatermen. Despite her enormous size — only a handful of ships ever exceeded her tonnage — *Roanoke* had a reputation for good speed. She sailed most frequently in the California grain trade, although she also carried case oil to Shanghai, sugar from Honolulu, and canned fish from Seattle. After a long voyage from Baltimore with coal, *Roanoke* was at San Francisco on September 5, 1900, the day that Arthur Sewall died in Maine. This was also the first time that four Sewall ships were together in port at the same time, the other vessels being the steel-hulled DIRIGO, *Edward Sewall,* and *Erskine M. Phelps.* On the following voyage, from Norfolk for San Francisco, *Roanoke*'s cargo of coal began burning, and the ship was only saved by pouring a continuous stream of water on the coal — and pumping out again — while

making for Honolulu, which she reached thirteen days later. In 1904, *Roanoke* collided with the British steamer *Llangibby* and spent six months in Rio de Janeiro for repairs before proceeding to Sydney. From there she sailed to New Caledonia for chrome ore. On August 10, 1905, a fire broke out in the hold and despite the best efforts of her crew, assisted by the crews of *Susquehanna* and the Norwegian bark *Arabia, Roanoke* was a total loss. Her crew shipped aboard *Susquehanna* when she sailed on August 23, only to see that vessel founder three days later. Of Sewall's noble foursome, only *Shenandoah* survived, *Rappahannock* having burned at Juan Fernández Island in 1891.

Lubbock, *Down Easters.* Matthews, *American Merchant Ships.*

ROB'T. E. LEE

Sidewheel steamer (4f/2m). *L/B/D:* 285.5′ × 46′ × 9′ dph (87m × 14m × 2.7m). *Tons:* 1,456 grt. *Hull:* wood. *Mach.:* high-pressure steam engines, sidewheels. *Built:* DeWitt Hill, New Albany, Ind.; 1866.

The steamboat *Rob't. E. Lee* was built so soon after the end of the Civil War that when the name of the Confederate general was painted on her paddleboxes, Captain John W. Cannon moved his vessel across the Ohio River to Kentucky to avoid offending the nonsecessionist Hoosiers. Built for the cotton trade between Vicksburg, Mississippi, and New Orleans, *Rob't. E. Lee* had a reputation as a fast, comfortable boat distinguished especially by "the rich deep tone of her bell, and the loud noise produced by the escapement of steam from her cylinders." Cannon's greatest competition — unfriendly at that — was with Captain Thomas P. Leathers, whose most celebrated steamer was NATCHEZ of 1869. Shortly after the latter broke a quarter-century-old record between New Orleans and St. Louis, the two vessels were loading at New Orleans for departure the same day, *Natchez* for St. Louis while *Lee* was advertised for Louisville.

Word of the impending race spread quickly, although the captains denied their intentions vigorously even as they prepared for departure. Neither vessel loaded cargo, but Cannon took additional measures, removing excess wood paneling and timbers to lighten her, loosening the hog chains to make the hull more limber, and opening the windows and doors in the wheelhouse to reduce wind resistance. On June 30, 1870, at 1658, *Lee* pulled away from St. Mary's Market in New Orleans, 3 minutes, 45 seconds ahead of *Natchez.* There was no starting line and the boats operated under different principles: *Natchez* stopped several times along the way to board or disem-

Perhaps the most celebrated steamer ever to ply the Mississippi River, the sidewheeler ROB'T. E. LEE *is seen here loading bales of cotton. Courtesy Murphy Library, Univ. of Wisconsin, La Crosse.*

bark passengers, while *Lee* did not. The latter, in fact, discharged her Louisville-bound passengers onto another steamer that ran alongside for the purpose near Cairo, Illinois. Shortly thereafter, a fog descended on the river, but *Lee* passed through it much faster than *Natchez*, and she arrived at St. Louis on the morning of July 4 after a new and enduring record run of 3 days, 18 hours, 14 minutes. Along the way she also broke records from New Orleans to Vicksburg (previously set by Leathers's *Princess* in 1855), and to Cairo.

Though she was badly damaged in a collision later that year, *Rob't. E. Lee* continued working until 1876, carrying more than 5,000 bales of cotton on her regular runs from Vicksburg to New Orleans. Dismantled at New Albany in 1876, her hull became a wharf boat at Memphis.

Barkhau, *Great Steamboat Race.* Way, *Way's Packet Directory.*

ROBERT F. STOCKTON

(later *New Jersey*) Steam tug (1f/2m). *L/B/D:* 70′ × 10′ × 6.8′ (21.3m × 3m × 2.1m). *Tons:* 32 burthen. *Hull:* iron. *Comp.:* 5. *Mach.:* direct acting, 50 hp, 2 screws; 6 kts. *Des.:* John Ericsson. *Built:* John Laird, Birkenhead, Eng.; 1838.

In 1837, the Swedish engineer John Ericsson launched the small experimental screw vessel *Francis B. Ogden* in England. Though she performed as expected, the British Admiralty were unimpressed. (Ericsson's American biographer later explained that his ideas were "so novel they confused the mind of the average Englishman.") Shortly thereafter, Ericsson was introduced to Lieutenant (later Captain) Robert F. Stockton, USN, who was in England seeking financial backing for his family's Delaware and Raritan Canal in New Jersey. Stockton invited Ericsson to build a second screw propeller vessel, named for himself. The machinery comprised a two-cylinder, direct-acting steam engine driving a two-screw system patented by Ericsson. Originally there was one screw on a solid shaft slipped inside a hollow outer shaft mounting another screw that turned in the opposite direction; this proved unwieldy, and one screw was later removed. On trials, the machinery proved remarkably efficient. Towing a 650-ton ship against a 2-knot current, *Robert F. Stockton* covered 3.5 miles in 40 minutes, or better than 4.5 knots.

Rigged out as a schooner, *Robert F. Stockton* sailed to New York in April 1839 and arrived after a voyage of 46 days. Renamed *New Jersey* in 1840, the towboat worked on the canal for 30 years. Somewhat belatedly, the British Patent Office sought to buy the original machinery for its museum for exhibition alongside Henry Bell's engine for the COMET and other revolutionary inventions, but *New Jersey* and its machinery were scrapped in 1871.

Brown, "*Robert F. Stockton.*"

HMS RODNEY

Nelson-class battleship (1f/2m). *L/B/D:* 710′ × 106′ × 30′ (216.4m × 32.3m × 9.1m). *Tons:* 38,000 disp. *Hull:* steel. *Comp.:* 1,361. *Arm.:* 9 × 16″ (3 × 3), 12 × 6″, 6 × 4.7″, 8 × 2pdr, 2 × 20mm, 8 × 0.5″; 2 × 24.5″TT. *Armor:* 14″ belt, 6.25″ deck. *Mach.:* geared turbines, 45,000 shp, 2 shafts; 23 kts. *Built:* Cammell Laird & Co., Birkenhead, Eng.; 1927.

Named after Admiral Sir George Brydges, Rodney, who commanded the British fleet at the Battle of the Saintes, *Rodney* was one of two NELSON-class battleships. Assigned to the Atlantic Fleet from 1928, *Rodney* transferred to the Home Fleet in 1932. During the German invasion of Norway in April 1940, *Rodney* sustained bomb damage. Repaired at Boston, Massachusetts, in 1941, in May she was escorting the troopship BRITANNIC when HMS HOOD was sunk by BISMARCK. Detached to prevent *Bismarck*'s return to France, at 0847 on May 27, *Rodney* and KING GEORGE V opened fire on the German battleship at 16,000 yards, quickly closing to "point blank target practice" range. *Bismarck* sank less than two hours later. Assigned to Admiral Sir James Somerville's Force H based at Gibraltar, *Rodney* helped maintain the vital lifeline to Malta; she sailed in support of the Operation Torch landings in North Africa in November 1942, and again during the invasion of Sicily in July 1943. During Operation Neptune — the naval end of the D-day Normandy landings — she bombarded Caen in June 1944. In September,

she sailed on the Murmansk convoy run. *Rodney* was broken up in 1948.

Raven, *Battleships "Rodney" and "Nelson."* Thompson, *HMS "Rodney" at War.*

ROEBUCK

5th rate 26 (3m). *L/B/D:* 96′ × 25.5′ × 9.8′ (29.3m × 6.9m × 3m). *Tons:* 292 bm. *Hull:* wood. *Comp.:* 50–125. *Arm.:* 12 guns. *Built:* Snelgrove, Wapping, Eng.; 1690.

Originally commissioned as a fireship, HMS *Roebuck* (the seventh ship of the name) is best known for her part in the exploration of Australia and New Guinea under the journal-keeping buccaneer and explorer William Dampier. In 1688, Dampier had sailed from Mexico to the Philippines in *Cygnet,* subsequently landing on the coast of Australia for repairs. Although he returned to England penniless, the competence of his *New Voyage around the World* in 1697 impressed the Admiralty, and he was given command of *Roebuck* for a voyage to Australia, or New Holland. Departing the Downs on January 14, 1699, he called at Bahia, Brazil, and from there proceeded east to arrive on August 7 at Shark's Bay, near where Dirck Hartog had landed in EENDRACHT in 1616. A week later he sailed north, following the coast as far as Roebuck Bay

HMS RODNEY *in late May 1944, just before the D-day landings in Normandy. Her nine guns were mounted in three turrets forward. In this photo, two guns in each turret are elevated to near the maximum 40° angle.* RODNEY *could hurl her 2,461-pound shells 35,000 yards, or 32 kilometers. Courtesy the Admiralty.*

(near Broome) before quitting the coast of New Holland on September 5. After calling at Timor on September 15, *Roebuck* was off the New Guinea coast by December. Dampier rounded north of New Britain, which he named after determining that it "does not join to the main Land of New Guinea, but is an Island, as I have described it in my Map."

Returning to Batavia, *Roebuck* was fitted out for the passage to England and sailed on October 17 via the Cape of Good Hope and "Santa Hellena." On February 21, 1700, about a mile from Ascension Island, the ship sprang "a Leak which could not be stopped, [and] foundered at Sea." The crew landed on Ascension and were rescued five weeks later by a British convoy.

Beaglehole, *Exploration of the Pacific.* Dampier, *Voyages.*

ROOSEVELT

Steam schooner (3m). *L/B/D:* 185′ × 35.6′ × 16′ (56.4m × 10.8m × 4.9m). *Tons:* 1,600 disp. *Hull:* wood. *Comp.:* 20. *Des.:* Robert E. Peary. *Built:* McKay & Dix Shipyard, Bucksport, Me.; 1905.

Designed specifically for Arctic expeditions, auxiliary schooner *Roosevelt* was named for President Theodore Roosevelt, who helped Commander Robert Peary obtain leave from the U.S. Navy to pursue his ambition of being the first man to reach the North Pole. Built along the lines of Roald Amundsen's FRAM, *Roosevelt's* rounded hull enabled her to be pushed up by the encroaching ice rather than be crushed by it. On the first voyage, *Roosevelt* departed New York in July 1905 and sailed through the Davis Strait and on to Cape Sheridan at the northern end of Ellesmere Island on the Arctic Ocean. Peary attempted to reach the Pole over the ice, but he only reached 87°6′N before being forced to turn back on April 21, 1906. Meanwhile, *Roosevelt* had been badly damaged in the ice. Captain Bob Bartlett wrestled her back to New York where she underwent extensive repairs that postponed Peary's next expedition by a year.

On July 8, 1908, Peary began his most famous expedition. At Etah, Greenland, *Roosevelt* embarked 69 Eskimos and 246 sled dogs for the final push north to Cape Sheridan, Ellesmere Island, where the ship arrived on September 5. After setting up supply depots along their prospective route north, on March 1, 1909, Peary set out from Cape Columbia, 90 miles northwest of Cape Sheridan. A total of 24 men blazed the trail north, but the final assault on the Pole was left to Peary, Matthew Henson, and the Eskimos Egingwah, Seeglo, Ootah, and Ooqueah. They reached their goal on April 6 and returned to the ship without serious incident on April 23. Peary's return to the United States was met with great acclaim, and Congress made him a rear admiral.

In 1910, the Peary Arctic Club sold *Roosevelt* to John Arbuckle, who sold her to the U.S. Fisheries Commission in 1915. Employed by the Navy on the West Coast during World War I, she was later bought for use as a tug, first by the West Coast Tug Company and, from 1924, the Washington Tug & Barge Company. She was abandoned in 1942.

Peary, *Nearest the Pole; North Pole.*

ROSCIUS

Packet ship (3m). *L/B/D:* 167.5′ × 36.4′ × 21.6′ dph (51.1m × 11.1m × 6.6m). *Tons:* 1,030 bm. *Hull:* wood. *Des.:* N. B. Palmer. *Built:* Brown & Bell, New York; 1838.

A forerunner of the swift clipper ships that would capture the world's imagination in the 1850s, packet ship *Roscius* was ordered for Edward Knight Collins's Dramatic Line, founded the previous year for service between New York and Liverpool. Most of Dramatic's ships bore the names of playwrights and actors — the first four were *Garrick, Siddons, Sheridan,* and *Shakespeare* — and *Roscius* was named for the Roman comic actor of antiquity. The ship's design owed much to that of the cotton droughers that plied between New Orleans and New York. Because of the shallow bar at the mouth of the Mississippi River, cotton ships had to be relatively shallow, so rather than having V-shaped hulls with a sharp deadrise, they had nearly flat floors. This design had the added benefit of increasing the ships' tonnage, which meant they could carry more cargo, and *Roscius* was the first packet to exceed 1,000 tons capacity. *Roscius's* massive rig was comparable to that of the extreme clipper FLYING CLOUD, which was almost 700 tons bigger. No less an authority than Commodore Isaac Hull claimed that she could outsail any ship in the U.S. Navy. In general, ships were becoming faster, and the average westbound speed for the Dramatic Line ships in 1839 was twenty-eight days — twelve days faster than the average for the Black Ball Liners that opened regular service between New York and Liverpool with JAMES MONROE twenty years before.

Dramatic Line was acquired by Spofford Tileston and Company in 1848, and four years later *Roscius* was sold. After service between New York and Mobile for the Pelican Line, *Roscius* returned to the transatlantic trade, foundering at sea on August 26, 1860, en route from Liverpool to New York.

Albion, *Square-Riggers on Schedule.* Cutler, *Greyhounds of the Sea; Queens of the Western Ocean.*

HMS ROSE

Seaford-class 6th rate 20 (3m). L/B/D: 108′ × 30.1′ × 9.5′ (32.9m × 9.2m × 2.9m). Tons: 430 tons. Hull: wood. Comp.: 160. Arm.: 20 × 9pdr. Built: Hugh Blades, Hull, Eng.; 1757.

Bearing one of the most common names in the Royal Navy (first used as early as 1322), HMS Rose was one of a class of the Royal Navy's smallest-rated vessels. Built at the outset of the Seven Years' (French and Indian) War, Rose served on patrol along the coast of France and in the Caribbean. In 1768, the Board of the Admiralty considered the ship for Captain James Cook's first South Seas expedition, but as she could not be made ready in time, he sailed in ENDEAVOUR instead. Later that year, Rose was dispatched to the coast of North America where she was active in impressing sailors from merchant ships for the Royal Navy. In 1774, Rose was dispatched to Narragansett Bay to suppress the very active and lucrative smuggling trade that had helped make Newport the fourth wealthiest city in the colonies. Captain James Wallace was so successful that the merchants of Newport were forced to appeal to Rhode Island's colonial legislature for the formation of a navy to combat the frigate, while they themselves fitted out the merchant sloop Katy — which they renamed PROVIDENCE — to patrol their waters. Rhode Island, in turn, asked the Continental Congress for the creation of a Continental Navy. In July of 1776, Rose took part in the British campaign to expel General George Washington's Continental Army from New York and saw action against shore batteries along the Hudson. Three years later Rose took part in the defense of Savannah, which the British had just captured and which was under threat of attack from a French fleet commanded by Comte Jean-Baptiste d'Estaing. On September 9, 1779, Rose was scuttled to prevent the French fleet from advancing upriver. The city remained in British hands until the end of the American Revolution in 1782, when the hulk was broken up so that regular commerce could be resumed.

In 1970, John Fitzhugh Millar built a replica of the ship in anticipation of the U.S. Bicentennial. At this writing, the ship is used as a sail-training vessel and dockside attraction, sailing to ports from the Great Lakes to Europe from her homeport of Bridgeport, Connecticut.

Bailey, Manual for Sailing aboard the American Tall Ship "Rose." Lyon, Sailing Navy List.

ROYAL CAROLINE

(later Royal Charlotte) Royal yacht (3m). L/B/D: 90.1′ × 24′ × 12.1′ (27.4m × 7.3m × 3.7m). Tons: 232 bm. Hull: wood. Comp.: 70 crew. Arm.: 24 guns. Des.: Joshua Allin. Built: Deptford Dockyard, Eng.; 1750.

Royal Caroline was a royal yacht built for the use of George II and his wife, Queen Caroline. She was sailed for pleasure cruises by the royal family, and as a transport for members of court sailing between England and Holland. On the latter assignments, she was usually escorted by as many as four frigates and, when the King was aboard, accompanied by the First Lord of the Admiralty. Her distinguished captains included Sir William Cornwallis and Sir Hyde Parker, both of whom rose to flag rank. In 1761, the vessel was renamed Charlotte (later Royal Charlotte) for George III's prospective bride and Queen, Princess Sophie Charlotte of Mecklenburg-Strelitz. Little used by the royal family after 1806, she was broken up in 1821.

Royal Caroline's design was based on that of a ship built in 1700 as Peregrine Galley and later named Carolina and Royal Caroline. Ordered by William III, this vessel was designed by Peregrine, Lord Danby, an admiral who had designed several vessels for Peter the Great, but whose efforts were not initially appreciated by the Admiralty. His success is seen not only in the similarity of the second Royal Caroline's design, but in the fact that the later ship was, in turn, the prototype for a long line of 20-gun and 32-gun ships, including the Richmond-class frigates, the last of which were ordered in 1804.

Bellabarba & Osculati, Royal Yacht "Caroline": 1749.

HMS ROYAL CHARLES

(ex-Naseby) 1st rate 80 (3m). L/B/D: 162′ × 42.5′ × 11′ (49.4m × 13m × 3.4m). Tons: 1,230 bm. Hull: wood. Arm.: 80 guns. Des.: Peter Pett. Built: Woolwich Dockyard, Eng.; 1655.

Two years after he assumed the title of Lord Protector of England, Oliver Cromwell authorized the construction of three "great ships" for the Navy: the 80-gun Naseby (so named for his victory over the Royalists in 1645), and the 64-gun London and Dunbar (subsequently renamed Henry). Naseby's original adornments included a figurehead portraying, according to Samuel Pepys, "Oliver on horseback trampling 6 nations under foote, a Scott, Irishman, Dutch, French, Spaniard and English as was easily made out by their several habits: A Fame held a laurell over his insulting head, & the word God with us." When Charles II returned from exile in the Naseby, he ordered the ship named for himself as well as a new figurehead of Neptune, an act that irritated the parsimonious Pepys, who complained, "God knows, it is even the flinging away of £100 out of the King's purse."

Commercial rivalry between England and the Dutch Republic led to the start of the Second Anglo-Dutch War in 1665. At the Battle of Lowestoft, *Royal Charles* was flagship of the Duke of York (later James II), Lord High Admiral. The two fleets — each numbered over 100 ships — met before dawn on June 13. Although the English had superior organization and more powerful guns, the Dutch fought well. By midafternoon, *Royal Charles* was in danger of being sunk or surrendered to *Eendracht* when the Dutch flagship exploded, killing all but five of her 400 crew, including the Dutch Admiral Wassenaer van Obdam. *Royal Charles* was so damaged that the Duke of York shifted his flag to the *St. Michael* and later still the *James.* Nonetheless, Lowestoft was a clear English victory, with only 250 dead compared with 4,000 Dutch dead. For his failure to pursue the retreating Dutch fleet, the Duke of York was obliged to pull down his flag after the battle, which was the last of the year.

In the spring of 1666, command of the fleet was divided between Prince Rupert and George Monck, Duke of Albemarle, in *Royal Charles.* At the end of May, with the Dutch fleet still in port, Charles unwisely divided his force and sent Rupert west to prevent a French force from joining Admiral Michiel Adriaanszoon de Ruyter. Monck was left with only 56 ships to oppose the 85 Dutch ships under de Ruyter. Nonetheless, Monck attacked the Dutch force as soon as it appeared on June 11. The English attack was impressive, and he renewed battle the next day. Early on the second day, he profited from a tactical error by Lieutenant Admiral Cornelis Tromp, until de Ruyter came to his countryman's assistance. Each side lost three ships. On June 13, Monck retreated to the west in hopes of joining Rupert, but in so doing the *Royal Prince* (90 guns) ran aground on Galloper Shoal and was burned by the Dutch. Battle was joined again on June 14, but by the end of the day, with the wind rising and supplies exhausted (to say nothing of the crews), both sides retired. The Four Days' Battle remains one of the longest fleet engagements on record. Although the English losses were more than double those of the Dutch — 20 ships lost, 5,000 crew killed, and 2,000 taken prisoner — the English regrouped fast, and the fleet put to sea again in July.

On August 4, the two fleets met in the North Sea off North Foreland, both Rupert and Monck flying their flags in *Royal Charles.* The battle proved disastrous for the Dutch, as usual because of the lack of discipline, although de Ruyter fought long and well. Dutch losses amounted to 20 ships, 4,000 dead, and 3,000 prisoners; the English lost three ships. (This battle was also known as the St. James' Day Fight because it took place on the Feast of St. James, July 24 in the Julian calendar, by which England still reckoned dates.)

In the spring of 1667, the English treasury was exhausted by a combination of Charles's extravagance and the lasting effects of both the Great Plague of 1665 and the London fire of September 1666. Charles decided to economize by laying up his fleet. Seeing their opportunity, the Dutch fleet attacked the fort at Sheerness on June 10 and advanced up the Medway. The English scuttled a number of ships in an effort to block the channel, and an iron chain was strung across the river between Upnor and Gillingham. Over the course of three days, twenty-three ships were lost, most intentionally sunk by the English and then burned by the Dutch. The losses included two first rates, three second rates, two third rates, six fourth rates, and one sixth rate. Orders were given to burn the *Royal Charles,* but at the approach of a Dutch boat from the *Bescherming,* the crew fled. As Pepys recounted,

> The Dutch did take her with a boat of nine men, who found not a man aboard her, and . . . presently a man went up and struck her flag and jack. . . . They did carry her down at a time when both for wind and tide, when the best pilot in Chatham would not have undertaken it, they heeling her on one side to make her draw little water.

Incompatible with the needs of the Dutch fleet, *Royal Charles* never fought again and the Dutch displayed her at Rotterdam as a war trophy. She was auctioned and broken up in 1673, during the Third Anglo-Dutch War.

Clowes, *Royal Navy.* Fox, *Great Ships.* Hepper, *British Warship Losses in the Age of Sail.* Pepys, *Pepys' Diary.*

ROYAL CHARTER

Screw steamer (1f/3m). *L/B:* 336′ × 22.5′ (102.4m × 6.9m). *Tons:* 2,719 tons. *Hull:* iron. *Comp.:* 112 crew; 400 pass. *Arm.:* 4 × 18pdr, 4 × 24pdr. *Mach.:* direct-acting trunk engines, 200 hp, single screw; 9 kts. *Built:* George Cramm, Sandycroft, Eng.; 1855.

Laid down by George Cramm and completed by William Patterson, who had overseen the building of Brunel's GREAT WESTERN and GREAT BRITAIN, *Royal Charter* was purchased by Gibbs, Bright & Company for its Australian Screw Steamship Company (later the Liverpool & Australian Navigation Company). One of the finest passenger ships of the day, *Royal Charter* was the first English ship to carry double topsails, and she performed well in the Australian passenger trade for three years. In August 1859 the ship left Melbourne with 511 passengers and crew aboard and bullion with an estimated value of £500,000. After 58 days at sea, she called at Queenstown, Ireland, and discharged 17 passengers. The following night, on October 26, *Royal Charter* encountered gales off Moelfre, Anglesey Island. Captain T. Taylor tried to anchor at 2245, but the cables parted at 0330 the next morning and the ship was driven ashore in Lligwy Bay, about four miles southeast of Point Lynus. She broke up with the loss of 455 people.

Hollett, *Fast Passage to Australia.* McKee, *Golden Wreck.*

HMS ROYAL GEORGE

(ex-*Royal Anne*) *Royal George*-class 1st rate 100 (3m). *L/B/D:* 178′ × 51.8′ × 21.5′ (54.3m × 15.8m × 6.6m). *Tons:* 2,047 bm. *Hull:* wood. *Comp.:* 850. *Arm.:* 28 × 42pdr, 28 × 24pdr, 28 × 12pdr, 16 × 6pdr. *Built:* Woolwich Dockyard, Eng.; 1756.

The first-rate ship HMS *Royal George* was laid down as *Royal Anne* in 1746 but renamed in honor of the reigning monarch George II before her launch ten years later. The first warship to exceed 2,000 tons burden, *Royal George* was commissioned at the start of the Seven Years' War with France and joined the Western Squadron in blockading the port of Brest and Quiberon Bay. On November 9, 1759, the British fleet was blown off station, and Vice Admiral Hubert de Brienne, Comte de Conflans, seized the opportunity to sortie from Brest with twenty-one ships of the line. This he did the same day that Admiral Sir Edward Hawke left Torbay, beating against the westerlies to regain his station. On the afternoon of November 20, 1759, the two fleets spotted each other off Brest, and Hawke ordered his ships to "form as you chase." Conflans decided to return to Brest, and despite the treacherous shoals and reefs of Quiberon Bay, Hawke ordered his ships to follow the French. As Conflans later wrote, "I had no reason to believe that if I went in first with my ships the enemy would dare follow, in spite of his superiority [of two ships] which must anyway restrict his movements."

The ensuing destruction of the French fleet was decisive. *Thésée* foundered when water rushed in through her lower gun ports, and *Héros* struck to HMS *Magnanime* (a French prize of 1748). As *Royal George* came up with Conflans's flagship *Soleil Royal* (80 guns), the French *Superbe* interposed herself but sank after one broadside from Hawke's flagship. The French *Formidable* also struck before darkness fell and Hawke ordered his fleet to anchor. The next morning revealed HMS *Resolution* and *Essex* driven ashore on Le Four shoal, but *Soleil Royal* was lost on Rouelle shoal and three other French ships were damaged beyond repair.

Hawke was knighted for his action, and *Royal George* spent the rest of the war on blockade duty off Brest. Peace came in 1763, and between that year and 1778, the Royal Navy laid up ninety-seven ships of the line, *Royal George* among them. When France threw in her lot with the American colonists and allied with Spain, *Royal George* recommissioned. In July 1778, she was under command of Sir Charles Hardy in his ignominious withdrawal before the combined Franco-Spanish fleet as it advanced up the Channel. (Sailors in *Royal George* are said to have blindfolded the figureheads, popularly believed to represent the former king, so that "George II should never see an English Fleet chased up their own channel.") In the event, Admiral Louis Guillouet, Comte d'Orvilliers, withdrew of his own accord, and England was spared further anxiety about the biggest invasion to threaten since the Spanish Armada in 1588.

At the end of 1779, *Royal George* sailed with Admiral Sir George Rodney's fleet to relieve Gibraltar and took part in the capture of two Spanish convoys, one guarded by nine ships under Admiral Don Juan de Langara; seven of these were captured or sunk. In 1782, she was part of another fleet, under Admiral Lord Howe, assembled for the permanent relief of Gibraltar. The ships were anchored at Spithead, taking on supplies, when on August 29 *Royal George* was being heeled at a slight angle to make some minor repairs below the waterline. At the same time, casks of rum were being loaded aboard and the lower deck gunports were not properly secured. At about 0920 the ship suddenly rolled over on her beam ends, filled with water, and sank, taking with her 800 people, including as many as 300 women and 60 children who were visiting the ship. A subsequent court-martial acquitted the ship's officers and crew (most of whom were dead) of any wrongdoing, and blamed the accident on the "general state of decay of her timbers."

Several attempts were made to salvage the ship. In 1783, William Tracey succeeded in moving the ship slightly before the Admiralty decided to abandon the project. In 1834, the pioneering diver Charles Deane recovered thirty guns before his work was interrupted to investigate a nearby wreck that turned out to be MARY ROSE. The remains of *Royal George* were eventually blown up by Royal Engineers in the early 1840s.

Hepper, *British Warship Losses.* Johnson, "*Royal George.*" Ker, "Loss of the *Royal George.*"

HMS ROYAL OAK

Revenge-class battleship (1f/2m). *L/B/D:* 624.3′ × 88.5′ × 30′ (190.3m × 27m × 9.1m). *Tons:* 33,500 disp. *Hull:* steel. *Comp.:* 997–1,247. *Arm.:* 8 × 15″ (4 × 2), 14 × 6″, 2 × 3″, 4 × 3pdr; 2 ×

21″TT. *Armor:* 13″ belt, 4″ deck. *Mach.:* geared turbines, 40,000 shp, 4 shafts; 21 kts. *Built:* Devonport Dockyard, Plymouth, Eng.; 1916.

Two weeks after commissioning, HMS *Royal Oak* sailed in the Grand Fleet's 4th Battle Squadron at the Battle of Jutland on May 31, 1916. She made no significant contribution to the fighting, but she remained with the Grand Fleet for the duration of the war. Following the scuttling of the German fleet at Scapa Flow in 1919, she was one of three battleships used to transport to Invergordon the nearly 2,000 German sailors now without ships. *Royal Oak* later served with the Atlantic Fleet (through 1926) and in the Mediterranean. Recalled to the Home Fleet in 1937, at the start of World War II, she was based at Scapa Flow, a huge naval anchorage the protection of which was made relatively simple thanks to the complex geography of the Shetland Islands. Admiral Karl Dönitz believed that sinking a British battleship there would undermine British morale, and he knew also that though easily defended, Scapa Flow was far from impregnable. Lieutenant Commander Gunther Prien in U-47 was chosen for the assignment, and on the night of October 13–14, 1939, the submarine slipped into Scapa Flow. *U-47* launched three torpedoes at two targets (the second was the seaplane tender *Pegasus,* which escaped unscathed). One torpedo hit *Royal Oak* and caused a small explosion attributed to spontaneous combustion in a paint locker. Fourteen minutes later, three more torpedoes hit *Royal Oak*'s starboard side. These caused massive magazine explosions that lifted the ship out of the water. A quarter of an hour later, she rolled over and sank with the loss of 24 officers and 809 other ranks; there were only 424 survivors.

Snyder, *"Royal Oak" Disaster.*

HMS ROYAL SOVEREIGN

1st rate 100 (3m). *L/B/D:* 184′ × 52′ (56.1m × 15.8m). *Tons:* 2,175 bm. *Hull:* wood. *Comp.:* 850. *Arm.:* 100 guns. *Built:* Devonport Dockyard, Plymouth, Eng.; 1787.

Launched in 1787, more than twelve and a half years after her laying down, the third HMS *Royal Sovereign* was a dull sailer known to her crews as "the West Country Wagon." Completed at the height of the Nootka Sound controversy, when Britain and Spain were poised for war over possession of the harbor on Vancouver Island, Canada, from 1790 to 1794 she was flagship of Vice Admiral Thomas Graves in the Channel Fleet. In 1794, she was part of Lord Howe's fleet against Admiral Louis-Thomas Villaret de Joyeuse's Brest Squadron at the Glorious First of June, during which she was hotly engaged by the French *Impetueux* and *Terrible* and suffered fifty-eight crew killed and wounded. *Royal Sovereign* remained with the Channel Fleet through 1803, and was caught up in the Spithead mutiny of 1797, for which two of her crew were hanged.

In 1804 *Royal Sovereign* joined the blockade of Toulon, and the following year became flagship of Vice Admiral Cuthbert Collingwood and Captain Edward Rotherham. She remained with Vice Admiral Lord Nelson's squadron in the long chase of Admiral Pierre de Villeneuve's Combined Fleet from the Mediterranean to the West Indies and back. At the Battle of Trafalgar on October 21, 1805, she led the lee column and was the first British ship to close with the Combined Fleet. Undermanned, her gun crews could only fire broadsides from one side of the ship at a time. After raking first Admiral Alava y Navarrete's flagship *Santa Ana* (112 guns), and then the French *Fougueux* (74), she came under the combined fire of *San Leandro* (64), *San Justo* (74), and *Indomptable* (80). The latter four ships moved on, leaving *Royal Sovereign* to grapple with *Santa Ana* alone, which struck to her at 1415 with casualties numbering 340 dead and wounded. *Royal Sovereign* lost her mizzen and mainmasts during the engagement and suffered 141 killed and wounded. Collingwood, who had succeeded to command of the fleet with the death of Nelson, had to shift his flag to the frigate *Euryalus,* and *Royal Sovereign* was towed to Gibraltar by HMS *Neptune.*

Royal Sovereign returned to duty in the Mediterranean the next year and remained on the blockade of Toulon until 1812, when she transferred to the Channel Fleet. Made a receiving ship at Plymouth in 1816, she was renamed *Captain* in 1825, and broken up at Pembroke Dockyard in 1849.

Mackenzie, *Trafalgar Roll.* Schom, *Trafalgar.*

ROYAL WILLIAM

(later *Isabella Segunda*) Steamer (1f/3m). *L/B:* 176′ × 28′ (44′ew) × 14′ (53.6m × 8.5m × 4.3m). *Tons:* 1,370 grt. *Hull:* wood. *Comp.:* 50 berths, 80 steerage; 36 crew. *Mach.:* side-lever engines, 300 ihp, sidewheels. *Built:* Black & Campbell, Quebec; 1831.

Designed for service between Quebec and the Maritime Provinces, *Royal William* (named for William IV) was built for the Quebec and Halifax Steam Navigation Company, of which Samuel Cunard was a part owner. After a successful first season during which she completed three roundtrips between Quebec and Halifax, *Royal William* was quarantined in 1832 because of a cholera epidemic. Sold the following year, she became the first British

An unknown artist's portrait of the ROYAL WILLIAM, *"the First Steamship to Cross the Atlantic." This attribution is inaccurate, given the fact of the steamship* SAVANNAH*'s crossing in 1819. Courtesy Peabody Essex Museum, Salem, Massachusetts.*

steamship to sail into Boston Harbor. Returning to Nova Scotia, she sailed from Pictou Harbor on August 18, 1833, for England, under Captain John McDougall, with seven passengers. Despite steaming on only the port engine for ten days, *Royal William* arrived at Cowes, Isle of Wight, on September 6, and at Gravesend on September 12, after a passage of twenty-five days. Sold to Spain and renamed *Isabella Segunda* in September 1834, she was the first steamship in the Spanish Navy. She was hulked at Bordeaux, France, in 1840.

Spratt, *Transatlantic Paddle Steamers.*

RUMSEIAN EXPERIMENT

Steamboat. *Hull:* wood. *Mach.:* steam engine, water jet. *Built:* James Rumsey, Shepherdstown, W. Va.; 1785.

One of the first Americans involved in the development and application of steam navigation was James Rumsey, an affable but secretive hotelkeeper from Bath, Virginia (now West Virginia). In 1785, one of his guests happened to be General George Washington, to whom he showed his model of a pole boat that used the river current to travel upstream. Later that year, Rumsey hit upon the idea of harnessing steam power for his engine, and he eventu-

ally dropped the pole boat idea for a boat driven by a water jet. Although technologically ahead of its time, the idea of jet propulsion had more support than the paddle systems devised by Rumsey's rival John Fitch. Benjamin Franklin had proposed the idea to the American Philosophical Society, and the machinery was relatively simple.

Rumsey's engine consisted of a single piston rod connecting two cylinders. The upper cylinder was part of the engine while the bottom cylinder acted as a pump, drawing water into the boat through valves in the keel on the up stroke and forcing water out through a tube in the stern on the down stroke. Rumsey tried his vessel for the first time on March 14, 1786. "The boat went against the current of the Potomac, but many parts of the machinery [were] imperfect, and some parts rendered useless by the heat of the steam." By the next year, Rumsey was in direct competition with Fitch for state monopolies and on December 3, 1787, he made a second demonstration during which his vessel was said to have gone at a rate of three miles per hour against the current; eight days later, his speed was estimated at four miles per hour. The vessel made no more trials, but Rumsey started the Rumseian Society and in 1788, he went to England bearing letters of introduction from Franklin and others. Patent negotiations with engine makers Matthew Boulton and James Watt collapsed. Construction of a vessel patriotically called *Columbia Maid,* but which Rumsey referred to as *The Rumseian Experiment,* was suspended for two years while the inventor staved off creditors. He had resumed work on the engine when, on December 18, 1790, he died just before he was to address the Society of Arts.

Flexner, *Steamboats Come True.*

RURIK

Brig. *Tons:* 180 bm. *Hull:* wood. *Arm.:* 8 guns. *Comp.:* 32–34. *Built:* Abo, Finland; 1815.

Named for the ninth-century founder of the Rurik dynasty that ruled Russia for eight centuries, *Rurik* was built for an expedition proposed by Count Nikolai P. Romanzof to sail through the Bering Strait and search for the Northeast Passage. Lieutenant Otto von Kotzebue, who had circumnavigated the globe in Krusenstern's NADEZHDA in 1803, commanded the expedition, whose members included the naturalists Adelbert von Chamisso and Johann Friedrich Eschscholtz. Sailing from Kronstadt on July 30, 1815, after stops at Copenhagen and Portsmouth, *Rurik* entered the Atlantic on October 5, 1815. While rounding Cape Horn in January 1816, Kotzebue sustained a chest injury that would plague him the rest of the voyage, and storm damage to the ship forced him to put into Talcahuano.

Heading west in March, *Rurik's* next Pacific landfall was at Easter Island on March 28. Sailing via the Tuamotus and Marshall Islands, the Russian ship arrived at Petropavlovsk, Kamchatka, on June 3. Over the course of the next twelve days, *Rurik* was sheathed in copper taken from the hull of Vasilii M. Golovnin's sloop DIANA. On July 30, *Rurik* sailed through the Bering Strait and, hugging the northern coast of the Seward Peninsula, she sailed into Kotzebue Sound, which at first Kotzebue believed might be an arm of the Northeast Passage. Heading east to Cape Dezhnev, the easternmost part of Asia, on

August 19 *Rurik* turned back from St. Lawrence Bay. Stopping at Yerba Buena (now San Francisco) for supplies in October, she sailed for the Sandwich Islands in November and thence on to the Marshall and Caroline Islands, which the expedition surveyed through March 1817.

On April 13, *Rurik* was pooped and lost her bowsprit; several sailors were also badly injured, including Kotzebue. A few days later, the ship was almost lost on Unimak Island, but after two months of repairs at Unalaska, she put to sea again on June 29, with fifteen Aleuts and equipped with *baidarkas* (skin boats) for coastal survey work. Greatly weakened by his Cape Horn injury, Kotzebue was forced to abandon the effort and return to Unalaska. By October 1, *Rurik* was back at Honolulu where the Russians gathered plants for transplantation in the Radak Island chain of the Marshall Islands, en route to Manila. At the end of March 1818, the Russians met the French ship URANIE at the Cape of Good Hope. After stops at Portsmouth and Copenhagen, *Rurik* arrived at the Neva on August 3, 1818. Kotzebue's account of the voyage was one of several. Chamisso and Friedrich Eschscholtz published studies of marine and animal life as well as ethnographic studies of the Siberian Chuchkis, California mission society, and the Sandwich Islands. (Eschscholtz sailed again with Kotzebue on the PREDPRIYATIYE expedition of 1823–26.)

Rurik was later purchased by the Russian-American Company and in 1821–22 made a second voyage under Navigator Klochov, in company with the ship *Elisaveta* in what was intended to be a second circumnavigation. The latter ship had to be sold at Cape Town, and *Rurik* proceeded alone to Novo Arkhangelsk (Sitka) where she was put into colonial service, in which she ended her days. Her officers and crew returned home via Okhotsk and thence overland.

Ivashintsov, *Russian Round-the-World Voyages.* Kotzebue, *Voyage of Discovery.*

HMCS Sackville

Flower-class corvette (1f/1m). *L/B/D:* 205.1′ × 33.1′ × 13.8′ (62.5m × 10.1m × 4.2m). *Tons:* 950 disp. *Hull:* steel. *Comp.:* 30–85. *Arm.:* 1 × 4″, 1 × 2pdr, 20mm; hedgehogs. *Mach.:* triple-expansion, 2,620 ihp, 1 screw; 30 kts. *Built:* St. John Shipbuilding & Drydock, Ltd., St. John, New Brunswick; 1941.

At the start of World War II, the British Admiralty decided to build as many warships as it could in Canada. Among the first vessels ordered were corvettes for convoy duty on the crucial North Atlantic run. Modeled on a British whale catcher, the corvettes had a smaller turning radius than a submarine and were the most famous escort class ever built, 261 of them being turned out for the British, Canadian, and Free French navies. The British-built corvettes were named for flowers and the Canadian corvettes for towns.

In April 1942, HMCS *Sackville* was assigned to Escort Group C-3, working out of St. John's, Newfoundland. She subsequently saw service with Escort Group C-2 until the summer of 1944 when a boiler explosion en route from Londonderry to Halifax put her out of commission. Refit as a minefield support vessel, after the war she removed the acoustic controlled-loop minefields off St. John, New Brunswick, and Sydney, Nova Scotia. After seven years in reserve, she was employed variously as a fisheries, oceanographic, and antisubmarine warfare research vessel. *Sackville* decommissioned in 1982 and was handed over to the Canadian Naval Corvette Trust for preservation at Halifax.

Lynch, "Saving the Last Flower-Class Corvette, HMCS *Sackville.*" Raven & Preston, *Flower Class Corvettes.*

Sacramento

Galleon (3m). *Tons:* 480 burden. *Hull:* wood. *Comp.:* 824–1,000. *Arm.:* 60 guns. *Des.:* Francisco Bento. *Built:* Francisco Bento, Oporto, Portugal; <1663.

The scene of one of the worst shipwrecks in colonial Brazil, *Sacramento* was the *almiranta* of a fleet maintained by the General Commercial Company of Brazil to escort transatlantic convoys. In early 1668, *Sacramento* sailed as flagship of a large fleet from Portugal to Bahía (Pernambuco). Her complement included two hundred friars, government officials, and other passengers. On the evening of May 5, the pilot attempted to enter All Saints Bay in rough weather, but at about 1800 the ship struck the Rio Vermelho Bank. Leaking badly, she fired her guns to signal for help, but no ships could leave the port. She drifted northward for five hours and sank in about thirty meters of water at 13°12′S, 38°30′W, taking with her all but 70 of her complement of 1,000.

Beginning in 1976, government-sponsored excavation of the site yielded an impressive trove of English, Dutch, and Portuguese iron and brass guns dating from between 1590 and 1653, as well as five brass compasses and other navigational instruments. Although the ship was primarily a warship, she apparently was carrying a cargo of brass thimbles, hundreds of which were found on the site. There were also large numbers of green jars and scores of Portuguese oil jars embellished with Chinese decorative motifs. The loss of the ship devastated Bahía, not only because of the human toll but, as Governor Francisco Correa da Silva wrote, due to the fact that "I was left without news because the letters were destroyed."

Mello, "Shipwreck of the Galleon *Sacramento.*"

St. Gabriel

(*Sviatoi Gavriil*) (1m). *L/B/D:* 60′ × 20′ × 7.5′ (18.3m × 6.1m × 2.3m) dph. *Hull:* wood. *Comp.:* 44. *Built:* Nizhnekamchatsk, Russia; 1728.

In the early 1700s, Czar Peter I conceived an expedition to find North America from Asia and determine the eastward extent of Asiatic Russia. The vessels were to be built on the Kamchatka Peninsula from where they would sail north. (That Asia and North America were not a contiguous landmass had been determined in a forgotten 1648 expedition by Semen Dezhnev; he explored in seven unnamed *koches,* a type of Siberian single-masted vessel well suited to sailing in ice-strewn waters.) As the commander for the First Kamchatka Expedition, Peter chose Vitus Bering, Danish born but in Russian service since 1703, with Alexei Chirikov as his second in command. They left St. Petersburg on January 25, 1725, to start a three-year journey that brought them to the Pacific shore. Reaching Okhotsk in October 1726, they built a small vessel named *Fortuna* in which they crossed the Sea of Okhotsk to the Kamchatka Peninsula. From there, supplies were carried by land and river to Nizhnekamchatsk at the mouth of the Kamchatka River on the Pacific in January 1728.

Here Bering built *St. Gabriel,* which put to sea for the first time on July 13, hugging the Asian coast. On August 1 he landed in Kresta Bay, at the base of the Chukotski Peninsula. Bering continued around the peninsula and sailed north through the Bering Strait to reach 67°18′N, 166°53′W, on August 16, when he turned back, having never seen the American continent. Retracing his course along the Asian shore, he returned to Nizhnekamchatsk on September 2. On June 5, 1729, Bering sailed about 130 miles east of Kamchatka in hopes of finding land — North America is about 1,500 miles away on that parallel — but as the boat was not designed for deep-sea voyaging, he turned back to Okhotsk. From here he returned to St. Petersburg.

In 1732, *St. Gabriel* undertook a second mission to explore the islands and "Big Land" known to lie east of the Chukotski Peninsula. Sailing on July 23 under Ivan Fedorov and Mikhail Gvozdev, the brig hugged the coast for two weeks before sailing east to Big Diomede Island, reached on August 17. Little Diomede Island came three days later, and on the following day the brig arrived at what is now called Cape Prince of Wales, Alaska. Although Bering and his crew did not land on the Big Land, before returning to Nizhnekamchatsk, they learned from Eskimos of its extensive forests and fur-bearing animals.

In 1738 and 1739, *St. Gabriel* was employed in two more expeditions to the south. The first, including three ships, resulted in the discovery of nearly thirty new islands in the Kurile chain between Kamchatka and Japan. On the second, the ships sailed over the nonexistent "Juan de Gama Land," believed to have been seen by a sixteenth-century explorer, before turning south and sailing to Matsmai Island, where they traded with the Japanese. *St. Gabriel*'s fate is unknown, although Russian support for exploration stopped after Bering's ill-fated expedition in ST. PETER and ST. PAUL in 1740.

Divin, *Great Russian Navigator, A. I. Chirikov.* Fisher, *Bering's Voyages.* Frost, *Bering and Chirikov.*

HMS ST. GEORGE

Duke-class 2nd rate 90 (3m). *L/B/D:* 177.5′ × 50′ × 21.1′ (54.1m × 15.2m × 6.4m). *Tons:* 1,932 bm. *Hull:* wood. *Comp.:* 750. *Arm.:* 28 × 32pdr, 30 × 18pdr, 30 × 12pdr, 2 × 6pdr. *Des.:* Sir John Williams. *Built:* Portsmouth Dockyard, Eng.; 1785.

The fourth Royal Navy ship of the name, HMS *St. George* was named for the patron saint of England. She participated in the action at Genoa following the French closure of that port to British shipping. In 1801, she was Rear Admiral Horatio Nelson's flagship prior to the Battle of Copenhagen; he transferred his flag to HMS *Elephant,* whose lighter draft enabled him to sail closer inshore for the bombardment of the Danish capital on April 2. In 1811, *St. George* was the flagship of Rear Admiral Robert Reynolds's Baltic Fleet. On November 1, she sailed with a number of other ships from Hano Bay to England. A merchant ship collided with her and she was driven aground on Låland Island, sustaining extensive damage. After major repairs, she got under way again with a jury rig on December 17, in company with HMS *Cressy* and DEFENCE. On Christmas Eve, the ships were off Jutland when a gale struck. Captain Daniel Guion attempted to anchor near Ringkøbing, Denmark, to await a favorable wind, but *St. George* ran aground before the anchors could be let go. Despite efforts to lighten the ship, she was pounded by the heavy seas and sank with the loss of all but eleven of her company. *Defence* was lost the same night.

Hepper, *British Warship Losses.*

ST. JEAN-BAPTISTE

Ship (3m). *Tons:* 650 bm. *Hull:* wood. *Comp.:* 172. *Arm.:* 26 × 12pdr, 10 × 6pdr. *Built:* Nantes, France; 1767.

St. Jean-Baptiste was a merchant ship built for trade between France and India following the collapse of the French East India Company. Jean-François-Marie de Surville was captain and part owner. On June 3, 1767, she sailed for the Ganges River on the Bay of Bengal and arrived in November 1768. The next spring, she traded between French-Indian ports at Madras, Chandernagore, and Binganapali before Surville began to ready her for a voyage east. Surville and his partners hoped to find a land rumored to have been discovered by the English — during Captain Samuel Wallis's cruise in HMS DOLPHIN — reports of which had been conflated with the century-old rumor of Davis Land, off the coast of Chile. Surville was also to "open trade with the Dutch and share it with the Dutch." If these plans failed, the enterprise might at least break even by selling off trade goods at Manila.

St. Jean-Baptiste sailed from the Hooghly River on March 3, 1769. After calling at Pondicherry, she crossed to Malacca and Trengganu, and then north to the Philippines and the Bashi Islands between Luzon and Formosa (Taiwan). From here she entered the Pacific and sailed southwest until, on October 8, she came to Choiseul Island, easternmost of the Solomon Islands (first identified by Alvaro Mendaña in 1568, though the French did not recognize them as such). Surville and his crew anchored at de Surville Island, east of Santa Isabel. On October 22, they sailed south through the Coral Sea and into the Tasman Sea in search of new lands. They narrowly missed New Caledonia, and after two months, during which scurvy ravaged the crew, they turned hopefully east to seek shelter on New Zealand, then known only from Tasman's 1642 voyage in HEEMSKERCK.

On December 12, they fell in with the land off Hokianga Harbor, about 100 miles below Cape Maria Van Diemen. Doubling the Cape, they came to anchor in what Captain James Cook had six days before named Doubtless Bay. One estimate suggests that *St. Jean-Baptiste* and Cook's ENDEAVOUR missed one another by as little as thirty miles, and certainly not more than a few days at Doubtless Bay. The Maoris proved helpful and the surviving crew soon regained their strength. After discussing the available options, Surville decided it was safer to run down the 5,000 miles to Chile before the prevailing westerlies than to risk the fickle winds and island-studded waters back to the Indies. Having kidnapped a Maori named Ranginui to retaliate for a stolen yawl boat, the French sailed on New Year's Eve 1769.

St. Jean-Baptiste crossed the Pacific in about 35°S, a higher southern latitude than any ship to that time, and thereby removed any lingering doubts about the existence of a Davis Land or Terra Australis in the central South Pacific. Nonetheless the journey took its toll, and many of the crew died, including Ranginui. The men were so enfeebled that Surville could not put ashore at Más Afuera, on March 24, 1770. Continuing to the Peruvian coast, on April 7 they made a landfall at Chilca, where Surville drowned in the surf when his boat capsized as he went ashore. First Officer Guillaume Labé took the ship to Callao, where the French were arrested and held for three years. With a crew that included 63 Spaniards recruited to make up for the 79 deaths and 23 desertions of the original crew, *St. Jean-Baptiste* sailed on April 7, 1773, and arrived back at Port-Louis, Brittany, on August 20. The voyage was a commercial disaster, and the ship and what cargo remained were auctioned.

Dunmore, *Expedition of the "St. Jean-Baptiste."*

USS ST. LÔ (CVE-63)

(ex-USS *Midway*) *Casablanca*-class aircraft carrier (1f/1m). *L/B/D:* 512.3′ × 65′ (108.1′ew) × 22.5′ (156.1m × 19.8m (32.9m) × 6.9m). *Tons:* 10,200 disp. *Hull:* steel. *Comp.:* 860. *Arm.:* 28 aircraft; 1 × 5″, 16 × 40mm. *Mach.:* geared turbines, 16,000 shp, 2 screws; 19 kts. *Built:* Henry J. Kaiser Shipbuilding Co., Inc., Vancouver, Wash.; 1943.

If renaming a ship confers bad luck on her, *St. Lô* was twice damned, having been laid down as *Chapin* and then commissioned as *Midway* before receiving the name by which she is best remembered. After ferrying aircraft to Pearl Harbor and Australia, USS *Midway* joined Rear Admiral G. F. Bogan's Carrier Support Group 1 in June 1944 and took part in the invasion of the Mariana Islands in June and July. In mid-August she was transferred to Manus, in the Admiralty Islands north of New Guinea, and from there supported Allied landings on Morotai, Moluccas, on September 15–23. On October 10, *Midway* was renamed *St. Lô*, for the site of a major Allied victory in France on July 18, and her old name was given to a new attack carrier (CVB-41).

Two days later, *St. Lô* sailed as one of six carriers of Rear Admiral C. A. F. Sprague's Task Force 3 for the invasion of Leyte, the Philippines. At dawn on October 25, Task Force 3 was about sixty miles east of Samar when it was attacked by Vice Admiral Takeo Kurita's Center Force. *St. Lô* launched her planes to attack the superior Japanese force — four battleships, eight cruisers, and eleven destroyers. Japanese surface forces sank the escort carrier GAMBIER BAY, destroyers JOHNSTON and *Hoel*, and destroyer escort *Samuel D. Roberts*. At 1050, the remaining ships came under air attack in the first kamikaze attack of the war. One plane crashed through *St. Lô*'s flight deck and detonated her magazine. Captain F. J. McKenna gave the order to abandon ship, and she sank half an hour later, in 11°10′N, 127°05′E.

U.S. Navy, *DANFS.*

ST. LOUIS

Liner (2f/2t). *L/B/D:* 543.8′ × 72.4′ × 42.1′ (165.8m × 22.1m × 12.8m). *Tons:* 16,732 grt. *Hull:* steel. *Comp.:* 973 pass. *Mach.:* oil engines, 3,060 nhp, 2 screws; 16 kts. *Built:* Bremer Vulkan Schiffban & Maschinenfabrik, Vegesack, Hamburg; 1928.

The passenger ship *St. Louis* was built for Hapag's transatlantic (Hamburg–New York) and cruising service. In May 1939, the German government decided to allow 933 Jews — some of whom had already been in concentration camps — to leave Germany. On May 13, the ship sailed from Hamburg. After a stop at Cherbourg, she arrived

The Hapag ocean liner ST. LOUIS, *scene of one of the most tragic, and easily avoidable, episodes involving Jewish emigrants in the years before World War I. Courtesy The Mariners' Museum, Newport News, Virginia.*

at Havana, Cuba, on May 27. The Cuban government, which had already accepted 2,500 refugees, had shortly before changed its immigration policy. It declined to accept the *St. Louis* passengers, 743 of whom had applied for U.S. visas and intended to remain in Cuba only until they could be admitted to the United States. While negotiations between Jewish leaders and the U.S. and Cuban governments dragged on, Captain Gustav Schroeder steamed slowly between southern Florida and Cuba until a shortage of supplies forced him back to Europe. President Franklin D. Roosevelt's draconian adherence to U.S. immigration quotas was the result of a number of factors, including overwhelming domestic — and congressional — opposition to any increase. As *St. Louis* made her way back to Europe, Jewish leaders redoubled their efforts to prevent the passengers from being returned to Germany. When the ship docked at Antwerp on June 17, 181 passengers went to the Netherlands, 288 to Britain, 224 to France, and the remainder stayed in Belgium.

St. Louis returned to regular service, and on August 27, 1939, was recalled from New York just before a run to Bermuda. The outbreak of World War II forced her to sail for Murmansk, USSR (newly allied with Germany), and she returned to Germany through Norwegian waters on New Year's Day. Severely damaged by the Royal Air Force bombing of Hamburg in 1944, the ship was broken up in 1950.

Thomas & Witts, *Voyage of the Damned.* Film: *Voyage of the Damned* (1976).

USS ST. MARY'S

Sloop-of-war (3m). *L/B/D:* 149.3′ × 37.3′ × 18′ (45.5m × 11.4m × 5.5m). *Tons:* 958 bm. *Hull:* wood. *Comp.:* 195. *Arm.:* 16 × 32pdr, 6 × 8″. *Built:* Washington Navy Yard, Washington, D.C.; 1844.

Named for the Maryland county, the U.S. Navy's second *St. Mary's* was originally slated for duty with the Mediterranean Squadron. Immediately before her departure, U.S. relations with Mexico began to deteriorate over the annexation of Texas, which Congress and President John Tyler had just approved. In March 1845, *St. Mary's* sailed in Commodore Robert Stockton's squadron to bolster U.S. forces in the Gulf of Mexico. In November, she carried John Slidell, the new minister to Mexico, to Vera Cruz, and she remained in the Gulf through the winter. When the Mexican-American War began in May 1846, she was assigned to blockade duty off Tampico and remained there intermittently through May 1847.

The following year *St. Mary's* was assigned to the Pacific Squadron, with which she cruised between California, Chile, and the Far East for five years. After a refit at Philadelphia, she returned to the Pacific for a further two years. In 1856, Commander Charles Davis took command of the ship at Panama City. His first assignment was to negotiate the surrender of William Walker, a U.S.-born buccaneer who had tried to established a personal empire in Nicaragua. Davis succeeded, but in 1860, when Walker attempted a similar intrigue in Honduras, he was captured and shot. *St. Mary's* remained on the West Coast through the Civil War. After a cruise to Australia and New Zealand in 1870, she returned to Norfolk in 1872.

Two years later, Congress transferred *St. Mary's* to the New York Nautical School. This, the first federally assisted merchant marine officer-training program, later evolved into the New York (State) Merchant Marine Academy, and formed the model upon which all other state merchant marine academies and the U.S. Merchant Marine Academy at Kings Point were modeled. *St. Mary's* served as a schoolship until 1908 when she was sold and broken up at Boston.

Mitchell, *We'll Deliver*. U.S. Navy, *DANFS*.

ST. PAUL

(*Sviatoi Pavel*) Brig. *L/B/D:* 80′ × 22.5′ × 12′ dph (24.4m × 6.9m × 3.7m). *Tons:* 360 dwt. *Hull:* wood. *Comp.:* 76. *Arm.:* 14 guns, 3 falconets. *Built:* Andrei Kuzmin, Okhotsk; 1737–40.

Sister ship of Vitus Bering's ST. PETER, after sailing from Petropavlovsk, Kamchatka (June 4, 1741), under command of Aleksei Chirikov, *St. Paul* was separated from the flagship on June 20 in about latitude 48°49′N. Steering east, on July 15, *St. Paul* reached the coast of North America near Dixon Entrance, in 54°25′N, 132°30′W. There Chirikov followed the coastline north, and three days later, he sent ashore a party of eleven men near Lisianskii Strait to get water and interview any natives about the surrounding country. Five days later, another boat was sent out to search for the men, but it too disappeared without trace. Forced to return to Kamchatka, Chirikov sailed through the Aleutian Islands and arrived at Petropavlovsk on October 12.

The following May, Chirikov once more sailed for America, to return to St. Theodore (Attu) Island, which he had seen the previous year. However, his crew were too weak to make the voyage and they returned to Okhotsk in August. Hereafter, government interest in the North Pacific waned, and *St. Paul* was laid up at Okhotsk. Chirikov and his officers returned to St. Petersburg.

Divin, *Great Russian Navigator, A. I. Chirikov*. Fisher, *Bering's Voyages*. Frost, *Bering and Chirikov*.

ST. PETER

(*Sviatoi Petr*) Brig. *L/B/D:* 80′ × 22.5′ × 12′ dph (24.2m × 6.9m × 3.7m). *Tons:* 360 dwt. *Hull:* wood. *Comp.:* 76. *Arm.:* 14 guns, 3 falconets. *Built:* Andrei Kuzmin, Okhotsk; 1740.

In 1730, fresh from his voyage in ST. GABRIEL through the Bering Strait, between Asia and North America, Vitus Bering wrote the Russian senate that "America is not far from Kamchatka, perhaps at a distance of 150 or 200 [German] miles. It is possible to arrange trade with people in America; so it is necessary to build a small cargo vessel in Kamchatka." Two years later he was authorized to build two vessels for an expedition "for the profit of the state and the enhancement of our interests." It was hoped that the core of this prosperity would be new sources of fur and gold. Recruiting master shipwright Andrei Kuzmin and mineralogist Georg W. Steller from St. Petersburg, Bering proceeded overland to Okhotsk where the ships *St. Peter* and ST. PAUL (*Sviatoi Petr* and *Sviatoi Pavel*) were built over the course of four years. In the fall of 1740, the ships departed Okhotsk and in October established winter quarters at Petropavlovsk — which takes its name from the two ships — on the Pacific coast of Kamchatka.

On June 4, 1741, the ships sailed east southeast as far as 46°N in search of the nonexistent Juan de Gama Land. Separated in a fog on June 13, *St. Peter* headed northeast, and on July 20 the Russians landed on Saint Elias (Kayak) Island. Although short of water, Bering was eager to return to Kamchatka and weighed anchor the next day. At the end of August, he was forced to stop again in the Shumagin Islands, but in his haste, he loaded brackish water, which further debilitated the weakened crew. Winter storms forced them to land on Bering Island on November 6, 400 miles from Petropavlovsk. Wracked with scurvy, by the summer the crew had lost thirty men, including Bering, who died on December 8. *St. Peter* was all but ruined, and the survivors broke her up and fashioned a smaller *St. Peter* (40 feet on the keel, 13 feet beam) in which they returned to Petropavlovsk on August 27 with 600 fur pelts.

Divin, *Great Russian Navigator, A. I. Chirikov*. Fisher, *Bering's Voyages*. Frost, *Bering and Chirikov*.

ST. PETER PORT WRECK

(1m). *L/B/D:* 82.0′ × 19.7′ × 9.8′ (25m × 6m × 3m). *Hull:* wood. *Comp.:* 3. *Built:* northwest Europe; 3rd cent. CE.

One of only two seagoing merchant vessels from the period of Roman rule in northern Europe found to date (the other is the BLACKFRIARS BARGE from London), the St. Peter Port wreck was discovered in the port of the same name on Guernsey, one of the Channel Islands off the coast of France. First identified by Richard Keen, the site was excavated by Margaret Rule and Jason Monaghan between 1984 and 1986. The dimensions cited here are interpolated from the existing remains of the vessel, which include a keel 14.1 meters long and bottom planks of a combined width of about 4 meters. From what survives of the vessel, which apparently burned sometime around the period 280–287 CE, the construction appears to resemble that of the ships of the Veneti described by Julius Caesar in his *Gallic Wars*:

> Their keels were considerably more flat than those of our own ships, that they might more easily weather shoals and ebb-tide. Their prows were very lofty, and their sterns were similarly adapted to meet the force of waves and storms. The ships were made entirely of oak, to endure any violence and buffeting. The cross-pieces were beams a foot thick, fastened with iron nails as thick as a thumb. . . . Our ships could not damage them with the ram (they were so stoutly built), nor, by reason of their height, was it easy to hurl a pike, and for the same reason they were less readily gripped by grapnels.

The vessel is of skeleton-first construction. That is, the frames were erected first and planks attached to them with iron nails. The nail holes were caulked with moss, while the builders employed a caulking of oak shavings between the planks, which were shaped by saws and adzes. Research on the ship is ongoing, and her origin is yet to be identified.

A study of the artifacts found on the site in the ship suggest that the vessel was sailed with a crew of three and traded as far south and west as the coast of Spain along the Bay of Biscay, and as far east as the North Sea. Among the finds in the ship were eighty Roman coins, the grouping of which suggests that they were originally held in a container of some sort, together with pottery amphorae, cooking pots, bowls and other vessels, fragments of wooden barrels, and Roman tiles (possibly from the deck house), as well as traces of grain and other foodstuffs.

Caesar, *Gallic Wars*. Rule & Monaghan, *Gallo-Roman Trading Vessel from Guernsey*.

ST. ROCH

Aux. schooner (1f/2m). *L/B/D:* 104.3′ bp × 24.8′ × 13′ (31.8m × 7.5m × 4m). *Tons:* 323 disp. *Hull:* wood. *Comp.:* 9. *Mach.:* diesel, 150 hp. *Built:* Burrard Dry Dock Co., Ltd., North Vancouver, B.C.; 1928.

Built for the Royal Canadian Mounted Police service in the Arctic, the patrol vessel *St. Roch* was named for the fourteenth-century French saint celebrated for his gift of healing. Norwegian-born RCMP Staff Sergeant Henry Larsen joined the ship on her first voyage and became

The Royal Canadian Mounted Police auxiliary schooner ST. ROCH, *on patrol in loose Arctic ice in northern Canada. Courtesy Vancouver Maritime Museum.*

master in August 1928. The first ten years of *St. Roch's* career were spent patrolling the Eskimo communities of the Western Arctic, returning to Vancouver via the Bering Strait for fresh supplies and crew every summer. In 1940, concerned about establishing uncontested sovereignty over the islands of the Canadian Arctic, the government ordered Larsen "to proceed, if possible, from Vancouver, British Columbia, on patrol to Halifax, Nova Scotia, via the Canadian Arctic, if there was sufficient time left after . . . duties in the Western Arctic."

On June 23, 1940, *St. Roch* sailed north through the Bering Strait into the Arctic Sea fully expecting to attempt the passage that year, but made it only as far as Victoria Island. The next spring, wartime shipping shortage obliged Larsen to return to Vancouver to load more supplies for the northern communities. Setting out from Cambridge Bay in August 1941, *St. Roch* made it as far as the Boothia Peninsula where the crew wintered in Pasley Bay. One of the crew, Albert Chartrand, died of a heart attack, and Larsen and two of the crew walked 1,140 miles to fetch a Catholic priest to conduct a funeral for him the following spring. When the ice broke up in August, they proceeded through Bellot Strait, a narrow defile measuring eighteen miles long and one mile wide. From there they made for Lancaster Strait, south into the Davis Strait, and put into Halifax, Nova Scotia, on October 11, 1942. *St. Roch* was the first ship to have made the Northwest Passage from east to west, and after Roald Amundsen's GJØA only the second ship to have made the passage in either direction.

In 1943, *St. Roch* was employed in servicing communities in the Eastern Arctic for a season before being fitted with a new 300-horsepower engine and rerigged as a ketch. In 1944, Larsen was ordered to return to Vancouver. Rather than go back by Amundsen's route, the way he had come, he decided to sail north around Victoria Island via the McClure and Prince of Wales Straits. From Holman Island, he raced the encroaching ice in a successful effort to avoid wintering in the Arctic. He sailed through the Bering Strait in September and was back in Vancouver on October 16. Having covered 7,295 miles in 86 days, *St. Roch* was the first ship to make the Northwest Passage in a single season. After two more voyages to the Western Arctic in 1945–46 and 1947–48, she returned to Halifax. Upon her arrival, it was decided that she was no longer fit for Arctic voyaging and she was laid up. In Vancouver, public sentiment for the ship was strong, and in 1954 funds were raised to return the ship to her homeport. Today the Arctic veteran is preserved in a tent-shaped building erected by the Vancouver Maritime Museum.

Delgado, *Dauntless "St. Roch."* Larsen, *The Big Ship.*

USS SALT LAKE CITY (CL-25)

Pensacola-class cruiser (2f/2m). *L/B/D:* 585.7' × 65.3' × 19.5' (178.5m × 19.9m × 5.9m). *Tons:* 11,512 disp. *Hull:* steel. *Comp.:* 631. *Arm.:* 10 × 8" (2 × 3, 2 × 2), 4 × 5", 2 × 3pdr; 6 × 21"TT; 4 aircraft. *Armor:* 3" belt, 1" deck. *Mach.:* geared turbines, 107,000 hp, 4 screws; 32.5 kts. *Built:* American Brown Boveri Electric Corp., Camden, N.J.; 1929.

Most of USS *Salt Lake City's* prewar career was spent with the Pacific Fleet, which she first joined in 1932. The Japanese attack on Pearl Harbor found her escorting the aircraft carrier ENTERPRISE en route from Wake Island to Hawaii. Following the fall of Wake at the end of December, she escorted supply forces bound for Midway. Arriving in the southwest Pacific in time to cover the withdrawal of YORKTOWN from the Battle of the Coral Sea in April, *Salt Lake City* was part of the rearguard at Midway in June. She then sailed in support of the Guadalcanal landings and helped rescue survivors of WASP when the carrier was torpedoed on September 15.

Assigned to Task Force 64 for the Solomons campaign, *Salt Lake City* was one of four cruisers — the others were *Boise, Helena,* and *San Francisco* — and five destroyers at the Battle of Cape Esperance on October 11–12. In a somewhat confused thirty-five-minute engagement, the Japanese lost one of three heavy cruisers and one of two destroyers, with two ships badly damaged. American losses included one destroyer, with several ships damaged, including *Boise* and *Salt Lake City,* which returned to Pearl Harbor.

In March 1943, under Captain Bertram J. Rodgers, *Salt Lake City* was dispatched together with light cruiser *Richmond* and four destroyers to thwart the reinforcement of Japanese bases in the Aleutian Islands. On the morning of March 26, the American fleet was engaged by a Japanese force of four cruisers and four destroyers at a range of 10,000 yards. In what Samuel Eliot Morison has called "the last heavy gunfire daylight action, with no interference by air power, submarines or torpedoes," *Salt Lake City* was brought to a standstill by eight-inch shells from *Maya* and *Nachi.* But aggressive maneuvers by *Bailey, Coghlan,* and *Monaghan* prompted Vice Admiral B. Hosogaya to withdraw his force, including the transports. Despite her damage, *Salt Lake City* remained in the Aleutians until the U.S. landings in May.

After repairs at San Francisco, she joined the forces gathering for the assault on the Gilbert Islands in October. The next year was spent in a variety of missions that took her from the Central Pacific to the West Coast and back to the Aleutians. Part of the Philippines invasion force in October 1944, *Salt Lake City* later provided fire support at Iwo Jima and Okinawa. In September, she sailed to northern Honshu to lend support to the Occupation. In 1946, *Salt Lake City* survived two atomic bomb tests at Bikini Atoll. She met her end as a target ship off southern California in 1948.

U.S. Navy, *DANFS.*

SAN ESTÉBAN

L/B: ca. 65.9′ × 21.3′ (20.1m × 6.5m). *Hull:* wood. *Comp.:* ca. 100. *Built:* Spain(?); <1550.

On November 4, 1552, fifty-four vessels under Captain General Bartolomé Carreño set sail from Sanlúcar de Barrameda, Spain. Twenty-four of the ships were bound for Tierra Firme (the mainland of South and Central America), sixteen for San Juan de Ulúa in Mexico, ten for Santo Domingo, and four for ports in Puerto Rico and Puerto de Plata. Of those bound for San Juan de Ulúa, the port for Vera Cruz, only four were slated for the return trip: *San Estéban,* probably the largest ship in the convoy, under Francisco del Huerto; *Espíritu Santo,* under Damián Martín; *San Andrés,* under Antonio Corzo; and *Santa María de Yciar,* under Alonso Ojos and her owner and pilot Miguel de Jáuregui. The ships carried a range of goods, including wine, clothing, textiles, vinegar, fruit, soap, olives, oils, lead, and wax for church candles. Despite the importance of these cargoes to Spain's outposts in the New World, and the ever-pressing need for gold and silver in Spain, in the 1550s the transatlantic passage was considered too hazardous to risk good ships, and only twelve of the fifty-four were due to return to Spain. The rest, worn out from hard service elsewhere, would be scrapped. It is not surprising, then, to read Fray Perpetuo's complaint to the Council of the Indies of ships "leaking water like sieves and so laden with merchandise and people that they could neither navigate nor defend themselves." The fleet was at the mercy of the elements and French corsairs, and eight were lost on the outward passage, among them Carreño's flagship, *Nuestra Señora de la Concepción,* which burned to the waterline with the loss of all but twenty (including Carreño) of her three hundred passengers and crew.

After watering at Dominica, the ships split up for the final leg of their respective voyages. Those bound for New Spain sailed between Cuba and Jamaica, through the Yucatan Channel and south along the coast to Vera Cruz. *Santa María de Yciar* and *San Andrés* arrived at San Juan de Ulúa on March 5, *San Estéban* and *Espíritu Santo* on March 25. Because the port had recently been ravaged by a hurricane, there were delays in unloading. They were unable to return to Spain that season, and had to wait for the arrival of the fleet in 1554. The only one of the four ships whose manifest for the return passage survives is that of *Santa María de Yciar.* She carried 243 individual shipments, including 25,000 pesos of the king's gold, the maximum amount that any one ship was legally allowed to carry. In addition to gold and silver, her cargo consisted of 22,000 pounds of cochineal (a red dyestuff derived from insects), cowhides, resins, sugar, silk, sarsaparilla root, and personal possessions. She also carried ten pieces of heavy ordnance, thirty-two swivels, and assorted smaller firearms, and her complement comprised twenty-seven crew and forty passengers, including six women.

On April 9, 1554, the four ships sailed for Havana to rendezvous with the ships returning to Spain from elsewhere in the Caribbean. Twenty days later, they were caught in a storm in the Gulf of Mexico and three of them wrecked on what is now Padre Island, Texas, about forty-five miles north of the Rio Grande. (Corzo's *San Andrés* weathered the storm, but was condemned upon her arrival in Havana.) A small number of survivors sailed to San Juan de Ulúa in one or two of the ships' boats, while the other two hundred or so began the long march overland. Beset by hostile Indians, environment, and terrain, only a handful reached Spanish territory. In the meantime, six ships were dispatched to salvage what they could of the gold and silver from *Santa María de Yciar, San Estéban,* and *Espíritu Santo.* Diving began on July 23, and the salvors recovered 35,804 pounds of the approximately 87,000 pounds of treasure now estimated to have been aboard the three ships.

In the 1950s, a navigation channel happened to be cut directly over the wreck of *Santa María de Yciar,* and in 1967 treasure hunters began diving on *Espíritu Santo,* though they were stopped by the Texas government. In 1972, the Texas Antiquities Commission authorized the archaeological excavation of the *San Estéban* site. Finds included seven anchors, iron fastenings, chains, rudder fittings, ship armament (including one verso and three bombards), navigational instruments (including sounding weights, dividers, astrolabes and sounding leads), pottery, small amounts of gold and silver bullion, and 358 silver and gold coins. Of the ship itself, only a few timbers survive, the most important of which comprise a 5.1-meter-long section of the keel and part of the sternpost. Based on these fragments, it has been estimated that the ship had a length of 20 to 21 meters and a beam of 5.5 to 5.6 meters.

Arnold & Weddle, *Nautical Archaeology of Padre Island.* Rosloff & Arnold, "Keel of the *San Estéban.*"

SAN FRANCISCO

Sidewheel steamship (2f/2m). *L/B/D:* 285' od × 41' × 12' (86.9m × 12.5m × 3.7m). *Hull:* wood. *Comp.:* 350 1st, 1,000 steerage. *Mach.:* oscillating engine, 2,000 hp, sidewheels; 8.5 kts. *Built:* William H. Webb, New York; 1853.

Built for W. H. Aspinwall & Company's Pacific Mail Steamship Company, *San Francisco's* patent condenser was removed after three trial runs. Despite the need to rework the engine, Aspinwall accepted a $75,000 contract to carry the U.S. Army's Third Artillery Regiment to California. Under Captain Watkins, *San Francisco* sailed from New York on December 22, 1853, with approximately 750 passengers and crew, including women and children, and so much coal that 300 of the soldiers were camped on deck. At 0330 on Christmas Day, the ship was laboring in a gale when the air pump broke and the engines failed. At 0700 the upper saloon and its 160 occupants were swept off the ship. To add to the terror, there were many cases of cholera and several children had come aboard with measles. On December 28, about 100 people were transferred to the bark *Kilby.* (They were taken to New York in the Down Easter *Lucy Thompson* on January 14.) On New Year's Day, the British clipper *Three Bells* under Captain Crighton hove to, and on January 3 the *Antarctic.* On January 4 the weather moderated and the remainder of the ship's company was transferred. *Antarctic* sailed for Liverpool with 192 people, and *Three Bells* landed at New York to a hero's welcome on January 13. All told, 246 people died, 60 succumbing to cholera.

Crichton, "Wreck of *San Francisco.*" Stackpole, *Wreck of the Steamer "San Francisco."*

USS SAN JACINTO

Screw frigate (3m). *L/B/D:* 237' × 37.8' × 17.3' (72.2m × 11.5m × 5.3m). *Tons:* 2,150 disp. *Hull:* wood. *Comp.:* 235. *Arm.:* 6 × 8″. *Mach.:* horizontal condensing engines, 500 hp, 1 screw; 11 kts. *Des.:* Hartt. *Built:* New York Navy Yard, Brooklyn, N.Y.; 1852.

The U.S. Navy's second screw frigate was named for the site of Sam Houston's victory over the Mexican Army in 1836. Built to an experimental design, USS *San Jacinto* was fitted with an off-center propeller shaft. Her greatest defect was her engines, which were replaced after only one year of faulty service. Recommissioned in 1854, she sailed in European and Caribbean waters for a year before assignment as flagship of the East India Squadron. Sailing via the Cape of Good Hope as flagship of Commodore James Armstrong, in April 1852, *San Jacinto* conveyed Townsend Harris to Siam (Thailand) to negotiate the first U.S. treaty with that country. From there she proceeded to Shimoda, where in August Harris established the first foreign consulate in Japan. *San Jacinto* remained in the Far East for two years, protecting U.S. merchant interests and landing marines to fight Chinese troops at Whampoa and Canton during the Second Opium War, which ended with the Treaties of Tientsin between China, Britain, the United States, France, and Russia in 1858.

Returning to the United States that same year, *San Jacinto* next joined the Africa Squadron, and on August 8, 1860, she captured the brig *Storm King* from which 616 slaves were freed at Monrovia, Liberia. She remained on station until August 27, 1861, when she sailed for the United States under Captain Charles Wilkes, returning via the Caribbean where she searched unsuccessfully for Captain Raphael Semmes's CSS *Sumter.* On November 8, Wilkes intercepted the Royal Mail steamer TRENT about 230 miles east of Havana and arrested the Southern diplomats James Mason and John Slidell who were en route to their posts in England. The *Trent* Affair strained relations between the United States and Britain until the Southerners' release in 1862.

In March 1862, *San Jacinto* took part in naval operations of the Peninsular Campaign in Virginia before proceeding to the East Gulf Blockading Squadron at Key West. From then on, her duties varied between blockade duty in the Gulf and off North Carolina, and the pursuit of ALABAMA (from October 1862 to January 1863), FLORIDA, and TALLAHASSEE. In the interim, she spent most of her time on blockade off Mobile, Alabama, where she captured four prizes. *San Jacinto* was lost on New Year's Day 1865 after hitting a reef near Great Abaco Island, Bahamas.

U.S. Navy, *DANFS.*

SAN JERÓNIMO

Tons: 150 tons. *Built:* Guayaquil, Ecuador(?); <1605.

Although Alvaro Mendaña sought to establish a colony in the Solomon Islands, which he discovered on his heroic but fruitless voyage of 1567–69 in LOS REYES and *Todos Los Santos,* it was not until 1574 that he secured in Spain authorization to take 500 men (50 of them with their wives and children), as well as cattle, horses, goats, sheep, and pigs for breeding, to fortify three cities within six years. No sooner was this done than Mendaña was arrested on a trumped-up charge. By the time he was free, Francis Drake had entered the Pacific in GOLDEN HIND, "whereupon commandment was given that [the Solomons] should not be inhabited; that the English, or others who pass the Straits of Magalhanes to go to the Malucas, might have no succour there but such as they got of the Indians."

Mendaña languished in Peru for the next fifteen years, but on April 5, 1595, he set sail with four ships — *San Jerónimo* (purchased from Sebastian de Goite y Figueroa), *Santa Ysabel,* the frigate *Santa Catalina,* and the galliot *San Felipe* — and 386 emigrants including his wife, Doña Ysabel de Barreto, and her three brothers. The chief pilot was Pedro Fernández de Quirós. The ships first sailed through the Marquesas Islands, which Mendaña named for the Viceroy Marquesas de Mendoza. Mendaña's lack of leadership plagued the expedition and contributed to the murder of 200 Marquesans, most of whom were killed with little or no provocation.

Running west in about 10°S, the ships next passed between the Ellice and Cook Islands, but before they reached the Solomons, they came to Santa Cruz Island, six degrees east of San Cristóbal. At the same time, *Santa Ysabel* disappeared, possibly sinking during an eruption of Tinakula volcano, fifteen miles away. After making a start at a colony, the soldiers — who treated the inhabitants ruthlessly — grew restive and decided they wanted to leave. Mendaña killed the camp master in an effort to restore order and allegiance to himself, but he was ailing and died a few days later, on October 18, leaving command of the expedition to his wife. Sickness descended on the camp, and it was not until November 18 that the three remaining ships sailed. On December 10, near the equator, *San Felipe* disappeared, only to arrive independently at Mindanao. Though those aboard *San Jerónimo* and *Santa Catalina* were starving or dying of thirst at the rate of more than one person a day, Mendaña's widow refused to share her provisions with the ship's company, and even used the scarce water to wash her clothes. On December 19, Quirós asked to bring the few survivors from *Santa Catalina* aboard his ship, but the governess refused and the frigate disappeared.

On December 23, the Spanish sighted Ponape, in the Carolines, but were unable to land here or, on January 1, 1596, at either Guam or Rota in the Marianas. Finally, on January 12, *San Jerónimo* reached the Philippines, where the crew found food. On February 11, Quirós's ship arrived at Manila; fifty of her complement died en route.

> There was not a yard that was not bent downward owing to parted lifts, the topsail ties were gone, and perhaps for three days at a time the sail was flapping in the waist because no one cared to hoist it with a rope that had been spliced thirty-three times.

Mendaña's widow remarried and, with her new husband, refit the ship for the return to Mexico on August 10, 1596; they arrived at Acapulco on December 11. *San Felipe* eventually reached Mindanao but neither the frigate *Santa Catalina* nor *Santa Ysabel* was ever heard from again, except for a vague report that the latter was run ashore on some unknown island and seen rotting with her crew.

Quirós, *Voyages of Fernández de Quirós.*

SAN JUAN

Galleon (3m). *L:* ca. 50′ (keel) (15m). *Tons:* 250–300 tons. *Hull:* wood. *Comp.:* 75. *Built:* Guipuzcoa, Spain(?); <1565.

San Juan was a Basque whaler lost in Red Bay, Labrador, in 1565. Owned by Ramos de Arrieta y Borda of Pasajes (de Fuenterrabia), she was part of the Basque fleet that sent as many as thirty ships a year in the mid-sixteenth century to work the Strait of Belle Isle whale fisheries between Newfoundland and Labrador. According to documents filed in Spain and archaeological evidence gathered in the 1980s, *San Juan* was apparently loading barrels of oil for the return to Spain when a strong northerly wind drove her onto the rocks near Saddle Island. Whether anyone was lost with the ship is unknown, but another whaler, *La Concepción,* embarked most of the crew together with what supplies could be salvaged from the ship. In addition, according to Simon de Echaniz, "the outfitter of the ship, Joannes de Portu, returned to Red Bay the following year in another ship . . . and took all the barrels that he could from the lost ship and sent them back to Spain and other places."

In 1978, government archaeologists located the wreck in Red Bay, near one of three known encampments that the whalers used during the whaling season. Parks Canada began excavation the next year. Finds on the site included barrel staves and tops, the jawbone of a whale (apparently stowed in the hold at the time of the sinking), the ship's capstan, fragments of ceramic pottery, and pieces of the ship's pump and pump well. Between 1979 and 1984, archaeologists carefully disassembled the remains of the ship for conservation and study ashore. These included approximately 3,000 individual timbers comprising 44 ceiling planks, 210 exterior planks, 230 futtocks, 50 floor timbers, and other structural and miscellaneous elements. At the same time, archaeologists from the University of Newfoundland have been studying the nearby Basque whaling station found on Red Bay.

Tuck & Grenier, "Sixteenth-Century Basque Whaling Station in Labrador." Waddell, "Disassembly of a Sixteenth-Century Galleon."

SAN MARTÍN

Galleon (3m). *Tons:* 1,000 tons. *Hull:* wood. *Comp.:* 650. *Arm.:* 48 guns. *Built:* Portugal(?); <1588.

Best known as the Duke of Medina Sidonia's *capitana general,* or flagship, in the Spanish Armada in 1588, the galleon *San Martín* was originally built as a Portuguese warship. Brought into the Spanish Navy following Philip II's annexation of Portugal in 1580, she sailed as *capitana* of Don Alonzo Bazan, Marqués of Santa Cruz, when the Spanish defeated a French fleet of 75 ships at the Battle of Terceiro in the Azores on July 25, 1582. Sometime thereafter, Philip began formulating his ambitious plan for an amphibious invasion of England using troops gathered under the Duke of Parma at Nieuport and Dunkirk in the Spanish Netherlands. To accomplish this, Medina Sidonia assembled a fleet of 130 ships. These included his own Squadron of Portugal with 12 ships; those of Biscay, 14; Castile, 16; Andalusia, 11; Guipuzcoa, 14; and Levant, 10. Other warships included 4 Neapolitan galleasses and 4 Portuguese galleys. In addition, the Spanish chartered from Hanseatic merchants in the Baltic 23 hulks (or *urcas*) as storeships, and they had 22 pinnaces — *zabras* and *pataches* — that served as dispatch boats and scouts. Of the 30,000 people in the Armada ships, more than 19,000 were soldiers intended to fight with Parma's forces. Ranged against this formidable assemblage, the English had about 197 ships: 34 royal ships belonging to the Crown, 105 merchant ships, and 58 victuallers and coasters, with a combined complement of just under 16,000 men.

La Felicissima Armada — "the most blessed fleet" — assembled at Lisbon in the spring of 1588, and on May 30, they sailed, but plagued by inadequate supplies of food and water (some had been poorly stowed, some had simply rotted over the winter), most of the fleet put into La Coruña. From there the fleet set out again on July 22. A week later, the Spanish were off Plymouth, minus the four galleys, which fled to port in the face of the Atlantic gales, and the Biscayan galleon *Santa Ana.* Medina Sidonia was intent on maintaining his ships in a defensive formation as they stood up the Channel, but they could not entirely avoid confrontations with the English. Al-

though the more numerous English ships were in general smaller and more lightly armed than their opponents, their guns had greater range and they could engage the Spanish without coming under fire or risking a boarding action, in which case the Spanish would certainly have had the upper hand.

On Sunday, July 31, the English ships made their first attack on the Spanish, but as it was evident from their actions that the English wanted to avoid a boarding action at all costs, Medina Sidonia ordered his ships to advance up the Channel. The English pursued them through the night, and although there were no significant engagements on August 1, Sir Francis Drake, in RE-VENGE, captured NUESTRA SEÑORA DEL ROSARIO. The next day saw major engagements off Portland Bill. The first, between Spanish and English galleons, was initiated by the Spanish, who had the weather gauge, but when the Spanish sought to close with Lord Howard of Effingham's ARK ROYAL, he stood out to sea to avoid a boarding action. The Mediterranean galleasses had meanwhile tried to cut out six English ships, including Martin Frobisher's *Triumph.* In the ensuing melee, *San Martín* herself was cut off for more than an hour and engaged closely by *Ark Royal.* By August 4, the Armada was south of the Isle of Wight when *San Martín* was again isolated and engaged by Frobisher. Damaged below the waterline, the Spanish flagship was eventually rescued by other ships in the squadron.

At this point, both fleets had spent a lot of gunpowder and ammunition, though to relatively little effect, and there were no ship actions for the next few days. By August 6, the Spanish had crossed the Channel to anchor in the exposed roadstead at Calais. The English fleet — now numbering about 140 ships, with the arrival of Seymour's fleet — gathered to the southeast and at a council of war determined to launch a fireship attack. On the night of August 7–8, eight ships were commandeered between 90 and 200 tons; the ships were loaded with combustibles and, with guns double-shotted, set on fire to sail downwind of the Spanish ships. Good seamanship enabled the Spanish to avoid the fireships in some order, and they lost only one ship to grounding — the galleass *San Lorenzo* — though many ships lost their anchors in their haste to get under way. More important, Medina Sidonia had lost an anchorage and there was nowhere his ships could go between Calais and Parma's (still unready) transports at Dunkirk.

The last and most hotly contested battle between the two fleets was fought off Gravelines on August 8. The initial focus of the battle was *San Martín,* which fought a rearguard action at the edge of the sandbanks that run from Calais up the Dutch coast. More units of both fleets joined the battle, fought at close range, and at least four Spanish ships were lost. When the battle was over, the Spanish fleet was kept off the coast by the shallows and the adverse wind and tide. By August 9, it was clear that there was little choice for the once "invincible" armada but to sail into the North Sea, around Scotland and Ireland, for home. Little did anyone imagine that only 67 Spanish ships would return to Spanish ports, nearly 50 having been lost at sea or wrecked on the rocky coasts that ring the British Isles. "Thus," as it is recorded in Hakluyt, "the magnificent, huge, and mighty fleet of the Spaniards (which themselves termed in all places invincible) such as sayled not upon the Ocean sea many hundreth years before, in the yeere 1588 vanished into smoke; to the great confusion and discouragement of its authors." *San Martín* returned to Santander on September 23, though 180 of her crew soldiers and crew who had survived the fighting succumbed to disease and privation. *San Martín*'s subsequent fate is unknown.

Hakluyt, *Principal Navigations*. Mattingly, *Armada*. Rodríguez-Salgado, *Armada: 1588–1988*.

SAN PEDRO

Nao (3m). *Tons:* 100 tons. *Hull:* wood. *Comp.:* 47. *Arm.:* 6 × 3pdr. *Built:* Peru(?); <1597.

In 1597, Pedro Fernández de Quirós, a veteran of Alvaro Mendaña's SAN JERÓNIMO, began planning an expedition to find Terra Australis. Seven years later he assembled three ships at Callao, the 100-tonners *San Pedro y San Pablo* and *San Pedro* (commanded by Luis Baéz de Torres and nicknamed *San Pedrico*), and the 20-ton *Los Tres Reyes*. The fleet sailed on December 21, 1605, and headed west along 26°S for thirteen weeks, when the ships arrived at the Duff Group (Taumaco Island). After nine days they turned south for the New Hebrides and Espiritu Santo, where they stayed six weeks. Here, on June 11, 1606, Quirós secretly withdrew from the expedition and returned to Mexico in *San Pedro y San Pablo*.

Command of the expedition fell to Torres, and on June 26, *San Pedro* and *Los Tres Reyes* sailed into the Coral Sea. Ten days later they turned north and on July 14 arrived in the Louisiade Archipelago. From here they made their way west along southern New Guinea, anchoring about August 28 off Port Moresby. Three days later they began threading their way across what Torres called "*el placer*," the shallow, coral-strewn waters of the Gulf of Papua, and about October 2, they sailed through the strait separating New Guinea from Australia's Cape York Peninsula. This transit established that New Guinea was not the "mainland of the summit of the antarctic pole," as had been thought. Unfortunately, Torres's official reports were filed in Spain to prevent any intelligence from the voyage falling into the wrong hands. They were not rediscovered until 1770, the same year that Cook passed through Torres Strait — as it became known after about 1775 — in ENDEAVOUR.

Once safely through, *San Pedro* and *Los Tres Reyes* sailed along southwestern New Guinea. On November 9, 1606, they arrived at Kepulauan Fam, between New Guinea and the Moluccas Islands. Here they met a Portuguese-speaking local who told them they were only five days from Ternate, which Philippines-based Spaniards had seized seven months before. Torres remained at Ternate from January 6 to May 1, 1607, before sailing for Manila, where *San Pedro* arrived on May 22; *Los Tres Reyes* had been left at Ternate. Remarkably, none of the crew had died from disease in the seventeen-month voyage. The ship also carried twenty New Guineans, one of whom is believed to have traveled to Spain and been painted by Velázquez. The subsequent careers of Torres and *San Pedro* are unknown.

Hilder, *Voyage of Torres*.

SAN PEDRO Y PABLO

Nao (3m). *Tons:* 100 tons. *Hull:* wood. *Built:* Peru; <1605.

The chief pilot and savior of Alvaro Mendaña's ill-fated expedition to the Santa Cruz Islands, Pedro Fernández de Quirós concluded that those islands, Mendaña's Solomons and New Guinea, must lie near one another, and that Terra Australis must be nearby as well. Backed by Pope Clement VIII and Philip III of Spain, the pious Quirós was given a fleet of three ships, *San Pedro y Paulo,* SAN PEDRO (under Luis Vaez de Torres), and the *zabra,* or launch, *Los Tres Reyes Magos*. Embarking 300 sailors, soldiers, and friars and sufficient provisions to establish a colony, the fleet sailed from Callao, Peru, on December 21, 1605. Quirós first sailed west-southwest to 26°S, then on January 22 turned west-northwest. Four days later he sighted Ducie Island (near Pitcairn) and on February 10 the ships landed briefly on Hao Island in the Tuamotus. Pressing on, in 10°40′S Quirós turned west, sailing through the Cook Islands in search of Santa Cruz where he knew he could get food and water for his restless crew. It was not until April that the ships anchored at Taumako atoll, where they learned they were five days from Santa Cruz (60 miles to the southwest). With his crews freshly provisioned, Quirós resumed his search for Terra Australis, heading first southeast then southwest, until on May 3 the ships came to what he believed to be the southern continent. He named it Austrialia (for Philip's House of Austria) del Espiritu Santo, the largest island in Vanuatu. Despite his initial enthusiasm, Quirós decided to leave after only three weeks. Once at sea, he changed his mind again, but foul weather prevented *San Pedro y Pablo* from regaining the land, and Torres was left with SAN PEDRO and *Los Tres Reyes Magos* to fend for themselves.

Quirós tried again to find Santa Cruz, but gave up and sailed north to the Marshall Islands. The inadequacies of seventeenth-century navigation and geographical knowledge can be judged from the fact that on July 23 Quirós and his pilots believed themselves about 2,700 miles from Mexico and 2,400 miles from the Philippines, which left about 4,000 miles of the Pacific unaccounted for. Nonetheless, they climbed into the high latitudes and turned for Mexico with the westerlies at their backs and arrived at Acapulco on November 23, 1606. Quirós had neither located Terra Australis nor founded a new settlement, and it was Torres who made the most significant — if not immediately appreciated — contribution to geography, by finding the passage between New Guinea and Australia. Quirós turned over *San Pedro y Pablo* to the Viceroy of Mexico, and the next year the ship was sent to the Philippines.

Beaglehole, *Exploration of the Pacific.* Kelly, *Austrialia del Espiritu Santo.* Quirós, *Voyages of Pedro Fernández de Quirós.*

SANTA MARÍA

Nao (3m). *L/B/D:* 58′–86′ × 19′–26′ × 10′–11′ dph (18–27m × 6–8m × 3m). *Tons:* 108–239 toneladas. *Hull:* wood. *Comp.:* 40. *Arm.:* 9cm lombard, 4.5cm falconets. *Built:* Galicia, Spain; 1492.

One of the single most important voyages in history was the first of Christopher Columbus's four voyages from Spain to the Americas between 1492 and 1502. Columbus had no intention of discovering anything other than a direct route to the Orient, "the land of India and the great island of Cipango [Japan] and the realms of the Great Khan," that is, Cathay, or China. His estimates of the distances involved — 2,400 miles from the Canary Islands to Japan and 3,550 miles to China — were wide of the mark. The actual distances are 10,600 miles and 11,766 miles, as the crow flies. Nonetheless, although Columbus landed in South America and Central America on his last voyage, he died in the belief that the Orient was only ten days from Honduras.

Columbus first approached João II of Portugal, who declined to sponsor him, although Portugal had been funding exploratory expeditions down the coast of Africa for about fifty years. In 1485, Columbus moved to Los Palos de la Frontera, Spain, with a view to interesting Ferdinand and Isabella of Castile in the same venture, and in this he was ultimately successful. When Columbus received his commission, the citizens of Palos furnished him with two caravels, NIÑA and PINTA, in satisfaction of a fine levied against the town by Ferdinand and Isabella. Columbus also hired the *nao Santa María,* a merchant ship from Galicia whose owner, Juan de la Cosa, sailed as pilot.

Although *naos* were larger than caravels, and *Santa María* was large enough for Columbus to make her his *capitana,* or flagship, she was not an especially large ship for her day. Sometimes called *La Gallega,* an epithet referring to her Galician origins, she had three masts. The mizzen carried a single fore-and-aft lateen sail, the main mast two square sails, a course, and a topsail, and the foremast a single square sail. There was also a square spritsail set from the bowsprit. In good weather, the area of the mainsail could be increased by the addition of two bonnets — spare lengths of canvas that could be laced to the foot of the course. The helmsman steered with a tiller that led to a rudder. With one deck and a year's provisions, there were few creature comforts, and sleeping quarters were fairly rude. (Crew accommodations in European ships improved markedly after Columbus's crew adopted the hammocks they found in the Caribbean.) For auxiliary power, the ship could be pulled by a heavy yawl boat or rowed by wooden sweeps. Columbus found *Santa María* a dull sailer, and he complained that her draft was too deep to make her useful for exploration.

Sailing from Palos on August 3, 1492, *Santa María* and *Niña* arrived at the island of Gomera in the Canary Islands on August 12. *Pinta*'s rudder trouble had forced her into Las Palmas, where *Santa María* and *Niña* put back to on August 25. The trio sailed for Gomera and finally resumed their westward voyage on September 6. Light airs kept them in sight of the Canaries until the 9th. Thereafter they met favorable winds. They reached the Sargasso Sea (about 32°W longitude) on the 16th, and three days later they were out of the trade winds. There followed about a week of light and variable winds. On September 25, *Niña*'s Vicente Yáñez Pinzón made the first false landfall. Conditions improved considerably between October 2 and 6, when they made 710 miles, including their best run of 182 miles in 24 hours. The next day, they made their second false landfall while still about 400 miles east of the Bahamas, but close enough to land to follow the path of birds heading southwest. Nonetheless, by the 10th the crew of *Santa María* were near mutiny and Columbus apparently agreed to put about within a few days if they did not sight land. The next day, the appearance of manmade artifacts and tree branches confirmed that land must be near.

All eyes strained to be the first to see the new shore (Ferdinand and Isabella had promised a reward of 10,000 maravedís, the equivalent of 10 months' pay for a seaman); at about 2200 that night Columbus believed he saw a light in the distance. Four hours later, at about 0200 on October 12, *Pinta*'s lookout Rodrigo de Triana saw the Taino Indian island of Guanahaní, in what is now the Bahamas, where they landed later that morning. Columbus gave this island the name San Salvador, although the English later renamed it Watlings Island. When it was realized that Watlings had a strong claim to a historical pedigree, they renamed it San Salvador. Most important, the Tainos wore jewelry made of gold — a chief object of the Spaniards' adventure.

Sailing through the Bahamas for two weeks, the little fleet crossed south to Cuba on October 27. They explored the north coast of that island for six weeks, sailing as far west as Puerto Padre. At the beginning of November, Columbus dispatched an embassy to the inland village of Holguín, hopeful that it would prove to be a major Asiatic capital. He was disappointed to learn that his interpreter, Luis de Torres — whose languages included Hebrew, Aramaic, and Arabic — could make no headway. On November 20, the three ships made a tentative foray in the direction of the Bahamas, but, while trying to return to Cuba, Martín Alonso Pinzón in *Pinta* split off from the others to investigate Great Inagua Island, and he was gone until the New Year.

After completing their investigation of northeast Cuba, on December 5 *Santa María* and *Niña* sailed east to Cape St. Nicholas, the northwestern tip of Hispaniola in what is now Haiti. On December 12 at Moustique Bay, they took possession of the land in the name of Ferdinand and Isabella. The presence of more gold artifacts and the friendliness of the local cacique, Guacanagarí, encouraged the explorers. But while working their way eastward, tragedy struck on Christmas Eve. The only man awake aboard the ship seems to have been a ship's boy at the tiller, for the master of midwatch, Juan de la Cosa, and the helmsman had fallen asleep. Shortly after midnight, *Santa María* grounded on a coral reef. No one was killed, but the ship was ruined and Christmas Day was spent salvaging what could be saved from the flagship. It would have been virtually impossible to cross the Atlantic with more than sixty men in *Niña*, so thirty-nine crew from *Santa María* and *Niña* volunteered to remain at La Navidad, in a fort fashioned from the flagship's timbers. *Niña* sailed on January 4, 1493, rejoining *Pinta* at Isla Cabra two days later for the voyage home. As fate would have it, none of the men who stayed in Hispaniola would survive to greet Columbus on his return in November 1493.

A number of replicas of Columbus's ships have been built since the 400th anniversary of the first voyage. As there are neither detailed descriptions nor plans of any of the ships — or their contemporaries — the dimensions have varied significantly. José Martínez-Hidalgo's designs for the 1992 replicas, based in part on the MATARÓ SHIP model, are described in Xavier Pastor's *Ships of Christopher Columbus*.

Morison, *Admiral of the Ocean Sea*. Pastor, *Ships of Christopher Columbus*. Philips, "Evolution of Spanish Ship Design." Smith, *Vanguard of Empire*.

SANTA MARIA

Liner (1f/1m). *L/B:* 608.9′ loa × 75.8′ (185.6m x 23.1m). *Tons:* 20,906 grt. *Hull:* steel. *Comp.:* 1st 156, cabin 228, tourist 800; crew 365. *Mach.:* steam turbines, 2 screws; 20 kts. *Built:* John Cockerill, Hoboken, N.J.; 1953.

One of two sister ships ordered for Companhia Colonial de Navegaçao (the other was *Vera Cruz*), *Santa Maria* was built for service between Lisbon, Madeira, Rio de Janeiro, Santos, Montevideo, and Buenos Aires. She remained on this route for only two years before making her first voyage to the Caribbean, calling at Madeira, the Canary Islands, La Guaira, Curaçao, Havana, and Port Everglades; her last scheduled stop, in Brazil, was in 1957.

Santa Maria leaped to the world headlines on January 22, 1961, when a band of twenty-six terrorists posing as tourists and under Portuguese Navy Captain Henrique Carlos Malta Galvao hijacked the ship just after she left Curaçao. The ship's third mate, Nascimiento Costa, was shot and killed during the takeover. Galvao's motive was to force the overthrow of the conservative and repressive government of Portugal's Antonio de Salazar, who had ruled without interruption for thirty-nine years. After eluding a search by ships of the U.S. and British navies for eleven days, *Santa Maria* was located and contact established with Galvao. Negotiations with Brazilian authorities resulted in the hijackers being given asylum in that country, and they were landed at Recife on February 2. *Santa Maria* landed her 600 passengers at Lisbon on the 16th and resumed service shortly thereafter. Later the same year, Havana was dropped from the itinerary; but *Santa Maria* continued to ply between Portugal and Caribbean ports until 1973, when she was retired and scrapped at Kao-Hsiung.

Bonsor, *South Atlantic Seaway*. Day, *Passage Perilous*. Rogers, *Floating Revolution*.

SANTÍSIMA TRINIDAD

Galleon (3m). *L/B/D:* 167.5′ (gundeck) × 50′ × 33′ (51.1m × 15.2m × 10.1m). *Tons:* 2,000. *Hull:* wood. *Comp.:* 400–800. *Arm.:* 54 guns. *Des.:* Don Domingo Nebra. *Built:* Bagatao, Manila, Philippines; 1750.

Officially named *Santísima Trinidad y Nuestra Señora del Buen Fin* ("Most Holy Trinity and Our Lady of the Good End") and optimistically nicknamed "El Poderoso" — the powerful one — *Santísima Trinidad* was the largest "Manila galleon" built for trade between the Philippines and Mexico. Modeled on the Spanish specification for a sixty-gun ship, she was pierced for only fifty-four broadside guns but never mounted a full battery. Despite ordinances limiting the size of the Manila galleons, authorities routinely overlooked most irregularities; but with her enormous draft, oversized top hamper, and pronounced sheer, her size was too great to be ignored. The Crown ordered her replaced or cut down, and in 1757 she had her bulwarks and upper decks reduced, further limiting the number of guns she mounted. These alterations did not affect her gargantuan hold nor did they much improve her poor sailing qualities.

On August 1, 1762, *Santísima Trinidad* departed Cavite for Acapulco. It was late in the season and contrary winds kept her from exiting the San Bernardino Strait until late September. On the night of October 2–3, a typhoon brought down her fore- and mainmasts, and she turned back for the Philippines under a jury rig. Unbeknownst to the ship's company, Spain and England were at war and Manila had fallen. As the ship passed through the strait, she was met by HMS *Panther* (60 guns) under Captain Hyde Parker (who had sailed in Commodore Anson's CENTURION during the capture of *Nuestra Señora de la Covadonga* in 1743) and the frigate *Argo* (28), under Captain Richard King. Although "the *Panther*'s shot was not able to penetrate" the galleon's hardwood hull, the crew of the overcrowded ship (she carried 800 people) was dispirited and soon surrendered, despite the loss of only eighteen killed and ten wounded to the thirty-five British dead and thirty-seven wounded. *Santísima Trinidad* remained in her captors' possession until their return to England in June 1764. She was sold at Plymouth the next year, and proceeds amounted to about £30,000 for the two captains — an enormous amount of money in those years — with smaller shares for the other officers and crew. The ship herself was probably broken up for her wood.

Marley, "Last Manila Galleon." Schurz, *Manila Galleon.*

SÃO GABRIEL

Nao (3m). *Tons:* 100. *Hull:* wood. *Comp.:* ca. 60. *Arm.:* 20 guns. *Des.:* Bartholomeu Dias. *Built:* Lisbon; 1497.

Although Christopher Columbus's transatlantic voyage of 1492 had incomparable consequences for world history, of more immediate significance to world trade of that time was the voyage of Vasco da Gama with four ships (from Portugal to India) five years later. Under Prince Henry the Navigator, Portugal had taken the lead in the systematic compilation of geographic knowledge and voyages of discovery down the coast of Africa. Portuguese ships pushed south beyond the Canary Islands and Cape Bojador — the Bulging Cape, in what is now Mauretania — to reach Madeira in 1420, Cape Bianco in 1441, and the Cape Verde Islands in 1445. The next year, they arrived at the Gambia River and thereafter developed a brisk West African trade in slaves, gold, and ivory.

During the reign of Henry's great-nephew João II, Bartholomeu Dias sailed with three ships — their names are unknown — on a voyage that first brought Europeans around the tip of South Africa, to land, on February 3, 1488, at Mossel Bay, 200 miles east of the Cape of Good Hope. Dias returned in December 1488 after an absence of more than sixteen months. At the same time, João had sent Pero da Covilhã eastward in search of the Ethiopian Christian king known as Prester John. (Several Ethiopian embassies visited Europe during the fifteenth century, including one to Lisbon in 1452.) Covilhã reached Calicut and Goa in India before returning to the court of Alexander, "Lion of the Tribe of Judah, and King of Kings." Letters back to Portugal revealed

> how he discovered cinnamon and pepper in the city of Calicut, and that cloves came from beyond, but that all might be had ... in the said cities of Cananor and Calicut and Goa, all on the coast, and that to this one could navigate by the coast and seas of Guinea [that is, from the west coast of Africa].

Domestic problems prevented the Portuguese from following up immediately on Dias's monumental achievement, but João ordered Dias to build two 100-ton square-rigged *naos*, *São Gabriel* and *São Rafael*, for a new voyage. In 1497, João's successor, Manoel, named the courtier Vasco da Gama to lead a four-ship expedition, including the 50-ton caravel *Berrio* and an anonymous storeship of perhaps 120 tons. Gama appointed his brother Paulo captain of *São Rafael* and Nicolau Coelho captain of *Berrio*. Provisioned for three years, the ships had a total complement of between 140 and 170 crew, including pilots, interpreters, and ten convicts for hazardous undertakings ashore.

On June 8, 1497, the fleet set out from the Tagus River

village of Restello, later named for the church of St. Mary of Bethlehem, or Belém. Sailing via the Canary and Cape Verde Islands, they came to Sierra Leone. To avoid the northerly Benguela Current, Gama turned west until he reached the southerly Brazil Current. He next steered southeast until, after three months at sea, the ships landed near the mouth of the Berg River on November 1, 1497. The Portuguese arrived at Mossel Bay on November 22 and on Christmas Day they were at Natal, farther east than Dias had gone. They first saw evidence of trade with the east at the Quelimane River where they stayed in January and February 1498, making repairs to the ships. Their next stop was at the island of Moçambique, where friction with Arabs of the town erupted into violence, as it would again at Mombasa, much of it instigated by the Portuguese. Unaccountably, the expedition's planners had provided Gama with only second-rate goods, and the Arab traders disdained the meager offerings of cotton, beads, tin ornaments, trousers, and hats. The Portuguese were better received at Malindi, a rival to Mombasa, and here they hired a pilot to guide them to India. The choice was a good one: Ahmad ibn Majid was the author of many pilot books and esteemed among Arab seafarers as "the most trustworthy of the many pilots and mariners of the west coast of India in the fifteenth and sixteenth centuries." The ships departed the African coast on April 24. Five days later they crossed the equator, and on May 20 ibn Majid brought them to the shores of Calicut. At long last, the Portuguese had opened the much sought-after sea route to the Indies.

Calicut was the most important and cosmopolitan trading center on the Malabar coast of India, midway along the flourishing trade route between Asia and the Middle East. Gama met the samorin of Calicut on May 28. Although the king was initially well disposed towards the Portuguese, his opinion was tempered by their paltry offerings and overbearing manner, together with the antagonism of the Muslim traders. On August 9 Gama decided it was time to leave, but the samorin insisted that the Portuguese pay a customs charge for the meager amounts of cinnamon, cloves, and precious stones they had managed to acquire. The unsold Portuguese goods were seized and members of the crew detained ashore, and in retaliation Gama took eighteen hostages. The crisis was resolved a week later and on August 29 Gama sailed with three ships. (He also kept a number of hostages, five of whom returned to India with Pedro Alvares Cabral in 1500.)

After final repairs in the Angevida Islands — where they embarked a Venetian-speaking pirate, a Polish Jew later known as Gaspar da India — they turned west on October 2 for a torturous three-month crossing of the Arabian Sea, during which thirty people died. Skirting the African coast, they came to Malindi on January 7, 1499. After only four days, they resumed their voyage, but by this time there were so few crew that off Mombasa, Gama decided to burn *São Rafael,* and he continued the voyage with only *São Gabriel* and *Berrio.* After stopping briefly near Moçambique, they doubled the Cape of Good Hope on March 20 and reached the Cape Verde Islands in mid-April. From here, *Berrio* sailed directly to Lisbon, where she arrived on July 10; *São Gabriel* arrived some time later. Gama had left his ship at Cape Verde to race for home in a hired caravel with his ailing brother, Paulo, who died and was buried at Madeira. Gama finally returned to Lisbon about September 1, 1499.

Gama's voyage was the culmination of the Portuguese age of discovery, and in one stroke it altered the pattern of European trade forever. Having broken the Arab-Venetian monopoly of the spice trade, Lisbon became, briefly, the most important entrepôt in Europe. Whether by good luck or design, Gama had also pioneered the standard sailing-ship route from Europe to the Indian Ocean. Although the Portuguese maintained colonies in India and Asia well into the twentieth century, their prosperity was undermined by ruthlessness towards their hosts and rivals. (On his second voyage in 1502, Gama showed uncommon savagery in the burning of a pilgrim ship from Mecca.) However brief, Portugal's golden age was well deserved, owing as it did not to luck but perseverance.

Hart, *Sea Road to the Indies.* Velho, *Journal of the First Voyage of Vasco da Gama.*

USS SARATOGA

Corvette (3m). *L/B/D:* 143′ bp × 36.5′ × 12.5′ (43.6m × 11.1m × 0.3m). *Tons:* 734 bm. *Hull:* wood. *Comp.:* 212. *Arm.:* 8 × 24pdr, 6 × 42pdr, 12 × 32pdr. *Des.:* Henry Eckford. *Built:* Noah Brown, Vergennes, Vt.; 1814.

During the American Revolution, the British were twice frustrated in their attempt to march from Canada down the Lake Champlain–Hudson River Valley to New York. In October 1776, General Benedict Arnold's autumn victory at the Battle of Valcour Bay had forced the postponement of the invasion, and in the following year General Horatio Gates won a crucial victory at the Battle of Saratoga. Late in the War of 1812, the British under General Sir George Prevost were ready to attempt the same strategy. Standing in his way was Master Commandant Thomas Macdonough who, aided by the New York shipbuilder Noah Brown, had built his flagship, the aptly named corvette USS *Saratoga,* in the remarkably fast time of only thirty-five days. After blockading the mouth of the Richelieu River during the summer, Macdonough was forced to drop down the lake as the British army began its advance in August. The army was accompanied by a naval force that included the thirty-six-gun HMS *Confiance,* the largest warship ever built on Lake Champlain. American forces withdrew to Plattsburg Bay, where Macdonough deployed his fleet of fourteen vessels across the mouth of Cumberland Bay, with kedge anchors and spring lines set so that each ship could turn on its own axis. Battle was joined when the British fleet rounded Cumberland Point on September 11. HMS *Linnet* opened fire first, followed by *Confiance,* which let loose her first broadside against *Saratoga* at point-blank range. After two hours, Macdonough brought his ship around to present a fresh broadside to *Confiance,* which was soon forced to strike; forty-one of her crew were killed, Captain George Downie among them, and a like number wounded. *Linnet* surrendered soon thereafter, as had *Finch* and *Chubb* earlier. The victory was decisive in ending the threat to the United States from Canada, and news of the victory influenced negotiations at the Treaty of Ghent, which was concluded on December 24.

Roosevelt, *Naval War of 1812.* U.S. Navy, *DANFS.*

USS SARATOGA (CV-3)

Lexington-class aircraft carrier (1f/1m). *L/B/D:* 888′ × 105.5′ (130′ew) × 24.2′ (270.7m × 32.2m (39.6m) × 7.4m). *Tons:* 33,000 disp. *Hull:* steel. *Comp.:* 2,951. *Arm.:* 81 aircraft; 12 × 5″, 48 × 1.1″ quad, 18 × 20mm. *Armor:* 7″ belt, 4.5″ deck. *Mach.:* turboelectric, 180,000 shp; 34 kts. *Built:* New York Shipbuilding Corp., Camden, N.J.; 1927.

Named for the site of an American Revolutionary War victory, USS *Saratoga* was a sister ship of USS LEXINGTON. Originally laid down as battlecruisers in 1921, the Washington Naval Conference that year led to agreements limiting the tonnage of battleships and battlecruisers. Under the so-called 5:5:3 formula, the United States and Britain were to reduce their capital tonnage to 525,000 tons each and Japan would reduce to 315,000 tons. France and Italy were both restricted to 175,000 tons. The United States and Japan were allowed to convert two battlecruisers currently under construction to aircraft carriers. The overall restrictions on carrier tonnage were 135,000 tons each for the United States and Britain, and 81,000 for the Japanese, carriers being described as ships built solely for carrying airplanes and armed with nothing larger than 8-inch guns.

Conversion of *Saratoga* and *Lexington* was authorized in 1922, but the ships were not completed for nearly six years. Unlike later carriers, they had enclosed hangar decks, and unlike their British counterparts, whose decks were steel, the *Lexington*-class ships had flight decks of steel with wood planking. With the most powerful engines of any contemporary U.S. warship, they were the largest aircraft carriers built until after World War II, with the exception of Japan's desperate end-of-war conversion of the *Yamato*-class battleship, *Shinano.* In addition to her 8-inch and 5-inch batteries, augmented by increasing numbers of antiaircraft guns as time went on, *Saratoga* was originally intended to carry 90 aircraft. Despite the dramatic increase in the size of carrier aircraft, by the opening of World War II, they could still carry 88 planes. On January 11, 1928, the first plane to land on *Saratoga*'s flight deck was flown by her air officer, Marc A. Mitscher, who would go on to become a carrier task force commander during World War II. The same year *Saratoga* was assigned to the Pacific Fleet and through the 1930s she participated in fleet exercises that helped develop and refine carrier strategy, tactics, and operations.

Japan's December 7 attack on Pearl Harbor found her at San Diego. She immediately sailed for Wake with Marine aircraft, though she was recalled to Pearl Harbor on December 22, the day before Wake fell. On January 11, 1942, en route to a rendezvous with *Lexington,* she was torpedoed by Japanese submarine *I-16,* 500 miles southwest of Oahu. She returned under her own power, offloaded her 8-inch guns, and proceeded to Bremerton, Washington, for repairs, arriving at Pearl Harbor on June 6, the day after the Battle of Midway. Flying the flag of Rear Admiral Frank J. Fletcher, *Saratoga* sailed for the southwest Pacific in mid-July, and on August 7 her planes flew cover for the first Allied landings on Guadalcanal and Tulagi in the Solomon Islands. On August 23, the Japanese launched a counterattack and in the Battle of the Eastern Solomons, *Saratoga*'s planes sank the Japanese carrier *Ryujo* and damaged *Chitose* while *Saratoga* herself remained undetected. More important, the Japanese transports were recalled from Guadalcanal.

On August 31, a torpedo from the submarine *I-26* left *Saratoga* dead in the water, and she was taken in tow by USS *Minneapolis* until she could again proceed under her own power. After repairs at Pearl Harbor, she returned to the southwest Pacific where she remained through 1943, joined by USS PRINCETON for the Bougainville landings on November 1, and staged a raid on Rabaul that resulted in heavy damage to six Japanese cruisers and a destroyer. After sailing as part of a Relief Carrier Group for the Gilbert Islands invasion on November 20, *Saratoga* steamed for the West Coast for overhaul. Returning to the central Pacific at the end of January 1944, she took part in the landings in the Marshall Islands before heading to the Indian Ocean to join Admiral Sir James Somerville's Eastern Fleet. This force comprised British aircraft carrier HMS VICTORIOUS, four British battleships, and, from April 12, the French battleship RICHELIEU. On April 15, the force launched an air raid on the Japanese-held port of Sabang at the northwest tip of Sumatra in the Dutch East Indies, followed by a second raid on Surabaya on May 17. Both of these attacks, from a completely unexpected quarter, caught the Japanese by surprise and resulted in heavy damage to crucial port facilities and oil depots. Returning once more to Bremerton for repairs that lasted through the summer, *Saratoga* began training pilots for night carrier operations. Returned to the front lines in February 1945, *Saratoga* flew raids against Tokyo and Yokohama on the 16th and 17th. Four days later, she was crashed by five kamikazes off Iwo Jima. The flight deck forward was destroyed, and she was hulled twice and lost 123 crew. Repairs lasted through June, when she resumed training operations in Hawaii.

During Operation Magic Carpet after the Japanese surrender in September, *Saratoga* repatriated 29,204 troops from the Pacific theater, more than any other ship. She also held the record for most carrier landings, with 98,549 since 1928. Decommissioned after the war, in 1946 she was used as a target ship for Operation Crossroads, the nuclear weapons tests at Bikini Atoll, where she was sunk on July 25.

Delgado, "Documenting the Sunken Remains of USS *Saratoga*." U.S. Navy, *DANFS*.

SS SAVANNAH

Steamship (1f/3m). *L/B/D:* 109′ × 25.8′ × 12′ (33.2m × 7.9m × 3.7m). *Tons:* 320 grt. *Hull:* wood. *Comp.:* ca. 20; 22 pass. *Mach.:* inclined single-cylinder, 72 hp, sidewheels; 8 kts. *Built:* Samuel Fickett & William Crockett, New York; 1819.

Savannah was the first steam-powered ship to cross the Atlantic Ocean or Baltic Sea in either direction. The ship was the inspiration of veteran steamboat captain Moses Rogers. In 1809 Rogers commanded John Stevens's PHOENIX on the Delaware River, and in 1818 he inaugurated the first steam service between Savannah and Charleston in *Charleston*. It took little to persuade the prosperous and civic-minded leaders of the Georgia port to finance what the London *Times* would call "the great experiment": the crossing of the Atlantic by a steam-powered vessel. Having secured capital of $50,000 for the project, Rogers proceeded to New York "to purchase a suitable ship of the first class, completely fitted and equipped in the ordinary manner — on board of which shall be placed a steam engine with the other necessary

apparatus." He found this ship on the stocks at the yard of Samuel Fickett and William Crockett. The engine was developed and built under the supervision of Stephen Vail, of special note being the five-foot-diameter piston, the largest of its day.

On March 28, 1819, *Savannah* began her maiden voyage for her namesake port under Captain Rogers. With neither passengers nor cargo, and with a slow time of 9 days, 6 hours, it was an inauspicious beginning. A week later, Rogers took his ship from Savannah to Charleston with three passengers, and returned with seven. On May 11, the ship hosted President James Monroe, who toured the city's harbor defenses in the company of Secretary of War John C. Calhoun and raised the possibility of acquiring *Savannah* for use against Cuba-based pirates. (The steam vessel *Sea Gull* was acquired for the purpose in 1823.)

Savannah was never a commercial success, though, and after failing to secure any business for New York, on May 22, 1819, she sailed for St. Petersburg, Russia, via Liverpool, again without freight or passengers. (The date is remembered in the United States as National Maritime Day.) Ireland was sighted on June 16, after 23 days, 4 hours, at sea, during which several vessels westbound saw *Savannah* steaming in midatlantic. As the ship approached the Irish coast with smoke pouring from her funnel, reports of a vessel on fire reached Queenstown and the revenue cutter *Kite* was dispatched to *Savannah*'s rescue. Rogers took the opportunity to demonstrate the ability of steam-powered vessels to outmaneuver sailing vessels by steaming into the wind. The ship proceeded to Liverpool, where her arrival made quite an impression. Steam propulsion was by no means new, but its use on the high seas was. Moreover, the display of Yankee ingenuity gave a tremendous boost to the morale of American citizens and diplomats both in England and elsewhere in Europe.

Savannah sailed for the Baltic on July 23, proceeding much of the way under steam alone, stopping at Helsingør in August for a week before sailing for Stockholm, where the ship was much admired; Charles XIV offered to purchase *Savannah* for $100,000 in hemp and iron. On September 5, Rogers and *Savannah* embarked the only paying passengers of their voyage, Sir Thomas Graham, Lord Lynedoch, and his cousin Robert Graham Roger. Five days later they anchored at Kronstadt, the port of entry for St. Petersburg; *Savannah*'s draft was too great to ascend the Neva River. As before, Rogers and his ship were well received, particularly by the American minister George M. Campbell, and there were three cruises for dignitaries on St. Petersburg Bay. Rogers had probably declined the Swedish king's offer of iron and hemp in anticipation of an even better one from the czar. But Alexander's suggestion that Rogers and *Savannah* remain in Russian waters with the exclusive right of steam navigation on the Baltic and Black Seas was more than Rogers could accept, and he decided to return to the United States.

On October 14, *Savannah* steamed away from St. Petersburg, making Copenhagen in four days and stopping briefly in Arendal, Norway, her last port of call in Europe. There are conflicting claims by members of the crew as to whether *Savannah* got steam up on her return trip — some say steam was used on 19 days, and one source says not at all. On November 30, she was back at Savannah, but sailed again on December 3 for Washington, where Rogers hoped the government would purchase his ship. Despite public interest in the ship, the Navy had no need of her. That winter she was moored at the Washington Navy Yard when the French naval engineer Jean Baptiste Marestier studied the ship and engines.

In the meantime, the Savannah Steam Ship Company was forced to dissolve, and in August 1820, Captain Nathan Holdridge of New York bought the ship at auction for an unknown amount. He removed the engines and used her as a packet between New York and Savannah, carrying 24 passengers and a full cargo on the first voyage. *Savannah* completed eight roundtrips in this trade, until November 5, 1821, when she ran aground on Fire Island opposite what is now Bellport, New York. There was no loss of life, but the ship was a total loss.

When larger vessels with more powerful engines — but still rigged as sailing ships — were built, *Savannah*'s claim to being the first steamship to cross the Atlantic began to erode. This would surprise the ship's contemporaries on both sides of the Atlantic. *Savannah* was designed and intended for transatlantic service; it is only due to a reluctant public that she did not succeed, and it would be another nineteen years before SIRIUS and GREAT WESTERN would herald the beginning of regular transatlantic steam service.

Braynard, *S.S. "Savannah."*

NS SAVANNAH

Passenger freighter (3m). *L/B:* 595.5′ × 78′ × 29.5′ (181.5m × 23.8m × 9m). *Tons:* 15,585 grt. *Comp.:* 1st 60. *Hull:* steel. *Mach.:* nuclear reactor and geared turbines, 22,000 shp, 1 screw; 21 kts. *Des.:* Messrs. George G. Sharp, Inc. *Built:* New York Shipbuilding Corp., Camden, N.J.; 1964.

Built and launched in Camden and fitted out in Galveston, the world's first commercial nuclear-powered ship owes her name largely to the enthusiastic lobbying of maritime historian Frank O. Braynard. He felt it would be an appropriate tribute to one of America's first great marine engineering achievements, the first transatlantic crossing by a steamship, SS SAVANNAH, in 1819. That ship's twentieth-century namesake was authorized by an Act of Congress in 1956, one year after the commissioning of USS NAUTILUS, the first nuclear-powered submarine, and she was launched in 1959, one year after the Soviet icebreaker *Lenin* became the world's first operational nuclear surface ship. A succession of technological difficulties and labor disputes delayed her commissioning until 1964. The United States Maritime Administration leased *Savannah* to American Export–Isbrandtsen Lines for $1 per year. The government was committed to promoting a policy of "atoms for peace," and the ship was operated under the strictest safety regulations that the Atomic Energy Commission could conceive. Despite all assurances, public fear of nuclear power worldwide restricted the number of ports *Savannah* could visit and this, combined with high manning requirements demanded by the AEC and other factors, made her economically unviable.

Savannah began her maiden voyage on May 5, 1964, sailing from the port of Houston for New Orleans, Baltimore, Boston, and New York. From there she continued on June 8 for Dublin, Bremerhaven, Hamburg, and Southampton before returning again to New York on July 20. A second voyage in July took her to the Baltic, as far as Mälmö, a third to the Netherlands and Belgium, while the fourth and fifth voyages took her into the Mediterranean and the Aegean as far as Istanbul. Though these were all accomplished without incident, passenger bookings were negligible and she eventually became a pure freighter. She remained in service as a cargo ship until 1968, when her nuclear fuel was replaced for the first time.

Savannah's fuel plant consisted of a pressurized water reactor built by Babcock and Wilcox Company, of New York, which drove a set of De Laval–built compound double-reduction geared turbines. Rated at 74 million watts, the reactor originally consisted of about 17,000 pounds (8.5 tons) of uranium 235 and was rated to last 1,230 days — almost three and a half years. During the same period of active service, a conventionally fueled freighter of the same size would have consumed 90,000 tons of fuel oil. One unique aspect of the ship's profile was the absence of even a single funnel, for with nuclear power, there is no exhaust.

In 1970, *Savannah* sailed from Baltimore for the Far East, but by the next year the government had decided it could no longer afford to subsidize her operations and she was laid up at Galveston. In the mid-1970s the city of

Savannah tried to operate her as a maritime museum, but she proved too costly and was transferred to the Patriots Point Maritime Museum in Charleston, South Carolina, in 1981. In 1994 she was taken to Baltimore for repair work. In 1995, she was laid up as part of the James River Reserve Fleet in Virginia.

Bonsor, *North Atlantic Seaway.* Braynard, *Famous American Ships.*

SMS SCHARNHORST

Scharnhorst-class armored cruiser (4f/2m). *L/B/D:* 474' × 70.8' × 26' (144.5m × 21.6m × 7.9m). *Tons:* 12,900 disp. *Comp.:* 860. *Hull:* steel. *Arm.:* 8 × 8.4", 6 × 5.9", 18 × 88mm; 4 × 18"TT. *Armor:* 6" belt, 2.4" deck. *Mach.:* triple expansion, 26,000 ihp, 3 screws; 22.5 kts. *Built:* Blohm & Voss, Hamburg; 1907.

The armored cruisers *Scharnhorst* (named for the Napoleonic-era Prussian General Gerhard von Scharnhorst) and GNEISENAU were the most powerful ships in the German Imperial Navy's East Asiatic Squadron stationed at Tsingtao, China. When World War I began, Vice Admiral Maximilian Graf von Spee was on a training cruise in the Caroline Islands, and fearing an engagement with a combined British and Japanese fleet, he abandoned the German base at Tsingtao (which fell on November 7, 1914) and took his squadron — including the light cruisers *Leipzig* and *Nürnberg* — across the Pacific to harass Allied coastal shipping on the west coast of South America. The squadron was joined by the light cruiser DRESDEN.

On October 31, 1914, the German and British squadrons were alerted to one another's presence off the coast of Chile, although each believed they were making contact with only one light cruiser. At 1620 on November 1, about 50 miles west of Coronel, Spee sighted Rear Admiral Christopher Cradock's force, consisting of armored cruisers HMS GOOD HOPE and *Monmouth,* light cruiser *Glasgow,* and armed merchant ship *Otranto.* After maneuvering for advantage — the German ships were faster, their guns were bigger, and their crews more experienced — the Battle of Coronel began at dusk. *Scharnhorst* concentrated her fire on *Good Hope,* which took at least 35 hits before being ripped apart by an internal magazine explosion at about 2000.

Coronel was a Pyrrhic victory for Spee, who had expended 42 percent of his ships' 8-inch ammunition — *Scharnhorst* had fired 422 shells and had only 350 remaining — and the nearest supply was in Germany. After a brief stop at Valparaiso, Spee sailed for the Atlantic on November 5. The next month his force was off the Falkland Islands when at about 0940 on December 8, *Gneis-*

enau and *Leipzig* reported the presence of two battle-cruisers at Stanley. With inferior speed, range, and weight of shell, Spee's ships had little or no chance against Admiral Sir Frederick Doveton Sturdee's battlecruisers HMS INVINCIBLE and INFLEXIBLE. *Scharnhorst* was engaged at about 1320, and although she managed to close and inflict some damage on her adversaries, by mid-afternoon she was all but finished. After refusing an order to surrender, she sank at 1617 in about 52°40′S, 55°51′W, with the loss of her entire crew. Of Spee's fleet, only *Dresden* and the collier *Seydlitz* escaped. The latter was interned in Argentina and the former was lost in Chile the following spring.

Yates, *Graf Spee's Raiders.*

SCHARNHORST

Scharnhorst-class battlecruiser (1f/2m). *L/B/D:* 770.5' × 98.4' × 32.5' (234.8m × 30m × 9.9m). *Tons:* 38,100 disp. *Comp.:* 1,800. *Hull:* steel. *Arm.:* 9 × 11.2" (3 × 3), 12 × 6", 14 × 10.5cm, 16 × 3.7cm, 34 × 2cm; 6 × 21"TT; 4 seaplanes. *Armor:* 14" belt, 2" deck. *Mach.:* geared turbines, 165,930 shp, 3 screws; 31.5 kts. *Built:* Kriegsmarinewerft, Wilhelmshaven, Germany; 1939.

Under the terms of the Versailles Peace Treaty, Germany was prohibited from laying down any warships with a displacement of more than 10,000 tons. The Anglo-German Naval Agreement of 1935 raised the maximum tonnage, and *Scharnhorst* and her sister ship GNEISENAU were laid down the same year with a nominal displacement of 26,000 tons. Commissioned two months before the German invasion of Poland, *Scharnhorst*'s first war cruise into the North Atlantic, with *Gneisenau,* resulted in the sinking of the armed merchant cruiser RAWALPINDI on November 23, 1939, southeast of Iceland. The following April the two ships took part in the German landing at Narvik; on April 9, 1940, they engaged HMS RENOWN, though *Scharnhorst* was unscathed. During the Allied withdrawal from Norway two months later, the ships sank aircraft carrier HMS GLORIOUS and destroyers *Acasta* and *Ardent* off Narvik. However, *Scharnhorst* was torpedoed by *Acasta* and was twice attacked by aircraft from HMS ARK ROYAL at Trondheim before she could return to Kiel. There she remained until January 22, 1941, when *Scharnhorst* and *Gneisenau* began a commerce-raiding cruise during which they sank a total of 22 ships totaling more than 105,000 gross tons. They returned on March 23 to Brest where they were joined by PRINZ EUGEN on June 1.

Though under periodic attack by British aircraft, the ships' greatest threat was that Hitler would order their

One of the luckiest German naval operations of World War II was Operation Cerberus, or the Channel Dash. On February 11, 1942, the battlecruisers SCHARNHORST *(second from right) and* GNEISENAU, *heavy cruiser* PRINZ EUGEN *and a host of escorts sailed in tight formation from Brest through the English Channel and the North Sea to Wilhelmshaven, some 675 miles away. Courtesy Imperial War Museum, London.*

guns removed for use as shore batteries in Norway. To effect their return to home waters, Admiral Erich Raeder ordered Operation Cerberus, a plan of dramatic simplicity. The ships would leave Brest, sail up the English Channel, through the 20-mile-wide Dover Strait, into the North Sea and home. The ships left Brest at 1930 hours on February 11, 1942. Though spotted by British patrols at 1042 the next morning, due to a series of errors they were not even challenged until after noon when shore batteries on South Foreland opened fire on the ships, then about 10 miles west of Calais. About 12 minutes later, a flotilla of seven motor gunboats and motor torpedo boats tried to work their way past the screen of E-boats and destroyers, but they were driven back or sunk without inflicting serious damage. A flight of six Swordfish attacked at 1245, with the loss of all planes and most of their crews. At 1432, *Scharnhorst* struck a mine that left her dead in the water for 17 minutes, though there were no British forces to take advantage of the situation. Six destroyers engaged the overwhelming German force starting at 1517 but to no effect, and a total of 242 bombers launched that afternoon likewise failed to damage the enemy. *Scharnhorst* hit a second mine at 2134 but docked under her own power at Wilhelmshaven the next morning.

Following lengthy repairs at Kiel, *Scharnhorst* was deployed to northern Norway, and she sailed with TIRPITZ to bombard Spitzbergen on September 6–8, 1943. She was not at Altenfjord when British midget submarines crippled *Tirpitz*. On Christmas Day, Germany's only operational capital ship, flying the flag of Rear Admiral Erich Bey (Captain Hintze commanding), was ordered to sea with five destroyers to intercept convoy JW55B. At 0820 the next morning, Bey inexplicably turned away from the destroyers, which took no part in the coming engagement. Within half an hour, *Scharnhorst* had been picked up on the radar of three British cruisers, HMS NORFOLK, BELFAST, and SHEFFIELD, which were escorted by four destroyers. At 0930, *Norfolk* opened fire and scored two hits that knocked out *Scharnhorst's* radar, and Bey withdrew; the three cruisers also turned away. Rather than return to base, Bey tried for a second attack on the cruisers. This began at 1221 — at this time of year it was virtually a night action — and knocked out *Norfolk's* "X" turret before breaking off again after 20 minutes.

All this time, Admiral Sir Bruce Fraser had been steaming to catch up with *Scharnhorst* in HMS DUKE OF YORK, which opened with accurate fire from her 14-inch guns at 1651, followed by the cruiser HMS *Jamaica;* this force was also accompanied by four destroyers. *Scharnhorst* was hit at least 13 times before getting out of range — or so the combatants thought. At 1820, a 14-inch shell fired at a range of more than 18,000 yards — more than 16 kilometers, or 10 miles — plunged into her boiler room, reducing her speed from 26 knots to about 10 knots. Although her speed was soon back up to 22 knots, within 20 minutes of this fatal blow, the destroyers had maneuvered into position. Four torpedoes struck home and *Scharnhorst* came under withering fire from *Jamaica, Belfast,* and *Duke of York,* which closed to 3,000 yards and only stopped firing at 1729. Fifteen minutes later, having been hit by eight more torpedoes, *Scharnhorst* exploded and sank in 72°16′N, 28°41′E, with the loss of 1,803 crew. There were only 36 survivors.

Gröner, *German Warships.* Kemp, *Escape of the "Scharnhorst" and the "Gneisenau."* Stephen, *Sea Battles in Close-Up.*

USS SCORPION (SSN-589)

Skipjack-class submarine. *L/B:* 251.8′ × 31.6′ (76.7m × 9.6m). *Tons:* 3,075/3,500 disp. *Hull:* steel. *Comp.:* 99. *Arm.:* 6 × 21TT″. *Mach.:* nuclear reactor, steam turbines; 20/30 kts. *Built:* Electric Boat Division, General Dynamics, Groton, Conn.; 1960.

One of six *Skipjack*-class submarines designed for antisubmarine warfare in defense of U.S. fleet ballistic submarines, USS *Scorpion*'s first assignment was in European waters, where she was deployed on exercises with NATO forces and with the Sixth Fleet in the Mediterranean. Homeported in Norfolk for the remainder of her career, she was used extensively in developing tactics for antisubmarine warfare, both as hunter and hunted. After duty in the Mediterranean during the spring of 1968, she was reported overdue at Norfolk on May 27, 1968, her last reported position having been about 50 miles south of the Azores, when she was making 18 knots submerged. A massive air and sea search was launched immediately, but on June 5, the Navy declared the submarine and her 99 crew under Commander Francis A. Slattery presumed lost. Subsequent investigation revealed that an underwater implosion had been recorded on May 21 about 400 miles southwest of the Azores. On October 24, the Navy's oceanographic research ship *Mizar* located parts of *Scorpion*'s hull lying at a depth of about 10,000 feet. Despite an exhaustive review of photographs taken by the submersible Trieste and other data, the cause of the disaster was never determined.

U.S. Navy, *DANFS.*

SCOTIA

Liner (2f/2m). *L/B/D:* 379.4′ bp × 47.8′ (76.5′ew) × 30.5′ (115.6m × 14.6m (23.3m) × 9.3m). *Tons:* 3,871 grt. *Hull:* iron. *Comp.:* 1st 573. *Mach.:* side-lever steam engine, sidewheel; 14 kts. *Built:* Robert Napier & Sons, Glasgow; 1862.

The last of the Cunard Line paddle steamers, *Scotia* was the first ship to set a new transatlantic record in eight years, and the first to make the westbound passage from the British Isles to the United States in under nine days. En route from Liverpool to New York, she steamed from Queenstown to Sandy Hook at an average speed of 14.46 knots (8 days, 3 hours; September 17–25, 1863). Three months later she set a westbound record of 14.16 knots (8 days, 5 hours, and 42 minutes; December 16–24). When *Scotia* first entered service, Cunard maintained a biweekly schedule between Liverpool and New York with her older consort, *Persia,* and *Africa,* a newer single-screw steamer. By the time she was withdrawn from service, Cunard's service was weekly; *Persia* had been withdrawn in 1867, and *Scotia*'s other consorts included *Java, Cuba, China,* and *Australasian.* By 1872, the side-wheeler was an anachronism, and *Scotia* was laid up. Two years later her paddles and one funnel were removed and she was fitted with twin screws. Thus transformed she began work as a cable-laying ship sailing under the flag of the Telegraph Construction and Maintenance Company. In 1896 her watertight bulkheads prevented her from sinking when an unexplained explosion blew out her bows, but she was repaired, and six years later, *Scotia* was sold to the Commercial Pacific Cable Company. Her end came on March 11, 1904, when she was wrecked accidentally on Catalan Bank, off Guam.

Baker, *Engine-Powered Vessel.* Bonsor, *North Atlantic Seaway.* Braynard & Miller, *Fifty Famous Liners.*

SCOTTISH MAID

Schooner (2m). *L/B/D:* 92.4′ × 19.4′ × 11.7′ dph (28.2m × 5.9m × 3.6m). *Tons:* 142 tons. *Hull:* wood. *Des.:* William Hall. *Built:* Alexander Hall & Sons, Aberdeen, Scotland; 1839.

In the 1940s, a keen debate between American and British historians erupted over the status of the Aberdeen-built schooner as the first true clipper. As the written use of the word "clipper" to describe fast ships (and horses) antedates *Scottish Maid,* and the first effort to forge a precise definition followed several years later, her claim to primacy seems weak; but in the arguments pro and con echo the rivalry of nineteenth-century British and American shipbuilders.

Ordered by the firm of Nicol and Munro, she was built to compete with steamers on the coastal run between Aberdeen and London. As freight rates were based on tonnage measurements, William Hall sought to achieve the greatest speed with the smallest tonnage. One of the earliest designers to develop models based on studies made in model tanks, Hall discovered that if the stem had a 50-degree forward rake, he could reduce the tonnage measurement while giving the hull a sharp entrance and hollow (or convex) waterline, a primary characteristic of later clipper ships. While this "Aberdeen bow" worked well in *Scottish Maid* and other relatively small vessels, larger square-riggers so modeled were wet ships and took excessive water over the bow.

Scottish Maid did well for her original owners, and shortly after her commissioning Hall and Sons built three more schooners for the same trade. She continued sailing for half a century before she was driven ashore and lost.

Cable, "World's First Clipper." Chapelle, "First Clipper." MacGregor, *Fast Sailing Ships.*

USS SCOURGE

(ex-*Lord Nelson*) Schooner (2m). *L/B:* 57′ × 20′ (17.4m × 6.1m). *Tons:* 110. *Hull:* wood. *Comp.:* 50. *Arm.:* 1 × 32 pdr, 8 × 12 pdr. *Built:* Asa Stanard, Niagara, N.Y., 1811.

Built for William and James Crooks, the Lake Ontario merchant schooner *Lord Nelson* was seized on June 5, 1812, by Lieutenant Melancthon Woolsey in *Oneida,* for violating the recently imposed Embargo Act. Thirteen days later the War of 1812 broke out, and Lieutenant Woolsey purchased *Lord Nelson* for the U.S. Navy at auction for $2,999.25. Renamed USS *Scourge,* the vessel was incorporated into Captain Isaac Chauncey's Lake Ontario squadron under Lieutenant H. McPherson. She took part in attacks on York (now Toronto) on April 27, 1813, and Fort George, on the Niagara River, on May 27. On the night of August 8, while off the Niagara River, *Scourge* was overwhelmed in a line squall and lost all but nine of her crew. The schooner USS HAMILTON was also lost.

In 1930, the U.S. government paid an indemnity to Crooks's descendants. In 1971, the same year that MARY ROSE was discovered, the Hamilton and Scourge Project was formed to locate the sunken ships. Two years later, they were located lying at a depth of 300 feet, both in a remarkable state of preservation.

Cain, *Ghost Ships "Hamilton" and "Scourge."* Nelson, *"Hamilton and Scourge."* Roosevelt, *Naval War of 1812.*

USS SCULPIN (SS-191)

Sargo-class submarine. *L/B/D:* 310.5′ × 27′ × 13.8′ (94.5m × 8.2m × 4.2m). *Tons:* 1,450/2,350 disp. *Hull:* steel; 256′dd. *Comp.:* 70. *Arm.:* 8 × 21″TT (4/4); 1 × 3″, 4 mgs. *Mach.:* diesel/electric,

5,500/3,300 hp, 20/9 kts; 2 screws. *Built:* Portsmouth Navy Yard, Kittery, Me.; 1939.

On her initial shakedown cruise on May 23, 1939, USS *Sculpin* was diverted to help in the search for her sister ship USS SQUALUS, which had sunk in about 240 feet of water off the coast of Portsmouth, New Hampshire. *Sculpin* established contact with the crew trapped aboard *Squalus* and assisted the submarine rescue ship USS *Falcon* during the subsequent recovery. *Sculpin* joined the Pacific Fleet in 1940 and was transferred to the Philippines in 1941. The start of World War II found her at Cavite. *Sculpin* completed eight war patrols: the first ended at Surabaya, Dutch East Indies, the next five were out of either Fremantle or Brisbane, and the last two out of Pearl Harbor.

On November 5, 1943, she sailed from Pearl Harbor as the lead boat of a three-submarine wolf pack ordered to patrol north of Truk in the Caroline Islands. While tracking a convoy on November 19, a depth-charge attack by a Japanese destroyer knocked out her sonar and depth gauge so that she alternately broached the surface or ran below a safe depth as she tried to evade her pursuer. Commander Fred Connaway ordered her to the surface in order to save his crew, 42 of whom were picked up by the destroyer *Yamagumo.* After a brief internment at Truk, the POWs were sent to Japan in two ships. At 0016 on December 4, one of these, the light carrier *Chuyo,* was torpedoed — by USS *Sailfish,* the renamed *Squalus,* as fate would have it — and all but one of the captured *Sculpin* crew aboard her died.

LaVo, *Back from the Deep.*

SEA CLOUD

(ex-*Sea Cloud of Grand Cayman, Patria, Antarna, Angelita, Sea Cloud, Hussar*) Bark (4m). *L/B/D:* 316′ × 50′ × 19.4′ (96.3m × 15.2m × 5.9m). *Tons:* 2,350 grt. *Hull:* steel *Mach.:* diesel, 3,200 ihp, 2 screws; 14 kts. *Mach.:* Friedrich Krupp Germaniawerft AG, Kiel, Germany; 1931.

Built as *Hussar* for the breakfast cereal heiress Marjorie Merriweather Post (then married to E. F. Hutton), this celebrated four-masted yacht was designed to carry twelve guests with a complement of sixty-six officers, crew, and staff. When Post married Ambassador Joseph E. Davies in 1935, she renamed her yacht *Sea Cloud* and took her first to Leningrad (now St. Petersburg) and then to Belgium, until Davies's recall in 1939. From 1942 to 1944, *Sea Cloud* (IX-99) served as a Coast Guard weather ship in the North Atlantic. Post sailed her again as a yacht from 1947 to 1955. Over the next twenty years, the bark had a succession of names and owners, including Dominican Republic's President Rafael Trujillo. In 1974, she was purchased by a German consortium and refitted for the Mediterranean and Caribbean cruise trade, in which she still sails today.

Leek, "Marjorie Hutton's Barque *Hussar* of 1931."

SEA VENTURE

Tons: ca. 240 burden. *Hull:* wood. *Comp.:* 150. *Arm.:* 8 sakers, 8 minions. *Built:* East Anglia(?); 1603.

One of the best-known shipwrecks in literature is that of the merchantman *Sea Venture* (sometimes called *Sea Adventure, Seaventure,* or *Seaventer*), whose loss on a Bermudan reef in 1609 became the subject of William Shakespeare's *Tempest.* Her early history is not known with certainty, but it is believed that she is the same *Sea Venture* owned by members of the Company of Merchant Adventurers, for whom she traded between London, the Elbe River port of Stade, and the Dutch market at Middleburg, carrying mostly wool and cloth. In 1609 she was purchased by or chartered to the Virginia Company to sail as flagship of the second supply mission sent out to the fledgling Jamestown colony since its establishment in 1607. The ship sailed from Plymouth on June 2 as flagship of the "Third Supply" (as it was known), which comprised six full-rigged ships and two pinnaces. On July 23, they were caught in a hurricane and *Sea Venture* became separated from the rest of the ships. After four days in midocean, when the ship "was growne five feet suddenly deepe with water above her ballast," Admiral of the flotilla Sir George Somers saw land. Soon thereafter, the ship lodged fast between two reefs about three-quarters of a mile from land, and the entire company of 150 rowed ashore on Bermuda, a place dreaded by mariners who knew it as "the Island of Devils." The ship remained afloat long enough for the crew to salvage most of her equipment and stores. They also built the pinnaces *Deliverance* and *Patience* in which all but two of the company continued their passage to Jamestown, arriving on May 10, 1610. The two men who remained at Bermuda were the first permanent settlers in what officially became an English settlement in 1612.

In 1610, William Strachey published an eyewitness account entitled "A True Repertory of the Wreck and Redemption of Sir Thomas Gates, Knight," and Silvester Jourdain published *Discovery of the Bermudas otherwise Called the "Isle of Devils."* It is believed that Shakespeare read both of these accounts in the course of writing his celebrated romantic drama *The Tempest* (1611), the last of his complete plays.

The wreck remained undisturbed until 1959 when American diver and amateur historian Edmund Dowling found it at a depth of 9.1 meters. The artifacts he retrieved suggested that the wreck was that of *Sea Venture,* until experts at the Tower of London misidentified one of the ship's guns as a saker dating from the eighteenth century, rather than a minion from the early seventeenth. Work on the site ceased and was not resumed until 1978, when divers working under the auspices of the Bermuda Maritime Museum Association resumed operations. The site yielded relatively few artifacts: some cannon shot and smaller weapons, fragments of ceramic plates and vessels of English, Rhenish, Spanish, and Chinese origin, and pewter spoons. Little of the hull remains apart from a 15-meter section of keel (which originally may have been as long as 25 meters), a few ceilings and outer planks, and some floors.

Peterson, "*Sea Venture.*" Winwood, "*Sea Venture.*"

SEA WITCH

Clipper (3m). *L/B/D:* 192′ × 34′ × 19′ (58.5m × 10.4m × 5.8m). *Tons:* 908 om. *Hull:* wood. *Built:* Smith & Dimon, New York; 1846.

Built to the order of the New York firm of Howland and Aspinwall for the Canton trade, *Sea Witch* was designed as a running mate for its clipper *Rainbow.* Though her hull was not as sharp as those of later extreme clippers, the *New York Herald* remarked on her "peculiar model and sharp bows [that] have for the past few months attracted so much attention." They went on to observe that "the *Sea Witch* is, for a vessel of her size, the prettiest vessel we have ever seen, and much resembles the model of the steamer GREAT BRITAIN, only on a smaller scale." Unconventional though she may have been, her sailing record over the course of ten voyages in as many years remains one of the most remarkable of that era.

For her first three voyages, *Sea Witch* was commanded by the hard-driving Captain Robert H. Waterman, famous for his handling of the fast packet NATCHEZ on the China run and later notorious for his handling of CHALLENGE on her maiden voyage. On her first voyage out, *Sea Witch* established a succession of records: 42 days from New York to the Cape of Good Hope and 70 days, 10 hours past Java Head, outbound, while returning against the monsoon, she was 26 days from Anjer to the

Unidentified Chinese artist's portrait of the clipper SEA WITCH, *flying the Howland and Aspinwall house flag. Courtesy Peabody Essex Museum, Salem, Massachusetts.*

Cape and 62 days to New York. On her second voyage, she nipped a day off her time from Java Head and the Cape of Good Hope and arrived at New York after a voyage of 77 days from Canton. Better things were still to come. On her third China voyage, *Sea Witch* sailed from New York to Canton and back in only 194 sailing days, with calls at Valparaiso and Callao on the outward passage. Departing Canton on January 8, 1849, she reached New York on March 25 after a passage of 74 days, 14 hours. "It was," as Carl Cutler emphasizes, "the World's First Permanent Sailing Record." A few days after her return, the *Commercial Advertiser* described the particulars:

> During the voyage she has made the shortest direct passages on record, viz.: 69 days from New York to Valparaiso; 50 days from Callao to China; 75 days from China to New York. Distance run by observation from New York to Valparaiso, 10,568 miles; average, 6 2/5 miles per hour. Distance from Callao to China, 10,417 miles; average, 8 5/8 knots per hour. Distance from China to New York, 14,255 miles; average, 7 7/8 knots per hour. Best ten (consecutive) days' run, 2,634 miles; average, 11 1/10 knots per hour.

Returning from China in April 1850, the year after the start of the California Gold Rush, *Sea Witch* was put on the berth for San Francisco, with Waterman relinquishing command in favor of his equally hard-driving first mate, George Fraser. Not surprisingly, she set a new record of 97 net sailing days for the outward passage, the first ship to make the run in less than 100 days. (Including four days at Valparaiso, she was 101 days from port to port.) It is interesting to note that the average time for 57 vessels

arriving from the East Coast at around the same time was 171 days. Just as remarkable, *Sea Witch*'s next two passages to San Francisco, in 1851 and 1852, were made in 111 days and 108 days, respectively. Her next voyage was via the Cape of Good Hope to Hong Kong, continuing eastward to South America, where she was forced to put into Valparaiso because of holes in the hull, possibly bored by a member of the crew.

The ship's ninth and last voyage began on April 5, 1855, when she sailed from New York. While still in the Atlantic, Captain Fraser was killed by one of his mates and the ship was forced into Rio de Janeiro, where Captain Lang assumed command. Continuing to China, *Sea Witch* embarked 500 Chinese workers — called coolies — bound for Havana. On March 28, 1856, after 99 days at sea, she struck a reef 12 miles from Havana and sank.

Cutler, *Greyhounds of the Sea.* Howe & Matthews, *American Clipper Ships.*

SECTOR

Rowboat. *L/B:* 26.3′ × 5.2′ (8m × 1.6m). *Tons:* 1,500 lb. (650 kg). *Hull:* carbon fiber. *Comp.:* 1. *Des.:* Jean Barret. *Built:* Bernard Fournier Le Ray, La Trinité-sur-Mer, France; 1991.

In 1990, veteran oarsman Gerard d'Aboville, who had rowed the single-handed *Captain Cook* across the Atlantic from Cape Cod to Brittany in 1980, determined to be the first person to row across the Pacific. His rowboat, *Sector* (named for the Swiss watch manufacturer that underwrote the venture), was built in France. There was an open cockpit for rowing, and watertight compartments forward, for supplies, and aft, for living quarters. The boat was fitted with telex communications, water desalinators and solar panels, and a case of wine. D'Aboville and the boat flew to Japan and set out from the port of Choshi on July 11, 1991, bound for San Francisco. Rowing ten hours, or about 7,000 strokes, a day, d'Aboville set sea anchors at night to prevent drifting backwards. But having left late in the season, *Sector* encountered contrary winds that for one two-week period prevented her from making any headway. Two days out the boat capsized for the first time, something that would happen frequently throughout the 134-day crossing. The boat had built-in ballast tanks that could be trimmed to right the boat, but *Sector* was once stuck upside down for an hour and a half. D'Aboville was amazed at the quantity of garbage he encountered on the lonely North Pacific sea route:

> Pollution was visible everywhere. I am not referring to those signs of terrible and perhaps irremediable pollution, such as the oil spills from the gigantic tankers, but of a rampant ordinary pollution that revealed itself in countless little ways: plastic bags, styrofoam packing, et cetera. Every twenty minutes or so I would come upon some sort or another of debris, which, considering my limited horizon, suggests the magnitude of the problem.

Sector met with a Russian ship on October 29, but refused any offers of assistance, and as d'Aboville neared the coast of Washington State on November 19, he was greeted by the trawler *Miss Mary*. He was taken in tow over the Columbia River bar on November 21, after a passage of 4,300 miles.

d'Aboville, *Alone*.

SEEADLER

(ex-*Pass of Balmaha*) Ship (3m). *L/B/D:* 245.5′ × 38.8′ × 22.5′ dph (74.8m × 11.8m × 6.9m). *Tons:* 1,571 grt. *Hull:* steel. *Comp.:* 63 crew. *Arm.:* 2 × 8.8cm. *Mach.:* diesel engine, 1 screw; 9 kts. *Built:* Robert Duncan & Co., Port Glasgow, Scotland; 1878.

Built for the River Plate Shipping Company of New York, at the beginning of World War I, *Pass of Balmaha* was sold to the Hunt Company. En route to Murmansk in July 1915, she was boarded by a British crew and ordered to the Orkneys for a search of her cargo. Released, the next day she was boarded by a crew from *U-36* and sent to Hamburg. Seized for contraband, she was eventually requisitioned by the Navy and fitted out as an armed merchant cruiser. Renamed *Seeadler* ("Sea Eagle"), Lieuten-

ant Commander Felix Graf von Luckner commanding, she sailed from Hamburg on December 21, 1916, disguised as the Norwegian-flag *Irma* bound for Australia. Between January 9 and March 11, 1917, she seized eleven ships, all of which were scuttled. In March, her 264 prisoners were sent to Rio de Janeiro aboard the French bark *Cambronne,* and *Seeadler* entered the Pacific where she captured three U.S. ships before putting into Mopelia, French Society Islands, on July 31. Two days later, she was driven onto a coral reef and wrecked. On August 23, Luckner and five others sailed in search of another ship in which to resume their raiding. On September 5, the remaining Germans seized the schooner *Lutèce,* which they renamed *Fortuna* and sailed to Easter Island. Luckner was captured in the Fiji Islands. The crew of the four ships seized in the Pacific were eventually rescued. After the war, Luckner became world famous for his exploits, which included the capture of sixteen ships of 30,099 gross tons without the death of one Allied sailor.

Hoyt, *Count von Luckner*. Thomas, *Count Luckner, the Sea Devil.* Walter, *Kaiser's Pirates*.

SEEANDBEE

(later USS *Wolverine*) Sidewheel steamer (2f/4m). *L/B/D:* 484.5′ × 58.1′ × 24′ (147.7m × 17.7m × 7.3m). *Tons:* 3,434 grt. *Hull:* steel. *Comp.:* 1,500 pass. *Mach.:* 1,596 nhp, sidewheels. *Des.:* Frank E. Kirby. *Built:* Detroit Ship Building Co., Wyandotte, Mich.; 1913.

The name of the Cleveland & Buffalo Transit Company's mammoth passenger steamer was chosen by a contest, the winner being a teenage girl who suggested the phonetic spelling of the company nickname, "C & B." Designed for the 189-mile overnight run between Cleveland and Buffalo, the steamer boasted 510 staterooms and could accommodate 1,500 passengers in addition to freight. Commissioned in late 1913, her early years coincided with a downturn in passenger traffic in the wake of the TITANIC and EASTLAND disasters, a problem aggravated by her enormous size. Paired with *City of Buffalo*, in addition to her regular Lake Erie route, she often ran overnight excursions to Niagara Falls on the weekends. Passenger shipping again ground to a halt during the depression and in 1932 she was laid up, being recommissioned for the run to Chicago during the World's Fair, and she afterward remained in interlake business until C&B's bankruptcy in 1939.

In the same year, Y. J. McGuire bought the old steamer for $135,000 and sold her to the U.S. Navy the following year for $750,000. Converted to a training aircraft carrier and renamed USS *Wolverine,* more than 18,000 naval aviators trained on her 550-foot-long flight deck during World War II. Sold in 1946, she was scrapped in 1947.

Hilton, *Night Boat*. U.S. Navy, *DANFS*.

SENYAVIN

Sloop of war (3m). *L/B/D:* 90′ bp × 29′ × 12.8′ (27.4m × 8.8m × 3.9m). *Hull:* wood. *Comp.:* 62. *Arm.:* 16 carr. *Built:* Okhta Shipyard, St. Petersburg, Russia; 1826.

In the early 1820s, relations between Russia and the United States were strained over the extent of czarist holdings in North America. Russia planned to send two warships to patrol its claims, but agreement on 54°40′N as the southern limit of its American territory in 1824 obviated the need for such a military presence, and the ships were ordered to explore the coasts of Russian America and Asia. Otto von Kotzebue returned to Kronstadt from his circumnavigation in PREDPRIYATIYE on July 10, 1826, and on August 16 *Senyavin* (Captain Lieutenant Fedor Petrovich Litke) sailed in company with *Möller* (Captain Lieutenant M. N. Staniukovich). Litke's orders were to

> reconnoiter, and describe, the coasts of Kamchatka, the land of the Chuchkis and the Koriaks (the coasts of which have not yet been described by anyone, and which are unknown except by the voyage of Captain Bering); the coasts of the Okhotsk Sea, and the Shantar Islands, which although they are known to us, have not been sufficiently described.

During the winter they were to cruise the western Caroline Islands as far south as the equator. (Staniukovich was to explore along the Alaskan coast but was lackluster in pursuit of his objectives.)

The vessels proceeded in company to Portsmouth, but they were separated soon after sailing from England. Rounding Cape Horn on February 24, 1827, *Senyavin* called at Concepción, Chile, in March before proceeding to Novo Arkhangelsk (Sitka), where the Russians remained from June 11 to July 19. After calling at Unalaska, they arrived at Petropavlovsk, Kamchatka, in mid-September. From November 1827 through April 1828, they cruised in the Caroline Islands and the Bonin-Jima group before returning to Kamchatka in May. That summer they surveyed the coast from Avacha Bay to Karaginskii Island and then sailed through the Bering Strait for a survey of the Chuchki coast from the East Cape to the Anadyr River. The ships left Petropavlovsk for the last time in October and rejoined *Möller* at Manila on January 1, 1830, before sailing for Europe via the Cape of Good Hope. *Senyavin* returned to Kronstadt on September 16, 1829.

Litke's voyage in *Senyavin* was among the most productive voyages of discovery sent out by any country in the nineteenth century. In addition to the survey work on the Asian coast, the expedition discovered twelve island groups and described another twenty-six in the Carolines. Experiments with an invariable pendulum enabled the company to determine the degree to which the earth flattens at the poles. Naturalist Karl Heinrich Mertens, ornithologist Baron von Kittlitz, and mineralogist Alexander Postels described over 1,000 new species of insects, fish, birds, and other animals, and more than 2,500 different types of plants, algae, and rocks. In addition, they also collected ethnographic artifacts and made more than 1,250 sketches of their findings.

Shortly after the conclusion of the voyage, *Senyavin* was dispatched on a second scientific expedition to Iceland, again under Litke. The expedition's chief scientist Mertens died two weeks after the ship's return to Kronstadt in September 1830.

Ivashintsov, *Russian Round-the-World Voyages*. Litke, *Voyage Round the World: 1826–1829*.

SERÇE LIMANI SHIP

Ship. *L/B/D:* 49.2′ × 16.7′ (15m × 5.1m). *Tons:* 30–40 burden. *Hull:* wood. *Built:* eastern Mediterranean; 11th cent. CE.

The earliest known ship incorporating "modern" shipbuilding techniques was discovered at a depth of 32 to 34 meters (100 feet) in the bay of Serçe Limani (Sparrow Harbor) on the coast of Turkey north of Rhodes (36°34′N, 28°05′E). First shown to George Bass in 1973 by Turkish sponge diver Mehmet Askin, the site was excavated between 1977 and 1979 under the direction of Bass and Frederick Van Doorninck, Jr. The lines of the Serçe Limani ship, as reconstructed by J. Richard Steffy, show a deep, full-ended vessel, rounded in profile, with a flat bottom, a sharp turn at the bilge, and a steep sheer. She was probably two-masted and lateen-rigged. The Serçe Limani ship may be called the first truly modern ship because its hull was built entirely onto a preexisting frame skeleton. By the beginning of the eleventh century, the transition in Mediterranean shipbuilding from the Greco-Roman "shell-first" to the modern "skeleton-first" construction technique was complete.

About 20 percent of the hull survived, primarily the bottom and a small area of the upper port stern. Widely scattered fragments represented various portions of the hull up to the deck level, and the keelson and some ceil-

After reassembling the remains of the 11th-century Serçe Limani wreck in the Bodrum Museum of Underwater Archaeology, J. Richard Steffy was able to draw a set of plans of the original ship. Upper left: the half-breadth or waterline plan shows half the hull as seen from above. Lower left: the sheer-and-profile plan shows the vessel in profile. Right: the body plan showing the view from the stern forward (left half) and from the bow sternward (right half). Photo courtesy Institute of Nautical Archaeology, College Station, Texas; plans courtesy of J. Richard Steffy.

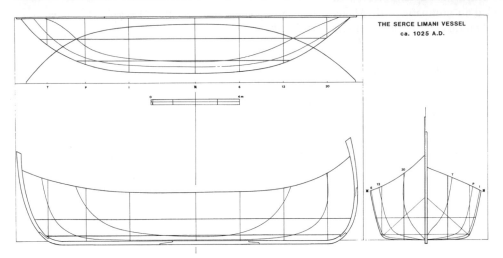

THE SERCE LIMANI VESSEL
ca. 1025 A.D.

ing planking were preserved in the after part of the hold. The keel — of which 11.3 meters (37 feet) survived — was hardwood; stringers and wales were all softwood, most likely pine. A single, flat scarf was located aft of amidships, but the foremost part of the keel curved into the stempost without the familiar keel-stempost scarf. There was no evidence for a false keel. The garboards were not rabbeted or attached to the keel in any way, but traces of pitch indicate that the keel-garboard seam was caulked. A keelson ran the length of the ship and was attached to the keel with iron bolts similar to those used in the Byzantine ship at YASSI ADA. The sternpost was a naturally curved timber rabbeted to receive the plank ends. The framing plan was complex and the spacing of the frames irregular. In the hold, floor timbers with long arms to port alternated with floors with long arms to starboard. V-floors and half-frames were used in the bow and stern. The hull was assembled by fastening planks to frames (both iron nails and wooden treenails were used) without any edge-joining of planks. The wales were logs sawn in half lengthwise, as in the Yassi Ada ship. The ceiling consisted of three elements: half-round longitudinal stringers, transverse boards, and standard longitudinal planks. The result was a strong flat floor in the hold

— perhaps, as has been suggested, intended to facilitate the transport of animals.

The ship carried an unusual cargo. Divers digging in the sand came up with hands cut and bleeding, and they soon realized they were excavating an enormous pile of glass — some three metric tons of broken glass vessels, raw glass, and factory waste. This consignment was undoubtedly en route to a glass-making center to be melted down — an early example of recycling. The glass vessels were deliberately smashed before being loaded into the hold, but many have now been reconstructed through painstaking work.

There is conflicting evidence about the origin of the ship and crew. One of the eight iron anchors was stamped with Arabic letters and a bronze bucket also bore an Arabic inscription. Among the ceramic finds were Islamic glazed bowls imitating Chinese Tang dynasty porcelain. Complete glass vessels found in the stern were also of Islamic type. On the other hand, Christian symbols were found on some of the net-weights, some amphorae and cooking pots had Greek graffiti, Byzantine coins were discovered as well as Islamic gold pieces, and pig bones were among the animal remains. This surprising cultural mixture suggests that commercial ties between the Byzantine and Arab worlds in the eleventh century may have been closer than is generally supposed.

A glass balance-pan of the Fatimid Caliph al-Zahir (1020–35) provides a terminus post quem for the wreck. The finds, including the preserved timbers, are displayed at the Bodrum Museum of Underwater Archaeology.

Bass, "Eleventh Century Shipwreck at Serçe Limani, Turkey." Steffy, "Reconstruction of the Eleventh Century Serçe Liman Vessel."

SMS SEYDLITZ

Battlecruiser (2f/2m). *L/B/D:* 658.0′ × 93.5′ × 30.5′ (200.6m × 28.5m × 9.3m). *Tons:* 28,550 disp. *Hull:* steel. *Comp.:* 1,143. *Arm.:* 10 × 11.2″ (5 × 2), 12 × 6″, 12 × 8.8cm; 4 × 20″TT. *Armor:* 12″ belt, 3.2″ deck. *Mach.:* turbines, 89,738 shp, 4 screws; 28.1 kts. *Built:* Blohm & Voss, Hamburg; 1913.

Essentially an improved *Moltke*-class cruiser and thus quite similar in appearance and design to SMS GOEBEN, SMS *Seydlitz* was one of the most battle-hardened ships of the Imperial German Navy. Named for the eighteenth-century cavalry officer Friedrich Wilhelm von Seydlitz, the cruiser was the flagship of Rear Admiral Franz von Hipper's First Reconnaissance Group, stationed at Wilhelmshaven. On November 3 and December 16, 1914, Hipper's battlecruisers bombarded British coastal defenses at Yarmouth and Hartlepool. On January 24, 1915,

Seydlitz sortied at the head of an eight-ship group, including the heavy cruisers MOLTKE, DERFFLINGER, and BLÜCHER, and four light cruisers. The British deployed Admiral David Beatty's First and Second Battle Cruiser Squadrons, supported by units from Rosyth, Harwich, and Scapa Flow. Action opened between light cruisers, and Hipper quickly realized that he was dangerously outgunned. In the ensuing chase, *Seydlitz*'s two after turrets were knocked out and she lost 165 crew; the older *Blücher* was sunk with the loss of 792 lives. British losses were light, although Beatty's flagship HMS LION required four months of repairs. But *Seydlitz*'s battle damage resulted in improvements to deck armor and antiflash protection in the magazines that gave the German fleet — and *Seydlitz* in particular — a dramatic advantage at the Battle of Jutland.

After repairs, *Seydlitz* served in the Baltic before returning to the North Sea. Damaged by a mine on an ineffectual raid against Lowestoft and Yarmouth on April 25, 1916, she was again battleworthy by the time the High Seas Fleet sallied in an effort to engage the Royal Navy's Grand Fleet. Hipper's battlecruisers fired the opening salvos of the Battle of Jutland at 1547. Shortly after 1600, *Von der Tann* sank HMS INDEFATIGABLE and fifteen minutes later, coordinated fire from *Seydlitz* and *Derfflinger* sank HMS *Queen Mary*. Before the afternoon was out, *Seydlitz* had received 23 hits and had been torpedoed by the destroyer HMS *Petard;* with 5,300 tons of water in her hull and well down at the head she limped back to port. Repairs lasted four months, but for all intents and purposes *Seydlitz*'s war was over, as it was for most of the German surface fleet.

On November 21, 1918, *Seydlitz* led 74 ships of the Imperial German Navy into internment at Scapa Flow under the armistice agreement that brought hostilities to a close. Weighed down by the humiliation of his ignominious surrender to the British, Admiral Ludwig von Reuter ordered the German Fleet to scuttle itself on June 21, 1919, one week before the Versailles Peace Treaty was ratified. *Seydlitz* rolled over and sank in about 70 feet of water. While British and French politicians decried the Germans' action, others were more accepting. Henry William Massingham, editor of the liberal British weekly the *Nation,* wrote:

> I have not spoken to a British sailor who did not heartily approve of the action of the German sailors in sinking their fleet. "I must admit I did not expect them to do it," said one naval officer to me, "but I know I should have done it in their place."

Seydlitz lay at Scapa Flow with about 25 feet of her hull exposed until November 2, 1928, when after more than

40 attempts she was refloated by the Cox and Danks Ltd. salvage company. Towed to Rosyth the following year, she was broken up in 1930.

Breyer, *Battleships and Battlecruisers.* Gröner, *German Warships.* Van der Vat, *Grand Scuttle.*

SHAMROCK V

(ex-*Quadrifoglio, Shamrock V*) J-class cutter. *L/B/D:* 119.8′ × 19.7′ × 14.7′ (36.5m × 6.8m × 4.5m). *Tons:* 104 grt. *Hull:* composite. *Built:* Camper & Nicholsons, Southampton, Eng.; 1930.

The most celebrated yachtsman ever to challenge for the America's Cup was the self-made millionaire Sir Thomas Lipton. Born to an Irish grocer in a Glasgow tenement, Lipton mounted the first of his five challenges under the auspices of the Royal Ulster Yacht Club in 1898. His William Fife–designed cutter *Shamrock,* the first challenger not to cross the Atlantic under its own power, lost to J. Pierpont Morgan's *Columbia* (designed by Nat Herreshoff) in three races. Gracious in defeat, Lipton was made an honorary member of the New York Yacht Club. Two years later, his George Watson–designed *Shamrock II* lost three races on corrected time to *Columbia,* though the margins were negligible and she actually crossed the line ahead by two seconds in the second race. The extreme limits of racing design were reached in 1903, when Fife's *Shamrock III* was pitted against Herreshoff's RELIANCE. The race conditions were mediocre, but in the contest between sail areas, *Shamrock*'s 14,154 square feet were no match for *Reliance*'s 17,730 square feet. These were the last America's Cup races for almost two decades, and when they resumed in 1920 it was with smaller yachts built to Herreshoff's International Rule. *Shamrock IV* and *Resolute,* both built before World War I, had the most exciting race series held to that time, and *Shamrock IV* won the first two of five races by decisive margins.

The rules changed yet again and the 1930 America's Cup races were the first of three between yachts designed to the J-class rule. The celebrated J-boats with their lofty rigs, Bermuda rigs, and Park Avenue booms were between 75 and 87 feet in length, with sail areas between 7,550 and 7,583 square feet, though this included three headsails — jib, jig, and topsail jib. *Shamrock V* was no match for *Resolute,* which was chosen from among four trial boats, and she lost the series in four straight races. So ended the racing career of Sir Thomas Lipton, "the world's best loser," who died the next year at the age of eighty-one.

Shamrock V was next purchased by T. O. M. Sopwith, who used her as a trial horse for his *Endeavour*s in 1933 (*Rainbow* vs. *Endeavour*) and 1937 (*Ranger* vs. *Endeavour II*). *Shamrock V* subsequently changed hands several times. An auxiliary diesel engine was installed and she was at one time rigged as a cruising ketch. While owned by the Immobiliare SIFI Spa in Sardinia, she was named *Quadrifoglio,* Italian for "shamrock." In the 1980s, she was acquired and restored to her original rig by the Museum of Yachting in Newport, Rhode Island, where she is maintained in sailing condition.

Leather, *Big Class Racing Yachts.*

The J-boat SHAMROCK V, *the fifth and last of Sir Thomas Lipton's America's Cup challengers, heels over on a port tack in a gentle breeze. Well into her seventh decade, the cutter still sails under the auspices of the Museum of Yachting in Newport, R.I. Courtesy New York Yacht Club.*

HMS SHEFFIELD

Southampton-class cruiser (2f/2m). *L/B/D:* 591.5′ × 61.7′ × 20.3′ (180.2m × 18.8m × 6.2m). *Tons:* 11,350 disp. *Hull:* steel. *Comp.:* 796. *Arm.:* 12 × 6″ (4 × 3), 8 × 4″, 8 × 2pdr, 2 × 0.5″; 6 × 21″TT; 3 aircraft. *Armor:* 4.5″ belt, 2″ deck. *Mach.:* geared turbines, 75,000 shp, 4 screws; 32 kts. *Built:* Vickers-Armstrong, Ltd., Newcastle-on-Tyne; 1937.

Originally assigned to the Home Fleet, at the start of World War II, HMS *Sheffield* was on the Northern Patrol almost continuously from November 1939 through February 1940. During the German invasion of Norway, she was deployed to Namsos in anticipation of a British counterattack, which never came, and she left Norwegian waters for the last time on May 2, evacuating troops and refugees from Narvik. Transferred to Force H in August, "Old Shiny" served as a convoy escort between Gibraltar and Malta. She was in the fleet engagement with the Italian battleships Vittorio Veneto and Giulio Cesare off Cape Spartivento on November 27, 1940, and she took part in the bombardment of Genoa on February 9, 1941, during which 5 merchant ships were sunk, 18 damaged, and 144 people killed.

In mid-May 1941, Force H headed into the North Atlantic to help search for the German battleship Bismarck, and on May 26 *Sheffield* was accidentally attacked by torpedo planes from HMS Ark Royal, but she escaped unscathed. En route to Britain later in June, *Sheffield* sank the tanker *Friedrich Breme*. By the following spring, *Sheffield* had rejoined the Home Fleet and the Arctic convoys, and on March 4, 1942, she was damaged by a mine off Iceland and returned to Britain. On November 8, 1942, the cruiser supported landings near Algiers during Operation Torch, the Allied invasion of North Africa, but she was soon recalled to Arctic duty. At the end of December 1942, the Germans mounted Operation Regenbogen, a failed attack led by the cruisers Admiral Hipper and Lützow on Convoy JW.51B. As part of the close escort, *Sheffield* sank the German destroyer *Friedrich Eckoldt*; British losses included the destroyer HMS *Achates* and minesweeper *Bramble*.

Captain Charles Larcom was replaced by Captain A. W. Clarke in February 1943, and shortly thereafter *Sheffield* sustained considerable storm damage off Iceland. After supporting antisubmarine operations in the Bay of Biscay, at the end of the year *Sheffield* was part of the cruiser force that brought to bay and helped sink the German battlecruiser Scharnhorst in the Battle of the North Cape on December 26. She remained in northern waters through the spring of 1944 and supported British naval air operations against Tirpitz in Norway.

From July 1944 through May 1945, *Sheffield* underwent an extensive refit at Boston, Massachusetts. In the postwar period she was stationed in the Mediterranean. Decommissioned in 1959, she was broken up at Faslane in 1967.

Bassett, HMS "Sheffield."

CSS SHENANDOAH

(ex-*Sea King*, later *El Majidi*) Commerce raider. *L/B/D:* 220′ × 36′ × 20′ (67.1m × 11m × 6.1m). *Tons:* 1,018 grt. *Hull:* steel. *Comp.:* 73. *Arm.:* 4 × 8″, 2 × 32pdr, 2 × 12pdr. *Mach.:* direct-acting engines, 1 screw; 9 kts. *Built:* Alexander Stephen & Sons, Ltd., Govan, Scotland; 1864.

The first ship designed solely as a troop transport, the composite-built auxiliary screw steamship *Sea King* made one voyage under the British flag before being purchased in September 1864 by Confederate agents in England. Sailing from London on October 8, *Shenandoah* met the supply vessel *Laurel* off Funchal on October 19 and was commissioned under Lieutenant J. I. Waddell. *Shenandoah* proceeded to Australia by way of the Cape of Good Hope, taking five prizes in the Atlantic and one in the Indian Ocean. Departing Melbourne on February 19, 1865, *Shenandoah* had spectacular luck against the American whaling fleet, burning five ships before sailing into the Bering Sea. On June 23, Waddell learned that the Civil War was over, but he continued his cruise and took twenty-one more prizes, eight of which were sunk. On August 2, a British ship informed Waddell of the war's end, at which point he converted *Shenandoah* to look as much like a merchantman as possible. *Shenandoah* arrived at Liverpool on November 6, 1865, having captured 38 prizes. Seized by the U.S. government, she was sold to the Sultan of Zanzibar and renamed *El Majidi*. She foundered at sea en route from Zanzibar to Bombay.

Horan, ed., CSS "Shenandoah." Silverstone, *Warships of the Civil War Navies.*

SHINAN WRECK

Junk (3m). *L/B/D:* 105.0′ × 32.8′ × 8.2′ dph (32m × 10m × 2.5m). *Tons:* 200 burden. *Hull:* wood. *Built:* southern China; 14th cent.

In 1975, Ch'oe Hyong-gun recovered a number of encrusted ceramic containers from a ship lying in about 20 meters of water off the coast of Shinan, South Korea (in 35°01′N, 126°05′E). These containers were positively identified as antiquities, and divers began to loot the site before government authorities put it under the auspices of the Cultural Property Preservation Office. Proper archaeological excavation began in 1976 and continued through 1984, culminating with the salvage and conservation of the ship's hull in a special shoreside facility.

The remains of the hull include 445 ship's timbers and 223 planks of Chinese red fir and Chinese red pine, both of which are native to southern China. The ship is similar to the thirteenth-century Quanzhou wreck, though there are differences in the construction details. In both ships, the bottom of the hull is V-shaped, and the hull planking is joined in a variety of ways. The Shinan wreck yielded the keel, fourteen starboard strakes, and six port strakes. The strakes were laid over one another in a rabbeted clinker construction, with the rabbet being cut out of the inner lower part of the plank. Towards the bow, this changes to a rabbeted carvel construction to give the hull a smooth side. Parts of two mast steps survive — a fore and a main — and the interior of the hull is divided by seven bulkheads.

Further study of the site revealed that the wreck was of a Chinese vessel en route from China, possibly Ningpo, towards Japan, when it sank in a storm. The cargo consisted of more than 12,000 pieces of Chinese ceramics, including celadon vases, plates and bowls, stoneware, incense burners, and *ching p'ai* (bluish white) porcelain pieces from the Yüan dynasty. Among other artifacts related to the cargo were numbered 729 metal objects, 45 stone objects, 20,000 individual Chinese copper coins, 1,017 pieces of red sandalwood measuring between 1 and 3 meters in length, and over 500 other objects, including the crew's personal possessions. Many of the finds were still packed in their shipping containers marked with the year, 1323, towards the end of the Yüan dynasty.

Green & Kim, "Shinan and Wando Sites." Kim & Keith, "Fourteenth-Century Cargo Makes Port at Last."

SHOHO

(ex-*Tsurugizaki*) *Zuiho*-class aircraft carrier. *L/B/D:* 671.9′ × 59.7′ × 21.75′ (204.8m × 18.2m × 6.6m). *Tons:* 11,262 disp. *Hull:* steel. *Comp.:* 785. *Arm.:* 30 aircraft; 8 × 5″, 8 × 25mm. *Mach.:* geared turbines, 52,000 shp, 2 screws; 26 kts. *Built:* Yokosuka Dockyard, Yokosuka, Japan; 1939.

Laid down as a submarine depot ship, *Shoho* ("Happy Phoenix") was converted to a light aircraft carrier in 1941. Four months after her commissioning, she was one of three carriers in the Japanese fleet sent to capture Port Moresby in the southeast corner of New Guinea. At about 0900 on May 7, 1942, planes from LEXINGTON and YORKTOWN were searching for the elusive heavy carriers SHOKAKU and ZUIKAKU in the opening stages of what became the Battle of the Coral Sea. Wandering off course, a flight of *Lexington*'s dive-bombers came across *Shoho* near Woodlark Island (in 10°29′S, 152°55′E) between New Guinea and the Solomon Islands. Hit by thirteen bombs and seven torpedoes, the small carrier sank within ten minutes, with the loss of about 600 crew. The loss of Japan's first aircraft carrier was reported in

Lieutenant Commander Robert E. Dixon's memorable signal: "Scratch one flattop."

Stephen, *Sea Battles in Close-Up.*

SHOKAKU

Shokaku-class aircraft carrier (2f/1m). *L/B/D:* 844.8′ × 85.3′ × 29′ (257.5m × 26m × 8.8m). *Tons:* 25,675 disp. (32,105 full). *Hull:* steel. *Comp.:* 1,660. *Arm.:* 84 aircraft; 16 × 5″, 42 × 25mm. *Armor:* 5.9″ belt. *Mach.:* geared turbines, 160,000 shp, 4 screws; 34.5 kts. *Built:* Yokosuka Dockyard, Yokosuka, Japan; 1941.

Shokaku, whose name means "happy crane," was among the most powerful Japanese carriers ever built, specifically designed to sail as a consort to the battleships YAMATO and MUSASHI. One of six carriers taking part in the December 7, 1941, attack on Pearl Harbor, she later sailed in support of operations against the Dutch East Indies and Ceylon. At the Battle of the Coral Sea on May 8, 1942, planes from *Shokaku* and her sister ship sank USS LEXINGTON and severely damaged YORKTOWN. However, planes from the American carriers also managed to score three bomb hits on *Shokaku,* and as a result she did not take part in the Battle of Midway in early June. At the Battle of Santa Cruz on October 26, 1942, dive-bombers from USS HORNET inflicted another nine months' worth of repairs on *Shokaku.* Just prior to the Battle of the Philippine Sea, *Shokaku* was struck by three torpedoes from the submarine USS CAVALLA and sank about 140 miles north of Yap Island (in 11°40′N, 137°40′E), with the loss of 1,263 crew.

Stephen, *Sea Battles in Close-Up.*

SILBERHORN

Bark (4m). *L/B/D:* 267.4′ × 40.2′ × 24′ dph (81.5m × 12.2m × 7.3m). *Tons:* 1,853 grt. *Hull:* iron. *Built:* Russell & Co., Port Glasgow, Scotland; 1884.

Silberhorn was one of three sister ships built for Charles E. de Wolf of Liverpool between 1882 and 1884 — the others were *Goldenhorn* and *Matterhorn*. One of the earlier four-masted iron barks, she was small in comparison with later vessels of the type, carrying single topgallants and royals. Her career was unexceptional, except for Bill Adams's remarkable account of his apprenticeship in her between 1897 and 1901. In that period, *Silberhorn* made four voyages: to Victoria, Astoria, and twice to San Francisco, where Adams's apprenticeship ended and a weak heart forced him to quit the sea. (In later years he became known for his sailing ship stories published in the *Saturday Evening Post*.) *Silberhorn* was lost in 1907 on a voyage bound from Newcastle for Iquique with coal. The German bark *Anny* reported seeing a ship on fire near Juan Fernández Island, but the only letters that could be read on her stern were "ool," thought to be the last letters of *Silberhorn*'s port of registry. In 1910, it was discovered that one of *Silberhorn*'s life buoys had washed ashore at Pitcairn Island.

Adams, *Ships and Memories*.

USS SILVERSIDES (SS-236)

Gato-class submarine. *L/B/D:* 311.8′ × 27.3′ × 15.3′ (95m × 8.3m × 4.6m). *Tons:* 1,256/2,410 disp. *Hull:* steel; 300′ dd. *Comp.:* 61. *Arm.:* 10 × 21″TT; 1 × 3″, 3 × mg. *Mach.:* diesel/electric, 5,400/2,740 hp, 2 screws; 20/9 kts. *Built:* Mare Island Navy Yard, Vallejo, Calif.; 1941.

One of the most successful U.S. submarines of World War II, USS *Silversides* (named for a fish) was commissioned only eight days after the Japanese attack on Pearl Harbor. Under Lieutenant Commander C. C. Burlingame, *Silversides* got off to an aggressive start, sinking four prizes in her first patrols, off the Japanese home islands. This was followed by a lackluster cruise in the Caroline Islands after which she put into Brisbane. On January 18, 1943, she scored her first of four hat-tricks, sinking three freighters; she did the same on October 24, off New Guinea, on December 29, 1943, in the Palau Islands, and on May 10, 1944, in the Marianas. The last took place on her tenth and most successful mission, during which she sank a total of six ships for 14,000 gross tons. Following another overhaul on the West Coast, *Silversides* returned to Japanese waters in September. There, she worked in concert with submarines *Trigger* and *Sterlet* to rescue *Salmon* after she was forced to the surface by depth charges. *Silversides*'s last three cruises were relatively uneventful. Used as a naval reserve training ship in Chicago from 1947 to 1962, in 1969 she was opened as a memorial and museum ship at the Great Lakes Naval and Maritime Museum in Muskegon, Michigan.

Roscoe, *United States Submarine Operations in World War II*. U.S. Navy, *DANFS*.

USS SIMS (DD-409)

Sims-class destroyer (1f/1m). *L/B/D:* 347.6′ × 36.1′ × 17.3′ (105.9m × 11m × 5.3m). *Tons:* 1,570 disp. *Hull:* steel. *Comp.:* 241. *Arm.:* 4 × 5″, 8 × 21″TT. *Mach.:* geared turbines, 44,000 shp, 2 screws; 36.5 kts. *Built:* Bath Iron Works, Bath, Me.; 1939.

Named for Canadian-born Admiral William S. Sims, a progressive gunnery officer who helped propel the U.S. Navy to the front rank of world navies in the early years of the twentieth century, USS *Sims* was the first of a twelve-ship class completed in 1939–40. As part of Destroyer Squadron 2, *Sims* was assigned to the Neutrality Patrol intended to keep European belligerents out of American waters. Following the Japanese attack on Pearl Harbor, Destroyer Squadron (DesRon) 2 was assigned to Task Force 17, centered on USS YORKTOWN. In January 1942, *Sims* helped convoy American troops to Samoa and took part in attacks on Japanese positions in the Marshall Islands.

That spring, TF 17 was deployed to the Coral Sea to check the Japanese advance towards Australia and New Zealand. On May 6, the eve of the Battle of the Coral Sea, *Sims* and the oiler USS NEOSHO were detached from the fleet. The next day, Japanese reconnaissance planes misidentified the pair as an aircraft carrier and her escort. Attacked by sixty-one planes, *Sims* was sunk in 15°10′S, 158°05′E when two bombs exploded in her engine room. Sixteen survivors were picked up by *Neosho*, which was intentionally sunk by USS *Henley* four days later.

U.S. Navy, *DANFS*.

HMS SIRIUS

6th rate 10 (3m). *L/B/D:* 110.4′ × 32.8′ × 12.9′ (33.7m × 10m × 3.9m). *Tons:* 512 bm. *Hull:* wood. *Comp.:* 50–160. *Arm.:* 4 × 6pdr, 6 × 18pdr. *Built:* Christopher Watson, Rotherhithe, Eng.; 1781.

The merchant ship *Berwick* was built for the Baltic trade, but while still on the stocks, she was purchased by the Royal Navy for use as an armed transport. After five years in service between Britain and North America, she was renamed HMS *Sirius* and fitted out for service as flagship of the "First Fleet" sent out to Botany Bay to establish a European settlement in Australia. While the expedition has often been derided as nothing more than an expedient measure to rid England of criminals, in fact it was part of a well-considered plan to establish a firm British presence in the Pacific as a counterweight to the Spanish in the Americas and the Philippines, and the Dutch in the East Indies. Nor was the idea of "transportation" of convicts new; the policy originated in 1717 and previous destinations included Africa and the American colonies.

On May 13, 1787, sixth-rate *Sirius* sailed from Portsmouth at the head of a fleet of eleven ships and a total complement of 1,350 people under Commander in Chief and Governor Arthur Phillip. These included the convict transports *Scarborough* (with 208 male convicts), *Alexander* (195 men), *Lady Penrhyn* (101 female convicts), *Charlotte* (88 men, 22 women), *Friendship* (76 men, 21 females) and *Prince of Wales* (1 man, 49 women). There were also the storeships *Fishburn, Golden Grove,* and *Borrowdale,* and the replenishment ship *Supply.* The convicts were given a certain amount of freedom in the ships, which the majority of them seem not to have abused. However, there was trouble not only from some of the prisoners but from the crew and guards as well, some of whom were disciplined for mutiny, disobedience, or sleeping with the women prisoners. The ships sailed via Tenerife, Rio de Janeiro (where they remained a month), and Cape Town. Shortly before their arrival at the latter port, convicts and members of *Alexander*'s crew conspired to seize the ship but were thwarted at the last minute, and the ships arrived without further incident on October 13.

Departing on November 12, the fleet broke into three separate squadrons. *Supply* and the faster transports would arrive early and make preparations for the arrival of the others. Bad weather slowed *Supply*'s progress, and she arrived at Botany Bay on January 18, 1788, only two days before the rest of the fleet, and eight months and one week since leaving Portsmouth. Dissatisfied with the situation at Botany Bay, Phillip reconnoitered Port Jackson ten miles to the north, which he found much more suitable for a colony, with a better anchorage and more fertile land. The first ships arrived on January 26 at Sydney Cove, named for Lord Sydney, Secretary of the Home Office, under whose auspices the First Fleet sailed. On the same day, *Sirius* and the nine remaining ships were attempting to leave Botany Bay when they encountered Jean-François de La Pérouse's ASTROLABE and BOUSSOLE. The French explorers remained at Port Jackson for several weeks before sailing to their doom.

The last convicts were finally landed on February 6, and after a night of debauchery among the newly released convicts, Phillip established a colonial government on the following day. Despite the rough material with which he had to work, he was inordinately optimistic about the potential for success. He wrote:

> We have come today to take possession of this fifth great continental division of the earth, on behalf of the British people, and have founded here a State which we hope will not only occupy and rule this great country, but also will become a shining light among all the nations of the Southern Hemisphere. How grand is the prospect which lies before this youthful nation.

A short time later, *Supply* sailed for Norfolk Island, about 1,500 miles northeast of Sydney, to establish another penal colony. In May, three ships sailed for China to load tea for London. By September, the colony was dangerously short of supplies, and under Captain John Hunter, *Sirius* sailed via Cape Horn for Cape Town, arriving back at Port Jackson on May 9, 1789. After four months of repairs, Phillip ordered *Sirius* and *Supply* to carry additional convicts to Norfolk Island to relieve the strain on the Port Jackson settlement. Forced by the weather to stand off the island for four days, on March 19, *Sirius* approached the settlement on Sydney Bay. The strong current and a sudden wind shift pushed her onto a reef. As her lieutenant related, "An Anchor was let go on Her first striking / in Less than 10 Minutes the Masts were all over the side, the Ship an intire Wreck."

Everything that could be salvaged was taken ashore, but the loss of the ship and her supplies, together with the addition of the survivors to the population, tested the island's resources to the limit. It was not until August 1791 that the next relief ships arrived. The location of the wreck of *Sirius* remained unknown. It was not until the 1980s that the Sirius Project excavated the site in anticipation of Australia's bicentennial. The ship has yielded hundreds of diverse artifacts, including iron and copper fastenings, navigational instruments, a pantograph (used for copying maps to scale), medical supplies, two carronades, personal effects, and an aboriginal stone ax, probably obtained as a souvenir at Port Jackson.

Henderson & Henderson, "*Sirius.*" Phillip, *Voyage of Governor Phillip to Botany Bay.* Stanbury, *HMS "Sirius."*

SIRIUS

Steamship (1f/2m). *L/B/D:* 208' × 25.8' (47.3'ew) × 15' (63.4m × 7.9m (14.4m) × 5.6m). *Tons:* 703 grt; 410 burden. *Hull:* wood. *Comp.:* 35 crew; 40+ pass. *Mach.:* side-lever engines, 320 nhp, 24' diameter paddles; 9 kts. *Built:* Robert Menzies and Son, Leith, Scotland; 1837.

Built for the St. George Steam Packet Company (later City of Cork Steam Packet Company), *Sirius* was the first ship to cross the Atlantic under sustained steam power. One of the ship's most important innovations was that she was fitted with surface condensers, patented by Samuel Hall in 1834, which meant that her boilers would not become caked with salt from the seawater used to cool the steam. Although built for service between Cork and London, the British and American Steam Navigation Company chartered *Sirius* (named for the Dog Star) for a transatlantic run with a view to beating GREAT WEST-ERN to New York. (Work on its *British Queen* would not be completed until after the *Great Western* was ready to sail.) Under Lieutenant Richard Roberts, RN, *Sirius* left London on March 28, 1838, and sailed from Cork on April 4 after stopping to load coal. Amid much expectation, she arrived at New York on April 22 after a passage of 18 days, 10 hours. Her average speed was 6.7 knots, and she logged an average daily distance of 161 miles per day. (*Great Western* arrived the next day, having sped at an average 8.8 knots.) *Sirius* departed New York again on May 1 and arrived at Falmouth on May 18. After a second roundtrip in July, she returned to her cross-Channel service. On January 29, 1847, while bound from Glasgow for Cork under Captain Moffett, she became a total loss in Ballycotton Bay, with the loss of 19 of her 90 passengers and crew.

Sheppard, "*Sirius*." Spratt, *Transatlantic Paddle Steamers.*

SIR LANCELOT

Clipper (3m). *L/B/D:* 197.6′ bp × 33.7′ × 21′ (60.2m × 10.3m × 6.4m). *Tons:* 886 net. *Hull:* composite. *Des.:* William Rennie. *Built:* Robert Steele & Co., Greenock, Scotland; 1866.

One of the longer lived of the British clippers, *Sir Lancelot* was a near, if not exact, sister ship of the celebrated ARIEL launched the year before. Built for James MacCunn of Glasgow, she had a mediocre first run under a Captain McDougall, and Captain Richard Robinson left FIERY CROSS to take command in 1866. His first voyage got off to a bad start when *Sir Lancelot* was dismasted off Ushant, but after rerigging at Falmouth, she eventually reached Shanghai to load tea, sailing again on June 16, 1867. Sixteen ships had departed in the previous two weeks, and most of them from Foochow, 440 miles to the south. *Sir Lancelot* beat all but *Taeping* and arrived on the same day as ARIEL and *Fiery Cross.* In 1869, she sailed from Foochow on July 17 and returned to London on October 14, a record run of only 89 days.

Following the opening of the Suez Canal in 1870, many clippers were forced to load tea for New York rather than London. To reduce manning requirements, *Sir Lancelot* was down-rigged to a bark in either 1874 or 1877, and by the 1880s, she was in trade between Europe and India. In 1886 she was bought by Viscount Ibrahim for trade between India and Mauritius. Nine years later she was sold to Persian interests, and on October 1, 1895, she sank off Calcutta in a cyclone.

Lubbock, *China Clippers.* MacGregor, *Tea Clippers.*

SIR ROBERT PEEL

Steamboat. *L/B/D:* 161′ × 30′ × 4′ (49.1m × 9.1m × 1.2m). *Comp.:* 350. *Built:* Brockville, Canada; 1837.

Named for the founder of Britain's Conservative Party and three-time prime minister, *Sir Robert Peel* was a passenger steamer built for service on Lake Ontario. The steamer's owner was Canadian John B. Armstrong, who was considered a spy by members of the Canadian Refugee Association, an underground group seeking to form an independent state for Upper and Lower Canada (now Ontario and Quebec) and based in New York. Seeking retribution for the destruction of the CAROLINE by Canadian troops, at 0300 on May 29, 1838, twenty-two members of the association seized *Peel* as the vessel stopped for wood on Wells Island en route to Oswego. Under Commodore William Johnson — Patriot Admiral of the Lakes, or Pirate of the St. Lawrence, depending on one's point of view — they rousted the fifty-nine passengers from their slumbers and sent them ashore. The vessel was plundered, towed into the stream, and burned. *Peel* capsized and was a total loss. Following the incident, government forces on either side of the border were reinforced in an effort to suppress the rebellion and relieve the threat to peace and commerce between the United States and Canada.

Musham, "Early Great Lakes Steamboats: The *Caroline* Affair."

USS SKATE

Skate-class nuclear submarine. *L/B/D:* 267.7′ × 25′ × 20′ (81.6m × 7.6m × 6.1m). *Tons:* 2,570/2,861 disp. *Hull:* steel; 700′ dd. *Comp.:* 93. *Arm.:* 6 × 21″TT. *Mach.:* 18+ kts. *Built:* Electric Boat Division, General Dynamics Corp., Groton, Conn.; 1957.

Named for a type of ray, USS *Skate* was the second submarine of the name. Assigned to the Atlantic for her entire career, on July 30, 1958, she began a voyage to the Arctic Circle under Commander James F. Calvert. Over the course of ten days during which she sailed 2,400 miles and surfaced through the ice nine times, she became the second ship after USS NAUTILUS to reach the North Pole. In March 1959, she headed to the Arctic for a second time to develop operational capabilities for submarines at periods of extreme cold and ice thickness. On March 17, *Skate* surfaced at the North Pole — the first ship to be on the surface at the Pole — and there committed the ashes of Arctic explorer Sir Hubert Wilkins. Three years later, she undertook a third Arctic mission, this time rendezvousing with USS *Seadragon.* The submarines surfaced together at the North Pole on August 2, 1962. In addition to normal operations with the Atlantic Fleet, *Skate* made three more voyages to the Arctic between 1969 and 1971. She was decommissioned in 1986 and held for disposal through the nuclear-powered ship and submarine recycling program in Bremerton, Washington.

Calvert, *Surface at the Pole*. U.S. Navy, *DANFS*.

SKULDELEV SHIPS

The Skuldelev find consists of the remains of five clinker-built Viking-era ships. These ships were loaded with rocks and sunk in the Peberrende narrows of Roskilde Fjord in an effort to prevent an enemy fleet from sailing up the fjord and attacking the town of Roskilde, Denmark. Long known as "Queen Margrethe's ship," in the belief that they were a single vessel sunk on orders of the Queen in about 1400, this dating proved wrong, although the purpose was not. Roskilde was a major trading center in the tenth and eleventh centuries, and its protection from seaborne raiders would have been of major importance, especially in the period of unrest between about 1040 and 1070.

Excavation of the site began in 1957 under Olaf Olsen and Ole Crumlin-Pedersen of the Danish National Museum. Two ships were identified in the first season, and in the second year a third ship was excavated together with what was initially called Wreck 4. These remains turned out to be part of Wreck 2, but because this was not discovered until 1959, the fourth and fifth ships have always been known as Wrecks 5 and 6. After excavation, labeling, and conservation, the fragmentary remains of the five vessels were erected on delicate metal frames that show the general shape of the complete ship. These are housed in the Viking Ship Museum in Roskilde, built on a site overlooking Roskilde Fjord. The five clinker-built ships include two warships (Wrecks 2 and 5), two knorrs (Wrecks 1 and 3), and a fishing boat (Wreck 6).

SKULDELEV 1

Trading vessel; knorr. *L/B/D:* 53.5′ × 14.8′ × 6.9′ (16.3m × 4.5m × 2.1m). *Hull:* deal, oak, lime. *Built:* 1010.

The larger of the two trading vessels found at Roskilde was in all likelihood built not in Denmark but in Norway, a theory supported by differences in detail and the fact that the pine planking used in building was probably unobtainable in Denmark during the period in question. In addition, the hull is of heavier construction and not suited to being driven ashore on the beaches of Denmark, as were the other vessels. With a capacity of 15 to 20 tons, this is the sort of ship that would have been used for long-distance trading to the British Isles, Iceland, Greenland, and beyond.

SKULDELEV 2

Longship. *L/B:* 95.1′ × 13.1′ (29m × 4m). *Comp.:* 50–100 men. *Hull:* wood. *Built:* ca. 930.

Wreck 2 is the least well-preserved of the Roskilde ships, with only about one-quarter of the original fabric surviving. Although her original length can only be approximated, this is the longest Viking ship yet found. According to the sagas, ships that carried between 13 and 23 pairs of oars were considered longships — of which this was probably one — while those that carried more than 25 pairs were called great ships. Built with thin oak planking (those that survive are only 2–2.5 centimeters thick), the bottom planks have been worn down from being repeatedly run up on beaches to discharge the ship's crews.

SKULDELEV 3

Trading vessel; knorr. *L/B/D:* 45.3′ × 11.2′ × 4.6′ (13.8m × 3.4m × 1.4m). *Hull:* wood. *Comp.:* 5–9. *Built:* 1030.

The best-preserved ship of the five ships at Roskilde, with approximately three-quarters of the original wood having survived, this vessel is the first Viking ship in which the whole stem has been preserved. It is similar in construction to Wreck 5, the chief difference being a broader length-to-beam ratio than that of the small warship, and the fact that the gunwale has only seven oar holes, five forward (three to port and two to starboard) and two aft. In addition, the vessel had a half deck and a 4-meter-long hold amidships with a total cargo capacity of about 5 tons.

SKULDELEV 5

Warship. *L/B/D:* 57.1′ × 8.5′ × 3.6′ (17.4m × 2.6m × 1.1m). *Hull:* oak and ash. *Comp.:* 25–30. *Built:* 960.

Known as the small warship, this ship is similar in form to the LADBY SHIP. Of particular note is the comparatively narrow length-to-beam ratio, a feature that had been considered an anomaly in the Ladby ship. However,

The reconstructed remains of Skuldelev 1, a Danish trading knorr of the early 11th century, on view at the Viking Ship Museum in Roskilde, Denmark. The silhouette profiles and overhead views of the actual remains show the different shapes and sizes of the five Skuldelev hulls. Courtesy Vikingskibshallen, Roskilde.

it is now accepted that Danish ships of the period were generally narrower than their Norwegian counterparts. The hull is pierced for 12 pairs of oars, and as with Wreck 2, it shows signs of repeated beaching. Vessels of this design seem to have been copied both in the Baltic as well as in Normandy, where descendants of the type are amply illustrated in the Bayeux tapestry showing William the Conqueror's Norman invasion of England in 1066.

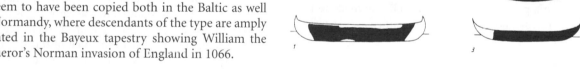

SKULDELEV 6

Fishing boat. *L/B/D:* 38.0′ × 8.2′ × 3.9′ (11.6m × 2.5m × 1.2m). *Hull:* pine.

The smallest of the five ships found at Roskilde, this vessel is often regarded as a fishing boat. She carried a mast and could probably be propelled by oars, although there are no oar holes in the remains of the ship.

Crumlin-Pedersen, "Skuldelev Ships." Olsen & Crumlin-Pedersen, *Five Viking Ships from Roskilde Fjord.*

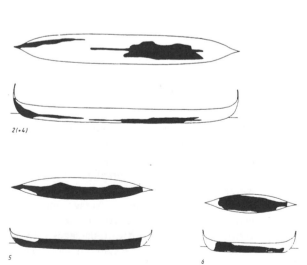

SNARK

Ketch. *L/B/D:* 55′ × 15′ × 7.7′ (16.8m × 4.6m × 2.3m). *Tons:* 10 net. *Hull:* wood. *Comp.:* 7. *Mach.:* gas, 70 hp, 1 screw; 9 kts. *Built:* San Francisco; 1906.

In 1904, Jack London, his wife, Charmian, and their friend Roscoe determined to sail around the world, paying for the adventure through the sale of magazine articles to be written by London along the way. So was born *Snark* and with her London's *Cruise of the "Snark,"* a collection of essays on a variety of topics. "We named her the *Snark,*" writes London, "because we could not think of any other name." (The name may have been borrowed from Lewis Carroll's poem "The Hunting of the Snark.") Much of London's book is concerned with their ports of call and what they found there — surfing and lepers in Hawaii, "Bêche de Mer English" spoken in the southwest Pacific, "Stone-Fishing in Bora-Bora," London's experience as "The Amateur M.D.," and his fascinating encounter with Ernest Darling, a 90-pound weakling from Oregon who had transformed himself into the robust "Nature Man" of Tahiti. The pieces about *Snark* and the voyage are humorous and somewhat carefree. The interminable delays in finishing the ketch are described in "The Inconceivable and Monstrous" and self-taught navigation in "Finding One's Way About" and "The Amateur Navigator." From Hawaii they sailed to Tahiti, the Fiji Islands, and the Solomons, before turning south for Australia, where London was subsequently hospitalized with a mysterious skin ailment that forced him to return to California prematurely. *Snark* herself eventually returned to California and ended her days hauled ashore near San Pedro.

London, *Cruise of the "Snark."*

SNOW SQUALL

Clipper (3m). *L/B/D:* 157′ bp × 32′ × 18.5′ dph (47.9m × 9.8m × 5.6m). *Tons:* 742 reg. *Hull:* wood. *Built:* Cornelius Butler, Cape Elizabeth, Me.; 1851.

Condemned at Stanley, Falkland Islands, in 1863, *Snow Squall* is often described as the last surviving American clipper ship. Purchased after her maiden voyage to New York by Charles R. Green, she remained under his flag for her entire career, carrying general cargo out and returning with silks and tea. She made on average one voyage per year between New York (once from Boston, in 1858) and the Orient, making three outward passages via Cape Horn, and the remainder via the Cape of Good Hope, often via Australian ports. An extreme clipper, she was described at her launch as "very sharp at the bows, with a lean but handsomely graduated run, but from her great breadth of beam, will be enabled to carry well, while at the same time she cannot fail of being a fast sailor." And indeed she made some very good times, posting near record runs between ports on all oceans.

Nowhere was her speed put to better use than on a 94-day transit between Penang and New York in 1863 under Captain James S. Dillingham, Jr. Near the Cape of Good Hope on July 28, 1863, the crew spoke the bark-rigged CSS *Tuscaloosa,* which closed flying the American flag. When alongside, the Confederate raider showed her true colors and opened fire with her stern gun. Nothing daunted, Dillingham hauled close to the wind and *Snow Squall* showed her heels until *Tuscaloosa* gave up the chase about four hours later. On her next voyage, *Snow Squall* sailed from New York for San Francisco, but on February 24, 1864, she was becalmed in the Straits of Le Maire east of Cape Horn and drifted ashore on Tierra del Fuego. Leaking badly, *Snow Squall* put back to Stanley, Falkland Islands, where she was condemned. Dillingham made his way to Rio de Janeiro; from here he sailed for home in *Mondamin,* only to have that ship captured and burned by the Confederate raider CSS FLORIDA.

Meanwhile, *Snow Squall* was incorporated into the Falkland Islands Company's makeshift jetty — which eventually comprised *Egeria* and *William Shand.* Over the next 122 years, her hull was loaded with ballast stone, punctured for pilings, and subjected to the harsh elements of the South Atlantic. In the early 1980s, Harvard University archaeologist Fred Yalouris launched the Snow Squall Project to save what remained of the Yankee clipper. The first of five visits to document the bow took place in 1982, just two weeks before Argentina invaded the British colony. Four years later, a thirty-five-foot section of the bow was cut free and transported to the Spring Point Museum in South Portland (formerly Cape Elizabeth), Maine, and eventually to the Maine Maritime Museum in Bath.

Bayreuther & Horvath, "*Snow Squall* Project." Howe & Matthews, *American Clipper Ships.*

SOBRAON

(later HMAS *Tingira*) Ship (3m). *L/B/D:* 272′ × 40′ × 27′ (82.9m × 12.2m × 8.2m). *Tons:* 2,131 net. *Hull:* composite. *Comp.:* 250 pass; 60–70 crew. *Built:* Alexander Hall & Co., Aberdeen, Scotland; 1866.

Sobraon was originally laid down as a steamship for Gellatly, Hankey and Sewell. While under construction, it was decided to finish her as a full-rigged ship, and when completed she was the largest ever built, with iron frames and wood planking. She set skysails on all three masts, and she carried fidded royal masts above her topgallant masts, an unusual rig for that late date. Named for the site of a British victory in the Punjab during the first Sikh War in 1846, she was owned by Lowther, Maxton & Company, but chartered to Devitt & Moore for passenger service to Sydney. In 1873, Devitt & Moore bought her outright and sailed her thereafter to Melbourne. A fast, comfortable ship, she was one of the most popular in the Australian immigrant trade; except for her first voyage, she sailed under command of Captain J. A. Elmslie. In addition to passengers, she carried general cargoes out, returning with grain and wool. In 1891, *Sobraon* was purchased by the government of New South Wales for use as a floating reformatory at Sydney. Twenty years later she became the stationary Navy training ship HMAS *Tingira* (an aborigine word meaning "open sea"). Sold in 1927, she remained at her moorings in Berry's Bay until broken up for scrap in 1941.

Course, *Painted Ports.*

SOHAR

Dhow (2m). *L:* 87′ (26.5m). *Hull:* wood. *Comp.:* 19. *Des.:* Colin Mudie. *Built:* Sur, Oman; 1980.

Inspired by *The Thousand and One Nights* (a collection of stories ascribed to Sinbad the Sailor, who was probably a mythic amalgam of Arab seafarers from between the eighth and eleventh centuries), Tim Severin decided to sail a dhow on a 6,000-mile voyage from the Persian Gulf to China. The design of *Sohar* (named for an ancient port said to have been the birthplace of the legendary Sinbad) was based on a drawing of a *boom* (a type of dhow) in a sixteenth-century Portuguese manuscript. The vessel's hull was built of aini wood from India sewn together with

The three-masted ship SOBRAON, *built for the Australian immigrant trade. This undated photo of the ship, taken off Gravesend, shows her with her upper yards sent down. Courtesy National Maritime Museum, Greenwich.*

400 miles of hand-laid coconut cord from Agatti in the Lakshadweep Islands (Laccadives) off southwest India. The 20,000 holes through which the coir passed were plugged with coconut husks and a mixture of lime and tree gum, and the hull's interior was preserved with vegetable oil.

Sohar's building and fitting out — paid for by Oman's Sultan Qaboos bin Said — took eleven months. When she sailed from Muscat on November 23, 1980, her crew included nine Omanis and ten Europeans, including Trondur Patursson, a veteran of Severin's BRENDAN voyage. The timing of the voyage was dictated by the availability of favorable winds, and Sohar ran off before the northwest monsoon, making four knots, or eighty miles per day, and arriving at Chetlat in the Lakshadweep Islands in mid-December. From there she sailed to the Indian mainland, stopping at Calicut and Beypore, where the ship was careened. The next port of call was at Galle, Sri Lanka, where she arrived on January 21, 1981. Severin had hoped to catch the southwest monsoon, but the winds were late and he was fifty-five days at sea before arriving at Sabang at the northern entrance to the Strait of Malacca on April 18. From there, he continued on to Singapore. Pressing on to avoid the typhoon season, in mid-June Sohar was hit by five days of vicious squalls in the South China Sea. She arrived off the Pearl River on June 28, and was greeted at Guanzhou (Canton) by Chinese and Omani officials. Sohar was later shipped back to Oman for display as a museum ship at Muscat.

Severin, Sinbad Voyage.

LE SOLEIL ROYAL

Vaisseau (1st rate) (3m). Hull: wood. Arm.: 104 guns. Built: Brest, France; 1669.

Named in honor of the Sun King, Louis XIV, Le Soleil Royal was one of the most powerful ships of her day. As flagship of the revitalized French Navy brought into being by Minister of Marine Jean-Baptiste Colbert, she was sumptuously decorated with wooden carvings depicting a variety of motifs emblematic of the French monarch. The taffrail was embellished with a rendering of the sun god drawn across the sky by a team of horses, while the ornate figurehead showed a seahorse flanked by winged maidens. The hull was painted a royal blue highlighted by the wales, strakes, and additional embellishments in gold. As the sculptures recovered from the Swedish warship WASA prove, such lavish ornament was not uncommon in seventeenth-century warships. Charles Le Brun's draw-

ings of the statuary for Le Soleil Royal are in the Louvre.

Details of the first decade of Le Soleil Royal's service are obscure, but after her refit in 1689, she flew the flag of Vice Admiral Anne-Hilarion de Cotentin, Comte de Tourville, Admiral of the French fleet. The year before, England's Catholic King James II had been overthrown in favor of the Dutch Protestant William III of Orange in the Glorious Revolution. In March 1689, a French fleet helped James II land in Ireland in the first of several failed efforts to regain his throne. In July 1690, Tourville led a fleet of seventy ships out of Brest and on July 10, he met a combined English and Dutch force of fifty-seven ships off Beachy Head. Ordered to engage the enemy against the larger fleet, Admiral Arthur Herbert, Lord Torrington, lost eight ships while the French lost none in a victory they called Béveziers.

Two years later, the position was reversed as Tourville, with a fleet of only forty-four ships — the remainder were with Vice Admiral Jean d'Estrées in the Mediterranean — was ordered to sail from Brest on May 12, 1692, to clear the English Channel for Louis XIV's invasion force of 30,000 men assembled near Cherbourg. On May 20, Tourville met an Anglo-Dutch fleet of eighty-eight ships off Pointe de Barfleur. By increasing the distance between his ships sailing in line ahead, Tourville prevented his fleet from being encircled or outflanked by the English and Dutch ships, under command of Admiral Edward Herbert, Earl of Orford, in HMS Britannia. But Le Soleil Royal was so badly damaged that Tourville was forced to transfer his flag to Ambiteux the next day. Ten French ships slipped away, but Le Soleil Royal, Admirable, and Conquerant were forced into Cherbourg where they ran aground and were destroyed by English fireships. Another twenty ships made for Brest, and Tourville ordered the remaining twelve to the shallow roads off La Hogue. There, on June 2, Tourville's brilliant handling of the fleet at Barfleur was obliterated, and as the French Army and James II (audibly proud of his disloyal subjects, to the chagrin of his allies) looked on from shore, the English fleet burned or sank a dozen ships.

Clowes, Royal Navy. Culver, Forty Famous Ships.

USS SOMERS

Brig (2m). L/B/D: 103′ × 25′ × 11′ dph (31.4m × 7.6m × 3.4m). Tons: 259 bm. Hull: wood. Comp.: 120. Arm.: 10 × 32pdr. Built: New York Navy Yard, Brooklyn, N.Y.; 1842.

USS Somers, the second ship of the name, was named for Richard Somers, who died while commanding the bomb

The Dutch painter Adriaen van Diest captures the destruction of Admiral Tourville's flagship SOLEIL
ROYAL *(104 guns) by British fireships, two days after she ran aground at the Battle of La Hogue, May
23, 1692. Courtesy National Maritime Museum, Greenwich.*

ketch INTREPID at Tripoli in 1804. A small, swift vessel, one of *Somer*'s primary missions was to train young naval ratings and officers for careers at sea, an idea fostered especially by Commodore Oliver Hazard Perry. Although designed to carry 90 officers and crew, on her second voyage, the brig carried a complement of 120. Although three-quarters of them were still teenagers, they included the scions of some distinguished families: two sons of Matthew Calbraith Perry, the son of Commodore John Rodgers, and Philip Spencer, the son of President John Tyler's Secretary of War, John Canfield Spencer.

Under command of Captain Alexander Slidell Mackenzie, *Somers* sailed from New York on September 12, 1842, bound for Monrovia with dispatches for the slave patrol frigate USS *Vandalia*. After calling at Madeira and the Canary Islands, the ship arrived at Cape Mesurado, the site chosen by Matthew Perry for the African-American colony of Liberia in 1822, only to find *Vandalia* had left. After only two days in port, *Somers* sailed for St. Thomas, Danish West Indies, on November 12. Two weeks later, on the strength of a report of a shipmate, Midshipman Philip Spencer, together with the boatswain's mate and another seaman, were placed under arrest for plotting a mutiny. Further investigation by Mackenzie and his officers revealed that Spencer intended to seize the ship and kill the officers and any who sided with them. For their crime, they were hanged, while still at sea, on December 1. Mackenzie was later court-martialed and, despite the standing of Spencer's father, acquitted of charges of illegal punishment, oppression, and murder.

Somers subsequently remained with the Home Squadron, cruising along the Atlantic and Gulf Coasts. During the Mexican-American War, she took up blockade duty

An anonymous woodcut of the brig USS SOMERS, *homeward bound from the coast of West Africa, December 1, 1842, with the bodies of alleged mutineers hanging from the main yard. Courtesy U.S. Naval Historical Center, Washington, D.C.*

off Vera Cruz, under command of Lieutenant Raphael Semmes, later captain of CSS ALABAMA. On December 8, 1846, while chasing a blockade-runner, *Somers* capsized in a squall and sank with the loss of 32 of her 76 crew. In 1986, her remains were found in 110 feet of water about a mile off Isla Verde.

Delgado, "Rediscovering the *Somers.*" McFarland, *Sea Dangers.*

SØRLANDET

Ship (3m). *L/B/D:* 186′ × 29′ × 16′ (56.7m × 8.8m × 4.9m). *Tons:* 577 grt. *Hull:* steel. *Comp.:* 107. *Built:* A/S Hoivolds Mek. Verksted, Kristiansand, Norway; 1927.

In 1922, Norwegian ship owner A. O. T. Skjelbred advanced £50,000 for the construction of a sail-training ship. The Norwegian Sail Training Association was organized, and it commissioned the full-rigged *Sørlandet,* a scaled-down version of a typical oceangoing merchant ship, designed exclusively for sail training with no thought to hauling cargoes. The ship's curriculum was the same as that of a shoreside high school, with additional instruction in all aspects of seamanship, including work in the galley. From April to September she engaged in long-distance cruising, and in 1933 she sailed up the St. Lawrence River and through the Great Lakes to visit the Chicago World's Fair.

During World War II she was used by the Norwegian

Navy, and after the occupation by German forces, as a prison ship. Sunk as a result of bomb damage, she was raised and converted to an accommodation hulk for submariners. The end of the war found *Sørlandet* in appalling condition, but her former owners lost no time in restoring her and, they reported, "She sailed in 1947 as a new and better ship." As the deed of gift stipulated that she be built without an engine, it was not until 1960 that an engine was finally installed. She continues to work as a sail-training ship out of Kristiansand.

Brouwer, *International Register of Historic Ships.* Underhill, *Sail Training and Cadet Ships.*

SORYU

Soryu-class aircraft carrier. *L/B/D:* 746.5′ × 69.9′ × 25′ (227.5m × 21.3m × 7.6m). *Tons:* 18,800 disp. *Hull:* steel. *Comp.:* 1,100. *Arm.:* 71 aircraft; 12 × 5″, 28 × 25mm. *Mach.:* geared turbines, 152,000 shp, 4 screws; 34 kts. *Built:* Kaigun Kosho, Kure, Japan; 1937.

Under Captain Ryusaku Yanagimoto, *Soryu* ("Blue Dragon") was one of six carriers (the others were AKAGI, HIRYU, KAGA, SHOKAKU, and ZUIKAKU) involved in the attack on Pearl Harbor on December 7, 1942. As the Pacific war unfolded, she took part in the capture of Wake Island on December 27, the campaign for the Dutch East Indies in February 1942, and the April strikes on Ceylon, after which she returned to Japan. On May 27, she was one of four carriers in Vice Admiral Chuichi Nagumo's First Carrier Striking Force as it sailed from Hashirajima en route for the central Pacific.

The Battle of Midway began on June 4, and *Soryu* aircraft were part of the first strike against the island base. The Japanese were preparing for a second strike when Nagumo learned of an American force that possibly included an aircraft carrier. Nagumo vacillated between arming his planes for another run against Midway or arming them with antiship bombs and torpedoes. In the meantime, Admiral Raymond Spruance had launched his attack. First in were the torpedo planes, though without fighter cover they were turned away handily. But at 1026, dive-bombers from USS YORKTOWN, ENTERPRISE, and HORNET began their attack from 14,000 feet. The attack was devastating, and within minutes, *Soryu, Akagi,* and *Kaga* were burning out of control. At 1913, *Soryu* sank in 30°42′N, 178°38′E, with the loss of 718 crew. Her sister ship *Hiryu* was not sunk until the next day.

Prange, *At Dawn We Slept; Miracle at Midway.*

SOUTHERN CROSS

(later *Calypso, Azure Seas, Ocean Breeze*) Cruise ship (1f/1m). *L/B/D:* 604′ × 76.8′ × 26′ (184.1m × 76.8m × 23.4m). *Tons:* 20,204 grt. *Hull:* steel. *Comp.:* 1,160 tourist. *Mach.:* geared turbines, 2 screws; 20 kts. *Built:* Harland & Wolff, Belfast, Northern Ireland; 1955.

One of the most innovative passenger ships of the 1950s, the Shaw, Savill & Albion Company's cruise ship *Southern Cross* was designed for round-the-world cruises with more than 1,000 passengers in a single class. As such, she was the first major passenger ship designed without provision for carrying cargo. She was also the first with engines, and thus her single funnel, aft. Her profile was somewhat unbalanced by the placement of her bridge slightly forward of amidships. A 100-foot-long sports deck ran between the funnel and the bridge superstructure.

Launched by the young Queen Elizabeth II, who praised her "entirely new and original design," *Southern Cross* made four circumnavigations from Southampton each year. The itinerary of her first voyage illustrates the pattern of the vacation cruise in the 1950s: Trinidad, Curaçao, Panama Canal, Tahiti, Fiji, Wellington, Sydney, Melbourne, Fremantle, Durban, Capetown, Las Palmas, and back to Southampton. One staple of her long-distance voyaging was the large number of emigrants bound from Great Britain to New Zealand and Australia. With the advent of jet transportation, this market declined in the 1960s. This and the rising labor costs led to her withdrawal from service in 1971.

Two years later, *Southern Cross* was purchased by the Greek Ulysses Line, and in 1975 she was recommissioned as the *Calypso.* Under her new owners, she cruised on a variety of different routes worldwide, in the Mediterranean, Scandinavia, the Pacific Northwest, West Africa, and the Caribbean. Five years later, she was sold again to the Western Cruise Lines and, renamed *Azure Seas,* began cruises from Los Angeles to Mexico. In 1992, she was sold to Dolphin Cruise Lines and began short-haul cruises along the East Coast of the United States as the *Ocean Breeze.*

Braynard & Miller, *Fifty Famous Liners 3.* Gardiner, *Golden Age of Shipping.*

HMS SOVEREIGN OF THE SEAS

(later HMS *Sovereign,* HMS *Royal Sovereign*) 1st rate 102 (3m). *L/B:* 232′ loa (128′ keel) × 48′ (70.7m (39.8m) × 14.6m). *Tons:* 1,141 bm. *Hull:* wood. *Arm.:* 102 guns. *Des.:* Phineas Pett. *Built:* Peter Pett, Woolwich Dockyard, Eng.; 1637.

In 1634, the ill-fated monarch Charles I informed the great English shipbuilder Phineas Pett of his "princely resolution for the building of a great new ship" as part of his overall effort to improve and expand England's navy, whose enemies and concerns included the Dutch — her most serious rival in overseas trade — France and Spain, and North African corsairs preying on vessels west of the English Channel. Though critics warned that "the art or wit of man cannot build a ship fit for service with three tier of ordnance," neither Charles nor Pett was to be dissuaded. Built at a cost of £65,586 — about ten 40-gun ships could have been built for the same amount — *Sovereign of the Seas* was intended as an instrument of propaganda as well as war. The Royal Navy's most lavishly ornamented vessel, her decorations were carved by the brothers John and Mathias Christmas and described in a booklet prepared by Thomas Heywood, who also managed to include a description of the ship itself:

> She hath three flush Deckes, and a Fore-Castle, an halfe Decke, a quarter Decke, and a round-house. Her lower Tyre [tier] hath thirty ports, which are to be furnished with Demy-Cannon [30-pdr.] and whole Cannon through out, (being able to beare them). Her middle Tyre hath also thirty ports for Demi-Culverin [10-pdr.], and whole Culverin: Her third Tyre hath Twentie six Ports for other Ordnance, her fore-Castle hath twelve ports, and her halfe Decke hath foureteene ports; She hath thirteene or fourteene ports more within Board for murdering peeces, besides a great many Loope holes out of the Cabins for Musket shot. She carrieth moreover ten peeces of chase Ordnance in her, right forward; and ten right aff, that is according to Land-service in the front and the reare. She carrieth eleven Anchors, one of them weighing foure thousand foure hundred, &c. and according to these are her Cables, Mastes, Sayles, Cordage; which considered together, seeing his Majesty is at this infinite charge, both for the honor of this Nation, and the security of his Kingdome, it should bee a great spur and incouragement to all his faithful and loving Subjects to bee liberall and willing Contributaries towards the *Ship-money.*

In fact, the ship-money tax levied by Charles for his naval program was much resented by his "faithful and loving subjects," and in *Sovereign of the Seas* can be seen some of the excess that contributed to his overthrow and execution in 1649. Under Oliver Cromwell's Commonwealth, the ship was renamed *Sovereign,* and following the restoration of Charles II in 1660 she was rebuilt and renamed *Royal Sovereign.* Despite her vast size, the ship was slow and of limited value in actual combat as she could not keep company with other ships. Nonetheless, during the three Anglo-Dutch Wars, she saw action at the

Battle of Kentish Knock in 1652, Orfordness (1666), Sole-bay (1672), Schoonveld (1673), and the Texel (1673). Following another rebuild in 1685, in the War of the League of Augsburg, she was at Beachy Head (1690) and Barfleur (1692). Eleven years later a misplaced candle set the ship on fire and she burned at Chatham.

Heywood, *His Majesty's Royal Ship.*

SOVEREIGN OF THE SEAS

Clipper (3m). *L/B/D:* 258.2′ × 44′ × 21′ (78.7m × 13.4m × 6.4m). *Tons:* 2,421 grt. *Hull:* wood. *Comp.:* 45 crew. *Built:* Donald McKay, East Boston, Mass.; 1852.

"Behold the modern *Sovereign of the Seas,* the longest, sharpest, the most beautiful merchant ship in the world, designed to sail at least twenty miles an hour with a whole-sail breeze. See her in the 'beauty of her strength,' the simplicity and neatness of her rig, flying before the gale and laughing at the rising sea." So wrote the *Boston Daily Atlas* upon the occasion of the launching of the new McKay clipper. Purchased by Funch and Meinke, New York, *Sovereign of the Seas* first sailed for San Francisco under Captain Lauchlan McKay, Donald's brother, who followed a route determined by careful study of Lieutenant Matthew Fontaine Maury's new wind and current charts. Sailing with a crew of 105, an unprecedented number, after rounding Cape Horn, *Sovereign of the Seas* encountered a gale that caused the loss of the main topmast, mizzen topgallant mast, the foretopsail yard, and all sails on the foremast. In a feat of seamanship rarely equaled, much less bettered, her officers and crew saved the spars and rerigged the ship so that she arrived at San Francisco in 103 days, exactly as Maury had predicted. Returning via Honolulu, where she shipped a cargo of whale oil, she sailed a record 411 miles in one 24-hour period, and had astounding runs averaging 378 miles a day over 4 days and 330 miles a day for 11 days. With unfavorable freight rates for San Francisco, she sailed for Liverpool and arrived at that port in a record 13 days and 23 hours. James Baines's Black Ball Line chartered *Sovereign of the Seas* for the Australia run and she was advertised with the singular offer: "Freight seven pounds a ton for Melbourne; forty shillings a ton to be returned if the *Sovereign* does not make a faster passage than any steamer on the berth" — which she did, although the run was a sluggish 78 days. She returned in 68 days, during which three members of the crew were arrested for threatening mutiny. Upon her return to Liverpool, she was sold to J. C. Godeffroy and Son, Hamburg, and sailed under its flag to Australia and the Far East. In 1859, on a voyage

from Hamburg to China, she ran aground on Pyramid Shoal and was a total loss, her crew being rescued by the American ship *Eloisa.*

Cutler, *Greyhounds of the Sea.* Hollett, *Fast Passage to Australia.* Howe & Matthews, *American Clipper Ships.*

HMS SPEEDY

Brig (14). *L/B:* 78′ × 26′ (23.8m × 7.9m). *Tons:* 208 bm. *Hull:* wood. *Comp.:* 90. *Arm.:* 14 × 4pdr. *Built:* King, Dover, Eng.; 1782.

European navies did not employ brig-rigged vessels in significant numbers until after the Seven Years' War. The Royal Navy introduced a new class of brig — the prototype was HMS *Childers* — in 1778. Fast and nimble, the two-masted square-riggers were used as dispatch boats and for convoy protection. Probably the most famous Royal Navy brig was HMS *Speedy.* Although remembered as the vessel in which Lieutenant Thomas Lord Cochrane acquired his reputation as one of the most enterprising officers of his day, her early career is illustrative of the variety of duties to which these vessels were assigned.

At the start of the French Revolutionary Wars in 1793, *Speedy* was dispatched to Gibraltar under Charles Cunningham. She undertook a variety of assignments around the Iberian peninsula and in the western Mediterranean for the next year. On June 9, 1794, she was looking for a British squadron off the coast of Nice when she closed with three French frigates that Commander George Eyre assumed to be British. He realized his mistake too late, and *Speedy* struck to the *Sérieuse* (36 guns). Taken into the French Navy, she was recaptured the following March by HMS *Inconstant* (36). *Speedy* remained in the Mediterranean, cruising with Commodore Horatio Nelson's squadron off the coast of Italy, and she took part in the capture of six vessels carrying arms for the siege of Padua.

On October 3, 1799, under command of Jahleel Brenton, *Speedy* attacked a convoy of eight merchantmen and two escorts. Though none were taken, six were forced ashore near Cape Trafalgar and destroyed. On November 6, *Speedy* fought off a flotilla of twelve Spanish gunboats while escorting a transport bound for Livorno with wine for the fleet. Although the Spaniards were driven off, *Speedy* suffered extensive damage to her hull and rigging. Shortly thereafter, Brenton was assigned to command the recently captured *Généreux,* and Lieutenant Cochrane assumed command of *Speedy* on March 28, 1800.

Speedy cruised off the Spanish coast with great success. In thirteen months under Cochrane's command, she captured upwards of fifty vessels, together with 122 guns and

534 prisoners. On December 21, 1801, Cochrane evaded a Spanish frigate detailed to capture her by flying the Danish flag and the quarantine flag and having a Danish-speaking officer explain that the ship had been at a North African port riddled with the plague. On May 6, 1802, *Speedy* fell in with the Spanish frigate *El Gamo* (32) off Barcelona. Although Cochrane had described *Speedy* as "crowded rather than manned" with a crew of ninety officers and men when he took command, nearly forty of these had been put aboard various prizes to be taken into port, and *Speedy*'s complement numbered only fifty-four. Nonetheless, Cochrane commenced an attack of unrivaled daring. Running alongside the larger ship, Cochrane fired a series of treble-shotted broadsides into *El Gamo,* whose twenty-two 12-pdr., eight 9-pdr., and two carronades were mounted too high to damage the smaller brig. Cochrane then led a boarding party and captured the frigate and her crew of 319. Spanish losses were fifteen killed (including Captain Don Francisco de Torris) and forty-one wounded, as against three British dead and eight wounded. Although outnumbered six to one, the British took *El Gamo* into Port Mahon, Minorca. To keep the Spanish crew below decks, their captors loaded *El Gamo*'s main-deck guns with canister and pointed them down the hatchways.

Instead of the honors he so richly deserved for such an unparalleled feat of arms, Cochrane was all but ignored. Although he was promoted to the rank of post-captain, his recommendation that Lieutenant Parker be promoted was overruled by Lord St. Vincent, First Lord of the Admiralty, on the grounds that "the small number of men killed on board the *Speedy* did not warrant the application." Cochrane imprudently observed that she had suffered more casualties than had HMS VICTORY at the Battle of Cape St. Vincent, for which Admiral Sir John Jervis had been made Earl St. Vincent and his first captain a knight.

Cochrane received more respect from his enemies. Ordered back to the Mediterranean, on July 3 *Speedy* was escorting a slow transport when she was set upon by three French frigates. After several hours of combat, Cochrane was forced to haul down his flag. The French captain of the *Dessaix* was so impressed by his enemy that he declined to accept Cochrane's sword in surrender. *Speedy*'s subsequent career is unknown, but it is doubtful that she entered French service.

Cochrane was soon exchanged and went on to further fame in the frigates *Pallas* and *Impérieuse*. His brazen and tireless campaigning against corruption in the service kept him out of favor with his superiors, and in 1814 he was disgraced because of his apparent complicity in a stock swindle perpetrated by a French refugee under his command. In 1816, Cochrane accepted an offer to command the Chilean Navy against the Spanish, and he sailed in the O'HIGGINS. He went on to serve in the Brazilian and Greek navies before his reinstatement as a rear admiral in the Royal Navy in 1832.

Clowes, *Royal Navy.* Cochrane, *Autobiography of a Seaman.* Phillips, *Ships of the Old Navy.*

SPRAGUE

Towboat (2f). *L/B/D:* 317.9' × 61' × 7.2' (96.9m × 18.6m × 2.2m). *Comp.:* 55. *Mach.:* compound engines, 2,720 hp, sternwheels. *Built:* Dubuque, Iowa; 1901.

Sprague, ordered for the Monongahela River Consolidated Coal and Coke Company and named for Captain Peter Sprague, was the largest steam sternwheel towboat ever built. Her hull was built in Dubuque and her sternwheel fitted at St. Louis. Popularly known as "Big Mama," *Sprague* was engaged in the towage of a variety of bulk cargoes on the Mississippi, including bauxite, coal, and crude oil, as well as general cargo southbound. In February 1907, "Big Mama" left Louisville with 60 barges carrying 67,307 tons of coal — then and for many years a record-sized tow. (Despite the name, towboats push, rather than pull, barges.) During the great Mississippi River flood of 1927, she evacuated 20,000 people from the levees of Greenville, Mississippi.

Retired from river traffic in 1948, *Sprague* was sold to the City of Vicksburg for $1. The site of the River Hall of Fame, *Sprague* was also used as a stage for the Showboat Players' melodrama *Gold in the Hills* and she was featured in MGM's musical movie *Showboat*. On April 15, 1974, the 73-year-old *Sprague* burned at her moorings.

Legler, "Percy Ruiz Visits Colorful Old Sternwheeler."

SPRAY

Sloop. *L/B/D:* 36.8' × 14.2' × 4.2' dph (11.2m × 4.3m × 1.3m). *Tons:* 13 grt. *Hull:* wood. *Comp.:* 1. *Built:* ca. 1800; rebuilt Joshua Slocum, Fairhaven, Mass., 1894.

Two years after completing his celebrated voyage from Argentina to the United States in LIBERDADE, Joshua Slocum was offered the use of a "ship" lying in a field in Fairhaven, Massachusetts. The vessel turned out to be *Spray,* the remains of a century-old Delaware oyster sloop. Nothing daunted, Slocum rebuilt *Spray* from the keel up. After a season as a fisherman, he "resolved upon a voyage around the world" and departed Boston on

One of the most powerful sternwheelers ever built, the towboat SPRAGUE *once pushed a raft of 60 barges. "Big Mama," as she was known, ended her days as a showboat. Courtesy Murphy Library, University of Wisconsin, La Crosse.*

April 24, 1895. Among his stores were a number of books given to him by Mabel Wagnalls, daughter of encyclopedia publisher Adam Wagnalls, and the person to whom he dedicated his memoir of the voyage: "To the one who said, 'The *Spray* will come back.'"

In no particular hurry, Slocum spent the next two weeks fitting out in Gloucester before sailing for his childhood home in Westport, Nova Scotia. From there he put to sea in earnest on July 2. Slocum's course took him first to the Azores, and from there to Gibraltar, where he arrived after a passage that included a night of delirium during which he believed he was being guided by the pilot of Columbus's PINTA. Well received at Gibraltar, he narrowly escaped capture by pirates as he made off southwest, reaching Pernambuco on October 5 after forty days at sea. After an unsuccessful bid to recoup some money he had forfeited on a previous voyage, he made his way south, calling at Rio de Janeiro and then, after running aground on the coast of Uruguay, Montevideo and Buenos Aires.

There next began the most difficult leg of his journey, through the Straits of Magellan. After calling at Punta Arenas on February 14, 1896, Slocum worked *Spray* through the Straits to Cape Pillar only to emerge into a furious gale that drove him southeast for four days to Fury Island: "This was the greatest sea adventure of my life." He sailed back into the Straits via Cockburn Channel, and this second time he sailed into the Pacific and

made for Juan Fernández Island. After a passage of one month to the Marquesas, he was seventy-two days to Apia, Samoa, where he visited with Fanny Stevenson, widow of Robert Louis Stevenson. From there he sailed to Australia, where he spent about five months visiting and frequently lecturing in Newcastle, Sydney, Melbourne, Tasmania, and Cooktown. He sailed from the last port on June 6, 1897, heading north and west through Torres Strait.

Throughout his memoir of his circumnavigation, Slocum is full of admiration for *Spray,* but at no point more so than in his description of the 2,700-mile run from Thursday Island to Keeling Cocos Islands. "It was a delightful sail!" he writes. "During those twenty-three days I had not spent altogether more than three hours at the helm, including the time occupied in beating into Keeling harbour. I just lashed the helm and let her go." He continued across the Indian Ocean to Mauritius and South Africa, arriving on November 17 at Port Natal. While in South Africa he had the run of the country, and he met with figures as distinct as the explorer Henry M. Stanley and President Paul Krüger, whose eccentric ideas — including a firm belief that the earth was flat — led Slocum to observe, with characteristic generosity, "Only unthinking people find President Krüger dull."

Departing Cape Town on March 26, 1898, Slocum called at St. Helena and Ascension Islands, then shaped a course for the Caribbean. While off the coast of Brazil

Photo by Willard B. Jackson of Marblehead showing Joshua Slocum's SPRAY *rigged as a yawl with a mizzen and shortened main mast. Courtesy Peabody Essex Museum, Salem, Massachusetts.*

just north of the equator, *Spray* encountered the battle-ship USS OREGON during that ship's dash from San Francisco to Florida on the eve of the Spanish-American War. Ever helpful, Slocum signaled his compatriots, "Let us keep together for mutual support." After calling at several Caribbean islands, he sailed from Antigua for Cape Hatteras and New York. Encountering a gale near his destination, he instead rounded Montauk Point and sailed up Narragansett Bay to Newport, Rhode Island, where he dropped anchor on June 27, 1898. The world's first solo circumnavigation had taken *Spray* and her crew on a 46,000-mile voyage lasting three years, two months, and two days. "My ship was also in better condition than when she sailed from Boston on her long voyage. She was still as sound as a nut, and as tight as the best ship afloat."

In 1901, Slocum exhibited *Spray* at the Pan-American Exposition in Buffalo, New York. Though he made an effort to settle down, the call of the sea was too strong. In 1906, he loaded *Spray* with a consignment of Caribbean orchids, which he delivered to President Theodore Roosevelt. Two years later he freighted a two-ton piece of coral from the Bahamas to New York for the Museum of Natural History. On November 14, 1909, Slocum sailed from Vineyard Haven, bound for the Orinoco River and, he hoped, the headwaters of the Amazon. Neither he nor *Spray* was ever seen again.

Slocum, *Sailing Alone around the World.* Teller, ed., *Voyages of Joshua Slocum.*

USS SQUALUS (SS-192)

(later USS *Sailfish*) *Sargo*-class submarine. *L/B/D:* 310.5′ × 27′ × 13.8′ (94.6m × 8.2m × 4.2m). *Tons:* 1,450/2,350 disp. *Hull:* steel; 256′ dd. *Comp.:* 59. *Arm.:* 8 × 21″TT; 1 × 3″, 4 mgs. *Mach.:* diesel/electric, 5,500/3,300 hp, 20/9 kts; 2 screws. *Built:* Portsmouth Navy Yard, Kittery, Me.; 1939.

Commissioned on March 1, 1939, USS *Squalus* was on her nineteenth test run, thirteen miles southeast of the Piscataqua River entrance light off the coast of New Hampshire (May 23), when the main induction valve leading to the engine room failed. She sank off Portsmouth, New Hampshire. Although twenty-three of her crew were lost immediately, the bulkhead door to the engine room was secured, and thirty-three crew members remained alive in the forward part of the submarine, which lay in about 240 feet of water. The stricken submarine was discovered by her sister ship USS SCULPIN, and with the assistance of submarine rescue ship USS *Falcon,* her survivors were brought safely to the surface by means of the McCann diving bell.

Three months later the hull was raised, and after an eleven-month refit at the Portsmouth Navy Yard, she was recommissioned as USS *Sailfish.* Attached to the Asiatic Fleet in the Philippines in early 1941, when the United States entered World War II in December, she embarked on the first of two patrols out of Manila, heading for the Dutch East Indies at the conclusion of the second. She sank her first ship on March 2, in the Java Sea, but had only two more confirmed kills in her next five patrols. Her tenth began at Pearl Harbor on November 17, 1943. While en route to her patrol area off the island of Honshu, Japan, she encountered a convoy about 250 miles southeast of Tokyo Bay on the night of December 3–4. *Sailfish* sank the light carrier *Chuyo,* whose complement included twenty-one POWs from USS *Sculpin,* twenty of whom died when the ship went down. Following the war, *Sailfish* was credited with sinking nine Japanese ships during her twelve patrols. She was sold for scrap at Philadelphia in 1948.

LaVo, *Back from the Deep.* U.S. Navy, *DANFS.*

STAFFORDSHIRE

Clipper (3m). *L/B/D:* 243′ loa (230′ keel) × 41′ × 19.5′ (74.1m × 12.5m × 5.9m). *Tons:* 1817 grt. *Hull:* wood. *Comp.:* 214. *Built:* Donald McKay, East Boston, Mass.; 1851.

Built by Donald McKay for Enoch Train & Company's White Diamond Line, the three-decker *Staffordshire* was one of the few clippers built for transatlantic packet service. On her first run in May 1851, she sailed from Boston to Liverpool in 14 days. In August of that year, Train hired veteran clipper captain Josiah Richardson to take *Staffordshire* to San Francisco, which he did in a brisk 103 days. From there they sailed to Singapore in 51 days, Calcutta (21 days), and thence to Boston in the then record time of 84 days, a pace that few sailing ships ever bettered.

Upon her return, she reentered the Boston–Liverpool run. *Staffordshire*'s tragic last voyage began at Liverpool on December 9, 1853, from where she departed with 214 passengers, most of them Irish emigrants. On December 24 the steering gear was disabled and the bowsprit and foremast were carried away. In the course of repairs, Captain Richardson was injured and a few days later, on December 30, 1853, the ship struck Blonde Rock off Seal Island (near Cape Sable) and sank quickly, bow first. Because there was not enough room in the boats to accommodate the passengers and crew, 170 people were drowned, including Richardson.

Cutler, *Greyhounds of the Sea.* Howe & Matthews, *American Clipper Ships.*

STAG HOUND

Clipper (3m). *L/B/D:* 215′ bp × 39.8′ × 21′ (65.5m × 12.1m × 6.4m). *Tons:* 1,534 om, 1,100 nm. *Hull:* wood. *Comp.:* 40. *Built:* Donald McKay, East Boston, Mass.; 1850.

Although the early nineteenth century saw the development of a variety of fast ship types in the United States, it was not until the California gold rush of 1849 that ships began sailing the 15,000 miles from New York around Cape Horn to California in significant numbers and the search for speed became an imperative. The first half of the 1850s saw the full flower of the clipper age, when speed generated higher profits than sheer volume. Considered the first extreme clipper ever built, *Stag Hound* was the pioneering creation of Donald McKay, who in subsequent years would launch FLYING CLOUD, SOVEREIGN OF THE SEAS, and GREAT REPUBLIC, among others of the best-known clipper ships. *Stag Hound* excited great interest at her launch, and the *Boston Atlas,* among other journals, was effusive in its praise:

This magnificent ship has been the wonder of all who have seen her. Not only is she the largest of her class afloat, but her model may be said to be the original of a new idea in naval architecture. She is longer and sharper than any other vessel of the merchant service in the world, while her breadth of beam and depth of hold are designed with special reference to stability. Every element in her has been made subservient to speed; she is therefore her builder's beau ideal of swiftness; for in designing her, he was not interfered with by her owners. . . .

She is, as we have already stated, an original, and to our eye, is perfect in her proportions. Her model must be criticized as an original production, and not as a copy from any class of ships or steamers. We have examined her carefully, both on the stocks and afloat, and are free to confess that there is not a single detail in her hull that we would wish to alter. We think, however, that she is rather too heavily sparred; but many New York captains, however, who have much experience in the China trade, say that she is just right aloft.

Considering her lines, marine underwriter Walter R. Jones reportedly remarked to Captain Josiah Richardson, "I think you would be somewhat nervous in going so long a voyage in so sharp a ship, so heavily sparred" (she carried 11,000 square feet of sail). "No, Mr. Jones," said Richardson, "I would not go in a ship at all, if I thought for a moment that she would be my coffin."

Stag Hound was built for the Boston merchants George B. Upton and Sampson & Tappan; they put her in the Cape Horn trade, from New York to San Francisco, thence to China and westward on to New York, sometimes via London. Although she was a fast ship — in a strong wind frequently logging as much as seventeen knots — an unfortunate schedule had her sailing mostly in the off-season and prevented her from setting any records. On her maiden voyage the main topmast and all topgallant masts were lost only six days out, but *Stag Hound* still made Valparaiso in sixty-six days, the second-fastest passage at the time. On her last voyage, *Stag Hound* sailed from Sunderland, England, with a load of coal for San Francisco. She was off Pernambuco (Recife), Brazil, when at about 0100 on October 12, 1861, her cargo of coal was found to be on fire, probably from spontaneous combustion. The ship was abandoned at 1700 and an hour later she burned to the waterline.

Cutler, *Greyhounds of the Sea.* Howe & Matthews, *American Clipper Ships.*

compartment, killing 37 and injuring 21. The Iraqi pilot claimed that he had fired at *Stark* because he believed her to be an Iranian vessel 20 to 25 miles inside the Iranian exclusion zone. *Stark*'s Captain Glenn Brindel was later relieved of command and his recent promotion to captain was never confirmed; he retired with the rank of commander. The frigate returned to Mayport in August, and after 15 months of repairs, she rejoined the Atlantic Fleet, where she remained through 1996.

"Attack on the USS *Stark*." Polmar, *Naval Institute Guide to Ships and Aircraft of the U.S. Fleet.* Press reports.

USS STARK (FRG-31)

Oliver Hazard Perry-class guided missile frigate. *L/B/D:* 413′ × 45′ × 22′ (125.9m × 13.7m × 6.7m). *Tons:* 3,658 disp. *Hull:* steel. *Comp.:* 214. *Arm.:* 1 × Harpoon SSM, 1 × 76mm, 1 × 20mm Phalanx, 6 × 12.75″TT; 2 helicopters. *Mach.:* gas turbines, 1 shaft; 29 kts. *Built:* Todd Shipyards, Seattle, Wash.; 1983.

USS *Stark* was named for Admiral Harold Stark, chief of naval operations, 1939–42. Stationed at Mayport, Florida, in February 1987 — the height of the Iran-Iraq War — *Stark* was assigned to the Middle East Force to protect shipping in the Persian Gulf. On May 17, *Stark* was on routine duty about 220 miles northeast of Bahrain, in or near an Iranian-declared exclusion zone. Advised of an Iraqi Mirage F-1 jet flying down the Persian Gulf at 1700, she first made radar contact at 1758, when the plane was 70 miles away. Eight minutes later the Mirage fired two Exocet missiles from a distance of about 10 miles. The missiles struck the port side and destroyed a crew

STAR OF INDIA

(ex-*Euterpe*) Bark (3m). *L/B/D:* 205.5′ × 35.2′ × 23.4′ (62.6m × 10.7m × 7.1m). *Tons:* 1,197 grt. *Hull:* iron. *Built:* Gibson, McDonald & Arnold, Ramsay, Isle of Man; 1863.

Built with a ship rig for trade to India for Wakefield, Nash and Company of Liverpool, *Euterpe* was sold in 1871 to Shaw, Savill & Company, who put her in the colonial trade to New Zealand and Australia. In 1898 she was sold to the Pacific Colonial Ship Company of San Francisco and registered at Hawaii. Registered in the United States the following year, on January 17, 1901, she was sold to the Alaska Packers Association, and became the first iron ship to join the Packers' fleet. Rerigged as a bark, she began a two-decade career carrying men and supplies to the salmon fisheries. She was renamed *Star of India* following the Packers' acquisition of four of the Belfast-built "Star" fleet of jute carriers. Laid up in Oakland in 1923, James Wood Coffroth bought her for use as a museum

Known to later generations as the bark STAR OF INDIA, *the iron-hulled museum ship now lying in San Diego began life as the iron ship* EUTERPE *in 1863. She traded throughout the world until sold to the Alaska Packers in 1901, who rerigged and renamed her and put her in the fish-packing trade. Courtesy National Maritime Museum, Greenwich.*

ship in San Diego. Although her rig was cut down during World War II, she was fully restored as a bark in the 1960s.

Arnold, ed., *Euterpe.* Huycke, "Colonial Trader to Museum Ship." MacMullen, "*Star of India.*"

STAR OF THE WEST

Sidewheel steamship (2m/1f). *L/B/D:* 228.3′ × 32.7′ × 24.5′ dph (69.6m × 10m × 7.5m). *Tons:* 1,172 grt. *Hull:* wood. *Arm.:* 2 × 68pdr; 4 × 32pdr. *Mach.:* 2 vertical beam engines; 11.5 kts. *Built:* Jeremiah Simonson, Greenpoint, N.Y.; 1852.

Laid down as *San Juan* but launched as *Star of the West,* this brigantine-rigged sidewheel steamship was built for the passenger trade between New York and California. In December 1860, the Buchanan administration chartered her to carry arms and men to Major Robert Anderson's garrison at Fort Sumter in Charleston, South Carolina, and on January 5, 1861, she left New York. Although Secretary of the Interior Jacob Thomson alerted authorities in Charleston of her impending arrival, President James Buchanan neglected to advise Anderson, and when *Star of the West* entered Charleston Harbor four days later, she came under fire. Receiving no support from Anderson, the captain of *Star* returned to New York. Anderson and South Carolina Governor Francis W. Pickens exchanged accusations of having committed acts of war, and Pickens began preparations to attack Fort Sumter.

Three months later the federal government again chartered *Star of the West,* to carry troops from Texas to New York. On April 17 — five days after the bombing of Fort Sumter and the outbreak of the Civil War — she was captured off Texas by the Confederate Army steamer *General Rusk.* Renamed *Saint Philip,* she sailed for two years under the Confederate flag. During Union operations to take Vicksburg in March 1863, she was scuttled in the Tallahatchie River to protect the approaches to Fort Pemberton, Mississippi.

Silverstone, *Warships of the Civil War Navies.* U.S. Navy, *DANFS.*

STATSRAAD LEHMKUHL

(ex-*Grossherzog Friedrich August*) Bark (3m). *L/B/D:* 258.2′ × 41.5′ × 21.4′ (78.7m × 12.6m × 6.5m). *Tons:* 1,701. *Hull:* steel. *Comp.:* 240. *Mach.:* aux. *Built:* J. C. Tecklenborg, Geestemünde, Germany; 1914.

Regarded by the naval architect and historian Harold Underhill as "the best-looking of all the three-posters of barque rig," *Grossherzog Friedrich August* was built for the German Sail Training Association, which already oper-

ated *Prinzess Eitel Friedrich* (later DAR POMORZA) and *Grossherzogin Elisabeth.* She made no training voyages before the start of World War I, and her career during the war is not known. Afterwards she was turned over to the British as part of reparations. There being no use for a sail-training ship in Britain at the time, she was sold to the Bergen Schoolship Association (Bergens Skoleskib) as a replacement for its training bark *Alfen,* built for the Norwegian Navy in 1853. Between 1923 and 1939, the renamed *Statsraad Lehmkuhl* made annual cruises lasting from April to September. Seized by German occupation forces in 1940, she spent the rest of World War II as a depot ship. Restored to sailing condition in 1946, from 1952 on the cost of sending her to sea was prohibitive, and so she has been kept at Bergen as a stationary schoolship.

Schäuffelen, *Great Sailing Ships.* Underhill, *Sail Training and Cadet Ships.*

STEAMBOAT

(1f) *L/B:* 60′ × 14′ (18.3m × 4.3m). *Hull:* wood. *Comp.:* 60. *Mach.:* horizontal cylinder, double-acting condensing steam engine, stern paddles. *Des.:* John Fitch. *Built:* John Fitch & Henry Voight, Philadelphia; 1790.

While Robert Fulton is popularly credited with developing the first working steamboat, John Fitch ran a steamboat on the Delaware River for an entire summer 17 years before Fulton's NORTH RIVER STEAM BOAT slid into the Hudson River. Fitch first conceived of employing steam for navigation in 1785; although he did so independently, he was not the first person to have the idea. After building a 23- by 4.5-inch model that featured a conveyor belt of paddles mounted on the side of the hull, he appealed to Congress for support of his "attempt to facilitate the internal navigation of the United States, adapted especially to the waters of the Mississippi." This was not forthcoming. Fitch also found General George Washington noncommittal (James Rumsey had confided in him his plans for a mechanical boat), and Benjamin Franklin, to whom Fitch later appealed, offered only tepid support.

Before the founding of the U.S. Patent Office, the best that would-be steamboat men could do to protect their inventions was to obtain a state monopoly. Supported by Colonel John Cox, in March 1786 Fitch secured from the New Jersey legislature exclusive rights to "all and every species or kinds of boats, or water craft, which might be urged or impelled by the force of fire or steam." Cox and his son-in-law John Stevens, Jr., failed to honor a commitment to fund Fitch, but he found financial support elsewhere. (The same Stevens, incidentally, later built the

PHOENIX and contended over monopoly rights on the Hudson River with another brother-in-law, Chancellor Robert Livingston, Fulton's partner.) At the same time, Fitch fell in with German watchmaker Henry Voight, who helped him build a 45-foot skiff for manual trials of various paddle systems. The most novel of these was a mechanism that mimicked the action of canoers. As Fitch described it,

> Each revolution of the axle tree moves 12 bars 5 1/2 feet. As six oars come out of the water, six more enter the water, which makes a stroke of about 11 feet each revolution. The oars work perpendicularly, and make a stroke similar to the paddles of a canoe.

In 1787, they applied a steam engine to this device, and the boat moved under her own power. Her speed of 3 knots could not compete with the stagecoaches that ran along the Delaware, much less stem the current of the Mississippi. The trials took place during the Constitutional Convention and were observed by many leading politicians. In November 1787 Fitch secured a Virginia monopoly valid for 14 years, provided that he had two vessels in operation by 1790.

In 1788, Fitch decided to use a tube boiler that lightened the engine plant by 3½ tons (most of it the brick support for the boiler). The engine now drove a system of vertical paddles at the stern. In July 1788, this boat steamed 20 miles to Burlington, New Jersey — by far the longest distance ever traveled by a steamboat. But misfortune plagued Fitch. An appeal to his backers for money to buy a larger vessel was rejected, and his collaboration with Voight collapsed over the winter for personal reasons.

During 1789, Fitch waited anxiously for a new 18-inch cylinder to be cast, but this proved to be no improvement before the boat was laid up for the winter. The following spring, Fitch hit on the idea of fitting the engine with a smaller condenser, as well as new air pumps, and on April 16, 1790, he and Voight steamed a measured mile at 8 miles an hour. On May 11, they sailed to Burlington "from Philadelphia in three hours and a quarter, with a head tide, the wind in their favor." On June 5, the boat traveled 90 miles in 12.5 hours, and on June 14, they began advertising in Philadelphia papers:

> The Steamboat is now ready to take passengers and is intended to set off from Arch Street Ferry in Philadelphia, every Monday, Wednesday, and Friday for Burlington, Bristol, Bordentown, and Trenton, to return on Tuesdays, Thursdays and Saturdays.

In the course of the first season of steam navigation, *Steamboat* made 14 trips and covered more than 2,000 miles. Despite competitive fares, a fair degree of reliability, and the provision of food and drink, the public remained apprehensive. The average passenger count was only seven and the boat ran at a loss. A second vessel — *Perseverance* — was not completed before the deadline stipulated in the Virginia monopoly, and just at the moment of success, Fitch's backers withdrew. In 1793, the luckless inventor attempted to build another vessel under patent in France, but his ambition was overwhelmed by the French Revolution. Returning to the United States, he died penniless and forlorn five years later.

Baker, *Engine Powered Vessel.* Boyd, *Poor John Fitch.* Flexner, *Steamboats Come True.*

STEPHEN HOPKINS

Liberty ship (1f/3m). *L/B/D:* 441.5′ × 57′ × 27.8′ (134.6m × 17.4m × 8.5m). *Tons:* 7,181 grt. *Hull:* steel. *Comp.:* 59. *Arm.:* 1 × 4″, 2 × 37mm; 6 mg. *Mach.:* triple expansion, 2,500 ihp, 1 screw; 11 kts. *Built:* Kaiser Permanente Yard No. 2, Richmond, Calif.; 1942.

Only four months after entering service in May 1942, the Liberty ship *Stephen Hopkins* was en route from Cape Town to Bahia and Paramaribo under Captain Paul Buck. Named for a Rhode Island delegate to the Continental Congress, the ship was under the management of the Luckenbach Steamship Company. On September 27, 1942, in an area of the South Atlantic "through which no ship ever passed," she stumbled upon the German commerce raider STIER and her consort *Tannenfels.* Because of the fog, the adversaries did not see each other until only two miles separated them. *Stier* opened fire at 0856; *Stephen Hopkins* returned fire at 0900, and five minutes later she scored two well-placed hits that stopped *Stier* dead in the water. But *Stier*'s six 6-inch guns were overwhelming, and by 0918 *Hopkins* was obviously sinking; she finally went down at 1000, with the loss of 42 crew, in position 28°08′S, 11°59′W. Her 19 survivors reached the coast of Brazil after 31 days. Unknown to the American seamen at the time, *Stier* also sank. So well had *Stephen Hopkins* acquitted herself that Captain Horst Gerlach claimed in his log that he had come under fire from a ship armed with "six 4.7″ guns and lighter weapons." *Stier* was the first German surface combatant in World War II sunk by an American surface ship of any kind.

Moore, *Needless Word.* Schmalenbach, *German Raiders.*

STIER

(ex-*Cairo*) Commerce raider (1f/2m). *L/B/D:* 439.5′ × 23.9′ × 23.6′ (134m × 7.3m × 7.2m). *Tons:* 4,778 grt. *Hull:* steel. *Comp.:*

324. *Arm.:* 6 × 6″, 1 × 3.7cm, 2 × 2cm; 2 × 21″TT; 2 seaplanes. *Mach.:* diesel, 3,750 bhp, 1 screw; 14 kts. *Built:* Friedrich Krupp AG Germaniawerft, Kiel, Germany; 1936.

Built for the Atlas-Levant Line for service between Bremen and the Mediterranean, *Cairo* was converted for use as a commerce raider in 1941–42 and renamed *Stier* ("Bull"). Under Captain Horst Gerlach, she slipped out of Rotterdam on May 12 and sailed down the English Channel into the Atlantic. *Stier* was an unlucky raider, sinking only three Allied ships — two in early June and a third on August 9. Seven weeks later, on September 27, while lying well off the sea lanes of the South Atlantic with her supply ship *Tannenfels,* she was surprised by the American Liberty ship STEPHEN HOPKINS, en route from Cape Town to Bahia. Because of the fog, the adversaries did not see each other until they were about two miles apart. *Stier* opened fire at 0854 and quickly reduced the lumbering American ship to a hulk. But *Hopkins* hit back with her single 4-inch gun and hit *Stier* 15 times, including two shots that knocked out her steering gear and started a fire in the engine room at 0905. *Stier* ceased fire at 0918, and *Hopkins* sank at 1000, with the loss of 42 crew. With his own ship ablaze, Gerlach gave the order to abandon ship and *Stier* sank at about 1140. *Tannenfels* returned to La Verdon, France, with the 320 survivors of the battle. *Stier* was the first German surface combatant sunk by an American surface ship during World War II.

Schmalenbach, *German Raiders.*

STOCKHOLM

Liner (1f/2m). *L/B/D:* 524.7′ × 69.2′ × 24.9′ (159.9m × 21.1m × 7.6m). *Tons:* 11,700 grt.. *Hull:* steel. *Comp.:* 1st 113; tourist 282. *Mach.:* oil engines, 2 screws; 19 kts. *Built:* A/B Gotaverken, Gothenburg, Sweden; 1948.

Stockholm was built for Swedish-American Line service between Gothenburg and New York, on a route she shared with *Gripsholm* (1925; the first passenger motorship in North Atlantic service) and later *Kungsholm.* At about 2100, on July 25, 1956, outward bound from New York with third officer Ernst Johannsen-Carstens at the helm, *Stockholm* rammed the luxury liner ANDREA DORIA. Her bows were horribly mangled, and five crew were killed in the accident. After standing by to take on survivors from the Italian Line ship, *Stockholm* returned to New York and after repairs to her bow, she reentered her old service. In 1958 she began sailing from Copenhagen, with stops at Gothenburg, Bremen, Halifax, and New York. Two years later, she was sold to the East German Freier Deutsche Gewerkschafts-Bund in Rostock.

Renamed *Völkerfreundschaft* ("International Friendship"), she was refitted to carry 568 passengers in one class on workers' holidays. She remained in that work through the 1980s.

Bonsor, *North Atlantic Seaway.* Hoffer, *Saved!*

STORNOWAY

Clipper (3m). *L/B/D:* 157.8′ × 28.8′ × 17.8′ dph (48.1m × 8.8m × 5.4m). *Tons:* 527 nm. *Hull:* wood. *Built:* Alexander Hall & Sons, Aberdeen, Scotland; 1850.

Named for Stornoway Castle on the Island of Lewis, *Stornoway* is often considered the first British clipper built expressly to bring tea from China to England. While *Stornoway* continued the tradition of the "Aberdeen bow" first seen in Hall's SCOTTISH MAID, she was a considerably larger ship than her immediate predecessors. The impetus for the development of such ships was the repeal of the Navigation Acts, which prohibited the importation of tea in foreign ships. When this happened, the large, fast American clippers would automatically dominate the trade. In fact, *Oriental* was the first American tea ship to arrive at London, only twenty days before *Stornoway*'s launch.

Despite the great promise of her design — she was advertised as "the far-famed, yacht-built clipper" — *Stornoway* never fulfilled her promise because her captains did not drive her hard enough. Under Captain John Robertson, she made five voyages, stopping at Bombay or Calcutta en route to China. Her return times were quite good and she averaged 119 days from China. She dropped out of the tea trade in 1860, when she made a roundtrip to Sydney, and spent the remainder of her career in the Australian and New Zealand trades. She was owned by Mackay & Company of London from 1861 to 1867, and after four years she passed to R. Chapman of Newcastle. Two years later, on June 7, 1873, she was wrecked on the Kentish Knock.

MacGregor, *Tea Clippers.*

STRASBOURG

Dunkerque-class battleship (1f/2m). *L/B/D:* 703.6′ × 102.0′ × 31.5′ (214.5m × 31.1m × 9.6m). *Tons:* 35,500 disp. *Hull:* steel. *Comp.:* 1,431. *Arm.:* 8 × 13″ (2 × 4), 16 × 13cm, 8 × 37mm, 32 mg; 4 aircraft. *Armor:* 9.6″ belt, 5.2″ deck. *Mach.:* steam turbines, 4 screws, 112,500 shp, 31 kts. *Built:* Chantiers & Ateliers de la Loire (Penhoët), St. Nazaire, France; 1938.

Under the terms of the Washington Naval Treaty, the French government was allowed to build a total of 70,000 tons of capital ships. Wary of German and Italian construction plans, but pressed by domestic financial considerations, France opted for the battleships *Dunkerque* and *Strasbourg* with a standard displacement of only 26,500 tons — considerably under the allowed limit. *Strasbourg* mounted eight 13-inch guns in two quadruple turrets, both mounted forward of the bridge structure. Assigned to the Atlantic Squadron, at the start of World War II, *Strasbourg* took part in the search for the German raider ADMIRAL GRAF SPEE in late 1939. Transferred to the Mediterranean following the French capitulation to Germany and the establishment of the Vichy government, she was sent to the Algerian port of Mers el-Kébir near Oran, together with her sister ship and the battleships BRETAGNE and PROVENCE. On July 3, the British government demanded that the French commanders disperse their fleet to overseas ports, disarm their ships, or surrender outright. Admiral Gensoul refused, and HMS HOOD, BARHAM, and *Resolution* opened fire; only *Strasbourg* escaped serious injury and made a run for Toulon. Scuttled in November 1942 and later raised, following the war she was used for weapons tests before being scrapped finally in 1955.

Breyer, *Battleships and Battle Cruisers.*

STRUMA

(ex-*Macedonian*) Cattle ship. *Tons:* 400 tons. *Built:* <1941.

Shortly after Kristallnacht, the Nazi-organized demonstrations in Germany that led to the destruction of thousands of Jewish-owned ships and businesses in November 1938, Jewish leaders called on the British government to increase the number of Jews eligible to immigrate to Palestine, then mandated to Britain by the League of Nations. When the British mandatory authority refused, Haganah, the underground Jewish military organization of Eretz Israel, formed Mossad le Aliyeh Beth ("illegal immigration bureau") to get Jews out of Europe. Many of these refugees made their way down the Danube to Black Sea ports, where they embarked in ships bound for Palestine.

Britain maintained its rigid immigration quotas even after the start of World War II. In December 1941, the diminutive Panamanian-flag freighter *Struma* — formerly a cattle boat named *Macedonian* — embarked more than 700 Jewish refugees in Bulgarian and Romanian ports. The ship made through the Sea of Marmara, but when Turkish officials learned that the illegals did not have appropriate visas, they first detained the ship at Istanbul, and then had her towed back into the Black Sea in February 1942. Five miles from the Bosporus, the ship hit a mine and sank with the loss of all but one of the 769 passengers and crew. Turkey's role was likened to that of the United States in the ST. LOUIS incident, but the British mandatory authority in Palestine came in for international censure. Officials claimed variously that immigrant quotas for the year had already been exceeded, that they were fearful of antagonizing Palestinian Muslims by admitting more Jews, and that they could not admit refugees from enemy territory. Chaim Weizmann, later the first president of Israel, denounced Britain's policy as "inimical to the Allied war effort," and Emmanuel Neumann, director of the American Emergency Committee for Palestine, said that it epitomized "the whole case of Jewish homelessness, the fate of the Jewish people after the war and the need for securing the establishment of a Jewish commonwealth in Palestine." The tragedy also led to calls for a more lenient immigration policy for refugees from countries under Nazi occupation, though after the war British intransigence led to other tragic incidents, such as the attack on the immigrant ship EXODUS 1947.

Holly, *"Exodus 1947."*

SUCCESS

Ship (3m). *L/B/D:* 117.3' × 26.8' × 22.5' (35.8m × 8.2m × 6.9m). *Tons:* 621 net. *Hull:* wood. *Built:* Natmoo, Tenasserim (Moulmein), Burma; 1840.

Once advertised as the oldest merchant vessel afloat and a convict ship from Australia's first fleet in 1790, *Success* was one of the earliest floating maritime exhibits in the United States. In fact, her origins were somewhat more prosaic than her promoters claimed. Built for Cockerell & Company of Calcutta, she was employed in trade around India for two years before being sold to Frederick Mangus & Company of London, who put her in the emigrant trade to Australia. Sold in 1845 to William Phillips and William H. Tiplady of London, she was in their service for seven years before being sold to the Victoria state government for use variously as a women's prison, a "reformatory ship for seamen," and as an explosives warehouse.

In 1885 *Success* sank in Sydney Harbor, but in 1890 she was purchased and fitted as a floating "convict ship" exhibit. After five years in Australia, she sailed for Europe and toured ports in Great Britain and on the continent for two decades. In 1912, her new American owners

Built as a merchant trader in Burma, the brigantine SUCCESS *came to a curious end as an amusement park sideshow at various ports in England and later the Great Lakes. Author's collection.*

rerigged her as a barkentine and sailed her to Boston where she arrived after a 92-day crossing. Over the next thirty-nine years she toured ports from New England to the Pacific Northwest and the Great Lakes. She attracted visitors at the 1915 San Francisco World's Fair and the Chicago World's Fair in 1933. Six years later she was laid up at Sandusky, Ohio, where she sank. In 1943, her last owner accidentally ran her aground outside Port Clinton, Ohio, and decided to break her up. Her remains were burned by local teenagers on the Fourth of July 1946.

Brouwer, "The 'Convict Ship' *Success.*"

SUHAILI

Ketch. *L/B/D:* 32′ × 11.1′ × 5′ (9.8m × 3.4m × 1.5m). *Tons:* 14 TM. *Hull:* wood. *Comp.:* 1–5. *Mach.:* aux. *Des.:* Production Promotions, Ltd. *Built:* Colaba Workshop Ltd., Bombay, India; 1964.

Merchant marine officer Robin Knox-Johnson was stationed in India with the British Steam Navigation Company when he built the teak-hulled ketch *Suhaili.* (The name is Arabic for the southeast wind.) Ordered home for work on the run between England and Africa, he sailed *Suhaili* the 12,000 miles back to London with his brother and a friend. A year later, motivated in part by rumors that the French yachtsman Eric Tabarly was planning a nonstop, solo circumnavigation — and determined that an English sailor should be the first — Knox-Johnson began preparing for the same. In the meantime, the *Sunday Times* put up the Golden Globe award for the first person to accomplish this feat. Between June 1 and October 31, 1969, six boats set sail: John Ridgway's *English Rose,* Chay Blyth's *Dytiscus, Suhaili,* the French Bernard Moitessier's JOSHUA, and two English trimarans, Donald Crowhurst's TEIGNMOUTH ELECTRON and Nigel Tetley's *Victress.*

Suhaili sailed third, departing Falmouth on June 14, 1968. Over the course of the next 310 days, she would log an average of 96.2 miles per day, following what Sir Francis Chichester had called the clipper route on his one-stop circumnavigation in GIPSY MOTH IV. *Suhaili* did not have an easy time of it. A knockdown off the Cape of Good Hope rendered her radio inoperable for most of the rest of the voyage. Crossing the Indian Ocean, Knox-Johnson decided to sail through Bass Strait rather than south of Tasmania, and there *Suhaili* took another knockdown that resulted in damage to the water tanks, tiller, and self-steering gear. Pressing on, he crossed the Tasman Sea and sailed through Foveaux Strait between New Zealand's South Island and Stewart Island, only to run aground on a sandbar near Dunedin. (The challenge judges determined that this did not constitute a stop.) Shortly after this he radioed his sponsors, the *Sunday Mirror* and *True* magazine:

> I am beginning to wonder how much of the original boat I am going to be left with by the time I reach home. So far I have written off the self-steering gear, two tillers, a jib, a spinnaker, half the cooking stove, and the water tank. The cabin has shifted and leaks, and its canvas cover is cracking up.

This upbeat transmission was his last for 134 days, during which *Suhaili* ran her easting down in the Roaring Forties, rounded Cape Horn on January 17, 1969, and sailed up the Atlantic. There was no word of *Suhaili* until April 5, when a British tanker spoke her about 500 miles west of the Azores. Thirteen days later she was off the coast of England, but four days of adverse gales kept Knox-Johnson from making port until April 22, when he landed at Falmouth, having sailed 30,123 miles in 313 days.

While his achievement garnered Knox-Johnson the Golden Globe, his fellow sailors seemed poised to complete the circuit in faster time. As it happened, none finished. Blyth was forced to land in South Africa. Having averaged 110.6 miles per day, Tetley's *Victress* broke up after 247 days at sea, 1,200 miles from Plymouth. After rounding Cape Horn, Moitessier thought better of racing and decided to stay in the Roaring Forties before turning north for Tahiti, sailing 37,455 miles in 301 days without touching land. Most curious of all was the fate of Donald Crowhurst, whose *Teignmouth Electron* was found drifting in the Atlantic on July 10, only days after he had slipped over the side.

Suhaili was repaired and Knox-Johnson resumed long-distance voyaging in her. In 1989, he crossed the Atlantic using only fifteenth-century navigational techniques and instruments. Two years later, *Suhaili* made her first voyage north of the Arctic Circle, when Knox-Johnson took a group of four climbers and photographers to attempt Cathedral Mountain, 30 miles inland from Greenland's Kangerdlugssuaq Fjord (68°12′N, 31°50′W). *Suhaili* is maintained in sailing condition at St. Katherine Dock, London.

Knox-Johnson, *A World of My Own.*

SULTANA

Packet boat. *L/B/D:* 260′ × 42′ × 7′ (79.2m × 12.8m × 2.1m). *Tons:* 660 grt. *Hull:* wood. *Comp.:* 376 (pass. & crew). *Mach.:* high-pressure engines, sidewheels. *Built:* John Litherbury, Cincinnati, Ohio; 1863.

Built for Captain Pres Lodwick of Cincinnati, who operated a fleet of boats on the Upper Mississippi and Ohio Rivers, *Sultana* was designed for the long route to New Orleans. Wartime conditions kept her on the Ohio River sailing between Cincinnati and Wheeling, West Virginia, for her first year, and it was not until January 1864 that she made her first voyage to New Orleans. The same year she was sold to a consortium of St. Louis owners, including Captain J. Cass Mason. Her last southbound journey began just after the assassination of President Abraham

A typical Mississippi River steamer of the mid-19th century, the SULTANA *was the scene of one of the most tragic peacetime accidents in U.S. history. On April 26, 1865, only two weeks after the end of the Civil War, she caught fire and burned with the loss of more than 1,500 passengers and crew — 1,200 more people than she was designed to carry — most of them Union Army veterans returning home. Courtesy Murphy Library, University of Wisconsin, La Crosse.*

Lincoln. Heading north again, she stopped at Vicksburg where Union Army Captain Speed ordered Captain Mason to embark 1,886 homeward-bound soldiers, more than five times the number of people *Sultana* was built to carry. She landed briefly at Helena, Arkansas, and Memphis on April 26, 1865. Early the next morning, a few miles above the latter port, three of her four boilers exploded. The heavily overloaded vessel burned and sank with the loss of 1,547 people — according to the official count — more than 1,100 of them Union veterans.

Potter, *The Sultana Tragedy.* Salecker, *Disaster on the Mississippi.* Way, *Way's Packet Directory.*

SULTAN OSMAN I

(ex-*Rio de Janeiro*, later HMS *Agincourt*) Battleship (2f/2m). *L/B/D:* 671.5′ × 89′ × 27′ (204.7m × 27.1m × 8.2m). *Tons:* 30,250 disp. *Hull:* steel. *Comp.:* 1,115–1,267. *Arm.:* 14 × 12″ (7 × 2), 20 × 6″, 10 × 3″. *Armor:* 9″ belt, 1.5″ deck. *Mach.:* geared turbines, 34,000 shp, 4 screws; 22 kts. *Des.:* Tennyson d'Eyncourt. *Built:* Sir W. G. Armstrong Co., Ltd., Newcastle-on-Tyne, Eng.; 1914.

Sultan Osman I was originally ordered for the Brazilian Navy and laid down in 1911 as *Rio de Janeiro*. The Brazilians dropped the project because her twelve-inch guns were considered inadequate, although with seven twin turrets, she was the most heavily armed big-gun ship built to date. The Ottoman Empire purchased the ship in January 1914 and crews arrived in Britain on July 27 to take delivery of her and *Reshadieh*, which had also been ordered from British builders in 1911. On August 2, the day Austria declared war on Serbia, First Lord of the Admiralty Winston Churchill requisitioned the ships for the Royal Navy and renamed them HMS *Agincourt* and *Erin*, respectively. Money for the new ships had been raised partly by public subscription in Turkey, and this move played into the hands of Turkey's pro-German faction. It removed all remaining objections to the Ottoman government's signing a mutual defense treaty with Germany, which it did the next day; two months later Turkey was officially at war with Britain. While Churchill has been criticized for his heavy-handed maneuver, such an alliance without ships was certainly preferable to one in which the Turks and Germans had two powerful new battleships to unleash in the Mediterranean. (In 1915, the British requisitioned a third ship, *Almirante Latorre*, being built for Chile. Commissioned as HMS *Canada*, she was handed over to Chile after the war.)

Named for the site of Henry V's victory over the French in 1415, HMS *Agincourt* was assigned to the Grand Fleet at Scapa Flow. She sortied with the First Battle Squadron at the Battle of Jutland on May 31, 1916, but she saw little action otherwise. Laid up in 1919, she was sold to Rosyth Shipbreaking Company and broken up in 1924.

Halpern, *Naval War in the Mediterranean.* Parkes, *British Battleships.*

CSS SUMTER

(ex-*Habana*, later *Gibraltar*) Commerce raider (1f/3m). *L/B/D:* 184′ × 30′ × 12′ (56.1m × 9.1m × 3.7m). *Tons:* 437 grt. *Hull:* wood. *Comp.:* 18. *Arm.:* 1 × 8″, 4 × 32pdr. *Mach.:* direct-acting engine, 1 screw; 10 kts. *Built:* Vaughn & Lynn, Philadelphia; 1859.

Built for the New Orleans & Havana Line, the auxiliary merchant bark *Habana* was purchased at New Orleans and commissioned as the auxiliary cruiser CSS *Sumter* on June 30, 1861. The first command of Captain Raphael Semmes, she captured eighteen prizes in a cruise that took her through the Caribbean and Atlantic as far south as Maranhão, Brazil, and which also tied up a considerable number of Union warships. While coaling at Martinique in December, she was discovered by USS *Iroquois*, but she eluded the blockade and escaped to Cadiz on January 4, 1862. The Spanish government allowed her only to make necessary repairs, and *Sumter* sailed for Gibraltar without refueling. Unable to escape, she was sold at auction to the Liverpool-based Fraser, Trenholm and Company, which served as financial agent for the Confederacy. (Semmes meanwhile preceded her to Liverpool to take command of CSS ALABAMA.)

Renamed *Gibraltar,* the ship sailed to Liverpool under the British flag. Sold back to the Confederate government, she sailed for Wilmington with a cargo of munitions including two Blakeley cannon. She arrived there in April 1863. Her subsequent service record is unknown. She was reported at Birkenhead in July 1864, and it is believed that in 1867 "she went down in a gale near the spot where the *Alabama* was sunk."

U.S. Navy, *DANFS.* Wise, *Lifeline of the Confederacy.*

SUNBEAM

Topsail schooner (3m). *L/B/D:* 170′ × 27.6′ × 13.5′ (51.8m × 8.4m × 4.1m). *Tons:* 334 grt. *Hull:* composite. *Comp.:* 41. *Mach.:* compound steam engine, 350 ihp, 1 screw; 10.3 kts. *Des.:* St. Clair Byrne. *Built:* Bowlder & Chaffers, Seacombe, Eng.; 1874.

One of the world's most renowned yachts, *Sunbeam* was built for British railroad magnate Thomas (later Earl) Brassey, who owned her for forty-five years. Intended for

Lord Brassey's SUNBEAM, *a 170-foot auxiliary topsail schooner, was manned by a crew of 36 who sailed her on all the world's oceans. Grand yachts remain, though differences in the price of technology and labor make such sights as this rare indeed. Courtesy New York Yacht Club.*

long-distance cruising on a grand scale, *Sunbeam* carried nine guests and a crew of thirty-two who sailed under Lord Brassey himself, an accomplished navigator and sailor who acted as ship's captain, unusual in an era when most yachts were handled entirely by professional crew. On July 1, 1876, *Sunbeam* sailed from England at the start of a 425-day circumnavigation that took her to Brazil, through the Straits of Magellan to Chile and on to Tahiti, Hawaii, and Japan. En route from the Orient, she called at Hong Kong, Macao, Singapore, and Penang before heading home via Ceylon, the Suez Canal, and Portugal. This and other voyages were popularized by Lady Brassey's accounts in *Sunshine and Storm in the East* and *A Voyage*

in the "Sunbeam," published in 1888, a year after her death aboard the great schooner during a circumnavigation of Australia.

Brassey himself returned to the Antipodes in *Sunbeam* to take up his post as governor of Victoria in 1895. In addition to these longer voyages, *Sunbeam* also made a number of voyages to North America, the most celebrated of which was in 1905 when she entered the Kaiser's Cup transatlantic race won by the three-masted schooner ATLANTIC. In 1916, Lord Brassey turned *Sunbeam* over to the Royal Indian Marine for use as a hospital ship. Following World War I, he presented her to Devitt & Moore's Ocean Training Ships Ltd., though she never sailed with cadets. In 1922 she was purchased by ship owner Walter Lord Runciman who sailed her as a yacht until 1929, when she was scrapped.

Brassey, *In the Trades; Last Voyage to India and Australia; Sunshine and Storm in the East; Voyage in the Sunbeam.* Hofman, *Steam Yachts.* Runciman, *Before the Mast and After.*

SUNNESHINE

Bark (3m). *Tons:* 50 tons. *Hull:* wood. *Comp.:* 16–23. *Built:* England; <1585.

John Davis in 1584 organized an expedition to search for the Northwest Passage. His supporters constituted the North-West Company and included Sir Humphrey Gilbert, Sir Francis Walsingham, and William Sanderson. The next year he sailed from Dartmouth with the ships *Sunneshine* and *Mooneshine,* the latter having a crew of 19. Adverse winds held them in the Scilly Islands until June 28. The ships rounded southern Greenland on July 20 and sailed up the west coast, which Davis called the Land of Desolation. On July 28 they landed in about 64°15′N, the area of modern Godthåb, then named Gilbert Sound. Here they encountered their first Eskimos, for whom the *Sunneshine*'s four musicians played their instruments and with whom they traded for furs, kayaks, and other items. On July 31, the English resumed their search to the northwest, reaching Baffin Island on August 6 in 66°40′N and studding the area with the names of patrons and familiars such as Mt. Raleigh, Exeter Sound, and Cape Walsingham. Turning south, they took their departure from Cape of God's Mercy and sailed across the opening of Cumberland Gulf, which Davis thought might be the Northwest Passage and which he named for George Clifford, Earl of Cumberland. The onset of winter forced their return before he could explore further, and the ships arrived in England in September.

The following year Davis undertook a second expedition, sailing on May 7 with the ships *Mermaid* (120 tons) and *North Star* (10 tons). Davis went with *Mermaid* and *Mooneshine* to explore again the shores of Davis Strait, while *Sunneshine* and *North Star* sailed north to Iceland in search of a strait between there and Greenland. This route was blocked by ice after only two days, but the two vessels followed the ice eastward back to Iceland, then westwards again for a rendezvous with Davis at Gilbert Sound; but Davis had chosen another route, and the two ships sailed for home at the end of August, though *North Star* and her crew were lost at sea. In the meantime, Davis sailed up the coast to about 66°33′N before crossing Davis Strait and sailing into Cumberland Gulf where "we plainely perceived a great current striking to the West. This land is nothing in sight but Isles, which increaseth our hope" of the existence of a passage west. They then sailed south along the Labrador coast before turning for home.

The next spring, Davis sailed with three ships, *Sunneshine, Elizabeth,* and *Helen.* After sailing to Greenland, *Sunneshine* and *Elizabeth* sailed for the Newfoundland fisheries — an easy way to earn back the expenses of the voyage. Davis resumed his exploring in *Helen,* sailing north through the Davis Strait to a point he called Hope Sanderson (72°46′N), arriving on June 30. From there he shaped a southerly course, passing the Cumberland Islands, Lumley's Inlet (Frobisher's Strait), and Cape Chidley in northern Labrador. *Helen* returned to Dartmouth in September; the fate of *Sunneshine* is unknown.

Hakluyt, *Principal Navigations.* Morison, *European Discovery of America.*

SUOMEN JOUTSEN

(ex-*Oldenburg, Laënnec*) Ship (3m). *L/B/D:* 262.5′ bp × 40.3′ × 17′ (80m × 12.3m × 5.2m). *Tons:* 2,260 grt. *Hull:* steel. *Built:* Chantiers & Ateliers de St. Nazaire, St. Nazaire, France; 1902.

Originally named for the eighteenth-century physician Laënnec, *Suomen Joutsen* is the last survivor of the so-called bounty ships, square-riggers whose construction and manning were subsidized by the French government. The subsidies (authorized in 1881, and again in 1892, and which applied to steamships as well) continued for the first ten years of the ship's life. The revival of world commerce in 1897 resulted in a burst of shipbuilding that saw the construction of 212 bounty ships in five years. By the start of World War I, there were still 140 French square-riggers working the long sea routes between Europe, Australia, Chile, and California.

Built for the Société des Armateurs Nantais, *Laënnec* entered the long-distance trade between Atlantic and Pacific ports. Her maiden voyage began badly when, bound for Cardiff in ballast, she rammed and sank a British collier in the Bristol Channel. Following repairs, she resumed her voyage and spent the next nineteen years in continuous service for her owners. Her only other major mishap occurred when she was badly damaged in a storm while discharging a cargo of nitrate at Santander, Spain, in 1911. Laid up near Nantes in 1921 during the postwar shipping slump, the following year she was purchased by H. H. Schmidt of Hamburg.

Renamed *Oldenburg,* she began a second career as a cargo-carrying training ship. In 1925 she was dismasted off Cape Horn and returned to Hamburg with nothing on her mainmast above the lower topsail. The next year she sailed for the West Coast for nitrate. She remained in the nitrate trade until 1928, when she was sold again, this time to the Seefahrt Segelschiffs Reederei of Bremen for whom she trained cadets of North German Lloyd. Her owners were not satisfied with her performance, and in 1930 she passed under the Finnish flag for work as a training ship for the Finnish Navy. Renamed *Suomen Joutsen* ("Swan of Finland"), her training voyages were suspended during World War II. After 1949 she rarely left the Baltic. Laid up as a stationary schoolship in 1956, she is presently owned by the Merchant Navy Seamen's School at Turku.

Underhill, *Sail Training and Cadet Ships.* Villiers & Picard, *Bounty Ships of France.*

SURCOUF

Cruiser-type submarine. *L/B/D:* 361′ × 29.5′ × 23′ (110m × 9m × 7m). *Tons:* 3,304/4,318 disp. *Hull:* steel; 214′ dd. *Comp.:* 130. *Arm.:* 10 × TT (2 × 8″ & 8 × 21″); 2 × 8″, 2 × 37 mm; 1 float-plane. *Mach.:* diesel/electric, 7,600/3,800 hp, 1 screw; 19/8 kts. *Built:* Cherbourg; 1931.

Named for Robert Surcouf, a nineteenth-century French corsair, *Surcouf* was built as a commerce-raiding submarine. Attached to the 2nd Submarine Flotilla at Brest, the two-decked submarine suffered from an excess of technological innovation. Her 8-inch guns were prone to flooding and her machinery was fickle. Cruising off Africa when World War II began, she was deployed to the Caribbean until recalled to Brest for a refit in October 1939. Following the German invasion of France, *Surcouf* escaped to Plymouth, England, but with a crew of divided loyalties. On July 3, 1940, the submarine was seized by the Royal Navy and turned over to the Free French Navy. After serving on convoy duty, *Surcouf* was dispatched to Bermuda in June 1941, but she had to undergo extensive repairs at Portsmouth, New Hampshire, and New London, Connecticut, from July 28 until November 27. *Surcouf* took part in the Free French Christmas Eve seizure of St. Pierre et Miquelon. Following further repairs at Bermuda, she was dispatched to Tahiti. Leaving Bermuda on February 12, 1942, en route to the Panama Canal, *Surcouf* was never seen again. Despite suggestions that she was deliberately sunk by the British or Americans, it is more likely that she was sunk after colliding with the American army transport *Thompson Lykes* in 10°40′N, 79°31′W on the night of February 18, or that she was mistakenly sunk by units of the U.S. Army Air Corps flying out of Rio Hato, Panama, on the morning of the 19th.

Rusbridger, *Who Sank "Surcouf"?*

SUSAN CONSTANT

Bark (3m). *L/B/D:* approx. 55.2′ × 22.8′ × 9.5′ (16.8m × 6.9m × 2.9m). *Tons:* 120. *Hull:* wood. *Comp.:* 85. *Arm.:* 4 minions, 4 falcons. *Built:* London; ca. 1605.

Originally owned by the merchant firm of Colthurst, Dapper and Wheatley, *Susan Constant* was probably built in or near London on the Thames River in about 1605. She is known to have made at least one voyage to Spain in 1606, the year in which she was purchased by the Virginia Company to sail as flagship of an expedition to take settlers to North America. In the same year, she is also known to have been in collision with a 100-ton merchant ship, *Phillip and Francis,* a case that was settled by the courts.

With Christopher Newport as captain of the expedition, *Susan Constant* embarked 71 colonists; her consort *Godspeed* carried 52 and *Discovery* 21. "On Saturday, the twentieth of December in the yeere 1606, the fleet fell from London." So wrote George Percy, one of the colonists. Storm-bound in the English Channel for nearly a month, they did not reach the Canary Islands until February 21. From there they headed west to the West Indies, where they landed to take on water and other provisions. Heading north, the ships entered Chesapeake Bay in mid-April and finally landed at Jamestown Island — named in honor of their King — on May 13, 1607. Although its early years were marked by illness and dissension, the colony weathered a succession of crises to become the first permanent English establishment in North America.

Susan Constant returned to England in May 1607 and as the Virginia Company had no further use for her, she resumed general trade. Her ultimate fate is not known, but there are records of her sailing from Bristol to Marseilles as late as 1615. The Jamestown-Yorktown Foundation at Williamsburg, Virginia, built replicas of the three ships in the 1980s. (The dimensions for the replica *Susan Constant* differ somewhat from published estimates.) Today these are used as living history exhibits and to teach people how seventeenth-century sailors made their way in the oceans.

Lavery, *Colonial Merchantman "Susan Constant": 1605.*

SUSSEX

Passenger ferry. *L/B/D:* 275' × 34.1' × 14' (83.8m × 10.4m × 4.3m). *Tons:* 1,353 grt. *Hull:* steel. *Comp.:* 450+ pass., 50 crew. *Mach.:* triple expansion steam, 292 nhp, 2 screws. *Built:* William Denny & Bros., Ltd., Dumbarton, Scotland; 1896.

Despite the threat of German submarines, civilian passenger service between England and France was not entirely interrupted during World War I. Following the sinking of the passenger ship ARABIC on August 19, 1915, the German government had pledged to refrain from sinking passenger ships without warning in the so-called Arabic Pledge. Those in the German high command favoring the position cited both humanitarian reasons and the desire to maintain U.S. neutrality. Nonetheless, on March 24, *UB-29* sank the London, Brighton & South Coast Railway Company's cross-Channel ferry *Sussex* about an hour outside Dieppe. Although the ship reached port, 50 people were killed in the attack, including some Americans. The cause was not immediately known — some thought the ship hit a mine — but analysis of fragments found in the hull proved that she had been torpedoed. Lieutenant Herbert Pustkuchen claimed that the ship appeared to be a troop transport and that his action was therefore justified, but President Woodrow Wilson threatened to sever diplomatic relations. The German government capitulated and agreed that U-boats would operate under traditional prize rules. Rather than condemn his submarines and crews to certain destruction, Admiral Reinhard Scheer recalled all attack submarines operating in British waters until October 1916. In January 1917 it was decided to allow unrestricted submarine warfare, and the United States broke diplomatic relations on February 3. Following the sinking of five U.S.-flag steamers, the United States declared war on April 6.

Grey, *U-Boat War.* Halpern, *Naval History of World War I.*

SUTIL

Brig. *L/B/D:* 45.8' × 11.8' × 4.6' (14m × 3.6m × 1.4m). *Tons:* 33 toneladas. *Hull:* wood. *Comp.:* 20. *Arm.:* 4 arrobas. *Built:* San Blas de California, Mexico; 1791.

In 1791, following his voyage of exploration in the corvettes DESCUBIERTA and *Atrevida,* Don Alejandro Malaspina dispatched his hydrographer, Frigate Captain Dionisio Alcalá Galiano, on a voyage to the Pacific Northwest. His primary objective was to sail through the Strait of Juan de Fuca "to decide once and for all the excessively confused and complicated questions" of whether a Northwest Passage existed from Hudson Bay in the east to somewhere near Vancouver on the west coast. This last Spanish voyage of discovery in the Pacific sailed from Acapulco on March 8, 1792, and the expedition arrived at the Spanish settlement at Nootka on May 12. In early June, *Sutil* and *Mexicana* entered the Strait of Juan de Fuca and proceeded north through the islands of the Strait of Georgia. Near the Fraser River, the Spanish encountered Captain George Vancouver's HMS DISCOVERY and *Chatham* with whom they exchanged information about their respective discoveries. Continuing around Vancouver Island, Galiano sailed west into Queen Charlotte Strait and back to Nootka, where the Spanish caught up with Vancouver's ships before returning to San Blas on November 25. Although the Galiano expedition was less significant than its immediate predecessor, because Malaspina was in disgrace, it received greater publicity.

Kendrick, *Voyage of "Sutil" and "Mexicana," 1792.*

SUTTON HOO SHIP

L/B/D: 88.6' × 14.8' × 4.9' dph (27m × 4.5m × 1.5m). *Hull:* wood. *Comp.:* 41+. *Built:* England(?); ca. 625.

Sutton Hoo is the name of a gravesite in East Anglia about eighty-six miles northeast of London near the town of Woodbridge. The area contains fifteen burial mounds dating from the early Anglo-Saxon period and is located a mile north of the River Deben about eight miles from the North Sea. In 1938, the owner of the land on which the site lies, Edith Pretty, commissioned archaeologist Basil Brown to excavate some of the mounds. While excavating mound 1 the following year, Brown discovered the remains of a ship that had been buried with the effects of an important chieftain, circumstantially identified as Raedwald, who ruled the East Angles from 599 to 625 and who was the acknowledged overlord of the other kings of England.

One interesting aspect of the ship is that at the time of its discovery, it no longer existed. In reacting with the soil, the ship's timbers and iron fastenings had dissolved, leaving very clear casts, traces and impressions of their actual form and placement. In outline, the Sutton Hoo ship is similar to, though longer than, the Norse OSEBERG or GOKSTAD ships, which date from the ninth century. The central keel was scarfed to long stem and stern posts that curved gracefully upward, increasing in thickness as they reached their ends. The hull consisted of nine strakes on either side of the keel, fastened to each other with iron rivets and strengthened by twenty-six transverse frames. There are traces of twenty-eight rowlocks in four groups, seven on either side of the hull forward and aft of amidships (a similar midships break in rowing positions can be seen in ships depicted in the Bayeux tapestry), and the helmsman probably steered the ship with an oar lashed to the starboard side of the hull about two meters forward of the sternpost. Although there is no evidence that the Sutton Hoo ship carried a sail, the hull shape and certain construction details suggest she could have sailed. *Sæ Wylfing,* a half-scale model built in 1993, demonstrated excellent sailing ability, achieving speeds of ten knots or better in Force 4 conditions. The ship was probably dragged from the river over rollers and then slid into the trench, during which process some of the stern planks appeared to have sprung. Evidence of repairs to the hull suggest that the ship saw many years of service prior to interment.

It is likely that the site was a burial mound whose inhumed body simply dissolved in the acidic soil. Alternatively, the mound may have served only as a cenotaph to the dead chieftain. Buried with the ship were the personal effects of a male warrior of some significance. Personal belongings included beautifully fashioned gold and garnet buckles and clasps, silver and brass buckles, an iron helmet and face mask, an otter skin hat, two pairs of leather shoes, bone combs, and a lyre wrapped in a beaver skin bag. Fighting implements included an iron sword and its scabbard, six spears, four iron knives, a mail shirt, an ax-hammer, three throwing spears, and a shield. In addition, there was a curious object that has been identified as a scepter; it consists of a long four-sided whetstone with four carved faces at either end, surmounted by a ring atop which stands a stag modeled in bronze.

While the Angles were Germanic in origin, other artifacts found with the warrior's personal possessions show that seventh-century England was by no means cut off from European trade. In addition to a variety of wood and horn drinking vessels, caldrons, and other containers of local provenance, there were sixteen silver artifacts of eastern Mediterranean origin. The largest of these is a seventy-two-centimeter-wide dish with maker's marks dating from the reign of the Byzantine Emperor Anastasius I (491–528). There was also a bronze bowl of a type known as "Coptic" because the principal site of manufacture for such vessels (20 of which have been found in England) was in Egypt's Nile Delta, though the same type of bowl was made elsewhere in the eastern Mediterranean. Two silver spoons inscribed with the names Saul and Paul in Greek letters, to which has been attributed a Christian significance, were also found. (Raedwald is thought to have converted briefly to Christianity, but reverted to paganism.) There were also thirty-seven gold coins from Merovingian Gaul, the earliest of which has

been dated to 575 and the latest to 625, the year of Raedwald's death and, presumably, the erection of the burial mound.

Evans, *Sutton Hoo Ship Burial.* Gifford, "Sailing Performance of Anglo-Saxon Ships."

HMS SWALLOW

Sloop 14 (3m). *L/B:* 92′ × 26.5′ (28m × 8.1m). *Tons:* 278 bm. *Hull:* wood. *Comp.:* 86. *Arm.:* 14 × 6pdr. *Built:* Rotherhithe, Eng.; 1745.

HMS *Swallow* spent her first twenty years' service lying in ordinary in the Medway. Surveyed in 1763, she was found in need of repairs, which were only carried out when it was decided that she sail as a consort to HMS DOLPHIN on that ship's second circumnavigation, under Captain Samuel Wallis. The ship was small and much slower than the copper-bottomed *Dolphin,* and Commander Philip Carteret described his new command as "a miserable tool" and "one of the worst if not the very worst of her kind; in his majesty's Navy." The ships left Plymouth on August 21, 1766. *Swallow*'s dull handling made progress down the Atlantic slow going, and she barely survived the agonizing four-month transit of the Strait of Magellan. As the two ships entered the Pacific on April 11, 1767, *Dolphin* vanished from sight, leaving Carteret and *Swallow* to carry on alone.

Contending with unseasonable gales, Carteret made first for the Juan Fernández Islands and then sailed west in latitude 28°S, "in as high, if not higher South latitude then Any men, before which have gon across this Ocean." In about 130°W longitude, Carteret headed north and on July 2 discovered an island that was named for Midshipman Robert Pitcairn. (Three decades later, the uninhabited island, "scarce better than a large rock," would shelter the BOUNTY mutineers.) Heading west in about 10°S, Carteret hoped to find Alvaro Mendaña's Solomon Islands, but running short of water, he gave up and continued west until coming to Egmont Island (named for the First Lord of the Admiralty) in the group he called the Queen Charlotte Islands. Only later did he realize that Egmont was the Santa Cruz Island of Mendaña and Pedro Fernández de Quirós's voyage in SAN JERÓNIMO in 1595. Unfortunately, eight of *Swallow*'s crew were wounded in a skirmish with the islanders, and four later died, including the master.

Although he had hoped to turn south to explore the eastern part of New Holland (Australia), with scurvy debilitating his crew Carteret was forced northwest. On August 20, *Swallow* was off Gower's, Carteret's, and Simpson's Islands, which he all but ignored, little realizing that they comprise the northern limit of the Solomon Islands. On August 26, *Swallow* came to New Britain where Carteret's crew was refreshed and the ship repaired, and which Carteret claimed for England. Sailing again on September 7, they passed through St. George Channel, identified by Carteret as a strait between New Britain and New Ireland and not a gulf as previously believed. *Swallow* reached the Dutch settlement at Macassar on December 27, 1767, and she remained there until the following May when favorable winds allowed for the passage to Batavia. After repairs to the ship, she sailed for England in September, stopping at Table Bay from November 28 to January 6, 1769. Three weeks north of Ascension Island, *Swallow* was hailed by the French ship LA BOUDEUSE, under Louis-Antoine de Bougainville, who was returning from his own expedition, and, having followed in *Swallow*'s wake since New Ireland, was well acquainted with Carteret's voyage. Bougainville's appreciation for Carteret was heartfelt, and as he sailed away he wrote, "His ship was very small, went very ill, and when we took leave of him, he remained as it were at anchor. How much he must have suffered in so bad a vessel may well be conceived."

Swallow finally straggled into Spithead on March 20, 1769, after a voyage whose results could be attributed only to Carteret's determination. *Swallow* had more than outlived her usefulness, and as she was "a leeward sloop, and bad sailor, merchant built and 24 years of age," she was sold on June 20.

Wallis, *Carteret's Voyage round the World.*

HMAS SYDNEY

Town-class cruiser (4f/2m). *L/B/D:* 457′ × 50′ × 18′ (139.3m × 15.2m × 5.5m). *Tons:* 5,400 disp. *Hull:* steel. *Comp.:* 450. *Arm.:* 8 × 6″ (8 × 1), 1 × 3″m 4 × 3pdr; 2 × 21″TT. *Armor:* 3″ belt. *Mach.:* geared turbines, 25,000 shp, 4 screws; 25.5 kts. *Built:* London & Glasgow Engine and Iron Shipbuilding Co., Ltd., Govan, Scotland; 1912.

HMAS *Sydney* was the Royal Australian Navy's first cruiser. After taking part in the capture of the German colony of Neu-Pommern (New Britain) at the start of World War I, on November 1, 1914, *Sydney* was one of four cruisers assigned to escort the first Australasian convoy — 29,000 Australian and New Zealand troops in 38 transports. Eight days later, *Sydney* was detached to investigate a mysterious ship in the Cocos Islands, 55 miles south of the convoy. At 0940, SMS EMDEN opened fire on the faster, better armed *Sydney*. By 1120, Germany's most successful raider had been driven ashore on North Keel-

ing Island with the loss of 134 dead, compared with 4 dead in *Sydney.*

For the rest of 1914 and 1915, *Sydney* patrolled the North and South Atlantic, and in November 1916, she joined the Second Light Cruiser Squadron based at Rosyth. On May 4, 1917, she became the first Australian unit to be attacked from the air when she was targeted by the Zeppelin L43 — without success — in the North Sea. Following the surrender of the German fleet, she returned to Australian waters in July 1919. She was broken up in 1929.

Bastock, *Australia's Ships of War.* Hoyt, *Last Cruise of the "Emden."*

HMAS SYDNEY

Sydney-class light cruiser (2f/2m). *L/B/D:* 562′ × 56.7′ × 19.5′ (171.3m × 17.3m × 5.9m). *Tons:* 8,850 disp. *Comp.:* 682. *Arm.:* 8 × 6″ (4 × 2), 8 × 4″, 12 × 0.5″; 8 × 21″TT; 1 aircraft. *Armor:* 4″ belt, 1.3″ deck. *Mach.:* geared turbines, 72,000 shp, 4 shafts; 32.5 kts. *Built:* Swan Hunter & Wigham Richardson, Ltd., Wallsend-on-Tyne, Eng.; 1935.

Essentially modified *Leander*-class cruisers (such as HMS AJAX and ACHILLES), the three *Sydney*-class cruisers had two funnels rather than one. Laid down as *Phaeton* for the Royal Navy, HMAS *Sydney* was acquired by the Royal Australian Navy while still on the stocks. She remained on duty in Australian waters until the late spring of 1940, when she was dispatched to bolster the British Mediterranean fleet. She arrived at Alexandria, Egypt, two weeks before Italy entered World War II on June 10. *Sydney*'s first action was a shore bombardment of Bardia, Libya, ten days later. On the 26th, while escorting one of the Malta convoys, she sank the Italian destroyer *Espero*. *Sydney* was also present at the Battle of Calabria on July 9, when the Italian battle fleet ran from the British fleet for Taranto at full speed.

Her most celebrated action came on July 19 when, off Crete, she took on *Bartolomeo Colleoni* and *Giovanni delle Bande Nere*. The Italian ships were soon in retreat, but *Sydney* scored crippling hits on the *Colleoni* (reputedly the fastest cruiser in the world, with a design speed of 36.5 knots), which was later sunk off Cape Spada by torpedoes from HMS *Hyperion, Ilex, Hero,* and *Hasty.* Of this notable achievement, the *Times* wrote that "the *Sydney* has thus demonstrated the hollowness of the claim of the Italian naval and air forces to dominate these [i.e., Mediterranean] waters." The following month, *Sydney* destroyed Italian airfields on the island of Scarpanto.

In the fall of 1940, the British were forced to reassess the threat to their interests in the Pacific, and on February

HMAS SYDNEY *at Alexandria, Egypt, in July 1940, shortly after the sinking of the Italian cruiser* BARTOLOMEO COLLEONI. *On November 19, 1941, the light cruiser and her entire complement were lost in an engagement with the German raider* KORMORAN *off the coast of Australia. Many believe that she was sunk by a Japanese submarine, although Japan did not officially enter World War II for another three weeks. Courtesy Imperial War Museum, London.*

9, 1941, *Sydney* returned to a hero's welcome in Australia. Under command of Captain J. Burnett, she was engaged primarily in escorting reinforcements for the garrison at Singapore. On November 19, 1941, about three weeks before Japan entered the war, *Sydney* was about 300 miles west of Carnarvon, Australia, in about 26°S, 111°E, when she encountered the German raider *Kormoran*. In the engagement that followed, *Kormoran* was sunk with the loss of about 60 of her 400 crew, the survivors later being interned in Australia. Of *Sydney* the only trace was two empty lifeboats and a Carley raft. The loss of such an accomplished ship and her entire complement to an opponent whose primary armament consisted of six 5.9-inch guns has never been satisfactorily explained. One theory is that the cruiser surprised the raider while she was rendezvousing with a Japanese submarine. To obliterate any evidence of the presence of one of their vessels in the area at all, it is believed that *Sydney* may have been sunk ultimately by a Japanese submarine — possibly *I-124* — and not by *Kormoran* alone.

Frame, HMAS *"Sydney."* Winter, *H.M.A.S. "Sydney."*

SYRACUSIA

(later *Alexandria*) Freighter (3m). *L/B/D:* 180′ × 45′ × 43′dph (55m × 14m × 13m). *Tons:* 1,228 burden. *Hull:* wood. *Comp.:* ca. 600. *Des.:* Archimedes. *Built:* Archias of Corinth, Syracuse, Sicily; ca. 240 BCE.

Although much of the power of the ancient Mediterranean states depended on maritime trade, until recently very little was known of the ships they sailed. Such literary fragments as survive seemed wildly exaggerated until the discovery of submerged shipwrecks provided hard evidence to confirm their size and nature. One of the most complete descriptions of a ship from antiquity is that described by the Greek writer Athenaeus. Writing in the second century CE, but basing his account on more contemporary descriptions (now lost), he described a huge grain ship built by Hieron II, king of Syracuse from 269 to 215 BCE. Lionel Casson considers this to be the largest ship built in antiquity.

The description attests to the sophistication of shipbuilding at the time, as specific materials used in construction were either obtained locally — pine and fir from the forests of Mount Etna — or imported — cordage from Spain and hemp and pitch for caulking from the Rhône Valley in France. The ship's designer was none other than the engineer and mathematician Archimedes, who employed a variant of his screw to pull the unfinished ship into the sea, after which work was completed. The hull was fastened with copper spikes weighing as much as 10 to 15 pounds, and the planks were sheathed in a tarred fabric covered by lead sheets.

There were cabins for 142 first-class passengers on the second deck in addition to accommodations for steerage, the lower deck being reserved for cargo and the upper deck for soldiers, said to number 400. The first-class passengers could use a library, a gymnasium, promenades lined with flower beds, a chapel dedicated to Aphrodite, a reading room, and a bath. Twenty horses could be carried in separate stalls, and there was ample provision for fresh water and a saltwater fish tank for the cook's use. The ship was also heavily armed, being defended by marines stationed in eight deck towers who could fight the ship from the bronze tops of the three masts or from a raised fighting deck. The latter was fitted with a catapult of Archimedes' design capable of hurling an 18-foot dart or 180-pound stone 600 feet. The number of crew is not specified, but the account says that "although the bilge was extraordinarily deep, it was bailed by only one man using a screw pump, one of Archimedes' inventions."

The dimensions of the ship are not given, but the cargo on the ship's maiden voyage to Alexandria is itemized as follows: 60,000 measures of grain, 10,000 jars of pickled Sicilian fish, 20,000 talents of wool, and 20,000 talents of miscellaneous cargo. Converting to modern equivalents yields a burden of about 1,900 tons, not including provisions for the large crew. It soon became apparent that the ship was too large to use many of the usual ports, and Hieron decided to rename his *Syracusia* for the main port of Egypt and to give *Alexandria* to his ally, Ptolemy III Euergetes.

Casson, *Ancient Mariners.*

Szent István

Tegetthof-class battleship (2f/2m). *L/B/D:* 499.3' × 89.7' × 29' (152.2m × 27.3m × 8.9m). *Tons:* 21,689 disp. *Hull:* steel. *Comp.:* 1,094. *Arm.:* 12 × 12.2" (4 × 3), 12 × 6", 18 × 66mm; 4 × 21"TT.

Armor: 11.2" belt, 1.9" deck. *Mach.:* geared turbines, 26,400 shp, 4 screws; 20 kts. *Des.:* Popper. *Built:* Stabilimento Tecnico Triestino, Trieste, Austria-Hungary; 1915.

Named for the king and patron saint of Hungary (975–1078), *Szent István* was the fourth and last *Tegetthoff*-class battleship built by Austria-Hungary. These ships spent most of World War I at Pola, a powerful fleet-in-being that contributed little offensively to the Axis war effort, but which the Allies could by no means ignore. In June 1918, Admiral Nikolaus Horthy de Nagybánya (later regent of Hungary) conceived a plan to destroy the Otranto barrage between the heel of the Italian boot and the coast of Albania, through which German and Austro-Hungarian submarines had to pass to reach the Mediterranean. On June 8 Horthy sailed with the dreadnoughts *Viribus Unitis* and *Prinz Eugen* down the Dalmatian coast. *Tegetthoff* and *Szent István* followed on the 9th, but at about 0330 on June 10, *Szent István* was torpedoed by the Italian Mas 15 (on exhibit at Rome since 1936) about nine miles southwest of Premuda Island. Despite efforts to take her in tow, she sank shortly after 0600 with the loss of 89 in about 44°20′N, 14°40′E. Lacking the element of surprise, Horthy canceled the attack on the Otranto barrage.

Halpern, *Naval History of World War I.* Sokol, *Imperial and Royal Austro-Hungarian Navy.*

T

CSS TALLAHASSEE

(ex-*Atalanta;* later CSS *Olustee,* CSS *Chameleon, Amelia, Haya Maru*) Steamship (2f/1m). *L/B/D:* 250′ × 23.5′ × 13.3′ (76.2m × 7.2m × 4.1m). *Tons:* 546 disp. *Hull:* iron. *Comp.:* 120. *Arm.:* 1 × 84pdr, 2 × 24pdr, 2 × 32pdr. *Mach.:* direct-acting engines, 1,220 ihp, 2 screws; 14 kts. *Built:* John & William Dudgeon, Millwall, London; 1863.

Later known as the ship with seven names, the *Atalanta* was built for Stringer, Pembroke and Company, as a cross-Channel steamer. In July 1864, after successfully running the Union blockade eight times, *Atalanta* was purchased and commissioned as a commerce raider in the Confederate Navy. Renamed CSS *Tallahassee* and later *Olustee,* she made two cruises off the New England and midatlantic coasts during which she captured thirty-seven prizes. Converted back to a merchantman and renamed *Chameleon,* she ran the blockade outbound but was frustrated in her attempts to return. Sailing for England, where she was given back her first name and then registered as *Amelia,* she was seized by the U.S. government, auctioned, and ended her career as *Haya Maru.* She was wrecked between Kobe and Yokohama on June 17, 1868.

O'Driscoll, "Ship with Seven Names." U.S. Navy, *DANFS.*

USS TANG (SS-306)

Balao-class submarine. *L/B/D:* 311.5′ × 27.2′ × 15.2′ (94.9m × 8.3m × 4.6m). *Tons:* 1,525/2,424 disp. *Hull:* steel; 400′dd. *Comp.:* 66. *Arm.:* 10 × 21″TT; 1 × 5″, 1 × 40mm. *Mach.:* diesel/battery, 6,500 bhp; 20/8.75 kts. *Built:* Mare Island Navy Yard, Vallejo, Calif.; 1943.

Named after a species of surgeonfish, in an active career that lasted less than thirteen months, USS *Tang* was credited with sinking 24 Japanese ships of 93,824 gross tons, earning two Presidential Unit Citations in the process. Only USS TAUTOG sank more ships, and only three submarines sank more in terms of tonnage. Commissioned in October 1943 under Lieutenant Commander Richard H. O'Kane, on January 22 she sailed from Pearl Harbor on her first war patrol, in the Caroline and Mariana Islands. Between February 17 and 26, *Tang* accounted for four Japanese merchant ships. Her second patrol was devoted to lifeguard duty during which she rescued 22 downed airmen in the waters around Truk during the Marshall Islands campaign.

Her third patrol, one of the most successful of any U.S. submarine during the war, took place in the East China Sea, north of Taiwan, and the Yellow Sea between China and Korea. Departing Pearl Harbor, on June 24 she closed with a convoy of 22 ships south of Kagoshima and was credited with sinking four merchant ships. Four days later, patrolling between Dairen and Kyushu, she began a five-day shooting spree during which she sank six more ships, including three on the Fourth of July.

Tang's fourth war patrol was conducted in Japanese home waters off Honshu. Between August 10 and 24, *Tang* sank six more ships, retiring, as always, only after she had expended the last of her 24 torpedoes. After a few weeks' overhaul at Pearl Harbor, *Tang* left on her last war patrol, heading for Formosa Strait between Taiwan and China. She sank two cargo ships on the night of October 10–11, and resumed her patrol until October 23. That night, near Turnabout Island, she sailed into the middle of a convoy comprising five merchantmen and their escort ships, sinking three merchant ships.

Tang resumed her search for Japanese shipping the next morning. That night she began trailing a convoy and fired six torpedoes at three targets, two of which were sunk. After standing off from the convoy to load her two remaining torpedoes, *Tang* closed to within 1,900 yards of a troop transport. The first torpedo ran true, but the second broached the surface, turned in an arc, and slammed back into *Tang* about 20 seconds after firing. The submarine sank in about 160 feet of water. Nine of the crew, including Lieutenant Commander O'Kane, survived their escape via the emergency hatch and were picked up by a Japanese destroyer escort the next morning.

O'Kane, *Clear the Bridge.* U.S. Navy, *DANFS.*

USS TAUTOG (SS-199)

Tambor-class submarine. *L/B/D:* 307.2′ × 27.3′ × 13.3′ (93.6m × 8.3m × 4m). *Tons:* 1,475/2,370 disp. *Hull:* steel; 250′dd. *Comp.:* 65. *Arm.:* 10 × 21″TT; 1 × 3″. *Mach.:* diesel/electric; 20/9 kts. *Built:* Electric Boat Co., Groton, Conn.; 1940.

One of the most successful submarines of World War II, USS *Tautog* (named for a North Atlantic fish) was credited with sinking 26 Japanese ships for a total of 72,606 tons — scoring first in number of ships and fourth in tonnage. Assigned to the Pacific Fleet in 1940, *Tautog* was at Pearl Harbor during the Japanese attack on December 7, 1941. Her first mission, for reconnaissance in the Marshall Islands, began three weeks later. En route to the Marshalls on her second patrol, on April 24, 1942, she sank her first target, the Japanese submarine *RO-30*. Operating out of Fremantle, *Tautog* spent five patrols in the East Indies and Indochina. Returning to the West Coast for a refit in June, after one patrol in the Caroline Islands she began a series of four patrols in Japanese home waters during which she ranged between Hokkaido in the south and the Kurile Islands in the north. She sank the destroyer *Shurakumo* as well as a variety of smaller merchant and support vessels. *Tautog*'s thirteenth patrol (between December 1944 and January 1945) took her into the South China Sea. *Tautog* ended the war as a training ship. Decommissioned in 1945, she was broken up at Manistee, Michigan, in 1959, after twelve years as a reserve training ship at Milwaukee.

Roscoe, *United States Submarine Operations in World War II.* U.S. Navy, *DANFS.*

TEGETTHOFF

Barkentine (3m). *Tons:* 220 burden. *Hull:* wood. *Comp.:* 24. *Mach.:* steam, 100 hp. *Built:* Germany; <1871.

As late as the second half of the nineteenth century, there was still a vestigial belief that north of the Arctic ice lay a warm "Polar Sea." In 1871, the Austrian government dispatched veteran Arctic explorers Julius von Payer and Karl Weyprecht to investigate this possibility. As Payer wrote, "Our ideal aim was the north-east passage, our immediate and definite object was the exploration of the seas and lands on the north-east of Novaya Zemlya." The ship chosen was *Tegetthoff*, a wooden steamship sheathed in iron and named for the nineteenth-century Austrian Admiral Wilhelm von Tegetthoff. With provisions for three years, the ship sailed from Bremerhaven on June 13, 1872. Rounding Norway and sailing into the Barents Sea, on August 20 she became icebound off No-

vaya Zemlya in 76°22′N, 63°3′E. By August 1873 she had drifted northwest to 79°43′E, 59°33′, near the previously unknown Franz Josef Land, a group of islands about 275 miles northeast of Novaya Zemlya. After exploring the islands, which they named for the Austrian emperor, and advancing as far north as 82°5′N, on May 20, 1874, Payer and Weyprecht decided to abandon *Tegetthoff* and sledge back to Novaya Zemlya with the ship's boats. Three months of sledging brought them to the edge of the ice pack in 77°40′N. Taking to their boats, they were rescued by the Russian whaleship *Nicholas* off Novaya Zemlya.

Payer, *New Lands within the Arctic Circle.*

TEIGNMOUTH ELECTRON

Victress-class trimaran. *L/B/D:* 41′ × 22′ (12.5m × 6.7m). *Hull:* fiberglass. *Comp.:* 1. *Built:* Brundall, Eng.; 1968.

Following the circumnavigations of Sir Francis Chichester's GIPSY MOTH IV and Sir Alec Rose's LIVELY LADY, the ultimate goal for solo yachtsmen was a nonstop circumnavigation of the globe. In 1968, the *Sunday Times* sponsored the Golden Globe challenge. Seven yachts entered, including Robin Knox-Johnston's SUHAILI and Donald Crowhurst's ketch-rigged trimaran *Teignmouth Electron,* named for his electronics company and homeport. Crowhurst set out on October 31, 1968, barely five weeks after his vessel's launch. He was ill-equipped from the start, and his boat's performance was lackluster. Crowhurst compensated for his boat's poor performance by making false claims — including a record day's run of 243 miles — and lying about his progress. Carefully monitoring broadcasts for the Southern Ocean from Cape Town and Melbourne, Crowhurst reported that he had rounded the Cape of Good Hope, sailed into the Roaring Forties, and rounded Cape Horn, though in fact he never got out of the South Atlantic. On March 6, 126 days out, he put in briefly at the small Argentine port of Rio Salado to repair his starboard float. On May 4, the time he felt he should have rounded Cape Horn, he began sailing north again. *Teignmouth Electron* was found on July 10 in 33°11′N, 40°28′W, by RMV *Picardy.* From his log entries, it is apparent that Crowhurst had begun to lose his mind a few weeks before; his last entry — dated June 29 — suggests that he simply let himself over the side of his boat. *Teignmouth Electron* was taken aboard *Picardy* and landed at Santo Domingo. Crowhurst's misadventure inspired an episode in Robert Stone's novel *Outerbridge Reach* (1992).

Tomalin & Hall, *Strange Last Voyage of Donald Crowhurst.*

HMS TÉMÉRAIRE

Dreadnought/Neptune-class 2nd rate 98 (3m). *L/B:* 185' × 51' × 21.5' (56.4m × 15.5m × 6.6m). *Tons:* 2,121 bm. *Hull:* wood. *Comp.:* 750. *Arm.:* 28 × 32pdr, 60 × 18pdr, 10 × 12pdr. *Des.:* John Henslow. *Built:* Chatham Dockyard, Eng.; 1798.

The second ship of the name, HMS *Téméraire* spent her first three years as flagship of the Channel Fleet and the Western Squadron during the War of the Second Coalition against France. At the end of 1801, she called at Bantry Bay bound for her new station in the Caribbean when the crew mutinied. Twenty were arrested and the ship returned to Spithead where eighteen were hanged at the yardarm. In 1803, *Téméraire* was assigned to blockade duty off western France. In 1805, she was one of eighteen ships detached from the Channel Fleet to a squadron under Admiral Sir Robert Calder in order to follow the Franco-Spanish Combined Fleet (Vice Admiral Pierre Villeneuve) to Spain. Vice Admiral Lord Nelson relieved Calder on September 28 and with his fleet stalked the Combined Fleet until it sailed from Cadiz on October 19–20. The following day, *Téméraire* was next astern of HMS VICTORY in Nelson's weather column at the Battle of Trafalgar. *Téméraire* relieved pressure on *Victory* by raking *Redoutable*'s starboard side. She was being mauled by the French 74 and *Neptune* (80 guns) when she was approached by *Fougueux* (80), against which she unleashed two devastating broadsides. The French ship drifted onto *Téméraire* and was swiftly captured by a British prize crew. With losses totaling 121 killed and wounded and her masts and rigging a shambles, *Téméraire* was unfit for further sea duty. She was employed as a prison ship from 1813 to 1815, and thereafter as a receiving ship at Devonport and Sheerness. In 1836 she was briefly recommissioned under Captain Thomas Fortescue Kennedy, who as her first lieutenant led in the capture of *Fougueux* at Trafalgar. Two years later she was en route to be broken up at Rotherhithe when J. M. W. Turner was inspired to paint "The Fighting *Téméraire*."

Longridge, *Anatomy of Nelson's Ships*. Mackenzie, *Trafalgar Roll*.

CSS TENNESSEE

Casemate ironclad (1f/2m). *L/B/D:* 217' × 48' × 14' (66.1m × 14.6m × 4.3m). *Tons:* 1,273 disp. *Hull:* wood. *Comp.:* 133. *Arm.:* 2 × 7"R, 4 × 6.4"R. *Armor:* 4"–6" casemate. *Mach.:* high-pressure engines, 1 screw; 6 kts. *Des.:* J. L. Porter. *Built:* Henry D. Bassett, Selma, Ala.; 1864.

Built at Selma, on the Alabama River, the ironclad ram CSS *Tennessee* was fitted out at Mobile. Her construction was hampered by shortages of material and manpower, and Admiral Franklin Buchanan had to conscript the civilians at Mobile in order to complete her fitting out. Her casemate was sheathed in layers of two-inch-thick iron. In addition to six rifled guns and a ram, she had "a hot water attachment to her boilers for repelling boarders, throwing one stream [of water] from forward of the casemate and one abaft." *Tennessee*'s engines were taken from a sidewheel steamer, and she had no living accommodations.

Tennessee became the flagship of Admiral Franklin Buchanan and in June 1864 she was stationed at the approaches to Mobile Bay, ninety miles south of the port. At 0530 on August 5, Flag Officer David G. Farragut's long-anticipated force of four ironclad steamers and fourteen gunboats ran past Forts Morgan and Gaines. In addition to *Tennessee*, Buchanan's fleet included the wooden gunboats CSS *Gaines, Morgan,* and *Selma. Tennessee* attempted to ram USS HARTFORD and ran down the Union line until abreast of Fort Morgan. At 0900, Buchanan turned for Farragut's ships, now anchored four miles into the bay. As the ironclad approached, she was rammed by USS MONONGAHELA, *Lackawanna* (twice), and *Hartford*. The worst damage was inflicted at close range by the fifteen-inch guns of the monitor *Manhattan* and eleven-inch guns of *Chickasaw*. With two crew killed and fourteen wounded, her exposed rudder chains shot away, and no means of escape, *Tennessee* surrendered. *Selma* did likewise, *Gaines* had sunk, and *Morgan* escaped. Union losses included the monitor *Tecumseh* and a supply vessel. Commissioned into the U.S. Navy the next day, USS *Tennessee* took part in the siege of Fort Morgan, which surrendered on August 28. After service on the Mississippi River, in 1867 she was sold for scrap.

Still, *Iron Afloat*. U.S. Navy, *DANFS*.

TERRA NOVA

Bark (1f/3m). *L/B/D:* 187' × 31.4' × 19' (57m × 9.6m × 5.8m). *Tons:* 744 grt. *Hull:* wood. *Comp.:* 65. *Mach.:* compound steam engine, 140 nhp, 1 screw. *Built:* Alexander Stephen & Sons Ltd., Dundee, Scotland; 1884.

Built for the Dundee whaling and sealing fleet, *Terra Nova* (Latin for Newfoundland) was ideally suited to the polar regions. Her first work in the cause of science was as a relief ship for the Jackson-Harmsworth Arctic Expedition of 1894–97. In 1903, she sailed in company with fellow Dundee whaler *Morning* to assist in freeing from McMurdo Sound the National Antarctic Expedition's DISCOVERY, under Commander Robert Falcon Scott.

In 1909, she was purchased from Messrs. C. T. Bowring

Would-be members of the Flat Earth Society peer over the bulwarks of the TERRA NOVA. *The bark was lodged in the Ross Ice Shelf during Captain Robert Falcon Scott's ill-fated British Antarctic Expedition of 1910–12. Courtesy National Maritime Museum, Greenwich.*

and Company for the British Antarctic Expedition, known also as the Terra Nova Expedition. Reinforced from bow to stern with seven feet of oak to protect against the Antarctic ice pack, she sailed from England in June 1910 under overall command of now Captain Scott, who described her as "a wonderfully fine ice ship. . . . As she bumped the floes with mighty shocks, crushing and grinding a way through some, twisting and turning to avoid others, she seemed like a living thing fighting a great fight."

Although the twenty-four officers and scientific staff made valuable observations in biology, geology, glaciology, meteorology, and geophysics along the coast of Victoria Land and on the Ross Ice Shelf, Scott's last expedition is best remembered for the death of Scott and four companions. After wintering at Cape Evans, on Ross Island, Scott, Henry Robertson Owers, Edgar Evans, Lawrence Edward Grace Oates, and Edward Adrian Wilson set out on a race to be the first men at the South Pole. Starting with tractors and Mongolian ponies, the final

800 miles had to be covered by man-hauling alone. Reaching the South Pole on January 17, 1912, they found that Roald Amundsen's expedition (based on FRAM) had beaten them by thirty-three days. Worse was to come, as all five men died on the return journey. Spurred by national pride, Edwardian propagandists romanticized the expedition and made Scott a hero. As Amundsen's success clearly showed, however, his planning and logistics were inadequate and the loss of the explorers avoidable.

After returning from the Antarctic in 1913, *Terra Nova* was purchased by her former owners and resumed work in the Newfoundland seal fishery. Her end came on September 13, 1943, when she foundered off Greenland; her crew were saved by a U.S. Coast Guard cutter.

Cherry-Garrard, *Worst Journey in the World.* Lubbock, *Arctic Whalers.* Wilson, *Diary of the "Terra Nova" Expedition to the Antarctic.*

HMS TERROR

Vesuvius-class bomb vessel (3m). *L/B/D:* 102′ × 27′ × 12.5′ (31.1m × 8.2m × 3.8m). *Tons:* 325 bm. *Hull:* wood. *Comp.:* 67. *Arm.:* 1 × 13″ mortar, 1 × 10″ mortar, 2 × 6″, 8 × 24″. *Des.:* Sir Henry Peake. *Built:* Davy, Topsham, Eng.; 1813.

Best known for two expeditions in company with HMS EREBUS, HMS *Terror* was a bomb ketch designed primarily for shore bombardment. *Terror* saw service during the War of 1812, but she was then laid up until 1828. Recommissioned for duty in the Mediterranean, she was damaged near Lisbon and withdrawn from service after repairs. To withstand the tremendous recoil of their three-ton mortars, such ships were powerfully built and therefore suitable for Arctic service. In 1836, *Terror*—under command of George Back—sailed to Hudson Bay with a view to entering Repulse Bay, from where shore parties were sent out to determine whether the Boothia Peninsula was an island or a peninsula. *Terror* failed to reach Repulse Bay and barely survived the winter off Southampton Island; at one point she was pushed forty feet up the side of a cliff before the ice subsided. After ten months in the ice, Back extricated his leaking command and limped to Ireland, where she was beached.

Following repairs, *Terror* sailed with James Clark Ross's expedition to Antarctica, under command of Francis Crozier. On a voyage lasting from September 1839 to September 1843, *Terror* and *Erebus* made three forays into the waters of Antarctica, crossing the Ross Sea south of New Zealand twice, and sailing once through the Weddell Sea southeast of the Falkland Islands. The next year, the two ships were fitted out with twenty-horsepower engines and single-screw propellers in preparation for a

Although best known for their tragic end in the Arctic wastes under Sir John Franklin, HMS TERROR *and* EREBUS *also spent time in the South Pacific during James Clark Ross's expedition to Antarctica. This painting by John Wilson shows the two ships surrounded by native craft in New Zealand in the early 1840s. Courtesy National Maritime Museum, Greenwich.*

voyage in search of the Northwest Passage under command of Sir John Franklin. The expedition sailed from Greenhithe on May 19, 1845, and it was last seen in Baffin Bay near the entrance to Lancaster Sound in August 1845.

Search parties later learned that the ships sailed through Lancaster Sound, and after going north through Wellington Channel and around Cornwallis Island, they headed into Peel Sound and Franklin Strait, which lie west of Somerset Island and the Boothia Peninsula. Continuing southwest, the ships became icebound in Victoria Strait between King William Island and Victoria Island. Franklin died on June 11, 1847, and command of the expedition fell to Crozier. By the following spring, twenty-three more men had died, and on April 22, 1848, the 105 survivors abandoned the ships and attempted to march to Fort Resolution, a Hudson's Bay Company outpost more than 600 miles to the southwest. None survived, and their fate was not learned until 1859, when notes and other artifacts from the expedition were found on King William Island by search parties from Francis M'Clintock's *Fox.*

Back, *Narrative of an Expedition in HMS "Terror."* Beattie & Geiger, *Frozen in Time.* Ross, *Ross in the Antarctic.*

TEUTONIC

Liner (2f/3m). *L/B:* 565.8′ bp × 57.8′ (172.4m × 17.6m). *Tons:* 9,984 grt. *Hull:* steel. *Comp.:* 1st 300, 2nd 190, 3rd 1,000. *Mach.:* triple expansion, 2 screws, 17,100 ihp; 19 kts. *Built:* Harland & Wolff Ltd., Belfast, Ireland; 1889.

White Star Line's sister ships *Teutonic* and *Majestic* have the distinction of being the first passenger ships built to an Admiralty specification that would allow for their quick conversion to armed merchant cruisers. In return, their operating costs were subsidized by the government. Though not known for their elegance, they were fast ships, and *Majestic* captured the Blue Riband with a westbound crossing speed of 20.1 knots. Two weeks later, *Teutonic* improved on this by a quarter knot and crossed from Queenstown to Sandy Hook in 5 days, 16 hours, 31 minutes (August 13–19, 1891). *Teutonic* remained in service between Liverpool and New York for the next 20 years, with Cherbourg replacing Queenstown as an intermediary stop in 1907. In 1911, *Teutonic* was switched to White Star–Dominion Line service to Quebec and Montreal. At the outbreak of World War I, *Teutonic* was requisitioned as an armed merchant cruiser and joined the Tenth Cruiser Squadron. The next August, she was bought by the Navy and worked as a troopship until 1918. She was finally scrapped at Emden in 1921.

Bonsor, *North Atlantic Seaway.*

USS TEXAS

Second-class battleship (1f/2m). *L/B/D:* 308.8′ × 61.1′ × 24.5′ (94.1m × 18.6m × 7.5m). *Tons:* 6,315 disp. *Hull:* steel. *Comp.:* 392. *Arm.:* 2 × 12″, 6 × 6″, 12 × 6pdr; 4 × 18″TT. *Armor:* 12″ belt, 3″ deck. *Mach.:* triple expansion, 8,600 ihp, 2 screws; 17.8 kts. *Built:* Norfolk Navy Yard, Portsmouth, Va.; 1895.

One of the first two armored cruisers built for the "New Navy," the primary armament of the first USS *Texas* consisted of two 12-inch guns mounted en echelon — that is, one to starboard and the other to port, but not on the same athwartships axis. Shortly after the sinking of her near sister ship MAINE at Havana on February 15, 1898, *Texas* was detached from the North Atlantic Squadron to join Commodore Winfield Scott Schley's Flying Squadron to guard the coast against a possible attack by Spanish ships. The Spanish-American War began on April 24, and on May 27 *Texas*, Captain John W. Philip commanding, began blockade duty along the coast of Cuba between Santiago de Cuba and Guantánamo Bay. There, she and *Marblehead* reduced the Spanish fort on June 16. On July 3, she was with the Flying Squadron off Santiago when Admiral Pascual Cervera y Topete was ordered to sortie with his fleet. Under withering fire from *Texas*, BROOKLYN, OREGON, and other ships, Cervera's four cruisers were run aground and two torpedo boats were sunk; 323 Spaniards died and 151 were wounded. After service as a station ship at Charleston, *Texas* was renamed *San Marcos* and converted to a target ship in 1911. She was sunk off Tangier Island, Maryland.

Trask, *War with Spain in 1898.* U.S. Navy, *DANFS.*

USS TEXAS (BB-35)

New York-class battleship (1f/2m). *L/B/D:* 572.7′ × 95.3′ × 28.5′ (174.5m × 29m × 8.7m). *Tons:* 27,000 disp. *Hull:* steel. *Comp.:* 1,530. *Arm.:* 10 × 14″ (5 × 2), 21 × 5″; 4 × 21″TT. *Armor:* 12″ belt, 2″ deck. *Mach.:* VTE engines, 28,100 shp, 2 screws; 21 kts. *Built:* Newport News Shipbuilding & Dry Dock Co., Newport News, Va.; 1914.

Between 1905 and 1916, Congress authorized twenty-four battleships in ten classes. The first to carry fourteen-inch guns were the two *New York*-class ships laid down in 1911; they were also the only capital ships ordered after 1906 to carry reciprocating engines rather than steam

The battleship USS TEXAS *in the graving dock at the New York Navy Yard, Brooklyn, during World War I. Seamen scrape the hull while standing on gangplanks hung over the side of the ship. As work progresses, water is pumped out of the dock and the gangs are lowered. When the dock is dry, the hull is completely exposed and can be painted. Photo by Burnell Poole, courtesy the family of Burnell Poole.*

turbines. Commissioned at a low point in Mexican-American relations, USS *Texas*'s first assignment was in support of U.S. troops landing at Veracruz in retaliation for the Tampico Incident, during which U.S. sailors had been detained by Mexican troops. Later stationed off Tampico, she resumed regular operations with the Atlantic Fleet in February 1915.

Following the U.S. entry into World War I, the ships of Battleship Division 9 were slated to join the Royal Navy's Grand Fleet at Scapa Flow, but *Texas* was detained after running aground on Block Island on September 26. After repairs at New York she joined the fleet in February 1918. Apart from convoy duty and a few forays into the North Sea, there was little activity for the American ships, which were present at Scapa Flow for the internment of the German High Seas Fleet on November 21, 1918.

Returning stateside, *Texas* was the first U.S. Navy ship to launch an airplane, on March 9, 1919. Assigned to the Pacific Fleet from 1919 to 1924, she returned to Norfolk for a rebuild during which her cage masts were replaced with tripod masts, her twin tunnels were replaced by one, and a plane catapult was added to "Q" (center) turret. During World War II, *Texas* sailed on convoy duty and provided gunnery support for Allied landings in Morocco and Algeria in November 1942, and at Normandy and in southern France in 1944. Reassigned to the Pacific, she did the same at Iwo Jima and Okinawa. In 1948, *Texas* became the first Navy warship to be transferred by act of Congress for use as a museum ship, and she is the centerpiece of the Battleship Texas State Historical Park at La Porte, Texas, on Galveston Bay.

Egan, Lott, & Sumrall, *USS "Texas" (BB-35)*. Power, *Battleship "Texas."*

T. F. OAKES

Ship (3m). L/B/D: 255′ × 40.6′ × 23.5′ (77.7m × 12.4m × 7.2m). Tons: 1,997 grt. Hull: iron. Comp.: 20. Built: American Shipbuilding Co., Philadelphia; 1883.

One of the few iron-hulled square-riggers built in the United States, *T. F. Oakes* was constructed for W. H. Starbuck. She proved a dull sailer — her first voyage took 195 days from New York to San Francisco — but is remembered for one passage from Hong Kong to New York. On July 5, 1896, she cleared Hong Kong with a cargo of hides and skins and a complement of twenty-seven, including Captain E. W. Reed and his wife, three mates, the cook, and twenty crew. A week out of Hong Kong, the *Oakes* was caught in a succession of typhoons that sent her 500 miles off course to the northeast. Reed decided to take his ship home via Cape Horn rather than the Cape of Good Hope as originally planned. Encountering nearly endless calms, she was 169 days to Cape Horn — almost six months — and many of her crew became ill with scurvy. The disease progressed rapidly, killing seven and debilitating everyone else but the second mate and Mrs. Reed, who all but assumed her husband's command. On March 15, *Oakes* was taken in tow by the British tanker *Kasbek*. For her skill in handling the ship, which had been posted missing well before its arrival in New York 249 days out from China, Lloyd's awarded Mrs. Reed its Silver Medal for Meritorious Service. *T. F. Oakes* was stranded near San Francisco in 1901.

Domville-Fife, *Epics of the Square-Rigged Ships*. Lubbock, *Down Easters*.

THERMOPYLAE

Clipper (3m). L/B/D: 212′ × 36′ × 20.9′ (64.6m × 11m × 6.4m). Tons: 991 grt. Hull: composite. Comp.: 36. Des.: Bernard Waymouth. Built: Hall, Russell & Co., Aberdeen, Scotland; 1868.

Built to the order of George Thompson & Company of London, the tea clipper *Thermopylae* was named for the site of the Greek victory over the Persians in 480 BCE, and her figurehead portrayed King Leonidas. The largest of the tea clippers, on her maiden run to Australia (her usual first stop outward bound) under Captain Robert Kemball, she was only 63 days from London to Melbourne, a record never beaten; the average of her first ten passages out was only 69 days. Continuing from Newcastle to Shanghai in only 31 days, *Thermopylae* loaded tea and took her departure from the River Min on July 3, 1869. She was 25 days to Anjer, 49 days to Cape Agulhas, and off the Lizard on September 30, completing her remarkable passage two days later after only 91 days out. This was the fastest of her eleven runs with tea from China, the average of which was under 107 days, and she was the first of the returning tea clippers in 1873, 1874, and 1877. *Thermopylae* is particularly remembered for her rivalry with CUTTY SARK. While *Thermopylae* generally performed better in the tea trade during the 1870s, when steamers on the tea route forced them into the Cape Horn wool trade from Australia, *Cutty Sark* proved an excellent heavy-weather sailer. *Thermopylae*'s best run from Sydney of 76 days in 1882 was two days shy of *Cutty Sark*'s seven-run average of under 74 days.

In 1890, *Thermopylae* was acquired by the Canadian firm of Mount Royal Milling and Manufacturing Company, and put in the rice trade between China and British Columbia. In 1892 she was down rigged to a bark and switched from the rice to the lumber trades. In 1896 she was sold to Portugal for use as a naval training ship and renamed *Pedro Nuñes,* for the sixteenth-century Portuguese cosmographer. A survey found her in worse condition than expected, and she spent her last years as a coal hulk on the Tagus. On October 13, 1907, in the presence of Amelia de Orleans, Queen of Portugal, she was given a naval funeral and torpedoed at sea.

Matheson, *Clippers for the Record*. MacGregor, *Tea Clippers*.

USS THE SULLIVANS (DD-537)

Fletcher-class destroyer. L/B/D: 376.4′ × 29.6′ × 13.8′ (114.7m × 9m × 4.2m). Tons: 2,050 disp. Hull: steel. Comp.: 329. Arm.: 5 × 5″ (5 × 1), 10 × 40mm, 7 × 20mm; 10 × 21″TT. Mach.: geared turbines, 60,000 shp, 2 screws; 36.5 kts. Built: Bethlehem Steel Co., San Francisco; 1942.

At the Naval Battle of Guadalcanal on November 12, 1942, the cruiser USS JUNEAU was lost with five brothers — George, Francis, Joseph, Madison, and Albert Sullivan, ages twenty-two to twenty-eight — from Waterloo, Iowa.

The family tragedy prompted the Navy to rule that brothers could no longer be assigned to the same ship. In memory of the five, the Navy renamed the destroyer *Putnam* while still on the ways, and she was commissioned as *The Sullivans,* under Commander Kenneth M. Gentry.

The destroyer's first assignment, as part of Task Group 58, was to screen the aircraft carriers INTREPID, *Cabot,* and ESSEX in their attack on Kwajalein atoll beginning on January 24, 1944. From this point on, *The Sullivans* took part in the long march across the central Pacific, seeing action in the Caroline Islands, the Palaus, and the Marianas. *The Sullivans* remained on duty around the Philippines until late January, and then sailed with the American carriers as they began to attack the Japanese mainland and Okinawa. Her last combat action of the war was on May 14, when she splashed a kamikaze off Okinawa, before returning to the West Coast.

Put in reserve from 1946, *The Sullivans* returned to duty in 1951. Between October 1952 and January 1953, she sailed in support of UN forces in Korea, returning thereafter to Newport in April. *The Sullivans* spent the varied remainder of her career in the Atlantic and Mediterranean, supporting the U.S. landings at Beirut during the Lebanon crisis in July 1958 and taking part in the blockade during the Cuban missile crisis in October 1962, among other assignments. After twelve years in reserve, she was transferred to Buffalo, New York, for use as a museum and war memorial.

U.S. Navy, *DANFS.*

HMS THETIS

(later HMS *Thunderbolt*) T-class submarine. *L/B/D:* 275′ × 26.5′ × 12′ (83.8m × 8.1m × 3.7m). *Tons:* 1,330/1,585 disp. *Hull:* steel. *Comp.:* 53. *Arm.:* 1 × 4″, 10 × 21″TT. *Mach.:* diesel/electric, 2,500/1,450 hp, 15/9 kts. *Built:* Cammell Laird & Co., Ltd., Birkenhead, Eng.; 1938.

On June 1, 1939, the British submarine *Thetis* was undergoing trials fourteen miles off Great Ormes Head in Wales with a total of 103 people on board — the fifty-three crew that she was designed to carry and fifty technicians and other naval and civilian crew. At 1340, she submerged for a three-hour test dive. During her descent, she was light in the bows because the bow caps had not opened to let water into the torpedo tubes. This was seen on the indicator dials, but a fifth dial was misread and a drop of paint over the opening of a test cock failed to show that the tube was filled with water. When the loading door was opened, water flooded in and the hatch

couldn't be closed. As a result, the submarine plunged bow first into the mud 165 feet below the surface. The stern of *Thetis* was seen from the surface at 0800 the next morning, at which point four men emerged from the submarine via the escape hatch. A series of errors led to the submarine's not being recovered in time to save the lives of the ninety-nine men still in the submarine, all of whom suffocated. The tragedy of the loss was heightened by the fact that only a week before, the U.S. Navy had rescued thirty-three men from USS SQUALUS in a similar incident.

The submarine was eventually recovered, refurbished, and, after the start of World War II, renamed *Thunderbolt*. On December 15, 1940, she was en route to Gibraltar when she sank the Italian submarine *Tarantini* returning from joint patrols with German U-boats in the Atlantic. Assigned to various stations in the Mediterranean, she sank a number of smaller vessels on patrols in 1942. On January 3, 1943, she and HMS *Trooper* launched six chariots (human torpedoes) into the harbor at Palermo, Sicily, where they damaged the cruiser *Ulpio Traiano* and the transport *Viminale*. After sinking several more small sailing vessels, on March 14, 1943, *Thunderbolt* was sunk by the Italian corvette *Cicogna* during an attack on a convoy bound for North Africa.

Van der Vat, *Stealth at Sea.* Warren & Benson, *Admiralty Regrets.*

THOMAS F. BAYARD

(later *Sandheads No. 16*) Pilot schooner (2m). *L/B/D:* 86′ × 21.1′ × 8.6′ (26.2m × 6.4m × 2.6m). *Tons:* 70 grt. *Hull:* wood. *Des.:* William Townsend(?). *Built:* C. & R. Poillon, Brooklyn, N.Y.; 1880.

Built for the Delaware Bay Pilots at Lewes and named for a U.S. senator from Delaware, *Thomas F. Bayard* was probably designed by the same man who designed the schooner *Sappho,* one of two successful defenders of the America's Cup in 1871. After six years as a pilot boat she was sold to the Alaska Transport, Trading and Mining Company, of Philadelphia, and sailed to San Francisco via Cape Horn, arriving on the West Coast in July 1888. Still with her original name (Bayard was now U.S. Secretary of State), she was sold to the White Star Steamship Company and spent nine years freighting people and supplies to the diggings in Alaska during the gold rush years. When that work ceased to be profitable, she was sold to Canadian sealers and sailed in that trade for five years.

In 1913, she was sold to Canada's Department of Marine and Fisheries for conversion into a lightship. Anchored at the mouth of the Fraser River near Vancouver, she was renamed *Sandheads No. 16* in 1921. She was driven ashore twice, neither time with any loss of life, in 1947 and 1955. The second time, repairs were determined to be too expensive, and she was replaced by a lighthouse. Plans by a succession of private owners sought to restore her to sailing condition, without success. In 1978, she was sold to the Vancouver Museums and Planetarium Association, which has been restoring her to her condition as a West Coast sealer.

Brouwer, *International Register of Historic Ships.* Vancouver Maritime Museum.

THOMAS W. LAWSON

Schooner (7m). *L/B/D:* 385′ × 50′ × 35′ dph (117.3m × 15.2m × 10.7m). *Tons:* 5,218 grt. *Hull:* steel. *Comp.:* 17. *Des.:* B. B. Crowninshield. *Built:* Fore River Shipbuilding Co., Quincy, Mass.; 1902.

The only seven-masted schooner — and one of the only seven-masted vessels of any rig — ever built, *Thomas W. Lawson* was an extreme attempt to keep sail viable in the coastal trade against competition from steam vessels. Carrying twenty-six sails — three each on her seven masts and five head sails — she was equipped with auxil-

iary steam winches for sail and cargo handling, as well as steam steering gear, economies that enabled her owners to run her with a minimum of crew. Nonetheless, she had no auxiliary propulsion. Her masts, each of which was 193 feet high, were called fore, main, mizzen, no. 4, no. 5, no. 6, and spanker. Built for the Coastwise Transportation Company of Boston, she was nearly 200 tons larger than the five-masted ship PREUSSEN, which was launched the same year. She was not an especially graceful vessel, and Basil Lubbock describes her as having "the lines of a canal barge, and about as sweet as a bath tub."

Named for a Boston businessman, *Lawson* was built for coal trade, for which she proved ill-suited because she drew too much water for the ports she was intended to serve. Converted for use as an oil tanker, she sailed between Texas and the Delaware River for a number of years before being chartered to the Sun Oil Company in 1907. On November 19 of that year, she sailed from Philadelphia for London with 2 million gallons of oil. Caught in a succession of winter gales, her hull and masts provided so much windage that she reportedly made twelve knots under bare poles. On December 13, she was riding out a gale off the Scilly Isles when she dragged her anchors and broke up on Hellweather's Reef, with the loss

THOMAS W. LAWSON's *seven masts required a unique nomenclature: fore, main, mizzen, no. 4, no. 5, no. 6, and spanker, though they seem also to have been named for the days of the week. Basil Lubbock may well have been referring to this photo when he compared her to a canal barge and a bathtub. Courtesy Peabody Essex Museum, Salem, Massachusetts.*

of all but Captain George Dow and one of her crew, Edward Rowe.

Ronnberg, "Stranger in Truth than in Fiction." Watts, "*Thomas W. Lawson.*"

USS THRESHER

Thresher-class submarine. *L/B/D:* 278.5′ × 31.7′ (84.9m × 9.7m). *Tons:* 3,700/4,300 disp. *Hull:* steel; 1,315′ dd. *Comp.:* 112. *Arm.:* 4 × 21″TT. *Mach.:* nuclear reactor, 15,000 shp, 1 screw; 20/27 kts. *Built:* Portsmouth Navy Yard, Kittery, Me.; 1960.

The second USS *Thresher* (named for a type of shark) was the first in a class of nuclear-powered, deep-diving attack submarines. Commissioned in 1960 under Commander Dean W. Axens, *Thresher* spent virtually the whole of her brief career undergoing trials and tests to improve the Navy's understanding of nuclear submarines in general and of her class in particular. On April 10, 1963, she left Portsmouth in company with USS *Skylark* (ASR-20) for a series of test dives about 220 miles east of Boston. In addition to her standard complement, she carried seventeen civilian technicians and observers. She submerged at about 0745, reporting back to *Skylark* every fifteen minutes. All went well for the first hour, but at 0902, *Thresher* reported, "Experiencing minor difficulties. Have positive angle. Am attempting to blow. Will keep you informed." A few minutes later, the radio operator aboard *Skylark* heard a sound "like air rushing into an air tank." A final transmission at 0917 was almost incomprehensible, and the only three words that could be distinguished were "exceeding . . . test depth."

A few items from the submarine were later found floating in the vicinity of where the submarine sank — these having surfaced when the hull was crushed under the intense water pressure. The remains of the submarine were eventually located by the deep-submergence vehicle TRIESTE II, in 8,400 feet, where the pressure exceeds 1,000 pounds per square inch. The submarine's loss was attributed to a failure of the saltwater induction system, which resulted in flooding of the engine room.

Hooke, *Modern Shipping Disasters.* U.S. Navy, *DANFS.*

THURSDAY'S CHILD

Sloop. *L/B/D:* 60′ × 15′ × 11.5′ (18.3m × 4.6m × 3.5m). *Tons:* 10 disp. *Hull:* fiberglass. *Comp.:* 1–3. *Des.:* Warren Luhrs. *Built:* Hunter Marine, Alachua, Fla.; 1988.

"The search for speed under sail," as Howard Chapelle elegantly described it, intensified enormously in the years immediately following the 1849 California gold rush. Scores of clippers were launched in eastern seaports, and as merchants settled down with larger, slower ships and eventually abandoned sails for steam, records set in the 1850s attained an almost mythic significance among seamen. Chief among these was that of FLYING CLOUD, which twice sailed from New York to San Francisco in 89 days, in 1851 and 1854. Given the number of variables over the 14,000-mile Cape Horn passage, it seemed that this time could never be bettered under sail. Starting in the 1970s, the development of high-tech building materials of light weight and great strength, coupled with electronic aids to navigation — including loran and weather faxes — made it increasingly likely that a blue-water

The ill-fated USS THRESHER *under way on the surface in the spring of 1961. Improved hydrodynamics in the atomic age led to the construction of submarines with rounded hulls instead of flat decks for mounting guns. Courtesy U.S. Naval Historical Center, Washington, D.C.*

yacht could do so. And between 1983 and 1988, there were three unsuccessful attempts to break the record.

In 1984, Hunter Marine Corporation chairman Warren Luhrs built *Thursday's Child* to compete in the OSTAR single-handed race and set a transatlantic east-to-west monohull record of 16 days, 22 hours, 27 minutes. Four years later, Luhrs took aim at the *Flying Cloud's* record. With Luhrs, Lars Bergstrom, and Courtney Hazelton as crew, *Thursday's Child* departed New York on November 24, 1988. She crossed the equator 14 days later, 3 days faster than *Flying Cloud* had in 1854, but 5 weeks out, she hit a submerged object and was forced back to the Royal Navy's base at East Cove, Falkland Islands. After four days of repairs, she rounded Cape Horn on January 4, 42 days out and 6 days ahead of *Flying Cloud*. Working up the Pacific, the crew increased their lead to sail into San Francisco Bay on February 12, 1989, 80 days, 20 hours out from New York.

Later that year, Georgs Kolesnikov's and Steve Pettengill's trimaran *Great American* bettered the time by four days. Five years later, this record was shattered by *Ecureuil Poitou Charentes 2*. Skippered by Isabelle Autissier with a crew of three, the monohull sloop roared into San Francisco Bay on April 22, 1994, after a passage of only 62 days, 5 hours, 55 minutes from New York, an average speed of better than 9 knots.

Bennett, "Isabelle's Excellent Adventure."

TICONDEROGA

Sidewheel steamer (1f). *L/B/D:* 220′ × 57.5′ × 11.5′ (67.1m × 17.5m × 3.5m). *Tons:* 892 disp. *Hull:* steel. *Comp.:* 1,050. *Mach.:* vertical-beam engine, 1,1150 hp, sidewheels; 20 mph. *Built:* Champlain Transportation Co., Shelburne, Vt.; 1906.

Ticonderoga is one of only two surviving vertical-beam, sidewheel steamers in the United States. Built for the Champlain Transportation Company, formed in 1826, she was employed as a ferry and excursion boat on Lake Champlain, in its heyday a major artery on the route between New York and Montreal, which were linked by a system of rivers and canals. The largest and last of the steamboats launched at Shelburne, *Ticonderoga* was a three-decked day boat that catered especially to the denizens of the summer colonies sprinkled throughout the islands of Lake Champlain. She also carried livestock, apples, and other freight for local farmers. In 1909, her pilothouse was host to President William Howard Taft and the ambassadors of France and Great Britain during the tercentenary celebrations of Samuel de Champlain's first expedition to the lake named for him.

Business declined rapidly before World War II, and by

Walking-beam steamers such as the TICONDEROGA *were once common on the inland lakes and rivers of the United States. Today* TI *is preserved ashore on the grounds of the Shelburne Museum. Courtesy Shelburne Museum, Shelburne, Vermont.*

1938 *Ti* was the only boat running on the lake. By war's end, she operated chiefly as a showboat, and in 1950 plans were made to scrap her. At this point, Vermont historian Ralph Nading Hill began a campaign to put *Ti* back to work as an excursion boat. The lack of qualified engineers and inadequate revenues led to the boat's sale to Electra Havemeyer Webb (granddaughter of pioneer steamboat man Commodore Cornelius Vanderbilt), who operated the boat for two more years. The ship's historical importance — especially in the form of her W. A. Fletcher–built engines — could not be overlooked, and Webb added *Ticonderoga* to the Shelburne Museum, which she and her husband had founded. In 1954–55, *Ticonderoga* was hauled two miles inland via a temporary double-track railroad to a field, where she remains today. In 1964, she was designated a National Historic Landmark.

Hill, *Sidewheeler Saga.* Williamson, "Sidewheeler SOS Call Answered."

TICONDEROGA

(ex-*Tioga*) Ketch. *L/B/D:* 72′ × 16.1′ × 7.9′ (21.9m × 4.9m × 2.4m). *Tons:* 39 grt. *Hull:* wood. *Mach.:* gasoline. *Des.:* L. Francis Herreshoff. *Built:* Quincy Adams Yacht Yard, Inc., Quincy, Mass.; 1936.

Built for Harry E. Noyes for cruising, the clipper-hulled *Tioga* (the Iroquois name means "swift current") soon established herself as one of the fastest racing yachts of all time. In her second season, she sailed the 171 miles between New London and Marblehead nearly two hours faster than the previous best time made by the 136-foot schooner *Elena* in 1911. Three years later, she began her quarter-century domination of the Southern Ocean Racing Circuit with a stunning time of 19 hours, 36 minutes on the 184-mile Miami–Nassau Race. Following the United States' entry into World War II, she was requisitioned by the Coast Guard for use as a submarine picket on the East Coast.

Purchased by Allan P. Carlisle in 1946, she was renamed *Ticonderoga* (another Iroquois word, for "between the lakes"). She resumed her winning ways with a record 50-hour, 16-minute run between Marblehead and Halifax, in 1947. Four years later, John Hertz, Jr., bought her and she sailed to a new best time for the Nassau Cup. She then shaved three and a half hours off the St. Petersburg–Havana run, thereby becoming the first boat to set records on all legs of the SORC. When Havana was closed to the SORC after Fidel Castro came to power, she set the record for the St. Petersburg–Fort Lauderdale Race in 1962.

In 1961, *Ticonderoga* placed second in her first showing on the 2,225-mile Transpac Race between Los Angeles and Honolulu. Two years later, Robert Johnson chartered her for the same race, which she won in a dramatic nighttime finish. The following year, she established a new record in the 3,600-mile Tahiti Race, which she sailed in 17 days, 6 hours — running under spinnaker for most of the way. Now owned by Johnson, *Ticonderoga* had her most brilliant year in 1965. Back in the Atlantic, she fell 32 seconds shy of her 1940 Miami–Nassau record, no doubt because a cruise ship blanketed her while steering close aboard for a better look at the race's finish. She followed up this disappointment with a record 4-day, 23-hour, 8-minute run from Miami to Montego Bay en route back to the West Coast. Later that season, in her second Transpac race, *Ticonderoga* pulled off an amazing victory in which she shaved an hour off *Morning Star*'s 1955 record. Making an average speed of 9.6 knots over the entire course, she thundered past Diamond Head after 9 days, 13 hours, 51 minutes at sea, and only 5 minutes, 48 seconds ahead of second-place finisher *Stormvogel*. *Ticonderoga* continued racing until 1968, when she was refitted for charter cruising.

Robinson, *Legendary Yachts*.

TIGRIS

Reed ship (1m). *L*: 60′ (18.3m). *Hull*: Berdi reed bundles. *Comp.*: 11. *Built*: Thor Heyerdahl, al-Qurna, Iraq; 1977.

Named for the Mesopotamian river along whose course the Sumerian civilization flourished about 3000 BCE, *Tigris* was built by Norwegian explorer Thor Heyerdahl, who intended to prove that Sumerians and their contemporaries could have navigated such craft over long distances. Heyerdahl had made previous similar investigations in KON-TIKI and RA II. Modeled on early renderings of seagoing craft from the Persian Gulf and Egypt, *Tigris* was built by so-called Marsh Arabs of Iraq's Shatt al-Arab, who bundled the reeds, and Aymara Indians from Lake Titicaca, Peru, who turned the reed bundles into "a sickle-shaped ship that would neither capsize nor lose its shape in the ocean waves." She carried a single mast from which were set two square sails.

Launched in November 1977, and flying the flag of the United Nations, *Tigris* had difficulty navigating through the Persian Gulf owing to unseasonably adverse winds and the tremendous amount of tanker traffic and offshore oil wells that had to be avoided. The first port of call was the island country of Bahrain, which many archaeologists have identified as Dilmun, the great seaport of the Gilgamesh epic. From there she sailed south and east out of the Strait of Hormuz before heading west along the coast of Oman. Landing at Muscat, the *Tigris* crew were among the first westerners to visit the remains of the ancient copper mining center at Shohar. After heading for Africa, a change in the wind enabled them to sail for Pakistan's Indus Valley, the site of an ancient civilization centered on Mohenjo Daro and Harappa that evidently traded with Sumer. From there they sailed west until they passed through the Bab al-Mandeb at the mouth of the Red Sea and on to Djibouti, where they arrived in March 1978. At Djibouti, on April 3, 1978, they burned *Tigris* to protest the conflicts that had prevented them from landing in North or South Yemen on the Arabian peninsula, or in war-torn Somalia or Ethiopia. Their five-month, 4,200-mile voyage through the Persian Gulf and across the Indian Ocean had proven both the navigability and the extreme seaworthiness of such reed craft and "shown that the ancient people in Mesopotamia, the Indus Valley and Egypt could have built man's earliest civilizations through the benefit of mutual contact with the primitive vessels at their disposal five thousand years ago."

Heyerdahl, *"Tigris" Expedition*.

TILIKUM

Schooner (3m). *L:* 30′ (9.1m). *Tons:* 3 grt. *Hull:* wood. *Comp.:* 2. *Built:* Vancouver Island, British Columbia; <1901.

Inspired in part by Joshua Slocum's account of his solo adventure in SPRAY, Captain John C. Voss rigged a Northwest Indian dugout canoe as a three-masted schooner rig for a circumnavigation and named her *Tilikum,* Chinook for "friend." On May 21, 1901, Voss left Victoria with journalist Norman Luxton, who stayed only as far as Samoa. He was succeeded by nine other crew, the first of whom, Louis Begent, was lost at sea. In Australia, the diminutive *Tilikum* was hauled 1,400 miles on trains as Voss ventured into the hinterland on the lecture circuit. *Tilikum* arrived in Margate, England, on September 2, 1904, having sailed 40,000 miles in three years, three months, and ten days. Voss eventually returned to Victoria, and *Tilikum* was exhibited at Earl's Court for two years before being purchased for use as a yacht. The boat lay in the mud of the Thames estuary from 1911 until H. T. Barnes bought it. The vessel's voyage around the world was finally completed aboard the Furness Lines' *Pacific Ranger* in 1930. Back in Victoria, *Tilikum* was exhibited first at the Crystal Gardens, later outdoors at the Thunderbird Park, and finally at the Maritime Museum of British Columbia.

Ross, "Travels of *Tilikum.*" Voss, *Venturesome Voyages of Captain Voss.*

TILLIE E. STARBUCK

Ship (3m). *L/B/D:* 270′ × 42.7′ × 21.5′ (82.3m × 13m × 6.6m). *Tons:* 2,750 dwt. *Hull:* iron. *Comp.:* 24. *Built:* John Roach & Sons, Chester, Pa.; 1883.

Tillie E. Starbuck was the first iron-hulled, full-rigged ship launched in the United States. Built for W. H. Starbuck, a railroad agent in Portland, Oregon, she was a profitable ship and made a record run of 106 days from New York to Portland. The *Nautical Gazette*'s summary of her manifest on the maiden voyage gives an idea of what sailing ships could carry towards the end of the age of sail:

> Her cargo consists of 22 locomotives, 1100 tons of railroad iron, the hull, engines, boilers, etc., for a side wheel steamboat; 40 bales of waste, 3 life boats, 1 life raft, 90 tons of car springs, 60 tons of railroad spikes, 1 turn table, 4 bridge girders, 3 barge loads of car wheels and axles, 15 tons of railroad bolts, 20 tons of stove coal, 80 cords of cord wood used as dunnage, 12,000 feet of lumber boards, 3,000 feet of hemlock joist.

The cost of transporting all this by ship was only $110,000, $40,000 less than by railroad. E. F. Luckenbach bought the *Starbuck* in the late 1890s, and after a few years, he sold her to Welch & Company of San Francisco. She had only three captains over her entire career, W. A. Rogers, Eben Curtis (1885–1902), and William Winn. Under the latter's command, she was bound from New York for Honolulu when on July 30, 1907, she was completely dismasted in 47°50′S, 81°35′W. After drifting north by west for eighteen days, her crew were taken off by the British ship *Cambuskenneth* and landed at Coquimbo, Chile.

Lubbock, *Down Easters.*

TINKERBELLE

Sloop. *L/B:* 13.5′ × 5.3′ (4.1m × 1.6m). *Hull:* wood. *Comp.:* 1. *Built:* Old Town; 1932.

Tinkerbelle was a thirty-year-old day sailer when Robert Manry bought her for recreational sailing with his wife and two children in 1962. After a few seasons of pleasure sailing on the lakes of Ohio, Manry, a copyeditor for the *Cleveland Plain Dealer,* determined to sail across the Atlantic Ocean. Following a winter of preparation, he trailered *Tinkerbelle* to Cape Cod, Massachusetts. *Tinkerbelle* departed Falmouth on June 1, 1965, provisioned for ninety days. As it happened, this was about two weeks more than necessary, not including the gifts of food and water he received from ships encountered en route. The longest period in which Manry did not spot another vessel was only nine days. After seventy-eight days at sea, he arrived at Falmouth, England, on August 17. *Tinkerbelle* was the smallest vessel to make the passage to that time.

Manry, *"Tinkerbelle."*

TIRPITZ

Bismarck-class battleship (1f/2m). *L/B/D:* 823.3′ × 118.1′ × 32.5′ (251m × 36m × 9.9m). *Tons:* 52,600 disp. *Comp.:* 2,608. *Hull:* steel. *Arm.:* 8 × 15.2″ (4 × 2), 12 × 6″, 16 × 10.5cm, 16 × 3.7cm, 78 × 2cm; 8 × 21″TT; 6 seaplanes. *Armor:* 12.8″ belt, 4.8″ deck. *Mach.:* geared turbines, 136,200 shp, 3 shafts; 30 kts. *Built:* Kriegsmarinewerft, Wilhelmshaven, Germany; 1941.

Named for Admiral Alfred von Tirpitz, the architect of Germany's Imperial Navy, *Tirpitz* was the largest and most feared surface unit in the German Navy. Following

The German battleship TIRPITZ *spent much of World War II tied up in Norwegian fjords; note the camouflage covers on her forward turrets. As a "fleet-in-being," she posed a significant threat to British planners, who expended countless resources in trying to destroy her. They finally succeeded on November 12, 1944. Courtesy Imperial War Museum, London.*

the loss of her sister ship, BISMARCK, in January 1942 *Tirpitz* was sent to Foettenfjord, Norway, about 40 miles from Trondheim. On March 6, 1942, *Tirpitz* sailed against convoys PQ12 (bound for the USSR) and QP8 (bound for Iceland); returning to base three days later, she was attacked by 12 planes from HMS VICTORIOUS. *Tirpitz* was unscathed, but the ship's vulnerability had been brought home to the German High Command, which became increasingly reluctant to risk its most powerful ship. As a fleet-in-being, she posed a threat that could not be ignored, and her destruction became a British obsession.

Raids by Halifax and Lancaster bombers later in March and April resulted in heavy losses for the British, but with no damage to the ship. In July 1942 the Germans

mounted Operation Rösselsprung, in which *Tirpitz*, ADMIRAL HIPPER, and ADMIRAL SCHEER were to attack convoy PQ17 in the Barents Sea. Held in the Altenfjord, near the North Cape, until July 5, *Tirpitz* was ordered back to base after only three hours at sea. But fear of encountering *Tirpitz* led Admiral Sir Dudley Pound to issue the catastrophic order for the convoy to scatter, which resulted in the sinking of 21 of 35 ships, the worst losses of any convoy of the war.

An effort to sink *Tirpitz* with chariots on October 28, 1942, failed when the two-man submarines sank before they could be launched. On September 6–8, 1943, she sortied with SCHARNHORST to bombard installations on Spitzbergen. Back at Altenfjord, on September 22 *Tirpitz* was attacked by two 51-foot-long midget submarines each carrying two 3,570-ton charges of high explosives. At least three charges were laid by *Pdinichthys* (X-6) and *Piker II* (X-7), and these put *Tirpitz* out of action for six months. An attack by Russian bombers on February 11, 1944, was ineffectual, and by March 15 *Tirpitz* was undergoing sea trials. On April 3, planes from HMS FURIOUS, *Victorious,* and four escort carriers inflicted another three months' worth of damage. Six more carrier-based attacks were mounted through the end of August.

On September 15, 1944, 27 Soviet-based British bombers dropped "Tallboy" bombs against *Tirpitz.* Only one hit, but it rendered the ship useless as a surface unit, and on October 15 she was moved down the coast to Tromsö, where she was reduced to a floating battery. British-based bombers attacked again on October 29, but it was not until November 12 that a raid by 39 Lancasters of the Fleet Air Arm succeeded in sinking *Tirpitz* in Operation Catechism. Hits from six Tallboys blew "C" turret off the ship, which then capsized at anchor (in 69°36′N, 18°59′E) with the loss of 1,204 officers and men; there were 680 survivors. The hulk was broken up between 1948 and 1957.

Kennedy, *Menace: The Life and Death of the "Tirpitz."*

RMS TITANIC

Liner (4f/2m). *L/B:* 852′ × 92′ (259.7m × 28m). *Tons:* 46,329 grt. *Hull:* steel. *Comp.:* 1st 1,034, 2nd 510, 3rd 1,026; 941 crew. *Mach.:* triple expansion & steam turbine, 50,000 hp, 3 screws; 24 kts. *Built:* Harland & Wolff Ltd., Belfast, Ireland; 1912.

The Royal Mail Ship *Titanic* was one of three sister ships laid down for Britain's White Star Line, then a subsidiary of American financier J. P. Morgan's International Mercantile Marine. Unlike their more utilitarian Cunard rivals, OLYMPIC, BRITANNIC, and *Titanic* were unabashed celebrations of opulence and technological wizardry. One of *Titanic*'s greatest innovations was the placement of fifteen watertight bulkheads (with electrically operated watertight doors) that extended from the ship's double bottom through four or five of her nine decks and were said to make the ship "unsinkable." Yet for all her safety features, *Titanic* carried just sixteen lifeboats and four collapsible boats, which could handle only 1,178 people, a meager 35 percent of the maximum passenger and crew complement of 3,511. Even so, this number exceeded the British Board of Trade's requirements, which dated from 1894 (when the largest ship afloat was 12,950 tons), under which *Titanic* was required to carry only enough lifeboats to seat 962 people.

Although her maiden voyage attracted an impressive roster of internationally known names, *Titanic* left Southampton on April 10, 1912, with relatively little fanfare. Among the 329 first-class passengers — whose aggregate wealth exceeded $500 million dollars — were John Jacob Astor, Isidor and Ida Strauss, Harry Widener (for whom Harvard University's Widener Memorial Library would be named), and, among the survivors, J. Bruce Ismay, Managing Director of the White Star Line, and Margaret "the Unsinkable Molly" Brown. There were also 285 second-class and 710 third-class passengers, and 899 crew on the ship's manifest.

Overseeing this small floating city was Commodore Edward J. Smith, a twenty-five-year veteran of the White Star Line who postponed his retirement to make the voyage. Smith had commanded *Olympic* since June 1911, and even after several peculiar accidents he was evidently unfazed by the superliner's power and size. During her August 10 departure from Southampton, the suction of *Titanic*'s propellers pulled the Inman Line's *New York* from her dock and snapped her mooring lines like string. Unscathed, *Titanic* proceeded first to Cherbourg and then Queenstown, where the last passengers were embarked.

On April 14, an aura of complacency pervaded the bridge, although *Titanic*'s wireless operators Jack Phillips and Harold Bride (employees not of Cunard but of the Marconi Wireless Company) received warnings of an ice field ahead of the ship. The first of the six messages came at 1340, but only one was formally posted on the bridge, and Smith neither slackened speed nor turned to the south. (The transmitting ships included *Baltic, Noordam, Amerika, Mesaba,* CALIFORNIAN, and CARONIA.) As *Titanic* plowed forward into the windless, moonless night at better than 22 knots, at 2340, lookout Frederick Fleet reported from the crow's nest: "Iceberg straight ahead."

First Officer William Murdoch immediately acted to leave the berg to starboard, but *Titanic* brushed 200 feet of her hull along a submerged spur that buckled her hull plates along the riveted seams. A hurried examination of the damage found that the six foremost watertight compartments had been breached; each would flood and spill successively into the next until she sank. In the wake of the collision, Captain Smith's behavior was vague, and it was only on his subordinates' initiative that distress rockets were fired or the lifeboats launched.

At 0015 on April 15, *Titanic* sent her first distress call and at 0045 she fired her first of eight distress rockets in an effort to bestir a mysterious ship, later thought to be the Leyland Line's *Californian,* lying about nineteen miles away. By 0220 the last of the lifeboats had pulled away and the ship was perpendicular to the water, her lights still blazing. Finally, she broke apart between the third and fourth funnels and sank in 13,000 feet of water in about 41°46′N, 50°14′W.

Many lifeboats left the ship partially full, and though 706 survivors were rescued by the Cunard Line's CARPATHIA — she arrived on the scene at about 0330, after speeding fifty-eight miles through the ice field — there were 473 empty seats. The death toll was estimated at between 1,500 and 1,635 people. Second Officer Charles H. Lightoller held firmly to the unwritten doctrine of "women and children first," and though they constituted only 24 percent of the ship's complement, they made up 53 percent of the survivors. There were also great disparities among the survivors by class. Only 25 percent of the third-class passengers and 24 percent of the crew survived, compared with 42 percent of the second-class and 60 percent of the first-class passengers.

The exact circumstances surrounding the tragedy created an orgy of press speculation. Because she was owned by an American consortium but regulated by the British Board of Trade, government inquiries into the disaster were convened in Washington and London. The politics of jurisdiction and liability were delicate, and neither inquiry assigned explicit blame for the disaster, except to the hapless *Californian.* Nonetheless, authorities in both countries sensibly addressed the fundamental safety issues of lifeboats for all, proper lifeboat drills and crew training, twenty-four-hour-a-day wireless operation, and the creation of the International Ice Patrol.

There the *Titanic* story seemed to end, though it went through a succession of interpretations in print and film, most notably Walter Lord's authoritative account, *A Night to Remember,* and a movie of the same name. Over the years, a variety of expeditions sought to locate the remains of the ship, but it was not until 1985 that an expedition led by Dr. Robert Ballard of the Woods Hole Oceanographic Institution succeeded. Working with the manned submersible ALVIN, the deep-towing camera sled *Argo,* and the remotely operated vehicle *Jason,* Ballard's team found and photographed *Titanic* in two sections — the stern engine room section, largely destroyed, and the bow section 1,930 feet away, more intact and surrounded by a huge debris field. In 1987, a French expedition removed artifacts from the site despite an international outcry that the wreck be respected as a mass grave and archaeological site. Others have visited the site, as treasure hunters, thrill seekers, or for documentaries, and part of James Cameron's *Titanic* (1997) was filmed on location inside the hull.

Ballard & Archibold, *Discovery of the "Titanic."* Lord, *Night to Remember.* Lynch & Marschall, *"Titanic."* Shipbuilder and Marine Engine-Builder, *White Star . . . Liners "Olympic" and "Titanic."* Film: *A Night to Remember.*

HMS TONNANT

3rd rate 80 (3m). *L/B/D:* 194.2′ bp × 51.8′ × 23.2′ (59.2m × 15.8m × 7.1m). *Tons:* 2,281 bm. *Hull:* wood. *Comp.:* 700. *Arm.:* 32 × 32pdr, 34 × 18pdr, 18 × 32pdr carr. *Built:* Toulon, France; 1792.

Launched in the first year of the French Republic, *Tonnant* ("Thundering") was commissioned as part of the Mediterranean fleet of Vice Admiral Comte Martin. Her first engagement was against Vice Admiral William Hotham's fleet off Genoa on March 14, 1795. Three years later, during Napoleon's Egyptian Campaign, she flew the flag of Commodore A. A. du Petit-Thouars at the Battle of the Nile on August 1, 1798. Directly astern of the flagship L'ORIENT, though completely dismasted, she was captured only after a protracted struggle, exemplified by the conduct of her captain, who, despite the loss of both arms and a leg, continued to exhort his crew until he died from loss of blood.

One of six French ships captured that day, *Tonnant* was taken into the Royal Navy and in 1803 became flagship of Commodore Sir Edward Pellew. In March 1805 she was detached from the Channel Squadron off Brest for blockade duty at El Ferrol, Spain. Vice Admiral Lord Nelson assumed command of her squadron in September, and at the Battle of Trafalgar, *Tonnant* sailed in the lee squadron led by Admiral Cornwallis's ROYAL SOVEREIGN. Going to the relief of HMS *Mars,* she engaged the Spanish *Monarca* and *San Juan Nepomuceno* and the French *Fougueux* and *Pluton* (all 74 guns). Captain Charles Tyler ran his ship into *Algesiras* (74), whose crew attempted to board *Tonnant.* They were repulsed, and at 1430 the French ship struck her colors. *Tonnant*'s casualties numbered 76 killed and wounded.

Assigned to the Channel Fleet from 1806 to 1809 un-

der Rear Admiral Eliab Harvey (captain of *Royal Sovereign* at Trafalgar), she later sailed on blockade off Cadiz. During the War of 1812, she was in Rear Admiral George Cockburn's squadron at the capture of Washington, D.C. In December, she was with Vice Admiral Sir Alexander Cochrane's squadron during the attack on New Orleans. She ended her career on the Irish station based at Cork from 1815 to 1818. Three years later she was broken up at Plymouth.

Longridge, *Anatomy of Nelson's Ships.* Mackenzie, *Trafalgar Roll.* Schom, *Trafalgar.*

TORREY CANYON

Tanker (1f). *L/B/D:* 974.4′ × 125.4′′ × 51.4′ (297m × 38.2m × 15.7m). *Tons:* 123,000 dwt. *Hull:* steel. *Comp.:* 36. *Mach.:* geared turbines, 25,000 shp, 4 screws; 16 kts. *Built:* Newport News Shipbuilding & Dry Dock Co., Newport News, Va.; 1959.

At 0850 on March 18, 1967, the crude-oil tanker *Torrey Canyon* ran aground on the Seven Stones Reef (50°02′N, 6°07′E) at the western entrance to the English Channel — eighteen miles west of Land's End and eight miles south of the Scilly Isles. At the time of the grounding, the ship was between the Scillies and Seven Stones, though common practice (and sense) dictated that ships pass either west of the Scillies or east of the Seven Stones. Manned by an Italian crew, the ship was owned by the Barracuda Tanker Corporation, a Liberian-based subsidiary of the Union Oil Company of California, and was en route from Mena al-Ahmadi, Kuwait, to Milford Haven, England, under charter to the British Petroleum Company. Investigators found Captain Pestrengo Rugiati solely responsible for the accident because he had kept the ship on automatic steering and steaming at its top speed of nearly sixteen knots. Captain Rugiati was also accused of failing to change course when advised to do so both by his third officer and by signals from the Seven Stones lightship.

Within seventy-two hours of the incident, which occurred in broad daylight, an estimated 37 million gallons of the tanker's 118,000-ton cargo of oil had spilled. In an effort to break up the slicks, Royal Navy ships sprayed a dispersal agent on the oil, and then sprayed the beaches when the oil began going ashore in Cornwall on March 24. Efforts to refloat the ship resulted in the death of one of the Dutch salvage crew and were ultimately a failure. As tugs attempted to pull the ship off the rocks on August 26, she broke in two; the following day the ship was declared a total loss. From March 28 to March 30, Royal Navy planes hit the ship repeatedly with 1,000-pound bombs and dumped aviation fuel, kerosene, and napalm on the wreck in an effort to start fires that would consume the remaining oil before it could spread.

Despite this drastic action, oil spread across 120 miles of southern England and 55 miles of the coast of Brittany in northwest France. The world's first major disaster involving one of the new breed of supertankers, the wreck of *Torrey Canyon* had a devastating effect on the environment — an estimated 15,000 birds died, as well as untold numbers of fish and shellfish — and on the $300 million tourist industry in southern England and northwestern France.

Cowan, *Oil and Water*. Petrow, *In the Wake of "Torrey Canyon."*

TRENT

Paddle steamer (1f/3m). *Tons:* 1,856 grt. *Hull:* wood. *Comp.:* 60 pass. *Mach.:* steam engine. *Built:* William Pitcher, Northfleet, Eng.; 1841.

In 1840, the Royal Mail Steam Packet Company secured a contract for subsidized mail service between the United Kingdom and the Caribbean. Within two years, they had built or otherwise acquired nineteen steam vessels on the various transatlantic routes, one of the last to enter service being RMS *Trent*. She operated on that route for twenty-four years except during the Crimean War (1854–55), when she was requisitioned for use as a troop carrier. Under Captain Robert Woolward, she carried 1,180 men and several horses of the Welsh Fusiliers to Istanbul, and while in the Black Sea, she towed ships (as many as seventy at one time) and ferried troops between the Crimea,

Istanbul, and Malta. Her return passage towing the monitor HMS *Meteor* lasted fifty-four days, after which she resumed her normal service.

Shortly after the start of the American Civil War in 1861, the Confederacy appointed James M. Mason and John Slidell as agents to Britain and France, respectively. The two men took a blockade-runner from Charleston to Havana, where they embarked on RMS *Trent* for the passage to England on November 7, 1861. The next day, USS SAN JACINTO, under Captain Charles Wilkes, stopped the ship at the entrance to the Bahama Channel, about nine miles from Cuba, and over the objection of Commander Moir, RN, and the naval agent, forcibly removed Mason, Slidell, and their assistants before allowing *Trent* to continue to England. While Wilkes was within his rights to stop the British ship on suspicion of her violating British neutrality, under the doctrine of freedom of the seas he should have brought *Trent* into port for adjudication by a prize court. The London *Times*'s reaction exemplified that of Britain as a whole: "By Captain Wilkes let the Yankee breed be judged. Swagger and ferocity, built on a foundation of vulgarity and cowardice, these are his characteristics, and these are the most prominent marks by which his countrymen, generally speaking, are known all over the world."

Appalled by the violation of its neutral status and in anticipation of hostilities with the Union, the British government formed a War Committee of the Cabinet to consider the defense of British Canada. At the same time, they sent a protest expressing the belief that the American government would "of its own accord offer to the British Government such redress as alone would satisfy the Brit-

W. Jefferson's 1846 painting of the Royal Mail steamship TRENT. *She was later the scene of an incident that nearly brought Great Britain into the Civil War against the North. Courtesy Peabody Essex Museum, Salem, Massachusetts.*

ish nation, namely the liberation of the four Gentlemen . . . and a suitable apology for the aggression which has been committed."

On Christmas Day 1861, the Lincoln administration agreed to release Mason and Slidell, who later sailed from Boston to England on another Royal Mail ship. *Trent* continued in service for another five years, when she was sold.

Bushell, *Royal Mail.* Warren, *Fountain of Discontent.*

TRIALL

Hull: wood. *Comp.:* 43+. *Arm.:* 5 guns+. *Built:* England; <1621.

On September 4, 1621, the British East India Company ship *Triall* sailed from Plymouth for the East Indies loaded with trade goods for the king of Siam. Though this was not the first English voyage to the Spice Islands, it was the first on the route pioneered by Hendrik Brouwer — west from the Cape of Good Hope and then north to Java. In 1622, the ship was wrecked on the Trial Rocks (20°16′S, 115°23′E) about thirty-eight leagues northeast of Northwest Cape. Captain Brookes and eight men sailed one of the ship's two boats, a skiff, and arrived at Batavia on July 5, followed by the longboat on the 8th with thirty-five of the crew. Brookes and the East India Company's factor John Bright both published accounts of their ordeal.

In 1969 archaeologists visited the oldest wreck site in Australian waters, and the oldest known wreck of an English East Indiaman. The site holds the remains of eleven anchors — some of which may have been carried as cargo — and five cannon. Nothing of the ship remains, the timbers and other light elements having been dispersed by the heavy sea surge.

Green, *Australia's Oldest Wreck;* "Survey and Identification of the . . . *Trial.*"

TRIESTE

Bathyscaph. *L/B/D:* 59.5′ × 11.5′ × 18′ (18.1m × 3.5m × 5.5m). *Tons:* 50 disp. *Hull:* steel. *Comp.:* 2. *Mach.:* electric motors, 2 hp; 1 kt. *Des.:* Auguste Piccard. *Built:* Navelmeccanica, Naples, Italy; 1953.

The creation of Swiss physicist and oceanographer Auguste Piccard, and a successor to his *FNRS-2* and *FNRS-3,* the bathyscaph *Trieste* was built in 1953. The vessel is named for the Adriatic port whose citizens supported his endeavors after disagreements with the French Navy arose over the fate of *FNRS-3.* (At the time the Free

Territory of Trieste was administered by Yugoslavia, the United States, and Britain; it passed to Italy in 1954.)

Trieste has two distinct components. The larger is a compartmentalized steel float with a capacity of 28,000 gallons (106 cubic meters) of gasoline used to provide buoyancy. Originally 50 feet long, it was lengthened to 59.5 feet; its diameter is 11.5 feet. The two end compartments are used for water ballast. In addition, the float holds solid ballast in the form of iron pellets; originally 9 tons, this was later increased to 16 tons. Attached to the bottom of the float is a steel passenger sphere. The original sphere, built by the Industrial and Electrical Company of Terni, Italy, was made of an alloy of nickel, chromium, and molybdenum. It had an exterior diameter of 7.2 feet (2.18 meters) and an interior diameter of 6.6 feet. There were two cone-shaped Plexiglas windows, 4 inches (10 centimeters) wide on the inside and 16 inches (40 centimeters) on the outside, and 6 inches (15 centimeters) thick. This sphere was later replaced by a Krupp-built sphere constructed especially for the U.S. Navy's Project Nekton. This had an interior diameter of 6.4 feet (1.9 meters). The windows were 2.5 inches (6 centimeters) on the inside and 16 inches (40 centimeters) on the outside. Not designed for horizontal movement, *Trieste*'s two electric motors generated 2 horsepower and could move the bathyscaph at about 1 knot. External light was provided by 500 mercury vapor lights.

Trieste first took the water in August 1953. After three shallow test dives around Castellamare, Piccard and his son Jacques took her down to 3,540 feet (1,080 meters), south of Capri, and then, on September 30, to a depth of 10,300 feet (3,150 meters) off Ponza Island. *Trieste* made a further eight dives in 1954, but a lack of funding forced her lay-up the following year. In 1956, she resumed oceanographic explorations and achieved a record depth of 12,110 feet (3,691 meters), south of Ponza Island in 40°37′N, 12°49′E.

By 1957, *Trieste*'s viability as a research vehicle had been firmly established and she was used in a number of experiments, including oceanographic and biological observation, underwater high- and low-frequency sound experiments, and light penetration measurements. The same year she was also chartered by the U.S. Navy, which was so pleased with the results that it purchased her from Piccard in 1958 and moved her to the Naval Electronics Laboratory in San Diego.

In anticipation of Operation Nekton, the Navy ordered the new passenger sphere from Krupp and lengthened the float by nine feet. In November 1960, *Trieste* was transferred to Guam in preparation for an attempt to descend to the bottom of the Marianas Trench. Jacques Piccard and Lieutenant Don Walsh piloted her on a succession of ever deeper dives that culminated in a descent to the bottom of the Nero Deep (23,000 feet, or 7,010 meters), and fifteen days later, on January 23, 1960, to the bottom of the Challenger Deep — 35,800 feet, or 10,912 meters — in position 11°18′N, 142°15′E, about 200 miles southwest of Guam — then the deepest known place on the planet. (The deepest point on earth is now believed to be 11,524 meters, in the Mindanao Trench off the Philippines.)

Subsequently used for oceanographic research off San Diego, in 1963 *Trieste* was sent to the East Coast to take part in the search for the lost submarine USS THRESHER. After ten dives under Commander Donald A. Keach, *Trieste* located wreckage from the ill-fated submarine, including the sail, in about 8,400 feet of water, 200 miles southeast of Boston. Retired after the commissioning of *Trieste II*, *Trieste* was put on exhibit at the Washington Navy Yard in 1980.

Piccard, *Earth, Sky, and Sea.* Piccard & Dietz, *Seven Miles Down.* U.S. Navy, *DANFS.*

The 5th-rate ship HMS TRINCOMALEE *as she looked in 1979 when she was cut down as a floating school, with windows fitted in the gunports. Note her Indian figurehead and the painted cathead — the beam along which the anchor chain was run in order to keep the anchor away from the hull when "catting" it (raising it) or letting it go. Courtesy Norman Brouwer.*

TRIESTE II (DSV-1)

Bathyscaph. *L/B/D:* 67′ × 15′ × 12.4′ (20.4m × 4.6m × 3.8m). *Tons:* 46 long tons. *Hull:* steel. *Comp.:* 2. *Mach.:* electric motors. *Des.:* Auguste Piccard. *Built:* Mare Island Navy Yard, Vallejo, Calif.; 1964.

Designed as a successor to the first bathyscaph to hold the name, *Trieste II* was built by the U.S. Navy and incorporated the original sphere built for her predecessor, combined with a longer but more maneuverable external float. Her first assignment was to investigate the area in which the submarine USS THRESHER sank in April 1963. (The original *Trieste* had already located parts of the submarine in 1963.) *Trieste II* was taken over by the Navy in 1966 and employed in a variety of deep-submergence operations. In 1971 she was reclassified as a deep-submergence vehicle. Experiments with *Trieste* have contributed especially to the design and construction of submarine rescue and comparable vessels. Taken out of service in 1984, she was put on display at the Naval Undersea Museum in Keyport, Washington.

U.S. Navy, *DANFS.*

HMS TRINCOMALEE

(ex-*Foudroyant, Trincomalee*) *Leda*-class 5th rate 46 (3m). *L/B/D:* 150.1′ × 39.8′ × 13.8 dph (45.8m × 12.1m × 4.2m). *Tons:* 1,052 disp. *Hull:* wood. *Comp.:* 284. *Arm.:* 28 × 18pdr, 8 × 32pdr, 10 × 9pdr. *Des.:* Sir Robert Seppings. *Built:* Wadia Shipyard, Bombay, India; 1817.

The oldest Royal Navy ship still afloat, *Trincomalee* was named for a port on the east coast of Ceylon (Sri Lanka) captured from the French in 1795. A *Leda*-class frigate built in response to the heavily built American frigates CONSTITUTION, PRESIDENT, and UNITED STATES, her hull was constructed of Malabar teak. With the advent of the Pax Britannica in the wake of the Napoleonic Wars, *Trincomalee* saw limited service before being laid up in England in 1819. Recommissioned as a sixth-rate, twenty-six-gun sloop in 1847, she served for three years on antislaving duty in the West Indies and off West Africa. After a refit, in 1852 she transferred to the Royal Navy base at Esquimault, Vancouver Island, and remained in the Pacific for four years. In 1857 she returned to England and became a training ship, stationed first at Sunderland and from 1861 as a reserve training ship at West Hartlepool and then Southampton. In 1897, the Royal Navy Reserve sold *Trincomalee* to G. Wheatley Cobb, a philanthropist who had earlier restored the second *Foudroyant,* which was lost in a storm in 1893. Cobb renamed *Trincomalee* in honor of that ship, and she continued as a training ship for boys and girls as young as eleven years old. Cobb's widow donated the ship to the Society for Nautical Research upon his death, and the new *Foudroyant* continued work as a sail-training ship until 1986. Handed over to the Trincomalee Restoration and given back her old name, *Trincomalee* is undergoing restoration to her 1817 appearance for use as a museum ship at Hartlepool.

Horton, HMS *"Trincomalee."* Marsh, *Story of a Frigate.*

TRINIDAD VALENCERA

Tons: 1,100. *Hull:* wood. *Comp.:* 360. *Arm.:* 32 guns. *Built:* Venice(?); <1587.

Trinidad Valencera was one of five Venetian traders requisitioned by Spanish authorities in Sicily for use as an armed transport with the Spanish Armada. Over the objections of her merchant captain Horatio Donai, she was fitted with twenty-eight bronze guns. When the fleet sailed, she was the most heavily armed ship in Martin de Bertendona's Levant Squadron, which included ten converted merchant ships from the Mediterranean. In addition to her own armament, she carried four of the King's guns, and a complement of 79 seaman, 281 Neapolitan soldiers, and a cadre of officers. During the Armada campaign, *Trinidad Valencera* (a Spanish corruption of her Venetian name, *Balanzara*) saw action off Portland Bill (August 1–2), the Isle of Wight (August 2–3), and in the crucial rearguard action fought at the Battle of Gravelines on August 7–9, just before the Armada sailed into the North Sea for the brutal return to Spain. On about August 20, *Trinidad Valencera*, GRAN GRIFÓN, and two other hulks separated from the main fleet off northern Scotland; none would return to Spain. On September 12, *Trinidad Valencera* was caught in a storm off the north coast of Ireland and, leaking badly, came to anchor in Kinnagoe Bay on the 14th. Two days later, she split in two and sank. Most of the ship's company seem to have made it safely to shore, but several days later they were tricked into laying down their weapons. Stripped of their clothes and other possessions by a nominally inferior force, three hundred of the soldiers and sailors were slaughtered by an Anglo-Irish force. Thirty-two of the surviving crew eventually made it to Scotland and, with safe passage from James VI, on to France. The officers were marched to Dublin, where all but two were murdered on orders from the Lord Deputy, Sir William Fitzwilliam.

Sport divers discovered the wreck site in 1971. As the crew had removed what they could from the ship, there are few substantial artifacts. Chief among them are the ship's guns, which have added considerably to the knowledge of naval gunnery in the sixteenth century. In addition, there are ship's fittings, a few dislocated structural timbers, and pieces of rigging and other cordage.

Martin, *Full Fathom Five;* "*La Trinidad Valencera.*"

USS TRITON (SSRN-586)

Triton-class submarine. *L/B/D:* 447.5′ × 37′ × 24′ (136.4m × 11.3m × 7.3m). *Tons:* 5,940/7,780 disp. *Hull:* steel; 985′dd. *Comp.:* 183. *Arm.:* 6″ TT. *Built:* Electric Boat Division, General Dynamics, Groton, Conn.; 1959.

The fifth U.S. Navy vessel of the name, USS *Triton* was named for a Greek demigod, the son of Poseidon and Amphitrite. *Triton* sailed into history on her maiden voyage when, in lieu of a shakedown cruise, she embarked on Operation Sandblast, the first underwater circumnavigation of the globe. Leaving New London, Connecticut, on February 15, 1960, under command of Captain Edward L. "Ned" Beach, *Triton* sailed south into the Atlantic, passing St. Peter and St. Paul's Rocks off Brazil on February 24. The effort was nearly jeopardized when a sailor suffering from kidney stones had to be transferred to the cruiser USS *Macon* off Montevideo on March 5. However, this was accomplished by surfacing only far enough for him to exit the sail, and *Triton*'s hull remained under water. Two days later she rounded Cape Horn, and from there she sped across the Pacific, passing Easter Island on March 13, and Guam on March 28. On April 1, *Triton* sailed into Magellan Bay off the Philippine island of Mactan, where Ferdinand Magellan was killed on April 27, 1521. After passing through Lombok Strait into the Indian Ocean, *Triton*'s next landfall was the Cape of Good Hope on Easter Sunday, April 17. Seven days later she was once again off St. Peter and St. Paul's Rocks, having sailed 27,723 miles in 60 days, 21 hours.

Although this landfall marked the official beginning and end of the circumnavigation, *Triton* had been submerged since departing New London, and would remain so until reaching her homeport on May 10. Her sail broke the surface only to take on a doctor off the Canary Islands, and again off the Virginia Capes so that Captain Beach could be flown to the White House for a ceremony with President Dwight D. Eisenhower. Although the voyage had been conceived as a way for Eisenhower to impress Soviet General Secretary Nikita Krushchev at the Paris Summit, this conference was canceled after U-2 pilot Francis Gary Powers was shot down over the Soviet Union on May 1. But coming less than two years after the transpolar expedition of USS NAUTILUS, *Triton*'s accomplishment was a clear reaffirmation of U.S. technological supremacy.

Nautilus next deployed as a radar picket vessel with NATO forces. In 1962 she was converted to an attack submarine, and from 1964 to 1967 she served as flagship of the Submarine Force, Atlantic Fleet, based at Norfolk. Decommissioned in 1969, in 1986 she entered the nuclear-powered ship and submarine recycling program in Bremerton, Washington.

Beach, *Around the World Submerged.*

TRUMBULL

Frigate (3m). *L/B/D:* 151' × 34' × 18' (46m × 10.4m × 5.5m). *Tons:* 682 bm. *Hull:* wood. *Comp.:* 199. *Arm.:* 24 × 12pdr, 6 × 6pdr. *Built:* John Cotton, Chatham, Conn.; 1776.

Named for Governor Jonathan Trumbull of Connecticut, Trumbull was one of the thirteen original frigates ordered by the Continental Congress in 1775. Under command of Captain Dudley Saltonstall, following her launch she was found to draw too much water to get over the bar at the mouth of the Connecticut River. It was not until Captain Elisha Hinman assumed command and girdled her with empty barrels to float her over the bar that she was moved to New London for fitting out. In late May 1780, *Trumbull* left New London and on June 1, 1780, she ran into the Liverpool privateer *Watt* (36 guns). In one of the bloodiest naval engagements of the war, the two ships fought to a draw, *Trumbull* losing her main and mizzenmasts, suffering eight crew dead and thirty-one wounded; *Watt* was set on fire and lost thirteen killed and seventy-nine wounded. Repairs and lack of funds kept her at Philadelphia until August 8, 1781, when she sailed as escort for a merchant convoy. On the night of August 28, she lost her foretop and topgallant masts in a storm, and the next morning she was set upon by HMS *Iris* (32) and *General Monk* (20). (*Iris* was Trumbull's sister ship, the former HANCOCK.) Although three-quarters of the crew refused to fight (many of them were originally British prisoners, as was common in the Continental Navy),

Nicholson engaged the enemy for an hour and a half before striking. The last of the original frigates was towed to New York and broken up.

Fowler, *Rebels under Sail.* U.S. Navy, *DANFS.*

TURBINIA

Steam launch (1f). *L/B/D:* 103.3' × 9' × 3' (31.5m × 2.7m × 0.9m). *Tons:* 44 disp. *Hull:* steel. *Mach.:* Parsons steam turbines, 2,100 shp, 1 screw; 32.75 kts. *Des.:* Charles A. Parsons. *Built:* Turbinia Works (Brown & Hood), Wallsend-on-Tyne, Eng.; 1894.

One of the most important developments in the history of steam power was Charles A. Parsons's steam turbine. Although the principle of the turbine is simpler than that of the reciprocating engine, in practice the reciprocating engine is simpler to build, which is why it developed first. Nonetheless, compound- and triple-expansion engines are less efficient, and their heavy cylinders, pistons, and bearings are subject to enormous stresses and cannot be driven at high speeds for long periods. Parsons's first working steam turbine was a six-horsepower engine developed in 1884, and the technology was quickly adopted for generating electric power on land. In its first twenty years, the turbine reduced coal consumption of electric generating stations by 75 percent. But it was not until Parsons's lithe *Turbinia* raced through the Spithead Naval

The world's first steam-turbine-driven vessel, Charles Parsons's TUBINIA *caught the attention of the maritime world when she sped through the international naval review gathered at Portsmouth for Queen Victoria's Diamond Jubilee in 1897. Courtesy National Maritime Museum, Greenwich, England.*

Review, held during Queen Victoria's Diamond Jubilee in 1897, that turbines first seized the public imagination.

Cognizant of the benefits of turbine engines in the more limited confines of a ship, Parsons had formed the Marine Steam Turbine Company for the specific purpose of building and testing a turbine-driven vessel. The company's prospectus clearly enumerated the benefits of the marine turbine:

> Increased speed, increased carrying power of vessel, increased economy in steam consumption, reduced initial cost, reduced weight of machinery, reduced cost of attendance on machinery, diminished cost of upkeep of machinery, largely reduced vibration, and reduced size and weight of screw propeller and shafting.

Parsons had difficulty in choosing the correct propulsion configuration and went through seven different propeller designs, including three screws on one shaft. Because the turbine turned the shaft faster than an expansion engine would, the screws were not as efficient as predicted due to cavitation. This phenomenon, the result of a vacuum forming around a screw turning at high speed, was first observed during tests on *Turbinia*. When the vessel failed to attain her design speed, Parsons replaced the single shaft with three separate shafts (initially, there were three screws on each shaft) and at the same time replaced the radial-flow turbine with a more efficient parallel-flow turbine. The results were spectacular, and in supervised trials *Turbinia* attained speeds of thirty-four knots.

Parsons labored in relative obscurity until June 26, 1897, during the international naval review held to celebrate the sixtieth year of Victoria's reign. After the royal yacht VICTORIA AND ALBERT had inspected the assembled ships, *Turbinia* romped through the anchored fleet with breathtaking speed and agility in a dramatic demonstration of the new technology. Shortly thereafter, the Parsons Marine Steam Turbine Company was formed. The Admiralty ordered its first turbine-powered vessel, the destroyer HMS *Viper,* in 1899, and soon purchased a second, *Cobra;* both achieved speeds of thirty-six knots. The light cruiser *Amethyst* was commissioned in 1903, but the technology received its greatest boost in 1905 when First Sea Lord John Arbuthnot Fisher decided on steam turbines for HMS DREADNOUGHT, the first all-big-gun battleship whose design revolutionized naval warfare.

Commercial interests were somewhat slower to embrace the new technology. The first merchant ship fitted with steam turbines, the 3,500-horsepower *King Edward,* was not ordered until 1901. A number of smaller vessels were built, and in 1904 Cunard Line ordered two ships that were identical except for their machinery. CARONIA, powered by triple-expansion engines, was consistently outperformed by her sister ship CARMANIA. As a result, the next year Cunard chose turbines for their new high-speed passenger liners MAURETANIA and LUSITANIA, whose 70,000-horsepower engines were three times more powerful than those of either *Carmania* or *Dreadnought.*

In 1900, *Turbinia* appeared at the Paris Exhibition; her last voyage was in 1907. Hauled by Parsons in 1927, she was cut in two and the aftermost forty-five feet was put on exhibit at the Science Museum in London. In 1944, about fifteen feet of the fore section was displayed at the Museum of Science and Engineering in Newcastle. Fifteen years later, Parsons reassembled the far-flung ship, which since 1960 has been exhibited at Turbinia Hall in the Tyne & Wear County Council Museum in Newcastle.

Brouwer, *International Register of Historic Ships.* Richardson, *Evolution of the Parsons Steam Turbine.*

USS TURNER JOY (DD-951)

Forrest Sherman-class destroyer. *L/B/D:* 418′ × 45′ × 22.5′ (127.4m × 13.7m × 6.9m). *Tons:* 4,200 disp. *Hull:* steel. *Comp.:* 360. *Arm.:* 3 × 5″, 2 × 3″; 6 × 15.5″TT; 1 dct, 1 dcp. *Mach.:* geared turbines, 70,000 shp, 2 screws; 33 kts. *Built:* Puget Sound Bridge & Dredging Co., Seattle, Wash.; 1959.

Named for Rear Admiral Charles Turner Joy, who served in the Pacific in World War II and commanded UN naval forces during the Korean War, USS *Turner Joy* entered service in 1960. Her front-line career began with her deployment in July 1960 in the Taiwan Strait following mainland China's bombing of Matsu and Quemoy Islands. In August 1964, while on her third overseas tour of duty, she was part of a task force built around USS *Ticonderoga* patrolling off Vietnam. On August 4, *Turner Joy* was ordered to join USS MADDOX, which had been fired on by three North Vietnamese torpedo boats two days before. On August 6, *Turner Joy* and *Maddox* believed themselves to be engaged by North Vietnamese vessels in a foul-weather night action lasting two and a half hours. There were no visual sightings of hostile craft, and it is possible that the destroyers were actually firing at radar echoes on *Turner Joy*'s screen caused by freak atmospheric conditions. The incident led to the passage of President Lyndon B. Johnson's Tonkin Gulf Resolution, which initiated full-scale U.S. military involvement in Vietnam. *Turner Joy* was stationed in Vietnamese waters off and on for the duration of hostilities, with returns to Long Beach. She was decommissioned in 1985–86 and stricken from the Navy list in 1990.

Jane's Fighting Ships. Marolda & Fitzgerald, *The United States Navy and the Vietnam Conflict.* U.S. Navy, *DANFS.*

TURTLE

Submarine. *L/D:* 7.5′ × 6′ dph (2.3m × 1.8m). *Tons:* ca. 2,000 lb. *Hull:* wood. *Comp.:* 1. *Arm.:* detachable mine. *Mach.:* 2 screws; 2–3 kts. *Des.:* David Bushnell. *Built:* David & Ezra Bushnell, Saybrook, Conn.; 1776.

Designed by David Bushnell and built by him and his brother Ezra at the latter's farm, *Turtle* took her name from her resemblance to "two upper tortoise shells of equal size, joined together." Conceived by Bushnell as a way of attacking the British fleet at Boston, Massachusetts, *Turtle* combined the four essential abilities of a true submersible. She could be propelled independently, dive below the surface of the water, provide thirty minutes of air for the one-man crew, and operate offensively against an enemy ship.

Diving was achieved by admitting water to the bilge; the water could be expelled by a foot-operated bellows. Light was admitted through watertight windows in the truncated conning tower; when submerged the interior was illuminated by a phosphorescent wood called foxfire. *Turtle* was powered by two manual screw-like devices, one for forward movement and the other for ascending and descending. She held 700 pounds of ballast, 200 pounds of which could be jettisoned in an emergency. Air was supplied through a pair of crude snorkel-like devices

fitted with check valves. In addition to a tiller-handled rudder, the operator was provided with a compass and a depth gauge. *Turtle*'s offensive capability was in the form of a detachable torpedo, or mine, of Bushnell's. This mine consisted of a casing filled with 150 pounds of gunpowder, which was to be attached to an auger that was bored into the underside of a ship's hull. The mine had a timer set to detonate an hour after the mine's release from *Turtle.*

When the British evacuated Boston, Bushnell offered his ingenious craft to General George Washington, who was desperate for something that might dislodge the British from New York and who agreed to provide funds to bring *Turtle* to the city. David Bushnell was too frail to operate the craft himself, and it was intended that his brother take her into battle, but he fell ill. In his place, Sergeant Ezra Lee, a Connecticut volunteer, was hastily trained.

Turtle's first target was the 64-gun HMS *Eagle,* flagship of Vice Admiral Richard "Black Dick" Howe, lying with the British squadron off Staten Island. At 2230 on the night of September 5, 1776, Lee and *Turtle* were towed as close to the fleet as possible before they were cast off on their own. Against the current, it took Lee two hours to maneuver *Turtle* alongside *Eagle.* Everything went according to plan, but for some reason Lee was unable to bore the auger into *Eagle*'s hull before he briefly lost control of *Turtle* and shot to the surface. Afraid of being detected, he decided to abandon the attempt and headed back to shore. As he passed Governors Island, a British cutter put out to investigate. As the cutter approached, Lee detached the mine, upon which the British returned the way they came. An hour later, the mine exploded in the British anchorage, throwing up a huge geyser of water

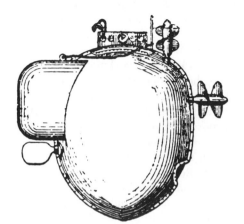
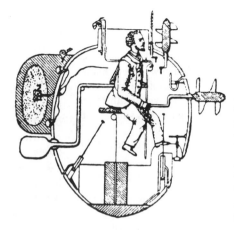

David Bushnell's submarine TURTLE *of 1776 came very close to destroying a British warship in New York Harbor. This 1885 drawing by F. M. Barber is based on Bushnell's written description of the vessel. Courtesy U.S. Naval Historical Center, Washington, D.C.*

that persuaded the British to slip their cables and flee. Two more attempts to use *Turtle* against the British were unsuccessful. The submarine's ultimate fate is not known, though it is believed that, after the British took New York, she was destroyed to prevent her falling into enemy hands.

Miller, *Sea of Glory*. U.S. Navy, *DANFS*.

TUSITALA

(ex-*Sophie, Sierra Lucena, Inveruglas*) Ship (3m). *L/B/D:* 260.4′ × 39′ × 23.5′ (79.4m × 11.9m × 7.2m). *Tons:* 1,684 grt. *Hull:* iron. *Comp.:* 22. *Built:* Robert Steele & Co., Greenock, Scotland; 1883.

Tusitala was among the last ships to fly the American flag on deep-sea routes. The last ship built by Robert Steel & Company, she was launched as *Inveruglas* and spent three years in the Australian grain trade before being sold to the Liverpool-based Sierra Shipping Company and re-named *Sierra Lucena*. In 1904, she was sold to Norwegian interests and renamed *Sophie*. While working in the Argentine grain trade, in 1916 her bow was badly damaged in a collision with an American tanker in the Plate River. She was soon back in service, and after World War I she hauled coal between the United States and Europe. Laid up at Hampton Roads during the postwar shipping slump, in 1923 she was purchased by the "Three Hours for Lunch Club," a New York syndicate of artists and writers. Rechristened *Tusitala*, the Samoan epithet for Robert Louis Stevenson meaning "Teller of Tales," she attracted the attention of deepwatermen the world over, and at her change-of-name ceremony, Christopher Morley read the following letter:

> I assume an ancient mariner's privilege of sending to the owners and the ship's company of the *Tusitala* my brotherly good wishes for fair winds and clear skies on all their voyages, and may they be many!
>
> And I would recommend to them to watch the weather, and keep the halliards clear for running, and to remember that "any fool can carry on, but only the wise man knows how to shorten sail in time," — and so on, in the manner of Ancient Mariners the world over. But the vital truth of sea life is to be found in the ancient saying that it is stout hearts that make the ship safe.
>
> Having been brought up on it, I pass it along to them in all confidence and affection.
>
> — Joseph Conrad

After two years in trade between New York and Rio de Janeiro, *Tusitala* was sold to James A. Farrell's Argonaut Line, under whose flag she sailed out to Honolulu in September 1924, returning via Seattle with magnesite and lumber for Baltimore. In 1925, she came under command of Captain James P. Barker, who sailed her on the same route, via the Panama Canal rather than Cape Horn, until 1933 when she was laid up at New York. Sold to ship breakers in 1938, she was instead taken over by the Coast Guard for use as a barracks ship, first at New London, Connecticut, and later Jacksonville, Florida. She was scrapped at Mobile, Alabama, in 1947.

Barker, "*Tusitala*." Lubbock, *Down Easters*. Meehan, "Vale *Tusitala*."

TZU HANG

Ketch. *L/B/D:* 46.2′ × 11.8′ × 7′ (14.1m × 3.6m × 2.1m). *Tons:* 18 disp. *Hull:* wood. *Comp.:* 2. *Mach.:* aux. *Des.:* H. S. "Uncle" Rouse. *Built:* Hop Kee, Hong Kong; 1938.

Named for the Chinese goddess of mercy and seafarers, *Tzu Hang* was built for British Army Lieutenant Colonel Denis Swinburne. He and his yacht — which had not yet been sailed — returned to England in 1939, but it was not until after the war that he could begin to sail *Tzu Hang*. In 1951, she was purchased by retired Brigadier Miles Smeeton and his indomitably peripatetic wife, Beryl Boxer Smeeton. Following his retirement from the army, Smeeton and his wife settled on a farm in British Columbia, and to circumvent British currency restrictions, they purchased *Tzu Hang* in England with the intention of selling her in Canada. In May 1951, they set sail with their ten-year-old daughter, Clio, on an eighteen-month passage home via the Panama Canal and the Galápagos Islands.

After several more years of farm life, they sold their farm and set out on an eighteen-month clockwise circuit of the Pacific. At San Francisco they met up with John Guzzwell in *Trekka* and sailed in company with him as far as Australia. Clio was sent to boarding school in England, and the Smeetons decided to sail there via Cape Horn with Guzzwell as crew. About 900 miles west of Cape Horn, on February 11, 1957, *Tzu Hang* pitchpoled. They lost both masts and the rudder, and though Beryl was thrown 100 feet from the boat, she managed to clamber back aboard. With a jury rig and sixteen-foot steering oar, they were thirty-seven days to Coronel, Chile. Ten months later, with *Tzu Hang* rebuilt from the deck up, the Smeetons sailed again for the Horn. On December 26, they were back in the Roaring Forties, lying ahull in a hurricane, when *Tzu Hang* was completely capsized. Again the masts were ripped out, but thirty days later they limped into Valparaíso; from here *Tzu Hang* was shipped to England.

After a complete overhaul, and the publication of Miles's *Once Is Enough,* in May 1959 the Smeetons began cruising around Europe. In 1961, both age fifty-six, they turned south at the start of an unintended eight-year circumnavigation. This extended voyage took them first through the Mediterranean and the Suez Canal, down the coast of Africa, eastward across the Indian Ocean to Ceylon, and then through the East Indies. Along the way they made many extended detours to visit old friends and acquaintances from their years before World War II. They spent the winter of 1964–65 in Japan before sailing north and east through the Aleutian Islands — one of the first yachts to do so — en route to Canada, where they arrived on September 9, 1965. A year and a half later they decided to return to England, this time via the Panama Canal, the east coast of the United States, and Iceland.

The Smeetons' passages in *Tzu Hang* were normally characterized by an intention of going from one place to the other. When they decided to return to Canada, however, they were piqued by a letter in a yachting magazine suggesting that *Tzu Hang* was too small for the Cape Horn passage, and they immediately abandoned any thought of a transit of the Panama Canal. Sailing with Bob Nance, they departed England on August 18 and doubled the Horn the hard way — from east to west — between December 9 and 23, 1967. After a stop in Hawaii, they returned to Vancouver. Retiring from the sea, they sold *Tzu Hang* to Nance and established the Wildlife Reserve of Western Canada in Alberta.

Nance continued to sail *Tzu Hang* long distance, including another rounding of the Horn, and in 1979 the Smeetons joined him on a passage from New York to England via Labrador and the Faeroes. In 1982, *Tzu Hang* was bought by a drug dealer who used her to smuggle 20,000 pounds of marijuana from Colombia to Maryland. Six years later she was seized by federal agents in the Virgin Islands, and the next year she sank at her moorings in Hurricane Hugo. In 1990, she was ignominiously bulldozed for a landfill in San Juan.

Clark, *High Endeavours.* Smeeton, *Because the Horn Is There; Misty Islands; Sea Was Our Village; Sunrise to Windward.*

U

U-9

U3-class submarine. *L/B/D:* 188.3′ × 19.7′ × 10.2′ (57.4m × 6m × 3.1m). *Tons:* 493/611 disp. *Hull:* steel. *Comp.:* 29. *Arm.:* 4 × 18″TT; 3.7cm mg. *Mach.:* gasoline engines, 1,160 ehp; 14.2/8.1 kts. *Built:* Kaiserlich Werft, Danzig, Germany; 1910.

Under Lieutenant Otto Weddigen, *U-9* took part in German fleet maneuvers in 1912 during which she was credited with "sinking" three battleships. During the uneasy days after the assassination of Austrian Archduke Francis Ferdinand, *U-9* was the first submarine to attempt reloading torpedo tubes from a submerged position. One of the first German submarines on patrol during World War I, in September *U-9* rode out a two-day storm off the coast of the Netherlands. Surfacing again on the morning of the 22nd, the crew were "agreeably surprised," wrote Lieutenant Commander Johann Spiess, Weddigen's second-in-command. "The light streamed up from the eastern horizon and spread over a cloudless sky. . . . A fine day to sink a ship."

Shortly thereafter, smoke was seen on the horizon, and *U-9* submerged. Three cruisers soon came into view and, closing to a distance of only 500 yards from the cruiser HMS ABOUKIR, Weddigen fired one torpedo at 0720. Assuming that their sister ship had struck a mine, CRESSY and HOGUE closed to pick up survivors. Half an hour later, *U-9* fired two torpedoes into *Hogue,* only 300 yards away. Turning on her axis, *U-9* fired her two stern torpedoes at *Cressy,* one of which missed, then turned again and fired her last torpedo. In addition to the three outdated cruisers — First Lord of the Admiralty Winston Churchill had referred to the *Bacchante*-class cruisers as "live bait" — the Royal Navy lost 1,459 experienced crew. Weddigen and his crew were awarded Germany's highest honor, the Pour le Mérite.

A scant three weeks later, *U-9* sailed again from Wilhelmshaven to the Royal Navy's base at Scapa Flow. On October 15, *U-9* came across the cruisers HMS *Hawke* and *Endymion* in the North Sea. Again at a range of only 500 yards, Weddigen fired one torpedo into *Hawke,* which sunk eight minutes later with the loss of 544 of her crew; there were 52 survivors. A subsequent attack on a line of destroyers — the submarine's chief enemy — nearly ended in disaster for *U-9,* and the boat achieved sufficient depth to avoid ramming with just seconds to spare.

Outmoded by 1916, *U-9* was restricted to training duty until surrendered to the Allies on November 26, 1918. She was taken to England and broken up in 1919.

Coles, *Three before Breakfast.* Gray, *U-Boat War.* Gröner, *German Warships.*

U-21

U3-class submarine. *L/B/D:* 210.6′ × 20′ × 11.8′ (26.6′ high) (64.2m × 6.1m × 3.6m/8.1m). *Tons:* 650/837 disp. *Hull:* steel. *Comp.:* 35. *Arm.:* 4 × 18″TT (2 × 2); 1 × 8.8cm gun. *Mach.:* diesels/batteries, 1,700/1,200 ehp, 2 screws; 15/9.5 kts. *Des.:* Dr. Techel. *Built:* Kaiserliche Werft, Danzig, Germany; 1913.

Commissioned one year before the start of World War I, under Lieutenant Commander Otto Hersing, *U-21* was the first submarine to sink a warship on the high seas. While on patrol in the North Sea on September 5, 1914, *U-21* torpedoed HMS *Pathfinder* off St. Abb's Head in the Firth of Forth; the light cruiser sank in eleven minutes, taking down all but three of her crew of 350. On November 23, Hersing stopped the French merchant ship *Malachite*; an examination of the ship's papers revealed that she was bound from Liverpool to Le Havre with contraband, and she was sunk by gunfire. Germany's policy of "restricted" commerce warfare was aimed at keeping neutral countries from siding with Britain, and Hersing observed the letter of the law, even as he sank three ships in the Irish Sea barely twenty miles from Liverpool on January 30, 1915.

On April 25, 1915 — the day that Australian and New Zealand forces landed at Gallipoli — *U-21* departed Wilhelmshaven and sailed around Scotland bound for the eastern Mediterranean. After refueling from a Hamburg-Amerika Linie freighter in the lee of Cape Finisterre,

Spain (the fuel turned out to be useless), *U-21* slipped by Gibraltar on May 6. Evading several British and French patrols, *U-21* made the Adriatic port of Cattaro (Kotor) on May 13 with only 1.8 tons of fuel, enough for about half a day's steaming. A week later she sailed for Gallipoli where, on May 25, she sank the battleship HMS *Triumph* and two days later, the battleship *Majestic* off Cape Helles, after which the Royal Navy ordered its capital ships to Lemnos and Imbros.

Narrowly escaping from an underwater maelstrom in the Dardanelles that dragged her down 100 feet, *U-21* sailed into Istanbul on June 5. The Kaiser awarded *U-21*'s crew the Iron Cross First Class and the Pour le Mérite to Hersing, for whom the British offered a £100,000 bounty. A month later, *U-21* sank the French transport *Carthage*, but she was almost lost when forced to submerge in the midst of a minefield. Her next major success was the February 8 sinking of the French cruiser *Amiral Charner*, with the loss of 334 of 335 crew, and in April the destruction of the British merchantman *City of Lucknow*, about sixty miles east of Malta.

Recalled to Germany in 1917, *U-21* resumed patrol work around Britain, though she came close to being sunk herself during an attack on a convoy in August. Later used for U-boat training, she was turned over to the British after the war. The implacable Hersing scuttled *U-21* while in tow of a British ship en route to surrender, in position 54°19′N, 3°42′W, on February 22, 1919.

Gray, *U-Boat War.* Gröner, *German Warships.* Hoover, "Commander Otto Hersing and the Dardanelles Cruise of S.M. *U-21*." Terraine, *Business in Great Waters.*

U-30

Type VII submarine. *L/B/D:* 211.6′ × 19.4′ × 14.4′ (31.2′ high) (64.5m × 5.9m × 4.4m/9.5m). *Tons:* 626/745 disp. *Hull:* steel; 309′dd. *Comp.:* 44–56. *Arm.:* 5 × 21.3″TT; 1 × 37mm, 2 × 20mm. *Mach.:* diesel/electric, 2,310/750 ehp, 2 screws; 17/8 kts. *Built:* Deschimag AG Weser, Bremerhaven, Germany; 1936.

On the night of August 22–23, 1939, *U-30* departed Wilhelmshaven, one of eighteen German submarines to take up station in the North Atlantic on the eve of World War II. (Germany had only fifty-seven U-boats at the start of the war.) Although U-boats were ordered to conduct submarine operations "in accordance with international rules," shortly after Britain's declaration of war on Germany on September 3, 1939, *U-30* torpedoed the passenger ship ATHENIA in 56°44′N, 14°05′W. The ship, which Lieutenant Fritz-Julius Lemp said he mistook for an auxiliary cruiser, sank with the loss of 112 passengers

and crew; 1,300 people were rescued by HM destroyers *Electra* and *Escort,* merchant ships *Knute Nelson* and *City of Flint,* and yacht *Southern Cross.* As Adolf Hitler initially sought to avoid unrestricted submarine warfare, U-boats were reminded that "the Führer has forbidden attacks on passenger liners sailing independently or in convoy."

After a tour as a minelayer off Liverpool, on December 28, *U-30* torpedoed HMS BARHAM off the Firth of Clyde, forcing the battleship into dock until April. As part of a wolf pack operating in the Bay of Biscay, she sank six ships and was the first submarine to enter the submarine pens at Lorient in July 1940. Scuttled in Flensburger Förde on May 4, 1945, *U-30* was broken up in 1948.

Ministry of Defence, *U-Boat War in the Atlantic.* Rohwer & Hummelchen, *Chronology of the War at Sea.*

U-35

U-23-class submarine. *L/B/D:* 212.2′ × 20.7′ × 11.5′ (25.3′ high) (64.7m × 6.3m × 3.5m/7.7m). *Tons:* 685/878 disp. *Hull:* steel. *Comp.:* 35. *Arm.:* 4 × 20″TT; 1 × 8.8cm. *Mach.:* diesels/batteries, 2,000/1,200 ehp, 2 screws; 16.4/9.7 kts. *Built:* Friedrich Krupp AG Germaniawerft, Kiel, Germany; 1914.

One of the most successful submarines of World War I, *U-35* was the first command of Germany's "Ace of aces," Lothar von Arnauld de la Perière. After duty in the restricted waters around Great Britain, in the late summer of 1915 she was one of four long-range submarines ordered to the Mediterranean to assist the fledgling Austro-Hungarian fleet in operations against British and French shipping. Under Captain Waldemar Kophamel, she cruised the approaches to Salonika and Kavalla, Greece. She claimed her first victim on October 23, sinking the 1,000-ton troopship *Marquette* in the Gulf of Salonika, the staging ground for British troops bound to and from the Gallipoli campaign. *U-35* also contributed to the uprising of Senussi tribesmen in North Africa against Italian and British control. On November 15, 1915, she accounted for the 1,800-ton armed boarding cruiser *Tara* and, during the same patrol, the Egyptian gunboats *Abbas* and *Nuhr el-Bahr.* One week later, the British evacuated 4,500 troops from Salum, Egypt, to Mersa Matruh. It is said that an unforeseen result of this campaign was *U-35*'s employment as a transport for two camels, gifts from a grateful Senussi to the Kaiser. According to Edwyn Gray,

How the U-boat men managed to house two awkwardly shaped and ferocious beasts like the camel in the cramped confines of the *U-35* has never been revealed, but one story indicates that the smell of the animals so permeated the garments of the crew that sailors from the other U-boats at

Pola refused to allow their *U-35* comrades to share the same mess with them.

In early 1916, Kophamel was promoted to command the Mediterranean U-Boat Flotilla. His replacement was Commander Lothar von Arnauld de la Perière, fresh from training in Germany. On his first cruise, von Arnauld got off to a bad start. Attacking the Q-ship *Margit,* he found his own submarine under fire, after surfacing to investigate the "panic party" that had put off from the antisubmarine decoy ship at the start of his attack. Undeterred, von Arnauld went on to sink the French troop transport *Provence II* with 990 soldiers. On March 1, he had to fend off more unanticipated resistance off Port Said, when HMS *Primula,* with a torpedo in the bow, reversed engines and attempted to ram *U-35* stern first. In all, it took four torpedoes — two of which missed — to sink the British sloop.

In June 1916, von Arnauld received international press coverage for sailing *U-35* to Cartagena, Spain, to deliver a letter from the Kaiser to Alfonso XIII thanking the Spanish king for his country's dealings with German refugees. Following his departure after the 24-hour limit allowed to combatants in neutral countries, *U-35* sank or seized 39 ships worth 56,818 tons. In light of the submarine's next voyage, this was a modest achievement. On July 26, *U-35* sailed from Cattaro and over the next 25 days sank 54 ships — more than any other submarine commander of any country in either of the two world wars — with an aggregate tonnage of more than 90,150 tons. The vast majority of these sinkings were in surface attacks, and in the course of the cruise, von Arnauld used only four torpedoes. In terms of human life, though, it was a cruise in October that proved most fatal, when off Sardinia on October 4, *U-35* sank the French auxiliary cruiser *Gallia,* which was lost with 600 of her 2,000 embarked troops. Between his cruises in *U-35* and *U-139,* von Arnauld proved the most successful submarine commander in history, with ten patrols that accounted for the loss of about 400,000 tons of Allied shipping.

The Allies concluded an armistice with the Ottoman Empire on October 30 and the Austro-Hungarian Empire on November 3, 1918. One immediate result was the collapse of the German submarine campaign in the Mediterranean. Those submarines that could be moved were ordered home to Germany through the closely watched Straits of Gibraltar. *U-35* sailed only as far as Barcelona and was interned there on November 26, 1918. Following the war, she was broken up at Blyth in 1919.

Gray, *U-Boat War.* Halpern, *Naval War in the Mediterranean.*

U-47

Type VII-B submarine. *L/B/D:* 218.1' × 20.3' × 15.7' (31.2' high) (66.5m × 6.2m × 4.8m/9.5m). *Tons:* 753/857 disp. *Hull:* steel. *Comp.:* 44. *Arm.:* 5 × 21.3"TT; 1 × 88mm, 1 × 20mm gun. *Mach.:* diesel/electric, 3,200/750 ehp, 2 screws; 17.9/8 kts. *Built:* Friedrich Krupp AG Germaniawerft, Kiel, Germany; 1938.

Less than three weeks after the loss of the aircraft carrier HMS COURAGEOUS to *U-29* southwest of Ireland, the German submarine service scored what was probably the most brilliantly executed submarine kill of World War II. Acting on intelligence from aerial reconnaissance, Admiral Karl Dönitz ordered Lieutenant Commander Günther Prien to take *U-47* into the Royal Navy's northern base at Scapa Flow. Threading his way through the narrow, eddying channels of the Orkney Islands, Prien entered Scapa Flow shortly after midnight on October 14. As Prien himself described it:

> It is disgustingly light. The whole bay is lit up. . . .
>
> We proceed north by the coast. Two battleships are lying there at anchor, and further inshore, destroyers. Cruisers not visible, therefore attack on the big fellows. Distance apart, three thousand metres. Estimated depth, seven and a half metres. Impact firing. One torpedo fired on northern ship, two on southern. After a good three and a half minutes, a torpedo detonates on the northern ship; of the other two nothing is to be seen.
>
> About! Torpedo fired from stern; in the bow two tubes are loaded; three torpedoes from the bow. After three tense minutes comes the detonation on the nearer ship. There is a loud explosion, roar and rumbling. Then come columns of water. The harbour springs to life. Destroyers are lit up, signalling starts on every side, and on land, two hundred metres away from me, cars roar along the roads. A battleship [HMS *Royal Oak*] had been sunk, a second [actually seaplane carrier HMS *Pegasus*] damaged, and the three other torpedoes have gone to blazes.

U-47 and Prien returned to a hero's welcome in Germany. The submarine's next major undertaking was in support of the German invasion of Norway in April 1940. Attacks against British transports at Bygdenfjord and later against HMS WARSPITE were completely ineffectual. This was not a localized problem, but it was Prien who reported to Dönitz that German torpedoes had serious problems owing, as it was later discovered, to a faulty magnetic pistol and to the torpedoes' running at depths greater than intended.

In September 1940, Germany unleashed the first wolf packs of the war. On September 7, *U-47* sank three ships of convoy SC2, followed the next day by a fourth. On March 7, *U-47* took part in another attack on convoy OB293. In the decisive counterattack that followed, several boats were forced to withdraw, but Prien kept up pursuit and reestablished contact the next morning. Before she could inflict any damage on the convoy, *U-47* was set upon by destroyer HMS *Wolverine*. After a four-hour hunt, the submarine was destroyed by depth charges in 60°47′N, 19°31′W.

Bekker, *Hitler's Naval War*. Gröner, *German Warships*. Snyder, *Royal Oak Disaster*.

U-110

Type IX-B submarine. *L/B/D:* 250.9′ × 25.6′ × 15.4′ (31.5′ high) (76.5m × 6.8m × 4.7m/9.6m). *Tons:* 1,051/1,178 disp. *Hull:* steel; 100m dd. *Comp.:* 48. *Arm.:* 6 × 21.3″TT; 1 × 10.5cm, 1 × 3.7mm. *Mach.:* diesel/electric, 4,400/1,000 ehp, 2 screws; 18.2/7.3 kts. *Built:* Deutsche Schiff und Machinenbau, Bremen, Germany; 1940.

At the outbreak of World War II, the Germans had a commanding lead over the British in encoding technology. Several events enabled the British to thwart the Enigma machine, but none were as important as the capture, on May 9, 1941, of *U-110*. On that day, the German submarine was under command of Lieutenant Commander Fritz-Julius Lemp, who as master of *U-30* had sunk the British liner ATHENIA at the start of the war. *U-110* attacked convoy OB 318 south of Greenland but was forced to the surface by depth charges launched from the destroyer HMS *Bulldog*. Lemp gave the order to set scuttling charges and abandon ship, but he neglected to destroy or jettison the ship's secret documents. By an unfortunate coincidence, the scuttling charges failed to detonate. Boarders from *Bulldog* found the cipher machine and code books, which were laboriously transported to *Bulldog*. *U-110* sank in tow (in 60°22′N, 33°12′W), which was probably just as well because any report of her capture would have alerted the Germans to the fact that their cipher equipment had been captured.

The treasure-trove of machinery and documents had an almost instantaneous effect. U-boats were normally sent out with daily Enigma settings for about three months, and *U-110* was only halfway through her cruise when she was seized. Of more lasting benefit was the fact that having an actual Enigma machine enabled cryptanalysts to break a variety of German codes. The most important of these was Hydra, used by the German U-boats, then decimating the transatlantic convoys upon which Britain's survival depended. In February 1942, the German U-boat command began to use a new code, called Triton, which was not broken until December 1942.

Lewin, *Ultra Goes to War*.

U-505

Type IX-C submarine. *L/B/D:* 251.6′ × 22.3′ × 15.4′ (31.5′ high) (76.8m × 6.8m × 4.7m/9.6m). *Tons:* 1,120/1,232 disp. *Hull:* steel. *Comp.:* 48. *Arm.:* 6 × 21.3″TT; 1 × 3.7mm, 1 × 2cm. *Mach.:* diesel/batteries, 4,400/1,000 ehp, 2 screws; 18.3/7.3 kts. *Built:* Deutsche Werft, Hamburg; 1941.

Commissioned in August 1941, *U-505* spent four months on training cruises in the Baltic under Lieutenant Commander Löwe before transferring to the submarine base at L'Orient, France. On her first (and most successful) operational cruise off West Africa, from February 11 to May 7, 1942, she sank four ships — two British, one American, and one Dutch — with a combined tonnage of 25,041 tons. On her second cruise, to the southern Caribbean, she sank three ships (12,748 tons). The ailing Löwe was replaced by Lieutenant Commander Cszhech in October 1942, and during her next cruise, also to the Caribbean, she sank only one 7,173-ton freighter before sustaining severe damage that forced her home. Her next three missions resulted in no sinkings. They were all cut short by more depth charges — off the Orinoco River, Spanish Sahara, and the Azores. The last was so traumatic that even though *U-505* lost her pursuers, Cszhech shot himself in his cabin.

Refitted with electric motors on the return to L'Orient, *U-505* sailed around Christmastime under Lieutenant Harald Lange. On December 28, 1943, she rescued thirty-six German survivors of a destroyer action in the Bay of Biscay and returned them to Brest. In April, she sailed on a fruitless month-long mission off West Africa. While returning home at the end of May, the submerged submarine was kept under observation by antisubmarine aircraft and sonobuoys from Captain Daniel V. Gallery's hunter-killer group comprising escort carrier USS GUADALCANAL and five destroyer escorts. After a week of trying to elude her trackers, on June 4, 1944, *U-505* was finally brought to the surface by depth charges from USS *Chatelain, Pillsbury,* and *Jenks*. With her rudder jammed and leaking badly, Lange brought his boat to the surface and his crew abandoned ship at 1120 in position 21°30′N, 19°20′W, 150 miles west of Rio de Oro.

A boarding party under Lieutenant (j.g.) Albert L. David entered the submarine and shut off the seacocks. After salvaging the code books and assuring themselves that the scuttling charges had not been set, they repaired the damage and *Guadalcanal* began towing *U-505* to Bermuda. It was the first high-seas capture of an enemy fighting unit since USS PEACOCK captured HMS *Nautilus* in 1815. None of the crews revealed the secret of their success, and it was not until after the war that the Germans learned that *U-505* had been captured rather than sunk. The code books enabled the Allies to read German traffic for the rest of the war.

Following the war, *U-505* was renamed USS *Nemo,* and with an American crew cruised the Gulf and East Coasts in a publicity campaign to sell war bonds. Decommissioned at the Portsmouth Navy Yard in New Hampshire, she languished there until 1954 when the Chicago Museum of Science and Industry — supported by Rear Admiral Gallery — acquired her as a permanent exhibit. The submarine was towed down the St. Lawrence River and through the Great Lakes to Calumet City, Michigan, where she was refurbished. In an interesting feat of engineering, *U-505* was then rolled across Chicago's Outer Drive to dry berth in front of the museum, where she remains today. The same year, she was dedicated as a memorial to the 55,000 American sailors who lost their lives in the two world wars.

Gallery, *Twenty Million Tons under the Sea.* Gröner, *German Warships.*

Excavation in progress on the middle section of the Bronze Age shipwreck at Ulu Burun, Turkey. Above a stack of copper ingots lies a row of stone weight-anchors. Courtesy Institute of Nautical Archaeology, College Station, Texas.

ULU BURUN WRECK

Hull: wood. *Built:* eastern Mediterranean; 14th cent. BCE.

The Ulu Burun wreck is the most spectacular extant Bronze Age shipwreck — spectacular more for the quantity and quality of the finds than for any additional light shed on ancient shipbuilding. In 1983 a Turkish sponge diver told Dr. Don Frey about a heap of ingots — "metal biscuits with ears" — he had seen on the bottom just east of the steep promontory of Uluburun, about eight miles southeast of the town of Kas. A team of archaeologists from the Institute of Nautical Archaeology at Texas A & M University and the Bodrum Museum investigated, and excavations have continued ever since. Deep and dangerous, the wreck site is located in position 36°8′N, 29°41′E; the site begins at a depth of 140 feet and ends below 200 feet, with the sea floor sloping as much as 45 degrees. As of 1995, some 22,000 dives had been logged at the site over 11 seasons.

The bulk of the cargo consisted of metal ingots: more than 350 four-handled "ox-hide" ingots of copper, each weighing approximately 27 kilograms, as well as about a ton of tin ingots. The ingots were stowed in four rows, neatly packed to minimize shifting, and cushioned by a layer of brushwood dunnage. In addition to the metals, the cargo comprised about 170 glass ingots, mostly of a cobalt-colored glass probably produced in the Syria-Palestine region. Other luxury goods included logs of ebony and cedar wood, raw hippopotamus and elephant ivory,

ostrich eggs, Baltic amber, a gold chalice, an ivory writing tablet, a faience drinking cup in the shape of a ram's head, and many pieces of jewelry, most notably a scarab of the Egyptian Queen Nefertiti and a Canaanite gold pectoral in the shape of a falcon. Chemical studies of Canaanite amphorae found amidst the cargo revealed traces of terebinth resin, a valuable commodity used in the production of incense. One amphora contained orpiment (arsenic trisulfide), which was used as a pigment.

The large quantities of luxury goods and precious objects suitable for royal gifts suggest that the Ulu Burun ship's cargo was sent from one ruler to another, either as tribute or as a commercial venture. The cargo included objects of Mycenaean Greek and Cypriot manufacture, but the preponderance of objects of Near Eastern origin among the equipment and personal possessions of the sailors and merchants — tools, weapons, balance-pan weights, cylinder seals, and weapons — suggests that the ship was en route from a port on the Syro-Palestinian coast towards Crete or the Greek mainland. The date of the wreck, about 1325 BCE, was determined by examining the tree rings on wood carried on board, perhaps for use as fuel.

Some well-articulated remains of the vessel were found preserved beneath the cargo: part of the keel, edge-joined planking, and fragments of a wicker bulwark. The precise dimensions of the ship are impossible to determine, but her impressive size is suggested by the cargo capacity and by the 24 stone anchors found around the wreck site.

Bass, "Bronze Age Shipwreck at Ulu Burun (Kas): 1984 Campaign"; "Byzantine Trading Venture."

UNICORN

Frigate (3m). Hull: wood. Comp.: 49. Built: Bremerholm Navy Yard, Copenhagen; 1605.

One of the finest frigates in the navy of Christian IV, *Unicorn* (in Danish, *Enhjørning*) appears to have been so named because earlier in the year all Denmark had been excited by the sale, for 40,000 rix-dollars, of the six-foot-long horn of a narwhal caught off Iceland. The ship had an active career during Christian IV's campaigns in the Baltic, but she is most celebrated for her connection with Jens Munk's expedition in search of the Northwest Passage. Munk, a veteran of ocean voyaging from Brazil to Novaya Zemlya, was first associated with *Unicorn* in 1616. At that time, the ship was one of six in a failed expedition against pirates operating in the waters between Denmark, the North Cape, Iceland, and the Faeroe Islands. (In 1615, Munk had sailed as second in command of a two-ship expedition that captured the Spanish pirate Mendoza in the Kara Sea.) Three years later, *Unicorn* was made flagship of Munk's expedition in search of the Northwest Passage, one of two expeditions bound for China dispatched that year by Christian IV. Among her sixty-five crew were two English veterans of northern voyages: John Watson, who probably sailed with Thomas Button in DISCOVERY in 1613, and William Gordon, whose salary, advance, and bonus (were the Passage found) would have equaled about half the cost of the entire expedition.

On May 9, 1619, *Unicorn* and *Lamprey* sailed from Copenhagen with the personal blessing of Christian IV, but soon after their departure, one man threw himself overboard in the Kattegat, and the ships were forced into harbor in Norway for repairs to *Lamprey*. Putting to sea again on May 30, the ships passed Shetland and the Faeroes and by the end of June were off Cape Farewell, Greenland. They crossed the ice-strewn Davis Strait and fetched up in Frobisher bay at the southern end of Baffin Island. Working their way out of the bay, the ships rounded Resolution Island on July 11 only to drift in the ice for two days before resuming their westward course. Actual transit of Hudson Strait took nearly six weeks, as the ships were caught in drifting ice or came to anchor at various points along the southern shore of Baffin Island. They also lost ten days sailing through Ungava Bay (in

northern Quebec), which Gordon mistook for Hudson Bay. Finally, after passing The Sisters (Digges Islands), the ships turned southwest at the beginning of September. *Lamprey* and *Unicorn* were separated in a storm, and on September 7, Munk conned *Unicorn* through the shoal water at the mouth of the Churchill River in northern Manitoba, where they were joined two days later by *Lamprey*.

The unexpectedly cold weather left Munk no choice but to winter at Munk Haven. The ships were hauled over the shallows to be out of the way of the ice, which was already building up around the hulls. Although well provisioned, the men had no winter clothing, and as the weather tightened its grip it became increasingly difficult to hunt or gather fuel. The first death of a crewman came on November 21, followed two weeks later by a second. By February 20, 1620, twenty-one men were dead, and by June 4, when Munk had given himself up for dead, there were sixty-one dead. Munk wrote in his log, "Since I no longer have any hopes of living, . . . I say good-bye to the world and give my soul to God's keeping."

Five days later, he learned that two of his men were still alive ashore, in a destitute state: "we crept all about, wherever we saw the slightest green growing and coming out of the earth which we digged up and sucked the very root thereof . . . and thereafter we began to feel well." By June 18, they could fish a little, and a week later they began preparations for leaving Munk Haven in *Lamprey*. Having unloaded the vessel, hauled her over the rocks to deeper water, and reloaded her, the three men sailed on July 16, leaving *Unicorn* and their dead comrades behind. Miraculously, *Lamprey* and her enfeebled crew made the hazardous eastward crossing of the Atlantic to fetch up in Sognefjord, Norway, on September 20. Munk recovered well enough to remain in the king's service until 1628, two years after *Lamprey* sank following Christian IV's disastrous defeat at Lutter am Barenberge (August 1626) during the Thirty Years' War.

Hansen, *Northwest to Hudson Bay.*

HMS UNICORN

(ex-*Unicorn II, Cressy, Unicorn*) *Leda*-class 5th rate 46 (3m). *L/B/D:* 150.1′ × 39.8′ × 13.8 dph (45.8m × 12.1m × 4.2m). *Tons:* 1,052 disp. *Hull:* wood. *Comp.:* 284. *Arm.:* 28 × 18pdr, 8 × 32pdr, 10 × 9pdr. *Des.:* Sir Robert Seppings. *Built:* Chatham Dockyard, Eng.; 1824.

A member of one of the Royal Navy's most successful classes of heavy frigates, HMS *Unicorn* has the curious distinction of being one of the oldest, least used, and best preserved wooden ships in the world. Laid down in 1822 and launched two years later, the Royal Navy realized immediately that they had little use for another 46-gun frigate of the same class as HMS *Shannon* and TRINCO-MALEE, and she was immediately put in ordinary, un-rigged and disarmed. She was employed as a powder hulk at Woolwich from 1857 to 1862, when she was moved to Sheerness and laid up. Ten years later she was towed to Dundee for use as a drill ship. She remained in this line of work until 1967, and during both world wars served also as the Area Headquarters of the Senior Naval Officer, Dundee. In 1939, she was renamed *Unicorn II* to free the name for a new aircraft carrier, and in 1941 she became *Cressy*. When the carrier was scrapped in 1959, she took back her old name. The frigate was herself headed to the ship breakers in 1967 when former Captain J. C. L. Anderson initiated an effort to save the ship and have her restored and rigged in the manner originally intended.

Stewart, *Welcome Aboard the Frigate "Unicorn."*

UNION

Sloop (1m). *L/B/D:* 65.4′ bp × 19.8′ × 8.4′ dph (19.9m × 6m × 2.6m). *Tons:* 94 burden. *Hull:* wood. *Comp.:* 22. *Arm.:* 10 guns (6pdr & 3pdr), 8 swivels. *Built:* Somerset, Mass.; 1792.

In the annals of American seafaring, the voyage of the sloop *Union* stands out for its sheer audacity. In July 1794, John Boit took command of *Union* at Newport, Rhode Island, in preparation for a voyage to the Pacific Northwest to gather furs for the Canton market, a trade that attracted scores of Boston merchants in the late eighteenth century. Though only nineteen, Boit was a veteran of COLUMBIA REDIVIVA's second voyage to the Pacific Northwest in 1790–83 and an accomplished navigator. *Union* sailed on August 29, 1794, and after passing through the Cape Verde Islands, she came to the Falkland Islands where she remained from January 4 to 22, 1795. After a quick rounding of Cape Horn, *Union* headed directly for Columbia's Cove on Vancouver Island, landing on May 16. Over the course of the next four months, the crew gathered sea otter skins from the mouth of the Columbia River in the south to Dixon Entrance at the northern end of the Queen Charlotte Islands.

On September 12, *Union* sailed for the Sandwich (Hawaiian) Islands, which she reached on October 17. Here John Young, an Englishman serving as an adviser to King Kamehameha, warned Boit about the possibility of *Union*'s being seized. Boit took the advice and the next day sailed for Canton. *Union* reached the mouth of the Pearl River at the end of November and Boit sold his furs at Canton on Christmas Eve. After loading a cargo of nankeens (a type of cloth) and embarking a passenger for Ile de France, *Union* sailed on January 12, 1796. She reached Ile de France in mid-March and from there sailed directly for Boston, which she reached on July 8. *Union* was probably "the first sloop that ever circumnavigated the globe," but although Boit considered her "an excellent sea boat & . . . a very safe vessel, still I think it too great a risque for to trust to one mast on such a long voyage when a small Brig would answer on the East Coast." Shortly after the sloop's return, her Newport and Boston merchants sold her.

Boit, *Log of the "Union."*

USS UNITED STATES

Frigate (3m). *L/B/D:* 175′ × 43.5′ × 14.3′ (53.3m × 13.3m × 4.3m). *Tons:* 2,200 tons. *Hull:* wood. *Comp.:* 364. *Des.:* Joshua Humphreys, Josiah Fox, William Doughty. *Built:* Joshua Humphreys, Philadelphia; 1797.

One of the U.S. Navy's original six frigates, authorized by Congress specifically to combat the Barbary corsairs in the western Mediterranean, USS *United States* was launched in 1797, followed shortly by CONSTELLATION and CONSTITUTION. Heavily built with a flush spar deck above the gundeck, *United States, Constitution,* and PRESIDENT were rated as 44s and designed to carry thirty 24-pdr. and twenty to twenty-two 12-pdr. long guns; the latter were eventually superseded by the more powerful, short-range 42-pdr. carronades. (The 38s, including CHESAPEAKE and *Congress,* were designed to carry twenty-eight 24-pdrs and eighteen to twenty 12-pdrs.)

Commissioned under Captain John Barry, during the Quasi-War with France, in July 1798 *United States* sailed with USS *Delaware* for the Caribbean in search of French prizes. She captured two privateers on her first cruise, and three in the second, during which the West Indies squadron grew to two frigates, three ships, and four revenue cutters. With the conclusion of the war, the American Navy was practically disbanded, and *United States* was laid up at the Washington Navy Yard with four of her sister ships; *Constitution* was at Boston.

In June 1810, the recommissioned *United States* put to sea under Captain Stephen Decatur. Two years later the United States declared war on Great Britain and Decatur's ship joined Commodore John Rodgers's North Atlantic Squadron. Their second cruise began on October 8, 1812; three days later *United States* split off from the Squadron. On October 25, about 500 miles south of the Azores, *United States* engaged HMS MACEDONIAN (38 guns) under Captain John Surman Carden. Battle was

Painting of the action between the USS UNITED STATES and HMS MACEDONIAN on October 25, 1812, by Arthur N. Disney, Sr. The British frigate was dismasted and so badly damaged that repairs took two weeks at sea. Courtesy U.S. Naval Historical Center, Washington, D.C.

joined at about 0920, and Decatur positioned his ship on *Macedonian*'s quarter. By noon the British frigate was a dismasted hulk with 104 of her crew dead or wounded; American casualties were 12 dead and wounded. Mid-ocean repairs to the British prize took two weeks, and it was not until December that *United States* returned to New York, where *Macedonian* was brought into the U.S. Navy. In May 1813, the ships slipped out of New York with the sloop HORNET, but they were forced into New London where they were blockaded for the duration of the war.

No sooner was the War of 1812 over than Congress declared war on Algiers, and *United States* was sent to the Mediterranean. Although peace was quickly made, *United States* was kept on station until 1819. Laid up for five years, her subsequent career reflected the widening scope of American merchant and naval interests. She sailed variously with the Pacific Squadron (1824–27, 1841–42), Mediterranean Squadron (1833–38, 1847–48), Home Squadron (1839–40), and African Squadron (1846–47). It was on her second patrol in the Pacific that she was joined by ordinary seaman Herman Melville, who translated his fourteen-month experience into the novel *White-Jacket, or The World in a Man-of-War*, in which his ship is called USS *Neversink*.

Decommissioned in 1849, *United States* was captured (with the rest of the Norfolk Navy Yard) and commissioned as the Confederate receiving ship CSS *United States* (or sometimes *Confederate States*). Sunk as a blockship in the Elizabeth River, she was raised and broken up at Norfolk in 1865.

Chapelle, *History of the American Sailing Navy*. U.S. Navy, *DANFS*.

UNITED STATES

Liner (2f/1m). *L/B:* 990′ × 101.6′ × 31′ (301.8m × 31m × 9.4m). *Tons:* 53,329 grt. *Hull:* steel. *Comp.:* 1st 913, cabin 558, tourist 537; 1,036 crew. *Mach.:* steam turbine, 4 screws, 240,000 shp; 35 kts. *Des.:* William Francis Gibbs (Gibbs & Cox). *Built:* Newport News Shipbuilding & Dry Dock Co., Newport News, Va.; 1952.

In many respects the most advanced passenger ship ever built, the North Atlantic passenger liner *United States* was the creation of naval architect William Francis Gibbs more than of any other single person. Frank O. Braynard aptly described *United States* and Gibbs as "Super ship, superman and super merger of the two!" Ever since the clipper age, American shipping and shipbuilding technology had been eclipsed by European rivals, not only in England but in Germany, France, and Italy as well. The last U.S. ship to set a transatlantic speed record was the

Collins Line's *Baltic,* which made the crossing from Liverpool to Sandy Hook in nine days, sixteen hours in 1854. Gibbs began planning for a ship to rival the most opulent and powerful creations from Europe even before World War II, and in many respects his AMERICA (1940) was a preview of his concept of "the big ship." World War II merely postponed his interest in the project, and in the era of postwar prosperity, he began to plan his grandest creation. Braynard summarized the project:

> The new liner was a synthesis of all the experience gained by Gibbs & Cox from passenger ships such as the *Leviathan,* the *Malolo,* the four Grace liners and the *America,* of course, and then combined with the technical advances made in machinery, structure, materials and methods developed in their work for the U.S. Navy. The new ship had to be the fastest afloat, with standards of subdivision and fire resistance surpassing all others. She had to compete with the two Queens in luxury, accommodation and to be much faster — and all this at less fuel consumption. And, she had to be at the same time convertible to a troopship.

The last requirement was due to the involvement of the U.S. government. Because of the projected costs of building such a vessel, Gibbs decided to sell the Navy on the idea that in the event of a national emergency, the ship could serve as a transport. In exchange for a government subsidy, he built into the ship a number of special features, including greater speed than needed for service as a passenger ship and two engine rooms so that she could operate normally in the event that one engine was torpedoed. The government agreed to subsidize the cost of building and maintaining the ship, which would be leased to and operated by United States Lines. By far the most extraordinary aspect of the new liner was her incredible speed, but although she boasted the most powerful machinery of any passenger ship, the abundant use of aluminum in her construction kept her weight to a minimum. Although high speed was an obvious objective, it was also a closely guarded secret, and non–U.S. Lines personnel were barred from the engine room for well over a decade.

In trials off Virginia in June 1952, *United States* generated 241,785 shaft horsepower to step out at over 39.38 knots, and in one spurt she reportedly hit 43 knots — faster than an accompanying Navy destroyer. But with a view to enhancing interest and publicity, U.S. Lines claimed only that she attained speeds of better than 34 knots. On July 3, *United States* embarked passengers for her maiden voyage from New York to Southampton, under command of Commodore Harry Manning. Starting at Ambrose Light off New York Harbor, she was off Bishop Rock on July 7, having covered a distance of 2,942 miles in only 3 days, 10 hours, 40 minutes — an average speed of 35.59 knots. On her return against the prevailing westerlies, she crossed from Bishop Rock to Ambrose in only 3 days, 12 hours, 12 minutes, an average speed of 34.51 knots, the westbound track being 36 miles shorter than the eastbound. These speeds were 11 to 12 percent faster than those of QUEEN MARY, which in 1938 crossed at 31.69 knots eastbound and 30.99 knots westbound, and *United States* maintained an average service speed of 32 to 33 knots.

Most voyages included a stop at Le Havre, and she occasionally also called at Bremen. Although her passenger capacity was less than that of either *Queen Mary* or QUEEN ELIZABETH, as measured by occupancy rate she was a more popular ship. In her first full season, she filled 90 percent of her berths and carried 69,231 passengers, as compared with 70,775 for *Queen Elizabeth* and 63,443 for *Queen Mary.* By the end of the 1950s, however, the transatlantic passenger ship was doomed as the first jet airplanes cut travel times to only seven to eight hours. Also, skyrocketing labor costs and increasing numbers of strikes put severe economic pressures on U.S. Lines. On November 7, 1969, *United States* sailed from New York for what was to have been a routine overhaul in Newport News, but in the face of escalating costs and declining revenues, her return to service was canceled and she was laid up at Newport News.

Over the years, various plans were floated to restore the ship to operation, and she was acquired variously by the Federal Maritime Commission in 1973 and U.S. Cruise Lines in 1978. In 1992, she was purchased by Turkish interests who planned to convert her to a cruise ship. Four years later, she returned to the United States and was laid up in Philadelphia.

Braynard, *Big Ship.* Miller, SS *"United States."*

HMS UPHOLDER

U-class submarine. *L/B:* 191′ × 16.1′ (58.2m × 4.9m). *Tons:* 630/730 disp. *Hull:* steel; 200′ dd. *Comp.:* 31. *Arm.:* 4 × 21″TT; 1 × 3″. *Mach.:* diesel/electric, 615/825 bhp, 2 screws; 11/9 kts. *Built:* Vickers-Armstrong, Barrow-in-Furness, Eng.; 1940.

HMS *Upholder* was one of a class of coastal submarines built just before World War II and designed for training surface forces in antisubmarine warfare. Shortly before war began, the U-class boats were retroactively fitted with torpedo tubes. Difficult to trim at periscope depth, they were also the slowest submarines employed by the British during the war; their only advantage was their ability to submerge faster than any other. Stationed at Malta, the U-class boats were further hampered by the shortage of torpedoes, inadequate night-sights and fire director computers, and inexperienced commanders. One of the last was Lieutenant Commander David Wanklyn, who, in his first four patrols, damaged only one transport and drove his despairing commanding officer to ask whether "such a poor shot could be kept in command." Given one opportunity to redeem himself, Wanklyn sailed *Upholder* for Tunisia on April 21, 1941. Four days later off Kerkenah, he boarded and burned a merchantman, and on May 1, he sank two merchant ships from a homeward-bound convoy.

Wanklyn's sixth patrol in *Upholder* began on May 15. Five days out, Wanklyn sighted a 4,000-ton tanker, two supply ships, and an escort. He fired four torpedoes and the tanker was hit. The bow cap of the fourth tube had failed to open, and in the counterattack, depth charges knocked out *Upholder*'s Asdic and hydrophones. *Upholder* remained on patrol, and three days later Wanklyn torpedoed the Vichy French liner *Alberta*. Only two torpedoes remained, and although one was defective and the other was in the faulty tube, both were readied for firing. At about 2030 on May 24, *Upholder* was recharging her batteries on the surface when Wanklyn sighted three large troopships and four or five destroyers steaming at 20 knots — nearly twice *Upholder*'s operational speed. Slipping inside the screen, Wanklyn launched four torpedoes at the 18,000-ton troop transport *Conte Rosso*, which sank with the loss of about 1,200 Italian soldiers. Following a withering depth-charge attack, the submarine escaped to Malta. Wanklyn was awarded the Victoria Cross for his conduct on this patrol.

On September 17, *Upholder* attacked another troop convoy carrying reinforcements to Field Marshal Erwin Rommel's Afrika Korps. Shortly after midnight, Wanklyn sighted the ships and, firing two torpedoes with "devastating accuracy at 5,000 yards [twice the accepted distance for U-class submarines] in poor light and with his ship yawing badly," holed and sank transport *Neptunia* and destroyed the propellers of *Oceania*, which was finished off at dawn.

By April 1942, *Upholder* had sunk fifteen transports and supply ships, two submarines, two destroyers, and one armed trawler, and had damaged four transports and a cruiser. In early April 1942, she landed Arab agents in Tunisia and on the 11th transferred Special Commando Officer Captain Wilson to her sister ship HMS *Unbeaten*. She then disappeared, and it is believed that she was sunk by a mine or possibly by the Italian torpedo boat *Pegaso*, on April 14. The significance of *Upholder*'s

contribution to the war effort can be gauged from the Admiralty's unusual statement following her loss:

> It is seldom proper for Their Lordships to draw distinction between different services rendered in the course of naval duty, but they take the opportunity of singling out those of HMS *Upholder*, under the command of Lieutenant-Commander Wanklyn, for special mention. . . . Such was the standard of skill and daring, that the ship and her officers and men became an inspiration, not only to their own flotilla, but to the fleet of which it was a part, and Malta, where for so long HMS *Upholder* was based. The ship and her company are gone, but the example and inspiration remain.

Allaway, *Hero of the "Upholder."* Padfield, *War beneath the Sea.*

L'URANIE

(ex-*La Ciotat*) Corvette (3m). *Hull:* wood. *Comp.:* 126. *Arm.:* 20 guns. *Built:* France; <1816.

The last decade of the Napoleonic Wars forestalled all attempts by the French to dispatch any voyages of exploration, but in 1816, Captain Louis de Freycinet was appointed to command a one-ship scientific expedition in *L'Uranie*. Among the ship's company were Rose de Freycinet, the captain's wife (who was disguised as a midshipman until the ship reached Gibraltar). *Uranie* departed Toulon on September 17, 1817, en route for Australia. The primary aim of the expedition was more scientific than geographic, the emphasis being on studies of terrestrial magnetism and astronomical observation. The passage out took a year, as the French conducted exhaustive pendulum observations and collected specimens of flora and fauna at Rio de Janeiro, the Cape of Good Hope, and Mauritius. At Dirk Hartog's Island in Shark Bay, Australia, Freycinet found an inscribed pewter plate that Willem Vlamingh in 1697 used to replace one originally dedicated by Hartog, sailing in EENDRACHT in 1616. (The Vlamingh plate is now in the Western Australian Maritime Museum in Perth.)

From Australia, *Uranie* sailed to Dutch and Portuguese Timor and the Moluccas where the crew were afflicted with dysentery and, despite the frequent stops, scurvy. On March 18, 1819, *Uranie* arrived at the Spanish outpost on Guam, in the Mariana Islands, where the crew recuperated and the young Lieutenant Louis Duperrey (who later commanded two expeditions in L'ASTROLABE) conducted surveys of the island. In May, the ship headed for Hawaii, arriving in early August to an enthusiastic welcome by the Hawaiians and the fledgling European community in Honolulu. Sailing south and southwest, *Uranie* arrived at Sydney, New South Wales, where the French spent six weeks as guests of the English governor Lachlan Macquarie.

On Christmas Day, 1819, *Uranie* sailed for France via Cape Horn. Attempting to enter Berkeley Sound in the Falkland Islands, the ship ran aground and had to be abandoned. Assistance arrived in the form of two American vessels. The French were taken to Montevideo in *Mercury,* where they purchased the vessel and renamed her *Physicienne* before returning to Le Havre on November 13, 1820.

Brosse, *Great Voyages of Discovery.* Dunmore, *French Explorers in the Pacific.*

UTOPIA

Steamship (1f/3m). *L/B/D:* 350.3′ bp × 35.2′ (106.8m bp × 10.7m). *Tons:* 2,731 grt. *Comp.:* 1st 120, 2nd 60, 3rd 600; 60 crew. *Hull:* iron. *Mach.:* compound engine, single screw; 13 kts. *Built:* Robert Duncan & Co., Port Glasgow, Scotland; 1874.

Built for the Henderson Brothers' Anchor Line in 1874 to sail on the North Atlantic route between Glasgow and New York, in 1876 *Utopia* began sailing between London and New York. In 1882, she was briefly put into Anchor Line's triangular service between Glasgow, Calcutta, and New York, by way of the Suez Canal and Mediterranean ports. She later resumed service between Glasgow, the Mediterranean, and New York. Following a major overhaul in 1890, during which she was given triple-expansion engines and her passenger accommodations were modernized, *Utopia* entered the immigrant trade direct between New York and the Mediterranean. Having embarked more than 800 passengers at Trieste and Naples, *Utopia* stopped briefly at Gibraltar on March 16, 1891. During a gale, she was blown broadside on into the ram bow of HMS *Anson,* which was at anchor. The damage was devastating and *Utopia* sank within five minutes; a total of 576 passengers and crew were lost with the ship.

Raised the following July, *Utopia*'s hull was patched, towed to the Clyde, and laid up. She was finally broken up in 1900.

Bonsor, *North Atlantic Seaway.* McLellan, *Anchor Line.*

UTRECHT BOAT

Logboat. *L/B:* 45.6′ × 6.2′ (13.9m × 1.85m). *Hull:* wood. *Built:* Netherlands; ca. 1050 CE.

First discovered by workmen digging a canal along Utrecht's van Hoornekade in 1930, the Utrecht boat was immediately excavated and taken to the Centraal Museum for study and reconstruction. The vessel was initially thought to be a small-decked, seagoing sailing ship dating first from the second and later from the eighth century CE. She was also compared with renderings of ships found in the ninth-century Utrecht Psalter and on Carolingian coins.

Subsequent research in the 1980s revealed an altogether different vessel. More sophisticated dating systems place the Utrecht boat in the eleventh century. The hull consists of a single oak log that has been hollowed. This base was lengthened both fore and aft by wooden extension boards. To port and starboard, there were a garboard strake, a half-round wale, and a sheer strake. These overlapped clinker fashion and were fastened with treenails (iron nails were used only to hold patches over cracks in the log), and the sheer strake was reinforced with a rubbing strake. The vessel was reinforced by an estimated thirty-eight ribs, all but two of which were preserved. The Utrecht boat was probably used only in inland waters, and was either towed or punted over shallow waters. As such she is thought to represent the ultimate development of the logboat, the origins of which have been traced to about 7000 BCE.

Vlek, *Medieval Utrecht Boat.*

VANDERBILT

(later *Three Brothers*) Sidewheel steamer (2f/2m). *L/B/D:* 323′ × 38.4′ × 31.1′ (98.5m × 11.7m × 9.5m). *Tons:* 3,019 grt. *Hull:* wood. *Mach.:* vertical-beam engines, 2,800 ihp, sidewheels; 14 kts. *Built:* Jeremiah Simonson, Greenpoint, N.Y.; 1857.

Built for direct competition with the British Cunard Line, the passenger mail steamship *Vanderbilt* was named for ferry-captain-turned-railroad-baron Cornelius Vanderbilt. Flying the flag of the North Atlantic Mail Steamship Line, she sailed (in summertime only) until the Civil War. *Vanderbilt* was then chartered to the government as a transport, but when the Confederacy unveiled the CSS VIRGINIA, Vanderbilt offered the services of his ship — which had 50 feet of iron plating forward — as a ram to destroy the ironclad. Armed with two 200-pdr., twelve 9-inch, and one 12-pdr. guns, she arrived at Hampton Roads after the duel between *Virginia* and MONITOR. She then sailed in a yearlong search for the Confederate raider ALABAMA, during which time she captured several blockade-runners. (Vanderbilt was disquieted to learn, upon receipt of a testimonial from Congress, that he had donated his ship to the Navy, but he figured out how to parlay "their twenty-five-dollar gold medal" into good publicity.) In 1867, "Vanderbilt's Yacht" transferred to the Pacific Squadron at San Francisco, where she was placed in ordinary from 1867 to 1873.

In the latter year she was sold to Howe & Company of San Francisco, who removed her engines, gave her a clipper bow, and rerigged her as a three-masted ship for trade around Cape Horn to the East Coast and Europe. In 1885, she was sold to the Anchor Line for use as a coal hulk at Gibraltar, where she remained until 1928, when she was sold for scrap.

Braynard, *Famous American Ships*. Silverstone, *Warships of the Civil War Navies*.

HMS VANGUARD

3rd rate 74 (3m). *L/B:* 168′ × 47′ (51.2m × 14.3m). *Tons:* 1,664 bm. *Hull:* wood. *Comp.:* 530. *Arm.:* 28 × 32pdr, 30 × 24pdr, 16 × 9pdr. *Built:* Deptford Dockyard; 1787.

When France under the Directory declared war on Great Britain in 1793, the Kingdom of Naples allied itself with Britain, which was forced thereby to commit major resources to the Mediterranean. The British presence there intensified even more after Napoleon invaded Italy in 1796. The next year, Rear Admiral Horatio Nelson had his right arm amputated after an attempted landing at Santa Cruz de Tenerife, in the Canary Islands. His first flagship upon returning to duty was HMS *Vanguard*, Captain Edward Berry commanding, and he was immediately sent to cruise off Toulon to determine the intentions of the huge French fleet mustering there under Vice Admiral François Paul Brueys d'Aiguïlliers. On May 20, 1798, *Vanguard* was dismasted in a gale and made repairs at Sardinia, returning to Toulon to find that the French had sailed, also on the 20th. Earl St. Vincent then appointed Nelson — over two more senior officers — to search for and destroy the French armada, numbering some 75 warships, 400 transports, 10,000 sailors, and 36,000 soldiers.

By June 7, Nelson had a fleet of 14 ships of the line but, through a confusion of orders, no frigates, a situation that led him to declare, "Frigates! Were I to die this moment, *want of frigates* would be found engraved on my heart!" Lacking these "eyes of the fleet," he was unable to locate the French armada until after it had captured Malta, at which point he supposed it to be headed for Egypt to establish a bridgehead for the capture of British India. Finding no French in Alexandria, Nelson put back to Sicily for water and provisions. Setting to sea again, on July 28 he learned that the French had been seen bound for Egypt, to which he now returned. On August 1, the British were off Alexandria, and that same afternoon found the French fleet of thirteen ships of the line and four frigates anchored in line ahead in Aboukir Bay. Many of the crews were ashore watering ship, and though they were recalled immediately, Admiral Brueys seems to have believed that Nelson would attack the following morning and that he had a night to prepare.

Nelson felt that when the French cleared for battle, they would assume that his attack would come from the sea and not bother with the guns facing the shore. At 1630, five of Nelson's ships passed between the French van and the shore while *Vanguard* and five other ships anchored to seaward. Seven French ships were pummeled by thirteen British (*Culloden* had run aground and *Swiftsure* and *Alexander* did not arrive off Aboukir until 2000), while the rest of the French fleet remained out of action to leeward. Nelson described the action briefly in a letter to Lord Howe:

> I had the happiness to command a band of brothers; therefore, night was to my advantage. Each knew his duty, and I was sure each would feel for a French ship. By attacking the enemy's van and centre, the wind blowing directly along their line, I was able to throw what force I pleased on a few ships. This plan my friends readily conceived by the signals, . . . and we always kept a superior force to the enemy. At twenty-eight minutes past six, the sun in the horizon, the firing commenced. At five minutes past ten, when the *Orient* blew up, having burnt seventy minutes, the six van ships surrendered. I then pressed further towards the rear; and had it pleased God that I had not been wounded and stone blind [from a piece of scrap iron that hit him in the forehead], there cannot be a doubt but that every ship would have been in our possession.

In the event, the Nile proved the most decisive victory of its day, and Rear Admiral Comte de Villeneuve escaped with only *Généreux, Guillaume Tell,* and two frigates. Two ships of the line were sunk, three were beyond repair, and six were taken into the Royal Navy. Nelson was honored with a peerage (Baron Nelson of the Nile and Burnham-Thorpe) and with gifts from Czar Paul of Russia, Ottoman Sultan Selim III, and the East India Company, among others.

France's army in Egypt remained cut off in the Middle East until 1802, although Napoleon returned to Europe in October 1799. In the meantime, French continental armies advanced through Italy with little resistance from the fragmented republics. In December 1798, the Neapolitan royal family sailed to exile in Sicily aboard *Vanguard*. Shortly thereafter, Nelson commenced a blockade of Malta, which held out for two years. Nelson later shifted his flag to HMS *Foudroyant,* and in 1800 *Vanguard* returned to home waters. Though she remained in active service, she was not present at the other major battles of the Napoleonic Wars. Reduced to a prison ship in 1812

and a powder hulk in 1814, *Vanguard* was broken up in 1821.

Bennett, *Nelson the Commander.*

VEGA

Bark (1f/3m). *L/B:* 142′ × 26′ (43.3m × 7.9m). *Tons:* 357 grt. *Hull:* wood. *Comp.:* 35. *Mach.:* steam, 60 hp, 1 screw; 7 kts. *Built:* Bremerhaven; 1873.

In 1873, veteran polar explorer Adolf Nordenskiöld began studying the feasibility of a Northeast Passage from European waters across the top of Russia to the Bering Sea. His first two efforts, in 1873 and 1875 aboard *Pröven* and *Ymer,* demonstrated that the coast of the Kara Sea was relatively ice free, and he eventually received backing from Oscar II of Norway and Sweden, among others, to undertake an expedition in the converted German whaler *Vega.* Accompanied by three support ships, *Vega* departed Tromsø, Norway, on July 21, 1878. By August 19, they had passed Cape Chelyushkin at the top of the Taimyr Peninsula, the northernmost point of continental Eurasia, and nine days later *Vega* was off the mouth of the Lena River. From here Nordenskiöld tried to explore the New Siberian Islands to the north, but forced back by the ice, *Vega* continued her way east.

On September 27, 1878, *Vega* became icebound just east of North Cape and only 120 miles from the Bering Strait. The ship remained fast in the ice for the next ten months, during which time *Vega*'s ethnographic and scientific experts studied the Chuchki culture and collected fauna and flora specimens. Addressing the problem of pack ice head-on, Nordenskiöld wrote "On the Possibility of Commercial Navigation in the Waters off Siberia," a report that anticipated by several decades the development of such a route by Soviet planners. On July 18, 1879, *Vega* was free of the ice and resumed her way east, and on July 20 she cleared Bering Strait. "Thus," as Nordenskiöld observed, "at last the goal was reached that so many nations had struggled for, ever since Sir Hugh Willoughby [in EDWARD BONAVENTURE] ushered in the long series of voyages to the Northeast." Nordenskiöld continued to make scientific observations for several weeks before turning for Japan, where he arrived in September. *Vega* returned to Europe via the Suez Canal, Naples, and London, but the ship's arrival at Stockholm on April 24 was a momentous occasion. The date is still celebrated as Vega Day in Sweden.

Vega was sold following the voyage and returned to her work in the fisheries under the Swedish flag for two decades. She was lost off Greenland when she was trapped in the ice, and sank.

Kish, *North-east Passage*. Nordenskiöld, *Voyage of the "Vega" round Asia and Europe*.

VERGULDE DRAECK

Ship (3m). *L/B/D:* 125.4′ × 29.3′ × 12.3′ dph (38.2m × 8.9m × 3.8m). *Tons:* 260 tons. *Hull:* wood. *Comp.:* 193. *Arm.:* 24. *Built:* VOC, Zaandam, Netherlands; 1653.

On her second voyage to Batavia, the Verenigde Oostindishche Compagnie (VOC, or Dutch East India Company) retour ship *Vergulde Draeck* ran aground on a reef about 120 kilometers (75 miles) north of modern Perth, Australia, on April 28, 1656. Seventy-five of the crew landed safely, and a ship's boat with seven crew put out for Batavia, 1,600 miles away, which they reached on June 7. Two ships sent out for the survivors the next day found nothing. A second two-ship expedition was dispatched in January 1658, and on March 20 *Wackende Boey* came across flotsam from the ship near Rottnest Island. A few days later, she was driven offshore while fourteen men were ashore in the ship's boat. Captain Samuel Volkersen abandoned his men, and under Abraham Leeman the castaways returned to Batavia on September 13, though ten of the fourteen crew were killed on Java.

In 1931, coins from *Vergulde Draeck* were found in the sand near Cape Leschenault, but little more was thought of the wreck until 1963, when divers found elephant tusks, cannon, ship's fittings, and ballast bricks off Ledge Point. The subsequent frenzy of treasure seekers, some armed with dynamite, led to the passage of an act assigning all wrecks from before 1900 in Western Australia to the Western Australian Maritime Museum. Excavation of the site began in 1972, and although the hull had broken up, archaeologists found trade articles, bricks (for ballast and construction in Batavia), about 7,800 coins (about 17% of the total listed in the manifest), stoneware jugs, several hundred clay pipes, thirteen elephant tusks, resin, and personal possessions such as combs and shoes.

Green, "Loss of the V.O.C. Jacht *Vergulde Draeck*." Henderson, *Marooned*.

VESTA

Screw steamer (1f/2m). *L/B/D:* 152′ × 20.3′ × 10.4′ (46.3m × 6.2m × 3.2m). *Tons:* 250. *Hull:* iron. *Comp.:* 150 pass.; 50 crew. *Built:* Hernoux & Cie., Dieppe, France; 1853.

Named for the virgin goddess of the hearth in Roman mythology, *Vesta* was built for the Société Terreneuvienne of Granville, Normandy, to service the firm's Grand Banks fishing fleets based at St. Pierre and Miquelon off Newfoundland. On September 20, 1854, *Vesta* was homeward bound from Miquelon with 147 fishermen and salters and a crew of 50 under command of Captain Alphonse Duchesne. About 50 or 60 miles from Cape Race, in heavy fog, *Vesta* was rammed by the wooden paddle steamer ARCTIC. A ten-foot section of *Vesta*'s bow was shorn off, but thanks to her iron hull and watertight bulkheads, she was able to return to St. John's, Newfoundland, two days later; *Arctic* went down with appalling loss of life. *Vesta* sailed again on March 20 and was forced into Liverpool after being beset for 17 days by gales and ice.

In 1855, *Vesta* was bought by Compagnie Générale Maritime, Le Havre, and five years later by the newly formed Compagnie Générale Transatlantique, later known as the French Line. In 1863, she was sold to the Spanish firm of J. Ammann of Bilbao. Renamed *Amberes* and put in service between Spain and Antwerp, she is believed to have sunk at Santander in 1874 or 1875. (In later years, the distinguished Captain Duchesne commanded the fast steamer PÉREIRE prior to her conversion to the four-masted ship *Lancing*.)

Brown, "Steamer *Vesta*."

USS VESUVIUS

Dynamite gun cruiser. *L/B/D:* 252.3′ × 26.4′ × 9′ (76.9m × 8.1m × 2.7m). *Tons:* 930 disp. *Hull:* steel. *Comp.:* 70. *Arm.:* 3 × 15″, 3 × 3pdr. *Mach.:* steam, 2 screws; 21 kts. *Built:* William Cramp & Son Ships and Engine Building Co., Philadelphia; 1890.

Named for the Italian volcano, the third USS *Vesuvius* was a unique vessel developed during the transition from muzzle-loading guns to recoil-controlled breech-loaders. Her three 15-inch "pneumatic dynamite" guns were designed by U.S. Army Lieutenant E. L. Zalinski and used compressed air to propel the nitrocellulose/nitroglycerin shells. Mounted in parallel, the barrels led from just forward of the massive compressed air tanks on the lower deck amidships up through the foredeck. The range — up to 1.5 miles — varied according to the amount of compressed air admitted to the firing chamber. The direction of fire could be changed only by turning the ship, and aiming the guns was crude.

Vesuvius operated with the North Atlantic Squadron from 1890 to 1895, when she was decommissioned for a

The experimental gunboat USS VESUVIUS *in 1891. The barrels of the three pneumatic guns, just forward of the mast, pass through the deck to the bottom of the hull. Courtesy U.S. Naval Historical Center, Washington, D.C.*

refit. During the Spanish-American War, on June 13, 1898, *Vesuvius*'s guns were engaged in a night bombardment of Santiago. While they inflicted few casualties, the huge shells were nonetheless terrifying because the pneumatic propellant was barely audible ashore. Decommissioned at the end of the war, in 1904 she exchanged her gun barrels for torpedo tubes and was used as a torpedo vessel for two more years. From 1910 to 1921, *Vesuvius* served as a station ship at Newport. She was broken up in 1922.

Allen, "Story of the USS *Vesuvius* and the Dynamite Gun." U.S. Navy, *DANFS*.

VICAR OF BRAY

Bark (3m). *L/B/D:* 97′ × 24.2′ × 17′ (29.6m × 7.4m × 5.2m). *Tons:* 282 grt. *Hull:* wood. *Built:* Robert Hardy, Whitehaven, Eng.; 1841.

Vicar of Bray was built for the copper-ore trade between England and Chile where, thirty years after Chile's independence, there were still no copper smelters. In *The Mirror of the Sea,* Joseph Conrad describes the work for which she was intended:

> . . . the famous copper-ore trade of old days between Swansea and the Chilian coast, coal out and ore in, deep-loaded both ways, as if in wanton defiance of the great Cape Horn seas — a work, this, for staunch ships, and a great school of

staunchness for West-Country seamen. A whole fleet of copper-bottomed barques, as strong in rib and planking, as well found in gear, as ever was sent upon the seas, manned by hardy crews and commanded by young masters, was engaged in this now long-defunct trade.

The *Vicar* remained in this work until the late 1840s, when she was put in general trade between England and South America and, later, Australia. In 1849 she was chartered to carry two retorts to the New Almaden quicksilver mine in California. (Retorts are devices for distilling quicksilver, which is used to extract gold from its ore.) Even as she was being readied for this voyage, the discovery of gold at Sutter's Mill was being announced to the world. The *Vicar*'s charter for this voyage probably had nothing to do with the California gold strike per se. At the time, the Rothschilds had a near monopoly on Spanish quicksilver; the New Almaden mines in California were owned by Baring Brothers, the British banking house.

In the twelve-month period from April 1848 to April 1849, four vessels put into San Francisco; in all of 1849, nearly 800 vessels sailed from East Coast ports. Upon their arrival in San Francisco, most crews deserted their ships, and shortly after entering port on November 3, 1849, most of *Vicar of Bray*'s crew legged it for the diggings. It was several months before her captain recruited enough hands to sail again.

The *Vicar* continued trading through the 1870s when, outward bound from Swansea to Valparaiso, heavy damage forced her into Stanley, Falkland Islands, where she was condemned. Purchased and refitted by the Falkland Islands Company, she commenced sailing between the Falklands and England. In 1880 her entry is listed for the last time in *Lloyd's Register* and stamped "now a hulk." The thrifty Falklanders used the condemned *Vicar* as a storage depot. In 1912, she was blown ashore at Goose Green, at the head of Choiseul Sound about fifty miles west of Stanley, and her remains were eventually incorporated into a pier. Today, *Vicar of Bray* is the only ship still extant that is known to have called at San Francisco in 1849.

The *Vicar's* longevity echoes that of her namesake. The Tudor clergyman may have mistaken doing well for doing good, but he remained at his post, variously Protestant or Popish, as dictated by the persuasion of the four monarchs under whom he served. He is immortalized in this bit of doggerel:

> And this is law I will maintain
> until my dying day, sir;
> That whatsoever king may reign
> Still I'll be the Vicar of Bray, sir!

Conrad, *Mirror of the Sea*. Paine, "Bring Home the *Vicar!*"

VICTORIA

Carrack (3m). *Tons:* 85 tons. *Hull:* wood. *Comp.:* 60. *Built:* Spain(?); <1519.

By the 1490s, Spain and Portugal were the world's dominant sea powers, and it seemed reasonable for the Pope to be called upon to divide the world between the two competing kingdoms. In 1493, a papal bull drew a line 100 leagues west of the Cape Verde Islands, and the following year the Treaty of Tordesillas divided the world along a north-south line drawn 370 leagues (about 1,100 miles) west of the Cape Verde Islands. This gave Portugal a foothold in what is now Brazil, but it remained to be seen whether the Spice Islands, to which Portugal had established a claim, fell within Spanish territory. The enormous wealth to be made trading in pepper, cloves, and other spices was impetus enough for Magellan, but he was also determined to find a westward route to the Pacific and the Orient through the Americas — in essence, to continue the voyage upon which Christopher Columbus had embarked with NIÑA, PINTA, and SANTA MARÍA in 1492. Although such a route could easily have led to a circumnavigation of the globe, that was not Magellan's intent, as he believed that the westward route was

shorter than the Portuguese route via the Cape of Good Hope.

Spurned by Manoel I, the king of his native Portugal, Magellan (his Portuguese name is Fernão de Magalhães) turned to the Spanish court, where his seven years' experience in the East Indies and well-conceived plan won him the support of Charles V, who consented to the voyage in March 1518. Despite royal backing, it was not until September 20, 1519, that Magellan sailed from Sanlúcar de Barrameda on the Guadalquivir River; he headed 237 men in a fleet of five ships provisioned for two years: *San Antonio* (120 tons), commanded by Juan de Cartagena; *Trinidad* (110 tons), in which Magellan himself sailed; *Concepción* (90 tons), under Gaspar de Quesada; *Victoria* (85 tons), under Luis de Mendoza; and *Santiago* (75 tons), under Juan Serrano.

Early on Magellan learned that some of the Spanish captains were plotting his overthrow, but he did not move against them at the time. Sailing from the Cape Verde Islands on October 3, the ships ran along the African coast as far as Sierra Leone, a route that his Spanish captains did not understand, and which Magellan did not explain. When Cartagena protested by refusing to show the evening signal, Magellan had him arrested and put *San Antonio* under command of Antonio de Coca. After crossing the equator, the ships stood south southwest until they reached the coast of Brazil on November 29, staying two weeks in the area of what is now Rio de Janeiro. They next explored the Plate River, and from there continued south, finally putting into Puerto San Julian for the winter. Here they encountered the people they called Patagonians (Spanish for "big feet"), two of whom were kidnapped, though both subsequently died at sea. It was here also that the Spanish conspiracy against Magellan came to a head. On April 1, Quesada, Juan de Cartagena, and Juan Sebastian del Cano, *Concepción's* master, seized *San Antonio*. Magellan moved quickly to take *Victoria* and, outnumbered three ships to two, the mutineers surrendered. Quesada was decapitated and then drawn and quartered, and when the fleet sailed, Cartagena and a priest were marooned.

On May 22, *Santiago* was wrecked near the mouth of the Santa Cruz River, about 70 miles south of San Julian, without loss of life, and shortly thereafter Magellan shifted winter quarters to Santa Cruz, where they remained until October 18. Three days later, the ships rounded the Cape of the Eleven Thousand Virgins — named in honor of the Feast of St. Ursula — and *Concepción* and *San Antonio* were sent ahead to explore. *Concepción* confirmed that the passage to the west was a strait and the remaining ships — *San Antonio's* disgruntled pilot Estevão Gómez had turned back for Spain — began the arduous five-week journey through the fickle winds and currents of the Strait of Magellan between Patagonia and Tierra del Fuego. On November 28, the three surviving ships passed Cape Desire — that is, the thing they had so long desired — and entered the Pacific.

Magellan's route across the Pacific is unknown. The ships may have sailed north until about 20°N before turning west, or they may have sailed only to the latitude of Juan Fernández Island before heading roughly northwest. Whatever the case, it was not until March 6 — after fourteen weeks at sea — that the surviving crews, wracked with scurvy and on the brink of starvation, reached the Mariana Islands in the western Pacific. These they called the Ladrones ("thieves") because the islanders stole from the ships. In return, the Spanish burned forty or fifty houses and killed seven islanders. A week later they reached Samar in what eventually became the Philippines. At the island of Limasawa, Magellan's Malay slave Enrique could make himself understood in his native language. At this point, Enrique and Magellan had effectively circled the globe, though not all in a single voyage.

On April 7, the ships landed at the island of Cebu, the Philippines. Here Magellan became a blood brother of the local ruler, who converted to Christianity together with several thousand of his kinsmen. To impress his new ally with Christian might, Magellan led a small Spanish expedition against one of the rajah's reluctant vassals. On April 27, 1521, Magellan waded ashore on the island of Mactan, where he was killed, together with seven of the forty or fifty men who accompanied him. To make matters worse, his wounded slave Enrique plotted with the rajah against the Spanish, and twenty-four more men were killed by Magellan's erstwhile blood brother. Retreating to the island of Bohol, the Spanish burned *Concepción* and distributed the crew between *Trinidad* and *Victoria*. Command of the expedition passed to the ineffectual pilot João Carvalho. After several months aimlessly cruising the Philippines, Juan Sebastian del Cano and Gonzalo Gómez de Espinosa took charge.

On November 8, *Victoria* and *Trinidad* arrived at Tadore in the Moluccas, or the Spice Islands. Here the Spanish were warmly received by the local ruler, and traded red cloth, hatchets, cups, linen, and other items for cloves, mace, nutmeg, cinnamon, and sandalwood. Six weeks later, the ships were prepared to return to Spain, but *Trinidad* was detained for repairs. On December 21, *Victoria* sailed with forty-seven European crew and thirteen East Indians. Stopping at Timor towards the end of January, they ransomed a local chief's son for food before setting out southwest across the Indian Ocean on February 11. Their passage home was long and difficult. It took twelve weeks to double the Cape of Good Hope, and they did not reach the Cape Verde Islands until July 8. In their twenty-one weeks at sea, twenty-one crew died and they lost their foremast. Then, a watering party of thirteen men was arrested by the Portuguese at Santiago, and del Cano was forced to continue with his reduced and enfeebled crew. On September 6, 1522, eighteen Europeans limped ashore at Sanlúcar, accompanied by three East Indians, having completed the first single-voyage circumnavigation of the globe in two years, eleven months, and two weeks. (Espinosa attempted to sail *Trinidad* back across the Pacific but was forced to return to Tadore; only four of her crew returned to Spain, in August 1527.)

Despite the disastrous consequences for most of the participants, Magellan's voyage was a milestone in the history of navigation. In finding a water route from the Atlantic to the Pacific through the Americas, he had proven that the American continent was not attached to a southern Terra Australis, and that the Pacific could be crossed, if as yet only by brute determination. Yet in key particulars he was wrong: the westward route to the Spice Islands was not shorter than by way of the Cape of Good Hope, and the Moluccas were eventually found to lie within the Portuguese sphere described by the Treaty of Tordesillas.

Victoria made two voyages to Hispaniola, but she foundered on the return from the second with the loss of all her crew. In 1524 del Cano led a fleet of seven ships for the Spice Islands by way of the Strait of Magellan. The expedition was a disaster, and del Cano died in mid-Pacific.

Pigafetta, Maximilian & Corrêa, *Magellan's Voyage around the World*.

HMS VICTORIA

Sans Pareil-class battleship (1f/2m). *L/B/D:* 340′ × 70′ × 29′ (103.6m × 21.3m × 8.8m). *Tons:* 11,020 disp. *Comp.:* 430–583. *Arm.:* 2 × 16.25″, 1 × 10″, 12 × 6″, 12 × 6pdr; 6 × 14″TT. *Armor:* 18″ belt. 3″ deck. *Hull:* steel. *Mach.:* triple-expansion steam, 7,500 ihp, 2 screws; 15.3 kts. *Built:* Sir W. G. Armstrong, Whitworth & Co., Ltd., Newcastle-on-Tyne, Eng.; 1890.

The *Sans Pareil*-class was the first class of battleships built after the *Admiral*-class barbette ships, which included HMS CAMPERDOWN. The last single-turret ships built for the Royal Navy — and as such representing a step backward from the earlier class — they were the first to be driven by triple-expansion engines. *Victoria* was commissioned as flagship of the Mediterranean fleet, to replace *Camperdown,* and remained on that station the whole of her brief career. On June 22, 1893, en route from Beirut to Tripoli, the fleet was steaming north-northeast in parallel columns six cables (1,200 yards) apart. For reasons never adequately explained, Vice Admiral Sir George Tryon ordered the two divisions to turn 16 points towards each other. Although there seemed to be some concern over the outcome of the maneuver — which sent the ships towards each other at a combined speed of 10 to 12 knots — no one questioned the order. *Camperdown's* ram struck *Victoria* just abaft the anchors 12 feet below the waterline, making a breach nearly 28 feet long. Although *Victoria* was turned towards shore in an attempt to reach shallow water, the inrush of water was so great that she quickly went down by the bows, taking with her 22 officers and 336 men.

Mead, "Loss of the *Victoria.*" Parkes, *British Battleships.*

VICTORIA AND ALBERT II

Paddle schooner (2f/3m). *L/B/D:* 300′ bp × 40.3′ × 16.3′ (91.4m × 12.3m × 5m). *Tons:* 2,470 disp. *Hull:* wood. *Mach.:* oscillating steam, sidewheels, 2,980 ihp; 15.4 kts. *Des.:* O. Lang. *Built:* Pembroke Dockyard, Wales; 1855.

Victoria and Albert was the second of three royal yachts of the same name built during the reign of Queen Victoria. Her immediate predecessor, built in 1843, was the first steam-powered royal yacht. A replacement for George IV's full-rigged ship *Royal George,* she did much to legitimize the use of steam power in yachts. A comfortable vessel, *Victoria and Albert* spent much of her time at Cowes, Isle of Wight, where the Queen held court at Osborne House during the summer; here she presided over the festivities of Cowes Week, the premier annual yachting regatta in the nineteenth century. In addition, the ship carried the Queen on several state visits and was frequently put at the disposal of visiting European monarchs, many of whom were related to Victoria by blood or marriage. Victoria only reluctantly consented to the construction of a replacement vessel, informing Lord Salisbury that "*Victoria and Albert* is no longer in accord with our dignity as the head of a great maritime State, and is the subject of continuous comment among our relations on the Continent." The third *Victoria and Albert,* a twin-screw steamer measuring 430 feet overall, was not commissioned until the year of Victoria's death in 1901. The second *Victoria and Albert* was broken up in 1904, and her successor fifty years later.

Heaton, *Yachting: A History.* Hofman, *Steam Yachts.*

HMS VICTORIOUS

Illustrious-class aircraft carrier (1f/1m). *L/B/D:* 753.6′ × 95.9′ × 28′ (229.7m × 29.2m × 8.5m). *Tons:* 28,619 disp. *Hull:* steel. *Comp.:* 1,600. *Arm.:* 36 aircraft; 16 × 4.5″, 48 × 2pdr. *Armor:* 4.5″ belt, 3″ deck. *Mach.:* steam turbines, 110,000 shp, 3 screws; 31 kts. *Built:* Vickers-Armstrong Ltd., Walker-on-Tyne; 1941.

Launched two weeks into World War II, HMS *Victorious* was not completed for another eighteen months because of the urgent need for escort vessels to combat German submarines. Her first active mission was as part of the hunt for BISMARCK and PRINZ EUGEN, which had broken into the North Atlantic and sunk the battlecruiser HMS HOOD. She was barely combat-ready and put to sea with only one-quarter of her planes embarked. On the night of May 24, 1941, her nine Swordfish attacked *Bismarck,* but contact with the enemy was lost and *Victorious* played no further role in the battleship's sinking three days later. After ferrying aircraft for the defense of Malta, she returned to Scapa Flow. When Germany invaded the Soviet Union on June 22, 1941, *Victorious* took part in attacks on German-held ports in Norway and northern Finland, and then provided distant cover for the Murmansk convoys. On March 9, *Victorious* aircraft attacked the battleship TIRPITZ off Norway's North Cape. Although no hits were scored, Hitler ordered that capital ships not be risked in the presence of enemy aircraft. When the Arctic convoys were suspended following the horrific losses of PQ17, *Victorious* took part in a last-ditch effort to relieve Malta — remembered chiefly for the incredible survival of the oil tanker OHIO. *Victorious* was one of seven British carriers that returned to the Mediterranean to cover the Allied invasion of North Africa in November. Operation Torch was a dramatic success, and returning home, *Victorious* aircraft sank German submarines *U-331* and *U-517.*

From May to August 1943, *Victorious* operated with the U.S. Pacific Fleet in support of SARATOGA, which was for a time the only operational U.S. carrier. After a refit, she was back in action against *Tirpitz,* still a fleet-in-being at Kaa Fjord. (A fleet-in-being is a ship or group of ships that, though withheld from action, constitutes a potential threat that must be contained or neutralized.) On April 3, aircraft from *Victorious* and FURIOUS put the battleship out of service for three months at the expense of only five planes. Several other attacks in Norway followed before *Victorious* was ordered to join the Eastern Fleet at Trincomalee in June 1944. Over the next eight months, British naval forces attacked Japanese installations in Indonesia, scoring notable successes against the crucial oil refineries around Palembang in late January

1945. In the spring, the British Pacific Fleet — including *Victorious*'s sister ships *Formidable* and ILLUSTRIOUS — visited Sydney before proceeding to attack airfields on Sakashima Gunto and Formosa in support of the April invasion of Okinawa. *Victorious*'s last combat missions were flown against the Japanese home islands before she was released from duty on August 12, three days before the war's end.

Victorious helped repatriate prisoners of war, and from 1947 to 1950, she served as a training ship. From 1950 to 1958 she underwent a refit from which she emerged with an angled flight deck and capable of handling 72 carrier jets; her length was 781 feet and she displaced 37,000 tons. After nine years in the Indian Ocean and Far East, she was undergoing a refit at Portsmouth when a dockyard fire brought her career to a premature close. The last of the *Illustrious*-class carriers was broken up at Metal Industries, Faslane, in 1969.

Apps, *Send Her "Victorious."* Watton, *Aircraft Carrier "Victorious."*

HMS VICTORY

1st rate 100 (3m). *L/B/D:* 226.5′ × 52′ × 21.5′ dph (69m × 15.8m × 6.6m). *Tons:* 2,162 bm. *Hull:* wood. *Comp.:* 850. *Arm.:* 2 × 68pdr, 28 × 42pdr, 28 × 24pdr, 28 × 12pdr, 16 × 6pdr. *Des.:* Sir Thomas Slade. *Built:* Chatham Dockyard; 1765.

The seventh ship of the name and the third first-rate ship so called, HMS *Victory* was launched in 1765, two years after the conclusion of the Seven Years' War, but she was not commissioned until 1778. When France signed a treaty of cooperation with the American colonies, *Victory* was made flagship of Admiral Sir Augustus Keppel's Channel Fleet and, on July 23, took part in an indecisive battle off Ushant (or Ile d'Ouessant, off the western tip of Brittany), where she lost thirty-five killed and wounded. She remained in the Channel Fleet for the next two years and was briefly assigned to Vice Admiral Hyde Parker's North Sea convoy squadron designated to protect English shipping from the Dutch, now allied with the French. On December 12, flying the flag of Admiral Richard Kempenfelt, she captured a French convoy off Ushant bound for America. In 1782, *Victory* was Lord Howe's flagship in the relief of Gibraltar. Paid off at Portsmouth the following year, *Victory* remained in ordinary for eight years.

In 1792, *Victory* became flagship of Vice Admiral Sir Samuel Hood's Mediterranean Fleet, which occupied Toulon (surrendered to the English by Loyalist troops) and captured Bastia and Calvi, Corsica, which Hood sought to use as a British base in 1794. The next year, Admiral Sir John Jervis broke his flag in *Victory*. With only half as many ships of the line as the French and Spanish combined fleets, Jervis consolidated his force at Gibraltar. On February 14, 1797, he sailed with fifteen British ships to intercept a large Spanish convoy guarded by twenty-seven ships of the line. In the ensuing engagement off Cape St. Vincent, the British broke the Spanish line and inflicted terrible damage on the Spanish flagship, *Principe de Asturias* (112 guns) before forcing *Salvador del Mundo* (112) to strike. *Victory* lost only nine killed and wounded in the battle. The British also captured the first-rate *San Josef* and the two-deckers *San Nicolás* and *San Ysidro*. Their success was due in no small part to Admiral Lord Nelson, then in HMS CAPTAIN. In 1798 *Victory* returned to Portsmouth, where she was considered fit only for a prison hospital ship at Chatham.

In 1800 it was decided to rebuild *Victory*, a process that took three years. On May 16, 1803, she became flagship of Lord Nelson's Mediterranean Fleet, Captain Thomas Masterman Hardy commanding. At this time Napoleon had begun formulating elaborate plans for the invasion of England, and Nelson was ordered to contain Vice Admiral Pierre Villeneuve's squadron at Toulon. Flying his flag in *Bucentaure*, Villeneuve slipped out in January 1805, returned, and sailed again on March 30. After picking up Admiral Federico Carlos Gravina's Spanish fleet at Cadiz, Villeneuve sailed for a rendezvous with other French forces at Martinique. Learning of his move, Nelson set off in hot pursuit across the Atlantic. In June, Villeneuve learned that Nelson had followed him, and he returned to Europe almost immediately. Nelson followed close behind, arriving off southern Spain four days before the Combined Fleet skirmished with Admiral Sir Robert Calder's fleet off El Ferrol.

Villeneuve arrived at Cadiz on August 21, and remained there, blockaded first by Vice Admiral Sir Cuthbert Collingwood and then, in October, by Nelson, fresh from meetings in London with Prime Minister William Pitt and First Lord of the Admiralty Lord Barham. Daunted by the prospect of an engagement with the British fleet, Villeneuve stayed put until he learned that Napoleon was relieving him of his command. At 0600 on October 19, the Combined Fleet — eighteen French and fifteen Spanish ships of the line — weighed anchor, and within two and a half hours, the news had been signaled to Nelson, fifty miles to the southwest. The fleet took two days to straggle out of Cadiz, and at first it seemed as though Villeneuve was going to make a run for the Mediterranean. But at 0800 on October 21, he turned back to face Nelson. Twelve days before, Nelson had outlined his plan of attack, "the Nelson Touch," as he called it in a letter to Emma Hamilton:

The whole impression of the British Fleet must be to overpower from two or three ships ahead of their Commander-in-Chief, supposed to be in the Centre, to the Rear of their Fleet. . . . I look with confidence to a Victory before the Van of the Enemy could succour their Rear.

On the eve of the battle, he concluded his remarks to his officers with the encouraging observation, "No Captain can do very wrong if he places his ship alongside that of an enemy."

In a move that might well have failed under any other commander, Nelson divided his fleet into two divisions, the weather division headed by *Victory* and the lee by Collingwood in HMS ROYAL SOVEREIGN. As the British lines approached the Combined Fleet, at 1125 Nelson ordered his most famous signal run up *Victory*'s masts: "England expects that every man will do his duty." *Victory* failed to cut off *Bucentaure,* but she came under all but unchallenged broadsides from *Redoutable* for forty-five minutes. Finally, at 1230, *Victory* let off a broadside into the stern gallery of the French flagship, though she was soon enfiladed by *Bucentaure, Redoutable,* under Jean-Jacques Lucas, and the French *Neptune.* (The Roman sea god was impartial at Trafalgar, which also saw the participation of HMS *Neptune* and the Spanish *Neptuno.*) Nelson had insisted on wearing his full allotment of medals and decorations, and at 1325 he was wounded by a French sharpshooter as he paced the quarterdeck with Hardy. In the meantime, *Redoutable* and *Victory* lay side by side, exchanging murderous volleys until *Redoutable* drifted into HMS TÉMÉRAIRE. Stuck fast between the unrelenting broadsides of the two British ships, *Redoutable* finally surrendered and *Victory* was out of the battle by 1430. Her mizzen topmast was shot away, many of the other masts severely weakened, and her bulwarks and hull considerably shot up. Nelson had been taken below, and at 1630 — having first been informed of the capture of fifteen of the enemy ships — the hero of Copenhagen, the Nile, and now Trafalgar, died.

British prizes numbered more than nine French and ten Spanish ships, including *Bucentaure.* Of these, two escaped, four were scuttled, and eight sank in a storm that hit after the battle. Casualties in the Combined Fleet totaled 6,953, as against 448 British dead and 1,241 wounded; *Victory* lost 57 dead and 102 wounded. Towed to Gibraltar by HMS *Neptune, Victory* sailed for England, reaching Sheerness on December 22, from where Nelson's body was carried to St. Paul's Cathedral for a state funeral. His death was not in vain, for with Trafalgar he had destroyed the French and any threat of a Napoleonic invasion of Britain. England would rule the seas uncon-

tested for a century. Defeated at sea he may have been, but six weeks later Napoleon's armies won a crushing victory at Austerlitz, and Napoleon would try the fate of Europe for another decade.

After a refit at Chatham, in 1808 *Victory* reentered service as the flagship of Sir James Saumarez's Baltic Fleet, which blockaded the Russian fleet and kept open the supply of naval stores from Sweden. Except for a brief spell escorting a troop convoy for the relief of the Duke of Wellington's forces in the Peninsular Campaign, she remained in the Baltic until paid off in 1812. Since 1824, *Victory* has served as flagship of the commander in chief at Portsmouth. In 1922 she was dry-docked and opened as a museum. She received her last battle wound in World War II, when a German bomb exploded in her dry-dock.

Bennett, *Nelson the Commander.* Bugler, *HMS "Victory."* Fraser, *"H.M.S. Victory."* Longridge, *Anatomy of Nelson's Ships.* McKay, *100-gun Ship "Victory."* Mackenzie, *Trafalgar Roll.* Schom, *Trafalgar.*

VICTORY

Sidewheel steamer (3m). *Tons:* 85 tons. *Hull:* wood. *Comp.:* 23. *Mach.:* steam, sidewheels. *Built:* England; <1828.

In 1828, English gin distiller Felix Booth commissioned John Ross to sail in search of the Northwest Passage. Ross had not held such a command since the return of his controversial expedition in ISABELLA and *Alexander* in 1819. For the expedition, he purchased the paddle steamer *Victory,* originally built for service between Liverpool, the Isle of Man, and Ireland. Ross raised her sides by 5.5 feet, which increased her tonnage from 85 to 150 tons, and he ordered from John Ericsson a high-pressure boiler of new, unproven design. *Victory* sailed from England in the spring of 1829. Passing through Lancaster Sound (which Ross once thought blocked by a mountain range), the ship sailed south through Prince Regent Inlet between Baffin Island and the Boothia Peninsula. By October, *Victory* was icebound at Felix Harbor on the east coast of the Boothia Peninsula, both being named for the expedition's patron. Ross's nephew and second in command James Clark Ross made overland expeditions in search of the Magnetic North Pole, which he located on May 31, 1831, in 70°5′N, 96°46′W.

Victory remained fast in the ice through the next winter, and in the spring of 1832, after 136 days of temperatures below 0°F, Ross decided to abandon the ship in Felix Harbor and seek help from the whaleships that plied Lancaster Sound. After wintering at Fury Beach, near the wreck of William E. Parry's *Fury* (abandoned in the ice in

1825), the party reached Lancaster Sound. On August 26, 1833, about ten miles east of Navy Board Inlet, they were rescued by the crew of the whaleship *Isabella*, John Ross's command in 1818–19. Remarkably, three of the crew had died in the course of the voyage, and only one of them after abandoning ship.

Ross, *Narrative of a Second Voyage in Search of North-West Passage.* Ross, *Polar Pioneers.*

USCGC VIGILANT (WMEC-617)

Reliance-class cutter (1f/1m). *L/B/D:* 210.5′ × 34′ × 10.5′ (64.2m × 10.4m × 3.2m). *Tons:* 930 disp. *Hull:* steel. *Comp.:* 50. *Arm.:* 1 × 40mm. *Mach.:* diesel, 5,000 hp, 2 screws; 18 kts. *Built:* Todd Shipyard, Houston, Tex.; 1964.

The scene of what the *New York Times* described as "one of the most disgraceful incidents ever to occur on a ship flying the American flag," USCGC *Vigilant* was a medium-endurance Coast Guard cutter built for law enforcement and search-and-rescue operations. Stationed at New Bedford, Massachusetts, from 1964 to 1988, her normal duties included evacuating ill or injured seamen from their ships, towing or escorting disabled ships and vessels, intercepting drug smugglers, and monitoring domestic and international fishing fleets.

On November 23, 1970, she carried five American representatives and their interpreter for a rendezvous in international waters with the Soviet factory ship *Sovetskaya Litva* for a discussion on fisheries issues. Because of bad weather, the Soviet ship had anchored in Menemsha Bight, half a mile off the southwest tip of Martha's Vineyard (41°22′N, 70°47′W), a violation of U.S. territorial waters that was overlooked. At Captain Vladimir Popov's request, Commander Ralph W. Eustis moored *Vigilant* alongside *Litva*. As the negotiations went on aboard the Soviet ship, Simonas Kudirka, a Lithuanian-born seaman on the ship, told Coast Guard officers that he wanted to seek political asylum. When his intention became known, the ship's officers radioed for instructions. Captain Fletcher Brown, Jr., Acting Commander of Coast Guard District 1, in Boston, decided to call Rear Admiral William B. Ellis, who was on convalescent leave. Ellis told Brown that if anyone attempted to defect, he should be returned to his ship, orders that Brown relayed to Eustis.

The Soviets and Americans exchanged visits during the day, and after the American delegation left the Soviet ship, Kudirka leaped to *Vigilant*'s deck. When notified of the fact that Kudirka had jumped ship, Ellis ordered him removed, by force if necessary, and authorized Soviet seamen to board the cutter to reclaim him. While still aboard *Vigilant*, Kudirka was chased down and severely beaten by seven Soviet sailors as the American officers and crew stood by. Ellis moved his ship away from *Litva* at about 2300 hours, with Kurdika and his jailers still aboard, but they were eventually returned to *Litva* in one of the cutter's launches. After escorting the Soviet ship out of territorial waters, *Vigilant* returned to New Bedford at about 0300 on November 24.

News of the forced repatriation sparked demonstrations around the country. The *Washington Post* wrote, "No more sickening and humiliating episode in international relations has taken place within memory than the American government's knowing return of a would-be Soviet defector to Soviet authorities on an American ship in American territorial waters." President Richard M. Nixon, who only learned of the incident in the press, called for a full report. Captain Brown was court-martialed for dereliction of duty, Ellis was removed from his command and asked to retire, and Eustis was reassigned and issued an administrative letter of reprimand. The incident led to a clarification of U.S. policy towards defectors and others seeking political asylum, and it provided some impetus for the nascent human rights campaign in Lithuania and the other Soviet Baltic states. Kudirka was imprisoned in Siberia, but his fate was carefully tracked by U.S. authorities. His release was eventually effected and he immigrated to the United States.

Vigilant remained stationed at New Bedford until 1988. After a two-year overhaul, she was reassigned to the Coast Guard base at Cape Canaveral.

Rukenas, *Day of Shame.* Scheina, *U.S. Coast Guard Cutters and Craft.*

VIKING

Bark (4m). *L/B/D:* 287.6′ × 45.6′ × 23.2′ (87.7m × 13.9m × 7.1m). *Tons:* 2,760 grt. *Hull:* steel. *Comp.:* 32–160. *Built:* Burmeister & Wain, Copenhagen; 1907.

Originally built as training ship for the Danish Schoolship Association, *Viking* was manned by about 160 cadets of the Danish merchant marine, who were housed in a 200-foot deckhouse that ran from the poop to the midships bridge deck. She sailed in the Peruvian guano trade until World War I, when she was laid up in Copenhagen for the duration of hostilities. Sold in the meantime to Det Forenede Dampskibs Selskab to train cadets for their ships, she made only short cruises after the war and was eventually laid up for lack of freights. In 1925 she was acquired by Gustaf Erikson of Mariehamn and sailed in the annual "grain race" from Australia to Europe. Converted for use as a storeship at Stockholm at the start of World War II, in 1946 she made her last run to Australia, sailing via South Africa with a cargo of lumber, manned by a crew of 32. By now, the sailing ship grain trade was all but dead, and in 1949 Erikson sold her to the city of Göteborg, Sweden, for use as a stationary schoolship with accommodations for 120 cadets. She continued in that work for many years before being converted to a floating museum and restaurant.

Hutton, *Cape Horn Passage.* Underhill, *Sail Training and Cadet Ships.*

VILLE DE MULHOUSE

(later *Andalucia*) Bark (4m). *L/B/D:* 312′ × 45.5′ × 24.6′ (95.1m × 13.9m × 7.5m). *Tons:* 2,798 grt. *Hull:* steel. *Built:* Chantiers de la Méditerranée, Le Havre; 1899.

Built for the Compagnie des Voiliers Havrais of Le Havre, *Ville de Mulhouse* entered the nickel-ore trade between New Caledonia and Europe, carrying patent oil, coal, and other cargoes outward. As with all deep-water sailers, she occasionally took advantage of favorable rates in other cargoes, such as when she loaded wheat at San Francisco in 1900. Sold in 1909 to the Société Générale d'Armament, she remained in service through World War I, though by war's end her routes were less standardized. In 1919 she sailed between Dakar, West Africa, and Brazil, returned to France to load for Montevideo, and in 1921 returned to San Francisco for wheat. The slump in world shipping forced her lay-up at Nantes from 1921 to 1927, when she was purchased by the Societá Anonymo Ganadera y Comercial Menendez Behety of Punta Arenas, Chile, and renamed *Andalucia.* Loading coal at Cardiff, she made the passage round Cape Horn and then converted to a coal hulk. Except for service as a barge during World War II, by which point she was owned by the Compañía Chilena de Navegación Interoceánica, she remained in this work until abandoned to the elements in the 1970s.

Villiers & Picard, *Bounty Ships of France.*

VILLE DE PARIS

1st rate 104 (3m). *L/B/D:* 177′ × 48.5′ × 23′ (57.9m × 16.4m × 7.5m). *Tons:* 2,347. *Hull:* wood. *Arm.:* 90–104 guns. *Built:* Rochefort, France; 1764.

Following the French defeat in the Seven Years' War, Louis XV's Minister of the Marine Etienne-François de Choiseul set about to rebuild the French Navy. Between 1763 and 1771, the number of French ships of the line rose from about thirty-five to sixty-four, and in 1771 there were also fifty frigates operational. One of the first of the new ships was *Ville de Paris,* which had been laid down in 1757 but was not completed until after the war. Originally rated as a 90-gun ship, she was subsequently enlarged to carry 104 guns (some authorities say 120 guns) during the reign of Louis XVI.

Hostilities with Great Britain resumed in 1778, when France decided to support actively the aspirations of Brit-

Thomas Whitcombe's depiction of Admiral de Grasse's surrender of his flagship VILLE DE PARIS *to a fleet under Rear Admiral Sir George B. Rodney at the Battle of the Saintes, off the island of Dominica (April 12, 1782). Only seven months earlier, de Grasse's fleet had ensured a colonial victory in the American war of independence. Courtesy National Maritime Museum, Greenwich.*

ain's American colonies in their war of independence. The naval war was truly global, and there were major campaigns in North America, the West Indies, the Indian Ocean, and in European waters. On July 23, 1778, a French fleet under Comte d'Orvilliers sailed from Brest for a month-long cruise to watch the British. Two days later the French came in contact with a British fleet under Admiral the Honourable Augustus Keppel, flying his flag in HMS VICTORY. For two days d'Orvilliers tried to avoid battle, but the two fleets met in a bloody though inconclusive engagement on July 27. The French lost 161 dead and 513 wounded to 133 British killed and 373 wounded before the two fleets returned to their respective homeports.

In March 1781, *Ville de Paris* sailed from Brest as flagship of a convoy led by Admiral François Joseph Paul Comte de Grasse bound for the island of Martinique. On April 28 land was sighted, as was a British fleet under Rear Admiral Samuel Hood. A skirmish developed between the British and French fleets, but the French convoy reached Fort de France unscathed. De Grasse later attempted to land 1,200 troops on St. Lucia, immediately south of Martinique, but these were repulsed by the British. He had more luck at Tobago, which capitulated on June 2. On July 26, the French fleet arrived at Cap François, Haiti, to rendezvous with four ships under Rear Admiral Comte de Guichen (who had commanded *Ville de Paris* at Ushant) and to receive intelligence on the situation unfolding in North America.

The British Army under Major General Charles Cornwallis had been ordered into a defensive position on the Yorktown Peninsula of Virginia in Chesapeake Bay. Moving with dispatch, de Grasse sailed from Haiti on August 2 with twenty-eight ships of the line, and at the end of the month 3,300 French troops landed near the mouth of the James River. Four ships were detailed to guard the York and James Rivers and to prevent Cornwallis from fleeing south. On September 5, an English fleet of nineteen ships under Rear Admiral Thomas Graves arrived from New York. The French fleet stood out of the bay in some disorder, but Graves was unable to bring his ships to bear and the French led the British fleet away from the bay. Although they suffered more casualties — about 200 French dead to 94 British — light airs over the following few days prevented a renewal of the battle, and by September 10 de Grasse was back in the Chesapeake. Caught between the French fleet and the Continental Army, on October 19 Cornwallis surrendered. The independence declared by the United States five years before was now secure.

On November 5, de Grasse sailed for the Caribbean. Adverse winds twice kept him from an assault on Bar-

bados, and he had to content himself with taking the islands of St. Kitts and Nevis at the end of January 1782. On January 25, Admiral Sir Samuel Hood (flying his flag in the 90-gun HMS BARFLEUR) seized the anchorage at Basse Terre from de Grasse, although the English garrison on St. Kitts was forced to surrender on February 12. De Grasse's ultimate aim was to join a Spanish fleet at Cap François and invade Jamaica.

This plan was frustrated by a British fleet under Admiral George Brydges Rodney in HMS *Formidable* (98 guns), with Hood as second in command. On April 12, the British and French fleets met just south of the Iles de Saintes in the channel between Dominica and Guadeloupe. Failure of the French to avoid battle with a superior force, or to engage it on more equal terms, stemmed from de Grasse's decision to rescue the *Zélé* (74), which had been dismasted a few days before in collision with *Ville de Paris*. Battle was joined at about 0830. The British quickly broke the ragged French line and isolated a number of French ships. The battle continued until 1829 when *Ville de Paris,* her ammunition spent, surrendered, the last of five ships to do so. Hood complained that had Rodney given the signal for a general chase, "I am very confident we should have had twenty sail of the enemy's ships before dark." Although the remainder of the French fleet retired to Haiti in reasonably good order, plans for more campaigns in the West Indies were abandoned.

Ironically, the only French ships to reach Jamaica were those captured at the Battle of the Saintes, including *Ville de Paris.* On August 15, she sailed as part of a large convoy bound for England under Admiral Graves. From September 16 to 19, the fleet was overtaken by a hurricane in which a number of transports and fighting ships were lost, the latter including *Ville de Paris* (from which there was only one survivor), the French prizes *Glorieux, Centaur,* and *Hector,* Graves's flagship *Ramillies* (all 74-gun ships), and the storeship *Cornwallis.*

Clowes, *Royal Navy.* Gardiner, *Line of Battle.* Hepper, *British Warship Losses in the Age of Sail.*

USS VINCENNES

Sloop of war (3m). *L/B/D:* 127′ × 33.8′ × 16.5′ (38.7m × 10.3m × 5m). *Tons:* 780 reg. *Hull:* wood. *Comp.:* 80. *Arm.:* 20 × 32pdr. *Built:* New York Navy Yard, Brooklyn, N.Y.; 1826.

Named for the Indiana fort twice captured by American forces under George Rogers Clark during the American Revolution, the first USS *Vincennes* had one of the most extraordinary careers of any ship in the U.S. Navy. Dispatched to the Pacific Squadron under Master Comman-

Often attributed to Captain Charles Wilkes, this engraving of the USS VINCENNES *in Disappointment Bay, Antarctica, was probably based on a sketch by the commander of the U.S. South Sea Surveying and Exploring Expedition of 1838–42. Courtesy Peabody Essex Museum, Salem, Massachusetts.*

dant William Bolton Finch one week after her commissioning, in 1828 she was ordered to look after American merchant and whaling interests in the Marquesas, Tahiti, and Sandwich Islands (Hawaii). From Hawaii she sailed east, stopping at Macao, Manila, Cape Town, and St. Helena before returning to New York on June 8, 1830, the first U.S. Navy ship to circumnavigate the globe. The following year found her on patrol in the Caribbean under Commander Edward R. Shubrick. In 1833–34, she made a second circumnavigation, under Commander Alexander S. Wadsworth, calling at Guam and Sumatra, among other places, en route.

In 1838, *Vincennes* was chosen as flagship of Lieutenant Charles Wilkes's United States South Sea Surveying and Exploring Expedition, also known as the Great United States Exploring Expedition. The origins of the Wilkes expedition can be traced to John Cleves Symmes, Jr., who believed that "the earth is hollow and habitable within . . . and that it is open at the poles twelve or sixteen degrees." This theory attained widespread currency, but Congress declined to sponsor a voyage of exploration. Symmes and his theory eventually passed into memory, but the cause of a polar expedition was taken up by his erstwhile disciple, Jeremiah Reynolds. In 1836, Congress reversed itself, and Commodore Thomas ap Catesby Jones was appointed to lead the expedition. Exhausted by

the endless politics of the preparations, Jones resigned, and command eventually fell to Wilkes.

On August 18, 1838, the expedition sailed with six vessels, *Vincennes*, *Peacock* (under Lieutenant William Hudson), *Porpoise* (Lieutenant Cadwallader Ringgold), *Relief*, and schooners *Flying Fish* and *Sea Gull*. Calling at Madeira, Cape Verde, Rio de Janeiro, and Rio Negro, they rounded Cape Horn and put in at Orange Harbor on Tierra del Fuego. *Vincennes* remained here while *Relief* surveyed the Strait of Magellan and the four remaining ships sailed south on February 25, 1839. *Porpoise* and *Sea Gull* skirted the (unseen) southeast coast of the Palmer Peninsula as far as 63°10′S on March 15. *Flying Fish* knocked its way south through the ice to 70°S, 101°11′W on March 22, and *Peacock* attained 68°08′S, 97°58′W. *Sea Gull* was later lost in a storm, but the other ships rendezvoused at Valparaiso in May, before continuing to Callao.

The ships reached the Tuamotus group in mid-August and worked their way west towards Tahiti, arriving on September 11. A month later they continued to Samoa and from there to Sydney, Australia. *Relief* was sent home, and the other ships were readied for their second voyage south. On January 11, 1840, they encountered an ice barrier, and five days later in 65°18′S, 157°36′E, Henry Eld and William Reynolds in *Peacock* sighted two mountains (named for them), which confirmed the existence of a continental landmass. On January 28, land was also sighted from *Vincennes,* then in 66°35′S, 140°30′E. Wilkes wrote that "it could be seen extending to the east and west of our position, and now that all were convinced of its existence, I gave the land the name of the Antarctic Continent." By the next year, the region had appeared on German maps as Wilkes Land.

After regrouping in New Zealand, the expedition sailed for Hawaii, spending six months en route surveying the Fiji Islands before arriving at Honolulu on September 23, 1841. In December, *Peacock* and *Flying Fish* left to reconnoiter islands in the central Pacific before proceeding to a rendezvous at the Columbia River. In April 1842, *Vincennes* and *Porpoise* sailed for the Pacific Northwest and surveyed the waters around Vancouver Island and the Strait of Juan de Fuca. Returning to the Columbia River in August, Wilkes learned that *Peacock* had wrecked on the bar on July 17, though without loss of life. *Vincennes* was sent to San Francisco while a party of nine men, including the geologist James Dwight Dana, botanist William Dunlop Brackenridge, and naturalist-painter Titian Peale, marched overland to San Francisco. *Peacock*'s crew were put aboard a purchased vessel renamed *Oregon.* The squadron sailed for Hawaii in November, and from there the ships made their way west via Wake (where the islands of Wilkes and Peale were named), Manila, Singapore, Cape Town, and eventually New York, where they arrived on June 10, 1842.

Much of the expedition's collections had preceded the ships home, having been sent to Philadelphia from various ports en route. The task of conservation and display fell to the fledgling Smithsonian Institution, established with a half-million-dollar bequest from an Englishman, James Smithson. At first, the scientific achievements paled in comparison with the public enthusiasm for the various courts-martial that began shortly after the ship's return, all centering on the conduct of Lieutenant Wilkes. The choice of the relatively junior officer as expedition leader had been questioned early on, for despite his industry and scientific attainments, he was a poor commander whose conduct, in the words of William Stanton, "in one incident after another created a bond of unity [among his subordinates] that could hardly have existed under a more popular commander."

Little the worse for wear, *Vincennes* was soon assigned to the Home Squadron, and under Commander Franklin Buchanan, she cruised the West Indies and Caribbean until 1844. The next year *Vincennes* and USS *Columbus* were sent to the Orient with orders to open trade with Japan. The squadron arrived at Edo (Tokyo) on July 21, 1846, but they were denied permission even to land, much less negotiate; Commodore James Biddle was obliged to leave after ten days. *Vincennes* was laid up at New York from 1847 to 1849, when she sailed again for a two-year stint with the Pacific Squadron. The following year, she was named the flagship of the United States Surveying Expedition to the North Pacific Ocean. Under Commander John Rodgers, she sailed with *Porpoise* via the Cape of Good Hope to chart parts of the Indian Ocean, the Bonins, and Ladrones in the South China Sea, and the Ryukyu and Kurile Islands (south and north of Japan). In 1855, the expedition sailed through the Bering Strait and 400 miles west to 176°E, farther into the Bering Sea than any ships before them.

In 1857, *Vincennes* joined the antislavery patrol on the African station, and from June 1861 to the end of the Civil War she served with the Gulf Coast Blockading Squadron between Pensacola and the Mississippi River. She was sold at Boston in 1867.

Bartlett, "Commodore James Biddle and the First Naval Mission to Japan." Johnson, *Thence round Cape Horn.* Lundeberg & Wegner, "Not for Conquest but Discovery." Stanton, *Great U.S. Exploring Expedition.* U.S. Navy, *DANFS.*

USS VINCENNES (CG-49)

Ticonderoga-class guided-missile cruiser. *L/B/D:* 532.5′ × 55′ × 31.5′ (162.3m × 16.8m × 9.6m). *Tons:* 9,589 disp. *Hull:* steel. *Comp.:* 360. *Arm.:* 8 × Harpoon missile launchers (2 × 4), 2 × SAM/AS missile launchers; 2 × 5″, 2 × Phalanx, 4 × 12.7mm mg; 6 × 13″TT; 1–2 helicopters. *Mach.:* gas turbines, 86,000 shp, 2 screws; 30 kts. *Built:* Ingalls Shipbuilding, Pascagoula, Miss.; 1983.

The advent of missiles has had a profound impact on military technology in the last twenty years, but it is nowhere more dramatically seen than in the design of surface warships. Even as the World War II–era 16-inch-gun battleships IOWA, *New Jersey,* MISSOURI, and *Wisconsin* were being recommissioned in the 1980s, the Navy was launching the *Ticonderoga*-class guided-missile cruisers, whose largest guns were only 5 inches. Rather, their primary armament consisted of surface-to-surface, surface-to-air, and antisubmarine missile systems, supplemented by six 324-millimeter torpedo tubes and two Phalanx guns capable of firing 3,000 rounds per minute. Their real strength was in their Aegis fire-control system, which is named for Zeus's shield. As a result, introduction of *Ticonderoga*-class ships enabled carrier groups to reduce the number of combat air patrols flown to protect the task force.

Assigned to the Sixth Fleet in the Mediterranean, the fourth USS *Vincennes* first saw active service in March and April of 1986. At that time she was deployed in operations off Libya in the Gulf of Sidra during which time U.S. land- and carrier-based aircraft destroyed military installations in Tripoli. This action was in retaliation for Libyan involvement in a terrorist attack on a nightclub in Berlin, in which a U.S. soldier was killed. In May 1988, USS *Vincennes* was dispatched to the Persian Gulf in response to reports that the Iranian government was positioning Chinese-made Silkworm missiles near the Strait of Hormuz. On the morning of July 3, one of *Vincennes*'s helicopters was fired on by three Iranian gunboats. The gunboats were engaged by the cruiser and the frigate USS *Elmer Montgomery,* which sank two and damaged the third. Five minutes later, at 1047, *Vincennes* detected an aircraft taking off from the civilian-military Bandar Abbas airport. The ship radioed seven warnings to the plane, which apparently went unanswered. Subsequently identifying the plane as a hostile F-14 approaching at an altitude of about 7,000 feet and descending, Captain Will C. Rogers III ordered two surface-to-air missiles fired. Tragically, the aircraft was an Iran Air Airbus A300 civilian jetliner en route to Dubai, climbing at an altitude of about 12,500 feet. All 290 people aboard the plane — 66 of whom were children and 38 foreign nationals — were killed. An official inquiry reported that the mistake was due to human error and that identifying the type of

> aircraft being tracked . . . is still a matter for human judgment. . . . Because of its long-range radar, [Aegis] gives operators additional time to react, to gather data and to make considered judgments. Operating close-in to a land-based airfield, however, these advantages can be severely eroded.

The tragedy heightened tension between Iran and the United States, which professed neutrality but was seen as favoring Iraq in the eight-year-old Iran-Iraq War. Captain Rogers retired, and *Vincennes* returned to duty with the Atlantic Fleet, remaining in service through 1997.

Baker, *Naval Institute Guide to Combat Fleets of the World, 1995.* Rogers & Rogers, *Storm Center.*

fleet escorts rather than for commerce raiding on distant stations, the cruisers' customary role, the *Arrogant*s were probably intended to be used for finishing off ships already disabled in combat. The warship revolution touched off by the commissioning of HMS DREADNOUGHT in 1906 quickly rendered these ships obsolete, and by World War I they were relegated to work as depot ships. *Vindictive* was rescued from obscurity when in 1918 she was chosen for a series of raids against the destroyer, U-boat, and naval aviation bases at Zeebrugge, Bruges, and Ostend in German-held Belgium.

Commodore Roger J. B. Keyes's plan called for sinking blockships at the mouth of the canal connecting Zeebrugge and Bruges, and at the entrance to Ostend harbor, which was also connected to Bruges via canal. The combined operation on the night of April 22–23 involved 165 vessels of all descriptions. Under Captain Alfred Carpenter, *Vindictive* was one of three ships assigned to disembark men directly onto the mole at Zeebrugge. She lay under close fire from German positions on the mole and far shore for nearly an hour before being recalled. The British managed to partially blockade the Zeebrugge Canal, though the tactical effectiveness of the operation was considerably overrated. In terms of morale, however, it was a huge success for the Royal Navy, whose operations during the war were widely viewed as more reactionary than preemptive.

The Ostend operation was less successful, and on May 10–11, Keyes mounted a second expedition against that port, with *Vindictive* and *Sappho* chosen as the two blockships. *Sappho* never reached Ostend, and *Vindictive* was sunk so that only a third of the channel was obstructed. Her hulk was broken up after the war, though part of the bridge was maintained as a memorial at Ostend.

Chesneau & Kolesink, eds., *Conway's All the World's Fighting Ships, 1860–1905.* Halpern, *Naval History of World War I.* Pitt, *Zeebrugge.*

HMS VINDICTIVE

Arrogant-class second-class cruiser. *L/B/D:* 342′ × 57.5′ × 20′ (104.2m × 17.5m × 6.1m). *Tons:* 5,750 disp. *Hull:* steel. *Comp.:* 480. *Arm.:* 4 × 7″, 6 × 4.7″, 8 × 12pdr, 3 × 3pdr, 5 mgs; 3 × 18″TT. *Armor:* 2″ belt, 3″ deck. *Mach.:* triple expansion, 10,100 ihp, 2 screws; 19 kts. *Built:* Chatham Dockyard; 1900.

Although ramming as an offensive tactic was no longer creditable in the late nineteenth century, the four *Arrogant*-class cruisers, of which *Vindictive* was one, were fitted with heavy bow rams for just that purpose. Built as

CSS VIRGINIA

(ex-USS *Merrimack*) Casemate ironclad (1f). *L/B/D:* 262.8′ × 38.5′ × 22′ (80.1m × 11.7m × 6.7m). *Tons:* 3,200 burden. *Hull:* wood. *Comp.:* 320. *Arm.:* 2 × 7″, 2 × 6.4″, 6 × 9″, 2 × 12pdr howitzers. *Armor:* 4″ casemate. *Mach.:* horizontal back-acting, 1,200 ihp, 1 screw; 7 kts. *Des.:* John M. Brooke. *Built:* Gosport Navy Yard, Norfolk, Va.; 1862.

One of the first screw-propelled warships in the U.S. Navy, the ship-rigged screw frigate USS *Merrimack* (named for a New England river) was built at the Boston

Navy Yard and commissioned in 1855. After service in the Caribbean and Europe, she served as flagship of the Pacific Squadron from 1857 to 1859, when she returned to Norfolk and was laid up. On April 17, one day after Virginia seceded from the Union, engineers were able to light off *Merrimack*'s engines; however, blockships in the channel prevented her moving from Norfolk. As the Gosport Navy Yard was prepared for evacuation on April 20, *Merrimack* was put to the torch and scuttled to prevent her capture by the Confederacy.

Northerners and Southerners alike knew that success rested in their ability to either close or keep open Confederate ports, and that to do either required ships. Recognizing his country's deficiency in this regard, Confederate Navy Secretary Stephen Mallory wrote, on May 9,

> I regard the possession of an iron armoured ship as a matter of the first necessity . . . inequality of numbers may be compensated for by invulnerability; and thus not only does economy but naval success dictate the wisdom and expediency of fighting with iron against wood.

On July 11, he formally authorized that *Merrimack* be raised and converted. Working to plans prepared by Lieutenant John M. Brooke, and under the direction of Lieutenant Catesby ap Roger Jones, an army of workers was put to work to salvage the hull (which had burned to the waterline) and machinery, and to create the central battery frigate CSS *Virginia*. The 170-foot-long casemate consisted of a shell of oak and pine 24 inches thick, sheathed by two layers of 2-inch-thick rolled iron, one layer laid horizontally, the other vertically. Rising at an angle of about 36 degrees, the sides were pierced for four guns on either side and three at either end (though she mounted only twelve guns), and were rounded fore and aft. The slightly submerged hull was also fitted with an iron ram. Her greatest defects were her deep draft — which made her as impractical for shallow waters as her lack of freeboard made her unfit for the open sea — and her engines, which had been inadequate even in the unarmored *Merrimack*.

On February 24, 1862, the flag officer, Captain Franklin Buchanan, assumed command of *Virginia*, which had been commissioned on the 17th. Work was still not complete when she got under way for the first time on March 8 on what should have been a trial run. Instead, escorted by the steam tugs *Beaufort* and *Raleigh*, *Virginia* stood down the Elizabeth River for Hampton Roads. Six miles away lay the Yorktown Peninsula, the lower half of which was occupied by the Union army. Five ships of the North Atlantic Blockading Squadron stood at anchor between Newport News and Hampton. *Virginia*'s first victim was the 24-gun USS CUMBERLAND, which opened fire at 1400 at a range of 1,500 yards. *Virginia* poured broadsides into the wooden sloop of war, then rammed and sank her at 1530. *Virginia* next engaged USS CONGRESS (44 guns), which had grounded stern to and could bring only two guns to bear. She was set on fire with incendiary shells and blew up later that night. In the meantime, the captains of the other Union vessels were making for Newport News. *Merrimack*'s sister ship USS *Minnesota* grounded and came under fire from *Virginia*, though the water was too shallow for her to close, and she disengaged at about 1700.

The Confederate ironclad was not undamaged. The sinking *Cumberland* had snapped off her ram, two guns were knocked out, her funnel was riddled with shot, and Buchanan had been wounded, leaving Jones in command. Anchoring for the night off Sewell's Point, Jones planned to finish off *Minnesota* the next morning. Unknown to him, the ironclad USS MONITOR had arrived at Newport News during the night. As *Virginia* closed with the stranded frigate at 0800 on the morning of May 9, the "cheesebox on a raft" steamed out to meet her. For four hours the ships exchanged fire, but neither could inflict serious damage on the other. *Virginia* attempted to ram the more maneuverable *Monitor*, but she delivered only a glancing blow. Although she maintained her structural integrity, two of her crew were killed and nineteen wounded. The Battle of Hampton Roads finally broke off at about 1215 when *Monitor* was ordered into shallow water by Lieutenant John L. Worden, who was temporarily blinded by shell fragments. Jones also retired, and so the first battle between ironclads ended, and with it the age of wooden ships.

Virginia underwent repairs at Norfolk for about a month, during which time Flag Officer Josiah Tattnall made her flagship of the Confederate States Navy. On April 11, she escorted CSS *Jamestown* and *Raleigh* on a mission to capture three troop transports destined for General George McClellan's Yorktown campaign. There was no other engagement between *Virginia* and *Monitor*, as the former was charged with protecting the James River, and the latter the York. As McClellan advanced up the Yorktown Peninsula, Confederate General Joseph P. Johnson ordered the evacuation of Yorktown and Norfolk. *Virginia*'s deep draft precluded her moving up the James, and she was blown up on May 11, 1862.

Lambert, ed., *Steam Steel and Shellfire*. Still, *Iron Afloat*. U.S. Navy, *DANFS*.

VIRGINIAN

(later *Drottningholm, Brasil, Homeland*) Liner (1f/2m). *L/B:* 538' × 60.3' (164m × 18.4m). *Tons:* 10,754 grt. *Hull:* steel. *Comp.:* 1st 426, 2nd 286, 3rd 1,000; crew 250. *Mach.:* steam turbines, 15,000 shp, 3 screws; 18 kts. *Built:* Alexander Stephen & Sons Ltd., Glasgow; 1905.

Built for the Allan Line's service between Liverpool and Canada, *Virginian* worked steadily until September 1914. During World War I, she was briefly requisitioned as an armed merchant cruiser, sailed as a troop transport for the Canadian Expeditionary Force, and maintained sporadic transatlantic service for Canadian Pacific, which purchased Allan Line in 1915. In 1920, she was sold to Swedish-American Line, renamed *Drottningholm,* and put in service between Gothenburg and New York. Over the course of the next few years, *Drottningholm* received new geared-turbine engines and her passenger accommodations were redone to cater to the expanding tourist trade.

During World War II, *Drottningholm* and her running mate GRIPSHOLM repatriated prisoners of war and wounded under the auspices of the International Red Cross, continuing in this work through 1946. After two more years with Swedish-American, *Drottningholm* was sold to the Panama-based Home Lines. Renamed first *Brazil* and in 1951 *Homeland,* she began service as an immigrant ship plying between Mediterranean and German ports in Europe, and either South America or the United States. She was finally broken up at Trieste in 1955.

Bonsor, *North Atlantic Seaway.*

VIRGINIUS

(ex-*Virgin*) *L/B/D:* 216' × 24.5' × 10.9' (65.8m × 7.5m × 3.3m). *Tons:* 442 burden. *Hull:* iron. *Comp.:* 100+ pass.; 52 crew. *Mach.:* sidewheel. *Built:* Aitken & Mansel, Glasgow; 1864.

Built as a Confederate blockade-runner, *Virgin* made only one voyage out of Mobile between June and August 1864. Following the evacuation of Mobile, she was taken to Gainesville, Alabama, and was captured there on April 12, 1865. In 1870 she was purchased by John F. Patterson and renamed *Virginius.* Fraudulently registered in the United States, she was employed as a gunrunner, first for Venezuelan and then for Cuban revolutionaries.

After a succession of masters, Annapolis graduate and Confederate Navy veteran Captain Joseph Fry was hired to skipper the ship. With a crew of 52 and 102 passengers, *Virginius* sailed from Kingston, Jamaica, for Cuba, on

The career gunrunner VIRGINIUS *was lost shortly after this picture was drawn in the fall of 1873. Captured by Spanish authorities in Cuba, 37 of her crew were tried and shot.* VIRGINIUS *later sank en route to the United States. Courtesy U.S. Naval Historical Center, Washington, D.C.*

October 23, 1873. Forced to put into two Haitian ports in succession for minor repairs, on October 31 she was within 18 miles of Cuba when she was spotted by the Spanish warship *Tornado* — coincidentally built the same year, at the same yard, and for the same purpose as *Virginius.* After an eight-hour chase, *Virginius* was overtaken near Morant Bay, Jamaica, and taken to Santiago de Cuba. Ten days later, 37 of the crew were tried as pirates and shot. In the diplomatic uproar that followed, Spain surrendered *Virginius* and the ship sank in tow of USS *Ossipee* off Cape Hatteras on December 26, 1873.

Allin, "First Cubic War." Hill, "Captain Joseph Fry of SS *Virginius.*" Wise, *Lifeline of the Confederacy.*

VITTORIO VENETO

Vittorio Veneto-class battleship (2f/2m). *L/B/D:* 780.2' × 107.8' × 34.4' (237.8m × 32.9m × 10.5m). *Tons:* 45,752 disp. *Hull:* steel. *Comp.:* 1,920. *Arm.:* 9 × 15.2" (3 × 3), 12 × 6.1", 12 × 90mm, 20 × 36mm. *Armor:* 14" belt, 8" deck. *Mach.:* geared turbines, 140,000 shp, 4 screws; 30 kts. *Des.:* Umberto Pugliese. *Built:* Cantieri Riuniti dell'Adriatico, Trieste, Italy; 1940.

One of a four-ship class, *Vittorio Veneto* was the first battleship commissioned by the Italian Navy since *Caio Duilio* and *Andrea Doria* in 1915 and 1916. Named for an Italian victory over Austria-Hungary in World War I, *Vittorio Veneto* was completed shortly before Italy's entry

Her decks crowded with hundreds of her crew, the powerful battleship VITTORIO VENETO *is en route to Egypt following Italy's surrender to the Allies in September 1943. Courtesy Imperial War Museum, London.*

into World War II. She fared poorly against Force H and the Malta convoys and narrowly missed being hit during the British air raid on Taranto on November 11–12, 1940. On March 28, 1941, flying the flag of Admiral A. Iachino at the head of five cruisers and thirteen destroyers about fifty miles southwest of Cape Matapan, Crete, she was crippled by an aerial torpedo launched by an aircraft from HMS *Formidable,* and she spent four months in repair. On December 14, she was torpedoed by the submarine HMS *Urge* while escorting a troop convoy, and she sortied only once more. On June 5, 1943, she was hit during an air raid on La Spezia, but after the Italian armistice in September, she steamed under her own power to Malta. Interned in Egypt until war's end, she was stricken from the Italian Navy in 1948 and broken up at La Spezia.

Breyer, *Battleships and Battlecruisers.* Stephen, *Sea Battles in Close-Up.*

SMS VON DER TANN

Battlecruiser (2f/2m). *L/B/D:* 558′ × 86.5′ × 29.9′ (171.7m × 26.6m × 9.2m). *Tons:* 21,300 disp. *Comp.:* 998. *Hull:* steel. *Arm.:* 8 × 11.2″ (4 × 2), 10 × 6″, 16 × 12cm, 4 × 8.8cm; 4 × 18″TT. *Armor:* 10″ belt, 2″ deck. *Mach.:* Parsons turbines, 79,007 shp, 4 screws; 27.4 kts. *Built:* Blohm & Voss, Hamburg; 1910.

Named for Freiherr von und zu der Tann-Rothsamhausen, a nineteenth-century Bavarian general, SMS *Von der Tann* was the German Navy's first heavy cruiser. Deployed with Rear Admiral Franz von Hipper's First Scout-ing Group, *Von der Tann* took part in the bombardment of Yarmouth on November 3 and of Scarborough and Whitby on December 16, 1914. The following August she took part in the ineffective operation against Russian forces in the Gulf of Riga. Returning to Wilhelmshaven, nine months later *Von der Tann* was again in action. At the Battle of Jutland, on May 31, 1916, she played a decisive role in the fierce action against Vice Admiral Sir David Beatty's Battle Cruiser Fleet. Hipper's fleet was spotted at 1530 that afternoon and battle was joined at 1548. As the last ship in Hipper's line *Von der Tann* engaged HMS INDEFATIGABLE, which was blown apart by a magazine explosion at 1602 and sank with the loss of 1,015 crew. Minutes later *Von der Tann* came under fire from the Fifth Battle Squadron's BARHAM and *Valiant,* her main armament being silenced by 1730. After surviving the night engagement with the British fleet, she returned to the safety of Wilhelmshaven, her war all but over. Interned at Scapa Flow on November 24, 1918, *Von der Tann* was scuttled on June 21, 1919. Sold to Cox & Danks, Ltd., she was raised on December 7, 1930, and towed upside down to Rosyth and scrapped in 1933.

Gröner, *German Warships.* Halpern, *Naval History of World War I.* Macintyre, *Jutland.* Van der Vat, *Grand Scuttle.*

VOSTOK

Sloop-of-war (3m). *L/B/D:* 129.8′ × 32.7′ × 9.6′ (39.6m × 10m × 2.9m). *Tons:* 900 tons. *Hull:* wood. *Comp.:* 127. *Arm.:* 28 guns. *Built:* Stoke and Kolodnin, Okhta Shipyard, St. Petersburg, Russia; 1818.

In 1819, Czar Alexander I ordered the dispatch of two expeditions for polar exploration. The first, under Captain Fabian Gottlieb von Bellingshausen (a veteran of Adam von Krusenstern's NADEZHDA expedition of 1803–6), was to sail towards the South Pole with the flagship *Vostok* ("East") and the 120-foot transport-turned-navy-sloop *Mirny* ("Peaceful," ex-*Lagoda*). The other — comprising the sloops *Otkrytie* and *Blagonamerennyi* — was to sail through the Bering Strait to explore the Arctic Ocean. The primary object of Bellingshausen's two-year expedition was "to carry out a voyage of discovery in the higher southern latitudes, and to circumnavigate the ice-belt of the southern Polar Circle." During the southern winter, he was to withdraw to equatorial waters.

Vostok and *Mirny* departed Kronstadt on July 4, 1819, and after stops at Copenhagen and Portsmouth, they entered the Atlantic Ocean on August 29, 1819, arriving at Rio de Janeiro on November 2. From Rio, the two ships headed for the South Georgia Islands, along the way searching for several features that were indicated on charts but which did not, in fact, exist. Passing South Georgia on November 16, the Russians named several nearby islands before continuing to the South Shetlands, near which they discovered the Marquis de Traversay Islands. By January 4, 1820, they had sailed to 60°25′S, 27°58′E when heavy ice forced them eastward. Crossing the Antarctic Circle for the first time on January 15 in about 3°W, they were no more than twenty miles from the coast of what is now called Princess Martha Land. As Bellingshausen's English editor wrote, "A few hours of clear weather here on this day would have certainly antedated the discovery of land by 110 years." Though they were forced below the Antarctic Circle by heavy ice on several occasions, on February 13 the sight of shore birds indicated land was nearby, although the nearest known bodies — Prince Edward Island and the Kerguelen Islands — were 1,200 miles away. (It would be another eleven years before the sealer Captain John Biscoe, sailing with *Tula* and *Lively,* actually spotted and named Enderby Land.) Continuing in their circumnavigation of the as yet unseen Antarctica, the Russians encountered land birds for the second time on February 24 (in 62°32′S, 57°41′E). On March 5, *Vostok* and *Mirny* (commanded by Mikhail Petrovich Lazarev) separated for their return to Port Jackson (Sydney), Australia, so that their parallel courses would fall between those followed by Captain James Cook in HMS RESOLUTION and Captain Tobias Furneaux in HMS ADVENTURE during Cook's second voyage.

Vostok arrived at Port Jackson on March 30, and *Mirny* on April 7, both remaining in port until May 8. Intending to sail north of New Zealand, the ships were forced south by contrary winds, and they passed through Cook Strait between North and South Islands. From there, they headed northeast for the Tuamotu Islands, where in early July they confirmed the position of, or put on the map for the first time, fifteen islands between 15°5′E and 17°49′E in about as many days. On the 22nd they put into Matavai Bay, Tahiti, for five days. En route back to Port Jackson, the Russians discovered Lazarev (Matahiva), Vostok, and Grand Duke Alexander Islands, among others. Repairs to the masts and rigging kept the ships in port for seven weeks, and it was not until October 31 that they resumed their cruise in Antarctic waters. Encountering ice at 62°18′S, 164°13′E, they turned east again, being forced north intermittently because of the ice. On January 10, 1821, they spotted a coast that they could approach no closer than fourteen miles, but which they named Peter I Island (now the Norwegian territory Peter I Øy), in honor of the founder of the Russian Navy. On January 17 they again encountered land, which they called Alexander I Land. Skirting the unseen Antarctic Peninsula, *Vostok* and *Mirny* turned northeast, sailing through the South Shetland Islands, whose extent they determined to be about 160 miles.

After stops at Rio de Janeiro and Lisbon (to transfer the Russian ambassador from Brazil to Portugal), *Vostok* and *Mirny* returned to Kronstadt on August 28, having completed a voyage of 751 days. They had spent 224 days at anchor, 527 under sail, and sailed more than 57,000 miles in the course of which they discovered twenty-nine islands — two in the Antarctic — and one coral reef and a lagoon. That part of the Southern Ocean lying between the Antarctic Peninsula in the east and Thurston Island in the west was subsequently named the Bellingshausen Sea.

Bellingshausen, *Voyage of Captain Bellingshausen to the Antarctic Seas.*

VULCANIA

Liner (1f/2m). *L/B:* 631.4′ × 79.8′ (192.4m × 24.3m). *Tons:* 23,970 grt. *Hull:* steel. *Comp.:* 1st 310, 2nd 460, intermediate 310, 3rd 700. *Mach.:* motorship, 2 screws; 19 kts. *Built:* Cantiere Navale Triestino, Monfalcone, Italy; 1928.

The second of three near–sister ships built for Italy's Cosulich Line (the others were *Saturnia* and *Urania*), *Vulcania* is considered one of the most successful passenger ships ever built. During her career she carried more passengers than any other Italian-flag ship. In the prewar years she had four classes and regularly called at ten ports: Trieste, Venice, Patras, Messina, Palermo, Naples, Gibraltar, Lisbon, Halifax, and New York; in the mid-1930s she also undertook Caribbean cruises. In 1937, she was given new engines, then the most powerful diesel machinery ever fitted in a ship, which increased her service speed to twenty-one knots.

Vulcania's wartime service began with special trooping duties during the Italian-Ethiopian war in 1935. She resumed her transatlantic sailings until Italy entered World War II in June 1940. Requisitioned as a troop transport, she sailed in support of Italy's North African campaign, and in 1942, under charter to the Red Cross, she repatriated refugees from East Africa. Italy surrendered in 1943 and *Vulcania* later saw duty as a U.S. troopship. Formally requisitioned after the war, she made six voyages for American Export Line before reverting to Italia. *Vulcania* made one voyage to South America in 1947 before entering express service between Genoa, Naples, and New York. When ANDREA DORIA and *Cristoforo Colombo* joined the fleet in 1955, *Vulcania* and *Saturnia* resumed their prewar schedule until 1965.

Sold to Grimaldi-Siosa Line and renamed *Caribia*, she ran as an immigrant ship between Southampton, Vigo, and Lisbon, and various Caribbean islands, before being put into Mediterranean cruise service. After stranding near Nice, France, she was sold to three different ship breakers in turn — Italian, Spanish, and Taiwanese — and arrived at Kao-Hsiung for scrapping on July 20, 1974.

Bonsor, *North Atlantic Seaway.* Braynard & Miller, *Fifty Famous Liners 2.*

W

USS WACHUSETT

Iroquois-class screw sloop (3m). *L/B/D:* 201.3′ × 33.8′ × 13′ (61.4m × 10.3m × 4m). *Tons:* 1,488 disp. *Hull:* wood. *Comp.:* 123. *Arm.:* 3 × 100pdr, 4 × 32pdr, 2 × 30pdr, 1 × 12pdr. *Mach.:* horizontal steeple engines, 1 screw; 11.5 kts. *Built:* Boston Navy Yard, Boston, Mass.; 1862.

Named for the Massachusetts mountain, USS *Wachusett* was assigned to the Atlantic Blockading Squadron in 1862. After service in the James River during the Peninsular Campaign, in 1863 she was made flagship of a "Flying Squadron" assigned to hunt the Confederate raiders ALABAMA and FLORIDA. Following a six-month refit, *Wachusett*, Commander Napoleon Collins, was dispatched to the Brazil station. On September 26, 1864, she sailed into Bahia. A few days later, CSS *Florida* entered port. In an effort to prevent an incident, the Brazilians stationed their fleet between the two antagonists. At 0300, on October 7, *Wachusett* weighed anchor and slipped through the Brazilian fleet to ram *Florida*. The ship did not sink, but in the face of cannon fire, the outnumbered crew surrendered their ship, which Collins towed from Bahia to Hampton Roads. The flagrant violation of Brazilian neutrality was endorsed by everyone from Secretary of State William H. Seward to the U.S. Minister to Brazil J. Watson Ebb, who had encouraged the taking of Confederate cruisers in Brazilian ports for more than a year. Later deployed to the Orient to search for CSS SHENANDOAH, *Wachusett* remained in the Pacific until 1867. Thereafter she saw service in a variety of distant stations until 1885; she was sold out of service to W. T. Garrett & Company in 1887.

Owsley, CSS *"Florida."*

HMS WAGER

6th-rate 24 (3m). *L/B/D:* 123′ × 32.2′ × 14.3′ dph (37.5m × 9.8m × 4.4m). *Tons:* 559 bm. *Hull:* wood. *Comp.:* 180 crew. *Arm.:* 28 guns. *Built:* England; <1739.

HMS *Wager* was an East Indiaman purchased specifically for Commodore George Anson's ambitious but ill-fated expedition against Spanish Pacific outposts at the start of the War of Jenkins' Ear. Named for First Lord of the Admiralty Sir Charles Wager, the mission's prime mover, *Wager* was one of six warships in the squadron, which also included two victualers. When the undermanned squadron sailed from Portsmouth on September 18, 1740, the crews included 260 invalids from Chelsea Hospital and 210 untrained marines. The ships were forty days to Madeira and another seven weeks to St. Catherine's Island off the coast of Brazil, where they remained until January 18, 1741. Although they intended to sail directly from there for Cape Horn, the need for repairs forced them to put into deserted Port St. Julian, where *Wager* came under command of Lieutenant David Cheap, formerly First Lieutenant in Anson's flagship, HMS CENTURION.

The ships transited the Straits of Le Maire on March 7, whereupon they were at the mercy of furious and relentless storms that kept them from rounding Cape Horn for more than six weeks. On April 24, *Wager* lost sight of the other ships, and for the next four days Cheap lay to at night despite the danger of doing so on a lee shore and despite standing orders from Anson to rendezvous at Juan Fernández Island. On May 13, *Wager* was in the Bay of Peñas, but "with only thirteen sickly hands" to work the ship, at 0430 the next morning she struck a reef and came to rest "not above a musket shot from shore." At first the ship's company was divided between those who went ashore in the ship's boats and those who stayed aboard sating themselves with brandy and wine. Eventually the latter group landed, too, but the crew gradually broke into a number of factions; some were in a state of mutiny against Cheap's authority while others simply ignored their fellow castaways and went off on their own. For five months they remained on inhospitable and barren Wager Island until the carpenter finished enlarging the longboat to accommodate all the survivors.

A major point of contention was whether they should

sail north, to try to overpower an unsuspecting Spanish merchantman and resume their voyage, as Cheap proposed, or return home via the Strait of Magellan, as gunner John Bulkeley suggested. Bulkeley's view carried the day, and on October 14 most of the survivors embarked in the longboat (named *Speedwell*), cutter, and barge. Ten of the men volunteered to return to Wager Island in the barge for extra canvas, but instead they rejoined Captain Cheap and three others who had stayed behind. Five deserters came back as well, but of these twenty, only four — including Cheap and Midshipman John Byron (later to circle the world in DOLPHIN) — would survive the seemingly endless struggle up the coast. Arriving at Santiago in January 1743, Cheap and the others remained prisoners of the Spanish, with the freedom of the town, for more than two years. Though they sailed for England on March 1, 1745, they were not home until the following year.

In the meantime, *Speedwell* and the cutter continued south with eighty-one men. On the night of November 6, 1742, the cutter was lost and her ten crew embarked in *Speedwell*. On the 14th they entered the Strait of Magellan and reached Cape Virgin Mary on December 16 and Port Desire four days later. From there they sailed across Golfo San Giorgio, on whose uninhabited shores eight men were abandoned (three eventually returned to England, in 1746). After landing briefly near Montevideo, *Speedwell* sailed on to the Rio Grande in Brazil where she arrived on January 28, 1743, with only thirty men in her crew. Most of these men eventually returned to England. Upon their return, a court-martial was convened to inquire into the loss of the ship, and the mate on duty at the time was reprimanded. Thanks to Anson's intervention, neither Bulkeley nor any of the others who left Cheap on Wager Island were tried for mutiny. In addition to eyewitness accounts by the *Wager*'s survivors, Patrick O'Brian's *Unknown Shore* is a readable and accurate, though fictional, account of the voyage and its aftermath.

Bulkeley & Cummins, *Voyage to the South Seas.* Byron, *Narrative.* Shankland, *Byron of the "Wager."*

USS WAHOO (SS-238)

Gato-class submarine. *L/B/D:* 311.8′ × 27.3′ × 15.3′ (95m × 8.3m × 4.6m). *Tons:* 1,525/2,424 disp. *Hull:* steel; 300′ dd. *Comp.:* 60. *Arm.:* 10 × 21″TT; 1 × 3″, 2 × .30-cal. *Mach.:* diesel/electric, 5,400/2,740 shp, 2 screws; 20.25/8.75 kts. *Built:* Mare Island Navy Yard, Vallejo, Calif.; 1942.

Named for a tropical food fish, USS *Wahoo* was one of the most successful submarines in the U.S. fleet during World War II. *Wahoo*'s first two cruises, in the Marshall and Solomon Islands, were marked by a lack of aggressiveness, and at the conclusion of the second cruise, Lieutenant Commander Marvin Granville Kennedy was replaced by his executive officer, Lieutenant Commander D. W. "Mush" Morton on December 2, 1942. Morton's dynamic leadership was evident from the start, when he articulated his vision of his crew's duty: "*Wahoo* is expendable. We will take every reasonable precaution, but our mission is to sink enemy shipping. . . . Now, if anyone doesn't want to go along under these conditions, just see the yeoman." There were no transfers.

Wahoo sailed on January 16, 1943, to a station off the Japanese base at Wewak, northern New Guinea, using an Australian school atlas as a guide. Eight days later, she sailed into Victoria Bay and engaged a destroyer at a range of 800 yards. The following morning, while en route for Palau, *Wahoo* sank a Japanese troop transport and then proceeded to sink twenty lifeboats and their passengers, an action for which Morton received considerable criticism from some of his brother officers. Pursuing a crippled freighter and tanker from the same convoy, he sank them later that day with his remaining four torpedoes. In recognition of his outstanding patrol, Morton ("the One-Boat Wolf Pack") was awarded the Navy Cross.

After two weeks at Pearl Harbor, *Wahoo* sailed on February 23 for the previously untested waters of the shallow Yellow Sea. Patrolling along the trade routes between Formosa and Japan, between March 19 and 29, *Wahoo* sank nine ships totaling 26,826 grt, the single best patrol of the war to that date. After only two weeks at Midway, *Wahoo* was dispatched to the Kurile Islands to intercept a Japanese fleet bound for the Aleutian Islands. She damaged a seaplane tender near Etorofu Island and sank three merchant ships before returning to Pearl Harbor. A two-month overhaul at San Diego brought about a change in luck for *Wahoo,* and on her next patrol, in the Sea of Okhotsk and Sea of Japan, ten of her torpedoes either broached or failed to explode on impact. Returning to the Sea of Japan for her sixth patrol, *Wahoo* was apparently sunk by an antisubmarine aircraft patrol in the Strait of La Pérouse on October 11. Postwar analysis of Japanese and American records credited *Wahoo* under Morton with nineteen ships — including four on her last patrol — and two under Kennedy, a stunning achievement for only fourteen months of combat duty.

O'Kane, "*Wahoo.*" Sterling, *Wake of the "Wahoo."*

WALK-IN-THE-WATER

Steamboat (1f/2m). *L/B/D:* 145' od × 32' ew × 6.5' (44.2m × 9.8m × 2m). *Tons:* 338 om. *Comp.:* 150–200 pass. *Mach.:* high-pressure steam engine, 73 hp, sidewheels; 7 kts. *Built:* Noah Brown, Black Rock, N.Y.; 1818.

Built for passenger service between Black Rock, New York, and Detroit, *Walk-in-the-Water* was the first steamboat on the upper Great Lakes above Niagara Falls. Black Rock was the terminus for the portage of goods between Lake Ontario and Lake Erie, which are separated by a vertical drop of 325 feet over 27 miles. (The opening of the Welland Canal put an end to the portage in 1833.) The consortium that underwrote the construction of *Walk-in-the-Water* included Noah Brown, a noted New York shipbuilder with prior experience on the Great Lakes. He had supervised construction of SARATOGA, Lieutenant Thomas MacDonough's flagship at the Battle of Lake Champlain in 1814, and he and his brother had built the FULTON STEAM FRIGATE the same year. *Walk-in-the-Water*'s engine was built by Robert McQueen in New York City and transported via Hudson River sloop to Albany and from there overland to Buffalo.

Named for a Wyandotte Indian chief, *Walk-in-the-Water* entered service in the summer of 1818. With her low horsepower, she was unable to buck the current on the Niagara River and had to be towed by a span of oxen from Black Rock to Buffalo. On her maiden voyage, she left Black Rock on August 23, 1818, with 29 passengers, calling in Dunkirk, Erie, Cleveland, Sandusky Bay, and, on August 27, Detroit. The return trip was made in 44 hours. Fares between Buffalo and Detroit were $18 for cabin passengers (this was later cut to $15 in response to competition from Great Lakes schooners) and $7 for steerage. When full, the steamboat carried about 150 passengers, though she carried 200 passengers for Mackinac and Green Bay in August 1821 on her first trip into Lake Michigan. This proved to be *Walk-in-the-Water*'s last season. On October 31, she left Black Rock for Detroit with 18 passengers. Encountering a stiff gale just 20 miles out, Captain Rogers (who had held the post since 1819) put back to Buffalo, but he anchored offshore rather than risk running into the harbor. Before dawn the following morning, Rogers cut the anchor cables in the hope that the ship would be blown ashore rather than broken apart and sunk by the storm-lashed lake. *Walk-in-the-Water* fetched up on the Buffalo shore at the foot of what is now Main Street. The vessel was a total loss, but the Lake Erie Steamboat Company immediately contracted to build a replacement vessel.

Musham, "Early Great Lakes Steamboats — The *Walk-in-the-Water*."

WANDER BIRD

(ex-*Wandervogel, Elbe 5*) Pilot schooner (2m). *L/B/D:* 85' × 18.5' × 10.5' (25.9m × 5.6m × 3.2m). *Tons:* 71 grt. *Hull:* wood. *Comp.:* 26. *Built:* Gustav Junge, Wevelsfleth, Germany; 1879.

The German government's pilot schooner *Elbe 5* was named for the river in whose North Sea estuary she sailed for the first forty-three years of her career. For periods of two to eight weeks, she carried a crew of five and as many as twenty-one pilots, who would board incoming ships and guide them through the tricky waters leading from the North Sea to the Elbe River ports of Cuxhaven and Hamburg. In 1924, she and her sister ship *Elbe 6* were traded to a Cuxhaven firm for the steel schooner *Emden*. (By coincidence, this schooner would also become world famous sailing under Irving and Exy Johnson as YANKEE.) Over the next five years, she changed hands several times before she was bought by the journalist Warwick Tompkins and his wife. To help pay for their new boat, they carried paying trainees on passages to the Baltic, Mediterranean, and Caribbean.

In 1936 they decided to sail her to San Francisco, and so with their two children, ages four and six, they sailed from Gloucester, Massachusetts, to San Francisco. Their 121-day voyage — a respectable time even for a hard-driven clipper ship — included twenty-eight days rounding Cape Horn and was described in Tompkins's memoir *Fifty South to Fifty South. Wander Bird* sailed throughout the Pacific for the next five years before the Tompkinses laid her up in San Francisco, took out her masts, and put a cabin on deck aft. The old schooner took a beating over the years, especially after she was sold in 1969 and moved to the foot of Johnson Street. Nine years later, Harold and Anna Sommer purchased *Wander Bird* and began a decade-long project to restore her to sailing form. After thousands of hours from countless friends who contributed time, skills, and fittings to her restoration, on June 1, 1981, the century-old *Wander Bird* sailed for the first time in forty years.

Sutter, "Rebirth of *Wander Bird*." Tompkins, *Fifty South to Fifty South*.

WARREN

Frigate (3m). *L/B/D:* 152' × 34.4' × 17' (46.3m × 10.5m × 5.2m). *Tons:* 690 bm. *Hull:* wood. *Comp.:* 200. *Arm.:* 12 × 18pdr, 14 × 12pdr, 8 × 9pdr. *Built:* Sylvester Bowers, Providence, R.I.; 1775.

One of thirteen frigates ordered by the Continental Congress in December 1775, and one of five built along the same lines as John Wharton and Joshua Humphries's

RANDOLPH, *Warren* was named for Joseph Warren, a patriot killed at the Battle of Breed's Hill, Boston, in June 1775. Command of *Warren* — with 18-pdr. guns, the most powerful of the new frigates — was given to John B. Hopkins, son of Esek Hopkins, commander in chief of the Continental Navy. (The elder Hopkins also flew his commodore's pennant in *Warren* until his dismissal in February 1778.)

Warren finally sailed on March 8, 1778, quickly taking two British supply ships before returning to Boston on the 23rd. With the possible exception of a cruise with the Massachusetts State Navy brig *Tyrannicide,* she did not sail again until March 13, 1779, in company with *Queen of France* and RANGER. The three ships captured the armed schooner *Jason* and seven of a ten-ship convoy under her guard. Nonetheless, Congress dismissed Captain Hopkins because he ended his cruise too soon, thus allowing his men to jump ship; crew shortages were one of the worst problems facing the Continental Navy.

Warren's next commander was Captain Dudley Saltonstall. While the ship was fitting out at Boston, the British established a base on the Bagaduce Peninsula in Penobscot Bay, 175 miles northeast of Boston. Congress named Saltonstall to command a huge amphibious force consisting of 39 ships and about 300 marines. Arriving below Castine on July 25, the Americans seized Nautilus Island and three cannon the next day. On the 28th, the Americans landed on the mainland, but following their initial victory, cooperation between the navy and army collapsed, and there was no follow-up. While the commanders temporized, a British force consisting of HMS *Raisonnable* (64 guns) and *Blonde* and *Virginia* (32s) arrived from Boston on August 13. In the face of this intimidating British force, Saltonstall panicked and his undisciplined fleet scattered upriver. The Americans lost their forty ships, all burned by their own crews save two that were captured, and more than 500 soldiers and sailors were killed or captured. The Penobscot Bay expedition was one of the single worst defeats of the Revolution, for which Saltonstall was court-martialed and dismissed.

Millar, *Early American Ships.* Miller, *Sea of Glory.* U.S. Navy, *DANFS.*

HMS WARRIOR

(ex-Oil Hulk C77, *Warrior, Vernon III, Warrior*). Frigate (2f/3m). *L/B/D:* 418' × 58.4" × 26' (128m × 17.8m × 7.9m). *Tons:* 9,137 disp. *Hull:* iron. *Comp.:* 700–709. *Arm.:* 26 × 68pdr, 4 × 40pdr, 10 × 110pdr, 2 × 20pdr, 1 × 12pdr, 1 × 6pdr. *Armor:* 4.5" hull. *Mach.:* Penn double-acting, single-expansion horizontal-trunk engine, 1,250 nhp/5,267 ihp, 1 screw; 14.1 kts. *Des.:* Isaac Watts, Thomas Lloyd. *Built:* Thames Iron Works, Blackwall, Eng.; 1861.

Often called the world's first battleship and the first ironclad, the revolutionary HMS *Warrior* was a superlative ship — but she was neither the first battleship nor the first ironclad. In 1858, the French Navy had ordered six iron-hulled ships; however, her limited industrial base required that the first three — including LA GLOIRE — have wooden hulls sheathed in iron. The British response was decisive. On the initiative of First Sea Lord Sir John Pakington, Surveyor of the Navy Admiral Sir Baldwin Wake Walker developed plans for what would be the most powerful and heavily armored ship afloat.

Warrior's great innovation was in being the first ocean-going warship to have an iron hull. As a result, she was also the largest warship of her day — 140 feet longer than the 120-gun three-decker HMS *Howe* (1860), and 82 feet longer than HMS *Orlando* of 1858, the longest single-deck wooden frigate (40 guns) ever built. *Gloire* and her sisters were a mere 256 feet. Perhaps more distinctive was *Warrior*'s graceful 6.5:1 length-to-breadth ratio; even *Orlando* achieved a ratio of only 5.8:1. Despite her extreme size, *Warrior*'s primary armament consisted of twenty-six 68-pdr. breech-loading guns. Twenty-two of these — eleven per broadside — were on the main deck within a central citadel, essentially an armor-protected box in the middle of the ship. Also within the citadel were four 110-pdr. breech-loaders. Just forward of the citadel there were two 110-pdr. and just abaft, two 110-pdr. and four more 68-pdr. Upper deck armament included single 110-pdr. bow and stern chasers and, working aft, one 6-pdr. and one 12-pdr., two 20-pdr., and four 40-pdr. On the basis of the heaviest guns alone, *Warrior* was classified as a 40-gun ship.

Warrior was not intended as a line of battleship. Rather, her superior speed enabled her to outdistance and outmaneuver any steam battleship she might encounter. At this stage in its development, mechanical propulsion was unreliable and engines were too inefficient to allow coaling for long-range cruising. Although designed to fight under steam, *Warrior* was rigged as a three-masted ship, and her 10-ton, two-bladed propeller was designed to be lifted free of the water, to reduce drag when cruising under sail. Located between the fore and main masts, her funnels could also be lowered to reduce wind resistance.

HMS *Warrior* was commissioned as part of the Channel Fleet on August 1, 1861, by Captain A. A. Cochrane. During her trials she received the accolade that defined her threat to the existing naval order: "She looks like a black snake among the rabbits" — the rabbits being the stubbier, high-sided ships of the line that still symbolized the might of the Royal Navy. *Warrior*'s active-duty service was confined to the Channel Fleet, where she could best face the French threat based at Cherbourg. During her

Although her engines, iron hull, and heavy guns made her the most powerful ship afloat when she was commissioned in 1861, with only a single gun deck HMS WARRIOR *was officially classed as a frigate. Several times saved from the breakers, the ship regarded as the world's first battleship was restored in the 1980s and is open to the public at Portsmouth Navy Yard. Courtesy Imperial War Museum, London.*

first commission, she sailed as far as Lisbon and Gibraltar, and made a tour around Britain.

Warrior's first refit took place between 1864 and 1867, after which she was commissioned again with the Channel Fleet, Captain Henry Boys commanding. By this time *Warrior* had already been eclipsed by the next generation of British ironclads — including the four-masted *Achilles* and five-masted *Minotaur*-class broadside ships. Her most remarkable accomplishment was in 1869, when she was assigned to help tow the floating dry-dock HMS *Bermuda* to the Royal Navy base at Bermuda, together with her sister ship *Black Prince*. Decommissioned in 1871, she underwent a further four-year refit during which a poop deck was added, she received new boilers, and her bowsprit was shortened. Commissioned into the First Reserve Fleet for eight years, *Warrior* made eight summer cruises, usually in home waters or to Gibraltar and the western Mediterranean.

Paid off and reclassed as an armored cruiser in 1883, *Warrior*'s star quickly faded. In 1900 she was stricken from the lists and became a hulk, seeing duty as a torpedo depot ship. In 1904 she was renamed *Vernon III* to free her original name for an armored cruiser. This ship sank on June 1, 1916, following damage sustained at the Battle of Jutland, and in 1923 *Vernon III* again became *Warrior*. An attempt to sell the ship in 1925 was unsuccessful and in 1929 she became a floating oil jetty at Llanion Cove, Pembroke Dock. In World War II she was briefly used as a depot ship for mine-sweepers, and in 1942 her name was appropriated for a light aircraft carrier, and she became Oil Hulk C77.

Interest in preserving and restoring *Warrior* began in the 1960s, but the Navy held on to the ship until 1978. The following year she was towed to Hartlepool and placed under the aegis of the Maritime Trust (and later the Warrior Preservation Trust). Initial financing for the restoration came from John Smith's Manifold Trust. A large number of the workers and artisans employed in cleaning and restoring the ship to her 1861 condition were provided through the government-run Manpower Services Commission. In 1987, HMS *Warrior 1860,* as she is officially known, was towed to Portsmouth and put on permanent public display at the Portsmouth Naval Base.

Lambert, *"Warrior."* Wells, *Immortal "Warrior."*

HMS WARSPITE

Queen Elizabeth-class battleship (2f/2m). *L/B/D:* 645.8′ × 90.4′ × 30.7′ (196.8m × 27.6m × 9.3m). *Tons:* 33,000 disp. *Comp.:* 925–1,297. *Arm.:* 8 × 15″ (4 × 2), 14 × 6″, 2 × 3″, 4 × 3pdr; 4 × 21″TT. *Hull:* steel. *Armor:* 13″ belt, 3″ deck. *Mach.:* geared turbines, 75,000 shp, 4 shafts; 24 kts. *Built:* Devonport Dockyard, Plymouth, Eng.; 1915.

One of a class of fast battleships that were the first to mount fifteen guns, HMS *Warspite* was one of Britain's most decorated ships in the twentieth century. Her first action was as part of the Grand Fleet's Fifth Battle Squadron at Jutland on May 31, 1916. Damaged by thirteen heavy shell hits, she was on the verge of annihilation when her jammed steering gear reengaged — possibly thanks to another hit. After the war, *Warspite* served with the Atlantic Fleet from 1919 to 1924. Following the Washington Naval Treaty prohibiting construction of new capital ships, she was the first of her class to be modernized. She next served in the Mediterranean (1926–30), Atlantic (1930–32), and Home Fleets (1932–34). She emerged from a second refit (1934–37) with a single funnel, remodeled tower, and two observation planes; her torpedo tubes were also removed.

The outbreak of World War II found *Warspite* at Alexandria, Egypt. After escorting a Canadian troop convoy across the Atlantic, she flew Vice Admiral Jock Whitworth's flag at the battles for Narvik, on April 10–13, 1940. Redeployed to the Mediterranean, she flew the flag of Admiral Andrew Browne Cunningham, revered as the Royal Navy's most aggressive admiral and known affectionately as "ABC." At the Battle of Cape Matapan, on March 28–29, 1941, *Warspite* helped sink the Italian cruiser *Fiume,* but she was herself damaged by German fighter-bombers during the evacuation of Crete on May 22. Under her own power she sailed via Singapore and Pearl Harbor to Bremerton, Washington, for repairs. By September 1943 she was back in the Mediterranean in support of the Allied landings at Salerno, Italy. There, radio-controlled bombs blew out her bottom. Again the aptly named *Warspite* made it home for repairs. Reassigned to the Home Fleet in 1944, she was mined just after the Normandy invasion in June, but returned to the coast of France by August. With fourteen battle honors to her credit, HMS *Warspite* was sold out of the Navy in 1946; but on April 23, 1947, she defiantly went aground in Mounts Bay, Cornwall, while en route to the breakers.

Parkes, *British Battleships.* Roskill, *H.M.S. "Warspite."*

WASA

Royal ship (3m). L/B/D: 180′ × 38.3′ × 15.4′ (54.9m × 11.7m × 4.9m). *Tons:* 1,300 disp. *Hull:* wood. *Comp.:* 145 crew; 300 soldiers. *Arm.:* 48 × 24pdr, 8 × 3pdr, 2 × 1pdr, 1 × 16pdr, 2 × 62pdr, 3 × 35pdr. *Des.:* Henrik Hybertson de Groot & Henrik Jacobson. *Built:* Royal Dockyard, Stockholm; 1628.

When she set sail on her maiden voyage, the ship of the line *Wasa* was the most impressive ship in the Swedish

HMS WARSPITE, *one of five* QUEEN ELIZABETH–*class battleships, had a long and distinguished career in two wars. She was heavily damaged at Jutland, in World War I, and again during World War II while campaigning in the Mediterranean. Courtesy Imperial War Museum, London.*

Navy. She sank within minutes, not a mile from land, and it would be 333 years before her salvage amazed the world and ushered in a new age of nautical archaeology and historic preservation. Named for the royal house of Wasa, the *Wasa* was built for the navy of Gustavus Adolphus (Gustav II Adolf), then the dominant military force in the Baltic, at the height of the Thirty Years' War. Sweden was at war with Poland because the latter's emperor, Sigismund III, an older cousin of Gustavus, was a pretender to the Swedish throne. The campaign in the southern Baltic began early in 1628, and by May there were thirty-four ships blockading Danzig to prevent the anticipated reinforcement of the city by Austrian General Albrecht Wallenstein's ships — should they appear.

Wasa was scheduled to join the thirty-four as soon as she was ready, and on April 10, 1628, she sailed from Stockholm with about 250 people aboard. Orders of the day read, "If anyone wishes to have his wife with him, he is free to do so here in Strömmen [part of the Stockholm channel] or in the Skärgård but not on a voyage where the objective is the enemy." In the light airs, the crew had to warp the ship out of the harbor — carrying an anchor ahead of the ship in a longboat, dropping it, and then pulling the ship up to the anchor. They continued the process until they reached Slussen, when the fore and main topsails and courses were set to the faint wind. *Wasa* had gone no more than 1,500 yards when a sudden gust laid the ship on her beam ends. Water rushed in through the open gunports and she sank immediately. The exact death toll is not known, but contemporary estimates put it at about fifty people. Captain Söfring Hansson was among those saved, and during his subsequent court-martial the Navy tried to assign blame to the Dutch master builder, Henrik Hybertson de Groot. Although blame was not firmly assigned, construction of Swedish warships subsequently came under more direct control of the Navy.

Salvage of the wreck began soon after the sinking, and the Englishman Ian Bulmer succeeded in putting *Wasa* on an even — if still submerged — keel. Although many were willing, the technical apparatus for raising *Wasa* was too primitive to raise a ship of that size from a depth of 35 meters (115 feet). The most successful salvage operations came in 1663–64, when Hans Albrecht von Treileben and Andreas Peckell raised 53 of the bronze guns, most weighing 1.5 tons, all of which were exported to Lübeck in the following year. Having yielded its most valuable cargo, interest in the ship waned until the publication in the 1920s of an article about the ship's loss. *Wasa* remained undiscovered until 1956, when, working from a surface vessel, amateur archaeologist Anders Fran-

zén succeeded in extracting a core sample of the hull. Swedish naval divers quickly confirmed the find, and efforts were soon begun to raise the ship.

Navy divers dug six tunnels between the hull and the mud into which it had settled. Slings were passed beneath the ship and attached to the pontoon vessels *Oden* and *Frigg*. On August 20, 1959, *Wasa* was pulled from the mud, and four weeks later the ship was transferred — still submerged — to an area where the water was only 15 meters (50 feet) deep. Over the next eighteen months, holes in the hull were patched. These included the gunports and the 5,000 holes through which iron bolts had been passed to secure the hull and which had rusted away. On April 24, 1960, *Wasa* broke the surface, and two weeks later she floated into a dry-dock on her own hull. In preparation for conservation and display, ballast and artifacts were removed from the hull, and by autumn she was safely housed in a museum building, where she remained under continuous water spray to prevent her timbers from disintegrating.

Wasa had three masts, square rigged on fore and main, with a lateen mizzen. Among her most obvious and unusual features were the sharp aft rake of the mainmast (about 8 or 9 degrees) and her steeply sloping decks. Both features were known from contemporary illustrations and models, but historians and naval architects generally believed that these were inaccurate exaggerations. The quarterdeck was 20 meters (65 feet) above the keel, and her mainmast probably 55 meters (165 feet) high.

As *Wasa*'s was the first recovery of its kind, virtually everything that was done was precedent-setting. The wood and all artifacts were permeated with polyethylene glycol, a preservative. Leather was treated in a similar fashion, while six sails had to be painstakingly unfurled in a shallow pool. Divers also rescued an additional 3,000 artifacts of various kinds from the wreck site. These included sculptural pieces that had fallen off as the iron fittings rusted. The need for such elaborate decoration was articulated by Jean-Baptiste Colbert, Louis XIV's pro-navy Minister of Finance: "Nothing can be more impressive, nor more likely to exalt the majesty of the King, than that his ships should have more magnificent ornamentation than has ever before been seen at sea."

Wasa's more than a thousand sculptures and fragments constitute one of the largest collections of mannerist-style seventeenth-century wooden sculpture in the world. Individual pieces include the magnificent stern decoration showing two lions rampant — originally gilt, and regilded upon their recovery. In addition to the House of Wasa's coat of arms on the stern, the carvings include renderings of biblical and classical themes: a series of figures from the Book of Judges, a representation of Gideon's victory over the Midianites, an image of Hercules, and, lining the bulkhead, two rows of Roman emperors, ten on either side of the bow. The bowsprit portrays a forward-leaping gilded lion.

Among the other artifacts were ship's stores and sailors' personal effects, which give a clear picture of daily life aboard ship. These include wooden plates for the sailors and pewter dishes for the officers, ceramic bowls, leather and felt clothing in sea chests, and more than 4,000 square copper coins called *klippingar*. Among the human remains found on the site were those of women and children, members of the crew's family who had joined the ship for the brief passage. One of the most popular attractions in Sweden since her recovery, *Wasa* is the centerpiece of the Statens Sjöhistoriska Museum on the Stockholm waterfront.

Kvarning & Ohrelius, *Swedish Warship "Wasa."* Naish, *"Wasa."*

USS WASHINGTON (BB-56)

North Carolina-class battleship (2f/1m). *L/B/D:* 728.8′ × 108.3′ × 35.5′ (222.1m × 33m × 10.8m). *Tons:* 46,770 disp. *Hull:* steel. *Comp.:* 1,890. *Arm.:* 9 × 16″ (3 × 3), 20 × 5″, 16 × 1.1″. *Armor:* 12″ belt, 6.3″ deck. *Mach.:* geared turbines, 121,000 shp, 4 screws; 27.6 kts. *Built:* Philadelphia Navy Yard; 1941.

On March 26, 1942, USS *Washington* sailed for Britain as flagship of Rear Admiral John W. Wilcox's Task Force 39; the next day, Admiral Wilcox was lost overboard, presumably after suffering a heart attack. Following work with the Arctic convoys through June 1942, *Washington* (under Captain Glenn Davis) sailed for the South Pacific. During the night action of the Naval Battle of Guadalcanal, on November 14–15, *Washington* sank the Japanese battleship KIRISHIMA in the first battleship action of the war. As flagship of Rear Admiral Willis Lee, *Washington* continued operations in the Solomons through mid-1943. She then took part in the landings in the Gilbert Islands in November 1943 and the Marshall Islands in January 1944. On February 2, she collided with USS *Indiana* and was out of action until June, arriving back on station for the landings in the Mariana Islands. In October she supported landings on Palau and Leyte, before turning to the sea lanes in the South China Sea. During the final Allied assault on the Japanese home islands, *Washington* shelled positions on Kyushu and was part of the massive armadas marshaled in support of the landings on Iwo Jima and Okinawa. Withdrawn for refit in June 1945, in September she transferred to the East Coast and helped repatriate U.S. troops in Europe. Put in reserve in 1947, she was

decommissioned in 1960 and broken up at Newark, New Jersey.

Musicant, *Battleship at War.* U.S. Navy, *DANFS.*

WASP

(ex-*Scorpion*) Schooner (2m). *Hull:* wood. *Comp.:* 49. *Arm.:* 8 × 2pdr, 6 swivels. *Built:* Baltimore(?); <1775.

Built as a merchant schooner for Baltimore owners, the schooner *Scorpion* was purchased by the Continental Congress and commissioned in 1775 under Captain William Hallock. On January 16, she and HORNET became the first two ships of the Continental Navy to put to sea, sailing from Baltimore to join a squadron under Commodore Esek Hopkins in ALFRED. During an expedition to the Bahamas, *Wasp* took part in the capture of Nassau, which Hopkins held for two weeks. The squadron sailed on March 17 and *Wasp* returned to Philadelphia. Operating from that port for the remainder of the year, she patrolled in and around the Delaware Capes, capturing five prizes and recapturing the American *Success* from a British prize crew. Following the fall of Philadelphia and the collapse of American resistance on the Delaware on November 20, 1777, *Wasp* was probably burned — together with ANDREW DORIA and *Hornet* — to prevent capture by the British.

Miller, *Sea of Glory.* U.S. Navy, *DANFS.*

USS WASP

Sloop of war (3m). *L/B/D:* 105.6′ × 30.1′ × 14.2′ (32.2m × 9.2m × 4.3m). *Tons:* 450 bm. *Hull:* wood. *Comp.:* 140. *Arm.:* 2 × 12pdr, 16 × 32pdr. *Built:* Washington Navy Yard; 1806.

The U.S. Navy's second *Wasp* was commissioned in 1806 under Master Commandant John Smith. The record of her first years is obscure, but in 1808 she was certainly operating along the East Coast, and by 1810 she cruised out of Savannah and Charleston. The following year, *Wasp* joined Commodore Stephen Decatur's squadron — USS UNITED STATES, *Congress,* and the brig NAUTILUS — and at the beginning of the War of 1812, she was stationed with these ships at Hampton Roads. On October 18, off the entrance of Delaware Bay under Master Commandant Jacob Jones, she gave chase to a British convoy of six merchantmen escorted by the brig-sloop HMS *Frolic* (22 guns). The two ships engaged at about 1130, and in a hot engagement *Frolic*'s crew boarded. The British ship was saved only by the arrival of the third-rate HMS *Poictiers* (74). *Wasp* was taken into the Royal Navy as HMS *Peacock,* and was lost at sea off South Carolina in July 1814.

U.S. Navy, *DANFS.*

USS WASP

Sloop of war (3m). *L/B/D:* 117.9′ × 31.5′ × 14.5′ (35.9m × 9.6m × 4.4m). *Tons:* 509 bm. *Hull:* wood. *Comp.:* 173. *Arm.:* 2 × 12pdr, 20 × 32pdr. *Built:* Cross & Merrill, Newburyport, Mass.; 1814.

The fifth ship of the name, and the fourth to see service in the War of 1812, USS *Wasp* was a ship-rigged sloop of war commissioned under Master Commandant Johnston Blakeley, in 1814. Putting to sea on May 1, she sailed for the English Channel on a commerce-destroying mission. En route, she captured five ships, sinking four and dispatching one as a cartel ship. On June 28, she engaged the sloop-of-war HMS *Reindeer* (21 guns), capturing her in a short, sharp action during which she sustained heavy damage herself. En route to L'Orient for repairs, she managed to capture and sink two more prizes.

Resuming her cruise on August 27, she captured three prizes by September 1, including one taken from under the guns of the third-rate HMS *Armada* (74). That night, *Wasp* fought the eighteen-gun brig *Avon,* but she was prevented from boarding the sinking ship by the arrival on the scene of three British ships. Between September 12 and 21, she engaged three more ships, sinking two and dispatching the brig *Atalanta* (8) to the United States. All trace of *Wasp* disappeared after October 9, when she spoke a Swedish ship.

U.S. Navy, *DANFS.*

USS WASP (CV-7)

Wasp-class aircraft carrier (1f/2m). *L/B/D:* 741.3′ × 80.7′ (109′ew) × 19.9′ (226m × 24.6m (33.2m) × 6.1m). *Tons:* 21,000 disp. *Hull:* steel. *Comp.:* 1,889. *Arm.:* 8 × 5″, 16 × 1.1″; 84 aircraft. *Armor:* 4″ belt, 1.5″ deck. *Mach.:* geared turbines, 75,000 hp, 2 screws; 29.5 kts. *Built:* Bethlehem Steel Co., Quincy, Mass.; 1940.

The only vessel of her class built, the U.S. Navy's eighth *Wasp* was the last of the so-called "treaty carriers" whose size was limited by the Washington Naval Conference of 1922. *Wasp* entered service on the East Coast, and in July 1941, she ferried Army Air Force planes to Iceland when the United States occupied that country. The rest of the year she spent on the North Atlantic Neutrality Patrol between Newfoundland and the Caribbean. Following the U.S. entry into World War II, *Wasp* made two voyages from England to the western Mediterranean; from here she launched British Spitfire fighters for the relief of Malta. On June 6, 1942, she sailed from Norfolk for the Pacific in an effort to shore up the U.S. carrier fleet, weakened by the recent loss of USS LEXINGTON and YORKTOWN. Joining a Support Force under Rear Admiral Frank Fletcher, *Wasp* supported the first Marine landings on Guadalcanal on August 7–8. On September 15, HORNET and *Wasp* (then the only operational U.S. carriers in the South Pacific) were again covering Marine transports headed for Guadalcanal. While refueling planes about 150 miles southeast of San Cristobal Island, *Wasp* was hit by two torpedoes from the Japanese submarine *I-119.* The resulting fires were uncontrollable, and Captain Forrest P. Sherman ordered the ship abandoned. She was then torpedoed and sunk by USS *Landsdowne;* 193 of *Wasp*'s crew died.

U.S. Navy, *DANFS.*

USS WATER WITCH

Sidewheel sloop (1f/2m). *L/B/D:* 150′ × 23′ × 9′ (45.7m × 7m × 2.7m). *Tons:* 378 burthen. *Hull:* wood. *Comp.:* 77. *Arm.:* 4 × 32pdr, 1 × 24pdr. *Mach.:* inclined condensing engine, 180 hp, 2 sidewheels; 11.5 kts. *Des.:* John Lenthall. *Built:* Washington Navy Yard; 1853.

The first assignment for the gunboat *Water Witch* was to undertake an extensive survey of the region around the River Plate, and in particular the Paraná River in Argentina and Paraguay. The ship sailed under command of Lieutenant Thomas Jefferson Page on February 8, 1853, and after several stops, she arrived at Buenos Aires in May. After ensuring the safety of the Argentine Confederation's General Justo Urquiza following the siege of Buenos Aires, Page began his official assignment. *Water Witch* was the first steam vessel to ascend the Paraná, Paraguay, and Salado Rivers, and her three years of surveys showed that these rivers were navigable by large, powered vessels, a fact that had great implications for the growth of Argentina, Paraguay, and Brazil. Though the expedition was a success, on February 1, 1855, Page ignored a Paraguayan decree forbidding him to ascend the Paraná River, and one sailor was killed when the fort at Itapirú fired on the ship. *Water Witch* returned to the United States in 1856, and in 1858 returned to the Plate as part of Flag Officer W. B. Shubrick's Paraguay Expedition, one aim of which was to negotiate a treaty and compensation for the dead man's family.

At the start of the Civil War, *Water Witch* was assigned to the Gulf Blockading Squadron and operated between Pensacola, Florida, and the Mississippi River.

Transferred to the South Atlantic Blockading Squadron, she operated mostly around Ossabaw Island off mainland Georgia until June 3, 1864, when she was captured near Bradley's River. Taken into the Confederate Navy, on December 19, 1864, she was burned to prevent her capture by federal forces.

Silverstone, *Warships of the Civil War Navies.* Wood, *Voyage of the "Water Witch."*

WAVERTREE

(ex-*Don Ariano N, Wavertree, Southgate*) Ship (3m). *L/B/D:* 268.5′ × 40.2′ × 12′ (81.8m × 12.3m × 3.7m). *Tons:* 2,170 grt. *Hull:* iron. *Comp.:* 28. *Built:* Oswald Mordaunt & Co., Southampton; 1885.

Laid down as *Toxteth* for R. W. Leyland and Company of Liverpool, the ship eventually known as *Wavertree* was one of the last and largest iron-hulled full-rigged ships built. Her builders sold her to Chadwick and Pritchard shortly after her launch, and she spent three years in the jute trade as *Southgate.* Although she had already changed hands, in 1888 Leyland bought back their old ship and renamed her *Wavertree* (for a Liverpool suburb). An ocean wanderer, *Wavertree* loaded a wide variety of cargoes in ports the world over. On her first voyage for Leyland, she sailed from Port Pirie, Australia, with 28,748 bags (122,900 bushels) of wheat, the largest load ever carried in a sailing ship to that time. On other voyages, she freighted salt from Hamburg to Calcutta, guano from Chile to England, coal from Calcutta to Mauritius, and case oil from New York to the Orient.

In 1910, *Wavertree* changed hands twice, but on May 26 she sailed from Cardiff for Valparaiso with coal. Severely damaged while rounding Cape Horn, she put back to Montevideo for repairs. These completed, she headed for Cape Stiff — as the Horn was known — a second time, only to be driven back again, this time to the Falkland Islands, with five of her crew severely injured and her masts and rigging a shambles. Condemned at Stanley, in 1911 she was sold to Chilean interests and towed to Punta Arenas for use as a wool storage hulk. In 1948, her hull still sound, she was towed to Buenos Aires where she spent two decades as a sand barge.

In 1966, fresh from a survey of GREAT BRITAIN at Stanley, Karl Kortum found the old *Wavertree* in a backwater of the Riachuelo: "Black hulled, deep sheered, fore and mizzen lower masts still in place. Clamshell buckets were clanging in her hatches. She was in use, cared for, in a way alive. And big." Negotiations to save the ship were opened with the recently founded South Street Sea-

Launched into the jute trade, the long-lived ship WAVERTREE *almost ended her days as a sand barge in Argentina. Discovered there by ship preservationist Karl Kortum, she was rescued and brought to New York's South Street Seaport Museum. This picture, taken in 1983, shows her riding light with only her topmasts fitted. Courtesy Norman Brouwer.*

port Museum in New York City. The museum's chairman, Jakob Isbrandtsen, arranged for the ship's purchase and donation to the museum, and in August 1970, she was towed to New York. She has been undergoing restoration at the museum for the last quarter-century.

Brouwer, *International Register of Historic Ships.* Spiers, *"Wavertree."* Walker, *Champion of Sail.*

WESTWARD

Schooner (2m). *L/B/D:* 135′ × 27.1′ × 16.8′ (41.1m × 8.3m × 5.1m). *Tons:* 323 grt. *Hull:* steel. *Comp.:* 32. *Des.:* Nathanael G. Herreshoff. *Built:* Herreshoff Manufacturing Co., Bristol, R.I.; 1910.

Known as the "Herreshoff Flyer," *Westward* was designed by the "Wizard of Bristol" for New York industrialist Alexander S. Cochran. Under Charlie Barr, *Westward* compiled an astounding record in her first season. In April 1910 she sailed from Brenton Reef to Southampton in fourteen days. At the Kiel Regatta in June, she handily won the Emperor's Cup in a four-race series during which the Kaiser's *Meteor IV* suffered a broken bowsprit in a collision with *Westward* when the indomitable Barr refused to give way. That summer, Barr wrote to Nat Herreshoff,

> She is a splendid boat. Crossed over with some rather rough weather and got no water on deck, and practically on an even keel. She has not shown the least sign of strain and made no creaking inside, which I think is a rare thing in a boat crossing the Atlantic. She has started nine times and won eight without time allowance and one with time allowance.

Returning to Cowes, *Westward* continued her winning ways against British and German yachts until an arbitrary midseason change in her handicap rating made her unable to compete realistically.

Barr died suddenly the next year, and at the end of 1911 Cochran sold *Westward* to the Verein Seefahrt Hamburg. Renamed *Hamburg II,* she was laid up during World War I, and in 1919 she was purchased by Clarence Hatry, who restored her original name but raced her little. In 1923, she was purchased by the seaman-turned-millionaire Thomas Benjamin Davis, a native of the Channel Islands and holder of an Extra Master's ticket. Under Davis, *Westward* raced such celebrated competitors as BLUENOSE, BRITANNIA, and SHAMROCK V, and on August 5, 1935, she beat every other vessel in the Royal Yacht Squadron's Regatta, including a clutch of J-boats. When in 1936 his king, friend, and racing rival George V died, Davis declared *Westward*'s racing days at an end and cruised her. Davis died in 1942, and five years later, *Westward* was sunk in the English Channel, just as *Britannia* had been eleven years before.

Hamilton-Adams, *Racing Schooner "Westward."* Herreshoff, *Captain Nat Herreshoff.*

WHITE SWALLOW

Clipper (3m). *L/B/D:* 192′ × 37′ × 22.8′ (58.5m × 11.3m × 6.9m). *Tons:* 985 nm. *Hull:* wood. *Built:* Hayden & Cudworth, Medford, Mass.; 1853.

Built for the Boston firm of William Lincoln & Company in the year Carl Cutler called the "flood tide" of the clipper age, *White Swallow* was one of five clippers launched in or near Boston on March 26, 1853. Although of sharp design, her maiden voyage from Boston to San Francisco took 150 days. This was her worst run from an East Coast port, but her best time was only 110 days and the average for nine runs, 130 days. On many of her voyages she did return via other Pacific ports, including Honolulu, Manila, Hong Kong, and Shanghai. She also made several visits to Jarvis, Baker, and McKean's Islands in the mid-Pacific to load guano, and she made at least one call at Callao, Chile, for the same task. While she usually loaded finished goods for the passage out, on what turned out be her last passage, she was en route from Boston to Hong Kong with a cargo of ice. She sank about 170 miles southwest of Fayal on June 17, 1871.

Despite her unexceptional record, the "*White Swallow* case" gained notoriety for a passage from New York to San Francisco in 1865 under Captain Elijah Knowles. Although harsh treatment was not uncommon on clipper ships, Knowles and his officers ordered the crew to perform extremely dangerous work, such as working on stages hung over the side while the ship was rolling heavily at ten knots. After two of the men were lost overboard, the remaining crew seized Knowles and his officers and held them below for three days, only allowing the captain to take sights and make course corrections. Knowles finally signed an agreement that he would make no unnecessary demands and absolve the crew from responsibility for their actions. The ship arrived at San Francisco without incident after a passage of 136 days. Six of the crew were arrested and tried, but on the basis of the officers' own testimony and that of passengers who had witnessed the events, the judge found in favor of the crew, a verdict unique for the period.

Howe & Matthews, *American Clipper Ships.*

WHYDAH

Galleon (3m). *L/B/D:* ca. 100′ (30m). *Tons:* 300 bm. *Hull:* wood. *Comp.:* 50. *Arm.:* 18 guns. *Built:* 1716.

Named for the slave port in Dahomey, West Africa (now Ouidah, Benin), the merchant ship *Whydah* was a slaver that sailed between England, West Africa, and the Caribbean. At the beginning of March 1717, she was returning to London with a cargo "consisting chiefly of Sugar, Indigo, Jesuits Bark [the basis for quinine], Silver and Gold" (as much as £20,000 to £30,000 of the latter), when she was captured by the pirate Samuel Bellamy off Long Island, the Bahamas, after a three-day chase from the Windward Passage between Cuba and Hispaniola (Haiti). Bellamy made her his own flagship, and after taking a

French vessel in the Bahamas, he sailed for the Virginia capes. En route, *Whydah* was dismasted in a storm.

Bellamy captured a number of other vessels off the Virginia and Delaware capes and off Cape Cod. It was from one of these ships that he chose a pilot. The pilot agreed to guide the four ships to Provincetown, but on the night of April 26–27, 1717, the ships were caught in a furious storm off Wellfleet and ran aground. (Some say the pilot ran the ships ashore to save his fellow merchants from the pirates.) The pink *Mary Ann* ran aground off Eastham, while the snow together with the sloop *Fisher* sailed away. There were seven survivors from *Mary Ann* and only two from *Whydah*. About 130 crew were lost. The governor of Massachusetts dispatched Captain Cyprian Southack to oversee the salvage of the ship, but neither the weather nor the Cape Codders cooperated and after twelve days he gave up. The nine survivors were brought to Boston, and on October 18, 1717, eight were brought to trial for "Piracy, Robbery and Felony Committed on the High Sea . . . To the high displeasure of Almighty God, in open Violation and Defyance of His Majesty's good and wholesome Laws." Seven of them were found guilty and, after a month in prison during which the supremely pious Reverend Cotton Mather prepared them "for a return unto God," they were hanged on November 15.

In 1982, diver Barry Clifford began a quest to find the remains of *Whydah* and her cargo, which he estimated to be worth $80 million to $400 million dollars. On July 19, 1984, divers located a concentration of cannon and other artifacts from the ship, but it was not until September 1985 that he received the permits necessary to begin salvage of the wreck itself. Dozens of artifacts and millions of dollars in gold pieces were salvaged, but some historians and archaeologists criticized Clifford for putting treasure hunting — and profits — ahead of historic preservation. *Whydah* was one of several underwater sites in the 1980s that excited public indignation and led to passage of the Abandoned Shipwreck Act of 1987, which granted a measure of federal protection to historic shipwrecks.

Dethlefsen, *"Whidah": Cape Cod's Mystery Ship.* Vanderbilt, *Treasure Wreck.*

WIDDER

(ex-*Neumark*; later *Ulysses, Fechenheim*) Commerce raider. *L/B/D:* 498.6′ × 59.7′ × 27.2′ (152m × 18.2 × 8.3m). *Tons:* 7,851 grt. *Hull:* steel. *Comp.:* 364. *Arm.:* 6 × 6″, 1 × 3″, 2 × 3.7cm; 4″TT; 2 aircraft. *Mach.:* geared turbine diesel; 14 kts. *Built:* Howaldtswerke AG, Kiel, Germany; 1930.

Built as a freighter for Hamburg-Amerika Linie, *Neumark* was requisitioned by the German government for use as a commerce raider. Converted by Blohm and Voss, she entered service in December 1939, was renamed *Widder* ("Ram"), and was designated Schiff 21 by German intelligence. On May 5, 1940, she sailed under Lieutenant Commander Hellmuth von Ruckteschell (who later commanded the raider *Michel*). The fourth cruiser identified by the British (and thus known as Raider D), she was credited with the sinking or capture of ten Allied merchant ships totaling 58,645 grt. Among her victims were the Finnish bark KILLORAN (August 10) and the steamship ANGLO SAXON (August 21). *Widder* remained in the North Atlantic until returning to Brest on October 31. She spent the remainder of the war as a supply ship, and after the war she became a British prize. Sold back to Germany in 1950, *Widder* resumed work as a tramp steamer until she broke up off Norway on October 3, 1955.

Lund, *Raider and the Tramp.* Muggenthaler, *German Raiders of World War II.* Schmalenbach, *German Raiders.*

WILD WAVE

Clipper (3m). *L/B/D:* 207.8′ × 40′ × 20′ (63.3m × 12.7m × 2.1m). *Tons:* 1,547 om. *Hull:* wood. *Comp.:* 40. *Built:* G. H. Ferrin, Richmond, Me.; 1854.

Built for trade between the East Coast, West Coast, and England, the short-lived *Wild Wave* attained fame not for her own attributes but for those of her shipwrecked captain and crew. *Wild Wave* was owned by Benjamin Bangs of Boston, and her master was Josiah Knowles, whose most celebrated command was the Down Easter GLORY OF THE SEAS. On February 9, 1858, *Wild Wave* sailed from San Francisco bound for Valparaiso in ballast, with a cargo consisting of two chests filled with $18,000 in gold coins. Shortly after midnight on March 5, the ship ran aground on a reef off the uninhabited island of Oeno, about 80 miles from Pitcairn Island. The following day, her 30 crew and 10 passengers made it safely ashore, along with provisions, livestock, and sails. A week later, Knowles and six of his officers and crew sailed the ship's boat for Pitcairn, which they reached in three days, only to discover that it was abandoned. (The inhabitants had moved, temporarily, to Norfolk Island, 3,300 miles to the southwest.) As their boat was destroyed in the heavy surf shortly after their arrival, the seven men had no recourse but to make a new boat from local materials, using the few tools found in the islanders' abandoned houses, some of which they burned for the nails and other metal.

On July 23, they launched a schooner measuring 30

feet by 8 feet by 4 feet and which they named *John Adams,* the name taken by BOUNTY mutineer Alexander Smith after coming to Pitcairn. Embarking with three of the crew, Knowles sailed to Nuku Hiva on August 4, where his company found the USS *Vandalia.* Embarking in the sloop of war, they sailed for Oeno (where one of the castaways had died) and Pitcairn. The survivors were returned to Tahiti and eventually made their way back to New York.

Cutler, *Greyhounds of the Sea.* Howe & Matthews, *American Clipper Ships.*

WILHELM GUSTLOFF

Passenger ship. L/B/D: 683.9′ × 77.1′ × 47.6′ dph (208.5m × 23.5 m × 14.5m). *Tons:* 25,484 grt. *Comp.:* 1,465 pass; 420 crew. *Hull:* steel. *Mach.:* diesel, 9,500 hp, 2 shafts; 15.5 kts. *Built:* Blohm & Voss, Hamburg; 1938.

Named for a Swiss Nazi leader murdered in 1936, *Wilhelm Gustloff* was built for the German Nazi Party's Kraft durch Freude (Work through Joy) organization to provide low-cost vacations to German workers, a program initiated in 1934 in an effort to put ships and seamen laid up during the depression back in service. Following the success achieved with older vessels, *Wilhelm Gustloff* was the first ship built especially for the trade; passengers were accommodated in one class. Appropriated by the German Navy before she could enter her intended service, *Gustloff* sailed as a hospital ship and troop carrier in the Baltic throughout World War II. During the German retreat from the Eastern Front in 1945, she was employed in ferrying refugees from the advancing Red Army. At about 1900 on January 30, 1945, she left Gdynia, in German-occupied Poland, with a complement officially set at 6,600 people, although some estimates put the total at closer to 10,000. Only two hours out, *Gustloff* was torpedoed by the Soviet submarine *S-13* off what is now Ustka, Poland. The ship sank quickly. The number of survivors is estimated at between 650 and 1,252 people, but the official death toll is 5,348, making it the greatest loss of life associated with any maritime disaster.

Dobson, Miller, & Payne, *Cruellest Night.*

WILLIAM MITCHELL

Ship (3m). L/B/D: 272.7′ × 41′ × 23.7′ (83.1m × 12.5m × 7.2m). *Tons:* 2,035. *Hull:* steel. *Built:* Foyle Shipyard, Londonderry, Ireland; 1892.

Built for William Mitchell's Foyle Line, the full-rigger *William Mitchell* was a dull sailer whose greatest claim to fame is that she was the last square-rigged ship engaged in regular deep-sea trade under the British flag. In the meantime, she accumulated an unenviable record of long passages. Early in her career she posted 160 days from Antwerp to San Francisco and 199 days from New York to Japan. At the beginning of 1920, she sailed from Buenos Aires for England and was prevented from making Leith by winter gales that kept her in the North Sea for 40 days; after securing a tow, her final time was 107 days. In October of that year, she was caught in a hurricane at Gulfport, Missisippi. After two weeks of repairs, she sailed for Buenos Aires with timber. Light and contrary winds kept her at sea for 147 days before she made Barbados; she finally arrived at Buenos Aires 266 days out.

WILLIAM MITCHELL *enters Hobson's Bay, Melbourne, 158 days out from Wilmington, Del. Courtesy National Maritime Museum, Greenwich.*

Sold to Potter Brothers, London, in 1900, she passed under the flag of John Stewart and Company in 1909, and her last voyage for that company began in 1925. After sailing for Australia with a load of New Brunswick lumber, she spent two years trading in the Pacific. She returned to Antwerp with nitrate in 1927 and was sold shortly thereafter to German ship breakers.

Anderson, *Sailing Ships of Ireland*. Course, *Wheel's Kick and the Wind's Song*.

WINDSOR CASTLE

Liner (4f/2m). *L/B/D:* 661' × 72.5' (201.4m × 22.1m). *Tons:* 18,967 grt. *Hull:* steel. *Comp.:* 1st 235, 2nd 360, 3rd 275; 440 crew. *Mach.:* geared turbines, 15,000 shp, 2 screws; 17 kts. *Built:* John Brown & Co., Ltd., Clydebank, Scotland; 1922.

Formed in 1900 by the merger of the Union Steam Ship Company and the Castle Line, Union-Castle Line was the preeminent shipping line between Britain and African ports. Union Steam Ship had received a government mail contract for steam service to Cape Town in 1857, and it dominated that route for two decades. Donald Currie established the rival Castle Line in 1872, and in 1876, the mail subsidy was divided between the two companies. Currie was a great believer in the potential of South Africa, and it was at his instigation that the two companies merged. Castle Line square-riggers had been named for castles, and this tradition was continued by Union-Castle Line, whose service eventually included the entire continent, including a special "round-Africa" service via the Mediterranean and the Suez Canal.

Commissioned in 1922 and 1923, the sister ships *Arundel Castle* and *Windsor Castle* were the only four-funneled merchant ships built for other than transatlantic service. Although she was among the most luxurious ships on the South Africa run, *Windsor Castle* catered to a less fashionable clientele than her North Atlantic contemporaries, and her accommodations were less sumptuous than those of the celebrated express liners. Nor was speed a major consideration — at least at first — and at a stately 17 knots, she could make the 6,000-mile passage in about fifteen days. In 1937, *Windsor Castle* and her sister ship were refitted in order to fulfill the terms of a new mail contract calling for a service speed of 20 knots, which shortened the passage by three days. The ships were lengthened 25 feet (7.5 meters), and two funnels were removed.

The reengined *Windsor Castle* was in service only a short time when she was requisitioned by the Royal Navy for service as a troop transport during World War II. On November 3, 1940, she was hit by German bombers off the coast of Spain. After repairs, she reentered service, but she was not so lucky the second time. On March 23, 1943, she was torpedoed in the western Mediterranean in position 37°28'N, 1°10'E.

Kludas, *Great Passenger Ships of the World*.

WITTE LEEUW

Ship (3m). *L/B:* ca. 155' × 36' (70m × 11m). *Tons:* 700 gross. *Hull:* wood. *Comp.:* 190. *Arm.:* 24–30. *Built:* Amsterdam; 1609.

Built for the Verenigde Oostindische Compagnie (Dutch East India Company, VOC)'s East Indies trade, *Witte Leeuw* ("White Lion") sailed from the Netherlands on January 30, 1610, and was the first of her fleet to arrive at Bantam, Java, on November 11, 1611. Her complement included Pieter Both, the VOC's first Governor General to the Indies, and about 60 passengers and soldiers. After stops at Amboina and Banda, the Dutch captured five Spanish supply ships bound for the Philippines before loading cloves, nutmeg, pepper, and some 1,300 diamonds in the Moluccas and at Bantam for the return passage. In December 1612, *Witte Leeuw* sailed under the command of Roeloff Sijmonz Blom, in company with three other Dutch ships, and was later joined by two English ships. In mid-May, the fleet called at St. Helena for water and on June 1, 1613, all but the English *Pearl* weighed anchor. No sooner had they sailed then *Nossa Senhora da Nazareth* and *Nossa Senhora do Monte do Carmo* put into Jamestown Bay. The Dutch and English put back to attack the Portuguese carracks, and in the skirmish, according to *Pearl*'s master, John Tatton, "one of [the White Lion's] peeces broke over his Powder Roome, as some thought, and the shippe blew up all to pieces, the after part of her, and so sunke presently."

In 1976, French archaeologist Robert Sténuit found the remains of *Witte Leeuw*. In addition to ship's fittings, fifteen guns, personal possessions, and exotic sea shells from the Indian and Pacific Oceans, divers found more than 400 kilograms of Chinese porcelain (none was listed in the cargo manifest) the bulk of which has been identified as Wanli export porcelain.

Van der Pijl-Ketel, ed., *Ceramic Load of the "Witte Leeuw."*

WOLF

(ex-*Jupiter, Wachtfels;* later *Antinous*) Commerce raider (1f/2m). *L/B/D:* 442.8' × 56.1' × 25.6' (135m × 17.1m × 7.8m). *Tons:*

5,809 grt. *Hull:* steel. *Comp.:* 147. *Arm.:* 6 × 6″, 1 × 4.2″, 3 × 5.2cm; 4 × 20″TT; 1 seaplane. *Mach.:* triple expansion, 2,800 ihp, 1 screw; 10.5 kts. *Built:* Flensburger Schiffbau AG, Flensburg, Germany; 1913.

Launched as a freighter for the Bremen-based Deutsche Dampfschiffahrts Gesellschaft "Hansa," *Wachtfels* was requisitioned by the German Navy in 1916. After brief duty as the submarine depot ship *Jupiter,* she was fitted out for commerce raiding and renamed *Wolf.* Alone of the World War I German raiders, she was equipped with a Friedrichshafen FF.33e seaplane, which had extraordinary success as a scout plane. Under Commander Karl August Nerger, *Wolf* left Kiel on November 30 and reached the South Atlantic without incident. After laying mines off Cape Town, Bombay, and Colombo, she took her first prize west of the Maldives Islands on February 27. Other prizes came at a steady rate as *Wolf* made her way south of Australia and around New Zealand to the Kermadec Islands at the end of May. *Wolf* remained in the western Pacific through the summer, taking more prizes and laying mines in the waters around New Zealand. Passing into the Java Sea in September, *Wolf* laid mines off Singapore before beginning the long westward journey home. On October 15, Nerger seized the Spanish collier *Igotz Mendi* off the Maldives, which remained with *Wolf* until the end of the cruise, when she ran aground on the Danish coast and was seized on February 24. *Wolf* had returned to Kiel on February 19 after a voyage of 1 year, 7 months, and 3 days, during which she had steamed 64,000 miles and taken 13 prizes. After the war, *Wolf* passed to France as reparations and she ended her days as the Compagnie Messageries Maritimes freighter *Antinous.* She was scrapped in Italy in 1931.

Walter, *Kaiser's Pirates.*

W. R. GRACE

Ship (3m). *L/B/D:* 218′ × 42′ × 28′ (66.4m × 12.8m × 8.5m). *Tons:* 1,893 grt. *Hull:* wood. *Built:* Chapman & Flint Co., Bath, Me.; 1873.

Named for the founder of W. R. Grace Company, a merchant house prominent in trade to South America (Grace himself later served as mayor of New York City), the Down Easter *W. R. Grace* was built for Chapman & Flint Company. Intended for the California trade, she made eleven passages from New York, and one from Baltimore, to San Francisco. Her return passages included one to New York, ten to Liverpool, and one to Le Havre. She also made a single voyage from San Francisco to Sydney. She was not a fast ship, her average passages being 136 days westbound and 123 days eastbound. Her two masters were Captain Dudley O. Black and his brother-in-law Joseph W. Wallnutt.

The handsome Down Easter w. r. grace *tied alongside at Port Costa, Calif. Courtesy South Street Seaport Museum, New York.*

On August 3, 1889, *W. R. Grace* sailed from Le Havre bound for Philadelphia. Her crossing was uneventful, and on September 9 she was off the entrance to Delaware Bay. In rising seas, *Grace* was taken in tow by the tug *Battler* but was forced to anchor off Cape Henlopen as the winds rose to hurricane force. The veteran clipper ship master Arthur H. Clark was sailing as a passenger and recounted the struggle to save the ship in conditions he likened to the worst China Sea typhoons. In winds clocked at 104 miles per hour, the *Grace* dragged between two barks "which were lying so close together that I am sure that we would never have attempted to tow between them in fine weather." On September 11 the crew cut away the masts to reduce windage, but when they did so, "it was blowing so hard that we could scarcely hear the crash and the whole scene was so grand and terrible that our enormous masts and yards seemed like jackstraws going over the side." Men of the Henlopen lifesaving station managed to take off the crew via a breeches buoy later that day, though four remained, including Clark, who later "landed safely with my dog and all my baggage." In all, thirty-six ships were lost in Delaware Bay. But of the *Grace*'s end, Clark reported that "no vessel ever went on shore under better seamanship."

Matthews, *American Merchant Ships.*

USS WYOMING

Wyoming-class screw sloop (1f/3m). *L/B/D:* 198.5′ × 33.2′ × 14.8′ (60.5m × 10.1m × 4.5m). *Tons:* 1,457 disp. *Hull:* wood. *Comp.:* 198. *Arm.:* 2 × 11″, 1 × 60pdr, 3 × 32pdr. *Mach.:* horizontal direct-acting engine, 793 ihp, 1 screw; 11 kts. *Built:* Merrick & Sons, Philadelphia; 1859.

Named for a Pennsylvania valley, the first USS *Wyoming* began service with the Pacific Squadron at San Francisco in 1860. With the start of the Civil War, she was assigned to guard the mail ships, and their gold, running between San Francisco and Panama. In June 1862, she was ordered to the eastern Pacific to search for Confederate raiders. Although *Wyoming* crossed the track of CSS ALABAMA, the two ships failed to meet.

In addition to Confederate raiders, the United States also had to contend with the isolationist Mikado of Japan, who had ordered all foreigners expelled on June 25, 1863. Following an attack on the American merchantman *Pembroke* the next day, *Wyoming* sailed from Yokohama to Shimonoseki, and in an hour-long engagement on July 16, she bombarded Japanese shore positions and sank a Japanese steamer. After repairs at Philadelphia in 1864, *Wyoming* returned to the East Indies and in 1866 took part in a punitive expedition against Formosan pirates.

In 1868, she returned to the United States and remained in home waters for the next decade. After a two-year stint on the European station, she was transferred to the Naval Academy where she spent another ten years as a training ship. She was sold in 1892.

U.S. Navy, *DANFS.*

WYOMING

Schooner (6m). *L/B/D:* 329.5′ × 50.1′ × 30.4′ (100.4m × 15.2m × 9.3m). *Tons:* 3,730 tons. *Hull:* wood. *Comp.:* 13. *Built:* Percy & Small, Bath, Me.; 1909.

One of the largest wooden hulls ever built, *Wyoming* had the greatest tonnage of any wooden schooner built (the only larger schooner of any description was the steel-hulled THOMAS W. LAWSON), and she was the last of ten six-masted schooners built in New England. The year 1879 saw the coming of the first four-masted schooners as well as the introduction of donkey engines into schooners. By significantly reducing the schooners' manning requirements, the engine made possible a thirty-year quest for ever larger vessels. By the time *Wyoming* slipped down the ways, East Coast shipbuilders had launched 311 four-masted schooners, 45 five-masters, 10 six-masters, and, in solitary splendor, the seven-masted *Lawson.*

The big schooners were designed primarily for the Delaware and Chesapeake coal trade, which had become increasingly dominated by barges. Schooners were pushed out of the New York market first, and following the opening of the Sewall's Point coal facility in Norfolk, Virginia, shippers turned increasingly to steamships on their New England routes. World War I brought a brief reprieve for the windjammers, but many ships were laid up in the postwar shipping slump. *Wyoming* escaped this fate by sailing on ever longer routes. On March 3, 1924, she departed Norfolk for St. John, New Brunswick. On the 24th she anchored off the Pollock Rip Lightship to ride out a nor'easter, but she sank with the loss of her 13 crew, including Captain Charles Glaesel.

Haskell, "Glamorous Six-Masters." Parker, *Great Coal Schooners of New England.*

Y

YAMATO

Yamato-class battleship (1f/1m). *L/B/D:* 862.6′ × 127.6′ × 34.1′ (263m × 38.9m × 10.4m). *Tons:* 72,809 disp. *Hull:* steel. *Comp.:* 2,500. *Arm.:* 9 × 18.4″ (3 × 3), 12 × 6.2″, 12 × 5.1″, 24 × 25mm. *Armor:* 16.4″ belt, 9.2″ deck. *Mach.:* geared turbines, 150,000 shp, 4 screws; 27 kts. *Des.:* Hiraga Yuzuru & Fukuda Keiji. *Built:* Kure Kaigun Kosho, Kure, Japan; 1941.

First conceived in 1934, the *Yamato*-class battleships were the biggest ever built, and they were surpassed in size only by the American supercarriers built after World War II. The class was to have consisted of five ships, but only *Yamato* and Musashi were commissioned as battleships; *Shinano* was reconfigured as an aircraft carrier when she was half built, one hull was broken up before completion, and the fifth was never begun. Despite their enormous size and strength, there were many advocates of naval air power who believed that battleships were obsolete and that these ships were a waste of scarce resources. Ironically, one of the most vigorous opponents was the air-minded Admiral Isoroku Yamamoto, whose flagship *Yamato* would become, on February 12, 1942 — just two months after Japan had proven the tactical effectiveness of naval aviation against battleships with the attack on Pearl Harbor and the sinking of HMS Prince of Wales and Repulse off Singapore.

Four months later, it was upon *Yamato*'s bridge — 500 miles northeast of the actual fighting — that Yamamoto learned of the devastating defeat of Japan's Fast Carrier Force at the Battle of Midway on June 4, 1942, where the carriers Akagi, Hiryu, Kaga, and Soryu were sunk. Realizing his rearguard fleet was no match for the U.S. carriers, Yamamoto turned for home. With her radius of action severely curtailed by her limited usefulness and a critical shortage of fuel, *Yamato* saw little action. On December 24, 1943, she was victim of a torpedo attack by the submarine USS *Skate* at Truk Island, although the damage was relatively minor.

At the Battle of Leyte Gulf — Japan's effort to disrupt the American landings in the Philippines — *Yamato* and *Musashi* formed the core of Vice Admiral T. Kurita's Force

A. Sailing from Singapore, via Borneo, they were to cross the Sibuyan Sea in the central Philippines and through the San Bernardino Strait, between Luzon and Samar Islands. Following the Battle of the Sibuyan Sea, in which *Musashi* was lost to aircraft from Vice Admiral Marc A. Mitscher's Task Force 58, Kurita's ships slipped out of the strait, narrowly missing Vice Admiral Willis A. Lee's battle line, which included the battleships *New Jersey,* Iowa, Washington, *South Dakota,* Massachusetts, and Alabama. Such an encounter would have demonstrated *Yamato*'s superiority against other battleships, the contest for which she was intended. The next morning they engaged an escort carrier group consisting of six escort carriers, three destroyers, and four destroyer escorts in the Battle of Samar Island, from which *Yamato* escaped unscathed.

During the Allied assault on the island of Okinawa, south of the Japanese home islands, *Yamato* was designated as the center of Vice Admiral Seiichi Ito's Special Surface Attack Force, consisting also of eight destroyers and one light cruiser. The purpose of this suicide run to Okinawa — *Yamato* had only enough fuel for a one-way trip — was to disrupt the amphibious landings there. On April 6, 1945, the force was sighted coming out of the Inland Sea and tracked as it threaded its way west along the southern tip of Kyushu into the East China Sea. Planes from Task Force 58 began their attack at 1232 on April 7. *Yamato* was hit by 10 aerial torpedoes and 23 bombs, including near misses. The world's greatest battleship finally sank in 30°40′N, 128°03′E, with the loss 2,498 men. In the words of Samuel Eliot Morison, "When she went down, five centuries of naval warfare ended."

Agawa, *Reluctant Admiral.* Morison, *Two-Ocean War.* Skulski, *Battleship "Yamato."*

YANKEE

(ex-*Duhnen, Emden*) Brigantine (2m). *L/B/D:* 96′ × 21.5′ × 11′ (29.3m × 6.6m × 3.4m). *Tons:* 200 disp. *Hull:* steel. *Mach.:* diesels,

110 hp, 2 screws; 6.5 kts. *Des.:* Peterson. *Built:* Nordseewerke, Emden, Germany; 1913.

Authorized by the German government as a North Sea pilot schooner, *Emden* remained in that work until the end of World War I, when she was transferred to Cuxhaven and renamed *Duhnen.* In 1934 she was transferred to the German Navy and converted to a training vessel, and from 1936 to 1939 she was used almost exclusively by the naval branch of the Sturmabteilung (SA). At the start of World War II, in 1939, she was fitted with an engine and electricity for the first time and handed over to the Luftwaffe for training members of the Naval Air Service. *Duhnen* survived the war and was surrendered to Great Britain as part of war reparations. After two years as a Royal Air Force yacht, she was bought by the American sailor Irving Johnson.

Drawing on his experience rounding Cape Horn in the four-masted bark Peking in 1928, by the 1930s Johnson and his wife, Electa, had circumnavigated the world three times in their training schooner *Yankee.* Following the war, they wanted to resume that work and purchased the *Duhnen.* In England, the Johnsons rigged the renamed *Yankee* as a brigantine, rebuilt her interior with watertight bulkheads, and otherwise adapted her for cruising with trainees. In October 1947, she embarked on her first circumnavigation — a voyage of 45,000 miles, completed in 1949. Many of the trainees who shipped in *Yankee* were drawn from the Girl Scouts' Mariner program, and several built on their experiences with Skipper and Exy, as the Johnsons were known, to develop new sail-training programs. The ship and her mission were well known not only among sailors, but, thanks to the Johnsons' books and articles (especially in *National Geographic*), their adventures in the Galápagos Islands, New Guinea, and the Orient were known to millions of readers. The Johnsons acquired a third *Yankee,* a ketch, in which they cruised extensively throughout Europe and the Mediterranean.

Johnson, *"Yankee"'s People and Places; "Yankee"'s Wander World.* Marden, "Saga of a Ship." Underhill, *Sail Training and Cadet Ships.*

Yarmouth Castle

(ex-*Evangeline*) Passenger ship (1f/2m). *L/B:* 380′ × 57′ (115.8m × 17.4m). *Tons:* 5,002 grt. *Hull:* steel. *Comp.:* 176 crew; 379 pass. *Mach.:* geared turbines, 2 screws; 18 kts. *Built:* William Cramp & Sons Ship and Engine Building Co., Philadelphia; 1927.

Built for the Eastern Steamship Lines' intracoastal service, *Evangeline* originally ran between Boston and New York and the Canadian Maritimes with her sister ship *Yar-*

mouth. (While *Evangeline* was only renamed *Yarmouth Castle* in 1958, *Yarmouth* had a succession of names including *Yarmouth Castle, Queen of Nassau, Yarmouth Castle* again, and *Yarmouth* again in 1958.) During World War II, *Evangeline* served as a troop transport. She was laid up from 1948 to 1953, except briefly in 1950. Passing into Liberian and then Panamanian registry, in 1964 she was acquired by the Chadade Steamship Company, a subsidiary company owned by Canadian shipping magnate Jules Sokoloff, for service on the 186-mile run between Miami and the Bahamas. On November 12, 1965, *Yarmouth Castle* sailed from Miami. At 1230 on the 13th, a fire of uncertain origin was detected in cabin 610, then being used for storage. Captain Byron Voutsinas gave the order to abandon ship at 0125, but he did not order the radio operator to transmit a distress call. Voutsinas was in the first lifeboat, although after making contact with the Finnish freighter MV *Finnpulp* (Captain Lehto), which had come to *Yarmouth Castle*'s aid as soon as a crewman saw the fire, he returned to his ship. Twelve miles astern, the passenger ship *Bahama Star* (Captain Carl Netherland-Brown) also came to the ship's assistance. *Yarmouth Castle* sank at 0603 in 25°55′N, 78°06′W, with the loss of 87 people, all but two of them passengers; *Finnpulp* took off 51 passengers and 41 crew, *Bahama Star* 240 passengers and 133 crew. Following the *Yarmouth Castle* disaster, Congress enacted legislation requiring foreign-flag ships sailing from U.S. ports to have improved safety measures. The United States also prevailed upon the UN's Intergovernmental Maritime Consultative Organization (later the International Maritime Organization) to promulgate stricter regulations for shipping worldwide.

Brown, "*Yarmouth Castle* Inferno." Watson, *Disasters at Sea.*

Yassi Ada wreck A

Merchantman. *L/B/D:* 6.2m × 1.6m × 0.5m (20.5m × 5.2m × 1.8m). *Tons:* 60 burden; 73 disp. *Hull:* wood. *Built:* Byzantine empire; 7th cent. CE.

Yassi Ada ("Flat Island") lies between Kalimnos and the Turkish mainland in 36°59′N, 27°11′E. Over the centuries a number of ships have run onto the treacherous reef that extends from the island. The two most important are one dating from the seventh century — Yassi Ada A — and another only 15 meters away dating from the fourth century, known as Yassi Ada B. The seventh-century Yassi Ada wreck lies on the south side of the island, east of the reef, at a depth of between 32 and 39 meters. The site was first shown to American maritime photographer and adventurer Peter Throckmorton by Kemâl Aras in 1958,

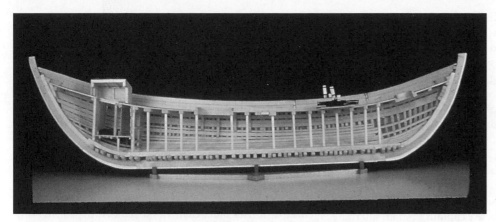

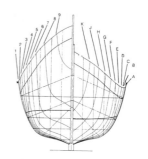

Top: A 1:10 scale model of the 7th-century wreck at Yassi Ada, found off the coast of Turkey. Bottom: Midships cross section and hull lines of the ship. Courtesy Institute for Nautical Archaeology, College Station, Texas.

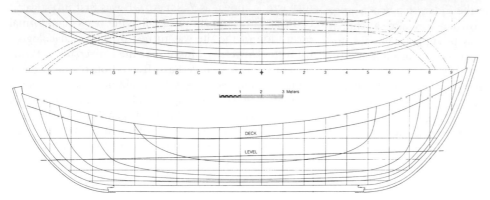

and it was completely excavated between 1961 and 1964 by an expedition from the University Museum of the University of Pennsylvania, led by George Bass. Significant parts of the hull had been preserved under sediment on the sea floor. The hull was deep and narrow. The length-to-beam ratio of approximately 4:1 is surprisingly slender for a cargo vessel. There is no surviving evidence for the rig, but given the hull shape and the probable locations of mainmast and steering oars, the ship would have sailed best with a fore-and-aft rig.

The excavated remains provide ample evidence for construction techniques, materials, and fastenings. The keel was probably hewn from a single log of cypress, and the wales and ceiling strakes were unfinished cypress logs sawn in half lengthwise. The sternpost and through-beams were also of cypress, the planking of pine, the frames elm, and the tenons oak. Only three types of fasteners were used: mortise-and-tenon joints, iron nails, and iron bolts. There is no evidence of dowels or treenails. The keel was a straight member 35.5 centimeters in height and from 22 centimeters to 13 centimeters in width, tapering sternward. A hook scarf fastened by a bolt

joined the keel to a high, curved sternpost. An outer, false sternpost was nailed to the main post, and probably a false keel, or "shoe," was similarly attached to the keel. The sternpost was not preserved. Rabbets were cut into the sides of the keel, the stempost, and (presumably) the sternpost for seating the garboard strakes. Strakes 2 through 16 were edge-lined with mortises and tenons that were small, loosely fitted, widely spaced, and not pegged with treenails. These joints thus did not contribute much to the strength of the hull. The planks below the waterline were thickly coated with pitch on both inboard and outboard surfaces. The framing consisted of short and long floors and half-frames, all approximately 15 square centimeters in section. The shipwrights put guidelines on the inboard surface of the planking to mark where frames were to be placed. Iron bolts as long as 72 centimeters were used to connect some of the frames to the keel. Through-beams, supported the deck and projected out through the hull. Steering oars were mounted between the two after through-beams and the helmsman probably steered from a raised helm-deck. Other topside features reconstructed by the excavators are a tile-roofed galley in the stern and hatches forward and amidships.

The ship carried eleven iron anchors when she went down: two were secured to the port gunwale, two to the starboard gunwale, and seven were stacked on deck forward of amidships. Among the shipboard gear recovered were terra-cotta lamps, steelyards and a steelyard counterweight, agricultural implements, and a variety of carpenter's tools. Galley equipment included fine tableware, pitchers, clay cooking pots, storage jars, a copper caldron, a stone mortar and pestle, a large water jar, and a "wine-thief" pipette for drawing liquid from amphorae. A Greek inscription punched into one of the steelyards reads: "Georgiou Presbyterou Nauklerou." Bass suggests the translation "George, senior sea captain," but an alternate reading is possible: "George the Elder, shipowner," suggesting that the merchant-owner was also a church official. This interpretation may be supported by the unexpected find of a bronze censer with a finial in the form of a cross.

The ship's cargo comprised between 850 and 900 amphorae. The origin of these storage vessels is uncertain, but the closest parallels for the forms are found at the port of Constanta (ancient Tomis) on the western Black Sea coast. The cargo consisted at least partly of wine, as the recovery of grape seeds from the sediment within some of the amphorae proves. If all the amphorae were filled with wine, the cargo would weigh some 37 tons. Seventy Byzantine coins were recovered, 54 copper and 16 gold. The latest datable coin is a copper *follis* struck in the sixteenth year of the reign of the emperor Heraclius, 625–626. In all likelihood the wreck occurred within a few years after that date. We do not know for certain where the Yassi Ada ship began her last voyage, but the evidence of the coins, the lamps, the amphorae, and the pottery all point to a northern homeport, perhaps in the northern Aegean, the environs of Constantinople, or the western Black Sea.

The Yassi Ada vessel belongs to a transitional phase in the history of shipbuilding from shell-first to skeleton-first construction. The shipwrights edge-joined the strakes in the lower part of the hull, but above the waterline, strakes and wales were simply nailed to existing frames. Using unpegged, widely spaced, mortise-and-tenon joints in the lower hull was doubtless faster and cheaper than the elaborate joinery of earlier vessels such as KYRENIA or ANTIKYTHERA. Similarly, the use of unfinished half-logs for wales and ceilings cut down on the investment in labor. These developments, appearing for the first time in the Yassi Ada ship, may have been motivated by economic conditions, as the reduced volume of maritime trade in the seventh-century Byzantine Empire led to an increase in small, independent shipowner-merchants. The unexpectedly sleek lines of this merchant vessel may have resulted from the need to avoid or outrun hostile ships during one of the many periods of insecurity for Mediterranean shipping.

Bass, "Byzantine Trading Venture." Bass & van Doorninck, *Yassi Ada.*

YASSI ADA WRECK B

Merchantman (1m). *L/B:* 62′ × 21.7′ (18.9m × 6.6m). *Hull:* wood. *Built:* 4th cent. CE.

Three centuries older than YASSI ADA A, the fourth-century wreck known as YASSI ADA B was first investigated by Peter Throckmorton in 1958. Nine years later, formal excavation of the site was turned over to archaeologists from the University Museum of the University of Pennsylvania, led by George Bass. Excavation of the site was undertaken in 1967, 1969, and again in 1974, after which time operations were suspended because of hostilities in Cyprus. Located at a depth of between 36 and 42 meters, the ship lay on its port side. Although the foremost ten feet of the nearly symmetrical hull had eroded, from the remains it is estimated that the complete hull was 62 feet long, with a maximum beam of about 22 feet amidships. The ship was of typical shell-first construction, with the planks joined first and frames inserted afterwards to strengthen the hull. The planking was edge-joined with mortise-and-tenon joints. Frames were inserted at intervals of about 24 centimeters — 45 of an estimated 68 frames survive — and they were fastened to the outer hull with oak treenails; iron nails were used to fasten the frames to the wales. Oak was also used for the keel, while the hull planks were of cypress.

The ship had a roofed galley aft equipped with a stone hearth, and divers found six storage vessels, as well as cooking pots, a funnel, drinking cups, four lamps, and other personal artifacts. The ship has been dated to the second half of the fourth century on the basis of an Athenian maker's mark on the bottom of a lamp. In addition to these remains, the site was littered with approximately 1,110 amphorae from the ship's cargo.

Bass & van Doorninck, "Fourth-Century Shipwreck at Yassi Ada." Van Doorninck, "Fourth-century Wreck at Yassi Ada."

USS YORKTOWN (CV-5)

Yorktown-class aircraft carrier (1f/2m). *L/B/D:* 809.5′ × 83′ (86′ew) × 21.5′ (246.7m × 25.3m (26.2m) × 6.6m). *Tons:* 25,500 disp. *Hull:* steel. *Comp.:* 1,889–2,919. *Arm.:* 72 aircraft; 8 × 5″ (8 × 1), 16

× 1.1″, 24 × 20mm. *Armor:* 4″ belt, 1.5″ deck. *Mach.:* geared turbines, 120,000 shp, 4 shafts; 32.5 kts. *Built:* Newport News Shipbuilding & Dry Dock Co., Newport News, Va.; 1937.

The third ship named to commemorate the site of the last battle of the American Revolution, USS *Yorktown,* along with ENTERPRISE and HORNET, constituted the second class of U.S. Navy ships designed as aircraft carriers from the keel up. Larger than their immediate predecessor, USS RANGER, but smaller than the cruiser-hulled SARATOGA and *Lexington,* the *Yorktowns* were built within the tonnage limits dictated by the Washington Naval Conference of 1922, which restricted total carrier tonnage to 135,000 tons and a per-ship maximum of 27,000 tons.

After a year and a half of training and fleet exercises in the Atlantic and Caribbean, in April 1939 *Yorktown* transferred to the Pacific and sailed out of San Diego and Pearl Harbor until April 1941. Returning to the Atlantic, she served on the Neutrality Patrol along the East Coast as a deterrent to German U-boats operating against British convoys in the Western Hemisphere. The Japanese attack on Pearl Harbor on December 7, 1941, found *Yorktown* at Norfolk; nine days later she sailed for the Pacific, where she became flagship of Admiral Frank Jack Fletcher's Task Force 17. After convoying American troops to American Samoa, she saw her first battle action in a series of attacks on Japanese installations on Jaluit, Makin, and Mili in the Gilbert Islands on January 31, 1942.

After replenishing at Pearl Harbor, *Yorktown* and *Lexington* left on February 14 bound for the Coral Sea to cover Allied landings on New Caledonia and to check the Japanese southward advance. On March 10, the carriers launched 104 planes from the Gulf of Papua and across the treacherous Owen Stanley Mountains to attack newly captured Japanese positions at Lae and Salamaua on the north coast of New Guinea. Surprise was complete, and only one plane was lost in the operation. *Yorktown* patrolled in the Coral Sea into April, when she put into the sheltered but undeveloped harbor at Tongatabu, Tonga Islands, for maintenance.

Weighing anchor on April 27, *Yorktown* returned to the Coral Sea, rendezvousing with *Lexington*'s Task Force 11 south of the New Hebrides on May 1, in anticipation of a Japanese thrust into the Solomon Islands. On May 4, *Yorktown* attacked a nascent Japanese seaplane base at Tulagi, Florida Island; her planes sank the destroyer *Kikuzuki,* three minelayers, and four barges, with the loss of three planes. At the same time the Japanese were sending 11 troop transports guarded by the light carrier SHOHO for a move against Port Moresby on the south coast of New Guinea; in the background lurked the carriers SHOKAKU and ZUIKAKU. On May 7, planes from

Lexington and *Yorktown* attacked the transports, sinking *Shoho,* while planes from *Shokaku* and *Zuikaku* sank the destroyer USS SIMS and the oiler USS NEOSHO, which the Japanese mistook for a carrier. The battle reached its climax the next day. Planes from *Yorktown* and *Lexington* struck first, causing serious damage to *Shokaku*'s flight deck. *Zuikaku*'s planes hit back, causing serious damage to *Yorktown* and sinking *Lexington.* The Battle of the Coral Sea was critical in several respects. Despite the loss of *Lexington,* the Japanese drive to Port Moresby had stalled. Moreover, it was the first naval battle in which the ships never established visual contact.

It took *Yorktown* 19 days to return to Pearl Harbor, where it was estimated she needed three months for repairs. But as the Japanese attack on Midway was imminent, Fleet Admiral Chester Nimitz allowed three days, and on May 30, she sortied to a rendezvous with *Enterprise* and *Hornet* northeast of Midway on June 4. The first U.S. strike against the Japanese fleet was a disaster, resulting in the loss of 35 of 41 Devastator torpedo planes. But, this attack had forced the Japanese combat air patrol down to near sea level, so when the Dauntless dive-bombers attacked, they met virtually no opposition. *Yorktown*'s planes landed three 1,000-pound bombs on SORYU, in the midst of rearming her planes, reducing her to a burning hulk; *Enterprise*'s planes inflicted comparable damage on AKAGI and KAGA. Meanwhile, HIRYU had launched 18 fighters and 18 dive-bombers, three of which scored crippling hits on *Yorktown,* which brought her to a dead stop by about 1440. Within an hour, though, she was again able to make 20 knots and her fires were under control. At 1620, though, Japanese torpedo planes scored fatal hits that knocked out her power and steering system. With the ship at a severe list, Captain Elliott Buckmaster was forced to give the order to abandon ship fifteen minutes later.

Meanwhile, planes from *Yorktown,* still pressing the attack on *Hiryu,* the last of the four Japanese carriers, were landing back on *Enterprise.* Despite her severe list, *Yorktown* refused to sink, and the following morning a salvage crew was put aboard. Taken in tow by the Navy tug *Vireo* on June 6, and receiving auxiliary power from the destroyer *Hammann,* which had come alongside, *Yorktown* was making her way slowly towards Pearl Harbor when the Japanese submarine *I-168* attacked. One torpedo hit *Hammann,* which sank within four minutes, taking with her 81 of her crew, and two more hit *Yorktown.* Abandoned once again, "Waltzing Mathilda" remained afloat until 0600 on June 7, when she rolled over and sank in 30°36′N, 176°34′W.

Cressman, *Gallant Ship.* U.S. Navy, *DANFS.*

USS YORKTOWN (CV-10)

Essex-class aircraft carrier (1f/2m). *L/B/D:* 872′ × 93′ (147.5′ew) × 28.6′ (265.8m × 28.3m (45m) × 8.7m). *Tons:* 34,346′ disp. *Hull:* steel. *Comp.:* 3,448. *Arm.:* 18 × 5″, 68 × 40mm. *Armor:* 3″ belt. *Mach.:* geared turbines, 150,000 shp, 4 screws; 33 kts. *Built:* Newport News Shipbuilding & Dry Dock Co., Newport News, Va.; 1943.

Laid down as *Bonhomme Richard* on December 1, 1941, the fourth USS *Yorktown* was so named following the loss of CV-5 at the Battle of Midway. Commissioned under Captain Joseph J. Clark, she was assigned to Fast Carrier Forces, Pacific Fleet. She took part in the invasion of the Gilbert Islands in November 1943, and of the Marshall Islands in January 1944. Through the spring, *Yorktown* ranged between New Guinea in the south and the Mariana Islands. The invasion of the latter began in June, and *Yorktown*'s aviators supported landings on Saipan and Guam, and fought with distinction during the Battle of the Philippine Sea. Following repairs on the West Coast, she resumed operations around the Philippines and in the South China Sea, where her planes sank 44 ships. Hit by a kamikaze on March 18, she remained on station, flying missions against Okinawa (March 30–May 11) and the Japanese mainland, being called off station only to help intercept the Japanese battleship YAMATO, which was sunk on April 7.

After a visit to Tokyo Bay following the peace, *Yorktown* returned stateside. Placed in reserve from 1947 to 1952, she went back on active duty in the Pacific for eighteen years. She was part of the U.S. response to the Communist Chinese shelling of Matsu and Quemoy in 1959, the year she first visited the waters off South Vietnam, where she would see duty intermittently until 1968. That same year, she was cast in the film *Tora! Tora! Tora!*, about the Japanese attack on Pearl Harbor. She was then transferred to the Atlantic Fleet. Decommissioned in 1970, five years later Congress authorized her transfer to the state of South Carolina where she was put on display at the Patriots Point Maritime Museum near Charleston.

Reynolds, *Fighting Lady*. U.S. Navy, *DANFS*.

YOUNG AMERICA

Clipper (3m). *L/B/D:* 243′ od × 43.2′ × 26.9′ (74.1m × 13.2m × 8.2m). *Tons:* 1,961 om. *Hull:* wood. *Comp.:* 75. *Des.:* William H. Webb. *Built:* William H. Webb, New York; 1853.

The name "Young America" belonged to an expansionist faction of the Democratic Party that advocated the doctrine of Manifest Destiny, and it was also perfectly suited to one of the strong, swift ships that helped the United States' westward push in the wake of the California gold rush of 1849. Built for New York merchant George B. Daniels, *Young America* was the last William Webb ship to leave the ways, and many considered her his crowning achievement. Built for trade between New York, San Francisco, and Liverpool, her size and great speed ensured her consistent command of the highest rates for freight and passengers, and in an age when clippers and their captains were household names, she was also a favorite among bettors. Over the course of twenty passages from New York to San Francisco, she averaged 118 days, while in thirteen return passages she averaged 98 days. In 1872–73, she established a westbound record between Liverpool and San Francisco of 99 days, and between San Francisco and New York her fastest times were 82 and 86 days, the two fastest times for a ship with cargo on that run.

Young America also called at stops throughout the Pacific and Indian Oceans, from Honolulu to Mauritius. On one passage she carried live sheep from Glasgow to New Zealand, and on another she transported 800 Chinese workers, known as coolies, from Hong Kong to Melbourne. Her other cargoes under the American flag included railroad iron, wheat, and general merchandise. Her last passage under U.S. ownership was from Portland, Oregon, to San Francisco and New York. A leak forced her into Rio de Janeiro for three weeks, but she managed to complete the passage in only 126 days between ports, or about 100 days under sail. Sold to Austrian owners at New York, she was renamed *Miroslav* and Buccari (now Bakar, Croatia) became her homeport. After two transatlantic voyages, on February 17, 1886, she departed Delaware and disappeared.

Cutler, *Greyhounds of the Sea*. Howe & Matthews, *American Clipper Ships*.

Z

ZEEWIJK

L: 148′ (45m). *Tons:* 70 tons. *Hull:* wood. *Comp.:* 212. *Arm.:* 36 guns; 6 swivels. *Des.:* Hendrik Raas. *Built:* VOC, Middleburg, Netherlands; 1726.

The Dutch East India Company (Verenigde Oostindische Compagnie, or VOC)'s ship *Zeewijk* sailed from Flushing on November 7, 1726, with a cargo that included 315,834 guilders destined for the company's coffers in Batavia. Separated from her consort *Barbesteyn,* she continued on alone for the Cape of Good Hope, where Captain Jan Steyns replenished his stores and recruited replacements for the twenty-eight crew who died in the first four and a half months at sea. Departing Table Bay, *Zeewijk* ran her easting down until the night of June 9, 1727, when she hit a reef in the Houtman Abrolhos off Australia, not far from where BATAVIA wrecked a century before. Over the next two weeks, the ninety-six survivors of the stranded ship moved to nearby Gun Island. Ten men sailed for Batavia in the ship's boat, but they were never heard of again. Despairing of rescue, after six months on the island, Steyns ordered a new boat to be built, and *Sloepie* ("Little Boat") was launched on February 28, 1728. On March 26, 1728, the vessel (12–16 meters × 2–7 meters × 2 meters) set sail with *Zeewijk*'s eighty-eight survivors and their provisions, and ten chests of VOC money, and arrived at Batavia on April 30. *Zeewijk*'s remains were found in 1972.

Sigmond & Zuiderbaan, *Dutch Discoveries of Australia.*

ZEVEN PROVINCIËN

Ship (3m). *L/B/D:* 146.7′ × 38.7′ × 14.4′ (44.7m × 11.8m × 4.4m). *Hull:* wood. *Comp.:* 450. *Arm.:* 80 guns. *Built:* Admiraliteit van de Maze, Delftshaven, Netherlands; 1664.

The commercial rivalry between English and Dutch merchants that led to the Anglo-Dutch War of 1652–54 reemerged in the early 1660s. In anticipation of renewed hostilities, the Dutch undertook a major building program; one of the largest vessels launched was the *Zeven Provinciën.* Admiral Michiel Adrienszoon de Ruyter was in the Mediterranean and then the Caribbean when war began, but upon his return to the Netherlands in late 1665 he was appointed commander in chief to succeed the late Admiral Jacob van Wassenaer van Obdam. Shifting his flag to the *Zeven Provinciën* in May, de Ruyter led the Dutch fleet for the first time in what became known as the Four Days' Battle. The Dutch had a slight numerical advantage in ships and men, though this was offset by the larger size and caliber of the English ships and guns of greater caliber. The fleets' parity was upset when Charles II ordered Prince Rupert's squadron to prevent a junction of a French fleet with de Ruyter. (France had declared war on England in January, but proved an indifferent ally.) Early in the morning of June 11, the Dutch arrived off the Downs with about eighty-five ships. They were met by an English force of about fifty-six ships under George Monck, Duke of Albemarle. The battle was marked by a lack of coordination on the part of the Dutch and stubborn determination by Monck, who after the second day's fighting turned west to link up with Rupert. *Zeven Provinciën*'s rigging was shot up and de Ruyter was unable to pursue. *Royal Prince* (90 guns) ran aground and was burned by the Dutch on the 12th, and Monck's ships were roughly handled by the Dutch on the 13th, but deteriorating weather and the imminent arrival of Rupert's squadron prevented further action.

The Dutch failure to achieve a decisive victory enabled the English to put to sea in force in mid-July, thus frustrating Dutch plans for a landing on the English coast. On July 25, the Dutch and English fleets met off North Foreland. As in the Four Days' Battle, Lieutenant Admiral Cornelis Tromp found himself cut off from the body of the Dutch fleet, and he was eventually forced to fly before a smaller English squadron. The heaviest fighting took place in the center and van of the opposing fleets; three Dutch flag officers were killed and *Zeven Provinciën* was completely dismasted. The English attempted to renew

The Dutch Admiral de Ruyter's favorite flagship in the Anglo-Dutch Wars, ZEVEN PROVINCIËN is "a vessel that deserves to rank with Nelson's VICTORY, according to British naval historian William Laird Clowes. A replica of ZEVEN PROVINCIËN is under construction in the Netherlands. Painting by the preeminent Dutch marine artist Willem van de Velde the Elder; courtesy Rijksmuseum, Amsterdam.

the battle in the evening, but de Ruyter managed a masterful withdrawal. All told, the Dutch lost twenty ships, 4,000 dead, and 3,000 prisoners.

The next spring, Charles decided to economize by laying up his fleet. In so doing he underestimated the determination of the Dutch. On June 14, they sailed into the Medway and Thames where they burned more than twenty ships and captured the ROYAL CHARLES (90), which they sailed back to Rotterdam. This was the last action of the war — which had been fought entirely at sea — and the Peace of Breda was signed on July 31.

Although the English and Dutch people would have preferred peace, Louis XIV had designs on Dutch territory and bribed Charles II to join an alliance against the United Provinces. With war imminent, the Dutch put seventy-five ships of the line into commission. Against this the French levied twenty-two and the English sixty-five ships. On June 7, 1672, de Ruyter followed the combined fleet to the English coast near Southwold Bay (or Solebay), 90 miles north of the Thames estuary. In the ensuing fight, the Dutch lost only two ships to three English; more important, they prevented the combined fleet from supporting the French army then infesting the Netherlands. The victory is also credited with helping to precipitate the overthrow of the United Provinces' ruling party and the accession of William of Orange. In England, passage of the Test Act barring Catholics from posi-

tions of trust or profit under the Crown forced the Duke of York (later James II) to resign from the Admiralty.

A year later, on June 7, 1673, and again on the 14th, the combined Anglo-French fleet tried to bring the Dutch fleet to battle in the shallows of the Schooneveld at the mouth of the Scheldt River, but they were beaten back by de Ruyter. In late July, the combined fleet put to sea again, and de Ruyter sailed north to join William at Scheveningen. On August 20, he met the combined fleet off Texel in the Frisian Islands. The allies had the advantage of the wind, so de Ruyter hugged the shore until the next morning, when he "made all sail and stood down boldly into action." The Battle of Texel had two major components. Lieutenant Admiral Adriaen Banckers, in the van, cut off a superior French squadron and then returned to help de Ruyter's center, which broke the English line in several places. In the rear, Admiral Sir Edward Spragge and the Dutch Tromp — "men of kindred kidney, brave, rash, and insubordinate" — fought an independent action in which Spragge was killed. Although neither side suffered heavy damage, the English were equally tired of war with the Dutch and of their alliance with Louis XIV, and the Treaty of Westminster was concluded in February 1674. (Three years later, William of Orange married Princess Mary, daughter of the Duke of York; in 1688, the pair acceded to the English throne.)

Zeven Provinciën's final naval action came during the

War of the League of Augsburg, which pitted an Anglo-Dutch alliance against France. On May 29, 1692, she was heavily damaged at the Battle of La Hogue — in which the French fleet was shattered — and returned to Rotterdam. She was broken up two years later. A replica is currently under construction in the Netherlands.

Clowes, *Royal Navy*. Mahan, *Influence of Sea Power*.

HMS ZUBIAN

Tribal-class destroyer. *L/B:* 288′ × 27′ (87.8m × 8.2m). *Tons:* 1,050 disp. *Hull:* steel. *Arm.:* 2 × 4″; 2 TT. *Built:* Chatham Dockyard; 1917.

HMS *Zubian* was a composite destroyer cobbled together — as was her name — from the forward end of HMS *Zulu* and the stern end of HMS *Nubian*. Originally built in 1909 and 1910, the Tribal-class destroyers were part of the Dover Patrol, a hard-pressed flotilla of smaller ships charged with protecting Allied shipping between England and the Continent from German submarines and destroyers operating out of Ostend and Zeebrugge, Belgium. Following a raid on the night of October 26–27, 1916, *Nubian* (Commander Montague Bernard) was dispatched with other destroyers to contact the Germans. Outmaneuvered by the faster German vessels, *Nubian*'s bow was blown off by a torpedo. Taken in tow, the rope broke and she went aground off Dover, eventually losing the rest of her forepart. Twelve days later, HMS *Zulu* struck a mine in mid-Channel and lost her stern, the remainder being taken in tow by a French torpedo-boat destroyer to Calais. The two halves were joined at Chatham in 1917, and *Zubian* served with distinction for the duration of the war. She was broken up at Sunderland in 1919.

Colledge, *Ships of the Royal Navy*. Mannering, "The Old Men and Their Ships Are Gone."

ZUIHO

Zuiho-class aircraft carrier. *L/B/D:* 671.9′ × 59.7′ (75.5′ew) × 21.8′ (204.8m × 18.2m (23m) × 6.6m). *Tons:* 11,260 disp. *Hull:* steel. *Comp.:* 785. *Arm.:* 30 aircraft; 8 × 5″, 8 × 25cm. *Mach.:* geared turbines, 52,000 shp, 2 shafts; 28 kts. *Built:* Yokosuka Dockyard, Yokosuka, Japan; 1940.

Laid down as a submarine tender and converted to an aircraft carrier in 1940, *Zuiho* ("Lucky Dragon") was completed only twenty days after the attack on Pearl Harbor. She was first deployed to help consolidate the

The Japanese carrier ZUIHO *under way after several hits at the Battle of Leyte Gulf, October 1944. The photo was taken from a carrier-based aircraft. Courtesy U.S. Naval Historical Center, Washington, D.C.*

Japanese gains in the Philippines. During the Japanese attack on Midway in June 1942, she sailed in support of the landing force. During the prolonged struggle for the Solomon Islands in the southwest Pacific, *Zuiho* was damaged at the Battle of the Santa Cruz Islands on October 26, 1942. Her next major engagement was at the Battle of the Philippine Sea in June 1944, where the Japanese carrier force was all but annihilated. On October 25, 1944, *Zuiho* was lost in about 19°20′N, 125°51′E, one of four Japanese carriers — with *Chitose*, ZUIKAKU, and *Chiyoda* — sunk by U.S. carrier-based planes at the Battle of Cape Engaño in one of the four actions that constituted the Battle of Leyte Gulf.

Grove, *Sea Battles in Close Up*. Stephen, *Sea Battles in Close-Up*.

ZUIKAKU

Shokaku-class aircraft carrier (2f/1m). *L/B/D:* 844.8′ × 85.3′ × 29′ (257.5m × 26m × 8.8m). *Tons:* 32,105 disp. *Comp.:* 1,660. *Arm.:* 84 aircraft; 16 × 5″, 96 × 25mm. *Armor:* 8.6″ belt, 6.8″ deck. *Mach.:* geared turbines, 160,000 shp, 4 shafts; 34.5 kts. *Built:* Kawasaki Dockyard Co., Kobe, Japan; 1941.

Zuikaku, whose name means "lucky crane," saw more action than any other Japanese aircraft carrier of World War II. Under Captain Ichibei Yokokawa, she sailed as part of the First Air Fleet in the December 7, 1941, attack on Pearl Harbor. The carrier later saw action in the Java Sea, and took part in the April 1942 attack on Ceylon. On May 8, at the Battle of the Coral Sea, planes from *Zuikaku* and SHOKAKU sank the aircraft carrier USS LEXINGTON and severely damaged YORKTOWN (CV-5), but at the expense of so many planes that she could not take part in the Battle of Midway.

Following that crushing defeat in June 1942, *Zuikaku* was the largest remaining Japanese carrier, but she saw little action over the next two years. At the Battle of the Philippine Sea, on June 19, 1944, *Zuikaku* was hit by dive-bombers from USS *Hornet* (CV-12), YORKTOWN (CV-10), and *Bataan.* Although she remained operational, that battle cost the Japanese nearly 405 of the 430 planes with which it had started the battle, as well as the carriers *Shokaku* and *Taiho.* Three months later, as the Japanese prepared their defense of the Philippines, *Zuikaku* sailed as the flagship of Admiral Jisaburo Ozawa's Northern Group. Assigned to draw American forces north while the Center Force closed in a pincer around the American landing force in Leyte Gulf, Ozawa's force comprised eighteen ships, including three smaller carriers; but by the evening of October 24, he had only 29 planes. The next day, planes from Admiral William F. Halsey's Third Fleet discovered the force about 200 miles north by east of Cape Engaño, the northeast tip of Luzon. The outcome was never in doubt, as Halsey had at his disposal 64 ships and 787 aircraft. Three torpedoes struck *Zuikaku,* and at 1310 she rolled over and sank in 19°20′N, 125°51′E. The Battle of Cape Engaño also cost the Japanese carriers ZUIHO, *Chitose,* and *Chiyoda,* together with two destroyers and a cruiser. It was the end of the Japanese carrier force.

Morison, *Two-Ocean War.*

ZUYTDORP

Ship (3m). *L/B/D:* 160.1′ × 39.4′ × 17′ (48.8m × 12.2m × 5.2m). *Tons:* 125 tons. *Hull:* wood. *Comp.:* 318. *Arm.:* 40 guns. *Built:* VOC, Master Shipwright Penne, Zeeland, Netherlands; 1702.

A retour ship built for the Dutch East India Company (Verenigde Oostindische Compagnie, or VOC) trade between the Netherlands and Batavia, *Zuytdorp* was an unlucky vessel. On her first voyage out, she suffered storm damage that required six weeks of repairs in Torbay, England, before she could proceed to Batavia. After trading in the Indies, she sailed for the Netherlands in December 1705, arriving at the Texel on July 26, 1706. Her second voyage lasted from 1707 to 1710. Her third passage out was a disaster from the start. She set sail on August 1, 1711, under Marinus Wysvliet, and it took her seven months to reach the Cape of Good Hope, during which time she lost 112 of her crew. *Zuytdorp* (named for a Dutch town) then sailed from Table Bay and vanished.

In 1927, Australian stockman Tom Pepper came across various artifacts — glass, coins, bronze breech-blocks, and a wooden statue — about 65 kilometers north of the Murchison River. Word of his discovery spread slowly, but eventually it was determined that the finds were from survivors of *Zuytdorp.* Because it is one of the world's most difficult wreck sites, it was not until 1963 that divers first saw the ship's remains, located in 27°11′S, 113°36′E. The site has yielded an impressive haul of silver coins, most minted in 1711.

Sigmond & Zuiderbaan, *Dutch Discoveries of Australia.*

MAPS

LITERARY SHIPS

CHRONOLOGIES

GLOSSARY

BIBLIOGRAPHY

INDEX

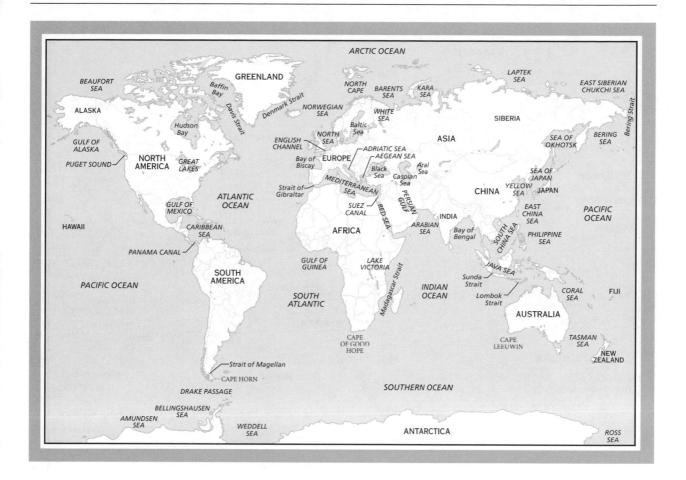

WATERS OF THE WORLD

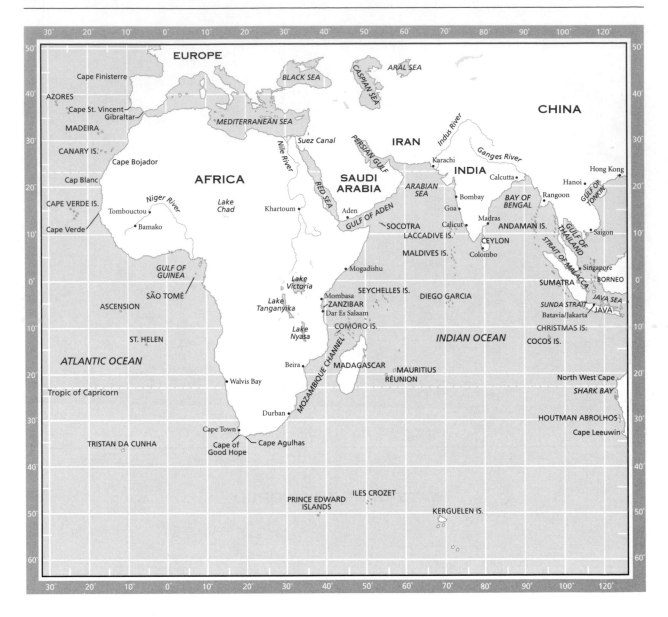

AFRICA AND THE INDIAN OCEAN

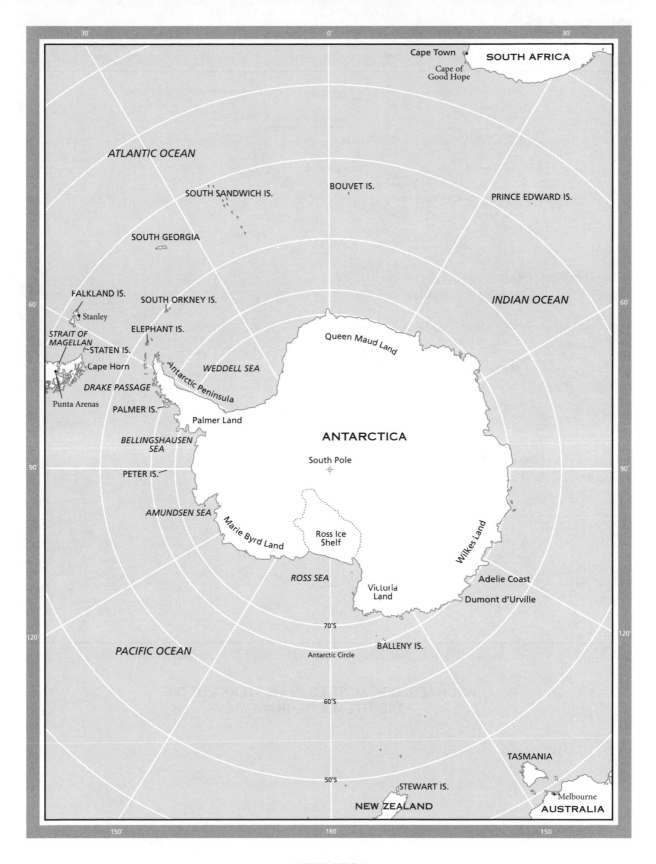

ANTARCTICA

ARCHAEOLOGICAL SITES IN WESTERN EUROPE
AND THE MEDITERRANEAN

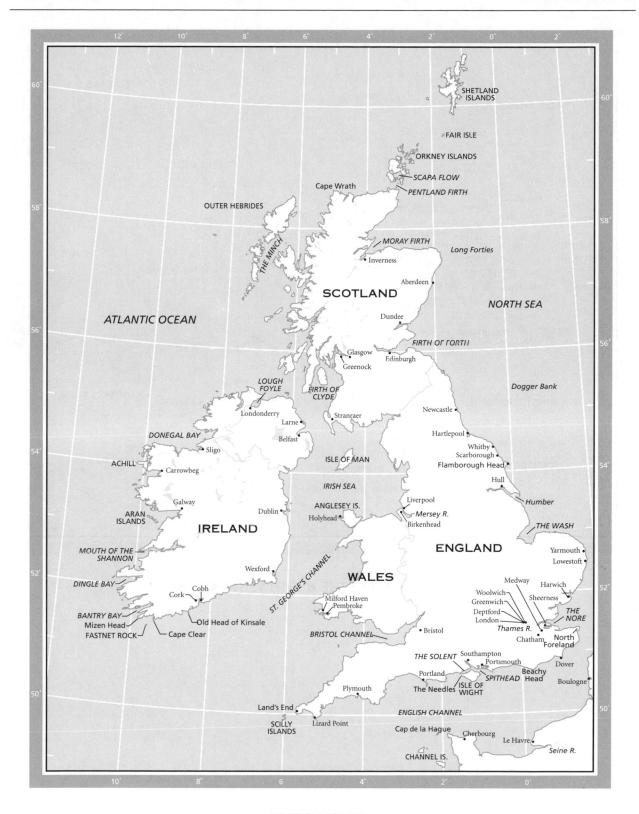

BRITISH ISLES

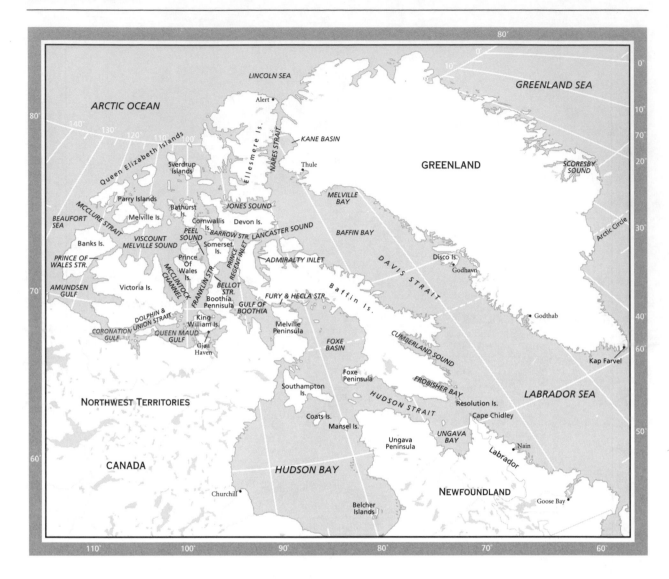

CANADIAN ARCTIC: THE NORTHWEST PASSAGE

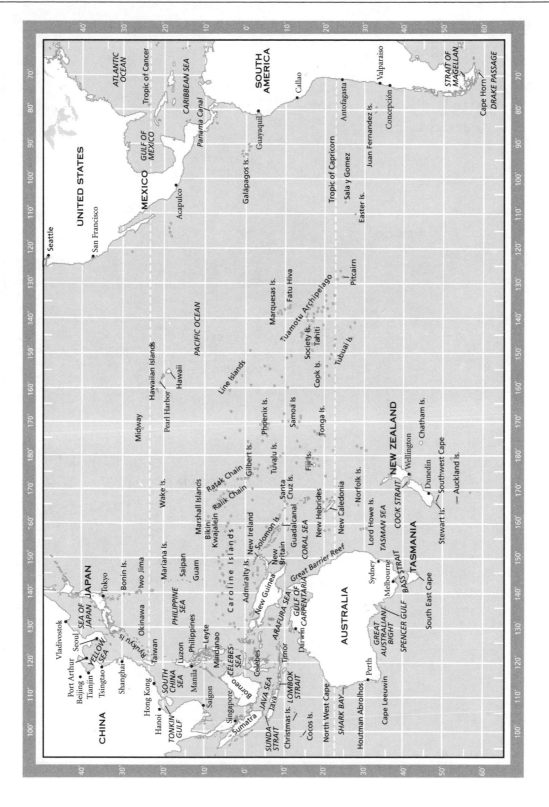

PACIFIC OCEAN

NORTH AND SOUTH AMERICA

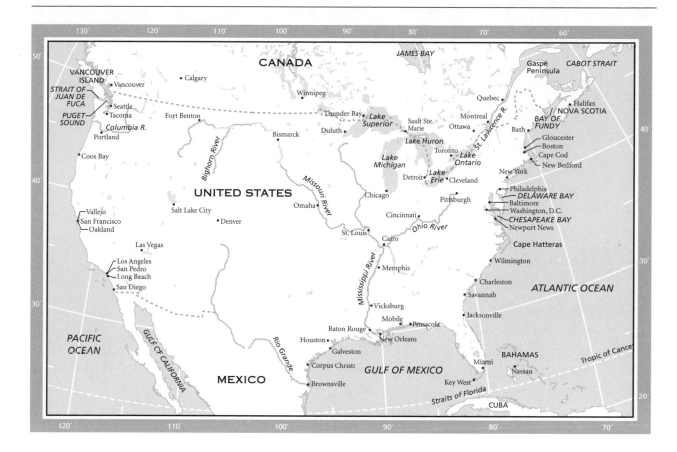

UNITED STATES

LITERARY SHIPS

HMS Achates (64) Richard Bolitho's flagship during the brief Peace of Amiens of 1803 in Alexander Kent's *Success to the Brave* (1983).

Adventure II A 350-tun merchantman from which Lemuel Gulliver is marooned in Brobdingnag — the land of the giants — in Jonathan Swift's *Gulliver's Travels* (1726). (See also **Antelope.**)

African Queen A river launch in C. S. Forester's novel *The African Queen* (1935), manned by the Cockney Charlie Allnutt and Rose Sayer, a missionary's sister. The two strike a blow for England by sinking the German gunboat *Königen Luise* on Lake Tanganyika in German Central Africa during World War I. John Huston's 1951 film starred Katharine Hepburn and Humphrey Bogart.

Amazon The sailing dinghy owned by the Blacketts (the Amazons) in Arthur Ransome's *Swallows and Amazons* (1930), *Swallowdale* (1931), and other books in the same series.

Antelope Ship in which Lemuel Gulliver, "First a Surgeon, and Then a Captain of Several Ships," is shipwrecked on Lilliput in Jonathan Swift's political satire *Travels into Several Remote Nations of the World*, better known as *Gulliver's Travels* (1726).

Arabella Buccaneer Peter Blood's command in Rafael Sabatini's Captain Blood novels: *Captain Blood* (1922), *The Chronicles of Captain Blood* (1931), and *The Fortunes of Captain Blood* (1933).

Archimedes Steamship that encounters a Caribbean hurricane in Richard Hughes's *In Hazard* (1938).

HMS Argonaute (74) Richard Bolitho's flagship in the Mediterranean in Alexander Kent's *Colors Aloft* (1986).

Ariel Sloop-of-war in which Jack Aubrey conveys Stephen Maturin to the Baltic in Patrick O'Brian's *The Surgeon's Mate* (1980).

HMS Artemis Light cruiser in C. S. Forester's *The Ship* (1943). The career of the *Artemis* was modeled on that of the World War II experience of HMS *Penelope,* particularly in the Second Battle of Sirte, March 1942.

HMS Atropos (22) Napoleonic-era sloop-of-war in C. S. Forester's *Hornblower and the "Atropos"* (1953).

Bachelor's Delight Captain Amasa Delano's sealer in Herman Melville's short story "Benito Cereno" (1855).

Balliol College British slaver commanded by a former Oxford don who shanghais Harry Flashman in George McDonald Fraser's novel *Flash for Freedom!* (1971).

USS Belinda Captain Hanks's attack transport in the Pacific theater from 1943 to 1945 in Kenneth Dodson's *Away All Boats* (1954); a movie of the same name followed in 1956.

HMS Bellipotent (74) Ship under Captain the Honorable Edward Fairfax Vere into which the foretopman Billy Budd is impressed from the merchantman *Rights of Man* and aboard which he inadvertently kills the treacherous Master-at-Arms John Claggart. Herman Melville's posthumously published *Billy Budd* (1924) was made into an opera by British composer Benjamin Britten (1951) and a film directed by Peter Ustinov (1962).

Black Swan Thomas Leach's 40-gun ship in Rafael Sabatini's novel *The "Black Swan"* (1932).

HMS Boadicea (38) Frigate in which Commodore Jack Aubrey must seize Mauritius Island from the French in Patrick O'Brian's *The Mauritius Command* (1977).

Broken Heart Captain Charles Margaret's ship in John Masefield's novel *Captain Margaret: A Romance* (1908).

Cachalot Whaleship in Frank T. Bullen's *Cruise of the "Cachalot"* (1898), the first of 36 novels by the veteran merchant seaman.

USS Caine Four-piper destroyer converted to a minelayer under the command of Captain Queeg in Herman Wouk's *The "Caine" Mutiny* (1951). The 1954 movie starred Humphrey Bogart and José Ferrer.

Caleuche Similar to the Flying Dutchman, fabled ship of the Chilean and Peruvian coasts.

HMS Calypso (36) Nicholas Ramage's ship in a number of Dudley Pope novels starting with *Ramage's Mutiny* (1977), in which the British cut out a captured frigate from a Spanish stronghold — a story based on the fate of HMS *Hermione.*

Cannibal Hogged barkentine attempting to cross the Pacific in Ernest K. Gann's novel *Twilight for the Gods* (1956).

HMS Carousel Cruiser in which First Lieutenant Robert Badger ("The Artful Bodger") sails in Robert Winton's *We Saw the Sea* (1960).

HMS Charybdis Obsolete armored cruiser in which Able Seaman Brown serves during World War I until she is sunk by the German SMS *Zeithen,* in C. S. Forester's *Brown on Resolution* (also published as *Single Handed,* 1929).

Clorinda Ship from which the Bas-Thornton children are kidnapped by pirates in Richard Hughes's *High Wind in Jamaica* (1929).

Compass Rose World War II *Flower*-class corvette in Nicholas Monsarrat's novel *The Cruel Sea* (1951). The book was turned into a movie of the same name (1953), written by Eric Ambler.

Covenant Brig in which the kidnapped David Balfour is sailing when she goes ashore on the Isle of Earraid in Robert Louis Stevenson's *Kidnapped: Being Memoirs of the Adventures of David Balfour in the Year 1751* (1886).

Das Boot Otherwise unidentified German submarine — "the boat" — aboard which 43 crew serve during the Battle of the Atlantic in 1941 in Lothar Gunther Buccheim's book (1973), and movie (1981), of the same name.

Das Feuerschiff Otherwise unnamed North Sea lightship in a story of the same name (1960) by Siegfried Lenz whose captain is mortally wounded after three gangsters board the ship and kidnap the crew.

Dawn Treader Galley in which Prince Caspian sails in search of the missing lords in C. S. Lewis's *Voyage of the "Dawn Treader"* (1952), the third volume in his six-part Chronicles of Narnia.

Dazzler Small boat in which a young boy sails through many adventures in and around San Francisco Bay in Jack London's *The Cruise of the "Dazzler"* (1902).

Death and Glory Pirate ship in Arthur Ransome's *Coot Club* (1934) used by members of the Coot Club in the Norfolk Broads in *The Big Six* (1940).

USS Delaware War of 1812–era frigate, similar to the USS *Constitution*, in C. S. Forester's *The Captain from Connecticut* (1941).

HMS Diane (36) Ship cut out of the French port of St. Martin, France, by Jack Aubrey in Patrick O'Brian's *The Letter of Marque* (1988). Aubrey and Steven Maturin later sail for the Indies in the *Diane* in *The Thirteen-Gun Salute* (1989), though the ship is wrecked there in *Nutmeg of Consolation* (1991).

HMS Dido (74) Nicholas Ramage's command in the West Indies in Dudley Pope's *Ramage and the "Dido"* (1989).

HMS Diomede In Frederick Marryat's *Peter Simple* (1834), a frigate commanded by Captain Savage, a character based on Lord Cochrane, under whom Marryat served on the French coast in HMS *Impérieuse.*

Dulcibella Cutter in which Davies and Carruthers reconnoiter Germany's North Sea coast shadowed by Herr Dolmann's galliot *Medusa* in Erskine Childers's *The Riddle of the Sands* (1906), often credited with being the first espionage novel. The 1984 film starred Michael York and Simon MacCorkindale. (See also, in main text, Childers's own *Asgard*.)

HMS Euryalus (100) Richard Bolitho's command in the western Mediterranean in Alexander Kent's *The Flag Captain* (1971).

Fidèle Ship aboard which occur the strange doings in Herman Melville's *The Confidence Man* (1857).

Flying Dutchman Legendary Dutch East Indiaman whose captain insisted on battling storms to round the Cape of Good Hope despite the entreaties of his crew and passengers. When God appeared in an apparition, the captain shot at him, and he was thus condemned to sail the seas forever as a torment to other sailors. The story has been interpreted in a variety of settings, notably Heinrich Heine's poem "Reisebilder" (1826), Frederick Marryat's novel *The Phantom Ship* (1839), Richard Wagner's opera *Der fliegender Holländer* (1843), and Washington Irving's "The *Flying Dutchman* of the Tappan Sea."

Goblin Yacht in which the Swallows sail from Harwich to Holland in Arthur Ransome's *We Didn't Mean to Go to Sea* (1937), and in which the Swallows, Amazons, and Eels have adventures in *Secret Water* (1939).

Golden Mary A three-masted ship sunk by an iceberg in *The Wreck of the "Golden Mary"* (1896), written by Charles Dickens and Wilkie Collins.

Happy Delivery Pirate ship in Sir Arthur Conan Doyle's short story "Captain Sharkey" (1897).

HMS Harpy Sloop-of-war in which Easy serves in Frederick Marryat's *Mr. Midshipman Easy* (1836). Easy's adventures are based on those of Lord Cochrane, under whom Marryat served in the frigate HMS *"Impérieuse"* from 1806 to 1809.

Hesperus The schooner of Henry Wadsworth Longfellow's ballad *Wreck of the "Hesperus"* (1840). The story is based on the events of a terrible gale in 1839 after which a young girl was washed ashore on Norman's Woe, near Gloucester, Massachusetts.

Highlander Merchant ship in which Wellingborough Redburn ships for a four-month voyage between New York and Liverpool in Herman Melville's *Redburn* (1849).

Hispaniola Ship used by Jim Hawkins and his confederates to seek Captain Flint's treasure in Robert Louis Stevenson's novel *Treasure Island* (1883).

Hopewell Ship on which Lemuel Gulliver sails as surgeon at the beginning of his third voyage in Jonathan Swift's political satire, *Travels into Several Remote Nations of the World,* better known as *Gulliver's Travels* (1726).

Hotspur (20) Horatio Hornblower's 6th-rate in C. S. Forester's *Hornblower and the "Hotspur"* (1962).

HMS Hyperion (74) Richard Bolitho's Napoleonic-era command in Alexander Kent's *Form Line of Battle!* (1969), *Enemy in Sight!* (1970), and *Honour This Day* (1987).

Inchcliffe Castle Tramp steamer that is the setting for Guy Gilpatric's stories about the Scots Chief Engineer Glencannon, including *Scotch and Water, Half Seas Over,* and *Three Sheets in the Wind.*

Isabel Kwel Oceangoing tug commanded by Martinus Harinxma in a series of Murmansk convoys in World War II in Jan de Hartog's *The Captain* (1966).

Ita Passenger ship commanded by the impostor master mariner Vasco de Aragão in Jorge Amado's *Home Is the Sailor: The Whole Truth Concerning the Redoubtful Adventures of Captain Vasco de Aragão from Bahía to Belém* (1964).

Judea Ship of about 400 tons, whose motto is "Do or Die," in Joseph Conrad's short story "Youth" (1898).

Julia Australian whaleship in which the crew mutiny against Captain Guy — "The Cabin Boy" — in Herman Melville's *Omoo, a Narrative of Adventures in the South Seas* (1847).

HMS Juno (32) Frigate in which Nicholas Ramage attacks a French convoy off Martinique in Dudley Pope's *Ramage's Diamond* (1976).

HMC Kathleen (8) Cutter in which Nicholas Ramage has a series of adventures — including the capture and recapture of his command — near the Spanish coast prior to the Battle of Cape St. Vincent in Dudley Pope's *Ramage and the Drumbeat* (1968).

USS Keeling *Mahan*-class destroyer under Commander George Krause, escort commander of an eastbound Atlantic convoy in the dark days of World War II, in C. S. Forester's *The Good Shepherd* (1955).

HMS Leviathan Aircraft carrier in John Winton's novel of the same name (1967).

HMS Lydia (36) Frigate in which Horatio Hornblower defeats the Spanish *Natividad* (50) on the Pacific coast of Central America in C. S. Forester's *The Happy Return* (also published as *Beat to Quarters*, 1938).

Mary Deare Liberty ship encountered by a salvage tug in the North Sea with only her captain aboard in Hammond Innes's *The Wreck of the "Mary Deare"* (1956); the 1959 movie starred Gary Cooper and Charlton Heston.

Mary Gloster Merchant ship named for Sir Anthony Gloster's wife, and in which Sir Anthony wishes to be buried, in Rudyard Kipling's poems "McAndrew's Hymn" and "The Mary Gloster" (1894).

SS Minnow Shipwrecked cabin cruiser in the 1960s television comedy *Gilligan's Island*.

Nan-Shan Captain McWhirr's stormbound steamship en route from Formosa to Fu-chau in Joseph Conrad's short story "Typhoon" (1902).

Narcissus The name of a real ship in which Joseph Conrad sailed from Bombay to Dunkirk and which he took for the setting for his novel *Nigger of the "Narcissus"* (1897). He probably retained the name — that of a white flower — to contrast with the title character, the black seaman James Wait. (See entry in main text.)

Narcissus Tug in which Tugboat Annie experiences her adventures on Puget Sound in Norman Reilly Raine's book of the same name (1934).

Natividad Old Spanish 50-gun two-decker captured on the west coast of Central America in the early 1800s by HMS *Lydia* in C. S. Forester's *The Happy Return* (or *Beat to Quarters*, 1938).

Nautilus Captain Nemo's submarine in Jules Verne's *Twenty Thousand Leagues beneath the Sea* (1869). Film versions include a silent movie made in 1916 and one starring James Mason and Kirk Douglas in 1954.

Nellie Cruising yawl aboard which Marlow tells the story of Mistuh Kurtz in Joseph Conrad's *Heart of Darkness* (1899).

USS Neversink American frigate in which the title character of Herman Melville's *White Jacket, or The World in a Man-of-War* (1850) sails from Callao to Norfolk. The novel is based on Melville's own experiences aboard the USS *United States* on a passage from Honolulu to Boston in 1843–44.

Nona Hilaire Belloc's actual yacht, aboard which he ponders "Reflections and Judgments on Life and Letters, Men and Manners" in *The Cruise of the "Nona": The Story of a Cruise* (1925).

Orca Whale-watching boat sunk by a great white shark off Long Island in Peter Benchley's novel *Jaws* (1974). The 1975 film directed by Steven Spielberg starred Richard Dreyfuss, Robert Shaw, and Roy Scheider.

Patna "A local steamer as old as the hills, lean like a greyhound, and eaten up with rust worse than a condemned water-tank" in Joseph Conrad's *Lord Jim* (1900). The *Patna* is based on the true story of the pilgrim ship *Jeddah* whose British officers abandoned her and 1,000 pilgrims bound from Singapore to Mecca, though the ship made it safely to Aden.

Pea Green Boat Otherwise unnamed vessel in which the title characters of Edward Lear's poem "The Owl and the Pussycat" (1846) put to sea.

Pequod Whaleship under command of Captain Ahab, whose relentless pursuit of the great white whale in Herman Melville's *Moby-Dick* (1851) leads to the loss of the ship and all her crew save Ishmael. Film adaptations include the 1926 silent film *The Sea Beast*, a 1930 sound remake called *Moby Dick*, and a *Moby Dick* directed by John Huston (1956), written by Ray Bradbury and starring Gregory Peck.

HMS Phalarope (36) Richard Bolitho's command during the American Revolution in Alexander Kent's *To Glory We Steer* (1968).

HMS Pinafore Captain Corcoran's "saucy ship" in the 1878 operetta of the same name by W.S. Gilbert and Arthur Sullivan.

HMS Polychrest (24) Jack Aubrey's brig to which Captain the Spanish Azema surrenders in Patrick O'Brian's *Post Captain* (1972).

Poseidon Passenger ship overwhelmed by a tidal wave in the Mediterranean in Paul Gallico's novel *The "Poseidon" Adventure* (1969). The 1972 movie starred Gene Hackman and Shelley Winters.

Pretty Jane Merchant brig in which Admiral Horatio Hornblower and his wife, Barbara, are nearly shipwrecked in C. S. Forester's *Admiral Hornblower in the West Indies* (1957).

PT-73 World War II–era PT boat commanded by Lieutenant Commander McHale in the 1960s television comedy *McHale's Navy*, starring Ernest Borgnine.

Red October Soviet submarine stalked by Soviet and U.S. forces in Tom Clancy's novel *The Hunt for "Red October"* (1984). The 1990 film starred Sean Connery.

USS Reluctant U.S. Navy transport in the backwaters of the Pacific during World War II in Thomas Heggen's novel *Mister Roberts.* The book was adapted for stage (coauthored by Joshua Logan) and film (1955), directed by John Huston and starring Henry Fonda and James Cagney.

S. A. Vera North German Lloyd passenger liner bound from Veracruz, Mexico, for Bremerhaven, Germany, in 1931 in Katherine Anne Porter's *Ship of Fools* (1945). The 1965 film starred Vivien Leigh and Oskar Werner.

San Dominick Slave ship commanded by Benito Cereno and visited by Captain Amasa Delano of the *Bachelor's Delight* in Herman Melville's "Benito Cereno" (1855).

USS San Pablos American gunboat on the Yangtze River in 1926 during the Chinese civil war in Richard McKenna's novel *The Sand Pebbles* (1962). The 1966 film starred Steve McQueen.

USS Scorpion American submarine in Nevil Shute's apocalyptic novel *On the Beach.*

Sea Bear An old Norwegian pilot cutter in which the Swallows, Amazons, and Scarabs sail to an island of the Outer Hebrides in Arthur Ransome's *Great Northern?* (1947).

Sephora Liverpool ship from which Second Mate Leggatt escapes after killing a member of the crew in Joseph Conrad's *Secret Sharer* (1910).

Ship of Fools A ship manned by fools of various sorts in Sebastian Brant's long satirical poem *Das Narrenschiff,* first published in Latin as *Stultifera Navis* (1494). The poem, which caricatures a wide variety of human vices, has been widely imitated. Alexander Barclay's *The Shyp of Folys of the Worlde* appeared in 1509, W. H. Ireland's *Modern Ship of Fools* in 1807, and Katherine Anne Porter's *Ship of Fools* in 1945 (see **S. A. Vera**). The Grateful Dead also wrote a song of the same name (1973).

Ship of State Literary metaphor for government widely employed since antiquity.

Sofala Steamer purchased by Captain Henry Whalley after selling the bark *Fair Maid* in Joseph Conrad's *End of the Tether* (1902).

HM Brig Sophie (14) Jack Aubrey's first command in Patrick O'Brian's *Master and Commander* (1970). Aubrey's exploits in the western Mediterranean are based on those of Lord Cochrane in HM Brig *Speedy.*

HMS Sparrow (20) Richard Bolitho's command in Alexander Kent's *Sloop of War* (1972), which takes place during the American Revolution.

HMS Sunderland (74) Horatio Hornblower's ship in C. S. Forester's *Ship of the Line* (1938).

HMS Surprise (28) Jack Aubrey's command on a voyage to India during which he fights the French *Marengo* (74) in Patrick O'Brian's *H.M.S. "Surprise"* (1973). Aubrey returns to command of the *Surprise* in *The Far Side of the World*

(1984), *The Reverse of the Medal* (1986), *Letter of Marque* (1988), *The Thirteen-Gun Salute* (1989), *The Truelove* (1992), and *The Wine-Dark Sea* (1994).

Swallow The 14-foot sailing dinghy owned by the Walkers (the Swallows) in Arthur Ransome's *Swallows and Amazons* (1930) and other books in the same series.

Taronga Park Tramp steamer owned by St. Vincent Halfhyde after his departure from the Royal Navy in Phillip McCutchen's turn-of-the-century series, including *The Halfhyde Line* (1984), *Halfhyde on the Amazon* (1988), and *Halfhyde and the Admiral* (1990).

HMS Temeraire Royal Navy Polaris submarine spying on the Soviet Union's Black Sea fleet in John Winton's *The Fighting "Temeraire"* (1971).

HMS Tempest (38) Richard Bolitho's command while searching the South Pacific for the *Bounty* mutineers in Alexander Kent's *Passage to Mutiny* (1976).

Titan Ill-fated unsinkable transatlantic liner that sinks on her maiden voyage after striking an iceberg at high speed in Morgan Robertson's *Futility, or Wreck of the "Titan"* (1898). The somewhat far-fetched story took on new significance following the loss of the similarly named *Titanic* in like circumstances fourteen years after the book appeared.

Triton (10) Brig in which Nicholas Ramage must sail to the Caribbean in the wake of the Spithead Mutiny in Dudley Pope's *The "Triton" Brig* (also published as *Ramage and the Freebooters,* 1969) and *Governor Ramage, R.N.* (1973).

HMS Ulysses Modified *Dido*-class cruiser in which the protagonists from Alistar MacLean's 1955 novel of the same name battle the Germans on the Murmansk convoy run.

HMS Undine (32) Richard Bolitho's East Indies command in Alexander Kent's *Command a King's Ship* (1973).

HMS Venus The first Royal Navy ship in which women sail as combatants in John Winton's novel *The Good Ship "Venus"* (1984). The Women's Royal Naval Service actually went to sea as combatants in 1990, and it was fully absorbed into the Royal Navy in 1994.

USS Walrus American submarine on patrol in the Pacific during World War II in *Run Silent, Run Deep* (1955), by Edward L. Beach; the 1958 movie starred Clark Gable and Burt Lancaster. (See also, in main text, Beach's command, USS *Triton.*)

We're Here Gloucester fishing schooner by whose crew spoiled rich kid Harvey Cheyne is rescued after falling from a luxury liner in Rudyard Kipling's *Captains Courageous* (1896). Victor Fleming's 1937 adaptation, with Spencer Tracy and Mickey Rooney, is notable for its footage of schooners under way.

Wild Cat Schooner in which Captain Flint, the Swallows, and the Amazons sail from Lowestoft to Crab Island, in the Caribbean, with able seaman Peter Duck in Arthur Ransome's *Peter Duck* (1932). She later burns in *Missee Lee* (1941).

Wonder Captain David Grief's interisland schooner in Jack London's South Pacific adventure *A Son of the Sun* (1911).

HMS Worcester (74) Ship of the line under Jack Aubrey's command in Patrick O'Brian's *Ionian Mission* (1981).

Yellow Submarine Submarine commanded by Old Fred in which The Beatles and the Lonely Hearts Club Band sail from Liverpool to the undersea kingdom of Pepperland "to rescue the pleasures of food and music and perpetual cele-bration and colorful beauty" from the Blue Meanies. The 1968 animated film is a psychedelic reinterpretation of the Old English epic, *Beowulf.*

SMS Zeithen German light cruiser damaged in action with HMS *Charybdis* in C. S. Forester's *Brown on Resolution* (also published as *Single Handed,* 1929). Her much needed repairs are hampered by Brown's intrigues, and she is later sunk by HMS *Leopard.*

CHRONOLOGIES

ARCHAEOLOGICAL SITES

2500 BCE Cheops ship; Egypt
2200 BCE Dokos wreck; Greece
1840 BCE Dahshur boats; Egypt
14th cent. BCE Ulu Burun wreck ("Kas wreck");
    Turkey
1300 BCE Ferriby Bronze Age wrecks; England
1200 BCE Cape Gelidonya wreck; Turkey
800–650 BCE Brigg boat; England
600 BCE Giglio ship; Italy
550–525 BCE Bon Porté wreck; France
400 BCE Porticello wreck; Italy
4th cent. BCE Kyrenia wreck; Greece
241 BCE Punic (Marsala) ship; Sicily
2nd cent. BCE Athlit ram; Israel
1st cent. BCE Mahdia wreck; Tunisia
    Galilee boat; Israel
    Albenga wreck; Italy
ca. 85 BCE Antikythera wreck; Greece
ca. 75 BCE Madrague de Giens wreck; France
2nd cent. CE Blackfriars barge; England
3rd cent. St. Peter Port wreck; Channel Islands
ca. 350 Nydam boats; Sweden
4th cent. Yassi Ada wreck B; Turkey
    Mainz ships; Germany
7th cent. Pantano Longarini wreck; Italy
    Yassi Ada wreck A; Turkey
ca. 625 Sutton Hoo ship; England
ca. 815–820 Oseberg ship; Norway
890–895 Gokstad ship; Norway
ca. 930 Graveney boat; England
10th cent. Agay wreck; France
ca. 1050 Utrecht boat; Belgium
11th cent. Skuldelev wrecks; Denmark
    Serçe Limani ship; Turkey
1277 Quanzhou wreck; China
1323 Shinan wreck; Korea
1379–80 Bremen Cog wreck; Germany
1418 *Grace Dieu*; England
16th cent. Highborn Cay wreck; Bahamas

1510 *Mary Rose*; England
    Molasses Reef wreck; Bahamas
ca. 1550 *San Estéban*; Texas
1565 *San Juan*; Labrador
1588 *Girona* & *Trinidad Valencera*; northern
    Ireland
1603 *Sea Venture*; Bermuda
1609 *Witte Leeuw*; Ascension
1620 *Nuestra Señora de Atocha*; Florida
    Nuestra Señora de la Concepción; West Indies
    Nuestra Señora de la Concepción; Saipan
1621 *Triall*; Western Australia
1628 *Batavia*; Australia
1653 *Vergulde Draeck*; Western Australia
1663 *Sacramento*; Brazil
1676 *Kronan*; Sweden
1686 *Belle*; Texas
1693 *Meresteyn*; South Africa
1695 *Adventure Galley*; Madagascar
1697 *Henrietta Marie*; Florida
1702 *Zuytdorp*; Australia
1713 *Risdam*; Malaysia
1716 *Whydah*; Cape Cod
1726 *Zeewijk*; Western Australia
1740 Brown's Ferry vessel; South Carolina
1742 *Hollandia*; England
1744 *Amsterdam*; England
1746 *Geldermalsen*; Malaysia
1758 *Machault*; Canada
1763 *Defence*; Maine
1779 HMS *Pandora*; Australia
1781 *Betsy*; Chesapeake Bay
1784 HMS *De Braak*; Chesapeake Bay
    HMS *Bounty*; Pitcairn Island
1787 HMS *Colossus*; England
1809 *Hamilton*; Great Lakes
1811 *Scourge*; Great Lakes
1843 HMS *Breadalbane*; Arctic
1848 *Indiana*; Great Lakes
1851 *Maple Leaf*; Florida
1864 *Bertrand*; Nebraska

MARITIME AND RELATED TECHNOLOGY

3000 BCE Oared galleys employing "shell-first" hull construction method appear in eastern Mediterranean. Galleys continue to be used for nearly 5,000 years.

8th cent. BCE Ships with 2 tiers of oars appear in eastern Mediterranean.

5th cent. BCE Triremes — galleys with 3 banks of oars — introduced in eastern Mediterranean.

4th cent. BCE Clinker-built, or lapstrake, hull planking (as opposed to edge-to-edge or carvel construction) found in Hjortspring boat from southeast Denmark.

4th cent. CE Lateen (fore-and-aft) sails begin to predominate over square sails in Mediterranean.

7th–14th cent. Cog develops in northern Europe: flat-bottomed, high-sided with edge-to-edge and clinker-laid planking.

9th cent. Shell-first, clinker-built Viking ships evolve in Scandinavia.

11th cent. Frame-first hull construction predominates in Mediterranean.

12th cent. Rudimentary compasses in Europe.

13th–15th cent. Caravels evolve in southern Europe. Two-masted, lateen-rigged vessels of frame-first construction, they were used extensively in the Portuguese voyages of exploration.

13th cent. Vertical-hinged rudder first appears in northern Europe, eventually to replace side-mounted steering oar. Cross staff for measuring altitudes of celestial bodies invented by Jacob ben Makir in southern France.

14th cent. Naval guns first used on ships.

14th–15th cent. Mediterranean *nao*, or carrack, merges Mediterranean and northern European shipbuilding practices. These forerunners of the full-rigged ship combine frame-first construction, high sides, center-line rudder, and mixed rigs of square and lateen sails.

15th cent. Quadrant first used by Portuguese navigators for measuring altitudes of celestial bodies.

16th–17th cent. Galleon — similar to a carrack, but with a lower forecastle that made it more weatherly — evolves in northern Europe.

1695–1712 Working independently, Denis Papin, Thomas Savery, and Thomas Newcomen develop low-pressure steam pump, or atmospheric engine, forerunner of the steam engine.

1757 Sextant invented in England; it is capable of measuring angles of up to 120°.

1759 John Harrison builds first marine chronometer, enabling mariners to determine longitude at sea.

1770 Grand Trunk Canal links England's industrial heartland to sea.

1776 David Bushnell builds submarine *Turtle* in New York.

James Watt develops steam engine, followed by double-acting expansion engine in **1782.** Commercial success begins with partnership with Matthew Boulton in **1785.**

1778 Scottish Carron Company develops large-caliber, short-range "ship-smashing" gun known as carronade.

1783 July 15 Marquis de Jouffroy d'Abbans's steamboat *Pyroscaphe* operates on Saône River, France, for 15 minutes.

1787–90 John Fitch's steamboat operates, albeit unprofitably, along the Delaware River.

1786–87 James Rumsey demonstrates water-jet-powered *Rumseian Experiment* on Potomac River.

1793 Claude Chappe develops semaphore signaling system in France.

1801 William Symington's *Charlotte Dundas* tows 2 barges 20 miles on Forth and Clyde Canal, Scotland.

1803 Robert Fulton builds early submarine *Nautilus* in France.

1807 Fulton's *North River Steam Boat,* first commercially successful steamer, begins service on Hudson River.

1808 June 10–23 *Phoenix* makes first sea passage of any steamship along coast of New Jersey.

1811–12 *New Orleans* first steamboat on the Mississippi.

1819 *Savannah* first steamship to cross the Atlantic.

1821 *Aaron Manby* first seagoing iron-hulled ship.

1824 Henri J. Paixhans experiments with shell guns; adopted by France in **1837.**

1825 Erie Canal links Hudson River and Great Lakes. First railway built in England.

1832 April 22–23 *Sirius* and *Great Western,* respectively, arrive at New York, completing first transatlantic passages under sustained steam power.

1833–36 Working independently, Robert Wilson, Francis Pettit Smith, Frédéric Sauvage, and John Ericsson develop screw propellers.

1836 *Beaver* first steamship in Pacific Northwest.

1837 Samuel F. B. Morse invents his telegraphic system and develops Morse code.

1839 John Ericsson's *Robert F. Stockton* first screw vessel in U.S.

1840 *Nemesis* first iron ship to round Cape of Good Hope, en route to India.

1840s–1850s Clippers developed for fast transport, especially between East Coast and San Francisco.

1843 Isambard Kingdom Brunel launches *Great Britain,* first oceangoing, iron screw-propeller ship.

1845 Tug-of-war between HMS *Rattler* & *Alecto,* which demonstrates superiority of screw over sidewheel propulsion.

1853 John Ericsson's "caloric ship" *Ericsson* proves unsuccessful.

1854 William Armstrong designs first breech-loading, rifled gun; Royal Navy first adopts them for shipboard batteries in **1860.**

1859 France launches first ironclad warship, *Gloire.*

1860s High-pressure compound steam engine developed.

1860 Britain launches HMS *Warrior,* first iron-hulled warship.

1862 Battle of Hampton Roads between USS *Monitor* & CSS *Virginia* is first between ironclad vessels. Steam-steering gear patented in Great Britain.

Banshee first steel-hulled ship to cross the Atlantic.

1864 Robert Whitehead develops self-propelled torpedo.

1869 Suez Canal opens, linking Mediterranean and Red seas.

1870s Triple-expansion steam engine developed.

1876 Plimsoll lines indicating levels to which a merchant ship can be safely loaded in different waters and at different seasons, adopted in Britain after passage of Merchant Shipping Act. The levels are tropical fresh water (TF); fresh water (F); tropical sea water (T); summer, sea water (S); winter, sea water (W); winter, North Atlantic (WNA). Alexander Graham Bell invents telephone.

1878–79 Electric lights invented in England and U.S.; pioneered aboard ship in *City of Berlin* (1879).

1881 John Holland builds Fenian Ram, early submarine, in U.S.

1885 Karl Benz develops prototype of automobile.

1894 Charles A. Parsons builds *Turbinia,* 10 years after patenting steam turbine.

1895 Kiel Canal through Schleswig-Holstein opens, linking Baltic and North seas.

1900 Holland builds first fully operational submarine, USS *Holland.*

1902 *Lake Champlain* first ship fitted with wireless telegraph.

1903 Orville and Wilbur Wright make first airplane flight at Kitty Hawk, North Carolina.

1906 HMS *Dreadnought* first "all-big-gun" battleship.

1910 **November 14** Eugene B. Ely flies Curtiss pusher biplane off anchored cruiser USS *Birmingham* in Hampton Roads, Virginia. On **January 18, 1911,** Ely lands on and takes off from anchored armored cruiser USS *Pennsylvania* in San Francisco Bay.

1914 Panama Canal opens, cutting distance between New York and San Francisco from about 13,100 miles (via Cape Horn) to about 5,300 miles.

1917 On **August 2,** E. H. Dunning lands Sopwith Pup on HMS *Furious* in the first landing of a plane on a ship under way.

1918 Allied Submarine Detection Investigation Committee (ASDIC) established to develop devices for determining range and bearing of submerged objects; later known as sonar (for SOund Navigation And Radar).

1919 Alexander Graham Bell's hydrofoil *HD-4* sets speed record of 70.86 mph.

1920 Anton Flettner launches rotor ship *Baden-Baden.*

1921 **July 21** Land-based Martin bombers sink deactivated German battleship *Ostfriesland* in first demonstration of aircraft's antiship capability.

1930s Radar (RAdio Direction And Range) developed in Britain, Germany, and U.S.

1942 Battle of Coral Sea between Japanese and American carriers is the first in which surface ships are not within visual range of each another.

Loran (LOng RAnge Navigation) hyperbolic navigation system developed in U.S.

1944 Decca hyperbolic navigation system used during D-day invasion of Normandy.

1945 Nuclear bombs dropped on Hiroshima and Nagasaki.

1952 *United States* captures Blue Riband, crossing Atlantic eastbound at 35.59 knots and returning at 34.51 knots.

1954 Submarine USS *Nautilus,* first commissioned nuclear-powered vessel; sails under North Pole in 1958.

1957 *Sputnik,* first manmade satellite, launched into orbit.

1958 First commercial transatlantic jet plane service.

1959 Soviet icebreaker *Lenin* first nuclear-powered surface ship.

St. Lawrence Seaway opens, enabling deep-water navigation between Great Lakes and Atlantic.

1960 USS *Triton* circumnavigates the world under water.

1964 *Savannah* commissioned as first commercial nuclear-powered ship.

1985 U.S. Department of Defense makes Navstar global position system (GPS) satellite data available to public.

VOYAGES OF DISCOVERY

ca. 1000 Leif Ericsson ("The Lucky") lands in North America; establishment of short-lived Viking outpost at L'Anse aux Meadows, Newfoundland.

1492 *Niña, Pinta,* & *Santa María.* Columbus's first voyage explores Bahamas, Cuba, and Hispaniola.

1497 *Mathew.* Cabot expedition to Newfoundland and Labrador.

1497–99 *São Gabriel.* Gama's flagship on first voyage round Cape of Good Hope to India.

1519–22 *Victoria,* etc. Magellan/De Elcano circumnavigation.

1524 *Dauphine.* Verrazzano explores North America from North Carolina to Maine and Newfoundland.

1534, 1535–36, 1541–42 *Grande Hermine.* Cartier expeditions to Canada.

1553–54 *Edward Bonaventure.* Borough/Chancellor expedition to Murmansk.

1567–69 *Los Reyes,* etc. Mendaña transpacific voyage to Solomon Islands and back.

1576 *Gabriel.* Frobisher's first search for Northwest Passage.

1577 *Aid, Gabriel,* etc. Frobisher's second expedition.

1577–80 *Golden Hind.* Drake circumnavigation.

1578 *Aid,* etc. Frobisher's third expedition.

1585 *Sunneshine,* etc. Davis expedition to Greenland.

1595–96 San Jerónimo, etc. Mendaña's second expedition, to colonize Solomon Islands.

1602 *Concord.* Gosnold expedition to New England.

Discovery. Weymouth expedition to Canada.

1605–6 *Duyfken.* Jansz explores northern Australia.

San Pedro y San Pablo, San Pedro, etc. Quiros expedition

to rediscover Solomon Islands. Torres transits strait between Australia and New Guinea in *San Pedro*.

1607 *Susan Constant*. Establishment of English colony at Jamestown, Virginia.

1609 *Sea Venture*. Shipwrecked on Bermuda.
Halve Maen. Hudson ascends Hudson River.

1610–11 *Discovery*. Hudson expedition to Hudson Bay.

1612–13 *Discovery*, etc. Exploration of Hudson Bay.

1615–16 *Discovery*. Bylot and Baffin voyages to Hudson Bay and Lancaster Sound.

1615–17 *Eendracht*, etc. Schouten and Le Maire first to round Cape Horn.

1616 *Eendracht*. Hartog lands in western Australia.

1619–20 *Unicorn*. Jens Munk's search for Northwest Passage in Hudson Bay.

1620 *Mayflower*. Pilgrims reach Plymouth (Massachusetts).

1642–43 *Heemskerck*, etc. Abel Tasman exploration of Australia.

1644 *Limmen*, etc. Tasman's second expedition to Australia.

1668–69 *Nonsuch*. Couart and Radisson voyage to Hudson Bay lays groundwork for Hudson's Bay Company.

1679 *Griffon*. La Salle's ship, first European vessel on the Great Lakes.

1684–86 *Belle*, etc. La Salle expedition to the Gulf Coast.

1698–1700 *Paramore*. Halley makes 2 voyages to South Atlantic for study of magnetic variation.

1699–1701 *Roebuck*. Dampier expedition to explore Australia and New Guinea.

1701 *Paramore*. Halley makes 4-month study of tides and tidal currents in English Channel.

1708–11 *Duke* et al. Rogers circumnavigation.

1721–22 *Arend*. Roggeveen's search for southern continent.

1728–29 *St. Gabriel*. Bering's first expedition, through Bering Strait.

1740–41 *St. Peter* & *St. Paul*. Bering's second expedition, in Alaska.

1740–44 HMS *Centurion, Wager*, etc. Anson circumnavigation; Byron shipwreck.

1764–66 HMS *Dolphin*, etc. Byron circumnavigation.

1766–68/69 HMS *Dolphin* & *Swallow*. Wallis and Carteret circumnavigations.

1766–69 *Boudeuse*, etc. Bougainville circumnavigation.

1768–71 HMS *Endeavour*. Cook's first expedition to Pacific.

1769–70 *St. Jean-Baptiste*. Surville commercial expedition from India to Peru.

1772–74 *Resolution* & *Adventure*. Cook's second expedition to Pacific.

1776–80 *Resolution* & *Discovery*. Cook's third expedition to Pacific.

1785–88 *Astrolabe* & *Boussole*. La Pérouse's ill-fated expedition.

1788 HMS *Sirius*. Establishment of British colony at Botany Bay, Australia.

1789–93 *Descubierta*. Malaspina exploration of Pacific Northwest and Australia.

1791–93 *Esperance*. Entrecasteaux expedition to Pacific in search of La Pérouse.

1791–95 *Discovery*, etc. Vancouver circumnavigation.

1792 *Sutil*, etc. Galiano explores Pacific Northwest for Spain.

1794–96 *Union*. Boit circumnavigation.

1800–4 *Géographe*, etc. Baudin exploration of Australia and circumnavigation.

1801–3 HMS *Investigator*. Flinders explores Australia.

1803–6 *Nadezhda*, etc. Krusenstern leads first Russian circumnavigation.

1805 *Joliba*. Park's boat on the Niger River.

1806 *Resolution*. Scoresby attains record farthest north in Greenland Sea.

1807–13 *Diana*. Golovnin voyage from Russia to Northwest Pacific and Japan.

1815–18 *Rurik*. Kotzebue circumnavigation.

1817–20 *Uranie*, etc. Freycinet circumnavigation.

1818 *Isabella*, etc. John Ross searches for Northwest Passage.

1819–20 HMS *Hecla*. Parry reaches Melville Island in Northwest Passage.

1819–21 *Vostok*. Bellingshausen expedition to Antarctica.

1820 *Hero*. American sealer under Nathaniel B. Palmer sails near Palmer (now Antarctic) Peninsula.

1821–23 *Hecla*, etc. Parry explores northern Hudson Bay.

1822–25 *Coquille* (later *Astrolabe*). Duperrey circumnavigation.

1823–26 *Predpriyatiye*. Kotzebue expedition to Pacific coast of North America.

1824–25 *Hecla*, etc. Parry explores Prince Regent Inlet in Northwest Passage.

1825–27 *Blossom*. Beechey expedition to Pacific and Arctic.

1826–29 *Astrolabe*. Dumont-D'Urville circumnavigation; finds relics of La Pérouse expedition.

1826–30 *Senyavin*. Litke scientific expedition to Pacific and circumnavigation.

1827 *Hecla*. Parry attempts to reach North Pole from Spitsbergen.

1829–33 *Victory*. John Ross's second expedition in quest of Northwest Passage.

1831–36 HMS *Beagle*. Fitzroy/Darwin circumnavigation via South America and Galapagos.

1836–37 HMS *Terror*. Back expedition to Hudson Bay.

1838–42 USS *Vincennes*. Wilkes circumnavigation.

1839–43 HMS *Erebus* & *Terror*. Ross Antarctic expedition.

1845–48 HMS *Erebus* & *Terror*. Franklin's ill-fated search for Northwest Passage.

1848–49 HMS *Investigator*. Ross expedition in search of Franklin.

1850–54 HMS *Investigator*. McClure establishes last link of Northwest Passage from west.
Advance. De Haven Arctic expedition.

1852–54 *Resolute*. Belcher expedition to find Franklin.

1857–59 *Fox*. M'Clintock finds remains of Franklin expedition.

1871–73 USS *Polaris*. Hall's third expedition in search of North Pole.

1871–74 *Tegetthoff*. Payer and Weyprecht Arctic expedition discovers Franz Josef Land.

1872–76 HMS *Challenger*. Nares oceanographic research expedition.

1875–76 *Alert,* etc. Nares Arctic expedition.

1878–79 *Vega*. Nordenskiöld circumnavigates Eurasia after becoming first to traverse Northeast Passage.

1879–82 *Jeannette*. Ill-fated De Long expedition in quest of North Pole.

1893–96 *Fram*. Nansen's drift in the Arctic Ocean.

1897–99 *Belgica*. Gerlache expedition first to winter in Antarctica.

1901–4 HMS *Discovery*. Scott leads British National Antarctic Expedition.

1903–6 *Gjøa*. Amundsen first to complete Northwest Passage.

1905–6 *Roosevelt*. Peary's fourth Arctic expedition establishes new farthest north.

1907–9 *Nimrod*. Shackleton's British Imperial Antarctic Expedition.

1908–10 *Pourquoi Pas?* Charcot leads first Antarctic expedition.

1909 *Roosevelt*. Peary & Henson first to reach North Pole.

1910–12 *Fram*. Amundsen first to reach South Pole.

1910–13 Terra Nova. Scott's ill-fated attempt to reach the South Pole.

1914–15 *Endurance*. Ship crushed in ice during Shackleton's Imperial Trans-Antarctic Expedition.

1921–54 *Bowdoin*. MacMillan's Arctic voyages.

1925–27 *Meteor*. Topographic survey of Atlantic Ocean floor.

1931 *Nautilus*. Wilkinson expedition first submarine under the ice pack.

1941–42 *St. Roch*. Larsen expedition second to traverse Northwest Passage, first from west to east.

1947 *Kon-Tiki*. Heyerdahl expedition from Peru to Tuamotus in reed raft.

1958 USS *Nautilus*. Anderson takes submarine to 90° N; first vessel at North Pole.

1969 *Manhattan*. First commercial vessel to transit Northwest Passage.

1970 *Ra II*. Heyerdahl transatlantic expedition from Morocco to Barbados in reed boat.

1975 *Arktika*. First surface ship to North Pole.

1976–77 *Brendan*. Severin re-creates legendary transatlantic voyage of St. Brendan in curragh.

1977–78 *Tigris*. Heyerdahl expedition from Persian Gulf to East Africa in reed boat.

1980 *Sohar*. Severin expedition from Oman to China in traditional dhow.

1984 *Argo*. Severin retraces Black Sea route of mythical Argonauts from Greece to Georgia.

1995 *Hawai'iloa*. Polynesian voyaging canoe re-creates traditional voyage from Hawaii to Tahiti.

NAVAL HISTORY

Antiquity to the Early Modern Period

480 BCE Battle of Salamis: Greek fleet led by Athenians defeats Persian invasion.

241 BCE Battle of the Egadi Islands (Sicily): Roman fleet wins decisive victory over Carthaginians to end First Punic War.

31 BCE **Sept. 2** Battle of Actium (Greece): Marc Antony and Cleopatra defeated by fleet under Octavian (later Augustus); date marks Rome's transition from republic to empire.

838 CE Vikings capture Dublin, Ireland.

1000 Battle of Øresund: Olaf Tryggvason killed; control of southern Norway passes to Eirik.

1066 Norman Conquest of England: William the Conqueror launches invasion across the English Channel and defeats King Harald at Battle of Hastings.

1340 **June 24** Battle of Sluys (Netherlands): English win control of the English Channel from French at start of Hundred Years' War.

1512 **Aug. 10** English defeat French in battle off Brest; *La Cordelière* sunk.

1544 **July 19** *Mary Rose* sunk at Portsmouth during French invasion.

1568 **Sept. 23** English ships under Hawkins, in *Jesus of Lubeck*, beaten by Spanish at San Juan de Ulloa, Mexico.

1571 **Oct. 7** Battle of Lepanto: Christian coalition defeats Turks at mouth of Gulf of Corinth, Greece.

1588 **July 31–Aug. 8** Spanish Armada against England ends in failure.

1591 **Sept. 8** Last fight of *Revenge* against superior Spanish force in the Azores.

1628 **Apr 10** Swedish flagship *Wasa* sinks off Stockholm on maiden voyage.

1651 **Oct. 9** Navigation Act restricts English trade to English ships and requires salute to English flag from foreign ships in the English Channel.

1652 **May 29** Battle of Dover (Downs): Tromp vs. Blake (prelude).
July 8 First Anglo-Dutch War officially begins.
Oct. 8 Battle of Kentish Knock: British fleet under Blake defeats Dutch under Witte de With.
Dec. 10 Battle of Dungeness: Dutch fleet under Tromp defeats English under Blake.

1653 **Feb. 28–Mar. 2** Three Days' Battle (Battle of Portland): English under Blake and Monck defeat Dutch under Tromp.
June 12–13 Battle of North Foreland (Gabbard Bank): English fleet under Monck and Deane defeats Dutch under Tromp.
Aug. 8–10 Battle of Scheveningen (or Texel): English under Monck defeat Dutch; Tromp killed.

Dec. 16 Cromwell made Lord Protector of the Commonwealth (until **Sept. 3, 1658**).

1654 Apr. 5 Treaty of Westminster ends war between England and the Netherlands.

1660 May 8 Charles II proclaimed King of England.

1664 Dec.–1666 Feb. Great Plague in London.

1665 Mar. 14 Second Anglo-Dutch War begins.
June 13 Battle of Lowestoft: English fleet under Duke of York defeats Dutch under van Obdam, who is killed.

1666 June 11–14 Four Days' Battle in the Channel: Dutch under de Ruyter defeat the English.
Aug. 4–5 St. James' Day Fight (Battle of North Foreland): English defeat Dutch.
Sept. 2–4 Great London fire.

1667 June 19–23 Dutch fleet sail into the Thames and up the Medway, capturing HMS *Royal Charles*.
July 21 Treaty of Breda ends war between England and the Netherlands.

1672 Mar. 17 Third Anglo-Dutch War begins.
June 7 Battle of Solebay: Dutch defeat the English.

1673 June 7 & 14 Battles of Schooneveldt: Dutch gain strategic victories over the English fleet.
Aug. 21 Battle of Camperdown (Texel): Dutch victory over combined French and English fleet.

1674 Feb. 9 Treaty of Westminster ends war between England and the Netherlands.

1676 June 1 Battle of Öland: Danish-Dutch fleet defeats Swedes; *Kronan* sunk.

1689 Feb. 13 William III and Mary proclaimed King and Queen of England.
May 7 War of the League of Augsburg starts. England and France at war until Peace of Ryswick, **Sept. 1697**.

1690 July 10 Battle of Beachy Head: French fleet defeats English.

1692 May 28-June 2 Battle of La Hogue (Barfleur): French fleet nearly destroyed by Anglo-Dutch fleet.

1702 May 4 War of the Spanish Succession makes England and France adversaries; Peace of Utrecht concluded in 1713.
Oct. 23 English defeat French fleet at Vigo, Spain.

1704 Aug. 4 English seize Gibraltar.

1756 May 20 Battle of Minorca: Byng fails to press home English attack on Port Mahon in first action of Seven Years' War; he is later hanged.

1759 Aug. 18–19 Battle of Lagos Bay: violating Portuguese neutrality, British destroy French squadron.
Nov. 20 Battle of Quiberon Bay: British best French fleet in home waters.

1763 Feb. 10 Treaty of Paris ends Seven Years' War.

Era of the American Revolution

1769 July 19 Merchants of Newport, Rhode Island, burn British customs boat *Liberty*.

1773 Dec. 16 Unknown parties stage the "Boston Tea Party" aboard the merchant ship *Dartmouth* to protest import duties.

1775 Apr. 19 American Revolution starts with the "Shot heard round the world" at the Battles of Lexington and Concord.
Sept. 5 Schooner *Hannah* embarks on first naval mission paid for by the Continental Congress.

1776 March Hopkins, with *Alfred, Providence, Hornet, Wasp*, & others, occupies Nassau, Bahamas, for 2 weeks.
Apr. 7 *Lexington* captures *Edward*, first victory of Continental Navy in single-ship action.
July 4 Declaration of Independence is approved by Congress.
Sept. 5 Bushnell's submersible *Turtle* attempts to sink HMS *Eagle* in New York Harbor.
Oct. 11–13 Americans gain strategic victory at Battle of Valcour Island, Lake Champlain, but lose *Philadelphia* & other vessels.

1777 Sept. 19 *Lexington* captured by HMS *Alert* off France.
Sept. 27 British seize Philadelphia.

1778 Jan. 27–30 Crew of *Providence* seize Fort Nassau, Bahamas.
Feb. 6 France signs Treaties of Commerce and Alliance with United States.
Feb. 14 *Ranger* first American warship saluted by a foreign vessel — LaMotte Piquet's *Robuste* — in Quiberon Bay, France.
Mar. 29 *Alfred* captured by HMS *Ariadne* & *Ceres* in West Indies.
Apr. 25 *Ranger* captures HMS *Drake* off Carrickfergus, Ireland.
July 27 Battle of Ushant: indecisive contest between British and French fleets off France.

1779 July 25–Aug. 13 American expeditionary force against British stronghold on Penobscot Bay ends in failure; *Defence* & *Warren* among 40 ships lost.
Aug. 14–Sept. 22 *Bonhomme Richard, Alliance*, & others raid British shipping in the Irish Sea.
Sept. 9 HMS *Rose* scuttled in Savannah River.
Sept. 23 *Bonhomme Richard* captures HMS *Serapis* off Flamborough Head, England. Jones sails to Netherlands in *Serapis* when his ship sinks.
Nov. 24 HMS *Hussar* sinks off Hell Gate, New York.

1780 Jan. 16 Battle of Cape St. Vincent: British fleet under Rodney breaks Spanish blockade of Gibraltar.
May 11 *Ranger*, etc. captured at fall of Charleston, South Carolina.

1781 Apr. 16 Suffren attacks English fleet anchored at Porto Praya, Cape Verde Islands.
May 27 *Alliance* captures HMS *Trepassy* & *Atalanta*.
Sept. 5 Battle of the Chesapeake: French fleet prevents British from relieving Cornwallis at Yorktown.
Oct. 19 Cornwallis surrenders British army to Washington at Yorktown, Virginia.

1782 **Feb. 17** French fleet under Suffren (in *Héros*) engages British fleet under Hughes at Madras, India.

Apr. 12 Battle of the Saintes: British fleet under Rodney defeats French under de Grasse in West Indies.

Battle of Providien: French fleet under Suffren seriously damages English fleet off Ceylon.

July 6 Suffren fails to dislodge English fleet from Negapatam, India.

Sept. 3 Battle of Trincomalee off Ceylon is strategically indecisive; Suffren withdraws to Sumatra for repairs.

1783 **Mar. 11** *Alliance* fights off HMS *Alarm, Sybil,* & *Tobago.*

June 20 Suffren breaks English blockade of Cuddalore, India, in last of 5 engagements with English fleet.

Sept. 3 Peace of Paris ends hostilities between Britain, the United States, France, and Spain.

French Revolution to the War of 1812

1792 **Sept. 21** France proclaims a republic.

1793 **Jan. 21** Execution of Louis XVI.

Feb. 1 French Revolutionary Wars start with French declaration of war against Great Britain.

Dec. 18 Aided by French royalists, British forces burn French fleet at Toulon.

1794 **Mar. 10** U.S. Congress authorizes construction of 6 frigates: *Chesapeake, Congress, Constellation, Constitution, President,* & *United States.*

May 28–June 1 Battle of the Glorious First of June: French gain strategic victory over the British.

1797 **Feb. 14** Battle of Cape St. Vincent: British defeat Spanish fleet off Portland.

Apr. 15 British sailors at the Spithead mutiny for better treatment; many demands are met.

June 30 Second British mutiny at the Nore put down by force.

Sept. 21 Mutiny aboard frigate HMS *Hermione* off Puerto Rico.

Oct. 11 Battle of Camperdown: British defeat Dutch fleet intending to assist French landing in Ireland.

1798 **Aug. 1–2** Battle of the Nile (Aboukir Bay): Nelson defeats Brueys.

1799 **Feb. 1** USS *Constellation* captures *L'Insurgente* off Nevis during Quasi-War with France.

1801 **Apr. 2** Battle of Copenhagen: British fleet under Hyde Parker and Nelson defeats Danish.

1802 **Mar. 27** Peace of Amiens between Great Britain and France.

1803–5 American fleet blockades North African coast between Tripoli and Tunis in effort to stop tribute payments to North African states.

1803 **Oct. 31** USS *Philadelphia* runs aground off Tripoli and is captured.

1804 **Feb. 16** Captured USS *Philadelphia* burned at Tripoli by American force under Decatur.

May 18 Napoleon proclaimed Emperor of France.

Sept. 4 Packed with gunpowder, USS *Intrepid* explodes prematurely at Tripoli, killing American crew.

1805 **Apr. 10–July 27** Villeneuve's fleet sails from Spain to West Indies and back, pursued by Nelson.

May 17 American marines and sailors capture Derna, Tripoli.

July 22 Battle of Cape Finisterre: Calder fails to press British advantage against Villeneuve's returning fleet.

Oct. 21 Battle of Trafalgar: British fleet demolishes Franco-Spanish fleet off Spain; Nelson killed.

Oct. 27 French occupy Berlin.

Nov. 4 Action off Cape Ortegal: British capture 4 French ships of the line; French and Spanish ships captured or sunk at Trafalgar and in related actions total 22 of 33.

Dec. 2 Napoleon wins decisive victory over Austrian and Russian armies at Battle of Austerlitz.

1807 **June 22** USS *Chesapeake* surrenders to HMS *Leopard* following unprovoked attack by the British during search for deserters.

1811 **May 17** USS *President* engages HMS *Little Belt* off the Chesapeake in retaliation for British impressment of American seamen.

1812 **June–December** French army shattered during disastrous invasion of Russia.

War of 1812 to Crimean War

1812 **June 18** U.S. declares war on Great Britain.

July 17–20 USS *Constitution* narrowly escapes British squadron after prolonged chase.

Aug. 19 USS *Constitution* defeats HMS *Guerriére;* the latter is sunk the next day.

Oct. 18 USS *Wasp* captures HMS *Frolic* east of the Chesapeake.

Oct. 25 USS *United States* captures HMS *Macedonian* south of the Azores.

Dec. 29 USS *Constitution* defeats HMS *Java* off coast of Brazil.

1813–14 British maintain tight blockade of American coast, especially off Connecticut and in Chesapeake Bay.

1813 **Feb. 24** USS *Hornet* sinks HMS *Peacock* off Demarara, British Guiana.

June 1 HMS *Shannon* captures USS *Chesapeake* off Boston, Massachusetts.

Aug. 8 Schooners *Hamilton* & *Scourge* sunk in squall off Niagara River in Lake Ontario.

Aug. 14 USS *Argus* captured by HMS *Pelican* after month-long spree against British commerce in Irish Sea.

Sept. 5 USS *Enterprise* defeats HMS *Boxer* off Portland, Maine.

Sept. 10 Battle of Lake Erie (Put In Bay): Americans under Perry defeat British.

Oct. 5 Battle of the Thames: Americans under Harrison defeat Tecumseh and Procter in Upper Canada (Ontario).

1814 **Mar. 28** HMS *Phoebe* & *Cherub* defeat USS *Essex* at Valparaiso.

Mar. 31 European allies enter Paris. Napoleon abdicates **Apr. 11**; retires to Elba **May 4.**

Apr. 29 USS *Peacock* captures HMS *Epervier.*

June 28 USS *Wasp* defeats HMS *Reindeer,* which is later sunk, off France.

July 25 Battle of Lundy's Lane: Americans defeat British in Ontario (Upper Canada).

Aug. 14 British burn Washington, D.C.

Sept. 1 USS *Wasp* sinks HMS *Avon* off France.

Sept. 11 Battle of Lake Champlain: Macdonough defeats Downie in "the greatest naval battle of the war" and a major American victory.

Sept. 13–14 Siege of Fort McHenry, Baltimore; Francis Scott Key writes national anthem.

Sept. 27 Privateer *General Armstrong* scuttled at Fayal after spirited defense against British attack.

Dec. 24 Treaty of Ghent ends War of 1812; ratified at Washington, D.C., **Feb. 18, 1815.**

1815 **Jan. 8** Battle of New Orleans: Jackson defeats British army.

Jan. 15 USS *President* captured after running battle with HMS *Majestic, Endymion, Pomone,* & *Tenedos.*

Feb. 20 USS *Constitution* captures HMS *Cyane* & *Levant* near Madeira.

Feb. 26 American privateer *Chasseur* captures schooner *St. Lawrence* off Cuba.

Mar. 23 USS *Hornet* captures HMS *Penguin* off Tristan da Cunha.

June 18 Battle of Waterloo: French defeated decisively; Napoleon abdicates a second time, **June 22.**

June 30 USS *Peacock* captures East India Company ship *Nautilus* near Anjer.

1853–56 Crimean War: Russians defeat Turks at Battle of Sinope (**Nov. 30, 1853**); British and French naval forces operate in Baltic and off Crimea; steam, screws, and shells are used extensively for the first time.

American Civil War

1860 **Nov. 6** Abraham Lincoln elected President of the U.S.

Dec. 20 South Carolina secedes from Union.

1861 **Jan. 9** Steamer *Star of the West* comes under fire while bringing arms and supplies to Fort Sumter at Charleston, South Carolina.

Feb. 8 Jefferson Davis elected President of the Confederate States of America.

Apr. 12 USS *Harriet Lane* fires first shot of the Civil War, trying to stop an inbound ship at Charleston, South Carolina, before the bombardment of Fort Sumter, which starts later that day.

Apr. 17 *Star of the West* captured off Texas and taken into Confederate Navy as *Saint Philip.*

Apr. 19 Union declares blockade of southern ports; blockading squadrons include North Atlantic (Virginia to North Carolina), South Atlantic (South Carolina to Key West, Florida), East Gulf (Key West to Pensacola, Florida), and West Gulf (Pensacola to Texas).

Apr. 20 Union soldiers burn ships in Gosport Navy Yard (Norfolk, Virginia) to prevent their capture by Confederate forces.

July 11 Confederate Navy Secretary authorizes conversion of burned hulk of USS *Merrimack* to central battery ship CSS *Virginia.*

July 21 Battle of Manassas, Maryland (1st Bull Run): Union Army routed.

Aug. 29 Federal forces capture Forts Clark and Hatteras at Hatteras Inlet, North Carolina.

Oct. 25 USS *Monitor* laid down.

Nov. 8–Jan. 1, 1862 *Trent* Affair: tensions between U.S. and Britain strained over arrest of Confederate agents aboard British ship on high seas.

1862 **Jan. 12** Semmes's CSS *Sumter* detained at Gibraltar after taking 18 prizes in 6 months.

February Western Gunboat Flotilla helps capture Forts Henry (**Feb. 6**) and Donelson (**Feb. 16**) on the Cumberland River in Tennessee.

Feb. 25 USS *Monitor* commissioned at New York.

Mar. 8 CSS *Virginia* sinks USS *Cumberland* & *Congress,* and engages USS *Minnesota* off Yorktown Peninsula. USS *Monitor* arrives 2 days out of New York.

Mar. 9 Battle of Hampton Roads: first ironclad battle, between USS *Monitor* & CSS *Virginia,* ushers in new era in naval warfare.

Apr. 6–7 Battle of Shiloh, Tennessee: Confederates defeated.

Apr. 24 West Gulf Blockading Squadron ascends Mississippi River and enters New Orleans, **May 1.**

May 11 CSS *Virginia* blown up in James River, Virginia, to prevent capture by Union forces.

June 6 Memphis, Tennessee, falls to Union forces.

Aug. 24 Confederate raider CSS *Alabama* commissioned off Azores by Semmes. Over the next 23 months she captures 55 ships.

Sept. 17 Battle of Antietam: Confederates defeated.

Sept. 22 Lincoln frees slaves with Emancipation Proclamation.

October Western Gunboat Flotilla command transferred from Army to Navy.

Oct. 4 West Gulf Blockading Squadron captures Galveston, Texas.

Dec. 12 USS *Cairo* mined and sunk on Yazoo River near Baines Bluff, Mississippi.

Dec. 31 USS *Monitor* founders off Cape Hatteras, North Carolina, while in tow of USS *Rhode Island.*

1863 **Jan. 1** Confederates retake Galveston; USS *Harriet Lane* captured.

Jan. 11 Confederate raider CSS *Alabama* sinks auxiliary schooner USS *Hatteras* south of Galveston.

Jan. 16 CSS *Florida* leaves Mobile for raiding cruise during which she takes 33 prizes in 7 months.

Apr. 9 CSS *Georgia* starts 6-month raiding cruise during which she takes 9 prizes.

May 1–4 Battle of Chancellorsville, Virginia: Confederates victorious but "Stonewall" Jackson fatally wounded.

June 25 Mikado of Japan orders expulsion of all foreigners from Japan.

June 27 Confederates working from captured schooner *Archer* seize revenue cutter *Caleb Cushing* in Casco Bay, Maine; vessel burned and crew captured the next day.

July 1–3 Union victory at Battle of Gettysburg, Pennsylvania.

July 9 Union takes control of Mississippi River after fall of Vicksburg, Mississippi (**July 4**), and Port Hudson, Louisiana (**July 6**).

July 16 USS *Wyoming* engages Japanese forts at Shimonoseki, Japan.

Oct. 5 CSS *David* attacks USS *New Ironsides* at Charleston, South Carolina.

Nov. 23–25 Battle of Chattanooga, Tennessee: Confederates defeated.

1864 **Feb. 17** Submarine *H. L. Hunley* attacks USS *Housatonic* with spar torpedo; both vessels sink.

June 18 Grant begins 10-month siege of Petersburg, Virginia.

June 19 USS *Kearsarge* sinks Confederate raider CSS *Alabama* off Cherbourg, France.

Aug. 5 Battle of Mobile Bay: Union forces capture CSS *Tennessee.*

Sept. 2 Union Army captures Atlanta, Georgia.

Oct. 7 USS *Wachusett* seizes CSS *Florida* at Bahía, Brazil.

Oct. 19 Commerce raider CSS *Shenandoah* begins 11-month cruise.

Dec. 21 Union Army captures Savannah, Georgia.

1865 **Jan. 15** Fort Fisher, North Carolina, captured by North Atlantic Blockading Squadron.

Apr. 9 Lee surrenders at Appomattox, Virginia, Court House, ending Civil War.

Apr. 14 Lincoln assassinated by John Wilkes Booth.

Apr. 27 *Sultana* burns on Mississippi River with loss of 1,547 people, mostly veterans.

Nov. 6 Commerce raider CSS *Shenandoah* ends cruise at Liverpool.

1872 **Sept. 14** "*Alabama* claims" settled by international tribunal; British government fined $15.5 million for losses to American shipping attributed to British-built Confederate raiders *Alabama, Tuscaloosa, Florida,* and *Shenandoah.*

The End of Pax Britannica

1877 **May 29** During Peruvian insurrection, *Huascar* engaged by HMS *Shah* & *Amethyst* off Ilo, Peru.

1879 **May 21** War of the Pacific: *Huascar* rams and sinks Chilean screw corvette *Esmeralda* off Iquique, Chile.

Oct. 8 *Huascar* captured after battle with *Cochrane* & *Blanco Encalada* off Antofagasta, Chile.

1898 **Feb. 15** USS *Maine* blows up at Havana, Cuba.

Mar. 19–May 24 USS *Oregon* steams 14,000 miles from San Francisco to Florida in record 66 days.

Apr. 24 U.S. declares war on Spain.

May 1 Battle of Manila Bay: U.S. fleet destroys Spain's Philippines fleet.

July 3 Battle of Santiago: U.S. destroys Spain's Cuban fleet.

Dec. 10 Treaty of Paris ends Spanish-American War.

1904 **Feb. 8–9** Japanese destroyers launch surprise attack on Russian fleet in Port Arthur, China.

Aug. 10 Battle of the Yellow Sea: Japanese engage Russian fleet.

1905 **May 27–28** Battle of Tsushima: Japanese annihilate Russian fleet, in transit from Baltic since October 1904.

June 27–July 6 *Potemkin* mutiny at Odessa, Russia.

Sept. 5 Treaty of Portsmouth ends Russo-Japanese War.

1909 **July 1** Agadir Crisis precipitated by arrival of German gunboat *Panther* at Agadir, Morocco.

World War I

1914 **June 28** Assassination of Austria-Hungary's Archduke Ferdinand in Sarajevo.

July 28 Austria declares war on Serbia; World War I begins.

July 31 SMS *Emden* begins 3-month commerce-raiding cruise in Pacific and Indian Oceans.

Aug. 2 British seize Turkish *Sultan Osman I* & *Reshadieh* on ways; later commissioned as HMS *Agincourt* & *Erin.*

Aug. 10 SMS *Goeben* & *Breslau* reach Constantinople and renamed *Yavuz Sultan Selim* & *Midilli.*

Aug. 21 Armed merchant cruiser *Kaiser Wilhelm der Grosse* attacked and scuttled at Rio de Oro, Spanish Sahara.

Aug. 26 Russians seize German code books from SMS *Magdeburg.*

Aug. 28 Battle of Heligoland Bight.

Sept. 5 *U-21* sinks HMS *Pathfinder,* first warship lost to submarine.

Sept. 14 Commerce raiders *Cap Trafalgar* sunk, and *Carmania* damaged, in action off Brazil.

Sept. 22 *U-9* sinks HMS *Aboukir, Cressy,* & *Hogue* off the Netherlands.

Oct. 27 Battleship HMS *Audacious* sunk after hitting mine north of Ireland.

Nov. 1 Battle of Coronel: German squadron under Graf Spee defeats British off Chile; HMS *Good Hope* & *Monmouth* sunk by SMS *Scharnhorst* & *Gneisenau.*

Nov. 3 German fleet raids Yarmouth, England.

Nov. 4 SMS *Karlsruhe* explodes in midatlantic.

Nov. 7 German colony at Tsingtao, China, surrenders to Japanese.

Nov. 9 HMAS *Sydney* sinks *Emden* at Direction Island, Indian Ocean.

Dec. 8 Battle of the Falkland Islands: SMS *Scharnhorst, Gneisenau, Leipzig,* & *Nürnberg* sunk by HMS *Invincible* & *Inflexible.*

Dec. 16 German fleet raids Scarborough and Hartlepool.

1915 Jan. 24 Battle of Dogger Bank: SMS *Blücher* sunk.

Feb. 18 Germany begins U-boat blockade of Britain.

Apr. 7 *Lusitania* torpedoed by *U-20* off Ireland; 1,201 lives lost.

Apr. 11 *Kronprinz Wilhelm* puts into Hampton Roads, Virginia, and interned.

Apr. 25 British Gallipoli campaign against Turkey begins.

May 13 Italy declares war on Austria-Hungary.

May 25–27 *U-21* sinks HMS *Triumph* & *Majestic* off Gallipoli.

June 11 SMS *Königsberg* sunk in Tanganyika.

Aug. 19 *Arabic* sunk by *U-24;* Germany issues "Arabic Pledge" to ease U-boat campaign.

1916 Jan. 9 Allies withdraw from Gallipoli.

Mar. 24 *Sussex* torpedoed by *UB-29;* Germany stops unrestricted U-boat warfare.

May 31 Battle of Jutland: losses include battlecruisers HMS *Indefatigable* & *Invincible,* armored cruisers *Defence,* etc. Germans lose battlecruiser SMS *Lützow,* etc.

June 5 HMS *Hampshire* mined off Orkneys; Minister of War Lord Kitchener killed.

1917 Feb. 3 Germany resumes unrestricted submarine warfare.

Mar. 12 Provisional government in Russia.

Apr. 6 U.S. declares war on Germany.

Aug. 2 *Seeadler* wrecked in Society Islands after 8-month commerce-raiding cruise.

Nov. 7 *Aurora* opens fire at start of Bolshevik overthrow of Russia's provisional government.

Dec. 6 Munitions freighter *Mont Blanc* explodes after colliding with *Imo* at Halifax, Nova Scotia; 2,000–3,000 people killed and 9,000 injured.

1918 Jan. 20 *Breslau* sunk & *Goeben* damaged by mines near Dardanelles.

Mar. 3 Treaty of Brest-Litovsk: Russia leaves the war.

Apr. 23 HMS *Vindictive* sunk as blockship at Zeebrugge, Belgium.

May 14 Germans occupy Sevastopol in the Crimea.

June 10 Italian *MAS-15* torpedoes Austro-Hungarian battleship *Szent István* in Adriatic.

Nov. 11 Germany signs armistice; German fleet interned at Scapa Flow, **Nov. 21.**

1919 June 21 German High Seas Fleet scuttled at Scapa Flow.

June 28 Treaty of Versailles signed.

Between the World Wars

1922 Feb. 6 Washington Naval Treaty imposes limits on fleet strengths: Britain and the U.S., 525,000 tons; Japan, 315,000 tons; France and Italy, 175,000 tons. No new capital ships (larger than 10,000 tons, with 8-inch guns) to be built for 10 years; maximum tonnage fixed for capital ships, aircraft carriers, and cruisers.

1930 Apr. 30 London Naval Conference confirms the 5:5:3 ratio in battleship construction (Italy and France refuse to sign) until 1936 and regulates submarine warfare.

1934 Dec. 19 Japan repudiates terms of Washington and London naval conferences to protest British and U.S. refusal to allow Japan to achieve parity with them in rearmament.

1936 Mar. 26 London Naval Treaty between Britain, France, and U.S. calls for exchange of information about construction details; German naval tonnage limited to 35 percent of Royal Navy.

1937 Apr. 30 Spanish battleship *España* mined and sunk during Spanish Civil War.

1939 May–June Jewish immigrants aboard *St. Louis* refused entrance to the U.S. in "voyage of the damned."

World War II

1939 Sept. 1 Germany invades Poland.

Sept. 3 *U-30* torpedoes steamship *Athenia.*

Sept. 17 HMS *Courageous* sunk by *U-29* off Ireland.

Oct. 14 HMS *Royal Oak* sunk by *U-47* at Scapa Flow.

Nov. 23 *Rawalpindi* sunk by *Scharnhorst* & *Gneisenau.*

Dec. 13 Battle of the River Plate between *Admiral Graf Spee* and HMS *Achilles, Ajax,* & *Exeter.*

1940 Feb. 16 HMS *Cossack* frees POWs from *Altmark* in Norwegian fjord.

Apr. 8–9 Operation Weserübung: *Blücher, Karlsruhe,* & *Königsberg* sunk during invasion of Norway; HMS *Glowworm* sunk ramming *Admiral Hipper.*

May 9 *U-110* captured with Enigma encoding machinery.

May 10 Germany invades France.

June 8 HMS *Glorious* sunk by *Scharnhorst* & *Gneisenau* off Norway.

July 3 British attack French fleet at Oran, Algeria; *Strasbourg* escapes.

Sept. 13 *City of Benares* sunk in convoy with loss of 73 children and 172 adults.

Sept. 25 British attack French fleet at Dakar.

Nov. 5 *Jervis Bay* sunk by *Admiral Scheer.*

Nov. 11–12 Raid on Taranto, Italy: carrier planes from HMS *Illustrious* sink battleship *Conte di Cavour* and damage *Littorio* & *Duilio.*

Nov. 25 Jewish resistance group accidentally kills 252 Jewish refugees in intentional bombing of refugee ship *Patria* at Haifa, Palestine.

1941 **Mar. 28** Battle of Cape Matapan: *Vittorio Veneto* damaged by British carrier aircraft.

May 18–27 *Bismarck* sorties with *Prinz Eugen;* sinks HMS *Hood,* **May 24;** *Bismarck* sunk, **May 27.**

May 27 Allies evacuate Crete.

June 22 German invasion of Soviet Union.

Aug. 14 Roosevelt and Churchill announce Atlantic Charter — the foundation of the United Nations — after meetings aboard USS *Augusta* & HMS *Prince of Wales.*

Sept. 4 USS *Greer* engages *U-652.*

Oct. 16 USS *Kearny* torpedoed by German U-boat.

Oct. 31 USS *Reuben James* sunk by *U-562.*

Nov. 13 HMS *Ark Royal* sunk in Mediterranean by *U-81.*

Nov. 19 HMAS *Sydney* sunk in action with *Kormoran* off Australia.

Nov. 25 HMS *Barham* sunk by *U-331* in Mediterranean.

Dec. 7 Japanese surprise attack on Pearl Harbor: U.S. losses include several battleships but no carriers.

Dec. 10 HMS *Repulse* & *Prince of Wales* sunk by Japanese planes off Malaya.

Dec. 19 HMS *Queen Elizabeth* & *Valiant* sunk by Italian frogmen at Alexandria, Egypt.

1942 **Jan. 29** USS *Yorktown* leads attack on Marshall Islands.

Feb. 11–13 Operation Cerberus: *Gneisenau, Prinz Eugen, & Scharnhorst* make Channel Dash from Brest to Kiel.

Feb. 18(?) Submarine *Surcouf* sunk in Caribbean.

Feb. 19 Japanese carrier raid on Darwin, Australia.

Feb. 27–28 Battle of Java Sea: Allied losses include *De Ruyter,* USS *Houston,* HMAS *Perth;* USS *Langley* sunk south of Java.

Apr. 5–9 Japanese raid Ceylon; HMS *Hermes* sunk.

Apr. 14 HMS *Upholder* lost in Mediterranean.

Apr. 18 Doolittle Raid on Japan launched from USS Hornet.

May 4 USS *Pigeon* sunk in Manila Bay; American forces surrender Philippines, **May 6.**

May 3–8 Battle of Coral Sea: first in which enemy ships are not visible to one another; carriers *Shoho* & USS *Lexington* sunk.

June 4–7 Battle of Midway: Japanese lose carriers *Akagi, Hiryu, Soryu,* & *Kaga;* USS *Yorktown* also sunk.

July 4 Convoy PQ17 scatters; 21 of 35 ships sunk in Barents Sea.

Aug. 7 U.S. Marines land on Guadalcanal.

Aug. 9 Battle of Savo Island: allies lose 3 cruisers off Guadalcanal.

Aug. 10–14 Operation Pedestal: tanker *Ohio* and 3 merchant ships reach Malta.

Aug. 23–25 Battle of Eastern Solomons: USS *Enterprise* & *Saratoga* vs. *Zuikaku* & *Shokaku.*

Sept. 27 Liberty ship *Stephen Hopkins* & German raider *Stier* sink each other in South Atlantic.

Oct. 11 Battle of Cape Esperance, Guadalcanal: U.S. claims first victory in night action.

Oct. 26–27 Battle of Santa Cruz Islands: carriers USS *Hornet* & *Zuiho* sunk.

Nov. 8–10 Operation Torch: Allied landings in North Africa.

Nov. 12–15 Naval Battle of Guadalcanal: USS *Juneau* sunk with 5 Sullivan brothers; USS *Washington* sinks *Kirishima.*

1943 **Feb. 2** German Army surrenders before Stalingrad.

February Japanese evacuate Guadalcanal.

May 9 Germans evacuate North Africa.

May 13 Hospital ship *Centaur* sunk by *I-177* off New Zealand.

July 6 Battle of Kula Gulf, New Georgia.

July 10 Allied landings in Sicily.

Aug. 2 *PT-109* sunk off Kolombangara, Solomon Islands.

Sept. 8 Italy surrenders.

Sept. 22 First attacks on *Tirpitz* at Altenfjord, Norway.

Nov. 20 U.S. landing on Tarawa and Makin, Gilbert Islands.

Dec. 26 Battle of North Cape: *Scharnhorst* sunk by HMS *Duke of York.*

1944 **Feb. 1–5** U.S. landing on Kwajalein, Marshall Islands.

Apr. 14 Explosion aboard *Fort Stikine* sinks 27 ships and kills 1,376 people in Bombay, India.

Apr. 28 *LST-507* & *LST-289* sunk off Slapton Sands, England.

May 19–31 USS *England* sinks 6 Japanese submarines in Marianas.

June 4 *U-505* captured in midatlantic.

June 6 D-day: Allied landings in Normandy, France.

June 15 U.S. landing on Saipan, Mariana Islands.

July 17 Explosions aboard *E. A. Bryan* & *Quinault Victory* kill 321 people at Port Chicago, California.

Aug. 15 Allied landings in southern France.

Aug. 19 Battle of the Philippine Sea ("Great Marianas Turkey Shoot"): Japanese lose more than 400 carrier aircraft and carriers *Shokaku, Taiho,* & *Hiyo.*

Oct. 23–25 Battle of Leyte Gulf, comprising Battles of Sibuyan Sea, Surigao Strait, Samar, and Cape Engaño.

Oct. 23 USS *Dace* & *Darter* attack *Atago, Takao,* & *Maya* in Palawan Passage.

Oct. 24 USS *Princeton* sunk east of Philippines, *Musashi* in Sibuyan Sea, USS *Tang* in Formosa Strait.

Oct. 25 *Fuso, Yamashiro,* & *Mogami* sunk in Surigao

Strait; USS *Gambier Bay, Hoel,* & *Johnston* sunk off Samar; USS *St. Lô* first ship sunk by kamikaze; carriers *Zuiho, Zuikaku, Chiyoda,* & *Chitose* sunk off Cape Engaño.

Nov. 12 *Tirpitz* sunk off Tromsø by bombers.

1945 Jan. 30 *Wilhelm Gustloff* sunk by *S-13* off Poland; more than 5,000 killed.

Feb. 19–Mar. 16 Allied landings on Iwo Jima.

Apr. 1–June 21 Allied landings on Okinawa.

Apr. 7 *Yamato* sunk by carrier aircraft off Japan.

Apr. 12 Pres. Roosevelt dies; succeeded by Truman.

Apr. 16 Kamikaze attacks on USS *Laffey* off Okinawa.

May 8 V-E Day: allies proclaim victory in Europe.

July 30 USS *Indianapolis* sunk by *I-58* off Tinian.

Aug. 6, 9 U.S. drops atomic bombs on Hiroshima and Nagasaki.

Sept. 2 Japanese surrender signed aboard USS *Missouri* in Tokyo Bay.

Oct. 24 UN charter ratified by 29 nations.

The Cold War

1950 June 25–July 27, 1953 Korean War.

1959 USS *George Washington* first ballistic missile submarine commissioned.

1962 October Cuban Missile Crisis: U.S. declares naval blockade of Cuba to secure removal of Soviet nuclear weapons.

1964 Aug. 2 Gulf of Tonkin incident precipitates Vietnam War.

1967 June 5–10 Six-Day War between Israel and Egypt, Syria, Jordan, & Iraq; Israelis attack USS *Liberty* **June 8.**

1968 Jan. 23–Dec. 22 USS *Pueblo* seized by North Korea.

1970 Nov. 23 Soviet defector Simonas Kudirka forcibly repatriated from USCGC *Vigilant* off Martha's Vineyard.

1975 May 12–16 *Mayaguez* seized by Cambodian gunboat.

1982 Apr. 2–June 14 Falkland Islands War between Argentina and Britain; *General Belgrano* sunk **May 2.**

1985 June 10 French secret service sinks *Rainbow Warrior* at dock in Auckland, New Zealand.

1987 May 17 USS *Stark* attacked by Iraqi jet during Iran-Iraq War.

1988 July 3 USS *Vincennes* shoots down Iran Air passenger jet during Iran-Iraq War.

SHIPWRECKS, HIGHJACKINGS, AND OTHER DISASTERS

1609 July 23 *Sea Venture* wrecks on Bermuda.

1629 June 4 *Batavia* hits reef off western Australia; more than 100 people killed after being marooned.

1656 Apr. 28 *Vergulde Draeck* wrecks off western Australia; 7 survivors reach Batavia.

1668 May 5 *Sacramento* runs aground off Bahía, Brazil, with loss of more than 900 people.

1707 Oct. 22 HMS *Association* & 3 other ships wreck on Scilly Isles; more than 1,500 dead.

1727 June 9 *Zeewijk* wrecks on western Australia; 88 of complement of 212 survive.

1741 May 14 HMS *Wager* wrecks on coast of Chile; only about 30 men survive ensuing hardships.

1743 June *Hollandia* runs aground in Scilly Isles; all 276 crew killed.

1782 Aug. 29 HMS *Royal George* capsizes while loading supplies at Spithead; 800 lives lost.

1791 March *L'Astrolabe* & *La Boussole* wrecked on Vanikoro Island.

1799 Oct. 9 HMS *Lutine* wrecks on coast of Holland with loss of 240 men and £2 million in gold.

1800 Mar. 17 HMS *Queen Charlotte* burns off Livorno, Italy, with loss of 690 crew.

1811 Dec. 24 HMS *St. George,* third-rate *Defence,* and brig *Fancy* lost in Baltic storm with death of more than 1,400 people.

1816 July 2 *Medusa* lost off coast of Mauritania; only 19 of 75 people abandoned by captain survive.

1820 Nov. 20 Whaleship *Essex* stove by a whale in mid-Pacific.

1838 Sept. 7 *Forfarshire* runs aground in North Sea.

1842 Nov. 26 Mutiny aboard USS *Somers;* 3 ringleaders hanged on **Dec. 1.**

1844 Feb. 29 Shell gun "Peacemaker" explodes aboard USS *Princeton* near Washington, D.C.; two cabinet officials among dead.

1852 Feb. 26 HMS *Birkenhead* runs aground in False Bay, South Africa; 438 of 631 drown.

1853 Dec. 25 Steamship *San Francisco* founders in gale with the loss of 246 of 750 passengers and crew.

1854 Sept. 27 Wooden steamship *Arctic* sinks after collision with iron-hulled *Vesta* off Newfoundland; 240–300 people lost.

1857 Sept. 12 Steamship *Central America* sinks in hurricane off South Carolina; 423 lives and $1.6 million in gold lost.

Dec. 25 Mutiny aboard whaleship *Junior* in Pacific.

1859 Oct. 26 Steamship *Royal Charter* sinks in Irish Sea with loss of 455 people and £500,000 in gold.

1863 Feb. 7 HMS *Orpheus* wrecks in Auckland, New Zealand; only 69 of 258 crew survive.

1870 Sept. 7 HMS *Captain* sinks in gale off Spain with the loss of 481 of 499 crew.

1872 Dec. 4 *Mary Celeste* found adrift in midatlantic with no sign of her complement of 10.

1873 Apr. 2 Steamship *Atlantic* wrecks on Nova Scotia with the loss of 585 lives.

1875 Dec. 6 Steamship *Deutschland* runs aground on Kentish Knock, England, with loss of 157.

1889 Mar. 14 HMS *Calliope,* only 1 of 7 warships to survive hurricane at Apia, Samoa.

1891 Mar. 16 Steamship *Utopia* blows onto ram bow of HMS *Anson* at Gibraltar and sinks with loss of 576 people.

1893 **June 22** HMS *Camperdown* rams and sinks HMS *Victoria* on maneuvers off Tripoli, Lebanon; 358 people drown.

1898 **July 4** Steel steamer *La Bourgogne* sinks off Cape Sable with loss of 549 after collision with iron ship *Cromartyshire*.
Nov. 26 Steamer *Portland* 1 of 400 vessels lost in New England during "Portland" Gale.

1904 **June 15** *General Slocum* burns in New York's East River with the loss of 1,031 lives.
June 28 *Norge* hits Rockall Island, 250 miles northwest of Ireland, and sinks with the loss of about 550 people.

1907 **Dec. 13** *Thomas W. Lawson* lost off Scilly Isles.

1909 **Jan. 23** *Republic* transmits first radio distress call after collision with *Florida; Republic* later sinks.

1912 **Apr. 15** RMS *Titanic* hits an iceberg in midatlantic and sinks with the loss of about 1,500 people; 706 survive.

1914 **May 30** *Empress of Ireland* sinks in Gulf of St. Lawrence after being rammed by *Storstad;* 1,024 people killed.
Nov. 26 HMS *Bulwark* destroyed at anchor off Sheerness by massive internal explosion with loss of 781.

1915 **May 6** *Lusitania* torpedoed by *U-20* off southern Ireland; 1,201 of complement of 1,965 killed.
July 24 Excursion steamer *Eastland* capsizes at dock in Chicago; 841 dead.

1916 **Aug. 29** USS *Memphis* thrown ashore at Santo Domingo by seismic waves caused by undersea earthquake; 40 crew killed.

1919 **March** USS *Cyclops* lost without trace en route from Barbados to U.S.

1920 **Jan. 12** French passenger ship *L'Afrique* sinks in Bay of Biscay with loss of all but 32 of 585 aboard.

1922 **May 20** P&O passenger ship *Egypt* sinks off Finistère, France, after ramming by icebreaker *Seine;* 86 lives lost.

1923 **Sept. 8** USS *Delphy* and 7 destroyers run aground north of Santa Barbara, California.

1934 **May 15** *Nantucket* lightship sunk by Cunard/White Star liner *Olympic*.

1935 **Sept. 9** *Morro Castle* burns off Atlantic City, New Jersey; 137 people killed.

1938 **Mar. 1** *Admiral Karpfanger* (ex-*L'Avenir*) lost en route from Australia to Europe.

1939 **May 23** Submarine USS *Squalus* sinks off New England.
June 1 Submarine HMS *Thetis* sinks during trials in Irish Sea; only 4 of 103 aboard survive.
June 15 Submarine *Phénix* sinks off Cam Ranh Bay, French Indochina, with loss of 71 crew.
May–June Jewish refugees aboard *St. Louis* denied entry into U.S. in "voyage of the damned."

1941 **Feb. 5** *Politician* runs aground on Eriskay Island, Outer Hebrides, with 22,000 cases of whiskey.

1942 **February** *Struma* hits a mine in Black Sea, sinking with loss of all but 1 of 769 Jewish refugees.
Feb. 9 *Normandie* burns and capsizes at New York pier.

1945 **Jan. 30** *Wilhelm Gustloff* sunk off Poland by Soviet submarine *S-13;* death toll put at 5,348.

1947 **Mar. 4** *Exodus 1947* forcibly boarded by British ships in Mediterranean.
Apr. 16 Explosion aboard *Grandcamp* kills 308 and injures 3,000 in Texas City, Texas.

1949 **Sept. 17** Great Lakes cruise ship *Noronic* burns at dockside in Toronto; 118 killed.

1952 **Jan. 10** *Flying Enterprise* sinks in English Channel after 2-week struggle to save freighter.

1953 **Jan. 31** *Princess Victoria* lost off Northern Ireland; 128 of 172 passengers and crew lost.

1954 **Mar. 1** Crew of Japanese trawler *Fukuryu Maru* ("Lucky Dragon") contaminated by fallout from hydrogen bomb test.

1955 **Oct. 29** Soviet battleship *Novorossisk* (ex-*Giulio Cesare*) sunk by mysterious explosion at Sevastopol; 600 dead.

1956 **July 25** *Andrea Doria* sinks off Nantucket after collision with *Stockholm;* 43 people killed.
Sept. 21 Merchant-training bark *Pamir* sinks in midatlantic hurricane; only 6 of 86 crew survive.

1961 **Jan. 22** *Santa Maria* hijacked by 26 terrorists seeking overthrow of Portugal's dictator Antonio Salazar.
May 3 Training brigantine *Albatros* sinks in Gulf of Mexico with loss of 4 crew and trainees.

1963 **April 10** Submarine USS *Thresher* sinks during trials off New England; 129 lost.

1965 **Nov. 12** *Yarmouth Castle* burns and sinks between Miami and Bahamas with loss of 87 passengers.

1967 **Mar. 18** *Torrey Canyon* runs aground off Land's End; massive oil slick coats English and French coasts.

1968 **May 21** Submarine USS *Scorpion* mysteriously sinks off Azores with loss of 99 crew.

1975 **Nov. 10** *Edmund Fitzgerald* sinks in Lake Superior off Michigan.

1976 **Dec. 15** *Argo Merchant* spills 7.7 million gallons of crude oil after running aground off Nantucket.

1978 **Mar. 16** *Amoco Cadiz* runs aground off coast of France and spills 223,000 tons of crude oil.

1985 **Oct. 7–9** *Achille Lauro* hijacked off coast of Egypt.

1987 **Mar. 6** *Herald of Free Enterprise* capsizes at Zeebrugge, Belgium, with loss of 135 lives.
Dec. 20 *Doña Paz* collides with tanker *Vector* in Tablas Strait, Philippines; death toll put at 4,375.

1989 **Mar. 24** *Exxon Valdez* runs aground in Prince Edward Sound, Alaska, spilling 260,000 barrels of oil.

1994 **Sept. 29** *Estonia* sinks in Baltic with loss of about 1,000 passengers and crew.

GLOSSARY

aircraft carrier A warship designed for carrying, launching, and landing aircraft.

amphora A large ceramic jar of the ancient Mediterranean used for bulk storage of olives, wine, fish sauce, and preserved fruit. The shape, design, and contents of amphorae (among other objects) found in ancient ships provide many clues about the extent and course of seaborne trade from the 3rd millennium BCE to the Byzantine era.

armor Extra iron or steel plate used to protect a ship from gunfire. The thickness of iron varied according to the part of the ship around which it was placed; vital areas included crew and engine spaces, magazines, and gun turrets.

bark A three-, four-, or five-masted vessel square rigged on all but the aftermost mast, which is fore-and-aft rigged.

barkentine A vessel of three to six masts, square rigged on the foremast, and fore-and-aft rigged on the others.

battlecruiser A hybrid capital ship of the early 20th century with the firepower of a battleship, but with armor protection sacrificed for greater speed.

battleship A ship fit to lie in the line of battle; the most heavily armed and stoutly built ship of the day. The battleship concept lasted from the 17th century until after World War II, when the development of torpedoes, naval aviation, and missiles rendered the battleship obsolete.

Bermuda rig A fore-and-aft rig in which the mainsail is triangular in shape; also called Marconi rig. (See also **gaff rig.**)

brig A two-masted vessel, square rigged on both masts.

brigantine A two-masted vessel, square rigged on the foremast, and fore-and-aft rigged on the main.

cable A unit of distance equal to one-tenth of a nautical mile, or approximately 200 yards or 200 meters.

capital ship The most important class of warship in a given era. The term originally referred to ships fit to sail in the line of battle, or battleships. In the 20th century, battleships were eclipsed by aircraft carriers.

caravel A relatively small Portuguese vessel of the 15th and 16th centuries setting lateen sails on two or three masts and sometimes a square sail on the foremast. Highly maneuverable, caravels helped to make possible the voyages of the early Portuguese and Spanish discoverers.

carrack A large seagoing vessel of the 14th century that combined northern European and Mediterranean ship-building techniques. Carracks resembled the northern cog, but they were constructed frame first and carried more than one mast. By the 16th century, they carried three masts and high stern and forecastles. Carracks were forerunners of galleons.

carronade A short-barreled ship's gun developed by the Carron Company in Scotland. Though of limited range, carronades were enormously destructive to ships' timbers and were originally known as "smashers." Within two years, 429 ships of the Royal Navy — "where a short range is ever the distance chosen" — carried carronades. The addition of carronades was not reflected in the nominal rate of a ship; a 54-gun ship mounting 10 carronades was still designated a "44." (See also **gun** and **rate.**)

carvel construction A method of hull construction in which the longitudinal strakes forming the skin of the hull are flush at the edges. In carvel construction, the planks are fastened to a pre-erected frame. (See also **clinker construction, frame-first construction,** and **shell-first construction.**)

casemate A fixed armored enclosure designed to protect a ship's guns from hostile fire.

clinker (or lapstrake) construction A method of hull construction in which the longitudinal strakes forming the hull overlap each other and are "clenched" to each other with iron nails. In clinker construction, the hull is built first; frames were sometimes inserted afterward. (See also **carvel construction, frame-first construction,** and **shell-first construction.**)

clipper The name given to a variety of square-rigged merchant ships built chiefly for speed. During the heyday of the American clipper ship, between 1845 and 1860, the term applied to "sharp-built" ships that sacrificed cargo capacity for speed and carried a maximum of canvas and correspondingly large crews. The primary impetus for the clipper era were the gold rushes in California and Australia. In the late 1860s the British built smaller clippers for the tea trade between China and England.

cog A type of capacious merchant vessel that originated in Germany and gradually spread throughout the Baltic and to the Mediterranean. It is characterized by high sides, a relatively flat bottom, and a single square sail.

composite construction A type of hull construction consisting of an iron or steel frame and wooden planking.

compound engine A steam engine in which the steam expands first in a high-pressure cylinder, and then in a low-pressure cylinder.

cruiser A type of warship falling between battleships and destroyers in size, armament, and speed. Cruisers were designed primarily for reconnaissance while with the fleet, or for commerce protection, commerce raiding, and patrolling on overseas stations.

cutter A single-masted vessel similar to a sloop but usually setting double headsails. Patrol vessels of the U.S. Coast Guard are also called cutters.

destroyer Relatively small warships, torpedo-boat destroyers originated as small, fast ships whose primary function was to protect larger ships from torpedo attack. Their roles later expanded to include antisubmarine and antiaircraft warfare and convoy protection.

displacement tonnage The standard method of measuring warships. Displacement tonnage is the volume of water displaced by a vessel, the weight of the water displaced being equal to the weight of the object displacing it. (See also **tonnage.**)

Down Easter A square-rigged merchant ship that combined large carrying capacity with relatively sharp hull design. Built especially for the California grain trade in the quarter century following the American Civil War (1865–1890), Down Easters were so called because they were built in Maine, which is downwind and east of the major East Coast ports.

escort carrier A small aircraft carrier designed chiefly to provide air cover for convoys and amphibious operations, and used also to ferry aircraft and train pilots.

fore-and-aft sail A sail set parallel to the centerline of a vessel. Fore-and-aft vessels are simpler to rig than square-rigged vessels, require a smaller crew, and can sail closer to the direction from which the wind is blowing.

forecastle Originally, a built-up structure comprising several decks in the forward part of a ship, from which archers or gunners could fire into an enemy ship. (A sterncastle aft served the same function.) In more modern usage, the forecastle (pronounced and often written "focsle") was the crew's quarters in the forward part of a ship.

frame A transverse rib that forms part of the skeleton of a ship's hull.

frame-first construction A method of construction in which the internal framework, or skeleton, of a ship's hull is constructed first, with the hull planking being attached afterward. (See also **carvel construction, clinker construction,** and **shell-first construction.**)

frigate A small combatant ship; a 4th- or 5th-rate ship in the Royal Navy. In the age of sail, frigates sailed with the fleet as reconnaissance vessels and were known as "the eyes of the fleet." In battle, they stood away from the line to relay signals from the flagship to other ships in the line who could not see the flagship because of gunsmoke. Frigates were also used for convoy protection and commerce raiding. In modern parlance, a frigate is a ship designed to protect shipping from aircraft and submarines.

gaff rig A fore-and-aft rig in which the primary sails abaft the mast are trapezoidal in shape: the bottom of the sail is attached to the boom, the luff (or forward edge) to the mast, and the head to a spar called a gaff. (See also **Bermuda rig.**)

galleasse A hybrid type of 16th-century vessel employing both a full sailing rig and oars for propulsion.

galleon A full-rigged vessel that evolved in Europe around the 16th century and is the immediate ancestor of the full-rigged ship. Galleons' higher length-to-beam ratio and lower fore- and sterncastles made them more maneuverable than carracks.

galley A relatively narrow vessel driven primarily by oars. Galleys evolved in the ancient Mediterranean, and the galley *par excellence* was the Greek "trieres," or trireme.

gun A generic term for a carriage-mounted gun in sailing warships. Guns were rated according to the weight of shot fired, anywhere from 1-pound antipersonnel guns to 42 pounders. In the sailing navy, guns were mounted in broadside, and the most effective use was to arrange the ship in a line to enable each to fire at the same target; hence the battle line, or line of battle. Developed in the 19th century, rifled guns (measured by the caliber, or internal diameter of the gun barrel) were housed in rotating turrets, which gave the guns wider arcs of fire. (See also **carronade** and **rate.**)

horsepower A measure of mechanical power. A vessel's horsepower is measured in various ways, depending on the type of engine. The power of a steam engine is expressed as *indicated horsepower* (ihp), the work of the steam in the cylinder, or *nominal horsepower* (nhp), an expression of power derived by formula. Steam turbines are measured by *shaft horsepower* (shp), the power at the crankshaft as indicated by a torsion meter. Diesel engines are often measured by *brake horsepower* (bhp), determined by a brake attached to the shaft coupling. *Effective horsepower* (ehp) is the actual work done by an engine propelling a vessel.

ironclad A warship with a wooden hull sheathed in iron for protection against gunfire.

jib A triangular fore-and-aft sail carried on a stay leading from the topmast head to the bow or bowsprit.

jury rig A temporary rig used to replace a damaged mast or spar.

ketch A two-masted yacht with a tall mainmast and a shorter mizzen mast.

knorr A Scandinavian seagoing cargo ship of the Viking era. Knorrs were shorter, beamier, and deeper than longships.

knot A unit of measure used to express the speed of a ship in nautical miles per hour. One international nautical mile is defined as 6,076.1155 feet, or approximately 1.15 statute (land) miles. A knot is generally taken to mean a rate of speed, and some argue that "knots per hour" is an incorrect expression. The argument is a pedantic one; many ship's logs record speeds in knots per hour. The accompanying table shows the time (in days and hours) required to travel a given distance at various speeds.

Nautical miles	SPEED					
	5 KTS.	10 KTS.	15 KTS.	20 KTS.	25 KTS.	30 KTS.
10	0d 02h	0d 01h	0d 01h	0d 01h	—	—
50	0d 10h	0d 05h	0d 03h	0d 03h	0d 02h	0d 02h
100	0d 20h	0d 10h	0d 07h	0d 05h	0d 04h	0d 03h
500	4d 04h	2d 02h	1d 09h	1d 01h	0d 20h	0d 17h
1,000	8d 08h	4d 04h	2d 19h	2d 02h	1d 16h	1d 09h
5,000	41d 16h	20d 20h	13d 21h	10d 10h	8d 08h	6d 23h
10,000	83d 08h	41d 16h	27d 18h	20d 20h	16d 04h	13d 21h

By custom, the speed of vessels on the Great Lakes and inland rivers of the United States is measured in statute miles per hour.

lapstrake See **clinker construction.**

lateen A triangular fore-and-aft sail set from a long spar attached to a short mast and found in traditional vessels of the Iberian Peninsula, Mediterranean, and Indian Ocean.

league A unit of distance equal to 3 nautical miles. The actual distance has varied at different times: Columbus's league was about 3.18 miles, that of Magellan 3.5 miles.

liner A passenger steam- or motorship that runs on an established route, such as between Europe and the United States.

mast A vertical pole or spar from which sails are set. In a square-rigged vessel, masts are often composed of separate sections: lower mast, topmast, topgallant mast, and royal mast. Masts are named, from bow to stern, foremast, mainmast, mizzen mast, and jigger mast. In some five-masted vessels, the middle mast is called, simply, a middle mast. Driver and spanker masts are also found on six-masted vessels.

packet The generic name for a ship that sails in regular service between two ports. The development of the transatlantic packet trade can be dated to 1817, when the Black Ball Line inaugurated service with ships sailing on a predetermined schedule regardless of whether they were booked to capacity.

paddle steamer A steamboat driven by a paddle wheel. The most common arrangement is a pair of wheels mounted on either side of the hull. American riverboats frequently have a single sternwheel.

piracy The unlawful seizure of property or ships on the high seas. Cf. *privateer.*

privateer One possessing a letter of marque from his government and thereby entitled to seize enemy shipping on the high seas. Under the Hague Convention of 1907, merchant-

men armed for purposes other than self-defense are classified as warships.

plank A long piece of sawn timber used in the construction of the hull and for decking. A **strake** can be made up of one or more planks.

quadruple-expansion engine A steam engine in which the steam expands through four cylinders.

rate A class of sailing warship, particularly in the Royal Navy, dependent on the number of guns mounted. The number of guns carried by a ship of a given rate changed from time to time. In 1779 it was as follows:

1st rate	100 guns
2nd rate	84–98 guns
3rd rate	64–80 guns
4th rate	50–60 guns
5th rate	32–44 guns
6th rate	20–30 guns

Ships of 60 guns and above were considered fit to lie in the battle line and referred to simply as vessels "of the line." Fourth and 5th rates were classed as frigates. Smaller combatants included sloops (ship-rigged, mounting 8–18 guns), bombs (fitted with mortars for bombing shoreside targets), and fireships (older vessels set on fire and sailed into an enemy fleet to destroy their ships). (See also **carronade** and **gun.**)

retour ship A capacious, heavily armed, and well-manned merchant ship of the Dutch East India Company (Verenigde Oostindische Compagnie, or VOC) designed for the long roundtrip (retour) voyage from the Netherlands to the East Indies.

round ship A medieval merchant sailing ship, as distinct from a longship or an oared galley.

rudder A device hung on the centerline at the stern and used to turn a vessel. (See also **steering oar.**)

schooner A vessel of two to seven masts, fore-and-aft rigged on each. A topsail schooner also sets square sails on the foremast. (See also **barkentine.**)

shell-first construction A method of hull construction in which the hull is formed without a frame. In shell-first construction, strakes either overlap, fastened to one another by clenched nails (clinker or lapstrake construction), or they form a smooth skin, fastened edge to edge by a complex system of mortise-and-tenon joinery. (See also **carvel construction, clinker construction,** and **frame-first construction.**)

ship A generic term usually referring to any large seagoing vessel.

ship of the line A full-rigged sailing ship fit to lie in the line of battle; a sailing battleship. A ship of the line carried 60 or more guns, and was rated as a 1st-, 2nd-, or 3rd-rate ship.

ship, full-rigged A vessel having three, four, or five masts and setting square sails on each. From the deck up, these are course, topsail (sometimes split into lower and upper), topgallant (sometimes split), royal, and skysail. In very light airs, some clipper ship captains would rig moonrakers above the skysails.

sloop A single-masted vessel setting a mainsail and a single jib, or headsail.

sloop-of-war A three-masted full-rigged warship, smaller than a frigate and rating 8 to 20 guns.

spar torpedo An explosive device carried at the end of a spar and placed against an enemy ship before being detonated.

square sail A quadrilateral sail set from a yard. Although a square-rigger can carry more sail than a fore-and-aft rigged vessel of comparable size, it is more dependent on favorable (following) winds.

staysail A triangular fore-and-aft sail set from a stay, a piece of standing rigging leading forward from, and providing longitudinal support for, a mast.

steering oar An oar mounted on the side of a ship (usually the right — steering board, or starboard — side) toward the stern and used for turning a ship. (See also **rudder.**)

strake A continuous row of hull planking (in a wooden ship) or plating (in an iron or steel ship) running fore and aft.

submarine A warship capable of operating underwater for long periods. During the two world wars, the submarine's primary armament consisted of torpedoes and small-caliber deck guns for work when surfaced. Many subs could be adapted for mine-laying operations, and a few also carried collapsible aircraft in deck hangars and midget submarines. In the nuclear era, strategic force submarines have been armed with intercontinental ballistic missiles that can be launched from underwater.

thole pin A vertical piece of wood against which a rowing oar pivots.

tonnage In merchant ships, tonnage is usually an expression of a ship's capacity or volume. The word has its origins in the medieval "tun," or wine cask, tunnage being the number of tuns a vessel could carry. Tonnage rules vary enormously. In the 18th century, tonnage was referred to as "burthen." This was replaced by "Builder's Old Measurement," abbreviated

"bm" or later "om," to distinguish it from new measurement (nm). One ton is now generally understood to equal 100 cubic feet.

Gross register tonnage (grt) is the whole cubic capacity of all enclosed spaces of a ship, including the entire room under the deck from stem to sternpost as well as that of the poop or bridge-house, a forecastle, or any other erection. *Net register tonnage* (nrt) is the capacity under deck available for stowing cargo only, and not including engine room spaces, passenger accommodations, or crew spaces.

Unlike cubic measures of tonnage, *deadweight tonnage* (dwt) is a measure of the weight of a vessel's cargo. This is determined by calculating the volume of water displaced by a vessel when "light" and when full of cargo. Because the water displaced is equal to the weight of the object displacing it, the difference in displacement figures is equal to the weight of the cargo. Deadweight tonnage is usually used only in reference to bulk cargo carriers such as oil tankers. (See also **displacement tonnage.**)

torpedo A self-propelled, underwater explosive device launched from surface ships, submarines, and aircraft. Developed in the late 19th century, torpedoes proved enormously effective against both merchant shipping and warships.

triple-expansion engine A steam engine in which the steam expands gradually and successively through three cylinders. Steam is first supplied to a high-pressure cylinder, then it passes into an intermediate-pressure cylinder at a lower pressure and finally into a low-pressure cylinder.

weather gauge In the age of fighting sail, if a ship was upwind of another it was said to have the weather gauge; the downwind or leeward ship had the **lee gauge.** The advantage of having the weather gauge was that a ship's guns could be aimed at the enemy's hull, often below the waterline. The guns of the leeward ship fired into the rigging, where damage was less serious.

yard A spar fastened to a mast perpendicular to the centerline of a vessel and from which square sails are set. The ends of a yard are called yardarms.

yawl A two-masted yacht similar in appearance to a ketch but with a smaller mizzen mast set abaft the rudderpost.

BIBLIOGRAPHY

The bibliography includes publication data for every work cited in the source notes of the articles. It should be noted that while there are more than a thousand titles listed, this bibliography can by no means be considered exhaustive. Taken together, the literature on the *Titanic, Bounty,* and Columbus's *Niña, Pinta,* and *Santa María* comprises hundreds of books and articles. Even a comprehensive listing of nautical bibliographies is impossible here, though four have been especially helpful in researching this book:

Bridges, R. C., and P. E. H. Hair. *Compassing the Vaste Globe of the Earth: Studies in the History of the Hakluyt Society 1846–1896.* London: Hakluyt Society, 1996. Includes a list of the more than 300 titles that have appeared under the society's imprint.

Labaree, Benjamin W. *A Supplement (1971–1986) to Robert G. Albion's Naval & Maritime History: An Annotated Bibliography.* 4th edition. Mystic, Conn.: Mystic Seaport Museum, 1988.

Law, Derek G. *The Royal Navy in World War Two: An Annotated Bibliography.* London: Greenhill Books, 1988.

National Maritime Museum (Greenwich, England). *Catalogue of the Library, Volume I: Voyages and Travel.* London: Her Majesty's Stationery Office, 1968.

There are many interesting avenues of research in maritime history on the Internet. Two have been particularly useful:

Maritime History Virtual Archives, owned and administered by Lar Bruzelius.
URL: http://pc-78-120.udac.se:8001/WWW/Nautica/Nautica.html

Rail, Sea and Air InfoPages and FAQ Archive (Military and TC FAQs), owned and administered by Andrew Toppan.
URL: http://www.membrane.com/~elmer/
mirror: http:// www.announce.com/~elmer/.

In addition, there are a number of online discussion groups to which one may subscribe. Two excellent forums are the Marine History Information Exchange Group owned by the Marine Museum of the Great Lakes at Kingston, Ontario, and administered by Maurice D. Smith, curator of the museum (E-mail: MARHST-L@POST.QUEENSU.CA); and the Underwater Archaeology Discussion List, owned and administered by Anita Cohen-Williams (E-mail: SUB-ARCH @ASUVM.INRE.ASU.EDU).

Note: IJNA stands for the International Journal of Nautical Archaeology.

Abbott, John S. C. "Ocean Life." *Harper's New Monthly Magazine* 5 (June 1852): 61–66.

d'Aboville, Gerard. *Alone: The Man Who Braved the Vast Pacific and Won.* New York: Arcade, 1993.

Adams, Bill. *Ships and Memories.* Brighton: Teredo Books, 1975.

Agawa, Hiroyuki. *The Reluctant Admiral: Yamamoto and the Imperial Navy.* New York: Kodansha International, 1979.

Aimone, Alan Conrad. "The Cruise of the U.S. Sloop *Hornet* in 1815." *Mariner's Mirror* 61 (1975): 377–384.

Alaska Oil Spill Commission. *Spill: The Wreck of the "Exxon Valdez," Final Report.* State of Alaska, 1990.

Albion, Robert Greenhalgh. *The Rise of New York Port, 1815–1860.* 1939. Reprint, Boston: Northeastern Univ. Press, 1984.

———. *Square-Riggers on Schedule: The New York Sailing Packets to England, France and the Cotton Ports.* Princeton: Princeton Univ. Press, 1938.

Albright, Alan B., and J. Richard Steffy. "The Brown's Ferry Vessel, South Carolina." *IJNA* 8 (1979): 121–142.

"Alexander Graham Bell Museum." Baddeck, Nova Scotia: 1965.

Allaway, J. *Hero of the "Upholder": The Story of Lt. Cdr. M. D. Wanklyn VC DSO, the Royal Navy's Top Submarine Ace.* Shrewsbury, Eng.: Airlife, 1991.

Allen, Francis J. "The Story of the USS *Vesuvius* and the Dynamite Gun." *Warship* 45 (1988): 10–15.

Allen, Jerry. *The Sea Years of Joseph Conrad.* Garden City, N.Y.: Doubleday, 1965.

Allen, J. F. "Answers." *Mariner's Mirror* 79 (1993): 220–221.

Allen, Joseph. *Battles of the Royal Navy from A.D. 1000 to 1840.* 2 vols. London: A. H. Baily, 1842.

Allin, Lawrence Carroll. "The First Cubic War — The *Virginius* Affair." *American Neptune* 38 (1978): 233–248.

American Bureau of Shipping. *ABS Record.* New York: ABS, annual.

American Sail Training Association. *ASTA Directory of Sail Training Ships and Programs.* Newport: ASTA, occasional.

Lord Amherst of Hackney, and Basil Thomson. *The Discovery of the Solomon Islands by Alvaro de Mendaña in 1568.* London: Hakluyt Society, 1901.

Amundsen, Roald. *My Life as an Explorer.* New York: Doubleday, Page, 1927.

———. *The Northwest Passage: The Voyage and Explorations of the "Gjoa."* London: Constable, 1908.

———. *The South Pole: An Account of the Norwegian Antarctic Expedition in the "Fram" 1910–1912.* 1912. Reprint, Toronto: McClelland & Stewart, 1976.

Anderson, Bern. *By Sea and by River: The Naval History of the Civil War.* New York: Alfred A. Knopf, 1962.

Anderson, Ernest B. *Sailing Ships of Ireland: A Book for Lovers of Sail, Being a Record of Irish Sailing Ships of the Nineteenth Century.* Dublin: Morris, 1951.

Anderson, R. C. "Henry VIII's Great Galley." Mariner's *Mirror* 6 (1920): 274–281.

Anderson, William R. *"Nautilus" — 90 North.* London: Hodder & Stoughton, 1959.

Apollonius Rhodius. *Argonautica.* Cambridge: Harvard Univ. Press, 1967.

Appleyard, H. S. *Bank Line and Andrew Weir and Company 1885–1985.* Kendal, Eng.: The World Ship Society, 1985.

Apps, Michael. *Send Her Victorious.* London: William Kimber, 1971.

Ardman, Harvey. *"Normandie," Her Life and Times.* New York: Franklin Watts, 1985.

Arenhold, Capt. L. "The Nydam Boat at Kiel." *Mariner's Mirror* 4 (1914): 182–185.

Arnold, Craig, ed. *Euterpe: Diaries, Letters and Logs of the "Star of India" as a British Emigrant Ship.* San Diego, 1988.

Arnold, J. B., and R. S. Weddle. *The Nautical Archaeology of Padre Island: The Spanish Shipwrecks of 1554.* New York: Academic Press, 1978.

Asher, G. M. *Henry Hudson the Navigator — The Original Documents in which his Career is Recorded, Partly Translated, and Annotated.* London: Hakluyt Society, 1860.

"Attack on the USS *Stark* (FFG-31)." *Warship International* 3 (1987): 264–68.

Back, George. *Narrative of an Expedition in HMS "Terror" Undertaken with a View to Geographical Discovery on the Arctic Shores . . .* London: John Murray, 1838.

Bailey, C. H. *Down the Burma Road: Work and Leisure for the Belowdeck Crew of the "Queen Mary" (1947–1967).* Southampton, Eng.: Southampton Oral History Team, 1990.

Bailey, Richard. *A Manual for Sailing Aboard the American Tall Ship "Rose."* Bridgeport, Conn.: "HMS" Rose Foundation, 1994.

Baker, A. D., III. *Naval Institute Guide to Combat Fleets of the World, 1995: Their Ships, Aircraft, and Armament.* Annapolis: Naval Institute Press, 1995.

Baker, William F. *Running Her Easting Down: A Documentary of the Development of the British Tea Clippers Culminating in the Building of the "Cutty Sark."* Caldwell, Idaho: Caxton, 1974.

Baker, William A. *The Engine-Powered Vessel, From Paddle-Wheeler to Nuclear Ship.* New York: Grosset & Dunlap, 1965.

———. "Gosnold's *Concord* and Her Shallop." *American Neptune* 34 (1974): 231–242.

———. "The *Gjoa.*" *American Neptune* 12 (1952): 7–21.

———. *"Mayflower" and Other Colonial Vessels.* London: Conway Maritime, 1983.

———. *The New "Mayflower."* Barre, Mass.: Barre Gazette, 1958.

Ball, Adrian, and Diana Wright. *S.S. "Great Britain."* Newton Abbot, Eng.: David & Charles, 1981.

Ball, Stuart R. "The Life and Death of an Edwardian Flagship: A Case Study of H.M.S. *Bulwark.*" *Mariner's Mirror* 72 (1986): 189–198.

Ballard, G. A. *The Black Battlefleet.* Lymington, Eng.: Nautical / Greenwich: Society for Nautical Research, 1980.

———. *The Discovery of the "Bismarck."* New York: Warner, 1990.

Ballard, Robert D., and Rick Archbold. *The Discovery of the "Titanic."* New York: Warner, 1987.

———. *Exploring the "Lusitania."* New York: Warner, 1995.

Barker, James P. *The Log of a Limejuicer: The Experience under Sail of James P. Barker, Master Mariner, As Told to Roland Barker.* New York: Macmillan, 1936.

Barker, Ralph. *Children of the Benares: A War Crime and Its Victims.* London: Methuen, 1987.

Barker, Roland. *"Tusitala": The Story of a Voyage in the Last of America's Square Riggers.* New York: W. W. Norton, 1959.

Barkhau, Roy L. *The Great Steamboat Race between the "Natchez" and the "Rob't. E. Lee."* Cincinnati, Ohio: Cincinnati Chapter of the Steamship Historical Society of America, 1962.

Barrow, Sir John. *The Mutiny and Piratical Seizure of HMS "Bounty": Its Causes and Consequences.* 1886. Reprint, London: The Folio Society, 1976.

Bartlett, Merrill L. "Commodore James Biddle and the First Naval Mission to Japan, 1845–46." *American Neptune* 41 (1981): 25–35.

Basalla, George. "The Voyage of the *Beagle* without Darwin." *Mariner's Mirror* 43 (1962): 42–48.

Basch, Lucien. "The Athlit Basch: A Preliminary Introduction and Report." *Mariner's Mirror* 68 (1982): 3–9.

———. "A Historic Ship, the *Giorgio Averoff.*" *Mariner's Mirror* 71 (1985): 183.

———. "The Kadirga Revisited: A Preliminary Re-appraisal." *Mariner's Mirror* 65 (1979): 39–51.

———. "The Sewn Ships of Bon Porte." *Mariner's Mirror* 67 (1981): 244.

Bass, G. F. "Bronze Age Shipwreck at Ulu Burun (Kas): 1984 Campaign." *American Journal of Archaeology* 90 (1986) 269–296.

———. "A Byzantine Trading Venture." *Scientific American* 225 (Aug. 1971) 22–33.

———. "Cape Gelidonya: A Bronze Age Shipwreck." *Transactions of the American Philosophical Society.* New Series 57:8 (1967).

———. *A History of Seafaring Based on Underwater Archaeology.* New York: Walker & Co., 1972.

———. "Return to Cape Gelidonya." *INA Newsletter* 15 (1988): 2–5.

———. *Ships and Shipwrecks of the Americas: A History Based on Underwater Archaeology.* London: Thames & Hudson, 1988.

———. "The Shipwreck at Serçe Liman, Turkey." *Archaeology* 32 (1979): 36–43.

Bass, G. F., and F. H. van Doorninck, Jr. "An 11th century Shipwreck at Serçe Limani, Turkey." *IJNA* 7 (1978) 119–132.

———. "A Fourth-Century Shipwreck at Yassi Ada." *American Journal of Archaeology* 75 (1971): 27–37.

———. *Yassi Ada. Vol. 1. A Seventh-Century Byzantine Shipwreck.* College Station, Tex.: IJNA, 1982.

Bassett, Ronald. *Battle-Cruisers: A History 1908–48.* London: Macmillan, 1981.

———. *HMS "Sheffield": The Life and Times of "Old Shiny."* Annapolis: Naval Institute Press, 1988.

Bastock, John. *Australia's Ships of War.* Sydney: Angus & Robertson, 1975.

Baxter, James Phinney. *Introduction of the Ironclad Warship.* Cambridge: Harvard Univ. Press, 1933.

Bayreuther, William A., and Molly J. Horvath. "The *Snow Squall* Project: Saving the Last Yankee Clipper Ship." *Bermuda Journal of Archaeology and Maritime History* 5 (1993): 99–109.

Beach, Edward L. *Around the World Submerged.* New York: Henry Holt, 1962.

————. *The United States Navy: 200 Years.* New York: Henry Holt, 1986.

————. *The Wreck of the "Memphis."* New York: Holt, Rinehart & Winston, 1966.

Beaglehole, J. C. *The Exploration of the Pacific.* 3rd ed. Stanford: Stanford Univ. Press, 1966.

Bearss, Edwin C. *Hardluck Ironclad: The Sinking and Salvage of the "Cairo."* Baton Rouge: Louisiana State Univ. Press, 1966.

Beattie, Judith, and Bernard Pothier. "The Battle of the Restigouche." In *Canadian Historic Sites: Occasional Papers in Archaeology and History.* Ottawa: Parks Canada, 1977.

Beattie, Owen, and John Geiger. *Frozen in Time: The Fate of the Franklin Expedition.* London: Bloomsbury, 1987.

Beaver, Patrick. *The Big Ship: Brunel's "Great Eastern" — a Pictorial History.* London: Hugh Evelyn, 1969.

Becton, F. Julian. *The Ship That Would Not Die.* Englewood Cliffs, N.J.: Prentice-Hall, 1980.

Bednall, Warren. *Strange Sea Road: The Story of a Sea Venture.* London: Jonathan Cape, 1936.

Beebe, William. *Half Mile Down.* New York: Harcourt Brace, 1934.

Beechey, Frederick William. *Narrative of a Voyage to the Pacific and Beering's Strait, to cooperate with the polar expeditions; performed in His Majesty's ship "Blossom," under the command of Captain F. W. Beechey, R.N. F.R.S. F.R.A.S. and F.R.G.S. in the years 1825, 26, 27, 28.* London: Henry Colburn & Richard Bentley, 1831.

Bekker, Claus. *Hitler's Naval War.* Garden City, N.Y.: Doubleday, 1974.

Bellabarba, Sergio, and Giorgio Osculati. *The Royal Yacht "Caroline" 1749.* London: Conway Maritime Press, 1989.

Bellingshausen, F. G. von. *The Voyage of Captain Bellingshausen to the Antarctic Seas 1819–1821.* 2 vols. Edited by F. Debenham. London: Hakluyt Society, 1945.

Bennett, Geoffrey. *Battle of the River Plate.* Annapolis: Naval Institute Press, 1972.

————. *Coronel and the Falklands.* London: Batsford, 1962.

————. *The Loss of the "Prince of Wales" and "Repulse."* London: Ian Allan, 1973.

————. *Nelson the Commander.* New York: Charles Scribner's Sons, 1972.

Bennett, Isabelle. "Isabelle's Excellent Adventure: Her 1994 New York–San Francisco Record Run." *Cruising World* (July 1994): 50.

Berthold, Victor. *The Pioneer Steamer "California" 1848–1849.* Boston: Houghton Mifflin, 1932.

Berton, Pierre. *The Arctic Grail: The Quest for the Northwest Passage and the North Pole, 1818–1909.* New York: Viking-Penguin, 1988.

Bevan, David. *Drums of the "Birkenhead."* London: London Stamp Exchange, 1989.

Bixby, William. *The Track of the "Bear": 1873–1963.* New York: David McKay, 1965.

Blake, Joe. *Restoring the "Great Britain."* Bristol, Eng.: Redcliffe, 1989.

Bligh, William. *Narrative of the Mutiny on the "Bounty."* 1792. Reprint, New York: Airmont, 1965.

Blow, Michael. *A Ship to Remember: The "Maine" and the Spanish-American War.* New York: Morrow, 1992.

Blyth, Chay. *The Impossible Dream.* London: Hodder & Stoughton, 1971.

Boit, John. *Log of the "Union": John Boit's Remarkable Voyage to the Northwest Coast and around the World, 1794–1796.* Edited by Edmund Hayes. Portland: Oregon Historical Society, 1986.

Bombard, Alain. *The Voyage of the "Hérétique."* New York: Simon & Schuster, 1953.

Bonde, Niels, and Arne Emil Christensen. "Dendrochronological Dating of the Viking Age Ship Burials at Oseberg, Gokstad & Tune." *Antiquity* 67 (1993): 575–583.

Bonsor, N. R. P. *North Atlantic Seaway.* 5 vols. Jersey: Brookside, 1975.

————. *South Atlantic Seaway.* Jersey: Brookside, 1983.

Boroughs, Polly. *The Great Ice Ship "Bear": Eighty-Nine Years in Polar Seas.* New York: Van Nostrand Reinhold, 1970.

Boudriot, Jean. *John Paul Jones and the "Bonhomme Richard" 1779: A Reconstruction of the Ship and an Account of the Battle with HMS "Serapis."* Annapolis: Naval Institute Press, 1987.

Bougainville, Lewis de. *A Voyage round the World: Performed by Order of His Most Christian Majesty, in the Years 1766, 1767, 1768, and 1769.* London: J. Nourse & T. Davies, 1772.

Bound, Mensun. "The Dattilo Wreck (Panarea, Aeolian Islands): First Season Report." *IJNA* 18 (1989): 203–219.

————. "Early Observations on the Construction of the Preclassical wreck at Campese Bay, island."

————. "A Wreck at Dattilo, Panarea (Aeolian Islands): A Preliminary Note." *IJNA* 18 (1989): 27–32.

Bound, Mensun, and R. Vallintine. "A Wreck of Possible Etruscan Origin off Giglio Island." *IJNA* 12 (1983) 113–122.

Bovill, E. W. "The *Madre de Dios.*" *Mariner's Mirror* 54 (1968): 129–152.

Bowker, Francis E. *Atlantic Four-Master: The Story of the Schooner "Herbert L. Rawding" 1919–1947.* Mystic, Conn.: Mystic Seaport Museum, 1976.

Bowness, Edward. *Modelling the "Archibald Russell."* London: Percival Press, n.d.

Boxer, C. R. "The Taking of *Madre de Dios.*" *Mariner's Mirror* 67 (1981): 82–84.

Boyd, Carl, and Akihiko Yoshida. *The Japanese Submarine Force and World War II.* Annapolis: Naval Institute Press, 1995.

Boyd, Thomas. *Poor John Fitch.* New York: G. P. Putnam's Sons, 1935.

Bradford, Ernle. *The Story of the "Mary Rose."* London: Hamish Hamilton, 1982.

Bradford, Gershom. *The Secret of the "Mary Celeste."* Barre, Mass.: Barre Publ., 1966.

Bradford, Richard H. "And *Oregon* Rushed Home." *American Neptune* 36 (1976): 155–169.

Bradlee, Francis B. C. *The Ship "Great Republic" and Donald McKay Her Builder.* Salem, Mass.: 1987.

Brassey, Lady. *In the Trades, the Tropics, and the Roaring Forties: R.Y.S. "Sunbeam," 1876–77.* New York: Henry Holt, 1887.

————. *The Last Voyage to India and Australia in the "Sunbeam," 1887.* London: Longmans & Green, 1889.

————. *Sunshine and Storm in the East, or Cruises to Cyprus and Constantinople.* London: Longmans & Green, 1880.

————. *A Voyage in the "Sunbeam": Our Home on the Ocean for Eleven Months . . .* London: Longmans & Green, 1889.

Bray, Maynard, and Pinheiro, Carlton. *Herreshoff of Bristol: A Photographic History of America's Greatest Yacht and Boat Builders.* Brooklin, Maine: WoodenBoat, 1989.

Braynard, Frank O. *The Big Ship: The Story of the SS "United States."* Newport News: The Mariners' Museum, 1981.

———. *Classic Ocean Liners.* Wellingborough, Eng.: Patrick Stephens, 1990.

———. *Famous American Ships.* New York: Hastings House, 1978.

———. *"Leviathan": The World's Greatest Ship.* 6 vols. New York: 1972–1983.

———. *Lives of the Liners.* New York: Cornell Maritime Press, 1947.

———. *S.S. "Savannah": The Elegant Steam Ship.* New York: Dover, 1988.

Braynard, Frank O., and William Miller. *Fifty Famous Liners.* New York: W. W. Norton, 1982.

———. *Fifty Famous Liners 2.* New York: W. W. Norton, 1985.

Brennecke, Jochan. *The "Tirpitz": The Drama of the "Lone Queen of the North."* London: Hale, 1963.

Brettle, Robert E. *"Cutty Sark": Her Designer and Builder Hercules Linton 1836–1900.* Cambridge, Eng.: Heffer, 1969.

Breyer, Siegfried. *Battleships and Battle Cruisers 1905–1970.* London: Macdonald & Jane's, 1973.

Brice, Martin H. *The Tribals.* London: Ian Allan, 1971.

Brigham, Lawson W. "Arctic Icebreakers: U.S., Canadian, and Soviet." *Oceanus* 29:1 (Spring 1986): 47–58.

Broadwater, John D., Robert M. Adams, and Marcie Renner. "The Yorktown Shipwreck Archaeological Project: An Interim Report on the Excavation of Shipwreck 44Y088." *IJNA* 14 (1985): 301–314.

Brock, P. W. "Cook's *Endeavour* and Other Ships." *Mariner's Mirror* 54:2 (1968): 194–95.

———. "Dossier HMS *Blossom* 1806–1848." Victoria: Maritime Museum of British Columbia, n.d.

Brookes, Douglas S. "The Turkish Imperial State Barges." *Mariner's Mirror* 76 (1990): 41–49.

Brosse, Jacques. *Great Voyages of Discovery: Circumnavigators and Scientists, 1764–1843.* New York: Facts on File, 1983.

Brouwer, Norman. "The 'Convict Ship' *Success.*" *Seaport* (Winter 1977–1978): 21.

———. "The 1856 Packet Ship *Charles Cooper.*" *Seaport* (Fall 1981): 18–21.

———. "The Four-Masted Ship *County of Peebles.*" *Seaport* (Winter 1979–1980): 23–25.

———. *International Register of Historic Ships.* 2nd ed. London: Anthony Nelson, 1993.

———. "The Queen of Long Island Sound." *Seaport* (Spring 1985): 32–36.

Brown, Alexander Crosby. "The *Robert F. Stockton* and the Introduction of Screw Propulsion." *Steamboat Bill of Facts* 40 (Dec. 1951): 73–75.

———. "The Steamer *Vesta*: Neglected Partner in a Fatal Collision." *American Neptune* 20 (1960): 177–184.

———. *Women and Children Last: The Loss of the Steamship "Arctic."* New York: G. P. Putnam's Sons, 1961.

———. "The *Yarmouth Castle* Inferno." *American Neptune* 36 (1976): 5–31.

Brown, D. K. *Before the Ironclad: The Development of Ship Design, Propulsion, and Armament in the Royal Navy, 1815–1860.* London: Conway Maritime Press, 1990.

———. "The Design of HMS *Inflexible.*" *Warship* 4:15 (1980): 146–152.

———. "The Introduction of the Screw Propeller into the Royal Navy." *Warship* 1:1 (1970): 59–63.

———. "*Nemesis:* The First Iron Warship." *Warship* 2:8 (1978): 283–285.

———. "The Paddle Frigate *Guadeloupe.*" *Mariner's Mirror* 58 (1972): 221–222.

———. "Seamanship, Steam and Steel: HMS *Calliope* at Samoa, 15–16 March 1889." *Mariner's Mirror* 49 (1953): 193–208.

———. "*Tirpitz*": The Floating Fortress. London: Arms & Armour, 1977.

———. *Warship Losses of World War Two.* Rev. ed. Annapolis: Naval Institute Press, 1990.

Brownlee, Walter. *"Warrior": The First Modern Battleship.* Cambridge, Eng.: Cambridge Univ. Press, 1985.

Bryer, Robin. *"Jolie Brise": A Tall Ship's Tale.* London: Secker & Warburg, 1982.

Buchanan, J. Y., H. N. Moseley, J. Murray, and T. H. Tizard. *Narrative of the Voyage.* Vol. 1 of *The Report of the Scientific Results of the Exploring Voyage of HMS "Challenger" during the years 1873–1876.* London: 1885–1895.

Bugler, Arthur R. *HMS "Victory": Building, Restoration and Repair.* London: Her Majesty's Stationery Office, 1966.

Bulkeley, John, and John Cummins. *A Voyage to the South Seas in His Majesty's Ship the "Wager" in the Years 1740–1741.* New York: Robert M. McBride, 1927.

Bulkley, Robert J., Jr. *At Close Quarters: PT Boats in the United States Navy.* Washington, D.C.: Naval Historical Division, 1962.

Burdick, Charles B. *The End of the "Prinz Eugen" (IX300).* Menlo Park, Calif.: Markgraf Publications Group, 1996.

Burdick, J. W. *Our World Tour, 1922–23: An Account by the First Ever World Tour, by a Passenger Liner.* Liverpool, Eng.: National Museums and Galleries on Merseyside, 1990.

Burleson, Clyde W. *Jennifer Project.* Englewood Cliffs, N.J.: Prentice Hall, 1977.

Burroughs, Polly. *Zeb: A Celebrated Schooner Life.* Chester, Conn.: Globe Pequot Press, 1972.

Burton, Hal. *The "Morro Castle": Tragedy at Sea.* New York: Viking Press, 1973.

Bushell, T. A. *Royal Mail: A Centennial History of the Royal Mail Line 1839–1939.* London: Trade & Travel, 1939.

Butlin, C. M. *White Sails Crowding.* London: Jonathan Cape, 1935.

Byron, John. *Byron's Journal of His Circumnavigation, 1764–1766.* Ed. Robert E. Gallagher. Cambridge, Eng.: Hakluyt Society, 1946.

———. *The Narrative of . . . the Honourable John Byron . . . Containing an account of the great distresses suffered by himself and his companions on the coast of Patagonia.* 1768. Reprinted in *Voyage to the South Seas in the Years 1740–41.* London: Folio Society, 1983.

Cable, Boyd. "The World's First Clipper." *Mariner's Mirror* 29 (1943): 66–92.

Caesar, Julius. *The Gallic Wars.* Cambridge: Harvard University Press, 1917.

Caffrey, Kate. *The "Mayflower."* New York: Stein & Day, 1974.

Cain, Emily. *Ghost Ships "Hamilton" & "Scourge": Historical Treasures from the War of 1812.* New York: Beaufort Books, 1983.

Calvert, James P. *Surface at the Pole: The Extraordinary Voyages of the USS "Skate."* New York: McGraw-Hill, 1960.

Campbell, William C. "Until the Owners Return." In H. K. Rigg, ed., *Tales from the Skipper.* Barre, Mass.: Barre Publications, 1968.

Canney, Donald L. *The Old Steam Navy: Frigates, Sloops and Gunboats 1815–1885.* Annapolis: Naval Institute Press, 1990.

———. *U.S. Coast Guard and Revenue Cutters, 1790–1935.* Annapolis: Naval Institute Press, 1995.

Cantelas, Frank J., and Bradley A. Rodgers. "The *Maple Leaf:* A Case Study in Cost-Effective Zero-Visibility Riverine Archaeology." *IJNA* 23 (1994): 271–282.

Careless, Ronald. *Battleship "Nelson": The Story of HMS "Nelson."* Annapolis: Naval Institute Press, 1986.

Carr, William Guy. *By Guess and By God: The Story of the British Submariners in the War.* Garden City, N.Y.: Doubleday, Doran, 1930.

Carrick, Robert W., and Richard Henderson. *John G. Alden and His Yacht Designs.* Camden, Maine: International Marine, 1995.

Carter, Hodding. *Rivers of America: Lower Mississippi.* New York: Farrar & Rinehart, 1942.

Casson, Lionel. *The Ancient Mariners: Seafarers and Sea Fighters in Ancient Times.* 2nd ed. Princeton: Princeton Univ. Press, 1991.

———. "The 'Isis' and her Voyage." *Transactions of the American Philological Association* 81 (1950): 43–56.

Casson, Lionel, and J. Richard Steffy. *The Athlit Ram.* College Station, Tex.: Institute of Nautical Archaeology, 1991.

Chance, Franklin N., Paul S. Chance, and David L. Topper. *Tangled Machinery and Charred Relics: The Historical and Archaeological Investigation of the CSS "Nashville."* Orangeburg, S.C.: 1985.

Chapelle, Howard I. *The American Fishing Schooners, 1825–1935.* New York: W. W. Norton, 1973.

———. "The First Clipper." *Mariner's Mirror* 34 (1948): 26–33.

———. *Fulton's "Steam Battery": Blockship and Catamaran.* Washington, D.C.: 1964.

———. *The History of the American Sailing Navy: The Ships and Their Development.* New York: Bonanza Books, 1949.

Charcot, Jean. *The Voyage of the "Why Not" in the Antarctic: The Journal of the Second French South Polar Expedition, 1908–1910.* London: Hodder & Stoughton, 1911.

Chase, Owen. *Shipwreck of the Whaleship "Essex."* 1821. Reprint, New York: Corinth Press, 1963.

Chelminski, Rudolph. *Superwreck: "Amoco Cadiz" — The Shipwreck That Had to Happen.* New York: William Morrow, 1987.

Cherry-Garrard, Apsley George Benet. *The Worst Journey in the World: Antarctica 1910–1913.* 2 vols. London: Constable, 1922.

Chesneau, Roger, ed. *Conway's All the World's Fighting Ships 1922–1946.* London: Conway Maritime, 1990.

Chesneau, Roger, and Eugene M. Kolesink, eds. *Conway's All the World's Fighting Ships 1860–1905.* London: Conway Maritime, 1979.

Chichester, Sir Francis. *"Gypsy Moth" Circles the World.* New York: Coward-McCann, 1967.

Childers, Erskine. *The Howth Gun-Running and the Kilcoole Gun-Running, 1914: Recollections and Documents.* Dublin: Browne & Nolan, 1964.

———. *A Thirst for the Sea: The Sailing Adventures of Erskine Childers.* Edited by Hugh and Robin Popham. London: Stanford Maritime, 1979.

Churchouse, E. J. *The "Pamir" Under the New Zealand Ensign.* Wellington, Eng.: Milwood Press, 1978.

Clamp, Arthur L. *The Loss of the "Herzogin Cecilie."* Plymouth, Eng.: n.d.

Clark, Miles. *High Endeavours: The Extraordinary Life and Adventures of Miles and Beryl Smeeton.* London: HarperCollins, 1991.

Clarke, Arthur C. *Voice across the Sea: The Story of the Deep-Sea Cables and the Men Who Made Possible a Century of Ever-Improving Communication.* New York: Harper & Brothers, 1958.

Clements, Rex. *A Gipsy of the Horn: A Narrative of a Voyage round the World in a Windjammer.* 1924. Reprint, London: 1951.

Clifford, Robert L. "The Unexpected End to *Seeadler.*" *American Neptune* 36 (1976): 266–275.

Clowes, William Laird. *The Royal Navy: A History from Earliest Times to the Present.* 6 vols. London: 1897. Reprint, Annapolis: Naval Institute Press, 1996–98.

Coates, John F. "The Trireme Sails Again." *Scientific American* 260 (Apr. 1989): 96–103.

Cochrane, Thomas. *Autobiography of a Seaman, by Thomas, Tenth Earl of Dundonald.* London: 1869.

Coles, Alan. *Three before Breakfast.* Homewell, Hants.: Kenneth Mason, 1979.

Colledge, J. J. *Ships of the Royal Navy: The Complete Record of All Fighting Ships of the Royal Navy from the Fifteenth Century to the Present.* 2 vols. Annapolis: Naval Institute Press, 1987.

Colton, J. Ferell. "Bring *Moshulu* Home!" *Sea Breezes* 68 (Apr. 1984): 297–298.

———. *Last of the Square-Rigged Ships.* New York: G. P. Putnam's Sons, 1937.

———. *Windjammers Significant.* Flagstaff, Ariz.: 1954.

Columbus, Christopher. *The Four Voyages of Christopher Columbus.* Ed. Cecil Jane. New York: Dover, 1988.

Comee, Fred T. "The Last Days of the *Coriolanus.*" *Sea History* 39 (1986): 23–26.

Compton-Hall, Richard. *Submarine Boats: The Beginnings of Underwater Warfare.* London: Conway Maritime Press, 1983.

Conrad, Joseph. *The Mirror of the Sea.* New York: Doubleday, Page & Co., 1925.

———. *The Nigger of the "Narcissus": A Tale of the Sea.* Garden City, N.Y.: Doubleday & Page, 1925.

———. *The Shadow-Line and Two Other Tales.* 1917. Reprint, Garden City, N.Y.: Doubleday Anchor Books, 1959.

Conway's All the World's Fighting Ships . . . See Chesneau; Chesneau and Kolesink; Gardiner; and Gray.

Cook, Frederick Albert. *Through the First Antarctic Night, 1898–1899: A Narrative of the Voyage of the "Belgica" among Newly Discovered Lands and over an Unknown Sea about the South Pole.* London: C. Hurst; Canberra: Australian National Union, 1980.

Cook, James. *The Journals of James Cook on His Voyages of Discovery.* Ed. J. C. Beaglehole. 3 vols. Cambridge, Eng.: Hakluyt Society, 1955–56.

Cooke, Robert. "Divers Report Mystery Ship Found." *Newsday* (April 14, 1989).

Corner, George. *Doctor of the Arctic Seas.* Philadelphia: Childs & Peterson, 1972.

Cottell, G. A. "The Gokstad Viking Ship: Some New Theories concerning the Purpose of Certain of Its Construction Features." *Mariner's Mirror* 69 (1983): 129–142.

Course, A. G. *Painted Ports: The Story of the Ships of Messrs Devitt and Moore.* London: Hollis & Carter, 1961.

———. *The Wheel's Kick and the Wind's Song: The Story of the John Stewart Line of Sailing Ships.* Newton Abbot, Eng.: David & Charles, 1968.

———. *Windjammers of the Horn: The Story of the Last British Fleet of Square-Rigger Sailing Ships.* London: Adlard Coles, 1969.

Cowan, Edward. *Oil and Water: The "Torrey Canyon" Disaster.* Philadelphia: J. B. Lippincott, 1968.

Cox, Lee J., and Michael A. Jehle, eds. *Ironclad Intruder: USS "Monitor."* Philadelphia: Philadelphia Maritime Museum, 1988.

Crabtree, Reginald. *Royal Yachts of Europe: From the Seventeenth to Twentieth Century.* Newton Abbot: David & Charles, 1975.

Craig, Gavin. *Boy Aloft.* London: Nautical, 1971.

Craig, John. *The "Noronic" Is Burning!* Don Mills, Ont.: General Publications, 1976.

Crainer, Scott. *Zeebrugge: Learning from Disaster — Lessons in Corporate Responsibility.* London: Heritable Charitable Trust, 1993.

Cressman, Robert. *That Gallant Ship: USS "Yorktown" (CV-5).* Missoula, Mont.: Pictorial Histories, 1985.

Crichton, Richard E. "The Wreck of *San Francisco.*" *American Neptune* 45 (1945): 20–34.

Croall, James. *Fourteen Minutes: The Last Voyage of the "Empress of Ireland."* London: Michael Joseph, 1978.

Crockett, Fred E. *Special Fleet: The History of the Presidential Yachts.* Camden, Maine: Down East Books, 1985.

Cross, Wilbur. *Challengers of the Deep: The Story of Submarines.* New York: William Sloan Assoc., 1959.

Crowninshield, Francis B. *The Story of George Crowninshield's Yacht "Cleopatra's Barge" on a Voyage of Pleasure to the Western Islands and the Mediterranean, 1816–17.* Boston: privately printed, 1913.

Crumlin-Pedersen, Ole. "The Skuldelev Ships." *Acta Archaeologica* 38 (1967): 73–174.

Cullivan, Lynn. "*Eureka:* A Centennial Retrospective." *Sea Letter* (Spring/Summer 1990).

Culver, Henry B. *Forty Famous Ships: Their Beginnings, Their Life Histories, Their Ultimate Fate.* New York: Garden City Publ., 1938.

Culver, Henry B., and R. Morton Nance. "A Contemporary Fifteenth Century Ship." *Mariner's Mirror* 15 (1929): 213–221.

Cussler, Clive. *The Sea Hunters.* New York: Simon & Schuster, 1996.

Cutler, Carl C. *Greyhounds of the Sea: The Story of the American Clipper Ship.* Annapolis: Naval Institute Press, 1961.

———. *Queens of the Western Ocean.* Annapolis: Naval Institute Press, 1961.

Cutter, Donald C. *Malaspina & Galiano: Spanish Voyages to the Northwest Coast 1791 & 1792.* Seattle: Univ. of Washington Press, 1991.

Dampier, William. *Voyages.* Edited by John Masefield. London: E. Grant Richards, 1906.

Dana, Richard Henry, Jr. *Two Years Before the Mast: A Personal Narrative of Life at Sea.* 1840. Edited by John Haskell Kemble. 2 vols. Los Angeles: Ward Ritchie Press, 1964.

Darling, Lois. "HMS *Beagle:* Further Research or Twenty Years A-Beagling." *Mariner's Mirror* 64 (1978): 315–325.

Darrach, Claude. *Race to Fame: The Inside Story of the "Bluenose."* Hantsport, Nova Scotia: 1985.

Darroch, Vin. *Barque "Polly Woodside (Rona)."* Melbourne, Australia: 1979.

Darwin, Charles. *Diary of the Voyage of H.M.S. "Beagle."* New York: Cambridge Univ. Press, 1988.

Davidsson, Jan. "*Viking.*" Göteborg, Sweden: 1981.

Davison, Ann. *My Ship Is So Small.* New York: William Sloan, 1956.

Day, Beth. *Passage Perilous.* New York: Putnam, 1962.

Dear, Ian. "*Enterprise" and "Endeavour": The J-Class Yachts.* London: Editors, Inc., 1989.

de Bray, Emile Frédéric. *A Frenchman in Search of Franklin: De Bray's Arctic Journal 1852–54.* Toronto: Univ. of Toronto Press, 1992.

de Kay, James Tertius. *Chronicles of the Frigate "Macedonian."* New York: W. W. Norton, 1995.

De Latil, Pierre, and Jean Rivoire. *Sunken Treasure.* New York: Hill & Wang, 1959.

Delgado, James P. "*Beaver": First Steamship on the West Coast.* Victoria, British Columbia: Horsdal & Schubart, 1992.

———. *Dauntless "St. Roch": The Mounties' Arctic Schooner.* Victoria, British Columbia: Horsdal & Schubart, 1992.

———. "Documenting the Sunken Remains of USS *Saratoga.*" *U.S. Naval Institute Proceedings* 116: 10 (Oct. 1990).

———. "Murder Most Foul: San Francisco Reacts to the Loss of the S.S. *Central America.*" *The Log of Mystic Seaport* 35:1 (Spring 1983).

———. "Recovering the Past of USS *Arizona:* Symbolism, Myth and Reality." *Historical Archaeology* 26:4 (1992).

———. "Rediscovering the *Somers.*" *Naval History* 8 (Mar./Apr. 1994): 28–31.

———. *A Symbol of American Ingenuity: Historical Context Study, USS "Monitor."* Washington, D.C.: National Park Service/National Oceanic and Atmospheric Administration, 1988.

Delgado, James P., and J. Candace Clifford. *Great American Ships.* Washington, D.C.: Preservation Press, 1991.

Denham, H. M. "Caligula's Galleys: Notes on a Short Visit, Especially with regard to Their Construction." *Mariner's Mirror* 15 (1929): 333–346.

Dennis, D. L. "The Action between the *Shannon* and the *Chesapeake.*" *Mariner's Mirror* 45 (1959): 36–45.

Derby, W. L. A. *The Tall Ships Pass: The Story of the Last Years of Deepwater Square-Rigged Sail.* London: Jonathan Cape, 1937.

Dethlefsen, Edwin. "*Whidah": Cape Cod's Mystery Ship.* Woodstock, Vt.: Seafarers Heritage Library, 1984.

Dictionary of National Biography. 22 vols. and supplements. London: Oxford University Press, 1917–.

Dierks, J. C. *A Leap to Arms: The Cuban Campaign of 1898.* New York: Lippincott, 1970.

Dingemans. "The Search for the Etruscan Wreck of Giglio Island." *Sea History* 67 (1993): 16–20.

Divin, Vasilii A. *The Great Russian Navigator, A. I. Chirikov.* Fairbanks: Univ. of Alaska Press, 1993.

Dobson, Christopher, John Miller, and Ronald Payne. *The Cruelest Night.* London: Hodder & Stoughton, 1979.

Dodge, Ernest S. *Northwest by Sea.* New York: Oxford Univ. Press, 1961.

———. *The Polar Rosses: John and James Clark Ross and Their Explorations.* London: Faber & Faber, 1973.

Domville-Fife, Charles W. *Epics of the Square-Rigged Ships.* London: Seeley Service, 1958.

Donald, T. W. "The *Livadia.*" *Mariner's Mirror* 55 (1969): 324.

Doyle, Conan. "J. Habakuk Jephson's Statement." In *The Captain of the "Polestar," and Other Tales.* London: 1892.

Drake-Brockman, Henrietta. *Voyage to Disaster.* Sydney: Angus & Robertson, 1963.

du Boulay, Juliet. "Wrecks in the Isles of Scilly." *Mariner's Mirror* 46 (1960): 88–113.

Dugan, James. *American Viking: The Saga of Hans Isbrandtsen and His Shipping Empire.* New York: Harper & Row, 1963.

———. *The Great Iron Ship*. New York: Harper, 1953.

———. *The Great Mutiny*. New York: G. P. Putnam's, 1964.

Dulles, Foster Rhea. *The Old China Trade*. Boston: Houghton Mifflin, 1930.

Dumas, Robert. "The *King George V* Class." *Warship* 3:9–12 (1979).

Dumas, Vito. *Alone through the Roaring Forties*. London: Adlard Coles, 1960.

Dumont d'Urville, Jules-Sebastien-César. *Two Voyages to the South Seas by Captain . . . Jules S-C Dumont d'Urville*. Melbourne: Melbourne Univ. Press, 1987.

Duncan, Roland F. "*Chile* and *Peru:* The First Successful Steamers in the Pacific." *American Neptune* 35 (1975): 248–269.

Dunmore, John. *French Explorers in the Pacific*. Vol. 1, *The Nineteenth Century;* Vol. 2, *The Twentieth Century*. New York: Oxford Univ. Press, 1965, 1969.

Dunmore, John, ed. *The Expedition of the "St. Jean-Baptiste" to the Pacific 1769–1770*. London: The Hakluyt Society, 1981.

Dunne, W. M. P. "The Frigate *Constellation* Clearly Was No More: Or Was She?" *American Neptune* 53 (1993): 77–97.

Dye, Ira. *The Fatal Cruise of the "Argus": Two Captains in the War of 1812*. Annapolis: Naval Institute Press, 1994.

Dyson, John, with J. Fitchett. *Sink the "Rainbow"! An Enquiry into the Greenpeace Affair*. London: Victor Golancz, 1986.

Earle, Peter. *The Last Fight of the "Revenge."* London: Collins & Brown, 1992.

———. *The Wreck of the "Almiranta": Sir William Phips and the Search for the Hispaniola Treasure*. London: Macmillan, 1979.

Eaton, John P., and Charles A. Haas. *Falling Star: The Misadventures of White Star Line Ships*. Wellingborough, Eng.: Patrick Stephens, 1989.

Edwards, Bernard. *Salvo! Classic Naval Gun Actions*. Annapolis: Naval Institute Press, 1995.

Egan, Robert S., Arnold S. Lott, and Robert F. Sumrall. *USS "Texas" (BB35)*. Annapolis: Leeward, 1976.

Einarsson, Lars. "The Royal Ship *Kronan* — Underwater Archaeological Investigations of a Great Swedish 17th Century Man-of-War." *Seventh International Congress of Maritime Museums, Proceedings 1990*. Stockholm: National Maritime Museums, 1990.

Eiseman, Cynthia J. "The Porticello Shipwreck." *INA Newsletter* 2.1 (1975): 1–4.

Eiseman, Cynthia J., and Brunilde Sismondo Ridgway. *The Porticello Shipwreck: A Mediterranean Merchant Vessel of 415–385 B.C.* College Station, Tex.: Texas A&M Press, 1987.

Eliseo, Maurizio. *Rex: Regis Nomen, Navis Omen. Storia di un Transatlantico — The Greyhound of the Seas*. Parma, Italy: Labertelli, 1992.

Emerson, William C. "The Armoured Cruiser USS *Brooklyn*." *Warship 1991*. London: Conway Maritime Press, 1991.

———. "USS *Olympia*." *Warship 1989*. London: Conway Maritime Press, 1989.

Emmerson, George S. *John Scott Russell: A Great Victorian Engineer and Naval Architect*. London: John Murray, 1977.

Ennes, James M., Jr. *Assault on the "Liberty": The Story of the Israeli Attack on an American Intelligence Ship*. New York: Random House, 1979.

Ennis, John. *The Great Bombay Explosion*. New York: Duell, Sloan & Pearce, 1959.

Eriksson, Pamela Bourne. *The Life and Death of the Duchess*. Boston: Houghton Mifflin, 1959.

———. *Out of the World*. London: Geoffrey Bles, 1935.

Evans, Angela Care. *The Sutton Hoo Ship Burial*. London: British Museum Press, 1986.

Ewing, Steve. *American Cruisers of World War Two: A Pictorial Encyclopedia*. Missoula, Mont.: Pictorial Histories, 1984.

———. *USS "Enterprise" (CV-6): The Most Decorated Ship of World War II, A Pictorial History*. Missoula, Mont.: Pictorial Histories, 1982.

Fairburn, Thayer. *The "Orpheus" Disaster*. Waiuku: Western Publ., 1987.

Fairburn, W. A., et al. *Merchant Sail*. 6 vols. Fairburn Marine Educational Foundation, 1945–1955.

Fairfax, John, and Sylvia Cook. *Oars across the Pacific*. London: William Kimber, 1972.

Fanning, Edmund. *Voyages around the World, with Selected Sketches of Voyages to the South Sea, North and South Pacific, China, etc.* 1833. Reprint, Upper Saddle River, N.J.: 1970.

F.S. "Cook's *Resolution*." *Mariner's Mirror* 17 (1931): 84.

Farr, Grahame E. "The *Great Western*." *Mariner's Mirror* 24 (1938): 131–152.

Fay, Charles Edey. *"Mary Celeste" — The Odyssey of an Abandoned Ship*. Salem, Mass.: Peabody Museum, 1942.

Fenwick, Valerie, ed. *The Graveney Boat: A Tenth-Century Find*. Oxford, Eng.: British Archaeological Reports, 1978.

Ferguson-Innes, I. R. "*Killoran*." In *The Grain Races: The Baltic Background*. Edited by Basil Greenhill and John Hackman. London: Conway Maritime Press, 1984.

Finney, Ben R. *Voyage of Rediscovery: A Cultural Odyssey through Polynesia*. Berkeley: Univ. of California Press, 1994.

Fisher, Raymond H. *Bering's Voyages: Whither and Why*. London: C. Hurst, 1977.

Fisher, Robin. *Vancouver's Charting the Northwest Coast, 1791–1795*. Vancouver, British Columbia: Douglas & McIntyre, 1992.

FitzRoy, R., and P. P. King. *Narrative of the Surveying Voyages of Her Majesty's Ships "Adventure" and "Beagle" between the Years 1826 and 1838, Describing Their Examination of the Southern Shores of South America and the "Beagle"'s Circumnavigation of the Globe*. 3 vols. London: Henry Colburn, 1839.

Flackman, R. M. B. H. "Answers." *Mariner's Mirror* 79 (1993): 220–221.

Flanagan, Lawrence. *Shipwrecks of the Irish Coast*. London: Gill & Macmillan, 1988.

Flanders, Stephen, and Carl N. Flanders. *Dictionary of American Foreign Policy*. New York: Macmillan, 1993.

Flexner, James Thomas. *Steamboats Come True: American Inventors in Action*. New York: Viking, 1944.

Flinders, Matthew. *A Voyage to Terra Australis in 1801–3 in HMS "Investigator."* London: W. Bulmer & Co. and W. Nicol, 1814.

Flint, Willard. *Lightships of the United States Government*. Washington, D.C.: U.S. Coast Guard, 1989.

Foucart, Bruno. *"Normandie": Queen of the Seas*. New York: Vendome Press, 1985.

Fox, Frank. *Great Ships: The Battlefleet of King Charles II*. Greenwich, Eng.: Conway Maritime, 1980.

Fowler, William M., Jr. *Rebels under Sail: The American Navy during the Revolution*. New York: Charles Scribner's, 1976.

Fox-Smith, C. *The Return of the "Cutty Sark."* London, 1924.

Frame, Tom. *HMAS "Sydney": Loss and Controversy*. Sydney: Hodder & Stoughton, 1993.

Franzén, Anders. "*Kronan* — Remnants of a Mighty Warship." *National Geographic* (Apr. 1990): 438–466.

Fraser, Edward. "H.M.S. *Victory*." *Mariner's Mirror* 8 (1922): 194, 232, 258, 297, 337.

Fraser-Lee, Robert. "A Bluenose on the Great Lakes: The *J. T. Wing*." *Sea History* 47 (Summer 1988): 24–27.

Frazier, Donald A. "Cottonclads in a Storm of Iron." *Naval History* 8:3 (May/June 1994): 26–33.

Freeston, Ewart C. "His Majesty's Sloop *Resolution*, 1772." *Mariner's Mirror* 58 (1972): 337–338.

Friedman, Robert. "*Amsterdam II*." *Sea History* 50 (1989): 38–39.

Frischauer, Willi, and Robert Jackson. *The Navy's Here! The "Altmark" Affair*. London: Gollancz, 1951.

Frost, Honor. "How Carthage Lost the Sea: Off the Coast of Sicily, a Punic Warship Gives up Its Secrets." *Natural History* 12/87: 58–67.

———. "The Marsala Punic Ship, An Obituary." *Mariner's Mirror* 83:2 (May 1997): 207–211.

Frost, Honor, et al. *The Punic Ship: Final Excavation Report*. Rome: Lilybaeum, Notizie degli Scavi di Antichità, Serie ottava vol. 30, 1976 (1981).

Frost, O. W., ed. *Bering and Chirikov: The American Voyages and Their Impact*. Anchorage: Alaska Historical Society, 1992.

Fryer, John. *The Voyage of the "Bounty" Launch*. Introduction by Stephen Walters. Guildford, Eng.: Genesis, 1979.

Gallery, Daniel V. *Twenty Million Tons under the Sea*. Chicago: H. Regenery & Co., 1956.

Gardiner, Reginald, ed. *Conway's All the World's Fighting Ships 1946–1987*. London: Conway Maritime, 1985.

Gardiner, Robert, ed. *Cogs, Caravels and Galleons: The Sailing Ship 1000–1650*. Annapolis: Naval Institute Press, 1994.

———. *The Golden Age of Shipping: The Classic Merchant Ship 1900–1960*. Annapolis: Naval Institute Press, 1994.

———. *The Shipping Revolution: The Modern Merchant Ship*. Annapolis: Naval Institute Press, 1992.

———. *Navies in the Nuclear Age: Warships since 1956*. Annapolis: Naval Institute Press, 1993.

Garland, Vera. *Lady of the Lake: Ninety Years with the M.V. "Chauncey Maples" on Lake Malawi*. Blantyre, Malawi: Central Africana, 1991.

Garzke, William H., Jr., Robert O. Dulin, Jr., and Robert F. Sumrall. *Battleships: United States Battleships in World War II*. Annapolis: Naval Institute Press, 1976.

Garzke, William H., Jr., Robert O. Dulin, Jr., and Thomas G. Webb. *Battleships: Allied Battleships in World War II*. Annapolis: Naval Institute Press, 1980.

Garzke, William H., Jr., et al. *Battleships: Axis and Neutral Battleships in World War II*. Annapolis: Naval Institute Press, 1985.

Gawronski, Jerzy, Bas Kist, and Odilia Stokvis-van Boetzelaer. *Hollandia Compendium: A Contribution to the History, Archeology, Classification and Lexicography of a 150 ft. Dutch East Indiaman (1740–1750)*. Amsterdam: Rijksmuseum, 1992.

Gentile, Gary. *Shipwrecks of New Jersey*. Norwalk, Conn.: Sea Sports, 1988.

Gerard, Philip. *Brilliant Passage: A Schooning Memoir*. Mystic, Conn.: Mystic Seaport Publ., 1989.

German Naval History Series: The U-Boat War in the Atlantic 1939–1945. Ministry of Defence (Navy) [Fregattenkapitän Gunther Hessler]. London: Her Majesty's Stationery Office, 1989.

Gibbs, C. R. Vernon. *Passenger Liners of the Western Ocean: A Record of the North Atlantic Steam and Motor Passenger Vessels from 1838 to the Present Day*. London: Staples Press, 1952.

Gibbs, James A. *Shipwrecks of the Pacific Coast*. Portland, Ore.: Binfords & Mort, 1957.

Gifford, Edwin, and Joyce Gifford. "The Sailing Performance of Anglo-Saxon Ships as Derived from the Building and Trials of Half-Scale Models of the Sutton Hoo & Graveney Ship Finds." *Mariner's Mirror* 82 (1996): 131–153.

Gillmer, Thomas C. *Old Ironsides: The Rise, Decline, and Resurrection of the USS "Constitution."* Camden, Maine: International Marine, 1993.

Glasgow, Tom, Jr. "List of Ships in the Royal Navy from 1539 to 1588 — The Navy from Its Infancy to the Defeat of the Spanish Armada." *Mariner's Mirror* 56 (1970): 299–307.

———. "The Navy in the French Wars of Mary and Elizabeth I, Part III: The Expeditions of Le Havre 1562–1564." *Mariner's Mirror* 54 (1968): 281–296.

Goldberg, Joyce S. *The "Baltimore" Affair*. Lincoln: Univ. of Nebraska Press, 1986.

Golovnin, V. M. *Detained in Simon's Bay: The Story of the Detention of the Imperial Russian Sloop "Diana" April 1808–May 1809*. Cape Town: Friends of the South African Library, 1964.

———. *Memoirs of a Captivity in Japan during the Years 1811, 1812, and 1813; with Observations on the Country and the People*. 3 vols. London: Henry Colburn, 1824.

Gores, Joe. *Marine Salvage: The Unfortunate Business of No Cure, No Pay*. Garden City, N.Y.: Doubleday, 1971.

Gould-Adams, Richard. *The Return of the "Great Britain."* London: Weidenfeld & Nicholson, 1976.

Graham, Robin Lee. *Dove*. New York: Harper & Row, 1972.

Graham, T. "Queries: The *Lawhill* Figurehead." *Mariner's Mirror* 78 (1992): 490.

Gramont, Sanche de [Ted Morgan]. *The Strong Brown God: The Story of the Niger River*. Boston: Houghton Mifflin, 1976.

Gray, Edwyn A. *The U-Boat War 1914–1918*. 1972. Reprint, London: Leo Cooper, 1994.

Gray, Randal, ed. *Conway's All the World's Fighting Ships 1906–1921*. Annapolis: Naval Institute Press, 1985.

Green, J. N. *Australia's Oldest Wreck: The Loss of the "Trial," 1622*, BAR Supplementary Series 27. Oxford, Eng.: BAR, 1977.

———. *The Loss of the Retourship "Batavia," Western Australia 1629 — An Excavation Report and Artefact Catalogue*. Oxford, Eng.: BAR, 1989.

———. "The Shinan Excavation, Korea: An Interim Report on the Hull." *IJNA* 12 (1983): 293–302.

———. "The Song Dynasty Shipwreck at Quanzhou, Fujian Province, People's Republic of China." *IJNA* 12 (1983): 253–261.

———. "The Survey and Identification of the English East India Company ship *Trial* (1622)." *IJNA* 15 (1986): 195–204.

———. "The Survey of the VOC *fluit Risdam* (1727), Malaysia." *IJNA* 15 (1986): 93–104.

———. "The Loss of the Dutch East Indiaman *The Vergulde Draeck* 1656." *IJNA* 2 (1973): 267–289.

Green, J. N., and Zae Geun Kim. "The Shinan and Wando Sites, Korea: Further Information." *IJNA* 18 (1989): 33–41.

Greene, Letha C. *Long Live the "Delta Queen."* New York: Hastings House, 1973.

Greenhill, Basil. "The Schooner *Peggy:* An Eighteenth-Century Survival." *American Neptune* 29 (1969): 54–61.

Greenhill, Basil, and John Hackman. *The Grain Races: The Baltic Background.* London: Conway Maritime Press, 1986.

———. and John Hackman. *"Herzogin Cecilie": The Life and Times of a Four-Masted Bark.* London: 1991.

Griffiths, David W. "The Discovery of the *Ericsson.*" *Diver* (July/Aug. 1985): 42–45.

———. "Ericsson's Caloric Ship: An Historical Overview." Underwater Archaeological Society of British Columbia; 1989.

Griffiths, Denis. *Brunel's "Great Western."* Wellingborough, Eng.: Patrick Stephens, 1985.

Grissim, John. *The Lost Treasure of the "Concepción."* New York: William Morrow, 1980.

Gröner, Erich. *German Warships 1815–1945.* 2 vols. London: Conway Maritime, 1990.

Grove, Eric. *Sea Battles in Close-Up, World War 2,* vol. 2. Annapolis: Naval Institute Press, 1993.

Grover, David H. "The *Panay* Revisited." *American Neptune* 50 (1990): 260–269.

Guérout, Max. "The Engagement between the C.S.S. *Alabama* and the U.S.S. *Kearsarge* 19 May 1864: The Archaeological Discovery 1984–1988." *Mariner's Mirror* 74 (1988): 355–362.

Guravich, Don, Bern Keating, and John Olson. *North West Passage: Manhattan on the Tides of History.* New York: South Street Seaport Museum, 1970.

Gutteridge, Leonard F. *Icebound: The "Jeannette" Expedition's Quest for the North Pole.* Annapolis: Naval Institute Press, 1986.

Hackney, Noel C. L. *Mayflower — Classic Ships No 2. Their History and How to Model Them.* London: Patrick Stephens, 1970.

Hakluyt, Richard. *The Principal Navigations Voyages Traffiques & Discoveries of the English Nation.* 12 vols. 1598–1600. Reprint, Glasgow: James MacLehose & Sons, 1905.

Halpern, Paul G. *A Naval History of World War I.* Annapolis: Naval Institute Press, 1994.

———. *The Naval War in the Mediterranean, 1914–1918.* Annapolis: Naval Institute Press, 1987.

Hamilton-Adams, C. P. *The Racing Schooner "Westward."* London: Stanford Maritime, 1976.

Hampden, John. *Francis Drake, Privateer: Contemporary Narratives and Documents.* University, Ala.: Univ. Of Alabama Press, 1972.

Hancock, C. H. *"La Couronne," A French Warship of the Seventeenth Century: A Survey of Ancient and Modern Accounts of This Ship.* Newport News, Va.: The Mariners' Museum, 1973.

Hansen, Thorkild. *Northwest to Hudson Bay: The Life and Times of Jens Munk.* London: Collins, 1970.

Hardin, Craig. "Notes." *American Neptune* 11 (1951): 73–76.

Harlan, George H. *San Francisco Bay Ferryboats.* Berkeley: Howell-North Books, 1967.

Harris, Sheldon H. "Mutiny on *Junior.*" *American Neptune* 21 (1961): 110–129.

Hart, Henry. *Sea Road to the Indies: An Account of the Voyages and Exploits of the Portuguese Navigators, together with the Life and Times of Dom Vasco da Gama, Capitão-Mór of India and Count of Vidigueira.* New York: Macmillan, 1950.

Haskell, Loren E. "The Glamorous Six-Masters." *Down East* (Apr. 1965): 20–25.

Hastings, Max, and Simon Jenkins. *The Battle of the Falklands.* New York: W. W. Norton, 1983.

Hatcher, Michael, Max de Rham, with Antony Thorncroft. *Geldermalsen, The Nanking Cargo.* London: Hamish Hamilton, 1987.

Hauser. *Fair Winds & Foul: Ship Crew Sea Horizon.* London: Hurst & Blackett, 1934.

Heaton, Peter. *Yachting: A History.* New York: Charles Scribner's Sons, 1956.

Heckstall-Smith, Anthony. *Sacred Cowes, or the Cream of Yachting Society.* London: Allan Wingate, 1955.

Heine, William C. *Historic Ships of the World.* New York: G. P. Putnam's Sons, 1977.

Heinrichs, Waldo H., Jr. "The Battle of Plattsburg, 1814 — The Losers." *American Neptune* 21 (1961): 42–56.

Hemming, Robert J. *Gales of November: The Sinking of the "Edmund Fitzgerald."* Chicago: Contemporary Books, 1981.

Henderson, Graeme, and Kandy-Lee Henderson. *The "Sirius": Past and Present.* Sydney: Collins Australia, 1988.

Henderson, James A. *Marooned: The Wreck of the "Vergulde Draeck" and the Abandonment and Escape from the Southland of Abraham Leeman in 1658.* Perth: St. George Books, 1982.

Hendricks, Andrew A. "Construction of the 1988 *Half Moon.*" *de Haelve Maen* 66 (1993): 42–53.

Hennessey, Mark W. *The Sewall Ships of Steel.* Augusta, Maine: Kennebec Journal Press, 1937.

Hepper, David. *British Warship Losses in the Age of Sail, 1650–1859.* Rotherfield, Eng.: Jean Boudriot, 1994.

Herd, R. J. *HMVS "Cerberus": Battleship to Breakwater.* Sandringham, Eng.. City of Sandringham, 1986.

Herreshoff, Halsey C. "A History of America's Cup Yacht Racing." *Marine Technology* 29:2 (1992): 51–70.

Herreshoff, L. Francis. *Capt. Nat Herreshoff: The Wizard of Bristol.* Dobbs Ferry, N.Y.: Sheridan House, 1974.

———. *An Introduction to Yachting.* White Plains, N.Y.: Sheridan House, 1980.

Hetherington, Roy. *The Wreck of H.M.S. "Orpheus."* Auckland: Cassell New Zealand, 1975.

Heyerdahl, Thor. *"Kon-Tiki": Across the Pacific by Raft.* Chicago: Rand McNally, 1950.

———. *The "Ra" Expeditions.* Garden City, N.Y.: Doubleday, 1971.

———. *The "Tigris" Expedition: In Search of Our Beginnings.* New York: Doubleday, 1981.

Heywood, Thomas. *His Majesty's Royal Ship: A Critical Edition of Thomas Heywood's "A True Description of His Majesties Royall Ship."* Edited by Alan R. Young. New York: AMS Press, 1990.

Hezlet, Sir Arthur Richard. *Aircraft and Seapower.* New York, 1970.

Hilder, Brett. *The Voyage of Torres.* St. Lucia: The Univ. of Queensland Press, 1980.

Hill, J. R. *The Oxford Illustrated History of the Royal Navy.* New York: Oxford Univ. Press, 1995.

Hill, Jim Dan. "Captain Joseph Fry of SS *Virginius.*" *American Neptune* 36 (1976): 88–100.

Hill, Ralph Nading. *Sidewheeler Saga: A Chronicle of Steamboating.* New York: Rinehart, 1953.

Hilton, George W. *"Eastland": Legacy of the "Titanic."* Stanford: Stanford Univ. Press, 1995.

———. *The Night Boat.* Berkeley: Howell-North Books, 1968.

Hocking, Charles. *Dictionary of Disasters at Sea during the Age of Steam, Including Sailing Ships and Ships of War Lost in Action 1824–1962.* London: Lloyd's Register of Shipping, 1969.

Höckmann, Olaf. "Late Roman Rhine Vessels from Mainz, Germany." *IJNA* 22 (1993): 125–135.

———. "Late Roman River Craft from Mainz, Germany." In *Local Boats, Fourth International Symposium on Boat and Ship Archaeology, Porto 1985* (BAR-S), edited by O. L. Filgueiras, 438: 23–34.

Hodgson, Godfrey. *Lloyd's of London.* New York: Viking, 1984.

Hoehling, A. A. *The "Franklin" Comes Home.* New York: Hawthorn, 1974.

Hoffer, William. *Saved! The Story of the "Andrea Doria" — The Greatest Sea Rescue in History.* London: Macmillan, 1980.

Hofman, Erik. *The Steam Yachts: An Era of Elegance.* Tuckahoe, N.Y.: John de Graff, 1970.

Hollett, D. *Fast Passage to Australia: The History of the Black Ball, Eagle, and White Star Lines of Australian Packets.* London: Fairplay, 1986.

Holly, David C. *"Exodus 1947."* Rev. ed. Annapolis: Naval Institute Press, 1995.

Hood, Edwin P. *The Life and Death of HMS "Hood."* London: Arthur Barker, 1971.

Hooke, Norman. "Marine Casualties." *Lloyd's Nautical Year Book 1995.* London: Lloyd's of London Press, 1995.

———. *Modern Shipping Disasters 1963–1987.* London: Lloyd's of London Press, 1989.

Hoover, Karl D. "Commander Otto Hersing and the Dardanelles Cruise of S.M. *U-21.*" *American Neptune* 36 (1976): 33–44.

Hopkins, Fred. *"Chasseur:* The Pride of Baltimore." *Mariner's Mirror* 64 (1978): 349–360.

———. "The Six *Baltimores.*" *American Neptune* 39 (1979): 29–44.

Horan, James D., Jr., ed. *C.S.S. "Shenandoah": The Memoirs of Lieutenant Commander James I. Waddell.* New York: Crown, 1960.

Hornby, W. M. Phipps. "Grace Horseley Darling, 1815–1842: Northumbrian Heroine." *Mariner's Mirror* 54 (1968): 55–69.

Horton, Brian. HMS *"Trincomalee."*

Hough, Richard. *The "Potemkin" Mutiny.* 1960. Reprint, Annapolis: Naval Institute Press, 1996.

Houot, George S., and Pierre Henri Willm. *2000 Fathoms Down.* New York: E. P. Dutton, 1955.

Howarth, David, and Stephen Howarth. *The Story of P&O: The Peninsular and Oriental Steam Navigation Company.* London: Weidenfeld & Nicholson, 1986.

Howay, Frederic W., ed. *Voyages of the "Columbia" to the Northwest Coast 1787–1790 and 1790–1793.* Portland: Oregon Historical Society Press, 1990.

Howe, Octavius T., and Frederick G. Matthews. *American Clipper Ships.* 2 vols. 1926–1927. Reprint, New York: Dover, 1986.

Howland, Capt. Vernon W. "The Loss of HMS *Glorious:* An Analysis of the Action." *Warship International* (1994): 47–62.

Hoyt, Edwin P. *Count von Luckner: Knight of the Sea.* New York: McKay, 1969.

———. *Ghost of the Atlantic, The "Kronprinz Wilhelm" 1914–19.* London: Arthur Barker, Ltd., 1974.

———. *The Invasion before Normandy: The Secret Battle of Slapton Sands.* New York: Stein & Day, 1985.

———. *The Last Cruise of the "Emden."* New York: Macmillan, 1960.

———. *The Life and Death of HMS "Hood."* New York: Stein & Day, 1980.

———. *Men of the "Gambier Bay."* Middlebury, Vt.: P.S. Eriksson, 1979.

———. *The Phantom Raider.* New York: Crowell, 1969.

Hsû, Kenneth. *Challenger at Sea: A Ship That Revolutionized Earth Science.* Princeton: Princeton Univ. Press, 1992.

Huchthausen, Peter A. "Espionage or Negligence? A Sinking Mystery." *Naval History* 10:1 (Feb. 1996): 19–24.

Humble, Richard. *Before the "Dreadnought": The Royal Navy from Nelson to Fisher.* London: MacDonald & Jane's, 1976.

Humiston, Fred. *Windjammers and Walking Beams.* Portland, Maine: Blue Water Books, 1968.

Huntford, Roland. *Shackleton.* New York: Athenaeum, 1985.

Hurst, Alex. A. *Square-Riggers: The Final Epoch 1921–1958.* Sussex, Eng.: Teredo Books, 1972.

Hutchinson, Alan. *"Kaiulani —* The Last Yankee Square Rigger." *Explorers Journal* 44 (Mar. 1966): 42–50.

Hutchinson, Roger. *"Polly": The True Story behind Whisky Galore.* Edinburgh: Mainstream, 1990.

Hutton, W. M. *Cape Horn Passage.* London: Blackie & Son, 1934.

Huycke, Harold D. "Colonial Trader to Museum Ship: The Bark *Star of India.*" *American Neptune* 10 (1950): 108–122.

———. "The Ship *Pacific Queen.*" *American Neptune* 4 (1944): 199–206.

Inkster, Tom H. "McDougall's Whalebacks." *American Neptune* 25 (1965): 168–175.

Ivashintsov, N. A. *Russian Round-the-World Voyages, 1803–1849. Materials for the Study of Alaska History, No. 14.* Kingston, Ontario: The Limestone Press, 1980.

Jackson, Kenneth T. "The Forgotten Saga of New York's Prison Ships." *Seaport* (Summer 1990): 25–28.

Jacobsen, Betty. *A Girl before the Mast.* New York: Charles Scribner's Sons, 1934.

Jaffee, Walter W. *The Last Liberty: The Biography of the SS "Jeremiah O'Brien."* Palo Alto, Calif.: Glencannon Press, 1993.

James, Naomi. *Alone around the World: The First Woman to Sail Single-Handedly around the World.* New York: Coward, McCann & Geoghegan, 1979.

James, Wendy, Gerd Baumann, and Douglas Johnson. *Juan Maria Schiver's Travels in North East Africa, 1880–1883.* London: Hakluyt Society, 1996.

Jameson, Edwin Milton, and Sanford Sternlicht. *Black Devil of the Bayous: The Life and Times of the United States Steam Sloop "Hartford," 1858–1957.* Upper Saddle River, N.J.: Gregg Press, 1970.

Jameson, William. *"Ark Royal" 1939–1941.* London: Hart Davis, 1957.

Jamieson, Alan G. "American Privateers in the Leeward Islands." *American Neptune* 43 (1983): 20–30.

Jane's Fighting Ships. Coulsdon, Surrey: Jane's Informational Group. Annual, 1897–.

Jeal, Tim. *Livingstone.* New York: G. P. Putnam's Sons, 1973.

Jenkins, C. A. *HMS "Furious"/Aircraft Carrier 1917–1948.* Windsor: Profile, 1972.

Jenkins, Nancy. *The Boat beneath the Pyramid: King Cheops' Royal Ship.* New York: Holt, Rinehart and Winston, 1980.

Jentschura, Hansgeorg, Dieter Jung, and Peter Mickel. *Warships of the Imperial Japanese Navy.* Annapolis: Naval Institute Press, 1977.

Johnson, Donald S. *Charting the Sea of Darkness.* Camden, Maine: International Marine, 1993.

Johnson, Irving. *The "Peking" Battles Cape Horn.* New York: Sea History Press, 1977.

Johnson, Irving, and Electa Johnson. *Yankee's Wanderworld: Circling the Globe in the Brigantine "Yankee."* Hale, 1956.

Johnson, Irving, Electa Johnson, and Lydia Edes. *Yankee's People and Places.* New York: W. W. Norton, 1955.

Johnson, Robert Erwin. *Bering Sea Escort: Life aboard a Coast Guard Cutter in World War II.* Annapolis: Naval Institute Press, 1991.

———. *Thence round Cape Horn: The Story of United States Naval Forces on Pacific Station, 1818–1923.* Annapolis: U.S. Naval Institute, 1963.

Johnston, Hugh. *The Voyage of the "Komagata Maru": The Sikh Challenge to Canada's Colour Bar.* Bombay: Oxford Univ. Press, 1979.

Johnston, Paul Forsythe. "Downbound: The History of the Early Great Lakes Propeller *Indiana.*" *American Neptune* 55:4 (1995): 323–355.

Johnston, Paul Forsythe, John O. Sands, and J. Richard Steffy. "The Cornwallis Cave Shipwreck, Yorktown, Virginia." *IJNA* 7 (1978): 205–225.

Jones, G. P. *Two Survived.* London: Hamish Hamilton, 1940.

Jones, Geoffrey P. *Battleship "Barham."* London: William Kimber, 1979.

Jones, Gwyn. *A History of the Vikings.* New York: Oxford Univ. Press, 1968.

Jones, Howard. *Mutiny on the "Amistad": The Saga of a Slave Revolt and Its Impact on American Abolition, Law, and Diplomacy.* New York: Oxford Univ. Press, 1987.

Jones, J. Michael. *Historic Warships: A Directory of 140 Museums and Memorials Worldwide, with Histories.* Jefferson, N.C.: McFarland, 1993.

Jones, William H. S. *The Cape Horn Breed.* New York: Criterion Books, 1956.

Jorg, Christiaan J. A. *The "Geldermalsen": History and Porcelain.* Groningen, Netherlands: Kemper, 1986.

Jourdain, Silvester. *A Discovery of the Barmudas.* 1610. Reprint, New York: Scholars' Facsimiles and Reprints, 1940.

Kaharl, Victoria A. *Water Baby: The Story of "Alvin."* New York: Oxford Univ. Press, 1990.

Kane, Elisha Kent. *The U.S. Grinnell Expedition in Search of Sir John Franklin: A Personal Narrative.* New York: Harper & Row, 1854.

Karlsson, Elis. *Mother Sea.* London: Oxford Univ. Press, 1964.

———. *Pully-Haul: The Story of a Voyage.* New York: Oxford Univ. Press, 1966.

Katzev, M. L. "*Kyrenia II:* Building a Replica of an Ancient Greek Merchantman." In *First International Symposium on Ship Construction in Antiquity.* Edited by H. Tzalas. 1985: 163–175.

———. "Last Harbor for the Oldest Known Greek Ship." *National Geographic* (Nov. 1974): 618–625.

———. "Resurrecting the Oldest Known Greek Ship." *National Geographic* (June 1970): 841–857.

———. "Voyage of *Kyrenia II.*" *INA Newsletter* 16 (1989): 4–10.

Katzev, M. L., and S. W. Katzev. "*Kyrenia II:* Research on an Ancient Shipwreck Comes Full Circle in a Full-Scale Replica." *INA Newsletter* 13 (1986): 1–11.

Keeble, John. *Out of the Channel: The "Exxon Valdez" Oil Spill in Prince William Sound.* New York: HarperCollins, 1991.

Keith, D. H. et al. "The Molasses Reef Wreck, Turks and Caicos Islands, B.W.I.: A Preliminary Report." *IJNA* 13 (1984): 45–63.

Keith, Donald H., and Christian J. Buys. "New Light on Medieval Chinese Seagoing Ship Construction." *IJNA* 10 (1981): 119–132.

Kelly, Celsus, ed. *La Austrialia del Espiritu Santo: The Journal of Fray Martin de Munilla, OFM, and Other Documents Relating to the Voyage of Pedro Fernández de Quirós to the South Sea . . . and the Franciscan Missionary Plan.* 2 vols. Cambridge, Eng.: Hakluyt Society, 1966.

Kelly, Mary Pat. *Proudly We Served.* Annapolis: Naval Institute Press, 1995.

Kemp, Peter. *The Escape of the "Scharnhorst" and the "Gneisenau."* Annapolis: Naval Institute Press, 1975.

———, ed. *The Oxford Companion to Ships and the Sea.* New York: Oxford Univ. Press, 1976.

Kendrick, John, ed. *The Voyage of "Sutil" and Mexicana 1792: The Last Spanish Exploration of the Northwest Coast of America.* Spokane, Wash.: Arthur H. Clark, 1991.

Kennedy, Gavin. "Bligh and the *Defiance* Mutiny." *Mariner's Mirror* 65 (1979): 39–51.

Kennedy, Ludovic. *Menace: The Life and Death of the "Tirpitz."* London: Sidgwick & Jackson, 1979.

———. *Pursuit: The Chase and Sinking of the "Bismarck."* New York: Viking, 1974.

Kim, H. Edward, and Donald H. Keith. "A 14th-Century Cargo Makes Port at Last." *National Geographic* (Aug. 1979): 230–243.

King, Derek, and Peter Bird. *Small Boat against the Sea: The Story of the First Trans-World Rowing Concept.* London: Paul Elek, 1976.

King, Robert J. *The Secret History of the Convict Colony: Alexandro Malaspina's Report on the British Settlement of New South Wales.* Sydney: Allen & Unwin, 1990.

Kinney, Francis S. "*You Are First*": The Story of Olin and Rod Stephens of Sparkman and Stephens.* New York: Dodd, Mead, 1978.

Kish, George. *North-east Passage: Adolf Erik Nordenskiöld, His Life and Times.* Amsterdam: Nico Israel, 1973.

Kitz, Janet. *Shattered City.* Halifax, Nova Scotia,: Nimbus, 1989.

Kjølsen, F. H. "The Old Danish Frigate." *Mariner's Mirror* 51 (1965): 27–33.

Klare, Normand E. *The Final Voyage of the Central America, 1857: The Saga of a Gold Rush Steamship in a Hurricane, the Tragedy of Her Loss, and the Treasure Which Is Now Recovered.* Spokane, Wash.: Arthur H. Clark, 1992.

Klebingat, Fred. "*Falls of Clyde.*" *Oceans* 5:5 (1972): 41–48.

Kloepel, James E. *Danger beneath the Waves: A History of the Confederate Submarine "H. L. Hunley."* College Park, Ga.: 1987.

Kludas, Arnold. *Great Passenger Ships of the World.* 6 vols. Cambridge, Eng.: Patrick Stephens, 1975–1986.

Knight, C. "H.M. Armed Vessel *Bounty.*" *Mariner's Mirror* 22 (1936): 183–199.

———. "H.M. Bark *Endeavour.*" *Mariner's Mirror* 19 (1933): 292–302.

Knox-Johnston, Robin. *Beyond Jules Verne: Circling the World in a Record-Breaking Seventy-Four Days.* London: Hodder & Stoughton, 1995.

———. *A World of My Own: The Single-Handed, Nonstop Circumnavigation of the World in "Suhaili."* New York: Morrow, 1970.

Koginos, Manny T. *The "Panay" Incident: Prelude to War.* Lafayette, Ind.: Purdue Univ. Studies, 1967.

König, Paul. *The Voyage of the "Deutschland."* New York: Hearst International Library, 1916.

Koskie, Jack L. *Ships That Shaped Australia*. London: Angus & Robertson, 1987.

Kotzebue, Otto von. *A New Voyage round the World in the Years 1823–1826*. 1830. Reprint, New York: Da Capo, 1967.

———. *A Voyage of Discovery into the South Sea and Beering's Strait, for the Purpose of Exploring a North-East Passage, Undertaken in the Years 1815–1818*. 1821. Reprint, New York: Da Capo, 1967.

Kraft, Barbara S. *The Peace Ship: Henry Ford's Pacifist Adventure in the First World War*. New York: Macmillan, 1978.

Krancke, Theodor, and H. J. Brennecke. *Pocket Battleship: The Story of the "Admiral Scheer."* New York: W. W. Norton, 1958.

Krusenstern, Adam Johann von. *Voyage Round the World, in the Years 1803, 1804, 1805 & 1806 . . . on board the ships "Nadseha" and "Neva."* London: John Murray, 1813.

Kvarning, Lars Ake, and Bengt Ohrelius. *Swedish Warship "Wasa."* London: Macmillan, 1973.

Labaree, Benjamin Woods. *The Boston Tea Party*. New York: Oxford Univ. Press, 1964.

Lahn, Werner. *Die Kogge von Bremen — the Hanse Cog of Bremen*. Hamburg: Deutsches Schiffahrtsmuseum, 1992.

Lamb, W. Kaye. *Empress to the Orient*. Vancouver: Vancouver Maritime Press, 1991.

Lambert, Andrew. *Battleships in Transition: The Creation of the Steam Battlefleet 1815–1860*. London: Conway Maritime Press, 1984.

———. *The Last Sailing Battlefleet: Maintaining Sailing Mastery 1815–1850*. London: Conway Maritime Press, 1991.

———, ed. *Steam, Steel & Shellfire: The Steam Warship 1815–1905*. London: Conway Maritime Press, 1992.

———. *"Warrior": Restoring the World's First Ironclad*. London: Conway Maritime Press, 1987.

Landström, Björn. *Ships of the Pharaohs: 4000 Years of Egyptian Shipbuilding*. Garden City, N.Y.: Doubleday, 1970.

La Pérouse, Jean-François de Galaup de. *The Journal of Jean-François de Galaup de la Pérouse 1785–1788*. Edited by John Dunmore. 2 vols. London: Hakluyt Society, 1994–1995.

Lapp, Ralph E. *The Voyage of the Lucky Dragon*. New York: Harper & Brothers, 1957.

LaRoe, Lisa Moore. "La Salle's Last Voyage." *National Geographic* (May 1997): 72–83.

Larrabee, Harold A. *Decision at the Chesapeake*. New York: C. N. Potter, 1964.

Larsen, Henry A. *The Big Ship*. Toronto: McClelland & Stewart, 1967.

Laughton, L. G. "Report: The *Henry Grace à Dieu*." *Mariner's Mirror* 17 (1931): 174–180.

Lavery, Brian. *The Colonial Merchantman "Susan Constant" 1605*. Annapolis: Naval Institute Press, 1988.

LaVo, Carl. *Back from the Deep: The Strange Story of the Sisters Subs "Squalus" and "Sculpin."* Annapolis: Naval Institute Press, 1994.

Leary, William M., Jr. "*Alabama* vs. *Kearsarge*: A Diplomatic View." *American Neptune* 29 (1969): 167–173.

Leather, John. *The Big Class Racing Yachts*. London: Stanford Maritime, 1982.

———. *Colin Archer and the Seaworthy Double-Ender*. London: Stanford Maritime, 1982.

Leavitt, John F. *The "Charles W. Morgan."* Mystic, Conn.: Marine Historical Association, 1973.

———. *Wake of the Coasters*. Middletown, Conn.: Marine Historical Association, 1970.

Lech, Raymond B. *All the Drowned Sailors*. New York: Stein & Day, 1982.

Le Conte, Pierre. *Repertoire des navires de guerre français*. Cherbourg: Le Conte, 1932.

Leek, B. M. "Marjorie Hutton's Barque *Hussar* of 1931." *Sea Breezes* 68 (June 1994): 480–485.

Legler, Gene. "Percy Ruiz Visits Colorful Old Sternwheeler." *Esso Fleet News* 13:1 (1971): 1–4.

Lehmann. "Turkish Imperial State Barges." *Mariner's Mirror* 76 (1990): 254.

Lengerer, Hans. "*Akagi & Kaga*." Parts 1 & 2. *Warship* 6:22–23 (1982).

Lesure, Marie. "Unlikely Legend." *Cruising World* (Sept. 1994):21–28.

Levitt, Michael, and Barbara Lloyd. *Upset: Australia Wins the America's Cup*. New York: Workman, 1983.

Lewin, Ronald. *Ultra Goes to War: The Secret Story*. London: Hutchinson, 1978.

Lewis, Cam, and Michael Levitt. *Around the World in Seventy-Nine Days*. New York: Dell, 1995.

Lewis, Tom. "The Mysteries of IJN Submarine *I-124*." Forthcoming.

Li Guo-Qing. "Archaeological Evidence for the Use of 'Chu-Nam' on the 13th-Century Quanzhou Ship, Fujian Province, China." *IJNA* 18 (1989): 277–283.

Lille, Sten, and Lars Grönstrand. *The Finnish Deep-Water Sailers*. Pori, Finland: Eita Oy, 1981.

Linklater, Eric. *The Voyage of the "Challenger."* London: John Murray, 1972.

Lipke, Paul. "Retrospective on the Royal Ship of Cheops." In *Sewn Plank Boats*, S. McGrail and E. Kently, eds. Oxford: BAR, 1985.

———. *The Royal Ship of Cheops: A Retrospective Account of the Discovery, Restoration and Reconstruction, Based on Interviews with Hag Ahmed Youssef Moustafa*. Oxford, Eng.: BAR, 1984.

Liston, Robert A. *The "Pueblo" Surrender: A Covert Action by the National Security Agency*. New York: M. Evans & Co., 1988.

Litke, Frederic. *A Voyage round the World 1826–1829, Vol. 1, to Russian America and Siberia*. Kingston, Ont.: Limestone, 1987.

Lloyd's of London. *Lloyd's Register of American Yachts*. London, annual.

Lloyd's of London. *Lloyd's Register of Shipping*. London, annual.

Lloyd's of London. *Lloyd's Register of Yachts*. London, annual.

London, Jack. *Cruise of the "Snark."* 1911. Reprint, New York: Sheridan House, 1993.

Longridge, C. N. *The Anatomy of Nelson's Ships*. Annapolis: Naval Institute Press, 1981.

———. *The "Cutty Sark": The Ship and a Model*. London: Percival Marshall, 1933.

Loomis, Chauncey C. *Weird and Tragic Shores: The Story of Charles Francis Hall, Explorer*. Lincoln: Univ. of Nebraska, 1991.

Lott, Arnold S., and Robert F. Sumrall. *USS "Alabama" (BB60)*. Pompton Lakes, N.J.: Leeward Publ., 1974.

Loxton, Bruce, with Chris Coulthard-Clark. *The Shame of "Savo": Anatomy of a Naval Disaster*. Annapolis: Naval Institute Press, 1994.

Lubbock, Basil. *The Arctic Whalers*. Glasgow: Brown, Son & Ferguson, 1937.

———. *The China Clippers*. Glasgow: Brown, Son & Ferguson, 1914.

———. *The Colonial Clippers*. Glasgow: Brown, Son & Ferguson, 1921.

———. *The Down Easters: The Story of the Cape Horners*. Glasgow: Brown, Son & Ferguson, 1929.

———. *The Last of the Windjammers*. 2 vols. Glasgow: Brown, Son & Ferguson, 1927, 1929.

———. *Log of the "Cutty Sark."* Glasgow: Brown, Son & Ferguson, 1924.

———. *The Western Ocean Packets*. 1925. Reprint, New York: Dover, 1988.

Lucian of Samosata. *The Ship or the Wishes*. Cambridge: Harvard Univ. Press, 1959.

Lund, Alfred. *The Raider and the Tramp*. N.p., n.d.

Lundeberg, Philip K. *The Continental Gunboat "Philadelphia" and the Northern Campaign of 1776*. Washington, D.C., 1966.

Lundeberg, Philip K., and Dana M. Wegner. "Not for Conquest but Discovery: Rediscovering the Ships of the Wilkes Expedition." *American Neptune* 49 (1989): 151–167.

Lyford, Thaddeus M. C. "'Long Life and Success:' A History of *Dirigo,* the First Steel Sailing Vessel Built in America." Master's thesis, Univ. of Maine, 1990.

Lyman, John. "Five-Masted Square-Riggers." *American Neptune* 6 (1946): 135–136.

———. "The Largest Wooden Ship." *Mariner's Mirror* 29 (1943).

———. "The *Star of Scotland,* ex-*Kenilworth.*" *American Neptune* 1 (1941): 333–344.

Lyman, R. D. "The Day the Admirals Wept: *Ostfriesland* and the Anatomy of a Myth." In *Warship 1995*. London: Conway Maritime Press, 1995.

Lynch, Thomas G. "Saving the Last Flower-Class Corvette, HMCS *Sackville.*" *Warship* 32 (1984): 226–235.

Lyon, David. *The Sailing Navy List: All the Ships of the Royal Navy, Built, Purchased and Captured 1688–1860*. London: Conway Maritime Press, 1993.

Lyon, Eugene. "*Santa Margarita:* Treasure from the Ghost Galleon." *National Geographic* (Feb. 1982): 229–243.

———. *The Search for the "Atocha."* New York: Harper & Row, 1979.

McAdam, Roger Williams. *The Old Fall River Line*. New York: Stephen Daye Press, 1955.

———. "*Priscilla*" *of Fall River*. New York: Stephen Daye Press, 1947.

McBride, Peter W. J., "The *Mary:* Charles II's Yacht. 2. Her History, Importance and Ordnance." *IJNA* 2 (1973): 59–73.

McCall, Edith S. *Conquering the Rivers: Henry Miller Shreve and the Navigation of America's Inland Waterways*. Baton Rouge: Louisiana State Univ. Press, 1984.

M'Clintock, Francis Leopold. *The Voyage of the "Fox" in the Arctic Seas: A Narrative of the Discovery of the Fate of Sir John Franklin and his Companions*. 1860. Reprint, Rutland, Vt.: Charles E. Tuttle, 1973.

McClure, Robert John Le Mesurier. *The Discovery of the North-West Passage by H.M.S. "Investigator," Capt. R. M'Clure 1850, 1851, 1852, 1853, 1854*. Edited by Sherard Osborn. 1857. Reprint, Edmonton, Alberta: Hurtig, 1969.

McCready, Lauren S. "The *Emery Rice* Engine." *Sea History* 46 (Winter 1987–1988): 20–21.

McCusker, John J. "*Alfred,*" *The First Continental Flagship, 1775–1778*. Washington, D.C.: Smithsonian Institution Press, 1973.

———. "The American Invasion of Nassau in the Bahamas." *American Neptune* 25 (1965): 189–217.

M'Dougall, George F. *The Eventful Voyage of H. M. "Discovery" Ship "Resolute" to the Arctic Regions in Search of Sir John Franklin and the Missing Crews of H. M. "Discovery" Ships "Erebus" and "Terror," 1852, 1853, 1854*. London: Longman, Brown, Green, Longman & Roberts, 1857.

McFarland, Philip J. *Sea Dangers: The Affair of the "Somers."* New York: Schocken Books, 1985.

McGowan, A. P. "Captain Cook's Ships." *Mariner's Mirror* 65 (1979): 109–118.

McGrail, Sean. "The Brigg Raft: A Flat-Bottomed Boat." *IJNA* 23 (1994): 283–288.

McGrail, Sean, and Eric Kentley. *Sewn Plank Boats: Archaeological and Ethnographic Papers Based on Those Presented to a Conference at Greenwich in November, 1984*. Oxford: BAR, 1985.

MacGregor, David R. *British and American Clippers: A Comparison of Their Design, Construction and Performance in the 1850s*. London: Conway Maritime Press, 1993.

———. *Fast Sailing Ships: Their Design and Construction 1775–1875*. Annapolis: Naval Institute Press, 1988.

———. *The Tea Clippers: Their History and Development, 1833–1875*. Annapolis: Naval Institute Press, 1983.

MacInnis, Joe. *The Land That Devours Ships*. Montreal: CBC Enterprises, 1985.

Macintyre, Donald. *Jutland*. London: Evans, 1957.

McKay, John. *The 100-Gun Ship "Victory."* London: Conway Maritime, 1997.

McKay, John, and Ron Coleman. *The 24-Gun Frigate "Pandora," 1779*. London: Conway Maritime, 1992.

McKee, Alexander. *Death Raft: The Human Drama of the "Medusa" Shipwreck*. New York: Warner, 1975.

———. *The Golden Wreck: The Tragedy of the Golden Charter*. London: Souvenir, 1961.

———. *King Henry VIII's "Mary Rose" Its Fate and Future*. London: Souvenir, 1973.

MacKenzie, Compton. *Whisky Galore*. In *The Highland Omnibus: Monarch of the Glen, Whisky Galore, and Rival Monster*. New York: Penguin Books, 1983.

Mackenzie, John. "The Naval Campaigns on Lakes Victoria and Nyasa, 1914–1918." *Mariner's Mirror* 71 (1985): 169–182.

Mackenzie, Robert Holden. *The Trafalgar Roll: The Ships and the Officers*. Annapolis: Naval Institute Press, 1989.

McLaughlin, Redmond. *The Escape of the "Goeben": Prelude to Gallipoli*. London: Seeley Service, 1974.

McLellan, R. S. *Anchor Line 1856–1956*. Glasgow: Anchor Line, 1956.

MacMillan, Donald B. *Etah and Beyond, or Life within Twelve Degrees of the Pole*. Boston: Houghton Mifflin, 1929.

MacMillan, Miriam. *Green Seas, White Ice*. New York: Dodd, Mead, 1948.

MacMullen, Jerry. "*Star of India*": *The Log of an Iron Ship*. Berkeley: Howell-North, 1961.

———. "The Transpacific Voyages of *Pamir.*" *American Neptune* 6 (1946): 112–115.

Mahan, Alfred Thayer. *The Influence of Sea Power upon History 1600–1783*. 5th ed., 1894. Reprint, New York: Dover, 1987.

———. *Seapower in Its Relations with the War of 1812*. Boston: Little, Brown, 1905.

Mallard, Victor F. L. "Ships of India, 1834–1934." *Mariner's Mirror* 30 (1944): 144–153.

Maloney, Linda McKee. "A Naval Experiment." *American Neptune* 34 (1974): 188–196.

Mannering. "The Old Ships and Their Men Are Gone . . ." *Sea Breezes* 42:272 (Aug. 1968): 477–480.

Manry, Robert. *"Tinkerbelle."* New York: Harper & Row, 1965.

March, Edgar J. *British Destroyers.* London: Seeley Service, 1966.

Marden, Luis. "Saga of a Ship, the *Yankee.*" *National Geographic* (Feb. 1966): 263–269.

———. "Wreck of H.M.S. *Pandora.*" *National Geographic* (Oct. 1985): 423–451.

Marder, Arthur J. *From the "Dreadnought" to Scapa Flow.* 5 vols. New York: Oxford Univ. Press, 1961–1970.

Marley, David F. "The Last Manila Galleon." In *Warship 1991.* London: Conway Maritime Press, 1991.

Marolda, Edward J., and Oscar P. Fitzgerald, *The United States Navy and the Vietnam Conflict: From Military Assistance to Combat 1959–1965.* Washington, D.C.: Naval Historical Center, 1986.

Marsden, P. R. V. *A Ship of the Roman Period, from Blackfriars, in the City of London.* London: Guildhall Museum, 1966.

Marsden, Peter. "The *Meresteyn,* Wrecked in 1702, near Cape Town, South Africa." *IJNA* 5 (1976): 201–219.

———. *The Wreck of the "Amsterdam."* New York: Stein & Day, 1975.

Marsh, A. J. *The Story of a Frigate: H.M.S. "Trincomalee" to T.S. "Foudroyant."* Portsmouth, Eng.: Portsmouth Museum Society, 1973.

Martelle, Mickey. "*Novgorod* and *Rear-Admiral Popov,* the Black Sea's Round Battleships." *Nautical Research Journal* 39 (June 1994): 83–97.

Martin, Colin. *Full Fathom Five: Wrecks of the Spanish-Armada.* London: Chatto & Windus, 1975.

———. "*La Trinidad Valencera:* An Armada Invasion Transport Lost off Donegal. Interim site report 1971–76." *IJNA* 8 (1979): 13–38.

Martin, Paula. *Spanish Armada Prisoners: The Story of the "Nuestra Señora del Rosario" and Her Crew, and of Other Prisoners in England, 1587–1597.* Exeter Maritime Studies No. 1. Exeter: Univ. of Exeter, 1988.

Martin, Simon. *The Other "Titanic."* Newton Abbot: David & Charles, 1980.

Martin, Tyrone G. *A Most Fortunate Ship.* Chester, Conn.: Globe Pequot Press, 1980.

Masefield, John. *The "Conway": From Her Foundation to the Present Day.* New York: Macmillan, 1933.

Massie, Robert K. *Dreadnought: Britain, Germany and the Coming of the Great War.* New York: Random House, 1991.

Matheson, Marny. *Clippers for the Record: The Story of Ship "Thermopylae," S.S. "Aberdeen" and Captain Charles Matheson.* Melbourne: Spectrum, 1984.

Mathewson, R. Duncan, III. *Treasure of the "Atocha."* New York: E. P. Dutton, 1986.

Matthews, Frederick C. *American Merchant Ships, 1850–1900,* Series 1 & 2; 1930, 1931. Reprint, New York: Dover, 1987.

Mattingly, Garrett. *The Armada.* Boston: Houghton Mifflin, 1959.

Mawdsley, Evan. *The Russian Revolution and the Baltic Fleet: War and Politics, February 1917–April 1918.* London: Macmillan, 1978.

May, W. E. "The *Gaspee* Affair." *Mariner's Mirror* 63 (1977): 129–135.

Mead, Hilary. "The Loss of the *Victoria.*" *Mariner's Mirror* 47 (1961): 17–24.

Meehan, Robert H. "Vale *Tusitala.*" *Sea Breezes* 23 (1938): 224–225.

Mello, Ulysses Pernambuco de. "The Shipwreck of the Galleon *Sacramento* — 1668 off Brazil." *IJNA* 8 (1979): 211–223.

Merkel, Andrew, and Wallace R. MacAskill. *Schooner "Bluenose."* Toronto: The Ryerson Press, 1948.

Merriam, Charles. *Last of the Five Masters.* New York: Claude Kendall, 1936.

Merwin, Douglas. "Selections from *Wen-wu* on the Excavation of a Sung Dynasty Seagoing Vessel in Ch'üan-chou." *Chinese Sociology and Anthropology* 9 (Spring 1977).

Messimer, Dwight R. *The Merchant U-Boat: Adventures of the "Deutschland," 1916–1918.* Annapolis: Naval Institute Press, 1988.

———. *Pawns of War: The Loss of the USS "Langley" and the USS "Pecos."* Annapolis: Naval Institute Press, 1983.

Middlebrook, Martin, and Patrick Mahoney. *Battleship: The Loss of "Prince of Wales" and the "Repulse."* New York: Charles Scribner's, 1979.

Millar, John Fitzhugh. *Early American Ships.* Williamsburg: Thirteen Colonies Press, 1986.

Miller, Edward M. *USS "Monitor": The Ship That Launched a Modern Navy.* Annapolis: Naval Institute Press, 1978.

Miller, George L. "The Second Destruction of the *Geldermalsen.*" *American Neptune* 47 (1987): 275–281.

Miller, Nathan. *Sea of Glory: A Naval History of the American Revolution.* Annapolis: Naval Institute Press, 1974.

———. *War at Sea: A Naval History of World War II.* New York: Scribner, 1995.

Miller, William H. *SS "United States": The Story of America's Greatest Ocean Liner.* Sparkford: Patrick Stephens, 1991.

Millett, Richard. "The State Department's Navy: A History of the Special Service Squadron, 1920–1940." *American Neptune* 35 (1975): 118–138.

Milligan, John D. *Gunboats down the Mississippi.* Annapolis: Naval Institute Press, 1965.

Mills, Simon. *"Britannic": The Last Titan.* Hallenbrook, 1993.

Mitchell, C. Bradford. *We'll Deliver: Early History of the United States Merchant Marine Academy, 1938–1956.* Kings Point, N.Y.: U.S. Merchant Marine Academy Alumni Assoc., 1977.

Mitchell, Carleton. "Looking Back on *Finisterre.*" *Yachting* (July 1976): 58ff.

Mitford, Jessica. *Grace Had an English Heart.* New York: E. P. Dutton, 1985.

Mjelde, Michael J. *Glory of the Seas.* Middletown, Conn.: Marine Historical Assoc., 1970.

Mohr, Ulrich. *"Atlantis": The Story of a German Surface Raider, as told to A. V. Sellwood.* London: Laurie, 1955.

Moitessier, Bernard. *The First Voyage of the "Joshua."* New York: William Morrow, 1973.

———. *The Long Way.* New York: Doubleday, 1975.

Moore, Arthur R. *A Careless Word . . . A Needless Sinking.* Hallowell, Maine: Granite Hill Corp., 1984.

Morgan, Dodge. *The Voyage of "American Promise."* Boston: Houghton Mifflin, 1989.

Morison, Samuel Eliot. *Admiral of the Ocean Sea: A Life of Chris-

topher Columbus. Reprint, Boston: Northeastern Univ. Press, 1983.

————. *The European Discovery of America: The Northern Voyages.* New York: Oxford Univ. Press, 1971.

————. *The European Discovery of America: The Southern Voyages.* New York: Oxford Univ. Press, 1971.

————. *History of the United States Naval Operations in World War II.* 15 vols. Boston: Little, Brown, 1947–1962.

————. *John Paul Jones: A Sailor's Biography.* Boston: Little, Brown, 1959.

————. *The Two-Ocean War: A Short History of the United States Navy in the Second World War.* Boston: Little, Brown, 1963. (An abridgment of the *History of the U.S. Naval Operations,* above)

Morris, Paul C. *American Sailing Coasters of the North Atlantic.* New York: Bonanza Book, 1973.

————. *Four-Masted Schooners of the East Coast.* Orleans, Mass.: Lower Cape Publ., 1975.

————. *A Portrait of a Ship, the "Benj. F. Packard."* Orleans, Mass.: Lower Cape Publ., 1987.

Morris, Richard Knowles. *John P. Holland 1841–1914, Inventor of the Modern Submarine.* Annapolis: Naval Institute Press, 1965.

Morris, Roland. *HMS "Colossus": The Story of the Salvage of the Hamilton Treasures.* London: Hutchinson, 1979.

Morrison, J. S., and J. F. Coates. *The Athenian Trireme: The History and Reconstruction of an Ancient Greek Warship.* Cambridge: Cambridge Univ. Press, 1986.

Morton, Andrew. *The Royal Yacht "Britannia": Life on Board the Floating Palace.* London: Orbis, 1984.

Morton, H. V. *Atlantic Meeting.* New York: Dodd, Mead, 1943.

Mountfield, David. *A History of Polar Exploration.* London: Hamlyn, 1974.

Muggenthaler, August Karl. *German Raiders of World War II.* Englewood Cliffs, N.J.: Prentice Hall, 1977.

Müllenheim-Rechberg, Burkard von. *Battleship "Bismarck": A Survivor's Story.* Annapolis: Naval Institute Press, 1990.

Muncaster, Claude. *Rolling round the Horn.* London: Rich & Cowan, 1933.

Murdoch, Priscilla. *Duyfken and the First Discoveries of Australia.* Artarmon, New South Wales: Antipodean Publ., 1974.

Murfett, Malcolm H. *Hostage on the Yangtze: Britain, China and the "Amethyst" Crisis of 1949.* Annapolis: Naval Institute Press, 1991.

Murray, Timothy F. "*Coronet:* Whither Away?" *Wooden Boat* 32 (Jan.–Feb. 1980): 20–27.

Musham, H. A. "Early Great Lakes Steamboats: The *Caroline* Affair, 1837–38." *American Neptune* 7 (1947): 298–315.

————. "Early Great Lakes Steamboats — The *Ontario* and *Frontenac.*" *American Neptune* 3 (1943): 333–344.

————. "Early Great Lakes Steamboats — The *Walk-in-the-Water.*" *American Neptune* 5 (1945): 27–42.

Musicant, Ivan. *Battleship at War: The Epic Story of the USS "Washington."* San Diego: Harcourt Brace Jovanovich, 1986.

Naish, George P. B. *The "Wasa": Her Place in History.* London: HMSO, 1968.

Nansen, Fridtjof. *Farthest North: Being a Record of a Voyage of Exploration of the Ship "Fram" 1893–96 and of a Fifteen Months' Sleigh Journey by Dr. Nansen and Lieut. Johnson.* 2 vols. New York: Harper & Brothers, 1897.

Nares, George Strong. *Narrative of a Voyage to the Polar Sea during 1875–6 in HM ships "Alert" and "Discovery".* London: Sampson Low, 1878.

Nash, Howard P., Jr. "Civil War Legend Examined." *American Neptune* 23 (1963): 197–203.

Naylon, John. "The Full-Rigged Ship *Monkbarns.*" *Ships in Focus Record* No. 1. London: Ships in Focus, 1996.

Nelson, Daniel A. "*Hamilton* and *Scourge:* Ghost Ships of the War of 1812." *National Geographic* (Mar. 1983): 289–313.

Nerney, Michael T. *A History of Williams, Dimond & Co. since 1862.* San Francisco: Williams, Dimond, 1988.

Newby, Eric. *The Last Grain Race.* London: Secker & Warburg, 1956.

————. *Windjammer: Pictures of Life before the Mast in the Last Grain Race.* New York: E. P. Dutton, 1968.

Newhall, Scott. *The "Eppleton Hall": Being a True and Faithful Narrative of the Remarkable Voyage of the Last Tyne River Steam Sidewheel Paddle Tug Afloat — Newcastle-upon-Tyne to San Francisco, 1969–70.* Berkeley: Howell-North Books, 1971.

Niezychowski, Alfred von. *The Cruise of the "Kronprinz Wilhelm."* Garden City, N.Y.: Doubleday, Doran, 1929.

Nikolaysen, N. *The Viking Ship Discovered at Gokstad in Norway.* Christiania (Oslo): Alb. Cammermayer, 1882.

Nordenskiöld, A. E. *The Voyage of the "Vega" Round Asia and Europe with A Historical Review of Previous Journeys Along the North Coast of the Old World.* 2 vols. London: Macmillan, 1881.

Norton, William. *Eagle Seamanship: Square Rigger Sailing.* New York: M. Evans, 1969.

Nutting, Anthony. *Gordon of Khartoum: Martyr and Misfit.* New York: Clarkson N. Potter, 1966.

O'Connell, Robert L. *Sacred Vessels: The Cult of the Battleship and the Rise of the U.S. Navy.* New York: Oxford Univ. Press, 1991.

O'Driscoll, Patricia E. "The Ship with Seven Names." *Sea Breezes* 110 (1955): 134.

Oertling, Thomas J. "The Highborn Cay wreck: The 1986 Field Season." *IJNA* 18 (1989): 244–253.

————. "The Molasses Reef Wreck Hull Analysis: Final Report." *IJNA* 18 (1989): 229–243.

O'Kane, Richard H. *Clear the Bridge! The War Patrols of the U.S.S. "Tang."* Chicago: Rand McNally, 1977.

————. "*Wahoo*": *The Patrols of America's Most Famous World War II Submarine.* Novato, Calif.: Presidio Press, 1987.

Olsen, Olaf, and Ole Crumlin-Pedersen. *Five Viking Ships from Roskilde Fjord.* Copenhagen: The National Museum, 1978.

O Luíng, Seán. *Fremantle Mission.* Tralee, Ireland: Anvil Books, 1965.

O'Neill, Paul. *The Old West: The Rivermen.* New York: Time-Life Books, 1975.

Oosten, F. C. "Some Notes Concerning the Dutch West Indies during the American Revolutionary War." *American Neptune* 36 (1976): 155–169.

Osbon, H. A. "Passing of the Steam and Sail Corvette: The *Comus* and *Calliope* Classes." *Mariner's Mirror* 49 (1963): 193–208.

Oulié, Marthe. *Charcot & The Antarctic.* New York: E. P. Dutton, 1939.

Owen, D. "Excavating a Classical Shipwreck." *Archaeology* 24 (1971): 118–129.

————. "Picking Up the Pieces: The Salvage Excavation of a Looted Fifth Century B.C. Shipwreck in the Straits of Messina." *Expedition* 13 (1970): 24–29.

Owen, Roderic. *The Fate of Franklin*. London: Hutchinson, 1978.

Owsley, F. L., Jr. *The CSS "Florida": Her Building and Operations*. Tuscaloosa: Univ. of Alabama Press, 1987.

Padfield, Peter. *War beneath the Sea: Submarine Conflict 1939–1945*. London: John Murray, 1995.

Paine, Lincoln D. "Bring Home the *Vicar!*" *Sea History* 38 (Winter 1985–86): 12–16.

Paine, Ralph D. *The "Corsair" in the War Zone*. Boston: Houghton Mifflin, 1920.

Papathansopoulos, George. "Dokos Excavation '89." *Enalia Annual 1989*: 34–37.

Parker, A. J. *Ancient Shipwrecks of the Mediterranean & the Roman Provinces*. Oxford, Eng.: Tempus Reparatum, 1992.

Parker, W. J. Lewis. *The Great Coal Schooners of New England 1870–1909*. Mystic, Conn.: Marine Historical Assoc., 1948.

Parkes, Oscar. *British Battleships 1860–1950*. London: Seeley Service, 1957.

Parkinson, John, Jr. *The History of the New York Yacht Club from Its Founding through 1973*. New York: New York Yacht Club, 1975.

Parry, Ann. *Parry of the Arctic, 1790–1855*. London: Chatto & Windus, 1963.

Parry, William Edward. *Journal of a Voyage for the Discovery of a North-West Passage from the Atlantic to the Pacific; performed in the years 1819–1820, in His Majesty's ships "Hecla" and "Griper"*. . . . London: John Murray, 1821.

———. *Journal of a Second Voyage for the Discovery of a North-West Passage from the Atlantic to the Pacific; performed in the years 1821–22–23 in His Majesty's Ships "Hecla" and "Fury"*. . . . London: John Murray, 1824.

———. *Journal of a Third Voyage for the Discovery of a North-West Passage from the Atlantic to the Pacific; performed in the years 1824–25, in His Majesty's Ships "Hecla" and "Fury"*. . . . London: John Murray, 1826.

———. *Narrative of an Attempt to Reach the North Pole in Boats Fitted for the Purpose, and Attached to his Majesty's Ship "Hecla," in the Year MCCCXXVII*. London: John Murray, 1828.

Pastor, Xavier. "A Replica of the Nao Catalana (Catalan Vessel) of 1450 in the Prins Hendrik Maritime Museum, Rotterdam." Lecture read by M. Akveld, at the Sixth International Congress of Maritime Museums (1987).

———. *The Ships of Christopher Columbus: "Santa María," "Niña," "Pinta."* Annapolis: Naval Institute Press, 1992.

Paul, J. Harland. *The Last Cruise of the "Carnegie."* Baltimore: Williams & Wilkins, 1932.

Payer, Julius. *New Lands within the Arctic Circle: Narrative of the Discoveries of the Austrian Ship "Tegetthoff" in the Years 1872–1874*. London: Macmillan, 1876.

Payne, Alan. *H.M.A.S. "Perth."* Garden Island, NSW: Naval Historical Society of Australia, 1978.

Peabody, Robert E. *Log of the Grand Turks*. Boston: Houghton Mifflin, 1926.

Peard, Lieutenant. *To the Pacific and Arctic with Beechy: The Journal of Lieutenant Peard of H.M.S. "Blossom."* Edited by Barry M. Gough. Cambridge, Eng.: Hakluyt Society, 1973.

Peary, R. E. *Nearest the Pole: A Narrative of the Polar Expedition of the Peary Arctic Club in the S.S. "Roosevelt," 1905–1906*. New York: Doubleday, Page, 1907.

———. *The North Pole*. London: Hodder & Stoughton, 1910.

Pease, Zephaniah W. *The "Catalpa" Expedition*. New Bedford, Mass.: George S. Anthony, 1897.

Peillard, Leonce. *The "Laconia" Affair*. New York: Bantam, 1983.

———. *Sink the "Tirpitz."* London: Jonathan Cape, 1968.

Pelsaert, François. *The Voyage of the "Batavia."* 1647. Reissued with a translation from the original Dutch and a commentary by Martin Terry. Sydney, Australia: Hordern House, 1994.

Pemsel, Helmut. *A History of War at Sea: An Atlas and Chronology of Conflict at Sea from Earliest Times to the Present*. Annapolis: Naval Institute Press, 1989.

Perry, Hamilton Darby. *The "Panay" Incident: Prelude to Pearl Harbor*. New York: Macmillan, 1969.

Perry, Milton F. *Infernal Machines: The Story of Confederate Submarine and Marine Warfare*. Baton Rouge: Louisiana State Univ. Press, 1965.

Peterson, M. L. R. "The *Sea Venture*." *Mariner's Mirror* 74 (1988): 37–48.

Petrow, Richard. *In the Wake of "Torrey Canyon."* New York: David McKay, 1968.

Petsche, Jerome E. *The Steamboat "Bertrand": History, Excavation and Architecture*. Washington, D.C.: National Park Service, 1974.

Philip, Cynthia Owen. *Robert Fulton: A Biography*. New York: Franklin Watts, 1985.

Phillip, A., et al. *The Voyage of Governor Phillip to Botany Bay with an account of the establishment of the colonies of Port Jackson and Norfolk Island*. 1789. Australia: Hutchinson, Australian Facsimile Editions, 1982.

Phillips, Carla Rahn. "The Evolution of Spanish Ship Design from the 15th to 18th Centuries." *American Neptune* 53:4 (Fall 1993): 229–238.

Phillips, Michael. *Ships of the Old Navy*. Forthcoming.

Piccard, Auguste. *Earth, Sky, and Sea*. New York: Oxford Univ. Press, 1956.

Piccard, Jacques, and Robert M. Dietz. *Seven Miles Down: The Story of the Bathyscaphe "Trieste."* New York: G. P. Putnam's Sons, 1961.

Pigafetta, Antonio, et al. *The First Voyage Round the World, by Magellan*. London: Hakluyt Society, 1874 (first series, no. 52).

Pinheiro, Carlton J. "Herreshoff Catamarans — *Amaryllis*." *Herreshoff Marine Museum Chronicle* 1:3 (1991).

Pitt, Barry. *Zeebrugge: St. George's Day 1918*. London: Cassell, 1958.

Plowman, Peter, and Alan Zammit. "The Sinking of the *Centaur*." *Australian Sea Heritage* 34 (1993): 22–27.

Pollock, Bill. *Last Message 1358: Death of the "Princess Victoria."* Belfast, 1990.

Pollock, George. *The "Jervis Bay."* London: Kimber, 1958.

Polmar, Norman. *The Naval Institute Guide to Ships and Aircraft of the U.S. Fleet*. 15th ed. Annapolis: Naval Institute Press, 1993.

———. *The Naval Institute Guide to the Soviet Navy*. 5th ed. Annapolis: Naval Institute Press, 1991.

———. *Ships and Aircraft of the U.S. Fleet*. 14th ed. Annapolis: Naval Institute Press, 1987.

Pope, Dudley. *At Twelve Mr Byng Was Shot*. Philadelphia: J. B. Lippincott, 1962.

———. *The Battle of the River Plate*. Annapolis: Naval Institute Press, 1991.

———. *The Black Ship*. Philadelphia: J. B. Lippincott, 1964.

———. *The Devil Himself: The Mutiny of 1800*. London: Secker & Warburg, 1988.

Porter, David. *Journal of a Cruise.* 1815. Reprint, Annapolis: Naval Institute Press, 1986.

Potter, Jerry O. *The "Sultana" Tragedy: America's Greatest Maritime Disaster.* Gretna: Pelican, 1992.

Potts, W. H. *Wind from the East.* London: Blackie & Son, 1940.

Powell, J. W. Damer. "The Wreck of *Sir Cloudesley Shovell.*" *Mariner's Mirror* 43 (1957): 333–336.

Power, Hugh. *Battleship "Texas."* College Station, Tex.: Texas A & M Univ. Press, 1993.

Prager, Hans Georg. *Blohm + Voss.* London: Brassey's, 1977.

Prange, Gordorn. *At Dawn We Slept.* New York: McGraw-Hill, 1981.

———. *Miracle at Midway.* New York: McGraw-Hill, 1982.

Price, Derek. "An Ancient Greek Computer." *Scientific American* 200 (June 1959): 60–67.

Prynne, M. W. "Annual Lecture of the Society for Nautical Research: *Henry V's Grace Dieu.*" *Mariner's Mirror* 54 (1968): 115–128.

———. "Notes: The Dimensions of the *Grace Dieu* (1418)." *Mariner's Mirror* 63 (1977): 6–7.

Pullen, H. F. *The "Shannon" and the "Chesapeake."* Toronto: McClelland & Stewart, 1970.

Purchas, Samuel. *Hakluytus Posthumus, or Purchas His Pilgrims, Contayning a History of the World in Sea Voyages and Lande Travells by Englishmen and others.* 20 vols. 1625. Reprint, Glasgow: James MacLehose & Sons, 1906.

Putz, George. *"Eagle": America's Sailing Square-Rigger.* Chester, Conn.: Globe Pequot Press, 1986.

Quinn, David B., and Allison M. Quinn, eds. *The English New England Voyages, 1602–1608.* London: Hakluyt Society, 1983.

Quirós, Pedro Fernández de. *The Voyage of Fernández de Quirós, 1593–96.* London: Hakluyt Society, 1903.

Randolph, Evan. "Fouled Anchors? Foul Blow." *American Neptune* 52 (1992): 94–101.

———. "USS *Constellation,* 1797–1979." *American Neptune* 39 (1979): 235–255.

Ratigan, William. *Great Lakes Shipwrecks & Survivors* (Steamer Edmund Fitzgerald Edition). Grand Rapids, Mich.: Wm. B. Eerdmans, 1977.

Rattray, Jeannette Edwards. *The Perils of the Port of New York: Maritime Disasters from Sandy Hook to Execution Rock.* New York: Dodd, Mead, 1973.

Raven, Alan. *Battleships "Rodney" and "Nelson."* New York: RSV, 1979.

———. *Essex Class Carriers.* Annapolis: Naval Institute Press, 1988.

Raven, Alan, and Antony Preston. *Flower Class Corvettes.* Norwich: Bivouac Books, 1973.

Rawson, Geoffrey. *"Pandora"'s Last Voyage.* New York: Harcourt, Brace & World, 1963.

Reade, Leslie. *The Ship That Stood Still: The "Californian" and Her Mysterious Role in the "Titanic" Disaster.* Somerset, Eng.: Patrick Stevens, 1993.

Reynolds, Clark G. *The Fighting Lady: The New "Yorktown" in the Pacific War.* Missoula, Mont.: Pictorial Histories, 1986.

The Recovery of the Manila Galleon the "Nuestra Señora de la Concepción." Report prepared for the Commonwealth of the Northern Marianas.

Rich, E. E. *The History of the Hudson's Bay Company, 1670–1870.* London: Hudson's Bay Record Society, 1958.

Richards, Mose. "Sis and J-826." *Calypso Log* 9:2 (June 1982): 1–3.

Richardson, Alex. *The Evolution of the Parsons Steam Turbine.* London: Engineering, 1911.

Rickover, H. G. *How the Battleship "Maine" Was Destroyed.* Washington, D.C.: Naval History Division, Dept. of the Navy, 1976.

Rider, Hope. *Valour Fore and Aft.* Annapolis: Naval Institute Press, 1976.

Ridgely-Nevitt, Cedric. "The Steam Boat, 1807–1814." *American Neptune* 27 (1967): 5–29.

Ridgway, Brunilde Sismondo. Review of *Das Wrack. Der Antike Schiffsfund von Mahdia,* ed. Gisela Hellenkamper Salies. *Journal of Roman Archaeology* 8 (1995): 340–347.

Ridgway, John, and Chay Blyth. *A Fighting Chance: How We Rowed the Atlantic in 92 Days.* London: Paul Hamlyn, 1966.

Riesenberg, Felix. *Under Sail: A Boy's Voyage around Cape Horn.* New York: Macmillan, 1918.

Ringwald, Donald C. *The "Mary Powell."* Berkeley, Calif.: Howell-North, 1972.

Ritchie, G. S. *The Admiralty Chart: British Naval Hydrography in the Nineteenth Century.* London: Hollis & Carter, 1967.

Ritchie, Robert C. *Captain Kidd and the War against the Pirates.* Boston: Harvard Univ. Press, 1986.

Roberts, David. "In Texas, a Ship Is Found and a Grand Dream Recalled." *Smithsonian* (Apr. 1997).

Roberts, John. *The Aircraft Carrier "Intrepid."* London: Conway Maritime Press, 1982.

———. *The Battlecruiser "Hood."* Annapolis: Naval Institute Press, 1982.

———. *The Battleship "Dreadnought."* London: Conway Maritime, 1992.

Robertson, George. *The Discovery of Tahiti: A Journal of the Second Voyage of HMS "Dolphin" round the world, under the command of Captain Wallis RN, in the years 1766, 1767, and 1768.* London: Hakluyt Society, 1948.

Robinson, Bill. *Legendary Yachts: The Great American Yachts from "Cleopatra's Barge" to "Courageous."* New York: David McKay, 1978.

Robinson, Charles M., III. *Shark of the Confederacy: The Story of the CSS "Alabama."* Annapolis: Naval Institute Press, 1995.

Robinson, Gregory. "The Great Harry." *Mariner's Mirror* 20 (1934): 85–92.

Robinson, William Morrison, Jr. *The Confederate Privateers.* New York: Yale Univ. Press, 1928.

Rodgers, William Ledyard. *Naval Warfare under Oars 4th to 16th Centuries.* Annapolis: Naval Institute Press, 1940.

Rodríguez-Salgado, M. J., et al. *Armada 1588–1988: An International Exhibition to Commemorate the Spanish Armada.* London: Penguin Books, 1988.

Rogers, Stanley R. H. *Freak Ships.* London: John Lane, The Bodley Head, 1936.

Rogers, Warren, Jr. *The Floating Revolution.* New York: McGraw-Hill, 1962.

Rogers, Will, and Sharon Rogers. *Storm Center: The USS "Vincennes" and Iran Air Flight 655.* Annapolis: Naval Institute Press, 1992.

Rogers, Woodes. *A Cruising Voyage Round the World.* 1712. Reprint, New York: Dover, 1970.

Roggeveen, Jacob. *The Journal of Jacob Roggeveen.* Ed. Andrew Sharp. Oxford, Eng.: The Clarendon Press, 1970.

Rohrbach, H. C., et al. *FL: A Century and a Quarter of Reederei F.*

Laeisz (Owners of the "Flying P" Nitrate Clippers). Flagstaff, Ariz.: J. F. Colton, 1957.

Rohwer, J., and G. Hummelchen *Chronology of the War at Sea, 1939–1945: The Naval History of World War Two.* 2nd ed. Annapolis: Naval Institute Press, 1992.

Rolt, L. T. C. *Isambard Kingdom Brunel.* London: Penguin Books, 1989.

Rolt, Peter. "Eighty Years a Gaff Cutter." *The Boatman* 9 (Oct. 1993): 14–23.

Ronnberg, Erik A. R., Jr. "Stranger in Truth Than in Fiction: The American Seven-Masted Schooners." *Nautical Research Journal* 38 (1992): 5–41.

Roosevelt, Theodore. *The Naval War of 1812: or The History of the United States Navy during the Last War with Great Britain.* 1882. Reprint, Annapolis: Naval Institute Press, 1987.

Roscoe, Theodore. *United States Submarine Operations in World War II.* Annapolis: Naval Institute Press, 1949.

Rose, Sir Alec. *My Lively Lady.* New York: David McKay, 1968.

Rose, Lisle A. *The Ship That Held the Line: The USS "Hornet" and the First Year of the Pacific War.* Annapolis: Naval Institute Press, 1995.

Rose, Susan. "Henry V's *Grace Dieu* and Mutiny at Sea: Some New Evidence." *Mariner's Mirror* 63 (1977): 3–8.

Roskill, S. W. *H.M.S. "Warspite": The Story of a Famous Battleship.* London: Futura, 1954.

Roskruge, F. I. "The *Victory* after Trafalgar." *Mariner's Mirror* 7 (1921): 267.

Rosloff, Jay, and J. Barto Arnold III. "The Keel of the *San Esteban* (1554): Continued Analysis." *IJNA* 13 (1984): 287–296.

Ross, Al. *The Escort Carrier "Gambier Bay."* London: Conway Maritime, 1993.

Ross, James Clark. *A Voyage of Discovery and Research in the Southern and Antarctic Regions, During the Years 1839–43.* 2 vols. 1847. Reprint, New York: Augustus M. Kelley, 1969.

Ross, Sir John. *Narrative of a Second Voyage in Search of a North-West Passage, and of a Residence in the Arctic Regions during the Years 1829, 1830, 1831, 1832, 1833.* London: A. W. Webster, 1835.

———. *A Voyage of Discovery . . . in His Majesty's Ships "Isabella" and "Alexander" for the Purpose of Exploring Baffin's Bay, and Inquiring into the Probability of a North-West Passage.* London: John Murray, 1819.

Ross, Lillian. "Where Are They Now? The Kaiser's Yacht." *The New Yorker* (June 22, 1946): 66–80.

Ross, M. J. *Polar Pioneers: John Ross and James Clark Ross.* Montreal & Kingston: McGill-Queen's Univ. Press, 1994.

———. *Ross in the Antarctic: The Voyages of James Clark Ross in HMS "Erebus" and "Terror," 1839–1843.* Whitby: Caedmon of Whitby, 1982.

Ross, W. Gillies. "The Travels of *Tilikum.*" *American Neptune* 38 (1968): 53–65.

Rousmaniere, John. *The Low Black Schooner: Yacht "America" 1851–1945: A New History of the Yacht "America" Based on the Exhibit Held at Mystic Seaport Museum November 1986 through March 1987 Cosponsored by the New York Yacht Club.* Mystic, Conn.: Mystic Seaport Museum Stores, 1986.

Rowan, Roy. *The Four Days of "Mayaguez."* New York: W. W. Norton, 1975.

Rowland, K. T. *The "Great Britain."* Newton Abbot, Eng.: David & Charles, 1971.

Rowse, A. L. *Sir Richard Grenville of the "Revenge."* London: Jonathan Cape, 1935.

Rubin de Cervin, G. B. "Mysteries and Nemesis of the Nemi Ships." *Mariner's Mirror* 41 (1955): 38–43.

Ruffman, Alan, and Colin Howell, eds. *Ground Zero.* Halifax, Nova Scotia: Nimbus, 1994.

Rukenas, Algis. *Day of Shame: The Truth about the Murderous Happenings Aboard the Cutter "Vigilant" during the Russian-American Confrontation off Martha's Vineyard.* New York: David McKay, 1973.

Rule, Margaret. *The "Mary Rose": The Excavation and Raising of Henry VIII's Flagship.* London: Conway Maritime, 1982.

Rule, Margaret, and Jason Monaghan. *A Gallo-Roman Trading Vessel from Guernsey: The Excavation and Recovery of a Third-Century Shipwreck.* Guernsey, Channel Islands: Guernsey Museum Monograph No. 5, 1993.

Rusbridger, James. *Who Sank "Surcouf"? The Truth about the Disappearance of the Pride of the French Navy.* London: Century, 1991.

Rust, Claude. *The Burning of the "General Slocum."* New York: Elsevier/Nelson Books, 1981.

Rybka, Walter. "*Elissa* Sails: The Ship Is Now Real and Beautiful." *Sea History* 26 (Winter 1982–1983): 18–23.

Salecker, Gene Eric. *Disaster on the Mississippi: The "Sultana" Explosion, April 27, 1865.* Annapolis: Naval Institute Press, 1996.

Samuels, Samuel. *From the Forecastle to the Cabin.* 1887.

Sandler, Stanley. "'In Deference to Public Opinion': The Loss of HMS *Captain.*" *Mariner's Mirror* 59 (1973): 57–68.

Sands, John O. *Yorktown's Captive Fleet.* Newport News, Va.: Mariners' Museum, 1984.

Savigny, J. B. Henry, and Alexandre Corréard. *Narrative of a Voyage to Senegal in 1816; undertaken by order of the French Government, comprising an account of the shipwreck of the "Medusa," the sufferings of the crew, and the various occurrences on board the raft . . . and at the camp of Daccard.* London: Henry Colburn, 1818.

Savill, David, and Duncan Haws. *Aberdeen and Aberdeen & Commonwealth Lines.* Hereford: TCL, 1989.

Savours, Ann. *The Voyages of "Discovery": The Illustrated History of Scott's Ship.* London: Virgin Books, 1992.

Sawtelle, Joseph G., ed. *John Paul Jones and the "Ranger": Portsmouth, New Hampshire, July 12–November 1, 1777 and the Log of the "Ranger" November 1, 1777–May 18, 1778.* Portsmouth, N.H.: Portsmouth Marine Society, 1994.

Sawyer, L. A., and W. H. Mitchell. *The Liberty Ships: The History of the "Emergency" Type Cargo Ships Constructed in the United States.* Newton Abbot, Eng.: David & Charles, 1970.

———. *Victory Ships and Tankers: The History of the "Victory" Type Cargo Ships and of the Tankers Built in the United States of America during World War II.* Cambridge, Md.: Cornell Maritime Press, 1974.

Schäuffelen, Otmar. *Great Sailing Ships.* New York: Frederick A. Praeger, 1969.

Scheina, Robert L. "Twice Unique."

———. *U.S. Coast Guard Cutters and Craft, 1946–1990.* Annapolis: Naval Institute Press, 1990.

Schmalenbach, Paul. *German Raiders: A History of Auxiliary Cruisers of the German Navy 1895–1945.* Annapolis: Naval Institute Press, 1979.

Schofield, Bernard B. *Taranto.* Annapolis: Naval Institute Press, 1973.

Schom, Alan. *Trafalgar: Countdown to Battle, 1803–1805.* New York: Oxford Univ. Press, 1990.

Schurz, William Lytle. *The Manila Galleon.* Manila: Historical Conservation Society, 1985.

Seamer, Robert. *The Floating Inferno: The Story of the Loss of the "Empress of Britain."* Cambridge, Eng.: Patrick Stephens, 1990.

Seeger, Martin L. "The Ten-Cent War: Naval Phase." *American Neptune* 39 (1979): 271–288.

Selfridge, Thomas O., Jr. Memoirs of Thomas O. Selfridge, Jr.: Rear Admiral U.S.N.

Seligman, Adrian. *The Voyage of the "Cap Pilar."* London: Hodder & Stoughton, 1939.

Semmes, Raphael. *Memoirs of Service Afloat.* 1868. Reprint, Secaucus, N.J.: Blue & Grey Press, 1987.

Senior, William. "The *Bucentaur.*" *Mariner's Mirror* 15 (1929): 131–138.

Severin, Tim. *The Brendan Voyage: A Leather Boat Tracks the Discovery of America by the Irish Sailor Saints.* New York: McGraw Hill, 1978.

———. *The Jason Voyage: The Quest for the Golden Fleece.* London: Hutchinson, 1985.

———. *The Sinbad Voyage.* New York: G. P. Putnam's Sons, 1982.

Shackleton, Ernest Henry. *The Heart of the Antarctic: Being the Story of the British Antarctic Expedition of 1907–1909.* London: Heinemann, 1909.

———. *South: The Story of Shackleton's Last Expedition, 1914–17.* London: Heinemann, 1919.

Shackleton, Keith. *Wildlife and Wilderness: An Artist's World.* London: Clive Holloway, 1986.

Shankland, Peter. *Byron of the "Wager."* London: Collins, 1975.

Sharp, Andrew. *The Voyages of Abel Janszoon Tasman.* Oxford, Eng.: Clarendon Press, 1968.

Shelton, Russell C. *From Hudson's Bay to Botany Bay: The Lost Frigates of Laperouse.* Toronto: NC Press, 1987.

Sheppard, Thomas. "The *Sirius,* the First Steamer to Cross the Atlantic." *Mariner's Mirror* 23 (1937): 84–94.

Sheridan, Richard Brinsley. *Heavenly Hell: The Experience of an Apprentice in a Four-Mast Barque.* London: Putnam, 1935.

Sherman, Constance D. "An Accounting of His Majesty's Armed Sloop *Liberty.*" *American Neptune* 20 (1960): 243–249.

Shipbuilder and Marine Engine-Builder. *The Canadian Pacific Quadruple-Screw North Atlantic Liner "Empress of Britain."* May 1931. Reprint, London: Patrick Stephens, 1971.

———. *The Cunard Express Liners "Lusitania" and "Mauretania."* Reprint, London: Patrick Stephens, 1970.

———. *The Cunard Quadruple-Screw Atlantic Liner "Aquitania."* Reprint, London: Patrick Stephens, 1971.

———. *The Cunard White Star Quadruple-Screw North Atlantic Liner "Queen Mary."* June 1936. Reprint, London: Patrick Stephens, 1972.

———. *The French Line Quadruple-Screw Turbo-Electric North Atlantic Steamship "Normandie."* June 1935. Reprint, London: Patrick Stephens, 1972.

———. *The White Star Triple Screw Atlantic Liners "Olympic" and "Titanic."* Reprint, London: Patrick Stephens, 1970.

Shomette, Donald. *The Hunt for HMS "De Braak": Legend and Legacy.* Durham: Carolina Academic Press, 1993.

Sieche, Erwin F. "The German Heavy Cruiser *Prinz Eugen:* A Career under Two Flags." *Warship* 49 (Jan. 1989): 44–48.

Sigmond, J. P., and L. H. Zuiderbaan. *Dutch Discoveries of Australia: Shipwrecks, Treasures and Early Voyages off the West Coast.* Adelaide: Rigby, 1976.

Silverstone, Paul H. *Directory of the World's Capital Ships.* London: Ian Allen, 1984.

———. *Warships of the Civil War Navies.* Annapolis: Naval Institute Press, 1989.

Simpson, Colin. *The Ship That Hunted Itself.* New York: Stein & Day, 1977.

Sjøvold, Thorleif. *The Oseberg Find and the Other Viking Ship Finds.* Oslo: Universitets Oldsaksamling, 1966.

Skulski, Janusz. *Anatomy of the Ship: The Battleship "Yamato."* Annapolis: Naval Institute Press, 1988.

Sloan, Edward W. "The Wreck of the Collins Liner *Pacific.*" *Bermuda Journal of Archaeology and Maritime History* 5 (1993): 84–92.

Slocum, Joshua. *Sailing Alone around the World and Voyage of the "Liberdade."* London: Rupert Hart-Davis, 1948.

Smeeton, Miles. *Because the Horn Is There.* London: Nautical, 1970.

———. *The Misty Islands.* London: Nautical, 1969.

———. *The Sea Was Our Village.* London: Nautical, 1971.

———. *Sunrise to Windward.* London: Hart-Davis, 1966.

Smith, D. Bonner. "Some Remarks about the Mutiny of the *Bounty.*" *Mariner's Mirror* 22 (1936): 200–237.

Smith, Eugene. *Passenger Ships of the World Past and Present.* Boston: George H. Dean, 1978.

Smith, Peter C. *Hit First, Hit Hard: The Story of HMS "Renown," 1916–48.* London: Kimber, 1979.

———. *Pedestal: The Malta Convoy of August 1942.* London: Kimber, 1987.

Smith, Peter L. *The Naval Wrecks of Scapa Flow.* Kirkwall, Orkney, 1989.

Smith, Philip Chadwick Foster. *The "Empress of China."* Philadelphia: Philadelphia Maritime Museum, 1984.

Smith, Philip Mason. *Confederates Downeast: Confederate Operations in and around Maine.* Portland, Maine: Provincial Press, 1985.

Smith, Roger C. *Vanguard of Empire: Ships of Exploration in the Age of Columbus.* New York: Oxford Univ. Press, 1993.

Smith, Roger C., Donald H. Keith, and Denise Lakey. "The Highborn Cay Wreck: Further Exploration of a 16th-Century Bahamian Shipwreck." *IJNA* 14 (1985): 63–72.

Smith, Sheli. "Life at Sea." In *The Sea Remembers: Shipwrecks and Archaeology.* Edited by Peter Throckmorton. New York: Smithmark, 1991.

Smith, William D. *Northwest Passage: The Historic Voyage of the S.S. "Manhattan."* New York: American Heritage Press, 1970.

Snorri Sturluson, *Haemskringla,* "The Building of the Long Serpent," Olaf Tryggvison's Saga, chap. 95 (ca. 1225). Translations: S. Laing, 1844 and 1961–64; W. Morris and E. Magnusson, 1893; Erling Monsen, 1932; L. M. Hollander, Austin, 1964.

Snow, Ralph L. *Bath Iron Works: The First Hundred Years.* Bath, Maine: Maine Maritime Museum, 1987.

Snyder, Gerald S. *The "Royal Oak" Disaster.* San Rafael, Calif.: Presidio, 1978.

Snyder, J., and Keith Shackleton. *Ship in the Wilderness.* London: Dent, 1986.

Sokol, Anthony E. *The Imperial and Royal Austro-Hungarian Navy.* Annapolis: Naval Institute Press, 1968.

Somerville, Duncan S. *The Aspinwall Empire*. Mystic, Conn.: Mystic Seaport Museum, 1983.

Spathari, E., et al. *A Voyage into Time and Legend aboard the Kyrenia Ship*. Athens, Greece: 1987.

Spectre, Peter. "*Alvin Clark:* The Challenge of the Challenge." *WoodenBoat* 52 (May/June 1983): 59–65.

Spencer, Warren F. *The Confederate Navy in Europe*. University: Univ. of Alabama Press, 1983.

Speziale, G. C. "The Roman Anchors Found at Nemi." *Mariner's Mirror* 17 (1931): 309–320.

———. "The Roman Galleys in the Lake of Nemi." *Mariner's Mirror* 15 (1929): 333–346.

Spiers, George. *The "Wavertree": Being an Account of an Ocean Wanderer and Particularly a Voyage around the Horn in 1907–1908. . . .* New York: South Street Seaport Museum, 1969.

Spies, M. H. "*Liemba*." *Steamboat Bill* (Autumn 1968): 148–149.

Spiess, F. *The "Meteor" Expedition: Scientific Results of the German Atlantic Expedition, 1925–1927*. New Delhi: Amerind, 1985.

Spratt, H. Philip. "The First Iron Steamer." *American Neptune* 13 (1953): 157–161.

———. *Transatlantic Paddle Steamers*. Glasgow: Brown Son & Ferguson, 1951.

Stackpole, Edouard A. *The "Charles W. Morgan," The Last Wooden Whaleship*. New York: Meredith Press, 1967.

———. "Nantucket and Pitcairn: An Islander Unravels an Island Mystery Half a World Away." *Sea History* 42 (Winter 1986–1987): 16–17.

———. *The Voyage of the Huron and the Huntress: The American Sealers and the Discovery of the Continent of Antarctica*. Mystic, Conn.: Marine Historical Assoc., 1955.

———. *The Wreck of the Steamer "San Francisco"*. Mystic, Conn.: Mystic Seaport, 1977.

Stafford, Edward. *The Big E:* The Story of the USS "Enterprise." Annapolis: Naval Institute Press, 1988.

Stammers, Michael. *The Passage Makers: The History of the Black Ball Line of Australian Packets, 1852–1871*. Brighton, Eng.: Teredo Books, 1978.

Stammers, Michael, and John Kearon. "*Jhelum*": *A Victorian Merchant Ship*. Wolfeboro Falls, N.H.: Alex Sutton, 1993.

Stanbury, Myra. *HMS "Sirius": An Illustrated Catalogue of Artefacts Recovered from the Wreck Site at Norfolk Island*. Adelaide: Australian Institute for Nautical Archaeology, 1994.

Stanford, Don. *The "Ile De France."* New York: Appleton-Century-Crofts, 1960.

Stanford, Peter. "*Elissa:* The Long Sea Career." *Sea History* 15 (Fall 1979): 9–11.

Stanton, William. *The Great U.S. Exploring Expedition of 1838–1842*. Berkeley: Univ. of California Press, 1975.

Staples, William R., ed. *Documentary History of the Destruction of the "Gaspé."* Providence: Rhode Island Publ. Society, 1990.

Starbuck, Alexander. *History of the American Whale Fishery to 1872*. 1878. Reprint, New York: Argosy-Antiquarian, 1964.

Steele, James. "*Queen Mary*." London: Phaidon Press, 1995.

Stefansson, Vilhjalmur, ed. *The Three Voyages of Martin Frobisher*. 2 vols. London: Argonaut, 1938.

Steffy, J. Richard. "The Kyrenia Ship: An Interim Report on Its Hull Reconstruction." *American Journal of Archaeology* 89 (1985) 71–101.

———. "The Reconstruction of the 11th Century Serçe Liman Vessel. A Preliminary Report." *IJNA* 11 (1982): 13–34.

———. *Wooden Shipbuilding and the Interpretation of Shipwrecks*. College Station, Tex.: Texas A & M Univ. Press, 1994.

Steiner, Erich Gershom. *The Story of the "Patria."* New York: Holocaust Library, 1982.

Sténuit, Robert. *Treasures of the Armada*. New York: E. P. Dutton, 1971.

Stephen, Adrian. *The "Dreadnought" Hoax*. 1936. Reprint, London: Chatto & Windus, Hogarth Press, 1983.

Stephen, Martin. *Sea Battles in Close-Up: World War 2*. Annapolis: Naval Institute Press, 1991.

Stephens, Hawley. "C.S.S. *Georgia:* Memory and Calling." *American Neptune* 45 (1985): 191–198.

Sterling, *Wake of the "Wahoo."* Philadelphia: Chilton, 1960.

Stern, Philip Van Doren. *Prologue to Sumter*. Bloomington, Indiana: Univ. Press, 1961.

Stern, Robert. *U.S. Aircraft Carriers in Action, Part 1*. Carrollton, Tex.: Squadron, Signal, 1991.

Sternlicht, Sanford. *McKinley's Bulldog: The Battleship "Oregon."* Chicago: Nelson-Hall, 1977.

Stevenson, Paul E. *The Race for the Emperor's Cup*. New York: Rudder, 1907.

Stewart, W. Roderick. *Welcome Aboard the Frigate "Unicorn."* Dundee, Scotland: Unicorn Preservation Society, 1982.

Still, William N., Jr. *Iron Afloat: The Story of the Confederate Ironclads*. Columbia: Univ. of South Carolina Press, 1985.

———. "*Monitor* Companies: A Study of the Major Firms That Built the USS *Monitor*." *American Neptune* 48 (1948): 106–130.

Stillwell, Paul. *Battleship "Arizona": An Illustrated History*. Annapolis: Naval Institute Press, 1991.

———. *Battleship "Missouri": An Illustrated History*. Annapolis: Naval Institute Press, 1996.

Story, Dana. *Hail "Columbia"!* Barre, Mass.: Barre Publications, 1970.

Strachey, William. "A True Repertory of the Wreck and Redemption of Sir Thomas Gates, Knight." 1610. In Purchas, *Hakluytus Posthumus* (see above).

Street, Sean. *The Wreck of the "Deutschland."* London: Souvenir Press, 1992.

Strum, Harvey. "The *Leopard-Chesapeake* Incident of 1807: The Arrogance of Seapower." *Warship* 11:43 (1987): 157–164.

Sugden, John. *Sir Francis Drake*. New York: Simon & Schuster, 1990.

Sullivan, Catherine. *Legacy of the "Machault": A Collection of 18th Century Artifacts*. Hull, Quebec: Parks Canada, 1986.

Sullivan, George. *Slave Ship: The Story of the "Henrietta Marie."* New York: Penguin USA, Cobblehill Books, 1994.

Sumrall, Robert F. *Iowa-Class Battleships: Their Design, Weapons and Equipment*. Annapolis: Naval Institute Press, 1988.

Sutter, Annie. "Rebirth of *Wander Bird*." *WoodenBoat* 55 (Nov.–Dec. 1983): 56–67.

Sverdrup, Otto N. *New Land: Four Years in the Arctic Regions*. New York: Longmans, Green, 1904.

Switzer, David. "Privateers, Not Pirates." In *The Sea Remembers: Shipwrecks and Archaeology*, Peter Thockmorton, ed. New York: Smithmark Publ., 1991.

[Tacitus] *Tacitus on Britain and Germany*. Trans. H. Mattingly. Baltimore: Penguin Books, 1948.

Tarrant, V. E. *Battlecruiser "Invincible": The History of the First Battlecruiser, 1909–1916.* Annapolis: Naval Institute Press, 1986.

Tasman, Abel. *Abel Janszoon Tasman's Journal.* Edited by J. E. Heeres. Amsterdam: Frederick Muller, 1898.

Taylor, Joan du Plat, ed. *Marine Archaeology.* New York: Crowell, 1966.

Taylor, William H. "*Ranger,* The American Defender." *Yachting* 62 (Aug. 1937): 43–49.

Tchernia, André. "The Madrague de Giens Wreck: A Roman Freighter Yields Its Secrets." *UNESCO Courier* (Nov. 1987): 11.

———. "Roman Divers' Salvage at La Madrague de Giens." In *The Sixth International Scientific Symposium of the World Underwater Federation.* London, 1982.

Teller, Walter Magnes, ed. *The Voyages of Joshua Slocum.* New Brunswick, N.J.: Rutgers Univ. Press, 1958.

Tennyson, Alfred Lord. "Last Fight of the *Revenge.*"

Terraine, John. *Business in Great Waters: The U-Boat Wars 1916–1945.* London: Leo Cooper, 1989.

Thesleff, Holger. *Farewell Windjammer.* London: Thames & Hudson, 1951.

Thomas, Gordon W. *Fast & Able: Life Stories of Great Gloucester Fishing Vessels.* Gloucester, Mass.: Gloucester 350th Anniversary Celebration, 1973.

Thomas, Gordon W., and Max Morgan Witts. *Voyage of the Damned.* New York: Stein & Day, 1974.

Thomas, Hugh. *The Spanish Civil War.* 3rd ed. London: Penguin, 1986.

Thomas, Lowell. *Count Luckner, The Sea Devil.* New York: Garden City Press, 1927.

Thompson, Kenneth. *HMS "Rodney" at War: Being an Account of the Part Played in the War from 1939 to 1945.* London: Hollis & Carter, 1946.

Thomson, Keith S. *HMS "Beagle": The Story of Darwin's Ship.* New York: W. W. Norton, 1995.

Thorndike, Virginia. *The Arctic Schooner "Bowdoin": A Biography.* Unity, Maine: North Country Press, 1995.

Thornton, Tim. "Air Power: The Sinking of the IJN *Musashi.*" *Warship* 45: 27–33.

———. "The Sinking of the *Yamato.*" *Warship 1989.* London: Conway Maritime Press, 1989.

Throckmorton, Peter, ed. *The Sea Remembers: Shipwrecks and Archaeology.* New York: Smithmark Publ., 1991.

———. *Shipwrecks and Archaeology: The Unharvested Sea.* Boston: Atlantic Monthly Press, 1970.

Throckmorton, Peter, and Gerhard Kapitän. "An Ancient Shipwreck at Pantano Longarini." *Archaeology* 21 (1968): 182–187.

Thrower, Norman J. W. *The Three Voyages of Edmund Halley in the "Paramore" 1698–1701.* London: Hakluyt Society, 1981.

Tod, Giles M. S. *The Last Sail Down East.* Barre, Vt.: Barre Publ., 1965.

Tolley, Kemp. *Yangtze Patrol: The U.S. Navy in China.* Annapolis: Naval Institute Press, 1971.

Tomalin, Nicholas, and Ron Hall. *The Strange Last Voyage of Donald Crowhurst.* New York: Stein & Day, 1970.

Tompkins, Warwick. *Fifty South to Fifty South: The Story of a Voyage Westward around Cape Horn in the Schooner "Wander Bird."* New York: W. W. Norton, 1942.

Trask, David F. *The War with Spain in 1898.* New York: Macmillan, 1986.

Tsouchlos, Nikos N. "The Year of Dokos." *Enalia Annual* (1989). Athens, Greece: HIMA, 1990.

Tuck, James A., and Robert Grenier. "A Sixteenth-Century Basque Whaling Station in Labrador." *Scientific American* (Nov. 1981): 180–190.

Tucker, Spencer C. "U.S. Navy Steam Sloop *Princeton.*" *American Neptune* 49 (1989): 96–113.

———, and Frank T. Reuter. *Injured Honor: The "Chesapeake"-"Leopard" Affair, June 22, 1807.* Annapolis: Naval Institute Press, 1996.

Tunstall-Behrens, Hilary. "*Pamir*": A Voyage to Rio in a Four-Masted Barque.* London: Routledge & Kegan Paul, 1956.

Turnbull, Archibald Douglas. *John Stevens: An American Record.* New York: Century, 1928.

Turner, Gordon. *The "Empress of Britain": Canadian Pacific's Greatest Ship.* Erin, Ontario: Boston Mills Press, 1992.

Turner, Mrs. W. J. Carpenter. "The Building of the *Grace Dieu, Valentine* and *Falconer* at Southampton, 1416–1420." *Mariner's Mirror* 40 (1954): 55–72.

Twitchett, E. G. *Life of a Seaman: Thomas Cochrane, 10th Earl of Dundonald.* London: Wishart, 1931.

Tyler, David P. "Fulton's Steam Frigate." *American Neptune* 6 (1946): 253–274.

Uden, Grant. *The Fighting "Temeraire."* Oxford, Eng.: Blackwell, 1961.

Underhill, Harold A. *Deepwater Sail.* Glasgow: Brown, Son & Ferguson, 1952.

———. *Sailing Ship Rigs and Rigging: With Authentic Plans of Famous Vessels of the Nineteenth and Twentieth Centuries.* Glasgow: Brown, Son & Ferguson, 1938.

———. *Sail Training and Cadet Ships.* Glasgow: Brown, Son & Ferguson, 1956.

Unger, Richard W. *The Art of Medieval Technology: Images of Noah the Shipbuilder.* New Brunswick, N.J.: Rutgers Univ. Press, 1991.

U.S. Coast Guard. "U.S. Merchant Ship Losses" (unpublished).

U.S. Navy. *Dictionary of American Naval Fighting Ships.* 8 vols. Washington, D.C.: Naval History Division, Department of the Navy, 1960–1981.

———. *United States Naval Chronology World War II.* Washington, D.C.: Government Printing Office, 1955.

Vancouver, George. *A Voyage of Discovery to the North Pacific Ocean and round the World 1791–1795.* London: Hakluyt Society, 1984.

Vanderbilt, Arthur T., II. *Treasure Wreck: The Fortunes and Fate of the Pirate Ship "Whydah."* Boston: Houghton Mifflin, 1986.

van der Molen, S. J. *The "Lutine" Treasure: The 150-Year Search for Gold in the Wreck of the Frigate "Lutine."* London: Adlard Coles, 1970.

van der Pijl-Ketel, C. L., ed. *The Ceramic Load of the "Witte Leeuw" (1613).* Amsterdam: Rijksmuseum, 1982.

Van der Vat, Dan. *The Grand Scuttle: The Sinking of the German Fleet at Scapa Flow in 1919.* Edinburgh: Waterfront, 1986.

———. *The Last Corsair: The Story of the "Emden."* London: Hodder & Stoughton, 1983.

———. *The Ship That Changed the World: The Escape of the "Goeben" to the Dardanelles in 1914.* London: Hodder & Stoughton, 1985.

———. *Stealth at Sea: The History of the Submarine.* Boston: Houghton Mifflin, 1995.

van Doorninck, Frederick H., Jr. "The 4th century Wreck at Yassi Ada: An Interim Report on the Hull." *IJNA* 5 (1976): 115–131.

van Nouhuys, J. W. "The Model of a Spanish Caravel of the Beginning of the Fifteenth Century." *Mariner's Mirror* 17 (1931): 327–346.

Van Oosten, F. C. "Her Netherlands Majesty's Ship *De Ruyter*."

van Rooij, Hans H., and Jerzy Gawronski. *East Indiaman "Amsterdam."* Haarlem: H. J. W. Becht, 1989.

Varner, Roy, and Wayne Collier. *A Matter of Risk: The Incredible Inside Story of the CIA's Hughes Glomar Explorer Mission to Raise a Russian Submarine.* New York: Random House, 1978.

Vaughan, Thomas, E. A. P. Crowhart-Vaughan, and Mercedes Palau de Iglesias. *Voyages of Enlightenment: Malaspina on the Northwest Coast 1791/1792.* Portland: Oregon Historical Society, 1977.

Velho, Alvaro. *Journal of the First Voyage of Vasco da Gama.* Trans. E. G. Ravenstein. London: Hakluyt Society, 1898.

Vernon-Gibbs, C. R. *Passenger Liners of the Western Ocean.* New York: Staples Press, 1952.

Villiers, Alan. *By Way of Cape Horn.* New York: Henry Holt, 1930.

———. *The Cruise of the "Conrad."* London: Hodder & Stoughton, 1937.

———. *The "Cutty Sark": Last of a Glorious Era.* London: Hodder & Stoughton, 1953.

———. *Falmouth for Orders.* New York: Charles Scribner's Sons, 1972.

———. "How We Sailed 'Mayflower II' to America." *National Geographic* (Nov. 1957): 627–672.

———. "I Sailed with Portugal's Captains Courageous." *National Geographic* (May 1952): 565–596.

———. *Last of the Wind Ships.* London: George Routledge & Sons, 1934.

———. *Quest of the Schooner "Argus": A Voyage to the Grand Banks and Greenland on a Modern Four-Masted Fishing Schooner.* New York: Charles Scribner's Sons, 1951.

———. *The Set of the Sails.* New York: Charles Scribner's Sons, 1949.

———. *Stormalong: An Account of a Boy's Voyage around the World.* New York: Charles Scribner's Sons, 1937.

———. *Voyage of the "Parma": The Great Grain Race of 1932.* London: Geoffrey Bles, 1933.

———. *The Way of a Ship, the Set of the Sails: The Story of a Cape Horn Seaman.* London: Hodder & Stoughton, 1949.

Villiers, Alan, and Henry Picard. *The Bounty Ships of France: The Story of the French Cape Horn Sailing Ships.* London: Patrick Stephens, 1972.

Villiers, J. A. J., ed. *The East and West Indian Mirror: Being an Account of Joris Van Speilbergen's Voyage round the World (1614–1617) and The Australian Navigations of Jacob Le Maire.* London: Hakluyt Society, 1906.

Vlek, Robert. *The Medieval Utrecht Boat: The History and Evaluation of One of the First Nautical Archaeological Excavations and Reconstructions in the Low Countries.* Oxford, Eng.: BAR/Greenwich: National Maritime Museum, 1987.

Voss, John C. *Venturesome Voyages of Capt. Voss.* New York: Dodd, Mead, 1941.

Wachsmann, Shelley. *The Sea of Galilee Boat: An Extraordinary 2000-Year-Old Discovery.* New York: Plenum Press, 1985.

Waddell, James I. *CSS "Shenandoah": The Memoirs of Lieutenant Commander James I. Waddell.* New York: Crown, 1960.

Waddell, Peter J. A. "The Disassembly of a 16th-Century Galleon." *IJNA* 15 (1986): 137–148.

Walker, David. *Champion of Sail: R. W. Leyland and His Shipping Line.* London: Conway Maritime, 1986.

Wallace, Frederick William. *In the Wake of the Wind Ships.* London: Hodder & Stoughton, 1927.

———. *Under Sail in the Last of the Clippers.* Glasgow: Brown, Son & Ferguson, 1936.

———. *Wooden Ships and Iron Men: The Story of the Square-Rigged Merchant Marine of British North America, The Ships, Their Builders and Owners, and the Men who Sailed Them.* Boston: Charles E. Lauriat, 1937.

Wallis, Helen. *Carteret's Voyage round the World 1766–1769.* Cambridge, Eng.: Hakluyt Society, 1965.

Walsh, William B. *A Ship Called "Hope."* New York: Scholastic Book Services, 1964.

Walter, John. *The Kaiser's Pirates: German Surface Raiders in World War One.* Annapolis: Naval Institute Press, 1994.

Ware, Chris. *The Bomb Vessel: Shore Bombardment Ships of the Age of Sail.* London: Conway Maaritime Press, 1994.

Warren, C. E. T., and James Benson. *"The Admiralty Regrets": The Story of H.M. Submarine "Thetis" and "Thunderbolt."* London: Harrap, 1958.

Warren, Gordon. *Fountain of Discontent: The "Trent" Affair and Freedom of the Seas.* Boston: Northeastern Univ. Press, 1981.

Waters, Sidney D. *"Pamir": The Story of a Sailing Ship.* Wellington, 1949.

Watson, Milton H. *Disasters at Sea.* Wellingborough, Eng.: Patrick Stephens, 1987.

Watton, Ross. *The Cruiser "Belfast."* Annapolis: Naval Institute Press, 1985.

Watts, Antony J. *The Imperial Russian Navy.* London: Arms & Armour, 1990.

Watts, Simon. "The *Thomas W. Lawson:* First or Last of the Great Sailing Bulk Carrier?" *Sea History* 16 (Winter 1980): 24–25.

Way, Frederick, Jr. *Way's Packet Directory, 1848–1983: Passenger Steamboats of the Mississippi River System since the Advent of Photography in Mid-Continent America.* Athens: Ohio Univ. Press, 1983.

Wead, Frank. *Gales, Ice and Men.* New York: Dodd, Mead, 1937.

Weaver, H. J. *Nightmare at Scapa Flow: The Truth about the Sinking of H.M.S. "Royal Oak" in Scapa Flow in 1939.* London: Cressrelles, 1981.

Webber, Bert. *Battleship "Oregon" . . . Bulldog of the Navy (An Oregon Documentary).* Medford, Oreg.: Webb Research Group, 1994.

Weeks, Jane. "Notes and News." *IJNA* 11 (1982): 174.

Wegner, Dana M. "An Apple and an Orange: Two *Constellations* at Gosport, 1853–1855." *American Neptune* 52 (1992): 77–93.

Wegner, Dana M., Colan Ratliff, and Kevin Lynaugh. *Fouled Anchors: The "Constellation" Question Answered.* Washington, D.C.: Government Printing Office, 1991.

Weinberg, G. D. et al. "The Antikythera Wreck Reconsidered." *Transactions of the American Philosophical Society* 55, 3 (1965).

Wells, John. *The Immortal Warrior: Britain's First and Last Battleship.* Emsworth, Pa.: Kenneth Mason, 1987.

Weyher, Kurt, and Hans Jürgen Ehrlich. *The Black Raider.* London: Elek Books, 1955.

Whipple, A. B. C. *The "Challenge."* New York: William Morrow, 1987.

Whitehead, Walter Muir. "George Crowninshield's Yacht *Cleopatra's Barge.*" *American Neptune* 13 (1953): 235–251.

Whitley, M. J. *Destroyers of World War II.* London: Arms & Armour, 1988.

———. *German Cruisers of World War Two.* London: Arms & Armour, 1985.

Wilhelmsen, Frederick D. *"Omega": Last of the Barques.* Westminster: Newman Press, 1956.

Wilkins, Sir George H. *Under the North Pole.* New York: Brewer & Putnam, 1931.

Williams, Glyndwr. *A Voyage Round the World in the Years MDCCXL, I, II, III, IV.* Edited by George Anson. London: Oxford Univ. Press, 1974.

Williamson, James A. *The Cabot Voyages and Bristol Discovery under Henry VII.* Cambridge, Eng.: Hakluyt Society, 1962.

Williamson, Jane. "Sidewheeler SOS Call Answered." *Historic Preservation* (Nov. 1992).

Wilson, David M. *The Bayeux Tapestry: The Complete Tapestry in Color.* New York: Knopf, 1985.

Wilson, Edward. *Diary of the "Terra Nova" Expedition to the Antarctic 1910–1912.* Edited by H. G. R. King. London: Blandford Press, 1972.

Wilson, James Grant, ed. *Memorial History of the City of New York.* New York: New York History Co., 1895.

Wilson, Jon. "Sailing the Schooner *Brilliant:* A Passage to Nova Scotia." *WoodenBoat* 122 (Jan.–Feb. 1995): 32–44.

Wilson, Michael. *Baltic Assignment: British Submarines in Russia 1914–1919.* London: Leo Cooper, 1985.

Wilterding, John H., Jr. *McDougall's Dream: The American Whaleback.* Green Bay, Wis.: Lakeside Publications, 1969.

Wincott, Len. *Invergordon Mutineer.* London: Weidenfeld & Nicolson, 1974.

Wingate, John. *HMS "Campbeltown" (USS "Buchanan").* Windsor: Profile Publishers, 1971.

Winslow, John. *The Ghost That Died in Sunda Strait.* Annapolis: Naval Institute Press, 1984.

Winslow, Ron. *Hard Aground: The Story of the "Argo" Merchant Oil Spill.* New York: W. W. Norton, 1978.

Winter, Barbara. *H.M.A.S. "Sydney": Fact, Fantasy and Fraud.* Brisbane: Boolarong, 1984.

Winton, John. *Carrier "Glorious": The Life and Death of an Aircraft Carrier.* London: Cooper, 1986.

———. *Warrior — The First and the Last.* Liskeard, Cornwall: Maritime Books, 1987.

Winwood, Allan J. "*Sea Venture:* An Interim Report on an Early 17th Century Shipwreck Lost in 1609." *IJNA* 11 (1982): 333–347.

Wise, Stephen R. *Lifeline of the Confederacy: Blockade Running during the Civil War.* Columbia: Univ. of South Carolina Press, 1988.

Wittholz, Charles. "Aloha *Kaiulani!* Part II: Design & Construction." *Sea History* 9: 23–26.

Wood, Gerald. "The Ironclad Turret Ship *Huascar.*" *Warship* 10:37–38 (1986).

Wood, Herbert P. *Till We Meet Again: The Sinking of the "Empress of Ireland."* Toronto: Image Publ., 1982.

Wood, Robert D. *The Voyage of the "Water Witch": A Scientific Expedition to Paraguay and La Plata Region (1853–1856).* Culver City, Calif.: Labyrinthos, 1985.

Wright, Edward V. *The Ferriby Boats: Seacraft of the Bronze Age.* London, 1990.

———. "The North Ferriby Boats — A Final Report." In *Crossroads in Ancient Shipbuilding: Proceedings of the Sixth International Symposium on Boat and Ship Archaeology, Roskilde, 1991.* Edited by C. Westerdahl. Oxford, Eng.: BAR, 1994.

———. *The North Ferriby Boats — A Guidebook.* Greenwich: National Maritime Museum, 1976.

Wroth, Lawrence C. *The Voyages of Giovanni da Verrazzano, 1524–1528.* New Haven: Yale Univ. Press, 1970.

Wyllie, Harold. "H.M.S. *Implacable.*" *Mariner's Mirror* 34:3 (1948): 147–155.

Yanaway, Philip E. "The United States Revenue Cutter *Harriet Lane,* 1857–1884." *American Neptune* 36 (1976): 174–205.

Yates, Keith. *Graf Spee's Raiders: Challenge to the Royal Navy, 1914–1915.* Annapolis: Naval Institute Press, 1995.

Corrigenda

Allen, Robert L. *The Port Chicago Mutiny.* New York: Warner Books, 1989.

Beaver, Paul. *The British Aircraft Carrier.* Cambridge: Patrick Stephens, 1982.

Bessemer, Sir Henry. *An Autobiography.* 1905. Reprint London: Institute of Metals, 1989.

Horton, Brian. *HMS Trincomalee.* Windsor: Profile Publ., 1989.

Maxtone-Graham, John. *The Only Way to Cross.* New York: Macmillan, 1973.

Scheina, Robert L. "The Helicopter Goes to War." *Warship* 3:9 (1979): 168–173.

Sterling, Forest J. *Wake of the Wahoo.* Philadelphia: Chilton, 1960.

Van Oosten, F. C. *Her Netherlands Majesty's Ship "De Ruyter."* Windsor: Profile, 1974.

Ward, Cheryl. *Sacred and Secular: Ancient Egyptian Hull Construction.* Boston: Archaeological Institute of America, 1998.

INDEX

Page numbers in bold type indicate main entries. Page numbers in italics refer to illustrations.